Dictionary of Literary Biography

1. *The American Renaissance in New England*, edited by Joel Myerson (1978)
2. *American Novelists Since World War II*, edited by Jeffrey Helterman and Richard Layman (1978)
3. *Antebellum Writers in New York and the South*, edited by Joel Myerson (1979)
4. *American Writers in Paris, 1920–1939*, edited by Karen Lane Rood (1980)
5. *American Poets Since World War II*, 2 parts, edited by Donald J. Greiner (1980)
6. *American Novelists Since World War II, Second Series*, edited by James E. Kibler Jr. (1980)
7. *Twentieth-Century American Dramatists*, 2 parts, edited by John MacNicholas (1981)
8. *Twentieth-Century American Science-Fiction Writers*, 2 parts, edited by David Cowart and Thomas L. Wymer (1981)
9. *American Novelists, 1910–1945*, 3 parts, edited by James J. Martine (1981)
10. *Modern British Dramatists, 1900–1945*, 2 parts, edited by Stanley Weintraub (1982)
11. *American Humorists, 1800–1950*, 2 parts, edited by Stanley Trachtenberg (1982)
12. *American Realists and Naturalists*, edited by Donald Pizer and Earl N. Harbert (1982)
13. *British Dramatists Since World War II*, 2 parts, edited by Stanley Weintraub (1982)
14. *British Novelists Since 1960*, 2 parts, edited by Jay L. Halio (1983)
15. *British Novelists, 1930–1959*, 2 parts, edited by Bernard Oldsey (1983)
16. *The Beats: Literary Bohemians in Postwar America*, 2 parts, edited by Ann Charters (1983)
17. *Twentieth-Century American Historians*, edited by Clyde N. Wilson (1983)
18. *Victorian Novelists After 1885*, edited by Ira B. Nadel and William E. Fredeman (1983)
19. *British Poets, 1880–1914*, edited by Donald E. Stanford (1983)
20. *British Poets, 1914–1945*, edited by Donald E. Stanford (1983)
21. *Victorian Novelists Before 1885*, edited by Ira B. Nadel and William E. Fredeman (1983)
22. *American Writers for Children, 1900–1960*, edited by John Cech (1983)
23. *American Newspaper Journalists, 1873–1900*, edited by Perry J. Ashley (1983)
24. *American Colonial Writers, 1606–1734*, edited by Emory Elliott (1984)
25. *American Newspaper Journalists, 1901–1925*, edited by Perry J. Ashley (1984)
26. *American Screenwriters*, edited by Robert E. Morsberger, Stephen O. Lesser, and Randall Clark (1984)
27. *Poets of Great Britain and Ireland, 1945–1960*, edited by Vincent B. Sherry Jr. (1984)
28. *Twentieth-Century American-Jewish Fiction Writers*, edited by Daniel Walden (1984)
29. *American Newspaper Journalists, 1926–1950*, edited by Perry J. Ashley (1984)
30. *American Historians, 1607–1865*, edited by Clyde N. Wilson (1984)
31. *American Colonial Writers, 1735–1781*, edited by Emory Elliott (1984)
32. *Victorian Poets Before 1850*, edited by William E. Fredeman and Ira B. Nadel (1984)
33. *Afro-American Fiction Writers After 1955*, edited by Thadious M. Davis and Trudier Harris (1984)
34. *British Novelists, 1890–1929: Traditionalists*, edited by Thomas F. Staley (1985)
35. *Victorian Poets After 1850*, edited by William E. Fredeman and Ira B. Nadel (1985)
36. *British Novelists, 1890–1929: Modernists*, edited by Thomas F. Staley (1985)
37. *American Writers of the Early Republic*, edited by Emory Elliott (1985)
38. *Afro-American Writers After 1955: Dramatists and Prose Writers*, edited by Thadious M. Davis and Trudier Harris (1985)
39. *British Novelists, 1660–1800*, 2 parts, edited by Martin C. Battestin (1985)
40. *Poets of Great Britain and Ireland Since 1960*, 2 parts, edited by Vincent B. Sherry Jr. (1985)
41. *Afro-American Poets Since 1955*, edited by Trudier Harris and Thadious M. Davis (1985)
42. *American Writers for Children Before 1900*, edited by Glenn E. Estes (1985)
43. *American Newspaper Journalists, 1690–1872*, edited by Perry J. Ashley (1986)
44. *American Screenwriters, Second Series*, edited by Randall Clark, Robert E. Morsberger, and Stephen O. Lesser (1986)
45. *American Poets, 1880–1945, First Series*, edited by Peter Quartermain (1986)
46. *American Literary Publishing Houses, 1900–1980: Trade and Paperback*, edited by Peter Dzwonkoski (1986)
47. *American Historians, 1866–1912*, edited by Clyde N. Wilson (1986)
48. *American Poets, 1880–1945, Second Series*, edited by Peter Quartermain (1986)
49. *American Literary Publishing Houses, 1638–1899*, 2 parts, edited by Peter Dzwonkoski (1986)
50. *Afro-American Writers Before the Harlem Renaissance*, edited by Trudier Harris (1986)
51. *Afro-American Writers from the Harlem Renaissance to 1940*, edited by Trudier Harris (1987)
52. *American Writers for Children Since 1960: Fiction*, edited by Glenn E. Estes (1986)
53. *Canadian Writers Since 1960, First Series*, edited by W. H. New (1986)
54. *American Poets, 1880–1945, Third Series*, 2 parts, edited by Peter Quartermain (1987)
55. *Victorian Prose Writers Before 1867*, edited by William B. Thesing (1987)
56. *German Fiction Writers, 1914–1945*, edited by James Hardin (1987)
57. *Victorian Prose Writers After 1867*, edited by William B. Thesing (1987)
58. *Jacobean and Caroline Dramatists*, edited by Fredson Bowers (1987)
59. *American Literary Critics and Scholars, 1800–1850*, edited by John W. Rathbun and Monica M. Grecu (1987)
60. *Canadian Writers Since 1960, Second Series*, edited by W. H. New (1987)
61. *American Writers for Children Since 1960: Poets, Illustrators, and Nonfiction Authors*, edited by Glenn E. Estes (1987)
62. *Elizabethan Dramatists*, edited by Fredson Bowers (1987)
63. *Modern American Critics, 1920–1955*, edited by Gregory S. Jay (1988)
64. *American Literary Critics and Scholars, 1850–1880*, edited by John W. Rathbun and Monica M. Grecu (1988)
65. *French Novelists, 1900–1930*, edited by Catharine Savage Brosman (1988)
66. *German Fiction Writers, 1885–1913*, 2 parts, edited by James Hardin (1988)
67. *Modern American Critics Since 1955*, edited by Gregory S. Jay (1988)
68. *Canadian Writers, 1920–1959, First Series*, edited by W. H. New (1988)
69. *Contemporary German Fiction Writers, First Series*, edited by Wolfgang D. Elfe and James Hardin (1988)
70. *British Mystery Writers, 1860–1919*, edited by Bernard Benstock and Thomas F. Staley (1988)
71. *American Literary Critics and Scholars, 1880–1900*, edited by John W. Rathbun and Monica M. Grecu (1988)
72. *French Novelists, 1930–1960*, edited by Catharine Savage Brosman (1988)
73. *American Magazine Journalists, 1741–1850*, edited by Sam G. Riley (1988)
74. *American Short-Story Writers Before 1880*, edited by Bobby Ellen Kimbel, with the assistance of William E. Grant (1988)
75. *Contemporary German Fiction Writers, Second Series*, edited by Wolfgang D. Elfe and James Hardin (1988)
76. *Afro-American Writers, 1940–1955*, edited by Trudier Harris (1988)

77 *British Mystery Writers, 1920-1939,* edited by Bernard Benstock and Thomas F. Staley (1988)

78 *American Short-Story Writers, 1880-1910,* edited by Bobby Ellen Kimbel, with the assistance of William E. Grant (1988)

79 *American Magazine Journalists, 1850-1900,* edited by Sam G. Riley (1988)

80 *Restoration and Eighteenth-Century Dramatists, First Series,* edited by Paula R. Backscheider (1989)

81 *Austrian Fiction Writers, 1875-1913,* edited by James Hardin and Donald G. Daviau (1989)

82 *Chicano Writers, First Series,* edited by Francisco A. Lomelí and Carl R. Shirley (1989)

83 *French Novelists Since 1960,* edited by Catharine Savage Brosman (1989)

84 *Restoration and Eighteenth-Century Dramatists, Second Series,* edited by Paula R. Backscheider (1989)

85 *Austrian Fiction Writers After 1914,* edited by James Hardin and Donald G. Daviau (1989)

86 *American Short-Story Writers, 1910-1945, First Series,* edited by Bobby Ellen Kimbel (1989)

87 *British Mystery and Thriller Writers Since 1940, First Series,* edited by Bernard Benstock and Thomas F. Staley (1989)

88 *Canadian Writers, 1920-1959, Second Series,* edited by W. H. New (1989)

89 *Restoration and Eighteenth-Century Dramatists, Third Series,* edited by Paula R. Backscheider (1989)

90 *German Writers in the Age of Goethe, 1789-1832,* edited by James Hardin and Christoph E. Schweitzer (1989)

91 *American Magazine Journalists, 1900-1960, First Series,* edited by Sam G. Riley (1990)

92 *Canadian Writers, 1890-1920,* edited by W. H. New (1990)

93 *British Romantic Poets, 1789-1832, First Series,* edited by John R. Greenfield (1990)

94 *German Writers in the Age of Goethe: Sturm und Drang to Classicism,* edited by James Hardin and Christoph E. Schweitzer (1990)

95 *Eighteenth-Century British Poets, First Series,* edited by John Sitter (1990)

96 *British Romantic Poets, 1789-1832, Second Series,* edited by John R. Greenfield (1990)

97 *German Writers from the Enlightenment to Sturm und Drang, 1720-1764,* edited by James Hardin and Christoph E. Schweitzer (1990)

98 *Modern British Essayists, First Series,* edited by Robert Beum (1990)

99 *Canadian Writers Before 1890,* edited by W. H. New (1990)

100 *Modern British Essayists, Second Series,* edited by Robert Beum (1990)

101 *British Prose Writers, 1660-1800, First Series,* edited by Donald T. Siebert (1991)

102 *American Short-Story Writers, 1910-1945, Second Series,* edited by Bobby Ellen Kimbel (1991)

103 *American Literary Biographers, First Series,* edited by Steven Serafin (1991)

104 *British Prose Writers, 1660-1800, Second Series,* edited by Donald T. Siebert (1991)

105 *American Poets Since World War II, Second Series,* edited by R. S. Gwynn (1991)

106 *British Literary Publishing Houses, 1820-1880,* edited by Patricia J. Anderson and Jonathan Rose (1991)

107 *British Romantic Prose Writers, 1789-1832, First Series,* edited by John R. Greenfield (1991)

108 *Twentieth-Century Spanish Poets, First Series,* edited by Michael L. Perna (1991)

109 *Eighteenth-Century British Poets, Second Series,* edited by John Sitter (1991)

110 *British Romantic Prose Writers, 1789-1832, Second Series,* edited by John R. Greenfield (1991)

111 *American Literary Biographers, Second Series,* edited by Steven Serafin (1991)

112 *British Literary Publishing Houses, 1881-1965,* edited by Jonathan Rose and Patricia J. Anderson (1991)

113 *Modern Latin-American Fiction Writers, First Series,* edited by William Luis (1992)

114 *Twentieth-Century Italian Poets, First Series,* edited by Giovanna Wedel De Stasio, Glauco Cambon, and Antonio Illiano (1992)

115 *Medieval Philosophers,* edited by Jeremiah Hackett (1992)

116 *British Romantic Novelists, 1789-1832,* edited by Bradford K. Mudge (1992)

117 *Twentieth-Century Caribbean and Black African Writers, First Series,* edited by Bernth Lindfors and Reinhard Sander (1992)

118 *Twentieth-Century German Dramatists, 1889-1918,* edited by Wolfgang D. Elfe and James Hardin (1992)

119 *Nineteenth-Century French Fiction Writers: Romanticism and Realism, 1800-1860,* edited by Catharine Savage Brosman (1992)

120 *American Poets Since World War II, Third Series,* edited by R. S. Gwynn (1992)

121 *Seventeenth-Century British Nondramatic Poets, First Series,* edited by M. Thomas Hester (1992)

122 *Chicano Writers, Second Series,* edited by Francisco A. Lomelí and Carl R. Shirley (1992)

123 *Nineteenth-Century French Fiction Writers: Naturalism and Beyond, 1860-1900,* edited by Catharine Savage Brosman (1992)

124 *Twentieth-Century German Dramatists, 1919-1992,* edited by Wolfgang D. Elfe and James Hardin (1992)

125 *Twentieth-Century Caribbean and Black African Writers, Second Series,* edited by Bernth Lindfors and Reinhard Sander (1993)

126 *Seventeenth-Century British Nondramatic Poets, Second Series,* edited by M. Thomas Hester (1993)

127 *American Newspaper Publishers, 1950-1990,* edited by Perry J. Ashley (1993)

128 *Twentieth-Century Italian Poets, Second Series,* edited by Giovanna Wedel De Stasio, Glauco Cambon, and Antonio Illiano (1993)

129 *Nineteenth-Century German Writers, 1841-1900,* edited by James Hardin and Siegfried Mews (1993)

130 *American Short-Story Writers Since World War II,* edited by Patrick Meanor (1993)

131 *Seventeenth-Century British Nondramatic Poets, Third Series,* edited by M. Thomas Hester (1993)

132 *Sixteenth-Century British Nondramatic Writers, First Series,* edited by David A. Richardson (1993)

133 *Nineteenth-Century German Writers to 1840,* edited by James Hardin and Siegfried Mews (1993)

134 *Twentieth-Century Spanish Poets, Second Series,* edited by Jerry Phillips Winfield (1994)

135 *British Short-Fiction Writers, 1880-1914: The Realist Tradition,* edited by William B. Thesing (1994)

136 *Sixteenth-Century British Nondramatic Writers, Second Series,* edited by David A. Richardson (1994)

137 *American Magazine Journalists, 1900-1960, Second Series,* edited by Sam G. Riley (1994)

138 *German Writers and Works of the High Middle Ages: 1170-1280,* edited by James Hardin and Will Hasty (1994)

139 *British Short-Fiction Writers, 1945-1980,* edited by Dean Baldwin (1994)

140 *American Book-Collectors and Bibliographers, First Series,* edited by Joseph Rosenblum (1994)

141 *British Children's Writers, 1880-1914,* edited by Laura M. Zaidman (1994)

142 *Eighteenth-Century British Literary Biographers,* edited by Steven Serafin (1994)

143 *American Novelists Since World War II, Third Series,* edited by James R. Giles and Wanda H. Giles (1994)

144 *Nineteenth-Century British Literary Biographers,* edited by Steven Serafin (1994)

145 *Modern Latin-American Fiction Writers, Second Series,* edited by William Luis and Ann González (1994)

146 *Old and Middle English Literature,* edited by Jeffrey Helterman and Jerome Mitchell (1994)

147 *South Slavic Writers Before World War II,* edited by Vasa D. Mihailovich (1994)

148 *German Writers and Works of the Early Middle Ages: 800-1170,* edited by Will Hasty and James Hardin (1994)

149 *Late Nineteenth- and Early Twentieth-Century British Literary Biographers,* edited by Steven Serafin (1995)

150 *Early Modern Russian Writers, Late Seventeenth and Eighteenth Centuries,* edited by Marcus C. Levitt (1995)

151 *British Prose Writers of the Early Seventeenth Century,* edited by Clayton D. Lein (1995)

152 *American Novelists Since World War II, Fourth Series,* edited by James R. Giles and Wanda H. Giles (1995)

153 *Late-Victorian and Edwardian British Novelists, First Series,* edited by George M. Johnson (1995)

154 *The British Literary Book Trade, 1700–1820,* edited by James K. Bracken and Joel Silver (1995)

155 *Twentieth-Century British Literary Biographers,* edited by Steven Serafin (1995)

156 *British Short-Fiction Writers, 1880–1914: The Romantic Tradition,* edited by William F. Naufftus (1995)

157 *Twentieth-Century Caribbean and Black African Writers, Third Series,* edited by Bernth Lindfors and Reinhard Sander (1995)

158 *British Reform Writers, 1789–1832,* edited by Gary Kelly and Edd Applegate (1995)

159 *British Short-Fiction Writers, 1800–1880,* edited by John R. Greenfield (1996)

160 *British Children's Writers, 1914–1960,* edited by Donald R. Hettinga and Gary D. Schmidt (1996)

161 *British Children's Writers Since 1960, First Series,* edited by Caroline Hunt (1996)

162 *British Short-Fiction Writers, 1915–1945,* edited by John H. Rogers (1996)

163 *British Children's Writers, 1800–1880,* edited by Meena Khorana (1996)

164 *German Baroque Writers, 1580–1660,* edited by James Hardin (1996)

165 *American Poets Since World War II, Fourth Series,* edited by Joseph Conte (1996)

166 *British Travel Writers, 1837–1875,* edited by Barbara Brothers and Julia Gergits (1996)

167 *Sixteenth-Century British Nondramatic Writers, Third Series,* edited by David A. Richardson (1996)

168 *German Baroque Writers, 1661–1730,* edited by James Hardin (1996)

169 *American Poets Since World War II, Fifth Series,* edited by Joseph Conte (1996)

170 *The British Literary Book Trade, 1475–1700,* edited by James K. Bracken and Joel Silver (1996)

171 *Twentieth-Century American Sportswriters,* edited by Richard Orodenker (1996)

172 *Sixteenth-Century British Nondramatic Writers, Fourth Series,* edited by David A. Richardson (1996)

173 *American Novelists Since World War II, Fifth Series,* edited by James R. Giles and Wanda H. Giles (1996)

174 *British Travel Writers, 1876–1909,* edited by Barbara Brothers and Julia Gergits (1997)

175 *Native American Writers of the United States,* edited by Kenneth M. Roemer (1997)

176 *Ancient Greek Authors,* edited by Ward W. Briggs (1997)

177 *Italian Novelists Since World War II, 1945–1965,* edited by Augustus Pallotta (1997)

178 *British Fantasy and Science-Fiction Writers Before World War I,* edited by Darren Harris-Fain (1997)

179 *German Writers of the Renaissance and Reformation, 1280–1580,* edited by James Hardin and Max Reinhart (1997)

180 *Japanese Fiction Writers, 1868–1945,* edited by Van C. Gessel (1997)

181 *South Slavic Writers Since World War II,* edited by Vasa D. Mihailovich (1997)

182 *Japanese Fiction Writers Since World War II,* edited by Van C. Gessel (1997)

183 *American Travel Writers, 1776–1864,* edited by James J. Schramer and Donald Ross (1997)

184 *Nineteenth-Century British Book-Collectors and Bibliographers,* edited by William Baker and Kenneth Womack (1997)

185 *American Literary Journalists, 1945–1995, First Series,* edited by Arthur J. Kaul (1998)

186 *Nineteenth-Century American Western Writers,* edited by Robert L. Gale (1998)

187 *American Book Collectors and Bibliographers, Second Series,* edited by Joseph Rosenblum (1998)

188 *American Book and Magazine Illustrators to 1920,* edited by Steven E. Smith, Catherine A. Hastedt, and Donald H. Dyal (1998)

189 *American Travel Writers, 1850–1915,* edited by Donald Ross and James J. Schramer (1998)

190 *British Reform Writers, 1832–1914,* edited by Gary Kelly and Edd Applegate (1998)

191 *British Novelists Between the Wars,* edited by George M. Johnson (1998)

192 *French Dramatists, 1789–1914,* edited by Barbara T. Cooper (1998)

193 *American Poets Since World War II, Sixth Series,* edited by Joseph Conte (1998)

194 *British Novelists Since 1960, Second Series,* edited by Merritt Moseley (1998)

195 *British Travel Writers, 1910–1939,* edited by Barbara Brothers and Julia Gergits (1998)

196 *Italian Novelists Since World War II, 1965–1995,* edited by Augustus Pallotta (1999)

197 *Late-Victorian and Edwardian British Novelists, Second Series,* edited by George M. Johnson (1999)

198 *Russian Literature in the Age of Pushkin and Gogol: Prose,* edited by Christine A. Rydel (1999)

199 *Victorian Women Poets,* edited by William B. Thesing (1999)

200 *American Women Prose Writers to 1820,* edited by Carla J. Mulford, with Angela Vietto and Amy E. Winans (1999)

201 *Twentieth-Century British Book Collectors and Bibliographers,* edited by William Baker and Kenneth Womack (1999)

202 *Nineteenth-Century American Fiction Writers,* edited by Kent P. Ljungquist (1999)

203 *Medieval Japanese Writers,* edited by Steven D. Carter (1999)

204 *British Travel Writers, 1940–1997,* edited by Barbara Brothers and Julia M. Gergits (1999)

205 *Russian Literature in the Age of Pushkin and Gogol: Poetry and Drama,* edited by Christine A. Rydel (1999)

206 *Twentieth-Century American Western Writers, First Series,* edited by Richard H. Cracroft (1999)

207 *British Novelists Since 1960, Third Series,* edited by Merritt Moseley (1999)

208 *Literature of the French and Occitan Middle Ages: Eleventh to Fifteenth Centuries,* edited by Deborah Sinnreich-Levi and Ian S. Laurie (1999)

209 *Chicano Writers, Third Series,* edited by Francisco A. Lomelí and Carl R. Shirley (1999)

210 *Ernest Hemingway: A Documentary Volume,* edited by Robert W. Trogdon (1999)

211 *Ancient Roman Writers,* edited by Ward W. Briggs (1999)

212 *Twentieth-Century American Western Writers, Second Series,* edited by Richard H. Cracroft (1999)

213 *Pre-Nineteenth-Century British Book Collectors and Bibliographers,* edited by William Baker and Kenneth Womack (1999)

214 *Twentieth-Century Danish Writers,* edited by Marianne Stecher-Hansen (1999)

215 *Twentieth-Century Eastern European Writers, First Series,* edited by Steven Serafin (1999)

216 *British Poets of the Great War: Brooke, Rosenberg, Thomas. A Documentary Volume,* edited by Patrick Quinn (2000)

217 *Nineteenth-Century French Poets,* edited by Robert Beum (2000)

218 *American Short-Story Writers Since World War II, Second Series,* edited by Patrick Meanor and Gwen Crane (2000)

219 *F. Scott Fitzgerald's* The Great Gatsby: *A Documentary Volume,* edited by Matthew J. Bruccoli (2000)

220 *Twentieth-Century Eastern European Writers, Second Series,* edited by Steven Serafin (2000)

221 *American Women Prose Writers, 1870–1920,* edited by Sharon M. Harris, with the assistance of Heidi L. M. Jacobs and Jennifer Putzi (2000)

222 *H. L. Mencken: A Documentary Volume,* edited by Richard J. Schrader (2000)

223 *The American Renaissance in New England, Second Series,* edited by Wesley T. Mott (2000)

224 *Walt Whitman: A Documentary Volume,* edited by Joel Myerson (2000)

225 *South African Writers,* edited by Paul A. Scanlon (2000)

226 *American Hard-Boiled Crime Writers,* edited by George Parker Anderson and Julie B. Anderson (2000)

227 *American Novelists Since World War II, Sixth Series,* edited by James R. Giles and Wanda H. Giles (2000)

228 *Twentieth-Century American Dramatists, Second Series,* edited by Christopher J. Wheatley (2000)

229 *Thomas Wolfe: A Documentary Volume,* edited by Ted Mitchell (2001)

230 *Australian Literature, 1788–1914,* edited by Selina Samuels (2001)

231 *British Novelists Since 1960, Fourth Series,* edited by Merritt Moseley (2001)

232 *Twentieth-Century Eastern European Writers, Third Series,* edited by Steven Serafin (2001)

233 *British and Irish Dramatists Since World War II, Second Series,* edited by John Bull (2001)

234 *American Short-Story Writers Since World War II, Third Series,* edited by Patrick Meanor and Richard E. Lee (2001)

235 *The American Renaissance in New England, Third Series,* edited by Wesley T. Mott (2001)

236 *British Rhetoricians and Logicians, 1500–1660,* edited by Edward A. Malone (2001)

237 *The Beats: A Documentary Volume,* edited by Matt Theado (2001)

238 *Russian Novelists in the Age of Tolstoy and Dostoevsky,* edited by J. Alexander Ogden and Judith E. Kalb (2001)

239 *American Women Prose Writers: 1820–1870,* edited by Amy E. Hudock and Katharine Rodier (2001)

240 *Late Nineteenth- and Early Twentieth-Century British Women Poets,* edited by William B. Thesing (2001)

241 *American Sportswriters and Writers on Sport,* edited by Richard Orodenker (2001)

242 *Twentieth-Century European Cultural Theorists, First Series,* edited by Paul Hansom (2001)

243 *The American Renaissance in New England, Fourth Series,* edited by Wesley T. Mott (2001)

244 *American Short-Story Writers Since World War II, Fourth Series,* edited by Patrick Meanor and Joseph McNicholas (2001)

245 *British and Irish Dramatists Since World War II, Third Series,* edited by John Bull (2001)

246 *Twentieth-Century American Cultural Theorists,* edited by Paul Hansom (2001)

247 *James Joyce: A Documentary Volume,* edited by A. Nicholas Fargnoli (2001)

248 *Antebellum Writers in the South, Second Series,* edited by Kent Ljungquist (2001)

249 *Twentieth-Century American Dramatists, Third Series,* edited by Christopher Wheatley (2002)

250 *Antebellum Writers in New York, Second Series,* edited by Kent Ljungquist (2002)

251 *Canadian Fantasy and Science-Fiction Writers,* edited by Douglas Ivison (2002)

252 *British Philosophers, 1500–1799,* edited by Philip B. Dematteis and Peter S. Fosl (2002)

253 *Raymond Chandler: A Documentary Volume,* edited by Robert Moss (2002)

254 *The House of Putnam, 1837–1872: A Documentary Volume,* edited by Ezra Greenspan (2002)

255 *British Fantasy and Science-Fiction Writers, 1918–1960,* edited by Darren Harris-Fain (2002)

256 *Twentieth-Century American Western Writers, Third Series,* edited by Richard H. Cracroft (2002)

257 *Twentieth-Century Swedish Writers After World War II,* edited by Ann-Charlotte Gavel Adams (2002)

258 *Modern French Poets,* edited by Jean-François Leroux (2002)

259 *Twentieth-Century Swedish Writers Before World War II,* edited by Ann-Charlotte Gavel Adams (2002)

260 *Australian Writers, 1915–1950,* edited by Selina Samuels (2002)

261 *British Fantasy and Science-Fiction Writers Since 1960,* edited by Darren Harris-Fain (2002)

262 *British Philosophers, 1800–2000,* edited by Peter S. Fosl and Leemon B. McHenry (2002)

263 *William Shakespeare: A Documentary Volume,* edited by Catherine Loomis (2002)

264 *Italian Prose Writers, 1900–1945,* edited by Luca Somigli and Rocco Capozzi (2002)

265 *American Song Lyricists, 1920–1960,* edited by Philip Furia (2002)

266 *Twentieth-Century American Dramatists, Fourth Series,* edited by Christopher J. Wheatley (2002)

267 *Twenty-First-Century British and Irish Novelists,* edited by Michael R. Molino (2002)

268 *Seventeenth-Century French Writers,* edited by Françoise Jaouën (2002)

269 *Nathaniel Hawthorne: A Documentary Volume,* edited by Benjamin Franklin V (2002)

270 *American Philosophers Before 1950,* edited by Philip B. Dematteis and Leemon B. McHenry (2002)

271 *British and Irish Novelists Since 1960,* edited by Merritt Moseley (2002)

272 *Russian Prose Writers Between the World Wars,* edited by Christine Rydel (2003)

273 *F. Scott Fitzgerald's Tender Is the Night: A Documentary Volume,* edited by Matthew J. Bruccoli and George Parker Anderson (2003)

274 *John Dos Passos's U.S.A.: A Documentary Volume,* edited by Donald Pizer (2003)

275 *Twentieth-Century American Nature Writers: Prose,* edited by Roger Thompson and J. Scott Bryson (2003)

276 *British Mystery and Thriller Writers Since 1960,* edited by Gina Macdonald (2003)

277 *Russian Literature in the Age of Realism,* edited by Allyssa Dinega Gillespie (2003)

278 *American Novelists Since World War II, Seventh Series,* edited by James R. Giles and Wanda H. Giles (2003)

279 *American Philosophers, 1950–2000,* edited by Philip B. Dematteis and Leemon B. McHenry (2003)

280 *Dashiell Hammett's The Maltese Falcon: A Documentary Volume,* edited by Richard Layman (2003)

281 *British Rhetoricians and Logicians, 1500–1660, Second Series,* edited by Edward A. Malone (2003)

282 *New Formalist Poets,* edited by Jonathan N. Barron and Bruce Meyer (2003)

283 *Modern Spanish American Poets, First Series,* edited by María A. Salgado (2003)

284 *The House of Holt, 1866–1946: A Documentary Volume,* edited by Ellen D. Gilbert (2003)

Dictionary of Literary Biography Documentary Series

1 *Sherwood Anderson, Willa Cather, John Dos Passos, Theodore Dreiser, F. Scott Fitzgerald, Ernest Hemingway, Sinclair Lewis,* edited by Margaret A. Van Antwerp (1982)

2 *James Gould Cozzens, James T. Farrell, William Faulkner, John O'Hara, John Steinbeck, Thomas Wolfe, Richard Wright,* edited by Margaret A. Van Antwerp (1982)

3 *Saul Bellow, Jack Kerouac, Norman Mailer, Vladimir Nabokov, John Updike, Kurt Vonnegut,* edited by Mary Bruccoli (1983)

4 *Tennessee Williams,* edited by Margaret A. Van Antwerp and Sally Johns (1984)

5 *American Transcendentalists,* edited by Joel Myerson (1988)

6 *Hardboiled Mystery Writers: Raymond Chandler, Dashiell Hammett, Ross Macdonald,* edited by Matthew J. Bruccoli and Richard Layman (1989)

7 *Modern American Poets: James Dickey, Robert Frost, Marianne Moore,* edited by Karen L. Rood (1989)

8 *The Black Aesthetic Movement,* edited by Jeffrey Louis Decker (1991)

9 *American Writers of the Vietnam War: W. D. Ehrhart, Larry Heinemann, Tim O'Brien, Walter McDonald, John M. Del Vecchio,* edited by Ronald Baughman (1991)

10 *The Bloomsbury Group,* edited by Edward L. Bishop (1992)

11 *American Proletarian Culture: The Twenties and The Thirties,* edited by Jon Christian Suggs (1993)

12 *Southern Women Writers: Flannery O'Connor, Katherine Anne Porter, Eudora Welty,* edited by Mary Ann Wimsatt and Karen L. Rood (1994)

13 *The House of Scribner, 1846–1904,* edited by John Delaney (1996)

14 *Four Women Writers for Children, 1868–1918,* edited by Caroline C. Hunt (1996)

15 *American Expatriate Writers: Paris in the Twenties,* edited by Matthew J. Bruccoli and Robert W. Trogdon (1997)

16 *The House of Scribner, 1905–1930,* edited by John Delaney (1997)

17 *The House of Scribner, 1931–1984,* edited by John Delaney (1998)

18 *British Poets of The Great War: Sassoon, Graves, Owen,* edited by Patrick Quinn (1999)

19 *James Dickey,* edited by Judith S. Baughman (1999)

See also DLB 210, 216, 219, 222, 224, 229, 237, 247, 253, 254, 263, 269, 273, 274, 280, 284

Dictionary of Literary Biography Yearbooks

1980 edited by Karen L. Rood, Jean W. Ross, and Richard Ziegfeld (1981)

1981 edited by Karen L. Rood, Jean W. Ross, and Richard Ziegfeld (1982)

1982 edited by Richard Ziegfeld; associate editors: Jean W. Ross and Lynne C. Zeigler (1983)

1983 edited by Mary Bruccoli and Jean W. Ross; associate editor Richard Ziegfeld (1984)

1984 edited by Jean W. Ross (1985)

1985 edited by Jean W. Ross (1986)

1986 edited by J. M. Brook (1987)

1987 edited by J. M. Brook (1988)

1988 edited by J. M. Brook (1989)

1989 edited by J. M. Brook (1990)

1990 edited by James W. Hipp (1991)

1991 edited by James W. Hipp (1992)

1992 edited by James W. Hipp (1993)

1993 edited by James W. Hipp, contributing editor George Garrett (1994)

1994 edited by James W. Hipp, contributing editor George Garrett (1995)

1995 edited by James W. Hipp, contributing editor George Garrett (1996)

1996 edited by Samuel W. Bruce and L. Kay Webster, contributing editor George Garrett (1997)

1997 edited by Matthew J. Bruccoli and George Garrett, with the assistance of L. Kay Webster (1998)

1998 edited by Matthew J. Bruccoli, contributing editor George Garrett, with the assistance of D. W. Thomas (1999)

1999 edited by Matthew J. Bruccoli, contributing editor George Garrett, with the assistance of D. W. Thomas (2000)

2000 edited by Matthew J. Bruccoli, contributing editor George Garrett, with the assistance of George Parker Anderson (2001)

2001 edited by Matthew J. Bruccoli, contributing editor George Garrett, with the assistance of George Parker Anderson (2002)

2002 edited by Matthew J. Bruccoli and George Garrett; George Parker Anderson, Assistant Editor (2003)

Concise Series

Concise Dictionary of American Literary Biography, 7 volumes (1988–1999): *The New Consciousness, 1941–1968; Colonization to the American Renaissance, 1640–1865; Realism, Naturalism, and Local Color, 1865–1917; The Twenties, 1917–1929; The Age of Maturity, 1929–1941; Broadening Views, 1968–1988; Supplement: Modern Writers, 1900–1998.*

Concise Dictionary of British Literary Biography, 8 volumes (1991–1992): *Writers of the Middle Ages and Renaissance Before 1660; Writers of the Restoration and Eighteenth Century, 1660–1789; Writers of the Romantic Period, 1789–1832; Victorian Writers, 1832–1890; Late-Victorian and Edwardian Writers, 1890–1914; Modern Writers, 1914–1945; Writers After World War II, 1945–1960; Contemporary Writers, 1960 to Present.*

Concise Dictionary of World Literary Biography, 4 volumes (1999–2000): *Ancient Greek and Roman Writers; German Writers; African, Caribbean, and Latin American Writers; South Slavic and Eastern European Writers.*

Dictionary of Literary Biography® • Volume Two Hundred Eighty-Four

The House of Holt, 1866–1946:
A Documentary Volume

Dictionary of Literary Biography® • Volume Two Hundred Eighty-Four

The House of Holt, 1866–1946: A Documentary Volume

Edited by
Ellen D. Gilbert
Rutgers University

A Bruccoli Clark Layman Book

GALE®

THOMSON

GALE
ST. PHILIP'S COLLEGE LIBRARY

Detroit • New York • San Diego • San Francisco • Cleveland • New Haven, Conn. • Waterville, Maine • London • Munich

THOMSON
GALE

Dictionary of Literary Biography
Volume 284: The House of Holt, 1866–1946:
A Documentary Volume
Ellen D. Gilbert

Advisory Board
John Baker
William Cagle
Patrick O'Connor
George Garrett
Trudier Harris
Alvin Kernan
Kenny J. Williams

Editorial Directors
Matthew J. Bruccoli and Richard Layman

© 2003 by Gale. Gale is an imprint of The Gale Group, Inc., a division of Thomson Learning, Inc.

Gale and Design™ and Thomson Learning™ are trademarks used herein under license.

For more information, contact
The Gale Group, Inc.
27500 Drake Rd.
Farmington Hills, MI 48331-3535
Or you can visit our Internet site at
http://www.gale.com

ALL RIGHTS RESERVED
No part of this work covered by the copyright hereon may be reproduced or used in any form or by any means—graphic, electronic, or mechanical, including photocopying, recording, taping, Web distribution, or information storage retrieval systems—without the written permission of the publisher.

For permission to use material from this product, submit your request via Web at http://www.gale-edit.com/permissions, or you may download our Permissions Request form and submit your request by fax or mail to:

Permissions Department
The Gale Group, Inc.
27500 Drake Rd.
Farmington Hills, MI 48331-3535
Permissions Hotline:
248-699-8006 or 800-877-4253, ext. 8006
Fax: 248-699-8074 or 800-762-4058

While every effort has been made to ensure the reliability of the information presented in this publication, The Gale Group, Inc. does not guarantee the accuracy of the data contained herein. The Gale Group, Inc. accepts no payment for listing; and inclusion in the publication of any organization, agency, institution, publication, service, or individual does not imply endorsement of the editors or publisher. Errors brought to the attention of the publisher and verified to the satisfaction of the publisher will be corrected in future editions.

LIBRARY OF CONGRESS CATALOGING-IN-PUBLICATION DATA

The house of Holt, 1866–1946: a documentary volume / edited by Ellen D. Gilbert.
    p. cm. — (Dictionary of literary biography ; v. 284)
"A Bruccoli Clark Layman book."
Includes bibliographical references and index.
    ISBN 0-7876-6821-4
    1. Henry Holt and Company—History. 2. Publishers and publishing—New York (State)—New York—History—19th century. 3. Publishers and publishing—New York (State)—New York—History—20th century. 4. Authors and publishers—New York (State)—New York—History—19th century. 5. Authors and publishers—New York (State)—New York—History—20th century. 6. Henry Holt and Company—Bibliography. I. Gilbert, Ellen D., 1952– II. Series.

Z473.H45H68 2003
070.5'09747'1—dc21
                        2003009241

Printed in the United States of America
10 9 8 7 6 5 4 3 2 1

In loving memory of my grandmother, Bertha Wohlmuth Sherman (1900–1986).

Contents

Plan of the Series xv
Introduction xvii
Acknowledgments xx

Selected Holt Titles, 1866–1946 3
    Leypoldt & Holt 3

    Holt & Williams 5

    Henry Holt & Co. 6

Early Years 20
    Beginnings 20

    Holt and American Publishing 28

    Reminiscences 44

1900–1920: The Harcourt Years 52
    Alfred Harcourt and Henry Holt 52

    Doing Business 63

    Publicity and Press Announcements 74

    Publishers' Associations 77

    Holt and Writers 78

    Politics and World War I 93

    Harcourt's Departure 99

The 1920s 102
    The Early 1920s 102

    The Later 1920s 117

    Writers 133

The 1930s 147
    Doing Business 148

    Politics and the Advent of War 156

    Authors 162

The 1940s 173
    William Sloane 173
    World War II 183
    1946: Sloane's Departure and an Oil Man's Takeover 196

Holt and Company Textbooks 205
    The Sciences 205
    The Social Sciences 214
    The Textbook Business 224

Holt and Company Authors 227
    Ivan Sergeevich Turgenev 227
    Thomas Hardy 229
    William James 231
    Henry Adams 241
    Dorothy Canfield Fisher 246
    Robert Frost 254
    W. E. B. Du Bois 281
    Carl Sandburg 285
    Sinclair Lewis 290
    Stephen Vincent Benét 297
    Walter de la Mare 301
    A. E. Housman 306
    Romain Rolland 313
    Albert Schweitzer 323
    Mark Van Doren 328

Books for Further Reading 335
Cumulative Index 343

Plan of the Series

... Almost the most prodigious asset of a country, and perhaps its most precious possession, is its native literary product—when that product is fine and noble and enduring.

Mark Twain*

The advisory board, the editors, and the publisher of the *Dictionary of Literary Biography* are joined in endorsing Mark Twain's declaration. The literature of a nation provides an inexhaustible resource of permanent worth. Our purpose is to make literature and its creators better understood and more accessible to students and the reading public, while satisfying the needs of teachers and researchers.

To meet these requirements, *literary biography* has been construed in terms of the author's achievement. The most important thing about a writer is his writing. Accordingly, the entries in *DLB* are career biographies, tracing the development of the author's canon and the evolution of his reputation.

The purpose of *DLB* is not only to provide reliable information in a usable format but also to place the figures in the larger perspective of literary history and to offer appraisals of their accomplishments by qualified scholars.

The publication plan for *DLB* resulted from two years of preparation. The project was proposed to Bruccoli Clark by Frederick G. Ruffner, president of the Gale Research Company, in November 1975. After specimen entries were prepared and typeset, an advisory board was formed to refine the entry format and develop the series rationale. In meetings held during 1976, the publisher, series editors, and advisory board approved the scheme for a comprehensive biographical dictionary of persons who contributed to literature. Editorial work on the first volume began in January 1977, and it was published in 1978. In order to make *DLB* more than a dictionary and to compile volumes that individually have claim to status as literary history, it was decided to organize volumes by topic, period, or genre. Each of these freestanding volumes provides a biographical-bibliographical guide and overview for a particular area of literature. We are convinced that this organization—as opposed to a single alphabet method—constitutes a valuable innovation in the presentation of reference material. The volume plan necessarily requires many decisions for the placement and treatment of authors. Certain figures will be included in separate volumes, but with different entries emphasizing the aspect of his career appropriate to each volume. Ernest Hemingway, for example, is represented in *American Writers in Paris, 1920–1939* by an entry focusing on his expatriate apprenticeship; he is also in *American Novelists, 1910–1945* with an entry surveying his entire career, as well as in *American Short-Story Writers, 1910–1945, Second Series* with an entry concentrating on his short fiction. Each volume includes a cumulative index of the subject authors and articles.

Since 1981 the series has been further augmented by the *DLB Yearbooks*, which update published entries, add new entries to keep the *DLB* current with contemporary activity, and provide articles on literary history. There have also been nineteen *DLB Documentary Series* volumes, which provide illustrations, facsimiles, and biographical and critical source materials for figures, works, or groups judged to have particular interest for students. In 1999 the *Documentary Series* was incorporated into the *DLB* volume numbering system beginning with *DLB 210: Ernest Hemingway*.

We define literature as the *intellectual commerce of a nation:* not merely as belles lettres but as that ample and complex process by which ideas are generated, shaped, and transmitted. *DLB* entries are not limited to "creative writers" but extend to other figures who in their time and in their way influenced the mind of a people. Thus the series encompasses historians, journalists, publishers, book collectors, and screenwriters. By this means readers of *DLB* may be aided to perceive literature not as cult scripture in the keeping of intellectual high priests but firmly positioned at the center of a nation's life.

DLB includes the major writers appropriate to each volume and those standing in the ranks behind them. Scholarly and critical counsel has been sought in

*From an unpublished section of Mark Twain's autobiography, copyright by the Mark Twain Company

deciding which minor figures to include and how full their entries should be. Wherever possible, useful references are made to figures who do not warrant separate entries.

Each *DLB* volume has an expert volume editor responsible for planning the volume, selecting the figures for inclusion, and assigning the entries. Volume editors are also responsible for preparing, where appropriate, appendices surveying the major periodicals and literary and intellectual movements for their volumes, as well as lists of further readings. Work on the series as a whole is coordinated at the Bruccoli Clark Layman editorial center in Columbia, South Carolina, where the editorial staff is responsible for accuracy and utility of the published volumes.

One feature that distinguishes *DLB* is the illustration policy—its concern with the iconography of literature. Just as an author is influenced by his surroundings, so is the reader's understanding of the author enhanced by a knowledge of his environment. Therefore *DLB* volumes include not only drawings, paintings, and photographs of authors, often depicting them at various stages in their careers, but also illustrations of their families and places where they lived. Title pages are regularly reproduced in facsimile along with dust jackets for modern authors. The dust jackets are a special feature of *DLB* because they often document better than anything else the way in which an author's work was perceived in its own time. Specimens of the writers' manuscripts and letters are included when feasible.

Samuel Johnson rightly decreed that "The chief glory of every people arises from its authors." The purpose of the *Dictionary of Literary Biography* is to compile literary history in the surest way available to us—by accurate and comprehensive treatment of the lives and work of those who contributed to it.

The *DLB* Advisory Board

Introduction

It is edifying to study publishing history at any time. The current age of media conglomerates, spectacular advances to authors, and blockbuster best-sellers, however, makes it all the more interesting—compelling, even—to understand publishing as it went on in earlier times. This backward look is fascinating, too, with regard to the current electronic environment, with its questions about such issues as the "death" of books and intellectual-property concerns.

When primary materials are available to afford first-hand accounts of a publishing firm's history, researchers are truly lucky. This is the case with Henry Holt and Company, for which records exist from the time of the firm's founding in 1866 (as Holt and Leypoldt) until shortly after World War II. The cutoff for the period covered in the present volume is determined not only by the scope of the Holt archives but by the circumstance that 1946 marks the point at which trade-department head William Sloane left Holt following Texas oilman Clint Marchison's acquisition of a controlling interest in the firm. That these records belong to one of the most distinguished American publishing houses in history makes the documents presented in this volume indeed extraordinary. Henry Holt and Company was known, almost from its founding in 1866, as a publishing house of integrity that produced quality books. Quality is, of course, not synonymous with quantity; fewer than a dozen Holt titles appear in Alice Payne Hackett and James Henry Burke's *80 Years of Best Sellers, 1895–1975* (1977). Holt titles that achieved best-seller status included Anthony Hope's *The Prisoner of Zenda* (1894); Paul Leicester Ford's *The Honorable Peter Stirling* (1894); *The Princess Passes* (1905), by C. N. and A. M. Williamson; *Creative Evolution* (1911), a translation of a 1907 work by Henri Bergson; Mary Green's *Better Meals for Less Money* (1917), *Joseph and His Brethren* (1929), by H. W. Freeman; *See Here, Private Hargrove* (1942), by Marion Hargrove; Ernie Pyle's *Here Is Your War* (1943), *Brave Men* (1944), and *Last Chapter* (1946); and Bill Mauldin's *Up Front* (1945). (Hackett and Burke document only fiction best-sellers from 1895 until 1912. Both fiction and nonfiction best-sellers are included, in separate lists, from 1912. Thus, Holt's financial success with novels before 1895, and with nonfiction until 1912, is uncertain.)

As Frederic Melcher observes in his foreword to *80 Years of Best Sellers,* best-selling books are not necessarily the best books but simply those that people liked best. Critical, too, is the consideration that best-sellers are the books that people like best at a particular time. While Holt titles appear not to have fared well on annual best-seller lists, their durability over time suggests that they had greater intrinsic value than many long-forgotten titles that briefly achieved glory as best-sellers.

The list of "Outstanding Holt Books" in *The Owl among Colophons: Henry Holt as Publisher and Editor,* former Holt employee Charles A. Madison's 1966 account of the firm, ranges from Ivan Sergeevich Turgenev's 1862 novel *Fathers and Sons,* published by Holt and Leypoldt in 1867, to Sacheverell Sitwell's *Monks, Nuns, and Monasteries,* published by Holt, Rinehart, and Winston in 1965. Appearing in the list between Turgenev and Sitwell is a remarkable group of authors, including Thomas Hardy, William Graham Sumner, Henry Adams, William James, Jerome K. Jerome, John Stuart Mill, Ford, Dorothy Canfield Fisher, John Dewey, Romain Rolland, Robert Frost, Walter Lippmann, Carl Sandburg, Walter de la Mare, Bertrand Russell, Bergson, Albert Einstein, Frederick Jackson Turner, Stephen Vincent Benét, A. E. Housman, Albert Schweitzer, and Mark Van Doren. Holt's strength as a publisher of poets is noteworthy, as is the firm's diverse list, especially in its early years, when it published fiction in addition to scholarly nonfiction by up and coming thinkers of the day.

Many works originally published by Holt remain in print today. Among these are novels by Hardy, Turgenev, and Adams. James's *Principles of Psychology* (1890) and Bergson's *Creative Evolution* are still in print, as is Einstein's *Relativity: The Special and General Theory,* the 1920 translation of his 1917 study; *Out of My Life and Thought,* the 1933 translation of Schweitzer's 1932 autobiography; and Frost's first book with Holt (and his first American publication), *North of Boston* (1914).

Behind the publication of Holt's distinctive titles were people who, with their knowledge of publishing, love of good writing, idealism, and business acumen, shaped the Holt list and guided the company's development. The careers of such important writers as James, Hardy, and Adams were significantly influenced by their relationship with the founder of the firm, Henry Holt.

Introduction

While other nineteenth-century publishers were content to wait for authors and manuscripts to come to them, Holt aggressively pursued distinguished writers and thinkers of the day. Nor did he consider his job finished once a contract was signed. Holt's correspondence with zoologist William Beebe (whom he sought out for a book after reading an article by Beebe about birds' beaks in the *New York Post*) reveals the thorough knowledge of animal anatomy that he brought to bear as he guided Beebe's writing. Indeed, Holt's careful reading of both fiction and nonfiction manuscripts and his suggestions for revisions earned him a reputation as an expert editor as well as an important publisher. In his role as a publisher he masterminded two of his greatest achievements, the Leisure Hour series and the American Science series, which brought both high-quality fiction and some of the best scientific writing to American readers before the end of the nineteenth century.

Holt will also be remembered for his passionate adherence to principles of proprietorship and fair play among authors and publishers in the years preceding the 1891 international copyright law. At a time when American publishers reprinted books from abroad without regard for the author's and the original publisher's interests, Holt steadfastly stood by the "courtesy of the trade" principle (a gentlemen's code; Holt is sometimes referred to as "the dean of gentlemen publishers"). His later unwillingness to conform to changes in the American publishing scene, particularly with regard to the use of literary agents, and his failure to appreciate new authors and their ideas led to a decline in his influence at the firm. Holt lived until 1926, staying, for the most part, at Fairholt, his home in Burlington, Vermont, and keeping in touch with office affairs through the mail (with twice-a-day deliveries in those years). Distance and his own intransigence diminished his effectiveness, however, especially when the able editor Alfred Harcourt joined the firm.

Sandburg, Lippmann, and Sinclair Lewis are among the American men of letters whose early careers were immeasurably helped by the attentions of Harcourt, who was with Henry Holt and Company from 1904 until 1919. Harcourt's appreciation of Frost helped to establish that great poet's long-lived (albeit stormy) relationship with Holt. Harcourt succeeded, to a degree, in bringing the firm into the twentieth century, in the face of considerable opposition from Henry Holt. Harcourt left the firm in 1919, taking with him his friend Donald Brace, head of Holt's production department, to found their own publishing house.

Lincoln MacVeagh's brief tenure (1919–1925) as head of Holt's trade department was highlighted by his reaffirmation of the firm's goodwill and interest in Frost, a significant accomplishment in the face of the departure of Frost's good friend Harcourt. Einstein, Thomas Mann, Benét, and Housman gave luster to Holt's list under MacVeagh, who brought an unusual degree of cosmopolitanism and scholarship to the job of editor.

The momentum established by the achievements of Holt, Harcourt, and MacVeagh stood the firm in good stead during the 1920s and 1930s. Although without distinguished leadership, the firm managed to do fairly well thanks to the strength of its highly regarded backlist, which included works by Rolland, Fisher, Frost, Sandburg, de la Mare, Louis Untermeyer, and Bergson. Holt's sons (Roland, Elliot, and Henry Jr.), who headed the firm from 1923 until 1928, did little to add to this list. The firm changed to public ownership at the end of this period and proceeded through the 1930s under the stronger, but not particularly innovative, leadership of E. N. Bristol.

Van Doren, Hargrove, John Ciardi, and, again, Frost were among the authors who flourished under the guidance of William Sloane, Holt trade-department head from 1939 until 1946. Like Harcourt before him, Sloane had an easy rapport with writers, editors, and agents. His literary interests included both scholarly and popular works, and Holt and Company gained renewed visibility during his tenure. An idealist whose career included a trip to China during World War II for the Council on Books in Wartime, Sloane left Holt in 1946 in the face of a takeover by businessmen whose priorities he disliked. The company archives essentially end at this point.

The Henry Holt and Company papers were donated to Princeton University in 1952. An item in *The Princeton University Library Chronicle* that year noted the significance of this gift:

> During the past few years, literary manuscripts, correspondence, and extensive groups of personal papers have been added to the Library's collections of original materials for the study of modern literature. The recent gift of the records of the publishing firm of Henry Holt and Company brings a new type of source material and thus broadens the scope of the existing collections. The Holt archives, roughly estimated to include some four hundred thousand letters and documents, were formally presented to the Library on April 14....
>
> The Holt records, strictly speaking, begin with the firm's establishment in 1866, although there are included in the gift to Princeton some records of Holt's predecessor, Frederick Leypoldt, dating back to 1859. Daybooks, ledgers, and inventory books provide a nearly complete record of the firm's publishing activities. The correspondence files are unfortunately less complete. Prior to about 1900 these are in the form of press copies of outgoing letters gathered together in bound volumes. Incoming letters for this early period

are only occasionally to be found. This fact should cause no surprise in view of the statement made by Henry Holt himself in a letter dated 1911: "Unfortunately as so much time has elapsed (over nine years), during which we have moved, and on moving placed many of our old records in a storehouse outside of our office–that it is difficult and perhaps in some cases impossible to recover all those bearing on this case; but we have unearthed all that seem essential to giving you a clear understanding of it. . . ."

As in the case of any similar extensive group of archival material, the value of the Holt records will depend upon the use made of them by scholars. From a cursory examination it would appear that they contain material of great interest not only for the study of individual authors, but also for the history of publishing methods and problems, of changing tastes in reading, of textbooks and teaching, and of such matters as international copyright and Anglo-American literary exchanges. In lieu of any formal history of the firm of Henry Holt and Company, the memoirs of the firm's founder, published under the title *Garrulities of an Octogenarian Editor* (Houghton Mifflin, 1923), may serve as guidepost to some of the personalities and questions touched upon in the extensive collection of papers now in the Princeton Library.[1]

The archives of Henry Holt and Company are in the Department of Rare Books and Special Collections at Princeton University's Firestone Library. Physically, the archives comprise some 126 cubic feet; inclusive dates of the records are 1859 (thus predating the firm's formal establishment by seven years) to 1962, with the bulk of the material falling between 1890 and 1943. The collection has been divided into ten series: Letterbooks; Correspondence; Robert Frost–Secondary Material; Permissions to Reprint; Miscellaneous Material; Correspondence–Holt, Harcourt, and Brace, 1909–1913; Financial Material; Inventory and Depository Records, 1859–1962; Copyright Records, 1900–1912 and 1935–1946; and Advertising Records. While the correspondence has been put into alphabetical order and an unpublished list of names and file locations has been created, the balance of the collection remains largely unprocessed.

This volume offers a selection of primary documents taken, for the most part, from the Henry Holt and Company papers at Princeton. The correspondence and other materials chosen were those that shed light on the firm, its authors, and American publishing concerns over several eras. The book is divided into two parts. In the first, Holt's general history is followed chronologically. Appearing in the chapters comprising this part are representative letters to and from authors of the day as well as other materials relevant to the times. Also included in this part is a chapter on textbooks, which were an important aspect of Holt's list from the beginning.

The second part of the book is devoted to those authors whose careers or notoriety are of particular interest in relation to Holt. (Obviously, the availability of correspondence and other documents relating to these writers played a role in their selection.) Frost, the firm's longest-standing "employee," commands the longest of these sections. Holt's special strength in publishing poets is also represented by sections on Sandburg, Benét, de la Mare, Housman, and Van Doren. Fiction writers for Holt in this part of the volume include Turgenev, Hardy, Adams (author of the infamous 1880 novel *Democracy*, which Henry Holt agreed to publish anonymously), Fisher, and Rolland. Nonfiction authors James, W. E. B. Du Bois, and Schweitzer round out the list. In the belief that those who were turned down may be as interesting, in some respects, as those who were published, a selection of rejection letters from Holt and Company to various authors through the years serves as the last word.

It is hoped that this volume provides the sense of immediacy and kinds of knowledge that can be achieved by using only primary sources. Changing letterheads alone–Holt and Company's own, as well as various correspondents'–provide a fascinating world of information. J. W. Arrowsmith, the British firm from which Holt obtained Jerome's *Three Men in a Boat* (1889), Hope's *The Prisoner of Zenda*, and books by Hugo Conway, cautioned in its letterhead, "We do not hold ourselves responsible for customers' goods or manuscripts injured or destroyed by fire." Striking green and black bands with white lettering gave verve to correspondence from *The Southern Review* during the 1930s. "Received" stamps, franking on envelopes, and, critically, marginal annotations and doodles reveal much about the times in general and the circumstances of a specific book in particular. One wonders whether such nuances are being–or will be–lost as more and more primary documents are being created in electronic formats.

From the messages conveyed by rubber stamps (for example, a call for the wider use of paper after years of war-related restrictions) to the text of authors' letters–business-like or casual, sharp or funny, awkward or eloquently to the point–these documents are important reflections of the people who wrote them and the times in which they lived. It is hoped that publishing houses today are routinely collecting their own records–including electronic documents–for similar consideration in the future.

–Ellen D. Gilbert

1. "Archives of Henry Holt and Company," *Princeton University Library Chronicle*, 13 (Spring 1952): 208–209.

Acknowledgments

This book was produced by Bruccoli Clark Layman, Inc. R. Bland Lawson was the in-house editor.

Production manager is Philip B. Dematteis.

Administrative support was provided by Ann M. Cheschi and Carol A. Cheschi.

Accountant is Ann-Marie Holland.

Copyediting supervisor is Sally R. Evans. The copyediting staff includes Phyllis A. Avant, Caryl Brown, Melissa D. Hinton, Philip I. Jones, Rebecca Mayo, Nancy E. Smith, and Elizabeth Jo Ann Sumner. Freelance copyeditor is Brenda Cabra.

Editorial associates are Amelia B. Lacey, Michael S. Martin, Catherine M. Polit, and William Mathes Straney.

In-house prevetting is by Nicole A. La Rocque.

Permissions editor and database manager is Amber L. Coker.

Layout and graphics supervisor is Janet E. Hill. The graphics staff includes Zoe R. Cook and Sydney E. Hammock.

Office manager is Kathy Lawler Merlette.

Photography supervisor is Paul Talbot. Photography editor is Scott Nemzek.

Digital photographic copy work was performed by Joseph M. Bruccoli.

Systems manager is Donald Kevin Starling.

Typesetting supervisor is Kathleen M. Flanagan. The typesetting staff includes Patricia Marie Flanagan, Mark J. McEwan, and Pamela D. Norton. Freelance typesetters are Wanda Adams and Rebecca Mayo.

Walter W. Ross did library research. He was assisted by Jo Cottingham and the following other librarians at the Thomas Cooper Library of the University of South Carolina: circulation department head Tucker Taylor; reference department head Virginia W. Weathers; reference department staff Brette Barron, Marilee Birchfield, Paul Cammarata, Gary Geer, Michael Macan, Tom Marcil, Rose Marshall, and Sharon Verba; interlibrary loan department head John Brunswick; and interlibrary loan staff Robert Arndt, Hayden Battle, Alex Byrne, Bill Fetty, Marna Hostetler, and Nelson Rivera.

Dictionary of Literary Biography® • Volume Two Hundred Eighty-Four

The House of Holt, 1866–1946:
A Documentary Volume

Dictionary of Literary Biography

Selected Holt Titles, 1866–1946

LEYPOLDT & HOLT

1866
Baldwin, John Loraine. *The Laws of Short Whist, Ed. by J. L. Baldwin, and a Treatise on the Game, by J.C.*
Barber, Joseph. *Crumbs from the Round Table: A Feast for Epicures.*
Bellenger, W. A. *New Guide to Modern Conversations in French and English; or, Dialogues on Ordinary and Familiar Subjects,* revised and enlarged by C. Witcomb and H. Witcomb.
Eichendorff, Joseph, Freiherr von. *Memoirs of a Good-for-Nothing,* translated by Charles G. Leland, illustrated by E. B. Bensell.
Heine, Heinrich. *Pictures of Travel,* translated by Leland.
Hertz, Henrik. *King Rene's Daughter: A Danish Lyrical Drama,* translated by Theodore Martin.
Kingsley, Charles. *Hereward the Wake, "Last of the English."*
Kingsley. *Yeast, a Problem.*
La Bédollière, Emile Gigault de. *Histoire de la Mère Michel et de son Chat.*
Mendelssohn-Bartholdy, Felix. *Letters of Felix Mendelssohn Bartholdy from 1833 to 1847,* edited by Paul Mendelssohn-Bartholdy and Karl Mendelssohn-Bartholdy, translated by Lady Grace Wallace.
Porchat, J. Jacques. *Trois Mois sous la neige: Journal d'un jeune habitant du Jura,* revised edition.
Pylodet, L. (Frederick Leypoldt). *Beginning French: Exercises in Pronouncing, Spelling and Translating, with a Vocabulary of Familiar Words and a Collection of Easy Phrases and Dialogues, in French and English.*
Pylodet, ed. *Gouttes de Rosée: French Lyric Poems.*
Thackeray, William Makepeace. *The Adventures of Philip on His Way through the World.*
Thackeray. *The Great Hoggarty Diamond; and, The Book of Snobs.*
Thackeray. *The History of Pendennis, His Fortunes and Misfortunes, His Friends and His Greatest Enemy.*
Thackeray. *Men's Wives.*
Thackeray. *The Newcomes.*
Thackeray. *The Tremendous Adventures of Major Gahagan, to Which Are Added, The Fatal Boots, and Ballads.*
Thackeray. *Vanity Fair: A Novel without a Hero.*
Thackeray. *The Virginians: A Tale of the Last Century.*
Thackeray. *The Yellowplush Papers: Consisting of the Memoirs of Mr. Charles J. Yellowplush, and the Diary of C. Jeames De La Pluche, to Which Is Added, Cox's Diary.*
Weeks, Robert Kelley. *Poems.*

1867 About, Edmond. *The Man with the Broken Ear,* translated by Henry Holt.
Bristed, Charles Astor. *The Interference Theory of Government.*
Carlier, Auguste. *Marriage in the United States,* third edition, translated by B. Joy Jeffries.
Craik, Georgiana Marion. *Faith Unwin's Ordeal.*
Critical and Social Essays Reprinted from the New York Nation.
Guérin, Maurice de. *The Journal of Maurice de Guérin, with an Essay by Matthew Arnold, and a Memoir by Sainte Beuve,* edited by G. S. Trébutien, translated by Edward Thornton Fisher.
Kortum, Karl Arnold. *The Jobsiad: A Grotesco-comico-heroic Poem,* translated by Charles T. Brooks.
Lessing, Gotthold Ephraim. *Nathan the Wise: A Dramatic Poem,* translated by Ellen Frothingham.
Marteilhe, Jean. *The Huguenot Galley-slave: Being the Autobiography of a French Protestant Condemned to the Galleys for the Sake of His Religion.*
Otto, Emil. *German Conversation-grammar: A New and Practical Method of Learning the German Language,* ninth revised edition.
Percy, Thomas. *Reliques of Ancient English Poetry.*
Pylodet. *Leçons de Littérature Française Classique, Précédées de Lecons de Littérature Francaise Depuis ses Origines.*
Reuter, Fritz. *In the Year '13: A Tale of Mecklenburg Life,* translated by Charles Lee Lewes.
Richter, Eugene. *Co-operative Stores: Their History, Organization, and Management.*
Sadler, Percy. *Petit cours de versions; or, Exercises for Translating English into French,* sixth American edition, revised by C. F. Gillette.
Shute, Samuel M. *A Manual of Anglo-Saxon for Beginners, Comprising a Grammar, Reader, and Glossary, with Explanatory Notes.*
Smollett, Tobias. *The Expedition of Humphry Clinker.*
Sterne, Laurence. *The Life and Opinions of Tristram Shandy, Gentleman.*
Sterne. *A Sentimental Journey through France and Italy.*
Storme, George. *Easy German Reading, after a New System,* revised by Edward A. Oppen.
Tegnér, Esaias. *Frithiof's Saga,* translated by William Lewery Blackley, edited by Bayard Taylor.
Thackeray. *The Kickleburys Abroad, to Which Are Added: A Legend of the Rhine, Rebecca and Rowena, The Second Funeral of Napoleon, and The Chronicle of the Drum.*
Thackeray. *A Little Dinner at Timmins's, to Which Are Added, The Bedford Row Conspiracy, The Fitz-Boodle Papers, and A Shabby Genteel Story.*
Thackeray. *Sketches and Travels in London.*
Turgenev, Ivan Sergeevich. *Fathers and Sons,* translated by Eugene Schuyler.
Vacquerie, Auguste. *Jean Baudry: Comédie en quatre actes.*
Yonge, Charlotte Mary. *Landmarks of History, II: Middle Ages, from the Reign of Charlemagne to That of Charles V,* revised by Edith L. Chase.

1868 Borel, Eugène. *Cours de Thèmes Français: Progressive Exercises for Translating English into French, Suitable for Use with All Grammars.*
Borel. *Grammaire Française à l'Usage des Anglais,* revised by Edward B. Coe.
Brinton, Daniel G. *The Myths of the New World: A Treatise on the Symbolism and Mythology of the Red Race of America.*
Cox, George W. *A Manual of Mythology in the Form of Question and Answer.*
Delille, C. J. *Condensed French Instruction, Consisting of Grammar and Exercises with Cross References.*
Fisher, Edward Thornton. *Easy French Reading.*
Hunter, William Wilson. *The Annals of Rural Bengal,* second edition.
Jenkin. *A Psyche of To-day.*
Lamé Fleury, Jules Raymond. *L'histoire de France, racontée à la jeunesse,* revised edition.
Pylodet. *La Littérature Française Contemporaine, recueil en prose et en vers de morceaux empruntés aux écrivains les plus renommés du XIXe siècle.*
Rau, Heribert. *Mozart: A Biographical Romance,* translated by Edward Rowland Sill.
Selections from the Kalevala, translated by John A. Porter.

Sill, Edward Rowland. *The Hermitage, and Other Poems.*

Souvestre, Emile. *Un Philosophe sous les Toits: Journal d'un Homme Heureux.*

Taine, Hippolyte-Adolphe. *Italy: Rome and Naples,* translated by John Durand.

Yonge. *Landmarks of History, III: Modern History, from the Beginning of the Reformation to the Accession of Napoleon III.*

1869 Auerbach, Berthold. *Black Forest Village Stories,* translated by Charles Goepp.

Auerbach. *The Villa on the Rhine,* translated by Taylor.

Bjørnson, Bjørnstjerne. *The Fisher-Maiden: A Norwegian Tale,* translated by M. E. Niles.

Evans, Edward Payson. *Abriss der deutschen Literaturgeschichte.*

Fiske, John. *Tobacco and Alcohol.*

Jenkin. *Madame de Beaupré.*

Martineau, Harriet. *Biographical Sketches.*

Pylodet. *New Guide to German Conversation.*

Saxton, Robert. *Mental Photographs: An Album for Confessions of Tastes, Habits, and Convictions.*

Schmid, Herman. *The Habermeister: A Tale of the Bavarian Mountains.*

Spielhagen, Friedrich. *Problematic Characters,* translated by Maximilian Schele De Vere.

Taine. *The Ideal in Art,* translated by Durand.

Taine. *Italy: Florence and Venice,* translated by Durand.

1870 Pumpelly, Raphael. *Across America and Asia.*

Spielhagen. *Through Night to Light,* translated by De Vere.

1871 Taine. *Art in the Netherlands,* translated by Durand.

HOLT & WILLIAMS

1872 Taine. *History of English Literature,* translated by Henri Van Laun.

Turgenev. *Smoke,* translated by William F. West.

1873 Turgenev. *Dimitri Roudine.*

Turgenev. *On the Eve,* translated by C. E. Turner.

Title page for the second edition of the study of Native American mythology first published by Leypoldt & Holt in 1868 (Rutgers University Library)

HENRY HOLT & CO.

1873
Hardy. *A Pair of Blue Eyes.*
Hardy. *Under the Greenwood Tree: A Rural Painting of the Dutch School.*
Maine, Henry Sumner. *Ancient Law: Its Connection with the Early History of Society.*
Turgenev. *Liza,* translated by W. R. S. Ralston.

1874
Auerbach. *Waldfried,* translated by Simon Adler Stern.
Hardy. *Desperate Remedies.*
Richardson, Samuel. *Clarissa; or, The History of a Young Lady,* abridged by C. H. Jones.
Sumner, William Graham. *A History of American Currency.*
Tylor, Edward Burnett. *Primitive Culture: Researches into the Development of Mythology, Philosophy, Religion, Language, Art, and Customs.*

1875
Erskine, Thomas, Mrs. *Wyncote.*
Gift, Theo. *Pretty Miss Bellew: A Tale of Home Life.*
Taine. *Lectures on Art,* translated by Durand.

1876
Hardy. *The Hand of Ethelberta: A Comedy in Chapters.*
Maine. *Village-Communities in the East and West.*
Taine. *The Ancient Regime,* translated by Durand.
Walker, Frances A. *The Wages Question: A Treatise on Wages and the Wages Class.*

1877
Morgan, Lewis Henry. *Ancient Society; or, Researches in the Lines of Human Progress from Savagery, Through Barbarism to Civilization.*
Richter, Jean Paul Friedrich. *Campaner Thal and Other Writings,* translated by Juliette Bauer, Thomas Carlyle, and Thomas De Quincey.
Richter. *Flower, Fruit and Thorn Pieces; or, The Married Life, Death, and Wedding of the Advocate of the Poor, Firmian Stanislaus Sienbenkäs,* translated by Edward Henry Noel.
Richter. *Titan.*
Turgenev. *Virgin Soil,* translated by T. S. Perry.
Wallace, Donald Mackenzie, Sir. *Russia.*
Wright, Chauncey. *Philosophical Discussions.*

1878
Hardy. *The Return of the Native.*
The Prince of Argolis: A Story of the Old Greek Fairy Time, illustrated by J. Moyr Smith.
Tylor. *Researches into the Early History of Mankind and the Development of Civilization.*
Walker. *Money.*

1879
Farrer, James A. *Primitive Manners and Customs.*
Kemble, Fanny. *Records of a Girlhood.*
Newcomb, Simon, and Edward S. Holden. *Astronomy for Schools and Colleges.*
Rydberg, Viktor. *The Magic of the Middle Ages,* translated by August Hjalmar Edgren.
Symonds, John Addington. *Renaissance in Italy: The Fine Arts.*

1880
Adams, Henry. *Democracy: An American Novel.*
Hardy. *The Trumpet-Major.*

TRADE LIST OF
HENRY HOLT & CO.
No. 25 Bond Street, New York.

JULY, 1876.

☞ *All books in this list are bound in cloth, lettered, unless otherwise expressed. Titles followed by the sign † are in the Leisure Hour Series. Those followed by the sign § are among the Condensed Classics.*

MISCELLANEOUS.

About, Edmond.
   The Man with the Broken Ear. 16mo. † $1 25
   The Notary's Nose. 16mo. † . . . 1 25
Adams, C. K.,
   Democracy and Monarchy in France.
   Large 12mo. 2 50
Africa. See Jones.
Alcestis. A Novel. 16mo. † . 1 25
Alexander, Mrs.
   The Wooing O't. 16mo. † 1 52
   Which Shall It Be? 16mo. † . . . 1 25
   Ralph Wilton's Weird. 16mo. † . . 1 25
   Her Dearest Foe. 16mo. † . . . 1 25
Arnold, Matthew.
   Essays in Criticism. 12mo. 2 00
   Literature and Dogma. 12mo. . . 1 50
   God and the Bible. 12mo. . . . 1 50
Albemarle, Geo. Thos., Earl of.
   Fifty Years of My Life. Large 12mo.
Allen, Professor Geo.
   Life of Philidor. 12mo. 1 50
Amateur Series.
   1. Moscheles' Recent Music and Musicians. 2 00
   2. Chorley's Recent Art and Society. . 2 00
   3. Wagner's Art Life and Theories. . . 2 00
   4. Berlioz' Autobiography and Musical Grotesques. (*In Press.*)
Auerbach, Berthold.
   Waldfried. A Novel. 12mo. . . . 2 00
   Villa on the Rhine. 2 vols. 16mo. †
    Per vol. 1 25
   Pocket Edition. 4 Parts. 16mo. Paper. Per Part, 40c. Complete, 1 50
   On the Heights. 12mo. Library edition, $2.00. Two vols. 16mo. †
    Per vol. 1 25
   Black Forest Village Stories. Illus. 16mo. † 1 25
   Joseph in the Snow. Illust. 16mo. † . 1 25
   Little Barefoot. Illust. 16mo. † . . 1 25
   German Tales. 16mo. † 1 25
   Edelweiss. 16mo. † 1 25

*Austin, John.
   Lectures on Jurisprudence, Abridged by Robert Campbell. 8vo. . . . $3 00
Baldwin, J. L.
   Laws of Short Whist. 16mo. . . 1 00
Björnson, B.
   The Fisher-Maiden. 16mo. † . . . 1 25
Bristed, Chas. Astor.
   Pieces of a Broken-down Critic. 8vo. 2 50
Brinton, D. G.
   Myths of the New World. Large 12mo. 2 50
   *Large paper. 8vo. First ed. Uncut. 6 00
   The Religious Sentiment. Large 12mo. 2 50
Busch, Wilhelm.
   Buzz a Buzz; or, The Bees. With colored illustrations. 8vo. . . . 1 50
Bulwer (Lord Lytton).
   Last Days of Pompeii. 18mo. § . . 1 00
Butt, Beatrice M.
   Miss Molly. 16mo. † 1 25
Cadell, Mrs. H. M.
   Ida Craven. 16mo. † 1 25
Calverly, C. S.
   Fly Leaves. 16mo. † 1 25
Carlier, A.
   Marriage in the United States. 16mo. 1 00
Cherbuliez, Victor.
   Joseph Noirel's Revenge. 16mo. † . 1 25
   Count Kostia. 16mo. † 1 25
   Prosper. 16mo. † 1 25
Chesney, Chas. C.
   Military Biography. Large 12mo. 2 50
Chorley, H. F.
   Recent Art and Society. 12mo. . . 2 00
Clough, Arthur Hugh.
   Poems. (*A new Revised Edition in Preparation.*)
Coleridge, S. T.
   Biographia Literaria. 2 vols. 8vo. . 5 00

First page of the Holt and Company trade list from The Publishers' Trade List Annual *(1876)*

1881	Dostoevsky, Fyodor. *Buried Alive; or, Ten Years of Penal Servitude in Siberia,* translated by Marie von Thilo. Fyffe, C. A. *A History of Modern Europe.* Hardy. *A Laodicean; or, The Castle of the De Stancys,* illustrated by George Du Maurier. Norris, W. E. *Matrimony.* Symonds. *Renaissance in Italy: The Age of the Despots.*
1882	Hardy. *Two on a Tower.* Heine. *The Romantic School,* translated by S. L. Fleishman. Kemble. *Records of Later Life.* Mill, John Stuart. *Dissertations and Discussions: Political, Philosophical, and Historical,* 5 volumes (1874–1882). Norris. *Heaps of Money.*
1883	Gosse, Edmund. *On Viol and Flute: Selected Poems.* Norris. *No New Thing.* Walker. *Political Economy.*

Cover design and title page for the 1797 German study on the immortality of the soul that was first published in America by Ticknor & Fields in 1864. The same cover design was used for other Richter titles published by Holt (Rutgers University Library).

1884	Adams. *Esther: A Novel*, as Frances Snow Compton. Sylva, Carmen. *Pilgrim Sorrow: A Cycle of Tales*, translated by Helen Zimmern.
1885	Holland, Frederic May. *The Rise of Intellectual Liberty from Thales to Copernicus*. Turgenev. *Annals of a Sportsman*, translated by Franklin Pierce Abbott.
1886	Adams, Charles F., Jr., and Henry Adams. *Chapters of Erie, and Other Essays*. Hardy. *The Mayor of Casterbridge*. Norris. *A Bachelor's Blunder*. Remsen, Ira. *An Introduction to the Study of Chemistry*. Symonds. *Renaissance in Italy: The Catholic Reaction*.
1887	Norris. *Major and Minor*.
1888	Norris. *The Rogue*. Symonds. *Renaissance in Italy: Italian Literature*.
1890	James, William. *Principles of Psychology*. Jerome, Jerome K. *The Idle Thoughts of an Idle Fellow*. Jerome. *Stage-land*. Jerome. *Three Men in a Boat (To Say Nothing of the Dog)*, illustrated by A. Frederics.
1891	Duruy, Victor. *The History of the Middle Ages*, translated by Emily Henrietta Whitney and Margaret Dwight Whitney. Jerome. *Diary of a Pilgrimage*. Jerome. *On the Stage—and Off*. Jerome. *Told after Supper*. Kemble. *Further Records, 1848–1883*. Meyer, Annie Nathan, ed. *Woman's Work in America*.
1894	Duruy. *History of Modern Times, from the Fall of Constantinople to the French Revolution*, translated by Edwin A. Grosvenor. Ford, Paul Leicester. *The Honorable Peter Stirling and What People Thought of Him*. Hope, Anthony. *A Change of Air*. Hope. *The Dolly Dialogues*. Hope. *The Indiscretion of the Duchess: Being a Story Concerning Two Ladies, a Nobleman, and a Necklace*. Hope. *The Prisoner of Zenda: Being the History of Three Months in the Life of an English Gentleman*, illustrated by Charles Dana Gibson. Jerome. *John Ingerfield, and Other Stories*. Johnson, Samuel. *History of Rasselas, Prince of Abyssinia*, edited by Oliver Farrar Emerson.
1895	Hope. *A Man of Mark*. Hope. *Sport Royal, and Other Stories*. Nevinson, Henry Woodd. *Neighbors of Ours: Slum Stories of London*. Paulsen, Friedrich. *Introduction to Philosophy*, translated by Frank Thilly. Wells, H. G. *The Time Machine*.
1896	Buchan, John. *Sir Quixote of the Moors: Being Some Account of an Episode in the Life of the Sieur De Rohaine*.

Francke, Kuno. *Social Forces in German Literature: A Study in the History of Civilization.*

Gerstäcker, Friedrich. *Irrfahrten,* edited by Marian P. Whitney.

1897 Jerome. *Sketches in Lavender, Blue, and Green.*

Jhering, Rudolf von. *The Evolution of the Aryan,* translated by Adolphus Drucker.

Voynich, E. L. *The Gadfly.*

1898 Beers, Henry A. *A History of English Romanticism in the Eighteenth Century.*

Hope. *Rupert of Hentzau, from the Memoirs of Fritz von Tarlenheim.*

1899 James. *Talks to Teachers on Psychology, and to Students on Some of Life's Ideals.*

Lucas, E. V. *The Open Road: A Little Book for Wayfarers.*

1901 Beers. *A History of English Romanticism in the Nineteenth Century.*

Bücher, Karl. *Industrial Evolution,* translated by Samuel Morley Wickett.

Dowden, Edward. *Puritan and Anglican: Studies in Literature.*

Gissing, George. *Our Friend the Charlatan.*

Schiller, Friedrich. *Die Jungfrau von Orleans.*

1903 Norris. *Lord Leonard the Luckless.*
Owen, Rye. *Red-Headed Gill.*
Stevenson, Burton E. *The Holladay Case.*
Tarde, Gabriel. *The Laws of Imitation,* translated by Elsie Clews Parsons.
Townsend, Edward W. *A Summer in New York: A Love Story Told in Letters.*

1904 Bacon, John Harwood. *The Pursuit of Phyllis,* illustrated by H. Latimer Brown.
Loomis, Charles Battell. *More Cheerful Americans,* illustrated by Florence Scovel Shinn, Fanny Y. Cory, F. R. Gruger, and May Wilson Watkins.
Quick, Herbert. *Aladdin and Company.*
Sinclair, May. *The Divine Fire.*

Cover design for the Holt edition of the controversial first novel by the Irish writer, translator, and composer E. L. Voynich. The author's British publisher, William Heinemann, allowed the Holt edition to come out first (in June 1897) because he was concerned about public response in England to the anticlerical message of the novel (Princeton University Library).

1905   Brooke, Stopford A. *On Ten Plays of Shakespeare.*
       Deledda, Grazia. *After the Divorce: A Romance,* translated by Maria Hornor Lansdale.
       Hale, Edward Everett, Jr. *Dramatists of To-day.*
       Jackson, Charles Tenney. *Losers' Luck: Being the Questionable Enterprises of a Yachtsman, a Princess, and Certain Filibusters in Central America.*
       Williamson, C. N., and A. M. Williamson. *The Princess Passes: A Romance of a Motor-car.*

1906   Bacon, Dolores. *A King's Divinity.*
       Beebe, William. *The Log of the Sun: A Chronicle of Nature's Year,* illustrated by Walter King Stone.
       Brooks, Hildegard. *The Larky Furnace, and Other Adventures of Sue Betty,* illustrated by Peter Newell.
       De Morgan, William. *Joseph Vance: An Ill-written Autobiography.*
       Hobhouse, L. T. *Morals in Evolution: A Study in Comparative Ethics.*
       Lucas. *The Friendly Town: A Little Book for the Urbane.*
       Merriam, George Spring. *The Negro and the Nation: A History of American Slavery and Enfranchisement.*
       Olmsted, Stanley. *The Nonchalante: Casual Data Touching the Career of Dixie Bilton, Operettensängerin at Beilmar.*
       Sinclair. *Superseded.*
       Stevenson. *Affairs of State.*

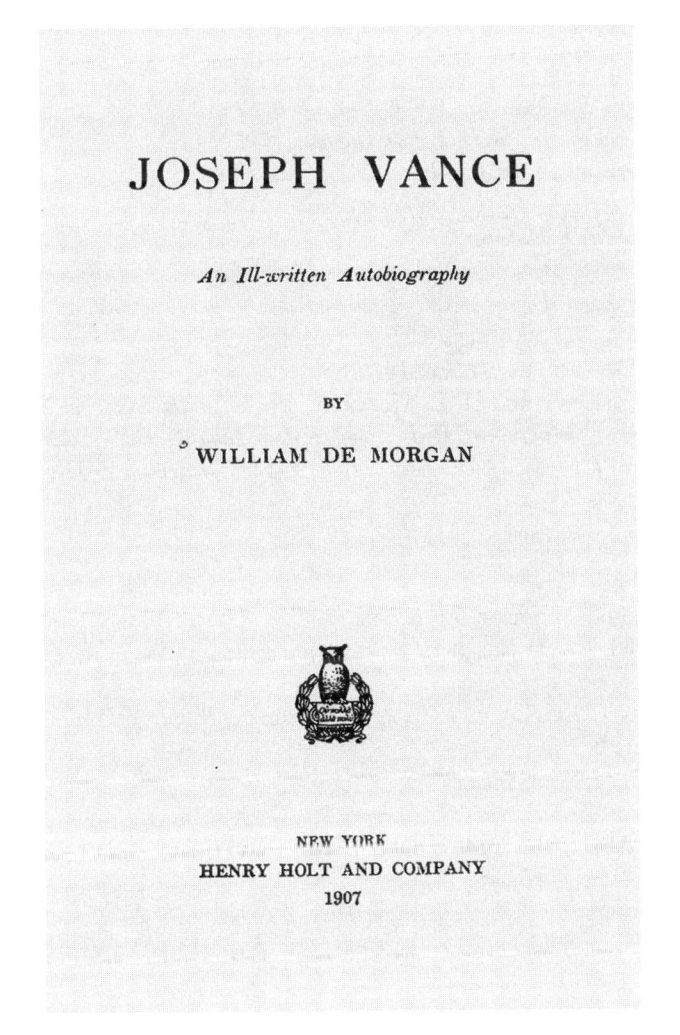

Title page for the first novel, originally published in 1906, by the British novelist for whom Holt was the American publisher (Rutgers University Library)

Selected Holt Titles, 1866–1946

1907
Benson, A. C. *Memoirs of Arthur Hamilton*.
De Morgan. *Alice-for-Short*.
Fisher, Dorothy Canfield. *Gunhild*.
Kellogg, Vernon L. *Darwinism To-day: A Discussion of Present-day Scientific Criticism of the Darwinian Selection Theories, Together with a Brief Account of the Principal Other Proposed Auxiliary and Alternative Theories of Species-forming*.
Neumann, Angelo. *Personal Recollections of Wagner*, translated by Edith Livermore.
Sinclair. *The Helpmate*.

1908
Barron, Edward. *The Lost Goddess*.
De Morgan. *Somehow Good*.
Dewey, John, and James H. Tufts. *Ethics*.
Krehbiel, Henry E. *Chapters of Opera*.

1909
Coolidge, Mary Roberts. *Chinese Immigration*.
De Morgan. *It Can Never Happen Again*.
Gordon, Kate. *Esthetics*.
Thomson, J. Arthur. *Darwinism and Human Life: The South African Lectures for 1909*.
Yung, Wing. *My Life in China and America*.

1910
Beebe, Mary Blair, and William Beebe. *Our Search for a Wilderness: An Account of Two Ornithological Expeditions to Venezuela and to British Guiana*.
Blackwood, Algernon Henry. *The Education of Uncle Paul*.
Brownell, Gertrude Hall. *The Unknown Quantity*.
De Morgan. *An Affair of Dishonor*.
Dewey. *The Influence of Darwin on Philosophy, and Other Essays in Contemporary Thought*.
Gillmore, Inez Haynes. *Phoebe and Ernest*, illustrated by R. F. Schabelitz.
Hamilton, Clayton. *The Theory of the Theatre, and Other Principles of Dramatic Criticism*.
Hazen, Charles Downer. *Europe since 1815*.
La Monte, Robert Rives, and H. L. Mencken. *Men versus the Man: A Correspondence between Robert Rives La Monte, Socialist, and H. L. Mencken, Individualist*.
Rolland, Romain. *Jean-Christophe: Dawn, Morning, Youth, Revolt*, translated by Gilbert Cannan.

1911
Bergson, Henri. *Creative Evolution*.
De Morgan. *A Likely Story*.
Geddes, Patrick, and Thomson. *Evolution*.
Haggard, H. Rider. *The Mahatma and the Hare*, illustrated by W. T. Horton and H. M. Brock.
Jacks, L. P. *The Alchemy of Thought*.
Jordan, David Starr. *The Stability of Truth: A Discussion of Reality as Related to Thought and Action*.
Macaulay, Rose. *The Valley Captives*.
Mercier, Charles. *Crime and Insanity*.
Middleton, George. *Embers, with The Failures, The Gargoyle, In His House, Madonna, The Man Masterful: One-act Plays of Contemporary Life*.
Myres, J. L. *The Dawn of History*.
Rolland. *Jean-Christophe in Paris: The Marketplace, Antoinette, The House*, translated by Cannan.
Semple, Ellen Churchill. *Influences of Geographic Environment on the Basis of Ratzel's System of Anthropo-geography*.
Yerkes, Robert M. *Introduction to Psychology*.
Yerkes. *Methods of Studying Vision in Animals*.

1912   Davids, Caroline A. F. Rhys. *Buddhism: A Study of the Buddhist Norm.*
Fisher. *A Montessori Mother.*
Fisher. *The Squirrel-Cage,* illustrated by John Alonzo Williams.
Housman, Laurence. *King John of Jingalo: The Story of a Monarch in Difficulties.*
Huxley, T. H. *Selections from Huxley,* edited by C. Alphonso Smith.
Macaulay. *Views and Vagabonds.*
Mather, Frank Jewett, Jr. *The Collectors: Being Cases Mostly under the Ninth and Tenth Commandments.*
Stevenson, ed. *The Home Book of Verse, American and English, 1580–1912.*
Strachey, Lytton. *Landmarks in French Literature.*
Thomson. *The Biology of the Seasons,* illustrated by William Smith.

1913   Benda, Julien. *The Yoke of Pity (L'Ordination),* translated by Cannan.
Dix, Beulah Marie. *Mother's Son.*
Lichtenberger, Henri. *Germany and Its Evolution in Modern Times,* illustrated by A. M. Ludovici.
MacDonald, William. *From Jefferson to Lincoln.*
Montague, C. E. *The Morning's War.*
Nexø, Martin Andersen. *Pelle the Conqueror: Boyhood,* translated by Jessie Muir and Bernard Miall.
Simkhovitch, Vladimir G. *Marxism versus Socialism.*

1914   De Morgan. *When Ghost Meets Ghost.*
Fisher. *Mothers and Children.*
Henderson, Archibald. *The Changing Drama. Contributions and Tendencies.*
Nexø. *Pelle the Conqueror: Apprenticeship,* translated by Muir and Miall.
Rolland. *Musicians of To-day,* translated by Mary Blaiklock.
Strunsky, Simeon. *Belshazzar Court; or, Village Life in New York City.*
Thomson. *The Wonder of Life.*

1915   Clark, Barrett H. *British and American Drama of To-day.*
Dewey. *German Philosophy and Politics.*
Du Bois, W. E. B. *The Negro.*
Fisher. *The Bent Twig.*
Fisher. *Hillsboro People.*
Frost, Robert. *A Boy's Will.*
Frost. *North of Boston.*
Kellogg and Rennie Wilbur Doane. *Elementary Textbook of Economic Zoology and Entomology.*

Title page for the 1910 edition of the first part (1905–1906) in the French writer's novel sequence presenting the life story of a German musician, Jean-Christophe Kraft (Rutgers University Library)

Lippmann, Walter. *The Stakes of Diplomacy.*
Morgan, T. H. *The Mechanism of Mendelian Heredity.*
Nexø. *Pelle the Conqueror: The Great Struggle,* translated by Muir and Miall.
Stevenson. *Little Comrade: A Tale of the Great War.*
Wald, Lillian D. *The House on Henry Street,* illustrated by Abraham Phillips.
Walling, William English. *The Socialists and the War.*

1916
Burke, Thomas. *Nights in London.*
Burton, Richard. *Bernard Shaw: The Man and the Mask.*
Charnwood, G. R. B., Baron. *Abraham Lincoln.*
Cleghorn, Sarah N. *The Spinster: A Novel Wherein a Nineteenth Century Girl Finds Her Place in the Twentieth.*
Colum, Padraic. *Wild Earth, and Other Poems.*
Cook, Edward, Sir. *Delane of the Times.*
Corbett, Elizabeth F. *Cecily and the Wide World: A Novel of American Life Today.*
de la Mare, Walter. *The Listeners, and Other Poems.*
Fisher. *The Real Motive.*
Francke. *The German Spirit.*
Frost. *Mountain Interval.*
Krows, Arthur Edwin. *Play Production in America.*
Nexø. *Pelle the Conqueror: Daybreak,* translated by Muir and Miall.
Rolland. *Handel,* translated by A. Edgefield Hull.
Sandburg, Carl. *Chicago Poems.*
Untermeyer, Louis. *"–And Other Poets."*
Yerkes. *The Mental Life of Monkeys and Apes: A Study of Ideational Behavior.*
Yost, Casper S. *Patience Worth: A Psychic Mystery.*

1917
Daudet, Alphonse. *Tartarin sur les Alpes.*
de la Mare. *Peacock Pie: A Book of Rhymes.*
Fisher. *Understood Betsy.*
Hamilton. *Problems of the Playwright.*
Hazen. *The French Revolution and Napoleon.*
Olgin, M. J. *The Soul of the Russian Revolution.*
Quiller-Couch, Arthur Thomas, Sir. *Notes on Shakespeare's Workmanship.*
Richardson, Henry Handel. *The Fortunes of Richard Mahony.*
Salter, William M. *Nietzsche, the Thinker.*
Sherman, Stuart P. *On Contemporary Literature.*

1918
Anthony, Joseph. *Rekindled Fires.*
Beebe, William. *Jungle Peace.*
Curran, Pearl Pollard. *Hope Trueblood, by Patience Worth, Communicated through Mrs. John H. Curran,* ed. by Casper S. Yost.
Davis, J. Frank. *Almanzar.*
Pumpelly. *My Reminiscences.*
Sandburg. *Cornhuskers.*
Strunsky. *Professor Latimer's Progress: A Novel of Contemporaneous Adventure,* illustrated by J. Ormsbee.
Trotsky, Leon. *Our Revolution: Essays on Working-class and International Revolution, 1904–1917.*
Widdemer, Margaret. *You're Only Young Once.*

1919
Burke. *Out and About London.*
De Morgan, William, and Evelyn De Morgan. *The Old Madhouse.*
Fisher. *The Day of Glory.*

Gillmore. *The Happy Years,* illustrated by R. M. Crosby, Gayle Porter Hoskins, and Harvey Dunn.

Hobson, J. A. *Richard Cobden, the International Man.*

Lippmann. *The Political Scene: An Essay on the Victory of 1918.*

Mackinder, H. J. *Democratic Ideals and Reality: A Study in the Politics of Reconstruction.*

Muir, Ramsay. *National Self-government: Its Growth and Principles, the Culmination of Modern History.*

Ransom, John Crowe. *Poems about God.*

Raymond, E. T. *Uncensored Celebrities.*

Robertson, C. Grant. *Bismarck.*

Rolland. *Colas Breugnon,* translated by Katherine Miller.

Russell, Bertrand. *Proposed Roads to Freedom: Socialism, Anarchism and Syndicalism.*

Thomson. *Secrets of Animal Life.*

Untermeyer. *The New Era in American Poetry.*

Wilson, Romer. *Martin Schüler.*

1920
Benét, Stephen Vincent. *Heavens and Earth.*

Bergson. *Mind-energy: Lectures and Essays,* translated by H. Wilden Carr.

Croce, Benedetto. *Ariosto, Shakespeare, and Corneille,* translated by Douglas Ainslie.

de la Mare, *Collected Poems, 1901–1918.*

De Morgan, William, and Evelyn De Morgan. *The Old Man's Youth and the Young Man's Old Age.*

Dewey. *Reconstruction in Philosophy.*

Einstein, Albert. *Relativity: The Special and General Theory,* translated by Robert W. Lawson.

Hewlett, Maurice. *The Light Heart.*

Nexø. *Ditte: Girl Alive!* translated by Richard Thirsk.

Raymond, E. T. *All and Sundry.*

Sarett, Lew. *Many, Many Moons: A Book of Wilderness Poems.*

Smith, Preserved. *The Age of the Reformation.*

Thomson. *The System of Animate Nature: The Gifford Lectures Delivered in the University of St. Andrews in the Years 1915 and 1916.*

Turner, Frederick Jackson. *The Frontier in American History.*

Yerkes and Clarence S. Yoakum, eds. *Army Mental Tests.*

1921
Adams, George Burton. *Constitutional History of England.*

Anthony. *The Gang.*

Beebe, William. *Edge of the Jungle.*

Benchley, Robert. *Of All Things!*

Benét. *The Beginning of Wisdom.*

Doolittle, Hilda (H.D.). *Hymen.*

Harrison, Frederic. *Novissima Verba: Last Words 1920.*

Hobhouse. *The Rational Good.*

Nexø. *Ditte: Daughter of Man,* translated by A. G. Chater and Thirsk.

Rolland. *Clerambault: The Story of an Independent Spirit during the War,* translated by Miller.

Thomson. *The Control of Life.*

Woodworth, Robert S. *Psychology: A Study of Mental Life.*

1922
Benchley. *Love Conquers All.*

Benét. *Young People's Pride.*

Croce. *The Poetry of Dante,* translated by Ainslie.

de la Mare. *Down-Adown-Derry: A Book of Fairy Poems.*

de la Mare. *The Veil, and Other Poems.*

Dewey. *Human Nature and Conduct: An Introduction to Social Psychology.*

Hobhouse. *The Elements of Social Justice.*

Housman, A. E. *Last Poems.*
Housman. *A Shropshire Lad,* authorized edition.
Jespersen, Otto. *Language: Its Nature, Development and Origin.*
Koch, Frederick H., ed. *Carolina Folk-plays.*
Nexø. *Ditte: Towards the Stars,* translated by Asta Kenney and Rowland Kenney.
Proust, Marcel. *Swann's Way,* translated by C. K. Scott Moncrieff.
Rolland. *Pierre and Luce,* translated by Charles de Kay.
Spitteler, Carl. *Two Little Misogynists,* translated by Mme. la Vicomtesse de Roquette-Buisson.
Stilson, Charles B., and Charles Beahan. *The Island God Forgot.*
Stirling, A. M. W. *William De Morgan and His Wife.*
Tyler, G. Vere. *Children of Transgression.*

1923
Benét. *Jean Huguenot.*
Benét. *King David.*
Frank, Tenney. *A History of Rome.*
Frost. *New Hampshire.*
Mann, Thomas. *Bashan and I,* translated by Herman George Scheffauer.
Mather. *A History of Italian Painting.*
Nevins, Allan, ed. *American Social History as Recorded by British Travellers.*
Nitti, Francesco Saverio. *The Decadence of Europe,* translated by Fred Brittain.
Rostand, Edmond. *Cyrano de Bergerac,* translated by Brian Hooker.
Sterling, George. *Selected Poems.*

1924
Forbes, Rosita. *The Sultan of the Mountains: The Life Story of Raisuli.*
Koch, ed. *Carolina Folk-plays: Second Series.*
Stern, William. *Psychology of Early Childhood up to the Sixth Year of Age,* translated by Anna Barwell.
Van Rensselaer, John King, Mrs., and Frederic Van de Water. *The Social Ladder.*

1925
Benchley. *Pluck and Luck.*
Harden, Maximilian. *I Meet My Contemporaries,* translated by William C. Lawton.
Locy, William A. *The Growth of Biology: Zoology from Aristotle to Cuvier, Botany from Theophrastus to Hofmeister, Physiology from Harvey to Claude Bernard.*
Morgan, C. Lloyd. *Life, Mind, and Spirit: Being the Second Course of the Gifford Lectures, Delivered in the University of St. Andrews in the Year 1923, under the General Title of Emergent Evolution.*
Rolland. *The Soul Enchanted: Annette and Sylvie,* translated by Ben Ray Redman.
Rolland. *The Soul Enchanted: Summer,* translated by Eleanor Stimson Brooks and Van Wyck Brooks.
Rostand. *The Far Princess,* translated by John Heard Jr.
Stevenson, ed. *The Home Book of Modern Verse.*
Ward, Christopher. *Foolish Fiction.*

1926
Bunin, Ivan. *Mitya's Love,* translated by Madeleine Boyd.
Manly, John Matthews. *Some New Light on Chaucer: Lectures Delivered at the Lowell Institute.*
Rolland. *The Game of Love and Death,* translated by Eleanor Stimson Brooks.
Sitwell, Edith. *Poetry and Criticism.*
Vidal de La Blache, Paul. *Principles of Human Geography,* translated by Millicent Todd Bingham.

1927
Benchley. *The Early Worm.*
Busbey, L. White. *Uncle Joe Cannon: The Story of a Pioneer American.*
de la Mare. *Selected Poems.*
de la Mare. *Stuff and Nonsense, and So On.*

Dewey. *The Public and Its Problems.*
Laski, Harold. *Communism.*
Lehmann, Rosamond. *Dusty Answer.*
Mather. *Modern Painting: A Study of Tendencies.*
Noyes, Alfred. *New Essays and American Impressions.*
Rolland. *The Soul Enchanted: Mother and Son,* translated by Van Wyck Brooks.
Salvemini, Gaetano. *The Fascist Dictatorship in Italy.*

1928
Benchley. *20,000 Leagues Under the Sea; or, David Copperfield.*
Davies, Rhys. *The Withered Root.*
Dewey. *The Philosophy of John Dewey,* edited by Joseph Ratner.
Frost. *West-Running Brook.*
Morand, Paul. *The Living Buddha,* translated by Boyd.
Read, Herbert. *English Prose Style.*
Robertson, E. Arnot. *Cullum.*
The Sacco-Vanzetti Case: Transcript of the Record of the Trial of Nicola Sacco and Bartolomeo Vanzetti in the Courts of Massachusetts and Subsequent Proceedings, 1920–7, 5 volumes.
Scott-James, R. A. *The Making of Literature: Some Principles of Criticism Examined in the Light of Ancient and Modern Theory.*
Squire, J. C. *Contemporary American Authors.*
Van Loon, Hendrik Willem. *Life and Times of Pieter Stuyvesant.*

1929
Dewey. *Characters and Events: Popular Essays in Social and Political Philosophy,* edited by Ratner.
France, Anatole. *Rabelais,* translated by Ernest Boyd.
Freeman, H. W. *Joseph and His Brethren.*
Hesse, Hermann. *Steppenwolf,* translated by Basil Creighton.
Pintner, Rudolf. *Educational Psychology.*
Reid, Forrest. *Walter de la Mare: A Critical Study.*
Valle-Inclán, Ramón del. *The Tyrant (Tirano Banderas), a Novel of Warm Lands,* translated by Margarita Pavitt.

1930
Langer, Susanne K. *The Practice of Philosophy.*
Lehmann. *A Note in Music.*
Mérimée, Ernest. *A History of Spanish Literature,* translated, revised, and enlarged by S. Griswold Morley.
Smith, Preserved. *A History of Modern Culture: The Great Renewal, 1543–1687.*

1931
Drinkwater, John. *Inheritance.*
Holt, Edwin B. *Animal Drive and the Learning Process: An Essay toward Radical Empiricism.*
Schweitzer, Albert. *The Mysticism of Paul the Apostle,* translated by William Montgomery.
Semple. *The Geography of the Mediterranean Region: Its Relation to Ancient History.*

1932
Chase, Mary Ellen. *A Goodly Heritage.*
Hazen. *The French Revolution.*
Komisarjevsky, Theodore. *The Costume of the Theatre.*
Lehmann. *Invitation to the Waltz.*
Petrie, Flinders. *Seventy Years in Archaeology.*
Tillich, Paul. *The Religious Situation,* translated by H. Richard Niebuhr.
Turner. *The Significance of Sections in American History.*
Wölfflin, Heinrich. *Principles of Art History: The Problem of the Development of Style in Later Art,* translated by M. D. Hottinger.

Selected Holt Titles, 1866–1946

1933 Gwynn, Stephen. *The Life and Friendships of Dean Swift.*
Kästner, Erich. *Emil und die Detektive,* edited by Lilian L. Stroebe and Ruth J. Hofrichter.
Murry, John Middleton. *Reminiscences of D. H. Lawrence.*
Rolland. *The Soul Enchanted: The Death of a World,* translated by Amalia De Alberti.
Schweitzer. *Out of My Life and Thought: An Autobiography,* translated by Charles Thomas Campion.
Tufts. *America's Social Morality: Dilemmas of the Changing Mores.*
Waddell, Helen. *Peter Abelard.*

1934 Jaspers, Karl. *Man in the Modern Age,* translated by Eden Paul and Cedar Paul.
Rolland. *The Soul Enchanted: A World in Birth,* translated by De Alberti.
Smith, Preserved. *A History of Modern Culture: The Enlightenment, 1687–1776.*

1935 Bergson. *The Two Sources of Morality and Religion,* translated by R. Ashley Audra, Cloudesley Brereton, and W. Horsfall Carter.
Finer, Herman. *Mussolini's Italy.*
Rader, Melvin M. *A Modern Book of Esthetics.*
Strong, Anna Louise. *I Change Worlds: The Remaking of an American.*
Turner. *The United States, 1830–1850: The Nation and Its Sections,* edited by M. H. Crissey, Max Farrand, and Avery Craven.

1936 Davenport, Charles B. *How We Came By Our Bodies.*
de la Mare. *Poems, 1919 to 1934.*
Frost. *A Further Range.*
Read, Conyers. *The Tudors: Personalities and Practical Politics in Sixteenth Century England.*
Schweitzer. *Indian Thought and Its Development,* translated by Lilian M. Rigby Russell.

1937 Van Doren, Mark. *The Last Look, and Other Poems.*

1938 de la Mare. *Memory, and Other Poems.*
Dewey. *Logic: The Theory of Inquiry.*
Duhamel, Georges. *The Pasquier Chronicles,* translated by Béatrice de Holthoir.
Stewart, George R. *East of the Giants.*

1939 Du Bois. *Black Folk, Then and Now: An Essay in the History and Sociology of the Negro Race.*
Gorki, Maxim. *A Book of Short Stories,* edited by Avrahm Yarmolinsky and Baroness Moura Budberg.
Mather. *Western European Painting of the Renaissance.*
Schweitzer. *Christianity and the Religions of the World.*
Smart, Christopher. *Rejoice in the Lamb: A Song from Bedlam,* edited by William Force Stead.
Van Doren. *Collected Poems.*
Van Doren. *Shakespeare.*

1940 Ameringer, Oscar. *If You Don't Weaken: The Autobiography of Oscar Ameringer.*
Ciardi, John. *Homeward to America.*
Duhamel. *Cécile Pasquier,* translated by Holthoir.
Guérard, Albert. *Preface to World Literature.*
Housman. *The Collected Poems of A. E. Housman.*

1941	de la Mare. *Collected Poems.* Sarett. *The Collected Poems of Lew Sarett.* Van Doren. *The Mayfield Deer.*
1942	Cannon, Le Grand. *Look to the Mountain.* Corwin, Norman. *Thirteen by Corwin: Radio Dramas by Norman Corwin.* Frost. *A Witness Tree.* Hargrove, Marion. *See Here, Private Hargrove.* Trumbull, Robert. *The Raft.*
1943	Frost. *Come In and Other Poems,* edited by Untermeyer. Pyle, Ernie. *Here Is Your War,* illustrated by Carol Johnson.
1944	Cohen, Morris Raphael. *A Preface to Logic.* Corwin. *More by Corwin: 16 Radio Dramas.* Cummings, E. E. *1 x 1.* Krutch, Joseph Wood. *Samuel Johnson.* Kunitz, Stanley. *Passport to the War.* Van Doren. *The Seven Sleepers, and Other Poems.*
1945	Frost. *A Masque of Reason.* Mauldin, Bill. *Up Front.* Pyle. *Brave Men.*
1946	Belloc, Hilaire. *The Servile State.* Cummings. *Santa Claus–A Morality.* Mauriac, François. *Woman of the Pharisees,* translated by Gerard Hopkins. Schorer, Mark. *William Blake: The Politics of Vision.* Van Doren. *The Noble Voice: A Study of Ten Great Poems.*

Early Years

BEGINNINGS

The New York Evening Post *recounted the history of Henry Holt's publishing firm in one of a series of articles on publishing houses that ran in the mid 1870s.*

Henry Holt and Company

The readers of these sketches have already observed that almost every publishing house has its peculiar inspiration; each was founded upon an idea differing from the ideas of other houses, and the ambition has been to excel in a certain line of publication, or in a certain style of conducting business.

Henry Holt, age twenty-five, in 1865, the year the publishing firm Leypoldt & Holt was established (from Henry Holt, Garrulities of an Octogenarian Editor, *1923; Thomas Cooper Library, University of South Carolina)*

There is a sort of mutual disagreement among the members of the book trade that really contributes to its harmony and success, for there is plenty of room for those who strive to do a great deal and do it as well as they can, as well as for those who strive to do well first and are satisfied to do only as much as is compatible with excellence. In bookmaking, as in almost every other kind of business, there may be said to exist two distinct classes, the æsthetic or eclectic and the commercial; and, although these are often subdivided or combined in the same house, these characteristics, as a rule, mark different publishing houses. We are strongly reminded of this by a survey of the work done by one of the youngest of the more respectable bookmaking houses of this century, Henry Holt & Co., a firm clearly belonging among the "eclectic philosophers" of the trade.

HENRY HOLT

Mr. Henry Holt was born in Baltimore in 1840. His family were among the early settlers of Connecticut, whence his father removed to Baltimore. Henry, when a child, was sent to New Haven, Conn., where he obtained most of his early education at General Russell's school. He was graduated from Yale College in the class of 1862. The next year he came to New York and studied law at the law school of Columbia College, from which he was graduated in 1864. While yet in the law school, unpractised in the mysteries of the legal profession, and literally briefless, Mr. Holt was married, and then he realized the disadvantage of waiting for clients. In fact he did not wait for them but cautiously turned his attention to other pursuits.

In 1863 he was introduced to Mr. George P. Putnam, who was then engaged in republishing Irving's "Sketch Book" in the elegant style which it finally assumed as the "Artist's Edition." The outlay was very heavy, and Mr. Putnam proposed to Mr. Holt to invest a few thousand dollars in the "Sketch Book" and receive a share of the profits. Mr. Holt accepted the offer, and after that he spent a part of his time assisting Mr. Putnam in his work and learning the trade which by the course of circumstances he was afterwards led to adopt as his profession. In fact, this was how and where Mr. Holt began as a publisher.

His intimate relations with Mr. Putnam led to further business connections. Mr. Putnam had begun the publication of the "Rebellion Record," having a joint interest with its editor, Mr. Frank Moore, and a Mr. Evans, who attended to the details of publishing. Mr. Evans desiring to leave New York, Mr. Holt purchased his interest, and became the active publisher, under Mr. Putnam's more experienced direction. Mr. Putnam was then in the internal revenue service, and devoted but little time to private business. This arrangement continued until the autumn of 1864, when both of them sold out their interest in the "Rebellion Record" to Mr. David Van Nostrand, who has since completed it and made it a special feature of his catalogues.

LEYPOLDT & HOLT

During the following year Mr. Holt remained out of business, and having the tastes and experience of a scholar rather than a man of affairs, succeeded in making some investments during that speculative period which reduced his patrimony to a figure that made business a pressing necessity. He had spent a part of his time in translating About's novel, "The Man with the Broken Ear." When completed he offered it to Mr. Frederic Leypoldt, who, while keeping a foreign bookstore in Philadelphia, had published a few books with such taste and discrimination as to give him a reputation among judicious people, and had just established a New York branch in a little room up-stairs at No. 646 Broadway. Mr. Leypoldt declined to publish it unless at Mr. Holt's risk, and so for a time the work was shelved. But this incident led to an acquaintance which ripened into business relations.

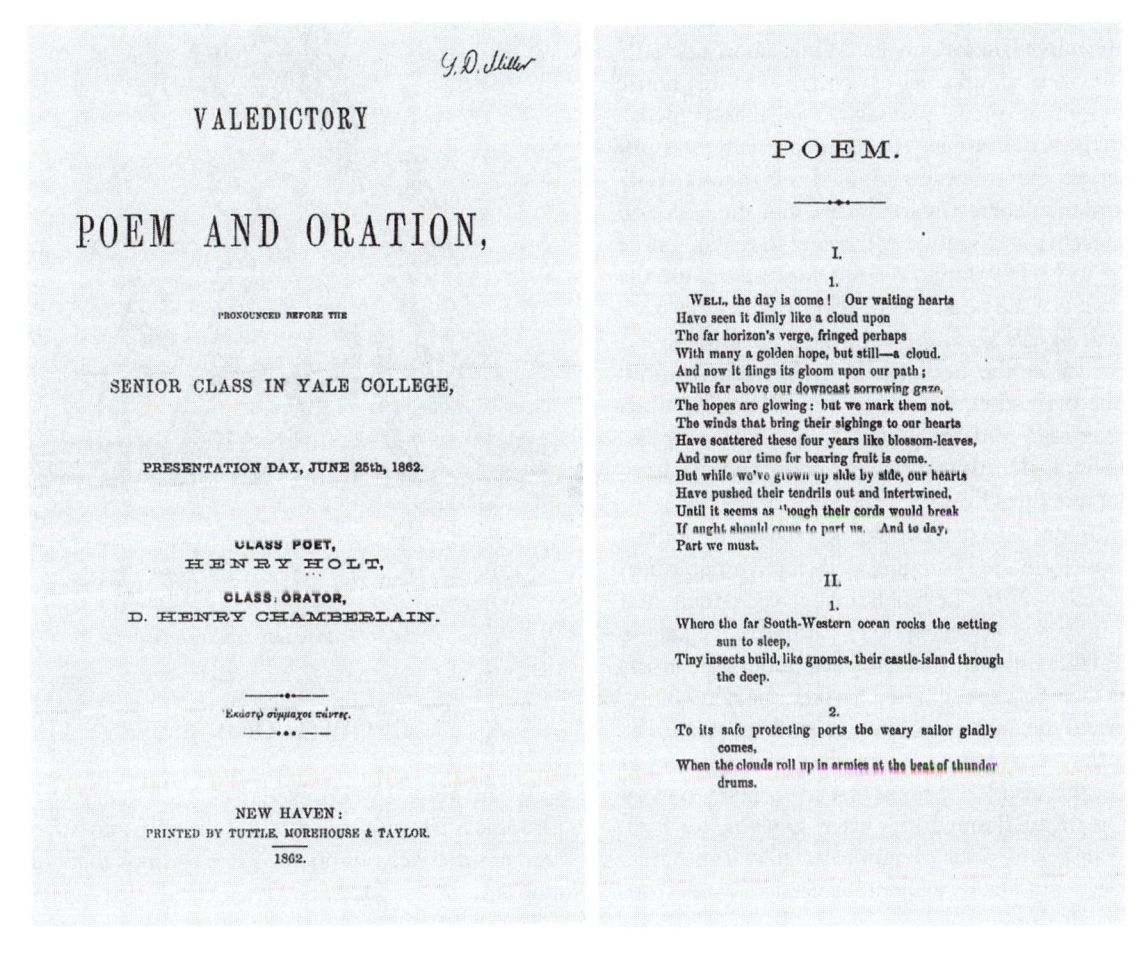

Title page and first page of the volume that includes Holt's poem for his graduating class at Yale. His eight-page valedictory is filled with expressions of affection for Yale, although he never got over not being invited to join the Skull and Bones senior society (Yale University Library).

In the fall of 1865, Mr. Holt entered Mr. Leypoldt's employment, and in January, 1866, they formed a partnership in the business of bookmaking. They began with about a score of their books upon their catalogue, but set sail with a flourish of trumpets which in after years caused them some amusement. For example, they announced several important works, which they had selected for early publication, but which further experience taught them would be utterly impracticable. Of the list then announced but a small part ever appeared, and they met with indifferent success. From the beginning, however, the house had the American agency for the Tauchnitz Collection of British Authors, which was of considerable relative importance in their early career, and has throughout all their vicissitudes been a source of steady, though now comparatively moderate, revenue.

They also, very early in their career, became (on account of the ill health of the owner) the active publishers of the standard school books for foreign languages, belonging to Mr. S. R. Urbino, of Boston, including Otto's French and German grammars, several series of French plays, Cuore's Italian grammar, and many miscellaneous books. While upon this subject of foreign textbooks, let us remark that this house has always made them a specialty, and has reaped a deserved reward from its efforts to present the most perfect series. The rule early adopted was to invite criticism in order to correct inaccuracies, and the attention of every teacher and scholar is directed to this in a note appended to each volume inviting suggestions for the improvement of the books. Whenever errors have been pointed out in this way, the publishers have made it a rule never to let the book go to press again without making the correction, if possible. It is a significant fact that the German and French courses at Harvard and Yale are supplied with text-books almost entirely from the catalogue of this house.

It was the fate of Leypoldt & Holt to be looked upon almost from the beginning as *the* foreign publishers and booksellers. Mr. Leypoldt being a German and being more or less versed in other European languages, while Mr. Holt was also well-informed, though he insists much less than his accomplished partner, the house naturally attracted the attention of foreign students and translators. As they good-naturedly observed of themselves in after years, this also led them at first to do many unwise things. They were flooded with letters applying for positions to translate all sorts of impracticable works–letters from college graduates without professions and from women of all degrees of inexperience. It soon became impossible to answer all these letters; they were forced to write a circular reply; and it is possible that that circular has passed through more editions than most of the publications of this or any other house.

The Holt Owl

Henry Holt and Company began using an owl device on title pages early in its history. Over the years the design changed, but the owl remained a constant. Although the owl has figured in several myths and legends with both good and bad connotations, it is probably correct to assume that in this instance the owl represents the "wise owl" associated with the Greek goddess Athena (known to Romans as Minerva). An "emblem of sagacity and bookish erudition," owls perching on books became a common motif in recent history, according to Jack Tresidder in *Dictionary of Symbols* (1998). Today Holt's paperback imprint is Owl Books.

Owl device from the title page of Aesop's Fables in French *(1864), which names Henry Holt and Company, F. W. Christern, and Carl Schönhof as publishers, although the copyright holder for the publication was Frederick Leypoldt*

GROWTH OF BUSINESS

In May, 1866, Leypoldt & Holt removed to 451 Broome Street, and entered more largely into the publication of miscellaneous books. The first book that bore their imprint was Charles G. Leland's translation of Eichendorff's "Aus dem Leben eines Taugenichts," under the name of "Memoirs of a Good-for-Nothing." The first edition is not yet sold, and a certain large dealer, with whom the name of the house is now good for thousands of dollars, requested payment for the paper in advance.

The first of the Turgénieff novels issued in this country was printed by them in the same year, and this list has proved to be one of the most creditable, though far from the most profitable of their ventures. They also concluded to print Mr. Holt's Translation of "The Man with the Broken Ear," which Mr. Leypoldt had before declined to do. When it came from the press the senior partner was surprised to find that it contained the following:

"DEAR LEYPOLDT:

"You have not forgotten that nearly two years ago, before our business connection was thought of, the risk of publishing this identical translation was 'respectfully declined' by you with that same courtesy whose exercise in frequent similar cases each one of us now tries so hard to shove on the other's shoulders. I hope that your surprise on reading this note of dedication will not interfere with your forgiving the pertinacity with which, through it, I still strive to make the book *yours*.

H.H.

"451 Broome street, May 16, 1867."

The book paid for itself in a reasonable time, and there has been a small but steady demand for it ever since.

Early in 1866 an agent of Bailliore of Paris applied for the co-operation of Leypoldt & Holt in selling their new edition of John Durand's translation of Taine's "Philosophy of Art," which had already been published in Europe. Later Mr. Durand, who was then in Paris, wrote to a friend in New York to find him an American publisher for a translation of the volume of Taine's "Italy" on "Rome and Naples," which he had already published in England. Leypoldt & Holt determined to take hold of these works, more as a labor of love than from the hope of profit. About the same time, Mr. Eugene Schuyler (whose translation of Turgénieff's "Fathers and Sons" had secured him the consulship to Moscow, and who is now secretary of the United States legation at St. Petersburg, and, by merit, a prospective Minister) and Mr. J. Safford Fiske (later consul at Edinburgh, and who has since translated Taine's "Pyrenees") began together the translation of Taine's "History of English Literature," which it was arranged that Leypoldt & Holt should publish, if the translators,

Title page for the second edition of Henry Holt's translation of the 1862 French novel L'Homme à l'oreille cassée, *with the dedication reprinted from the first edition (Rutgers University Library)*

who were then about going into foreign parts to take their respective offices, would find an English publisher to join in the enterprise. When they arrived in Europe they found that Mr. Henri Van Laun had also begun this translation. The three accordingly agreed to unite in the work, and estimates were sent for the American publishers' consideration. Later events prevented Messrs. Schuyler and Fiske from continuing the work, and it was left to Mr. Van Laun alone. Mr. Fiske, however, perfected the arrangement by which Leypoldt & Holt were to publish the book for this market, and it seems certain that had it not been for that arrangement no house in Great Britain could have been found to take it up, and that the English-speaking world would still be without it. There is reason to believe that it was refused by several British houses after Leypoldt & Holt expressed their readiness to undertake it, before Edmonstone & Douglas, of Edinburg, townsmen of the translator, went into it. In the summer of 1871, while Mr. Holt was then taking a vacation in the country, the plates of the book reached New York. He was written to for advice about the arrangements for publishing it. He had no confidence that it would ever be profitable, and expressed his disgust at having his quiet disturbed by so unimportant a project. There is an astonishing sequel to the story of this book. It has been one of the most successful works, in a pecuniary point of view, as well as one of the most meritorious, ever published by the house. M. Taine has been surprised by several voluntary remittances from the publishers, and recently said that the sums thus received from America amounted to four times as much as his profits on the English edition. He has paid the house the high compliment of confiding to them the arrangements for both Great Britain and America of his forthcoming work on the French Revolution. In connection with Taine's works the following extracts from a letter written by the house explain themselves:

"December 5, 1873.

"To the Editor of the Boston Advertiser:
"Sir: Your notice of Taine's Pyrenees, illustrated by Doré, contains the statement that Taine's works on Art and his History of English literature have been introduced to the American public *** in translations made in England.

"So far is this from being correct, that the first translation into English of a book by M. Taine was made by an American, Mr. John Durand. **

"Not only do we owe to an American the first translation of Taine ever made into English, but out of eleven volumes of his works now in English all published in America, seven are translated by Americans and only five have ever been published in England at all."

Another of the most notable and successful ventures of the house in its earlier days was Professor Pumpelly's account of his journey of five years around the world, called "Across America and Asia." Mr. Holt confesses that he undertook it with fear and trembling.

So much for some important and profitable books in which the house had no confidence. No less curious is the fact, which is, perhaps, characteristic of all publishing houses, that many books in which the firm professed the greatest confidence were scarcely heard of after they were printed. Indeed, Mr. Holt remarks that until an author's reputation is made, no one can prophesy what will be the fate of his or her books.

IMPORTANT CHANGES

Leypoldt & Holt remained in Broome street until May, 1870, when they removed to No. 25 Bond street, where the house has been situated ever since. Meantime they had begun the monthly publication of the "Literary Bulletin and Trade Circular," which has since absorbed the old "Publishers' Circular." This always has been under the exclusive management of Mr. Leypoldt, and so well has it been conducted that long ago it was recognised by all the book associations in this country as their official organ. As a guide to booksellers and book-buyers, it is almost infallible, and has no equal. Before this time, and before the removal from Broome street, Mr. R. O. Williams had been in the service of the house. In January, 1871, he took an interest in the business, and the name of the firm was changed to Leypoldt, Holt & Williams. In April of that year Mr. Leypoldt, who had become so absorbed in his work upon the *Literary Bulletin* that he had little time or inclination for other duties, retired from the firm and abandoned bookmaking in order to devote himself entirely to his chosen work. Before leaving this part of the subject we ought to say that Mr. Holt speaks in the warmest terms of his old friend and partner. "No man deserves more credit for elevating the character of the book trade in this country than Frederic Leypoldt," he remarks, enthusiastically, "and I hope you will honor him with a separate article. As a publisher of books, and as conductor of the book trade journal, he has done a grand service."

When Mr. Leypoldt retired the firm became Holt & Williams. In 1872 they entered upon a project which Mr. Holt had long meditated. This was a series of books containing the works of fiction of the better character, in a style that should be attractive and unique. After many experiments in various sizes and designs they at last decided upon some designs made by Mr. Holt and began the well-known "Leisure Hour Series," which is now so popular. In 1873 Mr. Williams retired from the firm, and Mr. Holt continued the business with a friend whose connection was neither long nor active, under the name of Henry Holt & Company, which the house still retains.

Column of listings from Goulding's Business Directory of New York *(1872–1873) in which Holt's name is misspelled "Hoet"*

GRAND PROJECTS

In the autumn of 1873, Mr. Holt undertook the publication of John Stuart Mill's "Autobiography." A number of Mr. Mill's works had already been published in this country. James R. Osgood & Company had issued his "Liberty;" Lee & Shepard (succeeding the late W. V. Spencer) his "Dissertations and Discussions," "Examination of Sir William Hamilton's Philosophy," and a volume on Comte; Appleton & Co., his "Subjection of Women" and "Political Economy;" and Harper & Brothers his "Logic," and "Representative Government." Mr. Holt, who had always been a student and almost a disciple of Mill, had long regretted, in common with most literary people, that there was no uniform edition of Mill's works published in this country, and set to work to find means for accomplishing that object. He offered to purchase the plates of all the publishers. Harper & Brothers however, had begun a new edition of Mill's "Logic" in a style which could not be made uniform with the others. Accordingly Mr. Holt modified his plan so that it included only the non-technical works, excluding the "Logic" and "Political Economy." He purchased the other volumes and had the plates worked over in uniform style. Now, since the appearance of the posthumous volume, "Essays on Religion," Mr. Holt has the satisfaction of knowing that his thirteen-volume edition of Mill's miscellaneous works is the only uniform one at all approaching completeness, and that it is far in advance of any English edition of the same works. His edition of the posthumous volume contains Mill's "Essay on Berkeley," which has not yet appeared in any of the English books.

At the suggestion of Mr. Charles Astor Bristed, and by an arrangement with Scribner, Armstrong & Co., Mr. Holt hopes soon to publish a complete and uniform edition of Maine's works on "Institutions," and "Ancient Law," which Mr. Holt says will live much longer than he will. Another important publication is "Tylor's Primitive Culture."

In 1869, Mr. Urbino's health continuing poor, Mr. Holt's firm purchased his publication outright, including Otto's French and German Series, Sewell's Dictation Exercises, and a large number of French and German reading books. A year or two afterwards Mr. G. H. De Vries, of Boston, for whom this house had also been publishing a series of similar works, died, and the firm purchased his books of the estate. This gives the house probably the most important list in this line of publications.

A FEW OF HOLT'S BOOKS

It is impossible, in the space at our command today, to give a full list of the publications of this house. We therefore merely mention About's, Mrs. Alexander's, Auerbach's and Hardy's novels; Bristed's pleasant sketches, called a "Broken-Down Critic;" Brinton's "Myths of the New World," Chesney's "Military Biography," M. D. Conway's "Sacred Anthology" and "Earthward Pilgrimage," Professor Hiram Corson's "Handbook of Anglo-Saxon and Early English," Freeman's Historical Course, Professor Hadley's "Essays, Philological and Critical," Heine's works, the "Library of Foreign Poetry," the "Mental Photography Album" of which a beautiful holiday edition has been issued; Professor William G. Sumner's "History of American Currency," Martineau's Essays, Strauss's "Old Faith and New," and Stahr's "Life of Lessing." Of text-books there are Professor W. D. Whitney's German series; the German Conversation Grammar of Dr. Otto, with a vocabulary by L. Pylodet; Otto's French Grammar, a large series of French instruction books, also by Pylodet; Dr. S. Deutsch's Hebrew books, the "Ordo Classics," the admirable Tauchnitz Collection of British Authors and Asher's "Collection of English Authors."

Messrs. Henry Holt & Co. have lately made arrangements to republish in this country the *Fortnightly Review,* one of the ablest and most entertaining of the more thoughtful periodicals. Among their very recent publications–that beautiful book, "Vers de Société" is specially prominent.

Title page for the first American edition of the final volume in the 1859–1875 collection of the British philosopher's writings. Volumes one through four were first published in the United States by the Boston publisher W. V. Spencer, 1864–1867 (Rutgers University Library).

A BOOKMAKING HOUSE

Although less than ten years old, the house of Henry Holt & Co. is among the leading bookmakers of this country. Their plan always has been to adhere strictly to one branch of business, that of bookmaking, and with the exception of the specialties with Tauchnitz and Asher, they sell no books except their own. Beginning with a score of books upon their list, they have now more than three hundred. Mr. Holt says that of their whole list probably one-fifth have paid a large profit, one-fifth have never paid for printing, and the rest have barely paid their own expense. This decision may not hold with other houses, for Mr. Holt has published many books having no commercial value except in the author's estimation, simply because of their intrinsic worth. So discouraging at first were the results of his theory of business that after a two years' trial he almost decided that, to say the least, it was not a profitable one. Indeed, he said at that time if the next year did not bring him a better reward, he would enter some other business. The following year the profits of the concern increased more than fifty per centum, and the business improved at about that rate up to the year of panic, 1873–a good lesson to "rolling stones." It is a cause of satisfaction to know that a house founded on correct principles has had such an experience.

–"The Bookmakers: Reminiscences and Contemporary Sketches of American Publishers," *New York Evening Post,* 1874–1876

Early Reviews

Early titles published by Holt and Company–including abridgments, translations, novels, and science texts–were well received.

Holt & Co. have done the lovers of old English literature a good service by publishing a well-executed abridgment of Richardson's *Clarissa Harlowe*. The original comprised about 2400 pages; the abridgment, which is made by simply leaving out superfluous portions, without the change of a single word or the alteration of a sentence, tells the whole story within the compass of about 500 small pages. In this new form we doubt not the pathetic story of "the admirable Clarissa" will become familiar to many readers who would have lacked the courage to take it up in its original form. Too much praise can not be bestowed upon the skillful and conscientious manner in which the editor has performed a difficult and delicate task.

–*Harper's Weekly,* 8 August 1874

* * *

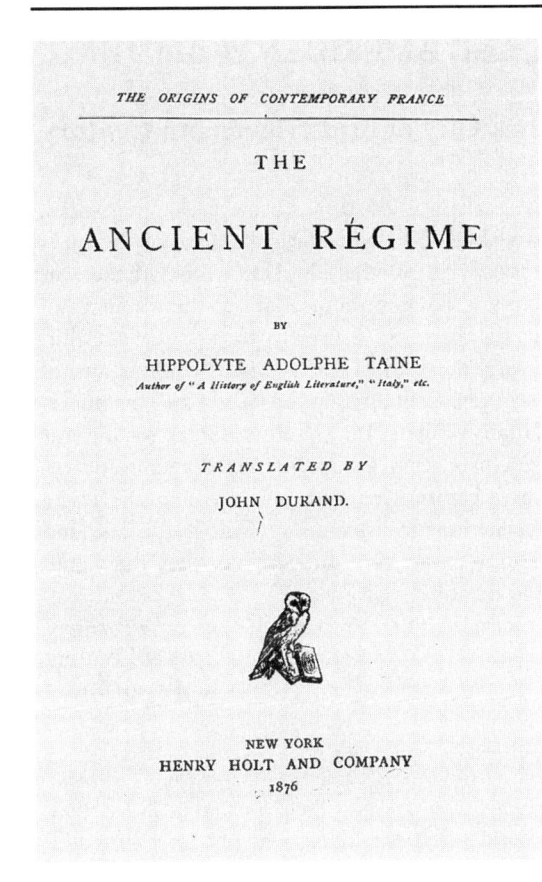

Title page for the first American edition of the first volume in Les Origines de la France contemporaine (1876–1885), which included an advertisement for other works by the French positivist that Holt published (Rutgers University Library)

A review of Jessie Fothergill's novel Probation, *published by Holt in 1879, appeared in the May 1880* Atlantic Monthly.

The writing of novels has come to be so definite a department of industry that idle people have begun to ask if there might not be some school or formal system by which young men and women of lively sensibilities could be trained as novelists. If any one wishes to be a painter or sculptor, it is argued, he enters a school of art, or places himself under the tuition of some master who will guide his talent and give him practical instruction in the laws of his art; why should not a novelist go to work in the same way, instead of blundering by himself and producing what any skillful master in the business could have shown was untrue and offensive to the canons of literary art? One could easily fancy a school of novel-writing, where the pupils would be set to work constructing tales . . . and were there such a school we think that Miss Fothergill would be recognized as one of the brightest and aptest scholars. *Probation* is a capital novel, well planned and well constructed, yet the incidents which make its crises are stock incidents which have been used again and again. A workman thrashes a rich man's son for insulting a young woman; the rich man gives a ball on his daughter's birthday, when he is on the eve of bankruptcy, and the festivities are arrested by the catastrophe; the favored lover overhears some words between his rival and the woman they love which he instantly misconstrues, and thereby spends two or three years in wretchedness; a young lady suddenly loses her property and station, and becomes a governess, to be accidentally discovered by her lover,—these are certainly not new inventions in novel-writing, and the plain catalogue of them here might easily persuade the reader that *Probation,* built upon such foundations, could hardly be more than a commonplace and conventional story. Conventional it may be called, but not commonplace, and it seems to us a singularly apt illustration of the truth that the inventive part of a story is really the least considerable part. It is like the underpinning of a house,—essential to the structure, but not very characteristic. A mature reader who takes up the Arabian Nights, for example, will very likely to be surprised at what he might call the poverty of invention and the simplicity of the expedients resorted to. A great number of modern stories are substantially the same in their groundwork; they use the common facts of the life they represent, and when a story is placed, as *Probation* is, in an English manufacturing town, one may look confidently for just such incidents as we have intimated, growing out of the relations between workmen and their employers. . . .

* * *

Eduard Hackel's Die natürlichen Pflanzenfamilien *(1887), translated by Frank Lamson-Scribner and Effie A. Southworth and published by Holt as* The True Grasses *in 1890, received a favorable notice in the November 1890* Atlantic Monthly.

[*The True Grasses* is a] special treatise, which, from the authority of the writer and the fullness of treatment, ought to be of great service in agricultural colleges. The editing and translating strike us as exceptionally good.

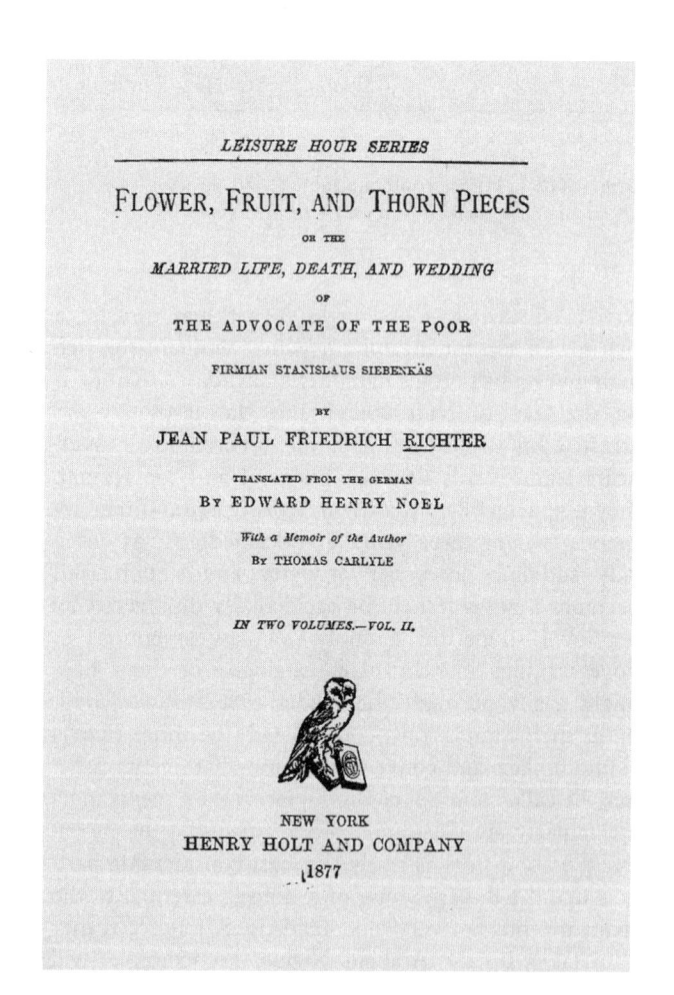

Title page for one of three books by the German Romantic writer that Holt published in 1877 (Rutgers University Library)

HOLT AND AMERICAN PUBLISHING

New York City at Mid Nineteenth Century

New York in 1866 showed many changes, social, political, and business, from the conditions of the quiet and more provincial city that I had known before the war. Notwithstanding the enormous losses to the resources of the country that had been caused by the waste of war during four years, the ruin of the Southern planters and of their business representatives in the North, and the undermining of many of their lines of business interests, the war had brought to certain groups of men larger resources than had ever before been known in the country. There was a great increase in ostentation of life in the city, and there came into existence a division of society that could be called plutocratic.

–George Haven Putnam, *Memories of a Publisher, 1865–1915* (New York & London: Putnam, 1915), pp. 21

* * *

The *Publishers' Weekly* office, located at 712 Broadway, just south of Astor Place, was not only functionally but geographically at the center of the American book-trade world. A few doors south were Henry Holt and Scribner's, across the street was E. P. Dutton; a few doors north were Dodd, Mead and Company and A. D. F. Randolph, and in near by Astor Place were Hurd and Houghton, John Wiley and Sons, and the site of the Leavitt Trade Sales. In the Bible House was the religious bookshop of Thomas Whitaker, while Macmillan's American agent was near by on Fifth Avenue. Farther away were the Harper House on Franklin Square, D. Appleton & Co. on lower Broadway, and G. P. Putnam's Sons at Fifth Avenue and Twenty-third Street. Such leaders as public-spirited William H. Appleton and the four enormously capable Harper brothers helped New York City to set the pace. Boston was second to New York as a publishing center, and Philadelphia third, with Cincinnati and Chicago the only other centers of note. [R. R.] Bowker estimated that in 1871 American book production was worth $40,000,000; and that in 1877 there were 800 publishers, 4,476 books copyrighted, and 10,000 retail bookstores. The book trade was still in the horse and buggy era, with no telephones or typewriters, but it was growing.

–E. McClung Fleming, *R. R. Bowker: Militant Liberal* (Norman: University of Oklahoma Press, 1952)

* * *

[The Holt & Co. office at 35 West Thirty-second Street was] much uptown, almost in a residential sec-

THE

MAGIC OF THE MIDDLE AGES

BY

VIKTOR RYDBERG

Translated from the Swedish

BY

AUGUST HJALMAR EDGREN

NEW YORK
HENRY HOLT AND COMPANY
1879

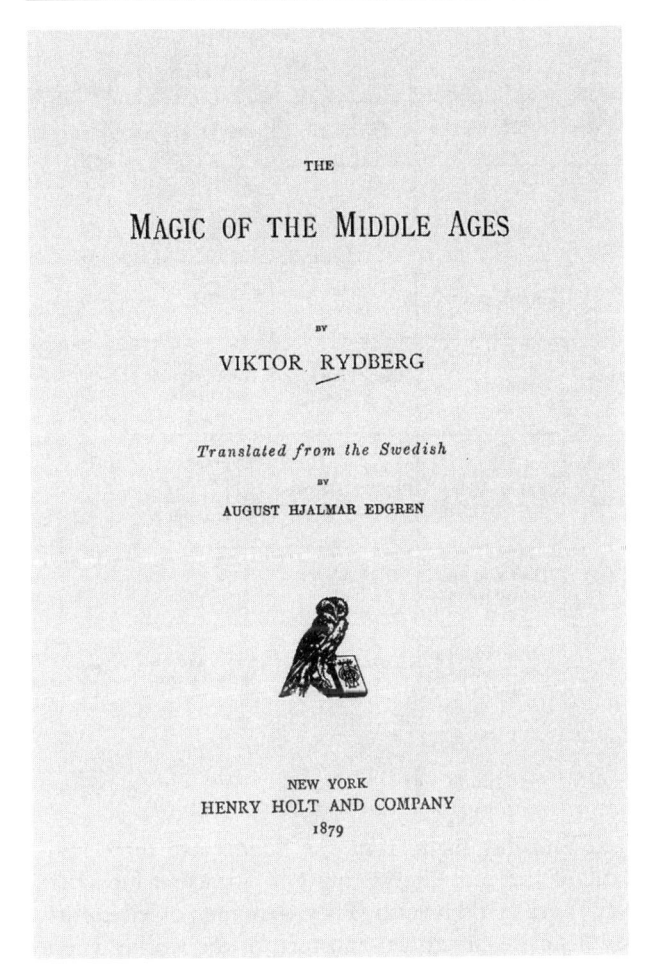

Title page for the only English-language edition of the Swedish writer's Medeltidens magi *(1865; Rutgers University Library)*

tion; for the great property movement at Forty-second Street had not yet begun, or at least the making of the Upton Centre was only at its beginning. Murray Hill was still the elect residential section. The Morgans, the Havemeyers, and many other magnates had their palatial residences on Madison Avenue from Twenty-eighth Street to Forty-second Street. In the same building were located . . . D. Appleton & Co., Henry Holt & Co., and the American branch of the Oxford University Press, making a representative publishing center.
–George H. Doran, *Chronicles of Barabbas, 1884–1934* (New York: Harcourt, Brace, 1935), pp. 35–36

* * *

When I bestowed the boon of my services on publishing at nine dollars a week in 1880–A.D. not B.C., as some might suspect–no association of publishers existed. The industry was then in "the horse and buggy era." It was also in what I might call the loving-cup era, for the relations between several of the leaders were so friendly that they dined together occasionally and drank from a loving-cup engraved with the names and common good wishes of–as I remember it–Harper, Scribner, Holt, Appleton and Putnam.

In those simple days publishers' letters were painfully written by hand in special copying ink and were then inserted between leaves of tissue paper which, after being wet with a brush and firmly pressed in a sort of vise, retained duplicates of the original letters. Manuscripts were manuscripts indeed, typewriters not being in common use. Telephones were hardly known and when they did come into general use required a vigorous cranking to get results.

* * *

The homes of New York's great publishing firms were then grouped together in the neighborhood of Astor Place and Broadway, where Appleton, Dodd, Mead & Co. and Scribner worked in friendly competition. Macmillan was near by in Fifth Avenue with Putnam and Dutton as pioneers northward in 23rd Street. Nearly all had flourishing retail departments, half of which have since been separated from them or abandoned. Frank N. Doubleday, then with Scribner, and later associated with S. S. McClure, Walter H. Page and other leaders, successfully conducted before long the daring venture of carrying publishing to Garden City. . . .

Individuals such as the heads of the houses just mentioned have been responsible for publishing successes more than has been the fact in many other activities, for the business is one that depends greatly on personality. Among the notable examples of this essential of great publishing in the '80s and '90s . . . were William W. Appleton . . . George P. Brett of Macmillan's, Thomas Y. Crowell, Frank H. Dodd, George H. Doran, E. P. Dutton and his associate John Macrae, Col. George B. Harvey of Harper's, Henry Holt, J. Bertram Lippincott, James W. McIntyre of Little, Brown & Co., George H. Mifflin, Charles J. Mills of Longmans, Green & Co., George Haven Putnam, Fleming H. Revell, Frank H. Scott of the Century Company and Charles Scribner 2nd.

* * *

From the leisurely days of long ago to the speed-loving present, bookmen have always been agog over what, with some approach to banality, have become known as "best sellers." The books contained in the lists of these today may not be wholly above suspicion as to high quality notwithstanding their glitter; but pure gold was certainly found in one product of the

	MOON.	MERCURY.	VENUS.	SUN.	MARS.	JUPITER.	SATURN.
ELEMENTS.	Earth, Water.	Water.	Air, Water.	Fire.	Fire.	Air.	Earth, Water.
MICROCOSMOS.	White juices.	Mixed juices.	Slimy juices.	Blood and vital power.	Acid juices.	Vegetative juices.	Gall.
ANIMALS.	Sociable and changeable.	Cunning and rapid.	Beautiful with strong sexual instinct.	Bold and courageous.	Beasts of prey.	Sagacious and gentle.	Crawling and nocturnal.
PLANTS.	Selenotrope, Palm, Hyssop, Rosemary, etc.	Little short leaves and many colored flowers.	Spices and fruit-trees.	Pine, Laurel, Vine, Heliotrope, Lotus, etc.	Burning, poisonous, and stinging.	Oak, Beech, Poplar, Cereals, etc.	Cypress and those of a gloomy aspect or foul odor.
METALS.	Silver.	Quicksilver, Tin, Bismuth.	Silver.	Gold.	Iron and sulphuric metals.	Gold, Silver, Tin.	Lead.
STONES.	All white stones and pearls.	Many colored.	Carnelian, Lazuli, etc.	Topaz, Ruby, Carbuncle, etc.	Diamond, Jasper, Amethyst, Magnet.	Green and air-colored.	Onyx and all brown clays.

Table from Viktor Rydberg's The Magic of the Middle Ages

'80s which was probably the first phenomenon of its kind. Strangely enough it narrowly escaped extinction in its youth, for it sold so slowly that Harper's hesitated as to letting it go out of print. This was, and is, for it still lives, *Ben Hur*. . . . Other large nuggets of the despised decade were *Treasure Island* and *Huckleberry Finn*. . . .

–Frederick Stokes, "A Publisher's Random Notes, 1880–1935," in *Bowker Lectures on Book Publishing* (New York: R. R. Bowker, 1957), pp. 8–9, 19–20, 23–24

Nicholas Murray Butler

Holt's friend Nicholas Murray Butler was a professor of education and philosophy at Columbia University and, later, president of the university (1901–1945). Columbia flourished under Butler, whose influence extended well beyond academe. An adviser to several American presidents and a well-traveled writer and speaker, he won the Nobel Peace Prize in 1931 (shared with Jane Addams) for his efforts on behalf of the Kellogg-Briand Pact.

Unfortunately, the famous Saturday nights at the Century Club exist no longer. . . . First in the old clubhouse on East 15th Street and afterwards in the new house on West 43rd Street, which is now about to complete its first half-century of occupancy, there gathered each Saturday night from one hundred to three hundred of the most interesting and attractive men that New York could furnish. They were men of letters, artists, scholars, statesmen and men of the world. There was no interest which they did not reflect and no form of public service or activity with which some of them were not in close contact. On Saturday evenings they used to sit together in casual groups, to smoke and to talk until midnight and long after. Indeed, Henry Holt once said that it should be made a misdemeanor to leave the Century on Saturday night before the hour arrived at which the clubhouse was to be closed. . . .

–Nicholas Murray Butler, *Across the Busy Years,* volume 2 (New York: Scribners, 1939), pp. 435–436

Holt's Century Club cronies sometimes became Holt and Company authors, reviewers, and unofficial consultants, Butler included.

Oct. 7, 1897.

Dear Mr. Holt:

In view of the prevailing and increasing interest in the study of children, it might be worth your while to look up a German book on this subject, that is rather well written in a popular vein. It is worth considering whether or not an English translation of it, perhaps with an adequate introduction by some American writer, would not be a profitable venture. The book is

Nicholas Murray Butler as a junior member of the Columbia University faculty, 1889 (from Butler, Across the Busy Years, *1939; Thomas Cooper Library, University of South Carolina)*

Pensig [Rudolph Penzig]–Ernste Autworten [sic] auf Kinderfragen. It is published in Berlin, 1897, by Dummler. Of course the title would have to be changed in the English version.

> Yours very truly,
> Nicholas Murray Butler
> Columbia University, New York
> Faculty of Philosophy

March 16, 1899.

Dear Mr. Holt:

I have yours of the 15th. Hereafter if you wish me to read manuscripts from time to time as a matter of business, I shall be glad to accept whatever honorarium custom and your sense of the importance of the particular undertaking, lead you to suggest.

I have no relations with any publishing house that will prevent me from rendering you the best service of which I am capable. I am called upon perhaps more frequently by the Macmillan Co. than by any other single house, for work of this kind, but I think it is safe to say that during the last six months I have read manuscripts and passed on literary projects for not fewer than eight different publishing firms.

With reference to the last paragraph of your letter: What are your relations to the principals of the New York and Brooklyn High Schools, and with the committee of the New York Board of Superintendents on High Schools, of which Dr. Marble is chairman? It is through these men that I could exercise more or less indirect influence in the selection of text-books. I do not wish, however, to enter into this matter personally (because it would prove in many ways embarrassing), unless it is to defend you from a blackmailing attack. If anything of that kind is in the air, it is then that I shall want to set counteracting forces in motion.

> Yours very truly,
> Nicholas Murray Butler

During the 1890s Holt published The Educational Review, *a monthly journal edited by Butler, who often used it to campaign for educational reform in New York City. When, in February of 1899, Butler published an article in the review describing the president of the school board as "that fine old educational mastodon," ward politicians had Butler indicted for criminal libel. Butler's sanguine reaction to the indictment is reflected in the following letter to Holt. The case was eventually laughed out of court.*

April 8, 1899

Dear Mr. Holt:

You will have seen from last night's paper that Judge Cowing granted our motion for an inspection of the Grand Jury minutes. Mr. Lindsay will have in his hands on Monday a copy of the stenographer's minutes showing exactly what Little and Fuller swore. He has prepared a very careful brief, which he expects to be able to buttress after inspecting the minutes, and will probably give notice that on Monday, April 17, he will move to dismiss the indictment chiefly on grounds of insufficient legal evidence.

Nothing will happen, therefore, until the last week in April. Under the circumstances it seems best to send you the indictment and some newspaper comments to be set up for the May [Educational] Review, in order that without any words of our own the matter may be put in just the right ridiculous light before the readers of school papers throughout the country.

Mr. Lindsay suggested yesterday to Mr. Pine that it was in order to pay him a proper retaining fee and he fixed $250 as the amount. If it meets your views to handle the matter in this way, I suggest your sending a check for that amount to him and charge it to the current expenses of the Review. His address is John D. Lindsay, 31 Nassau St., New York.

> Yours very truly,
> Nicholas Murray Butler

April 12, 1899

Dear Mr. Holt:

... I had already consulted several persons, including Bishop of the "Post," and Edwards of the Philadelphia "Press," about the advisability of publishing the indictment in full. They, as well as others, agree that it is a document of such a peculiar character that the best thing possible is to publish it in full and without comment. It will serve to show, as nothing else possibly can, the way in which the Tammany mind works in dealing with school affairs, and for this purpose all that irrelevant twaddle at the beginning about high school, etc., is quite as effective as anything else. . . .

Had the matter not become one of such public notoriety all over the country, and excited such wide comment, my own preference would be to say not a word in May or hereafter; but I am advised that the circumstances being as they are, such a course might render us liable to a misconstruction of our motives. . . .

There is no objection to my saying to you, although not to any one else, that I have seen the Grand Jury minutes, and that they render the whole proceeding more absurd than it was before. Somebody ought to print them, in order to throw light on what it is possible to do in this town.

Yours very truly,
Nicholas Murray Butler

William Graham Sumner

The distinguished economist and sociologist and Yale professor William Graham Sumner was among the notable thinkers of the day with whom Henry Holt enjoyed a friendship ("Billy" Sumner was in the class after his at Yale) as well as a publisher-author relationship. Sumner was a professor of political and social science at Yale from 1872 until his retirement in 1909. Holt published Sumner's A History of American Currency: With Chapters on the English Bank Restrictions and Austrian Paper Money *(1874) and* Protectionism: The -ism Which Teaches That Waste Makes Wealth *(1885). In 1897 Sumner looked forward to having Holt publish a work in progress called "The Dollar of the United States: Its Definitions and History," but this plan did not come to fruition.*

I/21/97

Dear Holt,
A man gave me $5000 for a department library & the work organizing it, choosing books *[illegible]* took all my spare time *[illegible]* Autumn. I was glad of the library, of course, but I begrudged the time. I turned to the book in Dec. I am giving all my spare time to it. I have altered my plan & am going to call it: "The Dollar of the United States; its Definition & History." Most of it will consist of the perils of the dollar since 1800.

Ysyly
W. G. Sumner

I am very well indeed—never better—provided that I keep within my *[illegible]*. I am able to do *[illegible]* of work within my rules. I cannot tell how much time I shall require to write the book. I have a course of lectures in Boston & another in Albany in Feb & Mch.

[Undated]

Dear Holt,
The "Dollar" has advanced little winter. I have had lots of interruptions. People come to me with all kinds of jobs wh. I "ought" to do, & all without pay (White Man's Burden). I throw off all I can & I reject all special engagements, but some I cannot escape.

William Graham Sumner (from Sumner, The Challenge of Facts, *1914)*

Title page for the German poet's critical essay that was originally published as Zur Geschichte der neueren schönen Literatur in Deutschland *in 1833 (Rutgers University Library)*

College work is more and more exacting. I have the first draft done for nearly all of it, but none of the final revision is done. Some new trouble arisen here in connection with the [Yale] "jubilee." We are all called upon to write great books as a part of the celebration. I cannot see my way clear, for this "Dollar" is hanging over me & will require a lot of work yet. I have had only one idea about it & that is to beg you to let me off so that I can put the "Dollar" into the Jubilee collection. What do you say to it? You will never make any money out of the "Dollar." It wd be a great relief to me if I cd use this to get out of my Jubilee obligation. Money will be no object there & I can make the book as stupid as I like.

[illegible]
W.G. Sumner

***

Sumner replied to Holt in response to his query about the reported publishing project in honor of Yale's bicentennial celebration.

III/7/99

Dear Holt,

I do not know details about the publishing project. One of the Bi-cent. Com. came to me & told me that there was such a project & asked me to consent to cooperate. I cd not do otherwise. I told him that was under an engagement to you. He thought that you wd consent to turn over this book of mine to the Com. for their enterprise. How they intend to publish I do not know. They will not publish for two or three years yet. I have one strong reason for preferring to give them this book. I want to make it technical & not popular. I have had great difficulty to plan it so as to strike a flame wh. wd make it suit you a [sic] yet be what I want to write. If I write a technical book there will be no money in it for you or me either, but this com. expects to beg money for these publications (since they will never pay) of the [illegible] are paid for by charity we may earn a little for our work.

[illegible]
W. G. Sumner

III/10/99

Dear Holt,

. . . I am nowadays entirely outside of all the projects & I get my information from newspapers and hearsay as much as you do. The man who came to me for the Com. was in a great hurry & only anxious to commit me to the plan. I try to economize all my time & strength. I never go anywhere & I never hear what is going on except by snatches & afterwards. Therefore I now find that, if I try to tell you anything about this matter, except the [illegible] in wh. I am as regards my own engagements, I may be in error. If you see your way to let me off, one trouble will be off my mind.

Ysvery sincerely,
W. G. Sumner

"Honor Among Thieves": Courtesy of the Trade

Before 1891 [the year that the international copyright law was enacted], British and European literature lacked copyright protection in America. If an American publisher issued such books as Kipling's *PLAIN TALES FROM THE HILLS* or Stevenson's *CHILD'S GARDEN OF VERSES,* he was soon confronted with a dozen pirated editions at continually lower prices. It is to the credit of the industry that gentlemen's agreements between such houses as Harper's, Scribner's, Holt's, and Appleton's worked as well as they did in such a situation, and that under the threat or direct competition of pirated editions, royalty payments were made so regularly.

–Alfred Harcourt, *Publishing Since 1900,* R. R. Bowker Memorial Lecture, no. 2 (New York: New York Public Library, 1937)

* * *

Sept. 12, 1868

Messrs. Harper & Bros.
Gentlemen:

We are in treaty for "Bramleigh's of Bishop's Folly." Since the negotiation began, we notice an announcement of the book by you. If you think the fact of your having announced it should preclude our consummation of arrangements with the author, please tell us. As we understand the usages of the trade, we are under no obligation to stop, but we don't feel quite big enough to fight you if you see fit to act on a different opinion.

We will be obliged if you will let us know your views in time for us to back out, if we've got to, by today's steamer.

Respectfully yours,
Leypoldt & Holt

* * *

Dec. 9, 1868

Dear Mr. Putnam:

Did you ever hear that if A announces an English book before he has a copy of it, and B makes a *subsequent* announcement after he (B) has received no copy meanwhile, B is not called upon to respect A's announcement?

Answer this by bearer and I'll do my best with the next conundrum you put to me.

Faithfully yours,
Henry Holt

* * *

Nov. 20, 1885

Dear Mr. Holt:

Yours of the 19th rec'd. I hasten to say that the Canadian firm did not intimate to me that there was to be any edition of Grimm published by either you or the Macmillans, & I found it out only after I had ordered duplicate plates from them. The publication of such a

Holt in 1887 (from Henry Holt, Garrulities of an Octogenarian Editor, *1923)*

book w'd have been a grim enough matter without two other good ones in the market. As it is, I am inclined to make a grim-ace at the whole business, give up publishing & go afishing. Well, of course my edition will be the best one, no matter how good yours & Macmillans are.

Long may you live!

Cordially yours,
D.C. Heath

* * *

November 27, 1885.

Gentlemen:

Yours of this date is at hand.

We observe that you did not see our announcement of Maine's *Popular Government* on the 19th inst. We send herewith our file copy of the *Commercial Advertiser* of that date in which you will find our announcement under the head of "New Publications." Please to return the paper to us.

Endpaper from the 1883 Holt edition of Richter's The Invisible Lodge *advertising other titles in the same series (Rutgers University Library)*

We do not stop to discuss the question whether or not this case is parallel with the recent case of *Healey*, but promptly stop work on our projected edition of *Popular Government*, and remain, once more,

      Your aggrieved friends,
      Harper & Brothers

* * *

      Jan. 24, 1891.

Dear Mr. Holt:—

   . . . .

I feel sure you have misjudged me if you have felt, or still feel, that we have other than the very best feelings towards you as a house, and I still insist that we have in no way sought to compete with you. We have simply published the books people have told us were needed. And wouldn't you have published books under the same circumstances? Of course you would, as you have. If we had wanted to compete with you, we should have taken your catalogue, looked it thro', found out which of your books sold the best, and made some editions of these very books. On the other hand, these are just the ones we have made no editions of, for the reason that yours were satisfactory to the schools: otherwise, they would not have sold so well. Even when we have been told that you were seeking direct competition with us we have not been influenced to retaliate; and we have been reminded a number of times that we ought to return the "favors."

The only reason I can see why you should understand that competition between us was to be limited to the classics is because when we began our correspondence with reference to the matter, I spoke of the Greek and Latin classics, among other things, and asked you if you thought that but one publisher had a right to print an edition of Caesar's Gallic War; you knew, as did I, that half a dozen publishers had made an edition of Caesar. And we probably remarked, also, that Arithmetics [sic], Geographies, and other books in classics were duplicated in the same way, and we could not see why you had any more right to the Modern Language field than Mr. Ginn has to the field of Mathematics or the Sciences. . . .

We feel sure that neither you nor we can get Mr. Ginn to confine himself to the classics. It was the understanding between him and me that when I left him we should steer clear of each other as much as possible, he confining himself to Latin, Greek, and Mathematics, and I to the Sciences and Modern Languages. Now that he has departed from the old agreement, I shall feel free to pitch into Mathematics, Latin, Greek, &c., so here goes. There is no great loss without some small gain. If you and I can't keep ahead of him in Modern Languages, then I am greatly mistaken. If you have been offered a good book like ours, take it: only don't take it simply to punish us, for we would not take one to punish you. We hated to see your edition of Grimm's Maerchen come out, as we saw pretty clearly that it would knock ours higher than a kite, as it has; but we never blamed you for bringing it out.

You must look out how you sass me now, for I weigh 183 lbs. When you last saw me I weighed about 150. I shall be sorry if you say sub voci that my mental and moral capacity has not grown in like proportion. Still, I believe you will find in the end that I am not half so bad a fellow as you think.

      Yours sincerely,
      D.C. Heath

* * *

      March 8, 1912.

Dear Sir:

As our House has almost reached the hundredth year of its existence, and during that time has fully borne its part in the literary growth and activities of the nation, it has seemed to us not unfitting that we should put into print some memorial of the men who established and have conducted this business. During these years they have had the honor of being the publishers of many of the most important works of the day, and have at the same time maintained cordial and in some cases intimate relations with the leading literary men of this country and England. Some of the English publishers have issued similar volumes relating to the history of their houses, and these have proved entertaining and in some cases have become what might be called in the language of the day "human documents."

One of the members of our House, the third in descent from the fourth of the original brothers, has prepared from a careful study of existing sources a volume detailing the history of the House of Harper, in the belief that to readers of the present day it would prove interesting and encouraging and would afford a valuable chapter in the record of successful and honorable industry.

This volume has just been published, and we have the pleasure of sending you a copy . . . some of its pages will awaken memories of persons or friends long since passed away who in their day filled an honorable place in society and literature. It has been a pleasure to us to be able to place before the public a record of these good men and true, and we trust that the perusal of its pages will be equally pleasant to you.

We remain, dear Sir,

      Sincerely yours,
      Harper & Brothers

* * *

THREE MEN IN A BOAT

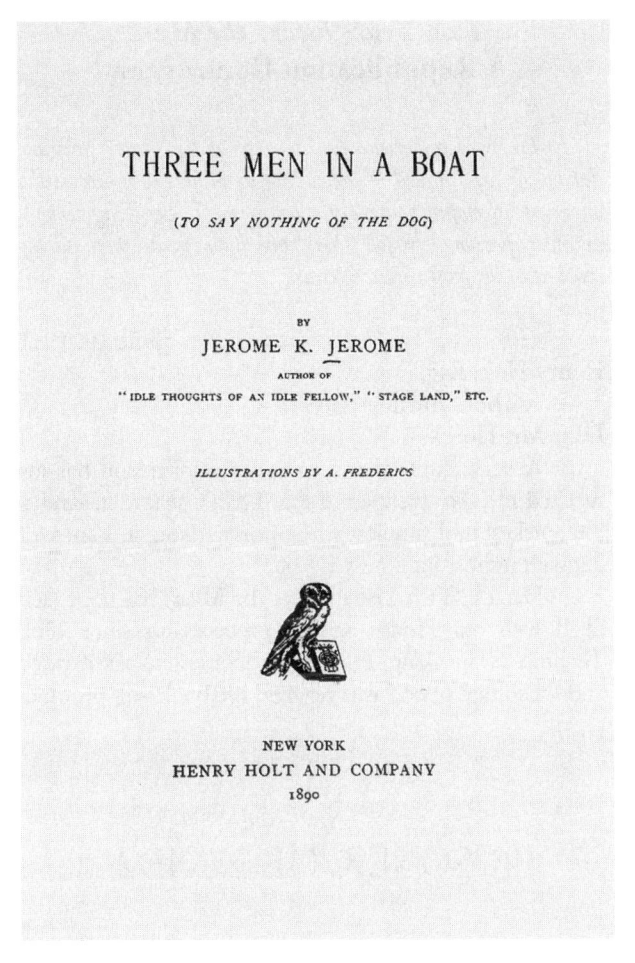

(TO SAY NOTHING OF THE DOG)

BY
JEROME K. JEROME
AUTHOR OF
"IDLE THOUGHTS OF AN IDLE FELLOW," "STAGE LAND," ETC.

ILLUSTRATIONS BY A. FREDERICS

NEW YORK
HENRY HOLT AND COMPANY
1890

Title page for the first American edition of the British humorist's 1889 account of a trip up the Thames to Oxford (Rutgers University Library)

May 20, 1912.

My dear Holt:

I returned last week from a winter's sojourn in Egypt, and have just read your very kind and generous notice of my book in the "Literary Digest"—doubly prized by me as coming from a fellow publisher.

In referring to Cousin Joe as Chairman of the Publishers' Copyright League I was in error, as you pointed out. In reading over some of the old copyright literature, I found him referred to as Chairman of the Publishers' Committee which went to Washington several times in the interest of International Copyright, and I inadvertently made him Chairman of the American Publishers' Copyright League, which I believe did not exist at that time. My mistake was rather in fact than in spirit, for the Committee of which he was Chairman represented all the leading houses of the day, as well as I can remember.

From the time I first went down to the office the firm favored International Copyright, either by treaty or legislation.

If you want to enjoy a winter holiday don't go West, but go to Egypt.

Always faithfully yours,
J. Henry Harper

* * *

Holt and his fellow publishers engaged in polite exchanges about their respective claims to various works.

June 29, 1914

Dear Mr. Dodd [Frank Dodd]:

I have always thought it for the highest interests of the trade that under all ordinary circumstances we should keep off each other's preserves, and that when we get onto them thru extraordinary circumstances, we should be prompt to explain. This opinion is kept alive in great part by the recollections of very scrupulous explanations volunteered to me by dear old Joe Harper many years ago. So I am troubling you with a spontaneous word of similar explanation.

As you probably know, I have for sometime had very little to do with the details of my business. So I was surprised, on looking over our Fall Announcement prospectus the other day in New York, to find on it a book by Strunsky, who I had supposed was your author, and had resisted the temptation to go for on that account.

On looking into the matter, I find that information was volunteered to our people that two houses other than yours were after his Atlantic papers, and that the book was certain to go to one of them unless we went for it; and on the strength of that situation they did not hesitate to go for it. Perhaps I had better add in all candor that their hesitation was less than it might have been if they hadn't had an impression that sometime ago you had outbid us on a book by Burton E. Stevenson, going so far even as to make a bid higher than they were able to reconcile with strict business. For myself, however, I had thrown what questions there were in that transaction, in your favor, and was satisfied to let it stand as O.K.; but my young folks brought it up to me as among the justifications for their action, though I should not have considered it myself.

I hate situations that even suggest explanation; but in a competitive world they are not to be entirely avoided. I do, however, try to avoid them as far as reason justifies, and I am glad there have been so few of them between us.

I trust you to take all this in the spirit that prompts it. . . .

Faithfully yours,
[Henry Holt]

* * *

Holt and Company vice president T. J. Wilson wrote publisher Frederick S. Crofts in 1936 to advise him of some rights to European works that Holt had secured.

June 10, 1936.

Dear Fred:

Just a brief note to inform you that we have secured the exclusive rights to publish a text edition in German for English speaking countries of Will Vesper's TRISTAN UND ISOLDE and PARZIVAL.

Henceforth we shall drop you a note like this whenever we secure rights from abroad, and we hope that you will give us the same information. It may help to avoid the continuous confusion and difficulty of more than one company securing "exclusive" permission for material.

Very sincerely yours,
[T. J. Wilson]

Two Years before the Mast: A Republication Controversy

Professed adherence to "courtesy of the trade" principles did not always succeed in precluding publishers' accusations that one was preempting another's territory. These disagreements, however passionately felt they may have been, were always couched in the most civilized terms.

June 19, 1911.

Henry Holt, Esq.
 Fairholt, Burlington, Vt.
Dear Mr. Holt:—

A very extraordinary piece of information has just reached me,—so unexpected that I can't believe it,—and as the quickest and simplest way of discrediting it, I am writing with utmost frankness to you.

Dana's "Two Years before the Mast" has been identified with our House and its predecessors since 1869. Technically speaking, the original copyright has expired, and when that period was reached the book was promptly

Frontispiece and title page for the first American edition of the 1894 British novel that was the author's most popular work (Rutgers University Library)

pirated by the usual crowd, who patiently and studiously wait and prepare for such events. This was expected, and caused no ripple of surprise. We ourselves continue to publish it in two trade, and two school editions.

This year we have been planning to issue an entirely new edition, from new plates, with illustrations, and with authoritative introductions, etc., by the author's son, Mr. Richard H. Dana. Our plans were just reaching a crucial point, when word comes to us that Henry Holt & Co. have announced a new edition of "Two Years before the Mast," with illustrations by E. Boyd Smith, uniform with our edition of "Robinson Crusoe"!! Now simply this can't be true,—can it? Or if so, it must have been done without any knowledge on your part, or on that of the Firm, of the actual conditions. The republication of a book so recently out of copyright, and so identified with its original authorized publishers, by a House of your character, would be so unprecedented, that I know it can only have been planned,—if at all,—under a complete misunderstanding on your part of the situation. This must justify this somewhat blunt letter, which please regard as personal, and written in full appreciation of our friendly relations.

Sincerely,
George H. Mifflin

P.S. Not being sure of your address, I am sending this letter in duplicate to your N.Y. office.

June 21, 1911

Dear Mr. Mifflin:

Yours of the 19th was as much of a surprise to me as the news that we were going to do a "Two Years Before the Mast" was to you.

You are right in your supposition that I went into the matter without knowing anything about your relations to the book. I had, oddly enough, never read it, and had no idea who was its original publisher, or when it went out of copyright.

I took the word of the energetic young man who suggested it, to the effect (I presume: for I have a memorandum to the same effect from the office in consequence of your letter being opened there before it was forwarded) that there were twenty editions from fourteen publishers, including Dutton, Macmillan and Eliot's Five-Foot-Shelf. Of course I supposed the book was *fera natura,* as much as "The Last of the Mohicans" with which we are making it uniform; and I confess that, except on some slight question of degree, I am of the same opinion still.

At the same time I think I appreciate and to a certain extent sympathize with your attitude. I can do that because I am old enough to recognize that in a good many instances—and in more probably than I can recognize, my own attitude has unconsciously been determined by my interests; and your interests have been affected more by expirations of copyright than those of any other American publisher.

I thought you were wrong in the "Sir Launfal" case, but I preferred to err on the side of literary property; I thought you were wrong regarding our forthcoming Anthology, but I still preferred to err on the same side; I think you are wrong now, but I still *prefer* to err in the same way. It is a question, though, whether I can with a reasonable regard to our own interests. I will write to the office and find out just how matters stand, and communicate with you later.

Which side I will prefer to err on next time, I don't know.

I take it for granted that your allusion to our edition being uniform with your "Robinson Crusoe," is merely "in passing." It is not strictly correct, and if it means anything critical, it means that you ought to have engaged the artist's whole output. We asked him specifically if he was under any obligation to you.

At one time I was distinctly in favor of perpetual copyright, and would vote for it now if I had to vote either way. One reason would be that it would obviate the danger of friends demanding from each other too much knowledge of ancient history, and save us all from some of our natural biases.

Always Faithfully Yours
(signed) Henry Holt

June 23, 1911.

Dear Mr. Holt:

Your frank letter of the 21st reached me yesterday, and was read with keen interest. Pending your later communication I venture to make some equally frank comments, but in no such skillful way. Few of us can keep step with you in this respect.

To me this is a question of publishing ethics, or, if you will, of "trade courtesy." If no such standard exists and business is business with no sentiment there is no argument. I shouldn't think of even raising the question with some firms, but with Henry Holt & Co.—well, it is quite different.

Now, really, what are the facts? You say there are twenty editions from fourteen publishers, but what kinds of editions and what kinds of publishers? I enclose a list of the latter, and I leave you to pass upon their character. The editions are mostly of the cheapest type and most of them simply variations in bindings. The only respectable name in the group (from my point of view) is Macmillan. And from a somewhat extended experience in this phase of the publishing business I think I can with truth say that Macmillan is the only house of any standing who does not recognize the principle I am contending for. With brutal indifference they reprint at will, whenever their convenience requires, anything from our list which is not legally protected, and this not only against our wishes but those of the representatives of the copyright to whom we continue our payments. This may be legal and may be business, but I shouldn't like to be associated in it. Doubtless I am influenced by selfish interests (Rochefoucauld, you know, says that selfishness is at the bottom of every human act), but trying to look at it from an impersonal standpoint I really believe that in the general interests of publisher and author it isn't right and it isn't wise.

Of course, there is a limit to this publishing courtesy. What is it? It generally defines itself without question, and one of the best ways to hasten it is the disregard of this trade courtesy by a house of real standing. The moment that is done without mutual consultation and agreement the first important step is taken.

However, I must not bore you with a sermon. I only wish we might talk it all over in leisurely and friendly fashion. Whatever happens with regard to "Two Years Before the Mast" the world will continue to revolve on its axis and Henry Holt & Co. and H. M. Co. will remain good friends. The business of neither will be perceptibly affected. Only I do wish before H. H. & Co. had put their imprimatur on a directly competing library edition of a book, which for so many years had been identified with our House, it had occurred to them to consider "Is this just the sort of thing we really want to do?" In a similar instance that I recall Mr. Scott of the Century Co., having unwittingly through the suggestion of one of their "energetic young men" issued an edition of an incomplete Longfellow in a single volume, willingly withdrew it when he understood the conditions. Perhaps some way out of this difficulty may occur to you, which will seem to you in harmony with your preferences and not unjust to your interests.

In the meantime pray excuse this hastily put together letter, and believe me in any event

Sincerely yours,
George H. Mifflin

June 24, 1911

Dear Mr. Mifflin:

I have yours of the 23rd.

I didn't know I had been writing a particularly good letter, but I am one of Houghton-Mifflin's authors, and have to live up to the part!

WOMAN'S WORK IN AMERICA

EDITED BY
ANNIE NATHAN MEYER

WITH AN INTRODUCTION
BY
JULIA WARD HOWE

NEW YORK
HENRY HOLT AND COMPANY
1891

Title page for the collection of writings on women in the labor force edited by one of the founders of Barnard College, the women's affiliate college to Columbia University (Wesleyan University Library)

You say: "To me this is a question of publishing ethics, or, if you will, of 'trade courtesy.' If no such standard exists and business is business with no sentiment, there is no argument."

Them's my sentiments exactly.

You also say that you wish before we had put our imprint on a directly competing library edition of a book, it had occurred to us to ask ourselves: "Is this just the sort of thing we really want to do?" My dear fellow, I have already plainly indicated to you that we did ask ourselves that. I asked my young man proposing it, what the status of the book in the market was, and he told me in effect (I don't vouch for the mathematical identity of his then statement and his recent one) that there were twenty editions from fourteen publishers, including Macmillan, Dutton and the Five-Foot Shelf, which last of course carried the sanction of President Eliot [Charles William Eliot, past president of Harvard]; and not until I had such evidence that the book had passed beyond the bounds of any question of trade courtesy, did we go in. Remember, I didn't then even know that the copyright had been yours. If I had, I probably should have at least ascertained when it expired. Though, on second thought, in view of the facts I did know, I doubt if I would have taken even that trouble.

The aforesaid young man says: "If it's not nice for us to do this book, why didn't Putnams object to our doing 'Mohicans'? They even carried 'Mohicans' in their retail store." I suppose your answer would be that "Mohicans" has been much longer out of copyright. I presume it has.

If Dutton, in addition to President Eliot (no publisher) and Macmillan (a putative foreigner) were in the field, it would be my clear opinion that the book had escaped from your bounds, even of courtesy, and become, as I said in my last, *fera natura;* but your letter and a letter just from the office, both look (altho the one from the office does not specifically say so) as if the young man who instigated our publication, in saying that Dutton had published it, really referred to another foreigner— Everyman's Library; and if so, I am willing to agree with you that the book is not clearly *fera natura* to publishers of our stamp, though it may be clearly so tomorrow.

If the question had come up before we had done anything in the matter, I should have retreated without a moment's hesitation. Or if this were a comparative trifle, as I assume the Century's incomplete Longfellow to have been, of course the question of disposing of it would be a much simpler one. But here we are with an elaborate and expensive idea which we have partly carried out, regarding which we have already in train several laborious and important arrangements, and which, through no fault of ours, has escaped your attention until we got in the fix. We have counted on the book as a leader for next Autumn, and if we hadn't got it more than half prepared, we should have had some other book more than half prepared to fill its exact place in that line: for the enterprise does not stand by itself, but "The Mohicans" we published last year, and another book in the same style (I really forget which of several we had named) we are going to publish this year, are materially influenced by the third, which you and I are discussing.

Now what is reasonable under the circumstances?

How does this strike you? We go ahead and put on the back of the title page something like *Published by arrangement with Messrs. Houghton, Mifflin & Company, original holders of the copyright, and representatives of the author's estate;* and put something to that effect in our catalogue and wherever else we legitimately can, and pay the author's estate, or you and the author's estate (for whatever rights or courtesies there are, you certainly share) a five per cent (5%) royalty after we have got our money back.

This royalty would of course be beggarly if the book were to be sold for a copyright price, but "The Mohicans" and the other books in this style are sold, I believe, for $1.35, largely because they are non-copyright, which is of course a ridiculously low price, and theoretically admits of no royalty at all: so if, after we get our money back, we pay 5% on that, I think we will be doing the liberal thing.

Such notice would perhaps be as effective a bit of bulwark for just the principles we both believe in, as could well be devised.

[Henry Holt]

June 27, 1911

Dear Mr. Mifflin:

I wrote a letter to you on the 24th, but thought best to submit it to the office before sending it to you. The telegram from the office which I told you of yesterday was in response, and the letter that follows it contains this passage:

"The arrangement to pay them a royalty seems a generous way out of the difficulty, but if we pay them a royalty and make the announcement you mention, shouldn't they allow us to reprint the additional matter which they added when the copyright reverted to the author, in order to make a copyright showing? Our edition at present lacks: 1st, the pages entitled "Twenty-four Years After" which the author put in place of the final chapter of the original edition; 2nd, various footnotes which he added chiefly to explain nautical terms (in the author's edition). The simplest way would be to ask H.-M. for permission to reprint their "new edition, with subsequent matter by the author."

As I told you, I had not read the book; still less had I known of an improved edition. Had I known that, we never would have got into the scrape.

Of course I would be glad to insert, instead of the mere acknowledgment I suggested in my letter of the 24th, your copyright notice of the improved edition, or that and acknowledgment both.

In view of such an arrangement, a 5% royalty seems to me more beggarly than ever. But you know

Advertisement in a New York literary magazine (Rutgers University Library)

what the enterprise can afford as well as I do. It's something like the rate of royalty on a cheap educational book, which I think I've heard of going down to one per cent.

Of course I like the spirit of your last letter—all your letters—very much, and I hope I am meeting it.

[Henry Holt]

June 29, 1911

Dear Mr. Mifflin:

I have yours of yesterday.

I have just telegraphed you: "Telegraph won't do justice to situation. Am writing."

This is partly because your letter seems to indicate that if we don't go ahead, you will use our edition in place of the one you contemplated. If you do that, you can afford to pay us for the not inconsiderable trouble of starting it and getting it half way through.

Another reason is that your letter reads a little as if you might *possibly* suppose that we had some idea that you would not go ahead with your new edition if we went ahead with ours. That would be incorrect.

A third reason is that after having the topic so long in mind, I have come to realize that for the sake of the two other books uniform with "Before the Mast" which we will have this Fall, it would pay us to publish that with no more profit than would cover actual outlays, of course including advertising, cataloguing, packing, collecting, etc. If we concede you a royalty that would leave us only that, I don't see how it could hurt you to make an arrangement with us for an edition bearing your copyright notice, any more than similar arrangements which are made every day, hurt the original proprietors. So I want you to send me the data for such an arrangement.

Then we'll all be happy!

Faithfully yours
[Henry Holt]

June 28, 1911.

Dear Mr. Holt:

Your two letters of the 24th and 27th are at hand. I accept all you write in the spirit in which clearly it was written. It is indeed an unfortunate "scrape," but we must get out of it in such seemly and friendly fashion as possible.

The suggestion of a royalty with the accompanying restrictions does not seem to me at all the solution. The real harm is done when Henry Holt & Co. put their imprint on a directly competing library edition of a book not only identified with our House, but actually in process of being republished in new form with fresh type, illustrations, and with introduction, notes, etc. by the author's son—clearly the authorized copyright edition.

The only way out would seem to be for you to turn over your material in the way of plates and illustrations to us at cost, a proposition we are not eager for, but which certainly we would consider.

Failing that, I see no way but for both of us to go ahead on our own individual lines. Certainly, being ourselves in medias res of revising and reissuing one of our own books, we cannot draw back. But if my suggestion does not meet the case from your point of view, we will dismiss all feeling and proceed as if we were issuing competing editions of, say, the Bible! In any event, we all appreciate the frank and friendly spirit of your letters....

[George H. Mifflin]

June 30, 1911.

Dear Mr. Holt:—

I duly received your telegram yesterday, and this morning your letter in further explanation comes.

I see no way but to accept your understanding that from *your* point of view you never entertained the idea that we should not go ahead with our edition, and we are accordingly proceeding on our own lines. Frankly, your alternative suggestions do not solve the problem from *our* point of view.

I am sorry we can't all be happy! But we must all, with good feeling, make the best that we can of the situation. In the meantime, you and I will take a vacation from our arduous correspondence, which we shall some day laugh over, and wonder that it interested us at all.

Sincerely yours,
George H. Mifflin

July 5, 1911.

Henry Holt, Esq.,

Dear Mr. Holt:

We celebrated the Glorious Fourth by closing on Monday so that it was not until this morning that your Sunday letter of the 2nd reached me.

We all heartily appreciate your sense of fairness and your desire to cooperate with us in the wisest solution of our problem. When I wrote you my last letter, we could see no way but for us both to go ahead on our individual lines and accordingly I started the necessary machinery, but your letter of the 2nd of course leads me to reconsider what seemed to us the only alternative. Accordingly I have wired you asking for a detailed statement as to the condition of the electrotype plates, illustrations, etc. of "Two Years" with the costs? I am of course without information as to how much of the type, if any, has already been set, and as to the number and cost of the illustrations together with their exact condition. Naturally we should prefer our own page, but if you have already made your plates, we certainly should take them off your hands.

Awaiting therefore full detailed information, and thanking you cordially for your letter of the 2nd, I am
    Sincerely yours,
    George H. Mifflin

        July 5, 1911

Dear Mr. Mifflin:

I have your telegram of today.

At the latest advices from New York (June 22nd), the contract with the artist was for everything at $900. About half of the illustrations had been received and processed. Composition or composition and electrotyping (I don't know which) was done for about half the book, at a cost of $120.

I don't know whether anything has been done since, but I am writing to New York to give you particulars.

I am glad to see from your telegram that you have lived through the past two or three days, and I hope you will get through this one—and a great many more not so hot!
    Faithfully yours
    [Henry Holt]

        July 7, 1911.

Henry Holt, Esq.
 Fairholt, Burlington, Vermont.
Dear Mr. Holt:—

You have doubtless receivd a copy of H. H. & Co.'s letter of July 6th from New York. To complete your information I enclose copy of my reply. Is this all right?
    Sincerely yours,
    G.H.M.

        July 11, 1911

Dear Mr. Mifflin:

I duly receivd yours of the 7th enclosing copy of yours of the same date to my concern. They didn't send me the letter to which yours was a response: their orders are never to send me anything not really necessary, which I don't suppose that was.

I understand yours to H. H. & Co., of the 7th, to mean in the passage: "We of course in asking this assume the cost on the basis of our correspondence with Mr. Holt," that you propose to take over the work and pay our outlay, all of which is satisfactory, and in doing which and the subsequent steps, you of course have my heartiest good wishes.
    Faithfully yours
    [Henry Holt]

        Dec. 13, 1911

Dear Mr. Mifflin:

I hav always had the feelings of a swel, but never the fortune of one, but I think I shal experience the sensations of one when I read "Two Years before the Mast" in the gorgeous edition you hav just so kindly sent me.

With all good wishes, as ever,
    Faithfully yours
    [Henry Holt]

REMINISCENCES

A congressional hearing on copyright in 1885 brought Holt to Washington, D.C., where he happened to room with Mark Twain, an incident Holt recalled in his memoir, Garrulities of an Octogenarian Editor *(1923). The memoir utilizes Holt's idiosyncratic spelling.*

About 1885 the Congressional Committee on Patents gave the Copyright Leaguers a hearing. I was one of the committee from the Publishers' League. Washington was crowded, but not of course because of our little interest. But other interests crowded Mark Twain and me into the same room and I believe the same bed at that good hotel then kept by a mulatto named Wormeley. There was no better hotel in Washington. About a year later I happend to occupy the same room on a honeymoon.

My occupancy of it with Mark is the first I remember of our acquaintance. He was great fun, as he always was before he lost his wife. The afternoon of that day in Washington was drizzly, and he and I took a constitutional under the same umbrella. He was most of the time talking about Blind Tom, a famous half-idiotic Negro pianist of those days. Mark said he never misst an opportunity to hear him. Tom, it appears, used to soliloquize about himself and his

> ## Maintaining Copyright
>
> December 13, 1935
>
> HENRY HOLT AND COMPANY
>
> Messrs. R. Bemporad and Figlio
> Via Cavour, 20
> Firenze, Italy
>
> R. Bemporad & F.
> Via Cavour, 20
> Firenze
>
> Dear Sirs:
>
> We have just seen a copy of the new translation of *Ciondolino,* by Vamba (Luigi Bertelli), which Messrs. Thomas Y. Crowell and Company have recently published here, in a new translation by Professor Nicola Di Pietro.
>
> Presumably, you gave your permission to Professor Di Pietro in September, 1931, and informed him that "these rights have never been ceded to any other person."
>
> We are very much astonished at this, as you granted us permission in September 1909 "the rights of translation into English for the United States of this volume (Ciondolino)." At the time we paid you One Hundred Dollars ($100.) for such rights, and also bought the right to use the illustrations. The book was published and copyrighted by us in 1910, under the title *The Prince and his Ants,* and it continues to find a sale. Furthermore, our copyright still holds on the book. The translator was Miss Sarah F. Woodruff, who also had correspondence with you in the matter.
>
> We should like to hear from you concerning this as soon as possible. Meanwhile, the sale of the Di Pietro translation (under the title *The Emperor of the Ants*) is hurting our own book very much.
>
> Very truly yours,
>
> Sgr. Signor
> Prof. Nicola Di Pietro
> Via S. Leonardo, 10
> Firenze
>
> Con la presente non abbiamo alcuna difficoltà a confermarLe che Ella ha regolarmente acquistato dalla nostra Casa Editrice, nel settembre del 1931, il diritto di traduzione in lingua inglese del libro "Ciondolino" di Vamba, di nostra proprietà. Dai nostri registri non resulta ohe tam le diritto sia stato ceduto precendentemente anche ad altri.
> Cei migliori saluti ci confermiamo
>
> (We have no difficulty in confirming to you that you have regularly acquired from our publishing house, in September, 1931, the right to translate into the English language the book "Ciondolino" by Vamba, the publishing rights of which belong to us. Our records do not show that these rights have ever been ceded to any other person.)
>
> R. BEMPORAD & FIGLIO
> SOCIETA ANONIMA PER AZIONI
> L'AMMINISTRATORE DELEGATO
> (signed) R. Bemporad

music, and Mark's memory was full of his quaint sayings, of which Mark poured out a stream to me, and so vividly that I can't tell today whether I ever saw and heard Tom, or whether my imagination has constructed him from Mark's account. I may as well tell here what more I can about Mark. He must have been a man of extraordinarily quick and broad sympathies: I don't remember any "getting acquainted" with him. He was one of those men whom from the start one seems to have always known well. I remember a wonderful Sunday afternoon in his pretty library at Hartford where Governor Jewell took Bill Fuller and me when we were spending a week-end with him about 1880. But I can't remember a thing that was said. I remember, too, a musical, much later, when Mark had a house on the southeast corner of Fifth Avenue and Ninth Street, where his daughter Clara, later Mme. Gabrilowitsch, among others, sang. On going away I said something to Mark that I thought was awfully funny, but his answer was so much funnier, that mine no longer seemd funny at all. What either of us said, I haven't the slightest idea. This is one of the moments when I half wish (not more than half) that I had kept a diary; but I'v always got to bed late enough without having that to make me later, and I'v always wasted time enough, without the large share of waste that a diary must inevitably involve.

One thing Mark said, I remember distinctly. When one of my boys who now measures six feet two or three, measured about two or three feet six, his mother on going out one afternoon told him she should be back to take him somewhere. She was detaind, and when she got home she found him drest and waiting on the stairs (it was a basement house) and he greeted her with: "It's dark now, and you're a liar." Mark and his surpassingly lovely wife dined with us that night, and my—may I say ditto?—told him the little story I've just written, when he almost jumpt around in his chair and

Title page for the first American edition of the German legal scholar's Vorgeschichte der Indoeuropäer *(1894; Rutgers University Library)*

flasht out: "You didn't punish that child?" I'm proud to tell that my wife was able to say she didn't.

The last time I remember seeing Mark was at a dinner given in the *Times* tower by the editors to the editor of the London *Times,* whose name, of course, I forget, but it was before the present management. If Mark said anything funny it was bitterly funny. His wife was dead. The burden of his talk was that he was growing old, that the future was dark, and that the heart was gone out of him. This has often puzzled me, in view of the printing of so much matter indicating that in his family were known psychical experiences which have convinced critics fully as exacting as he, that there is a prospect beyond this life brighter than any in it. That a nature so sunny as his should have found the prospect dark is doubly pathetic.

–*Garrulities of an Octogenarian Editor* (Boston & New York: Houghton Mifflin, 1923), pp. 99–100

* * *

In his memoir Holt quotes from a letter of his that had appeared in the 12 February 1910 issue of Publishers' Weekly.

Perhaps my colleagues in the book-trade may expect more reminiscences of it in this volume. Probably the best way I can supply them is to quote from a letter which I sent, by request, to *The Publishers' Weekly* about my seventieth birthday. My memories and my pen were then fresher than now, and the article will be new to the younger part of the trade, and nearly forgotten by the older.

Realizing, as I think I do somewhat, the danger of an old man overestimating the past, and also realizing that I looked upon the publishing world of forty-five (now, 1923, nearly sixty) years ago with the eyes of a novice, I suspect that some of my views must be taken with a grain of allowance. Perhaps the publishers of old loom large to me only because they loomed so large to my young eyes. But from any angle from which I am able to look, the publishing world seems to have occupied a much more important place in the community than it does now. (Yet it must not be forgotten that our great Ambassador [Walter H.] Page was a publisher of this later time.) Publishers' fortunes were relatively much larger. They have since stood at the same level or declined, while fortunes from other sources have enormously advanced, and men seem now to command an influence by brute force of dollars which then was more readily conceded to character and high tastes.

I did not really see much of [George Palmer] Putnam as a publisher, he being occupied with his internal revenue collectorship. I saw enough, however, to associate with the publishing business higher ideals than some I have known since. His place in the community was shown when his business came to grief through the sudden death, at a critical juncture, of a partner. He had such a host of influential friends among the best men, that he was at once made, under Lincoln's administration, collector of the most important revenue district in town. He interested himself from the outset in the work of organizing the Metropolitan Museum of Art, of which he became honorary secretary and, later, the first curator. He always held on to the framework of his publishing business, however, and after his lamented death it was reconstructed by his sons.

William H. Appleton was a financial magnate, at a time when that was an honor, and was vice-president of the Union Club when it was incontestably the best club in town. His was a heroic figure–literally one of the finest I ever saw, whose mere presence, not to speak of his character, always lent dignity to his surroundings. I used to meet him at the Century Club, where he talked to me about business as freely as if he were teaching me—as indeed he was, and invited me to dinner at his ample picture-lined house on Madison Square, accepting my modest hospitality in turn.

James Harper was mayor at a time when to be mayor was an honor. Joe Harper, as Joseph W. Harper, Jr., was affectionately and invariably known, must have become head of the old house in the seventies. The first time I remember talking with him was when I went down to Franklin Square to tell him that after he had bought the magazine right and book-right of one of Hardy's novels, trade courtesy required him to turn the book-right over to me, who had introduced Hardy here; and to turn it over, *not* at half the price he had paid for both rights, which my experience with Hardy demonstrated to be extravagant, but at the royalty (10 per cent. in those days) prevailing between me and Hardy; and to risk the deficit himself. If I remember rightly, the Harpers had offered the book rights to me before I knew they had bought them. Our discussion, as I remember, was only over terms. Joe nearly tired me out by talking all over Robin Hood's barn—a favorite trick of his—and then ended up by doing exactly what I wanted, and what the notions of honor then prevalent among publishers of standing required. Imagine in *these* days a youngster not a dozen years in the trade going to the head of the largest house, and calling him down, and the big man coming down as a point of honor!

I remember a similar interview with George Appleton—a warm-hearted man with a cold exterior, over some book of Baring-Gould's, and with similar results.

The *Atlantic* did the same that *Harper's Magazine* did regarding Hardy, at least twice, once even so recently as with a novel of May Sinclair.

By the way, I introduced Hardy here (at the suggestion of my friend of nearly forty [now over fifty] years, Fred Macmillan, now Sir Frederick). Subsequently, by an amicable arrangement, Harper took over certain relations with Hardy, yielding to me in return similar relations with [W. E.] Norris. But there was no "grabbing" on either side.

Prolixity was not Joe Harper's only weapon when he did not know his man; he used to affect pig-headedness and imbecility. Thus if there was anything rotten in his opponent's case, Joe would lead him to give it away. But if the case turned out sound, nothing could be more candid and generous than Joe's final treatment of it.

When the University Club was put on its feet in '79, he and I were together on the Council, and dined with it nearly every month during the season for eight years. Our business friendship became a very intimate personal one, and soon a word was enough to settle any differences.

He and William H. Appleton were both business geniuses—they both settled things offhand, nearly always settled them correctly, and never seemed to analyze their reasons or, perhaps, even to be able to give them.

Another admirable man in the trade of those days was Charles Scribner. When I was a youngster under thirty, I went to his office one day to ask him some business question; and when I turned to go, he stopped me, saying something like:

"Mr. Holt, I often thought, when I was a young fellow starting business, that I would give the world if I could have some experienced man to whom I could go with my questions and troubles. I should be very glad if you cared to come to me in that spirit."

I never discovered any weakness in the foundations which Mr. Scribner built for his great house with such material. He died comparatively early. The gods loved him, and so did men.

All those old publishers—Putnam, Appleton, Harper and Scribner—were incapable of petty or ostentatious things, and were much more inclined to friendly co-operation and mutual concession than to barbarous competition. The spectacle of a crowd of other men making fools of themselves exercised upon them no temptation to do as the herd did. No one of them, or of a few more, would go for another's author any more than for his watch; or, if he had got entangled with another's author through some periodical or other outside right, would no more hold on to him than to the watch if the guard had got caught on a button. They were wonderfully kind to me as a young fellow, and their kindness and example have been of inestimable value all my life. The idea of any knowledge that I might glean from them being used in rivalry against them, was too small for any of them to think of. In fact, any notion of the contemptible kinds of business rivalry, was too petty to find a place in their minds.

Those men were born in a less blatant, less extravagant, and therefore less competitive age. And yet I am not sure that it was not an age of greater elegance as well as of greater dignity and character.

The business of publishers does not throw them together much, and they are not apt to know each other well unless they have points of social contact. Moreover, there is a touch of natural aristocracy in such men as I have been telling about, though that they were far from exclusive is proved by their kindness to the young stranger I then was. Yet some publishers—more or less of specialties and sometimes of piracies, who did not know the leading group very well, supposed it to be a sort of trust, protecting each other and sharing all good things among themselves; and that the only way to get into the publishing business was to reprint books already published by these leaders. The lawyer for such a reprinter once asked me on the witness stand if there was not such a combination, and I was proud to tell him that I had seen no signs of it–that I had never been shut out or intrenched upon by men prominent in the trade, but had had only hospitality and kindness from them. That was a good many years ago.

A transition time between those days which I praise and these days which I do not, was in the late nineties, when Willie Appleton, Harry Harper, Haven Putnam, Charles Scribner, Jr., and I used to dine around at the clubs once a month every winter. We kept it up for several years. We had no rivalries, and it had not yet come quite time to fight each other at the instigation of the literary agent. Putnam got married, and at the dinner next before that happy event, we astonished him with a big loving-cup, filled with flowers, in the centre of the table. It had five handles, and bore on its five panels respectively the inscriptions, "With love of Appleton, With love of Harper, With love of Scribner, With love of Holt, For love of Putnam." Circumstances beyond the control of any of us made it our last dinner.

The foregoing says nothing of the Boston publishers. I was on excellent terms with Fields, Osgood, Houghton, Mifflin, and a few others. But though those were ornaments of the trade, I saw so little of them that I remember nothing worth telling beyond what I have told incidentally.

So far concerning its publishers' relations to each other. As to their relations with authors, I suspect, in fact I know, that the commercial turn given to their relations of late years has done them infinite harm. Authors now too often sell to whoever bids highest, and nobody has an interest in handling their books as a whole and with constant solicitude. It may be very stupid in publishers to lose such interest in the earlier books they retain, but human nature at best is often stupid, and it must be a rare publisher who feels a very active enthusiasm over what books he retains of an author who has left him.

Raphael Pumpelly on Henry Holt

Raphael Pumpelly, best known for his travel writing, was another Yale alumnus and close friend of Holt. In My Reminiscences *(1918) Pumpelly recalls his early association with Holt.*

In the winter of 1869-70 I had finished the manuscript of "Across America and Asia" and, with the help of my wife, had prepared it for publication. My friend and former schoolmate, Henry Holt, considered the question of bringing it out. However, the Appletons discouraged the venture, saying there was then small chance of success for books of travel. So I turned to the Harpers. When after sometime, at their request, I called at their office, Mr. Harper said they would like to publish the book, but would not be able to do so until after several months and would wish to bring it out in a cheap edition. When I objected that my plans made it necessary for me to get quickly through with the proof-reading, and that I had too many illustrations for a cheap form, Mr. Harper very kindly said:

"Think it over." Then handing me a paper he added, "I am doing an unusual thing. This is the very complimentary opinion of our best reader. Show it with your manuscript to other publishers and if you don't succeed come back to us."

I insert the "opinion" so courteously offered me by Mr. Harper. It bore no signature.

"Pumpelly's Tour round the World. A record of travel from the western terminus of the Missouri Railroad overland to San Francisco, thence to the Sandwich Islands, Japan, Russian Asia, and home to New York, by way of Paris. It consists of a copious and minute journal of adventure, exciting scenes and incidents, and geographical, historical and mercantile descriptions. The style is animated, though not in the least sensational, but on the whole rather more lively than Bayard Taylor. The information is abundant and apparently exact. Much of it is novel and all interesting. The author is a man of quick observation and sound reflection. His work is a large and important one, and will take the place of a standard book of travels. It might perhaps be more attractive to general readers if it were somewhat reduced in size, but its completeness would be impaired by any curtailment, but though long and costly it can scarcely fail of success."

Holt was captured and the book appeared in 1870, and went through at least nine editions. It has long been out of print, but, I am happy to be able to say, not out of memory; for even until now (1916) people who were then young or middle aged often introduce themselves on the strength of having enjoyed reading it.

–*My Reminiscences* (New York: Holt, 1918), II: 593-594

In support of the above statement, I have experienced since it was first written, a psychological phenomenon so remarkable as to be worth interpolating if only for its own sake. When *The Publishers' Weekly* sent me the proofs of its comments on my house's history, I added from memory the names of such distinguished authors whom we introduced here as I could think of. You will not find among them those of Anthony Hope, the Williamsons and May Sinclair. They simply did not come up in mind until later, when I was thinking the matter over in the night watches; the authors had been yanked away from me by their agents, with some help from very enterprising members of the trade; and my interest in their principal books, some of which I still publish, had simply followed the laws of mind (which are not of my making), and forgotten them, of course at my own expense as well as that of the authors. If I had voluntarily left out their names, of course I could have omitted them here too, making my point simply by blanks.

The same phenomenon would probably be as apt to take place in the mind of any other publisher, or any other human being, as in mine.

I see little in the present [1910] conditions of the trade that gives me very much satisfaction or hope–little but exaggerated competition in royalties, advances, discounts, drumming and advertising, all of which has brought the trade to a point where it takes many times as much effort and many times as much capital to make a dollar, as it did when I began business. Yet the insane extremes of advertising which set the proprietor of *The Times* to laughing at us a few years ago, seem to have outrun themselves, and the cringing before the lash of the literary agent may be less pronounced than it was; and perhaps there may be among some of us a little better realization than there was a few years ago, that we gain nothing by cutting each other's throats. But, take it all in all, my main hope for the future is that things must move–and as they cannot get very much lower than they are at present, possibly there may be a return, if even a forced one, toward the old spirit of co-operation, self-restraint and self-respect.

In publishing, the trust as a remedy for over-competition, as it is in many businesses, seems impracticable. With us competition can apparently be tempered only by character informed by broad views. I was not invited to attend the meeting which resulted in the foundation of the Publishers' Association, possibly because I am too "unpractical." But I have been invited to pay my share of the legal expenses and damages entailed by their policy of trying to control the book sellers instead of agreeing to control themselves–a policy that I don't think the fathers of any of them (so far as they had fathers in the trade) would have fallen into.

But, after all, the complexities in any form of human activity are greater than any one man's experience or intelligence can fathom. I am naturally anything but pessimistic, and notwithstanding the gloom of the outlook, I have optimism enough to think that things may turn out better than they seem to promise. They would if they could be shaped by my good wishes for my colleagues.

During the nearly fourteen years since the foregoing paragraph was written the note of hope which I managed to put after the Jeremiad paragraphs has been justified. Advertizing especially has been redeemed from the insanity then characterizing it, and competition has been brought more within reason.

This has largely been brought about by the publishers knowing each other better, and that has been chiefly due to the Publishers' Lunch Club, started some half dozen years ago. I being the oldest active member, they gave me during the first year the honor and pleasure of presiding at the monthly lunches.

–*Garrulities of an Octogenarian Editor*, pp. 206–213

***

In 1954 Holt's daughter Winifred Holt Bloodgood recalled her father and his times in "Notes on Henry Holt," which she recorded by hand in a spiral notebook now at the Rare Book and Manuscript Library, Columbia University. These notes shed an intimate–and not always flattering–light on Holt. Bloodgood's punctuation and grammar have been retained.

Henry Holt was born in Old Town, Baltimore January 3rd 1840. His father had left the Connecticut farm and worked his way to Baltimore selling tinware. The family had lived on the Grant from the Crown since 1640–ties seven generations–Selectmen etc.–See Holtbook [?] The first Holt was William.... There is a tradition that one of our Holts was in the first class at Yale. Father, his brother Charles and my brother Roland also were Yale graduates.... Dan Holt, Henry Holt's father, married Anne Zoe Seibold from Pennsylvania. Her people were "Pennsylvania Dutch"–she delighted us children giving us names of things in "Dutch."... Grandma was very beautiful all through her life as an old lady her white wavy hair and sparkling dark brown eyes were striking.

1851?

Grandpa died when father was 11 years old–Grandpa was killed by "a snakehead" on the B & O Railroad near Ellicot City. Note a "snakehead" was the end of an iron strip that was nailed onto the wooden rails of those days. The iron strip sometimes broke loose and shot up

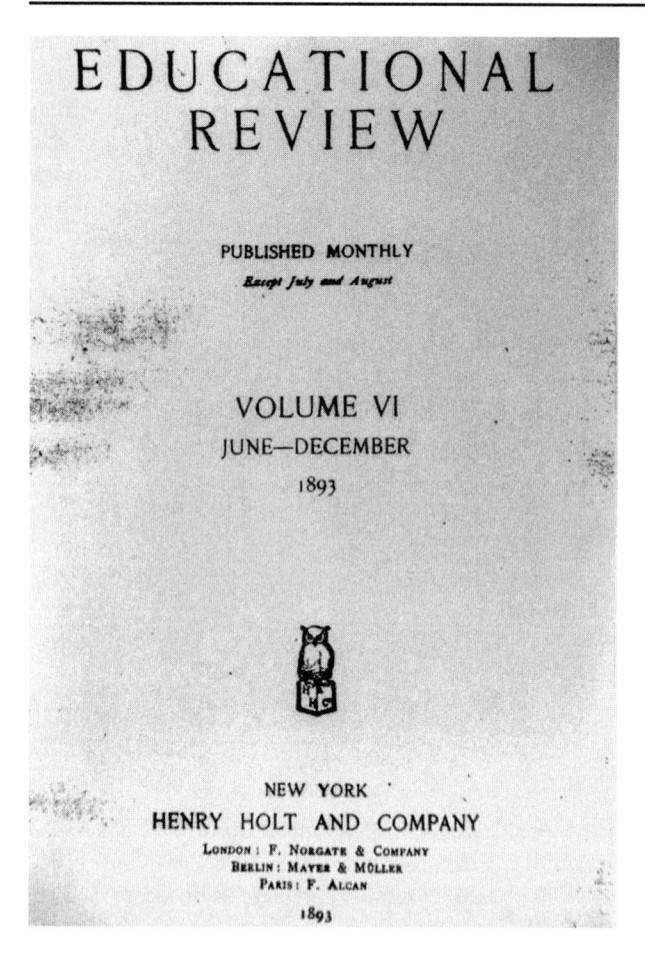

Title page for an issue of the review, edited by Nicholas Murray Butler, that Holt published from 1890 to 1899 (Rutgers University Library)

thru the floor of the railway carriage and stabbed the passenger sitting there.

1844?

At the age of 4 father smoked and read the newspaper. At the age of 6 he was lost much to the family's distress. He was found not far away sitting on the stoop of the house of a lady at home he had followed. He told me that it was his first love. She wore red shoes and was very beautiful! Father was 11 years old . . . when his father was killed in 1851. Henry Holt loved his father deeply and often spoke to me of him—I wish that I remembered just what father said—I merely know that he expressed love and admiration. His father had built a fine house in Baltimore on the corner of Lombard, and I think, Green Streets. It still stands. Brick with lovely ironwork—porch along the side—5 bathrooms—a great innovation for those days. Some people thought them indecent "such things should be outside of the house."

My daughter, Mrs. Samuel Hopkins (at 4302 Wendover Road, Baltimore 18) has beautiful portraits of Henry Holt's father and mother, painted by Tom Healy. Healy went to stay at Grandpa's house and painted the family while living there. Allen Dorsey was at the scene of the 1852 (?) accident when Grandpa was killed. He brought his body home to Grandma at the Lombard Street house. He fell in love with Grandma at first sight. A year later he married her. Her 4 Holt children—Henry the oldest, Ella next, Emma, and Charles the youngest. They all resented Grandma's marriage. . . . When Grandma returned from her wedding trip with Grandpa Dorsey—it was a freezing day, so the children poured water on the white marble steps hoping "that Allen Dorsey would break his leg."

"Allen Dorsey was known as Handsome Dorsey." He and Grandma must have been a wonderful couple to look at. He won his way with the children and saved the family financially. We grandchildren all loved him dearly. Dan Holt (Henry Holt's father) had built up a good business at the 1st oyster factory in the U.S.A. After his death his partner was taking advantage of Grandma. Grandpa Dorsey put a stop to that. When he had settled the Holt estate each child had a small inheritance. With their consent he invested that money in Indiana lands. I remember father's dictating letters to me about the sand that he was selling off of that land. Now the city of [illegible] built by Armour covers it and we grandchildren have added comfort from it. . . .

Grandpa Holt thought that "no gentleman was ever educated in the South" so at a very early age—6 or 8 years—father and Uncle Charles were shipped off to New Hampshire to live at Aunt English's house and to be educated "up North" then on to Yale. . . . At Yale he sat on the fence as a freshman. Joined (I think it was) "Keyes." Was not allowed to graduate with the class of 1861. As I remember it was because he differed with the strict Presbyterian authorities. He was allowed to graduate with the class of 1862. Thereafter, he always attended the reunions of '61 and '62. He helped start the first crew. . . .

1890s

"Educational Mastadon" is what Murray Butler called the head of [New York City's] Public School system—and it was published in Educational [Review]. Father was arrested and alarmed us at home by saying that he might have to spend the night in jail. The trial must have been wonderful! Butler and father were acquitted with reprimand on their language or some such thing. Father loved music—played the flute and at age of 40 took up playing the cello. My son irreverently said "Yes, played the cello but always out of tune.". . . We always had a box at the Philharmonic, after Carnegie Hall was built. Father and Charles had a wonderful time trying to reform English spelling.

[New York City:]

While we were still living at 54th Street and before father's second marriage–he used to take walks with his children on Sunday afternoons.... The idea of these walks was usually to teach us about the city of New York–I remember being taken to where 12th Street crosses 8th Street–most confusing! I also remember the goats and skeletons of hoop skirts on the cliffs of what is now Riverside Drive. We went to see "Industrial Exhibits" glass flowers *[illegible]* Peter Cooper Institute. We also went to work with father....

... Father did enjoy a good *[illegible]*. He couldn't find his ankle high boots one evening. I remember his calling over the bannister "Ella where has that damned nigger put my boots"! The boots were forthcoming from the cellar, nigger and all.

He called us children "Baboons and Monkeys." We adored him, but were a bit afraid of his flashing black eyes.

After his second marriage (1886?) everything changed. We saw little of him and he was preoccupied and didn't seem to notice us....

In [earlier] days he [Henry Holt] was absorbed in getting textbooks written by Americans for our American colleges. The people who visited us those days and filled the two guest rooms were John Fiske, historian, General [Francis Amasa] Walker, who founded M.I.T., Dr. [H. Newell] Martin who wrote "The Human Body," Dr. [Daniel Coit] Gilman, President of Johns Hopkins.... Professor William James I think came later. Professor Gildersleeve we saw in Baltimore. Also [Ira] Remsen. They wrote books for father.

... As I remember, but I could not swear to this Father met Oliver Lodge and Hodgson in London at the time [1890s] and that carried him into Psychical Research. This was a happy and absorbing interest to him.... The "Educational Review" was now absorbing him and the Psychological aspect of things was working in his dear mind. The World beyond was much in his thoughts.

... Father loved what he now called "The Unpopular Review" and wrote the "Psycic" articles for it. The Review became a financial burden to him. We hated to have him give up what was of so much interest to him but finally the decision was made and the last issue appeared.

Father's big book "The Cosmic Relations" was well on its way. He used to talk of it to me ... years later Edith would recall sitting with neighbors in the library at Fairholt where the "Omega Board" gave us a wonderful séance ... after father's death. I have a typescript in Baltimore.

... [Father] loved Roland, but never could understand his love of the theatre and theatrical people. He crushed a latent talent that might have gone far. Roland wanted to be a stage manager–the lighting and mechanics of the art absorbed him.

... I have always called father a "metior"–his thoughts carried one over the earth into the beyond and we had to rush along with him there.

P.S. Father's great friend over the years was Raphael Pumpelly. In the séance after father's death– we asked who had welcomed him in the beyond, he replied "Pompey of course." "Pompey" was father's nickname for Pumpelly....

I remember Williams [Ralph Williams, Holt's onetime business partner] as a disappointed little man, rather apologetic. He became the manager of a hotel.

Oil–Father told me that he had been asked to be one of the founders of Standard Oil he refused his friends as he said he loved books rather than oil and get rich quickly.

1900–1920: The Harcourt Years

ALFRED HARCOURT AND HENRY HOLT

Alfred Harcourt joined Holt and Company in 1904, along with fellow Columbia University graduate Donald Brace. While Brace assumed a quieter role in production, Harcourt began as a trade-department editor, happy to socialize with the writers and publishers, traveling abroad, and generally making it his business to know what was going on among the literati. Harcourt's defection from Holt in 1919 (along with Brace, to found their own firm) came about largely because of the discrepancy between his more-liberal attitudes and those of the elderly Henry Holt. Several Holt authors, including Carl Sandburg, Dorothy Canfield Fisher, and Walter Lippmann, left Holt to follow Harcourt. Robert Frost, who was close to Harcourt, did not.

Publishing Since 1900
Alfred Harcourt

When I entered publishing in 1904 with Henry Holt and Company, the center of gravity of American publishing of books in general literature was, in both senses of the word, only just moving from Boston and New England to New York. Chicago and Philadelphia were important centers, but the New England Brahmins–Longfellow, Whittier, Holmes– and their publishers set the standards of taste in literature and publishing practice for the whole country. Robert Grant and Margaret Deland were serious contemporary New England writers. Winston Churchill's *Coniston* was a sample of serious fiction.

The Holt and Company owl device, 1909 and 1912 (Rutgers University Library)

New York publishers were in general only following the best of the New England and British traditions.
–"Publishing Since 1900" in *Bowker Lectures on Book Publishing* (New York: R. R. Bowker, 1957)

Some Experiences
Harcourt

Harcourt included his recollections of Henry Holt in Some Experiences, *which he published privately with his wife, Ellen, in 1951.*

Mr. Holt was nearly seventy when I went to him, and his highly creative period was past, but the fearlessness was still there, the highest business principles, and an uncompromising loyalty to quality. Like all of us at seventy, this one-time "radical" was beginning to disapprove of some of the new ideas, and he gave me a lot of discipline in making me fight for a book or a policy that departed from what was considered "respectable and responsible." But when the new idea was really good, he let me go my way, sometimes with modifications. Perhaps he sneakingly relived his own youth as he watched my enthusiasms.
–Alfred Harcourt, *Some Experiences* (Riverside, Conn., 1951), pp. 13–14

An "Apprenticeship" in Letters

Harcourt's "apprenticeship" with Holt and Company took place mostly by mail, as the aging Henry Holt spent more and more of his time at Fairholt, his home in Burlington, Vermont. As Holt noted in a letter to Frederick Leypoldt's widow in 1911, "My own visits to the office since I was seventy are extremely uncertain. I am teaching the office to do without me, as they hav [sic] got to do before a great while." (He lived another fifteen years.) In the following letters Holt's idiosyncratic spelling will be reproduced without comment.

Alfred Harcourt (seated on cushion, right foreground) and Donald Brace (seated behind Harcourt to right) with other members of the Columbia University Spectator *board of editors, 1904 (from* The Nineteen Hundred and Four Columbian, *1904; Columbia University Library)*

Advertisement in the 1 May 1900 issue of a New York literary magazine (Rutgers University Library)

Undated photograph of Roland Holt, Henry Holt's son, who joined Holt and Company after graduating from Yale in 1890 but whose main interest lay in the theater (Princeton University Library)

Nov. 10, 1904

Dear Mr. Holt:

The questions you ask have been in my own mind for sometime, although they did not become clearly defined until after I had practically finished my traveling, and my answers are, at present, only rather clear-cut impressions, which I may or may not justify by the more intelligent questions that I can ask when I next go on the road.

I think we do sell less of a given book than publishers of our own weight or above, especially Scribners, Harpers, Doubleday-Page, McClure-Phillips, and Macmillan. I do not think Putnams or Appletons push their books to much better advantage than we; in fact, Mr. Baker last year told Mr. Roland [Holt, a son of Henry Holt] that they did not do so.

I do not think it costs the firms mentioned more than the difference to sell more books—for one thing, I think they make it easier than we do for the small jobbers (Claflin of New York, DeWolfe, Fiske & Co. of Boston, Western Book & Stationery Co. of Chicago, J. L. Boland of St. Louis, Macauley Bros. Of Detroit, St. Paul Book & Stationery Co. of St. Paul. Most of these houses not only have important retail trade, but supply most of the department stores of the country besides some other jobbing) to do business with them, by giving them 40% and 10% on all their fiction, conditioning this rate (as Doubleday-Page and Scribner's do *[illegible]*) on a certain amount of business each year. This enables dealers to push all their books all the time, instead of those they buy in 500 lots while that lot lasts. DeWolfe-Fiske did not have "Andrew Vane" in stock for over a month this fall: they were waiting till they could make up a 500 mixed order.

I have just shown your letter to Mr. Vogelius [Joseph Vogelius, a longtime Holt employee]. His answer to the first question is: "Yes, by a long way." To the second he expressed his opinion that we should publish more books by known authors, and spoke of the fact that good books take care of themselves. McClurg's and Burrows Bros.' first orders for "David Harum" were 3 and 10 copies, respectively; later they bought it in 10,000 lots.

In regard to the author's side of this question: I tell first or second book people, I think with truth, that they probably get as much or more advertising from us than from Macmillan, for instance, who advertises books by known authors, but with whom the new people get lost in the shuffle *[illegible]*.

As to how our sales of books by known authors compare with other houses: I think there is something radically wrong if we don't sell 50,000 "Princess Passes" and illustrated "Conductor" before publication. Mr. V. and I think Macmillan would sell from 75,000 to 100,000. I urge that the terms for such sales be settled as soon as possible. Samples of these books should be in dealers' hands by February 1st, for the books should be out March 1st, and the securing of 50,000 orders and manufacturing the books is at least a month's work.

As to a Boston trip: I was there quite recently, and sold the dealers enough books to keep them busy almost, if not quite, till Christmas. I think it would be better for me to go to Philadelphia, Baltimore and Washington. My two-days trip to Philadelphia was hurried, and I can do some business there with Wanamaker and Strawbridge & Clothier, and perhaps sell 500 more "Cheerful" or "Divine Fire" to Booklovers. I have not been to Baltimore or Washington. Our miscellaneous business in these three cities was more last year than that in those on the New England trip. Mr. Roland, Mr. Bristol [Holt employee Edward N. Bristol], Mr. Vogelius agree that the Southern trip is more important: so if you agree, I'll go down that way the week after Thanksgiving, for orders and information.

Frontispiece and title page for the autobiography of the first person from China to graduate from an American university (Rutgers University Library)

I fear my discount talk has gone farther than your questions warrant, but I feel it is not beyond what the conditions of our trade warrant. I also think our discounts are about o.k. for big jobbers and retailers.

Faithfully yours,
Alfred Harcourt

November 30, 1904

Dear Mr. Holt:

You wrote me some time ago in regard to the advertising done by Little-Brown, Appleton, and Longmans. At Mr. Bristol's suggestion, Morrison and I have been keeping track of these firms for the past month, and I send you an abstract of their recent advertising. It is not entirely complete for December as some of the magazines have not yet appeared, i.e., *The Bookman, Book Newsdealer, Book News*. Little-Brown does considerable [sic] more in the magazines than we. The use of *Scribner's* and the *Century* by all three houses is noteworthy, and I'm glad we have our page in the Christmas *Century*.

I wonder if we are not wasting money in the sort of newspaper advertising we are doing. The attached newspaper "Ads." are the usual forms for these houses. If we are to keep in their class, our policy would seem to be to use magazines for announcements, and an occasional splurge on a promising book, and the newspapers almost entirely in large enough space and type with popular books to make a showing among the other advertisers of various wares. Such a plan may seem to leave out our first book authors, but if we could have several books like *Vane, More Cheerful, Conductor,* and *Marathon* selling freely, it would be easier to get the new people's books in our assorted orders, where they will be taken to make up the quantity, and then get their chance on the dealer's counter.

Faithfully yours,
Alfred Harcourt

> Kegan Paul, Trench, Trübner & Co. Limited,
> Paternoster House, Charing Cross Road,
>
> *Telegraphic Address*
> COLUMNÆ LONDON
>
> London Dec 19th. 1900.
>
> Dear Mr Holt,
>
> I have yours of December 7th and 10th which arrived together, and thank you very sincerely for the pleasant things you say in the second of these letters with regard to our relations. No one can desire more cordially than I do myself that our relations should remain undisturbed, and I am hopeful that we may yet accomplish some of those big things which we so gaily set out to do three-and-a-half years ago, but which, so far, seem to have eluded us.
>
> With regard to your enquiry in the letter of December 7th. about "Adrian Rome", I do not think that Arthur Moore has any new book ready just now, but I am pretty sure that I can get the first chance of anything he writes. I must say that I have been rather disappointed at his failure to make any impression, not only on the public, but on the critics, and I am a little bit afraid that he is going to slip back into the army of the unsuccessful. I am sorry for many reasons, and principally because I know he is actuated by the highest literary ambition, that he never consciously writes below the demands of his literary conscience, and that he is in every way a true worker. I should not be surprised to see him arrive some day, but, on the other hand, I am afraid I must now confess that I should not be surprised either if he never got any further. He is too much of an artist to sink to the lower levels, and perhaps not quite enough of one to rise to the higher.

First page of a letter to Henry Holt from Arthur Waugh (father of the writers Evelyn and Alec Waugh), whom Holt retained in the late 1890s as his English agent. Despite Waugh's efforts, nothing was published out of this collaboration (Princeton University Library).

Author Mary Finley Leonard had already published several books with other publishers when Holt and Company rejected one of her manuscripts in 1909. The manuscript in question and Henry Holt's "personal mix-up in it" are not documented.

August 18, 1909

Dear Mr. Harcourt:

Please write Mary Finley Leonard that three readers fail to recommend us to undertake her book—tel her we ar very sorry. I don't want to hav any more personal mix-up in it.

. . . .

As to binding Yung Wing's Biography, the Chinese color is yellow. I would bind in the same yellow as Miss Perkins's Spanish book. Letter in gold on the back and side, and put on Yung Wing's name in Chinese characters somwhere from half an inch to an inch high. Giv his son the space it should occupy to look wel on the cover, and get him to use his judgment regrding size. I suspect we had better put it above the title on the side. *[illegible]*.

We can afford to make a handsom book out of that: for anybody who wants it is going to want it.

I do not see any popularity for Bennett's novel in the Tribune review you sent me, or in Garnett's recent letter to the Nation (#2281, Mch. 18) reviewing all the current English novelists. Somhow that letter gave me more of the feeling that English novels ar less likely to take here even than I had regarded them before. But I wil glance thru Bennett's novel when it coms.

I enclose an article from last Saturday's Times, apropos of which I hav to remark, 1st: the name of its writer should be on our cards for circulars, and the supplement of the Times should be searched through every Saturday for the names of its various correspondents interested in books;

2nd, Is Des Moines so much of a book place?

. . . .

. . . the fundamental reason why I am sending you this article: my general feeling about the miscellaneous business is, as you know, that it is not worth a man's doing . . . but reading this letter and reflecting that one of the oldest and best provincial bookstores here has just disposed of its general stock, while probably it ought to add to my conviction that the miscellaneous business is not worth doing, and tend to make me do less or none of it, takes me for a moment on the other side, as proving to me that while we are doing it, it is more necessary on account of the disappearance of the bookstores, to be in direct communication with book readers—if there ar any—if they are not all given over to the Sunday papers and other periodicals. . . .

[Henry Holt]

Title page for the Holt edition of the 1893 work on industrial development by a German economist (Rutgers University Library)

Mary and Jane Findlater's Crossriggs, *the novel mentioned in the following letter, was published in England in 1908 by Smith, Elder. E. P. Dutton eventually published the first American edition in 1913. The "forthcoming autobiography" by Jane Addams was* Twenty Years at Hull House, *published by Macmillan in 1910.*

August 21, 1909

Dear Mr. Holt:

I enclose correspondence and opinions in regard to "Crossriggs."

I also enclose a circular from the *American Magazine,* in which you will find marked a notice of Jane Addams forthcoming autobiography. Perhaps Miss [Ida] Tarbell knows all about it, and it ought to be a big book.

In regard to the *Times*'s letter about bookstores dying out: Des Moines was never very much of a book place. Since Baker & Trisler have gone out of business, the department store is the only bookstore there. There are good bookstores in Kansas City and Denver. They may not be so good, or so many as there were some time ago. . . .

There has been no complaint that we get out fifty cent editions too soon after our first editions. The trade have requested that publishers wait at least two years before getting out a cheap edition. As far as I can remember, we have always waited three or more.

. . . .

I should like to get out a fall circular similar to our last Christmas catalog, copy of which I am sending you, except that, in general, it would cover our fall announcements, and the live books on our list, with lists of standard sets, such as [John Addington] Symonds and [J. S.] Mill. I think it would pay to send these to 1,000 libraries, to the 3,600 names on our miscellaneous list, and to the artists, authors, college presidents, clergymen, educators, editors, lawyers and musicians in Who's Who. These classes comprise about 9,000 persons. . . .

Yours sincerely
Alfred Harcourt

* * *

According to Holt's daughter Edith Bloodgood, her father was asked to be one of the founders of Standard Oil. Bloodgood claims that Holt refused because he loved books more than business opportunities. Ida Tarbell wrote about American economics and industrial practices in magazines such as McClure's *and* The American Magazine. *Her volume* The History of the Standard Oil Co. *was published by Macmillan in 1937.*

Sept. 6, 1911

Dear Harcourt:

Glad you'r coming up: Bring me one piece of news, please–How Ida Tarbell happend to go to Macmillan.

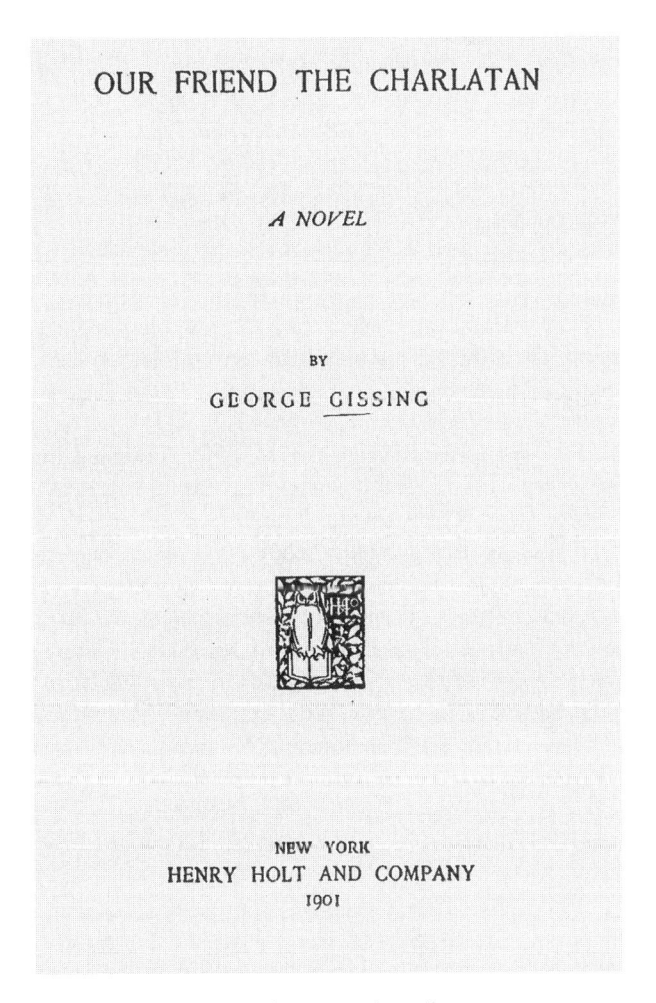

Cover design and title page for Holt's edition of the late-Victorian novelist and essayist's 1901 comic novel attacking the application of evolutionary theory to social issues (Rutgers University Library)

You know she came to me when I was in the midst of my Standard Oil row, and it was agreed that it would not be wel for me to take her; and she went over to Sturgis, Walton & Co. Why the change should hav been made after so brief a trial, puzzles me, and is wel worth our knowing....

Ar you aware that in yours of the 31st, you said "a memoranda"? Probably it is attributable to your stenographer and to haste on your part in not reading; or is it possible to get thru Columbia without knowing Latin? I got thru Yale, and printed in the Atlantic *vilum* as the neuter of *vilis;* and what is more, it past men who had got thru Dartmouth and Harvard. So we go!

....

[Henry Holt]

After publishing The Educational Review *in the 1890s, Henry Holt had been keen to publish another journal for some time. He began publishing* The Unpopular Review *as a quarterly in 1914. Harcourt's lack of enthusiasm for this endeavor may or may not have been responsible for its apparent lack of success. It certainly played a part, however, in driving Harcourt away from Holt. The* Unpopular Review *became* The Unpartizan Review *in 1919, retaining this title until publication ceased in 1921.*

October 8, 1912.

Dear Mr. Holt:

....

Personally, and very frankly, I should be sorry to see you try the [U]npopular Review unless you can secure a "first chop" editor who could, in the natural course of events, be permanently active....

I'd like to see the proposed tables of contents and *contributors* for the first few issues. The names you mention don't "thrill" me, though [Frank] Mather is good.

That is, if you really believe that America can supply enough notable contributors to give the necessary material for a permanent, *very* high class review, and you can secure an able, enthusiastic editor to share with you the very considerable labor of starting it, who could keep it going at your standard when you wish to become less active,—then I should be sorry if you did not try it....

Sincerely yours,
Alfred Harcourt

P.S. I hope the above expression on matters which you, of course, have considered, won't seem brash or rash;—but I couldn't very well express either enthusiasm or a lack of it without explaining why.

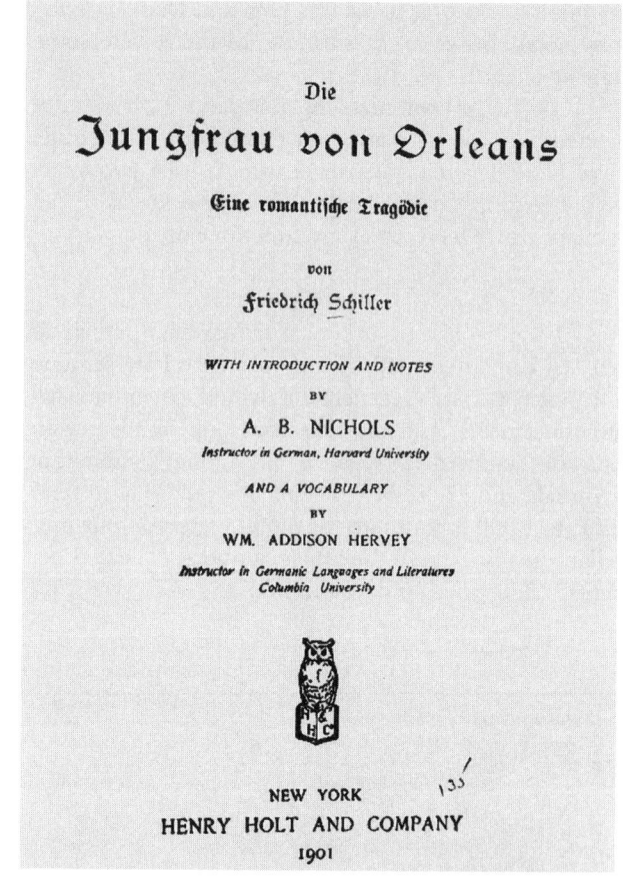

Title page for the student edition of the German dramatist's 1802 play (Rutgers University Library)

May 20, 1913

Dear Harcourt:

....

I think the main trouble is in the periodicals and the greater concentration of people's tastes upon money and the things they can buy with it.

I said at Yale som thirty years ago, that the libraries of the future wer going to consist of sets of bound periodicals. I was younger and bolder than I am now. I would not say it today: I would be more apt to say that people ar going without libraries—except public ones. But nevertheless there was an element of prophecy in it.

....

[Henry Holt]

Henry Holt's efforts to back out of a deal that Harcourt had already made were a precipitating factor in Harcourt's departure in 1918. (In that case Holt wanted to stop publication of Bertrand Russell's Proposed Roads to Freedom, *which Holt and Company published in 1919.) At least one earlier instance of a similar attempt at a retraction is documented, con-*

Holt and Company ledger sheet for July 1903 (Princeton University Library)

cerning Harold Fielding-Hall's The World Soul, *which Holt and Company published in 1913.*

June 15, 1913

Dear Harcourt:

We all need a margin for mistakes. I'm afraid "The World Soul" is another dog book.

Don't let any more of it go out until you hear farther from me. Meanwhile tel me what you no about it. Apparently some good English house has been fooled and fooled us.

Rite to the papers asking them not to review it til they hear farther from us, as there has been som mistake. Rite to the dealers to return their copies and charge bac.

That book cd easily prevent som real author from sending us a MS. It wil be cheaper to suppress it than to let it go.

Good Lord! How can we be *sure* of our advice?

Yrs. much
[Henry Holt]

Send me bac a copy of this. I'm riting on Sunday.

June 16, 1913

Dear Harcourt:

The plot thickens regarding "The World Soul."

This morning Mrs. Holt showd me a review of it in the English Nation, evidently by a person who is a little cract regarding the Oriental philosophers. The review does not really prais the book, tho it speaks of the author as having don good service in bringing accounts of Eastern matters to the Western world; but the review away the case when it shows that his book was publisht by Hurst & Blackett.

Mrs. Holt then said that his previous book, "The Soul of a People," had arousd great enthusiasm. I askt her how she knew of it, and she told that it was brought to her attention by an English actress!! I then turned to it and found that it was publisht by Macmillan.

Now my explanation of the hole business is that the man has a following among half-cract people in England, and that Macmillan got foold into publishing "The Soul of a People," and then found out what the man was, refused "World Soul," and the author had to go down the scale for a publisher until he came to Hurst & Blackett.

Advertisement for the second novel, published in 1907, of the British novelist for whom Holt and Company was the American publisher (Rutgers University Library)

I didn't read much of the book: I read only the introduction, when I found that he was a cranky ignoramus with all the conceit of a crank. He may hav a lot of the crazy knowledge about Oriental philosophies—the Blavatsky stuf and all that, but no scolarly knowledge.

I don't think it's possible that I can be doing the book injustice, but until I lern more about it, I certainly am not going to spend any more time in finding out.

Our getting out this shallow book on that subject just now is doubly hard luc on me, because in my forthcoming book [*On the Cosmic Relations,* 1914] there's going to be a great deal said about it, and I don't think I'm strong enuf to stand having such stuff as Hall's appears to be, associated with my name.

But as I'v read only his introduction, there is stil som margin left in my mind for any farther light you can throw on the situation. I guess, however, the early part of this letter contains all the light necessary.

[Henry Holt]

June 17, 1913

Dear Mr. Holt:

More about "The World Soul." Yours of the 16th crossed mine of the same date.

Hurst and Blackett is not *far* down the line from Macmillan. It is really Hutchinson and Company. The two firms use each other's name in some inexplicable fashion. Their offices are together, and the same people act for both. The correspondence I have had regarding "The World Soul" was all on Hutchinson and Company's stationery, and with the Vice-President and General Manager of Hutchinson and Company. He told that it was his strong personal interest in Fielding-Hall's work that had enabled them to get "The World Soul" from Macmillan; that they had published his first book or two, and that then Macmillan had taken him from them. According to the present publishing situation in England, it is no special come-down for Fielding-Hall to be published by "Hutchinson and Blackett." Personally, I do not believe Macmillan had a chance at this.

Scribners had ten copies on publication ten days ago, and sold them out, and ordered 15 more last week, and they have only a few of these to return. They have telephoned twice to-day to know whether it was really necessary to return, as their customers were calling for the book. The manager at Brentano's told Mr. Gehrs this morning that on the title and the author's name, it was, in his judgment, the most promising book on our spring list, and they have only a copy or two to return.

I do not look at the book as a work of philosophy so much as a personal, spiritual autobiography; that is, we do not stand sponsor for Fielding-Hall's ideas any more than we do for those of Mrs. Albee's "The Gleam." I do not see why we should not stand sponsor for both of these personal spiritual autobiographies as personal interpretations. That Fielding-Hall, through his long sojourn in the far east, does know Oriental modes of thought is hardly against the interest or value of his book.

I have had time to read only half of his book.

What shall I say to the English publishers and the author when they ask for American notices?

I anticipated, and so had the English publishers, and it seems with some reason from the trade experience so far, that we should use considerably more than the 750 copies we ordered to start with. We have about $600 invested.

Sincerely yours,
Alfred Harcourt

P.S. It is hard "luc" for H.H. & Co., as publishers, to cross you as author, but I hardly think this book will be read (would have been read) from at all the same point of view as yours.

DOING BUSINESS

Professor H. P. Trent of Columbia University was a good friend of Henry Holt and served the firm as a series editor and frequent manuscript reader.

Dec. 13, 1907

My dear Trent:

Yours of Thanksgiving Day is welcome.

I hope you had more festive functions in the course of the day, than writing to me, cheerful as your letter is.

. . . .

That is a very good joke of yours regarding my World's Series, that you "proposed a similar Series to a publisher except that it involved a volume to a man." The including of several men in a volume is the only justification that I see for my Series, for which you are hereby elected and confirmed as editor. . . . You observe that the generosity which characterized me in relation to the American Series, pervades my conduct regarding this Series too. Now these biographical series I think are going to be good things; and I should not be surprised if the World Series would turn out a big thing; so you may as well begin scratching your head at

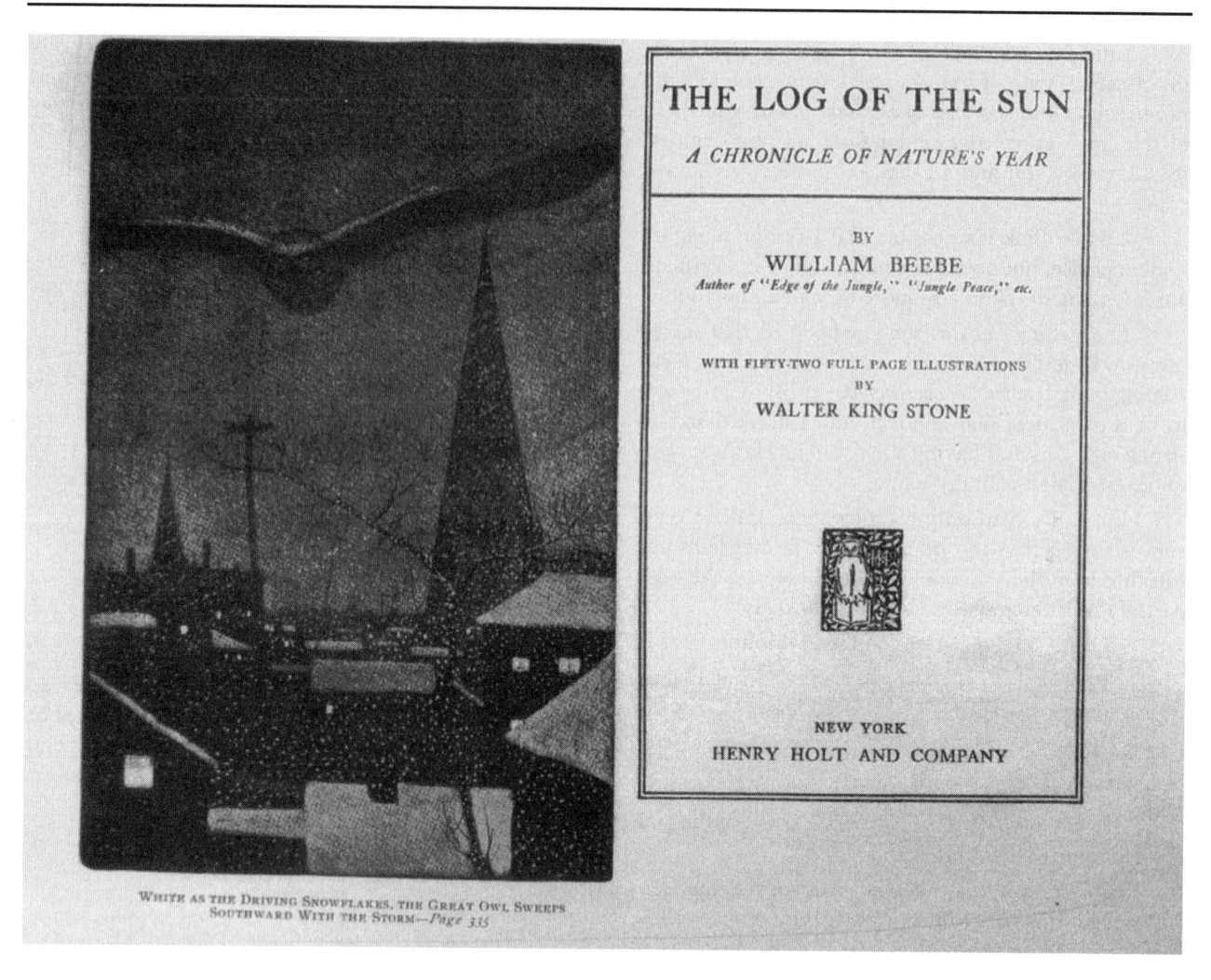

Frontispiece and title page for the naturalist's 1906 compilation of his articles on birding first published in the New York Tribune *(Rutgers University Library)*

once. As I understand it, I am to give $100 a volume for each volume of the World's Series which is really instigated and edited by you.

Suppose you address a letter to each of your minions . . . stirring him up? You know what awfully unreliable people you literary fellers are! And then give me your scheme for the World's Series, and I will give it fits, if I must, but I don't believe that I must.

First, last and all the time, bear in mind, in regard to all these Serieseses, that we have in mind the high-school library, or even the high-school library *[sic]*, without diluting below the interest of the intelligent adult—that we want the people treated as human beings as distinct from their purely professional functions, tho we want the genesis of their professional capacities as clearly marked as the material permits. In fact, I guess that the last clause embodies my subconscious root ideal, to teach youngish people how they can become great statesmen, soldiers, poets and sich, and how easy the trick is!! To become great prose writers, however, you and I know is difficult. But perhaps we hadn't better let out that secret.

By the way, what is your distinction between "hadn't better" and "wouldn't better"? Lounsbury has written me a couple of vitriolic letters on using "wouldn't better" at all, his only objection being that it is a neologism. Some people think the Sermon on the Mount was that, extending the definition of the term a little.

Profoundest to Madam!

Yours always
[Henry Holt]

* * *

Title page for the third volume in the Holt and Company series addressing contemporary social concerns, with an advertisement from the same volume for the books in the series (Rutgers University Library)

Henry Holt on the Publishing Business

October 20, 1911
Dear Putnam [George Haven Putnam]:

....

As I look bak over my life, among the things that I hav to regret is an inordinate amount of plain speaking, but I guess you won't giv me any occasion to regret my semi-humorous indulgence in it this time.

Good God, how I hate and despise the publishing business and everything connected with it, except you and one or two other good people!

....

But don't let my expression to you regarding the publishing business work in that way. I don't suppose it is my real chronic feeling: for even now when I am at my desk here and begin dictating my letters, I feel a pleasure in action and in the sense of competence that I don't feel for instance when I am studying Psychical Research, and that for any man to feel would simply demonstrate him a fool!

Giv my love to your wife and I wil risk saying my wife's love too.

Yours ever
[Henry Holt]

The Authors' Club was a favorite among the several clubs to which Henry Holt belonged. Among the contacts he met there was the writer William James Ghent, who approached Holt on behalf of a fellow Socialist who had written a book. Holt rejected the book, which was eventually published as Abraham Lincoln and the Working Class *(n.d.) in the Appeal Pocket Series (also known as the Ten Cent Pocket Series) by a publisher of some of Ghent's work, the Appeal Publishing Company (also known as the Haldeman-Julius Company) in Girard, Kansas.*

March 24 [1911]

Dear Mr. Holt:

Do you care to look at the manuscript of which I spoke to you once at The Authors Club–a work on "Lincoln, Labor & Slavery"? Its author is Hermann Schlueter, the Editor of The Volkszeitung of this city.

The work has been "turned down" by two or three publishers because, as it seems to me, it is written from a Socialist standpoint. The same publishers will publish a Socialist novel or a Socialist Exposition, but draw the line at a Socialist interpretation of a certain historical epoch. The why and wherefore of which I do not understand.

I shall be glad to send you the ms. if you care to take a look at it.

Sincerely yours,
W[illiam] J. Ghent

March 24, 1911

Dear Mr. Ghent:

Thanks for your favor of the 24th.

I try to keep as catholic as I can, and it wil help me to do so to hav the socialist work you speak of, examind. All the same, I tel you that I haven't any faith in it. Yet socialism, under a few of the million definitions, is very good for an ideal.

With all good wishes,

Faithfully yours
[Henry Holt]

April 24, 1911

My dear Mr. Ghent:

Your friend's first page is enuf to show me that it is not the kind of book I want. He speaks of the laboring classes being "deprived" of the means of production, as if sombody had robd them of somthing that they had ever had; and he also writes as if the means of production wer in the hands of a mass of men who prevented the working class from ever getting any possession of them; whereas the truth is that most of the men who own the means of production ar former members of the working class themselvs, and it is constantly demonstrated that there is nothing but any man's own laziness or incapacity to prevent his owning all the means of production that he needs. Your friend's views I consider utterly unjustifiable and the cause of a great deal of social trouble, and especially of a great deal of distress to the working classes; and of course I do not care to take any part in spreading them.

It may seem to you that it ought not to hav taken me so long to express this opinion, but it took me somtime to get around to the book.

With all good wishes, I am

Very truly yours
[Henry Holt]

What shal we do with the manuscript?

Ghent replied to Holt on the stationery of U.S. representative Victor L. Berger of the Fifth District of Wisconsin.

April 28 [1911]

My dear Mr. Holt:

I am sorry I haven't time to combat some of your opinions. But I haven't. I am down here as the secre-

William De Morgan, the English novelist who published seven titles with Holt and Company from 1907 to 1914

Title page for British novelist De Morgan's fifth book, an historical romance, and the advertisement from the same volume for the Holt and Company editions of his works (Rutgers University Library)

tary of the only Socialist Congressman, with a constituency of over 600,000 voters, and every minute is occupied.

Will you please send the ms. to Hermann Schlueter, The Volkszeitung, 15 Spruce St., New York?

With best wishes,
Very truly yours,
W. J. Ghent

The Literary Agency of London

The Literary Agency of London, headed by G. H. Perris and C. F. Cazenove, worked with Holt and Company at this time. Hilaire Belloc was a French-born British poet, essayist, satirist, and historian. At the top of the following letter Roland Holt wrote, "I think well of this. Perhaps L200 on receipt of completed ms. R.H."

Jan. 1st 1912

My dear Harcourt,

Hilaire Belloc:—We are arranging for him with [British publisher] Chapman & Hall an important book, running to some 200,000 words, which they will do in the first instance at 21/-, dealing with the History of France. It is a curious thing that there is no English book of any standing and literary value which gives a History of France. The only book we know of in England is by Dean Kitchen, but that is not regarded as in any sense a classic. What Belloc aims at is something comparable with Green's Short History of the English People. The claim is a bold one, but Belloc has undoubtedly the capacity to do really striking work, and something that will have a permanent sale.

We are reserving the American rights from Chapman, because we think the book too important to be treated in any casual way by a sale of sheets. I do not know how you have in the H.U.L. [Home University

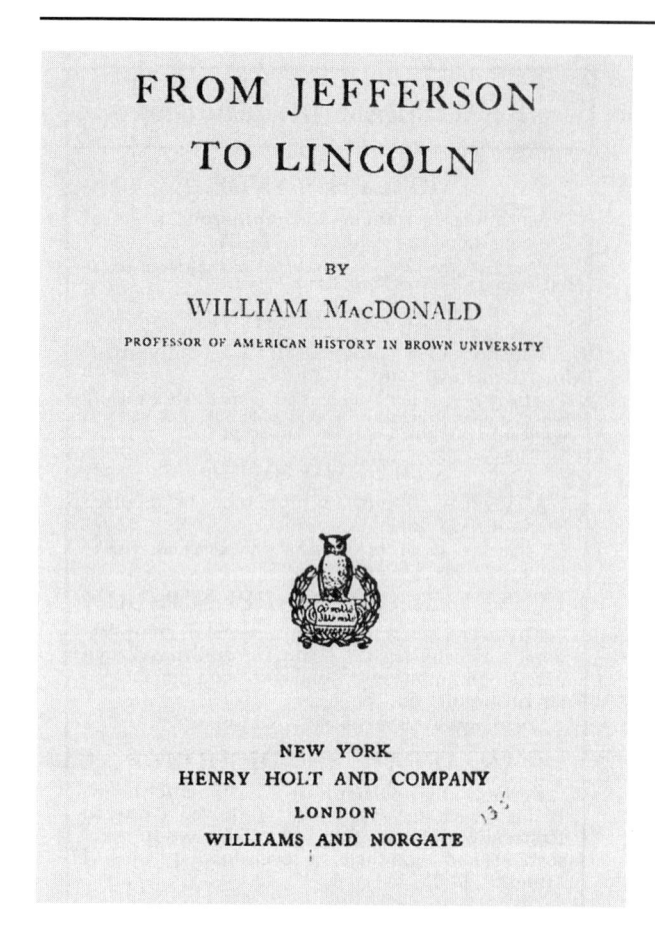

Title page for the 1913 historical study (Rutgers University Library)

Library series] with his little volume on the French Revolution. Here it has been by far the best seller. Belloc's standpoint, as you know, is at once Roman Catholic and democratic—a blend which we think should appeal to teachers in your country. It is impossible, of course, to write sympathetically in France if one has anything approaching a Protestant bias. At the same time, the book, to be regarded as valuable by modern eyes, must be written in sympathy with democratic ideals. Belloc wants an American commission to add to his English arrangement. Between ourselves, Chapman are covenanting to pay us an advance of L500 on account of royalties. A comparatively limited sale at a guinea will cover their outlay, and we reckon there should be a rich field in a reprint at say, 8/6d. net—the price at which Green has always appeared. And we want, of course, American copyright. I wish you would consider this carefully, and let us hear as soon as possible if you can agree to take the American end. The proposal seems to us safe, and as regards terms, Belloc will of course expect a decent advance on account of royalties. On this point we are content to receive any proposal you can make, and discuss it with Belloc. He reckons that if the matter is fixed quickly, he can finish it during the present year, as the ground he has to traverse is naturally very familiar to him. That would probably mean publication early in 1913.

I hope you will view the suggestion favourably. It is another of our own little ideas, and we are very keen on its going through.

With every good wish for the New Year,
Sincerely yours,
C. F. Cazenove

At the top of the following letter from Cazenove, Harcourt wrote, "Senate agreed to reject. AH." At the end of the same letter Roland Holt wrote, "Young Bell [a publisher referred to in the letter] seems to take to rather dreary subjects. I'd rather take this than the Jew book or the Pro-Catholic book he proposes, and which we rej'd, but it looks about as exciting as a sociological consideration of the Philippines, and I'd think 500 a risk. R.H." Sir Valentine Chirol's book, India, *was published in England by Ernest Benn in 1926 and in the United States by Scribners in 1930.*

May 24th 1912

Dear Harcourt,

Sir Valentine Chirol:—We have just fixed with your friends Bell's, an important book by Chirol on India. Chirol is, as I daresay you know, Foreign Editor of "The Times." He has done other books on India and the East, and besides being very well equipped as a writer, he is really a political force and an authority on his subject. In a word, we expect to have a book which shall do for India what Alfred Milner did for Egypt. I enclose with this a short precis of what Chirol wants to write, and shall be glad to know if you can take the American rights, which we have reserved. Chirol and we would much prefer a separate American copyright edition, but you might consider it and let us know what, if any, proposal you can make. Of course, it is evident that India means very much less to you than to us. At the same time, I fancy American interest in the East is growing, and the libraries ought to take a substantial number of copies.

I hope things are well with you, and that the H.U.L. has finally taken it into its head to move more quickly. Here, as you will have heard from [Geoffrey] Williams and Perris, we are continuing to do great things.

My normally tidy desk is still decorated with samples of your educational publications, in respect of which we have not done anything. . . .

Kindest regards,
Sincerely yours,
C. F. Cazenove

Advertisement in a New York literary magazine (Rutgers University Library)

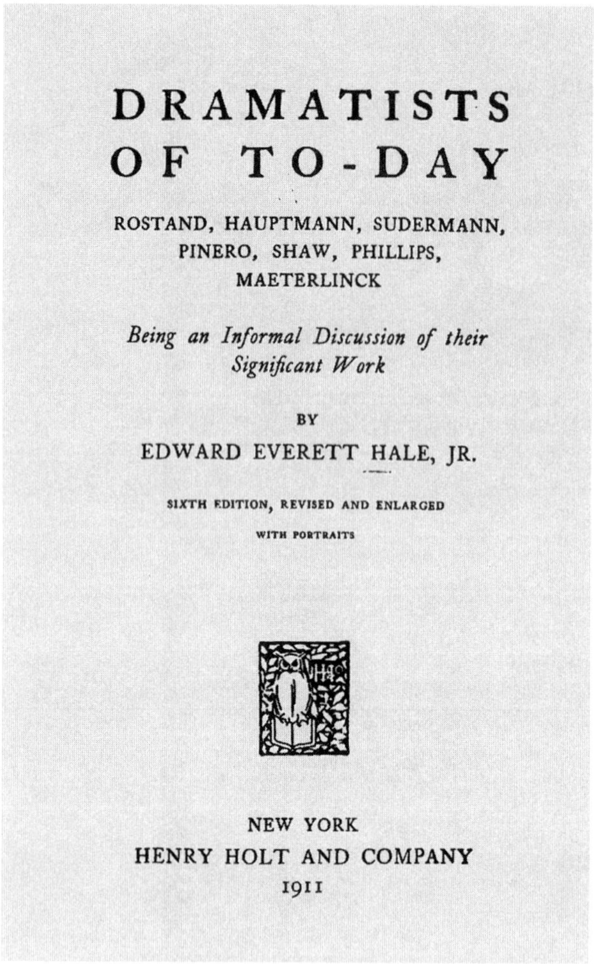

Russian men, who have reputations in Russia, but have not yet penetrated even to Germany.

The arrangements he has hitherto had have not, I gather, been entirely satisfactory. This is simply on what one may call intellectual rather than on commercial grounds. He has had all the money he wants—more, perhaps, than he would have been ready to accept. But the books have been split among a number of publishers. Mr. Rubinstein's feeling is that if a publisher finds he has paid more for an author than the result justifies, he ceases to have any interest in his work. Mr. Rubinstein himself is a man of culture, and prefers to see his authors published, first, by firms of distinctly intellectual quality, and secondly by firms who will take all an author's work.

During his visit to London, I have introduced him to Sidgwick & Jackson, whose list pleased him, and whom I think he liked personally. There is nothing definite concluded for the moment, but Sidgwick is interested in this newer and more striking Russian stuff, and will be very glad to go further into the matter.

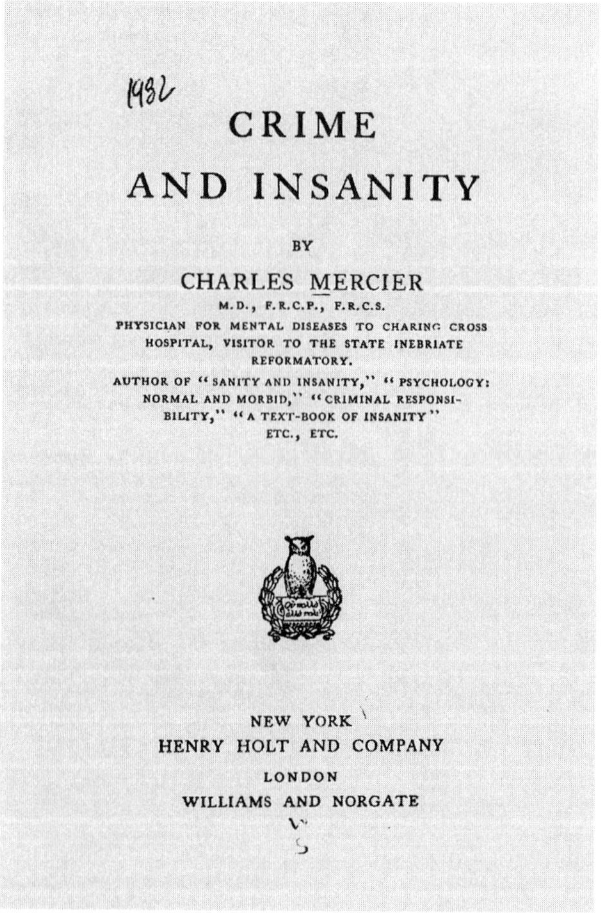

Title page for the sixth edition of the 1905 dramatic study by a professor of literature who was the son of the author of The Man without a Country *(1865; Rutgers University Library)*

August 2nd 1912

Dear Harcourt,

Geoffrey Williams has just introduced me to a German publisher named Rubinstein, who came to London to arrange for representation in the English speaking markets. The part of his business which more particularly concerns us is the work he does for Russian, Hungarian, and other novelists. You are, of course, familiar with the copyright difficulties in these countries, and these difficulties are overcome by publishing first in Berlin a month or so before the Russian edition appears. Editions are done both in German and in Russian, and, on the first, International Copyright, so far as it exists, is secured. Mr. Rubinstein assures me that he only touches the best of Russian and other fiction. For example, he has all Gorky and Andreyeff, anything there may be still to come from Tolstoy, and he is also concerning himself with some of the younger

Title page for the 1911 psychological study by a British physician and psychologist (Rutgers University Library)

The suggestion obviously is that, having considered the idea in its outline—at present necessarily vague—you should let me know whether or not it appeals to you, too. I may interject here that where Gorky, or, indeed, any of Mr. Rubinstein's authors, writes anything which, on grounds of taste or unconventional morality, is not likely to appeal to the English speaking world, there is full permission to omit offending passages. My next idea is that if you are interested a substantial saving could be effected by dividing the cost of the translations. Our present plan is to arrange to have early copies of both the Russian and German editions. The German editions can be read, but the actual translation would be made from the original Russian, and had, I suggest, perhaps better be made in London than in New York where the work is, I believe, very much more costly even than here.

If you are interested, we should propose to ask Mr. Rubinstein to let us have two copies of both editions of any books that come up, so that we can send them on to you without delay.

After you have considered the matter, you might write me your views. You might also touch on the question of serialising. Some of Gorky's stuff is quite suitable for serial. Would you interest yourself in this? If so, on what terms? Or would you let us act independently in this respect?

Sincerely yours,
C. F. Cazenove

August 15, 1912

Dear Cazenove:

Thanks for yours of August 2nd in regard to the German publisher, named Rubinstein.

To be frank, the proposal presents difficulties. Gorky and Adreyeff have not any such hold on this market as to warrant our obligating ourselves to undertake anything they might do, nor should we put ourselves in Mr. Rubinstein's hands with regard to the, at present, less important Russian novelists.

On the other hand, from what you say of him, and from what we know of Sidgwick and Jackson, the

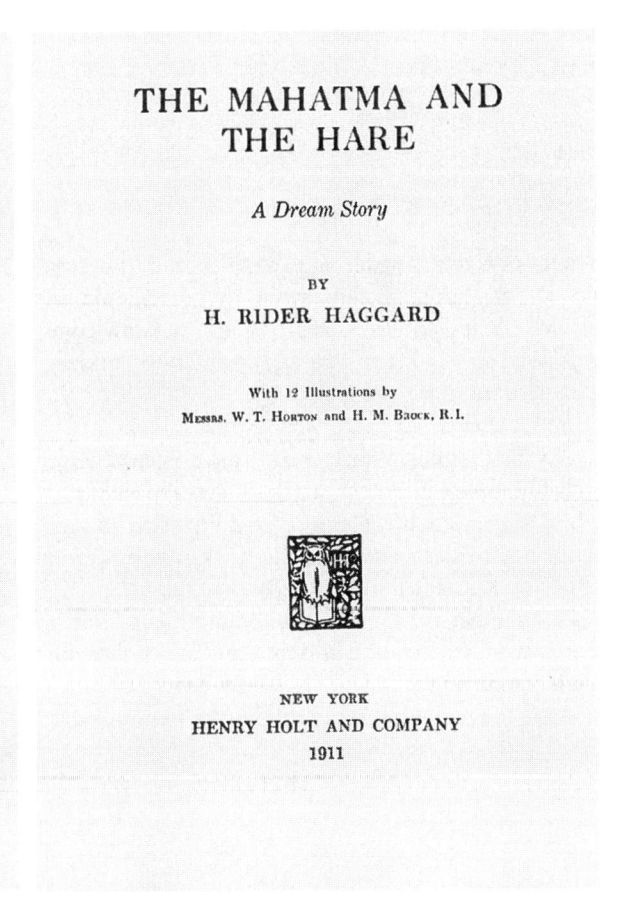

Frontispiece, illustrated by W. T. Horton, and title page for the only book by the prominent English novelist that was published by Holt and Company (Princeton University Library)

alliance would be an attractive one, but we do not see how it could be arranged on more than a book by book basis. If we could see the German version of anything which Sidgwick would be willing to take up with an estimate of our share of the cost of translation, we should be very glad to give the book the most careful consideration, and, of course, if the events should prove successful, it should naturally grow into a regular thing. Farther than this, we cannot go at the moment.

You might better act independently in respect to serialisation, though we should be glad to give you any assistance we can in this regard.

Your letter of August 6, reporting progress on those of our books which are in your hands is just in. Thanks for it. Do not go to too much trouble with what seem to you to be hopeless chances.

Sincerely yours,
AH

* * *

Holt and Company apparently rejected (though not on the basis of the following tongue-in-cheek letter) some early submissions from the Dutch-born, American-educated journalist and author of popular histories Hendrik Willem Van Loon. In 1928, however, they published his Life and Times of Pieter Stuyvesant.

April 11, 1913

My dear Mr. Van Loon:

On my return after a detour, I find the two books. It may take me little while to get an opinion regarding their publishability, but I acknowledge receipt now, so as to save you all possibility of anxiety on that account.

So far they seem to me very excellent fooling.

My first glance, which is all I have been able to give to the history, shows at the start a peculiarity which, if it prevails throughout, would be fatal to any desire I might have to publish the book: namely, you say that the Romans and Greeks only cared for eating and drinking. Now if for the sake of fun you say much of that sort of absolutely incorrect thing, of course the cautious parent would not let his child have the book; but it may be premature to say this before I know more about it.

[unsigned]

* * *

Irish poet and playwright Padraic Colum published two titles with Holt and Company in 1916, The King of Ireland's Son *and* Wild Earth, and Other Poems.

10th Feb 1916

My dear Mr. Harcourt,

I have just now received a letter from Maunsel's, my publisher in Dublin. They are willing to accept the terms you suggested, but they tell me they had offered Macmillan's the first refusal of my poems. If they have done this it has been without any authority from me, and I shall decline to be a party to it. Henry Holt are the publishers I want for America, and I am cabling Maunsel to this effect. I am telling him too that the sheets must be in your possession within a month.

Very sincerely yours,
Padraic Colum

* * *

Early in his career Edward L. Bernays, the "father of public relations," directed a publicity campaign for the first American tour of the Ballet Russe, which was sponsored by the Metropolitan

THE DAWN OF HISTORY

BY

J. L. MYRES, M.A.

WYKEHAM PROFESSOR OF ANCIENT HISTORY, OXFORD
AUTHOR OF "A HISTORY OF ROME," ETC.

NEW YORK
HENRY HOLT AND COMPANY
LONDON
WILLIAMS AND NORGATE

Title page for the twenty-sixth volume in the Home University Library of Modern Knowledge series, published in 1911 (Rutgers University Library)

Opera Company. Bernays wanted to use a forthcoming Holt and Company publication, Arthur Edwin Krows's Play Production in America (1916), in the promotion of the tour because the book cited the work of ballet authority Leon Bakst. Roland Holt, Bernays's correspondent, was not receptive to the idea.

August 14, 1916.

Dear Sir:

Pray accept our thanks, even tho somewhat tardy, for your favor of August 2nd, in which you kindly suggest cooperating with us in making Mr. Krows' PLAY PRODUCTION IN AMERICA known. Since, so far as the writer can say from memory (Mr. Krows now has his manuscript back in his hands) there will be but two or three pages devoted to Mr. Bakst, and but two or three plates devoted to his costumes and scenery, we doubt that there will be sufficient about him in this book for you to be encouraged to aid its distribution as you suggest. If, nevertheless, under these circumstances, you still would like to go ahead with it—we figure we will sell at a list price of $2.50 [illegible] would be glad to have some more definite details from you.

Very truly yours,
[Roland Holt]

August 17th, 1916.

My dear Mr. Holt:

In answer to your letter of the 14th relative to cooperative publicity on Mr. Krows' forthcoming book, I think that even with only two or three pages about Bakst, we could work on this book to our mutual advantage. This is the plan I have in mind:

In the fifty cities we are going to, and which will be surfeited with Ballet Russe and Bakst publicity, it is our intention to hold window exhibits in the largest book stores. For these exhibits it would be desirable for you to send a number of books on consignment, and to bring out the appealing Bakst factor by a poster which either you or we could send to these shops. That would make a selling point for the book, and the book gives point to the poster. At the same time, the book reviews gotten at the time in the various towns by our publicity staff on the road would attract attention to Bakst and the book.

Yours very truly,
THE METROPOLITAN
MUSICAL BUREAU.
Edward L. Bernays
Publicity Manager.

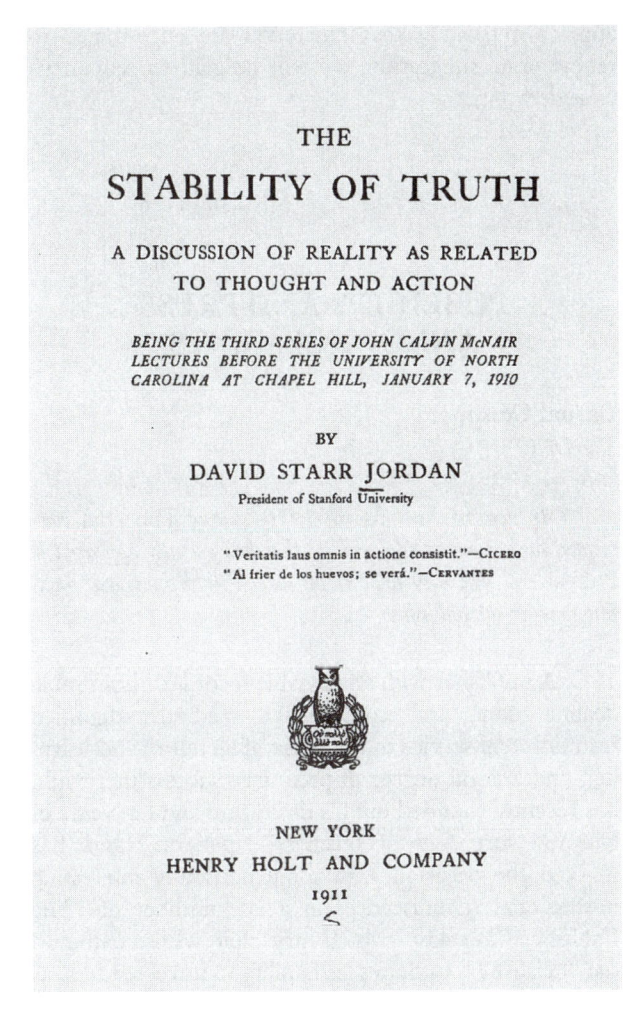

THE
STABILITY OF TRUTH

A DISCUSSION OF REALITY AS RELATED
TO THOUGHT AND ACTION

BEING THE THIRD SERIES OF JOHN CALVIN McNAIR
LECTURES BEFORE THE UNIVERSITY OF NORTH
CAROLINA AT CHAPEL HILL, JANUARY 7, 1910

BY

DAVID STARR JORDAN
President of Stanford University

"Veritatis laus omnis in actione consistit."—CICERO
"Al frier de los huevos; se verá."—CERVANTES

NEW YORK
HENRY HOLT AND COMPANY
1911

Title page for the essay by the scholar and peace activist who served as president of the World Peace Foundation from 1910 to 1914 (Rutgers University Library)

August 30, 1916.

My Dear Mr. Bernays:

Pardon my not having sooner acknowledged yours of August 17th and your willingness to offer for sale copies of Mr. Krows' PLAY PRODUCTION IN AMERICA by calling particular attention to the Bakst matter in it, despite the fact that we wrote you we thought there would not be more than two or three pages of such matter in this longish book.

We fear the book will not be ready until about the first of November, and we are very sorry to say that, so far as we can see, in view of the small amount of [B]akst material in it, we can have very little confidence that you could successfully handle it in the manner you kindly propose, and certainly we could scarcely afford to make a poster drawing particular attention to the "Bakst factor".

However, we are making a memorandum to send you a copy of the book with our compliments when it appears and if, at that time, you are encouraged to renew your suggestion, we will be glad to reopen its consideration.

We are,

                            Very truly yours,
                            [Roland Holt]

PUBLICITY AND PRESS ANUNCEMENTS

Casual Comment
The Dial

An item in the 1 March 1910 issue of The Dial *commented on a piece by Henry Holt that had recently appeared in* Publishers' Weekly *to mark his seventieth birthday and forty-five years in the publishing business.*

A publisher with an enviable record for honorable dealing, sane and conservative methods, dignified restraint, real service to the cause of literature and learning, and a good degree of pecuniary success therewith, has recently rounded out his threescore and ten years of life and forty-five of business experience, and has marked the occasion with some unusually interesting professional reminiscences in a late number of "The Publishers' Weekly." Mr. Henry Holt, whose name on the "Leisure Hour Series" is familiar to novel-readers, as it is to science-readers on the "American Science Series," and to naturalists on the "American Nature Series," and to other wide circles of readers on the works of [Hippolyte] Taine, Mill, [Henry Sumner] Maine, [Bernhard] ten Brink, Austin Dobson, and many other world-famous authors, relates how he (with abundant precedent and illustrious example to encourage him) forsook law for literature at an early age and became a manufacturer of books at the same time that he was, in a modest way, a writer of them. His authorship of two remarkably good novels, "Calmire, Man and Nature," and "Sturmsee, Man and Man," first issued anonymously, is now generally known. The rise of Mr. Holt's publishing house, under its various designations, is an instructive history of the increasing success and reputation of a wisely and honorably conducted business. Naturally enough, Mr. Holt dwells with fond retrospection upon the principles and policies of his earlier associates in publishing, and laments the competition and greed and questionable practices of these latter days, when the issuing of books is no longer the dignified profession it once was—to the present detriment of all concerned. "I suspect," he declares, "that whatever may be the case with the industrial and educational branches of publish-

EVOLUTION

BY

PATRICK GEDDES
PROFESSOR OF BOTANY, ST. ANDREWS UNIVERSITY

AND

J. ARTHUR THOMSON
REGIUS PROFESSOR OF NATURAL HISTORY, ABERDEEN UNIVERSITY

Joint Authors of " The Evolution of Sex," etc.

NEW YORK
HENRY HOLT AND COMPANY
LONDON
WILLIAMS AND NORGATE

Title page for the 1911 biological study by two Scottish scientists who were frequent collaborators (Rutgers University Library)

ing, the *belles-lettres* branch has got to be conducted as a profession, or there is no money in it. The old fortunes in the business were built up on this principle. Apparently the fine flavor of literature will not stand being dragged through the deeper mires of competition." All will join in Mr. Holt's hope that, despite his seventy years, he may "continue in evidence some time longer" in the trade which he has so long honored, and has done so much to elevate to the dignity of a profession.

—*Dial*, 48 (1 March 1910): 139

Not all of the responses to Holt's Publishers' Weekly *piece were as flattering, as is reflected by this letter to the editor published in the same magazine.*

. . . .

For some years people in our business have been reading with interest and a queer sort of pleasure Mr. Holt's statements about other publishers, literary agents, ungrateful authors and a degenerate trade spirit.

THE HOME UNIVERSITY LIBRARY OF MODERN KNOWLEDGE

16mo cloth, 50 cents *net*, postpaid

LITERATURE AND ART

Already Published

SHAKESPEARE	By John Masefield
ENGLISH LITERATURE—MODERN	By G. H. Mair
ENGLISH LITERATURE—MEDIEVAL	By W. P. Ker
LANDMARKS IN FRENCH LITERATURE	By G. L. Strachey
ARCHITECTURE	By W. R. Lethaby
THE ENGLISH LANGUAGE	By L. Pearsall Smith
WRITING ENGLISH PROSE	By W. T. Brewster
GREAT AMERICAN WRITERS	By W. P. Trent and John Erskine
DR. JOHNSON AND HIS CIRCLE	By John Bailey
THE VICTORIAN AGE IN LITERATURE	By G. K. Chesterton
THE LITERATURE OF GERMANY	By J. G. Robertson
PAINTERS AND PAINTING	By Frederick Wedmore
SHELLY, GODWIN, AND THEIR CIRCLE	By H. N. Brailsford
ANCIENT ART AND RITUAL	By Miss Jane Harrison
EURIPIDES AND HIS AGE	By Gilbert Murray
CHAUCER AND HIS TIMES	By Miss G. E. Hadow
WILLIAM MORRIS: HIS WORK AND INFLUENCE	By A. C. Brock
THE RENAISSANCE	By Edith Sichel
ELIZABETHAN LITERATURE	By J. M. Robertson

Future Issues

ITALIAN ART OF THE RENAISSANCE	By Roger E. Fry
SCANDINAVIAN HISTORY AND LITERATURE	By T. C. Snow
HISTORY AND LITERATURE OF SPAIN	By J. Fitzmaurice-Kelly
LATIN LITERATURE	By J. S. Phillimore
LITERARY TASTE	By Thomas Seccombe
GREAT WRITERS OF RUSSIA	By C. T. Hagberg Wright
MILTON	By John Bailey

Advertisement for books in a Holt and Company series that Henry Holt mentioned in his 4 April 1916 letter to The New York Times Book Review *on American and European reading tastes (Rutgers University Library)*

Of course, I do not mean to suggest that any one takes Mr. Holt's scoldings too seriously, but he has been having his fling at all the rest of us for so many years that it has just occurred to me that, after all, he does not speak exactly by divine right, and although he has assumed the pulpit, there is no law to prevent one from talking back to the minister occasionally.

There are people still living, beside Mr. Holt, who can remember back twenty years (and perhaps more), and I am one of these. I remember, for example, what violent statements Mr. Holt used to make in those days. He writes now as though publishing in the days long passed away had been a long summer holiday. In the good old times one would think that authors ate out of the hand, and publishers meeting on the street saluted with rapturous embraces and passed love tokens to each other on all occasions. Mr. Holt has surely overdrawn the picture....

[Mr. Holt] has abused us all for years, on the ground that we have tempted away the lambs from his flock, when, as a matter of fact, they have broken loose for reasons best known to themselves....

Cheer up, Mr Holt; the worst is passed, the best is yet to come; may you live and enjoy another full generation, and discover a hundred new authors bearing the flaming torch of genius and may you keep 'em, every one, is the wish of

A Hopeful Brother Publisher
New York, Feb. 21, 1910
—Publishers' Weekly (26 February 1910): 1079–1080

Forthcoming Titles

Publishers' Weekly ran the following item on forthcoming Holt titles in its 11 November 1911 issue.

HENRY HOLT & COMPANY expect to publish a number of books on November 4–including Lovat Fraser's "India Under Curzon and After," which is making quite a sensation in England; Joseph McCabe's "The Empresses of Rome," which gives a vivid idea of the luxury and decline of Roman society and has some striking illustrations; two noteworthy new volumes for young folk, being a fourth book by Mrs. Carroll Watson Rankin, "The Castaways of Pete's Patch" (in which she again introduces an interesting Indian, and among other characters, a mysterious shipwrecked boy and, of course, a group of good, wholesome girls[)], and another of Boyd Smith's inimitably illustrated books, this one being Marryat's "Children of the New Forest," which he has made a worthy companion to his last

BUDDHISM

A STUDY OF THE BUDDHIST NORM

BY

MRS. RHYS DAVIDS, M.A.
LECTURER IN INDIAN PHILOSOPHY, MANCHESTER UNIVERSITY
FELLOW OF UNIVERSITY COLLEGE
LONDON

NEW YORK
HENRY HOLT AND COMPANY
LONDON
WILLIAMS AND NORGATE

Title page for the 1912 study by a scholar of Pali, the language in which the sayings of the Buddha were first written down (Rutgers University Library)

year's "The Last of the Mohicans." Still another volume to appear on this date will be a sixth revised and enlarged edition of Edward Everett Hale, Jr.'s, standard work on "Dramatists of To-day," in which he gives particular attention to the more recent plays of Bernard Shaw, Maeterlinck and Pinero. Portraits of his seven dramatists are a further feature of this new edition.

—Publishers' Weekly (11 November 1911): 1961–1962

An item in the 20 January 1916 issue of The Nation *announced forthcoming Holt publications.*

Among the publications for early spring announced by Henry Holt & Co. are the following: "Fulfillment," by Emma Wolf; "The Socialism of To-day," by various authors; "Delane of the Times," by Sir Edward Cook (in the Makers of the Nineteenth

Century series); "Konversations und Lesebuch," by Edward Prokosch and C. M. Purin; "Commerce and Industry," by James Russell Smith.
–*Nation,* 104 (20 January 1916): 81

Henry Holt on Reading Tastes

April 4th 1916.
To the Editor of the Times Book Review
　Sir:
　　You ask me:
　"Judging the people of a country from the standpoint of the books they read–or, at least, buy–how do you think the people of the United States compare with those of the leading European nations?"

The people of the United States read many less books than they would if they did not read an enormous number of cheap periodicals which are supported by a government subvention in the shape of carriage by mail at less than cost of transportation, but at a very slow rate, because the cars are so overcrowded with such matter. Most of these periodicals, however, compare very favorably with those read by the same stratum of the public in England.

While we have solved, by a government subvention, the problem of the distribution of the cheap periodical, we have not found a way to distribute widely cheap books of information and cheap reprints. In England the news-stands display these, and there it is as easy to buy a volume of such a series as The Home University Library, for example, as it is here to buy the current issue of "Life". But here the periodicals crowd all books off virtually all the news stands. The British publisher of books can send his travelers to every town of a thousand inhabitants because the distances are so short. We cannot. Here only the mail order house and the ubiquitous subscription book agent can reach our small towns. Moreover, in England the government does not interfere with the publishers combining for the interests of their trade, while here only "Labor" is permitted to combine.

. . . .

　　You ask me further:
　"Are they (our people) as interested in books of all kinds that appeal to the intelligence and to cultivated taste?"

We have a large and commonplace audience for commonplace books that have wide human or sensational appeal. But the phenomenal "sellers" in this market do not completely overshadow the sales of works which appeal to cultured taste.

　　You ask me still further:
　"Do you think that the European war is having any effect, more than temporary and superficial, upon American taste in reading?"

A real taste in reading is usually too deeply and firmly grounded to be affected by anything short of death. It may be a trifling offset to the war that some thoughtless readers have been turned toward serious things and serious books.

　　　　　　　Your obedient servant,
　　　　　　　Henry Holt

PUBLISHERS' ASSOCIATIONS

The American Publishers' Association sent members this notice concerning an upcoming meeting in which Henry Holt was to be one of the speakers on the subject of the "Campaign for Better Books."

May 2nd, 1912.
Dear Sir:–
　At the informal meeting of publishers held at the Aldine Club in April, a Program Committee was appointed, consisting of Mr. Frank N. Doubleday, Chairman, Mr. Alexander Grosset and Mr. C. C. Shoemaker.

Another informal meeting will be held on Thursday, May 9th, at One P.M., at the Aldine Club, to which all publishers are cordially invited, without limitation as to the number of representatives of any one house. At this meeting, Mr. Doubleday will report for his Committee, and will add to this, comments on

THE CAMPAIGN FOR BETTER BOOKS

which will be the subject of discussion for the meeting.
　Mr. Henry Holt will comment on the subject under discussion; and others present will have an opportunity to take part in the debate.
　Luncheon will be served promptly at one o'clock; and, in accordance with the recommendations of the Committee, the cost of this ($1.25 for each person) will be paid by the individuals present.
　The real success of the April meeting should insure a large attendance on May 9th; and as arrangements must be made in advance, will you please notify me promptly how many from your house will attend the meeting?
　　　　　　　Yours very sincerely,
　　　　　　　F. C. J. Tessaro, Manager.

* * *

The Publishers' Cooperative Bureau was founded in August 1913. The original members of the executive committee were Harcourt, Frank N. Doubleday, Alexander Grosset, F. T. Leigh (Harper and Brothers), William Morrow (Frederick A. Stokes Company), Roger L. Scaife (Houghton Mifflin), and Charles C. Shoemaker (Penn Publishing), with Mr. Richard B. G. Gardner as manager. Headquarters were at 39 West Thirty-second Street in New York. An early brochure describes the function of the bureau.

The Publishers' Cooperative Bureau is an organization unique in purpose and scope, created and supported by more than a score of prominent American publishers actuated by a desire to bring into closer and more effective relationship the varying and yet allied interests of authors, publishers, booksellers and readers. . . . The Bureau was established in August of 1913. It provides, so to speak, a "clearing house" through which the publicity and market problems of its represented publishers can be studied, bookselling conditions and facilities bettered, and a wider knowledge and appreciation of contemporary literature on the part of the general reading public stimulated.

– *The Publishers' Cooperative Bureau* (n.d.)

***

The Publishers' Lunch Club, founded in 1915, consisted of "Partners, Directors, Officers, or Heads of Departments in any House in the United States publishing copyrighted books. The object of the club [was] to afford opportunities for social intercourse." The entrance fee for joining and the annual dues were both $5; the Club met on the first Thursday of each month, except in July, August, and September. Meetings were held at such places as the City Club and the Yale Club, with different publishers hosting each meeting. The following undated announcement is on George H. Doran letterhead.

THE PUBLISHERS' LUNCH CLUB

The first regular meeting of The Publishers' Lunch Club will be held on Thursday, May sixth, at twelve fortyfive, at The City Club, 55 West Forty-fourth Street, generously placed at our disposal through the courtesy of George Haven Putnam, Esq.

At the meeting called for Friday, April thirtieth, at The Century Club, a constitution was adopted and the following publishers were elected members:

President, Henry Holt; Vice President, Joseph Sears (D. Appleton & Company); Secretary-Treasurer, George H. Doran; Frank H. Dodd; George Haven Putnam; Frederick A. Stokes; F. A. Duneka (Harper & Brothers); W. W. Ellsworth (The Century Company); J. Bishop Putnam; Alfred Harcourt (Henry Holt & Company); Charles Scribner; F. N. Doubleday; George P. Brett (The Macmillan Company); A. F. Houghton.

At the meeting now called the completion of the organization and other important business will be transacted. Your presence is urgently desired.

THE PUBLISHERS' LUNCH CLUB
George H. Doran
Secretary-Treasurer.

HOLT AND WRITERS

H. L. Mencken

My Life as Author and Editor
H. L. Mencken

In 1910 Holt and Company published Men versus the Man, *a compilation of letters with opposing views on socialism, exchanged between H. L. Mencken and a lawyer named Robert Rives La Monte. In his posthumously published memoir,* My Life as Author and Editor *(1993), Mencken recalled how*

H. L. Mencken

Cover letter for a manuscript submitted to Holt and Company, with Harcourt's and Roland Holt's handwritten comments (Princeton University Library)

Men versus the Man *came to be placed with Holt. This recollection also provided an opportunity to comment on the Holt family itself. Mencken's feelings about Holt and Company may have been at least partially responsible for an unflattering newspaper piece about publishers that he wrote several years later.*

I must have told [Theodore] Dreiser about this project soon after it was launched, and La Monte must have spread news of it among his Socialist friends, for I find a letter from Dreiser, dated January 30, 1909, which indicates that he hoped to get the book for B. W. Dodge & Company and that an order for a thousand copies had already come in from a wholesaler of Socialist books. But La Monte, to whom I left the business of placing it, was eager to have it bear the imprint of a more distinguished publisher than Dodge, and some time toward the middle of 1909 he landed *Men vs. the Man* . . . with the old and rich firm of Henry Holt & Company. I had nothing to do with this, and my first letter from Henry Holt, dated December 21, 1909, shows that by that time all arrangements had been made. The book came out in March, 1910, and got, on the whole, a somewhat skeptical press.

The business brought me into contact with old Henry Holt, who was already close to seventy years old. Later on I got to know him pretty well, and saw him with some frequency, for one of his daughters was married to a Baltimore surgeon of my acquaintance, Joseph C. Bloodgood, and he often visited her. He was himself, in fact, a Baltimorean by birth, and one Sunday, when he and I were taking a walk, he showed me his childhood home at the northwest corner of Lombard and Penn Streets. In his youth that had been a fine neighborhood, but by 1910 it was much decayed, and we found the house occupied by Lithuanian immigrants. Holt was very tall and very slim, and with his large dark eyes showing curious dark pigmentation beneath he had an unusual appearance. He was a great talker, and loved to give advice to his authors.

He was an extraordinarily opinionated fellow, and most of his opinions, as I soon learned, were rubbish. His efforts to promote simplified spelling were ardent; in the later years of his long life he took to spiritualism, greatly to the horror of his surgeon son-in-law, Bloodgood. Bloodgood was himself an eccentric. He operated on me in the summer of 1910, and we became well acquainted.

. . . .

Bloodgood fitted into the Holt family admirably, for all of its members were uplifters of one sort or another. The son by the old man's first marriage, Roland, was a promoter of arty theatrical performances in New York; the eldest daughter, Winifred, devoted herself to succoring and harassing the blind; the younger daughter, Mrs. Bloodgood, was a do-gooder in general practice, and the old man himself whooped up not only simplified spelling and spiritualism, but also various other crazes. Only the young son of his second marriage, Eliot, showed any sign of normalcy—and Eliot was a drunkard.

Old Holt's publishing business was very profitable, and he had a large income from it. As he approached eighty his own share in its management grew less and less active, and he gave over most of his time to the various insane causes that he advocated. This left the conduct of affairs, at least in theory, to his son Roland, but Roland was virtually a half-wit, so the burden really fell on two employes *[sic]*, Alfred Harcourt and Donald C. Brace, both of them highly competent men. When, in 1919, the old man brought young Eliot into the office, Harcourt and Brace began to be uneasy, for it seemed to indicate that Eliot and Roland would share the business after their father's

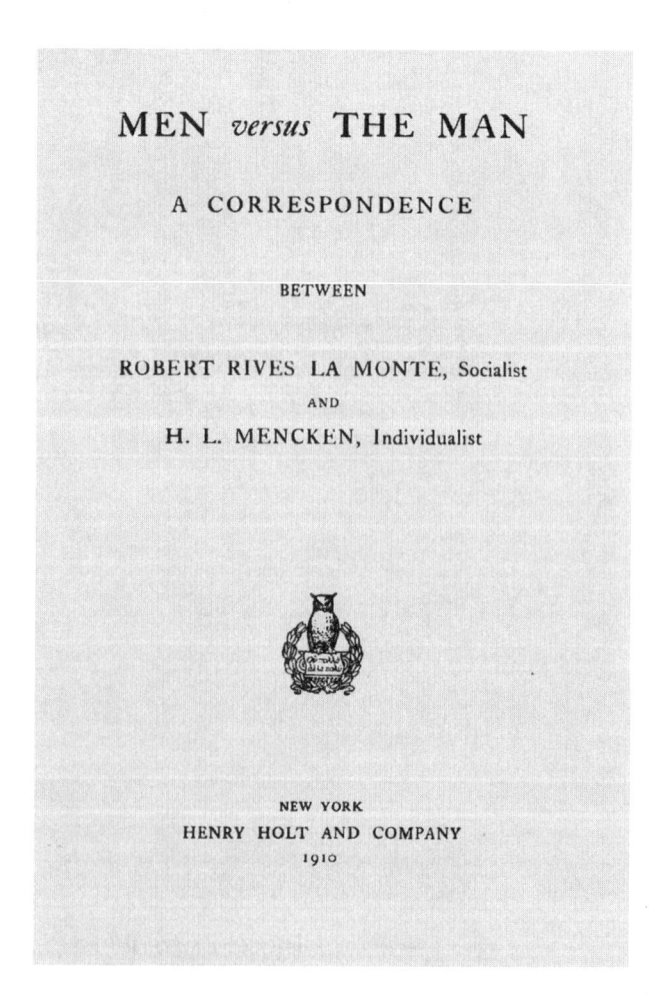

MEN *versus* THE MAN

A CORRESPONDENCE

BETWEEN

ROBERT RIVES LA MONTE, Socialist

AND

H. L. MENCKEN, Individualist

NEW YORK
HENRY HOLT AND COMPANY
1910

Title page for H. L. Mencken's only Holt and Company publication (Princeton University Library)

death. They accordingly tackled the old man on the subject, demanding immediate partnerships in the firm, and some insurance against the imbecilities of Roland and Eliot *post mortem*. But instead of giving them what they so plainly deserved Holt adopted a lofty attitude, and let them understand that they were still only employes and would remain so.

The upshot was that they withdrew, and, along with a pedagogue named Will D. Howe, organized the firm of Harcourt, Brace & Howe....

Curiously enough, Harcourt, years later, was to make precisely the same mistake that old Holt had made. He had only one son, but that son, Hastings, was quite as bad as Roland and Eliot Holt, and when he was introduced into the business and began to take a more and more active hand in it the father's partner, Brace (Howe had meanwhile retired), and the principal employes were full of disquiet. In the end Hastings became so obnoxious that they joined in a demand on his father that he be sent away, and, when the father refused, set up what amounted to a revolt. Its consequence was that not only was the son forced out, but also the father, who retired on the pretense of illness. Thus history repeated itself almost literatim, and Alfred Harcourt, despite his intelligence, added one more stone to the massive pile of proof that human beings learn nothing by experience.

Men vs. the Man was a complete failure. Holt's royalty reports show that, down to July, 1911, he had sold but 326 copies, and down to October 25, 1917, but 552. Inasmuch as La Monte and I were to receive no royalties until 1,000 had been sold, our receipts from the book were precisely nothing. This was discouraging....

–*My Life as Author and Editor,* edited by Jonathan Yardley (New York: Knopf, 1993), pp. 30–33

In My Life as Author and Editor *Mencken recalled how Henry Holt approached him to become a contributor to* The Unpopular Review *in September 1913.*

Apparently Bright [Johns Hopkins University English professor James W. Bright] suggested that I might make a good contributor to the *Unpopular Review,* for on September 12, 1913, Holt, who had published my *Men vs. the Man* in 1910, sent me a dummy of the magazine and proposed that I attempt something for it. He was then seventy-three years old, and September 12, 1913, was my thirty-third birthday. "Most every man to whom I have sent this dummy," he wrote, "is old enough to be your father; so I am running . . . risk of spoiling you . . . in telling you that I wish you would write for me an article on 'The Greek and the Puritan' which has been rattling about in my head for some time. But I have got enough else to do, and probably wouldn't do it as well as you anyhow. And now to counteract some of the tendencies to spoil you, and for other reasons, I must tell you that although the style of your article ["The American: His Morals"] was pretty well adapted for the *Smart Set* (in which, also in the direction of anti-spoiling, I will tell you I think it is a disgrace for any man to appear), I should want you to consent to do the one for the *Unpopular Review* in a rather different style, though I shouldn't want you to do it with any less humor. *Verb. sap. sat.* [*Verbum sapienti satis est, a word to the wise is sufficient*], I guess. If not, ask further particulars if you care to. The *Unpopular Review* will of course have a limited circulation, though I hope it will be read by people whose reading of one is an honor. Of course, such things can't compete with the *Smart Set* in prices paid for articles. The *Atlantic* manages to get itself filled up on $15 a thousand words–at least, that is what it has always paid me; but if there is so little unpopularity about you that must have more, pray let me know how much more, and I will think it over. Several

LANDMARKS IN
FRENCH
LITERATURE

BY

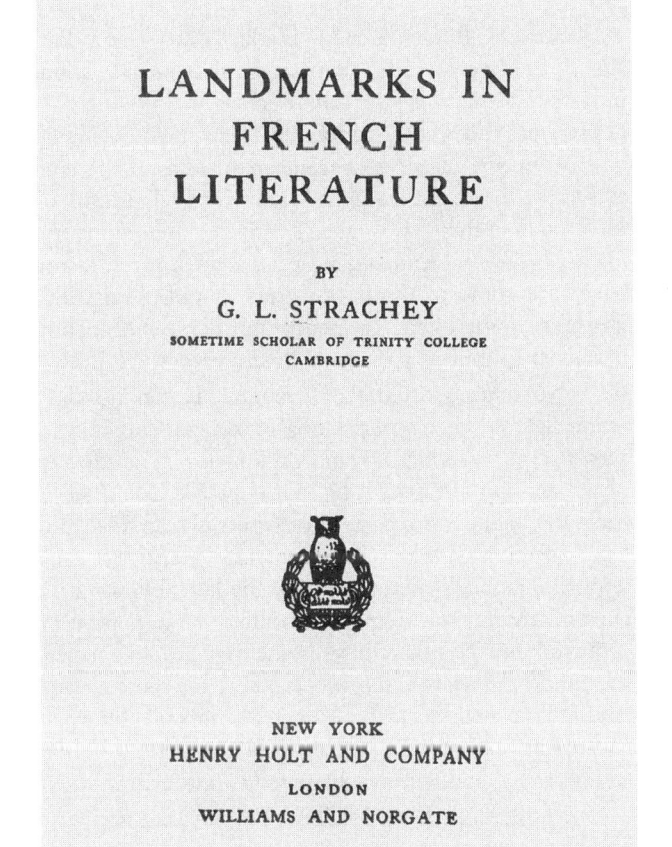

G. L. STRACHEY
SOMETIME SCHOLAR OF TRINITY COLLEGE
CAMBRIDGE

NEW YORK
HENRY HOLT AND COMPANY
LONDON
WILLIAMS AND NORGATE

Title page for the 1912 study of the classical spirit in French literature by the author best known for his Eminent Victorians *(1918; Rutgers University Library)*

very eminent men have pronounced the *Atlantic* terms satisfactory, but they have independent incomes from professorships and that sort of thing."

The pedagogical (and patronizing) tone of this was not reassuring, and I still remembered unpleasantly the trouble I had had with old Holt while *Men vs. the Man* was under way, but I was well aware that getting into so respectable a review as he seemed to have in mind might do me some good, so I fell on the proposed article at once and by the end of October had finished it. While it was being written Holt favored me with various admonitions. "It will certainly be more effective," he wrote to me on October 9, "the more you hold yourself in—not meaning necessarily that you should suppress anything worth saying; but the manner of saying and the degree of avalanche-like rush can of course influence the effect." By October 13 he was already so full of fears that he was talking of placing the article elsewhere—"if we can't agree on modifications, should I regard any as desirable." But by October 18 he was taking heart, and urging me to write "5,000 words or even more, if they come out naturally without padding."

By this time I had pretty well concluded that he would never print the article, but when it was finished I nevertheless sent it in, and at once my expectations were borne out. He not only had at me with a long letter on November 4, setting forth at least a dozen puerile objections to my argument; he also returned the typescripts with scores of even worse annotations. I refused, of course, to let him tell me how to write the article, and after a brief exchange of letters asked him to send it back. I preserved the annotated typescript for many years afterward as a shining example of editorial impudence and folly, but now (1943) it seems to have disappeared, for I can't find it.

I sent a carbon to the *Smart Set* at once, and Wright [*Smart Set* editor Willard H. White] printed it in February, 1914. . . .

—*My Life as Author and Editor,* pp. 175–177

In 1918 publisher Charles Boni wrote Harcourt proposing a public rejoinder to Mencken's negative portrayal of publishers in an Evening Mail *article. In a handwritten note attached to Boni's letter, Harcourt wrote that he "could not think of doing it. Perhaps Mr. [Frederick A.] Stokes might be interested to do this. He could do it very well."*

Feb. 19, 1918

Dear Mr. Harcourt:

I am enclosing an article by H. L. Mencken giving the author's side of the age-long controversy between publisher and author. In the article he attacks publishers for their mendaciousness, stupidity, and short-sightedness. He claims that, while always claiming to be acting for the benefit of literature, publishers destroy more potentially good authors than they welcome.

I believe that for the purpose of interest Mr. Mencken shows only one side of the picture. I should like to publish the publishers' side to this question. Will you present it?

Very truly yours,
Charles Boni, Jr.

"On Publishers"
By H. L. Mencken

Editor's note: In the first place, H. L. Mencken, by his own proclamation, has no pocketbook grouch against publishers, for he knows how to rough it with them, big and little. But if you've picked yourself to start out in the E. A. Poe–George Ade–Mark Twain class, the genial satirist strongly intimates, you'd better buy yourself a printing press and leave 'em all flat. Because they'll only save you cash and spoil your style.

Arnold Bennett's new book, "Books and Persons," is largely made up of waspish remarks about publishers; there is scarcely a chapter in which he doesn't pay his evil devotions to them. "A publisher," he says in one place, "is a tradesman; infinitely less an artist than a tailor is an artist." The word "Tradesman" must be read through English spectacles; Bennett is trying to be nasty. And nasty he is, God knoweth, and nasty are some of the back-waters of publishing, and nasty are some of the eminent publishers who posture before the public as patrons of lovely letters.

No other great trade, I venture, is conducted so unintelligently as this of printing books, and none other shows so many feeble and oafish chicaneries. The attorney of the Authors' League, if he would babble, could tell of tricks to pop the eye and start the sorrowful tear. The "Bulletin" of the league is full of warnings against new raids upon the author's meager pocket; the last, following the current custom, was disguised as public spirit, patriotism, sympathy for the gallant boys in the trenches. In England the Authors' Society is forever sounding the same alarms. And in France the Society of French Authors plays the part of an unsleeping police force, instantly alert for novel ganovries [*sic*] and immovably united to put them down.

But here, perhaps, I fall into the obvious, and even into the sentimental. Business is business; dog must eat dog. If publishers were not sharp traders they would soon come upon the rocks (most of them do, even as it is), and once they were on the rocks the authors would get nothing at all (many of them get it even now). Moreover, this sharpness seldom goes to the length of downright swindling. The author may have to make an atrociously bad bargain, but willingly or not, he actually makes it—and a bargain is a bargain, even when it is mayhem.

....

On the side of donkeyism there is more to be said, and it may be said more freely. In brief, it may be put thus: that the influence of publishers is exerted steadily in favor of what is flash and meretricious and against what is honest and sound, and that its effects upon a given author, supposing him to have talent to begin with, are invariably to wobble him and cheapen him. I could print a list of cases in point half as long as this column, but refrain in unaccustomed decency. The country, despite all the dismal croaking that one hears from college professors, fairly swarms with clever youngsters. They spring up on all sides; they write excellent first books; they somehow get their starts. And then some wise and wealthy publisher nabs them—and thereafter they write best-sellers.

I often wonder how many are thus ruined every year. Fully a dozen come under my personal observation. It is part of my business to unearth new authors of talent; I do it not only because I enjoy it, but because in my special case, it pays. Well, the thing I see is repeated over and over again. First the neophyte has his initial struggle, sometimes long, often very short. Then he makes his first success. Then some well-known publisher goes fishing for him. Then the publisher begins to advise him, and if he is very young and very green, to intimidate him. Then he begins writing in the way that the publisher thinks is nice. And then he blows up.

....

As I say, the list of slain is almost endless. It includes, to be specific, almost all the clever newcomers of ten years ago, with perhaps two or three exceptions—individuals of unusual toughness, egotists, monomaniacs. The rest have taken the veil. You hear a good deal about them. They are boomed like actors. The "Bookman" prints photographs showing them in labor or at golf. The New York "Times" reviews them oleaginously and at length. But what does one find in their books? One finds in their books a display of the particular sort of garbage that publishers currently and transiently esteem. One finds in their books a mess of balderdash.

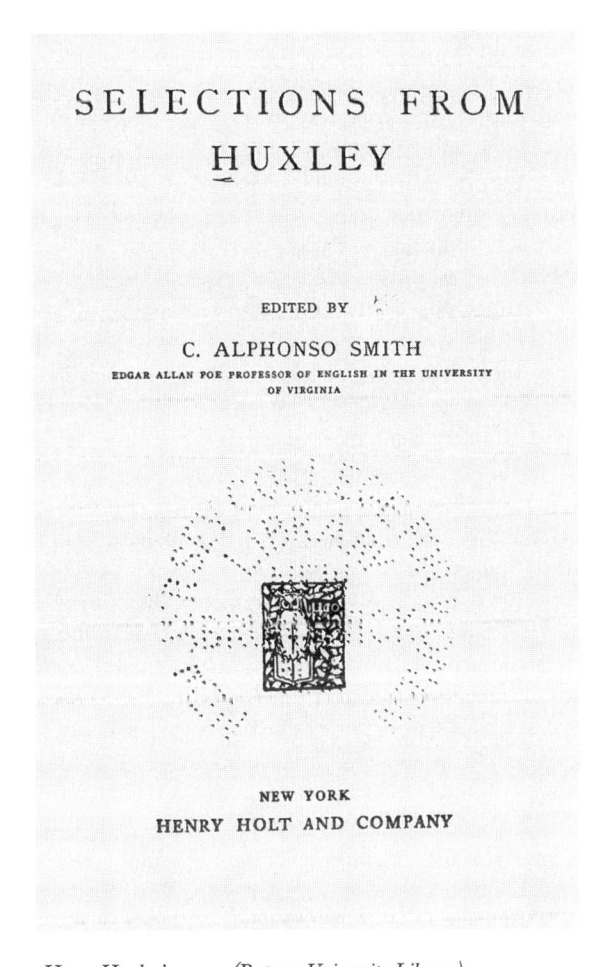

Author portrait and title page from the 1912 selection of Thomas Henry Huxley's essays (Rutgers University Library)

I speak here of publishers of wealth and reputation—the sort whose names are well known, and whose notice is thus bound to intrigue a young author, however well warned. What I say of them is that their influence upon the national letters is almost unqualifiedly pernicious—that they print, among them, at least nine-tenths of the rubbish that disgraces our book-counters—that they never take a chance on a good book if they can find a bad (and safe) one to print in place of it. These are what Bennett calls the mandarins of the craft. They have exactly the same sort of minds, and the same love and respect for the art they presumably serve, that one would look for in so many stockbrokers, delicatessen dealers or moving picture magnates.

. . . .

The history of American literature (and of English literature no less) is one long chronicle of the hunkerousness and stupidity of publishers. The early books of Edgar Allan Poe, now run up in the auction rooms to hundreds and even thousands of dollars, were brought out, not by any of the leading publishers of Poe's time, nor, indeed, by any recognized publisher at all, but by what were really no more than neighborhood job printers. So with the books of Whitman; even into our own day he was printed, not by the solemn Barabases who gobble about their devotion to literature, but by smaller, more obscure and far more intelligent fellows. Try to pick up the early books of Ambrose Bierce: you will find imprints you never heard of before. Look for the first edition of George Ade's "Fables in Slang"; you will not find a famous name on the title-page; you will find the name of young Herbert Stone, just out of Harvard.

As for Mark Twain, he had to start a publishing house of his own to get a free hand. True enough, when this venture failed (through no fault of his own books, surely) he went back to regular publishers—but with what result? With the result that it is impossible to buy a satisfactory edition of his collected works to-day. The only edition on the market contains many volumes that lack all, or a major part, of the original illustrations. Imagine "Huckleberry Finn" without Kemble's incomparable portraits of Huck, Tom Sawyer, the nigger Jim, the Duke, the King, and all the rest—the best illustrations, it seems to me, that any book in English has ever had. If you would get them with the text, you must hunt in second-hand bookstores for the first editions, now grown scarce and soaring in price.

. . . .

It would be easy to string out the tale to endless lengths. The first six books of Joseph Conrad were published in America by six different publishers. Each took one, and then returned to the Hall Caines and Corellis and Chamberses; not one had sense enough to recognize and make fast to the greatest romancer that England has ever seen; it is only with the past few years that he has reached the publishing dignity of Mrs. Humphry Ward, either in England or in America.

John Millington Synge had an even harder time of it. "Riders to the Sea" was brought out by a small London publisher, but after that masterpiece the whole book-selling fraternity washed their hands of him, and all his later books were printed obscurely and in Dublin. To this day no large and opulent house has ever set its imprint upon a single one of his books. As for Lord Dunsany, undoubtedly the greatest of the neo-Celts after Synge, he had to publish all his earlier books at his own expense.

. . . .

But the works of Beulah Pishposh get between covers instantly, and come out under the imprimatur of famous names. So do the shaggy, sweaty fictions of Hercules Mush, the prophet of red blood. So do the boudoir confections of Claude Talcum, the favorite of the finishing

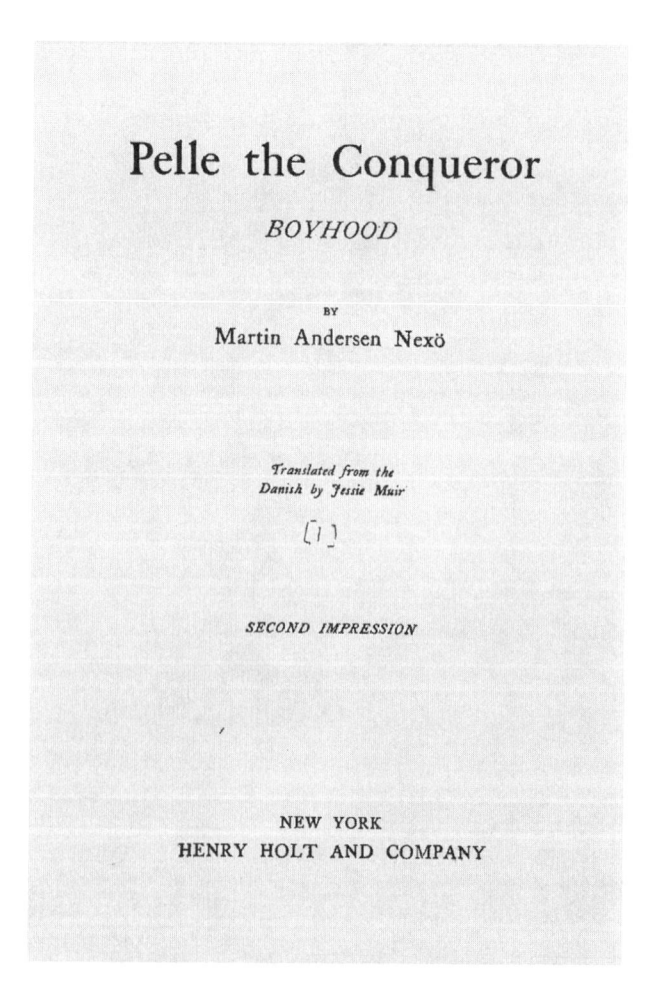

Title page for the first volume (1913) in the translated edition of the Danish writer's four-volume novel Pelle Erobreren *(1906–1910; Rutgers University Library)*

schools. If there exists a prominent American publisher (save perhaps one) who is ashamed to put his imprint upon such abominable rubbish, then I have yet to hear of him—and my ear is constantly open to the news. If there exists a publisher who would hold up such a piece of trash to make way for a new "Leaves of Grass" or "Riders to the Sea" or "Fables in Slang," then lead me to him and let me salute him.

. . . .

To avoid the obvious charge and retort, let me hasten to say that my own dealings with publishers have left no wounds. One of them, true enough, owes me a few dollars, and another has performed acts which cause me to cough deprecatingly, but none of them has ever tried to swindle me, nor have I ever detected any conspiracy among them against my compositions. On the contrary, they print my highly defective works very readily, and I have dealt agreeably with both big ones and little ones, resisting the effort of the former to teach me how to write profitably, and bearing the inability of the latter to overcome my deficiency by gaudy merchandising.

Nay, I do not bawl for myself, but for better men—better men who, at the same time, are less effectively equipped for making good bargains. What they need is recognition, encouragement, help to work out their ideas. What they get is such counsel as might just as well emanate from a cheesemonger, and such an impartial regard for their interests as one would confidently look for in a bookmaker. Among the smaller publishers, perhaps, they find some cheer, and maybe a bit of downright idealism. But among the big publishers what they principally find is an idiotic patronage that insults them, and a business theory that ranks them below the Caines, the Corellis and the manufacturers of the "glad" books.

. . . . . .

Some time ago, consulted by a beginning author, with a book of dignity and sound merit, I warned him solemnly against the sharks who would seek to hornswoggle him out of the cost of printing it, and gave him a list of the leading publishers of the nation. Well, three of those leading publishers of the nation, recognizing his inexperience, at once proceeded, by the most transparent devices, to try to shake him down. One tried to shake him down for a thousand dollars—a good deal less than the actual cost of manufacturing the book. I have the correspondence in the case in my archives. The next time certain Barabases begin talking about what they have done for literature I shall be sorely tempted to publish it.

—*Evening Mail*, 16 February 1918

Henri Bergson

In 1911 Holt and Company published the first American edition of French philosopher Henri Bergson's Creative Evolution *(1907).*

October 25, 1912

Dear Harcourt:

Pray find out at Columbia how long [Henri] Bergson is to be in this country, and what his engagements ar; also whether they hav found him a nice companionable gentleman. There was a great historian over here somtime since, who was not a gentleman, and whom I would not hav in my house. If Bergson is a gentleman, I would like to extend him a little courtesy. I mite ask him up here.

I take it for granted that a great many publishers wil be after him here, and I suppose Macmillan wil hav the inside trac. . . .

If you feel disposed to go to see him, and (always if he is a gentleman) to express my regrets at being out-of-town and my hope to see him when I return, (again, always if he is a gentleman) there might be no harm in your doing so.

I think I can depend upon your tact to judge just how far to go on business points. Probably it would be better to stop with the statement that we ar the publishers of [Bergson's] *Creative Evolution* than to barely allude incidentally to the Williams & Norgate books. Perhaps he wil go farther himself.

Of course you wil find out if he talks English, and post me on that point.

How about the American Home University Library [a Holt series]?

Good luc!

[Henry Holt]

Oct./28/12

Dear Mr. Holt—

Despite newspaper reports, Bergson isn't coming over till February. I'll try to find out about him before then. I've an idea he's a jew.

Ever yours,

A. Harcourt

Soon after writing the following letter, Holt changed his mind about Bergson after reading an article by George Moore in The Dial: *"Moore has opened my eyes to something well worth while and wil help people see the beautiful side of Evolution," Holt wrote to Harcourt on 28 November 1912.*

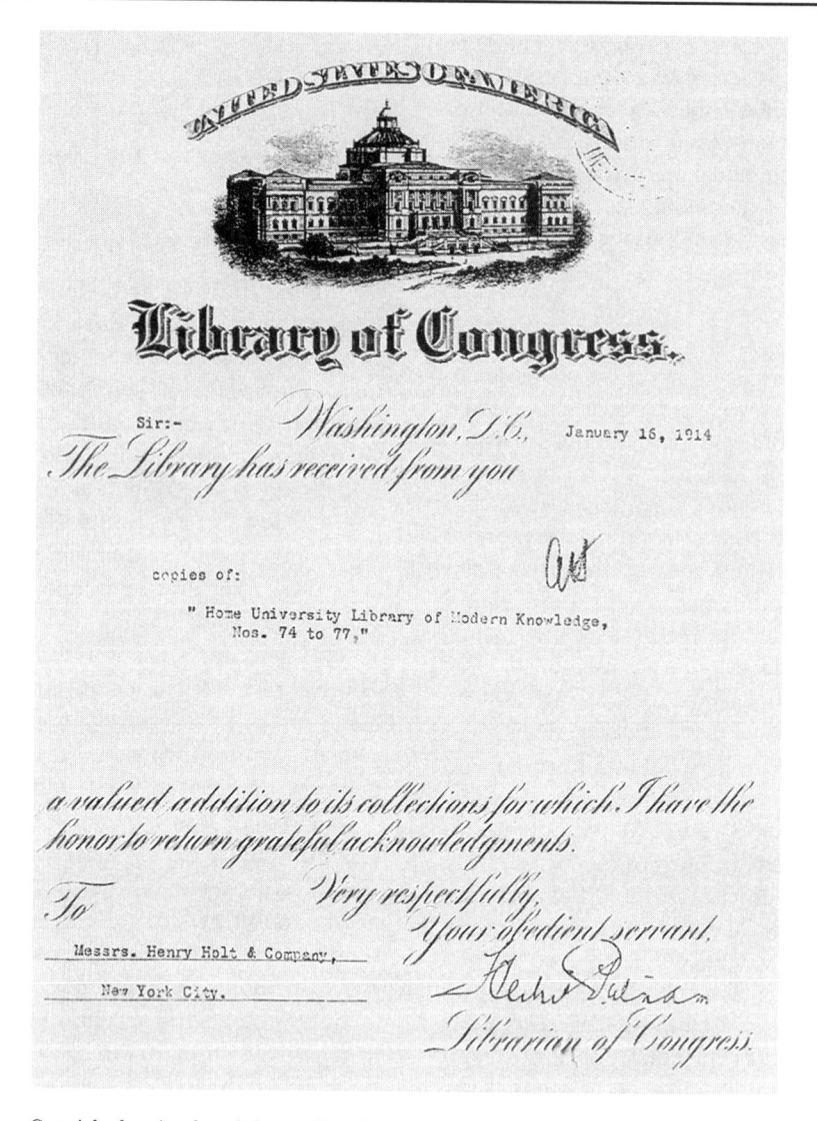

Copyright deposit acknowledgment from the Library of Congress for volumes in a Holt series, initialed by Alfred Harcourt (Princeton University Library)

Nov. 25, 1912

Dear Harcourt:

I came near saying that I had wasted som valuable hours over that "Bergson" thing, but I can't consider them wasted: for it gave me a little clearer notion of what generally passes for Philosophy, including Bergson's. The most I can make out of this (perhaps it's my own stupidity that prevents my making out more) is that it is an attempted short cut to knowledge, whose maker fols himself and his followers by a mass of words; and while admitting, or at least recognizing, that he hasn't got anywhere, says: "If you wil just fil your knapsac with these words, and keep traveling, you wil get somwhere."

I should even question my honesty in publishing Bergson, if it wer not that he seems to make a considerable intellectual stir among people who probably would not be capable of making any stir without such brilliant phrases as his to attract them.

....

[Henry Holt]

Ellen Glasgow

Holt's advice to the popular author Ellen Glasgow to "stick to one publisher" was—in spite of his apparent admiration for her work—characteristic of his publishing philosophy. Glasgow's American publishers at this time included Harper and Doubleday, Page.

August 19 '13

Dear Miss Glasgow:

I've just finisht Virginia and I am reminded of the ladies who have said to me: "I suppose you don't like my work, as you've never askt to publish it."

So I want to tell you that I do like your work, altho I wish your muse were not so inclined to be melancholy and would not rush your characters on the stage at the outset so fast that a reader finds it hard to distinguish them.

I even want to go so far as to say that if, among the unforeseeable mutations of life, you should ever want a new publisher, I should be proud to be the man, if I am here.

But saying this, I must say farther: Stick to one publisher unless you have very good reason to change. Your present one has publisht Virginia admirably.

With delightful recollections of our long talk, and hope of more, and all good wishes, I am,

Faithfully yours,
[Henry Holt]

August 29th 1913

Dear Mr. Holt,

It was a great pleasure to have your letter, and, indeed, I shall always remember your kind invitation to me to become one of your authors. Also, I may add, your good advice that I should stick to one publisher. It would be so nice to talk to you again. Perhaps, if you are not so very busy next winter, you will find time to come for another afternoon.

Sincerely yours,
Ellen Glasgow

Walter Lippmann

Holt and Harcourt simultaneously—though independently—identified Walter Lippmann as an important up-and-coming writer, although Holt's initial (and subsequent) interest in Lipp-

Frontispiece and title page for the first of two autobiographical works on the New York community center, established by the author in 1895, that eventually became known as the Henry Street Settlement (Rutgers University Library)

mann had largely to do with potential articles for The Unpopular Review, *and Harcourt had books in mind. Harcourt prevailed: Lippmann, who had been publishing with Mitchell Kennerley, moved to Holt and Company, with whom he published* The Stakes of Diplomacy *(1915) and* The Political Scene: An Essay on the Victory of 1918 *(1919). Lippmann also republished his 1913 Kennerley title,* A Preface to Politics, *with Holt in 1917.*

October 31, 1914

Dear Mr. Lippmann:

When Hackett [*New Republic* associate editor Francis Hackett] introduced me to you in his office the other day, he followed the formalities by asking me if I had read your book, and mea culpa, I hadn't.

I remedied that matter last night, at least as far as "Drift and Mastery" is concerned, and I hasten to write you that, without intending to disturb your relations with Mr. Kennerly, Henry Holt and Company would be very much honored to publish for you.

That is, if for any reason you should at some time change publishers, we should consider ourselves unusually privileged if you turned our way, and selfishly enough, be greatly disappointed if you didn't.

Sincerely yours,
[Alfred Harcourt]

Harcourt received a handwritten reply from Lippmann on New Republic *letterhead (421 West Twenty-first Street, New York).*

Nov. 4, 1914

Dear Mr. Harcourt,

I am very much flattered by your letter. For the present, however, I am not even contemplating another book. Do come in and lunch with us here some time.

Yours sincerely,
Walter Lippmann

December 4, 1914

Dear Mr. Harcourt:

Mrs. [Dorothy Canfield] Fisher's book [*Mothers and Children,* published by Holt in 1914] has just arrived, and I want to thank you and her for it. Back in the dark ages I used to cut 36-1/2 lines or so out of Mrs. Fisher's novel, "The Squirrel Cage", and I have known how valuable her work was ever since. I hope to get a chance to write about her book, which seems to be very interesting.

And we're not forgetting about your coming to lunch as soon as the atmosphere clears a little bit. Hackett or I will let you know.

Yours,
Walter Lippmann

Walter Lippmann (Gale International Portrait Gallery)

June 28, 1915

Dear Harcourt:

Who wrote the article on *The President's Responsibilities* and *Himself Again* (referring to Bryan) in a recent–probably the last–*New Republic?* They were fine articles, and I guess I want to get those cusses to writing for the Unpop!

Harcourt's handwritten reply appears on the same letter.

Dear Mr. Holt:

With Miss Eayrs [Ellen Eayrs, Harcourt's secretary, whom he later married] away it's easier to reply here than dictate.

Herbert Croly wrote *The President's Responsibilities* and Walter Lippmann wrote *Himself Again.* I happened to telephone Lippmann about your inquiry, and he was much gratified at the compliment it implied–all of which is fortunate as I hope we shall publish for him some day....

Sincerely yours,
Alfred Harcourt

P.S. I've just read the complete ms. of Miss [Lillian D.] Wald's "The House on Henry Street." I'm sure

Henry Holt (right) with Holt and Company author Raphael Pumpelly (center) and Ethan Allen Hitchcock, circa 1916 (Rutgers University Library)

you'll be proud of it, and I'm much gratified. There's a third more in the book than will be in the Atlantic, and all good stuff.

August 20, 1915

Dear Mr. Lippmann:

Haven't you the material for a new book? If you have, or when you have, we should be very glad indeed to talk with you about publishing it, and very much disappointed if, through any fault of omission on our part, we failed to have that privilege.

A publisher does his best work, and gets the most satisfaction from publishing for an author who furthers the interests the publisher has at heart as a human being. Publishing for you would be so especially satisfying to me in this respect that I am deeply interested.

Sincerely yours,
[Alfred Harcourt]

***

A "Real Feller"

Harcourt and Robert Frost enjoyed a close rapport early in their relationship. Florence Pillsbury was Henry Holt's secretary.

Sept-30-15

Dear Miss Pillsbury:

....

Have had such a good visit with Robert Frost this week. Had him out home and talked most of the night. He has more quality and a more loveable personality than anybody I've come at all close to for some time, and his character and brains have deepened my faith in his poetry. He's a "real feller"—no mere poet!

....

Sincerely yours,
Alfred Harcourt

Cover and title page for the second and final novel by the Virginia-born poet and novelist best known for her poems exploring social issues (Rutgers University Library)

Henry Holt's admiration for Lippmann was also considerable but not without qualification.

October 12, 1915

Dear Harcourt:

Coming up yesterday I read Lippmann's "Drift and Master," and like it better than the portion I read of "A Preface to Politics." In fact, I consider it worth reading, and from a man who reads as few books as I do and of the kind I do, that is pretty near as big a compliment as it would be possible for me to pay any book.

Has he been trying to get hold of the plates of both those books to have them publisht by us? If he succeeds, or if he doesn't succeed, he ought for his own sake to explain what he means on pages 108–9 where he says:

"Could the government make better use of Mr. Carnegie's huge fortune than Mr. Carnegie does? . . . Are there better uses to which it might be put than those which Mr. Carnegie has in mind? If there are, then the government is entirely justified in substituting itself for Mr. Carnegie as a dispenser of libraries and peace palaces."

Now of course if he wants to lay this down as a principle, there simply wouldn't be any Carnegie fortune or any other big fortune. No man would bother to make it if it were likely to be snapt up any time by the government. I think Lippmann has too much sense to have meant that, so it's important to say just what he does mean, and also to make his expression consistent with what he very sensibly says on page 317:

"There is, of course, no greater difficulty in thought than to attain a delicate adjustment of our own desires to what is possible."

He certainly has a wonderful grasp for so young a man, and for a young man of his general tendencies has kept better within the bounds of possibility than I expected to find him; and his gifts as a

October 13, 1915

Dear Harcourt:

I should have added to my letter about Lippmann's book that it had no index—a circumstance of which I think yu can make judicious use in conversation with him. Croly's latest book, which I began reading last night, has one. Lord! How few real publishers there are in the world! I haven't yet lived long enough to become one, I sometimes think.

Said Lippmann appears to believe in Mothers' pensions, old age insurance, unemployment insurance, workmen's compensation, etc., etc.; and I am not sure but that I do. But some of those dodges, the experience of the English Poor laws is dead against. I wonder if he wouldn't like to write the Unpop an article giving his impressions of those circumstances?

Yrs,
HH

Page from the back matter of Sarah N. Cleghorn's The Spinster *advertising Holt titles by the writer who collaborated with Cleghorn on a 1915 volume of poetry (Rutgers University Library)*

mere writer are even greater than I supposed from slight earlier knowledge. Of course I hope his new book will be better tempered still. Probably yu think it would be dangerous for me to read it in the proofs!

I haven't yet seen Thursday's Nation. I hope there's an advertisement of the Unpop in it.

I had rather expected this coming forward of the liquor dealers because of the articles on Prohibition in the October number. Certainly in some ways that number is making a hit. I haven't yet heard, however, from any of my expert contributors....

Yrs,
HH

Dorothy Canfield (later Dorothy Canfield Fisher), who published several fiction and nonfiction titles with Holt and Company beginning in 1907, shown as a senior at the University of Nebraska in 1899 (Bruccoli Clark Layman Archives)

Gentlemen:-

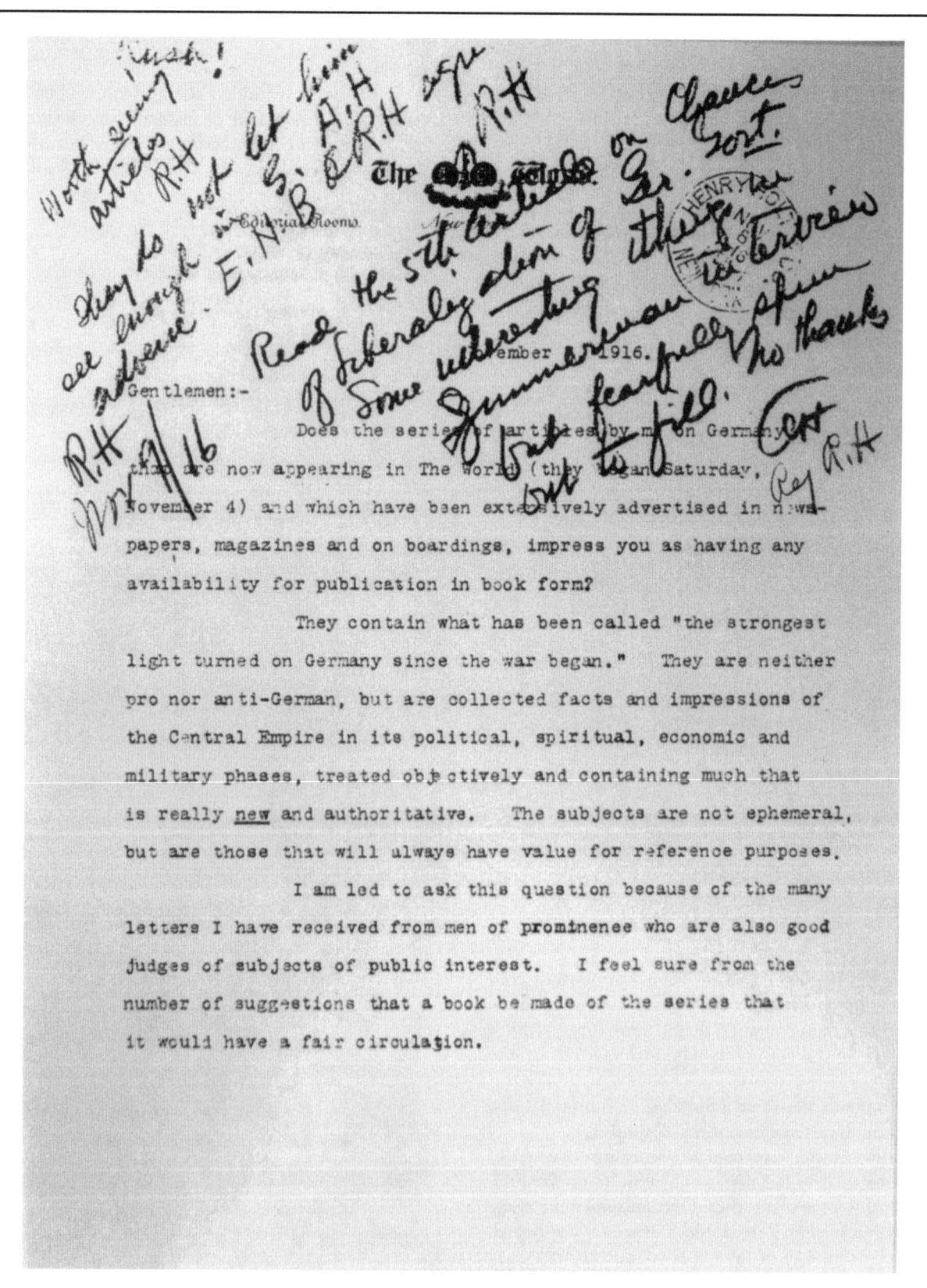

Does the series of articles by me on Germany that are now appearing in The World (they began Saturday, November 4) and which have been extensively advertised in newspapers, magazines and on boardings, impress you as having any availability for publication in book form?

They contain what has been called "the strongest light turned on Germany since the war began." They are neither pro nor anti-German, but are collected facts and impressions of the Central Empire in its political, spiritual, economic and military phases, treated objectively and containing much that is really <u>new</u> and authoritative. The subjects are not ephemeral, but are those that will always have value for reference purposes.

I am led to ask this question because of the many letters I have received from men of prominence who are also good judges of subjects of public interest. I feel sure from the number of suggestions that a book be made of the series that it would have a fair circulation.

Letter from Herbert Bayard Swope, city editor of The World, *offering his series of articles on wartime Germany to Holt and Company for book publication. The handwritten readers' comments are by members of Holt's "Senate," Harcourt, Roland Holt, and E. N. Bristol (Princeton University Library).*

October 14, 1915

Dear Mr. Holt:

I am immensely gratified that you think so well of Lippmann's "Drift and Mastery." The new book will, I think, please you even more.

He's been trying to get hold of his earlier books, but Kennerly wants $2,500 for them, and Lippmann and I are agreed to let Kennerly cool off before pressing the matter. He ought to sell for about $1000.

I'll tell Lippmann what you say about his inconsistencies. The questions of Carnegie, the government, the people, Carnegie's heirs and their rights to Carnegie's fortune etc. are so complicated that hardly anybody thinks plumb straight about them from page 108 to 317. Alvin Johnson's article in the Atlantic last year suggesting a way out by heavy inheritance taxes—the proceeds to furnish the capital for old age pensions etc. instead of going into the pot of current government income appealed to me strongly.

I'll also ask Lippmann about the Unpop article you suggest.

Sincerely,
Alfred Harcourt

* * *

In spite of Lippmann's defection from Holt and Company to join Harcourt, Brace and Company in 1919, Lincoln MacVeagh, Harcourt's successor at Holt, felt comfortable enough to ask Lippmann to comment on a prospective Holt title by the German philosopher and cultural historian Oswald Spengler.

February 17, 1923

Dear Mr. MacVeagh:

I read Spengler over a year ago for Harcourt and I can just tell you that I advised him against publishing it. It seemed to me rather pseudo.

Sincerely yours
Walter Lippmann

[n.d.]

Dear Mr. Lippmann

Thank you for telling us what your advice was on Spengler. We declined the first volume in April 1921, but the second volume, plus an English collaborator, revived the question. I think we can now give it its quietus, so far as we are concerned.

Sincerely yours,
[Lincoln MacVeagh]

I enclose a check for $10 which may go a little way toward expressing our appreciation.

Patriotic Publisher

May 3, 1918
Industrial Honor Flag Division
Liberty Loan Committee, 120 Broadway, New York

Dear Sirs:

We have on our New York pay-roll fifty-seven people, of whom 40 are takers of one or more bonds on the third Liberty Loan drive. This should entitle us to a flag with seven stars, and we beg to enclose check $1.75, requesting you to give bearer an order on the flag department. . . .

Respectfully yours
HENRY HOLT AND COMPANY

POLITICS AND WORLD WAR I

In a letter to Henry Holt, Harcourt expresses his qualified support for President Woodrow Wilson, running for reelection against the Republican candidate, U.S. Supreme Court Justice Charles Evans Hughes, in the 1916 race.

October 10, 1916.

Dear Mr. Holt:

Thanks for yours of the ninth.

I'll attend to the exchange advertising.

The October Unpop is, to me, about the best yet, though, as usual, and as is intended in the title, it gets my dander up about every third article.

I'm inclined to vote for Wilson, though without enthusiasm. Hughes has gone off too much like a giant firecracker that has been exposed to the weather. The income tax argument doesn't worry me. The dangers you point out seem to me to be minimized by the American habit of striving to get into the taxpaying class, and by the fact that (to my observation) men do their work more from interest in their job and from habit (see James's well-known chapter) than for the money they get. The exemptions will have to be lowered to pay for the social burdens the government is so rapidly assuming.

Wasn't Lincoln a gentleman, or do you mean "gentleman" merely as a tag of class? If the latter, hadn't we better take frequent chances on mere men for the sake of the better chance at an occasional demigod?

And I've bought two "honeless" razors (the first was so good I sent a second to my father), and they're only $3.00, if you buy 'em at Ferrieri's, 1589 Broadway.

. . . .

Advertisement for Holt titles from a 1918 issue of a New York literary magazine (Rutgers University Library)

[Sumner Locke's] "Samaritan Mary". . . sold 3,500 & dealers have cleaned up on it, which doesn't happen unless there's something in a book.

Sincerely yours,
Alfred Harcourt

***

Herbert Bayard Swope, city editor of The World, *offered his series of articles on Germany to Holt and Company in late 1916. Roland Holt replied to Swope explaining the firm's reasons for rejecting the proposed book.*

November 7, 1916.

Gentlemen:–

Does the series of articles by me on Germany that are now appearing in The World (they began Saturday, November 4) and which have been extensively advertised in newspapers, magazines and on boardings, impress you as having any availability for publication in book form?

They contain what has been called "the strongest light turned on Germany since the war began." They are neither pro nor anti-German, but are collected facts and impressions of the Central Empire in its political, spiritual, economic and military phases, treated objectively and containing much that is really *new* and authoritative. The subjects are not ephemeral, but are those that will always have value for reference purposes.

I am led to ask this question because of the many letters I have received from men of prominence who are also good judges of subjects of public interest. I feel sure from the number of suggestions that a book be made of the series that it would have a fair circulation.

I shall appreciate an early reply.

Faithfully,
Herbert Bayard Swope

P.S. It would not be a "war" book in the common understanding of that term.

November 8, 1916.

Dear Sir:

Pray accept our thanks for your very kind offer of your INSIDE THE GERMAN EMPIRE papers now appearing in The World. There is so much that is interesting in them that it increases our regret that, everything considered, we do not believe that the public would support us should we bring them out in book form, admirably as they are serving their purposes in The World.

While of course, as you say, this is not a war book from one point of view, still it is a result of the war, and most of the public would put it under the ban we find they are putting on war books.

We have only reached this conclusion reluctantly and after consideration here in council, and are,

Sincerely yours,
[Roland Holt]

Once the United States had entered World War I on 6 April 1917, questions about the propriety and marketability of war-related books became more urgent.

October 24, 1917.

Dear Mr. Holt:

. . . .

The back advertising pages of the latest edition of "Understood Betsy" on my shelves have a complete list of Mrs. Fisher's books, but there ought to be a list of her books facing the title page.

I have had the pretty distinct impression for years that the hullabaloo special book numbers of the Times Book Review, etc. are good things to stay out of, but only this year have I had the sufficient courage of my convictions to stay out. After I looked through the number I was not sorry.

Yes, there has been money made in military books, mostly, however, by people who had the makings of such a list started before the war. I have been looking into the field with considerable care, and it seems to be the general impression that the business is distinctly on the wane, as the government provides its own instructions, and the men are absorbed in actual practice instead of reading about it. We are now rushing through the press Professor Douglas W. Johnson's "Topography and Strategy in the War" which we hope to get started in military circles, and also to have some trade sale.

. . . .

Sincerely yours,
Alfred Harcourt

***

One effect of American involvement in the war was an increase in the price of materials and labor that affected much of the nation's economy, including the publishing sector.

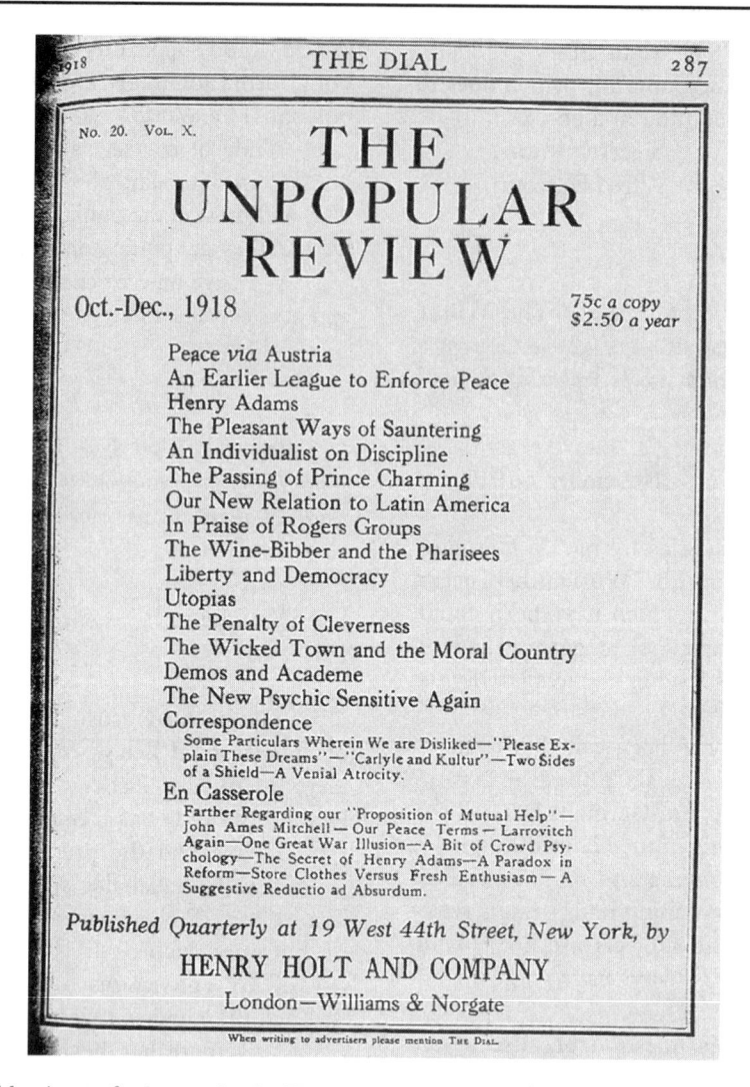

Advertisement for the magazine that Henry Holt started in 1914 (Rutgers University Library)

May 29, 1918

Henry Holt & Co.,
New York City.

Gentlemen:

The constantly increasing cost of materials and labor have made it necessary that printers increase prices in order to remain in business.

Aside from the increased cost of all materials, supplies and sundry expenses common to many lines of business, the printing industry has been most seriously hit by the condition of the labor market. Not only is labor demanding constantly increasing wages (there has just been another substantial increase in all departments), but there is a growing scarcity of experienced men. This has caused a serious decrease in output, which has the effect of greatly increasing the cost of the finished product. These conditions make it absolutely necessary that prices be increased. There is no other alternative if the firms who have been serving you these many years are to continue to do so.

All prices must increase at least 20% on the small runs and special work, and at least 15% on the larger runs.

This letter is written you in the interest and under the auspices of the Printers of New York City and vicinity, to acquaint you with the necessity for these increases in prices, hoping that, knowing the facts, you will feel that the increase which your printer must make is only fair, and forced by conditions beyond his control.

We shall be glad to go over the details of the increase in costs with anyone interested.

Yours very truly,
CONFERENCE OF THE
BOOK PRINTERS [of New York City]
Ralph C. Jappe
Secretary.

* * *

Henry Holt occasionally corresponded with U.S. senator Henry Cabot Lodge.

July 16, 1918

Dear Senator Lodge:

I suppose yu and other influential men in Washington are working on the theory that one of the very best things we can do to upset Germany, is to encourage with money, arms and everything we can, the disaffected peoples of the Austrian Empire.

Perhaps yu will forgive me, however, for begging your most serious attention to this point, if the point has not already secured it.

Faithfully yours,
[Henry Holt]

July 22, 1918

My dear Mr. Holt:

I have your note of the 16th. I am in most cordial agreement with you about the disaffected peoples of the Austrian Empire. To my mind perhaps the most essential thing, when we achieve victory, will be the establishment of Poland, of the Jugo-Slavs, and the Czecho-Slovaks, as independent States. It will do more to hold Germany in bonds than anything else, and moreover it is in the interest of freedom and justice. I have been doing what little I could in that direction for some months. It has been much on my mind. I think we are doing a little something as a Government now for the Jugo-Slavs and the Czecho-Slovaks. The Government is also interested in the Poles, but how far they have gone I am not aware.

With kind regards,

Very truly yours,
H. C. Lodge

***

Like other publishers, Holt and Company was subject to wartime regulations concerning books written by members of the military.

August 30, 1918

Adjutant General's Office
War Department
Washington, D.C.

Dear Sir:

We have your letter of August 23rd, referring to General Order, No. 168, forbidding the publication by members of the Military service of any matter without previously submitting it to the War Department for approval. We have the following books in preparation and in each case one of the authors is a member of the military service.

The Writing of English, by Captain John M. Manly and Edith Rickert. Captain Manly is in the military intelligence branch, office of the chief of staff. The book is a high school textbook of English composition.

Beginning French, by Professors W. F. Giese and Barry Cerf of the University of Wisconsin. Professor Cerf has just been commissioned a captain in the gas defense service. The book is a grammar for beginners in the study of French.

Neither of the books bears on military matters in any way, and we shall be glad to know whether special authorization is necessary.

Respectfully yours,
Henry Holt and Company

September 16, 1918

Dear Sirs:—

Your letter of August 30th has reached this office. Under the provisions of General Orders, No. 168, War Department, 1917, officers, enlisted men and other individual members of the service are prohibited from printing or distributing through publishing houses, or otherwise, any pamphlets or books not previously published or in process of being published, on any military subject whatever, except as authorized by the War Department.

However, as these books are not of a military nature, it is not deemed necessary to have them submitted to the War Department for approval.

Very truly yours,
Adjutant General

Even after the 11 November 1918 armistice that suspended hostilities, America was technically still at war with Germany and remained so until the signing of the Treaty of Versailles on 28 June 1919. As a reminder of this situation, Holt and Company received the following letter from the office of the Alien Property Custodian.

Jan. 15, 1919.

Dear Sir:

The Alien Property Custodian will greatly appreciate your assistance in locating patents, copyrights and trademarks, (together with applications therefor and rights to apply for the same), owing to or belonging to, or held for, by, or on account of, or on behalf of, or for the benefit of an enemy or an ally of an enemy. We are still at war with Germany. The Trading with the Enemy Act is still in force, with its penalties for failure to report enemy owned property to this office.

....

The Alien Property Custodian feels that he can count on your patriotic co-operation and will be pleased to receive from you any information that will lead to the detection of enemy property as outlined above. You will also be aiding your country in the most important task of emancipating American industry from the domination of the German monopolists....
Very truly yours,
Francis P. Gaway
Director, Bureau of Investigation.
Alien Property Custodian
Washington, D.C.

* * *

In 1919 Harcourt's successor at Holt and Company, Lincoln MacVeagh, tried to get his friend Franklin D. Roosevelt, at that time assistant secretary of the navy, to write a book for Holt and Company about the navy's role in the war. Although Roosevelt eventually wrote several books, none was published by Holt.

July 10, 1919

Dear Franklin:

I am just home from Europe and once more, as you see by the letter-head, in the game of publishing. This and the fact that peace has come at last gives me the opportunity of broaching a subject which, while I was in the army, I was unable to tackle. I realize, however, how busy you are so that I will set it out in the briefest manner possible and trust that you will give it consideration.

"Over there" we had a high opinion of and belief in the American navy and experienced its protection. In this country, however, people do not seem to have heard as much of the navy as they have of the army, though I believe there is a feeling that the navy was somehow the more efficient of the two. How did it become so? What were the workings behind the scene? These are questions which I think the country feels it has a right to have answered. These are certainly ones in which it is most deeply interested. Here in fact is a fine page of history to be written and one full of lessons for the future.

Of course the American navy in the war is a big subject, but it is fascinating and important, and so far virtually untouched. Furthermore, there is nobody who can handle the subject as you can. There is nobody who is credited by the country at large with a greater share in establishing the high record of the navy in this war, and nobody who possesses more solid claims to such credit.

I will not touch on the possible political value of such a book at this time. You can better determine that. But I will ask: Is there not a book in your kind [*sic*], or even on the tip of your pen?

Please give my best regards to Eleanor and believe me always
Yours very sincerely,
[Lincoln MacVeagh]

———◆———

March 24, 1920

Dear Franklin:

I am taking the liberty of sending you copies of a couple of small books we have just brought out. I think they will repay your trouble if you read them. At the same time I hope they will remind you of our previous correspondence. Smouch tells me you thought my ideas of your book (future) rather exaggerated. I still feel, however, that we need books dealing directly with present problems and written by men of your type. The presses are full of radical literature none the less dangerous for being half-baked. What the effect of such a book would be on your political future you can best decide. I am sure you would reach a very wide audience and do a great amount of good.
Sincerely yours,
[Lincoln MacVeagh]

———◆———

April 15, 1920.

Dear Lincoln:

Very many thanks for sending me the books. I am particularly interested in them, as they are of real value to me in some memoranda I am getting up on the work of the Marines on the other side. Some day, when this bad Spring and Summer are ended, I fully intend to rush into print, but just now it seems awfully hard to get any consecutive work accomplished.
Very sincerely yours,
Franklin D. Roosevelt

HARCOURT'S DEPARTURE

In the summer of 1918 Harcourt revealed to Henry Holt that he had received an offer from Doran and was considering leaving Holt and Company. Although Harcourt finally decided to decline Doran's offer and stay on at Holt, he and Donald Brace left the firm the following summer to found Harcourt, Brace and Company.

June 28 1918

Dear Mr. Holt:—

Entirely to my surprise, and out of a quite clear sky–I hadn't seen him for months except casually at a publishers' lunch–Doran offers me $10,000 a year and a commission which would amount to from three to five thousand more. I'd much rather stay with H.H. & Co., but I have financial responsibilities, since my father died land poor, which won't permit my being quixotic in the face of this proposal.

I have agreed with the others here to draw at the rate of $450 a month on the chance that commissions this year may not justify more, and to conserve the company's cash. This is, conservatively, $600 a month less than Doran assures me. I'd be quite willing to split this difference for the sake of my happiness here and my future here. Could you agree to guarantee that my salary and commissions would amount to not less than $750 a month? I should not want to draw over $450 a month, except in some personal financial emergency, until H.H. & Co.'s finances are easier.

Sincerely yours
Alfred Harcourt

Harcourt wired Henry Holt in Burlington, Vermont, on 1 July, three days after mailing his letter about the Doran offer.

After week end reflection I feel my roots are too deep in this business to be pulled out by dazzling schemes or immediate income please forget my letter unless it or anything else has distrubed [sic] you about my future here please wire me on this point
Harcourt

July 2, 1918

Dear Harcourt:

Your telegram did not reach me yesterday until after yu had left the office, and I wired a "night letter": "Am glad and proud of your decision, and hope and believe yu will never regret it."

Perhaps yu found my use of the word "proud" a little cryptic. It meant substantially that I was proud of whatever I had done to build a business that had led yu to such a resolution, and whatever influences I may have had on yu to make yu take it.

I hope I can safely say that I never made money a controling motive. Probably yu know cases where I disregarded it utterly, and yet thru an exceptionally long life I have had a reasonable amount of it, until this war pinch came.

Altho I so highly appreciate your withdrawing your letter, I am absolutely sincere in saying that the letter itself did not lower yu in my estimation; and that your withdrawal of it has raised yu. Yet I think that as the world goes, it was a rather handsome letter: the temptation was a strong and justifiable one. I should not have blamed yu one bit if yu had yielded to it, yet I believe that yu would have grown into a smaller man than yu will grow into now; and that even if yu have made, in some aspects, a serious mistake, there are other aspects making it plain that it can't fail to do yu good. I cannot tell yu how heartily I hope it will. I also think not only that it will do *yu* good, but I am sure it will do the rest of us good, and do the business good.

And to come to less speculative ground, isn't it the fact that before the war pinch, your income had got ahead of Doran's first offer, and that therefore there is reason to hope that after the war pinch, it may before long get ahead of his second offer?

. . . .

Yours more still
HH

July 5 /18

Dear Mr. Holt:

I can't tell you how much I value your letter of July 2nd.

I suppose Doran's schemes and pace fascinated me as much as his money. I suppose my anxieties about the long future of this business made Doran's uncertainties seem less uncertain. So I found myself quite unsettled. But reflection seemed to show clearly a surer happiness here and a more deeply rooted interest than I had realized. . . .

But I'm half glad I wrote to you, after all. Otherwise I couldn't have your letter, which I shall treasure.

Yours for good
Alfred Harcourt

***

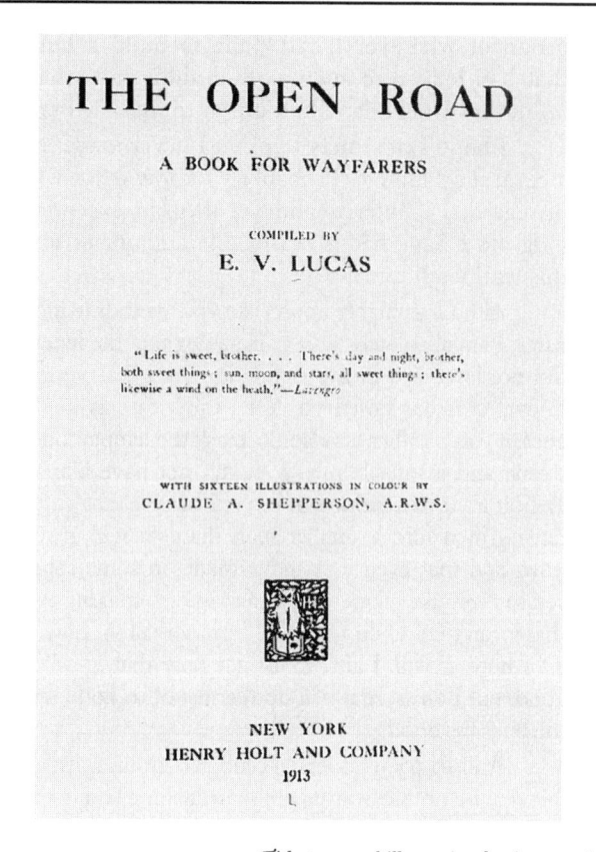

Title page and illustration for the seventh Holt and Company edition of the 1899 poetry and prose anthology (Rutgers University Library)

The departure of Harcourt and Brace from Holt and Company in 1919 occasioned the "special pressure of work" and "reorganizations" mentioned by Holt employee Edward N. Bristol in the following letter to James D. Phillips of the Houghton Mifflin Company.

Dec. 18, 1919.

Dear Mr. Phillips:

You have a right to be incensed at my not responding long ago to your letter about expense ratios; there is really no excuse for the delay. I can urge in palliation, however, that I made an excuse of not hearing from Mr. Stevenson of Silver Burdett and Company, and Mr. Nelson of The MacMillan Company, both of whom promised figures, but who have not yet furnished them. I suppose the real reason for the delay is that for two months I was under a special pressure of work, due partly to some reorganizations here, the brunt of which fell upon me, and partly to the complications of the printing situation in New York. Then I had to take a complete rest away from the office for a time.

The percentages of production expenses to net sales, as given me, were as follows:

Allyn and Bacon: "A fraction under 40%. This percentage includes all charges except manufacturing, plates, and royalties i.e., includes salaries of owners and managers as well as shipping, accounting, gift copy and branch office expenses".

D. C. Heath and Company: "A trifle over 40%", for the same items.

Henry Holt and Company: 36%, including all the items mentioned under Allyn and Bacon.

Benjamin Sanborn and Company: 43% including "agency, office, shipping, gift copy (at cost), freight, expressage and postage expense", but omitting "interest and discount, reserves for bad debts, insurance, depreciation of plates and publishing rights, and federal income tax."

Charles Scribners' Sons: 31% "as an average for ten years; in 1918 a fraction under this rate".

The ratio of agency expense to net sales:

> Allyn and Bacon: 20% excluding managers' salaries and branch office expense, but including gift copies at cost.

> D. C. Heath and Company: 15% excluding branch office expense, but including gift copies at cost.

> Henry Holt and Company: 15% including branch office expense, managers' salaries, and gift copies at cost.

> Benjamin Sanborn and Company: 19% on same basis as Holt.

> Charles Scribners' Sons give no separate agency percentage.

I have given the items as they came to me. You will see that they need analyzing in order to reach a sound basis of comparison, but that would require the services of an expert accountant, and involve, probably, not a little labor for each publisher's own accountant. There is also the added complication of the unusual conditions of 1918. I tried to see if this element could not be eliminated, but the attempt was not very successful. Allyn and Bacon said that the 1918 ratio was slightly under normal, but though the ratio had been declining steadily for several years, they expected some increase for this year, despite the large gain in sales. D. C. Heath's 1918 ratio was about normal, our own was something like 4% under normal, the difference lying almost entirely in agency expenses. It looks, however, as if this year our percentage would not be very different from 1918. In spite of the return of a number of our agents from public service, increased business and increased prices will probably keep us close to what we have for some time regarded as a maximum of 35%. Though the 15% allowance for agents' salaries and expenses, branch office expense, and gift copies, will probably hold, I think both the 35% and 15% are higher than educational publishing conditions in America warrant. . . .

Sincerely yours,

[E. N. Bristol]

The 1920s

The one-year-old firm of Harcourt, Brace and Company was the publisher of the number-two nonfiction book in the 1920 Publishers' Weekly annual best-seller list, John Maynard Keynes's The Economic Consequences of the Peace. The following year Harcourt, Brace had the top two titles in the fiction best-seller list: Main Street, by Sinclair Lewis, and The Brimming Cup, by Dorothy Canfield Fisher (a former Holt author). Holt and Company, meanwhile, had no books in the best-seller lists for either year. This situation reflects much about the success of the new publishing house—and the relative decline of the older one. This quietude was to characterize the following two and a half decades for Holt and Company. The void left by Alfred Harcourt's departure was never really filled; Henry Holt's sons, Henry Jr., Elliot, and Roland, were not inclined to take over the business. Lincoln MacVeagh, a trade-book editor of more promise, left the firm in December 1923 to become founder and president of the Dial Press. He also served as secretary and treasurer of Dial Publishing, publisher of The Dial. Henry Holt himself, who had long been removed from day-to-day business operations while living most of the year in Vermont, died in 1926.

THE EARLY 1920s

Lincoln MacVeagh

MacVeagh energetically tried to fill the gap left by Harcourt's departure, seeking to interest Carl Sandburg in publishing again with Holt and Company. Sandburg had published Chicago Poems (1916) and Cornhuskers (1918) with the firm. Although MacVeagh hoped for Sandburg's return, Sandburg never published with Holt again.

Holt and Company owl device, 1929 (Rutgers University Library)

Die cuts for Holt and Company titles, 1922 (courtesy of Princeton University Library)

102

Latter part of July 1920

Dear Mr. Holt:

I was in Chicago this week and saw [Carl] Sandburg. He was very cordial and seems to be exceedingly glad to have someone here take a personal interest in him. At the same time he says that it may be a number of years before he has another volume of poetry and he seems to be very thick with all Mr. Harcourt's crowd. This is especially understandable when you realize that Sandburg is strongly radical and is a personal friend of [William Z.] Foster who organized the late steel strike. Nevertheless, Sandburg is a fine upstanding fellow.

He told me that he had received several letters from you asking for something for The Unpartizan Review, but that he couldn't for the life of him see how his stuff would fit in with the general tenor of that paper. I told him that I thought that he wrote from time to time poems which did not treat of economic or social questions, and later when he read me some of his things, I suggested that he send you one which I enclose. He said, "Take it along with you and dedicate it to Robert Frost." I hope you may care to use it. I see no reason why we should not as time goes on get more out of Sandburg if we want to, but it will be a question of time and of fostering his friendship. Like most poets he is very sensitive.

I have just had breakfast with Mr. Theodore Stanton who is going to Paris for a year. He is going to keep us in touch with literary things over there and give us ideas and suggestions. He knows all the literary people in Paris and most of the publishers personally, and as he is a good friend of mine, I hope to make some valuable acquaintances through him. There is a lot of first-grade stuff being written in France, and so far we have had no way of getting directly in touch with it. When I go over next time, I shall run over to Paris and get Mr. Stanton to introduce me to Hachettes, the Alcans, etc. . . .

Frost wants me to come up and visit him at Franconia, and I shall be there a couple of days next week. The first two weeks in August I expect to be in Dublin [New Hampshire] with my family, and I hope to see you there.

With very best regards, I am

Sincerely yours,
[Lincoln MacVeagh]

**

Lincoln MacVeagh, a trade-book editor with Holt and Company in the early 1920s, in a photograph during his later career as a U.S. diplomat (from John O. Iatrides, ed., Ambassador MacVeagh Reports, *1980; Thomas Cooper Library, University of South Carolina)*

Frederic G. Melcher, for many years the editor of Publishers' Weekly *and, from 1920 to 1924, executive secretary of the National Association of Book Publishers, often acted as a liaison between publishers, the American government, and publishing-related industries.*

September 4th, 1920

Dear Sir [Holt employee Edward N. Bristol]:

The employing printers and binders of New York are facing demands for a 40% increase in wage scales. Whatever increases come to New York promptly affect wage scales in other cities, so that the whole publishing industry is vitally interested.

Under existing agreements the scale is submitted to readjustment on October 1st, the decision to rest on two factors; 1st, the cost of living as compared with last January; 2nd, the general economic conditions of the industry.

Government figures will be used as to cost of living, and figures as to the conditions in the industry must be promptly gathered for the use of the committees of the Employing Printers Association and the Employing Binders in presenting the arguments against such increases. The facts from the book publishers will be used in conjunction with similar facts from the periodical and job printing field.

One of the functions of the National Association of Book Publishers is the gathering of statistics vital to the industry, and we earnestly request your very prompt attention to the enclosed questionnaire.

Very truly yours,
Frederic G. Melcher
Executive Secretary

September 17, 1920

My dear Mr. Melcher:

I enclose a copy of your questionnaire with the best answers we can give. You will understand that the figures are all approximations, but I believe that in their entirety they represent very closely our situation. Just this afternoon we had to refuse a most attractive book which in former days we should have been glad to have; its small yearly sale would have been enough to justify publication. Now it is another story.

Very sincerely,
[Lincoln MacVeagh]

Title page for a collection of sketches of contemporary British political and literary figures, first published in England in 1919 (Rutgers University Library)

QUESTIONNAIRE ON THE SITUATION IN THE BOOK PUBLISHING FIELD AS AFFECTED BY INCREASED MANUFACTURING COSTS

Have present prices in printing and binding prevented you from undertaking any new enterprises this year? *Yes.*

About how many decisions have been affected by this since January 1st? *About ten.*

Estimate total number of volumes this left unprinted? *About 20,000.*

How many forms would that represent? *About 200,000.*

How much binding? *About 10,000 books.*

Has this affected the chances of new writers to get publication? *Yes.*

A book has to promise how large a scale before it can be undertaken? *About 5,000.*

How many formerly? *About 2,500.*

(This answer based on the $2.00 novel.)

Have you decided to discontinue from your list any titles this year on account of production costs? *Yes.*

How many since January 1st? *About 80.*

Estimate total number of volumes thus left unprinted? *About 40,000.*

How many 32 page forms would that be? *About 400,000.*

Are there other titles that will be discontinued if there are further increases? *Yes.*

Estimate how many? *Probably over 200.*

A reprinting has to be how large now to be profitably undertaken? *Average 1,000.* Under former conditions? *Average 250.*

Are you placing printing outside of your city? *Yes.* Binding? *Yes.*

Are present costs affecting your export opportunities? *Yes.* Give facts or figures that might be pertinent. *Present prices are stopping the taking of our sheets by English publishers. In general only such American books as the British can afford to print themselves have a chance abroad.*

Please give any further facts from your present business conditions that will throw light on the effect of increased costs in composition, electrotyping, printing, or binding? *Printing costs for editions of 1,000 are such as to make a reprinting of this number barely profitable. There is a great progressive increase of cost as the editions grow smaller, for which we hardly see the necessity, any more than for the great proportionate increase in cost of binding when anything but the standard 12mo is bound. These seemingly needless big increases are driving standard slow selling books from the market and tending to standardize the product to the detriment of quality and attractiveness.*

* * *

Advertisement from the 5 January 1929 issue of Publishers' Weekly
(Thomas Cooper Library, University of South Carolina)

When Harcourt acquired the American rights to Bertrand Russell's Proposed Roads to Freedom, *Henry Holt strenuously objected to the socialist sentiments expressed in the work and did not want to publish it. Harcourt prevailed, and the book was published by Holt and Company in 1919. This episode, however, strengthened Harcourt's resolve to leave the firm. When Holt and Company expressed interest in Russell's next book, Stanley Unwin of Allen and Unwin, Russell's English publisher, explained the author's preference for the new firm of Harcourt, Brace and Company.*

September 14, 1920

My dear Mr. Holt:

Here is Stanley Unwin's reply to my inquiry about Russell's new book:

"The articles, plus other material which has not yet appeared, will shortly be available for publication in book form and the entire rights will be under our control, but in accordance with the author's wishes the first offer of the book will have to go to Mr. Alfred Harcourt, who you will remember was responsible for the publications of "Roads to Freedom" at a time when you had definitely cabled to us that you did not wish to be associated with the book. In the event of Mr. Harcourt not being prepared to make a satisfactory proposal for the book we shall be only too pleased to let you have the offer of it. There is no doubt that it will be a big seller."

Very sincerely yours,
[Lincoln MacVeagh]

* * *

Henry Holt wrote MacVeagh in the fall of 1920 to complain about the actions of some of their competitors. Romain Rolland, like Sandburg, had published with Holt and Company earlier, but, unlike Sandburg, he continued to publish with Holt. Only one of Rolland's books, The Forerunners *(1920), was published by Harcourt, Brace and Howe.*

October 6, 1920

Dear Lincoln:

Do yu know how Mrs. [Edith] Wharton happened to go from Scribner to Appleton?

Do yu know how Harcourt gobbled up the new books of Romain Rolland and Carl Sandburg? I thought yu felt pretty confident we had the latter.

When I see the way Doran and Dutton are exploiting England, I am more and more convinced that we need an agent there, and that an inefficient one is worse than none at all. . . .

Yrs. much
HH

October 9, 1920

My dear Mr. Holt;

Thank you for your letter of October 6. I do not know why Mrs. Wharton left Scribner's to go to Appleton. I think as things go nowadays it might be a safe guess that Appleton bid higher for her work.

BRIEFER MENTION

The May 1920 issue of The Dial *included a capsule review of nature poet Lew Sarett's first book, published by Holt and Company.*

Many Many Moons, by Lew Sarett (12mo, 82 pages; Holt), is an attempt to reproduce in poetry "the loam and the lingo, the sand and the syllables of North America." More specifically it is a reproduction of Indian tribal chants, a task for which Mr. Sarett was eminently fitted. His predecessors were either anthropologists with little poetic ability, or poets with no authentic knowledge of the Indian. He has combined the merits of both.

–Dial (May 1920): 805

LAST POEMS

BY

A. E. HOUSMAN

NEW YORK
HENRY HOLT AND COMPANY
MDCCCCXXII

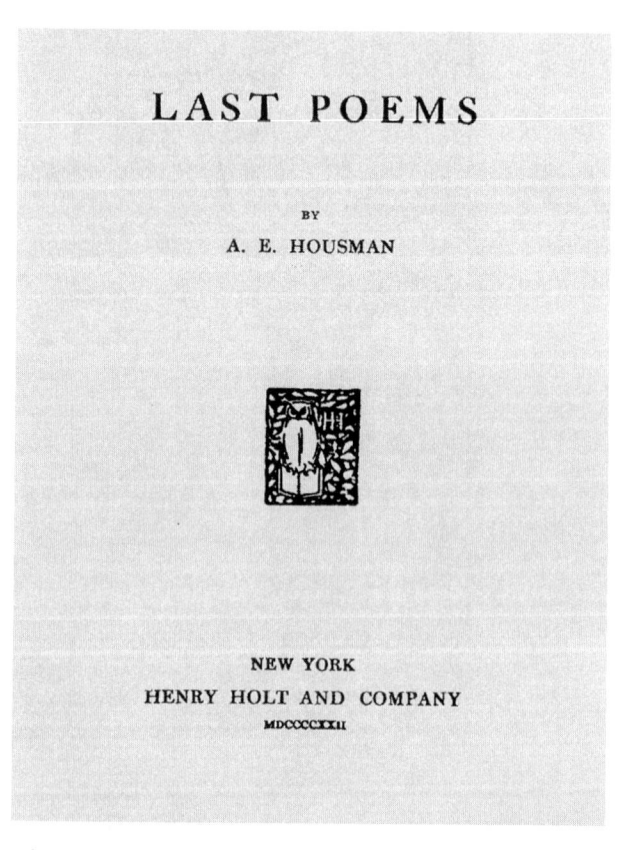

Title page for the American edition of the 1922 collection by the author of A Shropshire Lad *(1896; Rutgers University Library)*

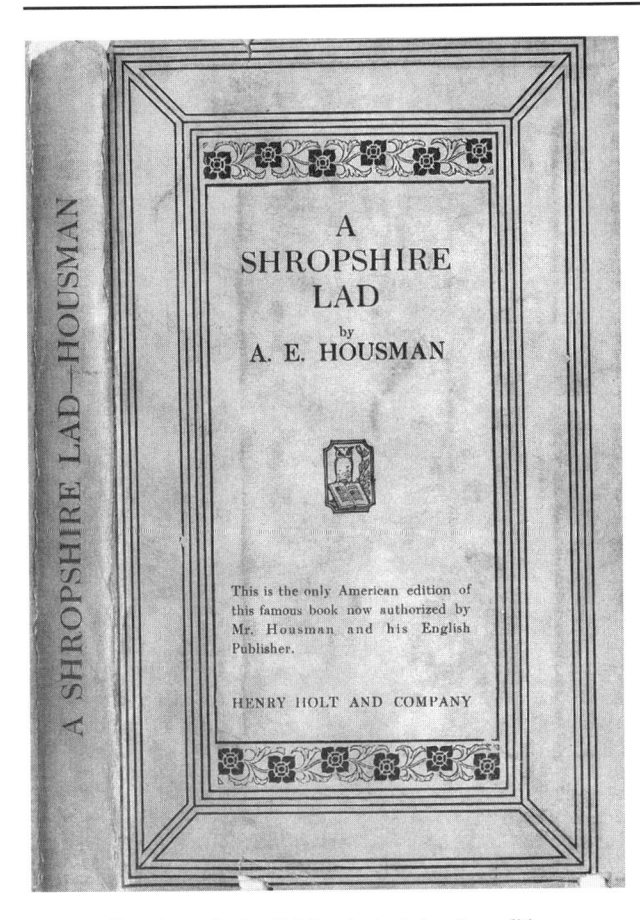

Dust jacket for the 1924 authorized American edition of the British poet's 1896 work (The Lilly Library, Indiana University)

We were not interested in Rolland's *Above the Battle* and would not have been in the *Forerunners*, its sequel. It is not an important book—a collection of radico-journalese papers—and I do not think we should have published it even had Harcourt remained with us. But as he is fixed now it is good grist for the particular mill he has set out to operate. Rolland's next big book after *Colas Breugnon*, a novel entitled *Clerambault*, came to us directly from the French publishers, and is now being translated for us. The French publishers (Ollendorff) state in their agreement that they will give us first chance at the author's future books. Rolland has written a number of books which we do not publish on this side and also a number that we would not publish.

As to Carl Sandburg, he naturally felt enough bound to Harcourt, who was his particular "friend" here, to desire to give him the book which Harcourt is now announcing. This was arranged for, of course, a long time ago. Knowing this feeling on his part, I did not disturb him until I heard that he and Harcourt had had a row. Harcourt based his royalty on the net wholesale price instead of the list price without saying anything to Sandburg, and this caused the row. Harcourt packed his bag and rushed to Chicago. He patched the trouble up, and when I saw Sandburg shortly afterwards I heard nothing but praise of Harcourt, but I left with the feeling that should Sandburg write any more, our chances are a good deal better of getting his work than they were before the break.

              Sincerely yours,
              [Lincoln MacVeagh]

* * *

In a ten-page letter to MacVeagh, Elliot Holt described his efforts on behalf of Holt and Company during a trip abroad.

              February 14th. 1923.

My dear Lincoln,

. . . .

At the present moment everything is in an awful mess in regard to Rolland and Proust. I arrived in Paris and went quietly to bed for four days with the 'flu. . . . On

Title page for the study of the evolution of language by the Danish linguist and authority on English grammar (Rutgers University Library)

Title pages for two novels by the writer who was later best known for his long narrative poems (Rutgers University Library)

getting up I got hold of Gibbs at Ollendorf's, who happens to be a most delightful and well mannered Mulatto. He told me there were four volumes of the new book, one written, as you know, one to be published in July, the third nearly done, and the fourth outlined. Unless Rolland gets some new bee in his bonnet that will be all. Gibbs insisted on a straight contract such as you received. I offered him $1500.00 for the whole business, at which he was astounded and mortified, and said there was not the possibility that Rolland would accept it. I said that was my bid and walked out, expecting to hear from him while I was still in Paris, or when I got to England. . . .

I met W. R. Bradley, who is Macmillan's Agent, and like a flash realised that he was bidding for the book, not for Macmillan but for Harcourt. He made a slip of the tongue after I had put quite a little Burgundy in him, which put me on to this. I had the suspicion before. The result of the matter was that he offered Gibbs . . . $1,000.00 down on Annette, 12½% to 5000, 15% straight afterwards. Gibbs fixed a date for my reply, and I telegraphed him the night before from London that I would accept Bradley's terms. I have the first volume. It has been most difficult. I hope you all will realise, despite the somewhat large advance, it would have been most unwise to let Harcourt get it. Now the position is this: I go to Paris Saturday to try and arrange for all volumes. Our position to do so at much less cost for the remaining books is infinitely better. I shall tell Gibbs that in all justification we can bring our Annette labelled "Volume I" giving the world in general the assumption that we shall do the series. This would mitigate against the possibility, as well as the agreeable probability for another publisher wanting to start with Volume II. Gibbs at Ollendorf's is keen about us, thinks us an "honourable house." I think I made a good personal impression, and cracked [*sic*] up the great machinery which we have established for selling Rolland as well as the assumption in America that he is our "goods." On this phase of things I hope to arrange for the rest at about $500.00 per, which I think would be doing well. . . .

Proust is in a worse mess. . . . Here is the situation: My bid in New York was the same as Seltzer's,—at the moment I forget exactly what it was, $275.00 down against normal percentage, I think. Well! Seltzer is going

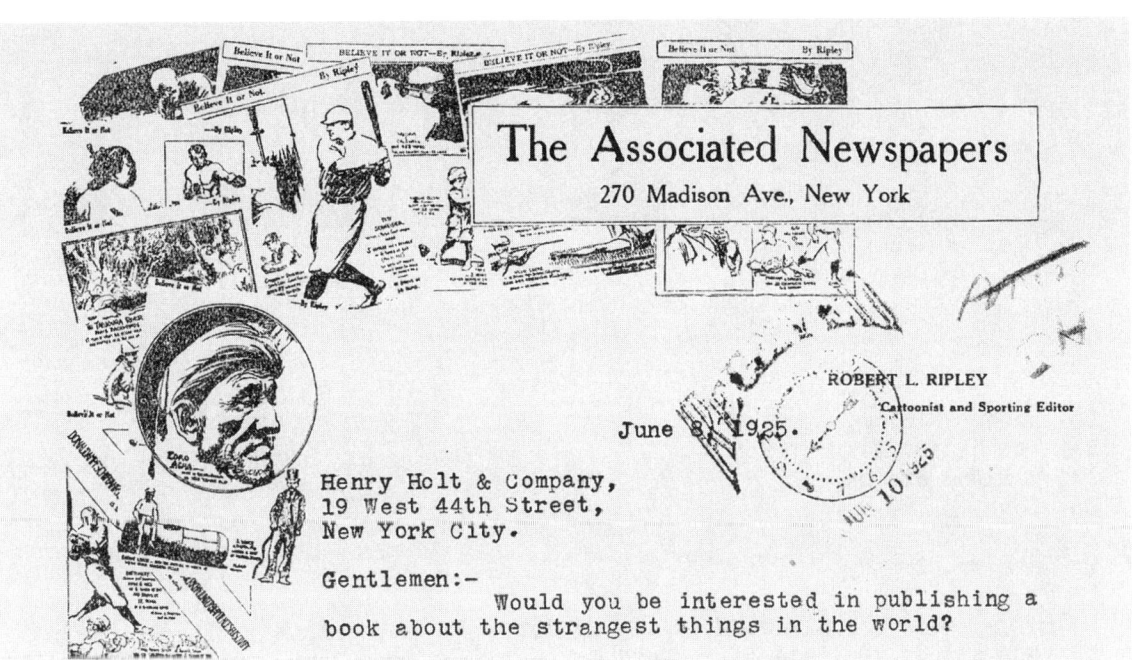

Letter to Holt and Company from Robert L. Ripley proposing the publication of a compilation of items from his syndicated newspaper feature Believe It or Not *(Princeton University Library)*

June 11, 1925.

Mr. Robert Ripley,
The Associated Newspapers,
270 Madison Avenue,
New York, N. Y.

My dear Mr. Ripley:-

    Both Mr. Elliot Holt and myself have been enthusiastic followers of your series "Believe It or Not" for a long time and we should both like to congratulate you on your energy and on the skill with which you have assembled all these facts. However, we cannot see that the series could be sold thru the regular book trade channels, and our advice would be to offer it to Reilly and Lee (536 Lake Shore Drive, Chicago) for sale thru the American News Company. I must admit that your letter of June 8th was an awful temptation to us. Both of us would like in the worst way to see the manuscript but it would hardly be fair to you to take advantage of your offer when we know that we could not possibly undertake its publication. I am particularly intrigued by the Moi-Boy with a tail, and wonder if he is the same one whom I saw described the other day by a Chinese traveller who related that the tail was "about eighteen inches long, slightly flat and a little too stiff for wagging." Then there's your postscript about driving a golf ball a distance of a mile up hill. I don't play golf, but I am going to file your name as a potential attraction for the next Charity Bazaar that comes along.

                      Faithfully and admiringly yours,

                      For HENRY HOLT AND COMPANY.

CB,Jr/t

Unsigned letter from Holt and Company declining Ripley's proposal for a Believe It or Not *book (Princeton University Library)*

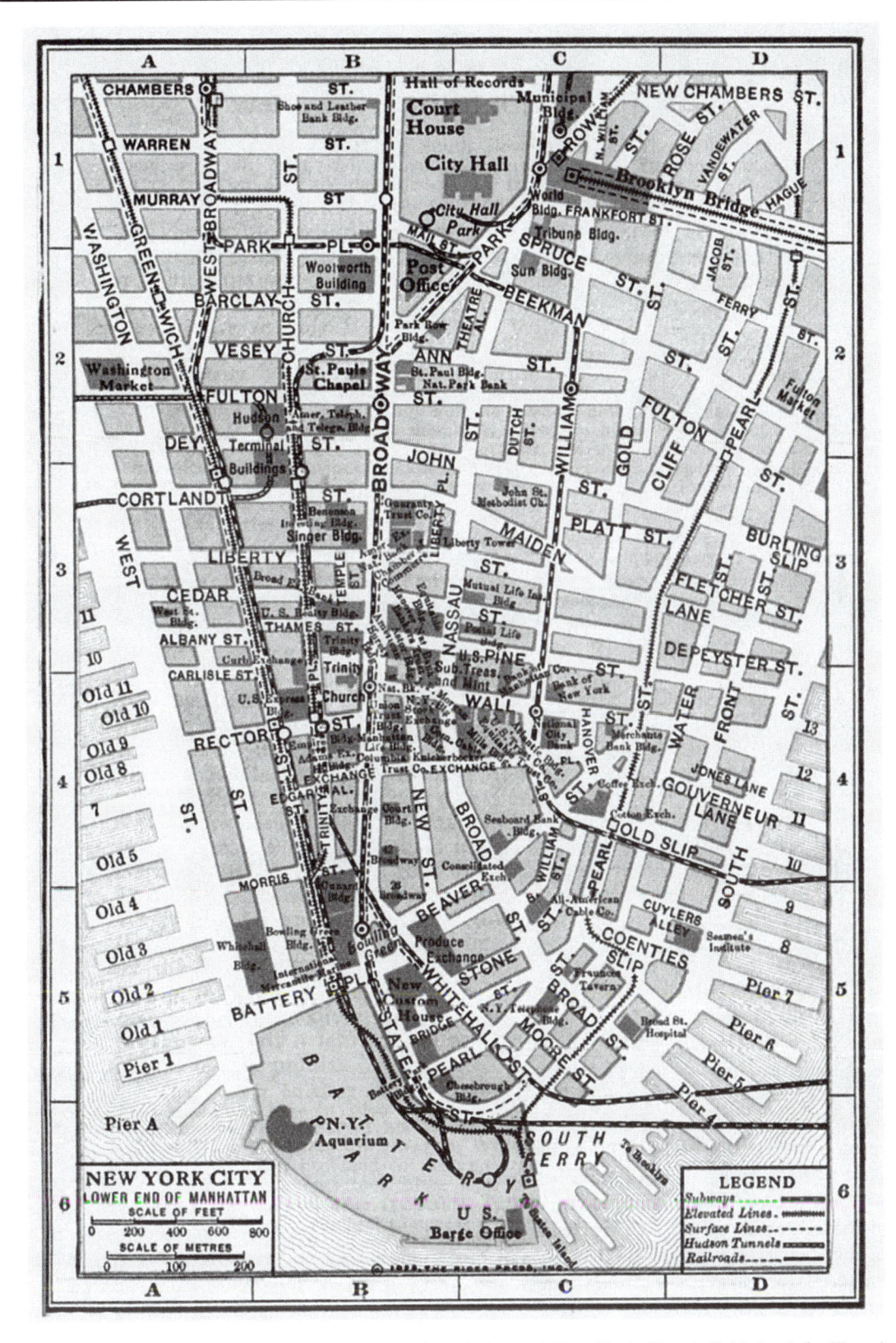

Map of the lower end of Manhattan, from the second edition (1923) of Rider's New York City: A Guide-book for Travelers
*(edited by Frederic Taber Cooper), a volume in the short-lived series of travel guides published by Holt and Company
under the general editorship of Fremont Rider (University of Kentucky Library)*

Advertisement for the Rider Guides, from the second edition of Rider's New York City
(University of Kentucky Library)

to try it on the assumption that he can do Sodom et Gomorre getting by censorship with it. . . .

I have bought 500 sheets of a sort of "just so" story type of thing for children from Duckworth. . . . Incidentally I feel from now on we'll have first crack with Butterworth—I am also hopeful that this situation has been enlarged with other publishers, and they will really look at us more favourably in future. Benchley, Benet, and Our Book of Boxing (sheets have gone forward) and Riding Astride for Girls, has given them a favourable shock. The attitude that Henry Holt & Co. was so completely conservative that they thought of nothing but serious books,—I find quite deep rooted. . . .

I very much appreciate now your remark that it would take two months to settle all this up, but unless you hear to the contrary I shall come back on the "Majestic" which sails in two weeks, and will arrive as I had hoped about the 1st. of the month. I cannot understand why you cabled Pollinger instead of me. Did you think I had joined the French army in the Ruhr? Pas encore. As you appreciate, it is mighty hard to give full particulars about everything. You all sent me over here, and I am working like the devil, and certainly not having much of a personally enjoyable time, aside from a couple of rides which I have taken in the Row when I got fed up with reading stuff, but so much of it is poor that it takes only a glimpse or so to decide, and I have not been roped in as yet by anything in Unwin's terrible first novel series. . . . Weather terrible; I've got a touch of trench mouth and am so keen to get good stuff that it's hard to sleep at nights thinking about it. . . . Everybody has been particularly kind. Geoffery Williams put me up at the Saville Club, and everybody else has lunched me most cordially, and with sincere friendly feeling, much of which, of course, I can thank Mr. H. H.

Title page for the illustrated volume tracing the history of people of "social distinction" in New York and Washington, D.C. (Rutgers University Library)

and you for. The only amusing aspect to this "lunching" is that Butterworth, as you forewarned me, tried to get me drunk, and because I am built as I am he ended up tight as a tick and I was perfectly normal. . . .

Yours
Elliot

. . . .

PP.S. The literary agents have it all their own way over here. I am flabbergasted by their power and am seeing them all. There is just the slightest possibility that I can get Rebecca West after her one book more contract with Doran runs out. . . .[1]

Note

1. This effort to sign West did not succeed.

* * *

Rogers MacVeagh, Lincoln MacVeagh's brother, was an attorney and author of a book on the 1920 Transportation Act published by Holt and Company in 1923.

April 4, 1923

Legal Department
Little, Brown & Co., Publishers
34 Beacon Street
Boston, MA

Gentlemen:

We are sending you a copy of *The Transportation Act–1920*, by Rogers MacVeagh, of the firm of Teal, Linfree, Johnson and McCulloch, Portland, Oregon. After considerable experience in dealing with matters of interstate transport Mr. MacVeagh comes to the conclusion that a handbook which brought together all the somewhat scattered material at present available dealing with the Transportation Act would be of great value to counsel for interstate shippers of all kinds. As you know, there are a great many questions raised by the provisions of the Act on which there has as yet been no legal decision but which must be solved every day in actual practice by hundreds of railroads and other concerns all over the country. Counsel are sometimes very much embarrassed in giving advice to such clients on account of the difficulty of obtaining all the material necessary to base a competent judgment on the legal aspects of a contemplated course of action. Mr. MacVeagh's book is prepared to meet real emergencies which arise every day.

Professor Homer Vanderblue, of Harvard University, an acknowledged expert on transportation, writes that he has found the book "An extremely elaborate and careful analysis of the Act, which should be of great use to students of recent railroad legislation."

We believe, therefore, that both to the lawyer who is occupied with problems of transportation and to the student this book will prove invaluable. We know that you have a large list of legal clients, and think that you might easily sell a number of these books among them. We should be glad to send you on sale a number of copies, allowing a discount from our list price of $6.50. Up to 10 copies we would suggest a discount of 25 percent, and above that, 33 percent. We believe that among your clients you could get rid of a good many more copies than this, but that if you care to take up the proposition at all you might prefer to begin with a small order.

Hoping to hear from you, we are

Very truly yours,
Henry Holt and Co.

* * *

Frontispiece from Mrs. John King Van Rensselaer and Frederic Van de Water's The Social Ladder *(1924), depicting guests at the 10 February 1897 party "which for vivid and sensational display of wealth still remain[s] unequaled in the annals of New York" (Rutgers University Library)*

MacVeagh had explored the possibility of publishing the work of Russian behaviorist Ivan Petrovich Pavlov and received the following letter from a member of the Harvard Medical School physiology department. Holt and Company ultimately did not publish any of Pavlov's work.

May 14, 1923.

My dear Mr. McVeagh [*sic*]:

Nearly a year ago you wrote to me about the possibility of publishing a book by Professor Pavlov of Petrograd detailing his very important investigations on the physiology of the nervous system. I answered your letter by stating that I should inform you on hearing from Professor Pavlov regarding his plans. A few days ago a letter from him was forwarded to me from London in which he stated that he had started writing the book, but had found that more experiments were necessary. On carrying them out still others appeared to be required, and now he is uncertain when he will be ready to put the work together as a whole.

Yours very truly,
W. B. Cannon

* * *

Journalist and historian Allan Nevins's request for a title-page correction to his American Social History as Recorded by British Travellers *(1923) generated consternation in the Holt and Company office. Several handwritten comments appear on the following letter, such as "Blizz! Return to me. E. H.," "Had to re-set 4 pages," and "Press-work will start—Friday. Title page was changed to end travellers. I am sending for a proof to make certain."*

Nov. 23, 1923

Dear Mr. [Elliot] Holt:

I understand printing of my book is likely to begin Monday or soon after. May I ask you to see that the title-page is correct? The title should not read as in your fall catalogue, but should be "American Social History Recorded by British Travellers." Mrs. Bromley and Mr. Roland Holt agreed with me that "travellers" is better than "observers." Also please see that my name is not misspelled.

I hope you noticed my editorial on Mrs. Harriman's book.

Sincerely yours,
Allan Nevins
New York Evening Post

Holt and the Movie Industry

By 1920 the movie industry was already on the lookout for literary properties, as is indicated by Holt's response to an inquiry from a representative of director D. W. Griffith's studio in Mamaroneck, New York.

January 27, 1920.

Dear Sir:

Pray accept our thanks for yours of the 26th.

We are sorry to have to write we publish extremely little that we think would be suitable for the "movies," but we shall try to keep you in mind to send you any material we think might prove of interest to you in this connection. If at any time you see a book of ours announced that you would care to examine with a view to purchasing the motion picture rights, we should be glad to hear from you.

Very truly yours,
HENRY HOLT AND COMPANY

One year later the situation was reversed when a studio declined to adapt a Holt and Company publication that it had been considering, Stephen Vincent Benét's The Beginning of Wisdom *(1921).*

December 4, 1921.

Dear Roland [Holt],–

Our editorial board has finally decided that we shall not be able to make a Goldwyn Picture out of "The Beginning of Wisdom." You will understand that, in the motion-picture business, decisions of this sort are affected much more by fluctuating commercial conditions than are decisions in the publishing business. At present, attendance at motion-pictures throughout the country is very bad; many studios are temporarily shutting down; and we have decided, for the next few months, to produce only "sure-fire stuff,"–for the most part, "melodrama with a punch."

. . . .

Ever yours faithfully,
Clayton Hamilton

* * *

Hollywood not only sought literary properties from publishers but also attempted to have novelizations of movies published. The following letter is from the Film Booking Offices of America.

May 29, 1923

Gentlemen:

I have just returned from Los Angeles after a number of conferences at the Thomas H. Ince Studios, where is now being completed Mrs. Wallace Reid's remarkable anti-narcotic picture "Human Wreckage" which as you may have possibly heard, promises to be the biggest motion picture sensation in fifteen years.

Because of the immensity of this production, Mr. James Kirkwood was induced to leave his leading role in "The Fool," the big Broadway success, right at the very height of the season to do his bit in the making of this marvelous picture which is Mrs. Reid's indictment against the narcotic evil.

A 60,000 word novelization of "Human Wreckage" has been written by C. Gardner Sullivan and is now in my hands here in New York, and as this picture is expected to show in more theatres and to gross more money than another motion picture ever filmed in all the history of the industry, you can readily understand that Mrs. Wallace Reid's story "Human Wreckage," published in a popular priced edition will be without question one of the most sensational sellers in years.

A national advertising campaign in which we have already scheduled two full pages and one one-half page of advertising in the Saturday Evening Post, together with full pages and half pages in such publications as the Literary Digest, Christian Herald, Messenger of the Sacred Heart, Union Signal and others, will create a nation-wide desire among millions of picture fans and in all other classes of society to read Mrs. Reid's story.

Backing up this campaign will be a campaign of 24-sheet posters all over America in all the principal cities and smaller communities as well, plus an avalanche of newspapers advertising in every city, town, village and hamlet throughout the United States which thousands of exhibitors will use in announcing and advertising Mrs. Wallace Reid in "Human Wreckage." Added to that will be an additional avalanche of news stories and pictures of Mrs. Reid in all newspapers throughout the United States of which we already have on file in our scrap books several thousand columns, and, besides that, 80% of these news stories have been front page stories, even on the largest metropolitan dailies.

Altogether the launching of this great picture "Human Wreckage," plus the giant campaign behind it, will stimulate the sales of the story of "Human Wreckage" in popular priced form to a record-breaking point.

If you are interested in the publication of this novelization, I will be glad to go into the details further with you. I must get action on this at once, as the Saturday Evening Post advertising begins in the June 23rd issue, also the other national advertising begins in June. The picture will be released and begin being shown in all the finest first run theatres throughout America in June and August, and I will appreciate your reply by return post.

Very truly yours,
Nat. G. Rothstein
Director of Publicity and Advertising

Publishers' Weekly *advertisement for the 1929 autobiographical account of service in the World War I French aviation unit staff comprised of American volunteers (Thomas Cooper Library, University of South Carolina)*

June 5, 1923

Dear Sir:

After due consideration, we do not feel like making an arrangement with you in regard to the story "Human Wreckage" by Mrs. Wally Reid.

Although this book is unquestionably of popular interest, it is not the type of story which we feel would fit into our regular line of publication, and for this reason, do not care to go further in making an offer.

Thank you for your courteous letter, and with all good wishes, we are

Sincerely yours,
[Elliot Holt]

THE LATER 1920s

The Death of Henry Holt

Henry Holt died on 13 February 1926. The New York Times *printed an editorial on his career.*

New York has lost one of its most distinguished citizens and the American publishing trade has lost its dean by the death of HENRY HOLT in his eighty-seventh year. His affiliation with the book world began during the Civil War and for fifty-three years he was at the head of his own firm. He carried on the business of publishing simultaneously with the practice of authorship in the field of philosophical speculation. His "Cosmic Relations and Immortality" appeared six years ago. It was followed, in 1923, by the "Garrulities of an Octogenarian Editor" in which were delightfully blended reminiscence and comment, mellow with years and experience and with a sense of quiet humor which made it possible for him to suggest, among the principal rules for the guidance of life, a firm belief in GOD and immortality and proper confidence in the future of New York real estate. Of the Victorian Age, he carried over into the second quarter of the twentieth century two traits which are apt to be overlooked in contemporary evaluations of Victorianism. One was a kindly courtliness of manner. The other was courage. At the age of 74 he became the founder and editor of The Unpopular Review, a title subsequently changed with much reluctance to The Unpartizan Review. It is not often given to a public figure to be at the same time distinguished and picturesque. The two qualities were combined in HENRY HOLT to make a striking personality.

He had an intellect both wide-ranging and daring. Not all could follow him in all his inquiries, but none could fail to admire his desire to learn, which was life-long. One

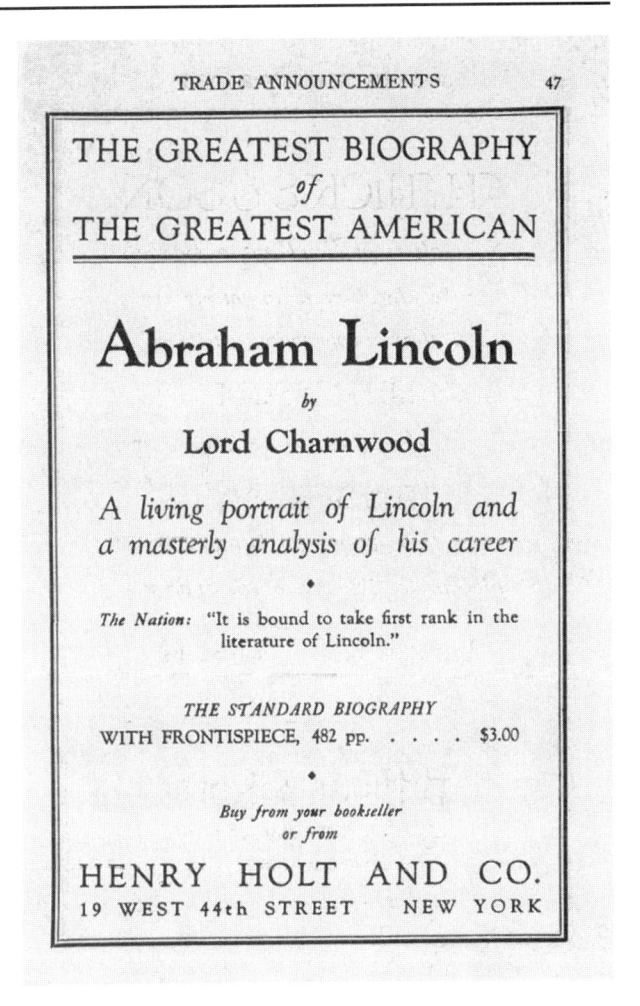

Advertisement for the influential biography of Abraham Lincoln published by Holt and Company in 1916, from the second edition of Rider's New York City
(University of Kentucky Library)

of the "Young Yale" movement of forty years ago, he was a gallant fighter with a youthful spirit to the very end.

—*New York Times*,
15 February 1926,
p. 18

Author and editor Christopher Morley wrote the following tribute to Henry Holt for The Saturday Review of Literature.

Henry Holt
Christopher Morley

Obviously the fitting tributes to that great gentleman, philosopher, and publisher, Henry Holt, will be paid by those who knew him closely; but I cannot refrain from recalling the thrill it was when I saw him for the first time, about the end of 1912. Partly because at school and college I had used so many

*Frontispiece and title page for the 1923 memoir by the founder of Holt and Company
(Thomas Cooper Library, University of South Carolina)*

books marked with the little owl of his firm, and partly because, to a youth speiring hopefully on the doorstep of the publishing business he was so plainly one of the dwellers on Olympus, I was filled with that tingling bashful excitement which is an excellent thing in young men. I can see him still as he was that evening–over seventy even then; the tall handsome figure, the fine grey head, the keen, quizzical, humane, and high-minded face; moving in evening dress in a roomful of people with some indescribable authority and charm that made the stranger instantly want to know who that was. I am just a little proud that of the very few times–perhaps half a dozen altogether–that I have deliberately asked anyone to autograph a book, his "Garrulities of an Octogenarian Editor" was one of them. He signed a copy for me last year, and I treasure it.

It was a chance remark of Daniel Coit Gilman, then librarian at Yale, that turned young Henry Holt toward publishing. Gilman said "If you find on a book the imprint of Ticknor and Fields it is probably a good book." This impressed Henry Holt with the idea that it would be a worthy ambition to have the same thing sayable of himself. It became equally true of his own imprint; and he chose Ticknor and Fields' successors (the Houghton Mifflin Company) as publishers of his own writings. Mr. Holt's career as a publisher, and the vigorous ethics of that career, have been certainly one of the heartening things to contemplate. Looked at from below, by men half a century his junior, he seems to have been so delightful a mixture of the radical free-thinker and the "old-fashioned" cultivated gentleman. There seemed to be, even for a young observer who saw him only a few times, absolutely nothing to be done about him but to love him. When someone said of St. Gaudens "His face looks as if he had made it himself," Holt replied "Of course! Everybody's does." Certainly that was true of him, for his whole bearing was so expressive of a generous, sensitive, and fearless spirit.

> **Funeral of Henry Holt**
>
> *Holt left his estate, valued at $1 million, to his widow and six children. He left his collection of books on psychical research, a longtime interest, to the Authors' Club, along with $1,000.00 for the upkeep of the collection.*
>
> Only Relatives and Intimate Friends at the Services
>
> Funeral services for Henry Holt, founder of the publishing house of Henry Holt & Co. were held yesterday at his late residence, 57 East Seventy-second Street, the Rev. Dr. Karl Reiland, rector of St. George's Church, officiating. Dr. Reiland read the twenty-third Psalm, selections from Tennyson's "In Memoriam" and the same poet's "Crossing the Bar." He also read Emily Bronte's "Last Lines." The male quartet from St. George's Church sang a choral by C. Kreutzer, "Das Ist der Tag," and the hymn of John Bunyan, "He Who Would Valiant Be."
>
> Those present, besides members of the family, were intimate friends including Dr. Nicholas Murray Butler, Elihu Root, Cass Gilbert, Henry James, Dr. Walter B. James, Mrs. Annie B. Jennings, John I. Burlingham, John Hiltman, Arthur Scribner, and Frederick Stokes. Interment was in Greenwood Cemetery.
>
> –*New York Times,* 26 February 1926, p. 25

monstrous creeds you don't believe, and begging for things you know no begging will ever bring; or whether you're an humble searcher in the new mysteries of energy and soul, the quiet meditative hours of the night are better for communion with the gods, than are the jocund hours of the morning.

I place the ordinary literary immortality at not over twenty-five years after the author passes on. From, say, 1850 to 1900 I must have known personally half a dozen American authors whose names were in everybody's mouth. Bryant and Mark Twain are the only ones of them that I hear mentioned now. The others that I recall at the moment are Stedman, Stoddard, Paul Ford, Frank Stockton, Howells, John Hay, and Warner. No one but us old people knows now that John Hay wrote "Jim Bludso" and "Little Breeches." Then a few of the great Boston group survive in men's memories, but I don't know how many read them—or read anything but the Sunday newspapers.

The one crying social need of America is cultivated men of leisure. Beyond commuting distance from home, it is next to impossible to get up a dinner party, with the sexes balanced; every man, hardly excepting

Those who knew him will honor themselves by recalling his virtue as a man and his honor as a publisher; all I have any right to do is give you a taste of his busy mind by quoting a few passages from his "Garrulities." It is a book full of charming crotchets and many matters for possible disagreement, but it is one of the perfect autobiographies because it gives the very form and pressure of its author's temperament.

> To what was due the astounding vitality, intellectual as well as physical, of the ancient Greeks? Obviously, for one thing, it had to be paid for by the enslavement of enough aliens to make the effective Greeks a leisured class. But they used to *sprawl* more than any civilized people does now. We sit on chairs, and not even at table on easy ones, but bolt upright. The Greeks used to sprawl on couches.
>
> In confirmation of the foregoing I have learned since it was written that the best preserved old man I know always has done a great deal of sprawling, especially after exercise.
>
> Pardon my taking the liberty of saying that you are apt to live longer if, when bedtime comes, you say your prayers. Whether you're a Thibetan with a praying machine, or a Catholic with a rosary, or a Jew groveling before the vindictive tyrant you've set up in your temple, or a Protestant given to the public recitation of

Dust jacket for the 1925 Holt and Company edition of the 1895 play by the author of Cyrano de Bergerac *(Bruccoli Clark Layman Archives)*

men of fortune, is almost required by public opinion to be at work in some money-making pursuit.

All those old publishers [he is speaking of publishing in the '70's]–Putnam, Appleton, Harper, and Scribner–were incapable of petty or ostentatious things, and were much more inclined to friendly coöperation and mutual concession than to barbarous competition. The spectacle of a crowd of other men making fools of themselves exercised upon them no temptation to do as the herd did. No one of them, or of a few more, would go for another's author any more than for his watch; or, if he had got entangled with another's author through some periodical or other outside right, would no more hold on to him than to the watch if the guard had got caught on a button. They were wonderfully kind to me as a young fellow, and their kindness and example have been of inestimable value all my life. Those men were born in a less blatant, less extravagant, and therefore less competitive age.

When the plates of Taine's "English Literature" were in the custom house, and I had to raise money to pay duty on them, I cursed the whole transaction. It turned out my first important business success.

The day when "The Home Book of Verse" was published, I would have sold out of it for twenty-five cents on the dollar.

The brushing up of wits that has so much to do with the dialogues of Socrates, is inherent to the dinner party, and is absent from cold-water feasts. Of them the kind gods have saved me from all but very few, and they were dismal affairs. Wine maketh glad the heart of man, and the hearts there were not glad. Where Prohibition prevails, if it does anywhere, groups of people may eat together, but they will not constitute dinner parties. Yet in America dinner parties have been largely wiped out by people who never saw one, or ever heard of those which were among the most important occurrences in history.

I would rather part with consciousness than with the faith that this life is but a culture-bed whence we are transplanted into a better and fuller life, where we will have free exercise and development for such capacities of knowing and thinking and loving as we are wise enough to develop here.

Reverence for the creeds is developing a great many people into liars.

Dust jackets for the Holt and Company editions of two 1928 British novels (Books Between the Covers Rare Books, Inc.; Babylon Revisited Rare Books)

The best solvent for questions of duty that I have been able to find, is to consider what would be the result of a given policy if it were followed by everybody under similar circumstance.

What usually passes for love is a desire for a beautiful member of the opposite sex to amuse oneself with.

There is only one virtue which cannot be carried to an extreme; that is temperance–the virtue placed at the summit by even the passionate Greeks, who perhaps knew it least, and therefore gave it a scarcity value.

I never hear "Sartor Resartus" mentioned now. When I was young, it was the salvation of most of the young men who did any thinking. But their troubles were different from those of the young people now.

There ought to be no difficulty, though some is alleged, in deciding what is not proper to literature. Obviously, the functions of the body which even savages consign to privacy, are not fit subjects for literature, nor is any allusion to them which is avoided in polite society. They are germane to science, but certainly not to art.

I have seldom used tobacco to excess. I never smoked before I was six years old, and thence only at rare intervals until I was nearly eleven.

Unwise eating has more to do with the dumps than most folks realize. Don't try to reason them away, but divert your mind. If you can't do it, seek outer diversion–go to see the best woman you know outside of home, or if you can't do better, play solitaire.

There is one interesting observation that occurs to the reader of Mr. Holt's "Garrulities." Occasionally nowadays you hear Americans murmur a little because so much of our literary activity consists of making fortunes for British authors. It should be remembered that American publishing when Holt began, sixty years ago, still consisted very largely of the plunder of British authors who were unprotected by copyright. It was Mr. Holt who, with other honorable colleagues, was active in pioneering the notion that even a British author deserves his royalties.

–"The Bowling Green,"
Saturday Review of Literature, 2
(27 February 1926): 591

Muckraking author Ida M. Tarbell did not publish with Holt and Company but knew Henry Holt and his wife socially.

February 19, 1926.

My dear Dear Mrs. Holt:–

I heard only two days ago just as I was leaving for Chicago of your great sorrow. I should have wired you of my sympathy but did not have your address–and then I wanted to write.

I cannot think of Mr. Holt as gone. He seemed to me so vital and courageous when I saw him in your drawing room a few weeks ago that I truly believed he had years of life before him. I went away to talk about his humor and interest and to prophecy [*sic*] that he would recover from his indisposition, I did not realize the truth.

He has been a great and fine figure in the publishing world–no one better. He has left a tradition which will not be lost. No one was like him–such a delightful person. I treasure all my glimpses of him.

You have all my sympathy, dear Mrs. Holt–in this separation from a companion of rare quality and charm.

Always faithfully yours,
Ida M. Tarbell.

Naturalist C. William Beebe published five books with Holt and Company from 1906 to 1924.

February 24 [1926].

My dear Mrs. Holt:

My deepest sympathy goes to you, for only today had I heard of Mr. Holt's death. I loved him, and shall never cease to be grateful for coming up to my little office in the Zoological Park so many years ago, and persuading me to write my first book.

I send you my love and can only think the things which at such a time as this it is impossible to put into words.

Will Beebe.

Dorothy Canfield Fisher was a Holt and Company author from 1907 to 1919.

[Undated]

Dear Mrs. Holt:

I've just this moment seen the notice of the disappearance of my father's old friend, my old friend,–everybody's old friend. I suppose it ought not to be so great a shock and surprise as it is–Mr. Holt had lived a life as notably long as it was notably fine–but I find it hard to believe that death could lay a hand on that splendid vitality. How many lives were enriched by that generous vitality! Mine is one. I have been thinking of what Mr. Holt said to my husband and me one evening of our notable visit to you in Burlington, when the conversation turned on immortality, and when Mr. Holt said that as he grew older he believed more and more in personal immortality. I certainly do for him. It is inconceivable that that fine, keen, kind intelligence is not still living. It is certainly living in the hearts of all who knew him.

Dear Mrs. Holt, there are no words to say to you what is in my heart of sympathy for you. My

Advertisements for Holt and Company drama titles from the 1925 Holt edition of Edmond Rostand's
The Far Princess *(Rutgers University Library)*

husband joins me in sending you our deepest, most heart-felt sympathy.

> With affection,
> Dorothy Canfield Fisher.

Like Henry Holt, Melvil Dewey, creator of the Dewey Decimal Classification for library cataloguing, championed and practiced a simplified phonetic spelling system.

16 Feb 26

Dear Mrs. Holt:

The delayd sad news has just reacht us and we send heartfelt simpathy in yur great sorrow. My acquaintance and admiration for yur great husband began 50 years ago this summer. For the last 15 years we have been bro't stil closer together by our work on the Carnegie Spelling Board.

I count it one of the things to be grateful for in my life that I knew as much of him as I did.

If yu go back to Fairholt or to Stowe this summer, yu must plan to motor over and see us at the Club. It wil be such a pleasure to show yu the great developments since yu were there last.

> Cordially,
> Melvil Dewey.

Vernon Lyman Kellogg, a zoologist and an administrator with the American Relief Administration in Europe after World War I, was a longtime Holt and Company author.

Advertisement from Publishers' Weekly *(5 January 1929) for the book that became one of the best-selling novels of 1929 (Thomas Cooper Library, University of South Carolina)*

Table of contents for philosopher John Dewey's The Public and Its Problems, *published by Holt and Company in 1927, a work that originated in a series of lectures Dewey delivered for the Larwill Foundation of Kenyon College in January 1926 (Rutgers University Library)*

23 February 1926.

Dear Mrs. Holt:

I am just back this morning from a fishing trip to Florida—out on the Keys with no letters or telegrams reaching me—and find your son's telegram letting me know of Mr. Holt's death.

He did so enjoy life—but Providence was generous to him and to you and to all his family and friends in letting him live his wonderful life so long. It is that you and we must think of, and not his passing.

Yet you need sympathy and you have it warmly from us all. My wife is in Europe and will grieve when she gets my news. I send you her heartfelt sympathy, with mine.

Sincerely yours,
Vernon Kellogg

Frederick A. Stokes was a fellow New York publisher who founded his own firm in 1881 after working for Dodd, Mead and Company. Authors published by the Frederick A. Stokes Company included Stephen Crane and Edna Ferber.

[Undated]

Dear Mrs. Holt:

It must be a great consolation to you and yours to realize what a legacy your distinguished husband has left to his brother publishers. As the most eminent and admirable figure in the history of American book-publishing, he has bequeathed to us who survive him a memory of altruism, of high literary and ethical standards, and of service to the best interests of all those creating and distributing worthwhile books that cannot fail, for years to come, to influence for good our own ideals and activities.

I have sat at his feet for several decades, with admiration and affection, and I have many times regretted that I was unable to accept an opportunity for working under him shortly after I began my apprenticeship with Messrs. Dodd, Mead & Company.

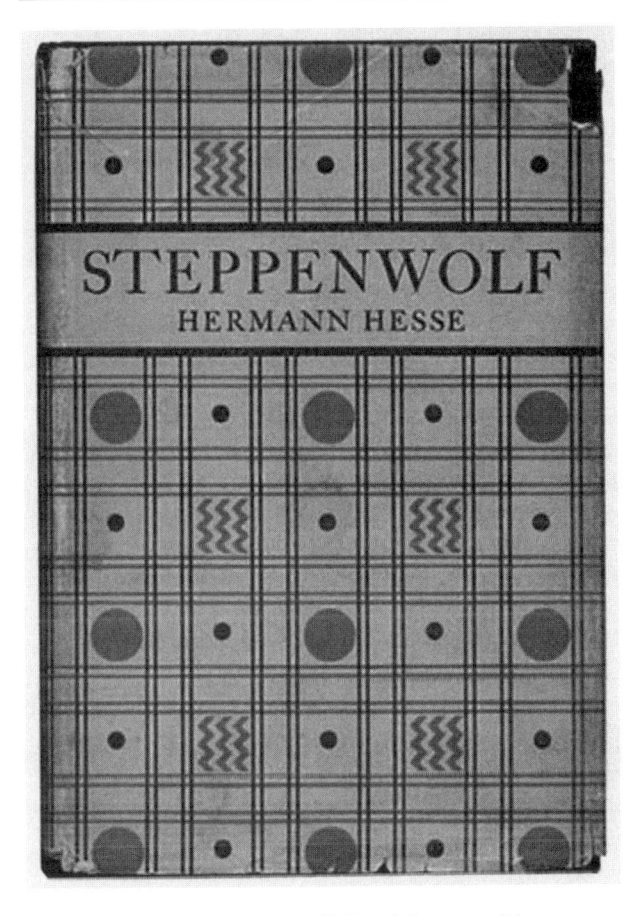

Dust jacket for the 1929 Holt and Company edition of the 1927 German novel (Ken Lopez, Bookseller)

I shall miss him greatly and constantly, but I shall have my highly prized remembrance of various associations with him.

With deep sympathy for you and the other members of his family and for those joined with him in business, I am

Yours most sincerely,
Frederick A. Stokes

The following is a translation of the letter Romain Rolland sent to Elliot Holt expressing his condolences for the death of Holt's father.

March 8, 1926.

Dear Mr. Elliot Holt:

As during my period of intensive work I read the papers little, I had not heard of the death of Mr. Henry Holt; I learn of it from your letter.

I regret it deeply, and, no less, not having had the opportunity of knowing more intimately a man whose personality seems to me, through those who have approached him, so attractive on account of its independence, its tolerance, its distinction of mind and its own originality. Music would have been the best of bonds between us.

It remains for me to express to you my sincere sympathy and the assurance of the faithful memory of gratitude that I hold for your father, who became, so early, my introducer to the United States and my firm supporter. I now transfer to the heirs of his house and his name the cordial sentiments that I had for him.

Please believe me, dear Mr. Elliot Holt, your very devoted

Romain Rolland.

The Holt Brothers

Henry Holt Jr. and his brother Elliot kept up with publishing-world news, looking for opportunities to recruit authors for Holt and Company.

January 13, 1926.

Dear Elliot:

On page 224 of the December issue of the London Mercury is a note that Williams and Norgate are issuing three of the H.U.L. [Home University Library, a series published by Williams and Norgate in England, and, selectively, by Holt and Company in America] in big editions at five shillings. Masefield's "Shakespeare", Chesterton's "Victorian Age in Literature", and Belloc's "French Revolution." They would all do well here too in a better edition. Do you want to look it up?

Did you know there has been a row at Stokes? Denhardt told me vaguely. Morrow is leaving, taking Honore Willsie. Mrs. Stokes is reported to be willing to sell out. This seems to leave Lawrence Bromfield open. Won't you go to see him in Paris and *buy him?* You may not like him, but he's really worth it. The "Beau Geste" man is free too. I'll go for him. Bromfield would be a great catch for us. We could afford to spend a lot of money on him.

Hatcher is out of the American Mercury.

Everything going well here. Please get some definite word from Pinker about the movie rights of "Volcano". Bettina Brown thinks she can sell them easily to Constance Talmadge, but I don't blame them for not wanting to do anything until they are sure all their time and trouble isn't going to be wasted. Will you let me know as soon as you can about it?

[Henry Holt Jr.]

* * *

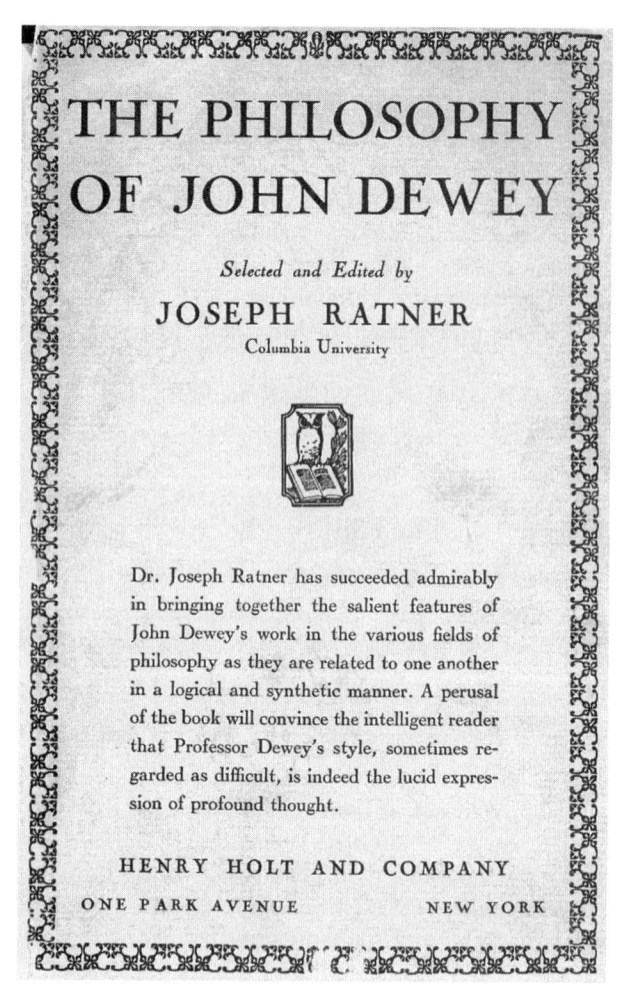

Dust jacket for the 1928 volume that provides a representative selection of the American philosopher's writings (Bruccoli Clark Layman Archives)

Harcourt, who had taken Sandburg with him when he left Holt and Company in 1919 to found Harcourt and Brace, attempted to consolidate his holdings of Sandburg's titles in early 1926.

January 15, 1926
Dear Mr. Butler [Holt employee Horace G. Butler]:

I am writing this on the chance that it may be convenient for you to send it on to Bristol if you are to bother him with the matter about which I spoke to you yesterday.

We intend to make rather unusual expenditures and efforts to develop a large market for Carl Sandburg's "Abraham Lincoln," which we shall publish on February fourth. We are finding it useful in our initial orders and shall find it even more so in our repeat orders to make combination offers of his other books which we publish at the same discount as the dealer receives on his orders for the "Lincoln." We are also devoting special attention to following up Sandburg's lecture trips with displays of all of his books which we publish. We have to send these "on sale" but the returns are insignificant, largely because we have developed a careful system to see that the books arrive on time and are available for Sandburg to autograph at his lectures. We are also working toward a collected edition of his works in the not too distant future, and, as Bristol knows, we have arranged with Henry Holt and Company for the publication by us of a selected volume of his poetry, which originated in England. In this situation, it seemed reasonable for us to follow Sandburg's suggestion to approach Henry Holt and Company with a proposal to buy the plates and rights of "Cornhuskers" and "Chicago Poems." I hope very much that you can see your way to set a price on these, as I am sure that we can do much more with all of Sandburg's books than we can with what we have. I remember Mr. Vogelius used to have a formula of two years' gross profits in arriving at a price for such a transfer. I think we could do a little better than that if you see your way to fall in with our suggestion. I do not foresee any great profit for us from this transfer, but I think it would pay out in the long run.

If Brace and I were not both leaving for a holiday the first of February, I would let the matter rest until after you were all moved, but I am afraid that Sandburg would blame us a little if we delayed the matter until the end of February.

Sincerely yours,
Alfred Harcourt

January 26, 1926
Dear Mr. Harcourt:

I am sorry that it has taken us so long to reach a decision with reference to the question raised in your letter of January 15. . . .

After careful consideration here . . . we cannot persuade ourselves to transfer to you our publishing rights in Sandburg's CHICAGO POEMS and CORNHUSKERS. It will be easily possible, however, to arrange terms for including these volumes in the collected edition of Sandburg which you say you are contemplating, and also to supply you with copies of the present printings for lecture sales on terms which would enable you to combine them with your "on sale" stock at a fair profit to you, if you care to consider such an arrangement for Mr. Sandburg's sake.

Very sincerely yours,
[Horace G. Butler]

* * *

Publisher Charles Boni Jr. of the firm Albert and Charles Boni took pleasure in sharing industry "news" with Elliot Holt.

Advertisement for a 1927 children's book that appeared in the 21 January 1928 issue of The Saturday Review of Literature *(Rutgers University Library)*

January 20, 1927.

Dear Elliot:

This is a letter of gossip in which I thought you might be interested. I had lunch with Mrs. Boyd yesterday and got quite a little. We went to your very nice joint at 34 East 40th. Christopher Morley and others of the brave were there.

Did you hear about this great book by Ludwig called *Napoleon, the Man of Destiny*, that Boni & Liveright have just published? George G. [sic] Nathan and Ernest Boyd were telling how fascinating it was when I was at the Boyds for tea a few weeks ago. I got a copy of it and found it was a superbly printed affair, two color title page, 700 pages of text, 24 illustrations, etc., and I was astonished that Boni & Liveright could sell it for $5. The day my copy arrived, the Publishers' Weekly came out with an announcement that the price had been reduced to $3. I took it this showed the result of the Book of the Month Club, and sure enough, yesterday Mrs. Boyd told me that it had been chosen. She added that she thought it had been bought outright which shows acumen. Nevertheless, I am afraid it is going to hurt the book business to publish such a magnificent affair at such a low price.

It seems that there has been a grand row between Knopf and Eleanor Wylie. When *The Orphan Angel* was chosen by the Book of the Month Club, Knopf tried to make her take a reduction in royalty, which she resented so highly that she's gone over to Harcourt. Of course,

Eleanor Wylie surely pulled strings to have her book chosen. . . .

Arnold Daly, the actor, got burned up in a fire the other night. Everybody else escaped, so considering his habits of life, the reasons were pretty obvious. Somebody went after Bernard Shaw for a statement of the affair and Shaw contented himself with saying that he judged it was the only case of spontaneous combustion on record.

[Charles Boni Jr.]

* * *

English writer Rosamond Lehmann's 1927 novel Dusty Answer *was a noteworthy success for Holt and Company.*

July 27, 1927

My dear Miss Lehmann:

I hope that you received my cable about *Dusty Answer*. I sent it off in a moment of exuberance when the news came in and I hadn't your address before me, so I trusted to memory, knowing that Chatto and Windus would forward the news in any case.

Since then I have taken up various business matters with Mr. [Harold] Raymond, but you might be interested to know that the initial order from the Book-of-the-Month Club is for 35,000 copies. You may realize that this should arouse attendant excitement enough to make a very pleasant general sale.

I am enclosing a copy of Mr. Christopher Morley's review, or sketch opinion. This is to be incorporated into his formal review to be published in *The Saturday Review of Literature*.

I am sorry that we are not able to keep your marriage and your married name quiet. So many of the English reviews have gone into many American papers as news notes. We shall, as we say, soft pedal the fact, but we are quite unable to hide it. . . .

We are glad to be the publishers of *Dusty Answer*, but we were as proud before we knew of its choice by the Book-of-the-Month as we could be now.

Faithfully yours,
[Unsigned]

Elliot Holt wrote Harold Raymond of Chatto and Windus, Lehmann's London publisher, regarding her views on selling the movie rights to Dusty Answer.

May 21, 1928

Dear Raymond:

Thanks for your letter about Rosamond Lehmann's reaction to the matter of selling DUSTY ANSWER for the movies. I can, in a sense, quite understand her point of view, but I must admit that

Form 101.   New York Charter.

REGISTRATION & TRUST COMPANY,
43 Cedar Street, New York.

THE

HENRY HOLT AND

COMPANY.

CERTIFICATE OF INCORPORATION.

Name.   ARTICLE I. The corporate name is

HENRY HOLT AND COMPANY.

Principal Objects.   ARTICLE II. The purposes for which the corporation is formed are:

To print, publish, bind, manufacture, issue, purchase, sell, deal in and otherwise turn to account books, magazines, publications, newspapers, pamphlets, maps, charts, engravings, lithographs, etchings, wood-cuts, electrotypes, stereotypes, photographic prints, photo-lithographs, pictures, and illustrations, whether colored or without color, and by whatsoever process or processes the same may be produced, whether now existing or hereafter to be discovered or invented; and generally, to carry on the business of printers, lithographers, stereotypers, engravers and publishers; to carry on the business of manufacturers of and dealers in photographs, pictures, prints, engravings and other works of art, and of photographers, paper makers, bookbinders, reproducers and publishers of works of art, books and other publications.

To carry on the business of stationers, electrotypers, die sinkers, envelope manufacturers, bookbinders and book manufacturers; to carry on the business of booksellers, and dealers in the materials used in the manufacture of paper, and dealers in or manufacturers of any other articles or things of a character similar or analogous to the foregoing, or any of them, or connected therewith.

C. of I. 1.

Holt and Company certificate of incorporation, issued when the Holt family had the firm incorporated in New York after Henry Holt's death in 1926 (Princeton University Library)

Advertisement from the 1 December 1928 issue of The Saturday Review of Literature
(Collection of Richard Layman)

Advertisement from the 28 January 1928 Saturday Review of Literature *for the American edition of the first book by the British novelist Rosamond Lehmann (her last name is misspelled in the ad), published in 1927 by Holt and Company (Rutgers University Library)*

the probability of an offer of fifteen thousand dollars would give me pause. At any rate I doubt if it will be possible to arrange any further development in the sale. We have done a lot of work in this connection and despite a number of refusals I had felt confident that Famous Players would consider the book at a fifteen thousand dollar figure, for the name alone. That chance now seems gone; so all I can say is that we have done our best, and if Miss Lehmann doesn't want to sell the book, we can do nothing further. Perhaps you can at least signify, in your talks with her, that we have not had a money-grabbing attitude in trying to further this sale for our commission, but that we've really gone at the matter with the idea of making money for one of our authors for whom we have every possible regard. I'll be in London the first part of July and if there are any further developments we can talk over the situation then.

Another matter that has come up recently—we both know how many times it has already been talked of—is the sale of our connection with the first two volumes of Proust's SWANN'S WAY. As you know, for a long time we were not interested in disposing of the books, but there seems to be a pretty well-founded general opinion that it is harmful to Proust's reputation that the volumes be split. After due deliberation, therefore, we made to Albert Boni the proposition contained in the copy of our letter to him which is enclosed. Our demand represents only the probable profits of three or four years sales if the ratio is maintained on about the same level as in former years. I think that unquestionably the Boni's are financially so fixed that you would not have any trouble in an eventual adjustment of the circumstances with them, and my own private opinion of Albert Boni is that he's a pretty decent little Jew and there could not be any similar unsatisfactory financial complications that might have held in the case of Thomas Seltzer.

To sum it all up, though we do not like to think of losing Proust's name from our list, I have been a bit sensitive over the fact that we are occasionally embarrassed somewhat by literary people who feel that we are jeopardizing the book's chances by splitting its entirety.

Boni is going to England shortly, and he will unquestionably talk the matter over with you. A transfer such as this would, naturally, preclude any possibility of our selling the book as a Modern Library edition.

I look forward heartily to seeing you in London. Perhaps you may have something, novel or otherwise, that you may care to hold for my consideration there. I'd appreciate it.

Sincerely
[Elliot Holt]

* * *

Elliot Holt later wrote Raymond describing his resignation from Holt and Company and announcing that he was considering going into publishing on his own.

December 21, 1928.

Dear Raymond:

I presume that by now you have heard that my Father's executor has sold the estate interests in Henry Holt and Company, including, with my assent, my chief share. A new corporation has been formed, with the old name and with the same general staff. Such a procedure appeared more favorable for the seven heirs of Mr. Holt's estate. I retire as a Vice-President of the company.

Leaving the business has seemed best for my own interests, both because I am the last member of the family in the organization and particularly as the attitude of the new owners could hardly approximate to me the old sentiments that I have entertained for the firm as a concern for so long identified with the Holt family interests.

I have no definite idea as to what I may do. It is possible I may start my own business, and in that case I may arrange to take with me some of the books I have been personally identified with here. Possibly I shall leave publishing entirely to enter "commerce" or even give up business altogether for country life.

If I remain with books it will be largely because of my interest in them, and the belief I like to feel that I have established regarding my personal relations to the business and the friendships it has brought me.

My leaving Henry Holt and Company, however, can in no way change any of your business relationships with them, as the trade department will continue as formerly.

As always,
[Elliot Holt]

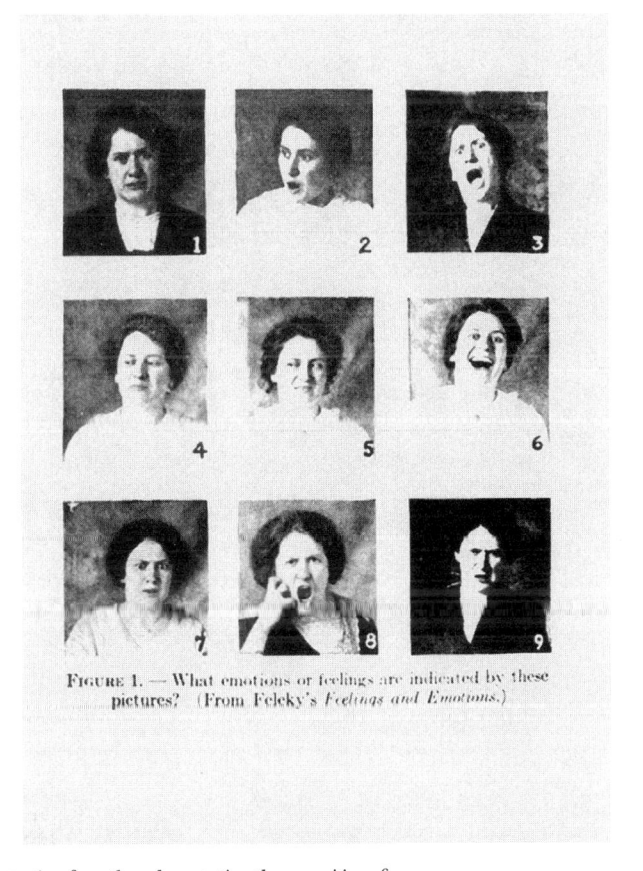

Title page for the 1929 psychological study and illustration from the volume testing the recognition of emotions from facial cues (Rutgers University Library)

40 EXCHANGE PLACE
NEW YORK CITY

December 20, 1929.

TO THE CONTRIBUTORS

To the Fund for the Publication of the Record of the Trial of Sacco and Vanzetti:

One thousand sets of the Record of six volumes containing 6,094 pages have been published. The volumes were printed and bound by the Lincoln Engraving and Printing Corporation at actual cost. The total cost of printing and distributing the volumes is $33,044.31.

The publication bears the imprint of Henry Holt & Company who generously contributed their services; through their efforts 164 sets at $25.00 per set were sold, yielding $4,100.00. The balance of the cost, to wit, $28,944.31, has been contributed by various donors so that the entire cost of the publication has been covered.

In addition to the sets sold by Henry Holt & Company the sponsors are distributing 611 sets and will retain 75 sets for further distribution.

A set of the Record has been sent to the following:

> Each Law School Library in the United States which is a member of the Association of American Law Schools
>
> Each State Library in the United States
>
> Each State University Library in the United States
>
> At least one important library in each state in the United States
>
> At least one public library in each country in the world
>
> The library of each United States Circuit Court of Appeals.

150 sets have been sent to individuals in this country and abroad, and to various journals.

On Behalf of the Sponsors.

Letter soliciting contributions to the fund that underwrote the publication by Holt and Company of The Sacco-Vanzetti Case: Transcript of the Record of the Trial of Nicola Sacco and Bartolomeo Vanzetti in the Courts of Massachusetts and Subsequent Proceedings, 1920–7 (1928–1929) in five volumes (Princeton University Library)

Elliot briefly pursued his plan of publishing. In March 1929 Bristol wrote to him regarding covers for a new book that Elliot was publishing, Con O'Leary's This Delicate Creature.

March 8, 1929

Dear Elliot:

Herbert telephoned you yesterday about the "This Delicate Creature" covers. . . .

Sorry you had this extra trouble when you must be having troubles enough getting under way. Luck to you.

Ever yours,
[Edward N. Bristol]

P.S. On my return I found a letter from your mother about your father's papers and have had a complete search made and expect the report this week. I'll give her all the details. The bulk is much less formidable than we had supposed. The labeled boxes contained much foreign stuff—old firm checks stubs and account books and the like.

WRITERS

H.D.

The American-born author "H.D." (Hilda Doolittle Aldington) was among the leading Imagist poets and, briefly, a Holt and Company author.

August 26, 1921

My dear Mrs. Aldington:

I am glad to get your letter of August 13th.

The sheets for *Hymen* have just arrived from the *Egoist Press,* and we are looking forward to getting out the book. We'll attend to sending out the copies to Miss Lowell, Miss Moore, and Mrs. Doolittle [*sic*], with Author's Compliments cards enclosed. We shall of course also send you a copy.

We agree with you that it is best to avoid the confusion of two names, and shall be careful to refer to you simply as H. D.

Mr. Frost has been intending to write you about the volume of Greek essays. I believe you will hear from him soon.

I am planning to sail for England the 17th of September, and hope to see you if you are back in England by that time. I shall also get to Paris.

Sincerely yours,
[Lincoln MacVeagh]

H. D., pen name of Hilda Doolittle Aldington (from Amy Lowell, Tendencies in Modern American Poetry, *1917; Thomas Cooper Library, University of South Carolina)*

September 25 [1921].

Dear Sir,

I find that there are several misprints in "Hymen" now that the bound copy has reached me. I was abroad when the proofs were sent me and as they followed me from place to place I had, at the end, to correct them in a great hurry and I was unable to see them afterwards.

I found that "Prayer", which should have come in the middle of the volume, had been omitted altogether. I wrote about it and it was printed from a magazine with several mistakes. In the third line from the end a syllable was missed out which completely destroys sense and rhythm. It should run,

"white silver with the *darker* hammered in,"
not "*dark,*" which is simply silly. I suppose it is too late to put in a slip to this effect or in some way to show that it is a misprint?

It should also have had a space in the middle, "Mistress,—be near" really began a separate stanza. There are several other slight mistakes . . . I mention this lest the volume should at any time be reprinted.

I know, of course, that you had nothing to do with the printing but had to let you know about the matter, for my own artistic satisfaction.

Yours sincerely,
Hilda Aldington
("H.D.")

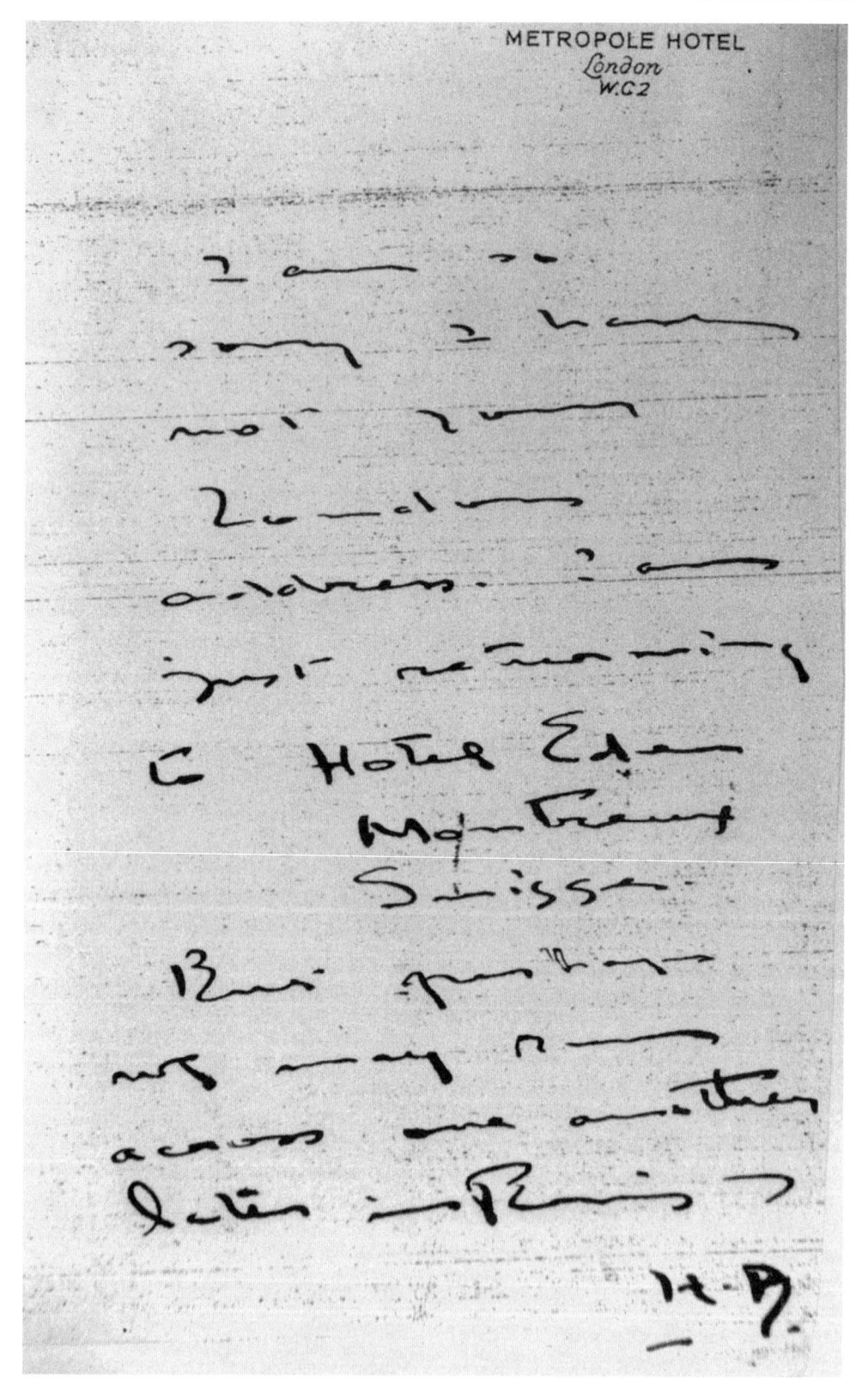

Undated note from H.D., the American-born Imagist poet who lived most of her life in Europe and published one of her books, Hymen (1921), with Holt and Company (Princeton University Library)

Will you let me know in good time, in case there may arise questions of reprinting, as I should be so glad to revise these and several other slight errors of punctuation etc.?

Dec. 1, 1921

My dear Mrs. Aldington:

The *Egoist Press* sold us five-hundred sheets of your *Hymen* on the understanding that the price we paid them was to include the royalty. We knew nothing about the agreement that you had with them, but we assumed that they were acting in their rights. They now however ask us to pay you a royalty besides paying them the sum they originally quoted, their reason being that the sheets cost them more than they thought they were going to! At the same time you inform us that they never had the American rights. I am sending you a copy of a letter I am writing them. It is my belief that they ought to live up [to] their undertaking. But I think it is only fair to say that should we import another edition in sheets from them, we would be glad to arrange with you to pay you a royalty on our sale of that edition. Or should the book have such a success here as to warrant our printing it, we would be glad to arrange that on a royalty basis with you.

Sincerely yours,
[Lincoln MacVeagh]

December 23rd [1921]

Dear Mr. MacVeigh [sic]:

I am sorry there seems to have been a misunderstanding about the royalties. I understood that, as I was abroad at the time, the Egoist Press were making all arrangements with you as regards royalties and so on. As it is, it seems I am to receive nothing from either publication for they write me from England they had understood you would pay me on the American edition.

I must admit I had counted on receiving a small sum for the book as some of the poems had not previously been published. However as there seems to have been confusion all round about the matter let us say no more about it. I must hope that the sales will warrant a reprint of the book. May I remind you again that in such an event there are several misprints I am anxious to correct.

Thank you for sending me the book by Stephen Benet which I have read with much interest. I should be glad to know how "Hymen" is selling in America.

Yours sincerely,
Hilda Aldington

My best wishes to you for the New Year.

February 21, 1923.

Dear Madam [H.D.]:

We are very sorry to have to write that, despite their beauty, we cannot see a market for your little fifty-two page volume of poems entitled

"WE TWO"

Although it had equal charm, we have not even been able so far to sell the five hundred copies of your HYMEN which we took. The writer of this letter has long been enthusiastic over classical poetry and mythology, and wishes to add his thanks for the pleasure you have given him and his regret for the conclusion to which we have been so reluctantly forced.

By the instructions of Mr. Louis Untermeyer, who so kindly gave us the poems, we are returning them to you enclosed by registered mail, and are, with appreciation and renewed regret,

Sincerely yours,
[Roland Holt]

Robert Benchley

Writer-humorist Robert Benchley published several books with Holt and Company during the 1920s.

Dec. 27, 1921

Dear B. Benchley:

You might take it ill if I expressed disappointment at your not saying hello when calling here recently, so won't express anything but merely remind you that some years ago I appealed to you for the MS which now as "Of All Things" appears—to judge from what some people say—to be doing very well. Looking at orders this morning makes me—oh so shrewdly—suspect that Christmas will prove no barrier and that "Bob Benchley's Book" is going to continue in popularity; and that brings me to fifthly: I would like another Benchley book for next fall and hope you will screw your courage up to the talking point at least. Please arrange a date—if you will—at your convenience. Will lunch at the Harvard Club, before all the waiters, embarrass you?

I had a characteristic but most unusual letter from Copey [Harvard English instructor Charles Townsend Copeland] about your book. He is reading it to his classes. If this goes on you will be too Great for me to write to, or speak to; so for mercy's sake arrange to lunch with me quick so that I can tell my grandchildren about it.

But seriously————

[Lincoln MacVeagh]

April 25 [1922?]

Dear Ellie [presumably Elliot Holt]:

I am going to be in Cleveland all next week at the Hotel Cleveland, and won't return to New York until Monday the fourth, and sail Tuesday the fifth. That won't give me much time to see you about the book [*Love Conquers All*]. But I will be back late in July and by then will have finished a series of scientific articles for Life which really ought to be the basis of the book anyway. I will have more than enough stuff and it will just be a question of getting it together. If the scientific articles work out as they ought to, it might be a burlesque scientific book entirely. I don't think that the Red Book stuff is good enough to go in.

Now Ellie. I probably have ten or fifteen dollars coming to me this month from my collected works, but that will not be enough to finance my trip abroad. I have got my passage paid for, but have nothing to eat on when I get over. Could you add to whatever my royalty check is enough advance on the next book to bring it up to a total of $500? It would ensure the little Benchleys getting enough good wholesome food and perhaps a little red wine in France. I don't bother you much about money, do I Ellie? So be a nice chap and just as soon as you get this tell someone in your office how things stand and see if they could get the check either to me at the Hotel Cleveland by Thursday, or up at Life office after Thursday so that I will be pleasantly surprised to find it when I get in there on Monday.

If I tell you how much I felicitate you and the bride, you will think that I am just after the five hundred.

Yours,
Bob Benchley

December 13, 1922

A CORRECTION

Henry Holt and Company have read with amazement a note in the *New York Times* of Sunday, December 10th, to the effect that Mr. Robert C. Benchley's new book is to be published by another house. Mr. Benchley authorizes Henry Holt and Company to qualify this statement as misleading. His arrangements with them provide for their issuing the next books he now contemplates writing.

December 7, 1925.

Dear Bob [Robert Benchley]:

The National Association of Book Publishers—which happens to be a somewhat profound and important body in either the publishing or marketing of a book–, wants you to be one of their two honored guests at their annual luncheon on Tuesday, January 19th, at one o'clock. I have a very nice letter from Frederick Melcher about it. He suggests (and I agree with him) that it might be a rather pleasant and informal way to eat a meal; from my own point of view, I am quite sure it would be a good thing for your books, as there will be a lot of booksellers there and they couldn't help but unconsciously react favorably towards selling your books, if you told them what wonderful men they were. I don't see why this should fall into the category of a complication with your fight manager. It would be a help to us and I know would have a tendency to increase your royalty statement. I've got to answer Melcher in a couple of days–this to him is really an important occasion....

As usual,
[Elliot Holt]

Robert Benchley (Bruccoli Clark Layman Archives)

20,000 Leagues Under the Sea, or, David Copperfield *(1928) turned out to be Benchley's last Holt and Com-*

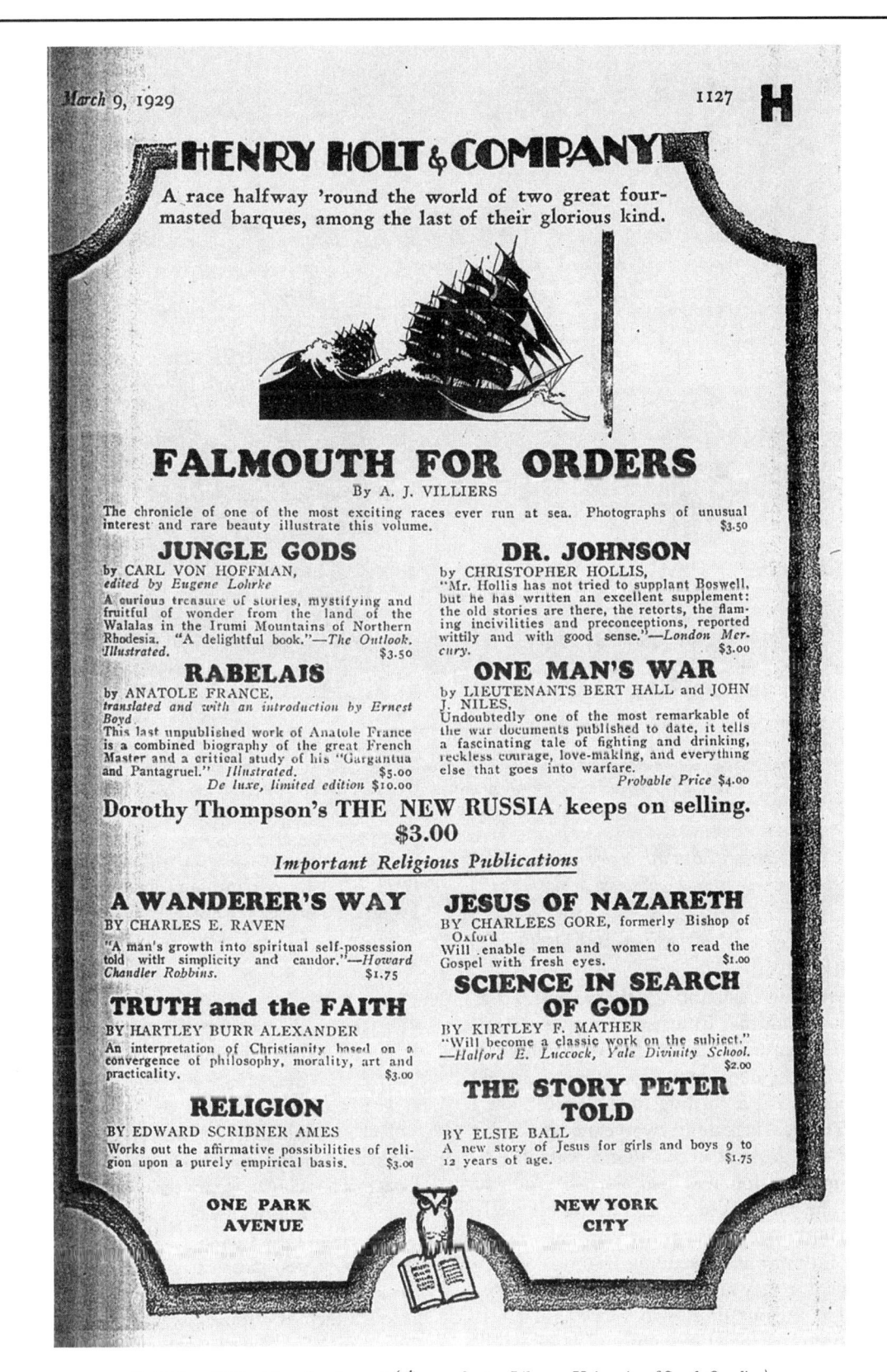

Publishers' Weekly advertisement (Thomas Cooper Library, University of South Carolina)

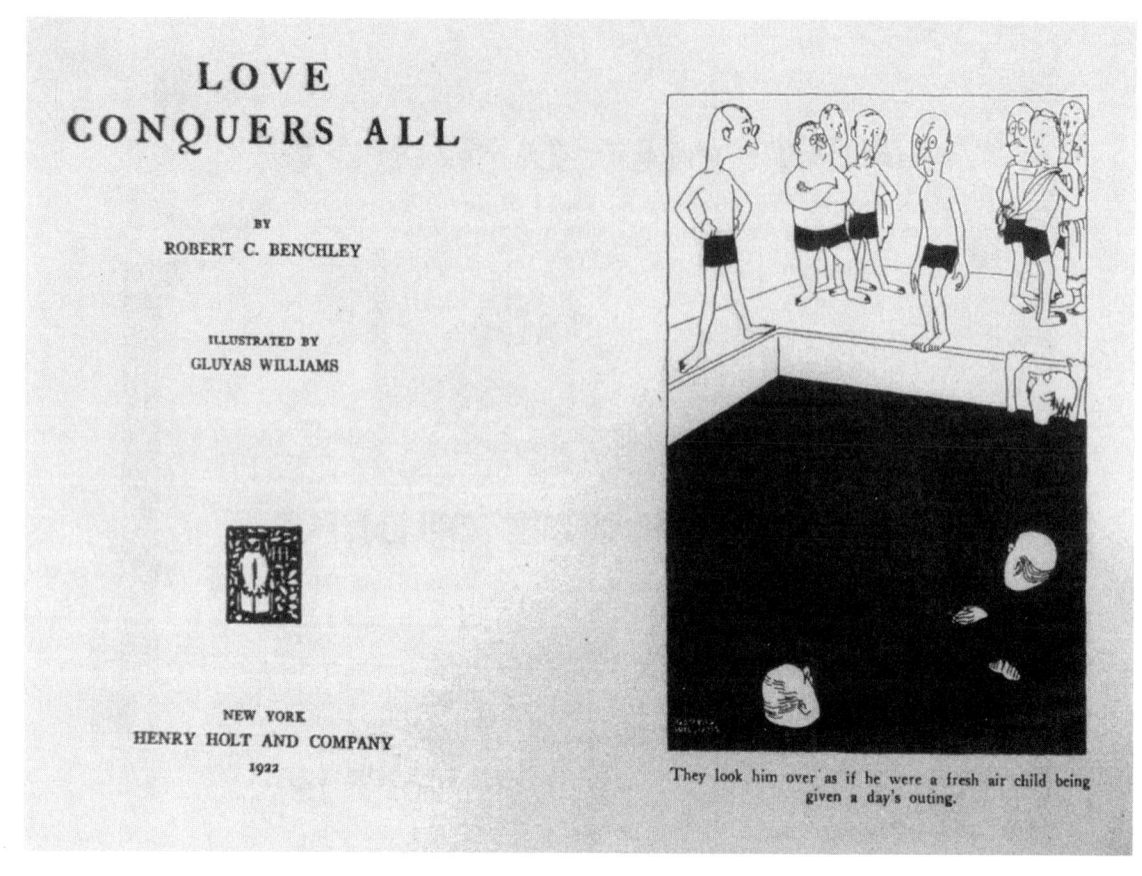

Title page for Robert Benchley's second Holt and Company publication, with drawings by Benchley's Harvard friend who illustrated all of his books (Rutgers University Library)

pany title. He wrote to Herschel Brickell, a member of the Holt trade department, explaining his prior obligation to Harper's.

March 10th, 1929

Dear Mr. Brickell:

I am sorry that I can not sign these contracts as they stand, as I find that I must give my next *book*, no matter what nature, to Harpers. As a matter of fact, I was supposed to have given them "20,000 David Copperfields", according to the agreement I made with Freddie Allen about two years ago, and it was only by the grossest deceit that I was able to convince him that Holt had had the material left over from "The Early Worm" and therefore really had to publish it. . . .

I am a little proud of sending back these contracts like this, for they are the first that I have ever refused to sign. At one time, two years ago, I was under obligation to Holt, Liveright and Harpers all at once. Like Serena Blandish, I find it hard to say "No". But I really am afraid of Harpers' this time.

Incidentally, when may I have some of my "David Copperfield" money? When I have signed the revised contracts you will send me? Please don't think I have any complaint against Holt. I just knew Freddie Allen very well.

Sincerely,
Robert Benchley

August 9th, 1929

Dear Mr. Carrick:

I am afraid that Mrs. Benchley didn't understand the situation when she intimated to you over the telephone that I was in a position to sign up again with Holt. I have already signed with Holt twice when I shouldn't have, and Harpers', to whom I was supposed to have given the book before "20,000 Leagues", are getting a little irked by my ingenuousness. I have *got* to give my next three books to Harpers, although there was some talk on Mr. Brickel's [*sic*] part of the possibility of Holt's getting out an "anthology" from all five books. I rather doubt that this would be a success, for it would make the third time that the pieces would have been published. I am afraid, however, that such is about the only book I can get out through you people until I have done

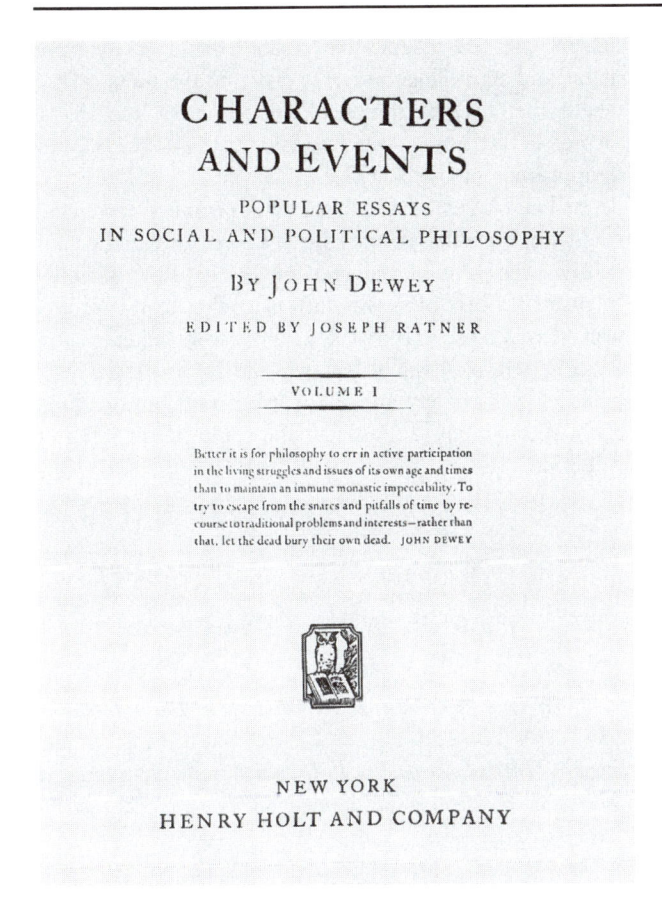

Title page for the first volume in the American philosopher's essay collection published in 1929 (Rutgers University Library)

three for Harpers' (which ought to bring us up to 1975 easily).

I don't suppose that this is a very opportune moment to say that I would like nothing better than to find some of the October "20,000 Leagues" money waiting for me at 44 West 44th Street [the Royalton Hotel, where Benchley kept a suite] when I get back on August 20th. What fun that would be!

I am sorry about this changing business, and assure you that it was because I roomed with Freddie Allen in college and when he went to Harpers' he signed me up (two years ago). Since then I have been publishing with Holt entirely illicitly.

Sincerely,
Robert Benchley

Ivan Alekseyevich Bunin

In 1926 Holt and Company published the novel Mitya's Love *(1925), by the Russian poet and novelist Ivan Alekseyevich Bunin. Bunin won the 1933 Nobel Prize in literature following the publication of his fictional autobiography* The Well of Days *(1930). An anti-Bolshevik, Bunin left Russia in 1919 and spent most of the rest of his life in France.* Mitya's Love *was translated from French by Madeleine Boyd. The following selection is from Ernest Boyd's introduction to the volume.*

Ivan Alexeyevich Bunin, whom Gorky has described as the greatest living Russian writer, was born at Voronezh, in 1870, the son of an old family of country gentry, distinguished in art and politics. "All my forebears were country gentlemen, closely attached to the soil and the people, and so were my parents, who owned property in central Russia, in those fertile steppes where the former Moscovite Tsars, as a protection against the Tartar invasions from the south, set up a rampart of colonies recruited from every province in the country. Thanks to that fact, this region saw the development of the richest of all Russian dialects and produced almost all our great writers beginning with Turgenev and Leo Tolstoy." Bunin's childhood and youth were spent almost entirely in the country on his father's estates, and in the town of Yelets, so frequently the scene of his stories, where he went to school before proceeding to the University of Moscow. "I began to write, in verse and prose, rather early, and my works were printed at an early date. When I published my books they were usually composed of prose

Ivan Alekseyevich Bunin (from Julian W. Connolly, Ivan Bunin, *1982)*

and poetry, some original, others translated (from the English). If these writings were divided according to kinds, I should have four volumes of my own verse, two of translations, and six of prose. Criticism was not slow to notice my works, and subsequently they were crowned several times, receiving in particular the Pushkin Prize, the highest award of the Russian Academy of Science. In 1909 that institution elected me one of its twelve honorary Academicians, a distinction corresponding to that of the forty French 'Immortals.'"

. . . .

[Bunin's] aloof, independent position [from the revolutionary school of writers in Russia] may explain, to some extent, his tardy recognition. . . . "For many reasons I waited a long time before achieving a certain popularity. After my first writings were published, during a considerable period, I wrote and published only poetry. I kept out of politics and did not touch in my work upon political questions. I belonged to no literary school, and did not call myself a Decadent or a Symbolist, a Romanticist or a Naturalist; I wore no mask and brandished no brightly colored banner. . . ."

. . . .

[In the] volume of short stories referred to as *The Dreams of Chang* . . . [the] best story . . . is *The Gentleman from San Francisco*. Independently of all his other work this story attained widespread recognition in English, and, until *Mitya's Love* appeared, it was the most famous. . . . In its sardonic simplicity this description of an American millionaire's journey alive to Capri and his return to his own country dead is a masterpiece which lingers in the memory with certain of Chekhov's austere marvels of artistic economy.

The transition from the skilful terseness of *The Gentleman from San Francisco* to the tender and romantic lyricism of *Mitya's Love* is abrupt, but readers of stories so various as *Brothers, The Dreams of Chang, Sukhodol* and *Kazimir Stanislavoch* do not need to be reminded of the great versatility of Ivan Bunin. . . .

–introduction to *Mitya's Love*
(New York: Holt,
1926), pp. 17–18

The following passage is taken from chapter 1 of Mitya's Love.

The ninth of March was Mitya's last happy day in Moscow, or at least, he thought so later.

He was walking up the Boulevard Tverskoy with Katya. It was midday. Winter was gradually yielding to spring; it was almost hot in the sun, as if the larks had really come back, bringing with them warmth, light and joy. The ice was melting and everything was damp, drops fell from the roofs, the caretakers were breaking the ice on the pavements and shovelling the wet snow from the roofs. Everywhere there were crowds of people. Even the clouds seemed to be melting away into thin white smoke and were disappearing into the soft blue of the sky.

The boulevard was black with people as far as one could see, Pushkin's statue rose in the distance, gentle and pensive, the roof of the convent of the Passion shone brightly. But best of all, Katya was lovelier than ever. She walked very close to Mitya, sometimes with childlike confidence; she took hold of his arm and looked up at him, while he, very happy and not a little proud, strode along, like a country boy, so fast that she could hardly keep up with him.

–*Mitya's Love*, p. 23

Hendrik Willem Van Loon

Historian, journalist, and illustrator Hendrik Willem Van Loon, whose Life and Times of Pieter Stuyvesant *was published by Holt and Company in 1928, maintained a lively correspondence with the firm in the months leading up to the planned publication of his book.*

22 June xxvii
Most indulgent of taskmasters and most agreeable of Publishers. . . .
I have just destroyed the work of two months,
not entirely
but almost entirely.
I had begun this book on old Pete Stuyvesant as a sort of Symphonia Eroica
a broad motive, broadly ausgekomponirt.
It just could not be done
the tinkly little tune sounded absurd "in the manner of Beethoven"
and so I have begun again
and this time it is a slight menuet
and that seems to be the right form
for it goes rapidly and well
(knock wood)
but listen dear Brethren
this will never make an imposing five dollar book
and if it were not damn hot
I would come and show you what has been done and what I hope to accomplish
but I think
three dollars will be about all the traffic can bear
unless you want a lot of pictures
and make it the sort of thing I have in mind
a very gay and amusing book

Hendrik Willem Van Loon in New York, 1939 (from Gerard Willem Van Loon, The Story of Hendrik Willem Van Loon, *1972; Thomas Cooper Library, University of South Carolina)*

the sort of thing that says "Good Lord, it might have been something
fine and grand and noble this Dutch American Empire but ouch what a fizzle,
phooey what a buttonhole."
My blessings, somewhat hot and frayed but sincere.

         Hendrik Willem van Loon

When Van Loon wired Holt and Company reporting his difficulties with research and proposing a title change, they responded with a short cable two days later, saying "ANYTHING YOU DO IS ALRIGHT AS LONG AS YOU DO IT."

WESTERN UNION CABLEGRAM
AUG. 27 1927
DESTRUCTION WEST INDIAN ARCHIVES 1825 FORBIDS FINDING NEW STUYVESANT MATERIALS MAKING BOOK REHASH SAME OLD YARNS MEANWHILE DISCOVERED NEVER CONSIDERED FACT THAT AMERICAN METROPOLIS OWES EXISTENCE DIRECTLY TO PROLONGED DUTCH QUEST INDEPENDENT INDIAN ROAD WHEREFORE SUGGEST CHANGE DULL STUYVESANT TITLE TO QUOTE NEW YORK AND THE QUEST OF CATHAY.

            April 4, 1928

My dear Mr. Holt,

 . . . .

We will have new care only for "philosophical discussions" or some such matter–: Geometry–Algebra" [*sic*] and therefor neglect Geography. You see, this Comic History is the only thing that ever came to me by spontaneous combustion and it was drawn right off–which accounts for all sorts of slips. I was in Dublin and had no books. For example: the amount of money given to Columbus . . . of course stated much too small. But I made it a ridiculously low amount to indicate something significant.

 Besides: this is merely the prospectus. Any detail will be changed to suit tenant. When I wrote about the eating and drinking of the Ancients I had probably in mind the materialism which wrecked the Old World and addressed it in the form of the pleasures of the Table.

        Sincerely yours,
        Hendrik Van Loon
        Washington DC

Elliot Holt addressed the following letter to Van Loon at the Hotel Bayerischer Hof in Munich.

           April 12, 1928

Dear Han:

 As yet the MS. is not in, nor are the illustrations, but we are well instructed to receive them like a Chicago Bomb, and I trust they'll be unrolled correctly. It's good to think the job is done.

 But, my boy, it seems absolutely suicidal to consider rushing the book out in the drab and heat of the early summer. You must realise that all books are sold on the road previous to the grand date of launching. Salesmen are glib and garrulous, but they must have a dummy of Pete, and a nice display to inveigle the bookselling fellers to buy. So it would seem (and it does to all of us) really foolhardy to publish before September 1. This allows us time for drumming it up, really selling it well beforehand, and whetting the appetites of the critic fellers for reviews on date of publication rather than months afterward. I phoned T. R. Smith and he says you have no volume with them for next autumn. I felt it would be foolish if both of us did not make some allowances for separate dates if you were doing another volume for them. Mayhap you have a book with others. Let me know of this in order for me to make any necessary adjustment.

 We've waited a long time as you know, and believe it would be unwise to rush Stuyvesant out without due combing of his whiskers beforehand.

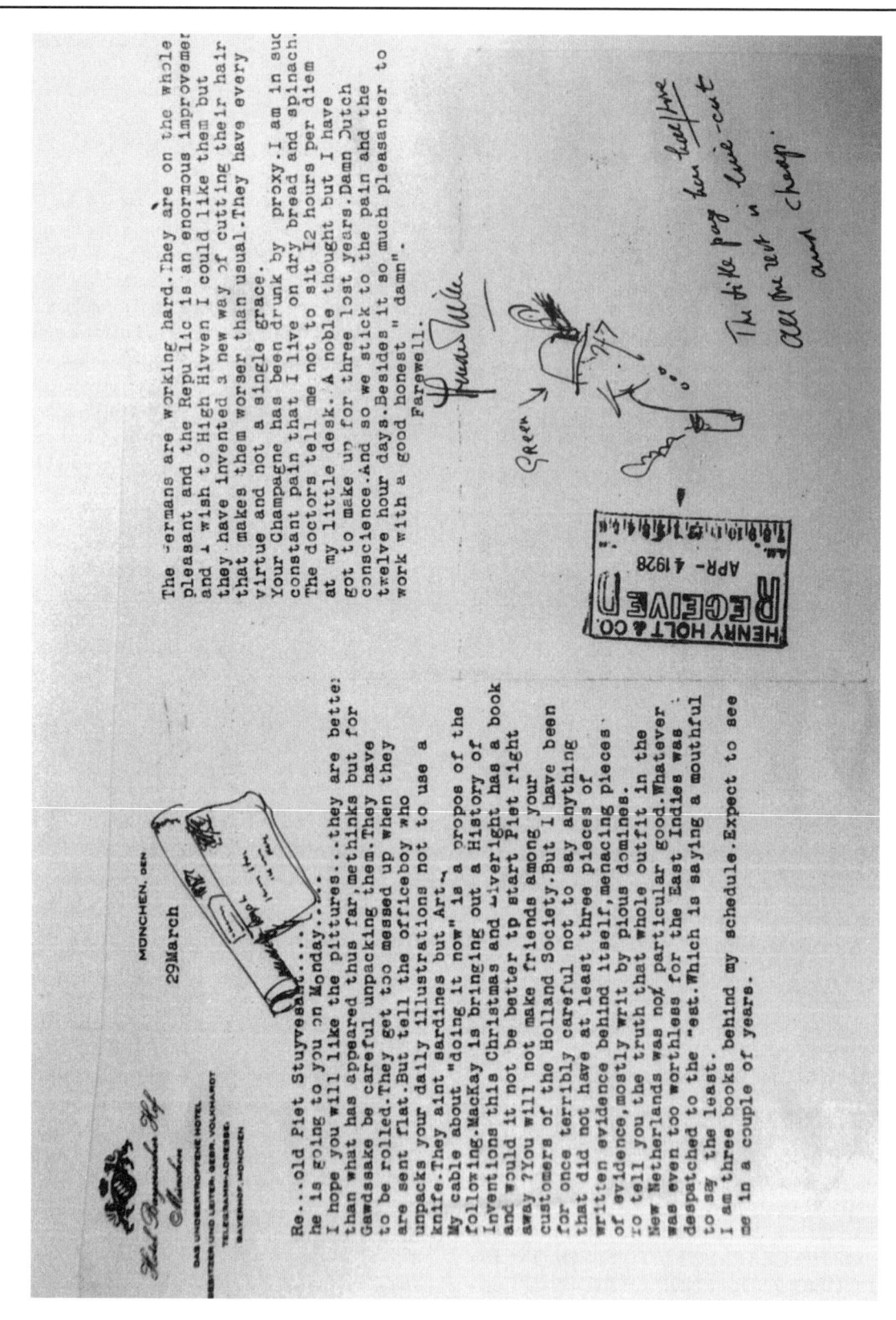

Letter from Hendrik Willem Van Loon to Elliot Holt informing him that the completed manuscript for Life and Times of Pieter Stuyvesant *(1928) had been sent (Princeton University Library)*

Frontispiece and title page for Van Loon's 1928 biography of the Dutch colonial governor who tried to resist the English seizure of New York in 1664 (Thomas Cooper Library, University of South Carolina)

I do hope you're feeling better. It is difficult to imagine you in frail condition. Continue the champagne.

      As usual,
      [Elliot Holt]

Holt and Company employee Herbert Bristol, son of Edward N. Bristol, wrote to Van Loon in Veere, Netherlands, apologizing for his failure to send him proofs for his book.

      July 17, 1928

My dear Mr. Van Loon:

  I have probably been as much distressed as you about the fact that proofs of "Peter [sic] Stuyvesant" were not sent to you. Exactly why this occurred I was not able to explain at the time your radiograms came in because Mr. Elliot Holt, who handled the arrangements for the book, as you probably know, is in London where he will be until September 1. I am sure there must have been some good reason in connection with the publication of the book which was responsible for your not seeing the proofs. They were read with a great deal of care in this office and I trust that you have not found any grievous errors in the copy which was sent on to you last week from Brandt & Brandt. I feel quite confident that there will be not only a second edition but several others and of course any errors that you may find will be corrected in subsequent printings.

  I read the book with a great deal of interest and think it one of the very best you have done. As you will see from the copy we have sent you, we took considerable pains with the design and we have an unusually good-looking jacket, a copy of which I shall forward to you when it is available.

  I hope you will be as patient as possible with us in the circumstances and that in due time the whole matter can be cleared up to your entire satisfaction.

      Sincerely yours,
      [Herbert Bristol]

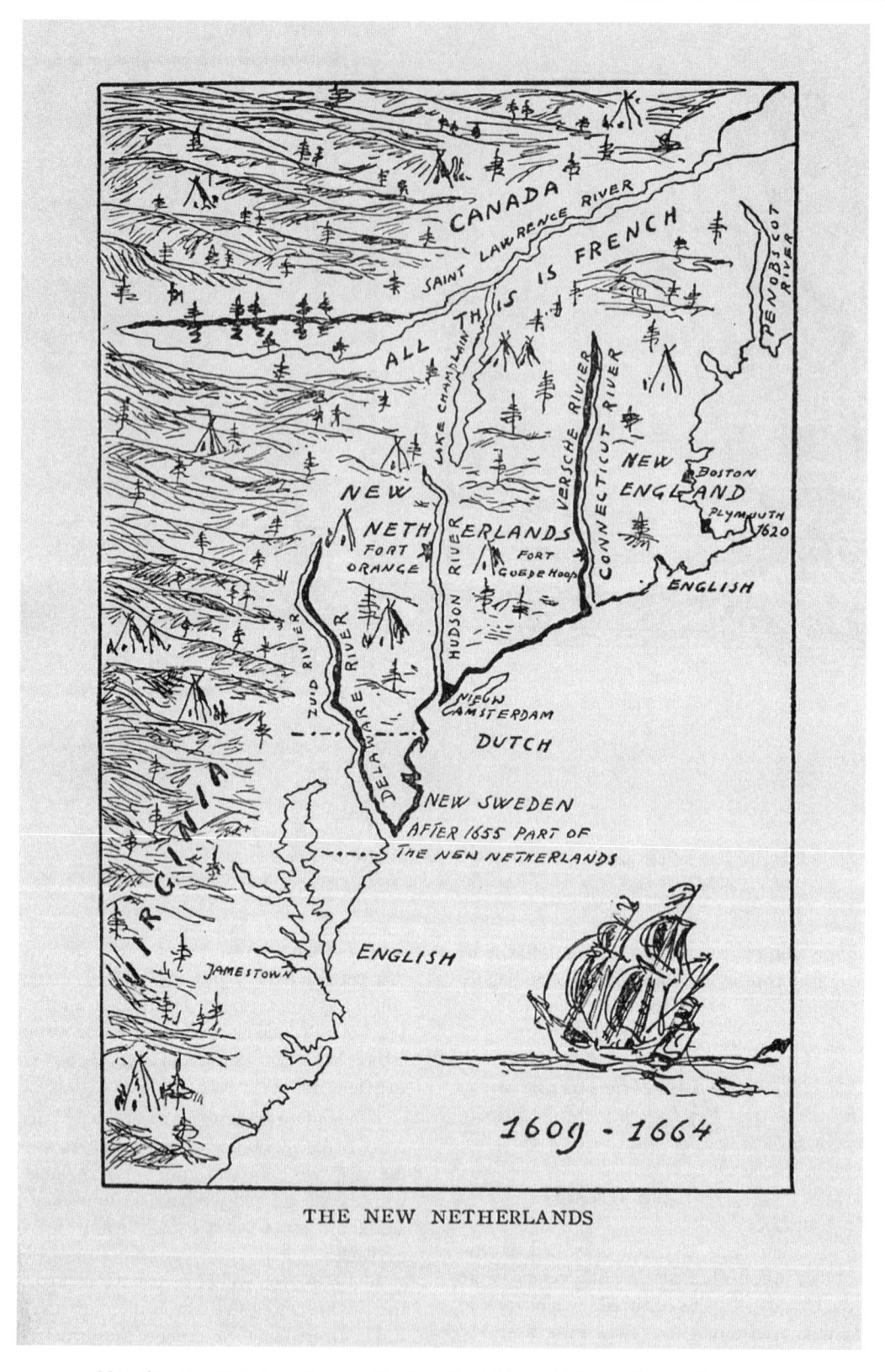

Map of the New Netherlands drawn by Van Loon for his Life and Times of Pieter Stuyvesant
(Thomas Cooper Library, University of South Carolina)

Advertisement from the 12 October 1929 issue of The Saturday Review of Literature
(Collection of Richard Layman)

Dust jacket for the first (left, 1922) and third (1928) volumes in the three-volume drama-collection series (Bruccoli Clark Layman Archives)

November 7, 1928

Dear Han:

Somehow or other Brandt & Brandt asked us to bill you for those two copies of Pete for which we sent you the memo. However, I have "adjusted" the circumstance.

Of course you have not heard from me lately, Old Timer, because I was abroad this summer in Europe trying to find books for the company, and if I hadn't been circumstanced by my wife and baby who accompanied me, I might have allowed myself the opportunity of convincing you that we did not have, as you express it, "a mad on."

Pete is not the flop that you suggest. It hasn't been, so far, a big seller, but it is continuing and we are hopeful of its doing well these coming Christmas months. Of course the subject has more or less identified the book with the New Yorker rather than the Oshkosh feller, but it's going pretty well throughout the country, and we haven't for a moment figured it in your expressive way.

Things go on much the same over here–endless books, useless reviews, the jargon of the literary group, the same quasi-idiocy. Doubleday-Doran appear to be the latest steam-rollers, though Horace [Liveright], with his change of name, is spreading his munificence to advertising agents with gusto. You have been missed, and expressions of this are not confined to smallish groups.

[Elliot Holt]

The 1930s

Robert Frost's books were a mainstay for Holt and Company during the Depression. Book-of-the-Month Club sales and the sale of Holt titles to the Modern Library, the series of classic reprints published by Random House, were also profitable at that time. The arrangement with the Modern Library began in 1928, when Holt trade-department head Herschel Brickell and Bennett Cerf of Random House came to an agreement on Brian Hooker's 1923 translation of Edmond Rostand's Cyrano de Bergerac. The agreement provided for Holt and Company to receive 8¢ per copy on the first 30,000 copies sold, and 10¢ per copy thereafter. Holt also received an advance of $3,400 against royalties. The Modern Library had to prepare new printing plates since the original Holt plates did not fit the Modern Library format. When the arrangement for republishing Cyrano de Bergerac in 1929 proved a success, other Holt titles from the Modern Library followed, including John Dewey's 1922 study Human Nature and Conduct, republished in 1930, and H. G. Wells's 1895 novel The Time Machine, republished in 1931. R. H. Thornton was named trade-department head after Brickell's departure in 1932 and later became president of the company. The arrival of William Sloane as the trade-department director in 1939 marked the beginning of a more dynamic era for the company.

Illustrated endpaper and title page for the first autobiographical work, published in 1932, by the Maine author who wrote extensively about her home state (Rutgers University Library)

DOING BUSINESS

International unrest early in the decade prompted Holt and Company insurers to recommend additional coverage for overseas shipments.

January 14, 1932

Dear Sirs:

Owing to the disturbed conditions in various parts of the world, we believe it to be advisable for your foreign shipments to be covered against the risks of war, and also against strikes, riots and civil commotion.

We are pleased to advise you that we have arranged with the Federal Insurance Company that until further notice these risks are insured without additional cost and we enclose herewith endorsement to be attached to your policy No. FO-61068 which we trust you will find in order.

This endorsement will include shipments to China and Manchuria, but such shipments are insured against war, strikes, riots, etc., at an additional rate. In reporting shipments by book post, parcel post etc., please keep a separate record of those shipments to China and Manchuria.

                Yours very truly,
                DESPARD & CO., INC.
                Samuel G. King

***

Rupert Grayson was the Holt and Company correspondent at Grayson and Grayson, a London literary agency.

October 27, 1932

Dear Mr. Grayson:

We hear of a rumor circulating in London (in New York, too, for that matter) that we are withdrawing from the "trade" publishing field, including fiction. May we assure you that there is no truth whatever in this rumor. We have no intention of diminishing our activities in any branch of the business. On the contrary we mean to extend them.

Mr. Brickell, of our editorial staff, and one of his assistants are leaving us at the end of the year; very likely the false rumor is merely a mistaken inference from this fact. We shall miss Mr. Brickell, but his going will not affect our policy, nor, we hope, cloud our friendly relations with you. The rest of the department staff, including salesmen, continues unchanged, and the editorial function we shall seek to develop and enlarge as we find occasion. In furtherance of this purpose Mr. Thornton, now president of the company, plans to call on you in person early next year.

                Very truly yours,
                [Unsigned]

***

When Anthony Hope's The Prisoner of Zenda, *first published in America by Holt and Company in 1894, was adapted as a motion picture, a representative of Grosset and Dunlap wrote Harmon Tupper of the Holt trade department confirming his firm's decision to publish a movie tie-in edition of the novel.*

December 28, 1936

Dear Mr. Tupper:

Confirming our recent telephone conversation, we will print an edition of 5000 copies of THE PRISONER OF ZENDA to be published in connection with the release of the photoplay which we understand will go into production about February 1. This is a David Selznick production, starring Ronald Colman and it should be one of the big pictures of the year.

If the picture clicks, we should do a great selling job on this perennial favorite.

                Yours very truly,
                E. Edelson
                GROSSET & DUNLAP, INC.

***

Late in 1938 Patricia Russell, wife of Bertrand Russell, wrote T. J. Wilson, head of Holt's college department, explaining that her husband declined to undertake the project of producing a revised edition of his Proposed Roads to Freedom, *published by Holt and Company in 1919.*

Trade Sales

Holt and Company reported 1934 sales figures to the New York accounting firm W. C. Heaton and Company.

March 18, 1935

Gentlemen:

At the request of the code Authority we are reporting that our trade sales for the year 1934 amounted to $94,287.46.

                Very truly yours,
                Henry Holt & Co.

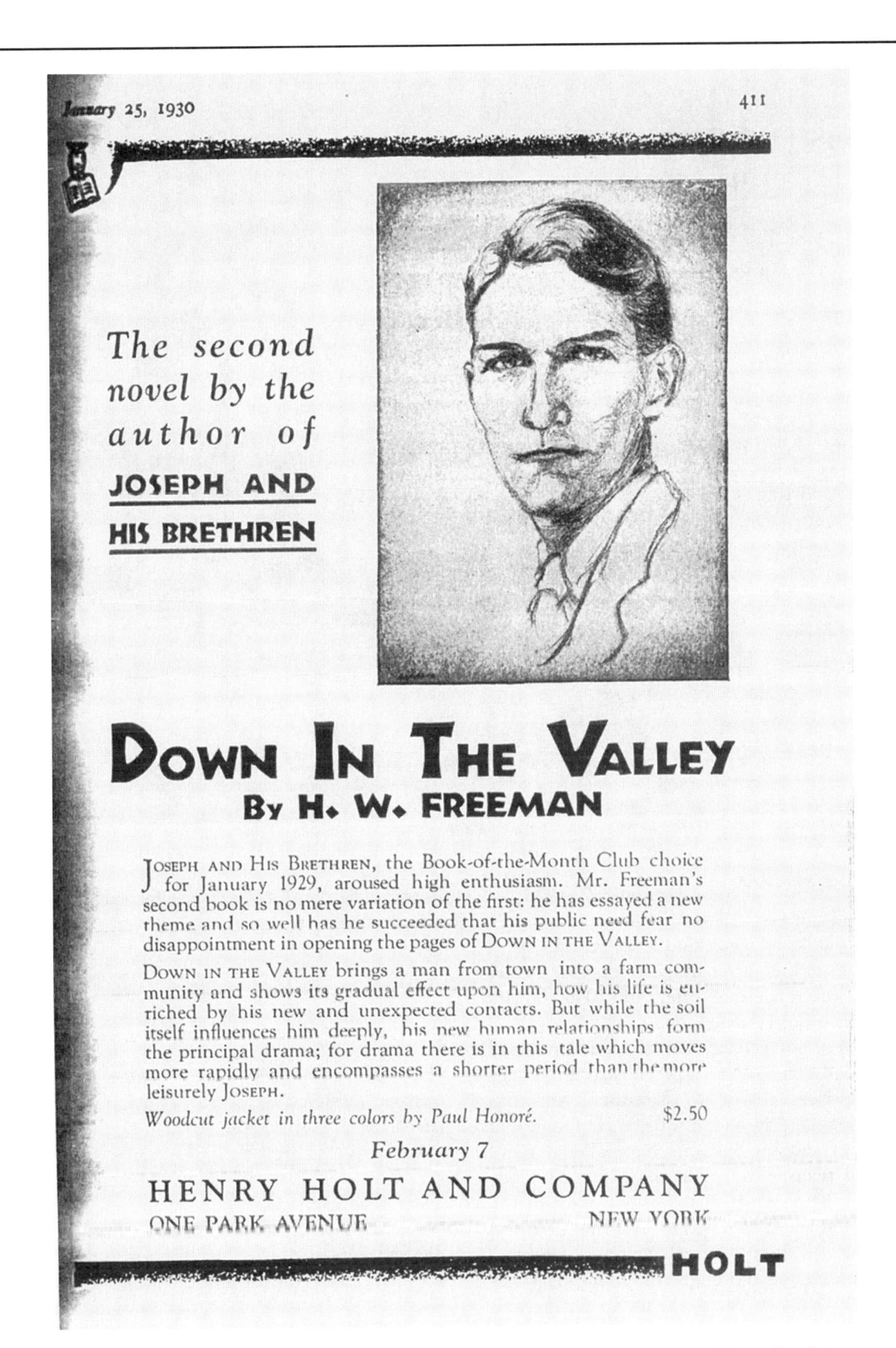

Publishers' Weekly *advertisement for the new book by the author whose first novel was the tenth-best-selling fiction title of 1929 (Thomas Cooper Library, University of South Carolina)*

Title page and illustration from the 1932 study by the Russian-born theater designer, producer, and director who spent most of his career in England and America (Rutgers University Library)

December 27 1938

Dear Mr. Wilson,

Many thanks for your kind letter with its list of Trade Unionism literature, and also for your earlier letter, with its generous offer of 1000 dollars advance, which Lord Russell much appreciates.

I am very sorry that, after all your trouble, I must now send you bad news. My husband has very carefully re-read "Roads to Freedom" and has thought a great deal about the subject. He found that circumstances and his opinions have altered more than he had realised, and that the necessary alterations would be so great that hardly a page of the old book could stand as it is. He feels that he could hardly tackle the subject afresh without involving himself in a long and thorough study and investigation which his present engagements do not permit. He would wish to spend at least two years on such a work. Perhaps some years hence this may be possible, now it is not. He is extremely sorry about this, and I am more sorry, as I have already done a good deal of reading and find the subject of absorbing interest. My husband asks me to send you his apologies and regrets.

Yours sincerely,
Patricia Russell

* * *

In late 1939 Sloane wrote to Elizabeth Strohecker, an employee at the Holt and Company office in San Francisco, about the state of the book business.

November 24, 1939

Dear Miss Strohecker:

Mr. Herbert Bristol has handed me your letter of the sixteenth and asked me to reply to certain parts of it. I have just returned to the office after two weeks in the field: that explains the tardiness of my reply.

The slump in business seems to be pretty general. New England and the Southwest give us our only sizeable gain this year. I have just been in Pennsylvania, New Jersey, and New York State. In the first two states I see possibilities of increased business in 1940;

MECHANICAL COSTUMES
Oscar Schlemmer

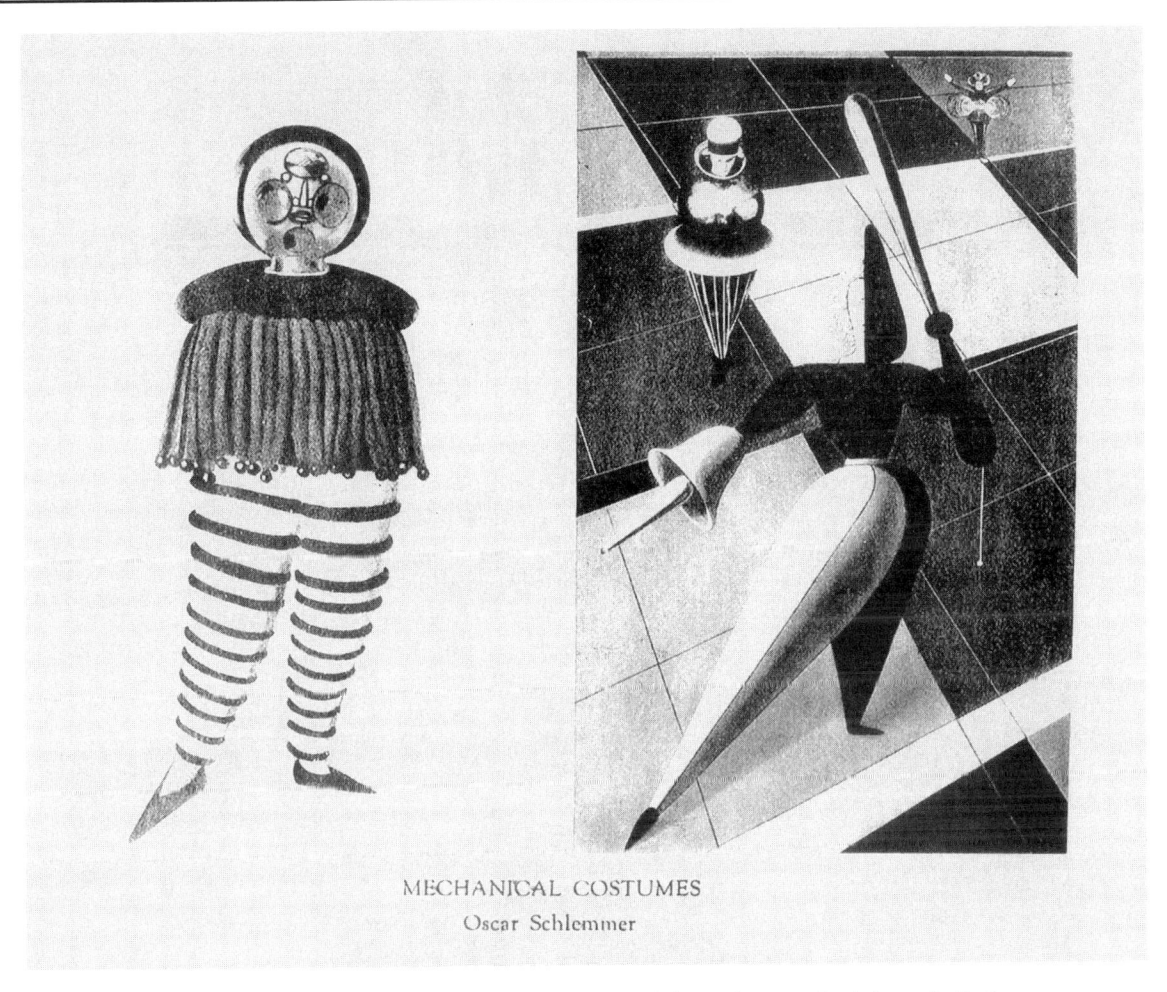

Costume illustrations by the German artist who taught stage design, sculpture, and painting at the Bauhaus, from Theodore Komisarjevsky's The Costume of the Theatre

in New York State, the whole situation is pretty sour, because of the tremendous cut of something like ten million dollars in 1939, and the threatened cut of an unknown amount in 1940, in state aid to public schools. We would as well admit that there are low-pressure areas in public-school purchasing power throughout the United States. Those areas make our work just that much harder. We cannot afford to take a decline in business. We've got to get the business even if budgets have been reduced.

As for your projected record system, I would be tempted to recommend something like the centralized Kardex system which we installed here in the New York office four years ago. That installation was the result of careful study lasting more than a year. We wanted to get all information in one place, have it quickly available and easy to see, and at the same time keep it in such a way as would not cause a great deal of clerical work. The girls who run the system and who use the system are still very fond of it, after these four years of experience with it. I shall ask Miss Braithwaite to write you a memorandum describing how it works. I understand that Mr. Herbert Bristol has given you samples of all forms. I am referring, of course, only to the Kardex system which is used in the School Division. The College Department uses quite a different system, one which has been developed through long years of experience.

Your question about the methods of following up sample copies I should like to answer myself. It is my conviction that we should spend more time and money following a sample than in getting people to ask for a sample. Thus, I feel inclined to economize on the kind of circulars which merely stimulate requests for examination copies; after all, our salesmen in the field ought to be able to put samples in the hands of the right people soon enough. But once that sample is placed in the hands of the right persons, I feel that we in the office have to bombard them with reminders that they have that book. . . .

[William Sloane]

Spring-list advertisements, 1933 and 1934, from Publishers' Weekly
(Thomas Cooper Library, University of South Carolina)

JANUARY 27, 1934   335 **H**

HENRY HOLT

1934 SPRING PUBLICATIONS

NON-FICTION

THE WHITE HILLS   by Cornelius Weygandt

The author of *A Passing America* and *The Red Hills* here does for New Hampshire and the White Mountains what he has previously done so successfully for Pennsylvania and the Wissahickon Hills. A delightful cross section of New England life in all its phases.   *Illustrated*   April $3.50

THE QUEST FOR SECURITY   by I. M. Rubinow

A clear presentation of the facts which a well-informed person needs to know about a vital question of the day—social insurance.   April $3.75

S. O. S., A Book of Sea Adventure   by David Masters

Thrilling tales of the sea and its heroes, by the author of *Wonders of Salvage, When Ships Go Down*, etc.   *Illustrated*   February $2.50

AMERICA'S SOCIAL MORALITY   by James H. Tufts

A revealing analysis of American social life, telling how we behave as a group and why.   January $3.00

A HISTORY OF MODERN CULTURE: Volume II, The Enlightenment
    by Preserved Smith

Deals with the period 1688–1776, discussing every phase of Western culture, especially as manifested in the fields of politics, science, philosophy and the arts.   February $5.00

PSYCHOLOGY, Third Edition   by Robert S. Woodworth

One of the most popular treatments of the subject, completely revised and brought up-to-date.   May $3.00

MORALS AND RELIGION   by Henri Bergson

"What Bergson has essentially done is to take the same critical guns which he formerly trained on scientism and turn them on traditional ethics and religion."
—*The Nation*   May $3.00

FICTION

THE SECOND DAY   by Ilya Ehrenbourg

The conflict between the old and the new Russia forms the background for this very human story of two men and a girl. A distinguished novel, highly praised by Romain Rolland. Together with the author's earlier *Street in Moscow*, it forms the basis for the moving picture *Red Square* to be released by Columbia this spring.   May $2.50

MIRACLE ON SINAI   by Osbert Sitwell

In this satirical novel, Osbert Sitwell tells the story of a modern "miracle" as witnessed by a group of tourists staying in a hotel at the foot of Mt. Sinai. Written with sly wit and humor.   February $2.00

A NOVEL   by Nicolai Gubsky

A sensitive and understanding portrayal of the lives of a young Russian couple living in England, and their efforts to adjust themselves to post-war conditions in a strange land.   March $2.00

All prices and dates subject to change

Henry Holt and Company   1 Park Avenue   New York

Sloane wrote Rupert Hart-Davis, his counterpart at Jonathan Cape Ltd., in London, regarding the publication of eighteenth-century English poet Christopher Smart's Rejoice in the Lamb, *a work written during Smart's confinement for mental illness but not published until Cape prepared an edition in 1939.*

May 12, 1939

Dear Mr. Hart-Davis:

We have decided to undertake a limited edition of Christopher Smart's REJOICE IN THE LAMB. Will you send us 400 flat sheets inclusive of royalty at 3s. 6d. as quoted in your letter to me of the 13th of April.

I have no idea what we shall be able to do with the book over here, but I would like to try at least to find a small market for it. Smart is one of my enthusiasms, and this book should also have an obvious interest for students and collectors of Blake.

Yours sincerely,
[William Sloane]

19th May 1939

Dear Mr. Sloane,

Very many thanks for your letter of May 12th. Naturally, I am delighted to hear of your decision, which I consider both admirable and courageous. Before dispatching the 400 sheets, there are one or two points on which I would like a definite ruling. I imagine that you would like a cancel title printed bearing your imprint. If so, perhaps you would let me have detailed copy for it. Secondly, what would you like done about the certificate which is at present printed on the reverse of the first half-title? It says:

"This edition of REJOICE IN THE LAMB is limited to eight hundred copies of which seven hundred and fifty numbered copies are for sale. This is copy number 000."

In view of the fact that the sheets that we shall send you will come out of these 750, they could be numbered straight on with our edition, if you so desire. In this case, it would be better perhaps to leave the imprint on the title page or to print a cancel with a joint imprint.

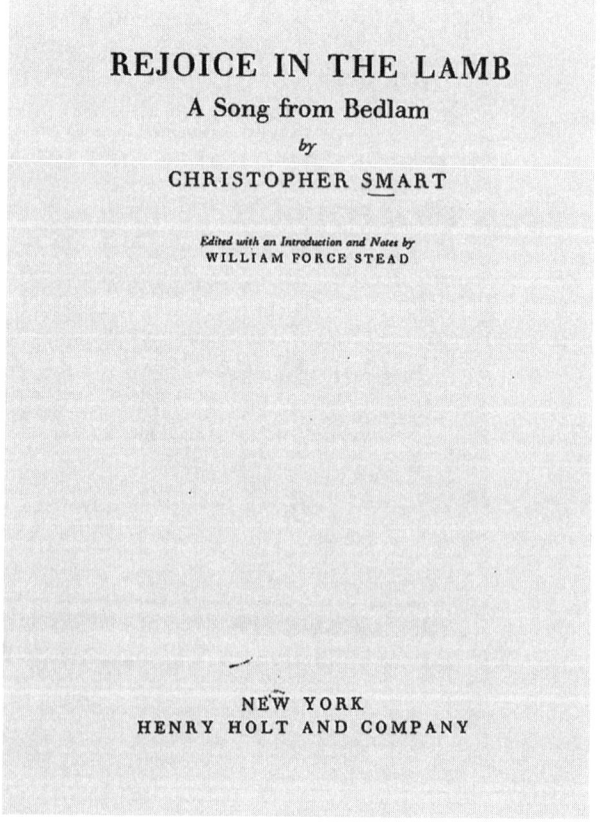

Frontispiece and title page for the American edition of the poem by the eighteenth-century British writer that was first published in England and the United States in 1939 (Rutgers University Library)

Alternatively, we could print a cancel half-title, leaving out the whole of the certificate. As soon as I have your instructions on these two points, we will go ahead with the shipment.

Yours sincerely,
Rupert Hart-Davis

May 26, 1939

Dear Mr. Hart-Davis:

Thank you for your letter of May 19. It never takes as much courage to do a book like REJOICE IN THE LAMB which one knows to be good of its kind, as to do something second rate which, if it fails, does not even leave you prestige.

Yes we should like a cancel title printed with our name. Copy for it is enclosed. I think you should also print a cancel half title without the certificate. I have been somewhat uncertain about this myself, but in view of the genuine importance of this book to college librarians and collectors, it is possible that we shall have to reorder it, and undoubtedly our lives will be simpler if we do not present it as a limited edition, even from the start.

. . . .

Sincerely yours,
[William Sloane]
MANAGER, TRADE DEPARTMENT

CONTENTS

INTRODUCTION	13
REJOICE IN THE LAMB	50
NOTES	183
APPENDIX I: A NOTE ON THE MANUSCRIPT	281
APPENDIX II: SMART'S LATIN WORDS	285
APPENDIX III: WHERE WAS SMART CONFINED?	292
APPENDIX IV: ON THE VERSE-FORM	296
APPENDIX V: LIST OF BOOKS CONSULTED	301

ERRATA

1. page 50, line 10, "let him at large" should be "set him at large."
2. page 126, line 28, "God is Contemplative" should be "Gad is Contemplative."
3. page 149, line 46, the Hebrew character ה should be ת.
4. page 154, line 39, Men should be Man.
5. page 161, line 19, "herb-germ" should be "herb-gem."
6. page 256, note on line 6, Sandares*os* should be Sandares*us*.

Contents page for the Holt and Company edition of Christopher Smart's Rejoice in the Lamb

Facsimile of a page from Smart's manuscript for Rejoice in the Lamb, *from the Holt and Company edition*

POLITICS AND THE ADVENT OF WAR

Federal Bureau of Investigation director J. Edgar Hoover wrote Tupper expressing his approval of the chapter on FBI activities in Alvin C. Eurich and Elmo C. Wilson's In 1936, *an overview of the current events of 1936 that was published by Holt and Company in 1937. A supplementary volume by Eurich and Wilson,* In 1937, *was published the following year.*

January 11, 1937.

Dear Mr. Tupper:

Your letter of December 29, 1936, has been received, together with the advance page proofs of "In 1936" which you forwarded under separate cover.

I have read the proofs and want to express my sincere appreciation for the commendatory manner in which the work of the Federal Bureau of Investigation is described in the chapter entitled "Crime and the G-Men." The chapter is indeed a good resume of our activities during the past year and I am sure it will give a better understanding of our efforts to improve the existing crime conditions.

. . . .

With best wishes and kind regards, I am
Sincerely yours,
J. Edgar Hoover

***

Cover of the issue of the trade magazine leading off with a series of advertisements for Holt and Company children's books (Thomas Cooper Library, University of South Carolina)

Dust jacket for the 1935 Holt and Company edition of the French philosopher's 1932 study Les Deux Sources de la morale et de la religion *(Bruccoli Clark Layman Archives)*

Holt and Company was one of several firms that no longer played an active role in the National Association of Book Publishers by the late 1930s.

April 28, 1937

Dear Mr. Thornton:

Mr. Stanley M. Rinehart, Jr., has asked the undersigned [Henry Hoyns of Harper and Brothers], who formed the original Committee of Organization [Frederick A. Stokes, Frank C. Dodd, and Hoyns] for the present NATIONAL ASSOCIATION OF BOOK PUBLISHERS, to meet with you informally and present briefly the present situation of the National Association.

It has become increasingly apparent that the present income is not sufficient to carry on this Association without the support of your house and a number of other important publishers who have, for one reason or another, retired from active participation. Our Committee is entirely open to any suggestions for re-organization, change of name, activities, etc. But the vital point for immediate settlement is whether or not there should be *an Association of any kind,* or whether it should disappear completely and we should revert to complete rugged individualism. Your reaction will very largely determine the issue.

. . . .

Please reply at once to Mr. Hoyns.

Yours, for the Committee,
Henry Hoyns

* * *

In 1937 Holt and Company was asked to endorse a declaration of intent to boycott the upcoming meeting of the International Congress of Publishers in Leipzig because of the press censorship then being practiced in Nazi Germany. The cover letter was signed by publishers B. W. Huebsch and W. W. Norton and by Paul Willert, an Englishman who was at that time working in New York as vice president and manager of the Oxford University Press.

December 13, 1937.

Dear Mr. Thornton:

The undersigned submit the accompanying declaration and hope that, if it represents your views, you may sign in the name of your firm; or, should that not be feasible, that such of your officers as sympathize with it may sign as individuals. The statement will be made public. . . .

It may seem to you that the matter is academic, since no American publisher is likely to go to Leipzig anyhow. We believe it important, nevertheless, to express our views, because silence may be misinterpreted as approval of a repugnant situation. . . .

Yours very truly,
B. W. Huebsch
W. W. Norton
Paul Willert

Sirs,

The undersigned authorize you to add their signature to the following statement for publication:

The next meeting of the International Congress of Publishers is to be held in Leipzig. We disapprove of a meeting in Germany at the present time and declare our intention not to participate.

Our admiration for Germany's publishing achievements remains unchanged; her methods have been a role model for the world. Those of us who have had relations with German publishers reiterate our

Advertisement for the new 1938 edition of the naturalist's 1906 book, from the 15 October 1938 issue of Publishers' Weekly *(Thomas Cooper Library, University of South Carolina)*

friendliness and appreciation of their straightforwardness and fair dealings. Our German colleagues are still our colleagues.

We in our country enjoy freedom of expression under the guarantee of the Bill of Rights. In Germany, under the present Government, the mere possession of certain books constitutes a criminal offense; no book may be published unless submitted in manuscript to a Government official and approved by him; the works of enlightened modern writers are forbidden. Recalcitrant booksellers and publishers are held guilty of treason. The book trade is gagged, as is the newspaper press. Censorship is not limited to political utterances but extends to the sciences, the arts, and culture in general. Works by Freud and Sinclair Lewis; Einstein and Bergson, Masaryk and Bertrand Russell; Professor Beard, Thomas Mann, Remarque, Zweig, (to cite, at random, well-known writers of our time), have been banned or publicly burned or both. The German Government strikes impartially at ideas whether those of Germans or foreigners. Just now the press announces the suppression of the Saturday Evening Post of November 27, presumably because the German Government dislikes an article by John Gunther. Nine-tenths of the modern German books successfully translated into English are unobtainable in Germany; if surreptitiously dealt in they imperil the lives of purchaser and seller.

Under the conditions that prevail in Germany no German publisher will dare at Leipzig to express opinions other than those dictated by the National Socialist officials who rule the publishers. It will be a display of ventriloquism....

We make this statement reluctantly. We imply no break with the International Congress or with the German publishers. On the contrary, in the course of time our ground for remaining away from Leipzig in 1938 may prove the basis for normal and fruitful cooperation.

December 14, 1937

Dear Mr. Norton:

We have the letter of December 13, signed by Mr. B. W. Huebsch, Mr. Paul Willert and yourself, relative to participation in the next meeting of the International Congress of Publishers to be held in Leipzig.

While for the most part we approve the position taken in the enclosed statement, we should not care to sign it as it stands. We do agree, however,

POEMS
1919 TO 1934
BY WALTER DE LA MARE

NEW YORK
HENRY HOLT AND COMPANY

Title page for the 1936 collection that was the tenth volume of the British poet's works published by Holt and Company (Rutgers University Library)

not to participate in this meeting, chiefly on the grounds stated in the last two paragraphs of the statement:

"Participation in a meeting in Germany, with all the implications of such cooperation, would be a contradiction of the very essence of our function as publishers. Our trade is a living symbol of the ideal of a free press and its corollaries, free speech and free assemblage...."

We hope this at least goes part of the way with you.

Sincerely yours,
[R. H. Thornton]
President,
HENRY HOLT
AND COMPANY

***

Advertisement for the 1938 historical novel by the author of the 1936 account of the Donner Party, from the 7 January 1939 issue of Publishers' Weekly *(Thomas Cooper Library, University of South Carolina)*

Frederic G. Melcher, editor of Publishers' Weekly, *asked Holt and Company to sign a letter from members of the publishing industry defending the publications of the Federal Writers' Project, a program of the Depression-era Works Progress Administration. The letter was addressed to Congressman Edward T. Taylor of Colorado, chairman of the House Subcommittee to Investigate the WPA.*

May 11, 1939

Dear Sir:

The undersigned members of the book publishing industry have followed with interest the reports printed in the press of the hearings before your Committee concerning the activities of the Federal Writers' Project.

We are concerned over what appears to be an erroneous impression concerning the Project, an impression which does not coincide with our knowledge of what has been done. The reports released say that the books which have been prepared by the Federal Writers' Project have been inferior in factual content and craftsmanship and have been marred by inclusion of radical propaganda.

We are convinced that neither of these allegations is true. . . .

These books can stand the closest examination and evaluation from any professional or literary standpoint as is attested by the universal acclaim which they have received from accredited critics of the newspapers and magazines of the entire country. . . .

So far as the charge of propaganda is concerned, we believe that these books contain far less personal bias than is usually found in books dealing with the American scene. We would certainly not have lent ourselves to the dissemination of propaganda and we do not feel that we have done so. On the contrary, in our considered opinion, these books represent a genuine, valuable and objective contribution to the understanding of American life.

. . . .

We should like also to point out that during a period of more than usual economic stress the production of these volumes has furnished the publishing industry with a most timely impetus which has enabled it to take up the slack of unemployment of workers. Industries related to book publishing have also benefited by the Government's establishment of the Federal Writers' Project. . . .

Aside from any question of necessity of maintaining this and the other Arts Projects as a means of self-respecting employment for writers and artists, we are convinced that the entire output of the Federal Writers' Project can stand scrutiny squarely upon its own merit. To hamper its program at this time would, in our opinion, be a severe deprivation to the reading public and to the enrichment of our national literature.

Yours truly,
Frederic G. Melcher,
Editor of Publishers' Weekly

———◆———

May 18, 1939

Dear Mr. Melcher:

The Board of Directors of Henry Holt and Company has requested me to inform you that we should like our signature added to that of the other firms subscribing to your letter of May 11 addressed to the Honorable Edward T. Taylor.

Sincerely yours,
[William Sloane]

AUTHORS

Susanne K. Langer

Susanne K. Langer was a distinguished philosopher of music and language. Holt and Company published one of her first philosophical treatises, The Practice of Philosophy *(1930). It included a prefatory note by Alfred North Whitehead, with whom Langer had studied at Radcliffe.*

February 20, 1930

Dear Mr. Thornton:—

It is hardly necessary to say how pleased I was to learn that you have found it possible to undertake the publication of my little book. I fully appreciate the risk involved in an enterprise of this kind, but I feel that you are rather underestimating the possible sales. I have shown the book to a number of people in the profession both here at Harvard and elsewhere, and after discussing it with them I am inclined to think that it has a very fair chance of a general sale. I wonder, therefore, whether some provision could not be made for an increasing royalty in the event of an unexpected success. A sliding

Dust jacket for the 1938 Holt and Company edition comprising the first five volumes in the ten-volume sequence of autobiographical novels by the French writer (Bruccoli Clark Layman Archives)

BOKFÖRLAGET NATUR OCH KULTUR

STOCKHOLM 3rd Febr. 1936.
Sveavägen 52

Messrs. Henry Holt and Co.,
1, Park Avenue,
New York City
/U.S.A./

Dear Sirs,

We beg to acknowledge with thanks the receipt of your letter of Jan. 20 with enclosed reviews and a picture of Prof. John Dewey.

We are glad to see that Prof. Dewey accepts the royalty proposed by us for a Swedish edition of HUMAN NATURE AND CONDUCT. $100:- we cannot pay when signing the agreement, however, but must insist on an advance payment of $50:-. For your guidance we may mention that this was the sum we paid for John Cowper Powys' THE MEANING OF CULTURE.

If an advance payment of $50:- is agreeable to Prof. Dewey, which we sincerely hope, we should thank you kindly to send us a formal agreement.

Yours very truly,

BOKFÖRLAGET NATUR OCH KULTUR

Letter from the firm planning to publish a Swedish edition of the John Dewey work that Holt and Company published in 1922 (Rutgers University Library)

scale of payments is, I believe, customary after the initial risks of publication have been overpassed. Would not a royalty of 10% of the *wholesale* price on copies up to 1000 or 1500, and a royalty of 10% of the *retail* price on all copies above that figure, be a reasonable and possible arrangement? In any event it is difficult for me to evaluate your proposal until I have a definite idea as to the wholesale price you intend to charge.

Will you please let me know more precisely what agreement we are about to enter? I trust that there will be no difficulty involved, and look forward with great eagerness to the opportunity of using my own book here at Radcliffe for the purpose which convinced me originally of its urgent need.

Yours sincerely,
Susanne K. Langer

February 25, 1930

Dear Mrs. Langer:

We are quite willing to grant you an additional royalty of three percent on all sales of your book (A Study of Philosophy) after the total sales have reached 1500. While we do not arrange royalties of educational books on the basis of the retail price, the three per cent additional on the wholesale price will amount to the same thing.

Our wholesale price is reckoned at twenty-five per cent less than the retail. If, therefore, we sell your book at $3.00, you would get $ .22½ a copy on the first 1500, and $ .29¼ (approximately) on all copies sold thereafter. If, of course, we thought it better to sell the book at $2.50, the royalties would be approximately $ .18¾ and $ .24⅓ respectively. We cannot well set the exact price on the book now, as we do not have cost figures on hand.

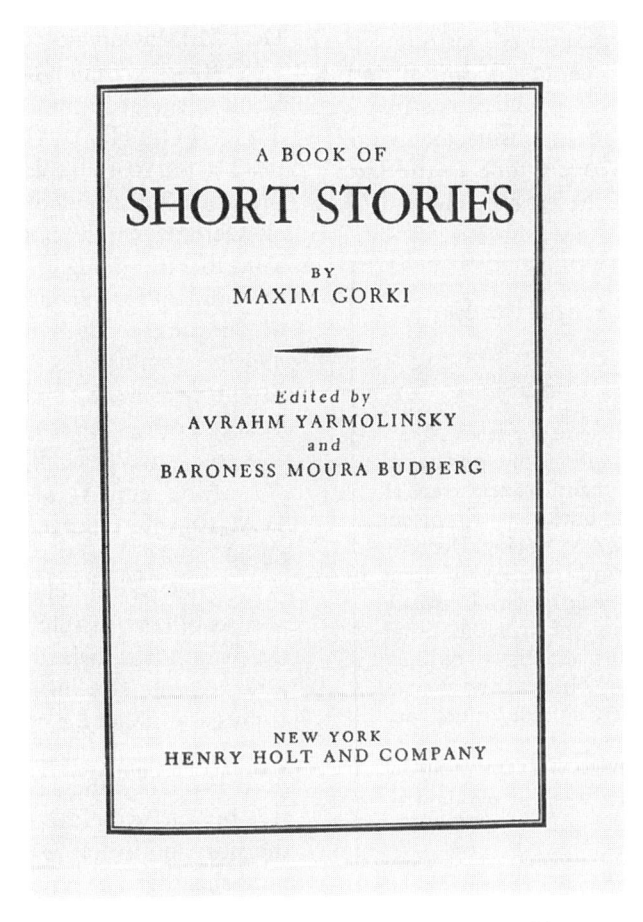

A BOOK OF
SHORT STORIES
BY
MAXIM GORKI

Edited by
AVRAHM YARMOLINSKY
and
BARONESS MOURA BUDBERG

NEW YORK
HENRY HOLT AND COMPANY

Title page for the 1939 book that is the only work of the Russian author published by Holt and Company (Rutgers University Library)

We like your book very much, and we shall certainly do all possible to secure for it a good sale. I am enclosing to you copies of our contract which the terms as outlined.

> Sincerely yours,
> R. H. Thornton
> Henry Holt & Co., Inc.

P.S. Would you object to our leaving out the last two or three pages of your manuscript? They do not seem to fit very well with the rest.

February 28, 1930

Dear Mr. Thornton:—

The contract which you have sent me, and which I am returning to you with signature, seems to me completely satisfactory. Thank you for your ready compliance in the matter of royalties, which removes my only misgiving.

In reading over my manuscript, I find myself slightly puzzled by your suggestion of "leaving out the last two or three pages," because I cannot find any paragraph prior to the end which seems like a possible *finis* am I mistaken in supposing that your objection to my concluding page is due to the fact that they cast aspersions on the current method of teaching. If so, I understand your feeling, and would be ready to rewrite the final passages. The pedagogical problem is really not in place, strictly speaking, and my comments might prejudice teachers against recommending the book to their students. Please let me know whether this or any other factor, in your opinion, ought to be remedied. I do think, at all events, that the last paragraphs might be improved upon.

> Sincerely yours,
> Susanne K. Langer

Rosamond Lehmann

Harold Raymond represented Rosamond Lehmann's British publisher, Chatto and Windus. Holt and Company published Lehmann's Invitation to the Waltz *in 1932.*

September 21, 1932

Dear Mr. Raymond:

By this time you have the big news of the Book-of-the-Month Club selection of INVITATION TO THE WALTZ. Perhaps the details may need a bit more explanation. What happened was that the Club decided definitely against the book as an October choice but there was so much enthusiasm for it among a minority group that it was brought up for reconsideration at the next meeting of the judges. They decided to take it along with another smallish book, WAH-KON-TAH by John Joseph Matthews, a publication of one of the University presses, offering the two to their subscribers at a combined price of $2.75.

Any copies of INVITATION TO THE WALTZ sold separately will be at our retail price of $2.00.

They pay $14,000 at present for a single selection and so offered to split this amount fifty-fifty between the two books, which seemed to me a satisfactory arrangement. The owner of the Club is unreservedly enthusiastic about the novel and will certainly do everything in his power to get it across....

Probably the matter of the Canadian rights will be settled before this letter can reach you, but the situation is that several times when an American publisher did not have all rights the Club has paid the English publisher or agent at the rate mentioned in my cablegram, namely, 20¢ a copy on all copies distributed in Canada. The Club has somewhere around a thousand subscribers in Canada and so is

---

War Books and Escape Books

Bookshops serving residential sections of New York apparently have not felt as direct a reaction from the war in Europe as some of the larger shops in the business districts, observations of a number of booksellers indicate. A good many readers seem to shy away deliberately from books on European affairs, while others are eagerly buying Dorothy Thompson's "Let the Record Speak," Vincent Sheean's "Not Peace but a Sword," Dr. Hermann Rauschning's "The Revolution of Nihilism," and related titles. Some bookshops, especially the midtown stores, have set up special counters and shelves of books on the crisis, displaying many titles, but even where these are in strong demand, books of general interest, not related to the war, seem to have held their own during the first week or ten days of conflict abroad.

....

—"Currents in the Trade," *Publishers' Weekly* (16 September 1939)

Rosamond Lehmann; dust jacket for the Holt and Company edition of her 1932 novel, which was a Book-of-the-Month Club selection that year (Bruccoli Clark Layman Archives)

willing to guarantee a minimum payment of two hundred dollars.

....

Even before the Book Club selection our salesmen were reporting an enthusiastic reception of the book, and I feel reasonably sure now that we should be able to accumulate a satisfactory subscription.

Faithfully,
[Herschel Brickell]

October Twentysixth
Nineteen Thirtytwo

Dear Brickell,

Rosamond Lehmann has been reading the American edition of her book, and rang me up with some perturbation over certain misprints which have occurred. I am afraid the fault is ours, and not yours. The fact was that at the eleventh hour she sent us a few corrections just in time for our own edition, and through some oversight they were not sent on to you. The most important corrections concern Mrs. Curtis's Christian name, which first appears on page 149 as Edith, and also on pages 150 and 175. As an Aunt Edith is mentioned on pages 32 and 82, the author to avoid confusion substituted Ethel for Edith as the Christian name of Mrs. Curtis. Personally I think that very few people will spot the mistake in your edition, since on pages 149, 150, and 175 it is perfectly clear that it is Mrs. Curtis who is being referred to under the name of Edith, and since Aunt Edith is only casually mentioned twice early in the book, and does not appear as a character. However, as the author is rather worried over the mistake, I have cabled you as follows today:

PLEASE NOTE CORRECTIONS FOR INVITATION FOR EDITH READ ETHEL PAGES 149, 150 AND 175. PAGE 221 LINE 12 FOR ONE READ ON, AND PAGE 164 FOR INCONSPICUOUS READ INCONSPICIOUS

hoping that it may reach you in time for the second impression. This last word is of course a deliberate

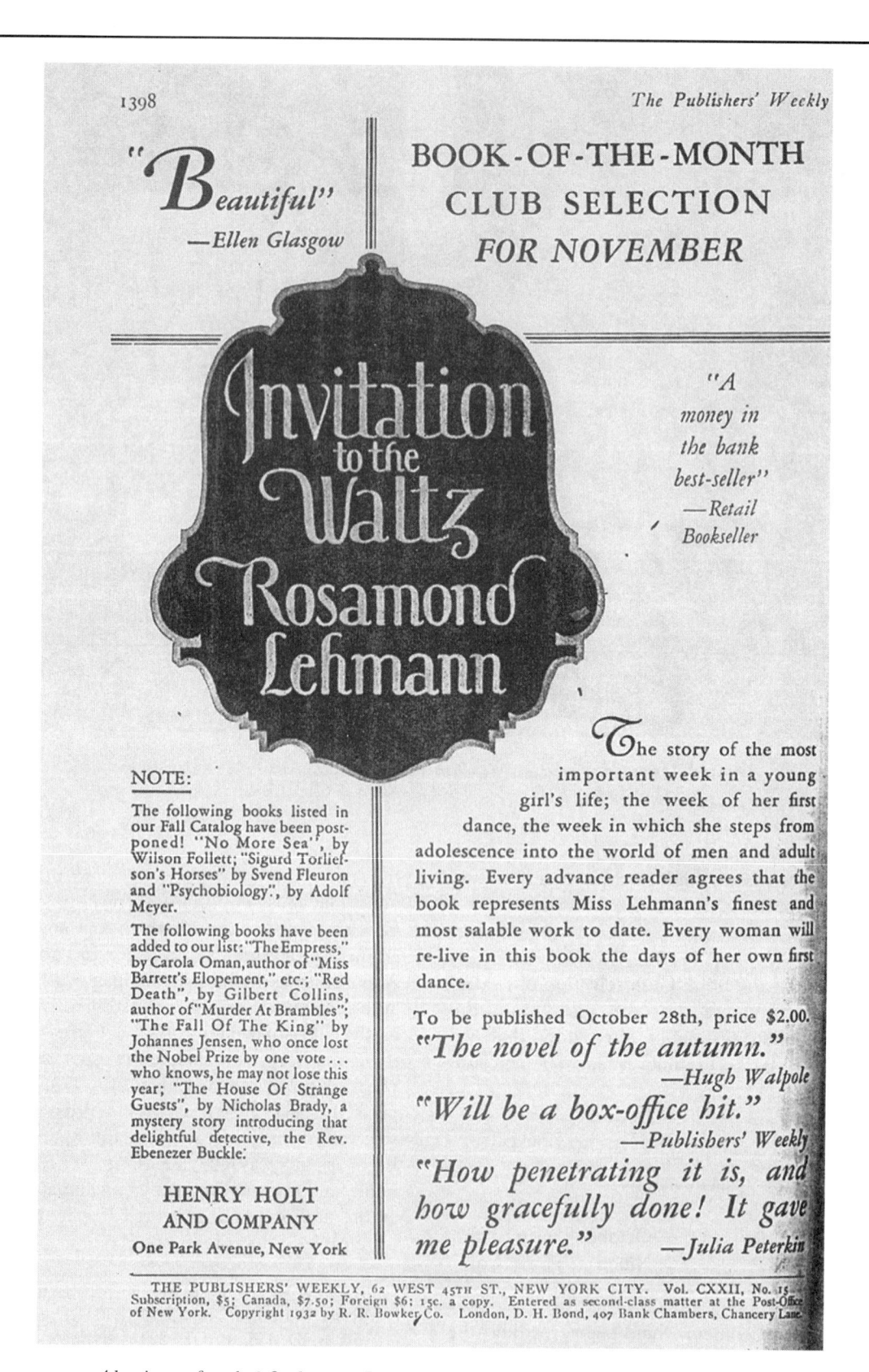

Advertisement from the 8 October 1932 Publishers' Weekly *for the British novelist's fourth book (Thomas Cooper Library, University of South Carolina)*

THE THEORY OF
THE THEATRE

AND OTHER PRINCIPLES OF DRAMATIC CRITICISM

Consolidated Edition Including
THE THEORY OF THE THEATRE
STUDIES IN STAGECRAFT
PROBLEMS OF THE PLAYWRIGHT
SEEN ON THE STAGE

BY
CLAYTON HAMILTON
WITH A FOREWORD BY
BURNS MANTLE

NEW YORK
HENRY HOLT AND COMPANY
1939

Title page for the theater study by the New York drama critic and playwright (Rutgers University Library)

printing of some 48,000 copies, and demands from subscribers still come to them. Our direct sales are now around 12,000 copies, and we shall probably have to make another printing soon (we have already made three). The success of the book has encouraged us to increase our advertising for it. We shall try to keep its merits before the public.

I am pleased to know that you like the special binding we made for you, and also our regular edition. We have received the corrections from Chatto, and have made the proper changes in the plates in time for the next printing.

The press notices of the book here have been uniformly good. It has been enthusiastically reviewed in most of the important journals, and, in many cases, by prominent people.

mis-spelling, and much of the point of the succeeding sentence is lost if the word is spelt correctly.

I hope you have made an auspicious start with the book, and that it will defy the slump with you. Over here it is doing splendidly, and the reviews are all that could be desired.

Yours sincerely,
Harold Raymond

When Thornton wrote Lehmann to tell her about the success of Invitation to the Waltz, *he addressed her by her married name, Mrs. Wogan Philipps.*

November 23, 1932

Dear Mrs. Philipps:

You will be pleased to know that *Invitation to the Waltz* is now on the "best seller" lists, and we expect its sale to hold up well for some time to come. The Book of the Month club has disposed of its entire

Christianity and the Religions of the World

BY
ALBERT SCHWEITZER
translated by JOHANNA POWERS

FOR the layman who wants a clear, simple account of the basic doctrines of other world religions, and their relation to Christianity this book will answer a real need. Dr. Schweitzer believes that Christianity is "the most profound religion, and at the same time the most profound philosophy." He contrasts its fundamental tenets with those of Brahmanism, Buddhism, and Hinduism.

Henry Holt and Company

Dust jacket for the 1939 Holt and Company edition of the German theologian's 1923 study Das Christentum und die Weltreligionen *(Bruccoli Clark Layman Archives)*

Advertisement for the 1939 autobiographical novel by the author of the fantasy novel that won the 1935 National Booksellers' Award, from the 7 October 1939 issue of Publishers' Weekly *(Thomas Cooper Library, University of South Carolina)*

We should like very much to have the additional photographs you mention. The clearer ones will undoubtedly serve best for the newspapers.

I shall be in London by January twenty-second, and shall look forward to seeing you while I am there.

Sincerely yours,
[R. H. Thornton]

John Ciardi

John Ciardi was to become a distinguished Holt and Company poet. He and Sloane participated for many years in the annual Bread Loaf Writers' Conference in Bread Loaf, Vermont. The following is an undated reader's report on the manuscript of Ciardi's first published collection, Homeward to America *(1940).*

These are the poems of a brilliant and precocious rather than a mature mind; precocious in that they are older than the years of the author might warrant, and lacking, perhaps, only the focus and solidity of maturity. This may sound like an adverse criticism at the beginning; it is not so intended. These are good poems for one of any age, but they are the work of an "old" boy rather than an adult. After all, Mr. Ciardi *is* young! He has youth's emotional intensity, he feels strongly and he reacts to the world around him. Sometimes he gropes and is not clear in expressing exactly what he feels, but he is aware and conscious of feeling, and that is good. If his premises are not always clear, at least his phrases and his technique are direct and sure. He has a freshness of image which is vivid and alive; one feels the sincerity behind his work. And he has the enthusiasm of an active and perceptive mind.

Some of these poems could be improved by condensation; their structure seems a bit loose, they ought to be tightened up. On the other hand, there are several admirably concise pieces, for example, that poem entitled "Anonymous", which is very fine. I don't quite like the line "beneath the purpling epiderm" which seems rather overloaded, but the concluding couplet is excellent.

"The hardy heart must come prepared
With more than love to travel long."

This is a fine instance of the use of suggestion and overtone, and Mr. Ciardi is good at turning such phrases.

There is a nice immediacy and warmth about his work; one feels that here is a poet who is really trying (to paraphrase his own poem "Continent's Edge") to find his America in his native world; to explore the longitudes and latitudes of his own mind. He remembers emotions, and translates those memories with simplicity and poignancy. (see "Letter to Those Who Grew up Together.")

The section "Nearly Rejected Poems" is the least good of the collection. I have the feeling that in these poems especially the emotion is not focused, and I find some of them obscure. Mr. Ciardi expresses himself in fine, capable and often beautiful lines, but sometimes I don't know what he means.

I detect some slight influence of T. S. Eliot and Archibald Macleish in this collection, but on the whole the idiom is the poet's own. These poems have personality. I think that Mr. Ciardi is probably one of the most promising young poets writing today. He is writing for the more intellectual audience, and writers especially will recognize how good he is. He needs self-criticism, he could take his own lines as warning:

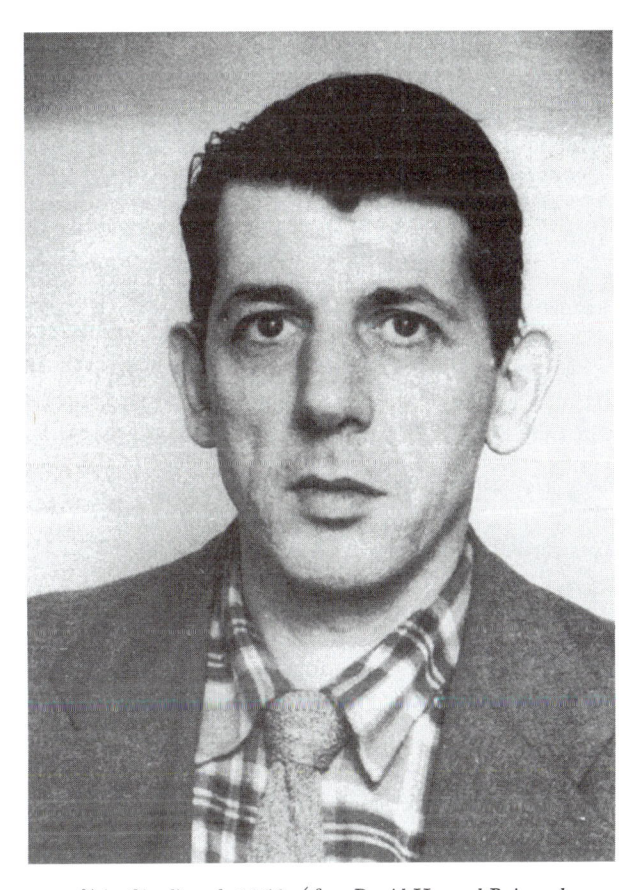

John Ciardi, early 1950s (from David Haward Bain and Mary Smyth Duffy, Whose Woods These Are, *1993; Thomas Cooper Library, University of South Carolina)*

"We have given our minds to reason in the night,
And were lost in too many causes, too many effects
And probabilities, till the mind sees but cannot choose..."

I hope he will guide his undoubted talent in the right direction. I hope he won't be swept up into the various schools and cults, or onto the bandwagon; I hope he will continue to say what he thinks and feels. He is a good poet now, and he has it in him, I believe, to be a very fine poet indeed.

Sara Henderson Hay

Poet, editor, and essayist Louis Untermeyer responded to Sloane's request for comments on Ciardi's first collection.

October 16, 1939

Dear Bill Sloane:

The Ciardi proofs are going back to you under separate cover–and here are my quick if incomplete reactions. If anything in the next paragraph can be used on the jacket, I will be perfectly willing–and a little surprised.

I wish there were another word for "promise." Promise is precisely what these poems by Ciardi have. They reveal the obvious influences, but this poet's taste is excellent, even in knowing what influences are best for him. But they show more than that; they show a spirit which is sensitive and yet tough, discriminating but by no means too delicate in its appetites. I should say that the best of Ciardi is this fusion, the paradox of sensibility and stubborn reality.

I rather think the book will have an effect on the reader as a whole rather than by virtue of any of its parts. But you asked me only for an opinion, not for a prognostication. Here, without further reservations, it is.

. . . .

Cordially,
Louis Untermeyer

Louis Untermeyer, 1929 (from Bain and Duffy, Whose Woods These Are, *1993; Thomas Cooper Library, University of South Carolina)*

The 1940s

WILLIAM SLOANE

Holt and Company was particularly successful during the World War II years thanks, in large part, to the efforts of William Sloane, who became head of the Holt trade department in 1939. Among Sloane's achievements was his successful promotion of poetry, including that of his friend John Ciardi. Sloane left Holt in 1946 to found his own publishing firm, William Sloane Associates, which was acquired by William Morrow in the early 1950s. He then became the director of the Rutgers University Press. Sloane was also the author of science-fiction novels and short stories.

May 2, 1940

Dear Bill Sloane,

Will you forgive my letter paper? Your letter deserves a soon answer, and to save my soul I can't find another unscrawled upon sheet of paper in these diggings. I hope no poems occur to me tonight, I'd have to write them on my cuff and my laundress would probably raise hell.

William Sloane (Photo by Blackstone)

Sloane on Editing

Sloane reflected on the role of the editor in a posthumously published guide to writing.

What is he and what does he do? He is a reader, perhaps the author's first real reader. The editor is a specialist about reading. His specialty is what is sufficiently general and common between a possible readership and what the author has to say. The tool he works with is himself. If the author cannot reach him, he can't reach the editor's readership either. That is the assumption. The editor is much more actively creative than the ordinary reader. He is not correcting themes or marking off for spelling. He is listening for the sound of people in what the author has submitted. He judges character by whether readers will recognize and believe. He judges dialogue by whether readers will hear it. And so on.

This does not mean literalism or realism of treatment. The editor knows that people also dream and sing and pray and hurt inside themselves and to themselves. He also knows that people will pretend, will make-believe, will go seek the hidden and not step on cracks because of their mother's backs, and invent dreamworlds, and play myriad games. He knows that the writer will find people to play his game if he makes the game a real game.

Editors also know that the people who are really readers want to read. They hunger to read. They will forgive a vast number of clumsinesses and scamped work of every sort if the author will delight them just enough to keep them able to continue.

My entire professional life has been spent as an editor, publisher, and writer, with teaching as its major public avocation. The professional editor and the teacher of writing are farther apart than is generally realized. The editor often works with accepted material or with accepted authors, and he works by definition with writers who have arrived—at least to the extent of a check or a publishing contract. The teacher works with beginners who have not yet reached the graduate world of the editor.

—*The Craft of Writing* (New York: Norton, 1979), pp. 22–23

Advertisement from the 10 August 1940 Saturday Review of Literature *for poetry volumes published by Holt and Company (Thomas Cooper Library, University of South Carolina)*

Advertisements for Holt and Company titles from a February 1940 issue of Publishers' Weekly
(Thomas Cooper Library, University of South Carolina)

I don't remember what I said in my last letter, but if it suggested that I expected to make money out of poetry, it didn't convey my intention. I'm afriad I haven't got the Millay sort of thing in my system. I don't say that scornfully, but regretfully. Shakespear [*sic*] was willing enough to give people what they wanted: whom am I not to wish I were able to?

Any inquiries of mine re sales have no cash register *double entendre*. I simply hate to think of myself as writing poetry in a vacuum. Pure poetry doesn't exist. It has to be read, and to be read it must reach people. With 125,000,000 people in the US by the last census, 500 copies would leave me 1/300,000 of an American poet more or less—1/250,000 to be exact. That's why I was delighted to have the book priced at $1.50. I like the idea of thin books at low prices. If I had my way I'd publish ten poems at a time for 50 cents per vol. A lot of people would risk 50 cents who won't risk $1.50 or $2.00, which no book of poems is really worth when one can buy a complete Shakespeare for $1.00 or less.

But as a matter of fact I have probably made to date more money on a first volume that I had a right to hope for. $1200 plus $100 from Holt's plus about $50 from magazines plus a job I never would have had without the book. Also I haven't a damn cent of it left, but it was fun while it lasted. Or should I say while it lasts.

Anyhow I'm beginning to see that it's close to the end. This job is up in August, and I'm going to take my life in my hands and go back to Boston jobless but brave. I still want to do a novel and maybe with time it will come. For the present I'm playing with fairly bad short stories. When I think I've tamed the cubs I'll be ready to be mangled by the mamma tiger.

But I suspect this chatter is taking more of your time than it deserves. Besides this sheet is giving out and there just ain't no more. All best and remember me to Madison.

Yrs.
John

* * *

Writer Charles G. Finney had published two novels, The Circus of Dr. Lao *(Viking, 1935) and* Unholy City *(Vanguard, 1937), before Holt and Company brought out his next book,* Past the End of the Pavement, *in 1939.*

May 3, 1940

Dear Mr. Finney:

I'm glad that our minute check on your book brought you a certain modest gratification. I have been looking over the sales thus far this year, and they have amounted to 165 copies. Unfortunately, we have had returns from booksellers amounting to 156 copies, so the net is pretty small. Nevertheless, the returns are now all in, and the novel has not yet ceased to sell in a slow but persistent way which leads me to believe that not all the book readers of America are dolts, but just about 99.8% of them. I do not think that I have ever been more disappointed in what a publisher could do for a good book than in the case of PAST THE END OF THE PAVEMENT. I still simply can't understand why it didn't sell five times what it did. Good reviews, lots of publicity, special promotion, advertising, special push from some reviewers like Lewis Gannett, and still the public would not believe that they ought to read it. Well, in this case it really is their loss, as well as yours and ours.

Well, I have reread MANHUNT, and our sales manager has read it, and my associate editor here has read it, and my wife, who is a shrewd judge, has read it, and we are stumped. The book is simply not publishable in its present form. It's got a fatal structural flaw which you've heard all about from John Farrar, and its loaded with language which would be all too true to life for the ordinary reader, and it isn't either fish, flesh, fowl, nor good red herring as far as the detective story market goes. And it's the kind of humor that I found out, in the case of Alan LeMay's BUG EYE, simply cannot be introduced to a profitably large audience.

Your notion that there is no reason to conform to the standard literary types is one that I personally believe in heartily. But I think perhaps that charter of liberty should not be attempted in a field where the traditional canons are so strict. Anyhow, I'll have to send the book back to you and admit I'm licked on it.

For some time I've had it in mind to send you some of our current books of which we are moderately proud. The first is Oscar Ameringer's IF YOU DON'T WEAKEN, and I am also sending along Mark Van Doren's last novel, and a detective story by our Mr. Healy, who is our sales manager and who thought PAST THE END OF THE PAVEMENT was a superb book. As a matter of fact, we all did, and we all curse when we look at the figures.

The new book is something for which I shall certainly wait with eagerness. Do you expect it will be done by the end of the summer? It would be a good thing if it could come out in the spring of 1941. . . .

Incidentally, THE ARK OF THE DESERT is an inspired title.

I take it that this new book is different from FUGUE, the opus about which you wrote me not so long ago, though longer than I like to recall. . . .

Eventually, I am convinced, you will want to do a book about the next stage of one or both of the Farrier boys. It will be a hard thing to bring off, but if you could do it, there is undoubtedly a superb book there.

Take care of yourself,
MANAGER, TRADE DEPARTMENT
[William Sloane]

THE
COLLECTED
POEMS OF
A. E. HOUSMAN

New York
HENRY HOLT AND COMPANY

Title page for the posthumously published 1940 edition of poems by the author of A Shropshire Lad *(1896) (Rutgers University Library)*

May 14, 1940

Dear Mr. Sloane:

Sorry no end to have delayed so long in acknowledging the books you sent and also your last letter. I don't blame Holt's a bit for being proud of these three particular volumes. WINDLESS CABINS I have just finished.... I enjoyed it immensely, and I don't wonder it went through three printings the first month. The only trouble is—and this hardly is a criticism—there is such little good poetry being published now, and so cockeyed many novels, and Van Doren is such a grand poet (even the Pulitzer judges seem to have caught on) that another novel of his seems just that much less poetry....

I imagine you intend in MR. SANDEMAN LOSES HIS LIFE to hint to me how a good detective yarn *should* be done, as against MANHUNT which, I gather, is all that one *shouldn't* be. Well, you are right; MANHUNT aint no classic of form and developement. Send the brute back and I'll file it away for my posterity to shudder at.

....

And so the literary work goes on, and will continue, I hope, till the parachutists land in Tucson and cut the power lines from Boulder dam. Incidentally, Tucson would be a hell of a place to dig bombproof shelters because the caliche is so tough it has to be dynamited. On the other hand, the cactus forests are poor places wherein to maneuver a field army and the mountains should act as natural tank barriers. Wouldn't it be funny if the Middlewest proved to be the safest place of all; and think how chagrined the Oakies would be at having migrated?

Dubiously,
Charles G. Finney

May 20, 1940

Dear Mr. Finney:

Your grand letter of May 14 has pleased all of us enormously. I may as well tell you that your letters are read around the office by the rest of the people here because when they know I have heard from you and don't show the letter I get accused of holding out. Anyhow it is grand you liked the Van Doren as much as you did. I feel myself that the next novel, when he writes it, is likely to prove a really remarkable piece of work. This one almost came off into a major volume, but not quite. It is a little special for that.

I meant nothing whatever about MR. SANDEMAN LOSES HIS LIFE. That was simply a courtesy volume and it happened to be written by our sales manager. I thought you might like to have a sample of the gent who is selling your books for you, and I also thought you might enjoy the humor. He enjoys yours.

I will look forward to reading FUGUE and to looking at the surrealist photos. If THE ARK OF THE DESERT is as nearly done as you say it is, which of these two numbers are you more interested in having published next? It sounds as if the second item would be easier to sell, if I may inject a commercial note at this point.

Your crack about the parachutists in Tucson is only half funny. Well as I remember the last war, I am still prejudiced about this one. Why the Germans should be so hell bent to conquer this particular world is beyon[d] me. What would they do with it after they got it?

Yours,
[William Sloane]
MANAGER, TRADE DEPARTMENT

Holt and Company employee Norman Hood sent Sloane a note about an incomplete Finney manuscript titled "The Magician from Manchuria." A shorthand note appearing underneath the text of the memo may be approximately translated, "No comment on this at all. Put in safe." A novel by Finney titled The Magician out of Manchuria *was published in England by Panther Books in 1968, suggesting that he held on to the manuscript that Holt rejected in 1942.*

10/19/42

That this book offers serious problems seems to me a gross understatement. It is good fun and has a flavor all its own, but I do not see from this present fragment how it could possibly be a profitable publishing venture. Perhaps you know more of Finney's plans. If so, I would like to hear about them.

* * *

Sloane sent the following figures to Meredith Wood of the Book-of-the-Month Club regarding Robert Trumbull's The Raft *(1942) when the book was chosen as a club selection.*

June 16, 1942

Dear Merry:

Here is our breakdown of the costs on the manufacture of THE RAFT:

Plates

    Composition $235.60
    Electros   155.40

	Reproduction rights of pictures	25.00	
	Line cut	8.45	
	Editorial	63.68	
	Plates total		$488.13

Binding dies   35.00

Jacket

	Artist	75.00	
	Wrapper plates	78.87	
	Jacket total		153.87
	TOTAL		$677.00

Our manufacturing man's estimate of the life of the plates is 350,000 impressions.

I hope this is the information that you require. If there is anything else, be sure to let me know.

                All best,
                [William Sloane]

* * *

A November 1942 Holt and Company shareholders' report noted the accomplishments of the trade department under Sloane's management.

To the Owners of Class "A" Stock of
HENRY HOLT AND COMPANY, INCORPORATED
REPORT OF TRADE DEPARTMENT

Its Trade Department (the department which produces novels, juveniles, books of poetry, and non-fiction titles for distribution through bookstores) has been an integral part of Henry Holt and Company throughout the more than three quarters of a century of the Company's existence. During that long period of time, the department's fortunes have varied considerably.

A successful trade department is a valuable component of the modern publishing house. Besides its direct contribution to the firm's income, a trade department can be a distinct asset to the varied activities of the company as a whole. Our earlier letters to you have mentioned the seasonal nature of sales of books to schools and colleges. The issuance of trade titles is not geared to the buying pattern of the school year, and there is no season of the year when a going concern in the trade field may not bring in a balancing revenue. Furthermore, authors of textbooks often prefer to be published by a house with an effective trade department. Certainly the general public's estimate of any publishing house is apt to be based largely on the company's reputation in the field of general, or trade, books rather than of educational books.

Advertisement for the third novel by Davis Dresser (who wrote under several pseudonyms) to feature the hard-boiled detective Mike Shayne, from the 20 July 1940 issue of Publishers' Weekly *(Thomas Cooper Library, University of South Carolina)*

But trade publishing is not wholly dissociated from educational publishing. Many books which are important in one field may have a large sale in another as well, and sometimes a book can be a best-seller simultaneously in more than one department. For example, our A MATHEMATICS REFRESHER by Alfred Hooper, which is currently appearing on most trade best-seller lists, is also enjoying a conspicuously fine sale in high schools and colleges.

Four years ago a more vigorous policy was inaugurated in our trade department which was placed under the management of William Sloane. His background included two years at Longman's,

Green and Company; five years as manager of a play-publishing concern in New York; and some time as associate editor at Farrar and Rinehart. Besides, he had done a good deal of book reviewing, ghost-writing, editorial free-lancing, and had written two successful novels.

During Mr. Sloane's first three years with us, he laid down the groundwork for a stronger Trade Department. Among the major book projects which he has initiated with us are LOOK TO THE MOUNTAIN by Le Grand Cannon, Jr., (the November selection of the Book-of-the-Month of which already 18,000 copies have been sold to bookstores and 287,000 copies printed for Book-Club subscribers); another, AMBASSADORS IN WHITE; and still others, the substantial and long-lived biographies of musicians, artists, and scientists for boys and girls. For several years our back-list sales tended to decline, as they are apt to in periods of crisis, so that the results of the new editorial policy, in terms of dollar volume, were not immediately apparent. But your management, watching the steady rise in the average sale of new trade titles, realized that sound progress was being made.

A nucleus of first-rate personnel was also being assembled. Advertising, publicity and promotion were put into the capable hands of Norman Hood, who had had five years of trade experience with the F. A. Stokes Company, and who had been that company's advertising manager at the time of its sale. When we lost Eugene Healy, our Sales Manager from 1939 to 1941, to the Army, his place was taken by Keith Jennison, whose background included a sales managership with A. S. Barnes and Company, and who had been with Harcourt, Brace and Company, in charge of New York City sales, for a number of years. We were fortunate, also, in having already on the staff an excellent manufacturer, Leonard W. Blizard, who is not only a fine designer in the sound tradition of bookmaking craftsmanship, but who also understands how often the profit of trade publishing depends upon conservative manufacturing specifications. Our trade books are frequently selected for commendation by the American Institute of Graphic Arts and by the Trade Book Clinic, and booksellers tell us that they are among the most attractive, as merchandise, of any offered to them.

With Mr. Sloane, this staff created a summer and fall list of books for 1942 which is the envy of our competitors in the trade field. It includes two selections of the Book of the-Month Club—THE RAFT, which has had a distribution of 20,000 to the general public and 238,000 to the Book-Club subscribers, and LOOK TO THE MOUNTAIN. It also includes the leading national best-seller in the non-fiction field, SEE HERE, PRIVATE HARGROVE (sales 150,000 copies so far), and A MATHEMATICS

> **Parenting**
>
> *Dr. Benjamin Spock was not the first author of books on child care. In 1940 Holt and Company published* Parents Can Learn, *by Helen Ellwanger Hanford. It was reviewed in the December issue of* The Atlantic *that year.*
>
> The immense number of books designed to lead stumbling parental feet along the dangerous path of parenthood are apt to recall the conversation between the frightened young mother whose baby had a chest cold and the amiable family doctor who was attending the patient. "But, Dr. Russell," she wailed, "why can't I rub camphor on his chest? Doesn't it do any good?" "Yes," said the doctor, "some. It relieves the mother's mind."
>
> Mrs. Hanford, however, does considerably better than that. Much of what she says in *Parents Can Learn*—particularly in the first few chapters, which deal with what might be called the pre-parent period—contains the hard sustaining core of good common sense. Her style is easy and humorous. She holds out hope, even to the parents of adolescents, of better times to come. She does not allow herself to use over-technical psychological terms. She conveys to the reader the warm and comforting assurance that the specific Jane or John who is causing two perfectly good adults to lie awake nights with anxiety is neither a unique case nor destined for the juvenile courts. A book which any woman in any one of the Seven Ages from expectant mother to grandmother of many can read with pleasure and profit.
>
> —*Atlantic* (December 1940)

REFRESHER, which stands high on most non-fiction best-seller lists, and has sold over 34,000 copies. In November we expect to have four volumes appearing simultaneously on national best-seller lists, a publishing feat which is seldom achieved by any publishing house, even those which issue several times the number of titles annually which we do.

These nation-wide successes are only a part of the solid publishing accomplishment which has been the result of several years of realistic trade planning. The *average* first-year sale of all new trade titles, except best-sellers, has been climbing steadily throughout the past three difficult years. It now stands at three times the figure which obtained in 1938. The department has balanced books-for-the-moment against books-for-permanence. As a result the average active sales-life of the list as a whole has continuously lengthened. This is a sure sign of a healthy publishing program, since it means that the books published each year add to the sales volume not only for that year but also during subsequent years.

The Company feels that the present program of the Trade Department is fully consonant with present-day policies of national interest. Our books are now manufactured on a strict wartime conservation basis. No Government agency has issued formal approval of any list of books, or of how they must be made, but the Holt lists are among the very best in the country from the standpoint of national morale and the war effort, as well as of conservation of materials.

Our recent gains have been accomplished without undue increase in the department's annual expenses. They will be consolidated by a continuation of the basic policies now in force, and, while we do not rely upon an unbroken continuation of our present unusual success, we are confident that our Trade Department is firmly established with authors, with agents, and with booksellers. The future should hold no more difficulties for this Company in the trade field than for any of our competitors.

While best-sellers are the more profitable and dramatic form of trade publishing success, the department is also proud of the recognition it has won in others ways. Holt trade books have won a Pulitzer Prize (Mark Van Doren's COLLECTED POEMS) and a National Booksellers' Award (Perry Burgess' WHO WALK ALONE). Several of our recent juveniles, including LAST SEMESTER, PACO GOES TO THE FAIR, HOW THINGS WORK, and HIGH HURDLES, have been selections of the Junior Literary Guild. Three of our titles already, in 1942, have been sold to major motion picture producers. *Parents' Magazine* awarded Helen Ellwanger Hanford's PARENTS CAN LEARN an Honorable Mention in its annual awards for excellent publishing in the field of parent-child relationships. Holt juveniles won two Honorable Mentions and one First Prize in recent *Herald-Tribune* Spring Book Festivals (STREET OF SHIPS, THAT MARIO, and FINLANDIA).

The department has not been forgetful of the old and valuable tradition of distinguished publishing which has been a part of the Henry Holt hallmark for a long time. Robert Frost's latest book of poems, A WITNESS TREE, published this year, has had a sale of over 11,000 copies already, thereby exceeding the record of any of his comparable recent volumes. THE COLLECTED POEMS OF A. E. HOUSMAN is another distinguished publishing venture which has been notably successful. It is part of our present trade policy to continue the publication of the kind of book which has earned the company so much prestige in past years.

In terms of practical results for the Company's stockholders, the work of the Trade Department since 1939 has increased its annual volume of sales by approximately 150%, and a branch of the business which for several years has barely paid its way has been made profitable.

A dividend of $1.80 per share, has been declared payable on December 8th to the holders of record of the Company's Class A stock at the close of business on November 18, 1942.

A. K. SHIELDS, *Secretary*
New York, N. Y.
November 10, 1942

BY ORDER OF THE BOARD OF DIRECTORS

* * *

Poet, editor, and essayist Louis Untermeyer, a good friend of Robert Frost, had close ties with Holt and Company and was consulted about a poetry collection submitted by Stanley Kunitz. Holt published Kunitz's Passport to the War, *his second book, in 1944.*

May 7, 1943

Dear Louis:

We have a volume of poetry in here by Stanley Kunitz, who is now in the Army. We all think well of it and are seriously considering adding it to our list for spring 1944. Bill [Sloane] and I were wondering whether you would take a look at it for us, and give us your judgement of the worth of the man and of this collection. . . .

Yours ever,
Helen K. Taylor
Trade Promotion and Advertising

May 8, 1943

Dear Helen,

I've seen a few poems by Stanley Kunitz, and to be frank, I have not been bowled over. They seemed adequate and even fluent, but they lacked that touch of originality which makes me stop, look, and listen. Nevertheless, I have seen only a few of Kunitz's poems, and it may well be that a volume may make a different impression. Send it along, and I'll look at it.

. . . .

Sincerely,
Louis U.

* * *

Advertisement from the 1 March 1941 Publishers' Weekly
(Thomas Cooper Library, University of South Carolina)

Advertisement from the 11 March 1944 Saturday Review of Literature *for the second Holt and Company publication by the radio dramatist (Thomas Cooper Library, University of South Carolina)*

In 1945 The Saturday Review *carried a full-page ad from Holt and Company touting a five-year-old book,* The Advance of the Fungi, *by E. C. Large.*

In defense of the beets and the broccoli. . . .

Now that the frost is out of the ground and we have got the fertilizer spaded into our garden patch—and even some of the seeds planted—we begin to think about a book that we published five years ago. It's something of a habit with us to reread it once a year at about this season because it keeps us from expecting too much from the seeds and the good earth in general. . . .

The book is E. C. Large's volume about man's unrelenting battle with all the diseases which attack his major food crops. The author gave it the unprepossessing title of THE ADVANCE OF THE FUNGI, a title that has helped to keep the book from reaching the audience that, in our opinion, it has always deserved. But we are no longer concerned about that because we imported it in sheets from Great Britain; there are only about 300 copies left, and when those are sold there will probably never be any more.

Large is one of the most brilliant of the younger English writers. He appeared first in this country as the author of a genuinely exciting first novel, SUGAR IN THE AIR, and a second, ASLEEP IN THE AFTERNOON. When he published this latter book we knew that he was working on a writing project which had occupied him, off and on, for most of his writing lifetime and an even larger proportion of his career as a research scientist. THE ADVANCE OF THE FUNGI turned out to be it, and when the first proofs reached us we knew at once two things about the book—the first that it would never have a large sale, the second that it was the kind of book that every publisher worth his salt would like to have on his list.

The multitudinous, minute, and baffling blights which attack the plants we hope to eat are among the most deadly enemies of mankind. They have changed the course of history many times in the past—the potato murrain in Ireland helped to populate the United States; phylloxera of the French grape vines shook the whole economy of France to its bottom and its effects were felt in Greece and California; wheat rusts affected the whole life of the middle ages; and the Leaf Disease, which put an end to coffee-growing in Ceylon, smashed the Oriental Bank and shifted the center of coffee production to Brazil.

At the very time THE ADVANCE OF THE FUNGI was being printed, the New York Times printed a news item from Berlin in which the British were accused of dropping hordes of Colorado beetles on the German potato crop. What had actually happened was that the German farmers were no longer able to get the chemical sprays which are necessary to make any potato crop in Europe possible.

The book ends with chapters on Fungi and the Great War, New Sprays for Old, and Towards Immunity. Large talks as many a scientist has, somewhat brusquely, against "the demented Thirties" when the "potato industry was not at all sure that it wanted blight-proof potatoes," and he suggests that after September 3, 1939, there might be a change in agricultural policy which would increase food production instead of attempting to restrict it.

Reading facts and seeing illustrations is of course educational, but what charms us about this book is the unique British approach. Not only is the research here, but so is the delicate appreciation of the old drawings and new microphotographs; here is the long view and the quiet humor.

In 1940, Large was in the service of his government, hoping to write when time allowed. We have not heard from him since, but we are hoping he will tell us more of plant blights when the retreating World Blight has been conquered completely. Meantime, we are oiling up the pressure sprayer and laying in the usual poundage of Bordeaux mixture. Advance fungi! We will give you a tussle for the beets and the broccoli. . . .

—Saturday Review (7 March 1945): 6

WORLD WAR II

Impact of the War on the Publishing World

Holt and Company editor Gilbert Loveland, a World War I pilot and air-travel advocate, wrote to New York mayor Fiorello H. La Guardia regarding training manuals for flight mechanics.

July 5, 1940

Dear Mayor LaGuardia:

In the past, my Company has not been very active in the field of vocational publishing; but in the present emergency we want to help all we can to implement, by the production of needed books, the new programmes that will gear vocational education to national defense.

So far, all we have done is to arrange the publication of two or three aircraft-training manuals by Clarence Chamberlin who, as you know, has his own school in the old Fokker plant at Bendix, N. J. Col. Chamberlin's engineers and mechanics have worked out, under his direction, a fine series of lessons for mechanics—whether service mechanics on engines or aircraft, or factory mechanics on engines or aircraft. But he puts his young men through the course in three months or less, and we think his materials need to be recast considerably to make them of the widest usefulness in the high schools and colleges where the expanded courses will be given. So we are seeking all the advice we can get to increase the practicality of these materials. As soon as Mr. Elliott V. Noska, principal of your Manhattan High School for the Aviation Trades, returns to the City, we hope to have a conference with him.

Do you wish to nominate another adviser or two for this job? I know how busy you are. But you are knowledgeable in this field of aircraft training, and are keenly interested in it, and I'd rather not go too far with this project without such advice or advisers as you can suggest. If you have any advice for us, won't you ask one of your staff to relay it to me?

With every good wish, I am
      Faithfully yours,
      [Gilbert Loveland]

* * *

July 9, 1940.

Dear Mr. Loveland:

I have your letter of July 5th, 1940. I agree with you that text books on aviation mechanics should be very carefully compiled....

If you have a good staff on the job and desire the reaction of practical men as to their own shop requirements, I would suggest Mr. O. M. Mosier of the American Airways and also Casey Jones who himself runs a very reputable and efficient school in Newark. Dr. Noska would be very helpful for he has developed an excellent high school and takes a very great interest in it. I would also suggest that you get in touch with the Curtiss Wright people and their engineers. Perhaps we are thinking about different things. What I have in mind is a real useful, accurate text book on the subject and not just popular reading, a sort of a bound correspondence school hodge podge.

      Very truly yours,
      F. H. La Guardia
      Mayor.

* * *

Sloane brought considerable success to Holt and Company with World War II–related books. Four such titles were Marion Hargrove's See Here, Private Hargrove *(1942), the* Publishers' Weekly *best-selling nonfiction book of 1942; Robert Trumbull's* The Raft *(1942); war journalist Ernie Pyle's* Here Is Your War *(1943); and cartoonist Bill Mauldin's* Up Front *(1945). Of these authors, Hargrove had the most extensive–and humorous–correspondence with Sloane.*

May 5, 1942

Dear Bill:

I am returning the proofs as a shaken and sobered man. I shall live long before I see anything else so merciless as the sight of them. They have all the irrevocable quality of the printed without its dignity and glamour. They're just naked.

I have tried to keep corrections to a minimum, but in three places, changes were necessary. Private Fink had to be changed, because he has been shanghaied as far as his gloating battery commander could manage and he would sue the bejesus out of me if he heard the crackle of currency. The sketch could as easily fit Sher and actually helps his characterization, so I made it Sher. The other two corrections in names call for a little more mechanical adjustment than the Fink-to-Sher, but all have been kept down as much as possible.

I am quite anxious about two things, Bill, and I wish you'd make sure of them yourself. They are the credit notice for The Charlotte News and the dedication, "For Michaele Fallon." I should also like to ask another boon. If you can manage it, may we have a little line of three-point type or something like that, under the jacket picture, crediting the picture to Bushemi? It would tickle the hell out of the lad.

Bushemi, by the way, is borrowing money again and is in real danger of being ousted from the Union. How long do I have to wait before he gets whatever you owe him and I can change the set-up. Please don't pay him without letting me know in advance, so I may have the first pounce at him.

Mademoiselle is calling the June article "The Life and Times of Private Jeep," which indicates that some mastermind is hidden away over there whose fiery genius should be turned to editing Sunday school weeklies. The New York Times has sent the second USO article back for certain revisions which they don't quite make clear, so that piece is postponed until May 16.

There was one thing else I wanted to request, which almost slipped my mind. Did you ever write excuses for the boys who skipped classes or cut whole days when you were in grammar school? Good. Well, here's the deal. I have a small sockful of money in my mattress and it is shrieking for active duty, as is found in three-day visits to New York, New York. I had thought of the last week of May, but Michaele plans to be in Canada then, so I would have to make it late in the week of May 10, early in the week of May 17, or more probably early in the first or second week of June.

The General wants me to take Duncan to New York with me the next time I go, so he won't be hard to crack for a three-day pass. If the manager of the

Dust jacket for the 1942 account of army life that was the number-one nonfiction title in the Publishers' Weekly *best-seller list for that year (Bruccoli Clark Layman Archives)*

trade department of Henry Holt & Co., Inc., were to write an informal little note to Corporal Hargrove—saying that certain conferences were necessary and asking that I try to get permission to come up for two or three days, even if I had to take a furlough—Corporal Hargrove could go running upstairs, all out of breath, and get a three-day pass just like that.

Will you do that much for me, Willyum? There are a couple of conferences I have to make with Michaele, after which I could give you the exact date these vital conferences should fall upon. Having acquired the pass and reached New York, I would not hang around the office and bother the boys, except maybe to mooch two drinks from Keith, one from Norm, and one from you.

Shower your blessings from your ivory tower, McGee. I will with you anon.

Marion

May 8, 1942

Dear Marion:

Well, under separate cover I am mailing you that letter for which you ask, and may the military police of Heaven have mercy on my soul when it gets there. See here, Corporal Hargrove, are you asking me to tamper with the discipline of the whole United States Army? How do you think that makes me feel? As a matter of fact, it makes me feel fine.

Personally I don't know what you mean by the dignity and glamour of the printed word. When you have spent a decade and a half in the book business you hope there is some dignity to the printed word, but you have begun to suspect that there is not. But if there is, I think your book has as much of it as is necessary.

Running rapidly over the points in your release of May 5, the changes you have made are going to be all right with us. If they are inexpensive it doesn't matter, and if they are expensive, I am sorry that your contract shows that you will get soaked for some of the changes yourself. But don't worry about it. You will be well under the maximum on that score.

I believe that both the credit notice to the Charlotte News and the dedication to Michelle Fallon are firmly in hand, but I will personally check on them at the proper point in the book's progress.

Of course we will credit Bushemi's picture to him. We almost always do that anyway. Please tell him that our consciences are very guilty about the check, which he should have received before now. It will go out *muy pronto*.

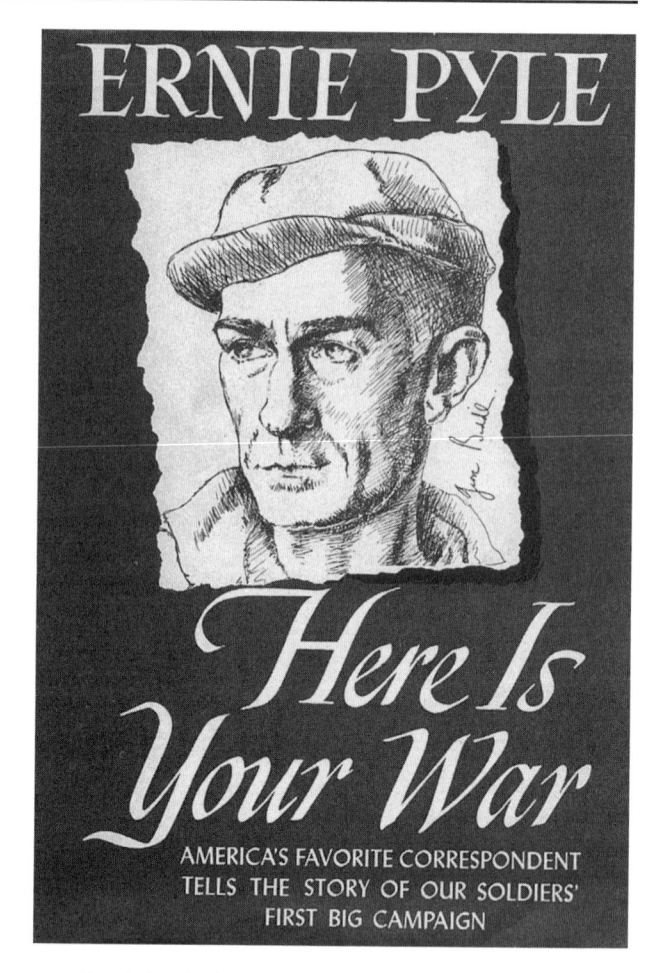

Dust jacket for the 1943 collection of war correspondence that was the ninth-best-selling nonfiction book of that year (courtesy of The Lilly Library, Indiana University)

Your report on Mademoiselle and the New York Times is interesting. Out upon you, Hargrove. What a fellow thou art. (Shakespeare.) You have made more of a career of writing from the army than any other private since history began, as far as I know. I do hope that these literary endeavors won't keep you from defending me and my whole family.

Last night was the annual banquet of the Booksellers' Association, so your remarks about mooching drinks come at an unfortunate time. However, by the time you get here my naturally rugged system will have thrown off the effects of last night and I shall be ready to be mooched upon—ready and willing.

All best,
[William Sloane]

* * *

With the wartime increase in the demand for metal, Sloane was compelled to write novelist Finney advising him that the printing plates for one of his books were scheduled to be melted down.

July 21, 1942

Dear Mr. Finney:

We are being asked these days to reduce the amount of plate metal which we are holding and help increase the turnover in what has come to be a valuable war resource. For that reason we are planning to melt down the plates of such of our books as will probably not require re-printing within the next two or three years. Your PAST THE END OF THE PAVEMENT is on this list.

If you do not care to have us melt down these plates, you can buy them from us for $6.00 plus the cost of boxing and transportation. Unless we hear from you shortly, we shall assume that we have your consent to this operation, much as we regret having to do so.

Yours,
[William Sloane]
HENRY HOLT AND COMPANY
Manager, Trade Department

P.S. Normally we should not be melting plates on this book, but we do have 309 copies on hand so it will continue in print for a good long time. Meanwhile, the government needs the metal.

July 27, 1942

Dear William:

Aye, melt those strategic PAVEMENT plates down! Who am I to withhold the foetal stuff of bullets? And after it is done, I can sleep better of nights, too, for then when the FBI comes around and points an accusing finger and asks: "What are you doing to help pommel Rommel, skin the Finns, slap the Japs, bop the Wops, and console the Communists?", I can always reply that I have destroyed my vanities and burnt my books. And then they will have to admit that where other men merely give their lives, Finney gives his soul.

Seriously, though, before you ship those poor plates off, sprinkle holy water on them and whisper reverently, "C'est le guerre."

Always
Charles G. Finney

In the fall of 1942 Bristol wrote the War Production Board asking for leniency in the matter of melting down printing plates.

October 5, 1942

Dear Sirs:

This company has melted or ordered melted between 68 and 70 tons of electrotype plates. It still has 7 sets of plates totalling approximately 2½ tons of metal which it requests permission to retain for six months more even though there is at present no "assured future use" for them. The sales of these 7 books has *[sic]* been very irregular ranging up and down from one year to another in amounts from 200 to 900 approximately. It is still too soon to be sure of 1942 sales but we believe that this will be one of the big years. If that turns out to be the fact, we shall reprint promptly. If the sales are small we shall, of course, order the plates melted. If the plates are melted now and the sales turn out to be large, we shall feel that the melting has worked an exceptional hardship upon us.

Yours truly,
Herbert Bristol
HENRY HOLT AND COMPANY, INC.

* * *

Sloane wrote Chester Kerr, book-section chief of the Office for Emergency Management, about an upcoming Holt and Company publication that he felt might attract the notice of the Office of War Information (OWI), a division of the Office for Emergency Management established on 13 June 1942. The book, Kwok Ying Fung's China, *was published in 1943.*

September 2, 1942

Dear Chester:

A very superb manuscript, including both text and pictures, has come in from a Mr. Kwok Ying Fung, a Chinese who runs a restaurant here in town and who is one of the officials of the China Benevolent Society. The book contains eighty odd magnificent photographs of China old and new and a really original running commentary of text. We are almost certainly going to contract for this book and publish it at the earliest possible moment. I assume that the OWI will feel as we do that such a book can have only a valuable propaganda effect toward the war effort.

. . . .

We are having a notable success with SEE HERE, PRIVATE HARGROVE. It has been sold to the motion pictures, will be the book feature in the October issue of the *Reader's Digest,* will run shortly as a feature in *Life Magazine,* and has just gone into a fifth printing of ten thousand copies. . . .

All best,
[William Sloane]
Manager, Trade Department

* * *

First page of Holt and Company report on paper use for 1942 and 1943 filed with the War Production Board (Princeton University Library)

Second page of Holt and Company paper-use report for 1942 and 1943 (Princeton University Library)

Publishers' Weekly editor Frederic G. Melcher periodically canvassed publishers to see how they were coping with wartime demands and restrictions. Holt and Company production head B. L. Stratton sent Melcher the following response.

March 25, 1943

Dear Mr. Melcher:

In answering your questions in regard to paper curtailment it seems easier to retype your questions along with our answers. I hope you will find them in a convenient form and satisfactory for your purpose.

1. In reprinting with the required 10% less weight
    a. By using lighter basic weights? *Yes*
    b. By lessening the margins? *Occasionally*
2. In Planning [*sic*] new titles
    a. By using lighter basic weights? *Yes*
    b. By planning more words to the page? *Yes*
    [c. crossed out on original form]
    d. Will you make fewer books but keep the old standards? *No*
    e. Shift paper from one department to another? *Yes*
3. Does the curtailment affect different classes of books differently and how? *No*

Very truly yours,
[B. L. Stratton]
HENRY HOLT AND COMPANY
Manager, Production Department

***

Bristol wrote the War Production Board in the summer of 1943 seeking approval for the purchase of an additional bookkeeping machine to handle the increased business volume arising from textbook orders placed largely by the armed services.

June 23, 1943

Gentlemen:

Because of our greatly increased volume of business in the past one and one half years, and because of the ever-increasing lack of man and woman power, we find ourselves greatly handicapped in our accounting department, and find no way of relieving the situation except by the purchase of an additional bookkeeping machine.

....

This volume of business for an article selling at a high price might not mean much of an increase in office work, but our business is school and college books and many, many entries are for the sale of a single book.

....

Since we have only one machine, we have attempted to hire an additional operator for a second shift, but have found this impossible as we cannot find girls who are willing to go home through the streets since the dim-out at night. The woman-power shortage is critical, as you know.

We are attaching hereto the two front pages of our weekly sales bulletin sent to our representatives, and this will give you an idea of the amount of our college book sales only for Army and Navy use.

We have orders from the United States Armed Forces Institute which, up to now, total 350,000 copies of our Dull's MODERN PHYSICS. All of this increases terrifically the amount of items to be posted, and we therefore believe that our need for an additional machine is a real and vital one.

We hope you will see your way clear to approve our purchase of this machine.

Yours very truly,
[Herbert Bristol]

***

One of the most successful ventures of the Council on Books in Wartime was the creation of the Armed Services Editions, specially printed and bound editions of a wide variety of titles sent to, and circulated among, soldiers abroad. Sloane was an original member of the council's advisory committee, which was responsible for selecting titles in the series. By the end of the war, it was estimated that 3,636,074 individual volumes had been shipped. Holt and Company titles published as Armed Services Editions included Frost's Come In *(1943); Finney's 1939 novel* Past the End of the Pavement *(1944); George R. Stewart Jr.'s* Ordeal by Hunger: The Story of the Donner Party *(1944), first published by Holt in 1936; and* The Selected Poems of A. E. Housman *(1944), drawn from* The Collected Poems of A. E. Housman *(1940). The following letter is from the general manager of the Armed Services Editions. The addressee was an associate editor with Holt.*

October 18, 1943

Dear Miss Lawton:

We are enclosing herewith jacket copy that was used on your book, ORDEAL BY HUNGER by George R. Stewart.

We thought you might like to look over your own jacket blurb and see whether you want to make any change[s] in it for Armed Services Editions. Generally speaking, we think it advisable to give the soldiers and sailors who will receive the book any interesting information about its publishing history. They are likely to be stationed overseas and consequently out of touch with things here. For instance, they might like to know what kind of reception the book got, that it may have become a best

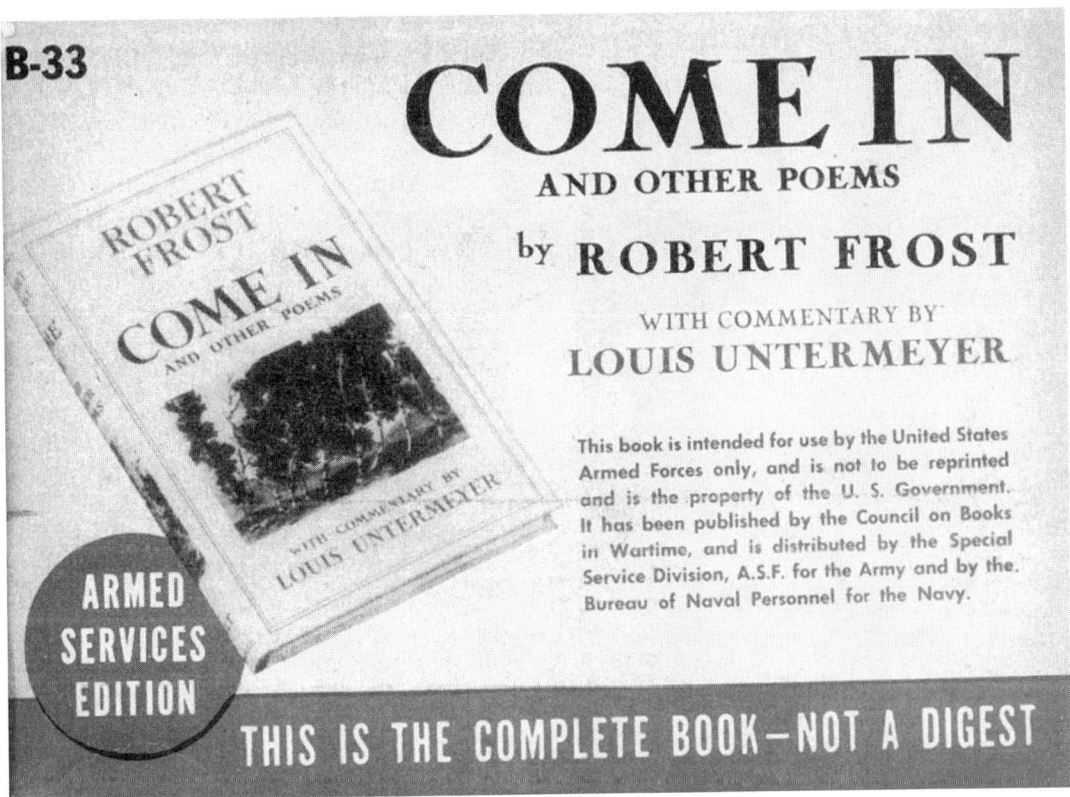

Cover of the 1943 Armed Services Edition of the poetry collection that Holt and Company first published that same year
(Bruccoli Collection, Thomas Cooper Library, University of South Carolina)

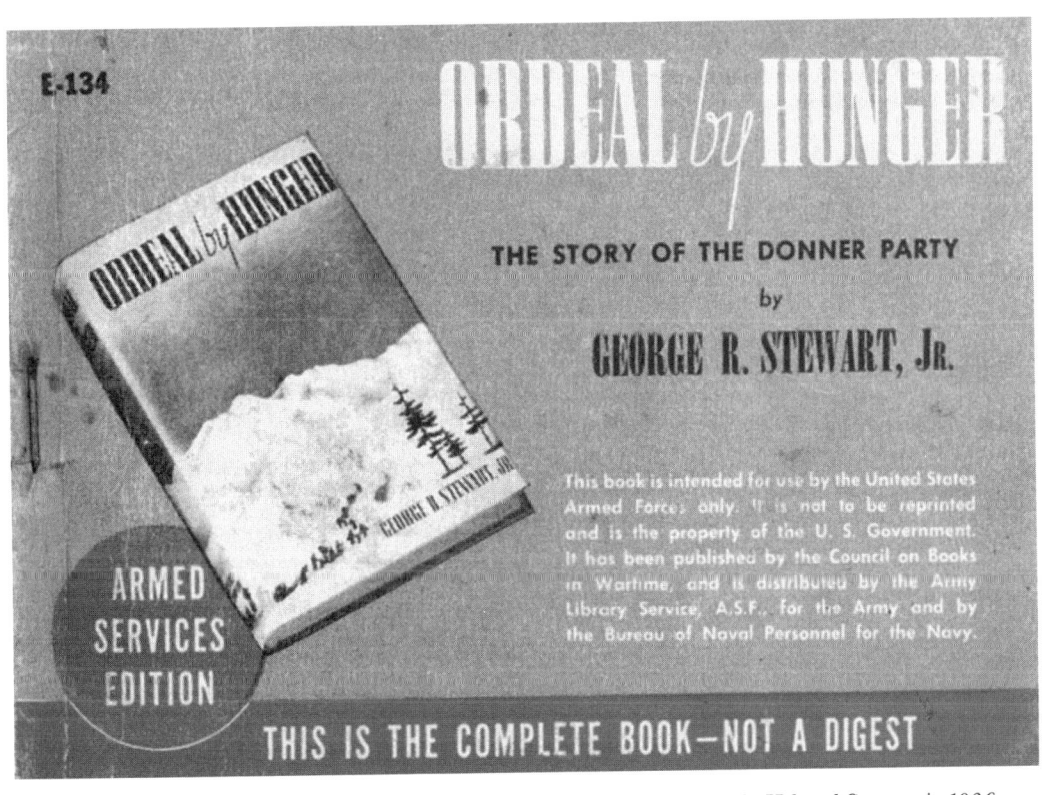

Cover of the 1944 Armed Services Edition of the historical account first published by Holt and Company in 1936
(Bruccoli Collection, Thomas Cooper Library, University of South Carolina)

Dust jacket for the war journalist's 1944 collection (Bruccoli Clark Layman Archives)

soundness of the book is the fact that, under present conditions, it is still in print. Since there is nothing sensational about the history of the book itself, it seems better to concentrate on the sensational nature of the theme.

In regard to this theme, I find myself in rather a peculiar position, since it occurs to me that, in view of what the readers of the Armed Services Editions may be asked to contemplate in the way of human behavior just now, the antics of the Donner Party may seem about as sensational as a tavern brawl. In 1936, the first paragraph of our jacket copy was possible justified; it seems meaningless now. I have deleted it, and have edited the rest to the required number of words with this point in mind. . . .
    Sincerely yours,
    [L. Lawton]
    HENRY HOLT AND COMPANY
    Associate Editor
    Trade Department

***

seller, that it has been sold to the motion pictures, that it was awarded some literary prize, etc.

We have space available for two hundred words of copy. Would you please let us have it at the earliest possible date?

    Most cordially yours,
    Philip Van Doren Stern

    October 20th, 1943
Dear Mr. Stern:
 ORDEAL BY HUNGER, by George R. Stewart, Jr., while it has always sold in respectable quantities, never reached the best seller class. It received very good reviews at the time of its appearance. There have been, as you probably know, a good many books based on the story,–novels, poems, historical chronicles of one sort and another. In going back over the clippings in our 1936 folder, I find enough to warrant leaving that word "definitive" in the jacket copy. Another tribute to the

Title page for the first full-length nonfiction work by the American critic and novelist, published in 1946 (Rutgers University Library)

Frances Pindyck was with Leland Hayward Inc., the A. E. Housman estate's American agent. The trade-department employee who wrote her was mistaken in referring to the earlier Holt book as The Complete Poems of A. E. Housman. *The volume was actually titled* The Collected Poems of A. E. Housman.

December 17th, 1943

Dear Miss Pindyck:

The Council on Books in Wartime would like to include our volume of the complete poems of A. E. Housman in The Armed Services Edition. You are perhaps familiar with this pocket edition, which is for the use of the United States Armed Forces and is distributed by the Army and the Navy without charge. The Council, a non-profit organization of publishers and booksellers, selects and publishes the titles. This company is represented on the board.

The contract for an Armed Services Edition of any title usually calls for a printing of 50,000 copies and the rate of royalty is 1¢ a copy. We do not wish to make any profit on the project, and expect to cover, from our share of the royalty, only the office expense and whatever fees may have to be met. The balance of the royalty check would of course, be paid in to the Housman estate as usual.

Will you advise me as to the necessary steps to take in order to clear the sections in our THE COMPLETE POEMS OF A. E. HOUSMAN entitled "More Poems" and "Additional Poems". We feel that the poems of A. E. Housman are particularly appropriate for this edition and hope that we can arrange for it. . . .

Very truly yours,
HENRY HOLT AND COMPANY
Trade Department

Bill Mauldin's Book
Herbert Lyons

Serviceman Herbert Lyons reviewed cartoonist Mauldin's Up Front *for* The New Republic.

It was a smallish, paper-bound book, and it cost 25 lire. Its title was *Mud, Mules and Mountains*, but nobody ever called it that. When the men came into Naples or Rome on pass, they would stop by the circulation office of *Stars and Stripes* and say: "Got any Mauldin books left? Sure would like to get a copy of that Mauldin book."

Often, there were none left. It was a hard book to keep in print. Even if the paper supply in Italy had been larger, it would have been a hard book to keep in print. To many men, it seemed the only thing in Italy worth having.

Now, for those men who have had to come home without one and for a great many persons who have never set foot in Italy, there is an American Mauldin book.[1] It is called *Up Front* after the heading used until recently on the Mauldin cartoons in *Stars and Stripes,* and it is clothbound. The paper, if somewhat better than that obtainable in Italy, is too thin, some of the plates are too small, and there appears to be none of Mauldin's pre-Italian work—which means that you cannot trace quite fully enough the development of Mauldin and his men. The next book, I hope, will carry dates under the cartoons and will include, by way of introduction, the admirable pieces that the late Ernie Pyle and the late Fred Painton wrote about the best United States cartoonist of this war.

This American Mauldin book contains some 160 cartoons—many more than in *Mud, Mules and Mountains,* and a number that you may have missed in the domestic newspapers that carry Mauldin's work—and some 30,000 words of text. The words are addressed mainly

Dust jacket for the blank-verse dramatic narrative published by Holt and Company in 1945 (The Book Guardian)

to civilians, who will be fools if they don't like them, but they will mean as much, or more, to Mauldin's overseas audience.

Mauldin, it turns out, writes almost exactly as he draws. When this book was first projected, some of us on *Stars and Stripes* thought it ill advised of the publishers to want text as well as pictures. We were somewhat snobbishly afraid that Mauldin the writer would look awkward beside so accomplished a guy as Mauldin the artist. By being casual, and himself, half brat and half sage, by ignoring the restraints of chapter divisions and the other paraphernalia of nice organization, he has put together the one indispensable book that any one man has so far published about Americans in action in this war.

The text, as he points out, is "pretty much background" for the drawings. It undertakes to explain why he draws the kind of pictures he does and why the men he draws deserve "to be appreciated a little by their countrymen." The whole is like listening to Mauldin talk while driving his jeep through Italy, except that only once does he halt to tell you that he has the most remarkable jeep in the Army.

He talks about Willie and Joe, his cartoon characters; about relations between officers and men (almost his most persistent theme); about the "battle of Naples," which was fought some time after the city fell into Allied hands; about Anzio; about the medics and, again and again, about the infantryman. It is a cocky and humble book, sly and wise, sardonic and humane—and wonderfully illuminating.

Nearly all the writing is deliberately non-professional, but the final episode—a night in a battalion medical-aid station south of Bologna—will probably find its way into all the war anthologies. It is a small miracle of unsentimental and compassionate reporting.

As Mauldin notes, he is a reporter in his cartoons. In his cartoons he is also unsentimental, compassionate and authentic. The usual explanation of his authenticity is that he has been most of the places that the sorely tried 45th Division has been and so has seen and been a part of the situations he describes. That is true as far as it goes, but other artists and other reporters have been to the front, and they did not see exactly what Mauldin saw. Authenticity is largely a matter of the spirit.

Though the cartoons drawn in Italy and France have more technical authority than those Mauldin drew for the 45th Division *News* when the division was still in training in the States, the earlier stuff is not much different in attitude from the later work. Mauldin's attitude is that of the young men who were thrown into camps before Pearl Harbor and became the American Army. Not members of the American Army—the Army itself.

Dust jacket for the 1946 Holt and Company edition of the British writer's 1912 political essay condemning the increasing power of the state and centralized economy in modern society (Bruccoli Clark Layman Archives)

The Army has other good cartoonists, but the essential humor of most of them is fantasy. It is the humor of those moments when the only way to make the Army tolerable is to daydream about it wildly. Mauldin's men, like everybody else, have such moments, and they admire cartoonists like *Yank's* George Baker (*The Sad Sack*). In the moments in which he catches them, however, Mauldin's men are usually too absorbed, or too tired, for fantasies.

Even when he is most high-spirited, Mauldin holds down the humor of exaggeration. He relies on a direct, uncompromising, sometimes brutal matter-of-factness. Mauldin's men may still be rubbed raw by the niceties of "military courtesy" in rear echelons, but they have long accepted combat. As he puts it, "they wish to hell they were someplace else, and they wish to hell they could get relief. They wish to hell the mud was dry and they wish to hell their coffee was hot. They want to go home. But they stay in their wet holes and fight, and they climb out and crawl through minefields and fight some more."

The aim of his cartoons, Mauldin says, is to enable such men to blow off steam. That is an okay explanation, if somewhat terse. There were times when not all the brass in Italy understood the medicinal and restorative qualities of Mauldin's stuff. From a Manhattan coign of vantage it is a little hard to recall why some gentlemen called Mauldin "seditious" during the "battle of Naples" in the early spring of 1944. That is because this is neither 1944 nor Naples. The men who came down from Anzio and incurred a base section's fury because on leave they forgot to "ack like sojers" have moved on some place else, or they are dead.

Some of the cartoons seem more mirthful than they did a year ago, and less biting and morose. But it is important to remember that it took courage as well as a tough critic's mind and an infallible eye and ear to do them. And it took intelligence on the part of the highest brass to recognize Mauldin's irreplaceable value to the infantryman. In its attitude toward Mauldin, the American Army in Italy did itself proud.

There are not enough books describing the relationship between a particular artist and a particular audience in a particular time. It would be good to be able to see some easy parallel and say that Mauldin meant to the men in Italy what this artist meant to that audience in some specified year. Perhaps there are no precedents. But during that first miserable winter in Italy–a winter that Mauldin says was worse than Valley Forge, and he seems to know–the men who came back from the front to buy Mauldin's book laughed like hell all over again at cartoons they had already seen in *Stars and Stripes,* and when they had finished laughing, they said: "This is just about the way it is."

Henry Holt and Company, Incorporated

BOARD OF DIRECTORS

Donald Carter	J. Patrick Lannan
Alfred C. Edwards	Gilbert Loveland
William L. Glenn	Robert H. MacMurphey
Alex L. Hillman	Edgar T. Rigg
Arnold M. Johnson	Benjamin Sonnenberg

William E. Stockhausen

OFFICERS

Edgar T. Rigg	President
Alfred C. Edwards	Executive Vice President and Treasurer
Gilbert Loveland	Vice President
Robert H. MacMurphey	Vice President
A. K. Shields	Vice President
Alden H. Clark	Secretary
James C. Hazelton	Assistant Treasurer
William J. Tribe	Assistant Treasurer
Florence B. Wolfe	Assistant Secretary

Transfer Agent and Trustee

Bankers Trust Company, 16 Wall Street, New York

Registrar

Guaranty Trust Company, 140 Broadway, New York

List of board members and officers from the Holt and Company annual report of 1949, the first year of Edgar T. Rigg's presidency (courtesy of Princeton University Library)

When an audience that knows laughs and then speaks those words about imitations of elemental actions, you have art as catharsis and as magic and as revelation. And leave us have no esthetic misunderstanding about it.

Mauldin has been drawing the kind of cartoons that have not been done by an American since the time of Art Young and the old *Masses*. He is probably the only cartoonist of his generation who owes nothing to the *New Yorker*. He is a very serious humorist and he deals principally with group contradictions–the contradiction between responsibility and privilege, between vocabulary and reality, between today's circumstance and yesterday's conditioning. The cartoon for which he recently received the Pulitzer Prize is an obvious example. A weary Joe walks head-down through the rain and some equally tired German prisoners walk in the same attitude beside him. The caption quotes a news item: "Fresh, spirited American troops, flushed with victory, are bringing in thousands of hungry, ragged, battleweary prisoners. . . ."

Mauldin may not have been consciously influenced by anybody, but whenever he sees the Art Young cartoon of the two kids and the stars as thick as bedbugs, he ought to say: "That's my boy."

He takes up where the cosy Bairnsfather left off, so he needn't say anything to the talented Britisher. And I think that those of his admirers who insist that Mauldin is in the tradition of Goya and Daumier are being too enthusiastic, though it's easy to see what they are driving at.

Like Young, Mauldin is often an indifferent craftsman. At his best, as in those two monumental little figures in the cartoon captioned, "How ya gonna find out if they're fresh troops if ya don't wake 'em up an' ask 'em?" he can achieve a harsh poignancy of line. He is a serious workman, as you will recognize if you ever hear him talk about why it is hard to draw a rifle so as to give it dramatic meaning. But like Young, he is primarily a cartoonist–a man who gets his effects by a combination of drawing and caption, who must make with words as well as line.

He seldom used to complain when Italian engravers did a sloppy job on his drawings, but the proofreader who omitted a single apostrophe, or altered the spelling of one word in a caption, risked his miserable neck.

In his audience, Mauldin has been luckier than Art Young. The latter mainly drew for a radical and highbrow little journal which, for all its influence, can seldom have been seen by the people who were Young's subjects. The artist who is separated from his natural audience is necessarily a lonely and to some extent a frustrated man. Between Mauldin and his men there have been no barriers.

The old question that men in the Army asked–"What did you do in civilian life?"–is now giving way to a new one, "What do you think you'll do when you get out?" Mauldin, of course, will go on being a cartoonist, and an able and famous one. But the civilian cartoonist who deals unsentimentally and almost never wistfully with social contradictions risks loneliness and frustration. Will Mauldin go on seeing contradictions?

His political convictions appear to be few and innocuous. It is a little embarrassing when he writes about the war, "I'm not old enough to understand what it is all about," but he is not being coy. As an Army cartoonist, he has maturity and an unassailable integrity. As a civilian, he will be a kid without much experience or education but with a great amount of fame. He is a complex figure, and it would be fatuous to try to see ahead for him. It is permissible, however, to think that while acclaim may dazzle his eye, no amount of money will be enough to stuff his ear.

Certain Army experiences with his audience should stand him in good stead. There was the time, shortly after the capture of Rome, when an epidemic of jeep-stealing broke out. Two tough characters came up to Mauldin as he was getting into his well loved jeep and told him to turn it over to them. Then one of them saw Mauldin's name on the jeep and yanked at his companion. "We don't want to take this guy's jeep," he said, and the two of them went away. Mauldin does a little quiet boasting about that incident. He has a right to, because he understands the implications.

–"Bill Mauldin's Book," *New Republic*, 112 (18 June 1945): 847–848

1946: SLOANE'S DEPARTURE AND AN OIL MAN'S TAKEOVER

Henry Holt and the Man from Koon Kreek
Robert Lubar

In 1946 Sloane left Holt and Company to found his own publishing firm, William Sloane Associates. His departure was precipitated by a stock takeover by Texas businessman Clint Murchison. In a letter dated 12 April 1946 to Holt staffer Horace G. Butler, Sloane described Murchison as "A Texas oil millionaire . . . with a very black record and absolutely no publishing interests whatsoever. I went down and saw this little man who is only a step ahead of the men who used to get sent away for long periods to the federal rest houses, known as penitentiaries. . . ." Murchison did indeed implement major changes at the firm. In a 1959 Fortune *magazine article Robert Lubar described both the transition effected by this "oil man" at Holt and Company, as well as the major changes occurring at that time in the publishing industry in general. Henry Holt regretfully referred* to "the commercialization of literature" at the beginning of the twentieth century; he probably could not have imagined just how commercial the world of publishing had become by mid century.

> Before a Texas oil millionaire got a Wall Street analyst to head Henry Holt, this old firm was run "like a literary tea party." Now it is being run like a business, and its financial reports make dandy reading.

Early this fall, Edgar T. Rigg, president of Henry Holt & Co., flew down from New York to visit Clint Murchison on his farm at Athens, Texas. Murchison took him over to the Koon Kreek Klub, a hangout of local oil and cattle millionaires, and they put out in a skiff on the artificial lake that the club stocks with bream. The fish were biting, and Murchison and Rigg were kept busy. But between fish, Rigg managed to get in the business that had brought him to Texas. He had come to tell Murchison, Henry Holt's controlling stockholder, of a decision reached by the venerable book company's board of directors a few days before. It had voted to split the common stock three for two and to declare a 10-cent quarterly dividend, the first cash dividend in many years.

"Fine, just fine," said oilman Murchison, and hauled in another bream.

The board's decision was amply justified. Holt's sales this year will amount to around $23 million, up $3,600,000 or 18.5 per cent over 1958 and more than seven times what they were in 1950. Net profit after taxes will come to $2 million, or 8.7 per cent of sales, well above the industry average and eleven times earnings of ten years ago.

Even more gratifying, from Murchison's standpoint as an investor, has been the spectacular performance of Holt common, now selling at around 30 on the American Stock Exchange. Taking into consideration a three-for-one split in 1957 and the one at three to two this year, the stock has appreciated 1,400 per cent in a decade. One lady stockholder recently calculated that, with a 10 per cent stock dividend each year since 1952, the $1,800 she put into Holt in 1949 has grown to $52,500. When Murchison first bought into Holt, back in 1945, a lot of people suspected he was seeking an outlet for some of the political views usually associated with Texas oil millionaires. Actually, although he is the dominant stockholder, he has been a model of unobtrusiveness. He does not sit on the board, although he is represented there by his son, John Dabney, and by Don Carter, a financial associate. In his fourteen-year association with the firm Murchison has never visited its offices.

Only once has he "interfered" in editorial operations. A robust sixty-four, Murchison some years ago became a disciple of a seventy-eight-year-old Vermont country doctor named DeForest Clinton Jarvis, who among other things advocates honey and apple-cider vinegar as an aid to human vitality. . . . Murchison thought the doctor's ideas worthy of wider circulation, and suggested to Rigg that Holt get out a book about them. Though some Holt editors expressed an expectable skepticism, *Folk Medicine* was duly published in a modest edition of 5,000. To date more than 235,000 copies have been sold at $2.95, and the book is still high on the best-seller lists.

But for the most part Murchison has been more than content to let Edgar Rigg run the show. Rigg came to Holt in 1949 from Wall Street, an unlikely background for a book publisher, but just the kind of background that was needed at Holt. When Rigg reflects on what he did at Holt, he says modestly, "All that was needed was someone to run the company as a modern business instead of a literary tea party."

"The industry capitalism forgot"

The fact is that book publishing as a whole has more nearly resembled a tea party than a modern business. It has long been known as "the industry capitalism forgot." Traditionally, publishing houses have been small, family-owned firms whose proprietors were really literary patrons, much more interested in cultivating talent than in operating in a businesslike fashion. Most of the illustrious founder owners are gone, leaving great names like Scribner, Putnam, and Dutton to adorn the industry, and publishing has long since passed into the hands of more frankly commercial minded people. But they have not come much nearer to solving the problem of how to merchandise their product, which, after all, is what any business is about.

Indeed, literature for the general reader, the so-called "trade" books that are the heart of publishing, might seem to defy effective merchandising. The business involves marketing thousands of separate new items each year, each with its own distinctive character and sales appeal (or lack of it), in thousands of small, often impoverished retail outlets. The great advances in market research elsewhere in the economy have left the book industry largely untouched. Nobody knows for sure what makes a book sell, how much good advertising or other forms of promotion will do it, or how many copies to print and distribute so as to have enough available to meet the potential demand without creating a glut of unsalable remainders. Yet publishers produce new books by the thousands each year and send them off to bookstore counters with the fervent hope that a TV plug, a spate of laudatory reviews, or a favorable display in a few big bookstores will somehow produce the money miracle of a smash best-seller.

The total market is alluring enough: last year $84 million worth of adult trade books were sold. The trouble is that the pie is cut into tiny pieces. There are about seventy-five firms in the business and somewhere in the neighborhood of 50,000 individual book titles in print, with about 5,000 new ones added every year. In the circumstances, a 450,000 sale, which was racked up by *Exodus,* Leon Uris' novel about Israel, is a historical event. Many a book pleases its publisher if it manages to sell 5,000 copies, and at 15,000 it has probably made the best-seller lists.

It would be incorrect to imply that the industry is complacent about its troubles. In the last few years some significant attempts have been made to do something about merchandising books as other industries merchandise their products. The cheap paperbacks, sold in supermarkets, drugstores, and other kinds of untraditional outlets, have opened up a vast new mass market; thirteen firms are currently in this fast-growing business, and last year their sales were a thumping 250 million. Some publishers, notably Simon & Schuster and Prentice-Hall, have specialized in mail-order selling in an effort to get at customers directly. Book clubs are another device to ensure a large and predictable sale for a small number of selected books.

The firm that has come closest to devising marketing techniques similar to those employed in other industries is Doubleday, the giant of the trade-book business. It maintains an unusually large sales force in order to achieve personal contact with thousands of bookstore owners, many of whom its competitors supply only indirectly, through jobbers. Some 450 of these bookstores, thus far, have enrolled in the Doubleday Merchandising Plan. Under this plan, salesmen visit the stores in their circuit at least once a month. They send back to Doubleday's New York office a steady flow of up-to-date information on the sales performance of Doubleday books in each store. With these figures and some application of the principles of mathematical probability, a merchandising staff in New York calculates how many additional copies of each title should be shipped to each store to keep its inventory at the proper level. Thus the Doubleday plan takes over from the bookstore proprietor the central, and vexing, problem of stock selection and inventory maintenance. (If it is possible, bookstores are even more backward and inefficient about such matters as inventory control than the publishers themselves. It is not unusual for a bookstore to wait until it runs out of stock before it reorders a book, or to return its copies just before a book catches on.)

Babies and Sputniks

Rather than challenge giant Doubleday in trade books, Holt expends its main effort on textbooks, where rational, or at least more rational, merchandising is possible and the growth of the market is as measurable as it is appetizing. . . . In fact, Murchison's canny foresight about this market was one of the big reasons for his investing in the publishing company in the first place. While others saw in the record mid-1940's birth statistics such obvious business implications as a boom in baby foods, baby clothing, and suburban housing, Murchison, though not a bookish man himself, looked further ahead to the fact that Americans would soon be buying a record number of schoolbooks.

Less than 10 per cent of Holt's sales are in trade books, while textbooks account for some 60 per cent. The company does not know its exact ranking among textbook publishers, because sales breakdowns are jealously guarded secrets in this highly competitive business, and most firms, being privately owned, do not release figures of any kind. But Holt is confident that it is first in the high-school field. In colleges, it has a high standing in the liberal arts, but trails in total sales behind McGraw-Hill and Prentice-Hall, with their vast output of technical and business texts.

Two recent developments in education have been right down Holt's alley. When the national shock over Sputnik I created a clamor for more and better science education, Holt was ahead of the field with an up-to-date series of high-school science textbooks. The new emphasis on teaching foreign languages found Holt with a full line of highly regarded texts based on the modern oral-aural method initiated in World War II Army courses. Holt was the first to introduce tapes as a complement to texts in classroom language instruction. And for the out-of-school student it has developed a successful line of self-teaching records and tapes, including such exotic tongues as Thai.

The remaining 30 per cent of Holt's gross comes from the third and newest branch of its operation, magazines. The company acquired *Field and Stream* in 1951 and has since lifted its circulation by 40 per cent to 1,100,000. In 1955, Holt bought the monthly *Popular Gardening,* whose current circulation is 300,000; and in 1958, two semi-annuals, *New Homes Guide* (500,000) and *Home Modernizing Guide* (300,000). All these acquisitions, of course, are addressed to the rapidly increasing number of leisure-conscious Americans.

No room for *Peyton Place*

As a textbook publisher, Rigg is as careful about the wholesomeness of Holt's reputation as a spinster teacher in a small town. Rigg is often asked whether he would have published *Peyton Place* (sales figures: 300,000 copies in the hard-cover edition by Messner at $3.95, eight million in 50-cent paperbacks by Dell) if it had been offered to him. He replies with a resounding "No." What would the teachers and school authorities who buy his text books think of a firm that published a book featuring incest and a school principal glorying in a lusty extramarital affair?

To build up Holt's prestige, Rigg began by building a formidable organization of editors and salesmen. When he came to Holt, he found the textbook staff small, and hobbled by an ill-considered policy that put arbitrary quotas on textbook production while money was frittered away on such whimsical projects as a Japanese-language Bible that had caught some editor's fancy. Rigg gave the textbook department more scope, more money, and more manpower. In ten years the editorial staff has more than quadrupled, the number of roving high-school "bookmen" (or "agents" as Holt now prefers to call them) has increased from thirteen to forty, and the college "traveler" force has grown from six to twenty-four.

In the high-school business, Holt believes in concentrating on a few fields where it knows the market and has established a well-known product line. Therefore it sticks to the five basic academic subjects: English, mathematics, science, foreign languages, and social studies. "Frill" subjects like home economics and stenography it is content to leave to competitors. (Holt also keeps out of the elementary field, though it may change this policy if the trend to science and language teaching in the lower grades gathers speed.) Some current Holt staples are old favorites—e.g., a high-school biology text first published in 1919, which had been allowed to get out of date and had lost its market in the firm's 1940's doldrums. Old books that have been extensively revised and "repackaged" in modern formats and bindings are once again selling briskly. Holt's new books are given every advantage of attractive design and lively illustrations—two features that have practically become a Holt trademark. In other words, Holt puts big money into packaging its product—but the payoff is big, too. For instance, North Carolina's recent adoption of Holt's Science I and Science II texts for all its junior high schools represents an order for 200,000 copies at $2.50 each.

Holt is also giving a lot of emphasis to new-product development. The foreign-language division, for instance, has developed tapes to promote its books. A school that adopts a Holt textbook gets a tape on loan, free, and can make as many copies as it needs. At present few schools have the equipment to take advantage of this offer, but many more soon will. Under Title III of the National Defense Education Act of 1958, the federal government is authorized to spend $280 million over four years "for strengthening science, mathematics, and modern language instruction." A substantial part of this money is going into school language labs fitted with tape recorders and players. Holt has its eye on some of those millions.

Gettysburg and Cleopatra

To be successful in the college-text business, a publisher has to contend with some uniquely difficult marketing conditions. He is offering a commodity that notoriously defies objective quality judgment—ideas. He has to deal with a lot of independent-minded, often cantankerous professors, each with his own concept of what his students should read. He has to keep up with constantly changing tastes and trends in college teaching. Consequently, the pressure is on the publisher to keep turning out a new line of original and striking books every year. Holt's college division has stepped up its new-book development from six titles in 1948 to sixty this year, and competitors concede that the books are generally setting a high standard. This is a notable performance, for a college book may require as much as three or four years of editorial preparation.

Holt is already preparing for the coming bulge in the college-age group. Next year it expects to enlarge its list of new college books to 100 titles. And anticipating that the future stampede of freshmen will overtax college library facilities, Holt is producing a new series of "controlled research manuals," which will contain packages of source material for term papers and enable the student to get his research in hand without going to the library. Topics include *The Third Day at Gettysburg, Shays' Rebellion,* and *Cleopatra's Lovers.*

Last year, to enhance its prestige in the college field, Holt purchased Dryden Books. This comparatively small publisher (annual sales: $1,500,000) of high-quality college texts was founded in 1939 by Stanley Burnshaw, an advertising man with an original flair for book design and typography. In acquiring Dryden, Holt augmented its product line with a new class of books and authors. Burnshaw himself came over in the merger and brought with him, among others, Lionel Trilling of Columbia University to advise and write on literature, and John Canaday, the art critic of the New York *Times,* as author and consultant on fine arts. Burnshaw also brought the Dryden techniques of printing and layout, which had become famous in the business. A few of the books published under the new joint Holt-Dryden label have such distinction and broad appeal that they have also been put out by the trade department for general sale.

"Sell hell out of it"

Rigg likes to cite the guiding principle he set for Holt: "Let's create the best product the market has ever seen, a product we're so proud of, we're busting out all over, and having done that, let's go out and sell hell out of it." But that is only part of what Rigg means when he talks about making publishing a modern business. Quality and salesmanship obviously count the most in the competitive textbook business, but to make money a firm needs to be soundly organized, too. Textbook publishing comes about as close to mass production as book publishing ever gets, and offers many opportunities for economy and bigger profits—but only if basic planning sees to it that deliveries aren't mixed up, copies overstocked, and money wasted on unnecessary transportation. These may seem to be the A B C's of business to most businessmen, but they are not to most publishers, and they certainly weren't to Holt pre-Rigg.

Rigg introduced a system of inventory control that was an innovation at Holt. Now the people in the company's Madison Avenue office actually know just how many copies of a book are available, exactly where they are stored, and how many more must be printed to meet upcoming deliveries, and they can coordinate print orders with anticipated sales. A Ramac data-processing unit will go into operation next April, and speed up the flow of this inventory information. Holt is also improving its warehouse facilities to get some economy into book storage. Its new warehouse is equipped with conveyers and fork-lift trucks, whose rarity in the industry is one measure of how backward this industry has been. And Rigg has familiarized the company with such previously foreign concepts as keeping departmental budgets and forecasting cash flow.

A new dollars-and-cents consciousness has also entered Holt's trade department. Money is no longer thrown away on an obvious loser just because some editor thinks it ought to be published, but Rigg frankly admits he has not turned the trade business into much of a profit maker. What is more, he doesn't think there's much possibility of important profit in trade books. The economics of the business are pretty forbidding. To begin with, discounts to middlemen and retailers usually come to 45 per cent of the sale price, so that a $5 book returns $2.75 to the publisher. Costs eat up practically all of this. On the average, 28 per cent of sales on a first edition goes to paper, printing, and binding, 34 per cent to so-called "departmental" costs including editing and shipping, 22 per cent to authors' royalties, and 14 per cent to overhead. These items add up to 98 per cent, and leave only 2 per cent profit for the publisher, or, on a $5 book, 5½ cents.

Paperbacks and dolls

How, then, do trade publishers make money? They run book clubs (Doubleday has twenty-four, ranging from the Literary Guild for general books to special clubs for garden and cook books) or go into paperbacks, where the possibilities of volume sales are much greater. And they rely on the gravy they get from "rights," meaning their percentage of income from reprints, magazine serialization, and special promotion tie-ins (e.g., Eloise dolls from Kay Thompson's *Eloise* books). However, movie sales, the richest source of side income for books, rarely benefit publishers; the big Hollywood money generally goes to "name" authors, whose hard-bargaining agents are able to exclude movie rights from the contract with the publisher.

To capitalize on all available sidelines for trade books, Rigg figures, he would need a much larger operation than he is prepared to commit himself to. He has no wish to see Holt become another Doubleday. While he has been building up his textbook business, he has been content that the Holt name still means something in the bookstores. Thanks to such authors as J. Edgar Hoover, Bernard Baruch, and Dr. Jarvis, the firm has made an impressive showing in best-sellers. But now that the finances of the company are in such good shape, Rigg is giving some consideration to improving the trade output and giving it better balance. He would like to be stronger in the inviting juvenile market and to develop a bigger back list of "bread and butter" books that sell year in and year out. Then Holt's trade editors could take greater risks on developing new authors, an area in which they have been notably unadventurous.

Yale and Hardy

Henry Holt & Co. began adventurously. The man who gave the firm his name founded it in 1866, after he had graduated from Yale. He soon became the most exciting publisher of his time. He introduced American readers to the daring (for their day) novels of Thomas Hardy, the tales of the then unknown Robert Louis Stevenson, the hot controversy over the Darwinian theory. He published John Dewey's *Human Nature and Conduct* and Albert Einstein's *Theory of Relativity,* and he commissioned William James to write his celebrated *Principles of Psychology,* the first textbook ever done on the subject.

As Henry Holt aged, the firm began to lose its eminence. By 1919, when the founder was approaching eighty, he no longer had a taste for new ideas. He got into a bitter dispute with his talented young editor, Alfred Harcourt, over a controversial Bertrand Russell book that Harcourt had bought. Harcourt quit and took along Donald Brace, the production chief, to found Harcourt, Brace. With them went Sinclair Lewis, Holt's most promising writer, who was then putting the finishing touches on *Main Street.*

Holt died in 1926, leaving three sons who had neither the interest nor the aptitude for publishing. At his widow's request, the company became a public corporation. Fortunately another strong man took hold. E. N. Bristol, whom Henry Holt had brought in as president a few years before he died, carried the firm safely if unspectacularly through the depression. In 1937, Bristol handed over the presidency to his son Herbert, a somewhat less effective executive. During the war, there was a brief and heady renaissance as Holt hit the jackpot with Marion Hargrove's *See Here, Private Hargrove,* Bill Mauldin's G.I. cartoon collections, and the works of Ernie Pyle. But when peace came, absence of strong leadership began to tell. The company was barely ticking over.

By that time, rescue was already on the way in the person of J. Patrick Lannan, the handsome and genial Chicago Irishman who was making a career of

Dust jacket for the 1947 printing of the historical novel that Holt and Company first published in 1933 (Bruccoli Clark Layman Archives)

easing himself into difficult corporate situations. Lannan has since become better known as an influential investor in enterprises such as International Telephone & Telegraph, Duquesne Light, and the Milwaukee Road. Lannan is also something of a literary buff (he has been, among other things, an important sponsor of *Poetry Magazine*) and that was the main reason he became involved with Holt. He thought it would be fun to be associated with a firm that published his favorite author, Ernie Pyle, and one of his favorite poets, Robert Frost. The stock was cheap and he bought a few shares, much as he might have backed a Broadway show whose star he admired. Despite several attractive opportunities, Lannan never invested heavily in Holt. He did join the board of directors in 1948, but he resigned a few months ago, stating as his reason the pressure of his other interests. He had had his fun as an insider in Holt's comeback, and now that the company was riding high, it no longer intrigued him.

Lannan's contribution, however, was far greater than the money he put into Holt or the advice he gave on its operation. It was he who brought in Clint Murchison. When Lannan first took an interest in Holt, he suggested to his friend Don Carter, who often acts as a financial representative for Murchison, that the oilman do the same. Murchison was in a very receptive mood for such advice. His two sons, John and Clint Jr., were then in college and he was thinking hard about their future. He thought there was "no finer heritage he could leave them than a publishing business." His first idea had been to put together a nice little chain of Texas newspapers as a graduation present, and he had asked Carter to scout around for some papers. Finding no good buys, Carter had broadened his search and was looking into New York publishing houses when Lannan came along with his recommendation. Soon afterward, when an investment trust called International Utilities put a 13 per cent block of Henry Holt common stock on the market, Carter bought it for Murchison.

As it turned out, neither of Murchison's sons was particularly interested in becoming a publisher (though John sits on the board and follows the company's affairs closely). But meanwhile Holt's promising textbook business offered Murchison reason enough to keep and enlarge his holdings in the company.

The editor meets the oilman

It was a few years, however, before the investment began to look good. At Holt, Herbert Bristol had finally been replaced as president by Joseph Brandt, who had headed the university presses successively at Oklahoma, Princeton, and Chicago. The firm's other important personality was William Sloane, the editor who was responsible for the wartime best-sellers. Soon after Murchison disclosed himself as the leading stockholder, he invited Brandt and Sloane down to Texas. Sloane came away with the impression that he was no longer wanted. Soon afterward he left Holt, and as Alfred Harcourt had done twenty-six years before, founded his own firm. He took away with him virtually the entire Holt trade-book staff and at least half of its authors.

Brandt, who stayed on as president, faced an imposing job. Even the best administrator would have had a hard time repairing the damage left by Sloane's departure, and administration wasn't Joseph Brandt's strong point. The Holt people who worked under him remember him as "a scholarly and delightful person" but unhappy with business responsibilities. In the chaos of his regime, Holt's 1947 profits dropped to $2,382 on sales of $3,400,000.

Casting about for help, Lannan asked his old friend Edgar Rigg (who also knew Murchison and Carter well) to look over Holt and determine if it could be salvaged. Rigg was not an obvious choice to call on for the salvage of a publishing house. He had started his working life as a technician in Lee De Forest's pioneer radio company. Later he had switched to Wall Street as a security analyst, eventually winding up as a vice president at Standard & Poor's. The nearest he had come to publishing was as supervisor of S. & P.'s *Corporation Records,* a responsibility that gave him, he says, "something of the smell of printer's ink." But what Lannan valued was Rigg's experience as a judge of corporate management.

Eager to help out his friends at Holt, with S.&P.'s permission, Rigg took a seat on the board. He went to his first board meeting resolved to keep quiet and listen. But there was such an obvious power vacuum that he was soon vigorously expounding his ideas about putting business methods to work for the company and proposing some of the specific changes, discussed earlier in this article, that he has since put into effect. The board was impressed, and he walked out as chairman of a newly formed executive committee. During most of 1948 he spent his evenings and weekends on Holt's problems. Finally, in 1949, he resigned from S.&P. and moved into the president's office at Holt.

Murchison expressed his confidence by acquiring more Holt common stock in the open market. He also advanced the firm $200,000 by buying its preferred stock, which was redeemed five years later. Rigg put some of his own money into Holt—he now has a 7 per cent holding—and suggested that some of his friends do the same. One who took his advice was Lannan's friend Arnold Johnson, now owner of the Kansas City Athletics baseball team. He is currently a member of Holt's board, along with such diverse personalities as Senator Clinton Anderson of New Mexico, and bibliophile C. Waller Barrett, of New York.

A favor for Murchison

While he was putting system and organization into Holt's book-publishing operations, Rigg began, quite by chance, to expand into magazines, a field that was entirely new to the company. Holt got into magazine publishing because Clint Murchison is an avid outdoorsman. For years he had been a regular reader of *Field and Stream* and an admirer of its staff

Dust jacket for the 1944 biography of the "Great Cham" of English literature (Bruccoli Clark Layman Archives)

of specialists on hunting, fishing, and wildlife conservation. One day in 1950, while he and Rigg were dove-shooting in Mexico, Murchison mentioned hearing that control of the magazine was for sale. He asked Rigg as a personal favor to buy it for him.

Rigg found that Eltinge Warner, who had run *Field and Stream* since 1906, was indeed willing to dispose of his 51 per cent holding; with magazine publishing entering an era of mounting production costs and hot competition for circulation, Warner was no longer getting the enjoyment out of it he once had. After many long bargaining sessions, Rigg and Warner finally met on a price slightly above what *Field and Stream* shares had been selling for over the counter–$12–and Murchison got control for about $950,000. He kept the magazine separate from Holt but asked Rigg to take over as chairman.

Rigg was soon struck by the idea that *Field and Stream* would fit nicely into the Holt organization. It would spread the overhead, and since the magazine's peak periods coincided with quiet periods in textbooks, it would even out the firm's income over the year. Murchison agreed to the integration, and the merger took place in 1951. Each *Field and Stream* share was exchanged for half a share of Holt common stock, three-tenths of a share of $10-par-value Holt preferred, and $7 in cash. This worked out to slightly less than Murchison had paid for the magazine a year before, but Rigg persuaded him to take a paper loss on the deal. The merger enabled Murchison to increase his Holt holding from 27 to 40 per cent, and all the former *Field and Stream* stockholders have since seen the value of the Holt common they received multiply fifteen times.

The magazine has helped Holt even more than Rigg expected. Not only has it added handsomely to profits and made possible the administrative economies he envisioned, but it has offered certain intangible advantages as well. Some *Field and Stream* pieces have led to popular Holt books. And some valuable authors have come to the publishing firm via the magazine. Robert Ruark submitted his current novel *Poor No More* to Holt after a warm association that began when he wrote some hunting stories for the monthly. And it was on a quail hunt with friends from Holt and *Field and Stream* that Bernard Baruch agreed to let the firm publish his autobiography.

Holt's expansion attic

Popular Gardening, New Homes Guide, and *Home Modernizing Guide* also came as full-grown successes into the Holt family. Rigg has made little change in their staffs or their formulas, though there is now somewhat more imaginativeness in their promotion. With their acquisition, the magazine division outgrew the space it had in Holt's main offices, and Rigg moved it to separate quarters on Fifth Avenue. The new offices have a sort of "expansion attic," an unoccupied wing ready in case the family increases again, as it probably will. Holt is looking for more publications in the hobby-and-recreation category to reach the ever rising number of Americans with longer weekends and vacations.

All together, Rigg estimates that he spends 30 per cent of his office time investigating possible acquisitions of all kinds. His search for merger situations is a constant subject of publishing gossip. Rigg is open about his intentions. He isn't interested in making Holt "the biggest frog in the pond," but he would welcome the addition of a publishing firm that would fill some of Holt's remaining weak spots. A few months ago he approached Random House with an offer to buy. This would have been an impressive acquisition indeed, for it would have brought Holt the very successful *American College Dictionary,* the widely esteemed and popular Modern Library, a wide range of juveniles, and a first-rate trade-book list. But Random's Bennett Cerf turned the proposition down because he didn't want to give up personal control.

Rigg may not come upon such a choice deal soon again. But he can afford to wait. Holt now has ample resources to expand in just about any direction it wants.

–"Henry Holt and the Man from Koon Kreek,"
Fortune (December 1959):
104–109, 230–240

Holt and Company Textbooks

THE SCIENCES

In 1874 Holt and Company launched the American Science Series. Henry Holt hoped to appeal to both students and general readers, so each title was produced in both full-length and abbreviated editions. American Science Series titles included works on astronomy, geology, botany, zoology, political economy, general biology, and human anatomy.

Ira Remsen

Ira Remsen was a scientist and educator who, beginning in the 1870s, led the way in establishing the place of scientific instruction in chemistry and chemical research in American universities. Johns Hopkins University president Daniel Coit Gilman recruited Remsen to head the university's chemistry department in 1879, the year Remsen founded the American Chemical Journal. *In 1885 Henry Holt asked Remsen to write a chemistry text for the American Science Series.* An Introduction to the Study of Chemistry, *published in 1886, proved to be an enduring success.*

Jan. 21/[18]86

My dear Mr. Holt:

I am pleased with the appearance of the Chemistry and am naturally relieved to have the birth process over. Several teachers of my acquaintance have written me regarding it, and some of them in this city *[Baltimore]* have spoken to me about using it. I send with this a list of names of teachers who are likely to use it, and to whom it would therefore be wise to send copies.

I would like to send some abroad to places where they will "do the most good." If you do not care to send these on your own account charge them to me. My only object in sending them abroad is to bring the book to the attention of the principal chemists of the world, as commendations from them will be of value in [illegible] the book here.

I enclose a card recently received from Heath which will give you an idea of the way my "Organic Chemistry" is going.

Yours cordially,
Ira Remsen

I will write you about the big book shortly.

———◆———

March 3 1886

My dear Mr. Holt,

I return herewith the letters touching my book. If they are fair average specimens of the others received, then the book is doomed. However much I may regret this, and I do regret it exceedingly, I could not conscientiously change the book, if I had the work to do over again; for any change in the fundamental principle of presentation would do violence to my own convictions.

. . . .

(Ira Remsen)

In spite of Remsen's initial misgivings, An Introduction to the Study of Chemistry *proved to be a great success, and he and Holt made plans for an expanded edition.*

Oct. 12/[18]88

My dear Mr. Holt,

Your letters of the 10th and 11th have been received, and I hasten to express my gratification at their contents. I enclose the contract signed. As regards the Macmillan matter, I fear I have produced the impression of being unduly anxious, in a case where my interests were being looked after, better than I could look after them myself. By way of excuse I now plead ignorance. I thought that Macmillan had simply taken the book, and that he would not pay anything in that account any longer. I am glad to learn that I was mistaken; and I am certainly entirely satisfied with the arrangement you have made. I am not grasping, but I am poor; and am desirous of getting all the income I can fairly get. I suppose that whatever arrangement may be made with Macmillan with reference to the Advanced

Chemistry, it is not likely to be a less advantageous one than the one made with reference to the Briefer Course, so I shall put my mind at ease. Before dismissing the subject, however, I beg to express my appreciation of your more than fair treatment of me in our business relations. I am inclined to think that the region of holiness has actually been entered. You may remember that in that silly play "The Professor," the principal character has a series of experiences which leads him to remark: "*Now* I believe there is a Hell." My own experiences would almost lead me to use the same phrase with the slight change of Heaven for Hell.–

The only reason why I thought it would be well to put the Appendix of the big book in smaller type, is that, without this, the book will be rather large, and may make the impression that it is larger and more advanced than it really is. Some might on this account be deterred from examining it and from using it. I do not know, however, whether this point is worth considering or not. You can judge of that better than I can.

Yours sincerely,
Ira Remsen

* * *

Title page for the second edition of the abbreviated version of the astronomy textbook in the American Science Series (Rutgers University Library)

Henry Holt and Textbook Publishing

In the early part of this century [the twentieth] the production of books for the higher educational institutions must have been comparatively limited....
[N]o publisher, so far as I can ascertain, had then a specially organized department to secure manuscripts in the college field and to promote the sale of the resulting books. Mr. Henry Holt, who by temperament and interest turned to college textbook publishing, had already published many distinguished books of that nature.

–Frederick S. Crofts,
"Textbooks Are Not Absolutely
Dead Things," in *Bowker Lectures
on Book Publishing* (New York:
R. R. Bowker, 1957),
pp. 43, 44

Existing copyright laws made it possible to secure British rights to a book by the author's being, however briefly, in Canada.

June 1, 1889

Dear Mr. Holt,
The author of the Advanced Chemistry to the Queen etc. greeting. Please inform her Imperial Majesty and all others interested in the matter that I shall use every effort to be on British soil on June 17. What method would you suggest to prove to the Queen that I was on her soil in the date mentioned? Will she believe me on my word alone? Hardly, for she is not a fool. Indeed the question suggests itself: How is anyone in Canada to *know* that I am I?

Yours sincerely,
Ira Remsen

* * *

In 1899 Holt and Company received an order from a Puerto Rican firm for copies of Remsen's The Elements of Chemistry *(1886), the second volume in the American Science Series. The letter was translated for Holt by the Languages Printing Company of New York.*

12 October 1899

Dear Sirs:
We being booksellers on a large scale, on this island, and finding ourselves in way of trade with the Board of Education for the supplying of books in the private schools for the whole island, we can do important business, and so we take the liberty to ask you for your general catalogue of your publications with the most liberal discounts which you can allow us. These discounts, natu-

Original Spanish text of the letter from the Puerto Rican firm ordering copies of Ira Remsen's 1886 book
The Elements of Chemistry *(Princeton University Library)*

rally are the primary basis of our dealings, for the reason that the main thing with the pupils is to sell them the books at the list prices, thus encouraging them to buy them freely, and getting for ourselves a larger profit.

We begin by ordering of you eighteen (18) copies [of] Remsen's Elements of Chemistry, which please send us at once to D. A. de Lima and Company, 17 State Street, New York, who are about to send us other goods, so that we wish to avail ourselves of the opportunity.

All the purchases that we make of you will be paid for [with] cash in New York, and the amount for the books that we now ask you for may be collected immediately of our bankers, Lawrence Turnure and Company, 50 Wall Street, New York, on presentation of the bill.

Awaiting your reply, etc., we are, etc.,
Yours, etc.,
A. Lynn e Hijos de Perez Moris

* * *

Through the years Holt and Company alerted Remsen to changes in the field of chemistry and the consequent need to update his books. Remsen responded with his own views.

April 27, 1900.

Dear Mr. Holt:

I do not understand how the statement can be made that the latest editions of my Chemistries say nothing about Argon. The last edition of the advanced book in my possession is the one with the imprint 1898. Page 259 gives a brief, but, it seems to me, entirely satisfactory account of this substance, in accordance with our present knowledge. The element is also included in the list on page 21, and it is also in the index, so that it would be very hard to miss it in case one were looking for it.

In the Briefer Course it is referred to on page 132, and in the index. To be sure the reference in the text is meagre, and that may be the point the critics have in mind. I have never taken out of these books anything that I have said about Argon. There is some misunderstanding somewhere. Please have the last edition of the big book examined. If there is no treatment of Argon in that book, I am entirely at a loss to explain the fact.

Within the last two years, that is in June, 1898, Ramsay announced the discovery of "three companions of Argon," as he calls them, in the air-minute quantities. These might be mentioned, but there is extremely little known about them and nobody else has thus far worked with them. Still, if I were writing the books to-day I should give these substances brief mention.

In connection with the work on Argon, Ramsay found evidences of the presence of a gas which had previously been found in the atmosphere of the sun, and therefore called Helium. In the edition of 1898 of the big book this discovery is presented on page 585. There is, however, no reference to this in the Briefer Course. It may be this the critics are carping at.

Yours sincerely,
Ira Remsen

Dec. 18, 1914.

Dear Sirs:

I am enclosing a review of the new edition of my Inorganic Chemistry which has just appeared in Germany. This leads me to raise the question whether anything can be done or, rather, whether you think I can do anything to put new life into my books on your list? They are plainly losing ground and, from the fact that you made no suggestions to me for some time past, I infer that you feel that resuscitation is out of the question.

My Organic Chemistry (Heath) more than holds its own. More copies were sold last year than in any previous year.

My Theoretical Chemistry (Lea) has been out of print for some time, and I have decided not to revise it as I should have to rewrite it from first to last, and that particular task does not appeal to me.

Germany seems to like my books. Is this to be ascribed to Militärismus or Kultur?

Yours very truly,
Ira Remsen

* * *

Holt and Company cited the views of schoolteachers (as reported by book salesmen) in asking Remsen for further revisions to his chemistry textbooks.

Nov. 26, 1900

. . . .

[S]ee if you cannot fit the new matter on physical chemistry on to the Briefer Course. The book ought to be rewritten, even if only for the name "new edition," and the sooner the better. You scientific gentlemen are responsible for the feeling that obtains among teachers that a book seven, or eight years old must necessarily be behind the times. . . .

Dec. 4, 1900

You won't forget, will you, to record the new ways of making sulphuric acid and aluminum. Some of the agents have apparently fixed on these 2 points as evidence that the book is not up to the times.

AMERICAN SCIENCE SERIES, BRIEFER COURSE

AN INTRODUCTION TO THE STUDY OF CHEMISTRY

BY

IRA REMSEN

President of The Johns Hopkins University

SEVENTH EDITION, REVISED AND ENLARGED

NEW YORK
HENRY HOLT AND COMPANY
1907

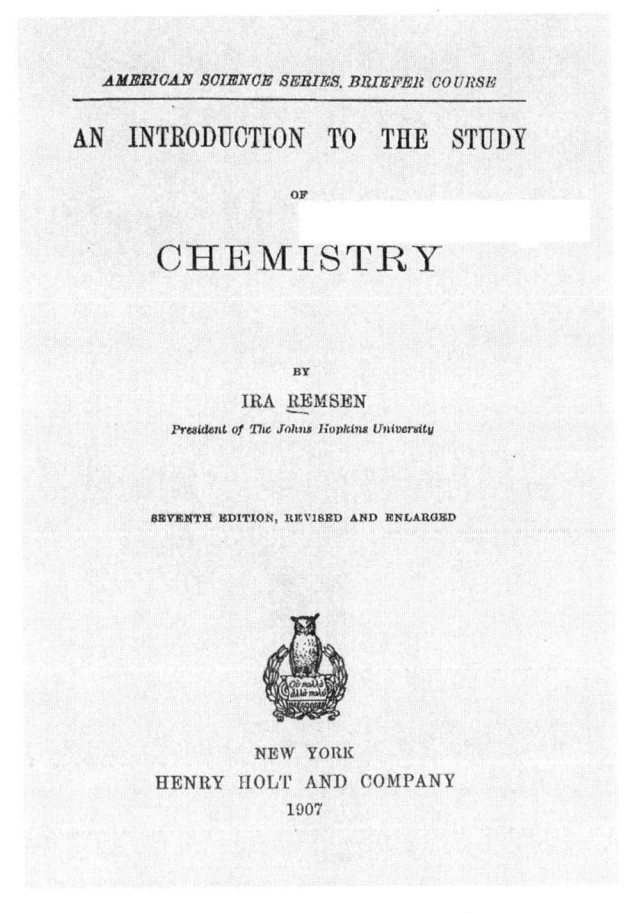

Title page for the seventh edition of the abbreviated version of Remsen's study that was first published in 1886 (Rutgers University Library)

Vernon L. Kellogg

The American zoologist Vernon Lyman Kellogg was trained as an entomologist and natural historian at the University of Kansas, Cornell University, and the University of Leipzig. He became professor of entomology at the newly formed Stanford University in 1894. Holt and Company published one of Kellogg's most popular books, Darwinism To-day *(1907), as well as other of his works, including* Elementary Zoology *(1901),* Insect Stories *(1908), and* Elementary Textbook of Economic Zoology and Entomology *(1915), which Kellogg co-wrote with Rennie Wilbur Doane.*

19 January 1901

Gentlemen:–

I have this morning received the second lot of picture proofs [for *Elementary Zoology*] and also your note of 14 January saying that the first installment of text proof had been sent. The picture proofs are for the most part satisfactory; in a few instances the rather free use of the engraver's tool has given a rather hard effect. In one instance especially is this noticeable, and I send you proof of the block to see whether you may not wish to ask the process people to make a new block in an attempt to get a softer and less staring picture. With regard to the dissection plates I quite agree with you with regard to the desirability of making the best of these drawings. The double plate scheme is an admirable one, and I am grateful to you for your hearty co-operation in the

---

Puff-Balls

In 1901 Holt and Company published Studies in American Fungi: Mushrooms, Edible, Poisonous, Etc., *by George Francis Atkinson, professor of botany at Cornell University and botanist of the Cornell Agricultural Experiment Station. The book had originally been published by Andrus and Church of Ithaca, New York, in 1900. The second Holt and Company edition, published in 1903, included "230 illustrations from photographs by the author, and colored plates by F. R. Rathbun." A domestic note was struck by the inclusion of "Recipes for Cooking Mushrooms" by Sarah Tyson Rorer.*

To be eatable, the puff-balls must be perfectly white to the very center. Pare off the skin; cut them into slices; dust with salt and pepper. Have ready in a large, shallow pan a sufficient quantity of hot oil to cover the bottom. Throw in the slices and, when brown on one side, turn and brown on the other; serve at once on a heated dish.

A la Poulette.–Pare the puff-balls; cut them into slices and then into dice; put them into a saucepan, allowing a tablespoonful of butter to each pint of blocks. Cover the saucepan; stew gently for fifteen minutes; lift the lid; sprinkle over a teaspoonful of salt and a dash of pepper. Beat the yolks of three eggs until light; add a half cup of cream and a half cup of milk; pour this into the hot mixture, and shake until smoking hot. Do not allow them to boil. Serve in a heated vegetable dish, with blocks of toast over the top. . . .

Puff-Balls with Agaricus campestris.–As the *Agaricus campestris* has a rather strong flavor and the puff-balls are mild, both are better for being mixed in the cooking. Take equal quantities of *Agaricus campestris* and puff-balls; pare and cut the puff-balls into blocks; to each half pound allow a tablespoonful of butter. Put the butter in a saucepan, add the mushrooms, sprinkle over the salt (allowing a half teaspoonful always to each pint); cover the saucepan and stew slowly for twenty minutes. Moisten a tablespoonful of flour in a half cup of milk, add it to the mixture, stir and cook for just a moment, add a dash of pepper, and serve in a heated dish.

–Studies in American Fungi: Mushrooms, Edible, Poisonous, Etc., second edition (New York: Holt, 1903)

treatment of the book. You suggest making double plates of the frog, sunfish, garter snake, mouse, sparrow, and mussel, six in all, and of cutting apart and making text figures of the earth worm, crayfish, and insect, and finally of putting the starfish on a single full-page. All these suggestions are entirely satisfactory. I think also with you that it would be well to reduce the frog a little more thus making it about life size. In the block (proof No. 3) as at present made, the engraver has cut off the word "rectum" at the end of the second line of leaders from the bottom on the right hand side.

I enclose herewith final account for drawings and photographs. . . .

                  Very sincerely yours,
                  V. L. Kellogg

* * *

Kellogg wrote from Honolulu regarding another series that Holt and Company was planning to launch, the American Nature Series. His Insect Stories *was published in 1908 as part of the series.*

                  29 May 1902

Gentlemen

Referring again to your favor of 14 May in regard to the "American Nature Series." (answered briefly from San Francisco on 21 May).

I am glad that you purpose undertaking such a series. A host of nature books has appeared in the last few years but so many are obviously ephemeral in character: and so many are more poetry than Nature: and so many are so uncertain in aim—that a series of seriously written and authoritative books—presenting known facts of natural history for non-specialized but educated and intelligent readers—is still a desideratum.

The Cambridge Natural History (English authors) does this well—but leaves American natural history so sadly out of account that the series only stimulates in American readers a desire for similar books using American animals and plants as subjects.

I shall be glad to modify my insect book to fit into this series—and especially gladly as it relieves me of a dilemma which has been the cause of my delay in going to work on the book: namely my hesitation to send out a book as a direct competitor of the college systematic manual of insects by my friend Prof. J. H. Comstock of Cornell.

The American Nature insect book will not offer itself as a college manual, but as a college reference, perhaps, and especially as a general account of American insect life.

ELEMENTARY TEXTBOOK OF
ECONOMIC ZOOLOGY
AND
ENTOMOLOGY

BY
VERNON LYMAN KELLOGG
PROFESSOR OF ENTOMOLOGY AND LECTURER IN BIONOMICS
IN STANFORD UNIVERSITY

AND

RENNIE WILBUR DOANE
ASSISTANT PROFESSOR OF ECONOMIC ENTOMOLOGY
IN STANFORD UNIVERSITY

NEW YORK
HENRY HOLT AND COMPANY

*Title page for Kellogg's 1915 textbook
(Rutgers University Library)*

I urge again your consideration of Professor W. H. Dudley as the author of your book on trees. He is absolutely competent both as authority and as an unusually graceful writer to make a splendid book for you.

I shall try by the way to make a number of photographs of the trees in these islands and in Samoa—which I shall be glad to turn over to you for the use of whomever undertakes the trees book. It should certainly include some account of the tropical flora which the possession of our few colonies enables us to include in American Nature.

                  Very truly yours,
                  V. L. Kellogg

William Beebe

Naturalist William Beebe's career provides a good example of Henry Holt's knack for identifying potential authors and suggesting the direction they might take in their writing. Holt and

Company titles by Beebe included The Bird: Its Form and Function *(1906);* The Log of the Sun: A Chronicle of Nature's Year *(1906);* Our Search for a Wilderness: An Account of Two Ornithological Expeditions to Venezuela and to British Guiana *(1910), cowritten with his first wife, Mary Blair Beebe;* Jungle Peace *(1918); and* Edge of the Jungle *(1921). Beebe had a particular genius for making technical scientific knowledge accessible to the layperson, a talent that Henry Holt, publisher of the Home University Library series, readily appreciated. In the summer of 1902 Holt, having read a newspaper article by Beebe about birds, asked Edward N. Bristol to approach the naturalist about publishing a book.*

June 4, 1902

Dear Mr. Holt:

As soon as I got your telegram Monday in regard to the Beebe bird article, I hunted up the paper and tried to hunt up the man . . . all that I did with him was to ascertain if he had thought of utilizing his various articles in the 'Tribune' and the 'Post,' or the material upon which they were founded in making a book. He had not thought of doing this. . . . Beebe said that Doubleday-Page had been after him for a book on birds, but that he did not take any stock in their series. Most of it was 'flea powder' he said."

Very truly yours,
E. N. Bristol

A week later Beebe wrote Holt on New York Zoological Society stationery.

June. 11. 1902.

My dear Sir:

Your letter of the 6th and the prospectus received yesterday, and I am very much interested in your plan.

Such a book as you speak of, has long been an ambition of mine, one to "answer the questions of unscientific, intelligent people." That expresses it exactly, and the majority of contemporary bird-books do this only to the extent of the birds names,—necessary, but which should be mere handles to facilitate their real study. After giving a series of lectures to teachers of New York State at the American Museum recently, I found that while many could identify fifty to one hundred birds, not *one* knew the significance of scales on a birds foot!

I should thoroughly enjoy undertaking such a book, and although I had not thought of doing so for a year or two, I am very happily situated to do the work thoroughly and with but little delay. But a book of such a character is a daring thing for a young man to attempt in the face of the overwhelming mass of ornithological literature, and the references and translating necessary to be able to compare all the latest researches will be a big undertaking, and I should be unwilling to attempt it

Naturalist William Beebe (from Stanley Kunitz, Living Authors, *1932; Thomas Cooper Library, University of South Carolina)*

unless it was to be as perfect scientifically as I could make it.

You ask, and rightly, for credentials. I have taken the entire three years course in Pure Science at Columbia under Profs. Osborn and Wilson. I took no degree for the reason that I preferred to devote all my time to science and literature, and nowadays the time gained in omitting mathematics, etc. is, I think, worth far more than a degree, at least it has proved so in my case. *Results* count most with a naturalist of the present day.

I have almost unprecedented opportunities for studying hundreds of varieties of birds, both living and in the flesh, and having full access to the museum collections and the Columbia laboratories, more advantages for study and research are accessible than I can ever avail myself of.

Last year I devoted my time to the diseases of birds, and succeeded in curing some twenty-seven out of thirty-five maladies. This year I am more carefully overseeing the rearing of young wild birds, which gives me plenty of time for dissection or study. In a way this is not foreign to our subject, so I have ventured to inflict an unpardonable amount of 'ego' upon you.

I should like, in a book of this character to have a generous supply of photographic illustrations, gross and microscopic, of the subjects treated.

The "Nature Photography" business has been run to death, but *really good* pictures are rare, and I have had very good success in obtaining unique ones. I send several untouched prints which even in their unfinished condition will illustrate what I mean. The swans breast-bone would come in among vocal organs, the California partridges as examples of ornaments, the snake-bird (in connection with dissections) showing the crook-trigger in the neck vertebrae, the Cassowarys tracks as comparable with those in the old sandstone, the owl under protective coloration, the young robin showing ancestral evolutionary characters and so on.

I agree with you that a more or less anatomical arrangement (eschewing the name) would perhaps be best, but if so, this must be closely interwoven with biological interests. There is a strong feeling (which I share) against wholesale killing and dissection and I should like to enable people (by descriptions and photographs) to be able to appreciate both the outer and inner structure of birds without their having to use laboratory guides.

My principal idea would be this. To interpret scientific facts which have been heretofore considered too dry to interest anyone but a specialist; to clothe these with the interest which is possible, and make them as interesting reading as they are scientifically correct.

The gulf between the public and the scientist proper, in spite of "popular nature books," is widening daily in all except trivial facts, and a bridge between would be welcome I am sure.

Seeing hundreds of people daily at the Zoological Park, and hearing their comments on the birds and animals, I think I can speak with some assurance.

Last but not least, I will have the benefit of Prof. Henry F. Osborn's sympathy and encouragement, whose help in difficult places will be of inestimable value.

I will make out a tentative working thesis, and submit it to you, when it assumes a satisfactory form.

Very truly yours,
C. William Beebe

Any hints you can give me in managing an 'embryo' book, will be of great assistance, as that species is new to me!

Oct. 25. 1902.

Dear Mr. Holt,–

Your letter of Thursday has just arrived. My conscience pricks me sorely that I left so many weak points for you to ferret out, but believe me the ferreting will do me much good and I am sure the errors which I made in preparing this book will help me greatly in another. I have been working very hard lately and before long will submit the feather chapters of the larger book.

Your re-arrangement idea came to me last week and I mentally made a recast which exactly agreed with yours, except the "perversities" division which I like very much.

The name is harder than anything else. All that has come to me is, "Birds in a Zoological Park;" "Bird Gossip from" or "Bird Notes from a Zoological Park."

I rather like the idea of bringing in the fact of a Zoo somewhere, as that would interest persons in many cities, but your suggestion appeals to me strongly.

I have some new photographs to go in the book, some very fine ones.

I shall begin a careful revision of the manuscript at once. Would it be necessary to type-write it again or insert new portions by cutting & pasting?

Sincerely yours,
C. William Beebe

Other Science Textbooks

Requests for translations of Holt and Company textbooks came in regularly. Edwin H. Hall was co-author, with Joseph Y. Bergen, of A Text-book of Physics, Largely Experimental *(1891).*

March 19, 1913

My dear Professor Hall:

We have just received the enclosed letter from Mr. Fitch of Hangchow, China, concerning the translation of your Text-book of Physics. As far as we are concerned, we would be only too glad to give him permission, and we suppose you will have no objection either. Do you think it would be worth while to send him a copy of the new edition? If so we will gladly do so, but we fear he has got along too far in the translation of the third edition to make it of any use to him. Kindly return Mr. Fitch's letter with your answer. We presume it will not be neces-

> ## Apologia of 1938
>
> William Beebe
>
> One-third of a century ago I wrote the two and fifty essays in this volume. At that time airplanes and radios were unknown; automobiles were the toys of wealthy men, as rare in the streets of New York as is the horse today. I might continue indefinitely, outlining a picture whose changes at first thought seem very radical.
>
> Together with the rush and worry of so-called progress, the violent vocal concussions of politics, the race for preparation to maim and kill as many fellow beings in as short a space of time as possible, I see (as Dooley would say in 1906), "I see by the papers" this morning that sixty-four species of migrating birds have been identified in Central Park within a week. Thirty-three years ago as a subject for early May I chose "The High Tide of Bird Life." Time has wrought no change at least in my facts.
>
> . . . .
>
> –"Apologia of 1938," in *The Log of the Sun: A Chronicle of Nature's Year* (New York: Holt, 1938), p. vii

sary to get Mr. Bergen's permission, as the third edition is practically all yours.

Very truly yours,
[Unsigned]

March 20, 1913

Gentlemen:

I am much set up over the idea of having the Hall and Bergen turned into Chinese, though it always has been Chinese to some people. I would send him, Mr. Fitch, a copy of the new book at once, for I think it would be a better one for his purpose. Couldn't you let him have duplicates of the cuts for Figures? I have a number of very small corrections to send you for the Hall's Physics

Very truly yours,
Edwin H. Hall

* * *

Another durable science textbook was chemist Charles Elwood Dull's Modern Chemistry, *published by Holt in 1931 and revised in 1950. Other Holt titles by Dull included* Essentials of Modern Chemistry *(1918) and* High School Chemistry *(1925).*

December 2, 1930

Gentlemen:

Your letter of November 18th to the Potash Importing Corporation of America has been referred to this company for consideration. Please be advised that we shall be glad to send you within the next few days copies of photographs showing the effect of potassium fertilizer on crop yield for publication in the new edition of High School chemistry text by C. E. Dull.

* * *

Yours very truly,
N. V. POTASH EXPORT MY. INC.
Agricultural and Scientific Bureau
New York Office
J. D. Romaine

* * *

William O. Brooks of the War Department's Chemical Warfare Service wrote to J. V. Crooks of Holt's school editorial department with corrections for Dull's Laboratory Exercises in Chemistry *(1943).*

June 5, 1942.

Dear Mr. Crooks:

Thank you for your letter of June 1, 1942. I realize what a turmoil exists when a new book is in the throes of childbirth.

Taking up the questions you raised, the term "oil gas" is satisfactory. I am not surprised that Mr. Dull prefers to use "adsorb". Of course, he is technically correct there. Taking up the galleys which you returned to me:

a. Page 79. Figure 6-4. I presume that diagram may be correct and that mercury does stay in the tube as Mr. Dull seems to think. Unfortunately, I do not have a laboratory here so that I could try out the experiment. Probably he has done so and found that it works.

b. Page 141. Section 179. "You are given a box full of marbles: 50% of the marbles are red and weigh 10 gm. each . . . etc." I do think that Mr. Dull is wrong in this section. I believe that as the statement is given in the book that the ratio must be 5-3-2, not 5-2-1. Several of my associates here agree with me. At any rate, if it is a point causing such controversy so that experienced chemists do not agree with the explanation which is given, I believe that that is sufficient in itself to cause the example to be changed. Otherwise, it will confuse high-school students.

c. Page 96. Mr. Dull raises the question as to the temperature of a magnesium incendiary bomb. We are in agreement here that its temperature is 3300 to 3500° F. However, I think his statement in the book is all right as the reaction is due to the high reaction rate of the magnesium uniting with the oxygen at the high temperature. No changes needed.

d. Page 81. I accept his explanation for the Boyle's Law curve.

e. Page 194. "Molasses, as used in baking cookies, unites with the sodium of baking soda . ." I maintain that Mr. Dull is wrong in this statement. Molasses is a mixture of sugar, acids, coloring matter, etc. Therefore, molasses cannot per se unite with anything but, rather, some of the materials in the mixture may unite with other substances. In this case, it is the acid which is present in the molasses that reacts with the sodium bicarbonate. His statement is absolutely wrong. My associates agree with me.

f. Page 194. "One type of baking power [sic] uses tartaric acid, or cream of tartar;". This statement, as given, is wrong. A student would get the impression from the wording that tartaric acid and cream of tartar are synonymous, which is not the case. It is true that a baking powder can be made using *either* tartaric acid or cream of tartar, but actually, as I stated on the galley, they usually contain both.

g. Page 192. Debatable point. Is sodium acid sulfate or neutral sodium sulfate produced in the soda-acid fire extinguisher? I have looked this up in a number of text-books and find a half-dozen that give the equation as Mr. Dull does, producing neutral sodium sulfate. However, I had read somewhere that the bisulfate is normally produced. I do know that the fluid from such an extinguisher is strongly acid and ruins clothing. If the sodium sulfate is neutral, how do you account for this acid reaction? My associates agree with me that bisulfate is produced in this fire extinguisher, but the text-books seem to disagree. Hence, I suggest that you leave the point as Mr. Dull has expressed it, but I go down still arguing.

h. Page 106. "An alcoholic solution of a nonvolatile substance is called a tincture. For example, tincture of iodine is principally . .". In one sentence, he gives a definition, then he selects an example, and picks for that example a substance which directly violates his definition. Common usage notwithstanding, he is violating the definition which he has given in the preceding sentence. I realize that students are familiar with tincture of iodine and that possibly it is the only "tincture" which they have heard mentioned, but I still prefer a change to tincture of Capsicum, or tincture of ginger. There are fifty-four official tinctures in the U.S. Pharamacopeia, and of these fifty-four, iodine is the only volatile substance, all the others are alcoholic solutions of nonvolatile materials in accordance with his definition.

I have enjoyed working on the book. I hope that Mr. Dull does not hold against me personally the criticisms which I have raised. An author inevitably is placed on the defensive when errors or suggested changes are made in his work, and it is only human to be somewhat hostile to such comments. I know, because I have gone through it myself from the author's viewpoint. However, Mr. Dull has written so many books over such a long period of years that he has doubtless grown hard boiled to criticisms and realizes that, in my case, I am merely trying to be helpful.

Best wishes.

Yours very truly,
William O. Brooks,
Major, C.W.S.

THE SOCIAL SCIENCES

Robert M. Yerkes

Holt and Company helped to pioneer modern developments in psychology with the publication of four books by the prominent American psychologist Robert M. Yerkes. These included Introduction to Psychology *(1911);* Methods of Studying Vision in Animals *(1911), by Yerkes and John B. Watson;* The Mental Life of Monkeys and Apes *(1916), published privately by Yerkes and distributed by Holt; and* Army Mental Tests *(1920), compiled and edited by Yerkes and Clarence Yoakum. These titles reflect Yerkes' major contributions to psychology: he helped to establish the field as an experimental science; he was among the first scientists to study animals in a laboratory setting; and he was a pioneer in the use of standardized intelligence tests. With Watson he founded* The Journal of Animal Behavior *in 1911.*

3/24/11.

My dear Mr. Bristol:

I enclose properly signed agreement. Thank you. I trust our relations may be long and profitably continued. My faith in the success of our publications is firm! Have just received entry notice of the Journal as second class matter in Cambridge.

Psychologist Robert M. Yerkes (© Bettman/CORBIS)

By all means take a look at [S. J.] Holmes Ms. He is a very able fellow, but his Ms. may be in bad form! I am surprised he did not offer the same for Animal Behavior Series. I had not heard even that he was writing the book. You know he is a member of the editorial board of the Journal of Animal Behavior.

What about a title for my attempt at a psychology? Your opinion I should prize. I am hoping to complete correcting my galley proofs before April 1st and hope that I may complete paper and index before April 17–as at that time I shall go to Ithaca for a few days.

      Yours cordially,
      Robert M. Yerkes

      May 23, 1911.

Dear Sirs:

I have samples of covers for my Introduction to Psychology and am returning the one which I prefer with this letter. I think this green cover will make up well. It has good "feel," is unlike any other American text-book of psychology, and certainly is not especially objectionable from the standpoint of appearance.

Your Mr. Burnett informed me the other day that I should receive 10 copies of my book free and could buy additional copies for presentation as half the retail price. I wish you would send me, as soon as the book is ready, fifteen copies in addition to the ten which you present. Twenty-five copies in all.

I am delighted with the prospect of having the book out by June first and am helping you to accomplish that end by sending my reply concerning cover thus promptly.

When you send me bill for books I should be obliged if you would let me know the total cost of corrections on my book. I do not think I overran your allowance, but I am curious to know just how much additional expense my changes caused.

With hearty thanks for your most satisfactory handling of the manufacture of my little book and for your uniform kindness, I am,

      Yours very truly,
      Robert M. Yerkes.

P.S. From Journal of Animal Behavior. Are we to understand, Mr. Vogelius [of the Holt and Company production staff], that you desire only one page of advertising in no. 4 of Journal of Animal Behavior? You are entitled to two pages at cost and have heretofore used two. Shall we not continue your second page as it stands? R.M.Y.[1]

Note

1. Directly below the postscript is written "Yes–Recent Bks on Darwinism."

* * *

Yerkes hoped to interest Holt and Company in a work in progress to be titled "Genetic Psychology," but it was never published in book form.

      February 25, 1914.

Dear Mr. Bristol:

I have been at work on my "Genetic Psychology" more or less during the past few months, and I have recently decided that it will be a considerable help to me to tie myself definitely to the publication of such a book. I am therefore writing to ask whether you care to make advance arrangements and to announce the book as you previously announced my "Introduction to Psychology" and Watson's "Comparative Psychology". This will obligate me and serve as pressure upon me, while at the same time supplying psychologists with the information that I am at work on a manual within my special field.

I have decided to give you the first chance at this book because of our pleasant and wholly satisfactory experiences. The Macmillan Company wants the book, and in case you do not desire it, I should naturally turn to them, I think.

Title page for the 1917 student edition of the French writer's 1885 novel (Rutgers University Library)

A word further about my plans.–I propose, as I wrote you some months ago, to write a manual which I should call "Genetic Psychology" in which, from the comparative point of view, I should deal, for the purposes of students, with materials of animal psychology, child psychology, social psychology, and abnormal psychology. I should hope that the bulk of the book might be limited to five or six hundred pages, but in any event it would be a substantial volume, perhaps similar to Titchener's [sic] textbook of psychology. There is no textbook of genetic psychology available today which is worth considering, and I am confident that in this case, if not previously, I am prepared to write a book which will be of distinct service to the public and which will find immediate use with teachers of psychology. I speak of it as "Genetic Psychology" rather than as "Comparative Psychology" because to many comparative psychology means the psychology of animals. Of course I shall be glad to give you more detailed information about the book, if you wish it, and certainly in the event of an announcement, I should wish the opportunity to prepare a statement.

With hearty thanks for your reaction to this proposal and the hope that I may be able to see you sometime during March when I shall be in New York for a few days, I am

Yours faithfully,
Robert M. Yerkes

March 23, 1916.

Dear Mr. Bristol:

I am just publishing in the Behavior Monographs an account of a study of the ideational behavior of monkeys and apes. It is doubtless the most interesting bit of scientific description I have ever written, and quite apart from my desire to get my money out of the publication, I think the monograph should sell fairly well!

I am writing to ask whether you will do me the favor, in connection with this publication, of giving it a page or half page in your catalogue, that is, listing it regularly among your publications, giving it such additional advertising as seems to you justified, and distributing for me, on the following terms.

I should supply you with bound copies, ready for the market, as needed at the rate of one dollar ($1.) while your listing price of the book should be one dollar and fifty cents ($1.50) postpaid, this being the price at which we list the monograph in our series. We should, of course, wish to retain the right of filling such orders for separate copies as come to the Cambridge office of the monographs.

I am making this request with the thought that it may be not only a favor to me and a means of enabling me to get at least some substantial part of my five or six hundred dollars investment out of the monograph, but that it may also prove commercially worth while to you. Should I attempt to advertise the book and have it sold from this office, I should soon expend half of the returns which I might reasonably expect. On the other hand, you can advertise so much more cheaply and distribute so much more satisfactorily that I very much hope for your coöperation.

The monograph, of which I shall be able to send you a bound copy in a few days if all goes well, consists of iv+145 pages, with six full page half tones and five text figures. It has been expensive of manufacture because of a number of complicated tables as well as illustrations. I believe that had you made a book out of the materials for me, you would doubtless have fixed a price above one dollar and fifty cents.

If my request appeals to you as reasonable and feasible, I should be very glad to hear from you at your earliest convenience and to enter upon agreement at once, having one hundred (100) bound copies sent to you within a few days.

Yours faithfully,
Robert M. Yerkes

Title

"The mental life of monkeys and apes: a study of ideational behavior."

* * *

Yerkes played the role of intermediary when Watson clashed with Holt and Company over the issue of corrections to his Behavior: An Introduction to Comparative Psychology *(1914).*

November 3, 1916

Dear Mr. Bristol:

Professor Watson of Johns Hopkins has just written, making a request which somewhat embarrasses me. He explains that he has had trouble with you and asks if I will act as an intermediary between your firm and himself. I fully realize the delicacy of the situation, and I shall try not to violate the rights or feelings of either party.

What I wish to ask is, not that you should issue a second edition of Professor Watson's book, unless your judgment dictates it, but instead that as soon as you can see your way to the publication of another edition, you give Professor Watson opportunity to make certain extremely important corrections in the book. As he says, there are several very bad slips, and these I am quite anxious to see corrected, for the sake of our science, as is he.

I am the more willing to write you in this way because our relations have been so wholly satisfactory to me. I feel sure that the blame is not chiefly yours, for I have had some experience with Professor Watson's manuscripts and proofs, and I know that he is liable to try the patience of editors, printers, and publishers. It will certainly be a great satisfaction to me if I can in any way help to reëstablish friendly relations between your firm and him. So if you see any way to use me in this connection, please feel wholly free to do so.

With apologies for thus butting in on your business affairs, I am

Cordially yours,
Robert M. Yerkes

I am working on my "Genetic Psychology"! so long delayed.

Watson thanked Yerkes for intervening with Holt and Company on his behalf.

21 November 1916

Dear Robert:

. . . .

I wish to thank you for your efforts in my behalf in settling the Holt difficulty. I think he has written a much more decent letter than I would have been willing to write some time ago; it must have been some little effort for him to do it. It would be more than indecent in me if I did not meet him at least half way. I wish you would say for me that however hot I might have felt about the charges there was no reason for me to lose my temper and write them the letter I did. If he and I could establish communications on purely objective grounds I should be very glad indeed. I note what they say about the sale of Behavior. I think Holts will undoubtedly get their money back and something besides. I should be greatly surprised if the sales did not really increase some in the next two or three years. The reason for the decline is that the Harvard purchase was very large at first, indeed unprecedented, and since that time there has been no extremely large order. I note too what they say about the corrections. I should not want them to discard the copies already printed. What I should like to do would be to pick up all of the actually necessary corrections, for example, a few stray "singulars" or "plurals," one or two sentences which will not parse, places where the printer pied the work in the foundry proof, etc. These I would keep to absolutely bare necessities. Then when the book paid out, as I am sure it will do in two or three years, I would like for them to let me bring it up to date. I do not yet feel like asking Holt to publish the objective psychology for me until they have paid out on the other book. Scribners have asked me for a book, and from what you say and from what others say I shall certainly not let Badger publish one for me. What would you think of that proposition of getting my own university press to publish it for me, taking all the profits until it is paid for and then giving them all to me less ten or fifteen per cent? They would be glad to do it for me.

The book I am planning will probably not sell very well because I am going to write the kind of book I want to write regardless of whether it will sell or not. It will be a book a little larger than my animal book and will be about the same level. If it meets with any success at all I will then prepare an introductory text from it. That ought to pay pretty well and I would want the publisher who published the first book to publish the introductory text as well.

Thanking you for your trouble and great consideration in this matter, I am

Sincerely yours,
John [Watson]

P.S. I shall be very glad to receive a letter from Bristol and shall be glad to answer it in kind.

* * *

The military's successful use of the tests in Yerkes and Yoakum's Army Mental Tests *during World War I marked the beginning of Americans' widespread use of standardized tests in other contexts.*

April 17, 1919

Dear Mr. Bristol:

The War Department yesterday approved request for authorization to publish a book on Army Mental Tests.

Yerkes' colleague and sometime co-author John B. Watson, with whom he founded The Journal of Animal Behavior *in 1911 (from Kerry W. Buckley,* Mechanical Man, *1989; Thomas Cooper Library, University of South Carolina)*

I shall submit the proposition with your proposed contract to the Chairman of the National Research Council at once hoping that satisfactory arrangements may be agreed upon. In the meantime, we shall proceed with preparation of manuscript. I hope that it may be ready for press very soon.

Cordially yours,
Robert M. Yerkes

Introduction to *Army Mental Tests*
Robert M. Yerkes

The introduction to Army Mental Tests *was reprinted, in part, from a lecture delivered by Yerkes in New York on 25 January 1919.*

The human factors in most practical situations have been neglected largely because of our consciousness of ignorance and our inability to control them. Whereas engineers deal constantly with physical problems of quality, capacity, stress and strain, they have tended to think of problems of human conduct and experience either as unsolved or as insoluble. At the same time there has existed a growing consciousness of the practical significance of these human factors and of the importance of such systematic research as shall extend our knowledge of them and increase our directive power.

The great war from which we are now emerging into a civilization in many respects new has already worked marvelous changes in our points of view, our expectations and practical demands. Relatively early in this supreme struggle, it became clear to certain individuals that the proper utilization of man power, and more particularly of mind or brain power, would assure ultimate victory. The war demanded of us the speedy mobilization of our military machine and in addition the organization and training of an immense supplementary armed force, the manufacture of ordnance and munitions of war in well-nigh unimaginable quantities, the construction of ships, motor transports, and of varieties of rolling stock in vast numbers. All this had to be done in the least possible time. Never before in the history of civilization was brain, as contrasted with brawn, so important; never before, the proper placement and utilization of brain power so essential to success.

Our War Department, nerved to exceptional risks by the stern necessity for early victory, saw and immediately seized its opportunity to develop various new lines of personnel work. Among these is numbered the psychological service. Great will be our good fortune if the lesson in human engineering which the war has taught is carried over directly and effectively into our civil institutions and activities.

PREFACE TO
WORLD LITERATURE

BY

ALBERT GUÉRARD
PROFESSOR OF GENERAL AND COMPARATIVE LITERATURE
STANFORD UNIVERSITY

NEW YORK
HENRY HOLT AND COMPANY

Title page for the 1940 literary study
(Rutgers University Library)

Scarcely had war been declared by our country before the psychologists were brought together in a plan to make their professional knowledge, technique, and experience useful in the emergency. In April, 1917, the American Psychological Association appointed numerous committees to study the situation and prepare for action. At the same time a Committee for Psychology was organized by the National Research Council. Thus it happened that from the outset American psychologists acted unitedly, whereas their professional colleagues in France and Great Britain served individually wherever they could discover opportunity. The Committee for Psychology of the National Research Council has continued active over a period of nearly two years. Almost all of the psychological contributions which the United States has made to the war are either directly or indirectly due to the efforts or the support of this body, the work of which has been carried on through conferences, sub-committees, or military appointees in the army and the navy.

In order that the psychological examining of the soldier may be seen in its proper setting, the various chiefly significant lines of psychological service will be enumerated and briefly characterized.

Under the Adjutant General, the Committee on Classification of Personnel in the Army, which was originally organized by a group of psychologists who were at the time serving as members of the Committee for Psychology of the National Research Council or of committees of the American Psychological Association for the furtherance of the military service, developed and introduced throughout the army methods of classifying and assigning enlisted men in accordance with occupational and educational qualifications and also methods of rating officers for appointment and promotion. The services of this Committee, to the work of which the War Department dedicated nearly a million dollars, ultimately touched and more or less profoundly modified almost every important aspect of military personnel.

To the Signal Corps, and subsequently to the Division of Military Aëronautics, psychological service was rendered in connection with measurement of the effects of high altitude and also in the selection and placement of men. Numerous important methods new or adapted, were introduced in this service by groups of psychologists whose primary concern was improved placement and the proper utilization and protection of the flyer.

The Committee for Psychology promoted effectively interest in measures for the control and improvement of both military and civilian morale. The interest and persistent activity of its members ultimately resulted in the organization of a Morale Branch within the General Staff of the Army. At various times as many as twenty-five officers and enlisted men trained in military psychology were engaged in the conduct of practical morale work.

For the Division of Military Intelligence psychological methods were devised or adapted to assist in the selection, placement and effective training of scouts and observers and in addition service of minor importance was rendered in numerous training camps.

In response to requests from the Chemical Warfare Service, psychological problems presented by the gas mask were studied and the major recommendations resulting from these investigations were embodied in the latest improved form of mask.

The psychological problems either partially or completely solved for the navy are comprehended in the proper selection, placement and training of gunners, listeners and lookouts. Numerous situations were carefully analyzed for the navy, and methods and mechanical devices which have achieved extensive application and appreciation were developed.

Within the Medical Department of the Army a Division of Psychology was organized for the administration of mental tests to enlisted men and commissioned officers in accordance with plans perfected during the summer of 1917. The history of this work will be briefly told as an introduction to the account of methods and results.

The chief purpose of the psychological assistance originally offered to the Medical Department was the prompt elimination of recruits whose grade of intelligence is too low for satisfactory service. It was believed by psychologists assembled in conference that their profession is better prepared technically and by practical experience to measure intelligence than are members of the medical profession and that psychologists therefore should be able in the military emergency to render invaluable assistance to medical officers by supplying reliable measures of intelligence which might be used as partial basis for rejection or discharge. Thus, it was thought, the efficiency of the service might be considerably increased and the costs materially diminished. As it happens, the purposes of this service as actually developed differ radically from that originally purposed; moreover they serve to identify this work even more closely with the personnel work of the Adjutant General's Office and the General Staff than with anything in the Medical Department of the Army aside from neuro-psychiatric work.

To meet the prospective need of psychological assistance a committee of seven experts in practical mental measurement was organized in the summer of 1917 and called together for the preparation or selection of suitable methods. This group of men worked almost continuously for a month, devising, selecting, and adapting methods. Another month was spent in thoroughly testing the methods in military stations in order that their value might be definitely established before they should be recommended to the Medical Department of the Army. The results were gratifying and the methods were therefore recommended to the Surgeon General of the Army in August, 1917, and promptly accepted for official trial. During October and November they were applied in four cantonments under conditions which could scarcely have been more unfavorable but with results which led the official medical inspector to formulate the following statements and recommendations:

"The purposes of psychological testing are (a) to aid in segregating the mentally incompetent, (b) to classify men according to their mental capacity, (c) to assist in selecting competent men for responsible positions.

"In the opinion of this office these reports (accompanying recommendation) indicate very definitely that the desired results have been achieved.

"The success of this work in a large series of observations, some five thousand officers and eighty thousand men, makes it reasonably certain that similar results may be expected if the system be extended to include the entire enlisted and drafted personnel and all newly appointed officers.

"In view of these considerations, I recommend that all company officers, all candidates for officers' training camps and all drafted and enlisted men be required to take the prescribed psychological tests."

In January, 1918, this new work of the Medical Department was extended in accordance with the above recommendation.

Placing psychological examining in the Medical Department naturally caused certain difficulties of administration. The confusion of psychological work with neuropsychiatry was one of the first difficulties met. The administration of psychological examining by a medical officer increased the work of this officer and at the same time added to his staff a group of psychologists with whose work he was unfamiliar and who were perhaps more interested in establishing their particular examinations than in correlating their work with the work of the Medical Department. Notwithstanding these and many other difficulties which the new methods met, official inquiry into the results of the examining made in the latter part of November and the early part of December, 1917, indicated that seventy-five per cent of the officers who had become even slightly acquainted with the work favored the continuation of psychological examining.

The original purposes of the committee in the preparation of methods for intelligence testing were less important than the uses actually made of the results. It was the intention of the committee as stated above to prepare an examination that would indicate the drafted men who were too low-grade mentally to make satisfactory privates in the Army; it was desired also to indicate, if possible, those who were mentally unstable or who might prove incorrigible so far as army discipline was concerned. In addition, the committee hoped to be able to pick out exceptional types of men who could be used for special tasks that demanded a high degree of intelligence. In interesting contrast with these original purposes of mental examining stand the results actually achieved.

1. The assignment of an intelligence rating to every soldier on the basis of systematic examination.

2. The designation and selection of men whose superior intelligence indicates the desirability of advance or special assignment.

3. The prompt selection and recommendation for development battalions of men who are so inferior intellectually as to be unsuited for regular military training.

4. The provision of measurements of mental ability which enable assigning officers to build organizations of uniform mental strength or in accordance with definite specifications concerning intelligence requirements.

5. The selection of men for various types of military duty or for special assignment, as for example, to military training schools, colleges, or technical schools.

6. The provision of data for the formation of special training groups within the regiment or battery in order that each man may receive instruction suited to his ability to learn.

7. The early discovery and recommendation for elimination of men whose intelligence is so inferior that they cannot be used to advantage in any line of military service.

It is of course unfortunate from the point of view of scientific research that many lines of investigation indicated by these general results could not be carried out. The psychological service existed in the Army for strictly practical purposes. The directors of the service emphasized continually the necessity for rendering immediate assistance in the organization of the Army and the setting aside of all investigations which did not further this practical end. The results given in the following chapter are therefore based almost entirely on military needs and indicate the success of this service in the Army. The more strictly scientific aspects of this type of examining can be considered in future studies when the practical aim is less insistent or can more readily be made subservient to scientific standards.

—introduction to *Army Mental Tests* (New York: Holt, 1920), pp. vii–xiii

Other Social-Science Textbooks

Psychologist Otto Klineberg's Social Psychology, *first published by Holt and Company in 1940, was revised and republished in 1954. The textbook was also translated into several languages.*

July 2, 1940

Dear Professor Klineberg:
   Professor J. McV. Hunt, of Brown University, has written to tell us that he is very pleased with your text and believes it to be "the most instructive book in the field."
   He has also included in his letter the following paragraph:

"A few minor errors have crept into the book. I give two which I noted in perusing it. On page 227, under *Inheritance of Acquired Characters:* 'The chromosomes and genes are located in the germ cells, and are not found elsewhere in the organism.' If I have not been misinformed all these years, every cell in the organism has the usual supply of chromosomes and genes in its nucleus. Klineberg's point depends upon the segregation of the germ plasm from the somatoplasm, not upon the absence of chromosomes and genes in the cells of somatoplasm. On pages 408 and 409, under *The Biological Approach to Personality:* '. . .Lavater (9), who in 1804 published four volumes of photographs and sketches with his own interpretative comments.' While the photographic process is supposed have been invented as early as 1802, Daguerre reported his process in 1839, and it did not become common for almost another decade. Such misstatements mar the volume only slightly, but they should be corrected before the book is reprinted."

Please check these two sentences and let me have the corrections if you agree with Professor Hunt that the wording requires changing.
   Sincerely yours,
   [Charles A. Madison]
   HENRY HOLT AND COMPANY

Robert H. MacMurphey, manager of the college department at Holt and Company, wrote Klineberg to report on the critical reception of Social Psychology.

September 6, 1940

Dear Professor Klineberg:
   We doubt that autumn sales will be very impressive, since Social Psychology is most frequently offered during the second semester, but criticism to date has been uniformly favorable . . . with one exception—a Catholic gentleman reviewing the book complains that God has been mentioned but once, and lightly at that. You can't please everyone!
   Cordially yours,
   Robert H. MacMurphey
   Manager, College Department

* * *

Holt and Company published Gordon W. Allport's Personality: A Psychological Interpretation *in 1937 but declined his next book.*

January 21, 1941

Dear Professor Allport:

We have gone over with the greatest interest your TENTATIVE SET OF RULES FOR THE PREPARATION AND EVALUATION OF LIFE HISTORIES AND CASE STUDIES, as well as the three mimeographed cases which you gave me when I saw you at Harvard in December. As a matter of fact, for several weeks my wife considered the case of Michael Flynn to be the most interesting thing she had read recently–but that was before she read FOR WHOM THE BELL TOLLS.

There can be no doubt that this material is of interest and of importance, but we are not at all certain that the market for such a work is large enough to justify the considerable investment involved in its publication. It has been our experience that this sort of book would not be likely to be required as a text in many courses, and that its sale would be confined mainly to individuals and to libraries. Be that as it may, the next time I am at Harvard, I should like to discuss this project with you further.

We are still hopeful that you will find the time before too long, to work on the abridged version of your PERSONALITY. All things considered, this seems to us a most excellent prospect, since it should be widely used in the rapidly increasing number of courses in Personality.

Cordially yours,
Robert H. MacMurphey
Manager, College Department

January 22, 1941

Dear Mr. MacMurphy [sic]:

Thank you for considering so carefully my projected volume on the case study in psychology. (Incidentally, please thank your wife for wading through some of the material. I am glad she liked Michael Flynn.) Your judgment as to the probable sales value of the book is no doubt entirely sound. Unfortunately however, I am the victim of an obsession and shall have to complete the job, whether or not I could find a publisher. And until this job is completed I doubt that I can clear my mind for work on a revision and simplification of my text, even though the latter would be financially more advantageous. If Herr Hitler would be so kind as to stay in Europe for a few years I hope I will finish both jobs, thereby satisfying you and myself.

Cordially yours,
Gordon W. Allport

January 24, 1941

Dear Mr. MacMurphey:

The enclosed documents from Dr. Donald Pierson explain his request for translation rights for my book *Personality* in the Portuguese language. Would you refer this matter to the proper authorities in your company and ask that they send their decision directly to Dr. Pierson?

It so happens that American psychologists are greatly interested in improving cultural relations with South America at the present time. Psychology in the southern hemisphere is almost totally undeveloped. I think it very brave of anyone to want to issue a Portuguese edition of my book. (Or any other technical book.) Because it is definitely in the sphere of our national defense program to further cultural relations with Latin America in every possible way, I am making bold to suggest that your company consider the possibility of granting these rights without expecting any financial return. I personally am willing to make this arrangement but have written Dr. Pierson that the final decision rests with your company.

Would you be so kind as to return the enclosures from Dr. Pierson as soon as the matter has received attention in your office? I shall be glad to hear what decision you have reached.

Very sincerely yours,
Gordon W. Allport

* * *

Clarence F. Jones, an authority on South America, was a professor of economic and commercial geography at Clark University in Worcester, Massachusetts. His Economic Geography *was published by Holt and Company in 1935.*

March 12, 1930

Dear Mr. Bristol:

I am sending you herewith the large colored map of South America entitled "South America, Relief and Geographic Regions," by Clarence F. Jones. Accompanying the map are two sheets of names, which are to be printed on the map. They include, as you will see, five different types of names to be printed in in different size type, of course. In the base map, which we have used, we have inked in the boundaries of the republics and the Guianas. Please note that the boundary of eastern Ecuador and Colombia has been corrected. The old one is crossed out with cross marks in ink. In the black plate I do not want the provinces of the different republics shown. That would just complicate the map unnecessarily.

. . . .

You will recall that we are planning to have this map appear in about the size that I am submitting it, either as an insert or as a folded map in a pocket on the back cover.

Cordially yours,
Clarence F. Jones

By 1941 Jones was thinking about revising Economic Geography.

October 4, 1941

Dear Mr. MacMurphey:

I returned to Clark University on September 23rd and two days later left for field work with the graduate students. I dropped into the office this morning for a few moments. I shall be engaged in field work until after October 16th. Until that time it will be impossible for me to do anything on the South American project. It certainly was a good thing that I made the trip before planning to revise the book. I found great changes in several parts of the continent. An adequate revision of the book is going to require a major operation. As soon as I return from camp, I shall give you a rather full report on what I believe is necessary in the revision.

With best of wishes, I am

Sincerely yours,
Clarence F. Jones

Oct. 19, 1942

Dear Mr MacMurphy [*sic*]:

A reply to your letter of Sept. 15 has been delayed because the government got after me to aid in the Amer. Hemisphere Division of the Board of Economic Warfare, which is under Vice Pres. Wallace's direction. I held off for weeks but finally gave in and came down Oct. 5. I'm here at a considerable financial sacrifice and on a temporary appointment for 90 days. Being away from Clark delays further work on South America until I return. I'm sorry

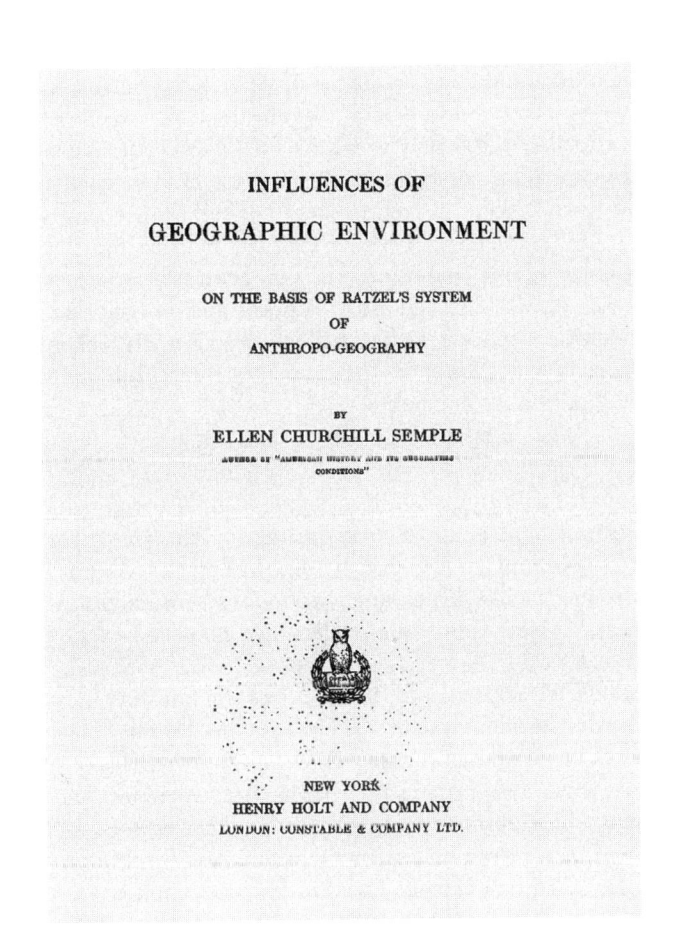

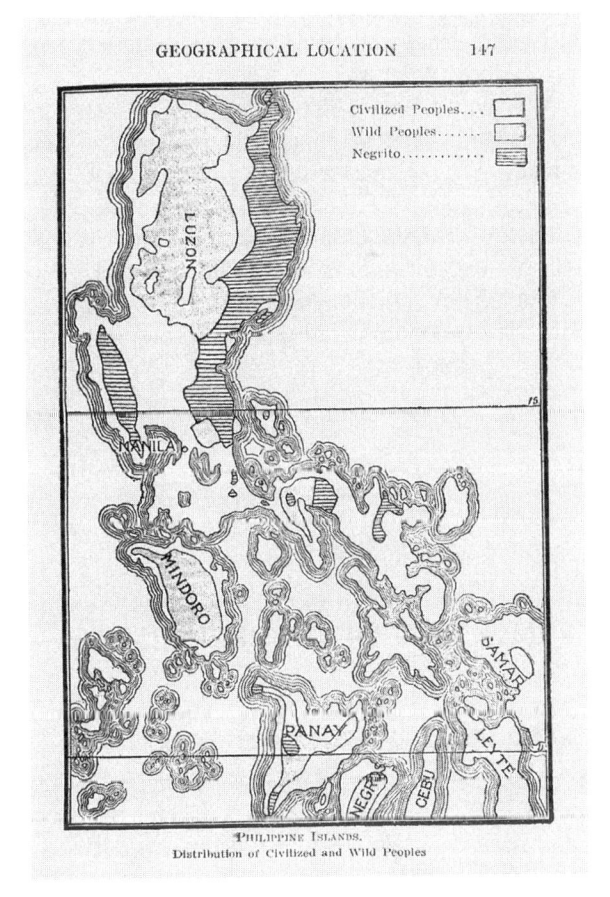

Title page and map from the 1911 study by the American geographer who promoted the idea that geographical environment has a deterministic effect on human culture and history (Rutgers University Library)

because I wanted to do that job this year and teachers want the revised copy. My plans now are to return to Clark after my temporary appointment here ends. I hope I can keep those plans, but, I think, all of us must realize that winning this war as soon as possible is the most important job for any American. It may be that pressure will be brought to keep me here, but I hope not.

Will you please tell the proper person in the company to send my next royalty statement and check to me at

1925 K Street N.W.
Washington D.C.

Cordially yours,
Clarence F. Jones

October 21, 1942

Dear Professor Jones:

Your letter has just arrived, and we are indeed sorry to learn that you have finally been drawn into the Washington maelstrom. On the other hand, since all of us have certain obligations to our country, you must be quietly pleased at your ability to contribute to the government knowledge and services which are of value in the prosecution of the war. . . .

We would like to thank you for notifying us that you have been taken off the revision for the time being. We regret as much as you the delay your Washington sojourn entails. Still, all that you or we can do is to make the best of an unfortunate circumstance. No organization is more willing than Henry Holt and Company to contribute to the war effort, either directly or indirectly, even though it frequently be painful.

. . . .

Cordially yours,
Robert H. MacMurphey
Manager, College Department

THE TEXTBOOK BUSINESS

McGuffey Was Never Like This
Robert Lubar

The textbook business was flourishing for Holt and Company a decade and a half later when Fortune *magazine published this report in its December 1959 issue.*

The textbook business, which is the foundation of Henry Holt's current prosperity, is the fastest-growing, most remunerative, and most fiercely competitive branch of book publishing. It is a far cry from the days when the famed McGuffey Readers were the staple of practically every American schoolhouse. Only about 1 per cent of U.S. outlays for education goes into books, but in dollar terms this 1 per cent now bulks to impressive proportions. Last year textbook sales amounted to $280 million; elementary schools accounted for $124 million, high schools for $71 million, and colleges and universities for $85 million.

The volume of textbook sales has just about doubled in ten years, largely because postwar babies have raised the elementary-schoolroom population by eight million. The future looks just as expansive. When the great population bulge moves from elementary schooling to secondary, in the early Sixties, book sales to high schools may be half again as high as they are now. And by 1970 the college market alone may well be worth $200 million.

This glittering prospect has drawn many general book publishers into the textbook field, which in less bustling times they had been content to leave to specialist firms. The American Textbook Publishers Institute, the industry's trade association, currently has eighty members, and there are about fifty-five firms outside it. No one house dominates the field. Holt excels in high-school texts and in books for college liberal-arts courses. McGraw-Hill, which has long dominated the advanced technical field, is only beginning to venture into the humanities. Prentice-Hall has built up most of its big volume in business books. Scott, Foresman, a lesser-known Chicago firm, concentrates on the vast elementary market. Others have done extremely well in specialties—for instance, Harcourt, Brace and Houghton Mifflin in English courses.

The textbook market offers publishers two advantages they do not have with general, or "trade," books: they can make direct personal contact with their customers; and most of their sales are in gratifyingly big lots. Elementary and high-school authorities contract for their books by making "adoptions" for each academic subject. This means selecting a book or series of books for all classes in the school system. It used to be customary for states to do the adopting, but now only North Carolina actually selects the books for all its schools. Other states either draw up approved lists of, say, four or five competing books in each subject and let the local authorities choose among them, or they use the "open territory" system, which allows localities to make all the decisions. Thus, in practice, book buying is in the hands of thousands of selection committees, usually composed of superintendents and teachers. In colleges, the "customers" are usually heads of departments or individual professors, who by placing a book

Advertisement for Holt and Company German-language textbooks (Rutgers University Library)

on the required lists for their courses compel the university bookstore to stock it, and students to buy it.

To sell their markets, publishers employ staffs of roving salesmen, called "bookmen" in the school trade and "travelers" at the college level. Holt and other leading houses require their bookmen to have previous experience as teachers or superintendents, so that they can speak with authority as educational advisers when they are promoting their books. Travelers, on the other hand, need not necessarily have had college-teaching experience, the reason given being that no traveler would presume to tell a professor how to teach his course. But a traveler has to be well educated and well informed on his own texts and those of his competitors. As one Holt editor puts it, "He has to be like the River Platte, thirty-six miles wide and six inches deep."

Neither the bookman nor the traveler actually makes a sale, or is so crude as to offer an order blank. His job is to get the prospect interested in the books; the firm then follows up with mailed promotion material and sample copies. He pounds his beat from September to June, then relaxes for the summer, hoping the selection committees or the professors will give him a favorable verdict.

The salesman's job also includes recruiting new authors. The competition among publishing houses for new book material is just as keen as it is for sales. The bookman or traveler is always looking for teachers with an urge to add to the literature on a subject. Holt likes to put several authors with different points of view to work on a new schoolbook. And many books are actually written from the authors' raw material, by the editors in the publishing house itself. With college professors, who usually prefer an individual stamp on their product but tend to be dilatory in production, the editors usually have the task of goading the author to the completion of his work.

The amount invested in the writing, editing, and designing of a major textbook sometimes exceeds $100,000. Setting it up in type and making plates may add

> ## Wartime Demand for Textbooks
>
> *Publisher James S. Thompson reflected on the enormity of the collaborative effort to produce huge numbers of technical books during World War II in the 1942 R. R. Bowker Memorial Lecture.*
>
> The vast upheaval in American education is vividly realized today in any technical publishing office. We are in a war of science. Ordinarily, the day's mail would contain pieces from M.I.T., Purdue, Cornell, and so on. But today—well, just consider these typical examples of the sources of demand for American technical books:
>
> *By Aircraft Companies:* Douglas, Grumman, Republic, Lockheed, Consolidated, North American, Vultee, Boeing, Bell, Curtiss-Wright.
>
> *By Arsenals:* Watervliet, Picatinny, Watertown, Springfield, Rock Island.
>
> *By Navy Training Schools:* Great Lakes Station, Radio Materiel School, Submarine School.
>
> *By Signal Corps Schools:* Fort Monmouth, Philadelphia, Lexington.
>
> *By Maritime Service Training Schools . . . Coast Guard Training Schools . . . Private Aviation Schools . . . By Manufacturers. . . .* [A]nd by shipyards, Army Service Schools, Navy Yard Apprentice Schools . . . and so on.
>
> This is not an inclusive list, it is not even an adequate list. To name all the branches of the mighty University for War that has been established in the United States during the last two years would require the afternoon. The courses of study draw from every technological field. The classrooms include factory storerooms, millionaires' estates, corners of airplane hangars, suburban cellar playrooms, lonely "toughening" camps high in the Sierra Nevada, training ships at sea. The students number millions. For this new university of war it is up to the authors and publishers of technical books to supply many of the texts. . . .
>
> —"The Technical Book Publisher in Wartimes,"
> in *Bowker Lectures on Book Publishing*
> (New York: R. R. Bowker,
> 1957), pp. 114–115

half again as much. All this money is spent before the presses turn and a single copy is actually sold; additional costs for the average $5 book come to about $1 per copy for printing and 36 cents for the author's royalty. But if the gamble is big, so are the stakes. A sale of 50,000 or more materially reduces the unit cost of development and plates and leaves the publisher a net of about 36 cents a copy, as compared to 5½ cents for a trade book. Sales of basic texts can be immense. It is not unusual for a well-established high-school book to sell more than 100,000 copies in one year—and it may have two or three years of good life in it before its publisher has to invest again in a revised edition.

How good are they?

The textbooks school children carry in their briefcases today are a far cry from the dreary tomes their fathers had to suffer through. They are more carefully and more imaginatively edited. Their bindings are gay, they are illustrated with lively four-color pictures instead of crude line cuts, and their typography makes for much easier reading.

But while there is no doubt about the advance in the bookmaking art, some critics question whether there has been any improvement in educational content. They contend that, in aiming for a mass market, publishers tend toward a low common denominator of uniformity. Stodgy textbook-selection committees, with backward ideas of what should be taught and how, impose a certain amount of stodginess on everyone. Moreover, the demand for quantity has resulted in some dilution of quality.

On the other hand, there is plenty of evidence that some textbooks are indeed pushing up the standards of education. Despite the resistance of old-fashioned teachers, the new language books steer away from monotonous vocabulary drills and ritual verb conjugation. They stress the kind of conversation a student would need if he traveled in a foreign country. The new science texts are making a notable effort to keep up with developments in technology, nuclear physics, and cosmology. A few enterprising editors are seeking new ways to make math more of an intellectual adventure and less of a boring discipline.

Textbook publishers are also giving the overworked teacher a helping hand. To supplement textbooks they are supplying teaching manuals, which organize the curriculum, and ready-made exams with accompanying answer sheets. Freed from tedious routine work, the teacher will presumably be able to devote more of her time and attention to teaching.

The industry is not ignoring the provocative new technical developments that may supplement and in some cases replace textbooks in the future—e.g., language tapes and filmed courses for classroom television. Yet, while the much-discussed "audio-visual aids" and devices like Professor B. F. Skinner's famous "teaching machine" . . . may find increasing application, it is safe to predict that for a long time to come children will get the bulk of their education the old-fashioned way—out of books.

—"McGuffey Was Never Like This,"
Fortune (December 1959): 109, 236, 240

Holt and Company Authors

IVAN SERGEEVICH TURGENEV

HOLT AND COMPANY BOOKS BY TURGENEV: *Fathers and Sons,* translated by Eugene Schuyler (New York: Leypoldt & Holt, 1867); **first edition,** *Ottsy i deti* (Moscow: Soldatenkov, 1862);
Smoke, translated by William F. West (New York: Holt & Williams, 1872); **first edition,** *Dym* (Moscow: Br. Salaevy, 1868);
Dimitri Roudine (New York: Holt & Williams, 1873); **first edition,** *Dimitri Roudine, suivi du Journal d'un homme de trop, et de Trois recontres* (Paris: Hetzel, 1862);
Liza, translated by W. R. S. Ralston (New York: Holt, 1873); **first edition,** *Dvorianskoe gnezdo* (Moscow: Glazunov, 1859); translated by Ralston as *Liza* (London: Chapman & Hall, 1869);
On the Eve, translated by C. E. Turner (New York: Holt & Williams, 1873); **first edition,** *On the Eve,* translated by Turner (London: Hodder & Stoughton, 1871);
Virgin Soil, translated by T. S. Perry (New York: Holt, 1877); **first edition,** *Nov',* 2 volumes (Leipzig: Gerhard, 1877);
Annals of a Sportsman, translated by Franklin Pierce Abbott (New York: Holt, 1885); **first edition,** *Zapiski okhotnika,* 2 volumes (Moscow: v Universitetskoi tipografii, 1852); translated by James D. Meiklejohn as *Russian Life in the Interior; or, The Experiences of a Sportsman* (Edinburgh: Black, 1855).

Henry Holt appears to have been responsible for introducing the popular Russian novelist Ivan Sergeevich Turgenev (1818-1883) to the American reading public. Holt was unusual among American publishers in his practice of paying royalties to foreign authors. Turgenev, who had apparently never before received remuneration for translations of his work, was amazed by the first checks he received from Holt. Turgenev scholar Avrahm Yarmolinsky describes how, upon receiving these checks, Turgenev immediately had a short story, "Living Relics" (1874), translated so he could send it to "this phoenix of an editor." ("Living Relics" was one of three stories that Turgenev added in the 1870s to the 1852 story collection that Holt and Company published in 1885 as Annals of a Sportsman.*)*

* * *

Turgenev wrote to author and critic Pavel Vasilyevich Annenkov in early 1874 recounting Henry Holt's graciousness in their business transactions.

Paris, 7 February 1874

Dear Pavel Vasilyevich,

. . . .

A funny thing happened to me yesterday, which I must tell you about. There is in America a certain publisher, Henry Holt, who has brought out a number of translations of my works over the past five years. As no copyright agreement exists between America and Europe, it never occurred to Holt to ask my permission, especially as other publishers have printed translations too. You can imagine my amazement when I received a letter from him yesterday where, after many compliments (he even used the word <enthusiasm!> [in English]), he reports that sales of my books have not gone very well, but as he managed to make some profit on them he is in the position to send me an honorarium of 1000 francs—and the letter actually contained a money order for this amount! This truly American graciousness really touched me. I must confess that throughout the whole of my literary career I have rarely felt so flattered. People have told me before that, if I may so express it, I am quite popular in America, but this living proof has made me very happy.

. . . .

Yours sincerely,
Iv. Turgenev

–A. V. Knowles, ed. and trans., *Turgenev's Letters* (London: Athlone Press, 1983), pp. 195–196

* * *

Ivan Sergeevich Turgenev, 1879 (from David Magarshack,
Turgenev: A Life, *1954; Thomas Cooper Library,*
University of South Carolina)

The works of Turgenev did not prove to be a commercial success for Holt and Company, but Henry Holt's great admiration for him appears to have transcended financial considerations. On 1 August 1878 he wrote to Turgenev that "there is some satisfaction in assuring you that our most cultivated public—a small one, it is true, continues to regard your writings with grateful enthusiasm." In his 1923 memoir Holt recalled meeting Turgenev in 1879.

I believe it was my privilege to be the publisher who introduced him [Turgenev] to English-speaking readers. In the late sixties, Eugene Schuyler, who graduated at Yale three classes ahead of mine, translated, and I published, *Fathers and Sons*. I followed it with three or four other Turgénief books, but had no encouragement to continue. A generation later, however, the public demand for high-class foreign literature began to increase rapidly. Apropos of those books, he wrote me a letter, of which the following passage seems to be of public interest. The English is his own:

My friend Mr. W. Ralston has transmitted to me your letter with the included check. Unexpected as it was to me, I can frankly tell you that seldom or never has anything during all my literary career given me such unmitigated pleasure. The deep sympathy I always felt for America and the Americans has been accrued by it; and the appreciation of your countrymen, testified by your amiable letter, makes me proud and happy.

Because of these publications, in the summer of '79 in Paris, Turgénief invited me to come to see him.

As I mounted a circular staircase to his apartment *au troisième,* he was leaning over the rail to greet me, and as I looked up at his full-bearded, strong, kind face, I seemed to be ascending to a prophet. He was a big but not very tall man, with blue eyes, as I remember.

We talked, or rather he did, for an hour or two, but the only thing that I remember of that interview was his saying: "I am no puritan." This is illustrated by the legend that when the Germans entered France in '70 a detachment of them took possession of a villa in which their commander recognized over the principal mantelpiece a portrait of Turgénief, and was told: "It is the father of Madame." I believe that he never was married. The German ordered that the place was to be unharmed and scrupulously guarded.

Turgénief must have found me an appreciative listener: he invited me to spend a day with him at his country home near Bougival. There I heard much more than I remember. By the way, he spoke much better English than I did, he having been at school in England and having had to *study* the language, which few American boys of my time did.

I reached Bougival towards noon. He was a wonderful host: for it was no small proposition to have on his hands, for five or six hours, a transatlantic stranger of whose tastes and ideas he knew so little. He received me in a second-story room surrounded by woods. It was evidently his work-room, and he showed me, with characterizations, an astonishing number of high-class Reviews published in Russia. There may have been half a dozen. I should not have felt confident beforehand that there was one.

After the samovar and some biscuits had been produced, he led me across the hall to another large room where he slept, and which, unlike his work-room, commanded a very wide and attractive prospect.

I said: "It's plain why you didn't make this your work-room: the view would have distracted your attention."

"No," he answered, "I don't react to it at all: it doesn't interest me; nothing without life does." (And I've just read his description of the graveyard at the end of *Fathers and Sons!*)

"But," I expostulated, "that's a singular instance of how little we know ourselves: for you have given virtually every one of your great scenes an appropriate natural background."

"Well," he said, "I hadn't realized it. So far as I know myself, if all being were arranged in orderly progression from inanimate matter up to the highest thought and feeling, my interest would begin where conscious life begins. I can sit for hours watching an ant, and taking the keenest interest in everything it does, and come home and, with interest just as keen, write out every detail." He paused a moment and then exclaimed: "And if I couldn't do that, I should die."
–*Garrulities of an Octogenarian Editor* (Boston & New York: Houghton Mifflin, 1923), pp. 202–204

THOMAS HARDY

HOLT AND COMPANY BOOKS BY HARDY:
Under the Greenwood Tree: A Rural Painting of the Dutch School (New York: Holt & Williams, 1873); **first edition**, *Under the Greenwood Tree: A Rural Painting of the Dutch School*, 2 volumes, anonymous (London: Tinsley, 1872);

A Pair of Blue Eyes (New York: Holt & Williams, 1873); **first edition**, *A Pair of Blue Eyes*, 3 volumes (London: Tinsley, 1873);

Desperate Remedies (New York: Holt, 1874); **first edition**, *Desperate Remedies*, 3 volumes, anonymous (London: Tinsley, 1871);

Far from the Madding Crowd (New York: Holt, 1874); **first edition**, *Far from the Madding Crowd*, 2 volumes (London: Smith, Elder, 1874);

The Hand of Ethelberta: A Comedy in Chapters (New York: Holt, 1876); **first edition**, *The Hand of Ethelberta: A Comedy in Chapters*, 2 volumes (London: Smith, Elder, 1876);

The Return of the Native (New York: Holt, 1878); **first edition**, *The Return of the Native*, 3 volumes (London: Smith, Elder, 1878);

The Trumpet-Major: A Tale (New York: Holt, 1880); **first edition**, *The Trumpet-Major: A Tale*, 3 volumes (London: Smith, Elder, 1880);

A Laodicean (New York: Holt, 1881); **first edition**, *A Laodicean*, 3 volumes (London: Sampson Low, Marston, Searle & Rivington, 1881; 1 volume, New York: Harper, 1881);

Two on a Tower: A Romance (New York: Holt, 1882); **first edition**, *Two on a Tower: A Romance*, 3 volumes (London: Sampson Low, Marston, Searle & Rivington, 1882);

The Mayor of Casterbridge (New York: Holt, 1886); **first edition**, *The Mayor of Casterbridge: The Life and Death of a Man of Character*, 2 volumes (London: Smith, Elder, 1886).

Thomas Hardy

When Henry Holt was seventy years old and had nearly forty years of experience as a publisher behind him, he liked to recall that he "introduced Hardy" to American readers. The Victorian novelist Thomas Hardy (1840–1928) had nothing to do with the introduction of his writing to America, and perhaps he never realized how much he owed to the energy, the critical insight, and the initiative of Henry Holt.

Copies of letters written to Hardy from Holt and Company were kept in letterpress books, identified by date ranges. Letterpress books were routinely used by the firm from the time of its founding until 1904, when they were replaced with vertical files. While the vertical-file system provides for the maintenance of incoming as well as copies of outgoing correspondence, letterpress books do not, and there are no letters from Hardy in the Holt archives.

Henry Holt apparently first became aware of Hardy through conversation with fellow publisher Frederick Macmillan. Subsequent reviews of Hardy's early work in London journals and newspapers, routinely read by Holt, reinforced his interest in Hardy. In 1873 Holt obtained publishing rights to Under the Greenwood Tree, *which had been published anonymously the previous year in London.*

May 29th/73.

My dear Sir,

My friend Mr. Frederick Macmillan has directed my attention to your writings with a favourable criticism which, coming from him, predisposed my own.

I have caused "Under the Greenwood Tree" to be prepared for publication, which will soon take place.

Should it be successful, you shall participate in the profits. I would then want to publish "A Pair of Blue Eyes," and it would be to the mutual advantage if you would let me know at once how much longer "A Pair of Blue Eyes" will run in *Tinsley* and, if practicable, send me at once proofs of all later than the May number.

Respectfully yours,
Henry Holt

—quoted in Carl J. Weber, *Hardy in America* (Waterville, Me.: Colby College Press, 1946), p. 15

Holt wrote in response to Hardy's reply, which included an inquiry regarding business arrangements and news of his writing progress. Holt subsequently arranged for the serialization of A Pair of Blue Eyes *in the* New York Tribune, *thus introducing Hardy to a wider American audience.*

July 27/73

My dear Sir,

Your letter was welcomed at this place where I spend the summer, excepting such runs to New York as business imposes.

I hope that "A Pair of Blue Eyes" will be issued by my house on the 26th and I have sent orders for a set of the Leisure Hour Series (in which it and "Under the Greenwood Tree" are included) to be sent you through Messrs. Macmillan and Co. with my compliments. I think that on seeing the series you will acknowledge that your books are in good company, and if, as is possible, the series shall introduce to you the novels of Turgénieff, Droz and Cherbuliez, I am confident that (especially in the case of the first writer) I shall have the satisfaction of affording you a very serious pleasure.

Much pleasure I certainly owe you for what, since I wrote you before, you have given me in "A Pair of Blue Eyes." Owing to my absence from New York, I have not as yet seen the last installment, but reading the rest prepared me to endorse the *Spectator*'s criticism (the receipt of a second copy of which I presume I owe to you) and also to have my tender faith in the gradual extinction of the fools sorely shaken by the wonderful article in the *Athenaeum*.

Perhaps you will pardon me for confessing that I learned your intention of so soon publishing again with regret. Probably no one but Shakespeare has ever been

Title page for the first Holt and Company Hardy novel, originally published in 1872 (Rutgers University Library)

able to accomplish the best class of work you are capable of with any rapidity; and there is, as far as I know, no certainty that he was. George Eliot (with whom I have been glad to see more than one point of resemblance traced in you) produces an average of about a 12mo page a day. If these remarks seem intrusive, excuse them as far as you can on the score of an interest in your work deeper than it is often the fortune of a jaded professional critic to be refreshed with.

It would be premature yet to speak, especially at this distance from my office, with any definiteness regarding business arrangements. *Greenwood Tree* is coming up to the modest expectations I could form for the work of a new author, but I cannot estimate the popular appreciation of your writing before the people have seen "A Pair of Blue Eyes." Should you propose some definite proposition from me before placing your next work in my hands, I will make one as soon as I have reasonable experience to make it on. English books not being protected by our copyright law, a publisher is never sure of holding the exclusive possession of one and therefore is forced to a degree of caution in his arrangements. . . .

Very truly yours,
Henry Holt
–quoted in Weber, Hardy in America, pp. 16–17

***

Hardy's journal entry for 8 or 9 July 1879 mentions his one meeting with Holt.

With E. [Emma, his wife] to Mrs. [Alexander] Macmillan's garden-party at Knapdale, near our house. A great many present. Talked to Mr. White of Harvard University, and Mr. Henry Holt the New York publisher, who said that American spelling and idiom must prevail over the English, as it was sixty millions against thirty. I forgot for the moment to say that it did not follow, the usage set up by a few people of rank, education, and fashion being the deciding factor.
–quoted in *The Life and Work of Thomas Hardy*, edited by Michael Millgate (Athens: University of Georgia Press, 1985), p. 131

***

In all, Holt and Company published ten Hardy titles. Although publication of Hardy's books preceded passage of international copyright law, Henry Holt paid Hardy 10 percent royalties, and his goodwill extended to the placing of Hardy's shorter works with various periodicals. In 1878, for example, Holt informed Hardy that he had sold "Indiscretion in the Life of an Heiress" to Harper and Brothers for publication in their weekly for £20. Letterpress Book 92 in the Holt and Company Archives includes a ledger page with figures for Hardy's books, indicating number of copies sold, royalty rate, and the royalty paid for each book.

May 25, 1882
Thomas Hardy Esq.
L5.5.5   25.90
   Dec. 31 '81
16 Greenwood Tree   10   1.60
59 Blue Eyes   10   5.90
16 Desperate Remedies   10   1.60
29 Madding Crowd   10   2.90
126 Trumpet Major   10   12.60
13 Ethelberta   10   1.30
                                  25.90

WILLIAM JAMES

HOLT AND COMPANY BOOKS BY JAMES: *The Principles of Psychology*, 2 volumes (New York: Holt, 1890; London: Macmillan, 1890); abridged as *Psychology* (New York: Holt, 1892; London: Macmillan, 1892);

Talks to Teachers on Psychology and to Students on Some of Life's Ideals (New York: Holt, 1899; London: Longmans, Green, 1899).

William James (1842–1910), brother of the novelist Henry James, agreed to write The Principles of Psychology *for the Holt and Company American Science Series in 1878, but the work was not completed until 1890. James warned Henry Holt from the start that finishing the book was going to take a long time. James began teaching anatomy at Harvard in 1873. Over the next several years he became increasingly interested in the relationship between physiology and psychology. The field of psychology was new, and James's own ideas were just coalescing when he agreed to write* The Principles of Psychology. *This situation, along with James's scrupulousness and ill health, made for slow going. The tenacity with which Holt stood by James during the twelve years he took to produce the book attests to the great confidence the publisher had in James. Their relationship was not without wrinkles, however. In his 1923 memoir Holt recalled, "James did the Psychology, as the world knows to its great advantage. For years I was greatly influenced, especially regarding Psychical Research, by a close friendship with him, which, I grieve to say, was somewhat clouded toward his end, by misunderstandings which were largely due to outside influences."*

March 21, 1890

My dear Holt:

Publishers are demons, there's no doubt about it. How silly it is to fly in the face of the accumulated wisdom of mankind, and think just because one of them appears genial socially that the great natural law is broken and that he is also a human being in his professional capacity. Fie upon such weakness! I shall ne'er be guilty of it again. I had thought I should expedite matters by getting the woodcuts read–and as I can't–*send* the Harvard Library books, and this next week is vacation and I can accompany them I tho't you would vehemently applaud the exhibition of energy on my part and let me get through as much business as possible in the time. Later it will be less convenient for me to go to N. Y. It may delay things. It may result in the things having to be made here. It is all on your "head."

As for the MS. I confess I don't know why you need the whole of it en bloc in your own hands, before printing begins. After this week of recess I shall write a

Henry and William James in England, 1902 (Houghton Library, Harvard University)

chapter which may take 3 weeks at the outside and complete the book. Some 1700 pp. of MS. will then be ready for the printer without an other [sic] touch from me. There will remain 5 or 6 chapters, some of which need slight retouches and additions, which can be added by me perfectly well in the intervals of correcting proofs, thereby enabling the latter to begin about the first of May. The *whole* work as I said will then be *written,* only those few chapters not *revised.* Time is so precious now that I don't see what possible thing is risked by proceeding to press with the revised mass. The rest *could* be printed without revision, but it will be better to go over it again. Write and tell me what is your decree. I want to get forward now with the last possible delay.

My visit to N. Y. was altogether for the sake of those woodcuts. For hygienic purposes just now I shall gain more by taking my week away from the garish gas lights and excitements of the metropolis, and so, my wife agreeing, I have decided after getting your note, to keep New York till later and spend the week in exploring the wilderness of Connecticut and Rhode Island. That was the meaning of my telegram this P. M. We will debit you with one dinner for some future day. I find that I have lost the contract which you sent me last spring. I did not even examine it then. Pray send another that I may see what to do.

Yours always
Wm. James

April 5, 1890

My dear Holt:

Your letter awaits me on my return from Newport. Poor publishers, poor fellow, poor human being, ex-demon! How those vermin of authors must have caused you to suffer in your time to wring from you such a tirade! Well, it has been very instructive to me to grasp the publishers point of view. Your fatal error however has been in not perceiving that I was an entirely *different kind* of author from any of those whom you had been in the habit of meeting, and that *celerity,* celerity incarnate, is the motive and result of all my plans and deeds. It is not fair to throw that former contract into my face, when you know or ought to know that when the ten years or a little more from the time of its signature had elapsed I wrote to you that you must get another man to write this book for you, and that, as things were then going, I didn't see how I could ever finish it.

I would return these contracts signed, herewith, but for two points. First the provision that the author "shall prepare" matter for new editions "whenever called on" by publishers. I should naturally hope to do that, but certainly can't pledge myself. And as the text stands it seems to me useless, for no penalty is attached to my disobedience in case I fail to comply. Shall we strike it out?–Secondly, I find in the former contract a MS. addition to the effect that on publication you deliver me 20 copies free of charge. That seems fair enough. I was calculating the other day that I should have in all to give away at least 75 copies of the book, most of them to professors here and abroad. As this helps your interest in the work as well as mine the 20 copies (or even more) provision seems fair.

Let me know about these points and I will sign.

Yours always
Wm. James

Apl, 8'90

My dear Holt:

Here goes a copy of the contract signed by me. Your copy found again. I add as you suggest, the clause about 20 copies; and I leave the clause about new matter for new editions; but I warn you clearly that I shall only consent to furnish such new matter in case it involves no great sacrifice. I can easily imagine myself engrossed in some other work hereafter, and having grown into such a state of disgust for my old psychology book as to find the re-handling of it an intellectually impossible task. In that case I should calmly fold my arms and say "the book has had its day–let it be republished if at all as an historical monument, not as a show exhibition of my present opinions." There comes a time in all books when a man can't tinker them; he must write a new work altogether.

Every [sic] truly yours,
Wm. James

Apr. 14, 1890

My dear James:

The copy of the contract got here duly. What a bold man you are! You may get yourself in that condition where, in my professional character of demon, I shall have to poison you in order to get onto a new edition of the book, which the contract allows me to do. Don't tamper too much with evil spirits. If you don't have your manuscript ready May 1st, let that day be a day of fasting over your sins, and you shall have the additional benefit of my demoniacal prayers.

Yours ever,
H. Holt

May 5, 1890

My dear James:

I have given you three day's grace since May first, and one over. Who's the demon now?

Yours ever,
H. Holt

May 7, 1890

My dear Holt:

If you will look at our contract I think you will see that it has yet over three weeks to run. I shall however be through in less than two, and as I am anxious, on every account, not to lose a single day, I don't see why we shouldn't be beginning already to decide on the page. The MS., to my great regret, is panning out bigger than I thought it would. I fear there will be no less than about 460,000 words, which would require 575 words on a page to make a book of 800 pp. I can't possibly cut this thing down, as it all belongs together; and I trust this bulk will not unfit it for the "series." It is a disappointment to me not to have made a smaller book, that having been my aim all along.

My calculation isn't *close*, as the pages are very irregularly written, and there are many notes, internal headings etc. But I feel pretty confident now, that taking the "Miad" page, or the page of Ladd's Physiol. Psych (strange to say they contain each just about the same no. of words (460) although the Miad p. is so much smaller and handsomer looking to my eye) my book will hardly fall inside of a 1000 of 'em! What shall be done? Two vols? or publish outside of the series? or what? let me know please, forthwith. It is only this A. M. that I have been able to make the calculation with any definiteness, owing to the broken up condition of the MS. hitherto.

Meanwhile I send you some of the first sheets, to be used if you wish to make experiments.

Always yours
Wm. James

May 8 [1890]

[Holt to James:]

We must get it into one volume, and I think we can do so without having you realize that it looks any worse than [Ira] Remsen's chemistry. If fellows will write such long books, however, they must not expect beautiful big margins and wide spaces. . . .

April 25, 1891

My dear James;

Here's the account of royalties for your book up to Jan. 1st.

If we were to make the royalty out according to our contract, on the sheets sent to England, it would be only 14-3/10 cents for you.

This, I think, would not be fair. It is impossible, apparently, to get any formula that always works justice in such cases. I have ordered that it should be made out so that your profits are reduced in the same proportions as ours are, which leaves your royalty at 33-1/3 cents, which I trust will be sanctified to your temporal and spiritual welfare.

Yours as ever,
Henry Holt

Dec. 13, 1893.

My dear Holt:

I dare say you've been wondering for a long time what has become of my famous book. About ten days ago I signed a contract for it with Longmans. When I last wrote you it was in Houghton's hands, but as their offer did not please me I called the manuscript back, and it has lain untouched until a month ago or more when I sent it to Longmans. It is now hurrying through the press, and I hope may be out by Feb. 1. I told you in my last letter that I should send it to you after Houghton. But on revolving in my mind the Scribner-Holt complication, I found it was too deep waters for me to stir up again, and as I was cut off from Scribner, I thought I would just cut myself off from you as I had previously announced. As I said before, I don't harbor a particle of resentment, and when I have got ready a manuscript on Talks to Teachers on Psychology which I expect to do by next summer, I will offer the same to you.

. . . .

I was called on by Mr. Hitchcock of the Appleton firm this morning, who once again asked me if I didn't have anything for them. Publishers dont seem to me very averse to interfering with each other's authors; and although the Scribners may have repudiated the action of Mr. Lord when you protested, I very much question whether they would have done anything of the kind otherwise.

The college year is wearing on, thank Heaven, with no lack of work to do. [George Trumbull] Ladd's Psychologies are, I imagine, the chief rivals of mine.

Scribner pushes them with great energy and copious critical notices in their support. I could give you a very much more imposing set of notices of my Psychology than those which you print. I don't know whether you think it might pay to get out a leaflet devoted to puffing it in this way, as an offset to Scribner's on Ladd. Believe me with best regards to Madame,

Always truly yours,
Wm. James

I have taken to a Stenographer at last. *What* a relief! I don't see how I ever wrote letters with a pen.

***

In an 1894 postcard to Henry Holt, James inquired about progress on a translation of Friedrich Paulsen's Einleitung in die Philosophie *(1892) that Holt and Company planned to publish.* Introduction to Philosophy, *translated by Frank Thilly, was published in 1895 and included a preface by James.*

May 25 [1894]

How does the Paulsen's "Einleitung" translation plan come on? Any chance of publication by Jan. 1? It is a wonderful book, and I should like to use it then in classes. But it would be a great shame to spoil the beauty by a poor translator's work.–Hope the world goes well with you.

Wm. James

***

Letter of Introduction

James sought to help a pupil obtain a start in the publishing business with a note of introduction to Holt. The student, Ellery Sedgwick, never worked for Holt and Company but did go on to a distinguished career in magazine journalism, becoming editor and publisher of The Atlantic Monthly *in 1908.*

July 8, 94

My dear Holt,

My friend and pupil Mr. Ellery Sedgwick, of Stockbridge, Mass, tells me that he aspires, after his college course, to employment of some sort in a publishing house.

I have no hesitation in offering him this note of introduction to you. He is of good "stock," and a most intelligent, upright, and agreeable fellow in every respect. Any help you may give him, in the way of advice if you have nothing better, will, I am sure, be well bestowed.

Always truly yours,
Wm. James

THE AMERICAN SCIENCE SERIES
FOR SCHOOLS AND COLLEGES.

The principal objects of the series are to supply the lack—in some subjects very great—of authoritative books whose principles are, so far as practicable, illustrated by familiar American facts, and also to supply the other lack that the advance of Science perennially creates, of text-books which at least do not contradict the latest generalizations. The books of this series systematically outline the field of Science, as the term is usually employed with reference to general education. The scheme includes an Advanced Course, a Briefer Course, and an Elementary Course.

☞ *In ordering be careful to state which course is desired—Advanced, Briefer, or Elementary.*

Physics.
By GEORGE F. BARKER, Professor in the University of Pennsylvania.
In preparation.

Chemistry.
By IRA REMSEN, Professor in the Johns Hopkins University.
Advanced Course, 850 pp.
Briefer Course, 387 pp.
Elementary Course, 272 pp.

Astronomy.
By SIMON NEWCOMB, Professor in the Johns Hopkins University, and EDWARD S. HOLDEN, Director of the Lick Observatory.
Advanced Course, 512 pp.
Briefer Course, 352 pp.

Biology.
By WILLIAM T. SEDGWICK, Professor in the Massachusetts Institute of Technology, and EDMUND B. WILSON, Professor in Bryn Mawr College.
Part I.—Introductory, 193 pp.

Botany.
By C. E. BESSEY, Professor in the University of Nebraska; formerly in the Iowa Agricultural College.
Advanced Course, 611 pp.
Briefer Course, 292 pp.

Zoology.
By A. S. PACKARD, Professor of Zoology and Geology in Brown University.
Advanced Course, 722 pp.
Briefer Course, 338 pp.
Elementary Course, 290 pp.

The Human Body.
By H. NEWELL MARTIN, Professor in the Johns Hopkins University.
Advanced Course, 631 — 34 pp. Copies without the Appendix on Reproduction will be sent when specially ordered.
Briefer Course, 377 pp.
Elementary Course, 261 pp.

The Principles of Psychology.
By WILLIAM JAMES, Professor of Psychology in Harvard University.
Advanced Course, in 2 vols. Vol. I, 689 pp.; Vol. II, 704 pp.

Political Economy.
By FRANCIS A. WALKER, President Massachusetts Institute of Technology.
Advanced Course, 537 pp.
Briefer Course, 415 pp.
Elementary Course, 323 pp.

HENRY HOLT & CO., PUBLISHERS, NEW YORK.

Advertisement including the first William James title (1890) published by Holt and Company (Princeton University Library)

James strongly resisted providing a photograph of himself for his Holt and Company publications.

Jan. 14, '96

Dear Holt:

Thank you for your compliments, but as aforesaid, *I have no photograph,* so the thumbnail must be lacking to the world. I would send you my wife's but she has none either, and I suppose the baby's won't do. We are a non-photographic family, on the whole.

. . . .

Yours as ever,
Wm. James

Jan. 19.96

My dear Holt:

At the risk of displeasing you, I think I won't have my photograph taken, even at no cost to myself. I abhor this hawking about of everybody's phiz which is growing on every hand, and don't see why having written a book should expose one to it. I am sorry that you should have succumbed to the supposed trade necessity. In any case, I will stand on my rights as a free man. You may kill me, but you shan't publish my photograph. Put a blank "thumb nail" in its place. Very very sorry to displease a man whom I love so much.

. . . .

Always lovingly yours
Wm. James

***

In the summer of 1896 James wrote Holt informing him of his plan to put together a collection consisting of previously published essays. The collection, The Will to Believe, and Other Essays in Popular Philosophy, *was published later that year by Longmans, Green, and Company.*

June 19.96

Dear Holt,

. . . .

I am just now putting together for republication a lot of my essays. There are 15 of them–eno' to form a vol. of 400 12° pp. or less, called "The Will to Believe, and other Essays in Popular Philosophy." A Mr. Lord from Scribners called on me twice last winter, urging me to give them something, and that brought this long-rumbling project to a head. I don't suppose there's any money in such a volume, but I told him I would send him the MS. and then get a bid from you, and give it to the highest! Isn't that good business? If you receive such an MS. from Scribner any time you will understand.

I also told Lord I was going to get ready for the press this summer my "Talks to Teachers on Psychology" a very small volume. It will consist of 6 lectures I have been giving outside the college for several years past. They have been well received and will doubtless sell, though of course it will be a low priced book. N. M. [Nicholas Murray] Butler has also applied for them for a certain "Series" he is interested in. I will, here also, send them to all three of you and see if anyone promises to make me richer than another. Wealth is now my only ideal.

College work *just* done, Gottlob! I hope that you and the fair lady who presides over your destinies are well. We have let our little N.H. place and are going to have a scattered summer. I give those lectures in three places.

Always truly yours,
Wm. James

July 2, '96

My dear Holt:

I got your letter last night on my return from the country, having already received one from Scribners in which they said that my having introduced the element of an "open competition" made it impossible, etc. I replied that there were delicacies among publishers that I couldn't fathom, so would they please send my Ms. back, and here I find it along with your letter. So much for the state of the outward facts.

Now for the inward ones. There is no chance of my feeling humanly put out in any way with you for the position you take up–the case lies between our *professional me's* which any student of my psychology will tell you are but small parts of our total selves. So filled am I with admiration of the literary genius of your epistle, from the first to the last line of it, that I feel that you should have been an "author" and I with my newly developed ruthlessness for gold should be your "publisher"–but the square pegs always get into the round holes, and this time there is no remedy. I admit and sympathize *in abstracto* most heartily with your ideal of the father-and-son relation between P. & A., their inseparable loyalty and all that, but concretions are always tripping up abstractions, and among the concretions here I find quite a 'bellious little feeling of *amour propre* stirred up by your action, which stands now much in the way of accommodation. It is obvious to my perception that the whole trouble lies in the word "open," coupled with the competition, and that the Scribners would have made me an offer instantly, had I not simultaneously notified you. It is morally inconceivable to me that a publisher with any ambition should *not* like to steal his rival's authors away from him, provided it be fairly done. As a matter of fact Appleton, Scribner, and Longmans have all spontaneously solicited me for "copy," with no reference made to you. Of course I am sensible of the advantages of continuity, and in spite of bruises (which I don't mind) I like to stay with you. But this isn't an absolute sentiment. It enters as a factor into a sum of considerations, one of which is percentages, and in the particular instance another is the great advertizing pertinacity with which I am struck in the Scribners, and the superior beauty of some of their publications. The simple and normal way seems to me an "auction" as regards the percentages, and the judgment of the poor devil (who altho an author needn't necessary be an *absolute* idiot) as to the total balance of his advantages when the element is known. There is no money in this present adventure–I shall be sincerely surprised if 2000 copies ever get sold to the end of time, but there is to me now a principle involved which you seem to deny, namely the right of an adult being to have some voice in the management of his own affairs. This is a paltry pride, to be sure, and we all know that free will is an illusion; nevertheless as a point in man's psychology great historic events have turned on it. There is an aesthetic enjoyment in a man's first little wiggle of pretense to take care of himself of which it is dangerous to interrupt the current, even by the most fatherly intended vetoes. Your veto on the auction business has roused in me all the freeman-blood of my ancestors, and makes it now quite impossible to publish the book with you, when before it was not only possible, but probable.

Surely the auction was the more natural way! The best of it is, my dear Holt, that I know that in your non-professional heart of hearts you entirely sympathize with me, and would, in a parallel conjunction act exactly as I am acting, only with ten times more cussedness. And as *men,* we shall love each other far more after this exchange of letters than we ever did before.

Always affectionately and admiringly yours,
William James

* * *

In spite of Holt and James's inability to reach agreement over the publication of The Will to Believe, *the two did come to terms over a later collection,* Talks to Teachers on Psychology and to Students on Some of Life's Ideals *(1899). James, however, took responsibility for the production of the book, with Holt publishing and distributing it on commission.*

Nov. 5, '98

Dear Sirs:

I shall send you tomorrow the manuscript of a small book I have finished, entitled "Talks to Teachers on Psychology, followed by three addresses to students of Women's Colleges." The three addresses cannot be sent at present. You can judge of their length by their falling inside of an hour in the delivery. The Atlantic Monthly is to publish about 2 thirds of the "Talks" which I send. Scribner's Magazine will publish one of the addresses, possibly more. The book can therefore hardly appear before next fall. But I send the manuscript now for your inspection and decision, because a certain business reason obliges me to fix upon my publisher at a very early date. I may say that the lectures have stood very well the test of repeated audiences to whom they were delivered. Suspicious at first of anything so unpedantic, the teachers at the close of the course have always been enthusiastic in their thanks and praise.

What I wish is that you would kindly look over the MS. to gain some idea of its value, and then if you wish it, name the most favorable contract with me which you are willing to accord. I am sorry to hurry you so, but the MS. and your reply must positively be back in my hands by the 15th.

If your reply is impossible by that date, let me know beforehand and I will see what can be done. The Atlantic Monthly in any case will require the first 40 pp. by that date.

Truly yours,
Wm. James

Nov. 19, 1898

Dear Holt:

I have received your 2 letters and the manuscript and thank you for all three.

The 3 addresses to "refined females" contain about 24,000 words or less. I think the volume ought not to sell for more than a dollar; and do not feel drawn by the idea of the 1st edition being *de luxe,* though I am willing to be guided in that matter by you, and profit accordingly.

I have decided that I had better manufacture the book myself, and publish it on commission. Will you take it thus, fully advertising it in your routine ways, and taking 10% of the list price for the handling? If you will, you may have the work, as I had rather you should publish it than another.

Always truly yours,
Wm. James

Feb. 3. 99

Dear Holt,

Your epistolary manners are so rough that unless I had had already some acquaintance with them, I should have supposed that your effusion of the first was meant as a notification that you don't care for the book.

I asked you a civil question about whether by "market" you meant the trade market or the public market. I had been told by Longmans that they send samples of all their new books to the trade before the "publication" thereof, and that much of their custom comes in this way. The agents for this are what I meant by "travellers." If this is not your method, I can only beg pardon; for no offense was tended, and certainly I never meant to imply that you were sending peddlers at $25.00 a day to send single copies to teachers, or that you are going to give my book any "special attention."

For any special pushing I expect to to [*sic*] be advised by you, and to pay. But I certainly expect publicity by all your general channels.

The book will D.v. be in your hands (1000 bound copies) by April 20th—It will be printed by Ellis in Boston. I will send you a specimen page in a day or so, and consult later about paper and binding.—All this on the continued supposition that you want it, & will do the fair thing by it, which of course I trust you to do, if you say so. But this last letter of yours reminds me of certain other letters I got during the Psychology time—well and humorously meant no doubt, but *rough!*—and I tremble at the prospect of their continuance!

Truly yours
Wm. James

March 22. 99

Dear Sirs:

I have examined the contract form sent me by you in duplicate and signed, and should return you a copy signed by myself, save for one or two doubts, etc.

Naturally the author should keep you in stock, due notice being given.

The right to sell your interest stays over from the royalty contract form. I am not sure that it is just. Do you care much for it?

It carries with it, in my opinion, the right on my part to terminate the contract at will so as to get the business away from anyone who might buy it from you and yet be obnoxious to me. Indeed in any case it seems to me that a contract like this should be terminable at will by either party, after six months notice to the other.

Will you agree to have it thus?

In the matter of advertising, I think the amount and kind of work which you expect to do gratis should be stated. For the rest I am in your hands, both as to judgment and execution. Being as ignorant as I am, I can name no sum for insertion. And ought not the first thousand be advertized considerably more than the later ones? Pray tell me what seems to you an *ample* sum for the first year, to expend *profitably* and I will see how it looks. I ought to have some account of what is done, and vouchers when practicable. Pray think a little of all this and write me what seems to you fairest and cheapest. Of course our interest in the *returns* of the advertizing is so identical that a publisher's commission on the advertizing itself doesn't seem called for. Moreover in principle it seems vicious, as possibly leading in unconscientious hands to extravagance for the author.

Apart from these points, the contract seems ultra simple and acceptable.

Truly yours,
Wm. James

P.S. I have pencilled a possible turn to give to the advertizing clause in the contract-blank.

* + *

March 24. 1899

Dear Sirs,

I have yours of the 23rd., and am glad your estimate of the advertising expenses is so low. You may fill in fifty dollars; or leave the pencilled emendation which I marginally suggest. The latter would seem better to cover all eventually [sic] possibilities.

I see that your right to sell signifies more than I supposed, though I should imagine this particular contract not to have any great market value. So I agree to it.

The terminability of the contract seems to me however an absolutely fair mutual provision, and I hope you will agree to it—six months notice being given by either of us to the other.

No matter for the voucher clause since the advertizing is so inconsiderable. The commission notion was my own idea, which I discussed as a possible alternative.

I corrected the last page proofs today, and the plates will soon be all cast.

On Monday I will send you the "Talks to Students" part. It has a somewhat different character from the teachers part, and might possibly justify a slightly different advertizing. The book will cost me, bound, 56 cents per copy at the present estimate, and contain 317 pp. all told. How many copies ought I to give away for publicity?—And can you judge of the right price from these facts? or must you have the book in your hands? I will send you dummies of binding as soon as they are got out.

Truly yours,
Wm. James

P.S. I send the last pp. *now* instead of Monday.

* * *

Charles Holt, Henry Holt's brother and, briefly, a business associate in Holt and Company, was quick to try to mollify James when an accounting error was discovered.

Nov. 21, 1902

Dear Sir:—

We are shocked at the contents of your letter of Nov. 19th. Someone in our receiving department evidently signed Mr. Ellis's receipts, and did not enter the shipments in our receiving book, consequently your account was not credited with them. Such errors could not occur with books we manufacture, as we have a long tried system of treble checks against them. In the case of the "Talks" we have been without such checks, you having the only means of comparing your printer's and binder's bills with our reports of books received and accounted for.

In future we shall ask Mr. Ellis for a statement each six months to compare with our entries.

We enclose account covering the books in question and our check to balance, with interest added from date when the accountings were due to to-day.

Will you kindly send the four receipts referred to in your letter, that we can place the responsibility upon the proper person?

We regret this matter more than you can imagine, and can only beg you to be as charitable as possible.
      Very truly yours,
      [Henry Holt & Co.]

      November 22, 1902

Dear James:

  I hope you will realize my surprise and disgust at learning of the discrepancies between our accounting and our receipts for your book. Fortunately the blunder is too absurd to make it possible that any thought of intention should cross a reasonable mind, in addition to certain other unfavorable impressions that were given you sometime ago by an erroneous coloring of the facts of my conference with Scribner.

  I write now merely to say that so far as I can recall, your "Talks to Teachers" is the *only* book that was delivered to us manufactured without any previous function of our own. With our other publications, the orders to paper-makers, printers, binders, etc., are constant checks against any failure to make the receipts of the completed work consistent with them, and by the aid of these checks, such receipts in other cases have always been so accurately kept that, apparently, there was no realization of the danger of their being overlooked with a book where we had no counter-check whatever. This experience was probably bound to come sooner or later, and I trust its arrival is safe to prevent its recurrence. I am only sorry that the necessary experience occurred with a client of so much importance as yourself, and for your own comfort's sake hope that it has occurred with some earlier client in the other houses with which you may be having similar dealings.

  In all this of course you won't understand me as claiming that the slip is not blameworthy, but only that it is not *as* blameworthy as would at first appear.

  I trust that counter-checks for the years preceding 1901 have already been applied (I believe 1901 was not the first year of the book's life), but even if they have, and no discrepancy was then unearthed by them, the discrepancies of 1901 are a little more puzzling, tho there are many ways of accounting for them—most prominent of course the changes among the clerks signing receipts, a grade of clerk which the inevitable checks in our usual business prevent the need of having as high and as permanent as those performing most other functions.

  As my brother said in a letter which he dictated from New York, I hope you will be "as charitable as possible."

      Faithfully yours,
      Henry Holt

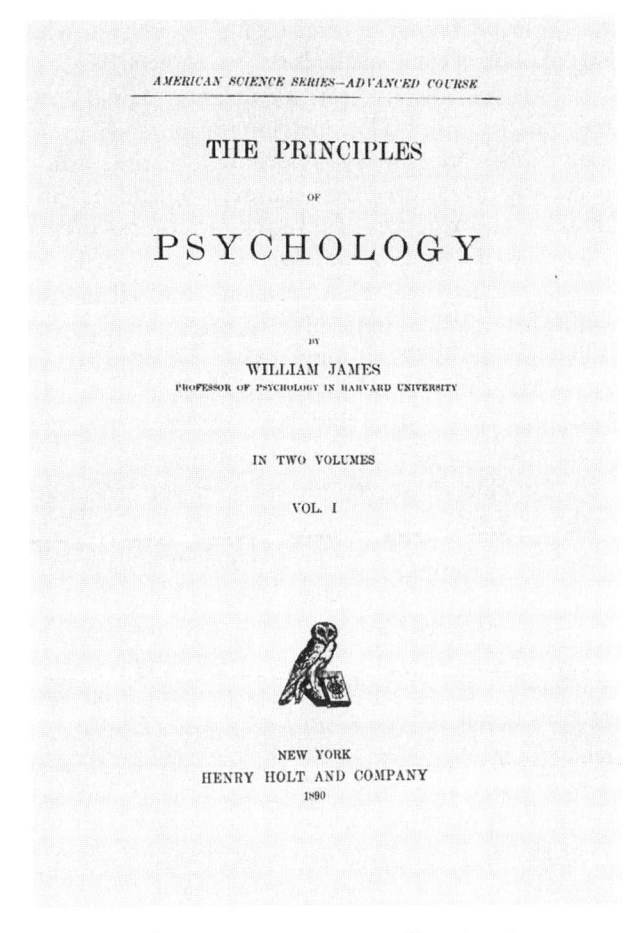

Title page for the first volume of James's study (Princeton University Library)

      Nov 24th. 1902

Dear Holt,

  Your letter from Burlington of the 22nd startles me, I confess, and since it comes as a sort of personal interlude to the business correspondence I shall respond in kind, & be absolutely candid.

  You make the whole business a more perfect abyss of unintelligibility than before, by repeating what I can only call the utterly *silly* explanations of the letter which accompanied the check.

  The plain and flagrant fact is that in your last two ½ yearly accounts the *sales were falsified* to correspond to a false number of copies received. The error was systematic. You say in explanation "change of receipt signing clerk" (*all* the receipts are by the same hand) and "no counter-check whatever," as if your own orders to printer, his letters of invoice, and your own sales-books didn't exist. When you add that such an "experience was probably bound to come sooner or later," to what sort of book keeping methods do you confess?!!

Am I a baby six years old that you should write me such rubbish? The only impression such irrelevant explanations can *possibly* arouse is that the firm is nervously concerned to conceal something, and thinks that for a man of my lack of business experience that kind of thing will do as a sop.

Now, my dear Holt, stand up and tell me the whole truth. What, until this last correspondence was only a puzzle, has been converted *by your letters* in[to] a grave suspicion of dealings which will not bear the light. It is up to you to dispel the suspicions by something more serious than what you write.

Confident that you can do so if you will, I am faithfully yours,

Wm. James

Several letters between Holt and James—with each insisting that he was right—were exchanged in rapid order at this time. In his retrospective scrutiny of James's accounts, Holt discovered an error in not paying James his due from sales of The Principles of Psychology. *His prompt payment to James, along with evidence regarding the truly accidental nature of the error regarding payments for* Talks to Teachers on Psychology and to Students on Some of Life's Ideals, *seem to have marked a turning point in the argument.*

Dec 14 '02

My dear Holt,

Yours of the 9th. came duly–this is the first moment I have had for a reply, both to it, and to what has gone before.

It is shameful that I should not have wound up the whole matter sooner, but after receiving yours of the 3rd. enclosing a check for $53.27 on acct. of an error discovered by yourselves in the past psychology accounts, I simply cashed the check provisionally, and resolved that, since the wine was poured out, I would drink it to the dregs, and wait till I could inform you of the complete annihilation of my suspicions, after examination of the binder's returns. These didn't come till last Sunday; and since then I have been kept too busy otherwise to think about this matter at all, until last night. It then took but a very short time to compare Valentine's report of shipments with your return of copies received during those years for which I have it, to ascertain the latter's absolute correctness save in two instances where you seem to have paid me too much. I have written to Valentine to repeat his record for those half years, and if he adds no new shipment, it will be I who must send you the check, probably. I confess that, to even up my side, I hope that this may prove to be the case.

The whole thing is perfectly simple to me now, but so long as I conceived of the return of sales being based only on positive entries of all sales made, I [*sic*] threw me into a greater perplexity than I ever remember being thrown into before. If I had only waited a couple of hours before writing that letter on which you animadvert so gracefully in your last, or if you and the firm had truly been at the outset as explicit as you afterwards became about your usual methods of book keeping, that letter would certainly never have been written, nor should I now have to apologize for it, as I hereby do. I always explode too abruptly; & I certainly did so in this case. Your tone with me on the contrary has been exemplary, and I only pray you to forgive and forget,

Yours repentantly,

W.J.

Dec 17/2

Dear James:

It's all right and you make it right so manfully that one can hardly regret the occasion.

"Yours as ever" and, I suspect, a little more so

H. Holt.

Dec. 27, 1902.

Dear James:

The spirit moves me to tell you that the discovery of our bookkeeper's little blunder in going over your accounts, led us to begin a thorough search for similar errors, with the result in 18 books–including those of all our Cambridge and Boston authors, some of the books nearly 20 years old–that we have discovered just one error, where we overpaid $26.

My conscience says we have gone far enough.

Wishing you a Happy New Year, where publishers shall not vex nor moths break in and steal,

Yours ever,
Henry Holt

Dec 31.

Rest, perturbe'd spirit! and pardon a mind "perplexed in the extreme" for stirring up so much trouble for you. I feel ashamed of the inordinate extension of my business "enterprise."

Yours as ever,   faithfully,

Wm. James

HENRY ADAMS

HOLT AND COMPANY BOOKS BY ADAMS:
Democracy, anonymous (New York: Holt, 1880; London: Macmillan, 1882);
Esther, as Frances Snow Compton (New York: Holt, 1884; London: Bentley, 1885).

Historian Henry Brooks Adams (1838–1918), grandson of President John Quincy Adams, was born in Boston, Massachusetts, and educated at Harvard University. After studying law in Germany, he served as secretary to his father, Charles Francis Adams, during Charles's term as ambassador to England (1861–1868). After a teaching stint at Harvard (1870–1877), Adams settled in Washington, D.C., where he wrote and enjoyed the company of an elite circle of friends. After the suicide of his wife in 1885, Adams traveled extensively, although he continued to make Washington his home.

* * *

In his 1923 memoir Henry Holt recalled how Adams approached him with the manuscript of his first novel, which Holt and Company published anonymously as Democracy *in 1880. Holt was so scrupulous about keeping the authorship of* Democracy *a secret that he wrote "Author of Democracy" rather than "Adams, Henry" in the index to the letterpress book in which there is a copy of a royalty statement dated 25 October 1893. Unfortunately, the letters from Holt to Adams copied into letterpress books during these years are almost completely faded.*

In the spring of '79 Henry [Adams] sent me the manuscript of *Democracy,* under a pledge of dead secrecy. I read it myself and accepted it at once. The secret inevitably got out to one or two men in my office, and in time to three or four, but it never got farther until [William Roscoe] Thayer told it in his biography of [John] Hay, and even to this day people ask me if Adams wrote the book, or even "who" wrote it.

We must have rushed it out regardless of season, which we would not be apt to do now, but possibly Adams may have been eager for it, or taken the risk himself. I think he did. At all events the book was out, and had created some sensation in England, tho not yet in America, when I met Adams and his wife in Paris in July or August. I need not tell anyone who has read his letters that they were very exceptionally good company. . . .
–*Garrulities of an Octogenarian Editor* (Boston & New York: Houghton Mifflin, 1923), pp. 136–137

The question of the authorship of Democracy *was still a source of amusement for Adams more than thirty years after the novel was published, as is seen in a July 1911 letter to Mary Cadwalader Jones, Edith Wharton's sister-in-law.*

Henry Adams (Massachusetts Historical Society)

Two years ago a gentleman called on me (sent by Henry Holt) to ask whether I wrote Democracy. I told him I did not. He went off, and wrote a book in which he said that I said I did. . . . If it pleases him to think I wrote Shakespeare and Mother Goose *tant mieux!* Really, of course Henry James wrote it, in connection with his brother Willy, to illustrate Pragmatism.
quoted in Joanne Jacobson, *Authority and Alliance in the Letters of Henry Adams* (Madison: University of Wisconsin Press, 1992), p. 90

On 23 August 1901 Adams wrote to Elizabeth Cameron describing a plan for the dramatization of his first novel.

I have . . . a note from Henry Holt offering to dramatise Democracy! I thought my old–five-and-twenty-year old–sins were long dead and buried, but they rise like Mrs. Bigelow Lawrence who will die convinced that she was meant as the heroine of that scandalous work. I saw it in her eye at Bayreuth. It would be fun for her to see herself on the stage.
–Ernest Samuels, ed., *Henry Adams: Selected Letters* (Cambridge, Mass.: Belknap Press of Harvard University Press, 1992), p. 410

* * *

Holt agreed to publish Esther, *Adams's second novel, in 1884 under the pseudonym Frances Snow Compton and further agreed to Adams's wish that, as an experiment, the book not be publicized.*

Before many years he brought me his second novel, *Esther*. That, too, he wanted kept anonymous, and for a new set of reasons. He wrote me that he was at the time especially averse to being talked about. This was, I think, because of the peculiar circumstances of his wife's death. . . .
He wanted to test how much the success of a book depends on pushing—how far a book can make its own publicity. He didn't want *Esther* advertised, or, I think, tho it hardly seems possible, even any copies sent to the press. Of course he took the risks himself. The result was *nil*. But who can tell if it would have been enough to pay for the advertising if any had been done. There are many respectable books that don't, and *Esther* was not *Democracy*.
—*Garrulities of an Octogenarian Editor,* pp. 138, 139

***

The 1885 suicide of Adams's wife, Marian ("Clover"), the inspiration for Esther in the novel of that title, devastated him. In March 1886 he wrote to Holt about his despondency.

I am almost amused at the idea of my caring now for anything that so-called critics could say. When the only chapter of one's story for which one cares is closed forever, locked up, and put away, to be kept, as a sort of open secret, between oneself and eternity, one does not think much of newspapers.
—quoted in Jacobson, *Authority and Alliance in the Letters of Henry Adams,* p. 90

On 23 August 1886 Adams wrote to his friend John Hay about his feelings of privacy regarding the identity of his wife as the model for Esther.

My poor boy, how very strong you do draw your vintage for my melancholy little Esther. . . . Perhaps I made the mistake even to tell [Clarence] King about it; but having told him, I could not leave you out. Now, let it die! To admit the public to it would be almost unendurable to me. I will not pretend that the book is not precious to me, but its value has nothing to do with the public who could never understand that such a book might be written in one's heart's blood.
—Samuels, ed., *Henry Adams: Selected Letters,* p. 192

***

In 1871 the Boston firm of James R. Osgood and Company had published Chapters of Erie, and Other Essays, *a collection of political essays by Adams and his brother Charles Francis Adams Jr. Holt and Company took over the book from Osgood in 1886.*

5 March, 1890

Dear Holt:

Thanks. I am concerned only in the larger volume called "Chapters of Erie," but I guess my brother Charles feels as I do about it, so you might as well melt up the plates of both. Credit me with whatever is proper, and send me a bill of sale. I will pay the balance by check.

Perhaps I would do well to take a few of the "Chapters of Erie" myself. I have now no copy of my own essays in that volume. You might send me half a dozen copies in place of royalty.

With the year 1890 I shall retire from authorship. As an occupation I can recommend it to the rich. It has cost me about a hundred thousand dollars, I calculate, in twenty years, and has given me that amount of amusement. In July I sail from San Francisco for new scenes and adventures, leaving to younger and better men whatever promotion my vacancy may cause in the service. I hope they will enjoy it as much as I have done.

Ever yrs
Henry Adams

***

In 1913 Holt wrote Adams requesting a copy of The Education of Henry Adams, *which had been privately printed in 1907 and was published commercially by Houghton Mifflin in 1918 after Adams's death. Adams's autobiographical work won the Pulitzer Prize in 1919.*

Sept. 3, 1913

My dear Historian:

Can you remember as far back as when you were that to me, and I was your dear philosopher to you? I remember the time so vividly that I find no difficulty in telling you that [Raphael] Pumpelly spoke to me the other day about your book "The Education of Henry Adams" in such a way that I want you to send me a copy. He also spoke about your *Letters to Teachers* or *To a Teacher,* ditto ditto ditto. I don't know whether it's a book or a pamphlet.

I understand that the book at least is privately printed, or else I would have self-respect enough to send to a dealer for a copy, although I don't object at all to this fashion of saying Hello to you across the ages and distances!

I hope all is well with you, and that you are confidently expecting more fun after something happens which is sure to happen before many years to you and me.

> Faithfully yours
> [Henry Holt]

> 22 Sept. 1913

My dear Holt

I was moved to a laugh when I read your letter yesterday. That three old men like Pumpelly, you and me should go muddling about each others' forgottennness still, after we were dead and forgotten these thousand years, seems a merry, young jest, but Shakespeare said something about comparing him with the bettering of the time as an excuse for such behavior in his own case, and although no one has yet found the betterment he kindly promised, no doubt everyone revels now in plenty of Shakespeares and such to encourage you to read me. Unluckily I don't carry my immortal works in my pocket. I must wait for winter, but if I survive till December I will try to bind a copy of my immortal thoughts. But pray remind me of it, for I remember nothing overnight;—least of all, about myself, which is a subject fit only for the ghosts. Oh, yes!—I like it! but I think even the ghosts are rather bored. Well they may be!

It is no great use wishing you all the blessings of youth and loveliness, but whatever falls in your way I trust will do you good. For my own part I want only personal beauty. It has such a good influence on my contemporaries!

> Ever yrs
> Henry Adams

***

Holt was still interested in publishing The Education of Henry Adams *after Adams's death on 27 March 1918, as is evidenced by this letter, dated 6 April 1918, from U.S. senator Henry Cabot Lodge of Massachusetts.*

. . . .

Mr. Adams left in my charge the "Education of Henry Adams," which is an Autobiography and a very remarkable book, about which he gave me full directions. He wished to have it published under my supervision and charge, through the Massachusetts Historical Society, and of course I shall simply follow his directions, which he gave me not only verbally but in a letter which accompanies the copy of the book in which he made certain corrections and additions. I have therefore no choice . . . except to bring it out in the manner in which he requested.

I am much interested in the note from the Evening Post. Mr. Adams was undoubtedly the author of "Democracy," as I have known for a great many years, but "Esther" is new to me. I have never heard of it and as I have been an intimate friend of Mr. Adams for nearly half a century I am a little surprised that I never saw it or heard a word from him in regard to it.

> Very truly yours,
> Henry Cabot Lodge

> June 11, 1918

Dear Senator Lodge:

I have uneartht a copy of "Esther" in the possession of an old member of our staff.

There is no question whatever about its having been the work of Mr. Adams. He and I had several conferences about it, and if necessary, the correspondence could be uneartht—if it has escaped two fires, to confirm my statements; but my recollection is as distinct about it as it is about "Democracy."

My immediate object in writing yu is to ascertain if yu care to read thru "Esther" and to try the other half of Adams's experiment. The first half was to find out if it would go without any public attention whatever being

---

Authorship Revealed

Literary Note
THE LITERARY OUT-PUT OF HENRY ADAMS

That Henry Adams was the author of DEMOCRACY was a well kept secret for over a generation, and was only lately revealed in "The Life of John Hay." It is now revealed by his publishers that he was also the author of ESTHER, a novel published in 1884. He insisted on the book not being advertised or even sent out for review. He wanted to test the possibility of a book succeeding absolutely on its merits. Esther did not, but Esther was not Democracy. Democracy has gone through sixteen editions, but was advertised and sent to the press, which Esther was not. Both of these novels were published here by Henry Holt and Company, and also in England. Mr. Adams was co-author with his brother, Charles Francis, of CHAPTERS OF ERIE (dealing with the Erie R.R. scandals) and other essays (1871), originally published by Ticknor and Fields, and later by Henry Holt and Company.

22 Sept. 1913
8, SQUARE DU BOIS DE BOULOGNE

My dear Fritz:

I was amused to laugh when I read your letter yesterday. That there are many like Pumpelly, you and me, should go muttering about each others forgivenness still, after we were dead and forgotten these thousand years, seems to many young jests, but Shakespeares did something about comparing him with the better-

ing of the tories as an example in such behavior in his own case, and although no one has yet found the document he kindly promised, no doubt everyone needs one in penny if Shakespeares and such. To encourage you to read me, unluckily I don't carry my monumental works in my pocket. I must wait for winter, but I survive till december

Four-page letter from Adams to Henry Holt (Princeton University Library)

I will try to send a copy of my immortal thoughts. But pray remind me of it, for I remember nothing now—look of all, and of myself, which is subject fit only for the ghosts. Oh, yes! — I take it! but I think even the ghosts are rather bored. Well they may be!

It is no great use wishing you all the blessings of your and sweetness, but whatever falls in your way I will do you good. For my own part I want only personal beauty. It has such a good influence on my contemporaries!

Ever yrs
Henry James

called to it. Now, it might be interesting to determine whether it would go *with* public attention called to it.

Do yu care to read it? If so, I will send it to yu.

Very truly yours,
[Henry Holt]

June 13, 1918

My dear Mr. Holt:

I know that Mr. Adams wrote Esther and I know the facts as to his experiment to be as you describe them. As for reprinting the book, the family are entirely opposed to it. They do not wish it reprinted, and personally I sincerely hope it will not be attempted. I have talked with members of the family about it and I speak with knowledge of their feelings. Mr. Adams left no directions to me about his two novels, but he did say in substance to his niece that they were things not to be revived.

Very truly yours,
H. C. Lodge

June 15, 1918

Dear Senator Lodge:

Thanks for yours of the 13th.

The slightest objection on your part or that of any of the family, would be abundantly sufficient to prevent our reprinting "Esther," even were we strongly inclined that way—which we are not.

Very truly yours,
[Henry Holt]

DOROTHY CANFIELD FISHER

HOLT AND COMPANY BOOKS BY FISHER: *Gunhild, a Norwegian-American Episode* (New York: Holt, 1907);

The Squirrel-Cage (New York: Holt, 1912);

A Montessori Mother (New York: Holt, 1912; London: Constable, 1913);

Mothers and Children (New York: Holt, 1914; London: Constable, 1915);

The Bent Twig (New York: Holt, 1915; London: Constable, 1922);

Hillsboro People, with occasional verses by Sarah N. Cleghorn (New York: Holt, 1915);

Fellow Captains, by Fisher and Cleghorn (New York: Holt, 1916);

The Real Motive (New York: Holt, 1916);

Understood Betsy (New York: Holt, 1917);

Home Fires in France (New York: Holt, 1918);

The Day of Glory (New York: Holt, 1919);

American Portraits (New York: Holt, 1946).

The American novelist Dorothy Canfield Fisher (1879–1958) enjoyed noteworthy popularity during her writing career, which spanned the early to mid 1900s. (Although she married in 1907, she continued to publish under her maiden name, Dorothy Canfield, until 1940.) Fisher moved easily back and forth between fiction and nonfiction. She influenced American reading taste when, from 1926 until 1950, she served as a member of the first selection board of the Book-of-the-Month Club. Although Henry Holt himself guided Fisher's early career and enjoyed her affectionate allegiance to him, she came to rely more and more on Alfred Harcourt, especially as the elder Holt retreated to Fairholt, his home in Vermont. Fisher's unease with Holt's son Roland, who now spent more time at the office, is apparent in the following letter to Harcourt. Fisher was among those authors who left Holt and Company to follow Harcourt when he and Donald Brace founded Harcourt, Brace and Company in July 1919.

October 4th 1911

My dear Alfred:

A letter from Mr. Holt (Roland) received yesterday, happens to mention that you are in town now and I hasten to seize the opportunity to write you, before (for all I know) you may be off in the wilds again. There are a lot of things I've been wishing to ask you . . . they've been piling up . . . and now's my time. I'll jumble them in together pell-mell, as I write with one eye on my bubbling grape-juice (its the jelly-making season at its heigth [*sic*])

. . . .

Next (confidential) I left out one chapter of "The Squirrel Cage" and sent it on yesterday to Mr. R. Holt, not knowing you were there. *Will* you, to ease my mind just make sure he received it and inserted it in the right place. Its to go at the very beginning of the second book, before the chapter called "a sop to the wolves." I was so foolish not to have an extra copy of that Mss. made! I'm as nervous as a witch about it until I know its safe. I followed your suggestion and cut it in various and sundry places, about (I suppose) five or six thousands words . . . maybe a little more.

. . . .

[A]fter the thing was set up, they made me cut the galleys a lot more than they specified at first. I was for a time quite disheartened and cast down about it. It seemed to me that nobody would care to read such a bare and bald outline of the story as they were going to print. . . . but a letter received as soon as the first installment came out, has quite set me up again, and made me think that maybe my little decorations which hurt so to

Dorothy Canfield Fisher (who continued to write under her maiden name until 1940) and her son, Jimmy, pictured on an undated promotional brochure (mid 1920s) published by the firm for which she began to write after leaving Holt and Company in 1919 (Princeton University Library)

cut out, weren't so dern important after all. I'll send you the letter herewith. . . . Don't bother to send it back. I've taken a copy of the man's name and address to write him my old formula of "no thank you sir. . .I'm engaged to Mr. Holt." But the letter did please me very much, as the first indication from the public of how The Squirrel Cage really looks in print.

And now before I arouse a busy man to rise and throw his ink-pot at the head of a too loquacious correspondent, I'd better stop, with much love to Sue [Harcourt] from us all and whatever is correct and proper in the way of greetings to her two men-folks! How good you all were to come to see us this summer!

      Faithfully and cordially yours,
      Dorothy C. F.

P.S. I didn't know I *was* such a womanly woman! . . here is one of the important things I meant to ask you shoved into the postscript! I've looked over my collection of printed short stories (they're about a million! I have been an awful chatter-box!) and find I have eighteen or twenty which deal with the life up here, most of which have met with a very friendly reception, and which could be entitled, after an essay on country life I did for Scribner's a year or two ago, "At the Foot of Hemlock Mountain." They would make a book about ninety thousands words long. Now the question is, would it be worth while to put them together now before we sail, and send them down for your readers to look over, with a view to possible publication some time next year, or would we better bide a wee? It might very well be, you know, that a disinterested set of readers would find them not worth permanent publication. . . . but of late I've had quite a number of letters asking if the "Hillsboro stories" had been published in book form. Will you give this matter a few minutes thought and decide it for me? I'll be much obliged.
      D. C. F.

***

The Natural Man Growing
Bolton Hall

In 1912, while wintering in Italy, Fisher met and befriended educator Maria Montessori. The first of Fisher's three nonfiction works on the Montessori method was A Montessori Mother, *published in 1912 and reviewed the following year in* The Public.

. . . .

Michelet's saying that "no consecrated absurdity could have stood its ground if the man had not silenced the objections of the child," is as true of secular as of religious thought; and the method of Mme. Montessori, so charmingly described in this book, is to avoid all dominating over the mind and the actions of the child—to let him learn, as he loves to do, instead of wearying him with teaching. The results in the automatic attainment of "the three R's" are most surprising.

. . . .

Mrs. Fisher sees clearly and shows plainly that such letting alone without steering is the way to teach self government, to build up the self reliant and self restraining person. We are not all blessed with children, nor does everyone realize that "all the babies in the world are mine," but we all have to teach, consciously or unconsciously, and we are all victims of the desire to make people think and act as we think and act, instead of allowing them to think and act for themselves. Big people and little people will work for the joy of the working, the pleasure of overcoming difficulties, and the happiness of creation, and, given liberty, have far more tendency to do right than wrong.

Mrs. Fisher leads us gently up to the startling conclusion that *there are no naughty children;* there are only mistreated and irritated children who can be set right loving wisdom. And she does not hesitate to show how the same principles apply to the "children of a larger growth."

On the last page, however, the author says:

> Here is the opportunity for us, mothers, perhaps among the last of the race who will be allowed the inestimable delight and joy of caring for our own little children, a delight and joy of which society, sooner or later, will consider us unworthy on account of our inexpertness, our carelessness, our absorption in other things, our lack of wise preparation, our lack of abstract good judgment.

This conclusion seems unwarranted. Because we do our education badly by using too much authority now, would the State do it better by using the horrible authority which Mrs. Fisher anticipates? Or is her prophecy intended as a wholesome warning?

–"The Natural Man Growing," *Public,* 16 (7 March 1913): 234–235

* * *

Henry Holt's letters to Fisher include much detailed editorial advice (as well as his idiosyncratic "progressive" spelling). He offered the following critical advice on the manuscript of her novel The Bent Twig *(1915).*

Fisher on Henry Holt

May 24, 1915

Dear Alfred [Harcourt]:

Who should suddenly drop in yesterday for a two-minute call but Mr. Holt himself. . . . I found the same astonishing fondness for the old gentleman spring up at the sight of him . . . although I don't suppose I agree with him about any single thing. But he's a wonderfully fine old specimen, isn't he, and I do love to see him!

[Dorothy Canfield Fisher]

Sept. 15, 1915

Dear little Lady:

Yu will find your proofs which I am returning, very full of comments, but it may help for me to sum up and emphasize a little. I take it for granted the book wouldn't have got into my hands unless yu cared for my impressions; and I also take it for granted that yu have too much sense and strength to be hurt by anything I honestly say. It will be but the opinion of one man anyhow, tho of course that man will be glad and flattered if he finds that in the main yu agree with him.

I welcome criticism so much myself, and act upon it so much, that perhaps I tend to underrate the sensitiveness of other people to it, but I don't really expect yu to be hurt, tho I shall be awfully sorry if yu are.

It is a good book, but seems to be encrusted with rather more superfluous matter than equally good books often are, some of which matter might be good if it were not superfluous; but nothing superfluous is ever good, especially in a work of art. In fact I have had beauty defined as freedom from superfluity.

It looks to me as if when your pen got to going with things with which yu were very familiar, yu yielded pretty freely to the pleasure of letting it go. I think the book would greatly gain by filing and sand papering off from, perhaps, a fifth to a quarter.

It is very difficult to kill one's own creations, but yu can probably bring a somewhat fresh mind to this one now. I would certainly take out most if not all of the department store business, unless there may be a few lines essential to the plot and characters; ditto the high school building, etc., and I think I would take out even the rather interesting matter regarding the two octoroon girls, unless you want them badly for the development of the characters.

There is also a good deal of a good housekeeper's interest in domestic affairs that will not interest a good many of your readers, especially those who are going to form public opinion: for the majority of them, being men, are presumably not interested in such affairs. But of course keep all really needed for the character development.

I think that the writer of a book ought to look at every sentence and every word with the question: Can I do equally well without this? Of course the standards on which such a question would be judged must not be too severe; but it is better that they should be too severe than that they should be too slack.

Possibly yu have trusted to the perspicacity of your readers too much—in leaving so many motives to be inferred from conduct. I think yu could give a slight touch of explanation here and there without doing the work any harm, and possibly doing it a great deal of good.

Yu essayed a heavy job in keeping Sylvia hesitating so long between the two men, and taxt somewhat at least my interest in her character and respect for her. But perhaps I'm too romantic for a real world.

I have said more than once on the margin of the proof that I consider that whole letter business between Page and Sylvia impossible. Perhaps a man who was crank enough to put those mines in other hands instead of running them himself the best he knew how, would be crank enough to leave all that matter for a letter, without talking it over with Sylvia before he left her; but his leaving it for a letter is no more admirable than it is probable; and yet yu intend him of course to be a hero. I don't think, anyhow, that men worth their salt do much of their love-making by letter, where they have a chance to do it any other way. But as I said, I'm romantic, and perhaps I'm particularly sore on this point, because a rather good friend of mine lost his girl by it, as I think he deserved to.

I think the condition of Sylvia's family, especially of her father after her mother's death, is good and strong, and yet if yu can find that yu can shorten it without lacerating yourself, I would do so. Of course yu want your book attractive, and I am the last one to deny that "Macbeth" and "Othello" are attractive; but with painful things, of course it is a question of how much.

And now may all good influences bless and guide you!

[Henry Holt]

September 16 1915

Dear Mr. Holt:

I pity you with all my heart if you have never known the exciting pleasure you have just given me, if you've never had the electrifying experience which has just ended for me with the last page of the proofs! Its been one of the dreams of my life, to have just such a criticism as that, illuminating, full, precise and accurate as a surgeons scalpel. And now I've had it. And I am, to express myself with genuine Vermont reserve, very much obliged to you. Indeed I am!

You're not to think from this that I'm at all intended to swallow whole the entire pungent pellet of your criticism! Some of your suggestions come too late for me to use, because to take advantage of them the book would have to be hatched over and hatched different; other suggestions have already been covered by other friendly readers, and have already been corrected; and I wouldn't use a few of your suggestions if I could, because I don't agree with you as to the principle involved. But I tell you what! For the most part I can scarcely wait for the proofs to come back in order to get into them the improvements made possible by your comments!

The subject of the punctuation of the book is one for laughter and tears! Those aren't *my* commas! I won't *have* them wished on to me! They're Holt and Co. commas! When Mr. Brace and Mr. Harcourt came up here in the summer, they insisted that they had read with ease the interlined, cued-in and cut-to-pieces Mss. I then had, and that it would need no retyping for the printers. I protested that John [Fisher, her husband] had typed part of it, and I part, and that the punctuation had had little attention and certainly wouldn't be consistent, because John punctuates prayerfully and well, and I carelessly and ill. They said, "Oh we'll send directions out to Rahway to have it punctuated consistently according to their usual formulae, the way they do all our books." Yessir! That's the way it was. I myself, vague as I am on the subject of punctuation, noticed a good many commas and took out a lot in my copy of the galley, but I thought (what little I thought about it) that the professional proof-readers of such a big printing establishment must know more about usage than I, and I didn't cut out any of those between adjectives because I was brought up to leave them in. . . . not that I have any fixed conviction on the subject! What shall we do about it? . . .

[I]n case you might be interested to know how some of the suggestions struck me, I set a few notes down, pell-mell. . . . Yes, of course the first third must be cut. Its been cut already to about half the original form, but I agree with you that more excisions would help it. I was about to begin a vigorous pruning when I heard you were to see the book and thought I'd wait to see if you thought it was necessary. Almost everybody else advises against cutting out things . . . for instance the chapter on the public school, which I have been waving my scissors over for months. Everybody says, "Oh no, all your middle-aged readers will enjoy the reminiscences it brings up." But now you've spoken, out it goes. Matrigna means stepmother in Italian, a horrid word which means cruelty and all dreadfulness. Mrs. Marshall-Smith would never have had Arnold call her that. Madrina is god-mother, which she might very well have been literally, and which is a pleasant, neutral title she might have chosen. Of course the cigarette-stained fingers are on the right hand! I will never make *that* mistake again, having been loudly corrected by every single person who has read the Mss.

Of course Sylvia brushes her teeth at night! She never smoked enough to get throughly [*sic*] inoculated to tobacco—kept a child-clean physique in that regard. Just once when I spent three or four months steadily in Norway where, as in Russia, everybody smokes, even to the dowager grandmothers, I grew really incoulated [*sic*], so I can believe what you say about your dozen cigars. But in ordinary, respectable American or French feminine life where smoking is a rather rare incident (and that would be Sylvia's experience) no amount of tooth-brushing has been sufficient to save me from the furry taste. And on this subject what a curiously imperfect sentence of mine about Arnold's not being able to remember that any sane man did not smoke; and what a comic misinterpretation you insisted upon! Of course you know that I did not mean that nobody who is sane, smokes. That would bar out nearly every man I know. I meant to indicate Arnold's surprise that every sane man does not smoke. You are right, English is a tuf [*sic*] language! There do be times when it seems to me it would be easier to do washings for one's living than to try to write it correctly. But on the other hand Flaubert and de Maupassant both went insane over writing French!

About Morrison. Yes surely, I meant him to be (like every merely aesthetic man I ever met) something of an intellectual prig and somewhat conscious of his own perfections. But [I] wanted him to seem so only to the mature and discerning reader not at all to Sylvia who was, for all her ideas of her cleverness, really very unsophisticated; nor to Aunt Victoria who was looking for leisurely and intelligent and sophisticated men so diligently that she would overlook self-consciousness and aesthetic priggishness. But in my little Sally's [Fisher's daughter] phrase, it was as hard as the dickleums to walk that tight-rope, to make him not wholly a cad or an aesthete, to make him really enough of a man to take Sylvia in, with his fine phrases, and yet to make him sufficiently less of a man to throw Austin into relief. . . .

But this getting too outrageously long. . . . I'll leave the other points, even the vital vital one of the deus ex machina thrust (which went to my heart with a nasty accuracy). That was not kind of you! Of course you must have known how many many times I'd examined my conscience on the use of Mrs. Marshall's death. But though you gave me a turn, I still stick to my guns. I have a reasoned belief on the subject of accidents in fiction which I want to talk to you about, some day. . . .

Which brings me naturally again to one more expression of my wonder at your being able to take the time to read it, and my great gratitude that you did! I'll do the next one a lot better because you did.

Always gratefully and affectionately,
Dorothy Canfield Fisher

Illustration from Fisher's The Squirrel-Cage, *published by Holt and Company in 1912 (Rutgers University Library)*

Oh, what *funny* mistakes you did put your ironic finger on—of course Aunt Victoria wouldn't say "*gold* watch." Why did nobody else notice that! And yes, of course again, its positively Ouida-ish to mention Aunt Victoria's expensive bric-a-brac . . . and to be sure, the Grand Canal *does* sound like Venice, rather than Versailles—and so on, and so on, and so on—blessings on your keen eye.

The Bent Twig *went on to achieve some popularity on the strength of favorable reviews, as is indicated by an order Holt and Company received from the librarian of the National Cash Register Company.*

August 28, 1916.

Gentlemen:

Under separate cover a copy of Fisher's "Bent Twig" published by your company is being ordered for the factory library. The library is mainly a technical one. It may interest you to know that this book has been ordered because of the demand created among our women employees by the weekly reviews given by Mrs. Charlotte Reeves Conover. Her reviews of books carry great weight with the reading people of Dayton.

    Yours very truly,
    Edith Phail,
    Librarian,
    The National Cash Register Company.

* * *

During World War I, Fisher went to live in France to help with the war effort. Among her projects was the establishment of a home for needy children. She and Harcourt continued to correspond about both personal and professional concerns. He sent her the following report on how the war was affecting daily business at Holt and Company.

    Dec. 17, 1917
. . . .

  Two more of our young men have decided to go to war, and we are thinking of trying women as salesmen to the high schools and colleges. It has really been a very tumultuous business year, moving office, moving the stockroom, some disheartening changes in the staff, the promising youngsters going off to war, and back of it all there has been the feeling that . . . it doesn't make much difference what happens to Henry Holt & Co. . . .

Shortly after the end of the war Harcourt wrote to Fisher following a buying trip to London. The plan for a Holt and Company book on General John J. Pershing never came to fruition.

    January 27, 1919
Dear Dorothy:
  I have been home a week after a long and rough voyage. We went from Liverpool to Brest for a fine load of returning soldiers, and then had a rough and slow voyage home. But the emotion with which those boys saw the harbor and their delight at the fuss made over them by the Committee of Welcome with its two bands, pretty Red Cross nurses, etc. thrilled me to my toes. You can look forward to coming up the harbor with all the spinal thrills that you are capable of.
  It is very good to be home. You know I am a man that likes his victuals. I am staying at the Columbia Club for a few weeks, leaving Sue and Hastings on an island in the Gulf of Mexico off the Florida coast, where they are in wonderful health and having lots of fun.

The Club is on 43rd St. just around the corner from the office, and a few weeks of being able to be here night and day will get work so cleaned up and things so started as to relieve the pressure all summer.
  I found twenty or thirty books in London, and got several schemes well started, the most important and interesting of which is, of course, the Pershing one. Will you keep your eye on that, and if you can, let me know the upshot of your talk with the General? Of course, the book will be written earlier than he now thinks, and that date and the consequent income from it will be hastened when and if he signs a contract. If you should ever find him in such a mood that you think he might be willing to make a bargain, even if only to be rid of the pestering that he will be having from all sides, and will cable me, I'll go straight to Paris, or wherever he is and have Curtis Brown meet me there, and get the whole thing in order. I don't see any reason why he shouldn't tie up to us all, as I have no doubt that we are making a proposal which, in the long run, will be as good as any he will receive. Of course it is slow work getting to France, and will be for six months or more, and perhaps Curtis Brown could settle the matter alone. All this is jumping ahead of even the probabilities a little bit, but it is wise to have the ground cleared for action, if action should suddenly become possible. Of course, in London I was talking somewhat off my own bat. I find the others here are as much interested in the scheme as I am, and are not staggered unduly by the figures mentioned.

. . . .

Harcourt wrote to Fisher in Versailles informing her that Holt and Company was planning to publish a second book of her short stories based on her wartime experiences as a follow-up to Home Fires in France *(1918). The second collection,* The Day of Glory, *came out in 1919.*

    January 30, 1919.
Dear Dorothy:
  This is just to say in a casual sort of fashion that you are to have a new book entitled "The Day of Glory," published by H. H. and Co. within a couple of months, and that your publisher hopes you don't mind.
  You will remember that I wrote you from London rather dubiously about business conditions here. I come back to find our business booming. "Home Fires" seems to have sold to the first of January 29,638 copies, and now after the usual slow-up of January business, when booksellers are taking inventory and keeping their stock down, we have about a thousand copies this month and reorders are beginning to come in for quantities. Women have stopped knitting and begun to read, and the book business is really fine. If we are ever to

cash in on the sketches from France that didn't get into "Home Fires," now is the time to do it, and our salesmen take the view that having the new book will enable them to make combination offers of it and "Home Fires" to the great advantage of "Home Fires" and not at all to the disadvantage of the new book. That is, we give a 40% discount on 150 copies. A typical bookstore would take 100 copies of "Home Fires" and if published next fall, would take 100 copies of the new book, but now we can get 250 of the combination. My experience would clearly show that the books will help each other, rather than get in each other's way. So after a good deal of cogitation, and a good deal of regret that I can't talk the matter over with you, we have decided to go ahead with the new book on the understanding that you have been leaving such matters to my judgment. Looking at it from your point of view, I think we will make a thousand dollars or two, or three for you that you might as well have as not. As to the book itself, though I shall reread the material before finally deciding, it shapes itself as follows now:

    Title----The Day of Glory

    Contents-----

        On the Edge; The Woman Doctor story; Some Confused Impressions; It is rather for us to be here Dedicated; The Day of Glory.

If it were not for the convention that the title story of a collection should be either the first or the last, I should be more inclined to put "It is rather, etc." at the end, though the last few paragraphs of "The Day of Glory" are so glowing as to be the proper ending for the book.

Communications are so slow and we are going to push the manufacture of the book so hard, that I doubt if there is time to hear from you. If what we are doing should meet with your real disapproval, we will do all we can to stop on receipt of a cable. Of course, what we can't stop is the announcement in our spring list which is just going to the printer and which, within a week, will be in the mail to go to all the literary editors, librarians, booksellers, etc.

As to the business arrangement: it is simplest and, I think, quite equitable to have all the terms and conditions of the agreement for "Home Fires" apply to this new book. If this seems right to you, as I think it will, and you will write, agreeing to it, we can attach your letter to the agreement for "Home Fires" and make a note on that agreement that it also applies to the book "The Day of Glory" and have the matter all in order.

I must say that going ahead like this for an author is not the most comfortable way to do things, but the author and the circumstances are both unusual.

Your mother came in to see me yesterday, looking very well. She has had influenza but says that several weeks ago she turned the corner and now is feeling fine, with her usual appetite and strength.... I spoke to her about the idea of this book and, of course, she was delighted. She is in town at her studio, and I hope to have the pleasure of taking her to dinner some evening before long.

                  Always sincerely yours,
                  [Alfred Harcourt]

. . . .

* * *

When Holt and Company employee E. N. Bristol sent Fisher a royalty payment five years after she had left Holt to publish with Harcourt, Brace, she responded warmly.

                      November first 1924

Dear Mr. Bristol:

I was very much pleased to hear from you personally.... such a kind letter, too! And I was as much astonished as pleased to have still some more royalties coming in. The English rights on books seldom amount to much and this is really a sizable amount to come from that source.

Thanks for your generous words about my new books. I'm touched that you have taken the time to read them (both *because of the special circumstances,* and because I should think publishers would be sick and tired of the very sight of books) and very much pleased that you like them.

And as to the continued sale of my books on your list being due to what's in the books, I still attribute a large share of it to your good management. I've had my fair share of experience now, with various books and various publishers, and I know what happens to a book when it is just left on the list, without anybody's making an effort to keep it in circulation. Bobbs-Merrill have a book of mine "Self-Reliance" (I forget by what mistake in judgment I wrote it for them rather than for you) which is just as good as Mothers and Children, and as The [*sic*] Montessori Mother, and whenever known is used as much, if not more by teachers and educators. They paid an advance royalty of $300 on that publication, and it was years before they sold enough to make up that immense sum! And since then, the royalties have been to [*sic*] small to meantion [*sic*], *quite literally.* There is a very good comparison, right there.... And I just made the comparison, when the check for your royalties came in.

Give my best regards, please, to Mr. Holt. I was very much interested to learn from the slip in your letter, that Mr. Roland Holt is not now in the Firm. Living out of New York, I never hear any such news, until it is brought directly to me.

Sincerely yours,
Dorothy Canfield Fisher

***

In 1942 Holt and Company trade-department manager William Sloane wrote Miriam Howell of the Myron Selznick talent agency about the terms for a stage adaptation of Fisher's children's book Understood Betsy, *which Holt had published in 1917.*

February 13, 1942

Dear Miss Howell:

I have had an opportunity today to talk to Mrs. Fisher about the dramatization of UNDERSTOOD BETSY, by Miss Catherine Turney.

Mrs. Fisher agrees with us to the general purport of your letter of January 27 addressed to Grosset and Dunlap. That is, Miss Turney to enter into the Dramatic Guild's standard form of agreement and to share equally in any rights which may arise in connection with a motion picture or stage presentation of her dramatization.

Both Mrs. Fisher and we ourselves feel that there are two points of safeguard which we should require in any transaction of this sort. First of all, it should be clearly understood that the dramatization should be in the spirit of the original and it should be entitled and generally handled in such a way that the people who have known and loved Mrs. Fisher's books and writing for many years will not be disappointed to find that the sweet and charming book has been turned into a sophisticated drama of a sort very different from the original book.

Second, we both feel that there should be not only a limit to the time during which Miss Turney can have the exclusive dramatization rights but that if she fails to dispose of them all copies of the dramatization and all further interest in it shall terminate completely—the copies being either returned to us or destroyed, as the case may be. Mrs. Fisher and ourselves, therefore, are willing to grant exclusive option on the dramatic and motion picture rights to UNDERSTOOD BETSY for a period of six or eight months under the Dramatic Guild's standard form of agreement.

There is only one point in your letter of January 27 which seems to require a certain amount of correction. It is true that UNDERSTOOD BETSY has been on the market for a long time, but let me assure you that this does not mean that its value is less. On the contrary its value has been enhanced with the passage of time. The book is a part of the heritage of many living Americans and remains a very important publishing property to us as well as a successful title on the Grosset and Dunlap list.

Sincerely yours,
[William Sloane]
Manager, Trade Department

***

Book-Clubs
Dorothy Canfield Fisher

In the eleventh R. R. Bowker Memorial Lecture, delivered at the New York Public Library in 1947, Fisher, drawing on her experiences as a Book-of-the-Month Club board member, expressed her regret at what she perceived as a less-than-enthusiastic American reading public and reminisced about her early days with Henry Holt.

. . . .

[P]ublishers are as much interested in the problem of getting books into the hands of American readers, as librarians or educators. If we believe in the profit motive as the real mainspring of human activity, probably a good deal more so. I remember my first publisher, old Mr. Henry Holt, standing toe-to-toe with this baffling mystery of why literate Americans don't read books as Danes and Germans and other literate modern peoples do, and slugging it out, year after year, with various publishing devices. He was, at first, absolutely certain that the reason why Americans did not read more was because books cost too much in this country. This theory in fact has been the first obvious one to be held by most intelligent and conscientious men who go into the publishing business. Not only Mr. Holt but many and many other publishers have tried to solve the problem by presenting cheaper books to the American public. The names of some of these may come readily to your minds. Yet compared to the total number of the population of the United States the numbers of these books were still negligible, twenty years ago. If it had not been for those disconcerting figures about the numbers of books read in other modern civilized countries, we might have thought this inevitable—inherent in human nature. But the figures seemed to show that it was, to speak unscientifically, considerably more inherent in U.S.A. human nature than elsewhere.

. . . .

–"Book-Clubs," in *Bowker Lectures on Book Publishing* (New York: Bowker, 1957), pp. 206–207

ROBERT FROST

HOLT AND COMPANY BOOKS BY FROST (THROUGH 1947): *North of Boston* (New York: Holt, 1914); **first edition,** *North of Boston* (London: D. Nutt, 1914);
A Boy's Will (New York: Holt, 1915); **first edition,** *A Boy's Will* (London: D. Nutt, 1913);
Mountain Interval (New York: Holt, 1916);
New Hampshire: A Poem, with Notes and Grace Notes (New York: Holt, 1923; London: Richards, 1924);
Selected Poems (New York: Holt, 1923; London: Heinemann, 1923);
Several Short Poems (New York: Holt, 1924);
Selected Poems (New York: Holt, 1928);
West-Running Brook (New York: Holt, 1928);
Collected Poems (New York: Holt, 1930; London: Longmans, Green, 1930);
Selected Poems (New York: Holt, 1934);
From Snow to Snow (New York: Holt, 1936);
A Further Range (New York: Holt, 1936; London: Cape, 1937);
Collected Poems (New York: Holt, 1939; London: Longmans, Green, 1939);
A Witness Tree (New York: Holt, 1942; London: Cape, 1943);
Come In and Other Poems, edited by Louis Untermeyer (New York: Holt, 1943; London: Cape, 1944);
A Masque of Reason (New York: Holt, 1945);
Steeple Bush (New York: Holt, 1947);
A Masque of Mercy (New York: Holt, 1947).

Holt and Company was the first American publisher of Robert Frost (1874–1963). He remained with Holt even after the departure in 1919 of Alfred Harcourt, with whom he enjoyed a close relationship. Through various ups and downs with the company, Frost stayed with Holt until the end of his life. Frost was first brought to the attention of the firm by Henry Holt's wife, Florence Taber Holt, who had read with enthusiasm Frost's North of Boston, *first published in England by David Nutt in 1914.*

September 2, 1914.

Dear Sir:

Mrs. Henry Holt, who is very enthusiastic over Robert Frost's NORTH OF BOSTON, has very kindly loaned us her copy. The two readers we had look at these poems found them uncommonly interesting and, while we cannot see a paying market here for this particular volume, still we are so interested in this author's work that if you have some later book of his for which you would care to offer

Robert Frost (Gale International Portrait Gallery)

us the American rights, we would be most happy to consider it.

With best wishes,

Sincerely yours,
[Roland Holt]

---

12 September 1914

Dear Sir:

We are in receipt of your letter concerning "North of Boston." We think that if you recognise the value of Mr. Frost's work you must also see that his books will make their way steadily. We could not offer you rights of his new book if you do not push the present volume to some extent. We can offer you 250 in sheets at 1/ and bound at 1/6.

We consider that under present political circumstances American publishers ought to show some willingness to help English publishers who have had sufficient daring and intelligence to recognize the talent of one of their own countrymen.

Faithfully yours,
David Nutt

September 12, 1914.

Dear Sir:

Following our letter of September 2nd in regard to Robert Frost's "North of Boston;" we are inclined on further consideration to take a small edition of this book, say 150 copies in sheets, if it has not already been placed in the American market, and if you can supply them at a reasonable price.

Of course, while we admire this book, it would not, we fear, be worth our while to take it up unless you could assure us that we can have the refusal of the American market on the author's next book.

Very truly yours,
Henry Holt and Company.

September 25th, 1914.

Dear Sir,

We are in receipt of your letter of September 13 and in answer we can give you a positive assurance that "North of Boston" has not been placed on the American market. We are willing to give you the refusal of the authors next book if you will buy now 150 copies in sheets at 1/– any further supply to be on the same terms.

Faithfully yours,
David Nutt.

October 5, 1914.

Dear Sir:

We have your favor of September 25th. In accordance with it, you may send us 150 copies in sheets of "North of Boston" at 1/–. Of course, you will put in, say 10 review copies without charge. It is understood that this charge includes royalty, and that it insures our having the refusal of the author's next book.

We wish we knew your published price.

Please ship these sheets through Thomas Meadows and Company. We enclose copy for our imprint and an electro of the owl cut.

Of course, you will accompany the shipment with the usual consular certificate and duplicate invoices.

Please let us have a line by return mail as to when the sheets will be shipped.

Very truly yours,
Henry Holt and Company

January 29 1915

Dear Sirs:

We are not prepared to fall in with your proposal regarding "North of Boston" by Frost accompanied as

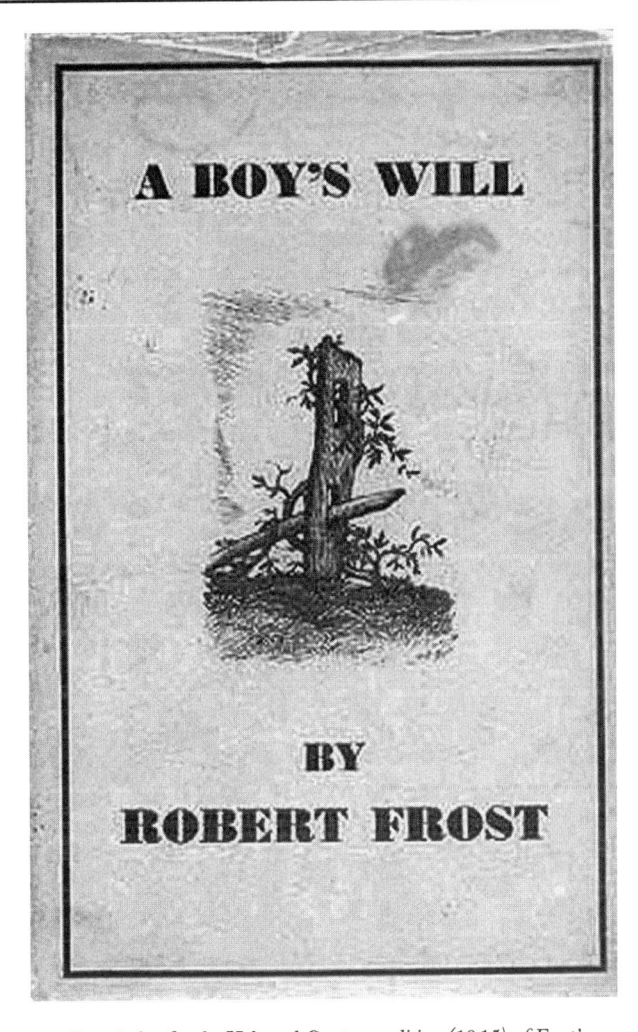

Dust jacket for the Holt and Company edition (1915) of Frost's first poetry collection, published in England in 1913 (Between the Covers Rare Books catalogue)

it is with the amending clause that should the volume be pirated your obligations concerning royalties would cease. But we are prepared to sell you sheets at a comparatively low price if we can make a sufficiently good contract with you, and this would allow you to sell the book to great advantage in America. We do not think this volume is likely to be pirated but even if it were you would be ahead of any competitors by the low price of the sheets. We are sending you a copy of "The Boys Will" [sic] with a quotation for sheets. If we come to a satisfactory arrangement we shall see about the possibility of making arrangements for your copyrighting Mr. Frosts further work in America.

In the meantime will you send us the cheque due to us for the sheets sent to you.

Faithfully yours,
David Nutt

February 19, 1915.

Dear Sir:

We have your favor of January 29th in regard to the possibility of our reprinting Robert Frost's "North of Boston." We also thank you for the copy of "A Boy's Will" which has just come to hand.

We shall be interested to know the "comparative low price" at which you can continue to supply sheets, and we trust that you will allow this price on the 200 copies for which we have just cabled. We have never before paid more than ten pence for sheets including royalty on a book of which the English price was 3/6.

Please realize that we are working in your interests and those of the author in whatever we do for this book. We enclose proofs of some of our advertisements in which you will see the way we are listing it. We are also sending out a number of copies for review. You will remember that you did not supply us with any review copies.

We are surprised that you do not realize that it would be impossible for us to meet the competition of a pirated edition by the importing of English sheets. The only way to combat piracy effectively is to a little more than meet the price of the pirated edition, and sheets of this book could be printed here for about three pence. We trust that you will reconsider your refusal to let us set up the book in case of success here, trusting us to treat your interests and those of the author fairly in case the book were pirated, which we think highly unlikely. If it were pirated, you would of course be unable to give us the exclusive right, for which we are now paying you. In that event, we should probably have to meet competition as best we could.

We should be glad to have quotations on "A Boy's Will" or your permission to set that upon a ten percent royalty of our list price. We should like to be in a position to handle Mr. Frost's work in this country as liberally and effectively as possible. We cannot do so without your cooperation.

We had sent you a check for the last shipment before the arrival of your letter, despite the fact that bills for importations are not regularly due until after six months, and despite the fact that you have never anticipated payments to us.

Very truly yours,
Henry Holt and Company.

March 23, 1915.

Dear Sir:

You will remember that we cabled for 200 more copies of "North of Boston" on February 19th, and we wrote you at length about the situation in regard to this book on the same date. We have had no word from you since then.

We published "North of Boston" February 20th, and our first supply was immediately exhausted. Now we find ourselves without any supply for a month, and piracy threatened. So to protect your interests and those of the author, we are forced to reset both of Mr. Frost's books here in order not only to forestall piracy but also to take advantage of the present interest in Mr. Frost's work. Of course, we will pay a royalty of 10% of our published price on the conditions outlined in our letter of February 19th.

Since the price of our edition of "North of Boston" is $1.25 net, your royalty would be 12½ cents a copy and since we can supply editorial copies and do a considerable amount of advertising on a book which we print here, we feel very sure that you are likely to realize more from this royalty arrangement than from the sale of sheets.

We trust that you will approve of the action we have been reluctantly forced to take. In times of normal communication both of mail and freight, we could very probably have kept our market supplied sufficiently well to protect our mutual interests by the importation of sheets, but in the present state of ocean mails and freight, it has not seemed possible to do so.

Of course, we assume that since we are making so much heavier investment in Mr. Frost and his future, the understanding that we are to have the first chance at his future work in this market will still hold.

Very truly yours,
Henry Holt and Company.

* * *

Critical Acclaim

Charles Hanson Towne, managing editor of McClure's Magazine, *warmly endorsed Frost's poetry.*

March 24, 1915.

Dear Mr. Harcourt:—

Here is a paragraph that you may wish to quote:

The discovery of Robert Frost's poetry was to me a spiritual experience. Nothing has come out of America since Whitman, so splendid, so real, so overwhelmingly great. We should rejoice in the definite arrival of this poet of the people.

Very truly yours,
Charles Hanson Towne.

A New American Poet
Edward Garnett

Edward Garnett, whom Frost considered "the greatest of English critics" at this time, wrote enthusiastically about North of Boston *in* The Atlantic Monthly.

....

[A] literary friend chanced to place in my hands a slim green volume, *North of Boston,* by Robert Frost. I read it, and reread it. It seemed to me that this poet was destined to take a permanent place in American literature. I asked myself why this book was issued by an English and not by an American publisher. And to this question I have found no answer.... [In a note Garnett explains that he learned of the Holt and Company edition after writing the review.]

....

[S]uch an authentic original force to me speaks from *North of Boston.* Surely a genuine New England voice, whatever be its literary debt to old-world English ancestry. Originality, the point is there,—for we may note that originality of tone and vision is always the stumbling-block to the common taste when the latter is invited to readjust its accepted standards.

On opening *North of Boston* we see the first lines to be stamped with the magic of *style,* of a style that obeys its own laws of grace and beauty and inner harmony.

....

–"A New American Poet," *Atlantic Monthly,* 121 (August 1915): 214, 215

* * *

Frost's correspondence with Harcourt reveals the closeness that quickly developed between the men.

[Undated]

Dear Harcourt:

We don't know definitely about Carol [Frost's son, born in 1902] yet. We hope to hear from the doctor's examination that there is nothing worse the matter with him than bad tonsils—as I think I told you. One thing is sure: I shan't try to winter with him at this altitude another year.

We are just off for the Phi Beta Kappa festival at Harvard. Some of our great neighbors of the summer colony are taking care of the girls. We are taking Carol with us. So-called festival.

Introducing Madame Nutt the Avenger. [The Nutts were challenging Holt and Company on copyright issues.] I almost welcome her as a diversion in the present circumstances. Wonder what she will do to me....

Always yours,
R.F.

May 28, 1916

Dear Frost:

About Madame Nutt's letter, our attorney says: "I advise you that in my opinion it is not necessary for Mr. Frost to reply to the letter to him from David Nutt, dated May 15, 1916, and that it does not seem advisable at the present time for him to make any reply thereto."

June 29 1916

Dear Harcourt:

You can't come a minute too soon for us. I've seen and heard so much of you on your home grounds that I can't help wondering how you will look and sound on mine. You are coming to camp down and stay with us some days, n'est-ce pas? Let it be "yes," and be damned to those who will protest that in indulging us you will be denying them. There are things that may not be transacted in less than days. I should like it if our differences touching the next book would resolve into a sort of powwow or battle of wits like a horse trade in which time is no object and in which the decision goes to the best talker. The decision once reached we would climb Lafayette on it.

You see the two big arguments against my giving you a book to publish this year? I may as well let them out of the bag now so that you may be ready to meet them when we meet. The first is that perhaps I shan't have the book and the second that perhaps I shan't dare to give it to you with Mrs. Nutt hanging over me in the way she undeniably is. I can see that she is going to cost me a penny before all is said and done and I begin to think it might be more restful to have her over with before I go much further with you and Co. I confess I rather hate the prospect of having to divide all I am ever likely to earn by writing between her and the lawyers. It would put me all out of sorts quite fundamentally out of sorts.

Carol is going to be an anxiety—that much is settled by our conference with the doctors.... The one certainty is that I shall have to be making money somehow to provide for the family in new quarters next winter.

First page of a letter from Frost to Alfred Harcourt (Princeton University Library)

Come for the earlier part of your vacation. I shall be teaching in Plymouth for the week, July 24–30.

And may the best man have his way.

Always yours,
Robert Frost

Will you cause someone to send me a copy of de la Mare?

December 1916

Dear Alfred:

. . . .

Tell me about de la Mare. It comes to me round the ring that you are to have another book of his. Is that right? I mustn't be too hard on de la Mare either. I have little enough to go on with regard to him.

. . . .

Always yours
Robert

* * *

Poet, editor, and critic Louis Untermeyer, an early champion of Frost and a lifelong close friend, agreed to Harcourt's request to provide biographical details on Frost.

Nov. 24, 1916

Dear Mr. Harcourt:

Some day, when I am forty-four years old and my fifth book has gone into its fifteenth edition, I shall forget my respect for my elders and betters, and call you Alfred, quite casually. In the meanwhile I answer your note with dignity and promptness.

I will, of course, be glad to write a brief biography of Robert, one which I hope will not be too dull on the one hand, or too scandalous on the other. Before I go ahead with it, can you tell me these statistical data:

Where, exactly was he born? Wasn't it San Francisco? How old was he when he moved to New England? When did he marry? Was Elinor a teacher and what is her full name? The children are Lesley, Carol, Irma and Marjorie, are they not? Lesley the eldest, is about eighteen and the youngest is–? Robert attempted Harvard for a short time. Did it give him a degree, other than the Phi-Beta-Kappa Key? What was the other college Robert tried? Was it Dartmouth? Where did he teach? Exactly how long was he in England? Did he publish any unheard-of volume, previous to "A Boy's Will?"

I know these things in a general way, but for a circular of this sort, it is well to be as precise as possible. There is always some meticulous statistician who lies in wait to trip you up! If there is any other secret vice that Robert is addicted to, don't fail to let me know. Meanwhile, may God protect you from a further rise in the price of coal.

Yours forever,
Louis

* * *

Briefer Mention

An anonymous reviewer in The Dial *provided capsule reviews of two Holt and Company volumes of Frost's poetry published in 1928,* Selected Poems *and* West-Running Brook.

WEST RUNNING BROOK, by Robert Frost (10mo, 64 pages; Holt: $2.50). In the most recent volume of poems Robert Frost has written in a manner that is quite different from that of the poems in North of Boston and Mountain Interval. These are not poems about people; they are, in the main, gnomic verses that read as if the poet had entered a world where words and movement do not matter so much, and where there is "no devotion Greater than being curve to ocean." A few of these poems appear to have been written at an early date, but even these have the gnomic quality. There are two poems in the collection which are probably the most poignant that Robert Frost has written, Acquainted with the Night, and The Thatch.

SELECTED POEMS, by Robert Frost (10mo, 213 pages; Holt: $2.50). Robert Frost is the one American poet whose poetry contains a particular landscape–we see New England with its stone walls and its waste farmlands when we read North of Boston or Mountain Interval. He has created a blank-verse form of his own through which he is able to give us something of the secret life of the earth, the secret life of men and women. The Death of the Hired Man, The Self-seeker, Mending Wall are poems which are already classic; they are idylls of a kind; they have a remote affinity with Virgil's eclogues; in them are elements of narrative and drama. Robert Frost can condense an experience into a brief and vivid expression such as the incandescent short poem, Fire and Ice. This selection gives us the most valuable of Frost's poems.

–"Briefer Mention," *Dial*, 86 (May 1929): 436

* * *

Herschel Brickell became manager of the Holt and Company trade department in 1928, working with Frost in the same capacity that Harcourt and others had done before him. The Spiral Press, founded by printer Joseph Blumenthal in 1926, was a specialty press that printed a limited advance edition of Frost's Collected Poems *(1930), provided the printing plates for the trade edition, and for many years produced illustrated editions of individual Frost poems as Christmas cards. At the bottom of the following letter is a handwritten note: "Answered by Herschel Brickell July 1. Spiral all okay and ready to print. Longmans asked to take . . . plates at $1000 as compromise." Despite Frost's complaints about working with Longmans, Green, and Company, the firm published the British edition of his* Collected Poems *in 1930.*

June 27, 1930

Dear Mr. Brickell:

The printing of the book still drags on with the Spiral Press. They say I am holding them up with one last poem they sent me the proof of a month ago. To the best of my recollection I sent it back O.K.'d. I can't find hide or hair of it round here. Of course I may have lost it in our moving. Anyway please ask them to conclude. I have had this business on my mind for six months now and I'm so sick of it I feel as if I never wanted to see my own works again. It is a perturbing thing with me to be having a book published—it always puts me off everything else—and I'm grateful to anyone who gets through the agony with despatch. How little fuss Updyke made over West-Running Brook.

I can see the book is going to be too late for the season in England. I have a telegram from Longmans asking if I will be satisfied to let them take sheets from you. I assume their idea is to save time. But this is utterly inconsistent with what R. G. Longman impressed on me, namely, that the proud firm of Longmans never took sheets from anyone: they published outright or not at all. (I had casually proposed their taking sheets of West-running Brook.) The entanglement with them has become a distasteful mess that I should value your advice about getting out of. Perhaps the collected poems had better wait another year—at least till next Spring both here and in England.

Don't let my troubles trouble you too much.

Sincerely yours,
Robert Frost

July 3 1930

Dear Mr. Brickell:

Your letter makes everything all right. I'm content to let you and R. G. Longmans arrange the business between you. Of course it won't do to have the book cost too much over there. Any compromise to prevent having it. The telegram threatened with having to charge 26 shillings if Longmans set up and printed the book themselves. I wonder why paper and print cost more in England than in America. But perhaps I'm not getting the idea. Well as I say I am willing to leave it to your discretion. I can see you know more about it than I do.

I'm glad you think so well of what Blumenthal has made of the book. Mind you it is not what others do but what I do myself that I get sick of when it is too long drawn out.

I've been thinking I'd run down to talk things over with you. But it is hard to pull out once I get into this retirement.

Always yours faithfully,
Robert Frost

July 15, 1930

Dear Mr. Brickell:

Suppose we leave it this way then that you are to let Longmans have sheets if they will take what you consider a large number of them; but if they seem afraid of me and cautious in their buying, you are to give them a chance to get out altogether. I'm disappointed in them. They kept me from everybody else and now they dont want me themselves. They are an infirm firm. I'd rather give them their money back than be their unwanted child. In other words t'Hell wit them. This is a fine day in Vermont anyway and ought to make it up to us for a lot of little annoyances. I hope it is a fine day in your office.

Sincerely yours,
Robert Frost

* * *

Holt and Company employee R. H. Thornton was Brickell's successor as head of the Holt and Company trade department.

[Undated]

Dear Mr. Thornton:

It is good to hear from you again. I have had half a mind to run down to see you. But I am trying to stay in one place as long as possible before the inevitable winter wandering. I shall be in and out with you in January February and March when I shall be giving Thursday evenings in poetry at the New School of Social Research. I may even set up a tent in Central Park or the Bronx Zoo for part of the job.

It would relieve me of something distasteful if you would deal with this Committee of Vermont Traditions and Ideals (tell it to Mencken!) Have I not put it in plenty good blank verse that the ideals will bear some keeping still about. The Walter J. Coates you mention is no friend of mine. I sat in an audience of twenty-five at Arlington Vermont two years ago and heard him read me out of the State and out of the ranks of important poets. Afterward ashamed of himself, he climbed all over me with adulation. I have become an issue in their local literary politics. It makes you laugh. They say I'm a foreigner because I came only ten years ago from New Hampshire. The leaders of this purging movement—I say leaders but should say cathartics are this Coates, an unfrocked parson from New York State, a Rutland (Vt) editor from Ohio and the reformed-radical Welsh Jew John Spargo. I don't know what their ideals may be, but possibly one of them is to stay black Republican, set the nigger free and elect Taft retroactively as of 1912. Vermont and Utah were the only states Taft carried in that election. I can barely stand such people. And still I must be careful not to get tarred and feathered and ridden on a rail by them some fine night lest I be suspected of doing it for the advertisement. If you act between us it will be all right probably. Tell them they can have the poems. I'll pretend not to know whats going on. If they send me their Anthology I'll burn it privately only in one of our three open fireplaces or the kitchen stove. All this sounds more like a mountain feud than it really is. I manage not to seem to notice most of the time.

Lets think of something pleasanter, the book you have made of my Collected. I look forward to seeing it. We both do. Remember us both to Mrs. Thornton. Sincerely yours,

Robert Frost

Oct 31 1930

Dear Mr. Thornton:

I want to tell you how perfect a book I think you have made for me. I wouldn't have a thing different in the make-up, whatever I might want to blot or alter in the content.

There is the matter of that stock I have never settled with the firm for. I must see to it as soon as I get my money from the Random House. I shall do it in person I think in the near future.

My friends are going to expect gift copies of the book. I mustnt take too many of the first edition for them, but I should like thirty or forty copies if you didn't think that was greedy. Tell me just how it is

I tremble and am never too happy at being exposed to the public with another book. I hope this one won't be badly received. I should like to know in general, though it is better for me to shut my eyes and ears to the details.

Ever yours,
Robert Frost

* * *

Frost at the Bread Loaf Writers' Conference, 1920s (from David Haward Bain and Mary Smyth Duffy, Whose Woods These Are, *1993; Thomas Cooper Library, University of South Carolina)*

Frost's Collected Poems *received the 1931 Pulitzer Prize in poetry.*

May 13, 1931

Dear Mr. Frost:

We have all been delighted over the Pulitzer award to your *Collected Poems*. We have sold nearly a thousand copies, by the way, since the announcement was made, and sales of your other books have been stimulated also. We expect to advertise the book as much as possible and are urging bookstores to stock it.

[R. H. Thornton]

October 5 1931

Dear Mr. Thornton:

We are back from having sown children broadcast over the West. One thing it does for us whatever it may do for them: it makes us feel as if we inhabited the whole country and not just New England: and it reassures us of the uniformity of the American people, East and West. We saw a teacher out there who was doing a book for California children on California flowers. To make it interesting she had made it a story of two little children who had been moved from bleak bare Vermont to live in luxuriant California. We couldn't make the mistake about California now that she makes about Vermont. California is as flowery as Vermont.

I am enclosing the signed contract you should have years ago [sic].

And another matter of business. A Mr. Udo Rall of Los Angeles thinks we ought to let him have four of my poems for nothing to translate into German. Don't you think it might be good advertising? I told him his letter to you probably didn't fall into the hands of anyone empowered to make exceptions.

Our best to you and your family.

Ever yours
Robert Frost

* * *

Thornton wrote Frost in late 1932 about the impending departure of Brickell, mentioning also the publication that year by Holt and Company of A Woodcut Manual *by J. J. Lankes, Frost's friend and collaborator who had been illustrating the poet's work with woodcuts since 1923.*

November 2, 1932

Dear Mr. Frost:

I assume that you are now back in the East, although I have heard nothing from you since your arrival. I am sure you have had an interesting summer in California. I am hoping that you will come down our way before long and spend a few days.

You may have heard already that Mr. Brickell is leaving us at the beginning of the year. There are so many rumors afloat these days about nearly every publisher in the city that you may have heard a rumor to the effect that we are discontinuing our trade department. We shall of course continue the department in all its phases, and I hope make it a more important part of our business. I shall personally take charge of the department after January first, and shall direct the editorial work. I plan to go to England around the middle of January for a stay of several weeks. I have for some time wanted to get in more intimate touch with the leading English publishers and some of our authors on the other side.

Though the book business has been extremely poor this fall, we have done quite well with a few of our books. Possibly you have already seen Mr. Lankes' volume. If you do not have [Cornelius] Weygandt's book, *A Passing America,* I want you to have a copy of that too. Miss [Rosamond] Lehmann's new novel *[Invitation to the Waltz]* promises to be a best seller. We had an advance sale on it of some ten thousand copies, and as you perhaps know it was one of the November choices of the Book of the Month Club.

With best wishes for you and Mrs. Frost,

Cordially yours,
[R. H. Thornton]

* * *

Royalties

Feb. 27, 1931

Dear Mr. Frost:

In response to your telephone request, we are pleased to inform you that during 1930 we sent you royalty checks aggregating $3,722.57.

Very truly yours,
Henry Holt & Co., Inc.

November 6, 1933

Dear Mr. Frost:

Mr. Thornton is on his way to England (hunting books not birds) and your letter has come to me.

It was quite in character that you should have returned the royalty check, which, as you surmised, was sent by mistake. We meant to hand you, as heretofore, a statement of earnings for the accounting period. The check would have been fielded back to you if the royalties for 1933 promised to come to more than $3,000, but alas! they do not. May the N.R.A. boost poetry sales!

Your November and December stipend will go forward in due course. May I add that I am happy you consented to continuing the arrangement through 1934. We do ourselves the good turn of assuming all the risk, and shall be delighted if your royalties for the year add something–a good deal–to your income, as well as to ours.

For Heaven's sake do you stick to your poetry and let us look out for ourselves, even if we don't seem to have done so in this instance. A publisher's cupidity should be dependable.

With best wishes

Sincerely yours
[Unsigned]

Herbert Bristol, E. N. Bristol's son, followed his father in joining Holt and Company, eventually becoming president of the firm in 1937.

January 16, 1936

Dear Mr. Frost:

Because the copyright situation has become so complex due to movies, radio, etc., we think it indiscreet for your sake and for ours to include in SNOW TO SNOW your "Desert Places." We will use as the frontispiece a facsimile of your copy of "Unharvested." In the fifth line of your long hand copy of this poem it reads "But there there had been an apple fall." Did you intend to have two "there's"? I am not enough of a poet to be able to tell.

For the twelfth poem we will use "Stopping by Woods on a Snowy Evening." I hope you will have no objection to this change in plans because I have advocated it in order to avoid any possible future copyright applications. Incidentally, it will make it possible under this new scheme for us to advertise your new volume of poems as containing exclusively poems which have not before appeared in book form.

I am hoping to slip down to Florida during February for a short time and without invitation from you I hope to give myself the pleasure of saying Howdy-do. I hope you are getting the full benefit of the Florida sunshine.

Faithfully yours,
[Herbert Bristol]

* * *

Frost showed a generous interest in promoting the work of a younger poet, John Holmes. Holt and Company published two books of Holmes's poetry, Address to the Living *(1937) and* Fair Warning *(1939).*

[Undated]

Dear Mr. Thornton:

Don't you think it might be good policy to let the enclosed Oysterman have a poem or at most two? We don't want to seem snooty and scornful of the day of small things. We were once small things ourselves. I leave it to you to act on as you decide.

Very important: I have been so well treated by the big magazines of late that I should look ungrateful if I made them no acknowledgement in the book. On some last page please say, Many of these poems have had the advantage of previous publication in The Yale Review, The Saturday Review, Poetry, Scribners Magazine, The Southern Quarterly, The Atlantic Monthly, The American Mercury, Books Direction, and The New Frontier. The author wishes to make grateful acknowledgement. Be sure to get them all in. If you don't like the wording of my acknowledgement change it. Such formalities bother me a little. But they should be observed this time.

Well we are pretty near ready to climb in over the ropes.

Ever yours
Robert Frost

I am really in earnest about this young John Holmes. He is a good poet and he is a splendid person in literary society. You must have his first book and buckle him to you. He is a favorite young teacher at Tufts and something on The Transcript among other things. I should inveigle a man like that to make himself at home in my office.

* * *

Robert S. Newdick, an English professor at Ohio State University, was an early Frost scholar. The bibliography to which he refers, W. B. Shubrick Clymer and Charles R. Green's Robert Frost: A Bibliography, *was published in 1937. Newdick died of appendicitis in 1939 at the age of forty; his planned Frost biography was published posthumously as* Newdick's Season of Frost: An Interrupted Biography of Robert Frost, *edited by William A. Sutton, in 1976.*

October 10, 1935.

Dear Mr. Thornton:

. . . .

You may have heard by this time that I have joined forces with Messrs. Clymer and Green and that the bibliography will be published by The Jones Library, Inc., sometime this winter. I believe Mr. [Little Joseph] Blumenthal's Spiral Press is to do the printing of it.

I had a delightful four-day visit with Mr. Frost in Franconia [New Hampshire]. One result is this, that he has consented to my doing a full-length biography, now that the bibliographical tools are assembled and now that he has taken my measure in personal contact as to discernment, understanding, and so on. Such things as the bibliography and the biography do not interest him a great deal, but he cooperated generously in supplying me with facts and views, and will do so hereafter. The biography was the ultimate goal I had in mind all along.

He is coming on here to Columbus some time this autumn to lecture at the University and to conduct an informal writers' conference. We shall wish to give the lecture wide publicity not only in the Columbus papers but also in the papers of cities and towns within easy driving distance. Henry Holt and Company will doubtless come in for mention many times as Mr. Frost's publisher, and I am wondering whether on that basis I dare ask you for a number of gloss prints of photographs of Mr. Frost for distribution to the press. I should suppose there would be at least a cost charge for these prints, and if there is I shall be glad to guarantee the payment of it. . . .

I doubt that Mr. Frost can ever be induced to write his memoirs, but I hope that you persist in the efoort [sic] to persuade him to do so.

Sincerely yours,
Robert S. Newdick

Newdick wrote Thornton again in 1938 to report on prospects for the planned biography. Handwritten on Newdick's letter is a note by Holt and Company vice president T. J. Wilson: "Mr. Frost should see this. I don't know whether he is willing to have Newdick so completely in control of the biographical situation."

November 26, 1938.

Dear Thornton:

Enclosed with this letter are your pictures. Many thanks. It has been sheer inertia that has kept them here instead of back with you where they belong. Since RF left I have been in second, sometimes third, gear!

His twelve days here with us were glorious. There wasn't a single thing that went the least bit wrong, to my knowledge at least; and there was good reason to think that RF enjoyed himself as thoroughly as his tempestuous mind will allow him. Of course he'd withdraw into himself some few hours before a public appearance, and of course there was, as regular as clock motion, the aftermath of depression each time; but the intervals were capital, and there was talk nearly unceasing then. I believe we are closer than ever before. The very thought of a biographer at work is something to dismay him at a distance, but he finds me less fearful close-up!–I tell you all this because I think you'll be pleased to learn of it.

Among other things he told me that you are to sever relations with HH&Co. That leads me to a prayer: Won't you, before you go, help me to gain access to the files of RF's letters to his publishers, and generally to take from the records the facts that will be vital biographically? Or have the letters to Harcourt, Brickell, and MacVeagh–these three particularly, with yourself as the fourth–been removed from the records? All such that remain could be most economically copied photostatically. And they must contain a wealth of material, as I could point to in press releases from HH&Co. from time to time beginning in the winter and spring of 1914–1915.

Again, could the file of clippings possibly be sent to me to use here,–say, in the custody of the University librarian? Somewhere between New York and Columbus I lost the notes that I made those days in the office last spring!

If any or all of this is plain cock-eyed, you will of course let me down gently, understanding the reason and purpose behind the suggestions.

Sincerely yours,
Robert S. Newdick

* * *

Thornton wrote Green, the co-compiler of the 1937 Frost bibliography and a librarian at the Jones Library in Amherst, Massachusetts, about items that Frost thought had been left out of the bibliography.

August 24, 1937

Dear Mr. Green:

Do you happen to have a copy of the letter from the poet Maurice Thompson, written to William Hayes Ward, of *The Independent* in 1893? Robert Frost thinks this is the first recognition of his work. I do not see this cited in your bibliography. He also refers to a first review of A BOY'S WILL in *The Academy* (Eng.) 1913. Do you happen to have this, or can it be that Mr. Frost refers to *The Atheneum* article, which you cite on p. 113 of the bibliography? I find it a bit difficult to get these early items straight.

Sincerely yours,
[R. H. Thornton]
President [Holt and Company]

* * *

Herbert Bristol, now Holt and Company president, wrote Frost in late 1938 to reassure him that the firm had no intention of dropping its trade-book division.

December 5, 1938

Dear Mr. Frost:

It did my heart good to hear from Mr. Wilson of your chat over the phone while I was away. As he assured you, we have no thought of giving up the trade branch of our business. On the contrary we are seeking a man of enterprise to develop it from a source of annual loss of over $30,000 (the other branches prospering) to at least its pre-depression place. Otherwise we should not have been so firm in our response to your suggestion of withdrawing your books. When a publisher sells out his book rights, he confesses either to financial straits or to retiring from business in whole or in part. That is not at all our case. It may have meaning for you that our only difficulty in finding a successor to Mr. Thornton is in choosing between opportunities.

Now as to financial matters. I don't know what passed between you and Mr. Thornton when your monthly stipend was reduced from $250. Your royalty earnings by and large seemed to justify the larger sum, and we are of course ready to continue it until you would call for a change. It would, of course, make the future more certain if you cared to include your prose as well as poetry, so long as you are satisfied that we are doing our part well. Mr. Wilson is trying to see you personally shortly, and can arrange details in person. These can then be reduced to writing—"good fences."

Sincerely yours,
[Herbert Bristol]

Wilson wrote a week later to offer terms for the continued publication of Frost's books. Frost agreed to allow Holt and Company to publish all of his future work, prose and poetry.

December 12, 1938.

Dear Mr. Frost:

You understand, of course, that we are anxious to arrange a plan under the terms of which you will be willing to have us publish all your future books, whether in verse or in prose. You understand also that if we cannot persuade you to let us have your entire literary output, we still are anxious to publish your future verse. We are stating below, first, the provisions we are ready to make in return for your promise to give us all your future writings; second, failing that, we are stating the provisions we are ready to make in order to publish your future verse.

I

If you will give us all your future books, whether in verse or in prose, for publication by us, we will pay you a royalty of twenty per cent of the published price on all copies sold. We will also pay you henceforth a royalty of twenty per cent of the published price on all copies sold of those books by you which we published prior to the present date, December 12, 1938. Furthermore, we will pay you, during the remainder of your lifetime, the sum of $300 monthly, until you consider such a payment an unfair burden to us. These monthly payments to you shall not be considered returnable to us under any circumstances. As soon as possible after the end of each calendar year, we shall total up all sums paid during the calendar year to you by us and shall set this total against the total of all sums earned for you by your books during the same year; if the total of your earnings in the calendar year be greater than the total of the sums paid you during that calendar year, we shall at once pay the difference between these two totals to you

So far as promotion of your works is concerned, we will promise to promote their sales to the best of our ability through salesmen's efforts, space advertising, circulars and publicity. We will promise to spend, during the first two years after publication of any one of your books, not less than ten per cent of the receipts from the regular sales in the United States and Canada of our edition of this new book for space advertising in behalf of your works.

II

If you will give us all your future books of verse, for publication by us, we will pay you a royalty of twenty per cent of the published price on all copies sold. We will further agree to pay you the sum of $250 monthly during your lifetime, or until you shall consider that such payment is an unfair burden to us, or until publication of any new book in verse by you (with the exception of the second edition of your COLLECTED POEMS, which is to be published this spring). Upon our publication of any new book in verse by you, with the exception noted, we will pay you the sum of $300 monthly during your lifetime, or until you shall consider such a payment an unfair burden to us. These monthly payments to you shall not be considered returnable to us under any circumstances. As soon as possible after the end of each calendar year, we shall total up all sums paid during the calendar year to you by us and shall set this total against the total of all sums earned for you by your books during the same year; if the total of your earnings in the calendar year be greater than the total of the sums paid you during that calendar year, we shall at once pay the difference between these two totals to you.

So far as promotion of your works is concerned, we will promise to promote their sales to the best of our ability through salesmen's efforts, space advertising, circulars and publicity. We will promise to spend, during the first two years after publication of any new book in verse by you, not less than ten per cent of the receipts from the regular sales in the United States and Canada of our edition of this new book in verse for space advertising in behalf of your poetic works.

Very sincerely yours,
[T. J. Wilson]
Vice-President

* * *

34 Amity St.
Amherst Mass.
Feb. 19th

Dear Mr. Thornton,
          I have just this
minute done a most extraordinarily absent-minded thing.
In sorting out the mail
I put the letters I wished to
keep into the fire, instead of
the advertising &c— which
I wished to throw away.
Among them, was the Holt
letter containing check for
this month—   I have
never done anything like
that in my life before—

Letter from Frost's wife, Elinor, to R. H. Thornton of Holt and Company explaining that she accidentally disposed of the letter with the check for her husband's monthly stipend from the publisher (Princeton University Library)

As it happens, we have had extra expenses this month and rather need the money. Could you ask them to send another? I feel very much chagrined.

When do you think you will be able to come to Amherst for a little visit?

Yours very sincerely
Elinor Frost

When William Sloane took charge of the Holt and Company trade department after Thornton's departure, he wrote Newdick asking for information on his intentions concerning the prose works of Frost that he had been gathering in his research for the planned biography.

December 28, 1938

Dear Professor Newdick:

I don't know whether you have heard yet that Mr. Thornton's resignation from the Trade Department here took effect about two weeks ago, and I am now doing the work which was formerly his.

Last week, I spent a day in Boston with Robert Frost, and we had a long talk about [some] of the things mentioned in your letter of November 26th to Mr. Thornton. Mr. Frost said that you have been making a collection of his prose, prefaces, etc., but I did not get from him a clear idea of whether this was in connection with a biography or as a volume for separate publication. At any rate, I should very much like to see the collection if you would be willing to send it on here temporarily.

Could you give me some general information of the progress of your work on the biography, when you expect to have it finished, etc.?

If I get an opportunity later in the year, I hope to visit Columbus, and perhaps we shall be able to get together. Meantime, remember me please to one of your colleagues, Professor Percival, if you happen to see him.

Sincerely yours,
[William Sloane]

———◆———

January 17, 1939

Dear Professor Newdick:

I found your letter of January 3rd waiting for me on my return from the coast. I am sorry that my previous letter wasn't more specific, but it is pretty hard for me to be very definite about the whole thing at this point. However, the following information is certain: Mr. Frost is going to continue to publish with us everything which he writes in the future, whether prose or poetry. Further, he wants us to do the volume of stray papers and lectures rather than the Oxford University Press and this point you can, of course, check with him if you want. Third: yes, we should be interested in the volume of collected things for publication the end of this year or later. We are doing a new collected poems this spring and Blue Ribbon are also bringing out a volume of his verse. Naturally, we don't want to over-publish in the Frost market.

Mr. Frost seemed to me to be a trifle embarrassed by the idea of a biography while he is still in the full tide of his productive work. It is easy to understand while he is gratified by the honor of a biography that he doesn't feel quite sure that one should come out so soon. He wants us to do the book when it comes, and of course we want to do it. So far I have not had time to see what there is in the way of Frost material here—this being my first full time day in the office—but I will write you again and let you know what I do find. Naturally I want to be sure that we do the book when it comes out and we do have full access to such material as will make it definitive and complete.

Sincerely yours,
William Sloane
HENRY HOLT AND COMPANY

***

Early in 1939 Frost's secretary, Kathleen Johnston Morrison, sent Sloane the preface for the new edition of Frost's Collected Poems, *published that year. In a postscript to Morrison's letter Frost wrote, "Will you please see that in the poem An Old Man's Winter Night, third line from the end, the word 'fill' is changed to 'keep' in the new edition. I am very anxious about this. Best wishes from me too. R.F."*

January 11, 1939.

Dear Mr. Sloane:

I am enclosing the preface to the new edition of the collected works and promise that I shall send along pretty soon the names for the special copies and additional names for your promotion list. Christmas, colds, and visitors have disorganized my working hours.

Mr. Frost will be in New York at the Hotel Seymour on January 17 and part of January 18. He will come there from Norfolk to receive the gold metal [*sic*] presented by the National Academy. The sheets arrived today and he has started signing them. Some are damaged. I hope that they are not too accurately counted. If so, you may run short.

Was the Western trip a success? I hope so.

Sincerely yours
Kathleen Johnston Morrison
Secretary to Mr Frost

***

Sloane sent Frederic G. Melcher, publisher and co-editor of Publishers' Weekly, *a correction to a story in that magazine regarding the 1939 edition of Frost's* Collected Poems.

January 26, 1939

Dear Mr. Melcher:

Yesterday we got a very pained letter from Mr. Blumenthal of The Spiral Press objecting to one sentence in the P.W.'s story of January 21 about Robert Frost's Collected Poems. The sentence went as follows:

> "The book, like the previous one, is handset by the Spiral Press and will be a fine piece of bookmaking, handsomely bound."

The facts seem to be that we originally planned to do the book with the Spiral Press exclusively, but since we were collaborating with Blue Ribbon in manufacturing the book, it proved impossible to reach an agreement. The result is that the pages containing the poems of "Further Range" were done by Quinn [and] Boden. The book is still a fine piece of bookmaking, and still handsomely bound, but not by the Spiral Press, although the bulk of it will be done from the pages which the Spiral Press originally set up for us. It is quite complicated, but I wonder if you could find space for a short retraction of the line about the Spiral Press. It is our fault in all probability.

. . . .

Sincerely yours,
[William Sloane]
Manager, Trade Department

* * *

Newdick offered to proofread the new edition of Frost's Collected Poems.

January 28, 1939.

Dear Mr. Sloane:

Don't think I lie awake nights trying to think of excuses to write you letters! But it just occurs to me that possible [*sic*] I may be of some small service to you and Mr. Frost, *if* the type has not yet been set for the new edition of his *Collected Poems,* or even if the proofsheets have not yet been finally passed for press. In the past, the special and general editorial supervision of the text of Mr. Frost's poems has, in my opinion, been lax, permitting the intrusion of inaccuracies, inconsistencies, and confusion. But please don't misunderstand me to be legging in any way for myself: my sole concern is RF and his poems; but if you would care for my cooperation with regard to a number of textual points, it is yours for the asking.

And may I not ask your cooperation? In your file of clippings relating to Mr. Frost (a file that has never been kept in order and that I asked in vain to put in order) there is one of an interview he gave to Harry Saltpeter, headed "Robert Frost, Non-Professional." It was, I believe, in the New York *World* for January 13, 1928, though I do not have the page reference. The University has that issue wanting in its files. Would you let me have the clipping for a few days while I copy it for possible use in whole or in part, probably the latter, in the book of RF's prose? Or, a carefully typewritten transcript would suffice for a while.

Sincerely yours,
Robert S. Newdick

———◆———

February 1, 1939

Dear Professor Newdick:

It was interesting to hear that you have arranged for Robert Frost's appearance at Iowa State College next October. We will get started right away on sending out the publicity material which they want. As a matter of fact, Mr. Frost does not care much for his existing pictures, and it may be possible to send no more than one of them. However, we will do the best we can. It seems to me that the best and most authoritative of the things that have been said about Frost are in Thornton's "Recognition." Why don't they just use that volume as the basis for their quotes etc.?

What you have to say about the prose book is decidedly interesting. The royalty arrangement seems very generous on your part, and I think there will be no question of defraying your expenses in compiling the book. When I saw Robert Frost two weeks ago, he told me that he was in the embarrassing position of having about eight applicants for the honor of writing a preface to his own book, which will of course, itself, consist of a good many prefaces. I think we must be careful not to do a piece of unconscious humor here, and although I like the ring of your own job, all I am saying is that I cannot say yes or no to the preface idea until Robert Frost's own mind is more crystallized on the whole book.

By the time your letter of the 28th had arrived, the COLLECTED POEMS were already on the press. Furthermore, as you probably know, we had to make our edition in cooperation with the Blue Ribbon Book people, and I am afraid it would not have been possible to do anything along the lines which you suggest. I am sorry to hear that you feel the supervision of the text of Mr. Frost's poems has been lax. I have not heard that comment from anyone else, but of course it is important that they should be as perfect as possible. Nevertheless, and strictly between you and me, I should like to remark that one thing that causes errors in books is the author's making last minute

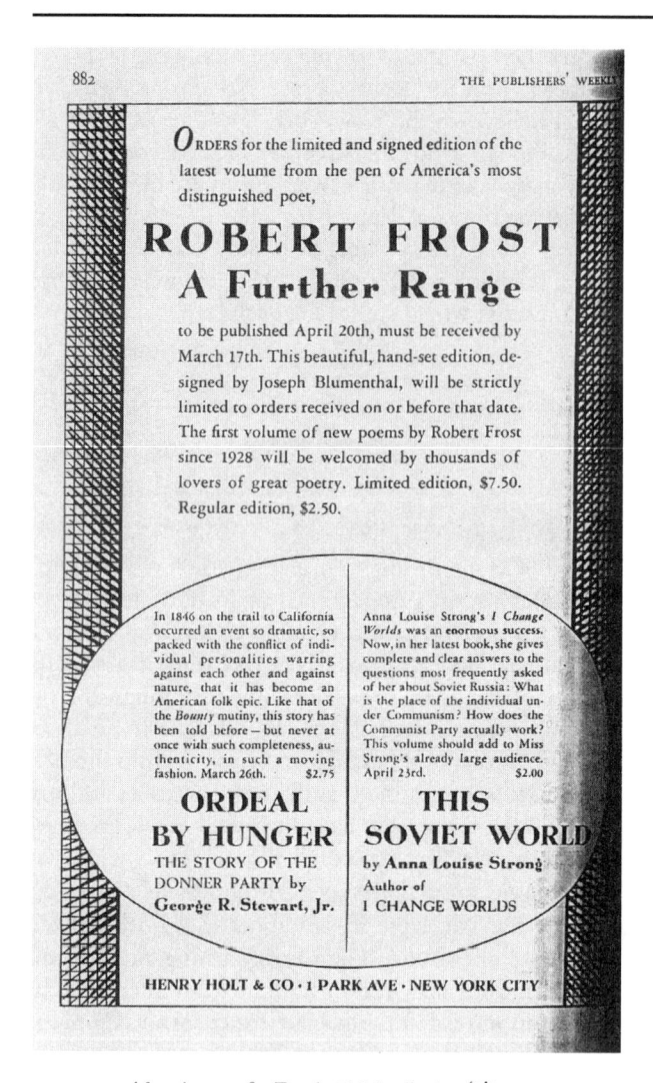

Advertisement for Frost's 1936 collection (Thomas Cooper Library, University of South Carolina)

changes by letter and telegram when the material is already on the bed of the press. However, your offer was most generous, and I wish we could have taken advantage of it.

                Cordially yours,
                [William Sloane]
                Manager, Trade Department

* * *

Sloane reported to Frost, then wintering in Florida, on the status of the new Collected Poems.

                February 14, 1939

Dear Mr. Frost:

    I have really owed you a letter for sometime and this is going to have to be a hasty note in spite of that delay. First of all the advance sale on the COL-LECTED POEMS has exceeded all our expectations. We have already received orders for the autographed edition which more than exhaust the total of 1200 signed pages, and they are stilling coming in by every mail. Under the circumstances, this is a remarkable testimonial to your poems. Anyhow we will need at least 350 more autographed copies to make good on our advertising commitment about them. . . .

    We shall not send you your six author's copies until you return North, but I am having one mailed today so that you can see what it looks like. There is one minor error in the jacket for which it is possible that I am to blame. That is in the reference to the new preface. I should have said "figure" instead of "shape." Naturally this will be corrected in subsequent editions.

                Cordially yours,
                [William Sloane]
                Manager, Trade Department

On 16 February 1939 Frost received an enthusiastic cable from Holt and Company upon the publication of the new Collected Poems. *The Latin statement translates as "You have built a monument more lasting than bronze."*

MR ROBERT FROST=
CARE OF HERVEY ALLEN ESQ= COCOANUT GROVE FLORIDA=
NO SATISFACTION COULD BE KEENER THAN THAT WITH WHICH WE PUBLISH TODAY YOUR COLLECTED POEMS STOP EXEGISTI MONUMENTUM PERENNIUS AERE=
        HENRY HOLT AND COMPANY

                February 17 1939

Dear Mr. Sloane:

    May I say through you to the firm that I have a great sense of being published? The telegram, particularly the Latin of it, gave me a thrill I had never expected to have again from being published. The book itself is here and in noble form. I see your taste and judgement in the text of both the fold-ins of the jacket. I am happy to be in your hands.

                Sincerely yours
                Robert Frost

. . . .

                February 20, 1939

Dear Robert Frost:

    Nothing in a long time has given me more pleasure than your letter of February 17th. It's so trite to say that publishing a poet like yourself is an honor that I hesitate to talk in those terms, but I feel that every editor I know would feel as I do about it.

Apparently it is not only an honor but good business as well. At any rate the advance demand for the book was twice what any of us had expected. The 350 sheets for future signature which we sent to Florida for you are really mortgaged against actual orders and this morning we had two poignant pleas, one from Baker & Taylor and the other from the Old Corner Bookstore, saying that in totaling their own advance orders they find that they will require a total of 125 copies more to fulfil their obligations. . . .

    With deep appreciation, faithfully yours,
    William Sloane
    HENRY HOLT AND COMPANY

***

Morrison, Frost's secretary, wrote conveying Frost's (and her own) misgivings about the prose collection that Newdick was planning.

    March 3, 1939.

Dear Mr. Sloane:

    . . . .

There is one other thing on my mind at the moment. It is that book which Mr. Newdick is planning. I have talked quite a bit to Robert since he has been back about it and see that he has deliberately left all that prose ungathered because he wants it to enter into later stuff and not be put together as sweepings from papers and badly reported speeches. Of course this objection does not hold for long and finished pieces—just to the snippets. I have urged him to come down and talk to you about it all and he says that he will come some week end very soon. In the meantime could you faintly discourage Mr. Newdick. It is all right for Mr. Newdick to have the collection out there in the library and as Robert says all right to use it if he gets run over by an automobile but it is a little mortuary to collect all these snippets and string them together in his clumsy way when the author of them can make much better use of them himself. But you will hear more of this yourself from the real boss himself.

I think the book is a lovely job. My only criticism—and it may just be fussiness—is that I should have liked to see more space between the title of the preface and the text of the preface. It seems crowded to my eye.

    Sincerely yours,
    Kathleen Morrison
    (Mrs Theodore Morrison)

    March 7, 1939

Dear Mrs. Morrison:

    . . . .

You say that the book Mr. Newdick is planning is on your mind! Well it's on my mind plus my neck I can tell you. I have no intention of sacrificing Mr. Frost's best interests either to Mr. Newdick's personal difficulties or to our own publishing exigencies. My feeling is that it will never be advisable to publish the trivial newspaper reports and the like. So far I have not had an opportunity to go over the whole of Mr. Newdick's collection. I won't comment on what he is doing until I have, but believe me I am not encouraging Mr. Newdick.

There is of course nothing more mortuary about publishing collected prose pieces than collected poems, but I am in complete agreement that only the best pieces, those deliberately designed for print in the first place, should appear. Robert Frost's prose is in many respects as remarkable as his poetry, and we have just as much at stake in keeping the quality of the included selections high as he has. Nothing is going to be done without his whole advice and consent. . . .

    Sincerely yours,
    [William Sloane]
    Manager, Trade Department

***

Sloane wrote Morrison's husband, Professor Theodore Morrison of the Harvard University English department, explaining why he preferred that Frost's "Geode" not be included in an anthology the professor was preparing with Little, Brown.

    March 29, 1939

Dear Professor Morrison:

A somewhat difficult matter has arisen in connection with your request for use of "Geode" for an Anthology to be published by Little, Brown and Company for college readings in English. The poem has not been published anywhere except in the Yale Review and its initial appearance in a book will of course make that book a collectors item. Robert has so many "supporters" who are trying to keep their libraries of his verses complete that I rather hesitate to confuse the issue by having "Geode" come out in your anthology.

Saturday night when Robert was at our house for dinner, he and Frederick [*sic*] Melcher were talking about cases in the past where Frost poems had appeared first in other books, and they agreed that the ultimate result is undesirable. For this reason it would ease my present feeling about the matter a lot if you would substitute some other poem for "Geode." Would this be possible?

I realize that my writing you affirmatively the first time puts you to a great deal of work unnecessarily, but please do what you can.

> Very sincerely yours,
> [William Sloane]
> Manager, Trade Department

March 30, 1939

Dear Mr. Sloane:

I do not wish to press any requests which would be really distasteful to Robert or to so good a friend of his as Frederick [sic] Melcher, and I should not wish to ask anything which would impair the interests of Robert's publishers. If any of these interests would really be injured, I should be glad to withdraw our request. At the same time there may be other considerations that you and Robert would wish to take into account.

I have a special sense of the value of the poem called "Geode" for our purposes. It represents the same Robert that we have always known, but with a difference. It is like and yet unlike; it compresses a whole cosmology almost into a single remarkable metaphor with a degree and kind of compression which is not a departure from his usual style but is, I think, an intensification and in a certain sense an advance into new territory. I therefore have a further desire to use the poem for particular reasons.

Would it carry any weight in your mind to reflect that this book will be used by almost one thousand of the newest and rising generation of readers at Harvard and Radcliffe?

. . . .

> Sincerely yours,
> Theodore Morrison

April 12, 1939

Dear Professor Morrison:

Go ahead and use *Geode* after all. I have just had a long distance call from Robert about the whole thing. He seems to have repented of his early feeling, and is now anxious to have you include the poem.

I am sorry about all the trouble over this matter, but such things can't be helped sometimes.

> Sincerely yours,
> [William Sloane]
> Manager, Trade Department

* * *

Advertisement from Publishers' Weekly *announcing the publication of the 1939 volume that collected Frost's poetry to that date (Thomas Cooper Library, University of South Carolina)*

When Newdick died unexpectedly, Sloane wrote Frost alerting him to the need to secure the Frost materials Newdick had in his possession.

July 27, 1939

Dear Robert:

. . . .

I am sure you will have heard of the recent death of Robert S. Newdick. It would be hypocritical for me not to admit that I think this simplifies your life and mine in certain ways, but we ought to between us take certain steps very soon about it. First, I believe that either you or I should write to Columbus to make sure that all his materials collected on your biography are carefully sequestered and reserved for whoever shall ultimately do the book. Perhaps you know better than I to whom such a letter should most suitably be written. Second, as regards your prose pieces which Mr. Newdick was collecting, it was far from clear to me who is to become the custodian of this material.

. . . .

<blockquote>
Yours with grateful affection,
[William Sloane]
MANAGER, TRADE DEPARTMENT
</blockquote>

Kathleen Morrison wrote Sloane saying she believed the situation with Newdick's materials was under control. Lawrance Thompson was the Princeton University professor Frost selected as his official biographer in 1939. His biography, which he agreed not to publish until after Frost's death, was eventually published in three volumes: Robert Frost: The Early Years, 1874–1915 *(1966),* Robert Frost: The Years of Triumph, 1915–1938 *(1970), and (with R. H. Winnick)* Robert Frost: The Later Years, 1938–1963 *(1976).*

August 3, 1939.

Dear Mr. Sloane:

. . . .

The Newdick situation seems to be shaking down. Mrs Newdick stopped here over the week-end and spent a great deal of time talking to Robert. They have reached an understanding about the life and papers related to it. Everything is coming to 88 Mt Vernon Street in the Fall. We shall look it over and probably deposit it in the Jones Library or some other place with suitable safeguards to keep it in R.F.'s control. . . .

Larry Thompson came up two week-ends ago to talk to Robert about the book he is working on. They had a very pleasant time and things went well between them. He is coming back the week-end you propose for your visit and will live down here in Robert's little house while he is up at the Inn for the [Bread Load Writers'] Conference. It might be good for you all three to meet and thrash things out while nothing is settled finally. . . .

<blockquote>
Sincerely yours,
Kathleen Morrison
</blockquote>

August 10, 1939

Dear Mrs. Morrison:

. . . .

I am glad the Newdick situation seem [*sic*] to you to be shaking down. Frankly, it does not quite seem so to me. The lady was in here the other day in what struck me as an overwrought state. She had apparently decided before she ever reached me that she was not going to part with Newdick's material after all. . . . The little book of essays is another headache. They are pretty damn bad if you ask me.

. . . .

<blockquote>
Yours in haste,
[William Sloane]
MANAGER, TRADE DEPARTMENT
</blockquote>

* * *

After the 1939 Bread Loaf Writers' Conference, Thompson reported to Sloane about the study of Frost that he had completed. Holt and Company published his Fire and Ice: The Art and Thought of Robert Frost *in 1942.*

September 22 [1939]

Dear Sloane,

Under separate cover I am sending you the "Introduction to Robert Frost" manuscript I told you about at Bread Loaf this summer. At that time, I said I thought I would not be able to get it done before school started, and hence feared I wouldn't get through with it before February or March. But the summer was kind to me, and I have had several weeks of solid work on it since I saw you. Now that it has gone through three revisions, I am willing to let you see it, although I shall be scouring my own copy up while your readers are considering the copy I send you. Several of my kind friends have said nice things about the essays in it which they have read. I hope you will like it.

I stayed at Bread Loaf for nearly a week after you left, and the ramifications of my activities will be kept in store for your ear whenever we can get together. You may imagine that there were sparks aplenty, what with [Bernard] DeVoto and [Louis] Untermeyer and the Dark Ladye all on Frost's tail (I use the word advisedly) at the same time.

Of course I am anxious to hear how you have been progressing with Mrs. Newdick. I think that I have solved the "Frost prose" book. First off, after looking over Newdick's "Frost Prose Parleyings," which I took along for that purpose at Frost's suggestion, I realized just why Frost didn't like the idea. The formal, dignified prose is not a very large section of the stuff Newdick had collected. You asked about his manuscript in comparison with mine. The answer is that I had notes on *almost* everything he had, although I had not included much of the junk he dignified with the name of prose. Frost knows that any book that included mere quotations of that stuff would look pretty silly. I agree, now that I have seen Newdick's plan. Eventually, a collection of the formal prose should be made. But at

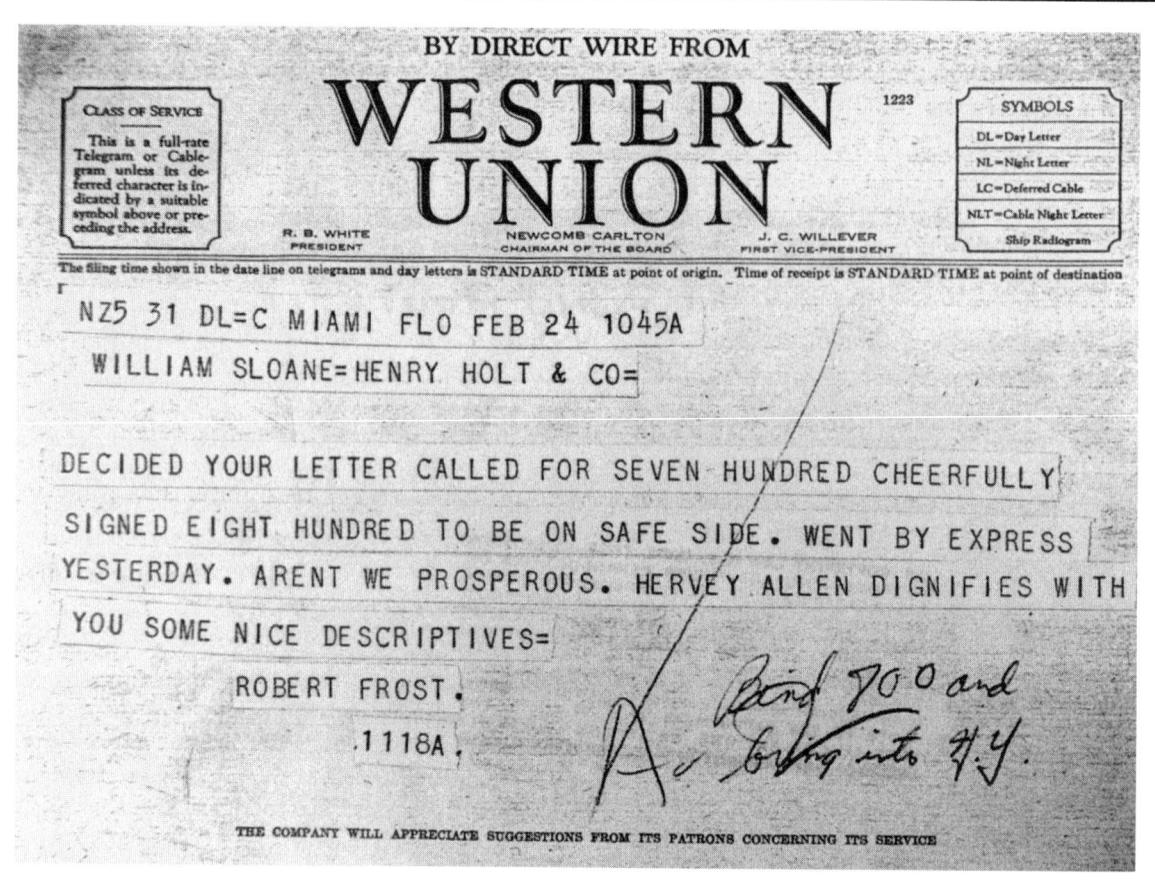

> **BY DIRECT WIRE FROM WESTERN UNION**
>
> NZ5 31 DL=C MIAMI FLO FEB 24 1045A
> WILLIAM SLOANE=HENRY HOLT & CO=
>
> DECIDED YOUR LETTER CALLED FOR SEVEN HUNDRED CHEERFULLY SIGNED EIGHT HUNDRED TO BE ON SAFE SIDE. WENT BY EXPRESS YESTERDAY. ARENT WE PROSPEROUS. HERVEY ALLEN DIGNIFIES WITH YOU SOME NICE DESCRIPTIVES=
> ROBERT FROST.
> 1118A.

24 February 1939 telegram from Frost to William Sloane, Holt and Company trade-department head, describing his progress in signing copies of his just-published Collected Poems *(Princeton University Library)*

present, it doesn't bulk large enough to be worth collecting.

It seemed to me, however, that there was real value in backing up my own statements of interpretation with proofs from Frost's own prose utterances, and consequently I have made what seems to me a sensible use of 30—no, about 25—quotations from Frost's prose in my 150-page manuscript which I am sending to you. It gives *authority* to what I have to say, and justifies using excerpts from certain of the newspaper articles, by carefully calling attention to the articles *as such*.

As such, also, Holt may feel that the manuscript offers not only a critical study of Frost but also a study which carries weight because it has enough of Frost in it to give it significance.

Furthermore, I understand exactly how you feel about your too-generous contract with Frost. I know that you must try to find sources of revenue which will help to counter-balance your "salary" paid to Frost annually. Hence I have no illusions about how much royalty you would be willing to pay me if you decide to you [sic] the "Introduction to Robert Frost." All I ask is that if you are interested in it, you give me a break by having it printed up attractively—a Holt tradition, but not a Macmillan tradition! I have a good friend at the Princeton University Press, and he is Joe Brandt's new layout man. I think that he would be willing, for the sake of friendship, to do the layout on the book outside of hours, free. He cares that much about layout. It would save you, and it would help me. Also, because he works for a University Press, he knows the necessity of keeping costs down. But he would make the job something a little out of the ordinary, I believe, if you would be willing to accept his suggestions as to type, paper, title-page, etc. And I think this would also give Holt & Company a chance to do well by the book not only for the trade but also for the collectors.

Well, this is probably silly for me to go shooting off my trap before you have even seen the manuscript. Forgive my particular interest in good printing. It comes from playing around the Treasure Room too much.

Yours,
Larry Thompson

September 28, 1939

Dear Lawrance Thompson:

This will be no suitable reply to your long and most entertaining letter of September 22. I just want to let you know that your manuscript has come in and I have read a good piece of it. So far as I personally am concerned, it convinces me that you could do a grand job although I may as well tell you right now that a book of this type will never sell much. Tom Wilson and I are interested in it however. We cannot bring it out instanter because we have Richard Thornton's RECOGNITION OF ROBERT FROST still technically current, but by next September the opus will be a possibility. This is not a promise but just an estimate of our feeling at the moment.

Can you let me know whether Robert has seen the book or not, and if the latter, whether you want him to see it?

. . . .

Yours in haste and with enthusiasm,
[William Sloane]
MANAGER, TRADE DEPARTMENT

———◆———

October 4, 1939

Dear William Sloane,

. . . .

I'm glad you liked your first glance at my manuscript. You asked if Frost had seen it. While I was at Bread Loaf, I worked on it steadily. But there was enough of the Yankee in me to keep me from ever mentioning it in any specific sense to him; so much of the Yankee in him that he never mentioned it to me, except to say, "We've talked long enough; you ought to go to work." He knew what my "work" was, but he never asked to see it; I never asked him to look at it.

I don't think that Robert, for all his natural vanity, ever reads through any book or article on him. [Handwritten in margin: "He used to; he doesn't, any more."] He would sniff around in it and then stop. In the present case, I don't think he wants to see it—although I was careful to secure his written permission to undertake the job before I started. Nevertheless, I think it would be a courteous thing for me to ask him if he wants to see it.

If you will give me a few days, I'll write to him, and then let you know that I've written. I'd rather you did not write and say, "The manuscript is in our hands; do you want to see it?" until I have said that much to him. Then I don't care what you do.

You say that Thornton's RECOGNITION is in the way of publication and I can understand that. While we have time to wait, I shall revise and enlarge certain sections of the manuscript. And because I have considerable admiration for your own critical attitude toward and understanding of Robert, I'd welcome any suggestions. If, on the other hand, you don't want to use the manuscript, our next question will be whether I can obtain permission from Holt to have someone like

---

Merry Christmas

Blumenthal prepared Frost Christmas cards for Holt and Company as well as for the Spiral Press. In the fall of 1940 Sloane wrote apprehensively to Kathleen Morrison about whether the content of the upcoming card would properly reflect the Christmas spirit.

September 6, 1940

Dear Mrs. Morrison:

. . . .

I approach this point with a lot of hesitation, and I want to leave it up to your own discretion as to how it should be handled. We have had such a desperate last minute rush always to get Robert's Christmas poem set up and distributed in reasonable time, that if he wants to do one for us this year I hope he can let us have it by the first of November at the very latest. Joe Blumenthal is a temperamental type setter, as you probably know. . . . Even more important than this point is the further one, that if Robert is going to release one of these things for our use—and you know that it is a pride and privilege for us to use it—I very much hope that it can be a poem in a mood which will not be too sharply in contrast to the Christmas one. I would not think of kibitzing in this way if I did not feel that these poems of Robert's have a good deal to do with the public feeling toward him, and if it did not seem to me essential to preserve the deep love, respect and affection with which he is held by practically everyone in America. I hope I can write frankly to you. Anyhow I shall have to. The thing we do not want is a bitter comment on the current political scene, or a disillusioned remark about humanity or something of that sort. It just does Robert harm rather than good for us to put out such a Christmas card, and I would rather not do one at all than do one which I think is not in his best interests.

. . . .

All best regards,
[William Sloane]
MANAGER, TRADE DEPARTMENT

Dust jacket for the Holt and Company edition of Frost's 1942 collection (from The Works of Robert Frost *in the Thomas Shelton Collection, n.d.; Collection of Donald J. Greiner)*

Joe Brandt bring it out. Frankly, I'd rather have Frost's publishers do it, and would go to Joe only as a last resort.

How is Mrs. Newdick?

Yours,
Lawrance Thompson

* * *

Untermeyer, at work compiling a new, combined edition of Modern American Poetry *and* Modern British Poetry, *reported to Frost that he was still lacking permission from Holt and Company for the Frost poems that he wished to use in the anthology.* Modern American Poetry, Modern British Poetry: A Critical Anthology *was published by Harcourt, Brace, and Company in 1942.*

July 21, 1941

Dear Rob:

No word from either Bristol or Bill Sloane. The formal permissions have finally come for two De la Mere [*sic*] poems, ditto Housman, and your "Departmental." Evidently the question of any of the new poems has not yet been settled. . . .

As I told you, I would rather not include any of the controversy-provoking poems than cause any trouble or any rift between you and Bill, or even (considering his position) between Bill and Bristol. I am still hoping that a compromise will permit me to include one of those desired poems, especially "Come In." The manuscript is finished and ready for delivery now—or will be when we have settled this last point.

Esther and I are coming over this Wednesday for the Elisabeth Schumann recital. We plan to arrive by six, and we will come to Ripton in the hope of seeing you first and possibly taking you to supper with us in Middlebury. We will drive home that night, but we will be back again Monday the 28th for my lecture with the new slides and the best of the old ones.

Forwardlookingly,
Louis

July 22, 1941

Dear Bill [Sloane]:

I am enclosing a letter from Louis about the permission to use one or two or three of the new poems. I trust there was nothing in what Robert said about the matter to give offense to either you or Mr. Bristol. He would of course leave the decision to you. The difficulty musn't [*sic*] be allowed to grow serious. All he meant was he would very much like to be in Louis' book with more poems than anybody else. We wish you could come up to talk over two or three things. We begin to wonder if there aren't enough poems for another book before the book of prose. He would rather let you hear the play up here than send it cold to New York. Please don't count too much on the play anyway. He thinks of it with misgivings.

Our best from here
Yours
Kathleen Morrison

* * *

The 1942 collection A Witness Tree *was Frost's fourth to win a Pulitzer Prize. At the beginning of the year Sloane wrote Frost to inform him of plans for the book.*

January 6, 1942

Dear Robert:

....

[P]lans for A WITNESS TREE are going ahead very nicely. You are, of course, getting the major place in our catalog, and Joe Blumenthal is hard at work on the typography and Norman Hood on the special circular.... I think it will be a beautiful book. All in all we are going to do our damnedest to give you a real publishing job here and see whether we cannot reach a larger audience for a new Frost book than has ever been reached before. If we don't it won't be for want of trying.

....

Kay [Kathleen Morrison] tells me that you are worried about the situation as regards the way it may effect [sic] the reception of this book. I want to give you an optimistic prognosis about that with the understanding that if I am wrong you won't hold it against me. I believe that the next months are going to see an intensification of the better kind of patriotism in this country, a renewal of the average American's love for the things which are distinctly his own. Your poetry is one of those things, and I do not believe that in the case of this book of all others the situation is going to prove unfavorable. Of course heavier taxes will mean less luxury money, and books are to a certain extent luxuries; but I think this will be more than offset by the other tendency which I have mentioned. We are planning our sales campaign so as to secure an *advance* sale of 7500 copies of THE [sic] WITNESS TREE if we can, and I can see no reason why we cannot.

....

Yours,
[William Sloane]
Manager, Trade Department

March 20, 1942

Dear Kay:

....

Everything ... is proceeding as well as could be expected, except for the fact that when you do a book with Joe Blumenthal only God and Joe know when the book will get finished....

The book is having a really strange and exciting advance sale. Everywhere we took it we sold fewer copies than we had hoped, and for a time we were disappointed. Now the stores are writing in every day to increase their advance orders, and we are going to have to make a very careful survey of the situation to see just how many first edition copies we shall have to print. I think, though, that considering everything, Robert will have reason to be proud and happy.

All best to you,
[William Sloane]
Manger, Trade Department

May 18, 1942.

Dear Bill:

Thank you for the reviews. Do you want them back? Could you possibly find out discreetly who wrote the review for TIME, May 18? Robert ran on to it unaware and it would help me a lot to know for my own guidance something about the author. Did you see the very excellent review by Wallace Stegner in the Boston GLOBE? It was only second to Mary Colum.

No books of the special edition have come except the first two which Jo [sic] Blumenthal sent early in the game. It is terrible to think of all those beautiful books roaming around the country—worth lots of money and not to be replaced. Can you get a tracer?

....

Cordially
Kathleen Morrison

* * *

Review of *A Witness Tree*

Like an ancient Vermont maple putting forth its leaf in due season, 67-year-old New England Poet Robert Frost this April brought out his seventh book of poems, his first new book in six years. During those years he lost his son (his youngest daughter died in 1935, his wife in 1938); yet the only lines in his book that refer to personal loss read as follows:

I could give all to Time except—except
What I myself have held. But why declare
The things forbidden that while the Customs slept
I have crossed to Safety with? For I am There,
And what I would not part with I have kept.

A Witness Tree is a testimony and a revelation of what Frost has managed to keep, through the happy and tragic years of his life. On the plus side is his

of Frost's unexampled historical poem, *The Gift Outright*, will quickly discern:–

The land was ours before we were the land's.
She was our land more than a hundred years
Before we were her people. She was ours
In Massachusetts, in Virginia,
But we were England's, still colonials,
Possessing what we still were unpossessed by,
Possessed by what we now no more possessed.
Something we were withholding made us weak
Until we found it was ourselves
We were withholding from our land of living,
And forthwith found salvation in surrender.
Such as we were we gave ourselves outright
(The deed of gift was many deeds of war)
To the land vaguely realizing westward,
But still unstoried, artless, unenhanced,
Such as she was, such as she would become.

Whatever America becomes, she will bear, to her lasting beautification, the pioneer trace of Robert Frost.
–"Poetry," *Time* (18 May 1942)

* * *

May 20, 1942

Dear Kay:

. . . .

The review in *Time* about which you inquire was a staff-produced review. I did everything I could to stem that thing, but there is never any possibility of handling the Luce organizations beyond a point. During its preparation they called here for various facts about Robert, and I gave them as little as possible. I also referred them to Fred Melcher for a good deal of the material because I thought that as a long standing friend of the family, so to speak, Fred would do the most discreet possible job. Speaking as a publisher, I can only say that that is a selling review of the book and will help continue the sales. The readers of *Time* are used to seeing people raked over the coals. One of the *Time*'s principal stocks in trade is the motto: "Nothing is sacred," and a Time-reader would not think he was getting his money's worth unless even Robert Frost were given at least one luceworthy kick in the teeth. Hence that jolting sentence to which I imagine Robert has taken justifiable offence. It is probably but poor comfort to tell him that the readers of the magazine will not see that sentence in the same light in which he will. It must have been a wounding one, especially for him to have come on; but the literary life is a fairly wounding one on occasion, anyhow. I have seen,

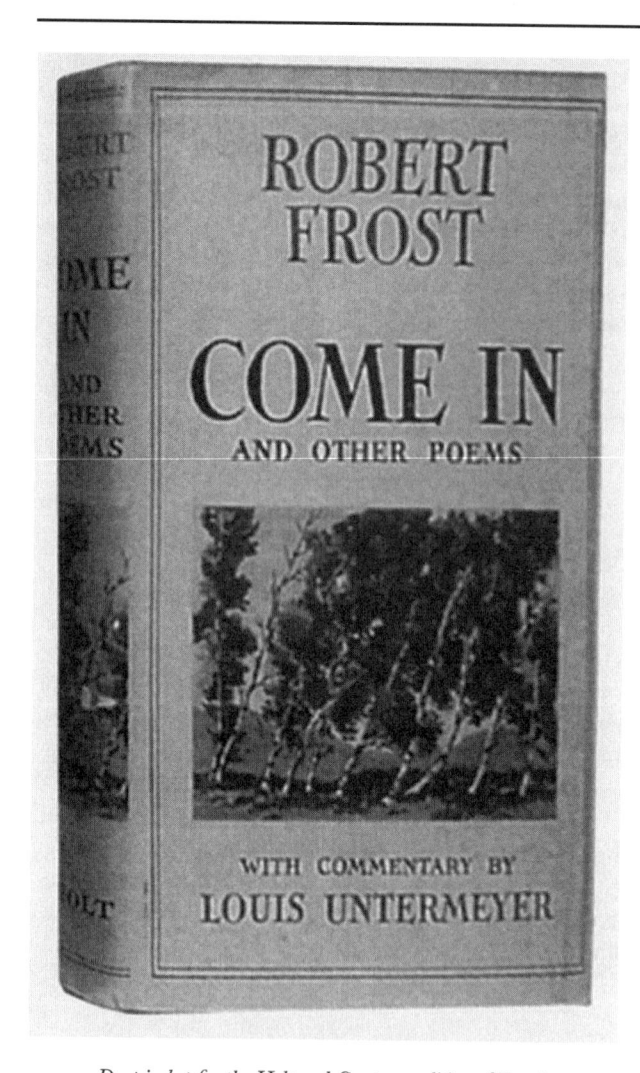

Dust jacket for the Holt and Company edition of Frost's 1943 collection (from The Works of Robert Frost in the Thomas Shelton Collection, n.d.; Collection of Donald J. Greiner)

passion for the passion that makes flowers bloom, trees scrape stars, and some people love each other. In his latest book, as in his first, Frost still goes for this heavenward earth-love as a horse goes for oats—see parts of his *Come In*, for instance. When he goes limpingly, as he does on many pages of his book, it is less because of his age than because he has come more and more to favor his worst poetical fault–his rascally independence, based on preternatural self-esteem. When full of this—and he is only occasionally entirely free of it—Frost writes like a wise man ensconced in a pickle jar.

But the plus outweighs the minus in *A Witness Tree,* and Frost remains in this book a first-rate poet and a natural American. How timely a thing this is, readers

and so have you, important and decent people absolutely pillored [sic] in that magazine, and I urge you both very strongly to do nothing except disregard it. Don't think about it or talk about it or pay any attention to it.

We do need the reviews back when you are through examining them. There are a good many more to paste in, including Wally Stagner's [sic] and Bill Snow's. The latter struck me as worthy but just dull. Please don't let either Robert or Bill know that I said that.

. . . .

Meantime, the sales are going on very much better than any of us had a right to hope; and the reorders are more than sixty copies for the first two days of this week. I think that Robert can feel confident that this book is going to be his most successful one in a long time.

Yours,
[William Sloane]
Manager, Trade Department

May 20, 1942

Dear Bill [Sloane]:

The review in TIME was done by Schuyler Jackson himself, the wretch, who had the affrontery [sic] to send it along with a personal letter to Robert this morning. But Robert feels better now he knows and can interpret Schuyler's phrases. He hated to think that a comparative stranger would have such personal information and make use of it in such a way.

Will you note that Robert's address will change? After May 26, Homer Noble Farm, Ripton, Vermont. How could I get the glad tidings to your banking department? Last summer the cheque was sometimes forwarded and sometimes left to languish in the summer heat of Brewster Street–depending on how bright the postman felt that morning. This year it is especially important to have letters go right to the farm because the war has successfully unmanned the Cambridge post office force and things go all over the lot.

He liked your letter this morning and thanks you for the good news.

Now, can you do a slight favor for him without breaking any policies. Mrs John Gould Fletcher is making an anthology and wants to use the following poems in it:–A PECK OF GOLD, THE TUFT OF FLOWERS, A TIME TO TALK, THE PASTURE, and MENDING WALL. She is paying her own permissions fees and wants to be lightly treated. Personally I don't see why people have the nerve to ask for such favors but when they do and when they are special friends of Robert's I feel we have to make a gesture. She has to live but so do you and so does Robert.

Dust jacket for Frost's 1947 poetry collection (from The Works of Robert Frost *in the Thomas Shelton Collection, n.d.; Collection of Donald J. Greiner)*

Still no books of the special edition. If they come after this house has been closed that will be a new headache.

All best,
Kathleen Morrison

* * *

In the summer of 1942 Frost wrote Sloane endorsing the plan for a collection of his work to be edited by Untermeyer. Holt and Company published Come In and Other Poems *the following year.*

Dust jacket for Frost's 1947 blank-verse dramatic narrative (from The Works of Robert Frost in the Thomas Shelton Collection, *n.d.; Collection of Donald J. Greiner)*

June 16, 1942.

Dear Bill:

This letter is to celebrate the ten thousandth [copy of *A Witness Tree* sold] by agreeing to your proposal about Louis' edition of me with pleasure and enthusiasm. Kathleen and I both think it a fine scheme worthy of the moment. Any royalties you name would be all right with us. There should be no talk of twenty per cent even for the trade edition, of course. And of course Louis should have his quarter. I wish we could see Louis for a good talk about one thing and another. Perhaps we can arrange a meeting on the battlefield of Ticonderoga which is about half way between us and divides the gas. It might be that he could see his way and you could see yours to having more of the commentary in the school book, less in the college, and less still in the trade. I am willing humbly to be explained behind my back but don't want to be explained too much, particularly to people who resent explanation. But I musn't [*sic*] seem too anxious in this matter. I know I can trust Louis' taste and I also know that much of his commentary will be something more and better than mere explanation. I have my doubts about that play on words in the title "Come In." It seems to Kathleen and me to take away from the poem. We might compromise by calling the book "Come In and Other Poems." Then we would have to start the book off with "Come In" made prominent in italics after a fashion I have used in some of my other books. I'd think Louis might get up a better title.

Really ten thousand in less than two months beats everything. Larry's book ahead, and then these books of Louis', and then my prose book, and then a volume of plays, and then another volume of poetry, and then somewhere in the middle of all this the definitive augmented "North of Boston," should assure us of sustaining this excitement for a while yet. You were right about publishing this Spring and we are glad you stuck to it—war or no war.

We are going to try to get Louis to meet us between June twenty fifth and June thirtieth.

. . . .

Yours always
Robert

* * *

In May 1943 Sloane congratulated Frost on winning the Pulitzer Prize for A Witness Tree. *Frost correspondence in the Holt and Company archives at Princeton University ends at this point. He was to remain with the firm, however, until his death in 1963. From 1958 until 1963 Stanley Burnshaw was Frost's editor at Holt. Their relationship is described in Burnshaw's* Robert Frost Himself *(1986).*

May 11, 1943

Dear Robert:

This is the first opportunity I have had to write you a real note about the Pulitzer Prize. You can imagine how happy we all feel about it here and how glad for you we are. It seems to me that the outcome could not have been happier: you and we did nothing to try to win the prize, but retired (so to speak) from the active lists. However, the book was so infinitely the best of the year that even the Pulitzer Prize judges could find no competitor—and that is that. Four times in a single lifetime is a tremendous honor. . . .

[William Sloane]

W. E. B. DU BOIS

HOLT AND COMPANY BOOKS BY DU BOIS: *The Negro* (New York: Holt, 1915; London: Williams & Norgate, 1915); revised and enlarged as *Black Folk, Then and Now: An Essay in the History and Sociology of the Negro Race* (New York: Holt, 1939).

Historian, educator, editor, and activist William Edward Burghardt Du Bois (1868-1963) was born in Great Barrington, Massachusetts. He was an early, highly influential writer on the history and concerns of black people, as well as editor of The Crisis, *a journal published by the National Association for the Advancement of Colored People (NAACP). Holt and Company published Du Bois's* The Negro *as volume ninety-one in the Home University Library series in 1915. His* Black Folk, Then and Now: An Essay in the History and Sociology of the Negro Race, *published in 1939, is a revised and enlarged version of* The Negro.

* * *

Professor William Tenney Brewster of Columbia University was a friend of Henry Holt and editor of the Home University Library series. Handwritten at the top of the letter, in apparent response to Du Bois's request for an advance, is "$150. OK."

Oct. 9, 1914.

Dear Mr. Brewster:

I am cutting the manuscript of "The Negro" down to the estimated length, 173 pages, and have finished 140 pages. I shall undoubtedly have it in your hands by November first, the date which the publishers set.

I write to ask if the publishers could not see their way clear to advance me $250 against future royalties when the manuscript is accepted. I have spent a great deal of time on the book—the spare time of over two years which has seriously interfered with other remunerative literary work. I had promised to finish a book for McClurg & Co., a year ago and on the strength of that bought $175 worth of books on Africa for use on this volume. They are naturally pressing for payment. The[n], too, I have had this manuscript copied three times beside other help from stenographers making a bill of over $100.

I have appreciated the privilege of writing this work and have been glad to spare no pains, but the financial burden has been a little too heavy for my straightened finances. I am aware that this advance was not in the contract and of course, the book will be finished under any circumstances; but the advance would be a very great favor.

Kindly take up this matter with the publishers.

Very sincerely yours,
W. E. B. Du Bois

W. E. B. Du Bois (Library of Congress)

* * *

In early 1916 the head of Negro Publications Exchange of Alexandria, Virginia, sent an inquiry to Holt and Company about the price of Du Bois's The Negro.

2-1-'16.

Gentlemen:

Please forward price of Du Bois' "The Negro." Terms to agents and price of cash purchases of lots of tens and twenty-fives.

Very truly,
C. Leslie Frazier

P.S.—Also include names of publications you have that are written *by* Negroes.

February 2, 1916.

Dear Sir:

We have your letter of February 1st. The price of Dr. DuBois's "The Negro" is 50 cents net, and we should be glad to sell copies to you at 37 cents a copy, transportation to be paid by you, cash with order. We are enclosing a circular in which you will find this book described. We have no other books by negro authors. We publish Professor [George Spring] Merriam's "The Negro and the Nation" but Professor Merriam is not a negro. The price of this latter title is $1.75 net, and we should be glad to give you a discount of 3/10 on single copies, 1/3 on quantity orders for this, transportation extra, cash with order.

Very truly yours,
Henry Holt and Company.

* * *

By the early 1930s Du Bois was anxious to revise The Negro *because of the advance of scholarship on Africa in the years since 1915. He wrote Holt and Company inquiring about the possibility of such a revision.*

April 27, 1932.

Gentlemen:

I wrote you some time ago concerning a revised edition of my book on "The Negro," Number 91, of the Home University Library. This book was published seventeen years ago. In the meantime, our knowledge of Africa has increased in general and in detail. These changes ought to be incorporated in a new edition. I believe that the little book has had a fair sale, but I have heard that it is not in good odor in England and is not mentioned in the English lists. Perhaps this has made you hesitate to re-issue it. At any rate, I should like very much to have your opinion on the matter, and if possible, your decision.

Very sincerely yours,
W. E. B. Du Bois

May 13, 1932

Dear Mr. DuBois:

Please pardon our delay in replying to your letter of April twenty-seventh. . . . We shall be very glad to consider the possibility of a new edition of your book on the Negro in our Home University Library. As you are perhaps aware, this is a joint enterprise between us and Thornton Butterworth, Ltd., of London, who now hold the English rights. We should have to take up the matter of a new edition with them.

Personally I know nothing of the attitude towards your volume in England, though I had not heard that it was in bad odor there. Certainly that has not made us hesitate in reissuing it. Unfortunately the sales for this volume have fallen off considerably in the last few years. The sales from 1927 have been as follows:–1927, 253; 1928, 209; 1929, 168; 1930, 190; 1931, 160; 1932 (to date) 58. We still have on hand 191 copies, which should be ample for the current year. We should probably find it necessary, however, to reprint the book next spring.

Meanwhile could you give us any specific suggestions as to the revision you contemplate, and whether this would involve rewriting the book. As soon as we hear from you, we shall be pleased to take the matter up with our English associates.

Very truly yours,
[R. H. Thornton]
HENRY HOLT AND COMPANY, Incorporated

October 20, 1937

Gentlemen:

Some years ago I took up with you the question of a revised edition of *The Negro,* Home University Library, but was unable to get your consent. This year I have been using the book in a little class in African Culture and I am more and more distressed by its shortcomings especially because of the fact that it is so far out of date. [C. G.] Seligmann, for instance, in the same library has a little book fifteen years later on the *Races of Africa* which gives a mass of information based largely on new material which has appeared in the last decade. At the same time even this is not the kind of book that can be used in classes. It is confined to a narrow field and not easily readable. I still think that a new edition of my book brought up to date by reference to the new work of the African Institute and men like Delafosse, Huxley, Windham, and a dozen others would have a distinct place and fill a want. A study of African history and African culture is beginning to spread especially in Negro schools and also in other schools. I am writing, therefore, to ask again that you consider a new edition of my book.

You will note from this letterhead that since speaking with you I have been elected Chairman of the Editorial Board of a projected Encyclopaedia of the Negro in four volumes. The funds for this project are not yet subscribed but we seem to have good prospects. The preparation of this Encyclopaedia would be a matter of four or five years. During 1936 I was in Europe and close touch with leading anthropologists like Malinowski, Westermann, Labouret, Von Eickstedt, De Cleene and others.

Very truly yours,
W. E. B. Du Bois

November 12, 1937

My dear Mr. Thornton:

I have your letter of November ninth and I am glad that you are willing to publish a book of 75,000 to 80,000 words on the Negro which will be in the nature of a revision or rewriting of my present volume in the Home University Library. I can have such a book in your hands in the summer of 1938 so that it can be ready for fall publication. Would this seem to be a proper time? The book ought to contain maps and possibly some illustrations, protraits [sic] of distinguished Negroes and possibly Negro cities or quarters of cities. I should be glad to have your judgment on these matters. Of course it should have an index.

I should be glad to receive from you at your convenience a contract for signature. I trust you will be able to make a payment of advanced royalties on the signing of the contract and on delivery of the manuscript....

Very sincerely yours,
W. E. B. Du Bois

* * *

Prior to the publication of Du Bois's Black Folk Then and Now: An Essay in the History and Sociology of the Negro Race, *the galley proof was sent for vetting to the New York law firm Campbell, Harding, Goodwin and Danforth. A representative of the firm wrote back advising various deletions to protect Holt and Company from action for libel.*

March 29, 1939.
Attention of Mr. Sloan [sic]

Dear Sirs:

We have read the galley proof of the book which we understand is to be published under the name "Black Folk," and we return the galley proof herewith.

We may assume as a general proposition that it is libelous to state erroneously that a white man or woman has colored blood. We may also assume that this statement is not libelous if it can be proven that a so-called white person has colored blood. Since in the event any action for libel is brought against you it would be incumbent upon you to prove the correctness of the statement made in order to sustain a defense of the truth, we feel it is incumbent upon you in publishing this book to ascertain if proof is available that the persons alleged in the book to have colored blood actually had or have such colored blood.

Ordinarily, descendants of a deceased person cannot bring an action for libel of their ancestor. However, in a case of a libelous statement that an ancestor had colored blood, an action would lie on behalf of descendants since by inference it is alleged that they have colored blood. Again, however, truth would be a defense. We do not attempt to pass upon the veracity of the statements in this book that certain people have or had colored blood or as to the question of whether or not proof of such fact is available. We leave this to you at this time.

In our opinion, the following should be deleted in the book:

(1) On galley page 69, the statement that Fulgencio Batista is a mulatto with white, negro and Indian blood, unless the same can be proven.

(2) The statement on page 70 that Alexander Hamilton and the forebears of Robert Browning were probably of negro descent.

(3) The statement on galley 88 that Governor Northey confiscated two million acres of land and that he so drew a native reserve boundary as to leave a million and a half acres open for European settlement and the further statements that the high lands and wood lands with water were taken for Europeans, unless Governor Northey is dead.

(4) The statements on galley 88 referring to Lord Delamere, unless he is dead.

(5) The last two sentences of the sixth full paragraph on galley 89, unless Delacasse is dead.

(6) All references to the Firestone Rubber Company in the last paragraph on galley 105 and the first paragraph on galley 106, unless the reference to forced labor and the implication of bribery of Liberian officials is eliminated on galley 105 and it is the fact that the rental for the million acres of land was six cents an acre, and unless the statement on galley 106 that the Firestone contract is unfair is eliminated as well as the statement that the insistence of the Firestone Company meant virtual surrender of Liberian autonomy.

(7) The references in the seventh and eighth full paragraphs on galley 117 to Lord Delamere and Sir Edward Grigg, unless these gentlemen are dead.

. . . .

We also wish to call your attention to the persons listed on galley 45 as being colored or of colored blood and feel that the name of any person should be deleted if that person is now alive or has descendants alive and it cannot be proven that that person is colored or has colored blood.

We also wish to point out that throughout the views and opinions of other scientists are referred to and it would be possible for a libel action by a scientist to be grounded on a distorted and ridiculous statement of his opinion. We call this to your attention, as we do not pass upon any of the statements ascribed to these various authors and scientists.

We wish to point out that when we use the word "descendants" on page 1 and page 3 of this letter, this term should be considered to cover not only direct descendants of the ancestor, but also descendants of any brothers and sisters of the ancestor.

We would be happy to discuss this matter with you at greater length, if you so desire.

Very truly yours,
CAMPBELL, HARDING,
GOODWIN & DANFORTH

Du Bois responded angrily to the forwarded copy of the attorneys' report, defending the veracity of his statements and attaching documentation backing up the disputed assertions.

April 4, 1939

My dear Mr. Sloane:

I am rushing this matter to you at the earliest possible moment. It has entailed a large amount of entirely unnecessary work, but you have a right to be assured on the facts. I have published ten volumes since 1903 not to mention innumerable pamphlets and articles on the controversial color question, and have never had to defend even an accusation of a libelous statement.

I do not think that in a single case cited by your attorneys, will it be necessary to change a word. Every assertion I have made, particularly as to Negro blood, has been made time and time again by the most reputable publishers in the land, including Henry Holt and Company. I especially resent the slur of your attorneys intimating that I have made "distorted and ridiculous" quotations from other authors. It is the first time that such an accusation has ever been made against me. I beg also to say that it may not be assumed "as a general proposition" that it is libelous per se to state erroneously that a white man has colored blood. However, in no case have I asserted this.

I would be very glad to make any further explanations or furnish further proof if you think it necessary. I have by no means exhausted the testimony, but have adduced such as was readily at hand.

Very sincerely yours,
W. E. B. Du Bois

MEMORANDUM TO HENRY HOLD [*sic*] AND COMPANY, ON POSSIBLE LIBELOUS STATEMENTS IN BLACK FOLK: THEN AND NOW

1. Galley 69. This statement is based on Carleton Beals' AMERICA SOUTH, Philadelphia, 1937, Lippincott, p. 161 (Note 1)

2. p. 70. References to the possible colored blood have often been published;

As to Hamilton: in Du Bois, THE NEGRO, Henry Holt and Co., New York, 1915, p. 141 (Note 2)

in Du Bois, THE GIFT OF BLACK FOLK, published for the Knights of Columbus, Stratford Company, Boston, 1924, pp. 174, 269 (Note 3)

in Lodge, ALEXANDER HAMILTON, American Statesmen Series, Houghton Mifflin, Boston, 1899, pp. 4, 5, 286 (Note 4)

....

3. Galley 88. Probably your attorneys are not familiar with the law in British colonies, and wrongly assume that I am accusing officials with illegal acts. In a British Crown colony, the governor has the right of legislation by ordinance; he has a council, but can override their advice. He himself can be overriden only by the Colonial Office in London.

....

April 6, 1939

Dear Professor Du Bois:

Your letter of April 4th and the notes you have forwarded to us are most welcome. I feel that with your explanations in hand we can safely proceed to publish the book as it stands but you will readily see that had any question arisen about any of these points things might be very difficult for us, and if your information were not here in our file we should be in a most embarrassing position.

I am sorry that anything in our attorney's letter should have given you occasion for distress. I don't believe that you ought to feel that way about it, because the paragraph to which you refer simply points out that the attorneys don't know about the quotations. They make no claim that they are garbled or even any insinuation; they simply say that if they are we should get into trouble. No doubt you know enough of the legal mind to know that this is the way in which lawyers always think, in which, as a matter of fact, they are paid to think, and that there is nothing personal in it.

I am certainly obliged for your courtesy and thoroughness in this matter.

Sincerely yours,
William Sloane

Carl Sandburg in a photograph from a 1922 issue of Vanity Fair *(Rutgers University Library)*

CARL SANDBURG

HOLT AND COMPANY BOOKS BY SANDBURG:
Chicago Poems (New York: Holt, 1916);
Cornhuskers (New York: Holt, 1918).

Holt and Company was an early publisher of the work of poet, writer, and folklorist Carl Sandburg (1878–1967). Harcourt established the connection, and Sandburg was among the Holt authors who left the company to publish for Harcourt's new firm in 1919. Sandburg's ties to Holt and Company were not completely severed at this point, however; he continued to receive royalties on the two books he published with them, something for which Sloane congratulated Sandburg years later. Sloane also attempted (apparently without success) to get Sandburg to comment on the work of a member of the newer generation of poets, Mark Van Doren.

A Chicago Poet
Alfred Harcourt

When I started selling the Holt line in the Middle West, Chicago was a center for young writers and artists. *Poetry,* a magazine published there under the editorship of Harriet Monroe, was flourishing. It was giving full representation to the poetry that was beginning to be written in America. Poems by two new Chicago poets were appearing in its pages: Edgar Lee Masters and Carl Sandburg. Harriet Monroe's assistant, Alice Corbin, and her artist husband, Will Henderson, became good friends of mine and brought me into their parties with the young group. Alice was also a friend of Carl Sandburg's, and I asked her to try to steer him my way when he had enough poems for a book.

In 1914, she came into my office in New York with a manuscript from Carl. It was entitled *Chicago Poems.* I was glad to see that it was a fat manuscript, for I have always felt that the first book of a new poet should be thoroughly representative of what he has to say, and be large enough to make a dent on the attention of an indifferent public. As soon as I read the manuscript, I knew it was of first-rate importance and quality, but I foresaw difficulties in getting it past the inhibitions and traditions of the Holt office. The best way to start, it seemed to me, was to go straight to Mr. Holt and say that I had turned up the manuscript of a volume of poems by Carl Sandburg, whose work had been appearing in *Poetry* as well as elsewhere, and I thought we should publish it. Mr. Holt said, "All right, if Trent agrees." "Trent" was Professor W. P. Trent of Columbia University, on whose advice Mr. Holt had depended for years. Professor Trent had a catholic taste and recognized new talent, but was of an older tradition, and I was afraid that some half dozen of the Sandburg poems would strike him as pretty raw meat for the Holt imprint. I puzzled over the problem and came to a decision about which I have had mingled feelings ever since. I took out the five or six poems which I knew would bother Trent, and sent the rest of the manuscript to him. His opinion, while he expressed some doubts, recommended publication. When Mr. Holt saw the opinion, he said "Go ahead." I put back the poems I had taken out and sent the whole manuscript to the printer, risking my job on the chance that Mr. Holt would never read the book, and that Professor Trent, having read the manuscript, wouldn't look at the book closely, if he ever saw it. I never told this to anyone until after Mr. Holt and Professor Trent were both dead. *Chicago Poems* was a distinguished success and was followed in a couple of years by *Cornhuskers.*

–*Some Experiences* (Riverside, Conn.: Privately printed, 1951), pp. 25–26

* * *

Nov. 11, 1915.

Dear Mr. Harcourt:

Your good letter should have been answered before this. I am helping build the Day Book here [in Chicago] into what we believe will be genuinely "the world's greatest newspaper," and recent live events in politics and labor have kept me out of poetry and art interests. I am putting into final form now however, a collection of writings I know will interest you personally and may win your decision that they will also interest the poetry-reading and poetry-buying public. I shall send you these in the next month.

     Yours sincerely,
     Carl Sandburg

     January 2, 1916.

Dear Mr. Harcourt:

 Under separate cover I am mailing you the manuscript of a book *[Chicago Poems]*. I am sorry I couldn't get it to you sooner. I have been fifteen years writing it. I wish you much joy reading it. I am willing to consider elimination or revision of any poems, lines or phrases.

     Yours faithfully,
     Carl Sandburg

     January 20, 1916.

Dear Mr. Sandburg:
 We like your
    Chicago Poems
And want to publish them.

 We would propose a royalty of 10% of the published price on sales up to 5,000 and 15% on sales thereafter.

 On commercial grounds, anyway, and probably for artistic reasons, we feel that there is too much in this manuscript to go into one book. Poems that are so much pictures need to be set off from each other, in good sized type and a poem to a page, unless two short ones naturally hang together, and this manuscript would make a book of about 350 pages of that character, which is, we fear, something like 150 pages too much with which to break in upon the public. Very likely most of those we would suggest omitting from this volume could find a place in the later volumes which, with the public favor, we would both want to do.

 You are the one to do the selecting and we are returning the manuscript for that purpose. We can give you two sorts of suggestions: notes on the manuscript and a general statement. We could advise you to omit those marked O in the manuscript; we would suggest omitting those marked X. Some marked "keep" seem, for one reason or another, to demand a place.

 As to the general principles of selection. For obvious reasons, we think the poems, the subjects of which are living people referred to by name should certainly be omitted. Some of the poems are a little too "raw."

These classes are small. The third class is larger. Often there are several poems with the same or very similar theme or written by the same formula. When these are read, as we have read them, one after another in the manuscript and as the public would read them in the book, the effect of repetition is unfortunate. There should be some careful winnowing with this effect, and with a probable second volume in mind.

 We believe you can arrange a volume which will have a much better commercial chance and which would mean "you" at your best more thoroughly. It is rare to have a manuscript in the shop which interests us as much as yours, and we think, too, it has a good chance of interesting the public.

 One thing more; If, as we hope, you find our proposals are satisfactory, will you let us know as soon as possible, as our spring list is on the verge of closing and, if we are to be your publishers, we should like to include your book in our regular first announcement list which has a very general circulation.

     Very truly yours,
     [Alfred Harcourt]
     Henry Holt and Company.

     Feb. 4, 1916.

Dear Mr. Harcourt:

 Of the poems you suggested for elimination from the present volume, all were left out from the manuscript of "CHICAGO POEMS" sent to you, with one exception. That was "Murmurings in a Field Hospital." That, I believe, has a present time value above that of others.

 You placed a question mark on "Dynamiter." I would say put it in. I believe the backing for this book will come from the younger, aggressive fellows, in the main. Without tying it up to any special schools or doctrines, the intellectual background of it takes color from the modern working class movement rather than old fashioned Jeffersonian democracy. Anton Johannsen of San Francisco, who was the model for "Dynamiter" probably commands more deep and genuine affection than any other man in the labor movement. Even those who want to jail him like the heart and wit of him. Some of his implacable enemies have known the motif I tried to catch in this poem.

 In "Buttons," I see where some folks might consider the phrase "by Christ" to be taking the name of the Son of God in vain. In this particular climax, however, I feel sure all readers with any true streak of religion in them will take this oath as the proper exclamation, a cry not lacking kinship with, "My God, why hast thou forsaken me?" It is the one oath in the book which has the best defense and justification.

I can readily see how the Billy Sunday excoriation may be accused of lacking the religious strain that should run through all real poetry. I saw clearly your points about certain words forming what might be taken as an irreverent contrast with the name of Jesus. And I made revisions that I believe put the Sunday poem in a class of reading enjoyable and profitable to all but the most hidebound and creed-drilled religionists. If necessary or important, which it is not, I could furnish statements from Protestant ministers and Catholic priests that this poem has more of the historic Jesus or the ideal Christ in it, than does a Billy Sunday series of exhortations. Mike Kenna (Hinky Dink) tells me that Sunday has bought stock in two Chicago hotels, one of them the Hotel Morrison, persistently notorious in Chicago courts for the studied and civilized vice, the commercialized night pleasure which is so much harder to look at than natural depravity. I used to lunch frequently with Sunday's Chautauqua booking manager, Harry Holbrook, and I know the opinions and convictions of those immediately around Sunday as to whether he is a salesman and crowd trickster or whether he is one sent from God. His own bunch privately admit that I have nailed his hide to the barn door and fixed him in correct historic perspective. There is terrific tragedy of the individual and of the crowd in and about Billy Sunday. He is the most conspicuous single embodiment in this country of the crowd leader or crowd operative who uses jungle methods, stark voodoo stage effects, to play hell with democracy. This is the main cause of the fundamental hatred which men have for Sunday. It isn't a hatred of Sunday so much as a flaming resentment against that type of human individual. The question is whether I have caught the values of it intensely enough. Such an apostrophe to Roosevelt or Bryan could not be tolerated because both of them are more or less prefigurations of the average man, the crowd man idealized and envisioned somewhat. The only other American figure that might compare with Sunday is Hearst. Both dabble in treacheries of the primitive, invoke terrors of the unknown, utilize sex as a stage prop, and work on elemental fears of the mob, with Hearst the same antithesis to Tom Jefferson that Billy Sunday is to Jesus of Nazareth.

I am writing about Sunday at this length, Mr. Harcourt, because I want you to know what sort of foundations I see the poem resting on. When your letter came saying the Billy Sunday poem with some revisions would be used, Mrs. Sandburg commented on that first of all. Edgar Lee Masters asked first of all, "Are they going to print Billy Sunday," and getting "Yes" for an answer, said "They are going after the soul of America."

If you think other changes are necessary to put across the Sunday poem, I'll co-operate. He is a type of crowd-faker the literature of democracy must handle.

Enclosed is what newspaper men call "personality dope." The newspaper sketch is by Chester M. Wright, editor of the New York Call. He and I have worked together on papers.

In two or three days I should find time to send on a "Who's Who" outline to you.

Yours faithfully,
Carl Sandburg

* * *

Edgar Lee Masters wrote the following text for the dust jacket of Sandburg's Chicago Poems *(1916). In pencil at top of the page Harcourt noted, "HH [Henry Holt] said use as he wrote it. AH."*

It is with high explosive that Carl Sandburg blasts from the mass of Chicago life these autocthonous masks and figures of modern circumstance. Poetry here prophesies of Industrial America, Business America, and its consummations. He is an observer with sympathy but without fear; compassionate but with an epic restraint, thoughtful without a synthetic purpose, philosophical and therefore without a solution, and comprehensive of a vast spectacle of restlessness, aspiration and pain. He puts words to the uses of bronze. His music at times is of clearest sweetness like the tinkling of blue chisels, at other times it has the appropriate harshness of resisting metal. He derives from no one, sees with his own eyes, touches with his own hands, is hearty, zestful, in love with life, full of wonder, fundamentally naive. He looks calmly on great blackness, poverty, sordidness, abject misery, hopeless agony, but with the self-possession of an artist. He loves stormy water like a Norseman, and the blue skies of Olympus like a Greek. He has a Slavic gaiety for pastoral delights

---

Sandburg on Frost

[Undated]

Dear Harcourt:

. . . .

Met Frost; about the strongest, loneliest, friendliest personality among the poets of today; I'm going to write him once a year; and feel the love of him every day.
Sandburg

```
              FOR HARCOURT'S DESK
      The screws of God are fastened on us
      And there is no getting away in the dawn
      And there is no getting away in the dusk.

      In the dim clamor of fresh labor pains,
      Long before the earliest milkman was born,
      Long before the night watchmen trod the sidewalks
      And the saloonkeepers turned the key on the last customer,
      The screws of God were fastened on us
      And there is no getting away in the dawn
      And there is no getting away in the dusk.
                                    Carl Sandburg
```

Poem by Sandburg for his friend Alfred Harcourt (Princeton University Library)

and the natural re-actions of healthy flesh. He is a comrade of great loneliness, has outstared Fate that thwarts, is a friend of Death as Nature's doorman at the house of Life. His book is sound, daring, inclusive of many types in the city, and makes a contribution to American literature of emancipating influence, and of permanent importance either in itself or in its effect.

***

Sandburg forwarded the following letter to Harcourt with the handwritten comment, "Harcourt: Have a laugh and chuck this. C S."

June 30, 1917

Dear Mr. Sandburg:

In reply to your note of the 19th, I have now to say that your publishers are not willing to let us use any of your good stuff except on terms that to us are prohibitive.

I am therefore reluctantly compelled to leave you out of our Anthology. It may be strange—and then again it may not be—but Elbert Hubbard's good stuff is used freely without let or hindrance on our part. But whenever we make any attempts at reciprocation, we either get the glassy eye and the marble heart, or are held up in true highwayman fashion. Such is commercialism!

Yours very sincerely,
John T. Hoyle
Managing Editor, THE FRA.

***

Sandburg sent Harcourt a second collection in May 1918. Cornhuskers was published later that year.

May 20, 1918.

Dear Harcourt:

The manuscript of CORNHUSKERS has gone forward to you by express. I hope reading of it gives you some joy and wins "the nod of inward approval" from you (1) as critic and (2) as publisher. There are more pieces than needed, probably, and if you should send me a list of those to be eliminated or return them intact, I suppose the reduction process would be accomplished.

....

Sandburg

July 27, 1918.

Dear Harcourt:

Please congratulate your mechanical department or proofreaders or both. I've never seen printers better at getting type and arrangement the form indicated by copy. A set of corrected sheets will be mailed to you today.

Enclosures herewith are for contingencies that may arise, in case pictures are asked for that haven't been used before. Not that I care to have my mug in newspapers blown by idle winds up dusty alleys. But these may be wanted and I'll be where I couldn't get 'em for you.

I'm not going to subscribe for any clip service on "Cornhuskers." If anything comes out that you think may have suggestions worth while—or some intensely human critic, not necessarily cordial, spills a real mouthful of pointed observation—send it on.

Cover, size and makeup of "Cornhuskers" I would suggest be like "Chicago Poems."

Sincerely,
Sandburg

Harcourt drafted a hasty note on 18 September 1918 to be cabled to Sandburg seeking a last-minute replacement for a poem in Cornhuskers.

All my associates very much desire to drop Steamboat Nights. Under the circumstances I hope you can mail at once special delivery a one page piece to replace it. Presses waiting. Sorry to bother you.

Alfred Harcourt

* * *

Sloane wrote Sandburg in 1941 with the welcome news that Chicago Poems *and* Cornhuskers *continued to sell, thus bringing Sandburg continued royalty payments.*

April 17, 1941

Dear Mr. Sandberg [sic]:

There is really no need for me to accompany this statement with any note of explanation except to tell you that it is pretty pleasant to keep on remitting royalties on books over as extensive a period of years as we have been doing with CHICAGO POEMS and CORNHUSKERS. You will see that they continue to sell and that, in particular, the reprint fees continue to come in.

As an editor I'm afraid I have a pretty commercial soul. At any rate, to me the ultimate endorsement of any poetry is that it continues to be in commercial demand two decades after its first appearance. You ought to feel very proud!

Yours,
[William Sloane]
Manager, Trade Department

* * *

In 1941 the German-born American composer, conductor, and pianist Lukas Foss approached Sandburg about the use of a poem from Cornhuskers, *"Prairie," as the text for a choral and orchestral composition. Foss's* Prairie Cantata *won the New York Music Critics' Award in 1944.*

July 1, 1941

Dear Mr. Sloane:

The enclosed letter speaks for itself. I would favor your letting him [Foss] have the use of this poem, without fee, until it should get into some real money. The chances are entirely that he has done this music in the same sporting approach that I had in writing the poem. He is not kidding us nor himself. Give him a break.

Sincerely yours,
[Carl Sandburg]

P.S. Please return letter.

July 11th, 1941

Dear Mr. Sandburg:—

Your letter of July 1st has waited this long for an answer because the absence occasioned by my father's death has put me far behind in my work. In reply to such a request as yours we are only too anxious to oblige Mr. Foss and I believe that we will make the release you request. However, I shall have to forward the correspondence to our person in charge of permissions, Miss Louise Lawton. She will notify you what final disposition we made and also return Mr. Foss' letter.

I approach this next point with a good deal of hesitation and this hesitation is due as much to the many kindnesses you have showed toward us in the past as any one other thing. I am much afraid I have abused your kindness but I believe that we are publishing this fall a book which is of rich American value and literary importance, and a copy of it is going forward to you today. It is Mark Van Doren's THE MAYFIELD DEER, which we shall be publishing in October. Perhaps I am wrong or no judge of poetry, but somehow I think this is a pretty large calibre thing and that it is also a thing which will have a great deal of personal meaning to you. It stems from a part of the world which you know, undoubtedly, and from a time which you understand. Its richness of overtones and depth of imagination will also, I think, appeal very strongly to you. If you don't like it for goodness sake say so and make no effort to gloss over the fact, but if you do I should very much like to hear that fact in some fashion which we could use in presenting the book later on.

      Cordially yours,
      [William Sloane]

      July 15th, 1941

Dear Mr. Sandburg:

Your letter of July 1st and that of Lukas Foss have been referred to this department by William Sloane. Mr. Foss spoke at length to the writer over the telephone as a preliminary to making formal application for permission to use the "Prairie" in the manner described. The impression he made then is the same to which your letter attests. He is genuine, and we should like to encourage him.

We are sorry that Mr. Foss has interpreted our designedly general statements and provisions in a manner so unfavorable to his project. The intention was quite the reverse. His plans are vague, and his opportunities for performance problematical, in his own words. We wish to give him the greatest leeway, and with your approval, will do so. We believe we can straighten that point out with him, without relaxing any of the safeguards necessary for the protection of copyrighted material in constant demand by people not so sincere nor so able as he appears to be.

In regard to changes in the text, we as publishers "of the word" were quite firm. We do not authorize changes, and if much cutting is to be done, we should like to have the poem, in the form in which it will be printed, submitted to you. Since he has assured us of his feeling for the spirit of the poem, there should be no difficulty there.

Our most recent letter from Mr. Foss states that he has not commenced work on the composition, as he must write ballet music "to order," for the present. It is our intention to write to Mr. Foss, to lessen his natural apprehension on the preliminary financial obligations that he will incur, and to assure him that there are no dragons in his path. Thank you for permitting us to see his letter. It is at no time an easy task to evaluate a proposal of this kind, but with your help, we can do a better job for you, and for Mr. Foss.

      Yours very truly,
      [Louise Lawton]
      HENRY HOLT AND COMPANY
      Permissions Clerk

Sinclair Lewis in a photograph from a 1928 issue of Vanity Fair *(Rutgers University Library)*

SINCLAIR LEWIS

Sinclair Lewis (1885–1951), novelist and limner of small-town American life, was born in Sauk Centre, Minnesota. Although he did not ultimately publish anything with Holt and Company, Lewis began his long association with Harcourt while Harcourt was still at Holt. Lewis's Main Street *was published in October 1920 and immediately became a best-seller for the new firm of Harcourt, Brace. Lewis went on to win the Pulitzer Prize (which he declined) in 1926 and the Nobel Prize (he was the first American recipient) in 1930.*

A New Novelist
Alfred Harcourt

My friendship with Sinclair Lewis started at about this time [circa 1915] when he was with the publishing house of George Doran. We fell into the habit of lunching together in the grillroom of the old Waldorf. He and Grace Hegger had just been married and were living on Long Island. He was spending all his time outside of office hours, on commuting trains, and at home, writing short stories and novels. He was beginning to sell stories to the *Saturday Evening Post*. His novels he had taken to Harper's because of Elizabeth Jordan, then in their editorial department, who was interested in his work. Those early novels, *Our Mr. Wrenn*, *The Trail of the Hawk,* and *The Job,* received scant attention, and their sales were small. Their unsentimental directness, the simple ordinary people he portrayed, the affectionate irony with which he treated them, made them ahead of their time.

We were both from small towns and swapped many a story about the people we had known—I in New Paltz, New York, and he in Sauk Center [*sic*], Minnesota. From those talks, I saw that he could write a first-rate novel about the small town, and I urged him to think about that. One day he came into my office at Holt's, closed the door, and said, "Alf, I am going to write that small-town novel which you have been pestering me about. I've got a title for it—'Main Street,' and don't you mention it to a single person. When it is done, you've got to publish it."

—*Some Experiences,* pp. 27–28

* * *

Lewis did not always date his letters, and when he did, he usually gave only the day of the week or day and month. These letters follow the order in which they appear in the Holt and Company Archives. Lewis biographer Mark Schorer has noted the difficulty of identifying which titles Lewis was referring to in some of the following letters.

March 31

Dear Alf [Harcourt]:
Excited to hear that maybe you'll be out in this wilderness. I'll probly be @above new (note it) address [in Chicago] for 3 weeks or a month. If you don't get here till after I've left for that dear Sauk Centre, Minn. I could come down from there to Minneapolis & we could meet there. Have met Sandberg. Rough but *real*. Lemme hear any news.

As ever,
Red [Lewis]

January 15

Dear Alf:
Naw, ain't writing a novel, writing a play, and when the managers have all turned that down with decision and contumely and the rest of Roget's Thesaurus I'll get some sense and write another novel. I started in gravely to write the Jim Hill novel—actually spent a couple weeks reading oceans of dope—and for the first time in trying to do a thing like that, turned back baffled—couldn't see my way out. So the novel when it does come will be either our old friend "Main Street"—of which you must be heartily sick by this time—or a novel about a traveling man—a man like Mr. Schwirtz in "The Job."

All goes well and cheerfully—we've made hundreds of good friends in St. Paul—enough parties, despite the war; skating and skiing; all feel well. Regards to your people and regrets we're not at Spuyten Dunvil to be near you—tho otherwise I'm more 'n happy in Sinpul.

Zever,
Sinclair Lewis

. . . .

Wednesday

Dammit, mit ad in last Sunday's Times and other plans, Harpers show signs of trying to live up to their feeble idea of trying to do something for Job, so as there is no real Overt Act I haven't been able to mail that letter asking for passports. You'll be getting damn tired of my feeble wriggles. But wait till you see that good and great masterpiece Main Street coming into you, and then all will be well, and MAYBE there'll still be an excuse for calling em off on Innocents.

In haste,
Sinclair Lewis

* * *

Ellen Eayres was Harcourt's secretary and later became his second wife. The address Lewis refers to in the following letter was that of the Holt and Company offices in New York.

September 10.

Dear Miss Eayrs:
You don't know it, but I live at 10 West 44th, with a Mr. Alfred Harcourt he probably is my landlord. Maybe I have a trundle bed under his desk, and keep my books (both of them) and the extra Sunday pants in his wastebasket. Cant you see him making up my bed every morning, and carefully sweeping the little space under the desk, which is my room, with a small whisk broom?

He must be my landlord, because he ain't my boss—yet—and I registered in the draft (in advance, up here, sending card down to NY) as from 19 W 44, c/o A.H.

Thank you for your bully letter. Re Carrington's war psychology book, sounds as if it needed editing. He's probably getting careless. I think a little encouragement and careful editorial attention would do wonders for him.

The novel, the great and only presumably-to-be-issued by Holt novel, is going strong. I've written eighty thousand words. Looks as though it would be about 130,000 in all. But that probably will be considerably cut.

As ever,
Sinclair Lewis

* * *

Harcourt reported to Lewis about a possible business takeover involving Harper, the publisher of his novels before Main Street, *and how it might affect plans for Lewis to move to Holt and Company.*

February 24, 1916.

Dear Red:

Although my information about Doubleday and Harpers came from a man who is intimately concerned in the deal, yet things I just hear from other sources indicate that it isn't all settled yet. I would guess that nothing is settled now. One says, "They've sold their printing plant and Franklin Square Agency and will move the publishing business and magazine up-town." Another says another thing, and so on. I would say that they probably have half a dozen propositions before them involving re-organization or sale and that the cat has not yet indicated which way it will jump. Naturally, the various interested parties are assuming its direction will be in line with their personal interests. I was on the point of writing the above when your letter came. I'll keep you informed of developments as they come to light. I just hear F.N.D. [Frank N. Doubleday] and the Morgan partner who attends to Harpers are at the Bahamas together, which confirms my first letter, somewhat.

I'm endlessly interested to hear of the progress of the new novel. If the change in Harper's ownership had matured as I expected it would when I wrote before, so as to free you to turn to us, and you wanted deliberately to come here, we should be glad to make a definite offer for your next book. But now the situation is very tangled. I can't ask the house to make a definite proposal for a book which is under contract to another house, and merely leave a disturbingly good offer hanging around loose. The situation will very likely untangle itself before you have to make a definite decision. Meantime, don't worry about it but put your best licks into the new book and have a good time.

Of course, if the air hasn't cleared when the time comes and you should definitely decide you wanted us to publish for you, there are ways enough to manage it. The situation at Harpers is likely to develop an easy way.

Do write when you can.

Ever yours,
AH.

Thursday

Dear old man:

If D-P [Doubleday, Page] or Brett buys Harpers, it does look zif the consummation devoutly hoped by me as well as by you, your taking over my novels, including I decidedly hope plates on Wrenn and Hawk, will eventuate. Please let me have the very latest on this. It's curious, two letters from Miss Jordan since you wrote me, and not a word about impending change. Would it let her out? For, as you know, tho I like Hoyns and Dunneke and Briggs and Miss Watson a lot, it's Miss Jordan who ties me up to Harpers.

I'm making "The Job," my next novel, just as big as I can, and may not get it finished till the end of the summer, simply shan't think of the element of time, for first of all I want it to be as big, as real, as sincere, as I possibly can.

I'm writing a long letter to Miss Jordan this morning, not mentioning Holt except in the following paragraph. I didn't want to mention Holt at all, but I had to give her some definite figures, and I hope that I fixed it so that there can be possible comeback. This paragraph will also give you the gloomy news of how much Harpers actually did sell of Hawk. (The rest of the letter is just travel news, etc.) You will note that I don't speak of any *present* Holt offer. Here's the paragraph:

"I was a good deal downcast to find that 'Hawk' had sold only 3665 copies up to January 1st–not because that gives me less money than I get for a single short story, but because that isn't much of an advance on the first season's sale of Our Mr. Wrenn–I haven't the Wrenn figures here, but I remember them as somewhat over 2000. And I was slightly surprised to find an item of $21.65 for author's corrections on Hawk. I hadn't thot they'd be anything like that much. I gave it exactly the kind of trained proofreader's corrections that I'd have given to a Doran book. . . . You see, Doran was ready to guarantee me a sale of 10,000 on Hawk, and that far more reliable firm–a firm without any of the earmarks of Bobbs Merrill or other author-snatchers–Henry Holt Co, were ready to guarantee me a sale of 20,000 on Hawk; and while of course I stuck to Harper–as indeed Holt advised me to, they being scrupulously fair in their dealings with other publishers, and asking for my book only if it was not pledged to Harpers (or rather to you, who are much the most important part of Harpers to me, as I once told you), yet in the light of these proffered guarantees, I can't help being sorrowful over 3665, even to [*sic*] I am aware that that must be equal to, or even greater than, the average sale on a second novel."

Gawk what a long sentence my damned old typewriter committed!

With the above, you know as much about the status as I do. Lemme hear. Harpers have the promise, in contract, to see my next novel first, but if Miss Jordan leaves, we could wriggle out of that, I hope. If the change in ownership leaves her still in power, she'd probly get the Job–tho not necessarily the one after that. But if she exits, then it's Harcourt ho! And let's see

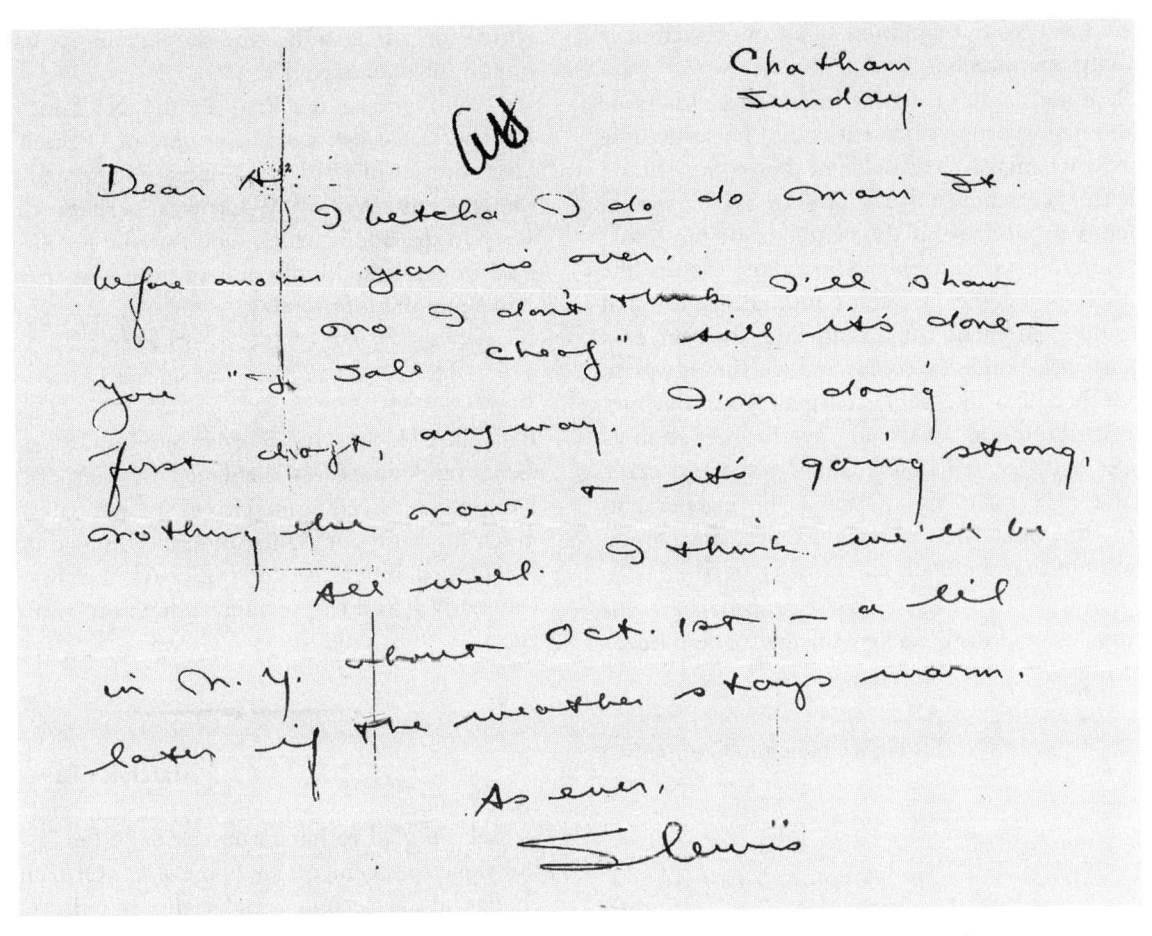

Note from Lewis to Harcourt promising to deliver Main Street *(Princeton University Library)*

if we can't give this damn province a real realistic novelist, Gawd and Alfred Harcourt assisting that poor boob Sinclair Lewis.

Been doing nothing but write, read, and bathe in the surf since last I wrote you, but now we're off for a little more hiking.

I'm leaving the whole question of what will actually become of The Job when it's done till then, but I do want to hear from you, and you might make your former verbal offer definite, if you'd like.... Between us, I don't expect The Job to sell 20,000, but I would like to see it go slightly more than 3 or 4 thou, I must say.

As ever,
Sinclair Lewis

If you took over Hawk, do you think you could get some more sale out of it, or is it dead? Oh yes! Can you send me all 3 vols of Martin Nexo & *third* vol of Jean Christophe to *Miami,* with bill & discount? Read Lippman. And, what would you do about English rights on my books?

April 4, 1917.

Dear Lewis:

I hope that this letter mirrors our understanding.

If, as we both hardly expect, your former publishers do not publish "The Innocents," we are ready to take over your contract with them for that book, or to make a new contract with you for its publication.

We are to publish for you the first novel which you write after "The Innocents." As your plans now shape themselves, this will be the novel about which we have talked as entitled "Main Street." We propose the following terms: A royalty of 15% to 10,000; 17½% to 20,000; and 20% after 20,000. You can have your choice of an advance of $1000 on publication, or what I prefer as fairer all around, what we call our prompt payment arrangement: i.e. we would pay within three weeks of publication, as soon as advance orders are all billed out, the royalty on all copies then sold. This is the most exact measure of what your reputation, plus our machinery for selling amounts to.

It is rather hard, so far in advance, to frame the advertising proposal, but it would be something like this: when we have read the book, we should decide that a certain sum, say $750 or $1000, should be spent on publicity. If the character of the book, our sales efforts, and this advertising carries the sales to 10,000 copies, we could mutually agree that we would then spend, on advertising, five per cent of the list price on 5000 copies and we should spend in your behalf a like sum, charging your five per cent contribution against your royalties. As soon as the sales had reached 15,000 copies, we could make the same agreement, or one for a varying percentage, on the next five thousand copies, and so on until we felt that the book would carry itself.

If you will write us that these proposals are satisfactory, we will draw up agreements for signature.

Sincerely yours,
AH
for Henry Holt and Company.

February 28, 1919.

Dear Miss Eayrs:

I am returning one of the agreements, signed. Please call to Mr. Harcourt's attention my addition at the top of page two of agreement. The Sat Even Post buys all fiction with the distinct understanding that there shall not be any second serial rights—tho, of course, they have no objection whatever to publication of extracts for advertising, or to such second use as the publication of a story in a book like O'Brien's "Best Short Stories" and that sort of thing. What they won't consent to is the sale of second serial rights to newspapers, etc. So I am forced to add this to contract.

I do hope it will be all right. I'm darn sorry to rob Holt's chance to sell 2nd rights, (if there ever is a chance!) but I'm powerless.

If it's all right, will you please have AH initial this new clause, so that it will stand in future?

He, poor patient man, may be glad to know that I'm already making plans for considerable addition to Free Air—distinctly NOT padding, but a whole new section, carrying on the story at the end, with the life of Claire and Milt in Seattle.

And that before the year is over, I'll probably have written a new novel—a hundred thousand words or more—and, one hopes, more basically important than Free Air.

Did you notice that in the NY Times Book Review of a week ago, in review of O'Brien's Best Short Stories of 1918, the reviewer suggested that he thought my Willow Walk was perhaps the best story in the book, which would make it—Oh, one is glad to get these kind woids of praise, after the generous panning of my play!

As ever,
Sinclair Lewis

PS Tell A.H. that, in accordance with the usual efficiency and quickness displayed by Harpers, I still have not received from Hoyns an estimate of how much he wants for rights on earlier books, though I telephoned him a second time, on the day before leaving NY, and was promised them for over a week ago.

March 5, 1919.

Dear Lewis,

I am glad to have your letter of the 28th with the signed agreement for "Free Air." Of course the change about second serial rights is correct, and I have initialed it.

Glad to know about all the rest of the things you mention.

Sincerely yours,
[Alfred Harcourt]

March 29

Dear Alf:

I'm enclosing the finally received letter from Hoyns about prices on earlier books. Will you have a copy of it made and send back either original letter or copy? A[n]d let me know what you want to do about this as soon as possible, so that I can answer Hoyns.

I am working on the new and extended end of Free Air now.

And I hope, before the year is over—MAIN STREET! I'm quite flush now, financially, and we're going to spend the summer in a Minnesota town called Fergus Falls, especially and exclusively to finish up my Main Street dope. I'm thinking about the plan of the thing all the time.

As ever,
Slewis

Lewis's 3 April 1919 letter mentioned by Harcourt in the following letter is not in the Holt and Company Archives.

April 10, 1919.

My dear Lewis:

I have been cogitating a good deal about the questions raised in your letters of March 29th and April 3rd. As the letter about postponing "Free Air" is the most important, and the answer to the other hangs a little on it, I'll let you have my views about that first.

I was inclined, at first, to the view that the order of publication is not particularly important. In the long run, each book would find its level, etc. But the upshot is that I agree with you. It will be better to have the next novel of more real significance than "Free Air" is likely to be, though that garage boy, given time, may grow into a really significant figure. That means a postponement anyway, and I'd like to have you put your best foot forward, especially on the first step with us, and have a book the whole organization will be crazy about and that will justify all the fuss we want to make over the first book you publish with us: in short, "Main Street."

As to the books that are already with Harpers. I think you could fairly reply to them that when and if the time comes when you want to dispose of them to another publisher, you couldn't fairly ask that publisher to pay the price they are asking you to pay now, and that you don't want to handle the transaction at a loss. The total sum called for is $1455, of which $888. is for plates. I have inquired at Baker and Taylor's as to what sale the books are now having. Their sales from the first of last September to the first of April are as follows: "The Innocents," 4; The Job," 1; "Mr. Wren," 1; "the Trail of the Hawk," 2. It's a crime to let books get as dead as that, and then to think of getting anything like cost out of the plates and stock. If Harpers sold those books in the market today, they would probably get $20 a set of plates as metal; 15 cents a copy for the bound books, and about 5 cents a copy for the sheets; roughly about $500 for the whole shooting-match, and I have used the top prices for plugs, in figuring. Why don't you write them that it is too much money for you to put into it now, but will they give you a last call before they melt the plates? Before you do this, look at your contract, and see if it doesn't give you the right of taking the plates back at their value as old metal if certain contingencies should arise. Such a letter would insure your having a last call at them. I think you could buy everything they have now for $700, and you can probably do better than that later, and I don't see why either of us should pay more or tie up money for a longer time than is necessary. I am returning a copy of Hoyns's letter, as I have figured out what the various quantities come to on the original.

You know, the more I have thought about it, the more encouraged I am by your letter about postponing "Free Air." It is a rare thing to find an author who hasn't the itch to get printed, and it is a mighty good sign.

Luck to us both!

Sincerely yours,
[Alfred Harcourt]

Following Harcourt's advice, Lewis wrote Henry Hoyns, an editor at Harpers, stating that the price demanded for the rights to his earlier books was too high.

April 14, 1919.

Dear Mr. Hoyns:

I have thought over your offer on prices of plates and sheets of my books pretty carefully, and it seems to me that it is pretty steep for books that are not selling at all.

I don't know just when I shall be able to get out another novel—none is scheduled yet. I had thought of publishing a serial that I have coming out in the Saturday Evening Post, but have decided not to. But when I do get ready to have another novel published, I wouldn't dare to ask the publisher to pay me back the total sum your figures amount to—$1455; and so I would have to handle the sale at a considerable loss. I had a little talk with Holt about taking over my novels, when I was in New York, and though they did seem rather interested, they were not so much so that they would be likely to pay more than half the amount asked. I am quite sure that they would think they were doing pretty well if they paid $700 for the whole thing. They were cautious, but their attitude seemed to be that they would be taking over books that are now not selling at all, and that anything they put into it would be something of a gamble.

I wonder if now, or sometime later, you would like to make me a new offer?

If not, won't you please make a note that before the time comes to melt the plates (which will be some years yet, even on Our Mr. Wrenn) I'd like to have you give me a last call on this. By that time I may have gotten away from my present absorption in writing short stories and plays, and really be doing novels again, and so more highly value previous novel rights. Of course, on the other hand, I may be still farther from the novel-writing game. But however it will be in the future, I can't begin to see $1455 now.

I hope you are having a good season, and that the Zane Grey book is selling a million an hour.

Sincerely yours,
Sinclair Lewis

April 14, 1919.

Dear Alf:

Here's the dirty lying scut letter I am sending to poor Mr. Hoyns today. I'll send his answer.

My contract merely gives me the right to take over plates at half the cost of making before melting up—in other words, just what their offer is now. I judge, tho, that they may come down. They were pretty anxious to sell.

We have been up to Fergus Falls—the Minnesota town where we hope to spend the summer, for Main Street—since I have written you, but we haven't yet been able to find a house. Of course the number of available furnished houses is limited. However we have a *chance* at three different ones, and I think we'll get one.

Will you make a note of this: When we get ready to republish my old books, wouldn't it be well to change the bum title of "The Train [sic] of the Hawk"? There are at least twenty recent novels with the word trail in 'em, and almost all of 'em are Zane Grey Wild West junk. I never did like the title, and wanted either "Hawk" or, still better, "This Young Man."

Your letter is a corker, and I'm glad you agree about Free Air postponement. The more I think about it, the more I'm sure that's a wise move.

As ever,
Sinclair Lewis

Can we copyright title Main St.?

———◆———

April 15

Dear Alf:

Off to Baltimore for a week, tomorrow. When I get back, we'll see about terms and agreement on Main Street, and mit pleasure view your new diggings, as suggested in yrs of day fore yesterday.

Zever,
Slewis

———◆———

April 17, 1919.

Dear Lewis:

We can't copyright the title "Main Street." There is no copyright on titles.

I think it would be well to change the title of "The Trail of the Hawk."

Let us know where and when you get settled for the summer.

Luck to us all!

Always sincerely yours,
[Alfred Harcourt]

P.S. I hear that Hoyns has gone away for a rest, so you may not have an early reply to your wise letter.

* * *

In July 1919, shortly after these negotiations for Lewis to begin publishing with Holt and Company, Harcourt and Donald Brace decided to leave Holt to establish their own firm. Lewis wanted to go with them and asked Roland Holt to be released from his Holt contract for Free Air.

Dear Mr. Holt:

I wonder if I can, without impairing our good personal relations, ask for the return of the contract on my book "Free Air"?

There are two disconnected reasons. First—as I wrote to Harcourt long before there was the slightest hint of his severing connections with Henry Holt Company—you'll find the letter in the files—when I started to work to add to the MS. to bring it from the present serial length of 56,000 words to a length suitable to book publication, I found that it would be such a long job that I couldn't, with the work already in hand, do it till sometime next year. And in its present short form it hasn't quite the dignity I want in my next book. Now as other tasks may keep coming in and preventing my properly enlarging and developing the book, I don't like to have a contract for it out, even with the understanding that it's not to be published till I do properly complete the work.

Second, despite my long and hearty respect for the Company and my personal liking for you and others, yet after all Harcourt has always been the man in the firm whom I have best known and with whom I have done business, as book-reviewer and fellow publisher and author, and while I don't know what his plans are, I want to be loyal to him and stick by him.

I understand that one of the fundamental principles of the Company has been to hold authors by their own desire rather than by the semi-compulsion of contracts, so I put this directly to you, and hope that you will see it in the decidedly friendly light in which I see it.

I am here in this Minnesota town [Mankato] for the summer—and I like it; like the friendliness, the neighborliness, and the glorious sweeps of country round about.

Sincerely yours,
Sinclair Lewis

———◆———

June 19, 1919.

Dear Mr. Lewis:

You ought to be a diplomat for in yours of the 16th you certainly have expressed a thing which I naturally regret with a charm that eases the matter.

Of course we do not want to hang on to your FREE AIR unless you are willing, and are sending you, enclosed, our copy of the contract, cancelled. Will you kindly write the words "Cancelled by mutual consent June 19, 1919" on your copy of the contract, sign it and send it along to us?

I wish I had more opportunity to see you, and especially appreciate your kind personal words. I still hope I may see more of you, and shall always be glad to hear from you.

With best wishes, I am,
Sincerely yours,
[Roland Holt]

June 25, 1919.

Dear Mr. Holt:

Thank you for the relinquishment of the Free Air contract—and still more for your charming letter. It's *you* who ought to be the diplomat!

I am, as you suggest, returning my copy of the contract, with the cancellation.

Thank you very much, and believe me to be,
As ever,
Yours sincerely,
Sinclair Lewis

STEPHEN VINCENT BENET

HOLT AND COMPANY BOOKS BY BENET: *Heavens and Earth: A Book of Poems* (New York: Holt, 1920);

The Beginning of Wisdom (New York: Holt, 1921; London & Sydney: Chapman & Dodd, 1922);

Young People's Pride (New York: Holt, 1922);

Jean Huguenot (New York: Holt, 1923; London: Methuen, 1925);

King David (New York: Holt, 1923).

Writer Stephen Vincent Benét (1898–1943) was born in Bethlehem, Pennsylvania, and educated at Yale. He traveled to France (1926), wrote screenplays in Hollywood (1929), and eventually settled in New York City. During his relatively brief life, Benét wrote many poems, short stories, historical works, novels, plays, and librettos. His best-known work is, perhaps, the Pulitzer Prize–winning epic poem John Brown's Body *(1928), published by Doubleday, Doran.*

* * *

Benét's initial contact with Holt and Company came about not through a query about a possible manuscript submission but through a letter asking about possible employment as a reader with the firm. He enclosed sample critiques of two novels with the letter.

Stephen Vincent Benét (Gale International Portrait Gallery)

[circa 25 November 1918]

Dear Sirs:—

Have you any vacancies open for readers on your staff? My qualifications are as follows.

I have read steadily and on an average of at least one hour a day for the last ten years, chiefly novels, poetry, biography and history. This is exclusive of any time spent in study at school or college. I read very fast; at one time when I had nothing else to do I read seven average-sized novels in one day; Mr. Wells' new book, "Joan and Peter," I read in three hours, travelling from New York to Hartford. I have had practical experience in writing for four years, taken part in managing two college papers, and published two volumes of verse. I spent three years in Yale College and left it to take a war-job in the State Department at a salary of $2000 a year. This position I resigned to enlist in the Heavy Artillery Preliminary Candidates' School but was honorably discharged on account of physical deficiency. I now wish to return to college for a special course to be run for men who have been absent or in service, but I shall largely have to work my way through if I do.

TO
ROSEMARY

If I were sly, I'd steal for you that cobbled hill, Montmartre,
Josephine's embroidered shoes, St. Louis' oriflamme,
The river on grey evenings and the bluebell-glass of Chartes,
And four sarcastic gargoyles from the roof of Notre Dame.

That wouldn't be enough, though, enough nor half a part;
There'd be shells because they're sorrowful, and pansies since
   they're wise,
The smell of rain on lilac-bloom, less fragrant than your heart,
And that small blossom of your name, as steadfast as your
   eyes.

Sapphires, pirates, sandalwood, porcelains, sonnets, pearls,
Sunsets gay as Joseph's coat and seas like milky jade,
Dancing at your birthday like a mermaid's dancing curls
— If my father'd only brought me up to half a decent trade!

Nothing I can give you — nothing but the rhymes —
Nothing but the empty speech, the idle words and few,
The mind made sick with irony you helped so many times,
The strengthless water of the soul your truthfulness kept true.

Take the little withered things and neither laugh nor cry
— Gifts to make a sick man glad he's going out like sand —
They and I are yours, you know, as long as there's an I.
Take them for the ages. Then they may not shame your
   hand.

Dedication page and dust jacket from Benét's 1922 novel (Rutgers University Library)

What I propose is this. It is only two hours by train from New Haven to New York. I could read and make a short typewritten report on a minimum of fifteen ordinary-sized novels—say 3000 pages—a week. Reading and reporting on what I have read are my greatest abilities—the things I do best. What are they worth to you? Considering the expenses of the trips to New York it seems to me that fifty dollars a week, to be increased at your discretion if I showed exceptional ability, is a fair price, though I should, of course, be very glad to discuss any other proposition you might care to make.

As for the most important and intangible thing of all—literary taste—for that it is, of necessity, impossible to give references. I enclose sample criticisms of "The Unwilling Vestal" by Edward Lucas White and "Java Head" by Joseph Hergesheimer. The following five names are those of people who know me and would give something more accurate than the usual laudatory and meaningless letter of recommendation.

   Sinclair Lewis
   Major Charles G. Norris, Camp Dix.
   Ellwood Hendrick, 139 E. 40 St.,
     New York City
   Professor C. B. Tinker, 1330 F. St.,
     Washington D.C.
   William Rose Benét

I can also refer you to Dean F. S. Jones of Yale College, Mr. Leland Harrison, Office of the Counsellor, State Department and Brig. Gen. O. C. Horney, Office of the Chief of Ordnance, Washington D.C.

As I wish to make a definite decision about re-entering college as soon as possible, I should greatly appreciate a prompt reply.

         Very sincerely yours,
         Stephen Vincent Benét

The Unwilling Vestal by Edward Lucas White. Good, exciting, rather machine-made historical romance. Point of view original in two respects, first, the quite colloquial and modern speech of the characters—there are no laborious "By Bacchus!"s dragged in for effect—second, the Christians and their persecutions do not take the center and most of the rest of the stage, as they have in nearly every other novel of ancient Rome. The plot is ingenious and holds the interest firmly, the people are either well-drawn or frankly types. Altogether a "good yarn" and hard to put down when once begun. Should be quite popular, though not a tremendous success as the public seems to be rather off historical romance *per se*.

Java Head by Joseph Hergesheimer. Should be very seriously considered. Hergesheimer's great quality is color, yet color with definiteness, there is nothing sloppy or splashy about his work. The plot is absorbing and adventurous—it alone is enough to keep you reading—but the people are the enduring success, for they are real. And more than this, when you finish the book you realize that an entire and amazing period of American life—that just at the beginning of the clipper-ship era has been reconstructed before you, almost unawares. The story is told without padding, yet so skillfully that it gives an effect of leisure and ease. A very near approach to a novel of the first rank. Should appeal to a not over-large but very worth-while audience, and while it probably won't exceed three editions at first, there will always be a small steady demand for it.

November 30, 1918.

Dear Sir:

We have been considering the proposition made in your recent letter, but we cannot at present avail ourselves of your services. All our reading is now done by our regular staff of readers, and there are not any vacancies on that staff. We thank you for writing to us, and we shall keep your name on file, so that we may address you later, if there should be a vacancy.

Very truly yours,
Henry Holt and Company.

* * *

Although Benét did not obtain a position as a reader for Holt and Company, his poetry collection Heavens and Earth *was accepted by the firm less than two years later and published in 1920. Benét had originally written the poems that make up* Heavens and Earth *as an alternative to the traditional M.A. thesis in graduate school at Yale. Trade-department head Lincoln MacVeagh wrote to inform Benét of the decision to publish his collection.*

March 31, 1920

Dear Mr. Benet:

It gives me great pleasure to say that we shall be glad to publish your volume at present entitled HEAVENS AND EARTH. We can give you a royalty of ten per cent on the published price of the book until two thousand

Illustration from Benét's Young People's Pride
(Rutgers University Library)

copies are sold and fifteen per cent afterwards, undertaking ourselves the cost of manufacture, distribution, advertising, etc. If this is satisfactory to you, will you let me know as soon as possible?

I should very much like to have you come to New York at the earliest opportunity, provided you care to have us publish the book on the terms above named, as I would like to go over the manuscript with you, poem by poem, in the hope that you may find to your liking a few suggestions I may be able to make from the publisher's point of view.

Hoping to hear from you, I am

Sincerely yours,
[Lincoln MacVeagh]

Mention of the Fifth Avenue jewelry store Black Starr and Frost in one of Benét's poems in Heavens And Earth *was a source of some concern for Holt and Company. Benét wrote in response to MacVeagh's request that the poem be omitted from the volume.*

[Undated]

Certificate of limitation and title page for the collector's edition of the long narrative poem that was Benét's last publication with Holt and Company (Princeton University Library)

I don't see any particular reason for omitting "Black Starr & Frost," it is as good as the rest of that bunch of poems. If I had used an imaginary and unromantic name instead of a real and attractive one, there would have been no question; when Vachel Lindsay writes poems to movie queens and Osbert Sitwell ones about prominent London restaurants by name, why can't I get away with one jeweller? Maybe they'll send me a platinum wrist-watch.

Still uncomfortable, MacVeagh wrote directly to the jeweler.

May 26, 1920

Gentlemen:

We have contracted to publish a book of poems by Mr. Stephen Vincent Benet entitled *Heavens and Earth*. The manuscript contains the poem typed below which we hesitate to include without knowing whether it would convey any offense to you. Will you kindly let us know if you are agreeable to the poem's being published?

Hoping to hear from you, we are
Very truly yours,
HENRY HOLT AND COMPANY

NAME OF A NAME
(5th Ave.)

"Like a bubble of ice through windy heavens tossed
Floats the name from the ringing sign, Black, Starr and Frost.
It is Winter's seal on the forehead of Earth embossed,
It is wolves in the snow and a lost wind mocking the lost,
It is mufflers of white on the stoop-roofed houses afar
Where the blue-black pines are lit by a frosty star,
It is ski-runners leaping the hills to the ice-bear's den—
I shall read and read and say it over again.
It whispers the air like a wave that a berg has crossed,
'Be patient awhile, for I give you black star, and frost.'
I am caught in the freezing wheels of the North's cold car!
'Black, Starr and Frost! Black, Starr and Frost! Black, Starr—!'"

May 28, 1920.

Gentlemen:— (Attention of Mr. Lincoln McVeagh [sic])

In answer to your favor of the 26th inst. in regard to a poem by Mr. Stephen Vincent Bennett [sic], would say that we have no objection to this being published.

For our own information, we would like to know the particular brand of "hootch" the author used which enabled him to evolve his ethereal effusion.

Yours very truly,
Black, Starr & Frost.
A. N. Frost
Vice-President

* * *

Late in 1923 Elliot Holt wrote with news of a royalty payment for Benét's second novel, Young People's Pride *(1922).*

November 2, 1923

Dear Steve:

I think all of us have a sort of fellow feeling about how hard it is to get money in this world. I know that nobody appreciates that exigency more than I do. So I thought you might like to have what royalty *Young People's Pride* has earned up to the first of the year over and above our advance to you of $750. I am accordingly forwarding through Brandt our check for $275., and I hope, Steve, it may come in handy and will constitute a bit of a New Year's surprise for you.

My very best to you and Rosemary.

Yours,
[Elliot Holt]

* * *

With the passage of years, sales of Benét's novels declined to the point that Herbert Bristol wrote him explaining that the printing plates were to be melted down.

May 6, 1936

Dear Sir:

We regret to report that the sale of BEGINNING OF WISDOM and YOUNG PEOPLE'S PRIDE, have fallen to such an extent that the electrotype plates must now be disposed of. We wish to give you the opportunity to buy these plates for $20.00 F.O.B., New York, N.Y. Since the storage vaults are badly crowded now, we must ask you to let us know your decision by June 1, 1936. If we do not hear from you by that date, we will assume you are not interested in purchasing the plates.

Yours truly,
[Herbert Bristol]
HENRY HOLT AND COMPANY

WALTER DE LA MARE

HOLT AND COMPANY BOOKS BY DE LA MARE: *The Listeners, and Other Poems* (New York: Holt, 1916); **first edition,** *The Listeners, and Other Poems* (London: Constable, 1912);

Peacock Pie (New York: Holt, 1917); **first edition,** *Peacock Pie* (London: Constable, 1913);

Motley, and Other Poems (New York: Holt, 1918); **first edition,** *Motley, and Other Poems* (London: Constable, 1918);

Collected Poems, 1901–1918 (New York: Holt, 1920); **first edition,** *Poems, 1901 to 1918,* 2 volumes (London: Constable, 1920);

Down-Adown-Derry (New York: Holt, 1922); **first edition,** *Down-Adown-Derry* (London: Constable, 1922);

The Veil, and Other Poems (New York: Holt, 1922); **first edition,** *The Veil, and Other Poems* (London: Constable, 1921);

A Child's Day (New York: Holt, 1923); **first edition,** *A Child's Day* (London: Constable, 1912);

Selected Poems (New York: Holt, 1927);

Walter de la Mare (BBC Hulton)

Illustration by Dorothy P. Lathrop for the poem "The Fairy in Winter," from the Holt and Company edition of de la Mare's 1922 collection Down-Adown-Derry
(Rutgers University Library)

Stuff and Nonsense, and So On (New York: Holt, 1927); **first edition,** *Stuff and Nonsense, and So On* (London: Constable, 1927);

Poems for Children (New York: Holt, 1930); **first edition,** *Poems for Children* (London: Constable, 1930);

Poems, 1919 to 1934 (New York: Holt, 1936); **first edition,** *Poems, 1919 to 1934* (London: Constable, 1935);

This Year, Next Year (New York: Holt, 1937); **first edition,** *This Year, Next Year* (London: Faber & Faber, 1937);

Memory, and Other Poems (New York: Holt, 1938); **first edition,** *Memory, and Other Poems* (London: Constable, 1938);

Collected Poems (New York: Holt, 1941; London: Faber & Faber, 1942);

Rhymes and Verse: Collected Poems for Children (New York: Holt, 1947); **first edition,** *Collected Rhymes & Verses* (London: Faber & Faber, 1944).

English novelist, poet, short-story writer, and children's author Walter de la Mare (1873–1956) was a Holt and Company author (though not exclusively) for many years. Much of de la Mare's work is characterized by dream-like, romantic imaginings. Unable to attend college after graduating from the St. Paul's Cathedral Choir School in London, de la Mare took a job in 1890 as a clerk in the statistics department of the Anglo-American Oil Company, a division of Standard Oil, in London. He remained there until 1908, when he was granted a Civil List pension of one hundred pounds a year. This pension enabled him to retire and devote himself completely to writing. Much of the correspondence in the de la Mare file of the Holt and Company Archives consists of reprint requests. De la Mare observed in 1932 that "[t]he fact that so many applications for permission to use poems are received suggests that they must be now fairly well-known in schools...."

* * *

Critic R. L. Mégroz describes de la Mare as he appeared in 1923.

Walter de la Mare at fifty years of age conveys by his personal presence first of all an impression of controlled power and an infinite catholicity of interests. He does not talk, and he does not look "like" the frail bloom of the dream-born poetry which is generally associated with his name. There is nothing obviously apparent of the seer's wildness about him which popular imagination has associated with the typical poet. But a recognition of the fitness of things follows the first shock of surprise which almost inevitably is experienced by an admirer of his poetry meeting him in the flesh. His square-set figure, about 5 feet 8 inches in height, and his strong face belong to a man possessing the tremendous energy which goes to work of creative imagination. Only gradually does one learn to see the shadowiness and haunted light of elusive moods which pass over his mind and conversation, or to perceive some of the remote associations of his casual remarks.

—*Walter De La Mare: A Biographical and Critical Study* (London: Hodder & Stoughton, 1924), pp. 1–2

* * *

De la Mare sent condolences to Henry Holt Jr. a month after his father's death. Eric Pinker was de la Mare's London agent. Otto Kyllmann was the chairman of de la Mare's English publisher, Constable.

29th March, 1926.

My dear Mr. Holt,

Thank you very much for your letter. I hope Eric Pinker gave you my message. I was grieved to hear of the death of your father. It was disappointing not to be able to see you again while you were in England, but I hope there will be another opportunity soon.

I doubt very much if I have sufficient material to make up a new volume of verse. But as soon as I get an opportunity, I will look through what there is, and let you have a definite reply. In any case I am grateful to you for the suggestion, and if it be possible should be delighted to take advantage of it.

I discussed with Kyllman [sic] some little time ago the possibility of bringing out in one volume, at a reasonable price, the poems as a whole. The debatable point being whether from a financial point of view this would be a good plan, as it would probably entail a loss of the current sales of the present volumes. The alternative would be to publish in one volume all, or most, of the poems *not* intended for children; i.e. excluding "A Child's Day," "Peacock Pie," and "Songs of Childhood." One advantage of that would be that it would not entail any arrangement with Longmans. Would you let me have your views about this. I might then have another consultation with Kyllmann.

With best wishes and remembrances from us all,

Yours sincerely
Walter de la Mare

* * *

De la Mare wrote Brickell in 1930 to correct the title on the forthcoming Holt and Company edition of Poems for Children, *first published that year by Constable. Brickell cabled in reply two weeks after de la Mare's letter: "SENDING THREE HUNDRED SHEETS POEMS FOR CHILDREN STOP TYPOGRAPHICAL ERROR SORRY."*

20th May, 1930.

Dear Brickell,

I was very much dismayed on opening the package of sheets for signature to find that the letter-press runs "Three Hundred Copies of 'Poetry for Children.'" The title we arranged was "Poems for Children," and I have a letter from you in which you actually mention this particular title. It looks as if the printers have made a mistake. You will agree, I know, that there is so great a difference between the two things, Poetry and Poems, that we can hardly allow it to stand.

There is no violent hurry, of course, so I am sending this and before returning the sheets will await your answer. If you cable *Yes* I will send them on, if *No* I shall take it that you are sending other sheets to sign.

All good wishes
Yours sincerely,
W. de la Mare

Dust jacket for de la Mare's 1927 collection (Between the Covers Rare Books catalogue)

Later that summer Brickell wrote to report on the progress of the American edition of Poems for Children, *informing de la Mare at the same time that the author photograph he had sent had already been used in the Holt and Company edition of Forrest Reid's* Walter de la Mare: A Critical Study *(1929).*

July 28, 1930

Dear Walter de la Mare:

The proofs have reached us and the book is underway. We are going to make it as good-looking as we possibly can.

> THIS collection includes all the poems that appeared in *The Veil* and in *The Fleeting*; also, with a few exceptions, the contents of *Flora*, a book of drawings by Pamela Bianco with illustrative poems, seven of which were reprinted in *The Veil* and one in *The Fleeting*. It also includes four songs from *Crossings: a Fairy Play* for children, and seven rhymes from *The Three Royal Monkeys* or *The Three Mulla-Mulgars*. The remainder of the volume consists of 'Occasional Poems' and 'Rhymes for Children,' which, with few exceptions, were written after the publication of *Poems 1901-1918*. No epitaphs have been included from *Ding Dong Bell*, and no rhymes from *A Child's Day* (which were written to accompany the illustrations), or from *Stuff & Nonsense*. Many of the poems, moreover, here reprinted, would have been omitted—for reasons which will be only too evident to the reader—had not the friend to whom this book is affectionately dedicated insisted that the term 'collected' means—just that.
>
> vii

De la Mare's prefatory note from the 1936 Holt and Company edition of his Poems, 1919 to 1934, *first published in England in 1935 (Rutgers University Library)*

I appreciate your sending me the photograph. It has been used here, however, as a frontispiece for Forrest Reid's book.

Faithfully yours,
[Herschel Brickell]

28th July, 1930.

Dear Brickell,

Your letter of July 17th has just reached me. You don't say whether you think the Introduction on the whole fits the case, but I hope this is so.

I agree with the alterations you suggest. But as you will see from the book-proof I am enclosing I have added a note of acknowledgments. This to all intents and purposes covers the same ground as the first paragraph of the introduction which you suggest printing separately. I think on the whole it would be better to use the new note, page vii, and to drop the first paragraph on Page xix altogether. In that case the first four lines of the Introduction, Page xix, might run as follows:

> Books, like most things in this world, have names given to them. But unfortunately their names—or, to give them a more high-sounding word, their titles—sometimes seem to claim a good deal more for their

If you agree, would you see that the printer makes this correction, as at present Page xix stands as it did. I have suggested to Kyllmann that the English edition follows suit, but it would not matter if to this extent the two differ.

You will notice that the page numbers have to be put in the "Contents." Two new poems have been added at the end of the book, but I think the proof I am sending you makes all this clear.

All greetings and remembrances,
Yours sincerely,
W. de la Mare

An exchange of cables settled a question of typographical style for the American edition of Poems for Children.

22 August 1930

PRINTER HAS FOLLOWED AMERICAN STYLE OF DOUBLE QUOTES THROUGH POEMS FOR CHILDREN STOP DO YOU MIND STOP IF SO WILL CHANGE PLEASE CABLE COLLECT.

---

25 August 1930

DOUBLE QUOTES ALL RIGHT DELAMARE.

***

In 1940 Sloane corresponded with Frances Pindyck, de la Mare's American agent, about a prospective volume of de la Mare's collected poems, which was published the next year. Alfred A. Knopf had published two of de la Mare's early books.

April 15, 1940

Dear Miss Pindyck:

Well I am glad to hear that the A. A. Knopf business was so easily settled. It seems to me that the next thing we need is a complete manuscript from Mr. De La Mare with all the changes and emendations that he wants made. You see, when one is doing a collected volume it is important to have it all letter-perfect the first time since it serves as the infinitive volume.

Naturally I would much prefer to do this volume without paying any advance for it since I think (a) we have done well by Mr. De La Mare's verse over the years and he has a continuing income from it, (b) the

THE APPLE CHARM

I PLUCKED an apple, sleek and red,
  I took his three black pips,
Stuck two upon my chin, and brow,
  And t' other on my lips.

Dick on my chin, the other Tom,
  But O—my loved to be—
Robin that couched upon my lip
  Was truest unto me.

SEEN AND HEARD

LOVELY things these eyes have seen—
  Dangling cherries, in leaves dark-green;
  Ducks as white as winter snow,
  Which quacked as they webbed on a-row;
  The wren that with her needle note
  Through blackthorn's foam will flit and float;
Clear dews whereon the moonbeams softly gloat
  And sun will sheen.

Lovely music my ears have heard—
  Catkined twigs in April stirred
  By the same air that carries true
  Two notes from Africa, 'Cuckoo';
  And then, when night hath darkened again,
  The love wail of the willow-wren,
And cricket rasping on, 'Goode'n—goode'n,'
  Shriller than mouse or bird.

Ay, and all praise would I, please God, dispose,
For but one faint-hued cowslip, one wild rose.

Two of de la Mare's "Rhymes for Children" from Poems, 1919 to 1934 *(Rutgers University Library)*

---

purpose of an advance is simply to enable the author to live and conduct his affairs while finishing the book. In this case, the book is finished and Mr. De La Mare is not in need of a subsidy, or so I presume. However, I suppose if worse came to worse, the directors here would be willing to advance $500 against the new book, or rather against the De La Mare royalties. A situation of this sort is one of the disadvantages of dealing through a third person—I cannot tell how the gentleman feels, and how urgent he believes an advance to be.

Once the manuscript is in hand we shall proceed to set the book. I suggest that you arrange with Mr. De La Mare to have us read the proof on it since shipping galleys back and forth right now is a chancey business. Until I see how many pages there are going to be in the whole book, and until we determine the format, I cannot make any very final offer on it in the way of a royalty scale. In general of course a big collection of poetry such as this would be is fairly expensive to make, and has a relatively small sale. It is quite important for us to recover our plate investment on the book, and the volume is not one which is going to sell willy nilly like the Housman. We are going to have to work on it quite hard.

           Sincerely yours,
           [William Sloane]
           MANAGER, TRADE DEPARTMENT

* * *

In 1941, in response to a query from University of Washington English professor Edward Wagenknecht, Sloane explained that Holt and Company was unable to come to terms with de la Mare for a collection of his children's poems. The next three American editions of de la Mare's books were published by different firms. In 1947, however, Holt did publish his Rhymes and Verse: Collected Poems for Children.

                        March 28th, 1941

Dear Professor Wagenknecht:

    . . . .

A very sad thing has just occurred between ourselves and Mr. de la Mare. We have been unable to come to an agreement on the terms for his book of Children's Poems and the upshot I am afraid will be that he will take it elsewhere. His minimum figures both for royalty and for advance are in excess of those we pay to any one on our list, and publishing Mr. de la Mare has been a losing proposition for us. Deeply as we esteem the honor of publishing him the present state of the book business is such that the one thing worse than losing a distinguished author is to enter into contracts which will simply constitute a continuing drain upon the resources of this department. I feel very unhappy about this and I think that Mr. de la Mare has made a mistake, one which he would not have made had it been possible for the two of us to sit down and talk the situation over. . . .

    Sincerely yours,
    [William Sloane]
    MANAGER, TRADE DEPARTMENT

A. E. HOUSMAN

HOLT AND COMPANY BOOKS BY HOUSMAN (THROUGH 1947): *Last Poems* (New York: Holt, 1922); **first edition**, *Last Poems* (London: Richards, 1922);

A Shropshire Lad, authorized edition (New York: Holt, 1922); **first edition**, *A Shropshire Lad* (London: Kegan Paul, Trench, Trübner, 1896; New York: John Lane/Bodley Head, 1897);

The Collected Poems of A. E. Housman (New York: Holt, 1940); **first edition**, *The Collected Poems of A. E. Housman* (London: Cape, 1939).

Questions of textual accuracy, sibling rivalry, a roguish English publisher, and competing American publishers figure in the story of the poet A. E. Housman's relationship with Holt and Company. Alfred Edward Housman (1859–1936) was an unassuming man who described himself as a professor of Latin and declined royalties on reprints of his poems. He was educated at St. John's College, Oxford University, and then went to work in London at Her Majesty's Patent Office as a civil servant from 1882 to 1892. He was professor of Latin from 1892 to 1911 at the University College, London. From 1911 until his death in 1936 Housman was the Kennedy Professor of Latin at Trinity College, Cambridge University. Housman is often referred to as a "scholar-poet," although he is probably best known for his poetry. His life was examined in the play The Invention of Love *(1997), by Tom Stoppard. The following letter to the editor of the* New York Herald Tribune *(11 May 1936) considers Housman's poetic reputation.*

 A letter is printed in your issue of May 10 in which Mr. George Meason Whicher suggests that con-

A. E. HOUSMAN, FROM A DRAWING BY FRANCIS DODD, 1926

Frontispiece for the Holt and Company edition of The Collected Poems of A. E. Housman, *published in 1940 (Rutgers University Library)*

trary to popular legend A. E. Housman did not become famous in a single night. He concludes with the question, "Will not some of the young men who used to murmur his verses in the '90s come forward with their testimony?" The '90s were over long before my time, but I come armed with facts to support Mr. Whicher's contention.

 Five hundred copies of the first edition of "A Shropshire Lad" were printed in 1896 at Mr. Housman's own expense. Mr. Grant Richards, who was later to publish the authorized English edition, was so deeply impressed by the poems that he tried to prevail upon the poet to give him the publication rights. Housman declined for the present, stating that when the first edition had been sold there would be time to talk about reprinting it. Two years passed, Mr. Richards tells us, before the 500 copies of the first edition of "A Shropshire Lad" were exhausted.

 There were some at the time, however, who were charmed by the poems. What is perhaps the first review of the book was written by Hubert Bland, the

Socialist, and was published in "The New Age" for April 16, 1896. Bland writes:

"The little volume before us contains, on well-nigh every page, essentially and distinctively new poetry. The individual voice rings out true and clear. It is not an inspiring voice, perhaps; it speaks not to us of hope in the future, of glory in the past, or of joy in the present. But it says and sings things that have not been sung or said before, and this with a power and directness, and with a heart-penetrating quality for which one may seek in vain through the work of any contemporary lyrist, Mr. Henley perhaps excepted. . . .

"This direct expression of elemental emotions, of heart-thoughts, if we may be permitted the phrase, is the dominant note of all Mr. Housman's work as it was of Heine's alone among modern singers. . . . Mr. Housman's artistic range is limited—it lies within narrow limits, even—but within those limits it is little short of consummate. In this small volume there are many flawless stanzas and not a few flawless poems. . . .

"As we have said, Mr. Housman's poetry is wanting in the note of gladness; that is to say, it is not the highest poetry. But it comes astonishingly near the highest."

These remarks, printed immediately upon publication of "A Shropshire Lad," apparently roused little curiosity in England. It is interesting to note that in a letter penciled from his hospital bed a few days before his death Housman wrote that Bland's was "the best review I ever saw of my poems."

It is to Mr. Richards that we owe the beginning of Housman's popularity. When the first edition was exhausted in 1898 the first authorized edition was published, bearing the imprint of Grant Richards, Ltd. Now that the book was officially launched upon its career, William Archer reviewed it in the "Fortnightly Review" for August 1, 1898:

"It is long since we have caught just this note in English verse the note of intense feeling uttering itself in language of unadorned precision, uncontorted truth. Mr. Housman is a vernacular poet if ever there was one. . . . But if he is vernacular he is also classical in the best sense of the word. His simplicity is not that of weakness, but of strength and skill. He eschews extrinsic and factitious ornament because he knows how to attain beauty without it. . . . He will often say more by a cunning silence than many another poet by pages of speech. That is how he has contrived to get into this tiny volume so much of the very essence and savour of life." In a note appended to a later issue of the review, Archer states that Housman's position among the English poets is secure.

The tinder of public curiosity was finally ignited. Slowly but surely, in the opening years of this century, Housman was coming into his own. The authorized edition had been reprinted several times.

The first American edition of "A Shropshire Lad" was published by Lane in 1897. The enthusiasm of Americans was aroused from the beginning, though it was not widespread. One of the first reviews of the book printed in this country was written by Louise Imogen Guiney and was published in "The Chap-book" for Feburary 1, 1897. The American poet writes of her English contemporary:

"Some of us, in these days of make-believe greatness, having given up the search for continents, are yet glad to cruise about painfully, on the chance of reaching one happy isle. Such an isle, rough rock below and flowered orchards above, is Mr. A. E. Housman's first book: a sort of careless, indignant jewel, bedded in the sea, asking for no mariner's eye. Surely, one of the finest distinctions left to the laity is such a lonely discovery, the identification of a bit of literature. And 'A Shropshire Lad' is literature. . . .

"*O Sancta Simplicitas!* Lovely verbal austerity, heroic, quiet, better than dramatic feeling! As old Basse, in his elegy, sweetly invited Spenser and Beaumont, in their Abbey graves, to lie nearer and make room for a greater third, so may our minor bards stand back a little for a young stranger who, in quality, has hardly a rival among them, and touch their rusty lances to the rim of his shining shield."

Reprints of the Lane edition followed in 1900 and 1901, and from 1906 to the present day there have been more than a dozen pirated editions. The authorized Holt editions (1922) of "A Shropshire Lad" and "Last Poems" have been reprinted many times.

The late Edwin Arlington Robinson told me a short time before his death that he found a copy of the first English edition of "A Shropshire Lad" in a Boston bookstore in 1896, before it was published in this country. He was immediately impressed, he said, by the beauty of the poems, and made numerous notes and allusions in his copy before passing it along to his friend, William Vaughn Moody. Robinson remarked of Housman in 1934 that he "could think of no other living writer whose work is likely to live longer, if as long."

Housman's fame was at its peak during the war. It has often been remarked that, excepting FitzGerald's "Omar Khayyam," no other poetry was oftener quoted in the trenches than the songs from "A Shropshire Lad." Something in them appealed essentially to the soldier.

"Oh tarnish late on Wenlock Edge,
Gold that I never see;
Life long, high snowdrifts in the hedge
That will not shower on me."

The demand for "A Shropshire Lad" and "Last Poems" increased immeasurably during the depression. No less than seven pirated editions of the former book have been printed in America alone since 1931. Despite the joyless note there is an ineluctable anodyne in every poem.

"Little is the luck I've had,
And oh, 'tis comfort small
To think that many another lad
Has had no luck at all."

Yes, Housman's fame grew slowly but surely. "The man of flesh and soul" is gone, but the thrilling "heart-thoughts," the marvelous quiet music which he left us will never be forgotten.

Houston Martin
Philadelphia, Pa.

* * *

*All of Housman's correspondence to Holt and Company was written from Trinity College, Cambridge. The question of whether or not to combine Housman's two volumes of poetry (*A Shropshire Lad *and* Last Poems*) into a single volume (he wished to keep them separate always) was touched on in his earliest correspondence with Holt.*

4 Jan. 1925.

Dear Sirs,

I have received a press-cutting from the New York Times of 7 Dec. 1924 which reads as follows:

"A. E. Housman's 'A Shropshire Lad' and 'Last Poems' have recently been published by Henry Holt & Co. in a limp leather edition, so that it is now possible to buy the complete works of the poet in a uniform de luxe edition."

I beg that you will inform me without delay whether this statement is true.

I am yours faithfully
A. E. Housman

January 16, 1925

Dear Mr. Housman:

We hasten to reply to your letter of the 4th of January and to inform you that we made up, for the Christmas season, a gift edition of 500 sets of "A Shropshire Lad" and "Last Poems" uniformly bound in red leather stamped with gold, with gold tops, and boxed. We realise with regret that owing to the rush of the Christmas season you were not apprised of this fact, and hope you will accept our apology. Under separate cover we take pleasure in sending you the two volumes with our compliments, and trust they will please you.

We are, with kindest regards,
Sincerely yours,
HENRY HOLT AND COMPANY

2 Feb. 1925

Dear Sir,

I am much obliged by your letter of the 16th Jan. and by the books you have been kind enough to send me, from which I see that the press-cutting gave me a false alarm. I have no objection at all to the issue of the two books as companion volumes (which seem to me, though I am no judge, to be very pretty): what I should have objected to, and not allowed in England, is the combination of the two sets of poems in a single volume.

If you reprint *A Shropshire Lad* I should be obliged if you would make two alterations which have been made in England since 1922:–No. XXXVIII line 10 for "Thick" read "Loose." No. LII line 9 for "long since forgotten" read "no more remembered."

I am yours very truly
A. E. Housman

In No. XXXIV line 3 there ought to be no inverted comma. The inverted comma in line 1 is right. Printers cannot understand this.

* * *

In acknowledging receipt of a royalty payment from Holt and Company, Housman explained that he did not want the firm to charge for the use of his poems in adaptations or anthologies.

13 May 1927

Dear Sirs:

I beg to acknowledge receipt of draft for £69.8.8 royalties.

I observe the item 20 dollars for "use of poems" Nov. 23. I suppose this is for poems included in an anthology or set to music. I do not make any charge for such use in England, and I do not wish to do so in America.

Yours faithfully
A. E. Housman

* * *

After Housman's death his heirs, his agent, Holt and Company, and Alfred A. Knopf engaged in an imbroglio over the disposition of subsequent American editions of his poems. Housman's brother Laurence wrote Thornton at Holt explaining the decision to place the American edition of More Poems *(1936) with Knopf.*

May 29th 1936

Dear Mr. Thornton

I am sorry you should be disappointed over the publication of the New Poems having gone to Messrs. A. Knopf. But when Mr. Pinker says this was done on *my* recommendation, he puts the cart before the horse. I am not my brother's executor: The executors put the whole business side of the publication of the selections I am empowered to make into the hands of Messrs. Pinker. *They* (Messrs. Pinker) recommended Messrs. Knopf as the publishers: and I acquiesced. I sent them word of your request for an interview directly on hearing from you; so there was no delay on my part over giving you the chance of placing your case before them.

I hear from Messrs. Pinker today that in the event of a complete edition of the poems being published, Messrs. Knopf will make arrangements with your firm.

Yours sincerely
Laurence Housman

Three years later Sloane, who had by this time replaced Thornton as Holt and Company trade-department head, wrote Alfred A. Knopf about the plan for Holt to publish a collected edition of A. E. Housman's poems.

March 30, 1939

Dear Mr. Knopf:

I have debated a considerable while before writing this letter, but it seemed to me that there could be no harm in sending it to you. It has to do with the A. E. Housman situation.

It seems a great pity that a poet like Mr. Housman whose total output is so small should not be available to poetry readers and libraries in a single collected volume. Such a volume would probably not be very large nor expensive to make, but I believe that it would have a good and continuing sale over a long period of time.

Whatever your feelings and the feelings of the people here may have been about the situation which arose at the time of the publication of "More Poems," it seems to me that this is water under the bridge, and I hope that you will not have any impression that this letter stems from that episode because it does not. I wasn't here then and my interest in suggesting that we get together to discuss the possibility of a single Housman volume is partly a business belief that such a book could be profitable to both of us, and partly a professional feeling that we rather owe it to Mr. Housman's public to get out such a book somehow or other.

Probably the Eric Pinker episode complicates the whole situation a good deal. Shortly before his incarceration I had lunch with him and asked what he thought Laurence Housman's reaction to such a project would be. He seemed to feel sure that it could be arranged and promised his cooperation. Probably any such idea as mine could not be accomplished in a hurry because I do not suppose Mr. Laurence Housman has found another agent, but I think that it is something we ought both to keep in mind, and some time when you are free why not give me a ring and let's get together on it, perhaps at lunch, I still owe you a lunch, incidentally, in return for a perfectly magnificent one which you once gave me two or three years ago.

. . . .

Sincerely yours,
[William Sloane]
Manager, Trade Department

Housman's sister Katharine, who did not know that Thornton had by this time left Holt and Company, wrote him in the summer of 1939 to discuss the plan for a collected edition of her late brother's poems.

4th July, 1939.

Dear Mr. Thornton.

I have some private information that I should like to send you, though I am not sure that it will interest you. I am not betraying any confidence in writing to you about it, but I do not want my name mentioned if you make any enquiries in connection with it.

A few weeks ago my brother Laurence Housman came to see me to ask whether I had any objection to a complete collection of poems by A. E. Housman being published? He consulted me because I share the copyrights with him and my sister. We all know that A.E.H. strongly objected to any proposal for printing *A Shropshire Lad* in one volume with his other poems; but that personal wish was not among the restrictions which he put upon his Executors; and now that poems have been printed in two others sources (*More Poems;* and *Additional Poems,* in Laurence Housman's *A.E.H.* Memoir;) it seems reasonable that a collected edition should be made. It is the publisher Cape who is pressing for this, and the Literary Agent James Pinker. I do not know how they would arrange with the Richards Press for their rights in *Last Poems;* but after I had given my consent to negotiations for a collected edition, I wrote to my brother Laurence and said that if an American edition was contemplated I wished Pinker to be asked to communicate with Henry Holt Ltd [*sic*], before arrangements were concluded elsewhere. I said that as A.E.H. had allowed that firm to publish the only *authorized* edition in America

A Shropshire Lad

LIV

With rue my heart is laden
    For golden friends I had,
For many a rose-lipt maiden
    And many a lightfoot lad.

By brooks too broad for leaping
    The lightfoot boys are laid;
The rose-lipt girls are sleeping
    In fields where roses fade.

A Shropshire Lad

XIII

When I was one-and-twenty
    I heard a wise man say,
'Give crowns and pounds and guineas
    But not your heart away;
Give pearls away and rubies
    But keep your fancy free.'
But I was one-and-twenty,
    No use to talk to me.

When I was one-and-twenty
    I heard him say again,
'The heart out of the bosom
    Was never given in vain;
'Tis paid with sighs a plenty
    And sold for endless rue.'
And I am two-and-twenty,
    And oh, 'tis true, 'tis true.

Two poems from The Collected Poems of A. E. Housman *(Rutgers University Library)*

of *A Shropshire Lad,* and *Last Poems,* I thought that consideration ought to be given to them—and I had thought so when Pinker disposed of the rights in *More Poems* to Knopf. My brother replies that no question of an American Edition has been raised, and he does not care about one. That is all very well for him, he is a rich man, but it seems to me it would be silly, if there is to be a collected edition, to forego American profits. The difficulty to me seems to be that Knopf's has rights in *More Poems;* & Henry Holt Ltd, I suppose has some rights as publishers of the only authorized edition in America of *A Shropshire Lad* and *Last Poems;* but I have no knowledge of how such interests work when there is a combined edition. I am anxious that you should be informed in good time that there may be such a project; and you are at liberty to make enquiries if you wish to—but without mentioning my name. I do not think that Knopf's knows anything about it yet.

    Yours faithfully,
    Katharine S. Symons (Mrs. E. W.)

    July 18, 1939

Dear Mrs. Symons:

    Your letter of the 4th of July addressed to Mr. Richard Thornton has come to my desk. Mr. Thornton is no longer connected with Henry Holt and Company so I am undertaking to answer the points which you raise.

    As a matter of fact, I wrote to Mr. Alfred Knopf some month's [*sic*] ago suggesting that he and I should have a long talk together about presenting a plan for a one volume edition of Mr. Housman's poetry to the English agent. I received no answer to this suggestion of mine, but the information conveyed in your letter indicates that the idea is in the air.

    Yes, I did know that A.E.H. was opposed to having all his poems collected in one place. At the same time, and with every respect to his memory, it seems to me that his poetry has taken such a notable place in English literature that the question is now out of the sphere of personal preferences. Undoubtedly the general public over here would like a single complete volume of Housman—I think that we should long ago have put the two books which we published together in a single set of covers if it had not been for the author's feeling, and now that there are three books, our unifying them seems even more important to me.

The general purpose of this letter then is to assure you that we are very much interested in doing a single complete Housman volume, and that we are willing to enter into any reasonable arrangement with Mr. Knopf about it, and that the whole project is one, which, as you see, we were already engaged upon before your letter arrived.

As you know, our own record in connection with the publication of A.E.H.'s poems is an honorable one. We have sold them very successfully, but more than that, we have paid royalties all the way through on the SHROPSHIRE LAD in spite of the copyright flaw. Mr. Housman himself recognized this position of ours when he granted the caption authorized edition to our publication of the book. Just how the details of a complete work could be arranged is not clear to me at the moment, and will not be until such time as I have had a chance to talk with Mr. Knopf at more length about it.

We are extremely grateful for your letter, and please feel sure that we shall keep in touch with you regarding the whole situation. I am today writing to Mr. James Pinker and no doubt his reply will clarify some of the moot points.

Rest assured that your name will be kept entirely confidential in this whole matter.

Sincerely yours,
[William Sloane]
MANAGER, TRADE DEPARTMENT

Private & confidential.

18th September, 1939.

Dear Mr. Sloane,

On July 18 last you wrote me a kind letter in reply to one that I had addressed to Mr. Richard Thornton. It did not need a reply, but I was much interested to know that the project of publishing a collected edition of the poems of my brother A. E. Housman had been raised by your firm before I wrote to you on the subject. Since then, difficulties arose between the English publishers, and it looked as though a collected edition could not be arranged. More recently, I have heard from my brother, Laurence Housman, that agreement has been reached, and also that an American edition is being arranged. This, I hope, means that your negotiations with Mr. Alfred Knopf have borne fruit, and that an American edition will be produced whether this dreadful War prevents publication in England or not. I do not see that the War should be detrimental to publication in America, but, in case publication comes there *first,* I want you to know the extent of the collection that has been projected by my brother Laurence or my sister and myself (jointly concerned in the copyrights). Our proposal is to let the collected volume contain, in separate sections, *A Shropshire Lad, Last Poems, More Poems,* and *Additional Poems.* The last section would comprise the poems in Laurence Housman's "A.E.H." memoir, together with some scattered poems previously published, and the three Greek Odes translated by A.E.H. for A. W. Pollard's Volume of Greek Odes. This means a very considerable assembly of poems from scattered sources, and I hope America will not have anything less than this complete collection.

Thanking you for the letter you wrote to me in July, I remain,

Yours sincerely,
Katharine E. Symons.

October 2, 1939

Dear Mrs. Symons:

Thank you for your letter of the 18th of September. I am happy to tell you that negotiations on the collected A. E. Housman are proceeding rather rapidly. It is our hope to publish the book next spring, and we are making what I regard an extremely generous offer to the Housman estate concerning royalties. This offer will no doubt reach you in due course through Mr. Ralph Pinker.

Today I have written to Mr. Jonathan Cape urging him to advise me in complete detail of the editorial structure of the Cape book so that our own may be as nearly like it as possible. It looks, too, as though we shall be able to reach an agreement with Mr. Knopf about the book.

Because you have been personally kind and thoughtful in this matter, I should like you to know that the total offer which we are making to the estate and to Mr. Knopf is one which is almost unjustifiably generous, and that we shall make almost no profit at all on the book. This is not the conventional publisher's cry of "wolf, wolf" but a genuine statement of the case.

We know these must be trying days for you and everyone in Britain. As you probably know already there are a great many people over here who are wishing you well and hoping for a speedy and victorious termination of the war.

Very sincerely yours,
[William Sloane]
MANAGER, TRADE DEPARTMENT

In a letter to Frances Pindyck, Walter de la Mare's American agent, Sloane mentioned the difficulties in proceeding with the collected edition of Housman's poems.

November 16, 1939

Dear Miss Pindyck:

....

[T]he A. E. Housman business is one of the reasons why editors slowly acquire softening of the brain. Every time I write to Cape they say "we shall be sending you preliminary galleys in a couple of weeks we hope," but they never tell me the precise editorial layout of the book, how many pages it is going to be, nor whether or not certain particular Housman items are in it etc. This is pretty nearly essential because our contracts and arrangements on the book preclude any additional editorial expense, and it would be almost folly to publish a collected Housman without being sure that it was editorially kosher.

    Sincerely yours,
    [Willliam Sloane]
    MANAGER, TRADE DEPARTMENT

***

The Collected Poems of A. E. Housman was finally published by Holt and Company in 1940, a year after the Jonathan Cape edition was published in England. A letter from a Housman enthusiast in Madison, Wisconsin, pointing out a minor error in the Holt edition inadvertently touched off concern about copyright.

March 7, 1940

Gentlemen:

I am very much interested in your *Collected Poems of A. E. Housman,* which I have recently been looking over. My interest is more than casual, for I have done quite a bit of work on Housman, both with his poetry and his classical papers, my chief bachelor work having to do with his poetic theory and practice.

Congratulations for having done so well in giving the public a definitive text, the one thing that would have most pleased the great poet. I notice, however, that you have used the 1890 text of the translations, which contains one error—an extremely minor one, to be sure, but one which obviously bothered Housman a great deal. In 1933—forty-three years after the publication of Pollard's *Odes*—Professor Housman wrote to Professor Agard of the University of Wisconsin classics department, giving him permission to reprint the translation of Euripides in an article he was then writing; "but," he adds, "if your text is that of A. W. Pollard's *Odes* I will ask you to make a correction. In the second line there is a misprint, *Far-seeking,* which should be *Far seeking,* as *seeking* is a noun substantive." Forty-three years after Pollard's *Odes* appeared Housman was still worrying about a hyphen!

I am sure, that if in succeeding editions you removed the hyphen the soul of Housman would rest more easily—and I would feel that I had a small part in helping to make Housman's text closer to the perfection he always strived for.

    Sincerely yours,
    Harry Runyan

P.S. The letter quoted from above is in the possession of Professor Walter R. Agard, Chairman of the Classics Department, The University of Wisconsin. . . .

March 13, 1940

Dear Mr. Runyan:

We certainly appreciate the spirit which prompted your recent letter about the Collected Poems of A. E. Housman. This book, as you probably surmised, was carefully edited by a number of the best Housman authorities in England, and we followed punctuation and design of the poems to the letter. It thus becomes a ticklish matter for us to know whether to leave off the hyphen which you suggest should be omitted. However, we shall probably do so since the point seems well taken.

Incidentally I am somewhat curious to know how a copy of the book fell into your hands so long in advance of publication. I sincerely trust that it was not a copy which you bought because the sale of books in advance of publication dates may invalidate a copyright in this country.

With many thanks for your kindness and the valuable information in your letter, I am

    Sincerely yours,
    [William Sloane]
    MANAGER, TRADE DEPARTMENT

3/19/40

Dear Mr. Sloane:

Regarding my access to *The Collected Poems of A. E. Housman* in advance of its publication date: I discovered through the monthly book news review that the book was to be published in March. So because I am extremely interested in everything relating to Housman, I asked the manager of a local book store if I could see a copy as soon as he received it, knowing that most publishers send several advance copies out to bookstores. In addition to being particularly interested in the writer, I also help review books for our local college daily. I was allowed to examine a copy sometime after they arrived, so I could gather material for a review. I was entirely ignorant of the factors governing copyright law, but even so, considering that the book was not purchased at the time, I hope there has been no invalidation of any regulations.

It was, I believe, ten days before official publication that I saw the book, and the translations were my immediate concern, for I knew that Housman's letter concerning the error was not known to anyone but Professor Agard and myself at the time, and I was curious to know if the original edition was used as the text for the new collected edition.

I hope that I have not unintentionally done anything seriously wrong, for I am too happy about the splendid new edition to feel that I was at fault concerning it.

Sincerely yours,
Harry J. Runyan

A representative of Brown's Book Shop in Madison, the store from which Runyan acquired an advance copy of The Collected Poems of A. E. Housman, *wrote Sloane to explain why the store had changed its policy on strict observance of publication dates.*

March 22, 1940

Dear Mr. Sloane:

Mr. Harry J. Runyan . . . has shown us your letter of March 13 which expresses surprise that he was able to see a copy of the new edition of Housman's Collected Poems so far in advance of actual publication date. Mr. Runyan was very much disturbed about the matter, and rather than put him to any unnecessary trouble, I have thought it best to write you and explain why the copy was sold before the day of publication.

Several years ago we scrupulously observed publication dates on all books. Our reason for discontinuing this practice was because we found that we were losing sales to other Madison book stores who were not as conscientious as we were in observing publication dates. Naturally this being the case, we had no choice but to put our books in stock as soon as they were received from the publishers.

I know that assurances have been given at various times that publication dates would be carefully observed, but I also know that such assurances were without foundation in fact and therefore quite worthless.

If the publication date is really an important matter to you in a town of this size, my suggestion would be that you ship your new books to your Madison accounts so that they arrive here on the date of publication. I know from experience that there is no other way in which the matter can be satisfactorily adjusted.

I assume, of course, that the various stores here are all buying from you direct as we are. If any of them are ordering through one of the wholesalers, then the matter of publication dates has practically no meaning. As an illustration of this, we were unable to obtain copies of the 69¢ edition of GONE WITH THE WIND from Macmillan's Chicago office until more than two weeks after they had been first offered for sale in Madison by another book store. Naturally in order to protect ourselves, we had to order copies from the same source which supplied this other store—namely the Western News Company in Chicago. It would seem to me that publishers should have absolute control over the distribution of their books or a complete elimination of publication dates as such.

I feel sure that you will appreciate our position in the matter and understand that we are quite helpless to do anything about it.

Very truly yours,
BROWN'S BOOK SHOP

March 25, 1940

Gentlemen:

We are most obliged for your courteous letter of March 22. My reason for writing to Mr. Runyan was merely to check up on the question of sales in advance of publication, because in the case of a book of English origin, such as the Housman, it is possible permanently to invalidate a copyright by selling it in advance of publication date. I am sorry to hear that other Madison book stores have been breaking publication dates, and may I say right now that it seems to me to be the worst sort of business policy? Publishers plan their whole campaigns on books to come to a peak on publication day, and it is silly to be offering for sale books about which the customer will have heard absolutely nothing.

We very much appreciate the kindness of your letter, and please believe that there was no criticism of you implied in our correspondence with Mr. Runyan.

Sincerely yours,
[William Sloane]
MANAGER, TRADE DEPARTMENT

ROMAIN ROLLAND

HOLT AND COMPANY BOOKS BY ROLLAND:
Jean-Christophe: Dawn, Morning, Youth, Revolt, translated by Gilbert Cannan (New York: Holt, 1910); **first edition**, *Jean-Christophe*, part 1, 4 volumes

Romain Rolland (Photograph by Almassy)

(Paris: Ollendorff, 1905–1906)—comprises *L'Aube, Le Matin, L'Adolescent,* and *La Révolte;*

Jean-Christophe in Paris: The Marketplace, Antoinette, The House, translated by Cannan (New York: Holt, 1911); **first edition,** *Jean-Christophe à Paris,* part 2 of *Jean-Christophe,* 3 volumes (Paris: Ollendorff, 1908)—comprises *La Foire sur la place, Antoinette,* and *Dans la maison;*

Jean-Christophe: Journey's End: Love and Friendship, The Burning Bush, The New Dawn, translated by Cannan (New York: Holt, 1913); **first edition,** *Jean-Christophe: La Fin du voyage,* part 3 of *Jean-Christophe,* 3 volumes (Paris: Ollendorff, 1910–1912)—comprises *Les Amies, Le Buisson ardent,* and *La Nouvelle Journée;*

Musicians of To-day, translated by Mary Blaiklock (New York: Holt, 1914); **first edition,** *Musiciens d'aujourd'hui* (Paris: Hachette, 1908);

Some Musicians of Former Days, translated by Blaiklock (New York: Holt, 1915); **first edition,** *Musiciens d'autrefois* (Paris: Hachette, 1908);

Handel, translated by A. Edgefield Hull (New York: Holt, 1916); **first edition,** *Haendel* (Paris: Alcan, 1910);

Beethoven, translated by B. Constance Hull (New York: Holt, 1917); **first edition,** *Vie de Beethoven* (Paris: Hachette, 1907);

The Fourteenth of July and Danton: Two Plays of the French Revolution, translated by Barrett H. Clark (New York: Holt, 1918); **first editions,** *Le Quatorze Juillet* (Paris: Editions des Cahiers, 1902) and *Danton* (Paris: Revue d'Art Dramatique, 1900);

The People's Theater, translated by Clark (New York: Holt, 1918); **first edition,** *Le Théâtre du peuple: Essai d'esthétique d'un théâtre nouveau* (Paris: Suresnes, 1903);

Colas Breugnon, translated by Katherine Miller (New York: Holt, 1919); **first edition,** *Colas Breugnon* (Paris: Albin Michel, 1919);

Clerambault: The Story of an Independent Spirit during the War, translated by Miller (New York: Holt, 1921); **first edition,** *Clerambault: Histoire d'une conscience libre pendant la guerre* (Paris: Albin Michel, 1920);

A Musical Tour through the Land of the Past, translated by Bernard Miall (New York: Holt, 1922);

Pierre and Luce, translated by Charles de Kay (New York: Holt, 1922); **first edition,** *Pierre et Luce* (Paris: Ollendorff, 1918);

Annette and Sylvie, translated by Ben Ray Redman (New York: Holt, 1925); **first edition,** *L'Ame enchantée,* part 1, *Annette et Sylvie* (Paris: Ollendorff, 1922);

Summer, translated by Eleanor Stimson and Van Wyck Brooks (New York: Holt, 1925); **first edition,** *L'Ame enchantée,* part 2, *L'Eté* (Paris: Ollendorff, 1923);

The Game of Love and Death, translated by Eleanor Stimson Brooks (New York: Holt, 1926); **first edition,** *Le Jeu de l'amour et de la mort* (Paris: Editions du Sablier, 1925);

Mother and Son, translated by Eleanor Stimson Brooks (New York: Holt, 1927); **first edition,** *L'Ame enchantée,* part 3, *Mère et fils,* 2 volumes (Paris: Albin Michel, 1927);

Palm Sunday, translated by Eugene Löhrke (New York: Holt, 1928); **first edition,** *Pâques fleuries* (Paris: Editions du Sablier, 1926);

Les Léonides, translated by Löhrke (New York: Holt, 1929); **first edition,** *Les Léonides* (Paris: Editions du Sablier, 1928);

The Death of a World, translated by Amalia De Alberti (New York: Holt, 1933); **first edition,** *L'Ame enchantée,* part 4, *L'Annonciatrice,* part 1, *La Mort d'un monde* (Paris: Albin Michel, 1933);

A World in Birth, translated by De Alberti (New York: Holt, 1934); **first edition,** *L'Ame enchantée,* part 4, *L'Annonciatrice,* part 2, *L'Enfantement,* 2 volumes (Paris: Albin Michel, 1933).

Books by the French writer, musicologist, and humanist Romain Rolland (1866–1944) helped to bring distinction to the Holt and Company list from 1910 to 1934. The remarkably prolific Rolland enjoyed wide popularity and official recognition in his time. In 1915 he won the Nobel Prize in literature for the multivolume novel Jean-Christophe *(1905–1912) and for his articles (collected as* Au-dessus de la mêlée *in 1915 and translated as* Above the Battle *in 1916) expressing his opposition to World War I. The terms of Rolland's first contract with Holt and Company stipulated that he was to see the translations of his work before they were published. This condition was not pro forma: Rolland made lists of detailed corrections for the translations.*

* * *

In 1927 Holt and Company published a thirty-one-page pamphlet titled Romain Rolland: A Brief Account of the Man and Critical Notes on His Novels. *In it a short biographical sketch is followed by selected reviews of several Rolland titles.*

Romain Rolland Writes a Charming Romance on Life in Burgundy
Edwin Francis Edgett

There is something especially gratifying finding at least a piece of fiction written by a European that is wholesome, vivid with the joy of life, in love with the sunshine and with work and play and trees and birds and tools and people. So many novels voicing the dreariness and weariness of life, jaded, cynical, and sneering, have come out of the various countries of Europe that American readers, with the brighter, more hopeful, and more youthful outlook upon life, have come to expect that kind of perverse and unwholesome picture from modern European writers, whatever the period of which they write. So accustomed to the point of view have they become that "Colas Breugnon" will be as surprising to them as it is delightful. It is true that the life it deals with is that of three hundred years ago, but it is good to find pictured such a character as old Colas, with his gay and sane outlook upon life, no matter in what period of world history he is placed.

The story recounts the life Colas Breugnon, carpenter and woodworker in a village of Burgundy, through a year or more, in his own language. As he writes he glances back over the fifty years he has covered, and remembers events and scenes in which he took joy at the time. He describes his work and his pleasure in it, his family, his surroundings, narrates some of his daily doings, tells of important events in the village life. And always he is gay, happy, good-natured, full of laughter and jest, so bubbling with delight in living, seeing, working, in whatever the day may bring forth, that his pleasure irradiates all that he writes. He loves his food and his wine, and he gets drunk occasionally, and this, too, he enjoys. He loves everything out of doors, sunshine and rain, birds, grass, trees, the soil of Mother Earth, and to be in intimate touch with them gives him keen pleasure. He loves his little grandchild and his daughter and, in less measure, his sons, and he talks and jests and laughs with them all. He does not love his wife and never has, but he feels for her respect and compassion and friendliness, and in his retrospective moods he tells the story of why he married her and why he did not marry the girl of his youthful choice. But most of all he loves his work, with tools and hands and sensitive touch, upon wood. It would be difficult to find anywhere a more graphic and more truthfully revealing depiction of the pleasure which the sane-minded worker can take in work than old Colas Breugnon sets down now and then in the course of history about himself....

He is a philosopher, too, and he makes himself many sane and wise observations, the basis of them being usually his own satisfaction in life, the world and himself....

Toward the end of his narrative misfortunes befall him, the plague sweeps the region and he falls ill of it; his beloved granddaughter almost dies, there are riots in the course of which much of the town is burned, he suffers a serious accident, his old wife dies. But through it all he keeps his gay good humor, his love of a joke, his pleasure in living and working, his philosophical habit of mind. And at the end he declares "The only fault I have to find with this good life of ours is that it is too short. I don't feel as if I had had my money's worth, and though I may be told that I ought to be satisfied with what has fallen to my lot, I can only say that I should like to have more, a second slice of cake, if I could get it without making too much fuss."

The story is as different from "Jean-Christophe" as one color is different from another, and the author explains in a little foreword that he wrote it in the reaction following the completion of the previous work, when he "felt in absolute need of something gay, in the true Gallic spirit." He had gone to his native place in Burgundy for the first time since his youth, and contact with the soil, he says, "roused all the Colas Breugnons under my skin, so that I was forced to speak for them." At any rate, M. Rolland has created a new and vital and most amusing and interesting character, of a sort that modern life very greatly needs to read about, that most healthily minded readers will find lovable and delightful. The book was written before the war and was printed and ready to appear, but was held back until the conflict was ended. "The grandchildren of Colas Breugnon," he says, "have just emerged as heroes and victims of a bloody epic, only to show an unquenchable flame to the world." And M. Rolland's book shows that their courage and spirit and undaunted souls were no new thing, but a part of that which is and has been France through all the centuries.

–"Romain Rolland Writes a Charming Romance on Life in Burgundy," *Boston Transcript,* 14 December 1910

The Story of a Temperament from Infancy to Manhood
Francis E. Regal

The six hundred pages of "Jean-Christophe" merely carry us across the threshold of the hero's life. One volume has been made of the four volumes in which the original French version of the story appeared, and there are, to come, we believe, two more in Mr. Cannan's highly commendable and effective translation. In Paris ten yellow-covered paper books will be necessary to bring Jean-Christophe's multitudinous adventures before the eager French public. In these first six hundred pages we accompany Jean-Christophe Kraft through the four early stages of his career, and as he is only twenty when the last word is said, it may easily be seen that his life and M. Rolland's record of it are very full.

In "Jean-Christophe" the novelist begins at the beginning, at the very moment when the new-born child is stirring in his cradle. "The child wakes and cries, and his eyes are troubled. Oh! How terrible! The darkness, the sudden flash of the lamp, the hallucinations of a mind as yet hardly detached from chaos, the stifling roaring night in which it is enveloped, the illimitable gloom from which, like blinding shafts of light, there emerge acute sensations. . . ." This is Jean-Christophe as we first see him, and through twenty years of infancy and youth he pursues an erratic course in which his ideals are paramount and continuously at odds with common sense.

Coming of artistic parentage, he could, perhaps, be none other than he is. His father and grandfather were musicians, both known to all the musicians of the country from Cologne to Mannheim, and at the time of his birth they were living in a little town on the Rhine, not far from the Belgian frontier. . . .

It is to show the contrast between the ideal and the real, between the efforts of a genius to keep his face to the future and the repressing force of a community that looks inevitably backward, that M. Rolland has undertaken to give us this finely particularized record and closely analyzed study of the progress of a youthful life and intellect. That his scenes and characters are German appears to have no national significance, for the novelist is not satirizing a people or a community. He is merely showing us a characteristic section of humanity, and it [is] mere chance that it happens to be German. "More than anywhere else there reigned the distrust, so innate in the German people, of anything new, the sort of laziness in feeling anything true or powerful which has not been pondered and digested by several generations." Of the French, he will doubtless have no less to say when Jean-Christophe begins, at the age of twenty, his life in Paris.

Varied is the course of Jean-Christophe through these twenty years, and unreserved is M. Rolland in his record and commentary. While scarcely more than a baby, he is taught the piano by Melchior [Jean-Christophe's father] who sees glorious visions of a great future for the boy and an equally auspicious old age for himself as the father of a prodigy and a genius. But drink soon ends him, and the boy goes his own way—which is the way of an irresponsible prodigy and a genius. . . . He is the type of the irresponsible artist whose conduct in all its extremes is due to an unquenchable egotism that, while it may be preposterous, is at the same time pardonable. He lives in a world for which he is unsuited, and he beats his feeble hands against its bars in a futile attempt to escape to his Utopia.

For no moment does the novelist lapse from his consistent view of Jean-Christophe's character. While he offers us at times his own opinions, he does not obtrude them. . . . Despite its length, the narrative does not seem unduly long. Six hundred pages is a small amount of space over which to spread the events of twenty years. . . . There can be no doubt that "Jean-Christophe" is the most momentous novel that has come to us from France, or from any other European country, in a decade. . . .

–"The Story of a Temperament from Infancy to Manhood," *Springfield Republican,* 3 December 1911

A Great Contemporary Novel
Waldo R. Browne

The first of the three volumes containing "Jean-Christophe" in its English version appeared during the winter of 1910; the last, something less than a year ago. If the book bore any relation to the generality of current fiction, some apology for dealing with it so tardily might be in order. But when one has to do with *a work of genius,* apologies may as well be dispensed with.

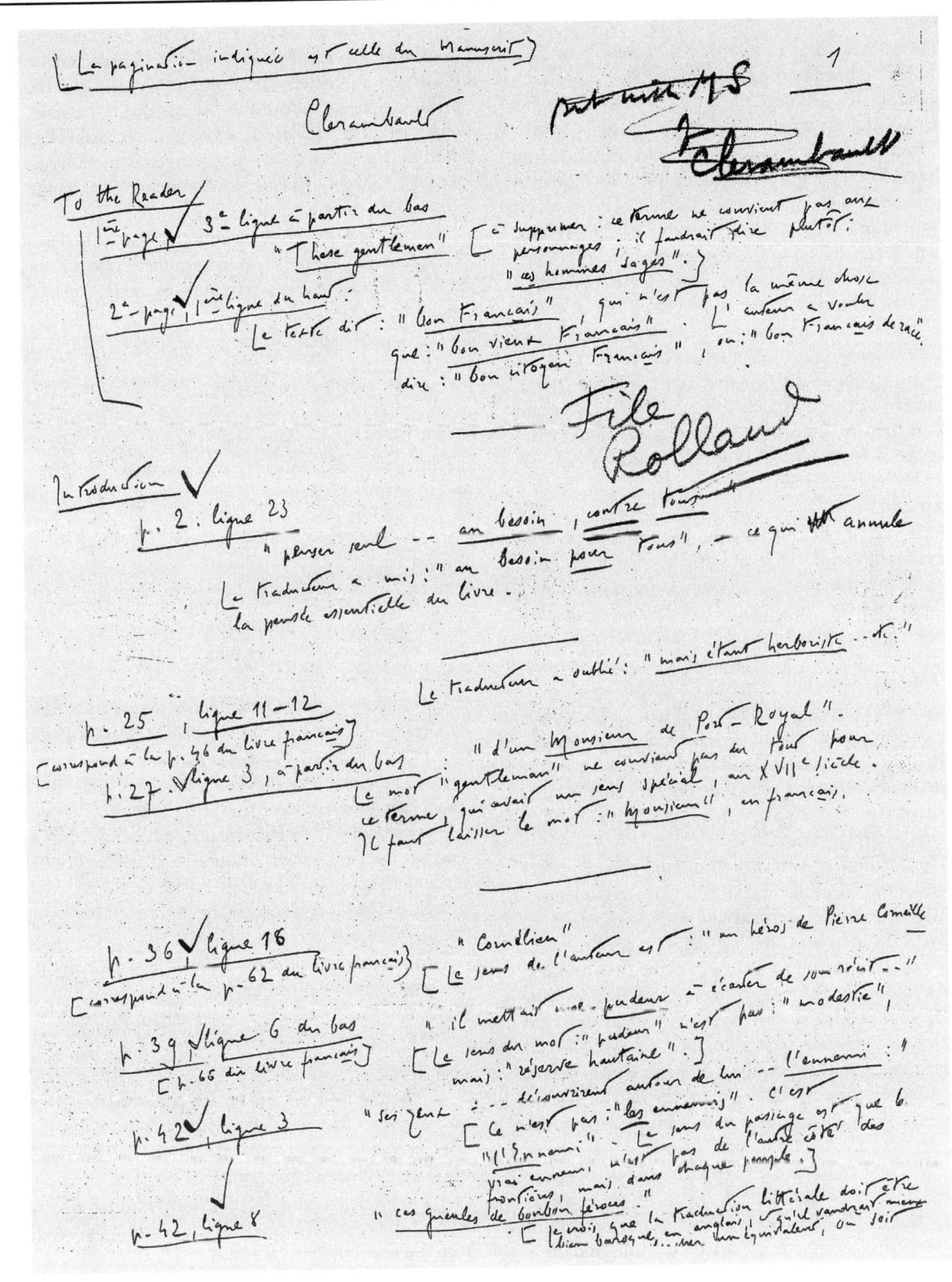

Page of Rolland's corrections for the 1921 Holt and Company edition of his 1920 novel Clerambault *(Princeton University Library)*

Compared with the great mass of current novels, "Jean-Christophe" is as an oak-tree rising above a field of summer grass. We should like to have been among the earliest to proclaim its qualities; that privilege having been missed, we can at least avoid a place among the tardiest.

Notwithstanding its recognition by Mr. Edmund Gosse and other high critical authorities as "the first great novel of the new century," the book seems as yet to have found only a small fraction of its destined English audience. Critical superlatives are too much soiled by ignoble use to carry much force nowadays; and as much as ever in the past, genius is still left to make its own way as it can. . . . Into the making of "Jean-Christophe" has gone the greater part of its author's life. The French original, in ten volumes, occupied nearly a decade in the publishing; and M. Rolland has said that the book was in conception many years before the first page was written—"Christophe only set out on his journey when I had been able to see the end of it for him.". . .

There is nothing of conventional plot in the book. Its connecting thread throughout is the history of a human soul. . . . But the book as a whole is far more than a biography of Jean-Christophe Kraft. It is an analysis, a synthesis, a criticism of present-day life in all of its most significant phases. It is an illuminating estimate of European culture, a sane and penetrative discussion of social tendencies, an inspiring handbook of ethics, a profound and eloquent treatise on music—and much else besides. . . . It is the ambition of M. Rolland's art to help the people "to live, to correct their errors, to conquer their prejudices, and to enlarge from day to day their thoughts and their hearts."

In conclusion, we shall venture the statement that with this work M. Rolland takes his place in contemporary literature as the spiritual and artistic successor of Tolstoy. He becomes the standard bearer around whom will rally the idealistic forces of the new century. More profoundly than any other yet offered by this century, the gospel he has given us will inspire and direct those who are toiling in the cause of human brotherhood,—"the free spirits of all nations who suffer, fight, and will prevail." That he assumes no authority, and claims no followers, only makes his leadership the more secure. He would have us understand almost before all else that human progress, like life itself, is not a smooth-flowing development, but a series of metamorphoses or transmutations; that each generation must wage its own battle for its own truth, and then without bitterness give place to a younger generation which perchance will carry the combat to a far different quarter of the field. . . . In no other way can we more fittingly take leave of *this noble book* than in the words of its author, appended as a preface to the final volume:

"I have written the tragedy of a generation which is nearing its end. I have sought to conceal neither its vices nor its virtues, its profound sadness, its chaotic pride, its heroic efforts, its despondency beneath the overwhelming burden of a superhuman task, the burden of the whole world, the reconstruction of the world's morality, its esthetic principles, its faith, the forging of a new humanity. . . .

"For myself, I bid the soul that was mine farewell. I cast it from me life [sic] an empty shell. Life is a succession of deaths and resurrections. We must die, Christophe, to be born again."
–"A Great Contemporary Novel," *Dial*, 1 March 1914

* * *

The following letter from Rolland was labeled "Une Copie," with a note that the original was in an "autograph box in Mr. H's room."

28 mars, 1913.

Cher Monsieur:

Je vous remercie de l'envoi des deux exemplaires do mon dernier volume de *Jean-Christophe*. Je trouve votre édition plus claire et plus soignée que l'édition de Londres.

Pourrais-je vous demander le premier volume? Je ne l'ai pas. Je n'ai reçu d'exemplaires de votre édition qu'à partir de *Jean-Christophe in Paris*.

Je suis en train de revoir, avec un ami, toute la traduction anglaise de M. Gilbert Cannan. J'enverrai mes corrections à M. Heinemann, qui m'a promis d'en tenir compte, dans ses rééditions de Jean Christophe. Je pense qu'il sera bon que vous fassiez de même. Malgré la valeur artistique, très réele, de la traduction, il y a un certain nombre d'erreurs.

Veuillez agréer, cher Monsieur, l'expression de mes sentiments très distingués.

Romain Rolland

(Dear Sir:

Thank you for sending two copies of the last volume of *Jean-Christophe*. I find your edition clearer and more carefully edited than the London edition [published by William Heinemann].

Could I ask you for the first volume? I do not have it. I have only received copies of your edition from *Jean-Christophe in Paris* [on].

I am currently reviewing, with a friend, all of Mr. Gilbert Cannan's English translation. I will send my corrections to Mr. Heinemann, who has promised to take them into account in future editions of *Jean-Christophe*. I think that it will be good if you do the same. In spite of

the indisputable artistic value of the translation, there is a certain number of errors.
    Faithfully yours,
    Romain Rolland)

* * *

MacVeagh wrote Rolland early in 1921 to thank him for his critique of Katherine Miller's translation of Clerambault: Histoire d'une conscience libre pendant la guerre *(1920), which Holt and Company published later that year as* Clerambault: The Story of an Independent Spirit during the War. *Ollendorff was Rolland's French publisher.*

                    February 2, 1921

Dear M. Rolland:
    Thank you very much for your criticisms of the translation of *Clerambault* which have arrived today. Doubtless the MS. will arrive shortly. We shall be glad to turn over your criticisms to the translator together with the general instructions contained in your letter, and we hope the result will be pleasing to you.
    We have just received from Ollendorff copies of their contract for the American edition of *Pierre et Luce*. We note that you desire the translation made by Miss Helena de Kaye, and we shall at once get in touch with her. Will you want to go over her translation as you have gone over the translation of *Clerambault?*
                      Sincerely yours,
                      [Lincoln MacVeagh]

* * *

Rolland wrote MacVeagh complaining about a negative review of the translated edition of Clerambeault *that also included an erroneous version of the subtitle.*

                    19 avril 1922

Cher M. MacVeagh
    Merci de votre lettre.
    Je lis, dans *The Freeman* du 12 avril, l'article . . . de Mrs. Elisabeth Shepley Sergeant sur *Clerambault.*
    C'est son droit de ne pas aimer l'oeuvre et de le dire. Mais est-ce aussi le droit de *The Freeman* de travestir du title du volume (en note de la p. 116), en sorte que "The Story of an *Independent* Spirit" devienne "The Story of an *Indifferent* Spirit"?
                    Bien cordialement à vous
                      Romain Rolland

Je quitte Paris, dans huit jours. A partir du 1er mai, veuillez m'adresser toute correspondence en Suisse, à Villeneuve (Vaud), Villa Olga.

Dust jacket for the 1925 Holt and Company edition of the 1922 novel that was the first volume in Rolland's novel sequence L'Ame enchantée *(Babylon Revisited Rare Books catalogue)*

(Dear Sir [MacVeagh],
    Thank you for your letter.
    I read Mrs. Elisabeth Shepley Sergeant's article on *Clerambeault* in the 12 April issue of *The Freeman.*
    It is her right not to like the work and to say so. But is it also the right of *The Freeman* to garble the title (on p. 116), so that "The Story of an *Independent* Spirit" becomes "The Story of an *Indifferent* Spirit"?
    Very cordially yours,
    Romain Rolland

I leave Paris in eight days. From May 1, please send any correspondence to me in Switzerland at Villeneuve (Vaud), Villa Olga.)

MacVeagh apologized to Rolland for the error in Sergeant's review in The Freeman, *including the text of a letter from Van Wyck Brooks, an associate editor for the journal (and, later, a translator of other novels by Rolland).*

May 12, 1922

Dear M. Rolland:

I have just received the following letter from "The Freeman"–

"My dear Mr. MacVeagh:

The error to which M. Rolland refers is, of course, a misprint, and I am extremely sorry that it should have occurred. I have looked the matter up and I find Miss Sergeant is in no way to blame for it: the title is correctly given in her manuscript, but the manuscript itself was copied by an outside typist, and the mistake is partly due to this fact. I do not wish to plead "not guilty" on our behalf ; but perhaps, if you are writing to M. Rolland, you will be so kind as to inform him that the error is ours and not Miss Sergeant's. In any case, I trust you will convey to him an expression of our regret.

Sincerely yours,"

(Signed) Van Wyck Brooks

I am also enclosing a number of duplicate copies of reviews of "Clerambault", which may interest you. "Pierre et Luce" having so recently appeared has not yet been reviewed in the important periodicals.

I wonder if you received, before you left Paris, a letter in which we requested a new photograph of yourself, if you could possibly arrange to send us one. We could make excellent use of it in the newspapers throughout the country.

Sincerely yours,
[Lincoln MacVeagh]

* * *

When the originally commissioned translation of Rolland's Annette et Sylvie *(1922), the first volume of his* L'Ame enchantée *(The Soul Enchanted, 1922–1933), turned out to be of poor quality, Elliot Holt wrote Rolland about their plans to hire a different translator. Holt and Company published* Annette and Sylvie, *translated by Ben Ray Redman, in 1925.*

May 16, 1924.

Dear M. Rolland:

We find ourselves in a most difficult quandary regarding Mrs. Victor Llona's translation of ANNETTE ET SYLVIE. We had, naturally, assumed this would be a capable and careful translation into English, which, in every way, would adhere to the true spirit of the original, and yet combine with it an idiomatic and gracefully contemporaneous use of English. We find that this is not the case. Not daring to trust entirely to our judgment in regard to the translation, although we felt it far from excellent, we sought the advice of some of the most noted critics in New York. Their opinions were the same as ours. One and all felt that it would be a grievous error to allow this translation to be printed. In the first place it would be most difficult for our public to fully appreciate and understand all the subtleties of French innuendoes and nuances which can be so well expressed in your language but are liable, unfortunately, to become banal and meaningless when changed to ours. In other words, it is almost necessary to reconstruct various adjectival and verbal phrases to fit what is customary in our own tongue. Mrs. Llona's translation is almost entirely literal. She uses, in adhering to this principle, phrases that are rough and abrupt and lack subtlety in English. Consequently, you can realize that our reading public would certainly not accept the book as favorably, in this condition, as they would if the translation were so smooth that they could forget it was a translation. When the manuscript first arrived, we felt that it was crude to the extent of needing at least slight revisions, and so we commissioned Miss Helen DeKay to read it carefully and make such suggestions here and there as might help the work, but she has now come to the decision that it is practically impossible to correct the text without having the whole book retranslated. We even went so far, in our hurry to issue the volume, as to have the type all set up. Of course, now, it must be entirely re-set.

For many reasons it seems best for us to have this done by a man, and now that we have discovered how very difficult the book is for translation, we should like to put it into the hands of no less an authority than Mr. Ernest Boyd. We are very desirous of having your permission to allow us to do this. Mr. Boyd is a linguist of the highest quality, being thoroughly familiar with seven languages. He has achieved great success with his translation of the complete edition of de Maupassant's work, recently published by Alfred Knopf in this country. Mr. Boyd is also a brilliant critic and is much sought after as a contributor to our literary magazines of the highest class. He has lived in France for a long time, is thoroughly in sympathy with French manners and customs, and, being so actively engaged in writing in America at the present time, he can, we feel, give us an excellent piece of work. He has a feeling for the rhythm and flow of sentences, and for poetic imagery that would enable him to render your French prose into English that would approximate it in beauty. That you may judge for yourself the high quality of his work, we are sending you one of his de Maupassant translations.

You appreciate, we trust, dear Monsieur Rolland, that all this places us in a most embarrassing situation.

Commercially, for you, naturally, as well as for ourselves, it would be more than unfortunate to adhere to Mrs. Llona's work. You understand, of course, that we have already paid her; that we have also paid Miss DeKay for editing a work with which she is herself not satisfied, and that we would be faced with a large additional expense in having Mr. Boyd do the whole work over again. But we feel that the future sales of the book would be greatly magnified by having such a prominent name as that of Mr. Boyd associated with the book, if you would allow us to have him do the entire series. He would deliver the translation to us so that we could publish the work early in August, and he would also be engaged on the second volume so that we might bring this out at the most favorable time, before Christmas. The books would then have the advantage of being both sold in the autumn season, which would be a material help, and the public would feel assured that the very best possible person had done the translation and was to continue L'Ame enchantée. If, however, we have to submit this translation for your revision it will, of course, delay us considerably. We assure you we will allow him to make no material omissions from the original. You could be confident that such a scholar as Mr. Boyd would always remain faithful to the spirit of your text if in some cases he had to deviate from the exact letter, in order to make the English graceful and idiomatic. We are therefore sincerely hoping that you will trust to our judgment in the matter, as it is to our mutual benefit to have the work done as well as possible. We therefore urge upon you the necessity of this course. We feel that our long association with you, and our reputation covering over fifty years, should assure you of satisfaction. We await your esteemed reply with interest.

    Sincerely,
    [Elliot Holt]
    HENRY HOLT AND COMPANY.

* * *

Elliot Holt wrote Rolland in September 1925 informing him of the publication of Summer, *the translated edition of the second volume in* L'Ame enchantée.

                      September 11, 1925

Dear Monsieur Rolland:—

    I have great pleasure in telling you that we published L'ETE (SUMMER) on the 8th of this month and we have received substantial assurances for an excellent sale. Our first printing was 10,000 copies, which I am sure you will realize at $2.50 for the volume is an excellent prognostication of its success. We personally are delighted with the book and feel that its substance lends itself, perhaps, to even more successful sales possibility than ANNETTE AND SYLVIE. We are reprinting ANNETTE AND SYLVIE for the third time, which constitutes 16,000 copies in all. . . .

    We were unable to procure Mr. Ben Ray Redman's services for the translation of the second volume. He has been complicated, unfortunately, by illness and divorce, as well as matters of business that have occupied him too much. However, we feel that Mr. Van Wyck Brooks has even a greater reputation in this country as a translator and is considered by all the critics as pre-eminently the one person in this country most suited to do your work. . . .

    We don't intend to bother you with signatures for the de luxe edition. Inasmuch as you have signed the books of the first volume, we feel confident that it will only be necessary to specify that this de luxe edition is identical with that of the first volume and it does not seem necessary to have it numbered. . . .

Dust jacket for the 1925 Holt and Company edition of the 1923 novel that is the second volume in L'Ame enchantée *(Bruccoli Clark Layman Archives)*

We have read with interest and pleasure your play, LE JEU DE L'AMOUR et DE LA MORT, and I have written today to Albin Michel asking if we might be considered for its publication in America. I hope that my writing direct to them has in no way complicated you Sir. I assume from the wording of our contracts that this was the correct procedure. We don't feel that we could offer an advance against royalties for the play, entirely on the basis that it is very hard to sell any plays, irrespective of their merit, in large quantities, but we told Messrs. Albin Michel that we would be very glad to pay a royalty of 10% and to publish the work as fittingly as we hope you have felt we have done with each of your works.

I am naturally most interested in the progress of the third volume of THE SOUL ENCHANTED, but I take from your letter that you will in all probability not finish it in time for publication next spring. . . .

With every good wish and expression of cordial feeling,

Sincerely yours,
[Elliot Holt]

* * *

Holt and Company received permission from Albin Michel to publish the American edition of Rolland's play Le Jeu de l'amour et de la mort *(1925) and submitted a translation to the author for his approval.* The Game of Love and Death, *translated by Eleanor Stimson Brooks (Van Wyck Brooks's wife), was published in 1926.*

December 29, 1925

My dear Mr. Rolland:

In accordance with the terms of our contract with you, we are submitting to you the translation of your play LE JEU DE L'AMOUR ET DE LA MORT. We feel that the translation is an excellent one and we hope that you will approve of it.

As we are trying to get our spring books to press as quickly as possible, may we request you to cable us the one word "approuve" if you are satisfied. We have retained a copy from which we shall print immediately upon word from you.

You will undoubtedly be glad to learn that we have sold 13,000 copies of ANNETTE AND SYLVIE and 9,000 copies of SUMMER.

We are, with our best wishes for a Happy New Year,

Faithfully yours,
HENRY HOLT AND COMPANY

December 30, 1925

My dear Mr. Rolland:

We are enclosing our draft for $60, as an advance on royalties on LE JEU DE L'AMOUR ET DE LA MORT. Albin Michel et Cie has asked us to send them their money in English pounds, but as we have instructions from you to send you yours in dollars, we are continuing to do so until we have further instructions from you. We should prefer, on account of our bookkeeping, always to send you American dollars.

Very truly yours,
HENRY HOLT AND COMPANY.

* * *

Eleanor Stimson Brooks also translated Mère et fils *(1927), the third volume of* L'Ame enchantée, *for Holt and Company.* Mother and Son *was published in 1927.*

22nd February, 1927

. . . .

I am returning you today the proofs of Mother & Son, and sorry that the holiday prevented them getting off sooner.

Since I have not my husband's experiences in proof-reading I shall be very glad to leave to your own judgement all such matters as initial letters, "End of book first" etc.

On page 126 I notice that in a speech of Annette's all the pronouns referring to the deity are spelled with a capital H. Of course this is the usual thing, but Annette speaks as a complete atheist and the mass of *Hs* gives an effect of exaggerated reference that seems at variance with the content of the paragraph. In the original French and in many of the new books the pronouns, used in this way, appear in lower case. However, I merely mention this, as I do not really feel competant [sic] to decide the question and will again be glad to trust to your judgement.

On pages 147 and 377 there are two expressions that I should be very grateful to have you verify for me in the original French.

On page 147 should not "*did*n't believe in the counqueror" [sic] be *did* believe?

On page 377 should not *replapla* be spelled *raplapla?*

I must apologize for giving you this trouble as in both cases you have followed the copy, but I have a horrid fear that the copy is wrong.

Very truly,
Eleanor S. Brooks
(Mrs. Van Wyck Brooks)

ALBERT SCHWEITZER

HOLT AND COMPANY BOOKS BY SCHWEITZER (THROUGH 1947): *The Forest Hospital at Lambarene,* translated by C. T. Campion (New York: Holt, 1931); **first edition,** *Mitteilungen aus Lambarene, Herbst 1925 bis Sommer 1927* (Strasbourg: Imprimerie alsacienne, 1928);

The Mysticism of Paul the Apostle, translated by William Montgomery (New York: Holt, 1931); **first edition,** *Die Mystik des Apostels Paulus* (Tübingen: Mohr, 1930);

Out of My Life and Thought: An Autobiography, translated by Campion (New York: Holt, 1933); **first edition,** *Aus meinem Leben und Denken* (Leipzig: F. Meiner, 1931);

Indian Thought and Its Development, translated by Lilian M. Rigby Russell (New York: Holt, 1936); **first edition,** *Die Weltanschauung der indischen Denker* (Munich: Beck, 1935);

African Notebook, translated by Russell (New York: Holt, 1939); **first edition,** *Afrikanische Geschichten* (Leipzig: F. Meiner, 1938);

Christianity and the Religions of the World, translated by Johanna Powers (New York: Holt, 1939); **first edition,** *Das Christentum und die Weltreligionen* (Bern: P. Haupt, 1924).

Although the books of theologian, medical missionary, and musician Albert Schweitzer (1875–1965) were not big moneymakers, Holt and Company considered it a privilege to be his publisher. Holt editor Gilbert Loveland was particularly supportive of efforts to raise money for Schweitzer's hospital in Lambaréné, in that part of French Equatorial Africa that is now Gabon. The hospital experienced devastating shortages during World War II. Holt and Company bound several copies of Schweitzer's The Forest Hospital at Lambarene *(1931) in special cloth to withstand the climate and insects of the tropics. The regular trade edition of the book was bound in a similar dark green cloth. Schweitzer's letters to Holt were written in German and subsequently translated for office use.*

4.9.30

Dear Mr. [Elliot] Holt,

I am answering your letter very late, but I think my friend Reiland will have kept you up to date on all questions which could interest you. Mr. Reiland manages all my affairs with editors, for I, unfortunately, have no time to concern myself with my business affairs. All that Mr. Reiland says and does in my name is therefore as if I myself say it and do it.

Since therefore you knew I have three English translations to offer you, on which I am now working, (1) a short biography with notes on the genesis of my various books, and with a résumé of the thoughts for which I

Albert Schweitzer at thirty-one (from James Brabazon, Albert Schweitzer, *1975; Thomas Cooper Library, University of South Carolina)*

strive. This will be translated by Mr. Campion. (2) The second volume of "On the Edge of the Primeval Forest," relating my activities in Africa from 1924–1929. Mr. Campion will translate this. (3) My work on St. Paul, which in English will be entitled "The Mysticism of St. Paul and of the Gospel According to St. John." The translation will be by the Rev. Montgomery, who translated my book on the Life of Jesus. I am asking my English editors, Mr. Black and Allen & Unwin to publish my books only in England and leave me free to publish them in America through an American publisher to be selected by Mr. Reiland. Please therefore show this letter to Mr. Reiland and discuss it with him. Thanks for your kind offer.

Yours very sincerely,
[Albert Schweitzer]

Please excuse a weary man for having written you so short a letter!

October 15, 1930

Dear Dr. Schweitzer:

We are happy to have your letter of the fourth of September, which names Dr. Karl Reiland as your literary manager in the States.

I have already conferred with Dr. Reiland. We have agreed as to the general procedure of bringing out your work in this country. Particular details in this procedure are being worked out now: Dr. Reiland is writing to both Mr. Montgomery and Mr. Campion; and our representative, Mr. Herschel Brickell, who goes to England within a fortnight, will seek an interview with Mr. Montgomery, and possibly will attempt to work out mutually acceptable terms with your English publishers.

We shall do all we can to meet Dr. Reiland's wishes for the American publication of your books.

Please accept an expression of our very great delight that we may have the privilege of publishing your work.

> Faithfully yours,
> [Gilbert Loveland]
> HENRY HOLT AND COMPANY

* * *

The following year Loveland sent Schweitzer the specially bound copies of The Forest Hospital at Lambarene.

August 18, 1931

We are sending to you, under separate cover, several copies of our edition of THE FOREST HOSPITAL AT LAMBARENE bound in a special cloth that will withstand the climate and insects of the tropics. Please accept these with our compliments.

The first copies of the regular trade edition, bound in a dark green cloth not greatly dissimilar from the cloth used in binding the special copies for you, have come from the printer last Friday.

Since Messrs. A. & C. Black had published the English edition, under the title MORE FROM THE PRIMEVAL FOREST, on April sixteenth, we were forced to publish our edition within four months of that date, or before August sixteenth, or lose the American copyright. The copy of the English edition which Frau Martin annotated was given to us by Dr. Reiland on the twenty-eighth of July. So you see that we had to make great speed, to get the book printed within three weeks! Mrs. Russell's photographs had not yet arrived (they are not here as I write), and we had to reproduce five illustrations from the half-tones of the English edition. Mrs. Russell's suggested emendations of Mr. Campion's translation we were able for the most part to incorporate. When we are ready to make the second printing—and that may be soon!—we shall make over several of the illustrations, and improve the style of the book in some respects. The edition as you receive it is the product of speedy work under great pressure.

Dr. Reiland has signed the various contracts as your American agent. Perhaps it would be well, however for us to draw new contracts, duplicates of those already executed by Mr. Reiland, and send them to you for your own signature. If that is your wish, please let us know.

Permit me to say to you that we are all of us delighted to have the privilege of publishing your books.

> Faithfully yours,
> Gilbert Loveland
> HENRY HOLT AND COMPANY

* * *

After Holt and Company published a third Schweitzer volume, Out of My Life and Thought: An Autobiography *(1933), Schweitzer wrote Loveland thanking him for a royalty payment.*

7th of May 1934

Dear Mr. Gilbert Loveland,

Thousand thanks for having sent the Royalty Statement of April 25, 1934 [and] for the cheque of 321 dollars. I acknowledge the receipt of both. I am happy to hear that "Out of My Life and Thought" has a good sale, I am glad for you too for you have taken the risk upon you for its publication. I wish you too will have satisfaction by it.—For the moment I stay in Günsbach where I may have rest whilst I am writing another philosophical book. Alas, I am not allowed to go over to America as I would like to do, before all I must do my work.

Dear Mr. Gilbert Loveland, when you send another Royalty Statement for me, would you have to kindness to add some commentary sentences to help me to understand better. It would be a great service for me. With kind thoughts

> Yours sincerely and thankfull [sic]
> [Albert Schweitzer]

* * *

Schweitzer's Indian Thought and Its Development *(1936) was not as successful for Holt and Company as his autobiography had been.*

31 October 1936

Dear Mr. Loveland:

A thousand thanks for your letter of the seventeenth of October and for the statement of account.

I am sorry that my book on Indian thought has not had the enthusiastic reception you had hoped. But I think it will still find its following in the States as it has in England, Germany, Sweden, and Holland. The people are not acquainted with such books in comparative philosophy, but I feel sure that this book will make its way.

My *Philosophy of Reverence for Life* has but taken its definitive form, but I will pursue my work on it diligently in Africa.

In the last few days I have made twenty-five records of Bach's organ music for the Columbia Gramophone Company (London) on a wonderful old organ here (in Günsbach.) It was very interesting to record these works on an organ which was in its prime in Bach's day[,] which for the main part dates from Bach's time.

Now another request, please. I am making use of the time before my departure for Africa to bring some order into my business affairs. Will you be good enough to tell me how much royalty Henry Holt and Company paid me in 1935, and also in 1936? I don't know whether my figures are exact. Then, about the accounts. I'm sorry to cause you so much trouble. But please send the statements to Herrn Dinner Obrist, Gotthardsstrasse 29, Basel, who is helping me bring order into my affairs. I shall be most of the time (up to my departure for Lambarene) in Switzerland. But the ordinary letters should be addressed to me always at Günsbach. Only the statements of account to Herrn Dinner.

With best wishes to you and colleagues, I am
Your devoted
Albert Schweitzer

* * *

Schweitzer continued to work at setting forth his philosophy of "reverence for life." Reverence for Life *(1965) was a posthumously published collection of his philosophical writings.*

October 27, 1937

Dear Mr. Loveland:

Thank you very much for your letter of the twenty-sixth of August, 1937. I am much indebted to you that you have gone to so much trouble for my wife and child. . . . Every evening I am working on my philosophy. It is something very beautiful to work and to write in complete quiet. That is essential to philosophy—no haste. Some of the chapters I have written over as many as six times since 1920. . . . Naturally I ask my publishers to give my wife, while she is in New York, whatever royalty may be earned by my books.

[Albert Schweitzer]

* * *

In what is annotated as a "rough translation of Dr. Alnert [sic] Schweitzer's letter of January 7 [1939] from Lambarene," Schweitzer speculated on the appropriate title for the forthcoming Holt and Company edition of his Afrikanische Geschichten (African Stories, 1938). *In the letter he erroneously refers to the title of the original edition as* Die Afrikanische Erzählungen (African Tales). *The Holt edition was published as* African Notebook *in 1939.*

Die Afrikanische Ergählungen [sic] have been published in Europe. I am very happy that they are selling well. Now the question of title for America. In the English edition *African Tales* was not considered interesting enough by Mr. Unwin and so at the suggestion of the translator, Mrs. Russell, *From My African Notebook* was substituted for that, which to me seems somewhat pretentious. Now Mr. Stanley Unwin writes that it would be a good thing if the American edition had the same title as the English edition. You can decide that. Naturally it would be a good thing if both editions had the same title. If you should use a different title from that of the English edition Mr. Unwin requests you to print the title of the English edition on the reverse of the title page. Then he might use the title of the American edition in his second printing. You can use your own judgment about which title to use. My principal with the translation is not to tamper with it very much, first because I don't know English very well, and second because all translators are terribly stubborn, so that the poor author has nothing to do but to remain in the background, which I for years have done and shall continue to do until my death.

Please greet all the gentlemen of the house, and give them my best wishes.

[Albert Schweitzer]

* * *

In 1939 Schweitzer wrote Loveland expressing his approval of the way Holt and Company brought out African Notebook *and* Christianity and the Religions of the World *(1939), the translation of* Das Christentum und die Weltreligionen *(1924).*

August 6, 1939

Dear Mr. Loveland:

Many thanks for your good letter of the ninth of January, 1939. I am in complete agreement with everything you have done in connection with the publication of *African Notebook* and *Christianity and the Religions* [sic]. I am delighted with the dress you have given to *African Notebook*. A thousand thanks for writing a Foreword to *Christianity and the Religions*.

> ### Cinematic Schweitzer?
>
> *William James Fadiman of M-G-M purchased a set of galley proofs of Schweitzer's* African Notebook *(1939) for consideration for a movie treatment. He wrote Holt and Company employee Eugene Healy with his assessment.*
>
> January 17th, 1939
>
> Dear Mr. Healy:
>
> I would like to express my appreciation for your kindness in permitting me to purchase a set of galleys on *African Notebook* by Albert Schweitzer.... This is an interesting and intelligently written anthropological study, bearing with it much of the wisdom and lore that life in Africa must have engendered in the author. It is definitely not screen fare except insofar as it presents isolated anecdotes and incidents that might be used in a picture with an African background; but I am nonetheless appreciative of your cooperation in letting me see it at such an early date.
>
> Yours sincerely,
William James Fadiman

My wife, who arrived here with Rhena [the Schweitzers' daughter] only a little time ago, has been telling me what you are doing for my work in the United States and how you are troubling yourself to win friends for it. My wife was deeply touched as she told me this. Thank you. In my anxieties and fatigue it is a comfort that my work and I can count on such friends.

I am glad that my daughter is seeing the hospital. She is having much fun with the six chimpanzees that play about the yard, and with the five antelopes. The youngest of the antelopes lives in my room. Even as I write this letter she is standing near my table. Recently she ate a page of my philosophical manuscript.

I am practicing again on the pedal-piano and am deep in the philosophical work.... Yes, I hope to come some day to the United States, to play Bach and Cesar Franck there. And it will be a great joy to see you.

I am sending this letter *via* Günsbach, as I always have the sad experience that letters which I send direct from here are frequently lost because of the valuable postage stamps.

My wife tells me that you are having trouble in reading my script (I have writer's cramp, inherited from my mother) and so I am having a copy of this letter made by typewriter.

With best wishes to you and yours,
Sincerely yours,
Albert Schweitzer

* * *

Early in 1940, at Schweitzer's request, Loveland sent him a summary of his Holt and Company publications, royalty rates, and royalties paid in 1938 and 1939.

January 18, 1940

Dear Dr. Schweitzer:

We have your letter of December 12, 1939, asking for certain information concerning the books which you have published with Henry Holt and Company. Below is a list of the seven books of your authorship which we have published, together with the date of the contract for each, the date of publication, the rate of royalty in per cent of catalogue price, and the royalty per copy in cents.

Title	Date of contract	Date of publication	Rate of royalty (Per cent of published price)	Royalty per copy (in cents)
THE FOREST HOSPITAL AT LAMBARENE	7/17/31	8/14/31	15%	.30
THE MYSTICISM OF ST. PAUL THE APOSTLE	7/17/31	12/14/31	12%	.36
OUT OF MY LIFE AND THOUGHT	7/17/31	2/14/33	15%	.37½
INDIAN THOUGHT AND ITS DEVELOPMENT	2/21/35	9/17/36	12%	.30
CHRISTIANITY AND THE RELIGIONS OF THE WORLD	1/13/39	3/22/39	10%	.12½
AFRICAN NOTEBOOK	8/25/38	4/5/39	12%	.24

The royalty clause in all your contracts states the royalty at a certain per cent of the published price. This published price is the list price, or catalogue price–the retail price which the individual purchaser must pay for the book at a bookstore. It is not the wholesale price which the bookseller pays us.

From January 1, 1938 to December 31, 1938, your books earned royalties amounting to $209.63. We withheld a ten per cent (10%) United States Government tax in the amount of $20.96. The net royalty paid to you in 1938 was, accordingly, $188.67. From January 1, 1939 to December 31, 1939, your books earned royalties amounting to $399.20. We withheld a ten per cent (10%) United States Government tax in the amount of $39.92. The net royalty paid to you in 1939 was, accordingly, $359.28.

We should like to call to your attention that these amounts were not paid to you entirely in cash. There were in both years deductions for books purchased by your wife and charged to your account.

We hope this information is clear and complete in order that you may make the necessary declaration to the French Government.

With all good wishes, we are
    Faithfully yours,
    HENRY HOLT AND COMPANY
    By
    [Gilbert Loveland]
    Vice President and Secretary

* * *

Gilbert Loveland was an active participant in organized efforts to send money and supplies to Schweitzer's hospital in Lamberéné, and the Holt and Company Archive includes copies of letters from Schweitzer (in translation) that were circulated among his supporters. A wartime letter to Reiland, his literary manager in the United States, was a cover letter for such a circular.

[Undated]

Dear Friend:

Yes, it has been a long time since we have exchanged letters. And you are so kind to write me. Since the war I have been so depressed that I am no longer writing. My energy is scarcely sufficient to do my work and to work at my philosophy book which I want to finish before dying. Therefore, thank you for your kind letter.

Meanwhile, you have certainly learned through friends that my daughter Rhena is married. It went very rapidly. The husband is a young Alsatian who works with a house that manufactures organs, Cavaille-Coll in Paris. For many years I have known him for he is a savant, as young as he is, in questions of organ construction, and he works according to my ideals. He came to Gumbail. There, my daughter became acquainted with him. He is a charming man. At the end of 1939 he was mobilized. But after having pneumonia, he is now in an office, where he has a very interesting job, thanks to his technical knowledge. As for myself, I have been at the Equator three years and I must remain here until after the war. The hospital continues to function, but naturally with great difficulty. We have three doctors, Dr. Goldschmid, myself, a lady doctor and nine nurses. To be able to help these poor sick people, in spite of the war, I count on my friends in America, because my friends in Europe aren't able to do much during the war. I am writing by the same mail to Prof. Everett Skillings, 47 South Street, Middlebury, Vermont. The most simple way to have gifts reach me is to make out a check in *dollars* to the name "Hospital of Dr. Schweitzer["] and to send the check by airmail to Lambarene. But indicate clearly that it should go directly from the U.S.A. by airmail via France to Africa, because otherwise it will be sent to France by ship. Then put on the envelope "By airmail from U.S.A. via France to Africa." At Port Gentil there is a bank where I am able to receive all checks.

I thank you again for all that you have done for my work and you are so good to take the trouble to send a circular to all my friends. My wife, as I have already written you in the summer, told me how my American friends are so good to my work. I am profoundly touched, because I must continue to help these unfortunate black people here. The misery is so great. Therefore, it isn't possible for me to come to the U.S.A. for lectures and concerts before the end of the war. Everything is so complicated here that it is necessary that I be at the head of my hospital to have it go on. But I believe I will have prepared several interesting philosophical and theological lectures to give in America, and also some good concert programs. Naturally I will play the great organ at St. George's Church. I rejoice greatly in anticipation.

    Your devoted,
    Albert Schweitzer

I am sending this letter via Switzerland.

NOTES FOR THE CIRCULAR

At the beginning of the war I didn't know whether I would be able to remain at Lambarene with my collaborators to continue our philanthropical work in my hospital, or whether we would have to close the hospital and return to Europe–and I didn't know how we could leave Africa, because at the beginning of the war there was no possibility of traveling as one wished. We remained, and the hospital continued to function because our conscience would not permit us to leave the poor black people who came from so far to be cared for by us. Therefore we have here two doctors and a lady doctor, and nine European nurses, the greater part of them Swiss. We have enough to eat, thanks to our garden and the hospital plantation. For months we have not had potatoes because they don't grow here and they cannot be shipped from

Europe because of the war. Our concern always is to have enough medicine and enough material for the operations. A great part of the sick people come to be operated on: it is especially a question of hernia and tumors. Some of these sick people come more than 400 kilometres by the paths of the virgin forest and by the river to be operated on by us. My colleague, Doctor Goldschmid, who has worked in my hospital since 1933, is an excellent surgeon. The great difficulty is to nourish the sick people. We buy salt in the factories. We don't have meat and salt fish for the sick people. We bought it for them before the war, but now it is too dear. Already rice is becoming very dear. For ourselves, we are obliged to have milk and butter brought from Europe because one is not able to raise cows in the virgin forest. That's what makes life so expensive here.

We have room to lodge 300 sick natives. We have also a maternity ward for the native women who come here to be delivered. As there is not enough cow milk in the country, the babies whose mothers are dead are brought to us to be raised by hand with the milk that comes from Europe. We have also room to lodge some of the insane, because in the villages no one wishes to keep them. They are feared, and then they are drowned in the river.

A great part of the sick people come because of great foot ulcers (tropical ulcers). To cure these ulcers takes weeks and months, and during this time we have to nourish the sick people.

Almost all of the sick people are so poor that they are not able to give anything for the medicine which they receive, the operations that are performed, and the nourishment that we are obliged to give them. It happens often that a sick person proudly brings us a chicken, believing that it is certainly enough for the cost of the operation.

Working side by side with the European nurses there are ten black internes. Since the beginning of the war we have not been able to pay them as we would wish. We aren't even able to give them enough to nourish themselves properly. But they remain with us by attachment. (because they become attached to us).

Those who are aiding my work from Europe are no longer able to do as formerly because of the war. In the name of the poor sick black people of the virgin forest I beg my friends of America to aid us by their gifts. All of us, the sick ones, the doctors, and the nurses are profoundly thankful to them. I hope that you find someone to translate these of French into English.

With my good wishes.
[Albert Schweitzer]

MARK VAN DOREN

HOLT AND COMPANY BOOKS BY VAN DOREN (THROUGH 1947): *The Last Look, and Other Poems* (New York: Holt, 1937);
Collected Poems, 1922–1938 (New York: Holt, 1939);
Shakespeare (New York: Holt, 1939);
The Transparent Tree (New York: Holt, 1940);
Windless Cabins (New York: Holt, 1940);
The Mayfield Deer (New York: Holt, 1941);
The Private Reader: Selected Articles and Reviews (New York: Holt, 1942);
Tilda (New York: Holt, 1943);
Liberal Education (New York: Holt, 1943);
The Seven Sleepers and Other Poems (New York: Holt, 1944);
John Dryden: A Study of His Poetry (New York: Holt, 1946); **first edition,** *The Poetry of John Dryden* (New York: Harcourt, Brace & Howe, 1920; Cambridge, U.K.: Minority Press, 1931);
The Noble Voice: A Study of Ten Great Poems (New York: Holt, 1946).

Mark Van Doren

Mark Van Doren (1894–1972) earned distinction as a poet, critic, teacher (he was an English professor at Columbia University), anthologist, editor, and reviewer (for The Nation). *Van Doren's association with Holt and Company began in 1937 but came to real fruition under the guidance of trade-department manager William Sloane, who joined the company in 1939. Van Doren followed Sloane when Sloane left Holt in 1947 to found his own firm, William Sloane Associates.*

* * *

In the spring of 1937 Van Doren wrote R. H. Thornton, Sloane's predecessor as Holt and Company trade-department head, arguing for the merits of a novel manuscript he had submitted–possibly Windless Cabins *(1940), his first novel published by Holt. Van Doren had published an earlier novel,* The Transients, *with Morrow in 1935.*

April 1, 1937

Dear Mr. Thornton:

When I said this morning that the novel was less important to me than the poetry I didn't mean it wasn't important. I believe in it very strongly, and if the question is still open when I see you I may want to argue with you a bit. It is of course an entirely separate matter from the poetry, which I am delighted to have you publish, with or without the novel. I must confess that I can't see how anyone can know that the novel is without commercial possibilities. Everyone who has read it among my acquaintance seems honestly to believe that it is exciting and original; and I should suppose that those qualities were more promising than many others. However.

Miss Joseph tells me that she will see you soon to make arrangements for "The Last Look" and the "Collected Poems." As I said this morning, I shall want the manuscript of the former for a few weeks, to see if any changes are necessary; they would be slight. . . .

As for future prose books, the volume on Shakespeare which I mentioned to you the other day is the only one I have definitely in mind; apart, of course, from further novewls. As for future work in poetry, there is the long poem I also mentioned; and that will take perhaps ten years.

Sincerely,
Mark Van Doren

* * *

Van Doren's older brother Carl had preceded him as literary editor and reviewer for The Nation. *Carl wrote Harmon Tupper of the Holt and Company sales department to thank him for a copy of* The Last Look, and Other Poems *(1937), his brother's first book with Holt.*

14 September 1937

Dear Mr. Tupper:

Thank you for the copy of my brother's book, which seems to me a very beautiful and very fitting dress for his poems. As he and I make it a rule not to review each other's work, which might seem too much like teamwork, I shall not be reviewing this. But I may say privately that I believe he is one of the few lasting poets of our time, strong, fresh, subtle, and witty. I know that he is very happy to have a place on your distinguished list, and I am happy to see him there. I believe this will bring the recognition his lovely art deserves.

Sincerely yours,
Carl Van Doren

* * *

Poet Marianne Moore thanked Sloane for a copy of Mark Van Doren's Collected Poems, 1922–1938 *(1939).*

January 28, 1939

Dear Mr. Sloane:

I thank you for the volume, COLLECTED POEMS, sent me by you at Dr. Van Doren's suggestion.

Although one can be at variance with Mark van [*sic*] Doren in certain respects and even question the lyric mode of certain poems, noone [*sic*] it seems to me, surpasses him in the unremitting and persuasive accuracy with which he portrays the American scene,—an apple tree in bloom, the impending snowstorm, the interior of house or barn, the domestic or woodland creature. The boldness of such diction as "the pond-dividing whiskers" (of the beaver), greatly delights me. His insistent sense of the inevitable, of the ghostly, and of the sombre, I respect; and I note that in the striking recurrence of certain themes and certain words, there is no effect of repetition for the reader, but continual freshness and interest; a most unusual triumph for a writer.

This work reiterates by implication that the author exigently labors to satisfy his own exacting mind, steeled as creativeness must be, to doubt or objection from others, and I notice as the book progresses, a certain gathering of forces interior and technical. I hope there will be grateful response from the public, to the unique gift presented here. Also may I say, regarding the pages themselves, there is a distinct beauty of physical presentment.

Very truly yours,
Marianne Moore

Advertisement from the 11 May 1940 Saturday Review of Literature for Van Doren's 1939 poetry collection (Rutgers University Library)

Van Doren was grateful to Sloane for his vigorous promotion of Collected Poems, 1922–1938.

February 8, 1939

Dear Mr. Sloane:

Your telegram today (I am sure it was yours), added to the letters I hear you sent with the copies I autographed, and to the ads in the *Times* and the *Saturday Review,* has set a record so far as I know for editorial courtesy, and this note is to say how deeply I feel such kindness. It is new to me, if not to Henry Holt and Company—long may the latter flourish. My hope for the *Poems,* now that they have been made into so beautiful a book, and now that they are in such hands as yours, is that they justify their existence in their publishers' eyes. Nothing could please me more than to have them do so.

. . . .

With best thanks again, and with my warmest personal regards,

Sincerely,
Mark Van Doren

* * *

Sloane explained to Van Doren the business realities behind the lack of a union label in Holt and Company books. "Jonathan Gentry," the poem mentioned in regard to a reviewer's comment, was a long narrative poem that Van Doren had first published in 1931.

February 15, 1939

Dear Mr. Van Doren:

Thank you for forwarding the Typographical Union No. 6 letter to me. I feel exactly the same way you do about wanting the Union Label books, but to explain very briefly, the situation is this: there is, or was last Spring, only one Union Bindery and its costs are 33 1/3% higher than anyone elses, [sic] in other words it exists to bind books which must contain the Union Label. The Quinn-Boden Company of Rahway, New Jersey, where our books are made is one of the most progressive printing shops in the country. It pays well over the Union scale in many departments, and never less than the Union minimum. It is partly organized, and the management has no objection to a closed job that the employees may have. None of the Quinn-Boden books can bear the Union Label for two reasons. First it is not a closed shop, second, we cannot have any of our books Union bound. I ought to add that all the binderies that I know of pay Union scale and work Union hours. There is no exploitation whatever at any point in the production of any of our books, unless it is here in our own office where everybody works harder than they ought to except me. I am returning the letter to you for such reply as you care to make. As a socialist of long standing, I can assure you that if we could put a Union Label on our books I would do it.

Meantime the sale of the poems continues, Union Label or none, and one or two reviews have come in. There is what I feel a stupid review in the Boston Herald which I will show you the next time you come in. The most quotable line is "Jonathan Gentry has a great deal of narrative power and is a truly find [sic] long poem."

I will keep in touch with you as further results come in. We have advertised the book in the Virginia Quarterly and the Yale Review. We are continuing to send out review copies really in excess of our proper budget.

Sincerely yours,
[William Sloane]
MANAGER, TRADE DEPARTMENT

* * *

In the summer of 1939 Van Doren forwarded Holt and Company a British scholar's plug for Shakespeare, *his critical study published later that year.*

July 22, 1939

Dear Bill [Sloane]:

G. Wilson Knight, of Trinity College, Toronto, has just sent me this opinion of the *Shakespeare* from England for you to use if you like. Please use it–there is almost nobody whose opinion I value more. He is the author of *The Wheel of Fire, The Shakespearian Tempest, The Imperial Theme,* and other works on Shakespeare.

Your fine letter came in the same mail–I am glad you are satisfied with the revision.

Don't let them work you to death.

Yours,
Mark

———◆———

This is a most important contribution to contemporary Shakespearian criticism. Mr. Mark Van Doren has a truly remarkable gift for defining, often through some uncannily well-chosen metaphor, Shakespeare's subtlest variations in language, characterization, and atmospheric quality; while leaving each a little more magic and mysterious than he found it. The treatment (of all the plays in turn) is rapid, concentrated, and strictly to the point. This is a most revealing and valuable book.

G. Wilson Knight

* * *

Sloane wrote Van Doren in the fall of 1939 to report strong sales for Shakespeare *and to discuss the upcoming publication of* Windless Cabins *and* The Transparent Tree *(1940), a children's story illustrated by Van Doren's niece, Margaret Van Doren.*

October 28, 1939

Dear Mark:

Well we have passed the 2,000 mark in the sale of the SHAKESPEARE, and after a couple of low days, orders came in this morning for nearly 200 copies. I believe we also got one order for your *Collected Poems!*

I wish you would tell Dorothy [Van Doren's wife, writer Dorothy Graffe Van Doren] for me that one of the responsibilities which publishers either take or have thrust upon them is the economic situations of their authors. In your case, you have a book currently selling and the advance on it has been doubtlessly more than earned back already. If your shoe string begins to rub thin she should give me a little notice and put at least part of the problem up to me. You are not holding us up in any way, it is just that at the peak of the season we do not get around to drawing up contracts, a time consuming business, as promptly as I know we ought to. Please do not feel embarrassed at asking us for help when you need it. It is foolishness not to try at least.

There are a couple of things which I should like to have from you if it is possible. One is a statement about WINDLESS CABINS from which I can write my copy. I have some pretty good copy of my own seething about in what I laughingly refer to as my mind, but your own taste and expression is so sure and good that I should like you to say something to me about the book as a cross reference for my own efforts. Secondly I seem to remember you showing me some quotes about THE TRANSIENTS. Anyhow I should like to use them if you have any available. By the way, how many copies did you say that book sold? Not that it makes any difference because we are going to sell plenty of WINDLESS CABINS under any circumstances, or I personally shall eat the overstock (I keep a bottle of rhubarb and soda on account of making statements like this every once in a while). I would very much like to get this material from you early next week if it is not going to crowd you too much.

THE TRANSPARENT TREE is going to be lovely. To straighten out the paging in relation to the illustrations I have had to add one five word sentence at one point, and your niece has taken out a single word at another. I bet you won't be able to tell. Her pictures are going to be beautiful and while the book

Advertisement from the 4 January 1947 Saturday Review of Literature *for Van Doren's 1946 work subtitled*
A Study of Ten Great Poems *(Rutgers University Library)*

is of a sort which may not sell extensively, it is solid aesthetic satisfaction to add it to the list.

Regards,
[William Sloane]

***

Sloane's prediction in a letter to Dorothy Van Doren that her husband would win the 1940 Pulitzer Prize in poetry for Collected Poems, 1922–1938 *turned out to be true.*

April 29, 1940

Dear Dorothy:

Well, we seem to have got things pretty well balled up about the money for you-all. I am now asking our royalty gal to send you the complete royalty due on the *Shakespeare* in one check next week, and to send Nannine [Nannine Joseph, Van Doren's agent] a check for the royalties on the poems.

Speaking of which, I regard it as absolutely essential that you let me know where you're gonna be between May first and May fifteenth, say. I honestly believe that Mark is leading the field for the Pulitzer, and attendance at that dinner will be obligatory if he wins. In fact, if he doesn't go to receive the prize—which is just as big a thing in terms of Cash as *Collier's* offers for short shorts—I shall be in a spot—having to receive thing on his behalf. So for the love of Mike be sure he takes along his dinner jacket and that I know where you are.

Yours in no small anxiousness,
[William Sloane]
MANAGER, TRADE DEPARTMENT

May 7, 1940

Dear Mark:

I am afraid I was in a pretty festive mood last night when you called up. In fact Gene and I, and two or three of the rest of us had been celebrating the prize with more enthusiasm than restraint. But then, it isn't every day that one of our authors wins a Pulitzer Prize, to say nothing of the fact that this time it was won by our favorite author.

I only hope at this point that you are not a subscriber to a clipping service. If you are, for heaven's sake telegraph them to discontinue the service.

We are proceeding at once with the second edition of the book, but I am afraid it is going to be some ten days before the new stock is on hand. We have 700 or 800 left of the first edition, and I anticipate that they will all be gone by the end of the week.

I hope you like the ad in the Times this morning. There will, of course, be subsequent ads in the Saturday Review of Literature in and the Sunday Times. I do wish Mr. Thornton had not printed the book from type because we would have more margin for advertising.

What a year this has been for the Van Dorens! Did I remember to write you that the Trade Book Clinic selected *The Transparent Tree* as one of the ten best pieces of book making for the month? That is only a minor scalp to hang on your belt, but still it is something.

All best,
[William Sloane]
MANAGER, TRADE DEPARTMENT

***

Holt and Company published The Mayfield Deer *(1941), another long narrative poem, but his next collection,* Our Lady Peace, and Other War Poems *(1942) was brought out by New Directions.*

September 30, 1941

Dear Mark:

I am returning herewith to you the manuscript of poems which it has been a privilege for me to read.

You are much too shrewd a guy for me to get by with anything half-baked in the way of comment about these things, so I will tell you that about half of them hit me where I lived, and of the remaining half some I thought were imperfect and others I just didn't understand.

I think a poem like "Down World," for instance, is magnificent. Some of "Armistice" I think is very good. However, in spite of what I said about the ones I didn't get or which I got and had to strain over, the fact is that this is an extraordinary body of work to have accomplished in a summer, and you have here more than the nucleus for a new volume of verse about which I shall want to talk to you one of these days.

We are now beginning our final sales campaign on THE MAYFIELD DEER, and a number of stores have asked for two or three autographed copies along with the rest of their orders. I wonder if you could let us know when you could come in and sign say twenty-five books. Ordinarily I don't approve of this, but in the case of poetry, which booksellers have such a hard time with anyway, I think it seems reasonable to cooperate with them whenever possible.

Tell Dorothy hello from me and also tell her I have been reading her previous novels with a lot of interest and some amazement at their failure to sell more widely than they did. Some time I want to have a talk with her, because she really has something.

          All best,
          [William Sloane]
          Manager, Trade Department

* * *

Stephen Vincent Benét's brother, writer and editor William Rose Benét, congratulated Sloane on Van Doren's Collected Poems, 1922–1938.

          [Undated; circa November 1941]

Dear Mr. Sloane:

You have made a fine looking book of Mark Van Doren's Collected Poems, a book worthy of the poetry. I am glad to have it. He is a remarkable poet and one of the few one can reread with satisfaction. Unobtrusively he has won a leading place in the literature of our time. His intellect and integrity, his deep knowledge of nature, his originality without affectation, his sagacity and humor, are elements that make a good deal of modern poetry seem, by comparison, flimsy and frenetic.

          Very sincerely yours,
          William Rose Benét

* * *

In Autobiography *(1958) Van Doren recalled working with Sloane in 1946, the final year of Sloane's association with Holt and Company. That year Holt published* The Noble Voice: A Study of Ten Great Poems *and* John Dryden: A Study of His Poetry, *Van Doren's master's thesis, which had first been published as* The Poetry of John Dryden *in 1920.*

I wrote *The Noble Voice: A Study of Ten Great Poems* in the summer of 1945. . . . William Sloane, who was my publisher for twelve years, first as editor in another house [Holt and Company] and then as master of his own [William Sloane Associates], and who throughout that time was generous beyond description, came to visit us in Cornwall just as the book was done. He insisted upon reading it at once, and did so in my study by the pond while I waited at the house for his verdict. He approved in the warm, intelligent way I was familiar with, but suggested that my title, *Calliope,* be changed; he said most people associated the name with circus origins. Calliope was the muse of epic poetry, and I had begun the preface with a reference to her noble voice. That phrase became the title, though I still think of the book as an examination of the ten poems, beginning with Homer's, in which she might have been most interested.

        . . . .

In the same year with *The Noble Voice* I published a third edition of the Dryden. It was out of print again, and Marjorie Nicolson at Columbia, widely known as a seventeenth-century scholar and a powerful person in her own right, was good enough to inform William Sloane that she thought it should be available. He agreed instantly, and I set about revising it—not much, but here and there I found I had used the word "cynical" as a term of praise, and since I no longer thought of it as that I took it out or modified it. In a new preface I spoke of Dryden's mastery in the art of verse, and said I still hoped his example would be followed in the interest of a greater firmness and resonance than modern poetry on the whole possessed. I was aware of no immediate response to the suggestion.

        . . . .

Meanwhile I was writing poems on my own account, and I was about to start on a headlong career with stories that still, whenever I think of it, astonishes me. But first, as to the poems. One thing I asked William Sloane to do he did with characteristic alacrity, but it was a mistake. I asked him to let me collect all of my poems again in the form of a series that might run to as many as five volumes, each one a unity with respect to subject matter. I proposed to begin with those, including of course *A Winter Diary,* which had to do with the country, whether Connecticut or Illinois. So in 1946 appeared *The Country Year,* with drawings of the house and lawn at Cornwall, and the study and the pond, which John O'Hara Cosgrave came to make. I still prize the drawings, as I do those of Waldo Peirce for the poems about children that appeared a year later in *The Careless Clock* (the title came from "Boy Dressing"). But by and large the public did not recognize that the volumes were collections of old pieces; and some reviewers, making the same error, were appalled because as a poet I had become so copious. I am copious, but not to the tune of a new book every year. So I abandoned the project, and to make things clear published in 1948 a volume labeled distinctly *New Poems.*

          —*Autobiography* (New York:
          Harcourt, Brace, 1958),
          pp. 285, 287-288

Books For Further Reading

Adams, Henry. *The Education of Henry Adams.* New York: Vintage/Library of America, 1990.

Allen, Gay Wilson. *William James.* New York: Viking, 1967.

Auchincloss, Louis. *The Vanderbilt Era: Profiles of a Gilded Age.* New York: Scribners, 1989.

Ballou, Robert Oleson. *A History of the Council on Books in Wartime, 1942-1946.* New York: Council on Books in Wartime, 1946.

Bender, Thomas. *New York Intellect: A History of Intellectual Life in New York City, from 1750 to the Beginnings of Our Time.* New York: Knopf, 1987.

Bentley, James. *Albert Schweitzer: The Enigma.* New York: HarperCollins, 1992.

Beswick, Jay W. *The Work of Frederick Leypoldt: Bibliographer and Publisher.* New York & London: R. R. Bowker, 1942.

Blumenthal, Joseph. *Robert Frost and His Printers.* Austin, Tex.: W. T. Taylor, 1985.

Brabazon, James. *Albert Schweitzer: A Biography.* Syracuse, N.Y.: Syracuse University Press, 2000.

Brain, Russell. *Tea with Walter de la Mare.* London: Faber & Faber, 1957.

Branshaw, Stanley. *Robert Frost Himself.* New York: Braziller, 1986.

Callahan, North. *Carl Sandburg: His Life and Works.* University Park: Pennsylvania State University Press, 1987.

Casper, Scott E., Joanne D. Chaison, and Jeffrey D. Groves. *Perspectives on American Book History: Artifacts and Commentary.* Amherst: University of Massachusetts Press, 2002.

Cerf, Bennett. *At Random: The Reminiscences of Bennett Cerf.* New York: Random House, 1977.

Chalfant, Edward. *Better in Darkness: A Biography of Henry Adams: His Second Life, 1862-1891.* Hamden, Conn.: Archon, 1994.

Chalfant. *Both Sides of the Ocean: A Biography of Henry Adams: His First Life, 1838-1862.* Hamden, Conn.: Archon, 1982.

Chalfant. *Improvement of the World: A Biography of Henry Adams: His Last Life, 1891-1918.* North Haven, Conn.: Archon, 2001.

Clark, Leonard. *Walter de la Mare.* New York: Henry Z. Walck, 1961.

Cole, John Y., ed. *Books in Action: The Armed Services Editions.* Washington, D.C.: Library of Congress, 1984.

Costlow, Jane T. *Worlds within Worlds: The Novels of Ivan Turgenev.* Princeton: Princeton University Press, 1990.

Books For Further Reading

Cousins, Norman. *Dr. Schweitzer of Lambaréné*. New York: Harper, 1960.

Dawidoff, Robert. *The Genteel Tradition and the Sacred Rage: High Culture vs. Democracy in Adams, James, and Santayana*. Chapel Hill: University of North Carolina Press, 1992.

Derby, J. C. *Fifty Years among Authors, Books and Publishers*. New York: Carleton, 1884.

Douglas, Ann. *Terrible Honesty: Mongrel Manhattan in the 1920s*. New York: Farrar, Straus & Giroux, 1995.

Dumenil, Lynn. *The Modern Temper: American Culture and Society in the 1920s*. New York: Hill & Wang, 1995.

Fenton, Charles A. *Stephen Vincent Benét: The Life and Times of an American Man of Letters 1898–1943*. New Haven: Yale University Press, 1958.

Fenton, ed. *Selected Letters of Stephen Vincent Benét*. New Haven: Yale University Press, 1960.

Fisher, David James. *Romain Rolland and the Politics of Intellectual Engagement*. Berkeley: University of California Press, 1998.

Fontenot, Chester J., Jr., and others, eds. *W. E. B. Du Bois and Race: Essays Celebrating the Centennial of the Publication of the Souls of Black Folk*. Macon, Ga.: Mercer University Press, 2001.

Francis, R. A. *Romain Rolland*. New York: Berg, 1999.

Gaige, Roscoe Crosby, and Alfred Harcourt, eds. *Books and Reading*. New York: Baker & Taylor, 1908.

Gibson, James, ed. *Thomas Hardy: Interviews and Recollections*. Basingstoke, U.K.: Macmillan / New York: St. Martin's Press, 1999.

Goldberg, David Joseph. *Discontented America: The United States in the 1920s*. Baltimore: Johns Hopkins University Press, 1999.

Graves, Richard Perceval. *A. E. Housman the Scholar-Poet*. New York: Scribners, 1979.

Harcourt, Alfred. *Some Experiences*. Riverside, Conn.: Privately printed, 1951.

Hardwick, Elizabeth, ed. *The Selected Letters of William James*. New York: Farrar, Straus & Cudahy, 1961.

Heller, Adele, and Lois Rudnick, eds. *1915. The Cultural Moment*. New Brunswick, N.J.: Rutgers University Press, 1991.

Holden, Alan W., and J. Roy Birch, eds. *A. E. Housman: A Reassessment*. London: Macmillan, 2000.

Holt, Henry. *Garrulities of an Octogenarian Editor*. Boston & New York: Houghton Mifflin, 1923.

Housman, Laurence. *My Brother, A. E. Housman: Personal Recollections, Together with Thirty Hitherto Unpublished Poems*. New York: Scribners, 1938.

Jacobson, Joanne. *Authority and Alliance in the Letters of Henry Adams*. Madison: University of Wisconsin Press, 1992.

Juguo, Zhang. *W. E. B. Du Bois: The Quest for the Abolition of the Color Line*. New York: Routledge, 2001.

Kent, Noel J. *America in 1900*. Armonk, N.Y.: Sharpe, 2000.

Kramer, Dale, ed. *The Cambridge Companion to Thomas Hardy*. Cambridge & New York: Cambridge University Press, 1999.

Langfeldt, Gabriel. *Albert Schweitzer; A Study of his Philosophy of Life,* translated by Maurice Michael. New York: Braziller, 1960.

Lewis, David Levering. *W. E. B. Du Bois: Biography of a Race, 1868–1919*. New York: Holt, 1993.

Lewis. *W. E. B. Du Bois: The Fight for Equality and the American Century, 1919–1963*. New York: Holt, 2000.

Lewis, R. W. B. *The Jameses: A Family Narrative*. New York: Farrar, Straus & Giroux, 1991.

Lingman, Richard R. *Sinclair Lewis: Rebel from Main Street*. New York: Random House, 2002.

Lopate, Phillip, ed. *Writing New York: A Literary Anthology*. New York: Library of America, 1998.

Lowe, David A., ed. *Critical Essays on Ivan Turgenev*. Boston: G. K. Hall, 1989.

Lutz, Tom. *American Nervousness, 1903: An Anecdotal History*. Ithaca, N.Y.: Cornell University Press, 1991.

Maas, Henry, ed. *The Letters of A. E. Housman*. Cambridge, Mass.: Harvard University Press, 1971.

Mallett, Philip, ed. *The Achievement of Thomas Hardy*. Basingstoke, U.K.: Macmillan / New York: St. Martin's Press, 2000.

March, Harold. *Romain Rolland*. New York: Twayne, 1971.

McCrosson, Doris Ross. *Walter de la Mare*. New York: Twayne, 1966.

Mégroz, R. L. *Walter de la Mare: A Biographical and Critical Study*. London: Hodder & Stoughton, 1924.

Menand, Louis. *The Metaphysical Club: A Story of Ideas in America*. New York: Farrar, Straus & Giroux, 2001.

Meyers, Jeffrey. *Robert Frost: A Biography*. Boston: Houghton Mifflin, 1996.

Morrison, Kathleen. *Robert Frost: A Pictorial Chronicle*. New York: Holt, Rinehart & Winston, 1974.

Murray, Michael. *Albert Schweitzer, Musician*. Brookfield, Vt.: Ashgate, 1994.

Niven, Penelope. *Carl Sandburg: A Biography*. New York: Scribners, 1991.

O'Toole, Patricia. *The Five of Hearts: An Intimate Portrait of Henry Adams and His Friends, 1880–1918*. New York: Clarkson Potter, 1990.

Page, Norman. *A. E. Housman: A Critical Biography*. New York: Schocken, 1983.

Page. *Thomas Hardy: The Novels*. New York: Palgrave, 2001.

Page, ed. *Oxford Reader's Companion to Hardy*. Oxford: Oxford University Press, 2000.

Perry, Ralph Barton. *The Thought and Character of William James*. Cambridge, Mass.: Harvard University Press, 1948.

Pritchett, V. S. *The Gentle Barbarian: The Life and Work of Turgenev*. London: Chatto & Windus, 1977.

Radway, Janice A. *A Feeling for Books: The Book-of-the-Month Club, Literary Taste, and Middle-Class Desire.* Chapel Hill: University of North Carolina Press, 1997.

Rolland, Romain. *Journey Within,* translated by Elsie Pell. New York: Philosophical Library, 1947.

Samuels, Ernest. *Henry Adams.* Cambridge, Mass.: Belknap Press of Harvard University Press, 1989.

Sandburg, Helga. *–Where Love Begins.* New York: Fine, 1989.

Schapiro, Leonard. *Turgenev, His Life and Times.* New York: Random House, 1978.

Schorer, Mark. *Sinclair Lewis: An American Life.* New York: McGraw-Hill, 1961.

Schweitzer, Albert. *Out of My Life and Thought: An Autobiography,* translated by A. B. Lemke. New York: Holt, 1990.

Seeley, Frank Friedeberg. *Turgenev: A Reading of His Fiction.* Cambridge & New York: Cambridge University Press, 1991.

Sherrick, Julie. *Thomas Hardy's Major Novels: An Annotated Bibliography.* Lanham, Md.: Scarecrow Press / Pasadena, Cal.: Salem Press, 1998.

Shi, David E. *Facing Facts: Realism in American Thought and Culture, 1850–1920.* New York: Oxford University Press, 1995.

Skrupskelis, Ignas K. and Elizabeth M. Berkeley, eds. *The Correspondence of William James.* Charlottesville: University Press of Virginia, 1992–   .

Sloane, William. *The Craft of Writing,* edited by Julia H. Sloane. New York: Norton, 1979.

Smith, Harrison. *From Main Street to Stockholm: Letters of Sinclair Lewis, 1919–1930.* New York: Harcourt, Brace, 1952.

Starr, William Thomas. *Romain Rolland and a World at War.* Evanston: Northwestern University Press, 1956.

Starr. *Romain Rolland: One against All.* The Hague: Mouton, 1971.

Symons, Katharine E., and others. *Alfred Edward Housman: Recollections.* New York: Holt, 1937.

Thompson, Lawrance. *Robert Frost: The Early Years, 1874–1915.* New York: Holt, Rinehart & Winston, 1966.

Thompson. *Robert Frost: The Years of Triumph, 1915–1938.* New York: Holt, Rinehart & Winston, 1970.

Thompson and R. H. Winnick. *Robert Frost: The Later Years, 1938–1963.* New York: Holt, Rinehart & Winston, 1976.

Thompson, ed. *The Selected Letters of Robert Frost.* New York: Holt, Rinehart & Winston, 1964.

Turgenev, Ivan. *Turgenev's Letters,* edited and translated by A. V. Knowles. London: Athlone Press, 1983.

Turton, Glyn. *Turgenev and the Context of English Literature, 1850–1900.* London & New York: Routledge, 1992.

Van Doren, Mark. *Autobiography.* New York: Greenwood Press, 1968.

Van Doren. *The Essays of Mark Van Doren (1924–1972),* selected, with an introduction, by William Claire. Westport, Conn.: Greenwood Press, 1980.

Van Doren. *The Private Reader: Selected Articles and Reviews*. New York: Kraus, 1968.

Van Doren. *The Selected Letters of Mark Van Doren,* edited, with an introduction, by George Hendrick. Baton Rouge: Louisiana State University Press, 1987.

Washington, Ida H. *Dorothy Canfield Fisher*. Shelburne, Vt.: New England Press, 1982.

Wasserstrom, William. *The Ironies of Progress: Henry Adams and the American Dream*. Carbondale: Southern Illinois University Press, 1984.

Weber, Carl J. *Hardy in America: A Study of Thomas Hardy and His American Readers*. New York: Russell & Russell, 1966.

Whistler, Theresa. *Imagination of the Heart: The Life of Walter de la Mare*. London: Duckworth, 1993.

Withers, Percy. *A Buried Life: Personal Recollections of A. E. Housman*. London: Cape, 1940.

Yarmolinsky, Avrahm. *Turgenev: The Man, His Art and His Age*. New York: Collier, 1958.

Young, James P. *Henry Adams: The Historian as Political Theorist*. Lawrence: University Press of Kansas, 2001.

Cumulative Index

Dictionary of Literary Biography, Volumes 1-284
Dictionary of Literary Biography Yearbook, 1980-2002
Dictionary of Literary Biography Documentary Series, Volumes 1-19
Concise Dictionary of American Literary Biography, Volumes 1-7
Concise Dictionary of British Literary Biography, Volumes 1-8
Concise Dictionary of World Literary Biography, Volumes 1-4

Cumulative Index

DLB before number: *Dictionary of Literary Biography,* Volumes 1-284
Y before number: *Dictionary of Literary Biography Yearbook,* 1980-2002
DS before number: *Dictionary of Literary Biography Documentary Series,* Volumes 1-19
CDALB before number: *Concise Dictionary of American Literary Biography,* Volumes 1-7
CDBLB before number: *Concise Dictionary of British Literary Biography,* Volumes 1-8
CDWLB before number: *Concise Dictionary of World Literary Biography,* Volumes 1-4

A

Aakjær, Jeppe 1866-1930 . . . . DLB-214
Abbey, Edward 1927-1989 . . . . DLB-256, 275
Abbey, Edwin Austin 1852-1911 . . . . DLB-188
Abbey, Maj. J. R. 1894-1969 . . . . DLB-201
Abbey Press DLB-49
The Abbey Theatre and Irish Drama,
  1900-1945 . . . . DLB-10
Abbot, Willis J. 1863-1934 . . . . DLB-29
Abbott, Edwin A. 1838-1926 . . . . DLB-178
Abbott, Jacob 1803-1879 . . . . DLB-1, 42, 243
Abbott, Lee K. 1947- DLB-130
Abbott, Lyman 1835-1922 . . . . DLB-79
Abbott, Robert S. 1868-1940 . . . . DLB-29, 91
Abe Kōbō 1924-1993 . . . . DLB-182
Abelard, Peter circa 1079-1142? DLB-115, 208
Abelard-Schuman DLB-46
Abell, Arunah S. 1806-1888 . . . . DLB-43
Abell, Kjeld 1901-1961 . . . . DLB-214
Abercrombie, Lascelles 1881-1938 . . . . DLB-19
  The Friends of the Dymock Poets Y-00
Aberdeen University Press Limited DLB-106
Abish, Walter 1931- DLB-130, 227
Ablesimov, Aleksandr Onisimovich
  1742-1783 . . . . DLB-150
Abraham à Sancta Clara 1644-1709 . . . . . DLB-168
Abrahams, Peter
  1919- DLB-117, 225; CDWLB-3
Abrams, M. H. 1912- DLB-67
Abramson, Jesse 1904-1979 . . . . DLB-241
Abrogans circa 790-800 . . . . DLB-148
Abschatz, Hans Aßmann von 1646-1699 . . DLB-168
Abse, Dannie 1923- DLB-27, 245
Abutsu-ni 1221-1283 . . . . DLB-203
Academy Chicago Publishers DLB-46
Accius circa 170 B.C.-circa 80 B.C. DLB-211
Accrocca, Elio Filippo 1923-1996 . . . . DLB-128
Ace Books DLB-46
Achebe, Chinua 1930- DLB-117; CDWLB-3
Achtenberg, Herbert 1938- DLB-124

Ackerman, Diane 1948- DLB-120
Ackroyd, Peter 1949- DLB-155, 231
Acorn, Milton 1923-1986 . . . . DLB-53
Acosta, Oscar Zeta 1935?-1974? DLB-82
Acosta Torres, José 1925- DLB-209
Actors Theatre of Louisville DLB-7
Adair, Gilbert 1944- DLB-194
Adair, James 1709?-1783? DLB-30
Adam, Graeme Mercer 1839-1912 . . . . DLB-99
Adam, Robert Borthwick, II 1863-1940 . . DLB-187
Adame, Leonard 1947- DLB-82
Adameşteanu, Gabriel 1942- DLB-232
Adamic, Louis 1898-1951 . . . . DLB-9
Adams, Abigail 1744-1818 . . . . DLB-183, 200
Adams, Alice 1926-1999 . . . . DLB-234; Y-86
Adams, Bertha Leith (Mrs. Leith Adams,
  Mrs. R. S. de Courcy Laffan)
  1837?-1912 . . . . DLB-240
Adams, Brooks 1848-1927 . . . . DLB-47
Adams, Charles Francis, Jr. 1835-1915 . . . . DLB-47
Adams, Douglas 1952-2001 . . . . DLB-261; Y-83
Adams, Franklin P. 1881-1960 . . . . DLB-29
Adams, Hannah 1755-1832 . . . . DLB-200
Adams, Henry 1838-1918 . . . . . . DLB-12, 47, 189
Adams, Herbert Baxter 1850-1901 . . . . DLB-47
Adams, James Truslow
  1878-1949 . . . . DLB-17; DS-17
Adams, John 1735-1826 . . . . DLB-31, 183
Adams, John Quincy 1767-1848 . . . . DLB-37
Adams, Léonie 1899-1988 . . . . DLB-48
Adams, Levi 1802-1832 . . . . DLB-99
Adams, Richard 1920- DLB-261
Adams, Samuel 1722-1803 . . . . DLB-31, 43
Adams, Sarah Fuller Flower
  1805-1848 . . . . DLB-199
Adams, Thomas 1582/1583-1652 . . . . DLB-151
Adams, William Taylor 1822-1897 . . . . DLB-42
J. S. and C. Adams [publishing house] DLB-49
Adamson, Harold 1906-1980 . . . . DLB-265
Adamson, Sir John 1867-1950 . . . . DLB-98
Adcock, Arthur St. John 1864-1930 . . . . . DLB-135
Adcock, Betty 1938- DLB-105

"Certain Gifts" DLB-105
  Tribute to James Dickey Y-97
Adcock, Fleur 1934- DLB-40
Addison, Joseph 1672-1719 . . . DLB-101; CDBLB-2
Ade, George 1866-1944 . . . . DLB-11, 25
Adeler, Max (see Clark, Charles Heber)
Adlard, Mark 1932- DLB-261
Adler, Richard 1921- DLB-265
Adonias Filho 1915-1990 . . . . DLB-145
Adorno, Theodor W. 1903-1969 . . . . DLB-242
Adoum, Jorge Enrique 1926- DLB-283
Advance Publishing Company DLB-49
Ady, Endre 1877-1919 . . . . . . DLB-215; CDWLB-4
AE 1867-1935 . . . . DLB-19; CDBLB-5
Ælfric circa 955-circa 1010 . . . . DLB-146
Aeschines circa 390 B.C.-circa 320 B.C. DLB-176
Aeschylus 525-524 B.C.-456-455 B.C.
  . . . . DLB-176; CDWLB-1
Aesthetic Papers DLB-1
Aesthetics
  Eighteenth-Century Aesthetic
    Theories DLB-31
African Literature
  Letter from Khartoum Y-90
African American
  Afro-American Literary Critics:
    An Introduction DLB-33
  The Black Aesthetic: Background DS-8
  The Black Arts Movement,
    by Larry Neal DLB-38
  Black Theaters and Theater Organizations
    in America, 1961-1982:
    A Research List DLB-38
  Black Theatre: A Forum [excerpts] . . . DLB-38
  Callaloo [journal] Y-87
  Community and Commentators:
    Black Theatre and Its Critics DLB-38
  The Emergence of Black
    Women Writers DS-8
  The Hatch-Billops Collection DLB-76
  A Look at the Contemporary Black
    Theatre Movement DLB-38
  The Moorland-Spingarn Research
    Center DLB-76

343

"The Negro as a Writer," by
 G. M. McClellan DLB-50
"Negro Poets and Their Poetry," by
 Wallace Thurman DLB-50
Olaudah Equiano and Unfinished Journeys:
 The Slave-Narrative Tradition and
 Twentieth-Century Continuities, by
 Paul Edwards and Pauline T.
 Wangman. DLB-117
PHYLON (Fourth Quarter, 1950),
 The Negro in Literature:
 The Current Scene. DLB-76
The Schomburg Center for Research
 in Black Culture DLB-76
Three Documents [poets], by John
 Edward Bruce. DLB-50
After Dinner Opera Company Y-92
Agassiz, Elizabeth Cary 1822-1907 . . . . . . DLB-189
Agassiz, Louis 1807-1873 . . . . DLB-1, 235
Agee, James
 1909-1955 . . . . DLB-2, 26, 152; CDALB-1
 The Agee Legacy: A Conference at
  the University of Tennessee
  at Knoxville Y-89
Aguilera Malta, Demetrio 1909-1981 . . . . DLB-145
Ahlin, Lars 1915-1997. . . . . DLB-257
Ai 1947- DLB-120
Aichinger, Ilse 1921- DLB-85
Aickman, Robert 1914-1981 . . . . DLB-261
Aidoo, Ama Ata 1942- DLB-117; CDWLB-3
Aiken, Conrad
 1889-1973. . . . . . . DLB-9, 45, 102; CDALB-5
Aiken, Joan 1924- DLB-161
Aikin, Lucy 1781-1864 . . . . DLB-144, 163
Ainsworth, William Harrison
 1805-1882 . . . . DLB-21
Aistis, Jonas 1904-1973 . . . . . DLB-220; CDWLB-4
Aitken, George A. 1860-1917 . . . . DLB-149
Robert Aitken [publishing house] DLB-49
Akenside, Mark 1721-1770 . . . . DLB-109
Akins, Zoë 1886-1958. . . . . DLB-26
Aksakov, Ivan Sergeevich 1823-1826 . . . . .DLB-277
Aksakov, Sergei Timofeevich
 1791-1859. DLB-198
Akutagawa Ryūnsuke 1892-1927 . . . . DLB-180
Alabaster, William 1568-1640 . . . . DLB-132
Alain de Lille circa 1116-1202/1203 . . . . . DLB-208
Alain-Fournier 1886-1914. . . . . DLB-65
Alanus de Insulis (see Alain de Lille)
Alarcón, Francisco X. 1954- DLB-122
Alarcón, Justo S. 1930- DLB-209
Alba, Nanina 1915-1968 . . . . DLB-41
Albee, Edward 1928- . . . DLB-7, 266; CDALB-1
Albert, Octavia 1853-ca. 1889 . . . . DLB-221
Albert the Great circa 1200-1280 . . . . DLB-115
Alberti, Rafael 1902-1999 . . . . DLB-108
Albertinus, Aegidius circa 1560-1620 . . . . DLB-164
Alcaeus born circa 620 B.C. DLB-176
Alcott, Amos Bronson
 1799-1888. . . . . DLB-1, 223; DS-5

Alcott, Louisa May 1832-1888
 . . . DLB-1, 42, 79, 223, 239; DS-14; CDALB-3
Alcott, William Andrus 1798-1859 . . . . DLB-1, 243
Alcuin circa 732-804 . . . . DLB-148
Alden, Henry Mills 1836-1919 . . . . DLB-79
Alden, Isabella 1841-1930. . . . . DLB-42
John B. Alden [publishing house] DLB-49
Alden, Beardsley, and Company DLB-49
Aldington, Richard
 1892-1962 . . . . .DLB-20, 36, 100, 149
Aldis, Dorothy 1896-1966 . . . . DLB-22
Aldis, H. G. 1863-1919. . . . . DLB-184
Aldiss, Brian W. 1925- DLB-14, 261, 271
Aldrich, Thomas Bailey
 1836-1907. . . . . DLB-42, 71, 74, 79
Alegría, Ciro 1909-1967 . . . . DLB-113
Alegría, Claribel 1924- DLB-145, 283
Aleixandre, Vicente 1898-1984. . . . . DLB-108
Aleksandravičius, Jonas (see Aistis, Jonas)
Aleksandrov, Aleksandr Andreevich
 (see Durova, Nadezhda Andreevna)
Aleramo, Sibilla (Rena Pierangeli Faccio)
 1876-1960. . . . . DLB-114, 264
Alexander, Cecil Frances 1818-1895. . . . . DLB-199
Alexander, Charles 1868-1923 . . . . DLB-91
Charles Wesley Alexander
 [publishing house] DLB-49
Alexander, James 1691-1756 . . . . DLB-24
Alexander, Lloyd 1924- DLB-52
Alexander, Sir William, Earl of Stirling
 1577?-1640 . . . . DLB-121
Alexie, Sherman 1966- DLB-175, 206, 278
Alexis, Willibald 1798-1871 . . . . DLB-133
Alfred, King 849-899 . . . . DLB-146
Alger, Horatio, Jr. 1832-1899 . . . . DLB-42
Algonquin Books of Chapel Hill DLB-46
Algren, Nelson
 1909-1981 . . . . . . DLB-9; Y-81, 82; CDALB-1
 Nelson Algren: An International
  Symposium. Y-00
Allan, Andrew 1907-1974 . . . . DLB-88
Allan, Ted 1916-1995. . . . . DLB-68
Allbeury, Ted 1917- DLB-87
Alldritt, Keith 1935- DLB-14
Allen, Dick 1939- DLB-282
Allen, Ethan 1738-1789 . . . . DLB-31
Allen, Frederick Lewis 1890-1954 . . . . . . DLB-137
Allen, Gay Wilson 1903-1995 . . . . .DLB-103; Y-95
Allen, George 1808-1876 . . . . DLB-59
Allen, Grant 1848-1899 . . . . .DLB-70, 92, 178
Allen, Henry W. 1912-1991 . . . . Y-85
Allen, Hervey 1889-1949 . . . . DLB-9, 45
Allen, James 1739-1808. . . . . DLB-31
Allen, James Lane 1849-1925 . . . . DLB-71
Allen, Jay Presson 1922- DLB-26
John Allen and Company DLB-49
Allen, Paula Gunn 1939- DLB-175

Allen, Samuel W. 1917- DLB-41
Allen, Woody 1935- DLB-44
George Allen [publishing house]. DLB-106
George Allen and Unwin Limited DLB-112
Allende, Isabel 1942- DLB-145; CDWLB-3
Alline, Henry 1748-1784. . . . . DLB-99
Allingham, Margery 1904-1966 . . . . DLB-77
 The Margery Allingham Society. Y-98
Allingham, William 1824-1889. . . . . DLB-35
W. L. Allison [publishing house] DLB-49
The Alliterative Morte Arthure and the Stanzaic
 Morte Arthur circa 1350-1400 . . . . DLB-146
Allott, Kenneth 1912-1973 . . . . DLB-20
Allston, Washington 1779-1843 . . . . . . DLB-1, 235
John Almon [publishing house] DLB-154
Alonzo, Dámaso 1898-1990 . . . . DLB-108
Alsop, George 1636-post 1673 . . . . DLB-24
Alsop, Richard 1761-1815. . . . . DLB-37
Henry Altemus and Company DLB-49
Altenberg, Peter 1885-1919 . . . . DLB-81
Althusser, Louis 1918-1990 . . . . DLB-242
Altolaguirre, Manuel 1905-1959. . . . . DLB-108
Aluko, T. M. 1918- DLB-117
Alurista 1947- DLB-82
Alvarez, A. 1929- DLB-14, 40
Alvarez, Julia 1950- DLB-282
Alvaro, Corrado 1895-1956 . . . . DLB-264
Alver, Betti 1906-1989 . . . . . DLB-220; CDWLB-4
Amadi, Elechi 1934- DLB-117
Amado, Jorge 1912-2001 . . . . DLB-113
Ambler, Eric 1909-1998 . . . . DLB-77
The Library of America DLB-46
The Library of America: An Assessment
 After Two Decades Y-02
America: or, A Poem on the Settlement
 of the British Colonies, by Timothy
 Dwight DLB-37
American Bible Society
 Department of Library, Archives, and
  Institutional Research. Y-97
American Conservatory Theatre DLB-7
American Culture
 American Proletarian Culture:
  The Twenties and Thirties. DS-11
Studies in American Jewish Literature Y-02
The American Library in Paris. Y-93
American Literature
 The Literary Scene and Situation and . . .
  (Who Besides Oprah) Really Runs
  American Literature? Y-99
 Who Owns American Literature, by
  Henry Taylor. Y-94
 Who Runs American Literature? Y-94
American News Company DLB-49
A Century of Poetry, a Lifetime of Collecting:
 J. M. Edelstein's Collection of Twentieth-
 Century American Poetry Y-02
The American Poets' Corner: The First
 Three Years (1983-1986) Y-86

American Publishing Company..........DLB-49

American Spectator

[Editorial] Rationale From the Initial
Issue of the *American Spectator*
(November 1932)............DLB-137

American Stationers' Company..........DLB-49

The American Studies Association
of Norway........................Y-00

American Sunday-School Union.........DLB-49

American Temperance Union...........DLB-49

American Tract Society...............DLB-49

The American Trust for the British Library..Y-96

American Writers Congress
The American Writers Congress
(9-12 October 1981)...............Y-81

The American Writers Congress: A Report
on Continuing Business............Y-81

Ames, Fisher 1758-1808................DLB-37

Ames, Mary Clemmer 1831-1884........DLB-23

Ames, William 1576-1633...............DLB-281

Amiel, Henri-Frédéric 1821-1881.........DLB-217

Amini, Johari M. 1935- DLB-41

Amis, Kingsley 1922-1995
......DLB-15, 27, 100, 139, Y-96; CDBLB-7

Amis, Martin 1949- DLB-14, 194

Ammianus Marcellinus
circa A.D. 330-A.D. 395............DLB-211

Ammons, A. R. 1926-2001...........DLB-5, 165

Amory, Thomas 1691?-1788..............DLB-39

Anania, Michael 1939- DLB-193

Anaya, Rudolfo A. 1937- DLB-82, 206, 278

Ancrene Riwle circa 1200-1225...........DLB-146

Andersch, Alfred 1914-1980............DLB-69

Andersen, Benny 1929- DLB-214

Anderson, Alexander 1775-1870........DLB-188

Anderson, David 1929- DLB-241

Anderson, Frederick Irving 1877-1947....DLB-202

Anderson, Margaret 1886-1973........DLB-4, 91

Anderson, Maxwell 1888-1959......DLB-7, 228

Anderson, Patrick 1915-1979............DLB-68

Anderson, Paul Y. 1893-1938............DLB-29

Anderson, Poul 1926-2001...............DLB-8

Tribute to Isaac Asimov.............Y-92

Anderson, Robert 1750-1830...........DLB-142

Anderson, Robert 1917- DLB-7

Anderson, Sherwood
1876-1941.....DLB-4, 9, 86; DS-1; CDALB-4

Andreae, Johann Valentin 1586-1654.....DLB-164

Andreas Capellanus
flourished circa 1185...............DLB-208

Andreas-Salomé, Lou 1861-1937.........DLB-66

Andres, Stefan 1906-1970...............DLB-69

Andreu, Blanca 1959- DLB-134

Andrewes, Lancelot 1555-1626......DLB-151, 172

Andrews, Charles M. 1863-1943..........DLB-17

Andrews, Miles Peter ?-1814............DLB-89

Andrews, Stephen Pearl 1812-1886......DLB-250

Andrian, Leopold von 1875-1951.......DLB-81

Andrić, Ivo 1892-1975......DLB-147; CDWLB-4

Andrieux, Louis (see Aragon, Louis)

Andrus, Silas, and Son..................DLB-49

Andrzejewski, Jerzy 1909-1983.........DLB-215

Angell, James Burrill 1829-1916..........DLB-64

Angell, Roger 1920- DLB-171, 185

Angelou, Maya 1928- DLB-38; CDALB-7

Tribute to Julian Mayfield............Y-84

Anger, Jane flourished 1589............DLB-136

Angers, Félicité (see Conan, Laure)

The Anglo-Saxon Chronicle circa 890-1154...DLB-146

Angus and Robertson (UK) Limited.....DLB-112

Anhalt, Edward 1914-2000.............DLB-26

Annenkov, Pavel Vasil'evich
1813?-1887........................DLB-277

Henry F. Anners [publishing house]......DLB-49

Annolied between 1077 and 1081.........DLB-148

Anscombe, G. E. M. 1919-2001.........DLB-262

Anselm of Canterbury 1033-1109........DLB-115

Anstey, F. 1856-1934.............DLB-141, 178

Anthologizing New Formalism..........DLB-282

Anthony, Michael 1932- DLB-125

Anthony, Piers 1934- DLB-8

Anthony, Susanna 1726-1791............DLB-200

Antin, David 1932- DLB-169

Antin, Mary 1881-1949..........DLB-221; Y-84

Anton Ulrich, Duke of Brunswick-Lüneburg
1633-1714........................DLB-168

Antschel, Paul (see Celan, Paul)

Anyidoho, Kofi 1947- DLB-157

Anzaldúa, Gloria 1942- DLB-122

Anzengruber, Ludwig 1839-1889........DLB-129

Apess, William 1798-1839........DLB-175, 243

Apodaca, Rudy S. 1939- DLB-82

Apollinaire, Guillaume 1880-1918......DLB-258

Apollonius Rhodius third century B.C....DLB-176

Apple, Max 1941- DLB-130

D. Appleton and Company.............DLB-49

Appleton-Century-Crofts................DLB-46

Applewhite, James 1935- DLB-105

Tribute to James Dickey.............Y-97

Apple-wood Books....................DLB-46

April, Jean-Pierre 1948- DLB-251

Apukhtin, Aleksei Nikolaevich
1840-1893........................DLB-277

Apuleius circa A.D. 125-post A.D. 164
.........................DLB-211; CDWLB-1

Aquin, Hubert 1929-1977..............DLB-53

Aquinas, Thomas 1224/1225-1274......DLB-115

Aragon, Louis 1897-1982............DLB-72, 258

Aralica, Ivan 1930- DLB-181

Aratus of Soli
circa 315 B.C.-circa 239 B.C.........DLB-176

Arbasino, Alberto 1930- DLB-196

Arbor House Publishing Company......DLB-46

Arbuthnot, John 1667-1735............DLB-101

Arcadia House.......................DLB-46

Arce, Julio G. (see Ulica, Jorge)

Archer, William 1856-1924.............DLB-10

Archilochhus
mid seventh century B.C.E.........DLB-176

The Archpoet circa 1130?-?............DLB-148

Archpriest Avvakum (Petrovich)
1620?-1682.......................DLB-150

Arden, John 1930- DLB-13, 245

Arden of Faversham...................DLB-62

Ardis Publishers......................Y-89

Ardizzone, Edward 1900-1979..........DLB-160

Arellano, Juan Estevan 1947- DLB-122

The Arena Publishing Company.........DLB-49

Arena Stage..........................DLB-7

Arenas, Reinaldo 1943-1990............DLB-145

Arendt, Hannah 1906-1975............DLB-242

Arensberg, Ann 1937- Y-82

Arghezi, Tudor 1880-1967...DLB-220; CDWLB-4

Arguedas, José María 1911-1969........DLB-113

Argueta, Manlio 1936- DLB-145

Arias, Ron 1941- DLB-82

Arishima Takeo 1878-1923.............DLB-180

Aristophanes circa 446 B.C.-circa 386 B.C.
.........................DLB-176; CDWLB-1

Aristotle 384 B.C.-322 B.C.
.........................DLB-176; CDWLB-1

Ariyoshi Sawako 1931-1984............DLB-182

Arland, Marcel 1899-1986...............DLB-72

Arlen, Michael 1895-1956......DLB-36, 77, 162

Armah, Ayi Kwei 1939- DLB-117; CDWLB-3

Armantrout, Rae 1947- DLB-193

Der arme Hartmann ?-after 1150........DLB-148

Armed Services Editions................DLB-46

Armitage, G. E. (Robert Edric) 1956- ..DLB-267

Armstrong, Martin Donisthorpe
1882-1974........................DLB-197

Armstrong, Richard 1903- DLB-160

Armstrong, Terence Ian Fytton (see Gawsworth, John)

Arnauld, Antoine 1612-1694............DLB-268

Arndt, Ernst Moritz 1769-1860.........DLB-90

Arnim, Achim von 1781-1831...........DLB-90

Arnim, Bettina von 1785-1859..........DLB-90

Arnim, Elizabeth von (Countess Mary Annette
Beauchamp Russell) 1866-1941.....DLB-197

Arno Press..........................DLB-46

Arnold, Edwin 1832-1904...............DLB-35

Arnold, Edwin L. 1857-1935...........DLB-178

Arnold, Matthew
1822-1888...........DLB-32, 57; CDBLB-4

Preface to *Poems* (1853).............DLB-32

Arnold, Thomas 1795-1842.............DLB-55

Edward Arnold [publishing house]......DLB-112

Arnott, Peter 1962- DLB-233

Arnow, Harriette Simpson 1908-1986.....DLB-6

Arp, Bill (see Smith, Charles Henry)
Arpino, Giovanni 1927-1987..........DLB-177
Arreola, Juan José 1918-2001.........DLB-113
Arrian circa 89-circa 155..............DLB-176
J. W. Arrowsmith [publishing house]....DLB-106
Art
   John Dos Passos: Artist................Y-99
   The First Post-Impressionist Exhibition....DS-5
   The Omega Workshops................DS-10
   The Second Post-Impressionist
     Exhibition......................DS-5
Artaud, Antonin 1896-1948...........DLB-258
Artel, Jorge 1909-1994...............DLB-283
Arthur, Timothy Shay
   1809-1885........DLB-3, 42, 79, 250; DS-13
Artmann, H. C. 1921-2000............DLB-85
Arvin, Newton 1900-1963.............DLB-103
Asch, Nathan 1902-1964..............DLB-4, 28
   Nathan Asch Remembers Ford Madox
     Ford, Sam Roth, and Hart Crane....Y-02
Ascham, Roger 1515/1516-1568........DLB-236
Ash, John 1948-....................DLB-40
Ashbery, John 1927-..........DLB-5, 165; Y-81
Ashbridge, Elizabeth 1713-1755........DLB-200
Ashburnham, Bertram Lord
   1797-1878.....................DLB-184
Ashendene Press....................DLB-112
Asher, Sandy 1942-....................Y-83
Ashton, Winifred (see Dane, Clemence)
Asimov, Isaac 1920-1992.........DLB-8; Y-92
   Tribute to John Ciardi................Y-86
Askew, Anne circa 1521-1546.........DLB-136
Aspazija 1865-1943.......DLB-220; CDWLB-4
Asselin, Olivar 1874-1937............DLB-92
The Association of American Publishers....Y-99
The Association for Documentary Editing....Y-00
The Association for the Study of
   Literature and Environment (ASLE)....Y-99
Astell, Mary 1666-1731..............DLB-252
Astley, William (see Warung, Price)
Asturias, Miguel Angel
   1899-1974............DLB-113; CDWLB-3
Atava, S. (see Terpigorev, Sergei Nikolaevich)
Atheneum Publishers.................DLB-46
Atherton, Gertrude 1857-1948.....DLB-9, 78, 186
Athlone Press......................DLB-112
Atkins, Josiah circa 1755-1781.........DLB-31
Atkins, Russell 1926-................DLB-41
Atkinson, Kate 1951-...............DLB-267
Atkinson, Louisa 1834-1872..........DLB-230
The Atlantic Monthly Press............DLB-46
Attaway, William 1911-1986...........DLB-76
Atwood, Margaret 1939-........DLB-53, 251
Aubert, Alvin 1930-.................DLB-41
Aubert de Gaspé, Phillipe-Ignace-François
   1814-1841......................DLB-99
Aubert de Gaspé, Phillipe-Joseph
   1786-1871......................DLB-99

Aubin, Napoléon 1812-1890............DLB-99
Aubin, Penelope
   1685-circa 1731..................DLB-39
   Preface to *The Life of Charlotta
     du Pont* (1723)................DLB-39
Aubrey-Fletcher, Henry Lancelot (see Wade, Henry)
Auchincloss, Louis 1917-......DLB-2, 244; Y-80
Auden, W. H. 1907-1973..DLB-10, 20; CDBLB-6
Audio Art in America: A Personal Memoir...Y-85
Audubon, John James 1785-1851.......DLB-248
Audubon, John Woodhouse 1812-1862..DLB-183
Auerbach, Berthold 1812-1882.........DLB-133
Auernheimer, Raoul 1876-1948.........DLB-81
Augier, Emile 1820-1889..............DLB-192
Augustine 354-430...................DLB-115
Aulnoy, Marie-Catherine Le Jumel de Barneville,
   comtesse d' 1650/1651-1705........DLB-268
Aulus Gellius
   circa A.D. 125-circa A.D. 180?......DLB-211
Austen, Jane 1775-1817......DLB-116; CDBLB-3
Auster, Paul 1947-..................DLB-227
Austin, Alfred 1835-1913..............DLB-35
Austin, J. L. 1911-1960...............DLB-262
Austin, Jane Goodwin 1831-1894.......DLB-202
Austin, John 1790-1859...............DLB-262
Austin, Mary Hunter
   1868-1934.........DLB-9, 78, 206, 221, 275
Austin, William 1778-1841.............DLB-74
Australie (Emily Manning)
   1845-1890.....................DLB-230
Authors and Newspapers Association....DLB-46
Authors' Publishing Company..........DLB-49
Avallone, Michael 1924-1999..............Y-99
   Tribute to John D. MacDonald.........Y-86
   Tribute to Kenneth Millar............Y-83
   Tribute to Raymond Chandler.........Y-88
Avalon Books.......................DLB-46
Avancini, Nicolaus 1611-1686.........DLB-164
Avendaño, Fausto 1941-...............DLB-82
Averroës 1126-1198..................DLB-115
Avery, Gillian 1926-.................DLB-161
Avicenna 980-1037...................DLB-115
Avison, Margaret 1918-1987............DLB-53
Avon Books.........................DLB-46
Avyžius, Jonas 1922-1999..............DLB-220
Awdry, Wilbert Vere 1911-1997........DLB-160
Awoonor, Kofi 1935-.................DLB-117
Ayckbourn, Alan 1939-..........DLB-13, 245
Ayer, A. J. 1910-1989.................DLB-262
Aymé, Marcel 1902-1967...............DLB-72
Aytoun, Sir Robert 1570-1638.........DLB-121
Aytoun, William Edmondstoune
   1813-1865..................DLB-32, 159

B

B.V. (see Thomson, James)

Babbitt, Irving 1865-1933..............DLB-63
Babbitt, Natalie 1932-................DLB-52
John Babcock [publishing house].......DLB-49
Babel, Isaak Emmanuilovich 1894-1940...DLB-272
Babits, Mihály 1883-1941....DLB-215; CDWLB-4
Babrius circa 150-200................DLB-176
Babson, Marian 1929-................DLB-276
Baca, Jimmy Santiago 1952-..........DLB-122
Bacchelli, Riccardo 1891-1985.........DLB-264
Bache, Benjamin Franklin 1769-1798....DLB-43
Bacheller, Irving 1859-1950...........DLB-202
Bachmann, Ingeborg 1926-1973.........DLB-85
Bačinskaitė-Bučienė, Salomėja (see Nėris, Salomėja)
Bacon, Delia 1811-1859............DLB-1, 243
Bacon, Francis
   1561-1626......DLB-151, 236, 252; CDBLB-1
Bacon, Sir Nicholas circa 1510-1579....DLB-132
Bacon, Roger circa 1214/1220-1292.....DLB-115
Bacon, Thomas circa 1700-1768........DLB-31
Bacovia, George
   1881-1957...........DLB-220; CDWLB-4
Richard G. Badger and Company.......DLB-49
Bagaduce Music Lending Library.........Y-00
Bage, Robert 1728-1801...............DLB-39
Bagehot, Walter 1826-1877............DLB-55
Bagley, Desmond 1923-1983...........DLB-87
Bagley, Sarah G. 1806-1848?..........DLB-239
Bagnold, Enid 1889-1981...DLB-13, 160, 191, 245
Bagryana, Elisaveta
   1893-1991............DLB-147; CDWLB-4
Bahr, Hermann 1863-1934.........DLB-81, 118
Bailey, Abigail Abbot 1746-1815.......DLB-200
Bailey, Alfred Goldsworthy 1905-......DLB-68
Bailey, H. C. 1878-1961................DLB-77
Bailey, Jacob 1731-1808...............DLB-99
Bailey, Paul 1937-................DLB-14, 271
Bailey, Philip James 1816-1902.........DLB-32
Francis Bailey [publishing house].......DLB-49
Baillargeon, Pierre 1916-1967...........DLB-88
Baillie, Hugh 1890-1966................DLB-29
Baillie, Joanna 1762-1851..............DLB-93
Bailyn, Bernard 1922-.................DLB-17
Bain, Alexander
   English Composition and Rhetoric (1866)
   [excerpt].......................DLB-57
Bainbridge, Beryl 1933-..........DLB-14, 231
Baird, Irene 1901-1981.................DLB-68
Baker, Augustine 1575-1641...........DLB-151
Baker, Carlos 1909-1987..............DLB-103
Baker, David 1954-..................DLB-120
Baker, George Pierce 1866-1935.......DLB-266
Baker, Herschel C. 1914-1990.........DLB-111
Baker, Houston A., Jr. 1943-..........DLB-67
Baker, Howard
   Tribute to Caroline Gordon...........Y-81
   Tribute to Katherine Anne Porter......Y-80

Baker, Nicholson 1957- DLB-227; Y-00
   Review of Nicholson Baker's *Double Fold: Libraries and the Assault on Paper* Y-00
Baker, Samuel White 1821-1893 .... DLB-166
Baker, Thomas 1656-1740 .... DLB-213
Walter H. Baker Company ("Baker's Plays") DLB-49
The Baker and Taylor Company DLB-49
Bakhtin, Mikhail Mikhailovich 1895-1975 .... DLB-242
Bakunin, Mikhail Aleksandrovich 1814-1876 .... DLB-277
Balaban, John 1943- DLB-120
Bald, Wambly 1902- DLB-4
Balde, Jacob 1604-1668 .... DLB-164
Balderston, John 1889-1954 .... DLB-26
Baldwin, James 1924-1987 ..... DLB-2, 7, 33, 249, 278; Y-87; CDALB-1
Baldwin, Joseph Glover 1815-1864 .... DLB-3, 11, 248
Baldwin, Louisa (Mrs. Alfred Baldwin) 1845-1925 .... DLB-240
Baldwin, William circa 1515-1563 .... DLB-132
Richard and Anne Baldwin [publishing house] DLB-170
Bale, John 1495-1563 .... DLB-132
Balestrini, Nanni 1935- DLB-128, 196
Balfour, Sir Andrew 1630-1694 .... DLB-213
Balfour, Arthur James 1848-1930 ...... DLB-190
Balfour, Sir James 1600-1657 .... DLB-213
Ballantine Books DLB-46
Ballantyne, R. M. 1825-1894 .... DLB-163
Ballard, J. G. 1930- DLB-14, 207, 261
Ballard, Martha Moore 1735-1812 ...... DLB-200
Ballerini, Luigi 1940- DLB-128
Ballou, Maturin Murray (Lieutenant Murray) 1820-1895 .... DLB-79, 189
Robert O. Ballou [publishing house] DLB-46
Balzac, Guez de 1597?-1654 .... DLB-268
Balzac, Honoré de 1799-1855 .... DLB-119
Bambara, Toni Cade 1939-1995 .... DLB-38, 218; CDALB-7
Bamford, Samuel 1788-1872 .... DLB-190
A. L. Bancroft and Company DLB-49
Bancroft, George 1800-1891 ... DLB-1, 30, 59, 243
Bancroft, Hubert Howe 1832-1918 ... DLB-47, 140
Bandelier, Adolph F. 1840-1914 .... DLB-186
Bangs, John Kendrick 1862-1922 ..... DLB-11, 79
Banim, John 1798-1842 .... DLB-116, 158, 159
Banim, Michael 1796-1874 .... DLB-158, 159
Banks, Iain (M.) 1954- DLB-194, 261
Banks, John circa 1653-1706 .... DLB-80
Banks, Russell 1940- DLB-130, 278
Bannerman, Helen 1862-1946 .... DLB-141
Bantam Books DLB-46
Banti, Anna 1895-1985 .... DLB-177
Banville, John 1945- DLB-14, 271

Banville, Théodore de 1823-1891 .... DLB-217
Baraka, Amiri 1934- DLB-5, 7, 16, 38; DS-8; CDALB-1
Barańczak, Stanisław 1946- DLB-232
Baratynsky, Evgenii Abramovich 1800-1844 .... DLB-205
Barba-Jacob, Porfirio 1883-1942 .... DLB-283
Barbauld, Anna Laetitia 1743-1825 .... DLB-107, 109, 142, 158
Barbeau, Marius 1883-1969 .... DLB-92
Barber, John Warner 1798-1885 .... DLB-30
Bàrberi Squarotti, Giorgio 1929- DLB-128
Barbey d'Aurevilly, Jules-Amédée 1808-1889 .... DLB-119
Barbier, Auguste 1805-1882 .... DLB-217
Barbilian, Dan (see Barbu, Ion)
Barbour, John circa 1316-1395 .... DLB-146
Barbour, Ralph Henry 1870-1944 .... DLB-22
Barbu, Ion 1895-1961 ...... DLB-220; CDWLB-4
Barbusse, Henri 1873-1935 .... DLB-65
Barclay, Alexander circa 1475-1552 ..... DLB-132
E. E. Barclay and Company DLB-49
C. W. Bardeen [publishing house] DLB-49
Barham, Richard Harris 1788-1845 ...... DLB-159
Barich, Bill 1943- DLB-185
Baring, Maurice 1874-1945 .... DLB-34
Baring-Gould, Sabine 1834-1924 .... DLB-156, 190
Barker, A. L. 1918- DLB-14, 139
Barker, Clive 1952- DLB-261
Barker, Dudley (see Black, Lionel)
Barker, George 1913-1991 .... DLB-20
Barker, Harley Granville 1877-1946 ...... DLB-10
Barker, Howard 1946- DLB-13, 233
Barker, James Nelson 1784-1858 .... DLB-37
Barker, Jane 1652-1727 .... DLB-39, 131
Barker, Lady Mary Anne 1831-1911 ..... DLB-166
Barker, Pat 1943- DLB-271
Barker, William circa 1520-after 1576 .... DLB-132
Arthur Barker Limited DLB-112
Barkov, Ivan Semenovich 1732-1768 ..... DLB-150
Barks, Coleman 1937- DLB-5
Barlach, Ernst 1870-1938 .... DLB-56, 118
Barlow, Joel 1754-1812 .... DLB-37
   The Prospect of Peace (1778) DLB-37
Barnard, John 1681-1770 .... DLB-24
Barnard, Marjorie (M. Barnard Eldershaw) 1897-1987 .... DLB-260
Barnard, Robert 1936- DLB-276
Barne, Kitty (Mary Catherine Barne) 1883-1957 .... DLB-160
Barnes, Barnabe 1571-1609 .... DLB-132
Barnes, Djuna 1892-1982 .... DLB-4, 9, 45; DS-15
Barnes, Jim 1933- DLB-175
Barnes, Julian 1946- DLB-194; Y-93
   Notes for a Checklist of Publications Y-01
Barnes, Margaret Ayer 1886-1967 .... DLB-9

Barnes, Peter 1931- DLB-13, 233
Barnes, William 1801-1886 .... DLB-32
A. S. Barnes and Company DLB-49
Barnes and Noble Books DLB-46
Barnet, Miguel 1940- DLB-145
Barney, Natalie 1876-1972 .... DLB-4; DS-15
Barnfield, Richard 1574-1627 .... DLB-172
Richard W. Baron [publishing house] DLB-46
Barr, Amelia Edith Huddleston 1831-1919 .... DLB-202, 221
Barr, Robert 1850-1912 .... DLB-70, 92
Barral, Carlos 1928-1989 .... DLB-134
Barrax, Gerald William 1933- DLB-41, 120
Barrès, Maurice 1862-1923 .... DLB-123
Barrett, Eaton Stannard 1786-1820 ...... DLB-116
Barrie, J. M. 1860-1937 .... DLB-10, 141, 156; CDBLB-5
Barrie and Jenkins DLB-112
Barrio, Raymond 1921- DLB-82
Barrios, Gregg 1945- DLB-122
Barry, Philip 1896-1949 .... DLB-7, 228
Barry, Robertine (see Françoise)
Barry, Sebastian 1955- DLB-245
Barse and Hopkins DLB-46
Barstow, Stan 1928- DLB-14, 139, 207
   Tribute to John Braine Y-86
Barth, John 1930- DLB-2, 227
Barthelme, Donald 1931-1989 .... DLB-2, 234; Y-80, 89
Barthelme, Frederick 1943- DLB-244; Y-85
Bartholomew, Frank 1898-1985 .... DLB-127
Bartlett, John 1820-1905 .... DLB-1, 235
Bartol, Cyrus Augustus 1813-1900 .... DLB-1, 235
Barton, Bernard 1784-1849 .... DLB-96
Barton, John ca. 1610-1675 .... DLB-236
Barton, Thomas Pennant 1803-1869 ..... DLB-140
Bartram, John 1699-1777 .... DLB-31
Bartram, William 1739-1823 .... DLB-37
Barykova, Anna Pavlovna 1839-1893 .... DLB-277
Basic Books DLB-46
Basille, Theodore (see Becon, Thomas)
Bass, Rick 1958- DLB-212, 275
Bass, T. J. 1932- Y-81
Bassani, Giorgio 1916-2000 .... DLB-128, 177
Basse, William circa 1583-1653 .... DLB-121
Bassett, John Spencer 1867-1928 .... DLB-17
Bassler, Thomas Joseph (see Bass, T. J.)
Bate, Walter Jackson 1918-1999 ..... DLB-67, 103
Bateman, Stephen circa 1510-1584 ...... DLB-136
Christopher Bateman [publishing house] .. DLB-170
Bates, H. E. 1905-1974 .... DLB-162, 191
Bates, Katharine Lee 1859-1929 .... DLB-71
Batiushkov, Konstantin Nikolaevich 1787-1855 .... DLB-205
B. T. Batsford [publishing house] DLB-106

Battiscombe, Georgina 1905- DLB-155	Becher, Ulrich 1910-1990 .... DLB-69	Bell, Vanessa 1879-1961 .... DS-10
The Battle of Maldon circa 1000 .... DLB-146	Becker, Carl 1873-1945 .... DLB-17	George Bell and Sons DLB-106
Baudelaire, Charles 1821-1867 .... DLB-217	Becker, Jurek 1937-1997 .... DLB-75	Robert Bell [publishing house] DLB-49
Bauer, Bruno 1809-1882 .... DLB-133	Becker, Jurgen 1932- DLB-75	Bellamy, Edward 1850-1898 .... DLB-12
Bauer, Wolfgang 1941- DLB-124	Beckett, Samuel 1906-1989 .... DLB-13, 15, 233; Y-90; CDBLB-7	Bellamy, Joseph 1719-1790 .... DLB-31
Baum, L. Frank 1856-1919 .... DLB-22	Beckford, William 1760-1844 ...... DLB-39, 213	John Bellamy [publishing house] DLB-170
Baum, Vicki 1888-1960 .... DLB-85	Beckham, Barry 1944- DLB-33	*La Belle Assemblée* 1806-1837 .... DLB-110
Baumbach, Jonathan 1933- Y-80	Bećković, Matija 1939- DLB-181	Bellezza, Dario 1944-1996 .... DLB-128
Bausch, Richard 1945- DLB-130	Becon, Thomas circa 1512-1567 .... DLB-136	Belloc, Hilaire 1870-1953 ....DLB-19, 100, 141, 174
Tribute to James Dickey Y-97	Becque, Henry 1837-1899 .... DLB-192	Belloc, Madame (see Parkes, Bessie Rayner)
Tribute to Peter Taylor Y-94	Beddoes, Thomas 1760-1808 .... DLB-158	Bellonci, Maria 1902-1986 .... DLB-196
Bausch, Robert 1945- DLB-218	Beddoes, Thomas Lovell 1803-1849 ..... DLB-96	Bellow, Saul 1915- ... DLB-2, 28; Y-82; DS-3; CDALB-1
Bawden, Nina 1925- DLB-14, 161, 207	Bede circa 673-735 .... DLB-146	Tribute to Isaac Bashevis Singer Y-91
Bax, Clifford 1886-1962 ....DLB-10, 100	Bedford-Jones, H. 1887-1949 .... DLB-251	Belmont Productions DLB-46
Baxter, Charles 1947- DLB-130	Bedregal, Yolanda 1913-1999 .... DLB-283	Bels, Alberts 1938- DLB-232
Bayer, Eleanor (see Perry, Eleanor)	Beebe, William 1877-1962 ....DLB-275	Belševica, Vizma 1931- ... DLB-232; CDWLB-4
Bayer, Konrad 1932-1964 .... DLB-85	Beecher, Catharine Esther 1800-1878 .... DLB-1, 243	Bemelmans, Ludwig 1898-1962 .... DLB-22
Bayle, Pierre 1647-1706 .... DLB-268	Beecher, Henry Ward 1813-1887 .... DLB-3, 43, 250	Bemis, Samuel Flagg 1891-1973 ....DLB-17
Bayley, Barrington J. 1937- DLB-261	Beer, George L. 1872-1920 .... DLB-47	William Bemrose [publishing house] DLB-106
Baynes, Pauline 1922- DLB-160	Beer, Johann 1655-1700 .... DLB-168	Ben no Naishi 1228?-1271? DLB-203
Baynton, Barbara 1857-1929 .... DLB-230	Beer, Patricia 1919-1999 .... DLB-40	Benchley, Robert 1889-1945 .... DLB-11
Bazin, Hervé (Jean Pierre Marie Hervé-Bazin) 1911-1996 .... DLB-83	Beerbohm, Max 1872-1956 .... DLB-34, 100	Bencúr, Matej (see Kukučin, Martin)
The BBC Four Samuel Johnson Prize for Non-fiction Y-02	Beer-Hofmann, Richard 1866-1945 ...... DLB-81	Benedetti, Mario 1920- DLB-113
Beach, Sylvia 1887-1962 .... DLB-4; DS-15	Beers, Henry A. 1847-1926 .... DLB-71	Benedict, Pinckney 1964- DLB-244
Beacon Press DLB-49	S. O. Beeton [publishing house] DLB-106	Benedict, Ruth 1887-1948 .... DLB-246
Beadle and Adams DLB-49	Bégon, Elisabeth 1696-1755 .... DLB-99	Benedictus, David 1938- DLB-14
Beagle, Peter S. 1939- Y-80	Behan, Brendan 1923-1964 .... DLB-13, 233; CDBLB-7	Benedikt, Michael 1935- DLB-5
Beal, M. F. 1937- Y-81	Behn, Aphra 1640?-1689 .... DLB-39, 80, 131	Benediktov, Vladimir Grigor'evich 1807-1873 .... DLB-205
Beale, Howard K. 1899-1959 .... DLB-17	Behn, Harry 1898-1973 .... DLB-61	Benét, Stephen Vincent 1898-1943 ....DLB-4, 48, 102, 249
Beard, Charles A. 1874-1948 .... DLB-17	Behrman, S. N. 1893-1973 ....DLB-7, 44	Stephen Vincent Benét Centenary Y-97
Beat Generation (Beats) As I See It, by Carolyn Cassady DLB-16	Beklemishev, Iurii Solomonvich (see Krymov, Iurii Solomonovich)	Benét, William Rose 1886-1950 .... DLB-45
A Beat Chronology: The First Twenty-five Years, 1944-1969 .... DLB-16	Belaney, Archibald Stansfeld (see Grey Owl)	Benford, Gregory 1941- Y-82
The Commercialization of the Image of Revolt, by Kenneth Rexroth .. DLB-16	Belasco, David 1853-1931 .... DLB-7	Benjamin, Park 1809-1864 .....DLB-3, 59, 73, 250
Four Essays on the Beat Generation .. DLB-16	Clarke Belford and Company DLB-49	Benjamin, Peter (see Cunningham, Peter)
in New York City DLB-237	Belgian Luxembourg American Studies Association Y-01	Benjamin, S. G. W. 1837-1914 .... DLB-189
in the West DLB-237	Belinsky, Vissarion Grigor'evich 1811-1848 .... DLB-198	Benjamin, Walter 1892-1940 .... DLB-242
Outlaw Days DLB-16	Belitt, Ben 1911- DLB-5	Benlowes, Edward 1602-1676 .... DLB-126
Periodicals of DLB-16	Belknap, Jeremy 1744-1798 .... DLB-30, 37	Benn, Gottfried 1886-1956 .... DLB-56
Beattie, Ann 1947- DLB-218, 278; Y-82	Bell, Adrian 1901-1980 .... DLB-191	Benn Brothers Limited DLB-106
Beattie, James 1735-1803 .... DLB-109	Bell, Clive 1881-1964 ....DS-10	Bennett, Arnold 1867-1931 .... DLB-10, 34, 98, 135; CDBLB-5
Beatty, Chester 1875-1968 .... DLB-201	Bell, Daniel 1919- DLB-246	The Arnold Bennett Society Y-98
Beauchemin, Nérée 1850-1931 .... DLB-92	Bell, Gertrude Margaret Lowthian 1868-1926 ....DLB-174	Bennett, Charles 1899-1995 .... DLB-44
Beauchemin, Yves 1941- DLB-60	Bell, James Madison 1826-1902 .... DLB-50	Bennett, Emerson 1822-1905 .... DLB-202
Beaugrand, Honoré 1848-1906 .... DLB-99	Bell, Madison Smartt 1957- DLB-218, 278	Bennett, Gwendolyn 1902-1981 .... DLB-51
Beaulieu, Victor-Lévy 1945- DLB-53	Tribute to Andrew Nelson Lytle Y-95	Bennett, Hal 1930- DLB-33
Beaumont, Francis circa 1584-1616 .... DLB-58; CDBLB-1	Tribute to Peter Taylor Y-94	Bennett, James Gordon 1795-1872 .... DLB-43
Beaumont, Sir John 1583?-1627 .... DLB-121	Bell, Marvin 1937- DLB-5	Bennett, James Gordon, Jr. 1841-1918 .... DLB-23
Beaumont, Joseph 1616-1699 .... DLB-126	Bell, Millicent 1919- DLB-111	Bennett, John 1865-1956 .... DLB-42
Beauvoir, Simone de 1908-1986 .....DLB-72; Y-86	Bell, Quentin 1910-1996 .... DLB-155	Bennett, Louise 1919- DLB-117; CDWLB-3
Personal Tribute to Simone de Beauvoir ... Y-86		Benni, Stefano 1947- DLB-196
		Benoit, Jacques 1941- DLB-60

Benson, A. C. 1862-1925 ... DLB-98
Benson, E. F. 1867-1940 ... DLB-135, 153
    The E. F. Benson Society ... Y-98
    The Tilling Society ... Y-98
Benson, Jackson J. 1930- ... DLB-111
Benson, Robert Hugh 1871-1914 ... DLB-153
Benson, Stella 1892-1933 ... DLB-36, 162
Bent, James Theodore 1852-1897 ... DLB-174
Bent, Mabel Virginia Anna ?-? ... DLB-174
Bentham, Jeremy 1748-1832 ... DLB-107, 158, 252
Bentley, E. C. 1875-1956 ... DLB-70
Bentley, Phyllis 1894-1977 ... DLB-191
Bentley, Richard 1662-1742 ... DLB-252
Richard Bentley [publishing house] ... DLB-106
Benton, Robert 1932- ... DLB-44
Benziger Brothers ... DLB-49
Beowulf circa 900-1000 or 790-825 ... DLB-146; CDBLB-1
Berent, Wacław 1873-1940 ... DLB-215
Beresford, Anne 1929- ... DLB-40
Beresford, John Davys 1873-1947 ... DLB-162, 178, 197
    "Experiment in the Novel" (1929) [excerpt] ... DLB-36
Beresford-Howe, Constance 1922- ... DLB-88
R. G. Berford Company ... DLB-49
Berg, Stephen 1934- ... DLB-5
Bergengruen, Werner 1892-1964 ... DLB-56
Berger, John 1926- ... DLB-14, 207
Berger, Meyer 1898-1959 ... DLB-29
Berger, Thomas 1924- ... DLB-2; Y-80
    A Statement by Thomas Berger ... Y-80
Bergman, Hjalmar 1883-1931 ... DLB-259
Bergman, Ingmar 1918- ... DLB-257
Berkeley, Anthony 1893-1971 ... DLB-77
Berkeley, George 1685-1753 ... DLB-31, 101, 252
The Berkley Publishing Corporation ... DLB-46
Berlin, Irving 1888-1989 ... DLB-265
Berlin, Lucia 1936- ... DLB-130
Berman, Marshall 1940- ... DLB-246
Bernal, Vicente J. 1888-1915 ... DLB-82
Bernanos, Georges 1888-1948 ... DLB-72
Bernard, Catherine 1663?-1712 ... DLB-268
Bernard, Harry 1898-1979 ... DLB-92
Bernard, John 1756-1828 ... DLB-37
Bernard of Chartres circa 1060-1124? ... DLB-115
Bernard of Clairvaux 1090-1153 ... DLB-208
Bernard, Richard 1568-1641 ... DLB-281
Bernard Silvestris flourished circa 1130-1160 ... DLB-208
Bernari, Carlo 1909-1992 ... DLB-177
Bernhard, Thomas 1931-1989 ... DLB-85, 124; CDWLB-2
Bernières, Louis de 1954- ... DLB-271
Bernstein, Charles 1950- ... DLB-169
Berriault, Gina 1926-1999 ... DLB-130

Berrigan, Daniel 1921- ... DLB-5
Berrigan, Ted 1934-1983 ... DLB-5, 169
Berry, Wendell 1934- ... DLB-5, 6, 234, 275
Berryman, John 1914-1972 ... DLB-48; CDALB-1
Bersianik, Louky 1930- ... DLB-60
Thomas Berthelet [publishing house] ... DLB-170
Berto, Giuseppe 1914-1978 ... DLB-177
Bertocci, Peter Anthony 1910-1989 ... DLB-279
Bertolucci, Attilio 1911-2000 ... DLB-128
Berton, Pierre 1920- ... DLB-68
Bertrand, Louis "Aloysius" 1807-1841 ... DLB-217
Besant, Sir Walter 1836-1901 ... DLB-135, 190
Bessette, Gerard 1920- ... DLB-53
Bessie, Alvah 1904-1985 ... DLB-26
Bester, Alfred 1913-1987 ... DLB-8
Besterman, Theodore 1904-1976 ... DLB-201
Beston, Henry (Henry Beston Sheahan) 1888-1968 ... DLB-275
Best-Seller Lists
    An Assessment ... Y-84
    What's Really Wrong With Bestseller Lists ... Y-84
Bestuzhev, Aleksandr Aleksandrovich (Marlinsky) 1797-1837 ... DLB-198
Bestuzhev, Nikolai Aleksandrovich 1791-1855 ... DLB-198
Betham-Edwards, Matilda Barbara (see Edwards, Matilda Barbara Betham-)
Betjeman, John 1906-1984 ... DLB-20; Y-84; CDBLB-7
Betocchi, Carlo 1899-1986 ... DLB-128
Bettarini, Mariella 1942- ... DLB-128
Betts, Doris 1932- ... DLB-218; Y-82
Beveridge, Albert J. 1862-1927 ... DLB-17
Beverley, Robert circa 1673-1722 ... DLB-24, 30
Bevilacqua, Alberto 1934- ... DLB-196
Bevington, Louisa Sarah 1845-1895 ... DLB-199
Beyle, Marie-Henri (see Stendhal)
Białoszewski, Miron 1922-1983 ... DLB-232
Bianco, Margery Williams 1881-1944 ... DLB-160
Bibaud, Adèle 1854-1941 ... DLB-92
Bibaud, Michel 1782-1857 ... DLB-99
Bibliography
    Bibliographical and Textual Scholarship Since World War II ... Y-89
    Center for Bibliographical Studies and Research at the University of California, Riverside ... Y-91
    The Great Bibliographers Series ... Y-93
    Primary Bibliography: A Retrospective ... Y-95
Bichsel, Peter 1935- ... DLB-75
Bickerstaff, Isaac John 1733-circa 1808 ... DLB-89
Drexel Biddle [publishing house] ... DLB-49
Bidermann, Jacob 1577 or 1578-1639 ... DLB-164
Bidwell, Walter Hilliard 1798-1881 ... DLB-79
Bienek, Horst 1930-1990 ... DLB-75
Bierbaum, Otto Julius 1865-1910 ... DLB-66

Bierce, Ambrose 1842-1914? ... DLB-11, 12, 23, 71, 74, 186; CDALB-3
Bigelow, William F. 1879-1966 ... DLB-91
Biggle, Lloyd, Jr. 1923- ... DLB-8
Bigiaretti, Libero 1905-1993 ... DLB-177
Bigland, Eileen 1898-1970 ... DLB-195
Biglow, Hosea (see Lowell, James Russell)
Bigongiari, Piero 1914-1997 ... DLB-128
Bilenchi, Romano 1909-1989 ... DLB-264
Billinger, Richard 1890-1965 ... DLB-124
Billings, Hammatt 1818-1874 ... DLB-188
Billings, John Shaw 1898-1975 ... DLB-137
Billings, Josh (see Shaw, Henry Wheeler)
Binding, Rudolf G. 1867-1938 ... DLB-66
Bingay, Malcolm 1884-1953 ... DLB-241
Bingham, Caleb 1757-1817 ... DLB-42
Bingham, George Barry 1906-1988 ... DLB-127
Bingham, Sallie 1937- ... DLB-234
William Bingley [publishing house] ... DLB-154
Binyon, Laurence 1869-1943 ... DLB-19
Biographia Brittanica ... DLB-142
Biography
    Biographical Documents ... Y-84, 85
    A Celebration of Literary Biography ... Y-98
    Conference on Modern Biography ... Y-85
    The Cult of Biography
    Excerpts from the Second Folio Debate: "Biographies are generally a disease of English Literature" ... Y-86
    New Approaches to Biography: Challenges from Critical Theory, USC Conference on Literary Studies, 1990 ... Y-90
    "The New Biography," by Virginia Woolf, *New York Herald Tribune*, 30 October 1927 ... DLB-149
    "The Practice of Biography," in *The English Sense of Humour and Other Essays*, by Harold Nicolson ... DLB-149
    "Principles of Biography," in *Elizabethan and Other Essays*, by Sidney Lee ... DLB-149
    Remarks at the Opening of "The Biographical Part of Literature" Exhibition, by William R. Cagle ... Y-98
    Survey of Literary Biographies ... Y-00
    A Transit of Poets and Others: American Biography in 1982 ... Y-82
    The Year in Literary Biography ... Y-83–01
Biography, The Practice of:
    An Interview with B. L. Reid ... Y-83
    An Interview with David Herbert Donald ... Y-87
    An Interview with Humphrey Carpenter ... Y-84
    An Interview with Joan Mellen ... Y-94
    An Interview with John Caldwell Guilds ... Y-92
    An Interview with Michael Reynolds ... Y-95
    An Interview with Stanley Weintraub ... Y-82
    An Interview with William Manchester ... Y-85
John Bioren [publishing house] ... DLB-49
Bioy Casares, Adolfo 1914-1999 ... DLB-113
Bird, Isabella Lucy 1831-1904 ... DLB-166

Bird, Robert Montgomery 1806-1854 ... DLB-202

Bird, William 1888-1963 .... DLB-4; DS-15

    The Cost of the *Cantos:* William Bird
      to Ezra Pound.................... Y-01

Birken, Sigmund von 1626-1681 .... DLB-164

Birney, Earle 1904-1995 .... DLB-88

Birrell, Augustine 1850-1933 .... DLB-98

Bisher, Furman 1918- DLB-171

Bishop, Elizabeth
    1911-1979.......... DLB-5, 169; CDALB-6

    The Elizabeth Bishop Society Y-01

Bishop, John Peale 1892-1944 ...... DLB-4, 9, 45

Bismarck, Otto von 1815-1898......... DLB-129

Bisset, Robert 1759-1805 .... DLB-142

Bissett, Bill 1939- DLB-53

Bitzius, Albert (see Gotthelf, Jeremias)

Bjørnvig, Thorkild 1918- DLB-214

Black, David (D. M.) 1941- DLB-40

Black, Gavin (Oswald Morris Wynd)
    1913-1998...................DLB-276

Black, Lionel (Dudley Barker)
    1910-1980....................DLB-276

Black, Winifred 1863-1936............ DLB-25

Walter J. Black [publishing house] DLB-46

Blackamore, Arthur 1679-? DLB-24, 39

Blackburn, Alexander L. 1929- Y-85

Blackburn, John 1923-1993 .... DLB-261

Blackburn, Paul 1926-1971........DLB-16; Y-81

Blackburn, Thomas 1916-1977 .... DLB-27

Blacker, Terence 1948- DLB-271

Blackmore, R. D. 1825-1900 .... DLB-18

Blackmore, Sir Richard 1654-1729 ...... DLB-131

Blackmur, R. P. 1904-1965............ DLB-63

Basil Blackwell, Publisher............ DLB-106

Blackwood, Algernon Henry
    1869-1951 ....DLB-153, 156, 178

Blackwood, Caroline 1931-1996..... DLB-14, 207

William Blackwood and Sons, Ltd. DLB-154

Blackwood's Edinburgh Magazine
    1817-1980.................... DLB-110

Blades, William 1824-1890............ DLB-184

Blaga, Lucian 1895-1961 .... DLB-220

Blagden, Isabella 1817?-1873 .... DLB-199

Blair, Eric Arthur (see Orwell, George)

Blair, Francis Preston 1791-1876......... DLB-43

Blair, Hugh
    Lectures on Rhetoric and Belles Lettres (1783),
    [excerpts] DLB-31

Blair, James circa 1655-1743 .... DLB-24

Blair, John Durburrow 1759-1823 .... DLB-37

Blais, Marie-Claire 1939- DLB-53

Blaise, Clark 1940- DLB-53

Blake, George 1893-1961 .... DLB-191

Blake, Lillie Devereux 1833-1913... DLB-202, 221

Blake, Nicholas (C. Day Lewis)
    1904-1972..................... DLB-77

Blake, William
    1757-1827 ...... DLB-93, 154, 163; CDBLB-3

The Blakiston Company DLB-49

Blanchard, Stephen 1950- DLB-267

Blanchot, Maurice 1907-2003 .... DLB-72

Blanckenburg, Christian Friedrich von
    1744-1796 .... DLB-94

Blandiana, Ana 1942- DLB-232; CDWLB-4

Blanshard, Brand 1892-1987 ....DLB-279

Blaser, Robin 1925- DLB-165

Blaumanis, Rudolfs 1863-1908......... DLB-220

Bleasdale, Alan 1946- DLB-245

Bledsoe, Albert Taylor
    1809-1877..................DLB-3, 79, 248

Bleecker, Ann Eliza 1752-1783 .... DLB-200

Blelock and Company DLB-49

Blennerhassett, Margaret Agnew
    1773-1842...................... DLB-99

Geoffrey Bles [publishing house] DLB-112

Blessington, Marguerite, Countess of
    1789-1849.................... DLB-166

Blew, Mary Clearman 1939- DLB-256

The Blickling Homilies circa 971 .... DLB-146

Blind, Mathilde 1841-1896............ DLB-199

Blish, James 1921-1975 .... DLB-8

E. Bliss and E. White
    [publishing house] DLB-49

Bliven, Bruce 1889-1977 .... DLB-137

Blixen, Karen 1885-1962 .... DLB-214

Bloch, Robert 1917-1994................ DLB-44

    Tribute to John D. MacDonald Y-86

Block, Lawrence 1938- DLB-226

Block, Rudolph (see Lessing, Bruno)

Blondal, Patricia 1926-1959 .... DLB-88

Bloom, Harold 1930- DLB-67

Bloomer, Amelia 1818-1894.......... DLB-79

Bloomfield, Robert 1766-1823 .... DLB-93

Bloomsbury Group.................DS-10

    The *Dreadnought* Hoax. DS-10

Blotner, Joseph 1923- DLB-111

Blount, Thomas 1618?-1679 .... DLB-236

Bloy, Léon 1846-1917................. DLB-123

Blume, Judy 1938- DLB-52

    Tribute to Theodor Seuss Geisel Y-91

Blunck, Hans Friedrich 1888-1961....... DLB-66

Blunden, Edmund 1896-1974 .... DLB-20, 100, 155

Blundeville, Thomas 1522?-1606 .... DLB-236

Blunt, Lady Anne Isabella Noel
    1837-1917.....................DLB-174

Blunt, Wilfrid Scawen 1840-1922.....DLB-19, 174

Bly, Nellie (see Cochrane, Elizabeth)

Bly, Robert 1926- DLB-5

Blyton, Enid 1897-1968 .... DLB-160

Boaden, James 1762-1839 .... DLB-89

Boas, Frederick S. 1862-1957.......... DLB-149

The Bobbs-Merrill Company DLB-46

The Bobbs-Merrill Archive at the
    Lilly Library, Indiana University Y-90

Boborykin, Petr Dmitrievich 1836-1921.. DLB-238

Bobrov, Semen Sergeevich 1763?-1810... DLB-150

Bobrowski, Johannes 1917-1965......... DLB-75

Bodenheim, Maxwell 1892-1954 ...... DLB-9, 45

Bodenstedt, Friedrich von 1819-1892.... DLB-129

Bodini, Vittorio 1914-1970 .... DLB-128

Bodkin, M. McDonnell 1850-1933....... DLB-70

Bodley, Sir Thomas 1545-1613 .... DLB-213

Bodley Head....................... DLB-112

Bodmer, Johann Jakob 1698-1783 .... DLB-97

Bodmershof, Imma von 1895-1982 ...... DLB-85

Bodsworth, Fred 1918- DLB-68

Boehm, Sydney 1908- DLB-44

Boer, Charles 1939- DLB-5

Boethius circa 480-circa 524........... DLB-115

Boethius of Dacia circa 1240-? DLB-115

Bogan, Louise 1897-1970 .... DLB-45, 169

Bogarde, Dirk 1921-1999 .... DLB-14

Bogdanovich, Ippolit Fedorovich
    circa 1743-1803 .... DLB-150

David Bogue [publishing house]........ DLB-106

Böhme, Jakob 1575-1624 .... DLB-164

H. G. Bohn [publishing house] DLB-106

Bohse, August 1661-1742 .... DLB-168

Boie, Heinrich Christian 1744-1806 ...... DLB-94

Boileau-Despréaux, Nicolas 1636-1711....DLB-268

Bok, Edward W. 1863-1930...... DLB-91; DS-16

Boland, Eavan 1944- DLB-40

Boldrewood, Rolf (Thomas Alexander Browne)
    1826?-1915.................... DLB-230

Bolingbroke, Henry St. John, Viscount
    1678-1751..................... DLB-101

Böll, Heinrich
    1917-1985.........DLB-69; Y-85; CDWLB-2

Bolling, Robert 1738-1775............. DLB-31

Bolotov, Andrei Timofeevich
    1738-1833.................... DLB-150

Bolt, Carol 1941- DLB-60

Bolt, Robert 1924-1995 .... DLB-13, 233

Bolton, Herbert E. 1870-1953 ....DLB-17

Bonaventura....................... DLB-90

Bonaventure circa 1217-1274 .... DLB-115

Bonaviri, Giuseppe 1924- DLB-177

Bond, Edward 1934- DLB-13

Bond, Michael 1926- DLB-161

Albert and Charles Boni
    [publishing house] DLB-46

Boni and Liveright DLB-46

Bonnefoy, Yves 1923- DLB-258

Bonner, Marita 1899-1971 .... DLB-228

Bonner, Paul Hyde 1893-1968........... DS-17

Bonner, Sherwood (see McDowell, Katharine
    Sherwood Bonner)

Robert Bonner's Sons................. DLB-49

Bonnin, Gertrude Simmons (see Zitkala-Ša)

Bonsanti, Alessandro 1904-1984 .... DLB-177

Bontempelli, Massimo 1878-1960 .... DLB-264

Bontemps, Arna 1902-1973 .... DLB-48, 51

The Book Buyer (1867-1880, 1884-1918,
    1935-1938) DS-13

The Book League of America DLB-46

Book Reviewing
    The American Book Review: A Sketch... Y-92
    Book Reviewing and the
        Literary Scene Y-96, 97
    Book Reviewing in America........ Y-87–94
    Book Reviewing in America and the
        Literary Scene Y-95
    Book Reviewing in Texas Y-94
    Book Reviews in Glossy Magazines..... Y-95
    Do They or Don't They?
        Writers Reading Book Reviews..... Y-01
    The Most Powerful Book Review
        in America [*New York Times
        Book Review*] Y-82
    Some Surprises and Universal Truths ... Y-92
    The Year in Book Reviewing and the
        Literary Situation............... Y-98

Book Supply Company DLB-49

The Book Trade History Group Y-93

The Booker Prize..................... Y-96-98
    Address by Anthony Thwaite,
        Chairman of the Booker Prize Judges
        Comments from Former Booker
        Prize Winners Y-86

Boorde, Andrew circa 1490-1549 .... DLB-136

Boorstin, Daniel J. 1914- DLB-17
    Tribute to Archibald MacLeish Y-82
    Tribute to Charles Scribner Jr......... Y-95

Booth, Franklin 1874-1948............. DLB-188

Booth, Mary L. 1831-1889 .... DLB-79

Booth, Philip 1925- Y-82

Booth, Wayne C. 1921- DLB-67

Booth, William 1829-1912............. DLB-190

Borchardt, Rudolf 1877-1945........... DLB-66

Borchert, Wolfgang 1921-1947 ...... DLB-69, 124

Borel, Pétrus 1809-1859................. DLB-119

Borges, Jorge Luis
    1899-1986 ... DLB-113, 283; Y-86; CDWLB-3
    The Poetry of Jorge Luis Borges Y-86
    A Personal Tribute................... Y-86

Borgese, Giuseppe Antonio 1882-1952 ... DLB-264

Börne, Ludwig 1786-1837 .... DLB-90

Bornstein, Miriam 1950- DLB-209

Borowski, Tadeusz
    1922-1951............. DLB-215; CDWLB-4

Borrow, George 1803-1881 ...... DLB-21, 55, 166

Bosanquet, Bernard 1848-1923 .... DLB-262

Bosch, Juan 1909-2001................. DLB-145

Bosco, Henri 1888-1976............... DLB-72

Bosco, Monique 1927 .... DLB-53

Bosman, Herman Charles 1905-1951 .... DLB-225

Bossuet, Jacques-Bénigne 1627-1704 ..... DLB-268

Bostic, Joe 1908-1988................. DLB-241

Boston, Lucy M. 1892-1990 .... DLB-161

Boston Quarterly Review.................. DLB-1

Boston University
    Editorial Institute at Boston University... Y-00
    Special Collections at Boston University . Y-99

Boswell, James
    1740-1795 .... DLB-104, 142; CDBLB-2

Boswell, Robert 1953- DLB-234

Bosworth, David Y-82
    Excerpt from "Excerpts from a Report
        of the Commission," in *The Death
        of Descartes* Y-82

Bote, Hermann circa 1460-circa 1520.... DLB-179

Botev, Khristo 1847-1876.............. DLB-147

Botkin, Vasilii Petrovich 1811-1869 ..... DLB-277

Botta, Anne C. Lynch 1815-1891 ..... DLB-3, 250

Botto, Ján (see Krasko, Ivan)

Bottome, Phyllis 1882-1963............ DLB-197

Bottomley, Gordon 1874-1948.......... DLB-10

Bottoms, David 1949- DLB-120; Y-83
    Tribute to James Dickey Y-97

Bottrall, Ronald 1906- DLB-20

Bouchardy, Joseph 1810-1870 .... DLB-192

Boucher, Anthony 1911-1968 .... DLB-8

Boucher, Jonathan 1738-1804 .... DLB-31

Boucher de Boucherville, Georges
    1814-1894 .... DLB-99

Boudreau, Daniel (see Coste, Donat)

Bouhours, Dominique 1628-1702 .... DLB-268

Bourassa, Napoléon 1827-1916 .... DLB-99

Bourget, Paul 1852-1935 .... DLB-123

Bourinot, John George 1837-1902 .... DLB-99

Bourjaily, Vance 1922- DLB-2, 143

Bourne, Edward Gaylord 1860-1908..... DLB-47

Bourne, Randolph 1886-1918 .... DLB-63

Bousoño, Carlos 1923- DLB-108

Bousquet, Joë 1897-1950 .... DLB-72

Bova, Ben 1932- Y-81

Bovard, Oliver K. 1872-1945 .... DLB-25

Bove, Emmanuel 1898-1945 .... DLB-72

Bowen, Elizabeth
    1899-1973 .... DLB-15, 162; CDBLB-7

Bowen, Francis 1811-1890........ DLB-1, 59, 235

Bowen, John 1924- DLB-13

Bowen, Marjorie 1886-1952 .... DLB-153

Bowen-Merrill Company............. DLB-49

Bowering, George 1935- DLB-53

Bowers, Bathsheba 1671-1718 .... DLB-200

Bowers, Claude G. 1878-1958 .... DLB-17

Bowers, Edgar 1924-2000 .... DLB-5

Bowers, Fredson Thayer
    1905-1991 .... DLB-140; Y-91
    The Editorial Style of Fredson Bowers .. Y-91
    Fredson Bowers and
        Studies in Bibliography Y-91

Fredson Bowers and the Cambridge
    Beaumont and Fletcher Y-91
Fredson Bowers as Critic of Renaissance
    Dramatic Literature............. Y-91
Fredson Bowers as Music Critic........ Y-91
Fredson Bowers, Master Teacher Y-91
An Interview [on Nabokov]........... Y-80
Working with Fredson Bowers Y-91

Bowles, Paul 1910-1999...... DLB-5, 6, 218; Y-99

Bowles, Samuel, III 1826-1878 .... DLB-43

Bowles, William Lisle 1762-1850.......... DLB-93

Bowman, Louise Morey 1882-1944....... DLB-68

Bowne, Borden Parker 1847-1919 .... DLB-270

Boyd, James 1888-1944 .... DLB-9; DS-16

Boyd, John 1919- DLB-8

Boyd, Martin 1893-1972 .... DLB-260

Boyd, Thomas 1898-1935 .... DLB-9; DS-16

Boyd, William 1952- DLB-231

Boye, Karin 1900-1941 .... DLB-259

Boyesen, Hjalmar Hjorth
    1848-1895 .... DLB-12, 71; DS-13

Boylan, Clare 1948- DLB-267

Boyle, Kay 1902-1992   DLB-4, 9, 48, 86; DS-15;
    .... Y-93

Boyle, Roger, Earl of Orrery 1621-1679 ... DLB-80

Boyle, T. Coraghessan
    1948- DLB-218, 278; Y-86

Božić, Mirko 1919- DLB-181

Brackenbury, Alison 1953- DLB-40

Brackenridge, Hugh Henry
    1748-1816 .... DLB-11, 37
    The Rising Glory of America........ DLB-37

Brackett, Charles 1892-1969 .... DLB-26

Brackett, Leigh 1915-1978 .... DLB-8, 26

John Bradburn [publishing house]........ DLB-49

Bradbury, Malcolm 1932-2000 ...... DLB-14, 207

Bradbury, Ray 1920- DLB-2, 8; CDALB-6

Bradbury and Evans DLB-106

Braddon, Mary Elizabeth
    1835-1915 .... DLB-18, 70, 156

Bradford, Andrew 1686-1742 .... DLB-43, 73

Bradford, Gamaliel 1863-1932........... DLB-17

Bradford, John 1749-1830 .... DLB-43

Bradford, Roark 1896-1948 .... DLB-86

Bradford, William 1590-1657 .... DLB-24, 30

Bradford, William, III 1719-1791... DLB-43, 73

Bradlaugh, Charles 1833-1891 .... DLB-57

Bradley, David 1950- DLB-33

Bradley, F. H. 1846-1924............... DLB-262

Bradley, Katherine Harris (see Field, Michael)

Bradley, Marion Zimmer 1930-1999....... DLB-8

Bradley, William Aspenwall 1878-1939..... DLB-4

Ira Bradley and Company............. DLB-49

J. W. Bradley and Company DLB-49

Bradshaw, Henry 1831-1886............ DLB-184

Bradstreet, Anne
    1612 or 1613-1672........ DLB-24; CDALB-2

Bradūnas, Kazys 1917- DLB-220
Bradwardine, Thomas circa 1295-1349 .. DLB-115
Brady, Frank 1924-1986............. DLB-111
Frederic A. Brady [publishing house] DLB-49
Bragg, Melvyn 1939- DLB-14, 271
Charles H. Brainard [publishing house] ... DLB-49
Braine, John 1922-1986 . DLB-15; Y-86; CDBLB-7
Braithwait, Richard 1588-1673 .... DLB-151
Braithwaite, William Stanley
  1878-1962................. DLB-50, 54
Bräker, Ulrich 1735-1798 .... DLB-94
Bramah, Ernest 1868-1942............. DLB-70
Branagan, Thomas 1774-1843 .... DLB-37
Brancati, Vitaliano 1907-1954......... DLB-264
Branch, William Blackwell 1927- DLB-76
Brand, Christianna 1907-1988 ....DLB-276
Brand, Max (see Faust, Frederick Schiller)
Branden Press..................... DLB-46
Branner, H.C. 1903-1966............. DLB-214
Brant, Sebastian 1457-1521..............DLB-179
Brassey, Lady Annie (Allnutt)
  1839-1887..................... DLB-166
Brathwaite, Edward Kamau
  1930- DLB-125; CDWLB-3
Brault, Jacques 1933- DLB-53
Braun, Matt 1932- DLB-212
Braun, Volker 1939- DLB-75, 124
Brautigan, Richard
  1935-1984 ....DLB-2, 5, 206; Y-80, 84
Braxton, Joanne M. 1950- DLB-41
Bray, Anne Eliza 1790-1883 .... DLB-116
Bray, Thomas 1656-1730 .... DLB-24
Brazdžionis, Bernardas 1907- DLB-220
George Braziller [publishing house] DLB-46
The Bread Loaf Writers' Conference 1983 ... Y-84
Breasted, James Henry 1865-1935 .... DLB-47
Brecht, Bertolt
  1898-1956 .... DLB-56, 124; CDWLB-2
Bredel, Willi 1901-1964 .... DLB-56
Bregendahl, Marie 1867-1940......... DLB-214
Breitinger, Johann Jakob 1701-1776 ..... DLB-97
Bremser, Bonnie 1939- DLB-16
Bremser, Ray 1934-1998 .... DLB-16
Brennan, Christopher 1870-1932 .... DLB-230
Brentano, Bernard von 1901-1964 ..... DLB-56
Brentano, Clemens 1778-1842 .... DLB-90
Brentano's..................... DLB-49
Brenton, Howard 1942- DLB-13
Breslin, Jimmy 1929-1996............. DLB-185
Breton, André 1896-1966.......... DLB-65, 258
Breton, Nicholas circa 1555-circa 1626... DLB-136
The Breton Lays
  1300-early fifteenth century DLB-146
Brett, Simon 1945- DLB-276
Brewer, Luther A. 1858-1933......... DLB-187
Brewer, Warren and Putnam DLB-46

Brewster, Elizabeth 1922- DLB-60
Breytenbach, Breyten 1939- DLB-225
Bridge, Ann (Lady Mary Dolling Sanders
  O'Malley) 1889-1974 .... DLB-191
Bridge, Horatio 1806-1893 .... DLB-183
Bridgers, Sue Ellen 1942- DLB-52
Bridges, Robert
  1844-1930 .... DLB-19, 98; CDBLB-5
The Bridgewater Library DLB-213
Bridie, James 1888-1951 .... DLB-10
Brieux, Eugene 1858-1932 .... DLB-192
Brigadere, Anna
  1861-1933 .... DLB-220; CDWLB-4
Briggs, Charles Frederick 1804-1877 .. DLB-3, 250
Brighouse, Harold 1882-1958............. DLB-10
Bright, Mary Chavelita Dunne (see Egerton, George)
Brightman, Edgar Sheffield 1884-1953....DLB-270
B. J. Brimmer Company............. DLB-46
Brines, Francisco 1932- DLB-134
Brink, André 1935- DLB-225
Brinley, George, Jr. 1817-1875 .... DLB-140
Brinnin, John Malcolm 1916-1998 .... DLB-48
Brisbane, Albert 1809-1890 .... DLB-3, 250
Brisbane, Arthur 1864-1936............. DLB-25
British Academy..................... DLB-112
The British Critic 1793-1843 .... DLB-110
British Library
  The American Trust for the
    British Library Y-96
  The British Library and the Regular
    Readers' Group Y-91
  Building the New British Library
    at St Pancras................... Y-94
British Literary Prizes..........DLB-207; Y-98
British Literature
  The "Angry Young Men" DLB-15
  Author-Printers, 1476-1599........ DLB-167
  The Comic Tradition Continued DLB-15
  Documents on Sixteenth-Century
    Literature DLB-167, 172
  Eikon Basilike 1649............... DLB-151
  Letter from London Y-96
  Literary Effects of World War II DLB-15
  A Mirror for Magistrates............. DLB-167
  "Modern English Prose" (1876),
    by George Saintsbury.......... DLB-57
  Sex, Class, Politics, and Religion [in the
    British Novel, 1930-1959]....... DLB-15
  Victorians on Rhetoric and Prose
    Style DLB-57
  The Year in British Fiction Y-99–01
  "You've Never Had It So Good," Gusted
    by "Winds of Change": British
    Fiction in the 1950s, 1960s,
    and After DLB-14
British Literature, Old and Middle English
  Anglo-Norman Literature in the
    Development of Middle English
    Literature DLB-146

The Alliterative Morte Arthure and the
  Stanzaic Morte Arthur
  circa 1350-1400 .... DLB-146
Ancrene Riwle circa 1200-1225 ...... DLB-146
The Anglo-Saxon Chronicle circa
  890-1154 .... DLB-146
The Battle of Maldon circa 1000...... DLB-146
Beowulf circa 900-1000 or
  790-825........... DLB-146; CDBLB-1
The Blickling Homilies circa 971 ... DLB-146
The Breton Lays
  1300-early fifteenth century DLB-146
The Castle of Perseverance
  circa 1400-1425 .... DLB-146
The Celtic Background to Medieval
  English Literature............. DLB-146
The Chester Plays circa 1505-1532;
  revisions until 1575.......... DLB-146
Cursor Mundi circa 1300.......... DLB-146
The English Language: 410
  to 1500 .... DLB-146
The Germanic Epic and Old English
  Heroic Poetry: Widsith, Waldere,
  and The Fight at Finnsburg DLB-146
Judith circa 930 .... DLB-146
The Matter of England 1240-1400 .. DLB-146
The Matter of Rome early twelfth to
  late fifteenth centuries......... DLB-146
Middle English Literature:
  An Introduction DLB-146
The Middle English Lyric........... DLB-146
Morality Plays: Mankind circa 1450-1500
  and Everyman circa 1500 ...... DLB-146
N-Town Plays circa 1468 to early
  sixteenth century............. DLB-146
Old English Literature:
  An Introduction DLB-146
Old English Riddles
  eighth to tenth centuries....... DLB-146
The Owl and the Nightingale
  circa 1189-1199 .... DLB-146
The Paston Letters 1422-1509 ...... DLB-146
The Seafarer circa 970............. DLB-146
The South English Legendary circa
  thirteenth to fifteenth centuries ... DLB-146
The British Review and London Critical
  Journal 1811-1825 .... DLB-110
Brito, Aristeo 1942- DLB-122
Brittain, Vera 1893-1970............. DLB-191
Brizeux, Auguste 1803-1858............DLB-217
Broadway Publishing Company......... DLB-46
Broch, Hermann
  1886-1951 ....DLB-85, 124; CDWLB-2
Brochu, André 1942- DLB-53
Brock, Edwin 1927-1997............. DLB-40
Brockes, Barthold Heinrich 1680-1747 ... DLB-168
Brod, Max 1884-1968................. DLB-81
Brodber, Erna 1940- DLB-157
Brodhead, John R. 1814-1873........... DLB-30
Brodkey, Harold 1930-1996........... DLB-130
Brodsky, Joseph 1940-1996 .... Y-87

Nobel Lecture 1987 .... Y-87

Brodsky, Michael 1948- DLB-244

Broeg, Bob 1918- DLB-171

Brøgger, Suzanne 1944- DLB-214

Brome, Richard circa 1590-1652 .....DLB-58

Brome, Vincent 1910- DLB-155

Bromfield, Louis 1896-1956.......DLB-4, 9, 86

Bromige, David 1933- DLB-193

Broner, E. M. 1930- DLB-28

    Tribute to Bernard Malamud......... Y-86

Bronk, William 1918-1999...........DLB-165

Bronnen, Arnolt 1895-1959..........DLB-124

Brontë, Anne 1820-1849 ....DLB-21, 199

Brontë, Charlotte
1816-1855 ....DLB-21, 159, 199; CDBLB-4

Brontë, Emily
1818-1848 ......DLB-21, 32, 199; CDBLB-4

    The Brontë Society Y-98

Brook, Stephen 1947- DLB-204

Brook Farm 1841-1847 ....DLB-1; 223; DS-5

Brooke, Frances 1724-1789..........DLB-39, 99

Brooke, Henry 1703?-1783...........DLB-39

Brooke, L. Leslie 1862-1940 ....DLB-141

Brooke, Margaret, Ranee of Sarawak
1849-1936 ....DLB-174

Brooke, Rupert
1887-1915 ....DLB-19, 216; CDBLB-6

    The Friends of the Dymock Poets Y-00

Brooker, Bertram 1888-1955..........DLB-88

Brooke-Rose, Christine 1923- DLB-14, 231

Brookner, Anita 1928- DLB-194; Y-87

Brooks, Charles Timothy 1813-1883...DLB-1, 243

Brooks, Cleanth 1906-1994........DLB-63; Y-94

    Tribute to Katherine Anne Porter Y-80

    Tribute to Walker Percy Y-90

Brooks, Gwendolyn
1917-2000 ....DLB-5, 76, 165; CDALB-1

    Tribute to Julian Mayfield Y-84

Brooks, Jeremy 1926- DLB-14

Brooks, Mel 1926- DLB-26

Brooks, Noah 1830-1903.........DLB-42; DS-13

Brooks, Richard 1912-1992..........DLB-44

Brooks, Van Wyck 1886-1963 ...DLB-45, 63, 103

Brophy, Brigid 1929-1995 ......DLB-14, 70, 271

Brophy, John 1899-1965 ....DLB-191

Brossard, Chandler 1922-1993 ......DLB-16

Brossard, Nicole 1943- DLB-53

Broster, Dorothy Kathleen 1877-1950 ....DLB-160

Brother Antoninus (see Everson, William)

Brotherton, Lord 1856-1930 ....DLB-184

Brougham, John 1810-1880..........DLB-11

Brougham and Vaux, Henry Peter
Brougham, Baron 1778-1868....DLB-110, 158

Broughton, James 1913-1999........DLB-5

Broughton, Rhoda 1840-1920 ....DLB-18

Broun, Heywood 1888-1939 ....DLB-29, 171

Brown, Alice 1856-1948................DLB-78

Brown, Bob 1886-1959 ....DLB-4, 45; DS-15

Brown, Cecil 1943- DLB-33

Brown, Charles Brockden
1771-1810 ....DLB-37, 59, 73; CDALB-2

Brown, Christy 1932-1981 ....DLB-14

Brown, Dee 1908-2002 .... Y-80

Brown, Frank London 1927-1962 ....DLB-76

Brown, Fredric 1906-1972 ....DLB-8

Brown, George Mackay
1921-1996 ....DLB-14, 27, 139, 271

Brown, Harry 1917-1986 ....DLB-26

Brown, Larry 1951- DLB-234

Brown, Lew 1893-1958 ....DLB-265

Brown, Marcia 1918- DLB-61

Brown, Margaret Wise 1910-1952........DLB-22

Brown, Morna Doris (see Ferrars, Elizabeth)

Brown, Oliver Madox 1855-1874 ....DLB-21

Brown, Sterling 1901-1989 ....DLB-48, 51, 63

Brown, T. E. 1830-1897 ....DLB-35

Brown, Thomas Alexander (see Boldrewood, Rolf)

Brown, Warren 1894-1978 ....DLB-241

Brown, William Hill 1765-1793 ....DLB-37

Brown, William Wells
1815-1884 ....DLB-3, 50, 183, 248

Brown University
    The Festival of Vanguard Narrative Y-93

Browne, Charles Farrar 1834-1867 ....DLB-11

Browne, Frances 1816-1879 ....DLB-199

Browne, Francis Fisher 1843-1913........DLB-79

Browne, Howard 1908-1999 ....DLB-226

Browne, J. Ross 1821-1875 ....DLB-202

Browne, Michael Dennis 1940- DLB-40

Browne, Sir Thomas 1605-1682 ....DLB-151

Browne, William, of Tavistock
1590-1645 ....DLB-121

Browne, Wynyard 1911-1964 ....DLB-13, 233

Browne and Nolan....................DLB-106

Brownell, W. C. 1851-1928 ....DLB-71

Browning, Elizabeth Barrett
1806-1861 ....DLB-32, 199; CDBLB-4

Browning, Robert
1812-1889 ....DLB-32, 163; CDBLB-4

    Essay on Chatterton DLB-32

    Introductory Essay: *Letters of Percy
    Bysshe Shelley* (1852) DLB-32

    "The Novel in [Robert Browning's]
    'The Ring and the Book'" (1912),
    by Henry James DLB-32

Brownjohn, Allan 1931- DLB-40

    Tribute to John Betjeman............ Y-84

Brownson, Orestes Augustus
1803-1876 ....DLB-1, 59, 73, 243; DS-5

Bruccoli, Matthew J. 1931- DLB-103

    Joseph [Heller] and George [V. Higgins] . Y-99

    Response [to Busch on Fitzgerald] Y-96

    Tribute to Albert Erskine............ Y-93

    Tribute to Charles E. Feinberg......... Y-88

    Working with Fredson Bowers Y-91

Bruce, Charles 1906-1971 ....DLB-68

Bruce, John Edward 1856-1924
    Three Documents [African American
    poets].........................DLB-50

Bruce, Leo 1903-1979 ....DLB-77

Bruce, Mary Grant 1878-1958..........DLB-230

Bruce, Philip Alexander 1856-1933.......DLB-47

Bruce-Novoa, Juan 1944- DLB-82

Bruckman, Clyde 1894-1955...........DLB-26

Bruckner, Ferdinand 1891-1958 ....DLB-118

Brundage, John Herbert (see Herbert, John)

Brunner, John 1934-1995 ....DLB-261

    Tribute to Theodore Sturgeon......... Y-85

Brutus, Dennis
1924- DLB-117, 225; CDWLB-3

Bryan, C. D. B. 1936- DLB-185

Bryant, Arthur 1899-1985 ....DLB-149

Bryant, William Cullen 1794-1878
.........DLB-3, 43, 59, 189, 250; CDALB-2

Bryce, James 1838-1922...........DLB-166, 190

Bryce Echenique, Alfredo
1939- DLB-145; CDWLB-3

Bryden, Bill 1942- DLB-233

Brydges, Sir Samuel Egerton
1762-1837 ....DLB-107, 142

Bryskett, Lodowick 1546?-1612 ....DLB-167

Buchan, John 1875-1940 ....DLB-34, 70, 156

Buchanan, George 1506-1582 ....DLB-132

Buchanan, Robert 1841-1901 ....DLB-18, 35

    "The Fleshly School of Poetry and
    Other Phenomena of the Day"
    (1872)........................DLB-35

    "The Fleshly School of Poetry:
    Mr. D. G. Rossetti" (1871),
    by Thomas Maitland............DLB-35

Buchler, Justus 1914-1991 ....DLB-279

Buchman, Sidney 1902-1975 ....DLB-26

Buchner, Augustus 1591-1661..........DLB-164

Büchner, Georg 1813-1837 ..DLB-133; CDWLB-2

Bucholtz, Andreas Heinrich 1607-1671 ...DLB-168

Buck, Pearl S. 1892-1973 ...DLB-9, 102; CDALB-7

Bucke, Charles 1781-1846 ....DLB-110

Bucke, Richard Maurice 1837-1902.......DLB-99

Buckingham, Edwin 1810-1833..........DLB-73

Buckingham, Joseph Tinker 1779-1861 ....DLB-73

Buckler, Ernest 1908-1984.............DLB-68

Buckley, William F., Jr. 1925- DLB-137; Y-80

    Publisher's Statement From the
    Initial Issue of *National Review*
    (19 November 1955)...........DLB-137

Buckminster, Joseph Stevens
1784-1812 ....DLB-37

Buckner, Robert 1906- DLB-26

Budd, Thomas ?-1698 ....DLB-24

Budrys, A. J. 1931- DLB-8

Buechner, Frederick 1926- Y-80

Buell, John 1927- DLB-53

Bufalino, Gesualdo 1920-1996 .... DLB-196

Job Buffum [publishing house].......... DLB-49

Bugnet, Georges 1879-1981 .... DLB-92

Buies, Arthur 1840-1901................ DLB-99

Bukowski, Charles 1920-1994 ... DLB-5, 130, 169

Bulatović, Miodrag
1930-1991 .... DLB-181; CDWLB-4

Bulgakov, Mikhail Afanas'evich
1891-1940 .... DLB-272

Bulgarin, Faddei Venediktovich
1789-1859..................... DLB-198

Bulger, Bozeman 1877-1932 .... DLB-171

Bullein, William
between 1520 and 1530-1576....... DLB-167

Bullins, Ed 1935- DLB-7, 38, 249

Bulwer, John 1606-1656............... DLB-236

Bulwer-Lytton, Edward (also Edward
Bulwer) 1803-1873................ DLB-21

"On Art in Fiction" (1838) DLB-21

Bumpus, Jerry 1937- Y-81

Bunce and Brother DLB-49

Bunner, H. C. 1855-1896............ DLB-78, 79

Bunting, Basil 1900-1985 .... DLB-20

Buntline, Ned (Edward Zane Carroll
Judson) 1821-1886................ DLB-186

Bunyan, John 1628-1688 ..... DLB-39; CDBLB-2

The Author's Apology for
His Book DLB-39

Burch, Robert 1925- DLB-52

Burciaga, José Antonio 1940- DLB-82

Burdekin, Katharine (Murray Constantine)
1896-1963 .... DLB-255

Bürger, Gottfried August 1747-1794 ...... DLB-94

Burgess, Anthony (John Anthony Burgess Wilson)
1917-1993 ..... DLB-14, 194, 261; CDBLB-8

The Anthony Burgess Archive at
the Harry Ransom Humanities
Research Center................ Y-98

Anthony Burgess's 99 Novels:
An Opinion Poll............... Y-84

Burgess, Gelett 1866-1951 .... DLB-11

Burgess, John W. 1844-1931 .... DLB-47

Burgess, Thornton W. 1874-1965 .... DLB-22

Burgess, Stringer and Company DLB-49

Burick, Si 1909-1986................... DLB-171

Burk, John Daly circa 1772-1808 .... DLB-37

Burk, Ronnie 1955- DLB-209

Burke, Edmund 1729?-1797 .... DLB-104, 252

Burke, James Lee 1936- DLB-226

Burke, Johnny 1908-1964............. DLB-265

Burke, Kenneth 1897-1993 .... DLB-45, 63

Burke, Thomas 1886-1945 .... DLB-197

Burley, Dan 1907-1962 .... DLB-241

Burley, W. J. 1914- DLB-276

Burlingame, Edward Livermore
1848-1922 .... DLB-79

Burman, Carina 1960- DLB-257

Burnet, Gilbert 1643-1715.............. DLB-101

Burnett, Frances Hodgson
1849-1924 .... DLB-42, 141; DS-13, 14

Burnett, W. R. 1899-1982 .... DLB-9, 226

Burnett, Whit 1899-1973 .... DLB-137

Burney, Fanny 1752-1840............... DLB-39

Dedication, The Wanderer (1814)..... DLB-39

Preface to Evelina (1778) DLB-39

Burns, Alan 1929- DLB-14, 194

Burns, John Horne 1916-1953 .... Y-85

Burns, Robert 1759-1796 .... DLB-109; CDBLB-3

Burns and Oates................... DLB-106

Burnshaw, Stanley 1906- DLB-48; Y-97

James Dickey and Stanley Burnshaw
Correspondence................ Y-02

Review of Stanley Burnshaw: The
Collected Poems and Selected
Prose............................ Y-02

Tribute to Robert Penn Warren........ Y-89

Burr, C. Chauncey 1815?-1883 .... DLB-79

Burr, Esther Edwards 1732-1758 .... DLB-200

Burroughs, Edgar Rice 1875-1950 .... DLB-8

The Burroughs Bibliophiles Y-98

Burroughs, John 1837-1921 ....DLB-64, 275

Burroughs, Margaret T. G. 1917- DLB-41

Burroughs, William S., Jr. 1947-1981 ..... DLB-16

Burroughs, William Seward 1914-1997
.... DLB-2, 8, 16, 152, 237; Y-81, 97

Burroway, Janet 1936- DLB-6

Burt, Maxwell Struthers
1882-1954 .... DLB-86; DS-16

A. L. Burt and Company DLB-49

Burton, Hester 1913- DLB-161

Burton, Isabel Arundell 1831-1896...... DLB-166

Burton, Miles (see Rhode, John)

Burton, Richard Francis
1821-1890 .... DLB-55, 166, 184

Burton, Robert 1577-1640.............. DLB-151

Burton, Virginia Lee 1909-1968......... DLB-22

Burton, William Evans 1804-1860 ...... DLB-73

Burwell, Adam Hood 1790-1849 .... DLB-99

Bury, Lady Charlotte 1775-1861 .... DLB-116

Busch, Frederick 1941- DLB-6, 218

Excerpts from Frederick Busch's USC
Remarks [on F. Scott Fitzgerald].... Y-96

Tribute to James Laughlin Y-97

Tribute to Raymond Carver.......... Y-88

Busch, Niven 1903-1991................ DLB-44

Bushnell, Horace 1802-1876............. DS-13

Business & Literature
The Claims of Business and Literature:
An Undergraduate Essay by
Maxwell Perkins.................. Y-01

Bussières, Arthur de 1877-1913......... DLB-92

Butler, Charles circa 1560-1647 .... DLB-236

Butler, Guy 1918- DLB-225

Butler, Joseph 1692-1752 .... DLB-252

Butler, Josephine Elizabeth
1828-1906 .... DLB-190

Butler, Juan 1942-1981................ DLB-53

Butler, Judith 1956- DLB-246

Butler, Octavia E. 1947- DLB-33

Butler, Pierce 1884-1953................DLB-187

Butler, Robert Olen 1945- DLB-173

Butler, Samuel 1613-1680..........DLB-101, 126

Butler, Samuel
1835-1902 .... DLB-18, 57, 174; CDBLB-5

Butler, William Francis 1838-1910...... DLB-166

E. H. Butler and Company DLB-49

Butor, Michel 1926- DLB-83

Nathaniel Butter [publishing house] DLB-170

Butterworth, Hezekiah 1839-1905 ...... DLB-42

Buttitta, Ignazio 1899-1997............ DLB-114

Butts, Mary 1890-1937................ DLB-240

Buzzati, Dino 1906-1972..............DLB-177

Byars, Betsy 1928- DLB-52

Byatt, A. S. 1936- DLB-14, 194

Byles, Mather 1707-1788 .... DLB-24

Henry Bynneman [publishing house] DLB-170

Bynner, Witter 1881-1968 .... DLB-54

Byrd, William circa 1543-1623..........DLB-172

Byrd, William, II 1674-1744 .... DLB-24, 140

Byrne, John Keyes (see Leonard, Hugh)

Byron, George Gordon, Lord
1788-1824 .... DLB-96, 110; CDBLB-3

The Byron Society of America Y-00

Byron, Robert 1905-1941.............. DLB-195

C

Caballero Bonald, José Manuel
1926- DLB-108

Cabañero, Eladio 1930- DLB-134

Cabell, James Branch 1879-1958 ....DLB-9, 78

Cabeza de Baca, Manuel 1853-1915..... DLB-122

Cabeza de Baca Gilbert, Fabiola
1898- DLB-122

Cable, George Washington
1844-1925 ....DLB-12, 74; DS-13

Cable, Mildred 1878-1952 .... DLB-195

Cabral, Manuel del 1907-1999 .... DLB-283

Cabrera, Lydia 1900-1991 .... DLB-145

Cabrera Infante, Guillermo
1929- DLB-113; CDWLB-3

Cadell [publishing house] DLB-154

Cady, Edwin H. 1917- DLB-103

Caedmon flourished 658-680 .... DLB-146

Caedmon School circa 660-899 .... DLB-146

Caesar, Irving 1895-1996............. DLB-265

Cafés, Brasseries, and Bistros...........DS-15

Cage, John 1912-1992 .... DLB-193

Cahan, Abraham 1860-1951 ...... DLB-9, 25, 28

Cahn, Sammy 1913-1993............. DLB-265

Cain, George 1943- DLB-33

Cain, James M. 1892-1977 .... DLB-226

Caird, Edward 1835-1908 .... DLB-262

Caird, Mona 1854-1932..............DLB-197

Čaks, Aleksandrs
1901-1950............DLB-220; CDWLB-4

Caldecott, Randolph 1846-1886........DLB-163

John Calder Limited
[Publishing house]................DLB-112

Calderón de la Barca, Fanny
1804-1882.....................DLB-183

Caldwell, Ben 1937-................DLB-38

Caldwell, Erskine 1903-1987..........DLB-9, 86

H. M. Caldwell Company..............DLB-49

Caldwell, Taylor 1900-1985.............DS-17

Calhoun, John C. 1782-1850.........DLB-3, 248

Călinescu, George 1899-1965..........DLB-220

Calisher, Hortense 1911-...........DLB-2, 218

Calkins, Mary Whiton 1863-1930.......DLB-270

Callaghan, Mary Rose 1944..........DLB-207

Callaghan, Morley 1903-1990.....DLB-68; DS-15

Callahan, S. Alice 1868-1894........DLB-175, 221

Callaloo [journal]........................Y-87

Callimachus circa 305 B.C.-240 B.C......DLB-176

Calmer, Edgar 1907-..................DLB-4

Calverley, C. S. 1831-1884.............DLB-35

Calvert, George Henry
1803-1889................DLB-1, 64, 248

Calvino, Italo 1923-1985..............DLB-196

Cambridge, Ada 1844-1926............DLB-230

Cambridge Press.....................DLB-49

Cambridge Songs (Carmina Cantabrigensia)
circa 1050......................DLB-148

Cambridge University
Cambridge and the Apostles...........DS-5

Cambridge University Press...........DLB-170

Camden, William 1551-1623...........DLB-172

Camden House: An Interview with
James Hardin......................Y-92

Cameron, Eleanor 1912-2000..........DLB-52

Cameron, George Frederick
1854-1885......................DLB-99

Cameron, Lucy Lyttelton 1781-1858.....DLB-163

Cameron, Peter 1959-..............DLB-234

Cameron, William Bleasdell 1862-1951 . . DLB-99

Camm, John 1718-1778................DLB-31

Camon, Ferdinando 1935-............DLB-196

Camp, Walter 1859-1925..............DLB-241

Campana, Dino 1885-1932............DLB-114

Campbell, Bebe Moore 1950-........DLB-227

Campbell, David 1915-1979.............DLB-260

Campbell, Gabrielle Margaret Vere
(see Shearing, Joseph, and Bowen, Marjorie)

Campbell, James Dykes 1838-1895......DLB-144

Campbell, James Edwin 1867-1896......DLB-50

Campbell, John 1653-1728..............DLB-43

Campbell, John W., Jr. 1910-1971........DLB-8

Campbell, Ramsey 1946-............DLB-261

Campbell, Roy 1901-1957..........DLB-20, 225

Campbell, Thomas 1777-1844.......DLB-93, 144

Campbell, William Edward (see March, William)

Campbell, William Wilfred 1858-1918....DLB-92

Campion, Edmund 1539-1581.........DLB-167

Campion, Thomas
1567-1620.........DLB-58, 172; CDBLB-1

Campo, Rafael 1964-...............DLB-282

Campton, David 1924-..............DLB-245

Camus, Albert 1913-1960..............DLB-72

Camus, Jean-Pierre 1584-1652.........DLB-268

The Canadian Publishers' Records Database . Y-96

Canby, Henry Seidel 1878-1961.........DLB-91

Candelaria, Cordelia 1943-..........DLB-82

Candelaria, Nash 1928-............DLB-82

Canetti, Elias
1905-1994.........DLB-85, 124; CDWLB-2

Canham, Erwin Dain 1904-1982........DLB-127

Canitz, Friedrich Rudolph Ludwig von
1654-1699.....................DLB-168

Cankar, Ivan 1876-1918......DLB-147; CDWLB-4

Cannan, Gilbert 1884-1955.........DLB-10, 197

Cannan, Joanna 1896-1961...........DLB-191

Cannell, Kathleen 1891-1974............DLB-4

Cannell, Skipwith 1887-1957...........DLB-45

Canning, George 1770-1827...........DLB-158

Cannon, Jimmy 1910-1973............DLB-171

Cano, Daniel 1947-................DLB-209

Old Dogs / New Tricks? New
Technologies, the Canon, and the
Structure of the Profession........Y-02

Cantú, Norma Elia 1947-............DLB-209

Cantwell, Robert 1908-1978............DLB-9

Jonathan Cape and Harrison Smith
[publishing house]................DLB-46

Jonathan Cape Limited...............DLB-112

Čapek, Karel 1890-1938....DLB-215; CDWLB-4

Capen, Joseph 1658-1725..............DLB-24

Capes, Bernard 1854-1918............DLB-156

Capote, Truman 1924-1984
.......DLB-2, 185, 227; Y-80, 84; CDALB-1

Capps, Benjamin 1922-..............DLB-256

Caproni, Giorgio 1912-1990..........DLB-128

Caragiale, Mateiu Ioan 1885-1936......DLB-220

Cardarelli, Vincenzo 1887-1959........DLB-114

Cárdenas, Reyes 1948-.............DLB-122

Cardinal, Marie 1929-2001.............DLB-83

Carew, Jan 1920-..................DLB-157

Carew, Thomas 1594 or 1595-1640.....DLB-126

Carey, Henry circa 1687-1689-1743......DLB-84

Carey, Mathew 1760-1839...........DLB-37, 73

M. Carey and Company...............DLB-49

Carey and Hart......................DLB-49

Carlell, Lodowick 1602-1675...........DLB-58

Carleton, William 1794-1869..........DLB-159

G. W. Carleton [publishing house].......DLB-49

Carlile, Richard 1790-1843........DLB-110, 158

Carlson, Ron 1947-................DLB-244

Carlyle, Jane Welsh 1801-1866..........DLB-55

Carlyle, Thomas
1795-1881.........DLB-55, 144; CDBLB-3

"The Hero as Man of Letters:
Johnson, Rousseau, Burns"
(1841) [excerpt]................DLB-57

The Hero as Poet. Dante; Shakspeare
(1841).......................DLB-32

Carman, Bliss 1861-1929..............DLB-92

Carmina Burana circa 1230............DLB-138

Carnap, Rudolf 1891-1970............DLB-270

Carnero, Guillermo 1947-...........DLB-108

Carossa, Hans 1878-1956..............DLB-66

Carpenter, Humphrey
1946-................DLB-155; Y-84, 99

Carpenter, Stephen Cullen ?-1820?.......DLB-73

Carpentier, Alejo
1904-1980............DLB-113; CDWLB-3

Carr, Emily (1871-1945)..............DLB-68

Carr, Marina 1964-................DLB-245

Carr, Virginia Spencer 1929-......DLB-111; Y-00

Carrera Andrade, Jorge 1903-1978......DLB-283

Carrier, Roch 1937-................DLB-53

Carrillo, Adolfo 1855-1926............DLB-122

Carroll, Gladys Hasty 1904-............DLB-9

Carroll, John 1735-1815...............DLB-37

Carroll, John 1809-1884...............DLB-99

Carroll, Lewis
1832-1898......DLB-18, 163, 178; CDBLB-4

The Lewis Carroll Centenary..........Y-98

The Lewis Carroll Society
of North America...............Y-00

Carroll, Paul 1927-................DLB-16

Carroll, Paul Vincent 1900-1968.........DLB-10

Carroll and Graf Publishers............DLB-46

Carruth, Hayden 1921-............DLB-5, 165

Tribute to James Dickey..............Y-97

Tribute to Raymond Carver...........Y-88

Carryl, Charles E. 1841-1920...........DLB-42

Carson, Anne 1950-................DLB-193

Carson, Rachel 1907-1964.............DLB-275

Carswell, Catherine 1879-1946..........DLB-36

Cărtărescu, Mirea 1956-............DLB-232

Carter, Angela 1940-1992......DLB-14, 207, 261

Carter, Elizabeth 1717-1806............DLB-109

Carter, Henry (see Leslie, Frank)

Carter, Hodding, Jr. 1907-1972........DLB-127

Carter, Jared 1939-................DLB-282

Carter, John 1905-1975...............DLB-201

Carter, Landon 1710-1778.............DLB-31

Carter, Lin 1930-1988..................Y-81

Carter, Martin 1927-1997....DLB-117; CDWLB-3

Carter, Robert, and Brothers...........DLB-49

Carter and Hendee...................DLB-49

Cartwright, Jim 1958-..............DLB-245

Cartwright, John 1740-1824...........DLB-158

Cartwright, William circa 1611-1643....DLB-126

Cumulative Index

Caruthers, William Alexander
    1802-1846 .... DLB-3, 248
Carver, Jonathan 1710-1780 .... DLB-31
Carver, Raymond 1938-1988 ... DLB-130; Y-83,88
    First Strauss "Livings" Awarded to Cynthia
      Ozick and Raymond Carver
    An Interview with Raymond Carver . Y-83
Carvic, Heron 1917?-1980 .... DLB-276
Cary, Alice 1820-1871................... DLB-202
Cary, Joyce 1888-1957 ... DLB-15, 100; CDBLB-6
Cary, Patrick 1623?-1657 .... DLB-131
Casal, Julián del 1863-1893 .... DLB-283
Case, John 1540-1600.................... DLB-281
Casey, Gavin 1907-1964 .... DLB-260
Casey, Juanita 1925- DLB-14
Casey, Michael 1947- DLB-5
Cassady, Carolyn 1923- DLB-16
    "As I See It" DLB-16
Cassady, Neal 1926-1968 .... DLB-16, 237
Cassell and Company................. DLB-106
Cassell Publishing Company DLB-49
Cassill, R. V. 1919- DLB-6, 218; Y-02
    Tribute to James Dickey Y-97
Cassity, Turner 1929- DLB-105; Y-02
Cassius Dio circa 155/164-post 229 ...... DLB-176
Cassola, Carlo 1917-1987 .... DLB-177
Castellano, Olivia 1944- DLB-122
Castellanos, Rosario
    1925-1974............ DLB-113; CDWLB-3
Castillo, Ana 1953- DLB-122, 227
Castillo, Rafael C. 1950- DLB-209
The Castle of Perseverance circa 1400-1425 . DLB-146
Castlemon, Harry (see Fosdick, Charles Austin)
Čašule, Kole 1921- DLB-181
Caswall, Edward 1814-1878 .... DLB-32
Catacalos, Rosemary 1944- DLB-122
Cather, Willa 1873-1947
    .... DLB-9, 54, 78, 256, DS-1; CDALB-3
    The Willa Cather Pioneer Memorial
      and Education Foundation Y-00
Catherine II (Ekaterina Alekseevna), "The Great,"
    Empress of Russia 1729-1796 .... DLB-150
Catherwood, Mary Hartwell 1847-1902 ... DLB-78
Catledge, Turner 1901-1983 .... DLB-127
Catlin, George 1796-1872 .... DLB-186, 189
Cato the Elder 234 B.C.-149 B.C. DLB-211
Cattafi, Bartolo 1922-1979 .... DLB-128
Catton, Bruce 1899-1978 .... DLB-17
Catullus circa 84 B.C.-54 B.C.
    .... DLB-211; CDWLB-1
Causley, Charles 1917- DLB-27
Caute, David 1936- DLB-14, 231
Cavendish, Duchess of Newcastle,
    Margaret Lucas
    1623-1673............. DLB-131, 252, 281
Cawein, Madison 1865-1914 .... DLB-54
William Caxton [publishing house] DLB-170

The Caxton Printers, Limited DLB-46
Caylor, O. P. 1849-1897.............. DLB-241
Cayrol, Jean 1911- DLB-83
Cecil, Lord David 1902-1986 .... DLB-155
Cela, Camilo José 1916-2002 .... Y-89
    Nobel Lecture 1989 .... Y-89
Celan, Paul 1920-1970 ...... DLB-69; CDWLB-2
Celati, Gianni 1937- DLB-196
Celaya, Gabriel 1911-1991 .... DLB-108
Céline, Louis-Ferdinand 1894-1961 ...... DLB-72
Celtis, Conrad 1459-1508.............. DLB-179
Cendrars, Blaise 1887-1961 .... DLB-258
The Steinbeck Centennial.................. Y-02
Censorship
    The Island Trees Case: A Symposium on
      School Library Censorship......... Y-82
Center for Bibliographical Studies and
    Research at the University of
    California, Riverside Y-91
Center for Book Research Y-84
The Center for the Book in the Library
    of Congress Y-93
    A New Voice: The Center for the
      Book's First Five Years........... Y-83
Centlivre, Susanna 1669?-1723.......... DLB-84
The Centre for Writing, Publishing and
    Printing History at the University
    of Reading Y-00
The Century Company DLB-49
A Century of Poetry, a Lifetime of Collecting:
    J. M. Edelstein's Collection of
    Twentieth-Century American Poetry Y-02
Cernuda, Luis 1902-1963.............. DLB-134
Cerruto, Oscar 1912-1981 .... DLB-283
Cervantes, Lorna Dee 1954- DLB-82
de Céspedes, Alba 1911-1997 .... DLB-264
Ch., T. (see Marchenko, Anastasiia Iakovlevna)
Chaadaev, Petr Iakovlevich
    1794-1856.................... DLB-198
Chabon, Michael 1963- DLB-278
Chacel, Rosa 1898-1994 .... DLB-134
Chacón, Eusebio 1869-1948 .... DLB-82
Chacón, Felipe Maximiliano 1873-? DLB-82
Chadwick, Henry 1824-1908 .... DLB-241
Chadwyck-Healey's Full-Text Literary Databases:
    Editing Commercial Databases of
    Primary Literary Texts Y-95
Challans, Eileen Mary (see Renault, Mary)
Chalmers, George 1742-1825 .... DLB-30
Chaloner, Sir Thomas 1520-1565 ...... DLB-167
Chamberlain, Samuel S. 1851-1916 ...... DLB-25
Chamberland, Paul 1939- DLB-60
Chamberlin, William Henry 1897-1969 ... DLB-29
Chambers, Charles Haddon 1860-1921 ... DLB-10
Chambers, María Cristina (see Mena, María Cristina)
Chambers, Robert W. 1865-1933 ...... DLB-202
W. and R. Chambers
    [publishing house] DLB-106
Chamisso, Adelbert von 1781-1838 ...... DLB-90

Champfleury 1821-1889............... DLB-119
Chandler, Harry 1864-1944 .... DLB-29
Chandler, Norman 1899-1973 .... DLB-127
Chandler, Otis 1927- DLB-127
Chandler, Raymond
    1888-1959 ... DLB-226, 253; DS-6; CDALB-5
    Raymond Chandler Centenary Y-88
Channing, Edward 1856-1931 .... DLB-17
Channing, Edward Tyrrell
    1790-1856 .... DLB-1, 59, 235
Channing, William Ellery
    1780-1842.............. DLB-1, 59, 235
Channing, William Ellery, II
    1817-1901..................... DLB-1, 223
Channing, William Henry
    1810-1884 .... DLB-1, 59, 243
Chapelain, Jean 1595-1674 .... DLB-268
Chaplin, Charlie 1889-1977 .... DLB-44
Chapman, George
    1559 or 1560-1634........... DLB-62, 121
Chapman, Olive Murray 1892-1977..... DLB-195
Chapman, R. W. 1881-1960 .... DLB-201
Chapman, William 1850-1917 .... DLB-99
John Chapman [publishing house] DLB-106
Chapman and Hall [publishing house] ... DLB-106
Chappell, Fred 1936- DLB-6, 105
    "A Detail in a Poem" DLB-105
    Tribute to Peter Taylor Y-94
Chappell, William 1582-1649.......... DLB-236
Char, René 1907-1988 .... DLB-258
Charbonneau, Jean 1875-1960 .... DLB-92
Charbonneau, Robert 1911-1967 .... DLB-68
Charles, Gerda 1914- DLB-14
William Charles [publishing house] DLB-49
Charles d'Orléans 1394-1465.......... DLB-208
Charley (see Mann, Charles)
Charteris, Leslie 1907-1993............ DLB-77
Chartier, Alain circa 1385-1430 .... DLB-208
Charyn, Jerome 1937- Y-83
Chase, Borden 1900-1971............. DLB-26
Chase, Edna Woolman 1877-1957 ...... DLB-91
Chase, James Hadley (René Raymond)
    1906-1985 .... DLB-276
Chase, Mary Coyle 1907-1981 .... DLB-228
Chase-Riboud, Barbara 1936- DLB-33
Chateaubriand, François-René de
    1768-1848................... DLB-119
Chatterton, Thomas 1752-1770......... DLB-109
    Essay on Chatterton (1842), by
      Robert Browning DLB-32
Chatto and Windus DLB-106
Chatwin, Bruce 1940-1989......... DLB-194, 204
Chaucer, Geoffrey
    1340?-1400............ DLB-146; CDBLB-1
    New Chaucer Society Y-00
Chaudhuri, Amit 1962- DLB-267
Chauncy, Charles 1705-1787 .... DLB-24

Chauveau, Pierre-Joseph-Olivier 1820-1890 .... DLB-99
Chávez, Denise 1948- DLB-122
Chávez, Fray Angélico 1910-1996 .... DLB-82
Chayefsky, Paddy 1923-1981 .... DLB-7, 44; Y-81
Cheesman, Evelyn 1881-1969 .... DLB-195
Cheever, Ezekiel 1615-1708 .... DLB-24
Cheever, George Barrell 1807-1890 .... DLB-59
Cheever, John 1912-1982
.... DLB-2, 102, 227; Y-80, 82; CDALB-1
Cheever, Susan 1943- Y-82
Cheke, Sir John 1514-1557 .... DLB-132
Chekhov, Anton Pavlovich 1860-1904 ... DLB-277
Chelsea House DLB-46
Chênedollé, Charles de 1769-1833 .... DLB-217
Cheney, Brainard
Tribute to Caroline Gordon Y-81
Cheney, Ednah Dow 1824-1904 ...... DLB-1, 223
Cheney, Harriet Vaughan 1796-1889 ..... DLB-99
Chénier, Marie-Joseph 1764-1811 .... DLB-192
Chernyshevsky, Nikolai Gavrilovich 1828-1889 .... DLB-238
Cherry, Kelly 1940 .... Y-83
Cherryh, C. J. 1942- Y-80
Chesebro', Caroline 1825-1873 .... DLB-202
Chesney, Sir George Tomkyns 1830-1895 .... DLB-190
Chesnut, Mary Boykin 1823-1886 .... DLB-239
Chesnutt, Charles Waddell 1858-1932 .... DLB-12, 50, 78
Chesson, Mrs. Nora (see Hopper, Nora)
Chester, Alfred 1928-1971 .... DLB-130
Chester, George Randolph 1869-1924 .... DLB-78
The Chester Plays circa 1505-1532; revisions until 1575 .... DLB-146
Chesterfield, Philip Dormer Stanhope, Fourth Earl of 1694-1773 .... DLB-104
Chesterton, G. K. 1874-1936
.. DLB-10, 19, 34, 70, 98, 149, 178; CDBLB-6
"The Ethics of Elfland" (1908) DLB-178
Chettle, Henry circa 1560-circa 1607 .... DLB-136
Cheuse, Alan 1940- DLB-244
Chew, Ada Nield 1870-1945 .... DLB-135
Cheyney, Edward P. 1861-1947 .... DLB-47
Chiara, Piero 1913-1986 .... DLB-177
Chicanos
Chicano History DLB-82
Chicano Language DLB-82
Chicano Literature: A Bibliography. DLB-209
A Contemporary Flourescence of Chicano Literature Y-84
Literatura Chicanesca: The View From Without DLB-82
Child, Francis James 1825-1896 .... DLB-1, 64, 235
Child, Lydia Maria 1802-1880 .... DLB-1, 74, 243
Child, Philip 1898-1978 .... DLB-68
Childers, Erskine 1870-1922 .... DLB-70

Children's Literature
Afterword: Propaganda, Namby-Pamby, and Some Books of Distinction DLB-52
Children's Book Awards and Prizes ... DLB-61
Children's Book Illustration in the Twentieth Century DLB-61
Children's Illustrators, 1800-1880 ... DLB-163
The Harry Potter Phenomenon Y-99
Pony Stories, Omnibus Essay on DLB-160
The Reality of One Woman's Dream: The de Grummond Children's Literature Collection Y-99
School Stories, 1914-1960 .... DLB-160
The Year in Children's Books Y-92-96, 98-01
The Year in Children's Literature Y-97
Childress, Alice 1916-1994 .... DLB-7, 38, 249
Childs, George W. 1829-1894 .... DLB-23
Chilton Book Company DLB-46
Chin, Frank 1940- DLB-206
Chinweizu 1943- DLB-157
Chitham, Edward 1932- DLB-155
Chittenden, Hiram Martin 1858-1917 ..... DLB-47
Chivers, Thomas Holley 1809-1858 ... DLB-3, 248
Cholmondeley, Mary 1859-1925 .... DLB-197
Chomsky, Noam 1928- DLB-246
Chopin, Kate 1850-1904 ... DLB-12, 78; CDALB-3
Chopin, René 1885-1953 .... DLB-92
Choquette, Adrienne 1915-1973 .... DLB-68
Choquette, Robert 1905-1991 .... DLB-68
Choyce, Lesley 1951- DLB-251
Chrétien de Troyes circa 1140-circa 1190 .... DLB-208
Christensen, Inger 1935- DLB-214
The Christian Examiner DLB-1
The Christian Publishing Company DLB-49
Christie, Agatha 1890-1976 .... DLB-13, 77, 245; CDBLB-6
Christine de Pizan circa 1365-circa 1431 .. DLB-208
Christopher, John (Sam Youd) 1922- ... DLB-255
Christus und die Samariterin circa 950 ...... DLB-148
Christy, Howard Chandler 1873-1952 ... DLB-188
Chulkov, Mikhail Dmitrievich 1743?-1792 .... DLB-150
Church, Benjamin 1734-1778 .... DLB-31
Church, Francis Pharcellus 1839-1906 .... DLB-79
Church, Peggy Pond 1903-1986 .... DLB-212
Church, Richard 1893-1972 .... DLB-191
Church, William Conant 1836-1917 ..... DLB-79
Churchill, Caryl 1938- DLB-13
Churchill, Charles 1731-1764 .... DLB-109
Churchill, Winston 1871-1947 .... DLB-202
Churchill, Sir Winston 1874-1965 .... DLB-100; DS-16; CDBLB-5
Churchyard, Thomas 1520?-1604 ...... DLB-132
E. Churton and Company DLB-106
Chute, Marchette 1909-1994 .... DLB-103

Ciardi, John 1916-1986 .... DLB-5; Y-86
Cibber, Colley 1671-1757 .... DLB-84
Cicero 106 B.C.-43 B.C. DLB-211, CDWLB-1
Cima, Annalisa 1941- DLB-128
Čingo, Živko 1935-1987 .... DLB-181
Cioran, E. M. 1911-1995 .... DLB-220
Čipkus, Alfonsas (see Nyka-Niliūnas, Alfonsas)
Cirese, Eugenio 1884-1955 .... DLB-114
Cīrulis, Jānis (see Bels, Alberts)
Cisneros, Sandra 1954- DLB-122, 152
City Lights Books DLB-46
Civil War (1861–1865)
Battles and Leaders of the Civil War .. DLB-47
Official Records of the Rebellion DLB-47
Recording the Civil War DLB-47
Cixous, Hélène 1937- DLB-83, 242
Clampitt, Amy 1920-1994 .... DLB-105
Tribute to Alfred A. Knopf Y-84
Clancy, Tom 1947- DLB-227
Clapper, Raymond 1892-1944 .... DLB-29
Clare, John 1793-1864 .... DLB-55, 96
Clarendon, Edward Hyde, Earl of 1609-1674 .... DLB-101
Clark, Alfred Alexander Gordon (see Hare, Cyril)
Clark, Ann Nolan 1896- DLB-52
Clark, C. E. Frazer, Jr. 1925-2001 .. DLB-187; Y-01
C. E. Frazer Clark Jr. and Hawthorne Bibliography DLB-269
The Publications of C. E. Frazer Clark Jr. DLB-269
Clark, Catherine Anthony 1892-1977 ..... DLB-68
Clark, Charles Heber 1841-1915 .... DLB-11
Clark, Davis Wasgatt 1812-1871 .... DLB-79
Clark, Douglas 1919-1993 .... DLB-276
Clark, Eleanor 1913- DLB-6
Clark, J. P. 1935- DLB-117; CDWLB-3
Clark, Lewis Gaylord 1808-1873 .... DLB-3, 64, 73, 250
Clark, Walter Van Tilburg 1909-1971 .... DLB-9, 206
Clark, William 1770-1838 .... DLB-183, 186
Clark, William Andrews, Jr. 1877-1934 ... DLB-187
C. M. Clark Publishing Company DLB-46
Clarke, Sir Arthur C. 1917- DLB-261
Tribute to Theodore Sturgeon Y-85
Clarke, Austin 1896-1974 .... DLB-10, 20
Clarke, Austin C. 1934- DLB-53, 125
Clarke, Gillian 1937- DLB-40
Clarke, James Freeman 1810-1888 .... DLB-1, 59, 235; DS-5
Clarke, John circa 1596-1658 .... DLB-281
Clarke, Lindsay 1939- DLB-231
Clarke, Marcus 1846-1881 .... DLB-230
Clarke, Pauline 1921- DLB-161
Clarke, Rebecca Sophia 1833-1906 ...... DLB-42
Clarke, Samuel 1675-1729 .... DLB-252

Robert Clarke and Company DLB-49

Clarkson, Thomas 1760-1846. . . . . DLB-158

Claudel, Paul 1868-1955. . . . . DLB-192, 258

Claudius, Matthias 1740-1815 . . . . DLB-97

Clausen, Andy 1943- DLB-16

Clawson, John L. 1865-1933 . . . . DLB-187

Claxton, Remsen and Haffelfinger DLB-49

Clay, Cassius Marcellus 1810-1903 . . . . . . DLB-43

Clayton, Richard (seed Haggard, William)

Cleage, Pearl 1948- DLB-228

Cleary, Beverly 1916- DLB-52

Cleary, Kate McPhelim 1863-1905. . . . . . DLB-221

Cleaver, Bill 1920-1981 . . . . DLB-52

Cleaver, Vera 1919-1992 . . . . DLB-52

Cleeve, Brian 1921- DLB-276

Cleland, John 1710-1789 . . . . DLB-39

Clemens, Samuel Langhorne (Mark Twain)
1835-1910 . . . . DLB-11, 12, 23, 64, 74,
186, 189; CDALB-3

Comments From Authors and
Scholars on
their First Reading of *Huck Finn*. Y-85

Huck at 100: How Old Is
Huckleberry Finn? Y-85

Mark Twain on Perpetual Copyright Y-92

A New Edition of *Huck Finn* Y-85

Clement, Hal 1922- DLB-8

Clemo, Jack 1916- DLB-27

Clephane, Elizabeth Cecilia 1830-1869. . . DLB-199

Cleveland, John 1613-1658. . . . . DLB-126

Cliff, Michelle 1946- DLB-157; CDWLB-3

Clifford, Lady Anne 1590-1676 . . . . DLB-151

Clifford, James L. 1901-1978 . . . . DLB-103

Clifford, Lucy 1853?-1929 . . . . DLB-135, 141, 197

Clift, Charmian 1923-1969 . . . . DLB-260

Clifton, Lucille 1936- DLB-5, 41

Clines, Francis X. 1938- DLB-185

Clive, Caroline (V) 1801-1873 . . . . DLB-199

Edward J. Clode [publishing house] DLB-46

Clough, Arthur Hugh 1819-1861 . . . . DLB-32

Cloutier, Cécile 1930- DLB-60

Clouts, Sidney 1926-1982. . . . . DLB-225

Clutton-Brock, Arthur 1868-1924 . . . . . . DLB-98

Coates, Robert M.
1897-1973 . . . . DLB-4, 9, 102; DS-15

Coatsworth, Elizabeth 1893-1986. . . . . . . DLB-22

Cobb, Charles E., Jr. 1943- DLB-41

Cobb, Frank I. 1869-1923. . . . . DLB-25

Cobb, Irvin S. 1876-1944 . . . . DLB-11, 25, 86

Cobbe, Frances Power 1822-1904 . . . . . . DLB-190

Cobbett, William 1763-1835. . . . . DLB-43, 107, 158

Cobbledick, Gordon 1898-1969 . . . . DLB-171

Cochran, Thomas C. 1902- DLB-17

Cochrane, Elizabeth 1867-1922. . . . . . DLB-25, 189

Cockerell, Sir Sydney 1867-1962 . . . . . . DLB-201

Cockerill, John A. 1845-1896 . . . . DLB-23

Cocteau, Jean 1889-1963 . . . . DLB-65, 258

Coderre, Emile (see Jean Narrache)

Cody, Liza 1944- DLB-276

Coe, Jonathan 1961- DLB-231

Coetzee, J. M. 1940- DLB-225

Coffee, Lenore J. 1900?-1984 . . . . DLB-44

Coffin, Robert P. Tristram 1892-1955 . . . . DLB-45

Coghill, Mrs. Harry (see Walker, Anna Louisa)

Cogswell, Fred 1917- DLB-60

Cogswell, Mason Fitch 1761-1830 . . . . . . DLB-37

Cohan, George M. 1878-1942 . . . . DLB-249

Cohen, Arthur A. 1928-1986 . . . . DLB-28

Cohen, Leonard 1934- DLB-53

Cohen, Matt 1942- DLB-53

Cohen, Morris Raphael 1880-1947. . . . . . DLB-270

Colbeck, Norman 1903-1987 . . . . DLB-201

Colden, Cadwallader 1688-1776. . . DLB-24, 30, 270

Colden, Jane 1724-1766 . . . . DLB-200

Cole, Barry 1936- DLB-14

Cole, George Watson 1850-1939 . . . . DLB-140

Colegate, Isabel 1931- DLB-14, 231

Coleman, Emily Holmes 1899-1974 . . . . . . DLB-4

Coleman, Wanda 1946- DLB-130

Coleridge, Hartley 1796-1849. . . . . DLB-96

Coleridge, Mary 1861-1907 . . . . DLB-19, 98

Coleridge, Samuel Taylor
1772-1834. . . . . DLB-93, 107; CDBLB-3

Coleridge, Sara 1802-1852 . . . . DLB-199

Colet, John 1467-1519. . . . . DLB-132

Colette 1873-1954. . . . . DLB-65

Colette, Sidonie Gabrielle (see Colette)

Colinas, Antonio 1946- DLB-134

Coll, Joseph Clement 1881-1921 . . . . . . DLB-188

A Century of Poetry, a Lifetime of Collecting:
J. M. Edelstein's Collection of
Twentieth-Century American Poetry Y-02

Collier, John 1901-1980 . . . . DLB-77, 255

Collier, John Payne 1789-1883 . . . . DLB-184

Collier, Mary 1690-1762. . . . . DLB-95

Collier, Robert J. 1876-1918 . . . . DLB-91

P. F. Collier [publishing house]. DLB-49

Collin and Small. DLB-49

Collingwood, R. G. 1889-1943. . . . . DLB-262

Collingwood, W. G. 1854-1932 . . . . DLB-149

Collins, An florunt circa 1653 . . . . DLB-131

Collins, Anthony 1676-1729 . . . . DLB-252

Collins, Merle 1950- DLB-157

Collins, Michael 1964- DLB-267

Tribute to John D. MacDonald Y-86

Tribute to Kenneth Millar Y-83

Why I Write Mysteries: Night and Day. . Y-85

Collins, Mortimer 1827-1876 . . . . DLB-21, 35

Collins, Tom (see Furphy, Joseph)

Collins, Wilkie
1824-1889 . . . . . . DLB-18, 70, 159; CDBLB-4

"The Unknown Public" (1858)
[excerpt] DLB-57

The Wilkie Collins Society Y-98

Collins, William 1721-1759. . . . . DLB-109

Isaac Collins [publishing house] DLB-49

William Collins, Sons and Company DLB-154

Collis, Maurice 1889-1973 . . . . DLB-195

Collyer, Mary 1716?-1763?. DLB-39

Colman, Benjamin 1673-1747. . . . . DLB-24

Colman, George, the Elder 1732-1794 . . . . DLB-89

Colman, George, the Younger
1762-1836. DLB-89

S. Colman [publishing house]. DLB-49

Colombo, John Robert 1936- DLB-53

Colquhoun, Patrick 1745-1820 . . . . DLB-158

Colter, Cyrus 1910-2002 . . . . DLB-33

Colum, Padraic 1881-1972 . . . . DLB-19

The Columbia History of the American Novel
A Symposium on Y-92

Columella fl. first century A.D. DLB-211

Colvin, Sir Sidney 1845-1927 . . . . DLB-149

Colwin, Laurie 1944-1992 . . . . DLB-218; Y-80

Comden, Betty 1915- DLB-44, 265

Comi, Girolamo 1890-1968 . . . . DLB-114

Comisso, Giovanni 1895-1969 . . . . DLB-264

Commager, Henry Steele 1902-1998 . . . . . DLB-17

Commynes, Philippe de
circa 1447-1511. . . . . DLB-208

Compton, D. G. 1930- DLB-261

Compton-Burnett, Ivy 1884?-1969. . . . . . . DLB-36

Conan, Laure (Félicité Angers)
1845-1924 . . . . DLB-99

Concord, Massachusetts
Concord History and Life DLB-223

Concord: Literary History of a Town DLB-223

The Old Manse, by Hawthorne DLB-223

The Thoreauvian Pilgrimage: The
Structure of an American Cult . . DLB-223

Conde, Carmen 1901-1996 . . . . DLB-108

Congreve, William
1670-1729 . . . . DLB-39, 84; CDBLB-2

Preface to *Incognita* (1692) DLB-39

W. B. Conkey Company DLB-49

Conn, Stewart 1936- DLB-233

Connell, Evan S., Jr. 1924- DLB-2; Y-81

Connelly, Marc 1890-1980. . . . . DLB-7; Y-80

Connolly, Cyril 1903-1974 . . . . DLB-98

Connolly, James B. 1868-1957 . . . . DLB-78

Connor, Ralph (Charles William Gordon)
1860-1937 . . . . DLB-92

Connor, Tony 1930- DLB-40

Conquest, Robert 1917- DLB-27

Conrad, Joseph
1857-1924. . . . DLB-10, 34, 98, 156; CDBLB-5

John Conrad and Company DLB-49

Conroy, Jack 1899-1990. . . . . Y-81

A Tribute [to Nelson Algren] Y-81

Conroy, Pat 1945- DLB-6

Considine, Bob 1906-1975 . . . . DLB-241

Consolo, Vincenzo 1933- DLB-196	Ćopić, Branko 1915-1984 .... DLB-181	Cortez, Jayne 1936- DLB-41
Constable, Henry 1562-1613 .... DLB-136	Copland, Robert 1470?-1548 .... DLB-136	Corvinus, Gottlieb Siegmund 1677-1746 .... DLB-168
Archibald Constable and Company DLB-154	Coppard, A. E. 1878-1957 .... DLB-162	Corvo, Baron (see Rolfe, Frederick William)
Constable and Company Limited DLB-112	Coppée, François 1842-1908 .... DLB-217	Cory, Annie Sophie (see Cross, Victoria)
Constant, Benjamin 1767-1830 .... DLB-119	Coppel, Alfred 1921- Y-83	Cory, Desmond (Shaun Lloyd McCarthy) 1928- DLB-276
Constant de Rebecque, Henri-Benjamin de (see Constant, Benjamin)	Tribute to Jessamyn West Y-84	Cory, William Johnson 1823-1892 .... DLB-35
Constantine, David 1944- DLB-40	Coppola, Francis Ford 1939- DLB-44	Coryate, Thomas 1577?-1617 ...... DLB-151, 172
Constantine, Murray (see Burdekin, Katharine)	Copway, George (Kah-ge-ga-gah-bowh) 1818-1869 .... DLB-175, 183	Ćosić, Dobrica 1921- DLB-181; CDWLB-4
Constantin-Weyer, Maurice 1881-1964 ... DLB-92	Copyright The Development of the Author's Copyright in Britain DLB-154	Cosin, John 1595-1672 .... DLB-151, 213
Contempo (magazine) Contempo Caravan: Kites in a Windstorm Y-85	The Digital Millennium Copyright Act: Expanding Copyright Protection in Cyberspace and Beyond Y-98	Cosmopolitan Book Corporation DLB-46
The Continental Publishing Company DLB-49	Editorial: The Extension of Copyright .. Y-02	Costain, Thomas B. 1885-1965 .... DLB-9
A Conversation between William Riggan and Janette Turner Hospital Y-02	Mark Twain on Perpetual Copyright ... Y-92	Coste, Donat (Daniel Boudreau) 1912-1957 .... DLB-88
Conversations with Editors Y-95	Public Domain and the Violation of Texts...................... Y-97	Costello, Louisa Stuart 1799-1870 .... DLB-166
Conway, Anne 1631-1679 .... DLB-252	The Question of American Copyright in the Nineteenth Century Preface, by George Haven Putnam The Evolution of Copyright, by Brander Matthews Summary of Copyright Legislation in the United States, by R. R. Bowker Analysis of the Provisions of the Copyright Law of 1891, by George Haven Putnam The Contest for International Copyright, by George Haven Putnam Cheap Books and Good Books, by Brander Matthews DLB-49	Cota-Cárdenas, Margarita 1941- DLB-122
Conway, Moncure Daniel 1832-1907 .... DLB-1, 223		Côté, Denis 1954- DLB-251
Cook, Ebenezer circa 1667-circa 1732 ..... DLB-24		Cotten, Bruce 1873-1954 .... DLB-187
Cook, Edward Tyas 1857-1919 .... DLB-149		Cotter, Joseph Seamon, Jr. 1895-1919 ..... DLB-50
Cook, Eliza 1818-1889................. DLB-199		Cotter, Joseph Seamon, Sr. 1861-1949 .... DLB-50
Cook, George Cram 1873-1924......... DLB-266		Joseph Cottle [publishing house] DLB-154
Cook, Michael 1933-1994 .... DLB-53		Cotton, Charles 1630-1687 .... DLB-131
David C. Cook Publishing Company DLB-49		Cotton, John 1584-1652 .... DLB-24
Cooke, George Willis 1848-1923 .... DLB-71		Cotton, Sir Robert Bruce 1571-1631 ..... DLB-213
Cooke, John Esten 1830-1886 .... DLB-3, 248		Coulter, John 1888-1980 .... DLB-68
Cooke, Philip Pendleton 1816-1850 .... DLB-3, 59, 248	Writers and Their Copyright Holders: the WATCH Project Y-94	Cournos, John 1881-1966 .... DLB-54
Cooke, Rose Terry 1827-1892 .... DLB-12, 74	Corazzini, Sergio 1886-1907 .... DLB-114	Courteline, Georges 1858-1929 .... DLB-192
Increase Cooke and Company DLB-49	Corbett, Richard 1582-1635 .... DLB-121	Cousins, Margaret 1905-1996 .... DLB-137
Cook-Lynn, Elizabeth 1930- DLB-175	Corbière, Tristan 1845-1875 .... DLB-217	Cousins, Norman 1915-1990.......... DLB-137
Coolbrith, Ina 1841-1928............ DLB-54, 186	Corcoran, Barbara 1911- DLB-52	Couvreur, Jessie (see Tasma)
Cooley, Peter 1940- DLB-105	Cordelli, Franco 1943- DLB-196	Coventry, Francis 1725-1754 .... DLB-39
"Into the Mirror" DLB-105	Corelli, Marie 1855-1924............ DLB-34, 156	Dedication, *The History of Pompey the Little* (1751) DLB-39
Coolidge, Clark 1939- DLB-193	Corle, Edwin 1906-1956 .... Y-85	Coverdale, Miles 1487 or 1488-1569..... DLB-167
Coolidge, Susan (see Woolsey, Sarah Chauncy)	Corman, Cid 1924- DLB-5, 193	N. Coverly [publishing house] DLB-49
George Coolidge [publishing house] DLB-49	Cormier, Robert 1925-2000.... DLB-52; CDALB-6	Covici-Friede DLB-46
Cooper, Anna Julia 1858-1964.......... DLB-221	Tribute to Theodor Seuss Geisel Y-91	Cowan, Peter 1914-2002 .... DLB-260
Cooper, Edith Emma 1862-1913 .... DLB-240	Corn, Alfred 1943- DLB-120, 282; Y-80	Coward, Noel 1899-1973 .... DLB 10, 245; CDBLB 6
Cooper, Giles 1918-1966............... DLB-13	Corneille, Pierre 1606-1684 .... DLB-268	Coward, McCann and Geoghegan DLB-46
Cooper, J. California 19??- DLB-212	Cornford, Frances 1886-1960 .... DLB-240	Cowles, Gardner 1861-1946 .... DLB-29
Cooper, James Fenimore 1789-1851 .... DLB-3, 183, 250; CDALB-2	Cornish, Sam 1935- DLB-41	Cowles, Gardner "Mike", Jr. 1903-1985 .... DLB-127, 137
The Bicentennial of James Fenimore Cooper: An International Celebration Y-89	Cornish, William circa 1465-circa 1524... DLB-132	Cowley, Abraham 1618-1667 ...... DLB-131, 151
	Cornwall, Barry (see Procter, Bryan Waller)	Cowley, Hannah 1743-1809 .... DLB-89
The James Fenimore Cooper Society Y-01	Cornwallis, Sir William, the Younger circa 1579-1614 .... DLB-151	Cowley, Malcolm 1898-1989 .... DLB-4, 48; DS-15; Y-81, 89
Cooper, Kent 1880-1965 .... DLB-29	Cornwell, David John Moore (see le Carré, John)	Cowper, Richard (John Middleton Murry Jr.) 1926-2002...................... DLB-261
Cooper, Susan 1935- DLB-161, 261	Corpi, Lucha 1945- DLB-82	Cowper, William 1731-1800 .... DLB-104, 109
Cooper, Susan Fenimore 1813-1894 ..... DLB-239	Corrington, John William 1932-1988 ..DLB-6, 244	Cox, A. B. (see Berkeley, Anthony)
William Cooper [publishing house] DLB-170	Corriveau, Monique 1927-1976 .... DLB-251	Cox, James McMahon 1903-1974 .... DLB-127
J. Coote [publishing house] DLB-154	Corrothers, James D. 1869-1917 .... DLB-50	Cox, James Middleton 1870-1957 .... DLB-127
Coover, Robert 1932- DLB-2, 227; Y-81	Corso, Gregory 1930-2001 ...... DLB-5, 16, 237	Cox, Leonard circa 1495-circa 1550 ..... DLB-281
Tribute to Donald Barthelme.......... Y-89	Cortázar, Julio 1914-1984 ... DLB-113; CDWLB-3	Cox, Palmer 1840-1924................. DLB-42
Tribute to Theodor Seuss Geisel Y-91	Cortéz, Carlos 1923- DLB-209	Coxe, Louis 1918-1993 .... DLB-5
Copeland and Day................... DLB-49		

Coxe, Tench 1755-1824 .... DLB-37

Cozzens, Frederick S. 1818-1869 .... DLB-202

Cozzens, James Gould
    1903-1978..... DLB-9; Y-84; DS-2; CDALB-1

    Cozzens's *Michael Scarlett*.............. Y-97

    Ernest Hemingway's Reaction to
        James Gould Cozzens............ Y-98

    James Gould Cozzens—A View
        from Afar.................... Y-97

    James Gould Cozzens: How to
        Read Him................... Y-97

    James Gould Cozzens Symposium and
        Exhibition at the University of
        South Carolina, Columbia......... Y-00

    Mens Rea (or Something).............. Y-97

    Novels for Grown-Ups............... Y-97

Crabbe, George 1754-1832............. DLB-93

Crace, Jim 1946- DLB-231

Crackanthorpe, Hubert 1870-1896...... DLB-135

Craddock, Charles Egbert (see Murfree, Mary N.)

Cradock, Thomas 1718-1770............ DLB-31

Craig, Daniel H. 1811-1895............ DLB-43

Craik, Dinah Maria 1826-1887...... DLB-35, 163

Cramer, Richard Ben 1950- DLB-185

Cranch, Christopher Pearse
    1813-1892............ DLB-1, 42, 243; DS-5

Crane, Hart 1899-1932..... DLB-4, 48; CDALB-4

    Nathan Asch Remembers Ford Madox
        Ford, Sam Roth, and Hart Crane.... Y-02

Crane, R. S. 1886-1967................. DLB-63

Crane, Stephen
    1871-1900........ DLB-12, 54, 78; CDALB-3

    Stephen Crane: A Revaluation, Virginia
        Tech Conference, 1989 .... Y-89

    The Stephen Crane Society......... Y-98, 01

Crane, Walter 1845-1915............... DLB-163

Cranmer, Thomas 1489-1556 ..... DLB-132, 213

Crapsey, Adelaide 1878-1914........... DLB-54

Crashaw, Richard 1612/1613-1649 ..... DLB-126

Craven, Avery 1885-1980.............. DLB-17

Crawford, Charles 1752-circa 1815 ...... DLB-31

Crawford, F. Marion 1854-1909.......... DLB-71

Crawford, Isabel Valancy 1850-1887 ..... DLB-92

Crawley, Alan 1887-1975 .... DLB-68

Crayon, Geoffrey (see Irving, Washington)

Crayon, Porte (see Strother, David Hunter)

Creamer, Robert W. 1922- DLB-171

Creasey, John 1908-1973 .... DLB-77

Creative Age Press.................. DLB-46

Creative Nonfiction Y-02

William Creech [publishing house]...... DLB-154

Thomas Creede [publishing house] DLB-170

Creel, George 1876-1953 .... DLB-25

Creeley, Robert 1926- DLB-5, 16, 169; DS-17

Creelman, James 1859-1915............ DLB-23

Cregan, David 1931- DLB-13

Creighton, Donald 1902-1979.......... DLB-88

Crémazie, Octave 1827-1879........... DLB-99

Crémer, Victoriano 1909?- DLB-108

Crescas, Hasdai circa 1340-1412?....... DLB-115

Crespo, Angel 1926-1995 .... DLB-134

Cresset Press..................... DLB-112

Cresswell, Helen 1934- DLB-161

Crèvecoeur, Michel Guillaume Jean de
    1735-1813..................... DLB-37

Crewe, Candida 1964- DLB-207

Crews, Harry 1935- DLB-6, 143, 185

Crichton, Michael 1942- Y-81

Crispin, Edmund (Robert Bruce Montgomery)
    1921-1978................... DLB-87

Cristofer, Michael 1946- DLB-7

Criticism

    Afro-American Literary Critics:
        An Introduction DLB-33

    The Consolidation of Opinion: Critical
        Responses to the Modernists DLB-36

    "Criticism in Relation to Novels"
        (1863), by G. H. Lewes DLB-21

    The Limits of Pluralism DLB-67

    Modern Critical Terms, Schools, and
        Movements................... DLB-67

    "Panic Among the Philistines": A Postscript,
        An Interview with Bryan Griffin.... Y-81

    The Recovery of Literature: Criticism
        in the 1990s: A Symposium Y-91

    The Stealthy School of Criticism (1871),
        by Dante Gabriel Rossetti DLB-35

Crnjanski, Miloš
    1893-1977............DLB-147; CDWLB-4

Crocker, Hannah Mather 1752-1829 .... DLB-200

Crockett, David (Davy)
    1786-1836.............DLB-3, 11, 183, 248

Croft-Cooke, Rupert (see Bruce, Leo)

Crofts, Freeman Wills 1879-1957 .... DLB-77

Croker, John Wilson 1780-1857 .... DLB-110

Croly, George 1780-1860 .... DLB-159

Croly, Herbert 1869-1930 .... DLB-91

Croly, Jane Cunningham 1829-1901 ..... DLB-23

Crompton, Richmal 1890-1969 .... DLB-160

Cronin, A. J. 1896-1981 .... DLB-191

Cros, Charles 1842-1888 .... DLB-217

Crosby, Caresse
    1892-1970............ DLB-4, 15, 48; DS-15

Crosby, Harry 1898-1929 .. DLB-4, 15, 48; DS-15

Crosland, Camilla Toulmin (Mrs. Newton
    Crosland) 1812-1895 .... DLB-240

Cross, Gillian 1945- DLB-161

Cross, Victoria 1868-1952 ....DLB-135, 197

Crossley-Holland, Kevin 1941- DLB-40, 161

Crothers, Rachel 1870-1958 ....DLB-7, 266

Thomas Y. Crowell Company DLB-49

Crowley, John 1942- Y-82

Crowley, Mart 1935- DLB-7, 266

Crown Publishers................... DLB-46

Crowne, John 1641-1712 .... DLB-80

Crowninshield, Edward Augustus
    1817-1859..................... DLB-140

Crowninshield, Frank 1872-1947 .... DLB-91

Croy, Homer 1883-1965 .... DLB-4

Crumley, James 1939- DLB-226; Y-84

Cruse, Mary Anne 1825?-1910 .... DLB-239

Cruz, Migdalia 1958- DLB-249

Cruz, Victor Hernández 1949- DLB-41

Csokor, Franz Theodor 1885-1969 ...... DLB-81

Csoóri, Sándor 1930- DLB-232; CDWLB-4

Cuala Press...................... DLB-112

Cudworth, Ralph 1617-1688.......... DLB-252

Cugoano, Quobna Ottabah 1797-? Y-02

Cullen, Countee
    1903-1946 .... DLB-4, 48, 51; CDALB-4

Culler, Jonathan D. 1944- DLB-67, 246

Cullinan, Elizabeth 1933- DLB-234

Culverwel, Nathaniel 1619?-1651?..... DLB-252

Cumberland, Richard 1732-1811 .... DLB-89

Cummings, Constance Gordon
    1837-1924.....................DLB-174

Cummings, E. E.
    1894-1962 .... DLB-4, 48; CDALB-5

    The E. E. Cummings Society Y-01

Cummings, Ray 1887-1957............. DLB-8

Cummings and Hilliard DLB-49

Cummins, Maria Susanna 1827-1866..... DLB-42

Cumpián, Carlos 1953- DLB-209

Cunard, Nancy 1896-1965............ DLB-240

Joseph Cundall [publishing house] DLB-106

Cuney, Waring 1906-1976 .... DLB-51

Cuney-Hare, Maude 1874-1936 .... DLB-52

Cunningham, Allan 1784-1842.....DLB-116, 144

Cunningham, J. V. 1911-1985 .... DLB-5

Cunningham, Peter (Peter Lauder, Peter
    Benjamin) 1947- DLB-267

Peter F. Cunningham
    [publishing house] DLB-49

Cunqueiro, Alvaro 1911-1981 .... DLB-134

Cuomo, George 1929- Y-80

Cupples, Upham and Company......... DLB-49

Cupples and Leon DLB-46

Cuppy, Will 1884-1949 .... DLB-11

Curiel, Barbara Brinson 1956- DLB-209

Edmund Curll [publishing house] DLB-154

Currie, James 1756-1805............... DLB-142

Currie, Mary Montgomerie Lamb Singleton,
    Lady Currie (see Fane, Violet)

Cursor Mundi circa 1300.............. DLB-146

Curti, Merle E. 1897-1996 ....DLB-17

Curtis, Anthony 1926- DLB-155

Curtis, Cyrus H. K. 1850-1933 .... DLB-91

Curtis, George William
    1824-1892 .... DLB-1, 43, 223

Curzon, Robert 1810-1873 .... DLB-166

Curzon, Sarah Anne 1833-1898 .... DLB-99

Cusack, Dymphna 1902-1981 .... DLB-260

Cushing, Eliza Lanesford 1794-1886 ......DLB-99
Cushing, Harvey 1869-1939 ....DLB-187
Custance, Olive (Lady Alfred Douglas)
  1874-1944 ....DLB-240
Cynewulf circa 770-840 ....DLB-146
Cyrano de Bergerac, Savinien de
  1619-1655 ....DLB-268
Czepko, Daniel 1605-1660...........DLB-164
Czerniawski, Adam 1934- DLB-232

D

Dabit, Eugène 1898-1936..............DLB-65
Daborne, Robert circa 1580-1628 ....DLB-58
Dąbrowska, Maria
  1889-1965............DLB-215; CDWLB-4
Dacey, Philip 1939- DLB-105
  "Eyes Across Centuries:
    Contemporary Poetry and 'That
    Vision Thing,'" DLB-105
Dach, Simon 1605-1659...............DLB-164
Dagerman, Stig 1923-1954............DLB-259
Daggett, Rollin M. 1831-1901 ....DLB-79
D'Aguiar, Fred 1960- DLB-157
Dahl, Roald 1916-1990 ....DLB-139, 255
  Tribute to Alfred A. Knopf Y-84
Dahlberg, Edward 1900-1977 ....DLB-48
Dahn, Felix 1834-1912................DLB-129
Dal', Vladimir Ivanovich (Kazak Vladimir
  Lugansky) 1801-1872 ....DLB-198
Dale, Peter 1938- DLB-40
Daley, Arthur 1904-1974 ....DLB-171
Dall, Caroline Healey 1822-1912......DLB-1, 235
Dallas, E. S. 1828-1879..............DLB-55
  The Gay Science [excerpt] (1866) DLB-21
The Dallas Theater Center DLB-7
D'Alton, Louis 1900-1951 ....DLB-10
Dalton, Roque 1935-1975 ....DLB-283
Daly, Carroll John 1889-1958 ....DLB-226
Daly, T. A. 1871-1948 ....DLB-11
Damon, S. Foster 1893-1971 ....DLB-45
William S. Damrell [publishing house] ...DLB-49
Dana, Charles A. 1819-1897 ......DLB-3, 23, 250
Dana, Richard Henry, Jr.
  1815-1882 ....DLB-1, 183, 235
Dandridge, Ray Garfield DLB-51
Dane, Clemence 1887-1965 ....DLB-10, 197
Danforth, John 1660-1730..............DLB-24
Danforth, Samuel, I 1626-1674 ....DLB-24
Danforth, Samuel, II 1666-1727........DLB-24
Daniel, John M. 1825-1865 ....DLB-43
Daniel, Samuel 1562 or 1563-1619 .....DLB-62
Daniel Press DLB-106
Daniells, Roy 1902-1979 ....DLB-68
Daniels, Jim 1956- DLB-120
Daniels, Jonathan 1902-1981 ....DLB-127
Daniels, Josephus 1862-1948..........DLB-29

Daniels, Sarah 1957- DLB-245
Danilevsky, Grigorii Petrovich
  1829-1890 ....DLB-238
Dannay, Frederic 1905-1982 ....DLB-137
Danner, Margaret Esse 1915- DLB-41
John Danter [publishing house] DLB-170
Dantin, Louis (Eugene Seers) 1865-1945...DLB-92
Danto, Arthur C. 1924- DLB-279
Danzig, Allison 1898-1987............DLB-171
D'Arcy, Ella circa 1857-1937 ....DLB-135
Dark, Eleanor 1901-1985.............DLB-260
Darke, Nick 1948- DLB-233
Darley, Felix Octavious Carr 1822-1888..DLB-188
Darley, George 1795-1846.............DLB-96
Darmesteter, Madame James
  (see Robinson, A. Mary F.)
Darwin, Charles 1809-1882..........DLB-57, 166
Darwin, Erasmus 1731-1802 ....DLB-93
Daryush, Elizabeth 1887-1977 ....DLB-20
Dashkova, Ekaterina Romanovna
  (née Vorontsova) 1743-1810 ....DLB-150
Dashwood, Edmée Elizabeth Monica de la Pasture
  (see Delafield, E. M.)
Daudet, Alphonse 1840-1897..........DLB-123
d'Aulaire, Edgar Parin 1898- DLB-22
d'Aulaire, Ingri 1904- DLB-22
Davenant, Sir William 1606-1668 ....DLB-58, 126
Davenport, Guy 1927- DLB-130
  Tribute to John Gardner Y-82
Davenport, Marcia 1903-1996............DS-17
Davenport, Robert ?-? DLB-58
Daves, Delmer 1904-1977 ....DLB-26
Davey, Frank 1940- DLB-53
Davidson, Avram 1923-1993............DLB-8
Davidson, Donald 1893-1968 ....DLB-45
Davidson, Donald 1917- DLB-279
Davidson, John 1857-1909..............DLB-19
Davidson, Lionel 1922- DLB-14, 276
Davidson, Robyn 1950-................DLB-204
Davidson, Sara 1943- DLB-185
Davie, Donald 1922- DLB-27
Davie, Elspeth 1919-1995 ....DLB-139
Davies, Sir John 1569-1626 ....DLB-172
Davies, John, of Hereford 1565?-1618....DLB-121
Davies, Rhys 1901-1978............DLB-139, 191
Davies, Robertson 1913-1995 ....DLB-68
Davies, Samuel 1723-1761 ....DLB-31
Davies, Thomas 1712?-1785 ....DLB-142, 154
Davies, W. H. 1871-1940...........DLB-19, 174
Peter Davies Limited DLB-112
Davin, Nicholas Flood 1840?-1901 ....DLB-99
Daviot, Gordon 1896?-1952 ....DLB-10
  (see also Tey, Josephine)
Davis, Arthur Hoey (see Rudd, Steele)
Davis, Charles A. (Major J. Downing)
  1795-1867 ....DLB-11

Davis, Clyde Brion 1894-1962 ....DLB-9
Davis, Dick 1945- DLB-40, 282
Davis, Frank Marshall 1905-1987 ....DLB-51
Davis, H. L. 1894-1960.............DLB-9, 206
Davis, John 1774-1854 ....DLB-37
Davis, Lydia 1947- DLB-130
Davis, Margaret Thomson 1926- DLB-14
Davis, Ossie 1917- DLB-7, 38, 249
Davis, Owen 1874-1956................DLB-249
Davis, Paxton 1925-1994.................Y-89
Davis, Rebecca Harding 1831-1910...DLB-74, 239
Davis, Richard Harding 1864-1916
  ....DLB-12, 23, 78, 79, 189; DS-13
Davis, Samuel Cole 1764-1809 ....DLB-37
Davis, Samuel Post 1850-1918..........DLB-202
Davison, Frank Dalby 1893-1970 ....DLB-260
Davison, Peter 1928- DLB-5
Davydov, Denis Vasil'evich 1784-1839...DLB-205
Davys, Mary 1674-1732................DLB-39
  Preface to *The Works of Mrs. Davys*
    (1725) DLB-39
DAW Books........................DLB-46
Dawson, Ernest 1882-1947 ......DLB-140; Y-02
Dawson, Fielding 1930- DLB-130
Dawson, Sarah Morgan 1842-1909......DLB-239
Dawson, William 1704-1752 ....DLB-31
Day, Angel flourished 1583-1599 ...DLB-167, 236
Day, Benjamin Henry 1810-1889 ....DLB-43
Day, Clarence 1874-1935................DLB-11
Day, Dorothy 1897-1980...............DLB-29
Day, Frank Parker 1881-1950 ....DLB-92
Day, John circa 1574-circa 1640..........DLB-62
Day, Thomas 1748-1789 ....DLB-39
John Day [publishing house] DLB-170
The John Day Company DLB-46
Mahlon Day [publishing house]..........DLB-49
Day Lewis, C. (see Blake, Nicholas)
Dazai Osamu 1909-1948 ....DLB-182
Deacon, William Arthur 1890-1977......DLB-68
Deal, Borden 1922-1985 ....DLB-6
de Angeli, Marguerite 1889-1987........DLB-22
De Angelis, Milo 1951- DLB-128
De Bow, J. D. B. 1820-1867.......DLB-3, 79, 248
de Bruyn, Günter 1926- DLB-75
de Camp, L. Sprague 1907-2000 ....DLB-8
De Carlo, Andrea 1952- DLB-196
De Casas, Celso A. 1944- DLB-209
Dechert, Robert 1895-1975 ....DLB-187
Dedications, Inscriptions, and
  Annotations...................Y-01–02
Dee, John 1527-1608 or 1609.......DLB-136, 213
Deeping, George Warwick 1877-1950 ....DLB-153
Defoe, Daniel
  1660-1731.......DLB-39, 95, 101; CDBLB-2
  Preface to *Colonel Jack* (1722) DLB-39

Preface to *The Farther Adventures of Robinson Crusoe* (1719) DLB-39

Preface to *Moll Flanders* (1722) DLB-39

Preface to *Robinson Crusoe* (1719) DLB-39

Preface to *Roxana* (1724) DLB-39

de Fontaine, Felix Gregory 1834-1896 .... DLB-43

De Forest, John William 1826-1906 .. DLB-12, 189

DeFrees, Madeline 1919- DLB-105

"The Poet's Kaleidoscope: The Element of Surprise in the Making of the Poem" DLB-105

DeGolyer, Everette Lee 1886-1956 ..... DLB-187

de Graff, Robert 1895-1981 .... Y-81

de Graft, Joe 1924-1978 .... DLB-117

De Heinrico circa 980? DLB-148

Deighton, Len 1929- DLB-87; CDBLB-8

DeJong, Meindert 1906-1991 .... DLB-52

Dekker, Thomas circa 1572-1632 ..... DLB-62, 172; CDBLB-1

Delacorte, George T., Jr. 1894-1991 ...... DLB-91

Delafield, E. M. 1890-1943 .... DLB-34

Delahaye, Guy (Guillaume Lahaise) 1888-1969 .... DLB-92

de la Mare, Walter 1873-1956 .... DLB-19, 153, 162, 255; CDBLB-6

Deland, Margaret 1857-1945 .... DLB-78

Delaney, Shelagh 1939- DLB-13; CDBLB-8

Delano, Amasa 1763-1823 .... DLB-183

Delany, Martin Robinson 1812-1885 ..... DLB-50

Delany, Samuel R. 1942- DLB-8, 33

de la Roche, Mazo 1879-1961 .... DLB-68

Delavigne, Jean François Casimir 1793-1843 .... DLB-192

Delbanco, Nicholas 1942- DLB-6, 234

Delblanc, Sven 1931-1992 .... DLB-257

Del Castillo, Ramón 1949- DLB-209

Deledda, Grazia 1871-1936 .... DLB-264

De León, Nephtal 1945- DLB-82

Delfini, Antonio 1907-1963 .... DLB-264

Delgado, Abelardo Barrientos 1931- DLB-82

Del Giudice, Daniele 1949- DLB-196

De Libero, Libero 1906-1981 .... DLB-114

DeLillo, Don 1936- DLB-6, 173

de Lint, Charles 1951- DLB-251

de Lisser H. G. 1878-1944 .... DLB-117

Dell, Floyd 1887-1969 .... DLB-9

Dell Publishing Company DLB-46

delle Grazie, Marie Eugene 1864-1931 .... DLB-81

Deloney, Thomas died 1600 .... DLB-167

Deloria, Ella C. 1889-1971 ....DLB-175

Deloria, Vine, Jr. 1933- DLB-175

del Rey, Lester 1915-1993 .... DLB-8

Del Vecchio, John M. 1947- DS-9

Del'vig, Anton Antonovich 1798-1831 ... DLB-205

de Man, Paul 1919-1983 .... DLB-67

DeMarinis, Rick 1934- DLB-218

Demby, William 1922- DLB-33

De Mille, James 1833-1880 .... DLB-99, 251

de Mille, William 1878-1955 .... DLB-266

Deming, Philander 1829-1915 .... DLB-74

Deml, Jakub 1878-1961 .... DLB-215

Demorest, William Jennings 1822-1895 ... DLB-79

De Morgan, William 1839-1917 .... DLB-153

Demosthenes 384 B.C.-322 B.C. DLB-176

Henry Denham [publishing house] DLB-170

Denham, Sir John 1615-1669 .... DLB-58, 126

Denison, Merrill 1893-1975 .... DLB-92

T. S. Denison and Company DLB-49

Dennery, Adolphe Philippe 1811-1899 ... DLB-192

Dennie, Joseph 1768-1812 ...... DLB-37, 43, 59, 73

Dennis, C. J. 1876-1938 .... DLB-260

Dennis, John 1658-1734 .... DLB-101

Dennis, Nigel 1912-1989 .... DLB-13, 15, 233

Denslow, W. W. 1856-1915 .... DLB-188

Dent, J. M., and Sons DLB-112

Dent, Tom 1932-1998 .... DLB-38

Denton, Daniel circa 1626-1703 .... DLB-24

DePaola, Tomie 1934- DLB-61

De Quille, Dan 1829-1898 .... DLB-186

De Quincey, Thomas 1785-1859 .... DLB-110, 144; CDBLB-3

"Rhetoric" (1828; revised, 1859) [excerpt] DLB-57

"Style" (1840; revised, 1859) [excerpt] DLB-57

Derby, George Horatio 1823-1861 .... DLB-11

J. C. Derby and Company DLB-49

Derby and Miller DLB-49

De Ricci, Seymour 1881-1942 .... DLB-201

Derleth, August 1909-1971 .... DLB-9; DS-17

Derrida, Jacques 1930- DLB-242

The Derrydale Press DLB-46

Derzhavin, Gavriil Romanovich 1743-1816 .... DLB-150

Desai, Anita 1937- DLB-271

Desaulniers, Gonzalve 1863-1934 .... DLB-92

Desbordes-Valmore, Marceline 1786-1859 .... DLB-217

Descartes, René 1596-1650 ....DLB-268

Deschamps, Emile 1791-1871 .... DLB-217

Deschamps, Eustache 1340?-1404 ...... DLB-208

Desbiens, Jean-Paul 1927- DLB-53

des Forêts, Louis-Rene 1918-2001 .... DLB-83

Desiato, Luca 1941- DLB-196

Desjardins, Marie-Catherine (see Villedieu, Madame de)

Desnica, Vladan 1905-1967 .... DLB-181

Desnos, Robert 1900-1945 .... DLB-258

DesRochers, Alfred 1901-1978 .... DLB-68

Desrosiers, Léo-Paul 1896-1967 .... DLB-68

Dessaulles, Louis-Antoine 1819-1895 ..... DLB-99

Dessì, Giuseppe 1909-1977 ....DLB-177

Destouches, Louis-Ferdinand (see Céline, Louis-Ferdinand)

DeSylva, Buddy 1895-1950 .... DLB-265

De Tabley, Lord 1835-1895 .... DLB-35

Deutsch, Babette 1895-1982 .... DLB-45

Deutsch, Niklaus Manuel (see Manuel, Niklaus)

André Deutsch Limited DLB-112

Devanny, Jean 1894-1962 .... DLB-260

Deveaux, Alexis 1948- DLB-38

De Vere, Aubrey 1814-1902 .... DLB-35

Devereux, second Earl of Essex, Robert 1565-1601 .... DLB-136

The Devin-Adair Company DLB-46

De Vinne, Theodore Low 1828-1914 ....DLB-187

Devlin, Anne 1951- DLB-245

DeVoto, Bernard 1897-1955 .... DLB-9, 256

De Vries, Peter 1910-1993 ....DLB-6; Y-82

Tribute to Albert Erskine Y-93

Dewart, Edward Hartley 1828-1903 ..... DLB-99

Dewdney, Christopher 1951- DLB-60

Dewdney, Selwyn 1909-1979 .... DLB-68

Dewey, John 1859-1952 ....DLB-246, 270

Dewey, Orville 1794-1882 .... DLB-243

Dewey, Thomas B. 1915-1981 .... DLB-226

DeWitt, Robert M., Publisher DLB-49

DeWolfe, Fiske and Company DLB-49

Dexter, Colin 1930- DLB-87

de Young, M. H. 1849-1925 .... DLB-25

Dhlomo, H. I. E. 1903-1956 ....DLB-157, 225

Dhuoda circa 803-after 843 .... DLB-148

The Dial 1840-1844 .... DLB-223

The Dial Press DLB-46

Diamond, I. A. L. 1920-1988 .... DLB-26

Dibble, L. Grace 1902-1998 .... DLB-204

Dibdin, Thomas Frognall 1776-1847 .... DLB-184

Di Cicco, Pier Giorgio 1949- DLB-60

Dick, Philip K. 1928-1982 .... DLB-8

Dick and Fitzgerald DLB-49

Dickens, Charles 1812-1870 ... DLB-21, 55, 70, 159, 166; DS-5; CDBLB-4

Dickey, James 1923-1997 ....DLB-5, 193; Y-82, 93, 96, 97; DS-7, 19; CDALB-6

James Dickey and Stanley Burnshaw Correspondence Y-02

James Dickey at Seventy–A Tribute Y-93

James Dickey, American Poet Y-96

The James Dickey Society Y-99

The Life of James Dickey: A Lecture to the Friends of the Emory Libraries, by Henry Hart Y-98

Tribute to Archibald MacLeish Y-82

Tribute to Malcolm Cowley Y-89

Tribute to Truman Capote Y-84

Tributes [to Dickey] Y-97

Dickey, William 1928-1994 .... DLB-5

Dickinson, Emily 1830-1886 .... DLB-1, 243; CDALB-3

Dickinson, John 1732-1808 .... DLB-31
Dickinson, Jonathan 1688-1747 .... DLB-24
Dickinson, Patric 1914- DLB-27
Dickinson, Peter 1927- DLB-87, 161, 276
John Dicks [publishing house] DLB-106
Dickson, Gordon R. 1923-2001 .... DLB-8
Dictionary of Literary Biography Annual Awards for Dictionary of Literary Biography Editors and Contributors Y-98–02
Dictionary of Literary Biography Yearbook Awards Y-92–93, 97–02
The Dictionary of National Biography DLB-144
Didion, Joan 1934-
 .... DLB-2, 173, 185; Y-81, 86; CDALB-6
Di Donato, Pietro 1911- DLB-9
Die Fürstliche Bibliothek Corvey Y-96
Diego, Gerardo 1896-1987 .... DLB-134
Dietz, Howard 1896-1983 .... DLB-265
Digby, Everard 1550?-1605 .... DLB-281
Digges, Thomas circa 1546-1595 .... DLB-136
The Digital Millennium Copyright Act: Expanding Copyright Protection in Cyberspace and Beyond Y-98
Diktonius, Elmer 1896-1961 .... DLB-259
Dillard, Annie 1945- DLB-275, 278; Y-80
Dillard, R. H. W. 1937- DLB-5, 244
Charles T. Dillingham Company DLB-49
G. W. Dillingham Company DLB-49
Edward and Charles Dilly [publishing house] DLB-154
Dilthey, Wilhelm 1833-1911 .... DLB-129
Dimitrova, Blaga 1922- ... DLB-181; CDWLB-4
Dimov, Dimitr 1909-1966 .... DLB-181
Dimsdale, Thomas J. 1831?-1866 .... DLB-186
Dinescu, Mircea 1950- DLB-232
Dinesen, Isak (see Blixen, Karen)
Dingelstedt, Franz von 1814-1881 .... DLB-133
Dintenfass, Mark 1941- Y-84
Diogenes, Jr. (see Brougham, John)
Diogenes Laertius circa 200 .... DLB-176
DiPrima, Diane 1934- DLB-5, 16
Disch, Thomas M. 1940- DLB-8, 282
Diski, Jenny 1947- DLB-271
Disney, Walt 1901-1966 .... DLB-22
Disraeli, Benjamin 1804-1881 .... DLB-21, 55
D'Israeli, Isaac 1766-1848 .... DLB-107
DLB Award for Distinguished Literary Criticism Y-02
Ditlevsen, Tove 1917-1976 .... DLB-214
Ditzen, Rudolf (see Fallada, Hans)
Dix, Dorothea Lynde 1802-1887 ..... DLB-1, 235
Dix, Dorothy (see Gilmer, Elizabeth Meriwether)
Dix, Edwards and Company DLB-49
Dix, Gertrude circa 1874-? DLB-197
Dixie, Florence Douglas 1857-1905 ..... DLB-174

Dixon, Ella Hepworth 1855 or 1857-1932 .... DLB-197
Dixon, Paige (see Corcoran, Barbara)
Dixon, Richard Watson 1833-1900 .... DLB-19
Dixon, Stephen 1936- DLB-130
DLB Award for Distinguished Literary Criticism Y-02
Dmitriev, Ivan Ivanovich 1760-1837 ..... DLB-150
Dobell, Bertram 1842-1914 .... DLB-184
Dobell, Sydney 1824-1874 .... DLB-32
Dobie, J. Frank 1888-1964 .... DLB-212
Dobles Yzaguirre, Julieta 1943- DLB-283
Döblin, Alfred 1878-1957 ..... DLB-66; CDWLB-2
Dobroliubov, Nikolai Aleksandrovich 1836-1861 .... DLB-277
Dobson, Austin 1840-1921 .... DLB-35, 144
Dobson, Rosemary 1920- DLB-260
Doctorow, E. L. 1931- DLB-2, 28, 173; Y-80; CDALB-6
Dodd, Susan M. 1946- DLB-244
Dodd, William E. 1869-1940 .... DLB-17
Anne Dodd [publishing house] DLB-154
Dodd, Mead and Company DLB-49
Doderer, Heimito von 1896-1966 .... DLB-85
B. W. Dodge and Company DLB-46
Dodge, Mary Abigail 1833-1896 .... DLB-221
Dodge, Mary Mapes 1831?-1905 .... DLB-42, 79; DS-13
Dodge Publishing Company DLB-49
Dodgson, Charles Lutwidge (see Carroll, Lewis)
Dodsley, Robert 1703-1764 .... DLB-95
R. Dodsley [publishing house] DLB-154
Dodson, Owen 1914-1983 .... DLB-76
Dodwell, Christina 1951- DLB-204
Doesticks, Q. K. Philander, P. B. (see Thomson, Mortimer)
Doheny, Carrie Estelle 1875-1958 .... DLB-140
Doherty, John 1798?-1854 .... DLB-190
Doig, Ivan 1939- DLB-206
Doinaș, Ștefan Augustin 1922- DLB-232
Domínguez, Sylvia Maida 1935- DLB-122
Donaghy, Michael 1954- DLB-282
Patrick Donahoe [publishing house] DLB-49
Donald, David H. 1920- DLB-17; Y-87
Donaldson, Scott 1928- DLB-111
Doni, Rodolfo 1919- DLB-177
Donleavy, J. P. 1926- DLB-6, 173
Donnadieu, Marguerite (see Duras, Marguerite)
Donne, John 1572-1631 .... DLB-121, 151; CDBLB-1
Donnelly, Ignatius 1831-1901 .... DLB-12
R. R. Donnelley and Sons Company DLB-49
Donoghue, Emma 1969- DLB-267
Donohue and Henneberry DLB-49
Donoso, José 1924-1996 .... DLB-113; CDWLB-3
M. Doolady [publishing house] DLB-49

Dooley, Ebon (see Ebon)
Doolittle, Hilda 1886-1961 ..... DLB-4, 45; DS-15
Doplicher, Fabio 1938- DLB-128
Dor, Milo 1923- DLB-85
George H. Doran Company DLB-46
Dorgelès, Roland 1886-1973 .... DLB-65
Dorn, Edward 1929-1999 .... DLB-5
Dorr, Rheta Childe 1866-1948 .... DLB-25
Dorris, Michael 1945-1997 .... DLB-175
Dorset and Middlesex, Charles Sackville, Lord Buckhurst, Earl of 1643-1706 .... DLB-131
Dorsey, Candas Jane 1952- DLB-251
Dorst, Tankred 1925- DLB-75, 124
Dos Passos, John 1896-1970 .... DLB-4, 9; DS-1, 15; CDALB-5
 John Dos Passos: A Centennial Commemoration Y-96
 John Dos Passos: Artist Y-99
 John Dos Passos Newsletter Y-00
 U.S.A. (Documentary) DLB-274
Dostoevsky, Fyodor 1821-1881 .... DLB-238
Doubleday and Company DLB-49
Dougall, Lily 1858-1923 .... DLB-92
Doughty, Charles M. 1843-1926 .... DLB-19, 57, 174
Douglas, Lady Alfred (see Custance, Olive)
Douglas, Gavin 1476-1522 .... DLB-132
Douglas, Keith 1920-1944 .... DLB-27
Douglas, Norman 1868-1952 .... DLB-34, 195
Douglass, Frederick 1817-1895 .... DLB-1, 43, 50, 79, 243; CDALB-2
 Frederick Douglass Creative Arts Center Y-01
Douglass, William circa 1691-1752 ...... DLB-24
Dourado, Autran 1926- DLB-145
Dove, Arthur G. 1880-1946 .... DLB-188
Dove, Rita 1952- DLB-120; CDALB-7
Dover Publications DLB-46
Doves Press DLB-112
Dowden, Edward 1843-1913 .... DLB-35, 149
Dowell, Coleman 1925-1985 .... DLB-130
Dowland, John 1563-1626 .... DLB-172
Downes, Gwladys 1915- DLB-88
Downing, J., Major (see Davis, Charles A.)
Downing, Major Jack (see Smith, Seba)
Dowriche, Anne before 1560-after 1613 .. DLB-172
Dowson, Ernest 1867-1900 .... DLB-19, 135
William Doxey [publishing house] DLB-49
Doyle, Sir Arthur Conan 1859-1930 ... DLB-18, 70, 156, 178; CDBLB-5
 The Priory Scholars of New York Y-99
Doyle, Kirby 1932- DLB-16
Doyle, Roddy 1958- DLB-194
Drabble, Margaret 1939- DLB-14, 155, 231; CDBLB-8
 Tribute to Graham Greene Y-91
Drach, Albert 1902-1995 .... DLB-85

Dragojević, Danijel 1934- DLB-181

Drake, Samuel Gardner 1798-1875 ...... DLB-187

Drama (See Theater)

The Dramatic Publishing Company DLB-49

Dramatists Play Service DLB-46

Drant, Thomas early 1540s?-1578 ...... DLB-167

Draper, John W. 1811-1882 .... DLB-30

Draper, Lyman C. 1815-1891 .... DLB-30

Drayton, Michael 1563-1631 .... DLB-121

Dreiser, Theodore 1871-1945
.... DLB-9, 12, 102, 137; DS-1; CDALB-3

 The International Theodore Dreiser
  Society Y-01

 Notes from the Underground
  of *Sister Carrie* Y-01

Dresser, Davis 1904-1977 .... DLB-226

Drew, Elizabeth A.
 "A Note on Technique" [excerpt]
  (1926) DLB-36

Drewitz, Ingeborg 1923-1986 .... DLB-75

Drieu La Rochelle, Pierre 1893-1945 ..... DLB-72

Drinker, Elizabeth 1735-1807 .... DLB-200

Drinkwater, John 1882-1937 ...... DLB-10, 19, 149

 The Friends of the Dymock Poets Y-00

Droste-Hülshoff, Annette von
 1797-1848 .... DLB-133; CDWLB-2

The Drue Heinz Literature Prize
 Excerpt from "Excerpts from a Report
 of the Commission," in David
 Bosworth's *The Death of Descartes*
 An Interview with David Bosworth Y-82

Drummond, William, of Hawthornden
 1585-1649 .... DLB-121, 213

Drummond, William Henry 1854-1907 ... DLB-92

Druzhinin, Aleksandr Vasil'evich
 1824-1864 .... DLB-238

Dryden, Charles 1860?-1931 .... DLB-171

Dryden, John
 1631-1700 ...... DLB-80, 101, 131; CDBLB-2

Držić, Marin
 circa 1508-1567 .... DLB-147; CDWLB-4

Duane, William 1760-1835 .... DLB-43

Dubé, Marcel 1930- DLB-53

Dubé, Rodolphe (see Hertel, François)

Dubie, Norman 1945- DLB-120

Dubin, Al 1891-1945 .... DLB-265

Dubois, Silvia 1788 or 1789?-1889 ...... DLB-239

Du Bois, W. E. B.
 1868-1963 ....DLB-47, 50, 91, 246; CDALB-3

Du Bois, William Pène 1916-1993 .... DLB-61

Dubrovina, Ekaterina Oskarovna
 1846-1913 .... DLB-238

Dubus, Andre 1936-1999 .... DLB-130

 Tribute to Michael M. Rea Y-97

Ducange, Victor 1783-1833 .... DLB-192

Du Chaillu, Paul Belloni 1831?-1903 .... DLB-189

Ducharme, Réjean 1941- DLB-60

Dučić, Jovan 1871-1943 .....DLB-147; CDWLB-4

Duck, Stephen 1705?-1756 .... DLB-95

Gerald Duckworth and Company
 Limited DLB-112

Duclaux, Madame Mary (see Robinson, A. Mary F.)

Dudek, Louis 1918-2001 .... DLB-88

Dudley-Smith, Trevor (see Hall, Adam)

Duell, Sloan and Pearce DLB-46

Duerer, Albrecht 1471-1528 ....DLB-179

Duff Gordon, Lucie 1821-1869 .... DLB-166

Dufferin, Helen Lady, Countess of Gifford
 1807-1867 .... DLB-199

Duffield and Green DLB-46

Duffy, Maureen 1933- DLB-14

Dufief, Nicholas Gouin 1776-1834 ...... DLB-187

Dugan, Alan 1923- DLB-5

Dugard, William 1606-1662 ....DLB-170, 281

William Dugard [publishing house] DLB-170

Dugas, Marcel 1883-1947 .... DLB-92

William Dugdale [publishing house]..... DLB-106

Duhamel, Georges 1884-1966 .... DLB-65

Dujardin, Edouard 1861-1949 .... DLB-123

Dukes, Ashley 1885-1959 .... DLB-10

Dumas, Alexandre *fils* 1824-1895 .... DLB-192

Dumas, Alexandre *père* 1802-1870 ..... DLB-119, 192

Dumas, Henry 1934-1968 .... DLB-41

du Maurier, Daphne 1907-1989 .... DLB-191

Du Maurier, George 1834-1896 .....DLB-153, 178

Dummett, Michael 1925- DLB-262

Dunbar, Paul Laurence
 1872-1906 ...... DLB-50, 54, 78; CDALB-3

 Introduction to *Lyrics of Lowly Life* (1896),
  by William Dean Howells DLB-50

Dunbar, William
 circa 1460-circa 1522 .... DLB-132, 146

Duncan, Dave 1933- DLB-251

Duncan, David James 1952- DLB-256

Duncan, Norman 1871-1916 .... DLB-92

Duncan, Quince 1940- DLB-145

Duncan, Robert 1919-1988 ...... DLB-5, 16, 193

Duncan, Ronald 1914-1982 .... DLB-13

Duncan, Sara Jeannette 1861-1922 ...... DLB-92

Dunigan, Edward, and Brother DLB-49

Dunlap, John 1747-1812 .... DLB-43

Dunlap, William 1766-1839 ....DLB-30, 37, 59

Dunlop, William "Tiger" 1792-1848 ..... DLB-99

Dunmore, Helen 1952- DLB-267

Dunn, Douglas 1942- DLB-40

Dunn, Harvey Thomas 1884-1952 ..... DLB-188

Dunn, Stephen 1939- DLB-105

 "The Good, The Not So Good" DLB-105

Dunne, Finley Peter 1867-1936 ...... DLB-11, 23

Dunne, John Gregory 1932- Y-80

Dunne, Philip 1908-1992 .... DLB-26

Dunning, Ralph Cheever 1878-1930 ...... DLB-4

Dunning, William A. 1857-1922 .... DLB-17

Duns Scotus, John circa 1266-1308 ..... DLB-115

Dunsany, Lord (Edward John Moreton
 Drax Plunkett, Baron Dunsany)
 1878-1957 .... DLB-10, 77, 153, 156, 255

Dunton, W. Herbert 1878-1936 .... DLB-188

John Dunton [publishing house] DLB-170

Dupin, Amantine-Aurore-Lucile (see Sand, George)

Dupuy, Eliza Ann 1814-1880 .... DLB-248

Durack, Mary 1913-1994 .... DLB-260

Durand, Lucile (see Bersianik, Louky)

Duranti, Francesca 1935- DLB-196

Duranty, Walter 1884-1957 .... DLB-29

Duras, Marguerite (Marguerite Donnadieu)
 1914-1996 .... DLB-83

Durfey, Thomas 1653-1723 .... DLB-80

Durova, Nadezhda Andreevna
 (Aleksandr Andreevich Aleksandrov)
 1783-1866 .... DLB-198

Durrell, Lawrence 1912-1990
 ....DLB-15, 27, 204; Y-90; CDBLB-7

William Durrell [publishing house] DLB-49

Dürrenmatt, Friedrich
 1921-1990 ....DLB-69, 124; CDWLB-2

Duston, Hannah 1657-1737 .... DLB-200

Dutt, Toru 1856-1877 .... DLB-240

E. P. Dutton and Company DLB-49

Duvoisin, Roger 1904-1980 .... DLB-61

Duyckinck, Evert Augustus
 1816-1878 .... DLB-3, 64, 250

Duyckinck, George L.
 1823-1863 .... DLB-3, 250

Duyckinck and Company DLB-49

Dwight, John Sullivan 1813-1893 ..... DLB-1, 235

Dwight, Timothy 1752-1817 .... DLB-37

 America: or, A Poem on the Settlement
  of the British Colonies, by
  Timothy Dwight DLB-37

Dybek, Stuart 1942- DLB-130

 Tribute to Michael M. Rea Y-97

Dyer, Charles 1928- DLB-13

Dyer, Sir Edward 1543-1607 .... DLB-136

Dyer, George 1755-1841 .... DLB-93

Dyer, John 1699-1757 .... DLB-95

Dyk, Viktor 1877-1931 .... DLB-215

Dylan, Bob 1941- DLB-16

E

Eager, Edward 1911-1964 .... DLB-22

Eagleton, Terry 1943- DLB-242

Eames, Wilberforce 1855-1937 .... DLB-140

Earle, Alice Morse 1853-1911 .... DLB-221

Earle, John 1600 or 1601-1665 .... DLB-151

James H. Earle and Company DLB-49

East Europe
 Independence and Destruction,
  1918-1941 .... DLB-220

 Social Theory and Ethnography:
  Language and Ethnicity in
  Eastern Europe DLB-220

 Western versus Eastern Man DLB-220

Eastlake, William 1917-1997 ....DLB-6, 206
Eastman, Carol ?- DLB-44
Eastman, Charles A. (Ohiyesa)
    1858-1939 ....DLB-175
Eastman, Max 1883-1969 ....DLB-91
Eaton, Daniel Isaac 1753-1814.........DLB-158
Eaton, Edith Maude 1865-1914........DLB-221
Eaton, Winnifred 1875-1954 ....DLB-221
Eberhart, Richard 1904- DLB-48; CDALB-1
    Tribute to Robert Penn Warren Y-89
Ebner, Jeannie 1918- DLB-85
Ebner-Eschenbach, Marie von
    1830-1916 ....DLB-81
Ebon 1942- DLB-41
E-Books' Second Act in Libraries........... Y-02
Ecbasis Captivi circa 1045...............DLB-148
Ecco Press DLB-46
Eckhart, Meister circa 1260-circa 1328 ...DLB-115
The Eclectic Review 1805-1868 ....DLB-110
Eco, Umberto 1932- DLB-196, 242
Eddison, E. R. 1882-1945 ....DLB-255
Edel, Leon 1907-1997.................DLB-103
Edelfeldt, Inger 1956- DLB-257
A Century of Poetry, a Lifetime of Collecting:
    J. M. Edelstein's Collection of Twentieth-
    Century American Poetry............. Y-02
Edes, Benjamin 1732-1803..............DLB-43
Edgar, David 1948- DLB-13, 233
    Viewpoint: Politics and
    Performance DLB-13
Edgerton, Clyde 1944- DLB-278
Edgeworth, Maria
    1768-1849 ....DLB-116, 159, 163
The Edinburgh Review 1802-1929.........DLB-110
Edinburgh University Press............DLB-112
Editing
    Conversations with Editors............ Y-95
    Editorial Statements DLB-137
    The Editorial Style of Fredson Bowers .. Y-91
    Editorial: The Extension of Copyright .. Y-02
    We See the Editor at Work Y-97
    Whose Ulysses? The Function of Editing .. Y-97
The Editor Publishing Company.........DLB-49
Editorial Institute at Boston University Y-00
Edmonds, Helen Woods Ferguson
    (see Kavan, Anna)
Edmonds, Randolph 1900-1983 ....DLB-51
Edmonds, Walter D. 1903-1998 ....DLB-9
Edric, Robert (see Armitage, G. E.)
Edschmid, Kasimir 1890-1966...........DLB-56
Edson, Margaret 1961- DLB-266
Edson, Russell 1935- DLB-244
Edwards, Amelia Anne Blandford
    1831-1892 ....DLB-174
Edwards, Dic 1953- DLB-245
Edwards, Edward 1812-1886 ....DLB-184
Edwards, Jonathan 1703-1758 ......DLB-24, 270

Edwards, Jonathan, Jr. 1745-1801 ....DLB-37
Edwards, Junius 1929- DLB-33
Edwards, Matilda Barbara Betham
    1836-1919 ....DLB-174
Edwards, Richard 1524-1566 ....DLB-62
Edwards, Sarah Pierpont 1710-1758......DLB-200
James Edwards [publishing house].......DLB-154
Effinger, George Alec 1947- DLB-8
Egerton, George 1859-1945............DLB-135
Eggleston, Edward 1837-1902 ....DLB-12
Eggleston, Wilfred 1901-1986 ....DLB-92
Eglītis, Anšlavs 1906-1993.............DLB-220
Ehrenreich, Barbara 1941- DLB-246
Ehrenstein, Albert 1886-1950 ....DLB-81
Ehrhart, W. D. 1948- DS-9
Ehrlich, Gretel 1946- DLB-212, 275
Eich, Günter 1907-1972 ....DLB-69, 124
Eichendorff, Joseph Freiherr von
    1788-1857 ....DLB-90
Eifukumon'in 1271-1342 ....DLB-203
Eigner, Larry 1926-1996 ....DLB-5, 193
Eikon Basilike 1649 ....DLB-151
Eilhart von Oberge
    circa 1140-circa 1195..............DLB-148
Einhard circa 770-840 ....DLB-148
Eiseley, Loren 1907-1977 .... DLB-275, DS-17
Eisenberg, Deborah 1945- DLB-244
Eisenreich, Herbert 1925-1986 ....DLB-85
Eisner, Kurt 1867-1919 ....DLB-66
Ekelöf, Gunnar 1907-1968.............DLB-259
Eklund, Gordon 1945- Y-83
Ekman, Kerstin 1933- DLB-257
Ekwensi, Cyprian 1921- ... DLB-117; CDWLB-3
Elaw, Zilpha circa 1790-? DLB-239
George Eld [publishing house]..........DLB-170
Elder, Lonne, III 1931- DLB-7, 38, 44
Paul Elder and Company DLB-49
Eldershaw, Flora (M. Barnard Eldershaw)
    1897-1956 ....DLB-260
Eldershaw, M. Barnard (see Barnard, Marjorie and
    Eldershaw, Flora)
The Electronic Text Center and the Electronic
    Archive of Early American Fiction at the
    University of Virginia Library Y-98
Eliade, Mircea 1907-1986....DLB-220; CDWLB-4
Elic, Robert 1915-1973.................DLB-88
Elin Pelin 1877-1949........ DLB-147; CDWLB-4
Eliot, George
    1819-1880 ......DLB-21, 35, 55; CDBLB-4
    The George Eliot Fellowship Y-99
Eliot, John 1604-1690 ....DLB-24
Eliot, T. S. 1888-1965
    .... DLB-7, 10, 45, 63, 245; CDALB-5
    T. S. Eliot Centennial: The Return
        of the Old Possum................ Y-88
    The T. S. Eliot Society: Celebration and
        Scholarship, 1980-1999 .... Y-99
Eliot's Court Press DLB-170

Elizabeth I 1533-1603 ....DLB-136
Elizabeth von Nassau-Saarbrücken
    after 1393-1456..................DLB-179
Elizondo, Salvador 1932- DLB-145
Elizondo, Sergio 1930- DLB-82
Elkin, Stanley
    1930-1995 .... DLB-2, 28, 218, 278; Y-80
Elles, Dora Amy (see Wentworth, Patricia)
Ellet, Elizabeth F. 1818?-1877 ....DLB-30
Elliot, Ebenezer 1781-1849............DLB-96, 190
Elliot, Frances Minto (Dickinson)
    1820-1898....................DLB-166
Elliott, Charlotte 1789-1871 ....DLB-199
Elliott, George 1923- DLB-68
Elliott, George P. 1918-1980 ....DLB-244
Elliott, Janice 1931-1995 ....DLB-14
Elliott, Sarah Barnwell 1848-1928 ....DLB-221
Elliott, Thomes and Talbot DLB-49
Elliott, William, III 1788-1863.........DLB-3, 248
Ellis, Alice Thomas (Anna Margaret Haycraft)
    1932- DLB-194
Ellis, Edward S. 1840-1916 ....DLB-42
Ellis, George E.
    "The New Controversy Concerning
        Miracles...................... DS-5
Ellis, Havelock 1859-1939 ....DLB-190
Frederick Staridge Ellis
    [publishing house]................DLB-106
The George H. Ellis Company DLB-49
Ellison, Harlan 1934- DLB-8
    Tribute to Isaac Asimov.............. Y-92
Ellison, Ralph
    1914-1994 ... DLB-2, 76, 227; Y-94; CDALB-1
Ellmann, Richard 1918-1987 ...... DLB-103; Y-87
Ellroy, James 1948- DLB-226; Y-91
    Tribute to John D. MacDonald Y-86
    Tribute to Raymond Chandler Y-88
Eluard, Paul 1895-1952...............DLB-258
Elyot, Thomas 1490?-1546 ....DLB-136
Emanuel, James Andrew 1921- DLB-41
Emecheta, Buchi 1944- ... DLB-117; CDWLB-3
Emerson, Ralph Waldo
    1803-1882......DLB-1, 59, 73, 183, 223, 270;
                                DS-5; CDALB-2
    Ralph Waldo Emerson in 1982 .... Y-82
    The Ralph Waldo Emerson Society Y-99
Emerson, William 1769-1811............DLB-37
Emerson, William R. 1923-1997 ....Y-97
Emin, Fedor Aleksandrovich
    circa 1735-1770 ....DLB-150
Emmanuel, Pierre 1916-1984 ....DLB-258
Empedocles fifth century B.C..........DLB-176
Empson, William 1906-1984.............DLB-20
Enchi Fumiko 1905-1986...............DLB-182
Ende, Michael 1929-1995 ....DLB-75
Endō Shūsaku 1923-1996 ....DLB-182
Engel, Marian 1933-1985 ....DLB-53

Engel'gardt, Sof'ia Vladimirovna 1828-1894 .... DLB-277
Engels, Friedrich 1820-1895 .... DLB-129
Engle, Paul 1908- DLB-48
    Tribute to Robert Penn Warren Y-89
English, Thomas Dunn 1819-1902 ..... DLB-202
Ennius 239 B.C.-169 B.C. DLB-211
Enquist, Per Olov 1934- DLB-257
Enright, Anne 1962- DLB-267
Enright, D. J. 1920- DLB-27
Enright, Elizabeth 1909-1968 .... DLB-22
Epictetus circa 55-circa 125-130 .... DLB-176
Epicurus 342/341 B.C.-271/270 B.C. DLB-176
Epps, Bernard 1936- DLB-53
Epstein, Julius 1909-2000 .... DLB-26
Epstein, Philip 1909-1952 .... DLB-26
Editors, Conversations with Y-95
Equiano, Olaudah
    circa 1745-1797 ..... DLB-37, 50; CDWLB-3
    Olaudah Equiano and Unfinished
    Journeys: The Slave-Narrative
    Tradition and Twentieth-Century
    Continuities DLB-117
Eragny Press DLB-112
Erasmus, Desiderius 1467-1536 .... DLB-136
Erba, Luciano 1922- DLB-128
Erdman, Nikolai Robertovich
    1900-1970 .... DLB-272
Erdrich, Louise
    1954- DLB-152, 175, 206; CDALB-7
Erenburg, Il'ia Grigor'evich 1891-1967 .. DLB-272
Erichsen-Brown, Gwethalyn Graham
    (see Graham, Gwethalyn)
Eriugena, John Scottus circa 810-877 .... DLB-115
Ernst, Paul 1866-1933 .... DLB-66, 118
Ershov, Petr Pavlovich 1815-1869 ..... DLB-205
Erskine, Albert 1911-1993 .... Y-93
    At Home with Albert Erskine Y-00
Erskine, John 1879-1951 .... DLB-9, 102
Erskine, Mrs. Steuart ?-1948 .... DLB-195
Ertel', Aleksandr Ivanovich 1855-1908 ... DLB-238
Ervine, St. John Greer 1883-1971 .... DLB-10
Eschenburg, Johann Joachim 1743-1820 ... DLB-97
Escoto, Julio 1944- DLB-145
Esdaile, Arundell 1880-1956 .... DLB-201
Eshleman, Clayton 1935- DLB-5
Espaillat, Rhina P. 1932- DLB-282
Espriu, Salvador 1913-1985 .... DLB-134
Ess Ess Publishing Company DLB-49
Essex House Press DLB-112
Esson, Louis 1878-1943 .... DLB-260
Essop, Ahmed 1931- DLB-225
Esterházy, Péter 1950- DLB-232; CDWLB-4
Estes, Eleanor 1906-1988 .... DLB-22
Estes and Lauriat DLB-49
Estleman, Loren D. 1952- DLB-226
Eszterhas, Joe 1944- DLB-185

Etherege, George 1636-circa 1692 .... DLB-80
Ethridge, Mark, Sr. 1896-1981 .... DLB-127
Ets, Marie Hall 1893-1984 .... DLB-22
Etter, David 1928- DLB-105
Ettner, Johann Christoph 1654-1724 .... DLB-168
Eudora Welty Remembered in
    Two Exhibits Y-02
Eugene Gant's Projected Works Y-01
Eupolemius flourished circa 1095 .... DLB-148
Euripides circa 484 B.C.-407/406 B.C.
    .... DLB-176; CDWLB-1
Evans, Augusta Jane 1835-1909 .... DLB-239
Evans, Caradoc 1878-1945 .... DLB-162
Evans, Charles 1850-1935 .... DLB-187
Evans, Donald 1884-1921 .... DLB-54
Evans, George Henry 1805-1856 .... DLB-43
Evans, Hubert 1892-1986 .... DLB-92
Evans, Mari 1923- DLB-41
Evans, Mary Ann (see Eliot, George)
Evans, Nathaniel 1742-1767 .... DLB-31
Evans, Sebastian 1830-1909 .... DLB-35
Evans, Ray 1915- DLB-265
M. Evans and Company DLB-46
Evaristi, Marcella 1953- DLB-233
Everett, Alexander Hill 1790-1847 ...... DLB-59
Everett, Edward 1794-1865 .... DLB-1, 59, 235
Everson, R. G. 1903- DLB-88
Everson, William 1912-1994 ..... DLB-5, 16, 212
Ewart, Gavin 1916-1995 .... DLB-40
Ewing, Juliana Horatia 1841-1885 ... DLB-21, 163
The Examiner 1808-1881 .... DLB-110
Exley, Frederick 1929-1992 .... DLB-143; Y-81
Editorial: The Extension of Copyright Y-02
von Eyb, Albrecht 1420-1475 .... DLB-179
Eyre and Spottiswoode DLB-106
Ezera, Regīna 1930- DLB-232
Ezzo ?-after 1065 .... DLB-148

F

Faber, Frederick William 1814-1863 ..... DLB-32
Faber and Faber Limited DLB-112
Faccio, Rena (see Aleramo, Sibilla)
Facsimiles
    The Uses of Facsimile: A Symposium Y-90
Fadeev, Aleksandr Aleksandrovich
    1901-1956 .... DLB-272
Fagundo, Ana María 1938- DLB-134
Fainzil'berg, Il'ia Arnol'dovich
    (see Il'f, Il'ia and Petrov, Evgenii)
Fair, Ronald L. 1932- DLB-33
Fairfax, Beatrice (see Manning, Marie)
Fairlie, Gerard 1899-1983 .... DLB-77
Fallada, Hans 1893-1947 .... DLB-56
Fancher, Betsy 1928- Y-83
Fane, Violet 1843-1905 .... DLB-35
Fanfrolico Press DLB-112

Fanning, Katherine 1927- DLB-127
Fanshawe, Sir Richard 1608-1666 ..... DLB-126
Fantasy Press Publishers DLB-46
Fante, John 1909-1983 .... DLB-130; Y-83
Al-Farabi circa 870-950 .... DLB-115
Farabough, Laura 1949- DLB-228
Farah, Nuruddin 1945- DLB-125; CDWLB-3
Farber, Norma 1909-1984 .... DLB-61
Fargue, Léon-Paul 1876-1947 .... DLB-258
Farigoule, Louis (see Romains, Jules)
Farjeon, Eleanor 1881-1965 .... DLB-160
Farley, Harriet 1812-1907 .... DLB-239
Farley, Walter 1920-1989 .... DLB-22
Farmborough, Florence 1887-1978 ...... DLB-204
Farmer, Penelope 1939- DLB-161
Farmer, Philip José 1918- DLB-8
Farnaby, Thomas 1575?-1647 .... DLB-236
Farningham, Marianne (see Hearn, Mary Anne)
Farquhar, George circa 1677-1707 ...... DLB-84
Farquharson, Martha (see Finley, Martha)
Farrar, Frederic William 1831-1903 ..... DLB-163
Farrar, Straus and Giroux DLB-46
Farrar and Rinehart DLB-46
Farrell, J. G. 1935-1979 .... DLB-14, 271
Farrell, James T. 1904-1979 ... DLB-4, 9, 86; DS-2
Fast, Howard 1914- DLB-9
Faulkner, William 1897-1962
    .... DLB-9, 11, 44, 102; DS-2; Y-86; CDALB-5
    Faulkner and Yoknapatawpha
    Conference, Oxford, Mississippi Y-97
    Faulkner Centennial Addresses Y-97
    "Faulkner 100—Celebrating the Work,"
    University of South Carolina,
    Columbia Y-97
    Impressions of William Faulkner Y-97
    William Faulkner and the People-to-People
    Program Y-86
    William Faulkner Centenary
    Celebrations Y-97
    The William Faulkner Society Y-99
George Faulkner [publishing house] DLB-154
Faulks, Sebastian 1953- DLB-207
Fauset, Jessie Redmon 1882-1961 ...... DLB-51
Faust, Frederick Schiller (Max Brand)
    1892-1944 .... DLB-256
Faust, Irvin
    1924- DLB-2, 28, 218, 278; Y-80, 00
    I Wake Up Screaming [Response to
    Ken Auletta] Y-97
    Tribute to Bernard Malamud Y-86
    Tribute to Isaac Bashevis Singer Y-91
    Tribute to Meyer Levin Y-81
Fawcett, Edgar 1847-1904 .... DLB-202
Fawcett, Millicent Garrett 1847-1929 ... DLB-190
Fawcett Books DLB-46
Fay, Theodore Sedgwick 1807-1898 ..... DLB-202
Fearing, Kenneth 1902-1961 .... DLB-9

Federal Writers' Project DLB-46

Federman, Raymond 1928- Y-80

Fedin, Konstantin Aleksandrovich
    1892-1977 . . . . DLB-272

Fedorov, Innokentii Vasil'evich
    (see Omulevsky, Innokentii Vasil'evich)

Feiffer, Jules 1929- DLB-7, 44

Feinberg, Charles E. 1899-1988 . . . . DLB-187; Y-88

Feind, Barthold 1678-1721 . . . . DLB-168

Feinstein, Elaine 1930- DLB-14, 40

Feirstein, Frederick 1940- DLB-282

Feiss, Paul Louis 1875-1952 . . . . DLB-187

Feldman, Irving 1928- DLB-169

Felipe, Léon 1884-1968 . . . . DLB-108

Fell, Frederick, Publishers DLB-46

Fellowship of Southern Writers Y-98

Felltham, Owen 1602?-1668 . . . . DLB-126, 151

Felman, Shoshana 1942- DLB-246

Fels, Ludwig 1946- DLB-75

Felton, Cornelius Conway
    1807-1862 . . . . DLB-1, 235

Mothe-Fénelon, François de Salignac de la
    1651-1715 . . . . DLB-268

Fenn, Harry 1837-1911 . . . . DLB-188

Fennario, David 1947- DLB-60

Fenner, Dudley 1558?-1587? DLB-236

Fenno, Jenny 1765?-1803 . . . . DLB-200

Fenno, John 1751-1798 . . . . DLB-43

R. F. Fenno and Company DLB-49

Fenoglio, Beppe 1922-1963 . . . . DLB-177

Fenton, Geoffrey 1539?-1608 . . . . DLB-136

Fenton, James 1949- DLB-40

    The Hemingway/Fenton
        Correspondence Y-02

Ferber, Edna 1885-1968 . . . . DLB-9, 28, 86, 266

Ferdinand, Vallery, III (see Salaam, Kalamu ya)

Ferguson, Sir Samuel 1810-1886 . . . . DLB-32

Ferguson, William Scott 1875-1954 . . . . DLB-47

Fergusson, Robert 1750-1774 . . . . DLB-109

Ferland, Albert 1872-1943 . . . . DLB-92

Ferlinghetti, Lawrence
    1919- DLB-5, 16; CDALB-1

    Tribute to Kenneth Rexroth Y-82

Fermor, Patrick Leigh 1915- DLB-204

Fern, Fanny (see Parton, Sara Payson Willis)

Ferrars, Elizabeth (Morna Doris Brown)
    1907-1995 . . . . DLB-87

Ferré, Rosario 1942- DLB-145

E. Ferret and Company DLB-49

Ferrier, Susan 1782-1854 . . . . DLB-116

Ferril, Thomas Hornsby 1896-1988 . . . . . . DLB-206

Ferrini, Vincent 1913- DLB-48

Ferron, Jacques 1921-1985 . . . . DLB-60

Ferron, Madeleine 1922- DLB-53

Ferrucci, Franco 1936- DLB-196

Fet, Afanasii Afanas'evich
    1820?-1892 . . . . DLB-277

Fetridge and Company DLB-49

Feuchtersleben, Ernst Freiherr von
    1806-1849 . . . . DLB-133

Feuchtwanger, Lion 1884-1958 . . . . DLB-66

Feuerbach, Ludwig 1804-1872 . . . . DLB-133

Feuillet, Octave 1821-1890 . . . . DLB-192

Feydeau, Georges 1862-1921 . . . . DLB-192

Fichte, Johann Gottlieb 1762-1814 . . . . DLB-90

Ficke, Arthur Davison 1883-1945 . . . . DLB-54

Fiction
    American Fiction and the 1930s DLB-9

        Fiction Best-Sellers, 1910-1945 . . . . DLB-9

        The Year in Fiction Y-84, 86, 89, 94–99

        The Year in Fiction: A Biased View Y-83

        The Year in U.S. Fiction Y-00, 01

        The Year's Work in Fiction: A Survey . . Y-82

Fiedler, Leslie A. 1917- DLB-28, 67

    Tribute to Bernard Malamud Y-86

    Tribute to James Dickey Y-97

Field, Barron 1789-1846 . . . . DLB-230

Field, Edward 1924- DLB-105

Field, Eugene 1850-1895 . . DLB-23, 42, 140; DS-13

Field, John 1545?-1588 . . . . DLB-167

Field, Joseph M. 1810-1856 . . . . DLB-248

Field, Marshall, III 1893-1956 . . . . DLB-127

Field, Marshall, IV 1916-1965 . . . . DLB-127

Field, Marshall, V 1941- DLB-127

Field, Michael (Katherine Harris Bradley)
    1846-1914 . . . . DLB-240

    "The Poetry File" DLB-105

Field, Nathan 1587-1619 or 1620 . . . . DLB-58

Field, Rachel 1894-1942 . . . . DLB-9, 22

Fielding, Helen 1958- DLB-231

Fielding, Henry
    1707-1754 . . . . DLB-39, 84, 101; CDBLB-2

    "Defense of *Amelia*" (1752) DLB-39

    The History of the Adventures of Joseph Andrews
        [excerpt] (1742) DLB-39

    Letter to [Samuel] Richardson on *Clarissa*
        (1748) DLB-39

    Preface to *Joseph Andrews* (1742) DLB-39

    Preface to Sarah Fielding's *Familiar
        Letters* (1747) [excerpt] DLB-39

    Preface to Sarah Fielding's *The
        Adventures of David Simple* (1744) . . . DLB-39

    Review of *Clarissa* (1748) DLB-39

    Tom Jones (1749) [excerpt] DLB-39

Fielding, Sarah 1710-1768 . . . . DLB-39

    Preface to *The Cry* (1754) DLB-39

Fields, Annie Adams 1834-1915 . . . . DLB-221

Fields, Dorothy 1905-1974 . . . . DLB-265

Fields, James T. 1817-1881 . . . . DLB-1, 235

Fields, Julia 1938- DLB-41

Fields, Osgood and Company DLB-49

Fields, W. C. 1880-1946 . . . . DLB-44

Fierstein, Harvey 1954- DLB-266

Figes, Eva 1932- DLB-14, 271

Figuera, Angela 1902-1984 . . . . DLB-108

Filmer, Sir Robert 1586-1653 . . . . DLB-151

Filson, John circa 1753-1788 . . . . DLB-37

Finch, Anne, Countess of Winchilsea
    1661-1720 . . . . DLB-95

Finch, Annie 1956- DLB-282

Finch, Robert 1900- DLB-88

Findley, Timothy 1930-2002 . . . . DLB-53

Finlay, Ian Hamilton 1925- DLB-40

Finley, Martha 1828-1909 . . . . DLB-42

Finn, Elizabeth Anne (McCaul)
    1825-1921 . . . . DLB-166

Finnegan, Seamus 1949- DLB-245

Finney, Jack 1911-1995 . . . . DLB-8

Finney, Walter Braden (see Finney, Jack)

Firbank, Ronald 1886-1926 . . . . DLB-36

Firmin, Giles 1615-1697 . . . . DLB-24

First Edition Library/Collectors'
    Reprints, Inc. Y-91

Fischart, Johann
    1546 or 1547-1590 or 1591 . . . . DLB-179

Fischer, Karoline Auguste Fernandine
    1764-1842 . . . . DLB-94

Fischer, Tibor 1959- DLB-231

Fish, Stanley 1938- DLB-67

Fishacre, Richard 1205-1248 . . . . DLB-115

Fisher, Clay (see Allen, Henry W.)

Fisher, Dorothy Canfield 1879-1958 . . . DLB-9, 102

Fisher, Leonard Everett 1924- DLB-61

Fisher, Roy 1930- DLB-40

Fisher, Rudolph 1897-1934 . . . . DLB-51, 102

Fisher, Steve 1913-1980 . . . . DLB-226

Fisher, Sydney George 1856-1927 . . . . DLB-47

Fisher, Vardis 1895-1968 . . . . DLB-9, 206

Fiske, John 1608-1677 . . . . DLB-24

Fiske, John 1842-1901 . . . . DLB-47, 64

Fitch, Thomas circa 1700-1774 . . . . DLB-31

Fitch, William Clyde 1865-1909 . . . . DLB-7

FitzGerald, Edward 1809-1883 . . . . DLB-32

Fitzgerald, F. Scott 1896-1940
    . . . . DLB-4, 9, 86; Y-81, 92;
        DS-1, 15, 16; CDALB-4

    F. Scott Fitzgerald: A Descriptive
        Bibliography, Supplement (2001) . . . Y-01

    F. Scott Fitzgerald Centenary
        Celebrations Y-96

    F. Scott Fitzgerald Inducted into the
        American Poets' Corner at St. John
        the Divine; Ezra Pound Banned . . . Y-99

    "F. Scott Fitzgerald: St. Paul's Native Son
        and Distinguished American Writer":
        University of Minnesota Conference,
        29-31 October 1982 . . . . Y-82

    First International F. Scott Fitzgerald
        Conference Y-92

    The Great Gatsby (Documentary) DLB-219

    Tender Is the Night (Documentary) . . . DLB-273

Fitzgerald, Penelope 1916- DLB-14, 194

Fitzgerald, Robert 1910-1985 . . . . Y-80

FitzGerald, Robert D. 1902-1987 .... DLB-260
Fitzgerald, Thomas 1819-1891 .... DLB-23
Fitzgerald, Zelda Sayre 1900-1948 .... Y-84
Fitzhugh, Louise 1928-1974 .... DLB-52
Fitzhugh, William circa 1651-1701 ...... DLB-24
Flagg, James Montgomery 1877-1960 .... DLB-188
Flanagan, Thomas 1923-2002............. Y-80
Flanner, Hildegarde 1899-1987......... DLB-48
Flanner, Janet 1892-1978.......... DLB-4; DS-15
Flannery, Peter 1951- DLB-233
Flaubert, Gustave 1821-1880 .... DLB-119
Flavin, Martin 1883-1967 .... DLB-9
Fleck, Konrad (flourished circa 1220) ... DLB-138
Flecker, James Elroy 1884-1915 ...... DLB-10, 19
Fleeson, Doris 1901-1970 .... DLB-29
Fleißer, Marieluise 1901-1974....... DLB-56, 124
Fleischer, Nat 1887-1972 .... DLB-241
Fleming, Abraham 1552?-1607......... DLB-236
Fleming, Ian 1908-1964 .. DLB-87, 201; CDBLB-7
Fleming, Joan 1908-1980 .... DLB-276
Fleming, May Agnes 1840-1880 .... DLB-99
Fleming, Paul 1609-1640 .... DLB-164
Fleming, Peter 1907-1971 .... DLB-195
Fletcher, Giles, the Elder 1546-1611 ..... DLB-136
Fletcher, Giles, the Younger
  1585 or 1586-1623 .... DLB-121
Fletcher, J. S. 1863-1935 .... DLB-70
Fletcher, John 1579-1625............... DLB-58
Fletcher, John Gould 1886-1950 ...... DLB-4, 45
Fletcher, Phineas 1582-1650 .... DLB-121
Flieg, Helmut (see Heym, Stefan)
Flint, F. S. 1885-1960 .... DLB-19
Flint, Timothy 1780-1840 .... DLB-73, 186
Flores-Williams, Jason 1969- DLB-209
Florio, John 1553?-1625 .... DLB-172
Fludd, Robert 1574-1637............... DLB-281
Fo, Dario 1926- Y-97
  Nobel Lecture 1997: Contra Jogulatores
    Obloquentes Y-97
Foden, Giles 1967- DLB-267
Fofanov, Konstantin Mikhailovich
  1862-1911...................... DLB-277
Foix, J. V. 1893-1987 .... DLB-134
Foley, Martha 1897-1977 .... DLB-137
Folger, Henry Clay 1857-1930 .... DLB-140
Folio Society DLB-112
Follain, Jean 1903-1971 .... DLB-258
Follen, Charles 1796-1840............. DLB-235
Follen, Eliza Lee (Cabot) 1787-1860 ... DLB-1, 235
Follett, Ken 1949- DLB-87; Y-81
Follett Publishing Company DLB-46
John West Folsom [publishing house]..... DLB-49
Folz, Hans
  between 1435 and 1440-1513....... DLB-179
Fontane, Theodor
  1819-1898........... DLB-129; CDWLB-2

Fontenelle, Bernard Le Bovier de
  1657-1757...................... DLB-268
Fontes, Montserrat 1940- DLB-209
Fonvisin, Denis Ivanovich
  1744 or 1745-1792 .... DLB-150
Foote, Horton 1916- DLB-26, 266
Foote, Mary Hallock
  1847-1938.......... DLB-186, 188, 202, 221
Foote, Samuel 1721-1777 .... DLB-89
Foote, Shelby 1916- DLB-2, 17
Forbes, Calvin 1945- DLB-41
Forbes, Ester 1891-1967 .... DLB-22
Forbes, Rosita 1893?-1967 .... DLB-195
Forbes and Company DLB-49
Force, Peter 1790-1868 .... DLB-30
Forché, Carolyn 1950- DLB-5, 193
Ford, Charles Henri 1913-2002 .... DLB-4, 48
Ford, Corey 1902-1969................ DLB-11
Ford, Ford Madox
  1873-1939....... DLB-34, 98, 162; CDBLB-6
  Nathan Asch Remembers Ford Madox
    Ford, Sam Roth, and Hart Crane.... Y-02
J. B. Ford and Company............... DLB-49
Ford, Jesse Hill 1928-1996 .... DLB-6
Ford, John 1586-? DLB-58; CDBLB-1
Ford, R. A. D. 1915- DLB-88
Ford, Richard 1944- DLB-227
Ford, Worthington C. 1858-1941....... DLB-47
Fords, Howard, and Hulbert DLB-49
Foreman, Carl 1914-1984............... DLB-26
Forester, C. S. 1899-1966 .... DLB-191
  The C. S. Forester Society............ Y-00
Forester, Frank (see Herbert, Henry William)
Anthologizing New Formalism DLB-282
The Little Magazines of the
  New Formalism DLB-282
The New Narrative Poetry............ DLB-282
Presses of the New Formalism and
  the New Narrative DLB-282
The Prosody of the New Formalism..... DLB-282
Younger Women Poets of the
  New Formalism DLB-282
Forman, Harry Buxton 1842-1917 ...... DLB-184
Fornés, María Irene 1930- DLB-7
Forrest, Leon 1937-1997 .... DLB-33
Forsh, Ol'ga Dmitrievna 1873-1961 .....DLB-272
Forster, E. M.
  1879-1970 ...... DLB-34, 98, 162, 178, 195;
                              DS-10; CDBLB-6
  "Fantasy," from Aspects of the Novel
    (1927)...................... DLB-178
Forster, Georg 1754-1794 .... DLB-94
Forster, John 1812-1876 .... DLB-144
Forster, Margaret 1938- DLB-155, 271
Forsyth, Frederick 1938- DLB-87
Forsyth, William
  "Literary Style" (1857) [excerpt] DLB-57
Forten, Charlotte L. 1837-1914 ...... DLB-50, 239

Pages from Her Diary............. DLB-50
Fortini, Franco 1917-1994............. DLB-128
Fortune, Mary ca. 1833-ca. 1910 ...... DLB-230
Fortune, T. Thomas 1856-1928 .... DLB-23
Fosdick, Charles Austin 1842-1915 ...... DLB-42
Foster, Genevieve 1893-1979 .... DLB-61
Foster, Hannah Webster 1758-1840 ...DLB-37, 200
Foster, John 1648-1681................ DLB-24
Foster, Michael 1904-1956 .... DLB-9
Foster, Myles Birket 1825-1899 .... DLB-184
Foucault, Michel 1926-1984 .... DLB-242
Robert and Andrew Foulis
  [publishing house] DLB-154
Fouqué, Caroline de la Motte 1774-1831 .. DLB-90
Fouqué, Friedrich de la Motte
  1777-1843 .... DLB-90
Four Seas Company DLB-46
Four Winds Press.................... DLB-46
Fournier, Henri Alban (see Alain-Fournier)
Fowler, Christopher 1953- DLB-267
Fowler and Wells Company........... DLB-49
Fowles, John
  1926- DLB-14, 139, 207; CDBLB-8
Fox, John 1939- DLB-245
Fox, John, Jr. 1862 or 1863-1919 ... DLB-9; DS-13
Fox, Paula 1923- DLB-52
Fox, Richard Kyle 1846-1922........... DLB-79
Fox, William Price 1926- DLB-2; Y-81
  Remembering Joe Heller.............. Y-99
Richard K. Fox [publishing house] DLB-49
Foxe, John 1517-1587 .... DLB-132
Fraenkel, Michael 1896-1957 .... DLB-4
France, Anatole 1844-1924............ DLB-123
France, Richard 1938- DLB-7
Francis, Convers 1795-1863 .... DLB-1, 235
Francis, Dick 1920- DLB-87; CDBLB-8
Francis, Sir Frank 1901-1988 .... DLB-201
Francis, Jeffrey, Lord 1773-1850..........DLB-107
C. S. Francis [publishing house] DLB-49
Franck, Sebastian 1499-1542 ....DLB-179
Francke, Kuno 1855-1930 .... DLB-71
Françoise (Robertine Barry) 1863-1910 ... DLB-92
François, Louise von 1817-1893 .... DLB-129
Frank, Bruno 1887-1945............... DLB-118
Frank, Leonhard 1882-1961........ DLB-56, 118
Frank, Melvin 1913-1988 .... DLB-26
Frank, Waldo 1889-1967 .... DLB-9, 63
Franken, Rose 1895?-1988 ......DLB-228, Y-84
Franklin, Benjamin
  1706-1790.... DLB-24, 43, 73, 183; CDALB-2
Franklin, James 1697-1735 .... DLB-43
Franklin, John 1786-1847 .... DLB-99
Franklin, Miles 1879-1954 .... DLB-230
Franklin Library.................... DLB-46
Frantz, Ralph Jules 1902-1979 .... DLB-4

Franzos, Karl Emil 1848-1904 ....DLB-129
Fraser, Antonia 1932- DLB-276
Fraser, G. S. 1915-1980 ....DLB-27
Fraser, Kathleen 1935- DLB-169
Frattini, Alberto 1922- DLB-128
Frau Ava ?-1127.....................DLB-148
Fraunce, Abraham 1558?-1592 or 1593...DLB-236
Frayn, Michael 1933- DLB-13, 14, 194, 245
Fréchette, Louis-Honoré 1839-1908.......DLB-99
Frederic, Harold 1856-1898....DLB-12, 23; DS-13
Freed, Arthur 1894-1973 ....DLB-265
Freeling, Nicolas 1927- DLB-87
   Tribute to Georges Simenon Y-89
Freeman, Douglas Southall
  1886-1953 .... DLB-17; DS-17
Freeman, Judith 1946- DLB-256
Freeman, Legh Richmond 1842-1915 .....DLB-23
Freeman, Mary E. Wilkins
  1852-1930 .... DLB-12, 78, 221
Freeman, R. Austin 1862-1943 ....DLB-70
Freidank circa 1170 circa 1233..........DLB-138
Freiligrath, Ferdinand 1810-1876 ....DLB-133
Fremlin, Celia 1914- DLB-276
Frémont, Jessie Benton 1834-1902.......DLB-183
Frémont, John Charles 1813-1890...DLB-183, 186
French, Alice 1850-1934 ....DLB 74; DS-13
French, David 1939- DLB-53
French, Evangeline 1869-1960..........DLB-195
French, Francesca 1871-1960 ....DLB-195
James French [publishing house] DLB-49
Samuel French [publishing house] DLB-49
Samuel French, Limited DLB-106
French Literature
  Epic and Beast Epic.................DLB-208
  French Arthurian Literature........DLB-208
  Lyric Poetry DLB-268
  Other Poets DLB-217
  Poetry in Nineteenth-Century France:
    Cultural Background and Critical
    Commentary.................DLB-217
  Roman de la Rose: Guillaume de Lorris
    1200 to 1205-circa 1230, Jean de
    Meun 1235/1240-circa 1305 ....DLB-208
  Saints' Lives DLB-208
  Troubadours, *Trobairitz,* and
    Trouvères..................DLB-208
French Theater
  Medieval French Drama DLB-208
  Parisian Theater, Fall 1984: Toward
    a New Baroque Y-85
Freneau, Philip 1752-1832 .... DLB-37, 43
  The Rising Glory of America........DLB-37
Freni, Melo 1934- DLB-128
Freshfield, Douglas W. 1845-1934.......DLB-174
Freyre, Ricardo 1866?-1933...........DLB-283
Freytag, Gustav 1816-1895 ....DLB-129
Fridegård, Jan 1897-1968 ....DLB-259

Fried, Erich 1921-1988 ....DLB-85
Friedan, Betty 1921- DLB-246
Friedman, Bruce Jay 1930- DLB-2, 28, 244
Friedrich von Hausen circa 1171-1190....DLB-138
Friel, Brian 1929- DLB-13
Friend, Krebs 1895?-1967? DLB-4
Fries, Fritz Rudolf 1935- DLB-75
Frisch, Max
  1911-1991 .... DLB-69, 124; CDWLB-2
Frischlin, Nicodemus 1547-1590 ....DLB-179
Frischmuth, Barbara 1941- DLB-85
Fritz, Jean 1915- DLB-52
Froissart, Jean circa 1337-circa 1404......DLB-208
Fromentin, Eugene 1820-1876 ....DLB-123
Frontinus circa A.D. 35-A.D. 103/104....DLB-211
Frost, A. B. 1851-1928..........DLB-188; DS-13
Frost, Robert
  1874-1963 ....DLB-54; DS-7; CDALB-4
  The Friends of the Dymock Poets Y-00
Frostenson, Katarina 1953- DLB-257
Frothingham, Octavius Brooks
  1822-1895 ....DLB-1, 243
Froude, James Anthony
  1818-1894 .... DLB-18, 57, 144
Fruitlands 1843-1844..........DLB-1, 223; DS-5
Fry, Christopher 1907- DLB-13
  Tribute to John Betjeman............. Y-84
Fry, Roger 1866-1934 .... DS-10
Fry, Stephen 1957- DLB-207
Frye, Northrop 1912-1991...... DLB-67, 68, 246
Fuchs, Daniel 1909-1993 ..... DLB-9, 26, 28; Y-93
  Tribute to Isaac Bashevis Singer Y-91
Fuentes, Carlos 1928- DLB-113; CDWLB-3
Fuertes, Gloria 1918-1998 ....DLB-108
Fugard, Athol 1932- DLB-225
The Fugitives and the Agrarians:
  The First Exhibition Y-85
Fujiwara no Shunzei 1114-1204.........DLB-203
Fujiwara no Tameaki 1230s?-1290s?.....DLB-203
Fujiwara no Tameie 1198-1275 ....DLB-203
Fujiwara no Teika 1162-1241 ....DLB-203
Fulbecke, William 1560-1603?..........DLB-172
Fuller, Charles 1939- DLB-38, 266
Fuller, Henry Blake 1857-1929 ....DLB-12
Fuller, John 1937- DLB-40
Fuller, Margaret (see Fuller, Sarah)
Fuller, Roy 1912-1991 ....DLB-15, 20
  Tribute to Christopher Isherwood...... Y-86
Fuller, Samuel 1912-1997 ....DLB-26
Fuller, Sarah 1810-1850 .... DLB-1, 59, 73,
          183, 223, 239; DS-5; CDALB-2
Fuller, Thomas 1608-1661............DLB-151
Fullerton, Hugh 1873-1945 ....DLB-171
Fullwood, William flourished 1568 .....DLB-236
Fulton, Alice 1952- DLB-193
Fulton, Len 1934- Y-86

Fulton, Robin 1937- DLB-40
Furbank, P. N. 1920- DLB-155
Furetière, Antoine 1619-1688...........DLB-268
Furman, Laura 1945- Y-86
Furmanov, Dmitrii Andreevich
  1891-1926.....................DLB-272
Furness, Horace Howard 1833-1912......DLB-64
Furness, William Henry 1802-1896....DLB-1, 235
Furnivall, Frederick James 1825-1910 ....DLB-184
Furphy, Joseph (Tom Collins)
  1843-1912 ....DLB-230
Furthman, Jules 1888-1966 ....DLB-26
  Shakespeare and Montaigne: A
    Symposium by Jules Furthman Y-02
Furui Yoshikichi 1937- DLB-182
Fushimi, Emperor 1265-1317...........DLB-203
Futabatei Shimei (Hasegawa Tatsunosuke)
  1864-1909 ....DLB-180
Fyleman, Rose 1877-1957.............DLB-160

G

Gadallah, Leslie 1939- DLB-251
Gadda, Carlo Emilio 1893-1973 ....DLB-177
Gaddis, William 1922-1998..........DLB-2, 278
  William Gaddis: A Tribute Y-99
Gág, Wanda 1893-1946................DLB-22
Gagarin, Ivan Sergeevich 1814-1882 .....DLB-198
Gagnon, Madeleine 1938- DLB-60
Gaiman, Neil 1960- DLB-261
Gaine, Hugh 1726-1807................DLB-43
  Hugh Gaine [publishing house] DLB-49
Gaines, Ernest J.
  1933- DLB-2, 33, 152; Y-80; CDALB-6
Gaiser, Gerd 1908-1976................DLB-69
Gaitskill, Mary 1954- DLB-244
Galarza, Ernesto 1905-1984............DLB-122
Galaxy Science Fiction Novels..........DLB-46
Galbraith, Robert (or Caubraith)
  circa 1483-1544..................DLB-281
Gale, Zona 1874-1938 .... DLB-9, 228, 78
Galen of Pergamon 129-after 210 ....DLB-176
Gales, Winifred Marshall 1761-1839.....DLB-200
Gall, Louise von 1815-1855............DLB-133
Gallagher, Tess 1943- DLB-120, 212, 244
Gallagher, Wes 1911- DLB-127
Gallagher, William Davis 1808-1894......DLB-73
Gallant, Mavis 1922- DLB-53
Gallegos, María Magdalena 1935- DLB-209
Gallico, Paul 1897-1976 ....DLB-9, 171
Gallop, Jane 1952- DLB-246
Galloway, Grace Growden 1727-1782 ....DLB-200
Gallup, Donald 1913-2000.............DLB-187
Galsworthy, John 1867-1933
  ......DLB-10, 34, 98, 162; DS-16; CDBLB-5
Galt, John 1779-1839 .... DLB-99, 116, 159
Galton, Sir Francis 1822-1911 ....DLB-166

Cumulative Index

Galvin, Brendan 1938- DLB-5
Gambit DLB-46
Gamboa, Reymundo 1948- DLB-122
Gammer Gurton's Needle.................. DLB-62
Gan, Elena Andreevna (Zeneida R-va)
   1814-1842..................... DLB-198
Gannett, Frank E. 1876-1957 .... DLB-29
Gao Xingjian 1940- Y-00
   Nobel Lecture 2000: "The Case for
     Literature"..................... Y-00
Gaos, Vicente 1919-1980 .... DLB-134
García, Andrew 1854?-1943 .... DLB-209
García, Lionel G. 1935- DLB-82
García, Richard 1941- DLB-209
García Márquez, Gabriel
   1928- DLB-113; Y-82; CDWLB-3
   The Magical World of Macondo Y-82
   Nobel Lecture 1982: The Solitude of
     Latin America.................... Y-82
   A Tribute to Gabriel García Márquez.... Y-82
García-Camarillo, Cecilio 1943- DLB-209
Gardam, Jane 1928- DLB-14, 161, 231
Gardell, Jonas 1963- DLB-257
Garden, Alexander circa 1685-1756 ...... DLB-31
Gardiner, John Rolfe 1936- DLB-244
Gardiner, Margaret Power Farmer
   (see Blessington, Marguerite, Countess of)
Gardner, John
   1933-1982 .... DLB-2; Y-82; CDALB-7
Garfield, Leon 1921-1996............. DLB-161
Garis, Howard R. 1873-1962 .... DLB-22
Garland, Hamlin 1860-1940...DLB-12, 71, 78, 186
   The Hamlin Garland Society Y-01
Garneau, François-Xavier 1809-1866..... DLB-99
Garneau, Hector de Saint-Denys
   1912-1943...................... DLB-88
Garneau, Michel 1939- DLB-53
Garner, Alan 1934- DLB-161, 261
Garner, Hugh 1913-1979 .... DLB-68
Garnett, David 1892-1981 .... DLB-34
Garnett, Eve 1900-1991 .... DLB-160
Garnett, Richard 1835-1906........... DLB-184
Garrard, Lewis H. 1829-1887.......... DLB-186
Garraty, John A. 1920- DLB-17
Garrett, George
   1929- DLB-2, 5, 130, 152; Y-83
   Literary Prizes..................... Y-00
   My Summer Reading Orgy: Reading
     for Fun and Games: One Reader's
     Report on the Summer of 2001 ..... Y-01
   A Summing Up at Century's End....... Y-99
   Tribute to James Dickey.............. Y-97
   Tribute to Michael M. Rea........... Y-97
   Tribute to Paxton Davis Y-94
   Tribute to Peter Taylor............... Y-94
   Tribute to William Goyen Y-83
   A Writer Talking: A Collage Y-00

Garrett, John Work 1872-1942......... DLB-187
Garrick, David 1717-1779 .... DLB-84, 213
Garrison, William Lloyd
   1805-1879....... DLB-1, 43, 235; CDALB-2
Garro, Elena 1920-1998 .... DLB-145
Garshin, Vsevolod Mikhailovich
   1855-1888 ....DLB-277
Garth, Samuel 1661-1719 .... DLB-95
Garve, Andrew 1908-2001 .... DLB-87
Gary, Romain 1914-1980 .... DLB-83
Gascoigne, George 1539?-1577........ DLB-136
Gascoyne, David 1916-2001............ DLB-20
Gash, Jonathan (John Grant) 1933- DLB-276
Gaskell, Elizabeth Cleghorn
   1810-1865 ..... DLB-21, 144, 159; CDBLB-4
   The Gaskell Society Y-98
Gaskell, Jane 1941- DLB-261
Gaspey, Thomas 1788-1871 .... DLB-116
Gass, William H. 1924- DLB-2, 227
Gates, Doris 1901-1987 .... DLB-22
Gates, Henry Louis, Jr. 1950- DLB-67
Gates, Lewis E. 1860-1924............ DLB-71
Gatto, Alfonso 1909-1976 .... DLB-114
Gault, William Campbell 1910-1995 .... DLB-226
   Tribute to Kenneth Millar Y-83
Gaunt, Mary 1861-1942..........DLB-174, 230
Gautier, Théophile 1811-1872 .... DLB-119
Gauvreau, Claude 1925-1971 .... DLB-88
The *Gawain*-Poet
   flourished circa 1350-1400 .... DLB-146
Gawsworth, John (Terence Ian Fytton
   Armstrong) 1912-1970 .... DLB-255
Gay, Ebenezer 1696-1787 .... DLB-24
Gay, John 1685-1732 .... DLB-84, 95
Gayarré, Charles E. A. 1805-1895 .... DLB-30
Charles Gaylord [publishing house]...... DLB-49
Gaylord, Edward King 1873-1974 .... DLB-127
Gaylord, Edward Lewis 1919- DLB-127
Gébler, Carlo 1954- DLB-271
Geda, Sigitas 1943- DLB-232
Geddes, Gary 1940- DLB-60
Geddes, Virgil 1897- DLB-4
Gedeon (Georgii Andreevich Krinovsky)
   circa 1730-1763.................. DLB-150
Gee, Maggie 1948- DLB-207
Gee, Shirley 1932- DLB-245
Geibel, Emanuel 1815-1884 .... DLB-129
Geiogamah, Hanay 1945- DLB-175
Geis, Bernard, Associates DLB-46
Geisel, Theodor Seuss 1904-1991....DLB-61; Y-91
Gelb, Arthur 1924- DLB-103
Gelb, Barbara 1926- DLB-103
Gelber, Jack 1932- DLB-7, 228
Gélinas, Gratien 1909-1999 .... DLB-88
Gellert, Christian Fürchtegott
   1715-1769 .... DLB-97

Gellhorn, Martha 1908-1998 .... Y-82, 98
Gems, Pam 1925- DLB-13
Genet, Jean 1910-1986 ....DLB-72; Y-86
Genette, Gérard 1930- DLB-242
Genevoix, Maurice 1890-1980 .... DLB-65
Genovese, Eugene D. 1930- DLB-17
Gent, Peter 1942- Y-82
Geoffrey of Monmouth
   circa 1100-1155 .... DLB-146
George, Henry 1839-1897 .... DLB-23
George, Jean Craighead 1919- DLB-52
George, W. L. 1882-1926.............DLB-197
George III, King of Great Britain
   and Ireland 1738-1820 .... DLB-213
Georgslied 896?..................... DLB-148
Gerber, Merrill Joan 1938- DLB-218
Gerhardie, William 1895-1977 .... DLB-36
Gerhardt, Paul 1607-1676............. DLB-164
Gérin, Winifred 1901-1981 .... DLB-155
Gérin-Lajoie, Antoine 1824-1882........ DLB-99
German Literature
   A Call to Letters and an Invitation
     to the Electric Chair........... DLB-75
   The Conversion of an Unpolitical
     Man DLB-66
   The German Radio Play.......... DLB-124
   The German Transformation from the
     Baroque to the Enlightenment ... DLB-97
   Germanophilism DLB-66
   A Letter from a New Germany......... Y-90
   The Making of a People DLB-66
   The Novel of Impressionism DLB-66
   Pattern and Paradigm: History as
     Design DLB-75
   Premisses DLB-66
   The 'Twenties and Berlin.......... DLB-66
   Wolfram von Eschenbach's *Parzival*:
     Prologue and Book 3 ...... DLB-138
   Writers and Politics: 1871-1918 ..... DLB-66
German Literature, Middle Ages
   Abrogans circa 790-800 .... DLB-148
   Annolied between 1077 and 1081 .... DLB-148
   The Arthurian Tradition and
     Its European Context......... DLB-138
   Cambridge Songs (*Carmina Cantabrigensia*)
     circa 1050.................. DLB-148
   Christus und die Samariterin circa 950 .. DLB-148
   De Heinrico circa 980? DLB-148
   Ecbasis Captivi circa 1045 .... DLB-148
   Georgslied 896?.................. DLB-148
   German Literature and Culture from
     Charlemagne to the Early Courtly
     Period............DLB-148; CDWLB-2
   The Germanic Epic and Old English
     Heroic Poetry: *Widsith*, *Waldere*,
     and *The Fight at Finnsburg* DLB-146
   Graf Rudolf between circa
     1170 and circa 1185.......... DLB-148
   Heliand circa 850 .... DLB-148

Das Hildebrandslied
circa 820 . . . . DLB-148; CDWLB-2

Kaiserchronik circa 1147 . . . . DLB-148

The Legends of the Saints and a
Medieval Christian
Worldview DLB-148

Ludus de Antichristo circa 1160 . . . . DLB-148

Ludwigslied 881 or 882 . . . . DLB-148

Muspilli circa 790-circa 850 . . . . DLB-148

Old German Genesis and *Old German Exodus* circa 1050-circa 1130 . . . . DLB-148

Old High German Charms
and Blessings DLB-148; CDWLB-2

The *Old High German Isidor*
circa 790-800 . . . . DLB-148

Petruslied circa 854? DLB-148

Physiologus circa 1070-circa 1150 . . . . . DLB-148

Ruodlieb circa 1050-1075 . . . . DLB-148

"*Spielmannsepen*" (circa 1152-
circa 1500) DLB-148

The Strasbourg Oaths 842 . . . . DLB-148

Tatian circa 830 . . . . DLB-148

Waltharius circa 825 . . . . DLB-148

Wessobrunner Gebet circa 787-815 . . . . . DLB-148

German Theater
German Drama 800-1280 . . . . DLB-138

German Drama from Naturalism
to Fascism: 1889-1933 . . . . DLB-118

Gernsback, Hugo 1884-1967 . . . . . DLB-8, 137

Gerould, Katharine Fullerton
1879-1944 . . . . DLB-78

Samuel Gerrish [publishing house] DLB-49

Gerrold, David 1944- DLB-8

Gershwin, Ira 1896-1983 . . . . DLB-265

The Ira Gershwin Centenary Y-96

Gerson, Jean 1363-1429 . . . . DLB-208

Gersonides 1288-1344 . . . . DLB-115

Gerstäcker, Friedrich 1816-1872 . . . . . . DLB-129

Gertsen, Aleksandr Ivanovich
(see Herzen, Alexander)

Gerstenberg, Heinrich Wilhelm von
1737-1823 . . . . DLB-97

Gervinus, Georg Gottfried
1805-1871 . . . . DLB-133

Gery, John 1953- DLB-282

Geßner, Solomon 1730-1788 . . . . DLB-97

Geston, Mark S. 1946- DLB-8

Al-Ghazali 1058-1111 . . . . DLB-115

Gibbings, Robert 1889-1958 . . . . DLB-195

Gibbon, Edward 1737-1794 . . . . DLB-104

Gibbon, John Murray 1875-1952 . . . . . . DLB-92

Gibbon, Lewis Grassic (see Mitchell, James Leslie)

Gibbons, Floyd 1887-1939 . . . . DLB-25

Gibbons, Reginald 1947- DLB-120

Gibbons, William ?-? DLB-73

Gibson, Charles Dana
1867-1944 . . . . DLB-188; DS-13

Gibson, Graeme 1934- DLB-53

Gibson, Margaret 1944- DLB-120

Gibson, Margaret Dunlop 1843-1920 . . . . DLB-174

Gibson, Wilfrid 1878-1962 . . . . DLB-19

The Friends of the Dymock Poets Y-00

Gibson, William 1914- DLB-7

Gibson, William 1948- DLB-251

Gide, André 1869-1951 . . . . DLB-65

Giguère, Diane 1937- DLB-53

Giguère, Roland 1929- DLB-60

Gil de Biedma, Jaime 1929-1990 . . . . . . DLB-108

Gil-Albert, Juan 1906-1994 . . . . DLB-134

Gilbert, Anthony 1899-1973 . . . . DLB-77

Gilbert, Sir Humphrey 1537-1583 . . . . . DLB-136

Gilbert, Michael 1912- DLB-87

Gilbert, Sandra M. 1936- DLB-120, 246

Gilchrist, Alexander 1828-1861 . . . . DLB-144

Gilchrist, Ellen 1935- DLB-130

Gilder, Jeannette L. 1849-1916 . . . . DLB-79

Gilder, Richard Watson 1844-1909 . . . . DLB-64, 79

Gildersleeve, Basil 1831-1924 . . . . DLB-71

Giles, Henry 1809-1882 . . . . DLB-64

Giles of Rome circa 1243-1316 . . . . DLB-115

Gilfillan, George 1813-1878 . . . . DLB-144

Gill, Eric 1882-1940 . . . . DLB-98

Gill, Sarah Prince 1728-1771 . . . . DLB-200

William F. Gill Company DLB-49

Gillespie, A. Lincoln, Jr. 1895-1950 . . . . . . DLB-4

Gillespie, Haven 1883-1975 . . . . DLB-265

Gilliam, Florence ?-? DLB-4

Gilliatt, Penelope 1932-1993 . . . . DLB-14

Gillott, Jacky 1939-1980 . . . . DLB-14

Gilman, Caroline H. 1794-1888 . . . . . . DLB-3, 73

Gilman, Charlotte Perkins 1860-1935 . . . . DLB-221

The Charlotte Perkins Gilman Society . . Y-99

W. and J. Gilman [publishing house] DLB-49

Gilmer, Elizabeth Meriwether
1861-1951 . . . . DLB-29

Gilmer, Francis Walker 1790-1826 . . . . . DLB-37

Gilmore, Mary 1865-1962 . . . . DLB-260

Gilroy, Frank D. 1925- DLB-7

Gimferrer, Pere (Pedro) 1945- DLB-134

Gingrich, Arnold 1903-1976 . . . . DLB-137

Prospectus From the Initial Issue of
Esquire (Autumn 1933) DLB-137

"With the Editorial Ken," Prospectus
From the Initial Issue of *Ken*
(7 April 1938) DLB-137

Ginsberg, Allen
1926-1997 . . . . DLB-5, 16, 169, 237; CDALB-1

Ginzburg, Natalia 1916-1991 . . . . DLB-177

Ginzkey, Franz Karl 1871-1963 . . . . DLB-81

Gioia, Dana 1950- DLB-120, 282

Giono, Jean 1895-1970 . . . . DLB-72

Giotti, Virgilio 1885-1957 . . . . DLB-114

Giovanni, Nikki 1943- DLB-5, 41; CDALB-7

Gipson, Lawrence Henry 1880-1971 . . . . . DLB-17

Girard, Rodolphe 1879-1956 . . . . DLB-92

Giraudoux, Jean 1882-1944 . . . . DLB-65

Girondo, Oliverio 1891-1967 . . . . DLB-283

Gissing, George 1857-1903 . . . . DLB-18, 135, 184

The Place of Realism in Fiction (1895) DLB-18

Giudici, Giovanni 1924- DLB-128

Giuliani, Alfredo 1924- DLB-128

Glackens, William J. 1870-1938 . . . . DLB-188

Gladkov, Fedor Vasil'evich 1883-1958 . . . DLB-272

Gladstone, William Ewart
1809-1898 . . . . DLB-57, 184

Glaeser, Ernst 1902-1963 . . . . DLB-69

Glancy, Diane 1941- DLB-175

Glanvill, Joseph 1636-1680 . . . . DLB-252

Glanville, Brian 1931- DLB-15, 139

Glapthorne, Henry 1610-1643? DLB-58

Glasgow, Ellen 1873-1945 . . . . DLB-9, 12

The Ellen Glasgow Society Y-01

Glasier, Katharine Bruce 1867-1950 . . . . . DLB-190

Glaspell, Susan 1876-1948 . . . . . . DLB-7, 9, 78, 228

Glass, Montague 1877-1934 . . . . DLB-11

Glassco, John 1909-1981 . . . . DLB-68

Glauser, Friedrich 1896-1938 . . . . DLB-56

F. Gleason's Publishing Hall DLB-49

Gleim, Johann Wilhelm Ludwig
1719-1803 . . . . DLB-97

Glendinning, Victoria 1937- DLB-155

Glidden, Frederick Dilley (Luke Short)
1908-1975 . . . . DLB-256

Glinka, Fedor Nikolaevich 1786-1880 . . . . DLB-205

Glover, Keith 1966- DLB-249

Glover, Richard 1712-1785 . . . . DLB-95

Glück, Louise 1943- DLB-5

Glyn, Elinor 1864-1943 . . . . DLB-153

Gnedich, Nikolai Ivanovich 1784-1833 . . . DLB-205

Gobineau, Joseph-Arthur de 1816-1882 . . . DLB-123

Godber, John 1956- DLB-233

Godbout, Jacques 1933- DLB-53

Goddard, Morrill 1865-1937 . . . . DLB-25

Goddard, William 1740-1817 . . . . DLB-43

Godden, Rumer 1907-1998 . . . . DLB-161

Godey, Louis A. 1804-1878 . . . . DLB-73

Godey and McMichael DLB-49

Godfrey, Dave 1938- DLB-60

Godfrey, Thomas 1736-1763 . . . . DLB-31

Godine, David R., Publisher DLB-46

Godkin, E. L. 1831-1902 . . . . DLB-79

Godolphin, Sidney 1610-1643 . . . . DLB-126

Godwin, Gail 1937- DLB-6, 234

M. J. Godwin and Company DLB-154

Godwin, Mary Jane Clairmont
1766-1841 . . . . DLB-163

Godwin, Parke 1816-1904 . . . . . . DLB-3, 64, 250

Godwin, William 1756-1836 . . . . . . DLB-39, 104,
142, 158, 163, 262; CDBLB-3

Preface to *St. Leon* (1799) DLB-39

Goering, Reinhard 1887-1936 . . . . DLB-118

Cumulative Index

Goes, Albrecht 1908- DLB-69
Goethe, Johann Wolfgang von
    1749-1832............. DLB-94; CDWLB-2
Goetz, Curt 1888-1960................ DLB-124
Goffe, Thomas circa 1592-1629 .... DLB-58
Goffstein, M. B. 1940- DLB-61
Gogarty, Oliver St. John 1878-1957 ... DLB-15, 19
Gogol, Nikolai Vasil'evich 1809-1852 ... DLB-198
Goines, Donald 1937-1974 .... DLB-33
Gold, Herbert 1924- DLB-2; Y-81
    Tribute to William Saroyan Y-81
Gold, Michael 1893-1967 .... DLB-9, 28
Goldbarth, Albert 1948- DLB-120
Goldberg, Dick 1947- DLB-7
Golden Cockerel Press DLB-112
Golding, Arthur 1536-1606 .... DLB-136
Golding, Louis 1895-1958 .... DLB-195
Golding, William 1911-1993
    .... DLB-15, 100, 255; Y-83; CDBLB-7
    Nobel Lecture 1993 .... Y-83
    The Stature of William Golding Y-83
Goldman, Emma 1869-1940............. DLB-221
Goldman, William 1931- DLB-44
Goldring, Douglas 1887-1960 .... DLB-197
Goldsmith, Oliver 1730?-1774
    .... DLB-39, 89, 99. 104, 109, 142; CDBLB-2
Goldsmith, Oliver 1794-1861 .... DLB-99
Goldsmith Publishing Company DLB-46
Goldstein, Richard 1944- DLB-185
Gollancz, Sir Israel 1864-1930 .... DLB-201
Victor Gollancz Limited DLB-112
Gomberville, Marin Le Roy, sieur de
    1600?-1674 .... DLB-268
Gombrowicz, Witold
    1904-1969 .... DLB-215; CDWLB-4
Gómez-Quiñones, Juan 1942- DLB-122
Laurence James Gomme
    [publishing house] DLB-46
Goncharov, Ivan Aleksandrovich
    1812-1891......................... DLB-238
Goncourt, Edmond de 1822-1896 ...... DLB-123
Goncourt, Jules de 1830-1870.......... DLB-123
Gonzales, Rodolfo "Corky" 1928- DLB-122
Gonzales-Berry, Erlinda 1942- DLB-209
    "Chicano Language".............. DLB-82
González, Angel 1925- DLB-108
Gonzalez, Genaro 1949- DLB-122
Gonzalez, Ray 1952- DLB-122
González de Mireles, Jovita
    1899-1983 .... DLB-122
González-T., César A. 1931- DLB-82
Goodis, David 1917-1967 .... DLB-226
Goodison, Lorna 1947- DLB-157
Goodman, Allegra 1967- DLB-244
Goodman, Nelson 1906-1998..........DLB-279
Goodman, Paul 1911-1972 .... DLB-130, 246
The Goodman Theatre DLB-7

Goodrich, Frances 1891-1984........... DLB-26
Goodrich, Samuel Griswold
    1793-1860....................DLB-1, 42, 73, 243
S. G. Goodrich [publishing house] DLB-49
C. E. Goodspeed and Company......... DLB-49
Goodwin, Stephen 1943- Y-82
Googe, Barnabe 1540-1594 .... DLB-132
Gookin, Daniel 1612-1687 .... DLB-24
Goran, Lester 1928- DLB-244
Gordimer, Nadine 1923- DLB-225; Y-91
    Nobel Lecture 1991 .... Y-91
Gordon, Adam Lindsay 1833-1870 ..... DLB-230
Gordon, Caroline
    1895-1981 .... DLB-4, 9, 102; DS-17; Y-81
Gordon, Charles F. (see OyamO)
Gordon, Charles William (see Connor, Ralph)
Gordon, Giles 1940- DLB-14, 139, 207
Gordon, Helen Cameron, Lady Russell
    1867-1949...................... DLB-195
Gordon, Lyndall 1941- DLB-155
Gordon, Mack 1904-1959 .... DLB-265
Gordon, Mary 1949- DLB-6; Y-81
Gordone, Charles 1925-1995 .... DLB-7
Gore, Catherine 1800-1861 .... DLB-116
Gore-Booth, Eva 1870-1926 .... DLB-240
Gores, Joe 1931- DLB-226; Y-02
    Tribute to Kenneth Millar Y-83
    Tribute to Raymond Chandler......... Y-88
Gorey, Edward 1925-2000 .... DLB-61
Gorgias of Leontini
    circa 485 B.C.-376 B.C. DLB-176
Görres, Joseph 1776-1848............. DLB-90
Gosse, Edmund 1849-1928...... DLB-57, 144, 184
Gosson, Stephen 1554-1624 ....DLB-172
    The Schoole of Abuse (1579) DLB-172
Gotanda, Philip Kan 1951- DLB-266
Gotlieb, Phyllis 1926- DLB-88, 251
Go-Toba 1180-1239 .... DLB-203
Gottfried von Straßburg
    died before 1230 ...... DLB-138; CDWLB-2
Gotthelf, Jeremias 1797-1854......... DLB-133
Gottschalk circa 804/808-869 .... DLB-148
Gottsched, Johann Christoph
    1700-1766...................... DLB-97
Götz, Johann Nikolaus 1721-1781....... DLB-97
Goudge, Elizabeth 1900-1984 .... DLB-191
Gough, John B. 1817-1886 .... DLB-243
Gould, Wallace 1882-1940............. DLB-54
Govoni, Corrado 1884-1965 .... DLB-114
Gower, John circa 1330-1408 .... DLB-146
Goyen, William 1915-1983 .....DLB-2, 218; Y-83
Goytisolo, José Augustín 1928- DLB-134
Gozzano, Guido 1883-1916 .... DLB-114
Grabbe, Christian Dietrich 1801-1836 ... DLB-133
García Marruz, Fina 1923- DLB-283
Gracq, Julien (Louis Poirier) 1910- DLB-83

Grady, Henry W. 1850-1889.......... DLB-23
Graf, Oskar Maria 1894-1967 .... DLB-56
Graf Rudolf between circa 1170 and
    circa 1185..................... DLB-148
Graff, Gerald 1937- DLB-246
Richard Grafton [publishing house]......DLB-170
Grafton, Sue 1940- DLB-226
Graham, Frank 1893-1965 .... DLB-241
Graham, George Rex 1813-1894 ...... DLB-73
Graham, Gwethalyn (Gwethalyn Graham
    Erichsen-Brown) 1913-1965......... DLB-88
Graham, Jorie 1951- DLB-120
Graham, Katharine 1917-2001 ....DLB-127
Graham, Lorenz 1902-1989 .... DLB-76
Graham, Philip 1915-1963 ....DLB-127
Graham, R. B. Cunninghame
    1852-1936 .... DLB-98, 135, 174
Graham, Shirley 1896-1977 .... DLB-76
Graham, Stephen 1884-1975............ DLB-195
Graham, W. S. 1918-1986 .... DLB-20
William H. Graham [publishing house] ... DLB-49
Graham, Winston 1910- DLB-77
Grahame, Kenneth 1859-1932 ...DLB-34, 141, 178
Grainger, Martin Allerdale 1874-1941 .... DLB-92
Gramatky, Hardie 1907-1979 .... DLB-22
Grand, Sarah 1854-1943............DLB-135, 197
Grandbois, Alain 1900-1975 .... DLB-92
Grandson, Oton de circa 1345-1397..... DLB-208
Grange, John circa 1556-? DLB-136
Granger, Thomas 1578-1627 .... DLB-281
Granich, Irwin (see Gold, Michael)
Granovsky, Timofei Nikolaevich
    1813-1855 .... DLB-198
Grant, Anne MacVicar 1755-1838 ...... DLB-200
Grant, Duncan 1885-1978 .... DS-10
Grant, George 1918-1988 .... DLB-88
Grant, George Monro 1835-1902....... DLB-99
Grant, Harry J. 1881-1963 .... DLB-29
Grant, James Edward 1905-1966 .... DLB-26
Grant, John (see Gash, Jonathan)
War of the Words (and Pictures): The Creation
    of a Graphic Novel Y-02
Grass, Günter 1927- ...DLB-75, 124; CDWLB-2
    Nobel Lecture 1999:
    "To Be Continued..." Y-99
    Tribute to Helen Wolff............. Y-94
Grasty, Charles H. 1863-1924 .... DLB-25
Grau, Shirley Ann 1929- DLB-2, 218
Graves, John 1920- Y-83
Graves, Richard 1715-1804 .... DLB-39
Graves, Robert 1895-1985
    ....DLB-20, 100, 191; DS-18; Y-85; CDBLB-6
    The St. John's College
    Robert Graves Trust Y-96
Gray, Alasdair 1934- DLB-194, 261
Gray, Asa 1810-1888 .... DLB-1, 235
Gray, David 1838-1861 .... DLB-32

Gray, Simon 1936- DLB-13
Gray, Thomas 1716-1771 .....DLB-109; CDBLB-2
Grayson, Richard 1951- DLB-234
Grayson, William J. 1788-1863 ....DLB-3, 64, 248
The Great Bibliographers Series Y-93
The Great Gatsby (Documentary).........DLB-219
"The Greatness of Southern Literature":
  League of the South Institute for the
  Study of Southern Culture and History
  ....Y-02
Grech, Nikolai Ivanovich 1787-1867 .....DLB-198
Greeley, Horace 1811-1872 ...DLB-3, 43, 189, 250
Green, Adolph 1915-2002 ....DLB-44, 265
Green, Anna Katharine
  1846-1935 ....DLB-202, 221
Green, Duff 1791-1875................DLB-43
Green, Elizabeth Shippen 1871-1954 .....DLB-188
Green, Gerald 1922- DLB-28
Green, Henry 1905-1973 ....DLB-15
Green, Jonas 1712-1767 ....DLB-31
Green, Joseph 1706-1780 ....DLB-31
Green, Julien 1900-1998 ....DLB-4, 72
Green, Paul 1894-1981 ......DLB-7, 9, 249; Y-81
Green, T. H. 1836-1882 ....DLB-190, 262
Green, Terence M. 1947- DLB-251
T. and S. Green [publishing house] DLB-49
Green Tiger Press DLB-46
Timothy Green [publishing house] DLB-49
Greenaway, Kate 1846-1901 ....DLB-141
Greenberg: Publisher..................DLB-46
Greene, Asa 1789-1838 ....DLB-11
Greene, Belle da Costa 1883-1950.......DLB-187
Greene, Graham 1904-1991
  ....DLB-13, 15, 77, 100, 162, 201, 204;
                          Y-85, 91; CDBLB-7
  Tribute to Christopher Isherwood......Y-86
Greene, Robert 1558-1592..........DLB-62, 167
Greene, Robert Bernard (Bob), Jr.
  1947- DLB-185
Benjamin H Greene [publishing house] DLB-49
Greenfield, George 1917-2000 ....Y-91, 00
  Derek Robinson's Review of George
  Greenfield's *Rich Dust*...........Y-02
Greenhow, Robert 1800-1854 ....DLB-30
Greenlee, William B. 1872-1953 ....DLB-187
Greenough, Horatio 1805-1852......DLB-1, 235
Greenwell, Dora 1821-1882.........DLB-35, 199
Greenwillow Books DLB-46
Greenwood, Grace (see Lippincott, Sara Jane Clarke)
Greenwood, Walter 1903-1974 ......DLB-10, 191
Greer, Ben 1948- DLB-6
Greflinger, Georg 1620?-1677 ....DLB-164
Greg, W. R. 1809-1881 ....DLB-55
Greg, W. W. 1875-1959.................DLB-201
Gregg, Josiah 1806-1850 ....DLB-183, 186
Gregg Press DLB-46
Gregory, Horace 1898-1982 ....DLB-48

Gregory, Isabella Augusta Persse, Lady
  1852-1932 ....DLB-10
Gregory of Rimini circa 1300-1358 ......DLB-115
Gregynog Press DLB-112
Greiff, Leon de 1895-1976 ....DLB-283
Greiffenberg, Catharina Regina von
  1633-1694 ....DLB-168
Greig, Noël 1944- DLB-245
Grenfell, Wilfred Thomason
  1865-1940.....................DLB-92
Gress, Elsa 1919-1988 ....DLB-214
Greve, Felix Paul (see Grove, Frederick Philip)
Greville, Fulke, First Lord Brooke
  1554-1628 ....DLB-62, 172
Grey, Sir George, K.C.B. 1812-1898.....DLB-184
Grey, Lady Jane 1537-1554 ....DLB-132
Grey, Zane 1872-1939 ....DLB-9, 212
  Zane Grey's West Society Y-00
Grey Owl (Archibald Stansfeld Belaney)
  1888-1938 ....DLB-92; DS-17
Grey Walls Press DLB-112
Griboedov, Aleksandr Sergeevich
  1795?-1829 ....DLB-205
Grice, Paul 1913-1988 ....DLB-279
Grier, Eldon 1917- DLB-88
Grieve, C. M. (see MacDiarmid, Hugh)
Griffin, Bartholomew flourished 1596....DLB-172
Griffin, Bryan
  "Panic Among the Philistines":
  A Postscript, An Interview
  with Bryan Griffin..............Y-81
Griffin, Gerald 1803-1840 ....DLB-159
The Griffin Poetry Prize Y-00
Griffith, Elizabeth 1727?-1793 .....DLB-39, 89
  Preface to *The Delicate Distress* (1769)...DLB-39
Griffith, George 1857-1906 ....DLB-178
Ralph Griffiths [publishing house] DLB-154
Griffiths, Trevor 1935- DLB-13, 245
S. C. Griggs and Company DLB-49
Griggs, Sutton Elbert 1872-1930 ....DLB-50
Grignon, Claude-Henri 1894-1976........DLB-68
Grigor'ev, Apollon Aleksandrovich
  1822-1864 ....DLB-277
Grigorovich, Dmitrii Vasil'evich
  1822-1899 ....DLB-238
Grigson, Geoffrey 1905-1985 ....DLB-27
Grillparzer, Franz
  1791-1872 ....DLB-133; CDWLB-2
Grimald, Nicholas
  circa 1519-circa 1562..............DLB-136
Grimké, Angelina Weld 1880-1958....DLB-50, 54
Grimké, Sarah Moore 1792-1873 ....DLB-239
Grimm, Hans 1875-1959 ....DLB-66
Grimm, Jacob 1785-1863 ....DLB-90
Grimm, Wilhelm
  1786-1859 ....DLB-90; CDWLB-2
Grimmelshausen, Johann Jacob Christoffel von
  1621 or 1622-1676......DLB-168; CDWLB-2
Grimshaw, Beatrice Ethel 1871-1953 .....DLB-174

Grin, Aleksandr Stepanovich
  1880-1932 ....DLB-272
Grindal, Edmund 1519 or 1520-1583 ....DLB-132
Gripe, Maria (Kristina) 1923- DLB-257
Griswold, Rufus Wilmot
  1815-1857 ....DLB-3, 59, 250
Grosart, Alexander Balloch 1827-1899 ...DLB-184
Grosholz, Emily 1950- DLB-282
Gross, Milt 1895-1953..................DLB-11
Grosset and Dunlap....................DLB-49
Grosseteste, Robert circa 1160-1253 .....DLB-115
Grossman, Allen 1932- DLB-193
Grossman, Vasilii Semenovich
  1905-1964 ....DLB-272
Grossman Publishers....................DLB-46
Grosvenor, Gilbert H. 1875-1966 ....DLB-91
Groth, Klaus 1819-1899 ....DLB-129
Groulx, Lionel 1878-1967 ....DLB-68
Grove, Frederick Philip (Felix Paul Greve)
  1879-1948 ....DLB-92
Grove Press.........................DLB-46
Grubb, Davis 1919-1980 ....DLB-6
Gruelle, Johnny 1880-1938 ....DLB-22
von Grumbach, Argula
  1492-after 1563?..................DLB-179
Grymeston, Elizabeth
  before 1563-before 1604 ....DLB-136
Gryphius, Andreas
  1616-1664 ....DLB-164; CDWLB-2
Gryphius, Christian 1649-1706 ....DLB-168
Guare, John 1938- DLB-7, 249
Guerra, Tonino 1920- DLB-128
Guest, Barbara 1920- DLB-5, 193
Guèvremont, Germaine 1893-1968.......DLB-68
Guglielminetti, Amalia 1881-1941 ....DLB-264
Guidacci, Margherita 1921-1992 ....DLB-128
Guillén, Jorge 1893-1984 ....DLB-108
Guillén, Nicolás 1902-1989 ....DLB-283
Guilloux, Louis 1899-1980 ....DLB-72
Guilpin, Everard circa 1572-after 1608?...DLB-136
Guiney, Louise Imogen 1861-1920 ....DLB-54
Guiterman, Arthur 1871-1943 ....DLB-11
Günderrode, Caroline von
  1780-1806 ....DLB-90
Gundulić, Ivan 1589-1638 ...DLB-147; CDWLB-4
Gunesekera, Romesh 1954- DLB-267
Gunn, Bill 1934-1989 ....DLB-38
Gunn, James E. 1923- DLB-8
Gunn, Neil M. 1891-1973 ....DLB-15
Gunn, Thom 1929- DLB-27; CDBLB-8
Gunnars, Kristjana 1948- DLB-60
Günther, Johann Christian 1695-1723....DLB-168
Gurik, Robert 1932- DLB-60
Gurney, A. R. 1930- DLB-266
Gurney, Ivor 1890-1937 ....Y-02
  The Ivor Gurney Society Y-98
Gustafson, Ralph 1909-1995 ....DLB-88

Gustafsson, Lars 1936- DLB-257	Hale, Nancy 1908-1988 .... DLB-86; DS-17; Y-80, 88	Hammett, Dashiell 1894-1961 ... DLB-226, 280; DS-6; CDALB-5
Gütersloh, Albert Paris 1887-1973. .... DLB-81	Hale, Sarah Josepha (Buell) 1788-1879 .... DLB-1, 42, 73, 243	An Appeal in *TAC* Y-91
Guthrie, A. B., Jr. 1901-1991 .... DLB-6, 212	Hale, Susan 1833-1910 .... DLB-221	*The Glass Key* and Other Dashiell Hammett Mysteries Y-96
Guthrie, Ramon 1896-1973 .... DLB-4	Hales, John 1584-1656 .... DLB-151	Knopf to Hammett: The Editoral Correspondence Y-00
Guthrie, Thomas Anstey (see Anstey, FC)	Halévy, Ludovic 1834-1908 .... DLB-192	Hammon, Jupiter 1711-died between 1790 and 1806 .... DLB-31, 50
The Guthrie Theater DLB-7	Haley, Alex 1921-1992 .... DLB-38; CDALB-7	
Gutzkow, Karl 1811-1878 .... DLB-133	Haliburton, Thomas Chandler 1796-1865 .... DLB-11, 99	Hammond, John ?-1663 .... DLB-24
Guy, Ray 1939- DLB-60		Hamner, Earl 1923- DLB-6
Guy, Rosa 1925- DLB-33	Hall, Adam (Trevor Dudley-Smith) 1920-1995 .... DLB-276	Hampson, John 1901-1955 .... DLB-191
Guyot, Arnold 1807-1884 ....DS-13	Hall, Anna Maria 1800-1881 .... DLB-159	Hampton, Christopher 1946- DLB-13
Gwynn, R. S. 1948- DLB-282	Hall, Donald 1928- DLB-5	Handel-Mazzetti, Enrica von 1871-1955... DLB-81
Gwynne, Erskine 1898-1948. .... DLB-4	Hall, Edward 1497-1547 .... DLB-132	Handke, Peter 1942- DLB-85, 124
Gyles, John 1680-1755 .... DLB-99	Hall, Halsey 1898-1977 .... DLB-241	Handlin, Oscar 1915- DLB-17
Gyllensten, Lars 1921- DLB-257	Hall, James 1793-1868 ....DLB-73, 74	Hankin, St. John 1869-1909 .... DLB-10
Gysin, Brion 1916-1986 .... DLB-16	Hall, Joseph 1574-1656 .... DLB-121, 151	Hanley, Clifford 1922- DLB-14
	Hall, Radclyffe 1880-1943 .... DLB-191	Hanley, James 1901-1985 .... DLB-191
H	Hall, Sarah Ewing 1761-1830 .... DLB-200	Hannah, Barry 1942- DLB-6, 234
	Hall, Stuart 1932- DLB-242	Hannay, James 1827-1873 .... DLB-21
H.D. (see Doolittle, Hilda)	Samuel Hall [publishing house] DLB-49	Hano, Arnold 1922- DLB-241
Habermas, Jürgen 1929- DLB-242	Hallam, Arthur Henry 1811-1833 .... DLB-32	Hansberry, Lorraine 1930-1965 ....DLB-7, 38; CDALB-1
Habington, William 1605-1654 .... DLB-126	On Some of the Characteristics of Modern Poetry and On the Lyrical Poems of Alfred Tennyson (1831) DLB-32	
Hacker, Marilyn 1942- DLB-120, 282		Hansen, Martin A. 1909-1955 .... DLB-214
Hackett, Albert 1900-1995 .... DLB-26		Hansen, Thorkild 1927-1989 .... DLB-214
Hacks, Peter 1928- DLB-124	Halleck, Fitz-Greene 1790-1867 ...... DLB-3, 250	Hanson, Elizabeth 1684-1737 .... DLB-200
Hadas, Rachel 1948- DLB-120, 282	Haller, Albrecht von 1708-1777........ DLB-168	Hapgood, Norman 1868-1937 .... DLB-91
Hadden, Briton 1898-1929 .... DLB-91	Halliday, Brett (see Dresser, Davis)	Happel, Eberhard Werner 1647-1690.... DLB-168
Hagedorn, Friedrich von 1708-1754 ..... DLB-168	Halliwell-Phillipps, James Orchard 1820-1889 .... DLB-184	Harbach, Otto 1873-1963 .... DLB-265
Hagelstange, Rudolf 1912-1984 .... DLB-69		*The Harbinger* 1845-1849 .... DLB-1, 223
Haggard, H. Rider 1856-1925 .... DLB-70, 156, 174, 178	Hallmann, Johann Christian 1640-1704 or 1716? DLB-168	Harburg, E. Y. "Yip" 1896-1981 .... DLB-265
Haggard, William (Richard Clayton) 1907-1993 ....DLB-276; Y-93	Hallmark Editions DLB-46	Harcourt Brace Jovanovich DLB-46
	Halper, Albert 1904-1984 .... DLB-9	Hardenberg, Friedrich von (see Novalis)
Hagy, Alyson 1960- DLB-244	Halperin, John William 1941- DLB-111	Harding, Walter 1917- DLB-111
Hahn-Hahn, Ida Gräfin von 1805-1880 .. DLB-133	Halstead, Murat 1829-1908 .... DLB-23	Hardwick, Elizabeth 1916- DLB-6
Haig-Brown, Roderick 1908-1976. .... DLB-88	Hamann, Johann Georg 1730-1788. ...... DLB-97	Hardy, Alexandre 1572?-1632 ....DLB-268
Haight, Gordon S. 1901-1985. .... DLB-103	Hamburger, Michael 1924- DLB-27	Hardy, Frank 1917-1994 .... DLB-260
Hailey, Arthur 1920- DLB-88; Y-82	Hamilton, Alexander 1712-1756 .... DLB-31	Hardy, Thomas 1840-1928 ...... DLB-18, 19, 135; CDBLB-5
Haines, John 1924- DLB-5, 212	Hamilton, Alexander 1755?-1804 .... DLB-37	"Candour in English Fiction" (1890) . DLB-18
Hake, Edward flourished 1566-1604 .... DLB-136	Hamilton, Cicely 1872-1952.........DLB-10, 197	Hare, Cyril 1900-1958 .... DLB-77
Hake, Thomas Gordon 1809-1895. ...... DLB-32	Hamilton, Edmond 1904-1977 .... DLB-8	Hare, David 1947- DLB-13
Hakluyt, Richard 1552?-1616 .... DLB-136	Hamilton, Elizabeth 1758-1816....... DLB-116, 158	Hare, R. M. 1919-2002................ DLB-262
Halas, František 1901-1949 .... DLB-215	Hamilton, Gail (see Corcoran, Barbara)	Hargrove, Marion 1919- DLB-11
Halbe, Max 1865-1944................ DLB-118	Hamilton, Gail (see Dodge, Mary Abigail)	Häring, Georg Wilhelm Heinrich (see Alexis, Willibald)
Halberstam, David 1934- DLB-241	Hamish Hamilton Limited DLB-112	
Haldane, Charlotte 1894-1969 .... DLB-191	Hamilton, Hugo 1953- DLB-267	Harington, Donald 1935- DLB-152
Haldane, J. B. S. 1892-1964 .... DLB-160	Hamilton, Ian 1938-2001 .... DLB-40, 155	Harington, Sir John 1560-1612......... DLB-136
Haldeman, Joe 1943- DLB-8	Hamilton, Janet 1795-1873 .... DLB-199	Harjo, Joy 1951- DLB-120, 175
Haldeman-Julius Company............. DLB-46	Hamilton, Mary Agnes 1884-1962 ...... DLB-197	Harkness, Margaret (John Law) 1854-1923 ....DLB-197
Hale, E. J., and Son................. DLB-49	Hamilton, Patrick 1904-1962 .... DLB-10, 191	
Hale, Edward Everett 1822-1909 ....DLB-1, 42, 74, 235	Hamilton, Virginia 1936-2002 ...DLB-33, 52; Y-01	Harley, Edward, second Earl of Oxford 1689-1741..................... DLB-213
Hale, Janet Campbell 1946- DLB-175	Hamilton, Sir William 1788-1856....... DLB-262	
Hale, Kathleen 1898-2000 .... DLB-160	Hamilton-Paterson, James 1941- DLB-267	Harley, Robert, first Earl of Oxford 1661-1724..................... DLB-213
Hale, Leo Thomas (see Ebon)	Hammerstein, Oscar, 2nd 1895-1960.... DLB-265	
Hale, Lucretia Peabody 1820-1900....... DLB-42		Harlow, Robert 1923- DLB-60

Harman, Thomas flourished 1566-1573 ..DLB-136
Harness, Charles L. 1915- DLB-8
Harnett, Cynthia 1893-1981 ....DLB-161
Harnick, Sheldon 1924- DLB-265
 Tribute to Ira Gershwin............. Y-96
 Tribute to Lorenz Hart Y-95
Harper, Edith Alice Mary (see Wickham, Anna)
Harper, Fletcher 1806-1877 ....DLB-79
Harper, Frances Ellen Watkins
 1825-1911 ....DLB-50, 221
Harper, Michael S. 1938- DLB-41
Harper and Brothers DLB-49
Harpur, Charles 1813-1868...........DLB-230
Harraden, Beatrice 1864-1943.........DLB-153
George G. Harrap and Company
 Limited DLB-112
Harriot, Thomas 1560-1621 ....DLB-136
Harris, Alexander 1805-1874 ....DLB-230
Harris, Benjamin ?-circa 1720 ....DLB-42, 43
Harris, Christie 1907-2002...............DLB-88
Harris, Errol E. 1908- DLB-279
Harris, Frank 1856-1931 ....DLB-156, 197
Harris, George Washington
 1814-1869 ....DLB-3, 11, 248
Harris, Joanne 1964- DLB-271
Harris, Joel Chandler
 1848-1908 ....DLB-11, 23, 42, 78, 91
 The Joel Chandler Harris Association ... Y-99
Harris, Mark 1922- DLB-2; Y-80
 Tribute to Frederick A. Pottle Y-87
Harris, William Torrey 1835-1909 ......DLB-270
Harris, Wilson 1921- DLB-117; CDWLB-3
Harrison, Mrs. Burton
 (see Harrison, Constance Cary)
Harrison, Charles Yale 1898-1954........DLB-68
Harrison, Constance Cary 1843-1920....DLB-221
Harrison, Frederic 1831-1923 .... DLB-57, 190
 "On Style in English Prose" (1898) ...DLB-57
Harrison, Harry 1925- DLB-8
James P. Harrison Company DLB-49
Harrison, Jim 1937- Y-82
Harrison, M. John 1945- DLB-261
Harrison, Mary St. Leger Kingsley
 (see Malet, Lucas)
Harrison, Paul Carter 1936- DLB-38
Harrison, Susan Frances 1859-1935.......DLB-99
Harrison, Tony 1937- DLB-40, 245
Harrison, William 1535-1593 ....DLB-136
Harrison, William 1933- DLB-234
Harrisse, Henry 1829-1910 ....DLB-47
The Harry Ransom Humanities Research Center
 at the University of Texas at Austin Y-00
Harryman, Carla 1952- DLB-193
Harsdörffer, Georg Philipp 1607-1658....DLB-164
Harsent, David 1942- DLB-40
Hart, Albert Bushnell 1854-1943 ....DLB-17

Hart, Anne 1768-1834 ....DLB-200
Hart, Elizabeth 1771-1833 ....DLB-200
Hart, Julia Catherine 1796-1867..........DLB-99
Hart, Lorenz 1895-1943..............DLB-265
 Larry Hart: Still an Influence Y-95
 Lorenz Hart: An American Lyricist..... Y-95
 The Lorenz Hart Centenary Y-95
Hart, Moss 1904-1961............. DLB-7, 266
Hart, Oliver 1723-1795 ....DLB-31
Rupert Hart-Davis Limited DLB-112
Harte, Bret 1836-1902
 .... DLB-12, 64, 74, 79, 186; CDALB-3
Harte, Edward Holmead 1922- DLB-127
Harte, Houston Harriman 1927- DLB-127
Hartlaub, Felix 1913-1945 ....DLB-56
Hartleben, Otto Erich 1864-1905 ....DLB-118
Hartley, David 1705-1757 ....DLB-252
Hartley, L. P. 1895-1972 ....DLB-15, 139
Hartley, Marsden 1877-1943 ....DLB-54
Hartling, Peter 1933- DLB-75
Hartman, Geoffrey H. 1929- DLB-67
Hartmann, Sadakichi 1867-1944 ....DLB-54
Hartmann von Aue
 circa 1160-circa 1205....DLB-138; CDWLB-2
Hartshorne, Charles 1897-2000 ....DLB-270
Harvey, Gabriel 1550?-1631 ... DLB-167, 213, 281
Harvey, Jack (see Rankin, Ian)
Harvey, Jean-Charles 1891-1967.........DLB-88
Harvill Press Limited.................DLB-112
Harwood, Lee 1939- DLB-40
Harwood, Ronald 1934- DLB-13
Hašek, Jaroslav 1883-1923...DLB-215; CDWLB-4
Haskins, Charles Homer 1870-1937 ......DLB-47
Haslam, Gerald 1937- DLB-212
Hass, Robert 1941- DLB-105, 206
Hasselstrom, Linda M. 1943- DLB-256
Hastings, Michael 1938- DLB-233
Hatar, Győző 1914- DLB-215
The Hatch-Billops Collection...........DLB-76
Hathaway, William 1944- DLB-120
Hauff, Wilhelm 1802-1827 ....DLB-90
Haugwitz, August Adolph von
 1647-1706....................DLB-168
Hauptmann, Carl 1858-1921 ....DLB-66, 118
Hauptmann, Gerhart
 1862-1946 ....DLB-66, 118; CDWLB-2
Hauser, Marianne 1910- Y-83
Havel, Václav 1936- DLB-232; CDWLB-4
Haven, Alice B. Neal 1827-1863 ....DLB-250
Havergal, Frances Ridley 1836-1879 .....DLB-199
Hawes, Stephen 1475?-before 1529 ......DLB-132
Hawker, Robert Stephen 1803-1875 ......DLB-32
Hawkes, John
 1925-1998 ....DLB-2, 7, 227; Y-80, Y-98
 John Hawkes: A Tribute Y-98
 Tribute to Donald Barthelme......... Y-89

Hawkesworth, John 1720-1773 ....DLB-142
Hawkins, Sir Anthony Hope (see Hope, Anthony)
Hawkins, Sir John 1719-1789.......DLB-104, 142
Hawkins, Walter Everette 1883-? DLB-50
Hawthorne, Nathaniel 1804-1864
 ...DLB-1, 74, 183, 223, 269; DS-5; CDALB-2
 The Nathaniel Hawthorne Society....... Y-00
 The Old Manse DLB-223
Hawthorne, Sophia Peabody
 1809-1871 ....DLB-183, 239
Hay, John 1835-1905........... DLB-12, 47, 189
Hay, John 1915- DLB-275
Hayashi Fumiko 1903-1951............DLB-180
Haycox, Ernest 1899-1950 ....DLB-206
Haycraft, Anna Margaret (see Ellis, Alice Thomas)
Hayden, Robert
 1913-1980 ....DLB-5, 76; CDALB-1
Haydon, Benjamin Robert 1786-1846 ...DLB-110
Hayes, John Michael 1919- DLB-26
Hayley, William 1745-1820..........DLB-93, 142
Haym, Rudolf 1821-1901 ....DLB-129
Hayman, Robert 1575-1629.............DLB-99
Hayman, Ronald 1932- DLB-155
Hayne, Paul Hamilton
 1830-1886.............. DLB-3, 64, 79, 248
Hays, Mary 1760-1843 ....DLB-142, 158
Hayward, John 1905-1965............DLB-201
Haywood, Eliza 1693?-1756 ....DLB-39
 Dedication of Lasselia [excerpt]
 (1723).......................DLB-39
 Preface to The Disguis'd Prince
 [excerpt] (1723)................DLB-39
 The Tea-Table [excerpt] DLB-39
Willis P. Hazard [publishing house].......DLB-49
Hazlitt, William 1778-1830 .... DLB-110, 158
Hazzard, Shirley 1931- Y-82
Head, Bessie
 1937-1986 .... DLB-117, 225; CDWLB-3
Headley, Joel T. 1813-1897 ... DLB-30, 183; DS-13
Heaney, Seamus 1939-...DLB-40; Y-95; CDBLB-8
 Nobel Lecture 1994: Crediting Poetry... Y-95
Heard, Nathan C. 1936- DLB-33
Hearn, Lafcadio 1850-1904 ...... DLB-12, 78, 189
Hearn, Mary Anne (Marianne Farningham,
 Eva Hope) 1834-1909 ....DLB-240
Hearne, John 1926- DLB-117
Hearne, Samuel 1745-1792..............DLB-99
Hearne, Thomas 1678?-1735 ....DLB-213
Hearst, William Randolph 1863-1951.....DLB-25
Hearst, William Randolph, Jr.
 1908-1993 ....DLB-127
Heartman, Charles Frederick 1883-1953..DLB-187
Heath, Catherine 1924- DLB-14
Heath, James Ewell 1792-1862..........DLB-248
Heath, Roy A. K. 1926- DLB-117
Heath-Stubbs, John 1918- DLB-27
Heavysege, Charles 1816-1876 ....DLB-99

Hebbel, Friedrich 1813-1863............ DLB-129; CDWLB-2
Hebel, Johann Peter 1760-1826.......... DLB-90
Heber, Richard 1774-1833 .... DLB-184
Hébert, Anne 1916-2000................ DLB-68
Hébert, Jacques 1923- DLB-53
Hecht, Anthony 1923- DLB-5, 169
Hecht, Ben 1894-1964 ....DLB-7, 9, 25, 26, 28, 86
Hecker, Isaac Thomas 1819-1888 .... DLB-1, 243
Hedge, Frederic Henry 1805-1890 .... DLB-1, 59, 243; DS-5
Hefner, Hugh M. 1926- DLB-137
Hegel, Georg Wilhelm Friedrich 1770-1831..................... DLB-90
Heide, Robert 1939- DLB-249
Heidish, Marcy 1947- Y-82
Heißenbüttel, Helmut 1921-1996......... DLB-75
Heike monogatari................... DLB-203
Hein, Christoph 1944- ... DLB-124; CDWLB-2
Hein, Piet 1905-1996 .... DLB-214
Heine, Heinrich 1797-1856 ... DLB-90; CDWLB-2
Heinemann, Larry 1944- DS-9
William Heinemann Limited DLB-112
Heinesen, William 1900-1991.......... DLB-214
Heinlein, Robert A. 1907-1988 .... DLB-8
Heinrich, Willi 1920- DLB-75
Heinrich Julius of Brunswick 1564-1613 . DLB-164
Heinrich von dem Türlîn flourished circa 1230 .... DLB-138
Heinrich von Melk flourished after 1160 .... DLB-148
Heinrich von Veldeke circa 1145-circa 1190 .... DLB-138
Heinse, Wilhelm 1746-1803 .... DLB-94
Heinz, W. C. 1915- DLB-171
Heiskell, John 1872-1972.............. DLB-127
Hejinian, Lyn 1941- DLB-165
Heliand circa 850..................... DLB-148
Heller, Joseph 1923-1999 ......DLB-2, 28, 227; Y-80, 99, 02
  Excerpts from Joseph Heller's USC Address, "The Literature of Despair".................... Y-96
  Remembering Joe Heller, by William Price Fox..................... Y-99
  A Tribute to Joseph Heller Y-99
Heller, Michael 1937- DLB-165
Hellman, Lillian 1906-1984 .....DLB-7, 228; Y-84
Hellwig, Johann 1609-1674............ DLB-164
Helprin, Mark 1947- Y-85; CDALB-7
Helwig, David 1938- DLB-60
Hemans, Felicia 1793-1835............. DLB-96
Hemenway, Abby Maria 1828-1890..... DLB-243
Hemingway, Ernest 1899-1961 .... DLB-4, 9, 102, 210; Y-81, 87, 99; DS-1, 15, 16; CDALB-4
  A Centennial Celebration Y-99
  Come to Papa Y-99

The Ernest Hemingway Collection at the John F. Kennedy Library Y-99
Ernest Hemingway Declines to Introduce *War and Peace* Y-01
Ernest Hemingway's Reaction to James Gould Cozzens............. Y-98
Ernest Hemingway's Toronto Journalism Revisited: With Three Previously Unrecorded Stories................ Y-92
Falsifying Hemingway Y-96
Hemingway Centenary Celebration at the JFK Library Y-99
The Hemingway/Fenton Correspondence Y-02
Hemingway in the JFK............... Y-99
The Hemingway Letters Project Finds an Editor.................. Y-02
Hemingway Salesmen's Dummies Y-00
Hemingway: Twenty-Five Years Later... Y-85
A Literary Archaeologist Digs On: A Brief Interview with Michael Reynolds Y-99
Not Immediately Discernible... but Eventually Quite Clear: The *First Light* and *Final Years* of Hemingway's Centenary Y-99
Packaging Papa: *The Garden of Eden* Y-86
Second International Hemingway Colloquium: Cuba Y-98
Hémon, Louis 1880-1913.............. DLB-92
Hempel, Amy 1951- DLB-218
Hempel, Carl G. 1905-1997 ....DLB-279
Hemphill, Paul 1936- Y-87
Hénault, Gilles 1920-1996 .... DLB-88
Henchman, Daniel 1689-1761 .... DLB-24
Henderson, Alice Corbin 1881-1949 ..... DLB-54
Henderson, Archibald 1877-1963 .... DLB-103
Henderson, David 1942- DLB-41
Henderson, George Wylie 1904-1965 .... DLB-51
Henderson, Zenna 1917-1983........... DLB-8
Henighan, Tom 1934- DLB-251
Henisch, Peter 1943- DLB-85
Henley, Beth 1952- Y-86
Henley, William Ernest 1849-1903 ...... DLB-19
Henniker, Florence 1855-1923 .... DLB-135
Henning, Rachel 1826-1914 .... DLB-230
Henningsen, Agnes 1868-1962......... DLB-214
Henry, Alexander 1739-1824 .... DLB-99
Henry, Buck 1930- DLB-26
Henry, Marguerite 1902-1997 .... DLB-22
Henry, O. (see Porter, William Sydney)
Henry, Robert Selph 1889-1970 .... DLB-17
Henry, Will (see Allen, Henry W.)
Henry VIII of England 1491-1547...... DLB-132
Henry of Ghent circa 1217-1229 - 1293 .. DLB-115
Henryson, Robert 1420s or 1430s-circa 1505 .... DLB-146
Henschke, Alfred (see Klabund)
Hensher, Philip 1965- DLB-267

Hensley, Sophie Almon 1866-1946 ...... DLB-99
Henson, Lance 1944- DLB-175
Henty, G. A. 1832-1902.......... DLB-18, 141
  The Henty Society Y-98
Hentz, Caroline Lee 1800-1856 ...... DLB-3, 248
Heraclitus flourished circa 500 B.C............DLB-176
Herbert, Agnes circa 1880-1960.........DLB-174
Herbert, Alan Patrick 1890-1971 .....DLB-10, 191
Herbert, Edward, Lord, of Cherbury 1582-1648 ....DLB-121, 151, 252
Herbert, Frank 1920-1986 ..... DLB-8; CDALB-7
Herbert, George 1593-1633 .. DLB-126; CDBLB-1
Herbert, Henry William 1807-1858 .... DLB-3, 73
Herbert, John 1926- DLB-53
Herbert, Mary Sidney, Countess of Pembroke (see Sidney, Mary)
Herbert, Xavier 1901-1984 .... DLB-260
Herbert, Zbigniew 1924-1998 .... DLB-232; CDWLB-4
Herbst, Josephine 1892-1969 .... DLB-9
Herburger, Gunter 1932- DLB-75, 124
Hercules, Frank E. M. 1917-1996 .... DLB-33
Herder, Johann Gottfried 1744-1803 ..... DLB-97
B. Herder Book Company............. DLB-49
Heredia, José-María de 1842-1905 .....DLB-217
Herford, Charles Harold 1853-1931 .... DLB-149
Hergesheimer, Joseph 1880-1954..... DLB-9, 102
Heritage Press...................... DLB-46
Hermann the Lame 1013-1054......... DLB-148
Hermes, Johann Timotheu 1738-1821 .... DLB-97
Hermlin, Stephan 1915-1997 .... DLB-69
Hernández, Alfonso C. 1938- DLB-122
Hernández, Inés 1947- DLB-122
Hernández, Miguel 1910-1942 .... DLB-134
Hernton, Calvin C. 1932- DLB-38
Herodotus circa 484 B.C.-circa 420 B.C. DLB-176; CDWLB-1
Heron, Robert 1764-1807 .... DLB-142
Herr, Michael 1940- DLB-185
Herrera, Juan Felipe 1948- DLB-122
E. R. Herrick and Company DLB-49
Herrick, Robert 1591-1674 .... DLB-126
Herrick, Robert 1868-1938..........DLB-9, 12, 78
Herrick, William 1915- Y-83
Herrmann, John 1900-1959 .... DLB-4
Hersey, John 1914-1993 ....DLB-6, 185, 278; CDALB-7
Hertel, François 1905-1985............. DLB-68
Hervé-Bazin, Jean Pierre Marie (see Bazin, Hervé)
Hervey, John, Lord 1696-1743 .... DLB-101
Herwig, Georg 1817-1875 .... DLB-133
Herzen, Alexander (Aleksandr Ivanovich Gersten) 1812-1870 ....DLB-277
Herzog, Emile Salomon Wilhelm (see Maurois, André)
Hesiod eighth century B.C. DLB-176

Hesse, Hermann 1877-1962 . . . DLB-66; CDWLB-2

Hessus, Eobanus 1488-1540 . . . . DLB-179

Heureka! (see Kertész, Imre and Nobel Prize in Literature: 2002) Y-02

Hewat, Alexander circa 1743-circa 1824 . . . DLB-30

Hewitt, John 1907-1987 . . . . DLB-27

Hewlett, Maurice 1861-1923 . . . . DLB-34, 156

Heyen, William 1940- DLB-5

Heyer, Georgette 1902-1974 . . . . DLB-77, 191

Heym, Stefan 1913-2001 . . . . DLB-69

Heyse, Paul 1830-1914 . . . . DLB-129

Heytesbury, William circa 1310-1372 or 1373 . . . . DLB-115

Heyward, Dorothy 1890-1961 . . . . DLB-7, 249

Heyward, DuBose 1885-1940 . . . DLB-7, 9, 45, 249

Heywood, John 1497?-1580? DLB-136

Heywood, Thomas 1573 or 1574-1641 . . . . DLB-62

Hibbs, Ben 1901-1975 . . . . DLB-137

"The Saturday Evening Post reaffirms a policy," Ben Hibb's Statement in *The Saturday Evening Post* (16 May 1942) DLB-137

Hichens, Robert S. 1864-1950 . . . . DLB-153

Hickey, Emily 1845-1924 . . . . DLB-199

Hickman, William Albert 1877-1957 . . . . . DLB-92

Hicks, Granville 1901-1982 . . . . DLB-246

Hidalgo, José Luis 1919-1947 . . . . DLB-108

Hiebert, Paul 1892-1987 . . . . DLB-68

Hieng, Andrej 1925- DLB-181

Hierro, José 1922-2002 . . . . DLB-108

Higgins, Aidan 1927- DLB-14

Higgins, Colin 1941-1988 . . . . DLB-26

Higgins, George V. 1939-1999 . . . . DLB-2; Y-81, 98–99

Afterword [in response to Cozzen's *Mens Rea* (or Something)] Y-97

At End of Day: The Last George V. Higgins Novel Y-99

The Books of George V. Higgins: A Checklist of Editions and Printings Y-00

George V. Higgins in Class Y-02

Higgins to Julian Symons [letter] Y-99

Tribute to Alfred A. Knopf Y-84

Tributes to George V. Higgins Y-99

"What You Lose on the Swings You Make Up on the Merry-Go-Round" Y-99

Higginson, Thomas Wentworth 1823-1911 . . . . DLB-1, 64, 243

Highwater, Jamake 1942?- DLB-52; Y-85

Hijuelos, Oscar 1951- DLB-145

Hildegard von Bingen 1098-1179 . . . . DLB-148

Das Hildesbrandslied circa 820 . . . . DLB-148; CDWLB-2

Hildesheimer, Wolfgang 1916-1991 . . DLB-69, 124

Hildreth, Richard 1807-1865 . . . DLB-1, 30, 59, 235

Hill, Aaron 1685-1750 . . . . DLB-84

Hill, Geoffrey 1932- DLB-40; CDBLB-8

George M. Hill Company DLB-49

Hill, "Sir" John 1714?-1775 . . . . DLB-39

Lawrence Hill and Company, Publishers . . DLB-46

Hill, Leslie 1880-1960 . . . . DLB-51

Hill, Reginald 1936- DLB-276

Hill, Susan 1942- DLB-14, 139

Hill, Walter 1942- DLB-44

Hill and Wang DLB-46

Hillberry, Conrad 1928- DLB-120

Hillerman, Tony 1925- DLB-206

Hilliard, Gray and Company DLB-49

Hills, Lee 1906-2000 . . . . DLB-127

Hillyer, Robert 1895-1961 . . . . DLB-54

Hilton, James 1900-1954 . . . . DLB-34, 77

Hilton, Walter died 1396 . . . . DLB-146

Hilton and Company DLB-49

Himes, Chester 1909-1984 . . . . . . DLB-2, 76, 143, 226

Joseph Hindmarsh [publishing house] DLB-170

Hine, Daryl 1936- DLB-60

Hingley, Ronald 1920- DLB-155

Hinojosa-Smith, Rolando 1929- DLB-82

Hinton, S. E. 1948- CDALB-7

Hippel, Theodor Gottlieb von 1741-1796 . . . . DLB-97

Hippocrates of Cos flourished circa 425 B.C. DLB-176; CDWLB-1

Hirabayashi Taiko 1905-1972 . . . . DLB-180

Hirsch, E. D., Jr. 1928- DLB-67

Hirsch, Edward 1950- DLB-120

Hoagland, Edward 1932- DLB-6

Hoagland, Everett H., III 1942- DLB-41

Hoban, Russell 1925- DLB-52; Y-90

Hobbes, Thomas 1588-1679 . . . DLB-151, 252, 281

Hobby, Oveta 1905-1995 . . . . DLB-127

Hobby, William 1878-1964 . . . . DLB-127

Hobsbaum, Philip 1932- DLB-40

Hobson, Laura Z. 1900- DLB-28

Hobson, Sarah 1947- DLB-204

Hoby, Thomas 1530-1566 . . . . DLB-132

Hoccleve, Thomas circa 1368-circa 1437 . . . . DLB-146

Hochhuth, Rolf 1931- DLB-124

Hochman, Sandra 1936- DLB-5

Hocken, Thomas Morland 1836-1910 . . . . DLB-184

Hocking, William Ernest 1873-1966 . . . . . DLB-270

Hodder and Stoughton, Limited DLB-106

Hodgins, Jack 1938- DLB-60

Hodgman, Helen 1945- DLB-14

Hodgskin, Thomas 1787-1869 . . . . DLB-158

Hodgson, Ralph 1871-1962 . . . . DLB-19

Hodgson, William Hope 1877-1918 . . . . DLB-70, 153, 156, 178

Hoe, Robert, III 1839-1909 . . . . DLB-187

Hoeg, Peter 1957- DLB-214

Hoffenstein, Samuel 1890-1947 . . . . DLB-11

Hoffman, Charles Fenno 1806-1884 . . . DLB-3, 250

Hoffman, Daniel 1923- DLB-5

Tribute to Robert Graves Y-85

Hoffmann, E. T. A. 1776-1822 . . . . DLB-90; CDWLB-2

Hoffman, Frank B. 1888-1958 . . . . DLB-188

Hoffman, William 1925- DLB-234

Tribute to Paxton Davis Y-94

Hoffmanswaldau, Christian Hoffman von 1616-1679 . . . . DLB-168

Hofmann, Michael 1957- DLB-40

Hofmannsthal, Hugo von 1874-1929 . . . . DLB-81, 118; CDWLB-2

Hofstadter, Richard 1916-1970 . . . . . . DLB-17, 246

Hogan, Desmond 1950- DLB-14

Hogan, Linda 1947- DLB-175

Hogan and Thompson DLB-49

Hogarth Press DLB-112; DS-10

Hogg, James 1770-1835 . . . . DLB-93, 116, 159

Hohberg, Wolfgang Helmhard Freiherr von 1612-1688 . . . . DLB-168

von Hohenheim, Philippus Aureolus Theophrastus Bombastus (see Paracelsus)

Hohl, Ludwig 1904-1980 . . . . DLB-56

Højholt, Per 1928- DLB-214

Holan, Vladimír 1905-1980 . . . . DLB-215

Holbrook, David 1923- DLB-14, 40

Holcroft, Thomas 1745-1809 . . . . . DLB-39, 89, 158

Preface to *Alwyn* (1780) DLB-39

Holden, Jonathan 1941- DLB-105

"Contemporary Verse Story-telling" . . DLB-105

Holden, Molly 1927-1981 . . . . DLB-40

Hölderlin, Friedrich 1770-1843 . . . . DLB-90; CDWLB-2

Holdstock, Robert 1948- DLB-261

Holiday House DLB-46

Holinshed, Raphael died 1580 . . . . DLB-167

Holland, J. G. 1819-1881 . . . . DS-13

Holland, Norman N. 1927- DLB-67

Hollander, John 1929- DLB-5

Holley, Marietta 1836-1926 . . . . DLB-11

Hollinghurst, Alan 1954- DLB-207

Hollingsworth, Margaret 1940- DLB-60

Hollo, Anselm 1934- DLB-40

Holloway, Emory 1885-1977 . . . . DLB-103

Holloway, John 1920- DLB-27

Holloway House Publishing Company DLB-46

Holme, Constance 1880-1955 . . . . DLB-34

Holmes, Abraham S. 1821?-1908 . . . . DLB-99

Holmes, John Clellon 1926-1988 . . . . . DLB-16, 237

"Four Essays on the Beat Generation" DLB-16

Holmes, Mary Jane 1825-1907 . . . . . DLB-202, 221

Holmes, Oliver Wendell 1809-1894 . . . . DLB-1, 189, 235; CDALB-2

Holmes, Richard 1945- DLB-155

Holmes, Thomas James 1874-1959 . . . . . . DLB-187

Holroyd, Michael 1935- DLB-155; Y-99	Tribute to Alfred A. Knopf............ Y-84	The William Dean Howells Society Y-01
Holst, Hermann E. von 1841-1904....... DLB-47	Horizon Press..................... DLB-46	Howitt, Mary 1799-1888 ....DLB-110, 199
Holt, John 1721-1784 .... DLB-43	Hornby, C. H. St. John 1867-1946 ...... DLB-201	Howitt, William 1792-1879............ DLB-110
Henry Holt and Company DLB-49, 284	Hornby, Nick 1957- DLB-207	Hoyem, Andrew 1935- DLB-5
Holt, Rinehart and Winston............ DLB-46	Horne, Frank 1899-1974............... DLB-51	Hoyers, Anna Ovena 1584-1655 .... DLB-164
Holtby, Winifred 1898-1935 .... DLB-191	Horne, Richard Henry (Hengist) 1802 or 1803-1884................ DLB-32	Hoyle, Fred 1915-2001................ DLB-261
Holthusen, Hans Egon 1913-1997 .... DLB-69	Horne, Thomas 1608-1654 .... DLB-281	Hoyos, Angela de 1940- DLB-82
Hölty, Ludwig Christoph Heinrich 1748-1776..................... DLB-94	Horney, Karen 1885-1952 .... DLB-246	Henry Hoyt [publishing house] DLB-49
Holub, Miroslav 1923-1998 .... DLB-232; CDWLB-4	Hornung, E. W. 1866-1921 .... DLB-70	Hoyt, Palmer 1897-1979 ....DLB-127
Holz, Arno 1863-1929 .... DLB-118	Horovitz, Israel 1939- DLB-7	Hrabal, Bohumil 1914-1997 .... DLB-232
Home, Henry, Lord Kames (see Kames, Henry Home, Lord)	Horton, George Moses 1797?-1883?...... DLB-50	Hrabanus Maurus 776?-856 .... DLB-148
Home, John 1722-1808............... DLB-84	George Moses Horton Society Y-99	Hronský, Josef Cíger 1896-1960........ DLB-215
Home, William Douglas 1912- DLB-13	Horváth, Ödön von 1901-1938 ..... DLB-85, 124	Hrotsvit of Gandersheim circa 935-circa 1000 .... DLB-148
Home Publishing Company DLB-49	Horwood, Harold 1923- DLB-60	Hubbard, Elbert 1856-1915 .... DLB-91
Homer circa eighth-seventh centuries B.C. DLB-176; CDWLB-1	E. and E. Hosford [publishing house]..... DLB-49	Hubbard, Kin 1868-1930 .... DLB-11
Homer, Winslow 1836-1910 .... DLB-188	Hoskens, Jane Fenn 1693-1770? DLB-200	Hubbard, William circa 1621-1704....... DLB-24
Homes, Geoffrey (see Mainwaring, Daniel)	Hoskyns, John 1566-1638 .... DLB-121, 281	Huber, Therese 1764-1829 .... DLB-90
Honan, Park 1928- DLB-111	Hosokawa Yūsai 1535-1610 .... DLB-203	Huch, Friedrich 1873-1913............. DLB-66
Hone, William 1780-1842......... DLB-110, 158	Hospers, John 1918- DLB-279	Huch, Ricarda 1864-1947.............. DLB-66
Hongo, Garrett Kaoru 1951- DLB-120	Hostovský, Egon 1908-1973 .... DLB-215	Huddle, David 1942- DLB-130
Honig, Edwin 1919- DLB-5	Hotchkiss and Company DLB-49	Hudgins, Andrew 1951- DLB-120, 282
Hood, Hugh 1928-2000 .... DLB-53	Hough, Emerson 1857-1923 .... DLB-9, 212	Hudson, Henry Norman 1814-1886 ..... DLB-64
Hood, Mary 1946- DLB-234	Houghton, Stanley 1881-1913 .... DLB-10	Hudson, Stephen 1868?-1944.........DLB-197
Hood, Thomas 1799-1845 .... DLB-96	Houghton Mifflin Company............ DLB-49	Hudson, W. H. 1841-1922......DLB-98, 153, 174
Hook, Sidney 1902-1989 ....DLB-279	Hours at Home DS-13	Hudson and Goodwin DLB-49
Hook, Theodore 1788-1841 .... DLB-116	Household, Geoffrey 1900-1988......... DLB-87	Huebsch, B. W., oral history Y-99
Hooker, Jeremy 1941- DLB-40	Housman, A. E. 1859-1936 ... DLB-19; CDBLB-5	B. W. Huebsch [publishing house]....... DLB-46
Hooker, Richard 1554-1600 .... DLB-132	Housman, Laurence 1865-1959 .... DLB-10	Hueffer, Oliver Madox 1876-1931 ....DLB-197
Hooker, Thomas 1586-1647 .... DLB-24	Houston, Pam 1962- DLB-244	Huet, Pierre Daniel Preface to *The History of Romances* (1715) DLB-39
hooks, bell 1952- DLB-246	Houwald, Ernst von 1778-1845 .... DLB-90	Hugh of St. Victor circa 1096-1141 ..... DLB-208
Hooper, Johnson Jones 1815-1862................. DLB-3, 11, 248	Hovey, Richard 1864-1900............ DLB-54	Hughes, David 1930- DLB-14
Hope, Anthony 1863-1933........ DLB-153, 156	Howard, Donald R. 1927-1987......... DLB-111	Hughes, Dusty 1947- DLB-233
Hope, Christopher 1944- DLB-225	Howard, Maureen 1930- Y-83	Hughes, Hatcher 1881-1945............ DLB-249
Hope, Eva (see Hearn, Mary Anne)	Howard, Richard 1929- DLB-5	Hughes, John 1677-1720 .... DLB-84
Hope, Laurence (Adela Florence Cory Nicolson) 1865-1904......... DLB-240	Howard, Roy W. 1883-1964 .... DLB-29	Hughes, Langston 1902-1967........ DLB-4, 7, 48, 51, 86, 228; ; DS-15; CDALB-5
Hopkins, Ellice 1836-1904 .... DLB-190	Howard, Sidney 1891-1939 ....DLB-7, 26, 249	Hughes, Richard 1900-1976 .... DLB-15, 161
Hopkins, Gerard Manley 1844-1889 .... DLB-35, 57; CDBLB-5	Howard, Thomas, second Earl of Arundel 1585-1646 .... DLB-213	Hughes, Ted 1930-1998 .... DLB-40, 161
Hopkins, John ?-1570 .... DLB-132	Howe, E. W. 1853-1937 .... DLB-12, 25	Hughes, Thomas 1822-1896 .... DLB-18, 163
Hopkins, John H., and Son............ DLB-46	Howe, Henry 1816-1893 .... DLB-30	Hugo, Richard 1923-1982 .... DLB-5, 206
Hopkins, Lemuel 1750-1801 .... DLB-37	Howe, Irving 1920-1993................ DLB-67	Hugo, Victor 1802-1885........DLB-119, 192, 217
Hopkins, Pauline Elizabeth 1859-1930.... DLB-50	Howe, Joseph 1804-1873 .... DLB-99	Hugo Awards and Nebula Awards DLB-8
Hopkins, Samuel 1721-1803 .... DLB-31	Howe, Julia Ward 1819-1910 .... DLB-1, 189, 235	Huidobro, Vicente 1893-1948 .... DLB-283
Hopkinson, Francis 1737-1791 .... DLB-31	Howe, Percival Presland 1886-1944..... DLB-149	Hull, Richard 1896-1973 .... DLB-77
Hopkinson, Nalo 1960- DLB-251	Howe, Susan 1937- DLB-120	Hulme, T. E. 1883-1917............... DLB-19
Hopper, Nora (Mrs. Nora Chesson) 1871-1906...................... DLB-240	Howell, Clark, Sr. 1863-1936 .... DLB-25	Hulton, Anne ?-1779?................. DLB-200
Hoppin, Augustus 1828-1896.......... DLB-188	Howell, Evan P. 1839-1905 .... DLB-23	Humboldt, Alexander von 1769-1859 .... DLB-90
Hora, Josef 1891-1945 ..... DLB-215; CDWLB-4	Howell, James 1594?-1666 .... DLB-151	Humboldt, Wilhelm von 1767-1835 ...... DLB-90
Horace 65 B.C.-8 B.C. DLB-211; CDWLB-1	Howell, Soskin and Company DLB-46	Hume, David 1711-1776 .... DLB-104, 252
Horgan, Paul 1903-1995......DLB-102, 212; Y-85	Howell, Warren Richardson 1912-1984.. DLB-140	Hume, Fergus 1859-1932 .... DLB-70
	Howells, William Dean 1837-1920 ....DLB-12, 64, 74, 79, 189; CDALB-3	Hume, Sophia 1702-1774 .... DLB-200
	Introduction to Paul Laurence Dunbar's *Lyrics of Lowly Life* (1896) DLB-50	Hume-Rothery, Mary Catherine 1824-1885 .... DLB-240

Humishuma (see Mourning Dove)

Hummer, T. R. 1950- DLB-120

Humor
    American Humor: A Historical
        Survey DLB-11

    American Humor Studies Association ... Y-99

    The Comic Tradition Continued
        [in the British Novel] DLB-15

    Humorous Book Illustration DLB-11

    International Society for Humor Studies . Y-99

    Newspaper Syndication of American
        Humor.....................DLB-11

    Selected Humorous Magazines
        (1820-1950) DLB-11

Humphrey, Duke of Gloucester
    1391-1447 ....DLB-213

Humphrey, William
    1924-1997 .... DLB-6, 212, 234, 278

Humphreys, David 1752-1818...........DLB-37

Humphreys, Emyr 1919- DLB-15

Bruce Humphries [publishing house] DLB-46

Huncke, Herbert 1915-1996 ....DLB-16

Huneker, James Gibbons 1857-1921 ......DLB-71

Hunold, Christian Friedrich 1681-1721 ...DLB-168

Hunt, Irene 1907- DLB-52

Hunt, Leigh 1784-1859 .... DLB-96, 110, 144

Hunt, Violet 1862-1942................ DLB-162, 197

Hunt, William Gibbes 1791-1833 ....DLB-73

Hunter, Evan 1926- Y-82

    Tribute to John D. MacDonald Y-86

Hunter, Jim 1939- DLB-14

Hunter, Kristin 1931- DLB-33

    Tribute to Julian Mayfield Y-84

Hunter, Mollie 1922- DLB-161

Hunter, N. C. 1908-1971 ....DLB-10

Hunter-Duvar, John 1821-1899..........DLB-99

Huntington, Henry E. 1850-1927 ....DLB-140

    The Henry E. Huntington Library Y-92

Huntington, Susan Mansfield 1791-1823 ..DLB-200

Hurd and Houghton DLB-49

Hurst, Fannie 1889-1968 ....DLB-86

Hurst and Blackett...................DLB-106

Hurst and Company DLB-49

Hurston, Zora Neale
    1901?-1960 ....DLB-51, 86; CDALB-7

Husson, Jules-François-Félix (see Champfleury)

Huston, John 1906-1987 ....DLB-26

Hutcheson, Francis 1694-1746.......DLB-31, 252

Hutchinson, Ron 1947- DLB-245

Hutchinson, R. C. 1907-1975 ....DLB-191

Hutchinson, Thomas 1711-1780 ......DLB-30, 31

Hutchinson and Company
    (Publishers) Limited DLB-112

Huth, Angela 1938- DLB-271

Hutton, Richard Holt 1826-1897.........DLB-57

von Hutten, Ulrich 1488-1523 ....DLB-179

Huxley, Aldous 1894-1963
    .....DLB-36, 100, 162, 195, 255; CDBLB-6

Huxley, Elspeth Josceline
    1907-1997 .... DLB-77, 204

Huxley, T. H. 1825-1895 ....DLB-57

Huyghue, Douglas Smith 1816-1891......DLB-99

Huysmans, Joris-Karl 1848-1907 ....DLB-123

Hwang, David Henry 1957- DLB-212, 228

Hyde, Donald 1909-1966................DLB-187

Hyde, Mary 1912- DLB-187

Hyman, Trina Schart 1939- DLB-61

I

Iavorsky, Stefan 1658-1722 ....DLB-150

Iazykov, Nikolai Mikhailovich
    1803-1846 ....DLB-205

Ibáñez, Armando P. 1949- DLB-209

Ibn Bajja circa 1077-1138 ....DLB-115

Ibn Gabirol, Solomon
    circa 1021-circa 1058...............DLB-115

Ibuse Masuji 1898-1993................DLB-180

Ichijō Kanera (see Ichijō Kaneyoshi)

Ichijō Kaneyoshi (Ichijō Kanera)
    1402-1481 ....DLB-203

Iffland, August Wilhelm 1759-1814.......DLB-94

Ignatieff, Michael 1947- DLB-267

Ignatow, David 1914-1997...............DLB-5

Ike, Chukwuemeka 1931- DLB-157

Ikkyū Sōjun 1394-1481 ....DLB-203

Iles, Francis (see Berkeley, Anthony)

Il'f, Il'ia (Il'ia Arnol'dovich Fainzil'berg)
    1897-1937 ....DLB-272

Illich, Ivan 1926-2002 ....DLB-242

Illustration
    Children's Book Illustration in the
        Twentieth Century DLB-61

    Children's Illustrators, 1800-1880 ...DLB-163

    Early American Book Illustration DLB-49

    The Iconography of Science-Fiction
        Art........................DLB-8

    The Illustration of Early German
        Literary Manuscripts, circa
        1150-circa 1300 ....DLB-148

    Minor Illustrators, 1880-1914 ......DLB-141

Illyés, Gyula 1902-1983 ..... DLB-215; CDWLB-4

Imbs, Bravig 1904-1946............DLB-4; DS-15

Imbuga, Francis D. 1947- DLB-157

Immermann, Karl 1796-1840...........DLB-133

Inchbald, Elizabeth 1753-1821..........DLB-39, 89

Indiana University Press Y-02

Ingamells, Rex 1913-1955 ....DLB-260

Inge, William 1913-1973 ... DLB-7, 249; CDALB-1

Ingelow, Jean 1820-1897 ....DLB-35, 163

Ingersoll, Ralph 1900-1985 ....DLB-127

The Ingersoll Prizes Y-84

Ingoldsby, Thomas (see Barham, Richard Harris)

Ingraham, Joseph Holt 1809-1860.....DLB-3, 248

Inman, John 1805-1850 ....DLB-73

Innerhofer, Franz 1944- DLB-85

Innes, Michael (J. I. M. Stewart)
    1906-1994 ....DLB-276

Innis, Harold Adams 1894-1952 ....DLB-88

Innis, Mary Quayle 1899-1972 ....DLB-88

Inō Sōgi 1421-1502 ....DLB-203

Inoue Yasushi 1907-1991 ....DLB-182

"The Greatness of Southern Literature":
    League of the South Institute for the
    Study of Southern Culture and History
    .... Y-02

International Publishers Company DLB-46

Internet (publishing and commerce)
    Author Websites....................Y-97

    The Book Trade and the Internet Y-00

    E-Books Turn the Corner Y-98

    The E-Researcher: Possibilities
        and Pitfalls................... Y-00

    Interviews on E-publishing............. Y-00

    John Updike on the Internet Y-97

    LitCheck Website Y-01

    Virtual Books and Enemies of Books ... Y-00

Interviews
    Adoff, Arnold Y-01
    Aldridge, John W. Y-91
    Anastas, Benjamin Y-98
    Baker, Nicholson Y-00
    Bank, Melissa Y-98
    Bass, T. J......................... Y-80
    Bernstein, Harriet.................. Y-82
    Betts, Doris Y-82
    Bosworth, David Y-82
    Bottoms, David Y-83
    Bowers, Fredson................... Y-80
    Burnshaw, Stanley Y-97
    Carpenter, Humphrey Y-84, 99
    Carr, Virginia Spencer.............. Y-00
    Carver, Raymond Y-83
    Cherry, Kelly..................... Y-83
    Conroy, Jack Y-81
    Coppel, Alfred Y-83
    Cowley, Malcolm.................. Y-81
    Davis, Paxton..................... Y-89
    Devito, Carlo Y-94
    De Vries, Peter.................... Y-82
    Dickey, James..................... Y-82
    Donald, David Herbert Y-87
    Editors, Conversations with.......... Y-95
    Ellroy, James Y-91
    Fancher, Betsy Y-83
    Faust, Irvin...................... Y-00
    Fulton, Len...................... Y-86
    Furst, Alan Y-01
    Garrett, George Y-83
    Gelfman, Jane.................... Y-93
    Goldwater, Walter................. Y-93

Gores, Joe Y-02	Schroeder, Patricia Y-99	Jackson, Angela 1951- DLB-41
Greenfield, George Y-91	Schulberg, Budd Y-81, 01	Jackson, Charles 1903-1968 .... DLB-234
Griffin, Bryan Y-81	Scribner, Charles, III Y-94	Jackson, Helen Hunt
Groom, Winston................ Y-01	Sipper, Ralph Y-94	1830-1885 .... DLB-42, 47, 186, 189
Guilds, John Caldwell........... Y-92	Smith, Cork Y-95	Jackson, Holbrook 1874-1948.......... DLB-98
Hamilton, Virginia Y-01	Staley, Thomas F................. Y-00	Jackson, Laura Riding 1901-1991....... DLB-48
Hardin, James Y-92	Styron, William................... Y-80	Jackson, Shirley
Harris, Mark................... Y-80	Talese, Nan..................... Y-94	1916-1965 .... DLB-6, 234; CDALB-1
Harrison, Jim Y-82	Thornton, John.................. Y-94	Jacob, Max 1876-1944 .... DLB-258
Hazzard, Shirley Y-82	Toth, Susan Allen Y-86	Jacob, Naomi 1884?-1964............ DLB-191
Herrick, William................ Y-01	Tyler, Anne Y-82	Jacob, Piers Anthony Dillingham
Higgins, George V............... Y-98	Vaughan, Samuel Y-97	(see Anthony, Piers)
Hoban, Russell Y-90	Von Ogtrop, Kristin Y-92	Jacob, Violet 1863-1946 .... DLB-240
Holroyd, Michael Y-99	Wallenstein, Barry Y-92	Jacobi, Friedrich Heinrich 1743-1819 ..... DLB-94
Horowitz, Glen Y-90	Weintraub, Stanley................ Y-82	Jacobi, Johann Georg 1740-1841......... DLB-97
Iggulden, John.................. Y-01	Williams, J. Chamberlain Y-84	George W. Jacobs and Company........ DLB-49
Jakes, John.................... Y-83	Into the Past: William Jovanovich's	Jacobs, Harriet 1813-1897........... DLB-239
Jenkinson, Edward B.............. Y-82	Reflections in Publishing Y-02	Jacobs, Joseph 1854-1916 .... DLB-141
Jenks, Tom Y-86	The National Library of Ireland's	Jacobs, W. W. 1863-1943............ DLB-135
Kaplan, Justin Y-86	New James Joyce Manuscripts Y-02	The W. W. Jacobs Appreciation Society . Y-98
King, Florence.................. Y-85	Irving, John 1942- DLB-6, 278; Y-82	Jacobsen, Jørgen-Frantz 1900-1938...... DLB-214
Klopfer, Donald S. Y-97	Irving, Washington 1783-1859	Jacobsen, Josephine 1908- DLB-244
Krug, Judith Y-82	.... DLB-3, 11, 30, 59, 73, 74,	Jacobson, Dan 1929- DLB-14, 207, 225
Lamm, Donald Y-95	183, 186, 250; CDALB-2	Jacobson, Howard 1942- DLB-207
Laughlin, James................. Y-96	Irwin, Grace 1907- DLB-68	Jacques de Vitry circa 1160/1170-1240... DLB-208
Lawrence, Starling Y-95	Irwin, Will 1873-1948............... DLB-25	Jæger, Frank 1926-1977.............. DLB-214
Lindsay, Jack.................... Y-84	Isaksson, Ulla 1916-2000 .... DLB-257	William Jaggard [publishing house] DLB-170
Mailer, Norman Y-97	Iser, Wolfgang 1926- DLB-242	Jahier, Piero 1884-1966 .... DLB-114, 264
Manchester, William.............. Y-85	Isherwood, Christopher	Jahnn, Hans Henny 1894-1959 ..... DLB-56, 124
Max, D. T. Y-94	1904-1986 ....DLB-15, 195; Y-86	Jakes, John 1932- DLB-278; Y-83
McCormack, Thomas.............. Y-98	The Christopher Isherwood Archive,	Tribute to John Gardner............. Y-82
McNamara, Katherine Y-97	The Huntington Library Y-99	Tribute to John D. MacDonald Y-86
Mellen, Joan Y-94	Ishiguro, Kazuo	Jakobson, Roman 1896-1982 .... DLB-242
Menaker, Daniel Y-97	1954- DLB-194	James, Alice 1848-1892............... DLB-221
Mooneyham, Lamarr Y-82	Ishikawa Jun 1899-1987 .... DLB-182	James, C. L. R. 1901-1989 .... DLB-125
Murray, Les Y-01	The Island Trees Case: A Symposium on	James, George P. R. 1801-1860 .... DLB-116
Nosworth, David Y-82	School Library Censorship	James, Henry 1843-1916
O'Connor, Patrick Y-84, 99	An Interview with Judith Krug	......DLB-12, 71, 74, 189; DS-13; CDALB-3
Ozick, Cynthia Y-83	An Interview with Phyllis Schlafly	"The Future of the Novel" (1899) ... DLB-18
Penner, Jonathan................ Y-83	An Interview with Edward B. Jenkinson	"The Novel in [Robert Browning's]
Pennington, Lee Y-82	An Interview with Lamarr Mooneyham	'The Ring and the Book'"
Penzler, Otto.................... Y-96	An Interview with Harriet Bernstein Y-82	(1912) DLB-32
Plimpton, George Y-99	Islas, Arturo	James, John circa 1633-1729 .... DLB-24
Potok, Chaim Y-84	1938-1991 .... DLB-122	James, M. R. 1862-1936 .... DLB-156, 201
Powell, Padgett Y-01	Issit, Debbie 1966- DLB-233	James, Naomi 1949- DLB-204
Prescott, Peter S. Y-86	Ivanišević, Drago 1907-1981 .... DLB-181	James, P. D. (Phyllis Dorothy James White)
Rabe, David Y-91	Ivanov, Vsevolod Viacheslavovich	1920- DLB-87, 276; DS-17; CDBLB-8
Rechy, John.................... Y-82	1895-1963 ....DLB-272	Tribute to Charles Scribner Jr. Y-95
Reid, B. L. Y-83	Ivaska, Astrīde 1926- DLB-232	James, Thomas 1572?-1629 .... DLB-213
Reynolds, Michael Y-95, 99	M. J. Ivers and Company DLB-49	U. P. James [publishing house] DLB-49
Robinson, Derek................ Y-02	Iwaniuk, Wacław 1915- DLB-215	James, Will 1892-1942 ....DS-16
Rollyson, Carl.................. Y-97	Iwano Hōmei 1873-1920............. DLB-180	James, William 1842-1910 ....DLB-270
Rosset, Barney Y-02	Iwaszkiewicz, Jarosław 1894-1980....... DLB-215	James VI of Scotland, I of England
Schlafly, Phyllis.................. Y-82	Iyayi, Festus 1947- DLB-157	1566-1625 ....DLB-151, 172
	Izumi Kyōka 1873-1939 .... DLB-180	*Ane Schort Treatise Conteining Some Revlis and Cautelis to Be Obseruit and Eschewit in Scottis Poesi* (1584) DLB-172

J

Jackmon, Marvin E. (see Marvin X)

Jacks, L. P. 1860-1955 .... DLB-135

Humishuma (see Mourning Dove)

Hummer, T. R. 1950- DLB-120

Humor
   American Humor: A Historical
     Survey.....................DLB-11

   American Humor Studies Association ... Y-99

   The Comic Tradition Continued
     [in the British Novel]..........DLB-15

   Humorous Book Illustration.......DLB-11

   International Society for Humor Studies . Y-99

   Newspaper Syndication of American
     Humor......................DLB-11

   Selected Humorous Magazines
     (1820-1950).................DLB-11

Humphrey, Duke of Gloucester
   1391-1447......................DLB-213

Humphrey, William
   1924-1997..........DLB-6, 212, 234, 278

Humphreys, David 1752-1818..........DLB-37

Humphreys, Emyr 1919-................DLB-15

Bruce Humphries [publishing house].....DLB-46

Huncke, Herbert 1915-1996............DLB-16

Huneker, James Gibbons 1857-1921.......DLB-71

Hunold, Christian Friedrich 1681-1721...DLB-168

Hunt, Irene 1907-....................DLB-52

Hunt, Leigh 1784-1859........DLB-96, 110, 144

Hunt, Violet 1862-1942............DLB-162, 197

Hunt, William Gibbes 1791-1833........DLB-73

Hunter, Evan 1926-....................Y-82

   Tribute to John D. MacDonald........Y-86

Hunter, Jim 1939-....................DLB-14

Hunter, Kristin 1931-................DLB-33

   Tribute to Julian Mayfield............Y-84

Hunter, Mollie 1922-................DLB-161

Hunter, N. C. 1908-1971..............DLB-10

Hunter-Duvar, John 1821-1899..........DLB-99

Huntington, Henry E. 1850-1927.......DLB-140

   The Henry E. Huntington Library.....Y-92

Huntington, Susan Mansfield 1791-1823..DLB-200

Hurd and Houghton....................DLB-49

Hurst, Fannie 1889-1968...............DLB-86

Hurst and Blackett...................DLB-106

Hurst and Company....................DLB-49

Hurston, Zora Neale
   1901?-1960..........DLB-51, 86; CDALB-7

Husson, Jules-François-Félix (see Champfleury)

Huston, John 1906-1987...............DLB-26

Hutcheson, Francis 1694-1746......DLB-31, 252

Hutchinson, Ron 1947-................DLB-245

Hutchinson, R. C. 1907-1975..........DLB-191

Hutchinson, Thomas 1711-1780......DLB-30, 31

Hutchinson and Company
   (Publishers) Limited............DLB-112

Huth, Angela 1938-..................DLB-271

Hutton, Richard Holt 1826-1897.......DLB-57

von Hutten, Ulrich 1488-1523.........DLB-179

Huxley, Aldous 1894-1963
   .....DLB-36, 100, 162, 195, 255; CDBLB-6

Huxley, Elspeth Josceline
   1907-1997..................DLB-77, 204

Huxley, T. H. 1825-1895...............DLB-57

Huyghue, Douglas Smith 1816-1891......DLB-99

Huysmans, Joris-Karl 1848-1907........DLB-123

Hwang, David Henry 1957-........DLB-212, 228

Hyde, Donald 1909-1966...............DLB-187

Hyde, Mary 1912-....................DLB-187

Hyman, Trina Schart 1939-............DLB-61

I

Iavorsky, Stefan 1658-1722............DLB-150

Iazykov, Nikolai Mikhailovich
   1803-1846......................DLB-205

Ibáñez, Armando P. 1949-.............DLB-209

Ibn Bajja circa 1077-1138.............DLB-115

Ibn Gabirol, Solomon
   circa 1021-circa 1058.............DLB-115

Ibuse Masuji 1898-1993...............DLB-180

Ichijō Kanera (see Ichijō Kaneyoshi)

Ichijō Kaneyoshi (Ichijō Kanera)
   1402-1481......................DLB-203

Iffland, August Wilhelm 1759-1814.....DLB-94

Ignatieff, Michael 1947-...............DLB-267

Ignatow, David 1914-1997..............DLB-5

Ike, Chukwuemeka 1931-...............DLB-157

Ikkyū Sōjun 1394-1481................DLB-203

Iles, Francis (see Berkeley, Anthony)

Il'f, Il'ia (Il'ia Arnol'dovich Fainzil'berg)
   1897-1937......................DLB-272

Illich, Ivan 1926-2002................DLB-242

Illustration
   Children's Book Illustration in the
     Twentieth Century............DLB-61

   Children's Illustrators, 1800-1880...DLB-163

   Early American Book Illustration....DLB-49

   The Iconography of Science-Fiction
     Art.........................DLB-8

   The Illustration of Early German
     Literary Manuscripts, circa
     1150-circa 1300..............DLB-148

   Minor Illustrators, 1880-1914.......DLB-141

Illyés, Gyula 1902-1983......DLB-215; CDWLB-4

Imbs, Bravig 1904-1946..........DLB-4; DS-15

Imbuga, Francis D. 1947-.............DLB-157

Immermann, Karl 1796-1840............DLB-133

Inchbald, Elizabeth 1753-1821.......DLB-39, 89

Indiana University Press...............Y-02

Ingamells, Rex 1913-1955.............DLB-260

Inge, William 1913-1973....DLB-7, 249; CDALB-1

Ingelow, Jean 1820-1897...........DLB-35, 163

Ingersoll, Ralph 1900-1985...........DLB-127

The Ingersoll Prizes.....................Y-84

Ingoldsby, Thomas (see Barham, Richard Harris)

Ingraham, Joseph Holt 1809-1860....DLB-3, 248

Inman, John 1805-1850................DLB-73

Innerhofer, Franz 1944-...............DLB-85

Innes, Michael (J. I. M. Stewart)
   1906-1994......................DLB-276

Innis, Harold Adams 1894-1952.........DLB-88

Innis, Mary Quayle 1899-1972..........DLB-88

Inō Sōgi 1421-1502..................DLB-203

Inoue Yasushi 1907-1991..............DLB-182

"The Greatness of Southern Literature":
   League of the South Institute for the
   Study of Southern Culture and History
   ....Y-02

International Publishers Company.......DLB-46

Internet (publishing and commerce)
   Author Websites...................Y-97

   The Book Trade and the Internet.....Y-00

   E-Books Turn the Corner............Y-98

   The E-Researcher: Possibilities
     and Pitfalls..................Y-00

   Interviews on E-publishing..........Y-00

   John Updike on the Internet.........Y-97

   LitCheck Website...................Y-01

   Virtual Books and Enemies of Books...Y-00

Interviews
   Adoff, Arnold......................Y-01
   Aldridge, John W...................Y-91
   Anastas, Benjamin..................Y-98
   Baker, Nicholson...................Y-00
   Bank, Melissa......................Y-98
   Bass, T. J.........................Y-80
   Bernstein, Harriet.................Y-82
   Betts, Doris.......................Y-82
   Bosworth, David....................Y-82
   Bottoms, David.....................Y-83
   Bowers, Fredson....................Y-80
   Burnshaw, Stanley..................Y-97
   Carpenter, Humphrey............Y-84, 99
   Carr, Virginia Spencer.............Y-00
   Carver, Raymond....................Y-83
   Cherry, Kelly......................Y-83
   Conroy, Jack.......................Y-81
   Coppel, Alfred.....................Y-83
   Cowley, Malcolm....................Y-81
   Davis, Paxton......................Y-89
   Devito, Carlo......................Y-94
   De Vries, Peter....................Y-82
   Dickey, James......................Y-82
   Donald, David Herbert..............Y-87
   Editors, Conversations with........Y-95
   Ellroy, James......................Y-91
   Fancher, Betsy.....................Y-83
   Faust, Irvin.......................Y-00
   Fulton, Len........................Y-86
   Furst, Alan........................Y-01
   Garrett, George....................Y-83
   Gelfman, Jane......................Y-93
   Goldwater, Walter..................Y-93

Gores, Joe Y-02	Schroeder, Patricia Y-99	Jackson, Angela 1951- DLB-41
Greenfield, George Y-91	Schulberg, Budd Y-81, 01	Jackson, Charles 1903-1968 .... DLB-234
Griffin, Bryan Y-81	Scribner, Charles, III Y-94	Jackson, Helen Hunt
Groom, Winston Y-01	Sipper, Ralph Y-94	1830-1885 .... DLB-42, 47, 186, 189
Guilds, John Caldwell Y-92	Smith, Cork Y-95	Jackson, Holbrook 1874-1948 .... DLB-98
Hamilton, Virginia Y-01	Staley, Thomas F. Y-00	Jackson, Laura Riding 1901-1991 ...... DLB-48
Hardin, James Y-92	Styron, William Y-80	Jackson, Shirley
Harris, Mark Y-80	Talese, Nan Y-94	1916-1965 .... DLB-6, 234; CDALB-1
Harrison, Jim Y-82	Thornton, John Y-94	Jacob, Max 1876-1944 .... DLB-258
Hazzard, Shirley Y-82	Toth, Susan Allen Y-86	Jacob, Naomi 1884?-1964 .... DLB-191
Herrick, William Y-01	Tyler, Anne Y-82	Jacob, Piers Anthony Dillingham
Higgins, George V. Y-98	Vaughan, Samuel Y-97	(see Anthony, Piers)
Hoban, Russell Y-90	Von Ogtrop, Kristin Y-92	Jacob, Violet 1863-1946 .... DLB-240
Holroyd, Michael Y-99	Wallenstein, Barry Y-92	Jacobi, Friedrich Heinrich 1743-1819 ..... DLB-94
Horowitz, Glen Y-90	Weintraub, Stanley Y-82	Jacobi, Johann Georg 1740-1841 .... DLB-97
Iggulden, John Y-01	Williams, J. Chamberlain Y-84	George W. Jacobs and Company DLB-49
Jakes, John Y-83	Into the Past: William Jovanovich's	Jacobs, Harriet 1813-1897 .... DLB-239
Jenkinson, Edward B. Y-82	Reflections in Publishing Y-02	Jacobs, Joseph 1854-1916 .... DLB-141
Jenks, Tom Y-86	The National Library of Ireland's	Jacobs, W. W. 1863-1943 .... DLB-135
Kaplan, Justin Y-86	New James Joyce Manuscripts Y-02	The W. W. Jacobs Appreciation Society . Y-98
King, Florence Y-85	Irving, John 1942- DLB-6, 278; Y-82	Jacobsen, Jørgen-Frantz 1900-1938 ...... DLB-214
Klopfer, Donald S. Y-97	Irving, Washington 1783-1859	Jacobsen, Josephine 1908- DLB-244
Krug, Judith Y-82	.... DLB-3, 11, 30, 59, 73, 74,	Jacobson, Dan 1929- DLB-14, 207, 225
Lamm, Donald Y-95	183, 186, 250; CDALB-2	Jacobson, Howard 1942- DLB-207
Laughlin, James Y-96	Irwin, Grace 1907- DLB-68	Jacques de Vitry circa 1160/1170-1240 ... DLB-208
Lawrence, Starling Y-95	Irwin, Will 1873-1948 .... DLB-25	Jæger, Frank 1926-1977 .... DLB-214
Lindsay, Jack Y-84	Isaksson, Ulla 1916-2000 .... DLB-257	William Jaggard [publishing house] DLB-170
Mailer, Norman Y-97	Iser, Wolfgang 1926- DLB-242	Jahier, Piero 1884-1966 .... DLB-114, 264
Manchester, William Y-85	Isherwood, Christopher	Jahnn, Hans Henny 1894-1959 ..... DLB-56, 124
Max, D. T. Y-94	1904-1986 .... DLB-15, 195; Y-86	Jakes, John 1932- DLB-278; Y-83
McCormack, Thomas Y-98	The Christopher Isherwood Archive,	Tribute to John Gardner Y-82
McNamara, Katherine Y-97	The Huntington Library Y-99	Tribute to John D. MacDonald Y-86
Mellen, Joan Y-94	Ishiguro, Kazuo	Jakobson, Roman 1896-1982 .... DLB-242
Menaker, Daniel Y-97	1954- DLB-194	James, Alice 1848-1892 .... DLB-221
Mooneyham, Lamarr Y-82	Ishikawa Jun 1899-1987 .... DLB-182	James, C. L. R. 1901-1989 .... DLB-125
Murray, Les Y-01	The Island Trees Case: A Symposium on	James, George P. R. 1801-1860 .... DLB-116
Nosworth, David Y-82	School Library Censorship	James, Henry 1843-1916
O'Connor, Patrick Y-84, 99	An Interview with Judith Krug	..... DLB-12, 71, 74, 189; DS-13; CDALB-3
Ozick, Cynthia Y-83	An Interview with Phyllis Schlafly	"The Future of the Novel" (1899) ... DLB-18
Penner, Jonathan Y-83	An Interview with Edward B. Jenkinson	"The Novel in [Robert Browning's]
Pennington, Lee Y-82	An Interview with Lamarr Mooneyham	'The Ring and the Book'"
Penzler, Otto Y-96	An Interview with Harriet Bernstein Y-82	(1912)" DLB-32
Plimpton, George Y-99	Islas, Arturo	James, John circa 1633-1729 .... DLB-24
Potok, Chaim Y-84	1938-1991 .... DLB-122	James, M. R. 1862-1936 .... DLB-156, 201
Powell, Padgett Y-01	Issit, Debbie 1966- DLB-233	James, Naomi 1949- DLB-204
Prescott, Peter S. Y-86	Ivanišević, Drago 1907-1981 .... DLB-181	James, P. D. (Phyllis Dorothy James White)
Rabe, David Y-91	Ivanov, Vsevolod Viacheslavovich	1920- DLB-87, 276; DS-17; CDBLB-8
Rechy, John Y-82	1895-1963 .... DLB-272	Tribute to Charles Scribner Jr. Y-95
Reid, B. L. Y-83	Ivaska, Astrīde 1926- DLB-232	James, Thomas 1572?-1629 .... DLB-213
Reynolds, Michael Y-95, 99	M. J. Ivers and Company DLB-49	U. P. James [publishing house] DLB-49
Robinson, Derek Y-02	Iwaniuk, Wacław 1915- DLB-215	James, Will 1892-1942 .... DS-16
Rollyson, Carl Y-97	Iwano Hōmei 1873-1920 .... DLB-180	James, William 1842-1910 .... DLB-270
Rosset, Barney Y-02	Iwaszkiewicz, Jarosław 1894-1980 ...... DLB-215	James VI of Scotland, I of England
Schlafly, Phyllis Y-82	Iyayi, Festus 1947- DLB-157	1566-1625 .... DLB-151, 172
	Izumi Kyōka 1873-1939 .... DLB-180	*Ane Schort Treatise Conteining Some Revlis*
		and Cautelis to Be Obseruit and
	# J	*Eschewit in Scottis Poesi* (1584) DLB-172
	Jackmon, Marvin E. (see Marvin X)	
	Jacks, L. P. 1860-1955 .... DLB-135	

Jameson, Anna 1794-1860 . . . . DLB-99, 166
Jameson, Fredric 1934- DLB-67
Jameson, J. Franklin 1859-1937 . . . . DLB-17
Jameson, Storm 1891-1986 . . . . .DLB-36
Jančar, Drago 1948- DLB-181
Janés, Clara 1940- DLB-134
Janevski, Slavko 1920- DLB-181; CDWLB-4
Jansson, Tove 1914-2001 . . . . DLB-257
Janvier, Thomas 1849-1913 . . . . DLB-202
Japan
  "The Development of Meiji Japan" . . . DLB-180
  "Encounter with the West" DLB-180
Japanese Literature
  Letter from Japan Y-94, 98
  Medieval Travel Diaries DLB-203
  Surveys: 1987-1995 . . . . DLB-182
Jaramillo, Cleofas M. 1878-1956 . . . . DLB-122
Jarman, Mark 1952- DLB-120, 282
Jarrell, Randall
  1914-1965 . . . . DLB-48, 52; CDALB-1
Jarrold and Sons DLB-106
Jarry, Alfred 1873-1907 . . . . DLB-192, 258
Jarves, James Jackson 1818-1888 . . . . DLB-189
Jasmin, Claude 1930- DLB-60
Jaunsudrabiņš, Jānis 1877-1962 . . . . DLB-220
Jay, John 1745-1829 . . . . DLB-31
Jean de Garlande (see John of Garland)
Jefferies, Richard 1848-1887 . . . . DLB-98, 141
  The Richard Jefferies Society Y-98
Jeffers, Lance 1919-1985 . . . . DLB-41
Jeffers, Robinson
  1887-1962 . . . . DLB-45, 212; CDALB-4
Jefferson, Thomas
  1743-1826 . . . . DLB-31, 183; CDALB-2
Jégé 1866-1940 . . . . DLB-215
Jelinek, Elfriede 1946- DLB-85
Jellicoe, Ann 1927- DLB-13, 233
Jemison, Mary circa 1742-1833 . . . . DLB-239
Jenkins, Dan 1929- DLB-241
Jenkins, Elizabeth 1905- DLB-155
Jenkins, Robin 1912- DLB-14, 271
Jenkins, William Fitzgerald (see Leinster, Murray)
Herbert Jenkins Limited DLB-112
Jennings, Elizabeth 1926- DLB-27
Jens, Walter 1923- DLB-69
Jensen, Johannes V. 1873-1950 . . . . DLB-214
Jensen, Merrill 1905-1980 . . . . DLB-17
Jensen, Thit 1876-1957 . . . . DLB-214
Jephson, Robert 1736-1803 . . . . DLB-89
Jerome, Jerome K. 1859-1927 . . . . DLB-10, 34, 135
  The Jerome K. Jerome Society Y-98
Jerome, Judson 1927-1991 . . . . DLB-105
  "Reflections: After a Tornado" DLB-105
Jerrold, Douglas 1803-1857 . . . . DLB-158, 159
Jersild, Per Christian 1935- DLB-257
Jesse, F. Tennyson 1888-1958 . . . . DLB-77

Jewel, John 1522-1571 . . . . DLB-236
John P. Jewett and Company DLB-49
Jewett, Sarah Orne 1849-1909 . . . . DLB-12, 74, 221
The Jewish Publication Society DLB-49
Studies in American Jewish Literature Y-02
Jewitt, John Rodgers 1783-1821 . . . . DLB-99
Jewsbury, Geraldine 1812-1880 . . . . DLB-21
Jewsbury, Maria Jane 1800-1833 . . . . DLB-199
Jhabvala, Ruth Prawer 1927- DLB-139, 194
Jiménez, Atonio Ávila 1898-1965 . . . . DLB-283
Jiménez, Juan Ramón 1881-1958 . . . . DLB-134
Jin, Ha 1956- DLB-244
Joans, Ted 1928- DLB-16, 41
Jōha 1525-1602 . . . . DLB-203
Johannis de Garlandia (see John of Garland)
John, Errol 1924-1988 . . . . DLB-233
John, Eugenie (see Marlitt, E.)
John of Dumbleton
  circa 1310-circa 1349 . . . . DLB-115
John of Garland (Jean de Garlande,
  Johannis de Garlandia)
  circa 1195-circa 1272 . . . . DLB-208
Johns, Captain W. E. 1893-1968 . . . . DLB-160
Johnson, Mrs. A. E. ca. 1858-1922 . . . . . . DLB-221
Johnson, Amelia (see Johnson, Mrs. A. E.)
Johnson, B. S. 1933-1973 . . . . DLB-14, 40
Johnson, Charles 1679-1748 . . . . DLB-84
Johnson, Charles 1948- DLB-33, 278
Johnson, Charles S. 1893-1956 . . . . DLB-51, 91
Johnson, Denis 1949- DLB-120
Johnson, Diane 1934- Y-80
Johnson, Dorothy M. 1905–1984 . . . . DLB-206
Johnson, E. Pauline (Tekahionwake)
  1861-1913 . . . . DLB-175
Johnson, Edgar 1901-1995 . . . . DLB-103
Johnson, Edward 1598-1672 . . . . DLB-24
Johnson, Eyvind 1900-1976 . . . . DLB-259
Johnson, Fenton 1888-1958 . . . . DLB-45, 50
Johnson, Georgia Douglas
  1877?-1966 . . . . DLB-51, 249
Johnson, Gerald W. 1890-1980 . . . . DLB-29
Johnson, Greg 1953- DLB-234
Johnson, Helene 1907-1995 . . . . DLB-51
Jacob Johnson and Company DLB-49
Johnson, James Weldon
  1871-1938 . . . . DLB-51; CDALB-4
Johnson, John H. 1918- DLB-137
  "Backstage," Statement From the
  Initial Issue of Ebony
  (November 1945) DLB-137
Johnson, Joseph [publishing house] DLB-154
Johnson, Linton Kwesi 1952- DLB-157
Johnson, Lionel 1867-1902 . . . . DLB-19
Johnson, Nunnally 1897-1977 . . . . DLB-26
Johnson, Owen 1878-1952 . . . . Y-87
Johnson, Pamela Hansford 1912-1981 . . . . DLB-15
Johnson, Pauline 1861-1913 . . . . DLB-92

Johnson, Ronald 1935-1998 . . . . DLB-169
Johnson, Samuel 1696-1772 . . . . DLB-24; CDBLB-2
Johnson, Samuel
  1709-1784 . . . . . . DLB-39, 95, 104, 142, 213
  Rambler, no. 4 (1750) [excerpt] DLB-39
The BBC Four Samuel Johnson Prize
  for Non-fiction Y-02
Johnson, Samuel 1822-1882 . . . . DLB-1, 243
Johnson, Susanna 1730-1810 . . . . DLB-200
Johnson, Terry 1955- DLB-233
Johnson, Uwe 1934-1984 . . . . . DLB-75; CDWLB-2
Benjamin Johnson [publishing house] DLB-49
Benjamin, Jacob, and Robert Johnson
  [publishing house] DLB-49
Johnston, Annie Fellows 1863-1931 . . . . . . DLB-42
Johnston, Basil H. 1929- DLB-60
Johnston, David Claypole 1798?-1865 . . . . DLB-188
Johnston, Denis 1901-1984 . . . . DLB-10
Johnston, Ellen 1835-1873 . . . . DLB-199
Johnston, George 1912-1970 . . . . DLB-260
Johnston, George 1913- DLB-88
Johnston, Sir Harry 1858-1927 . . . . DLB-174
Johnston, Jennifer 1930- DLB-14
Johnston, Mary 1870-1936 . . . . DLB-9
Johnston, Richard Malcolm 1822-1898 . . . . DLB-74
Johnstone, Charles 1719?-1800? DLB-39
Johst, Hanns 1890-1978 . . . . DLB-124
Jolas, Eugene 1894-1952 . . . . DLB-4, 45
Jones, Alice C. 1853-1933 . . . . DLB-92
Jones, Charles C., Jr. 1831-1893 . . . . DLB-30
Jones, D. G. 1929- DLB-53
Jones, David
  1895-1974 . . . . DLB-20, 100; CDBLB-7
Jones, Diana Wynne 1934- DLB-161
Jones, Ebenezer 1820-1860 . . . . DLB-32
Jones, Ernest 1819-1868 . . . . DLB-32
Jones, Gayl 1949- DLB-33, 278
Jones, George 1800-1870 . . . . DLB-183
Jones, Glyn 1905-1995 . . . . DLB-15
Jones, Gwyn 1907- DLB-15, 139
Jones, Henry Arthur 1851-1929 . . . . DLB-10
Jones, Hugh circa 1692-1760 . . . . DLB-24
Jones, James 1921-1977 . . . . . . DLB-2, 143; DS-17
  James Jones Papers in the Handy
  Writers' Colony Collection at
  the University of Illinois at
  Springfield Y-98
  The James Jones Society Y-92
Jones, Jenkin Lloyd 1911- DLB-127
Jones, John Beauchamp 1810-1866 . . . . . . DLB-202
Jones, Joseph, Major
  (see Thompson, William Tappan)
Jones, LeRoi (see Baraka, Amiri)
Jones, Lewis 1897-1939 . . . . DLB-15
Jones, Madison 1925- DLB-152
Jones, Marie 1951- DLB-233
Jones, Preston 1936-1979 . . . . DLB-7

Jones, Rodney 1950- DLB-120	Julius Caesar 100 B.C.-44 B.C. DLB-211; CDWLB-1	Kästner, Erich 1899-1974 .... DLB-56
Jones, Thom 1945- DLB-244	June, Jennie (see Croly, Jane Cunningham)	Kataev, Evgenii Petrovich (see Il'f, Il'ia and Petrov, Evgenii)
Jones, Sir William 1746-1794 .... DLB-109	Jung, Franz 1888-1963 .... DLB-118	Kataev, Valentin Petrovich 1897-1986 ... DLB-272
Jones, William Alfred 1817-1900........ DLB-59	Jünger, Ernst 1895- DLB-56; CDWLB-2	Katenin, Pavel Aleksandrovich 1792-1853..................... DLB-205
Jones's Publishing House DLB-49	Der jüngere Titurel circa 1275 .... DLB-138	Kattan, Naim 1928- DLB-53
Jong, Erica 1942- DLB-2, 5, 28, 152	Jung-Stilling, Johann Heinrich 1740-1817.... DLB-94	Katz, Steve 1935- Y-83
Jonke, Gert F. 1946- DLB-85	Justice, Donald 1925- Y-83	Kauffman, Janet 1945- DLB-218; Y-86
Jonson, Ben 1572?-1637 .. DLB-62, 121; CDBLB-1	Juvenal circa A.D. 60-circa A.D. 130 .... DLB-211; CDWLB-1	Kauffmann, Samuel 1898-1971.......... DLB-127
Jordan, June 1936- DLB-38	The Juvenile Library (see M. J. Godwin and Company)	Kaufman, Bob 1925-1986......... DLB-16, 41
Joseph, Jenny 1932- DLB-40		Kaufman, George S. 1889-1961 .... DLB-7
Joseph and George Y-99	**K**	Kaufmann, Walter 1921-1980 ....DLB-279
Michael Joseph Limited DLB-112		Kavan, Anna (Helen Woods Ferguson Edmonds) 1901-1968............. DLB-255
Josephson, Matthew 1899-1978 .... DLB-4	Kacew, Romain (see Gary, Romain)	
Josephus, Flavius 37-100 ....DLB-176	Kafka, Franz 1883-1924 ..... DLB-81; CDWLB-2	Kavanagh, P. J. 1931- DLB-40
Josephy, Alvin M., Jr. Tribute to Alfred A. Knopf Y-84	Kahn, Gus 1886-1941................ DLB-265	Kavanagh, Patrick 1904-1967....... DLB-15, 20
Josiah Allen's Wife (see Holley, Marietta)	Kahn, Roger 1927- DLB-171	Kaverin, Veniamin Aleksandrovich (Veniamin Aleksandrovich Zil'ber) 1902-1989 ....DLB-272
Josipovici, Gabriel 1940- DLB-14	Kaikō Takeshi 1939-1989............... DLB-182	
Josselyn, John ?-1675 .... DLB-24	Kaiser, Georg 1878-1945 ... DLB-124; CDWLB-2	Kawabata Yasunari 1899-1972 .... DLB-180
Joudry, Patricia 1921-2000 .... DLB-88	*Kaiserchronik* circa 1147 .... DLB-148	Kay, Guy Gavriel 1954- DLB-251
Jouve, Pierre Jean 1887-1976.......... DLB-258	Kaleb, Vjekoslav 1905- DLB-181	Kaye-Smith, Sheila 1887-1956 .... DLB-36
Jovanovich, William 1920-2001 .... Y-01	Kalechofsky, Roberta 1931- DLB-28	Kazin, Alfred 1915-1998............... DLB-67
Into the Past: William Jovanovich's Reflections on Publishing Y-02	Kaler, James Otis 1848-1912.......... DLB-12, 42	Keane, John B. 1928- DLB-13
[Repsonse to Ken Auletta]............Y-97	Kalmar, Bert 1884-1947 .... DLB-265	Keary, Annie 1825-1879.............. DLB-163
The Temper of the West: William Jovanovich Y-02	Kames, Henry Home, Lord 1696-1782................... DLB-31, 104	Keary, Eliza 1827-1918 .... DLB-240
	Kamo no Chōmei (Kamo no Nagaakira) 1153 or 1155-1216 .... DLB-203	Keating, H. R. F. 1926- DLB-87
Tribute to Charles Scribner Jr. Y-95		Keatley, Charlotte 1960- DLB-245
Jovine, Francesco 1902-1950 .... DLB-264	Kamo no Nagaakira (see Kamo no Chōmei)	Keats, Ezra Jack 1916-1983 .... DLB-61
Jovine, Giuseppe 1922- DLB-128	Kampmann, Christian 1939-1988....... DLB-214	Keats, John 1795-1821 ... DLB-96, 110; CDBLB-3
Joyaux, Philippe (see Sollers, Philippe)	Kandel, Lenore 1932- DLB-16	Keble, John 1792-1866 .... DLB-32, 55
Joyce, Adrien (see Eastman, Carol)	Kanin, Garson 1912-1999.............. DLB-7	Keckley, Elizabeth 1818?-1907 .... DLB-239
Joyce, James 1882-1941 .... DLB-10, 19, 36, 162, 247; CDBLB-6	A Tribute (to Marc Connelly) Y-80	Keeble, John 1944- Y-83
Danis Rose and the Rendering of *Ulysses*. . Y-97	Kant, Hermann 1926- DLB-75	Keeffe, Barrie 1945- DLB-13, 245
James Joyce Centenary: Dublin, 1982 ... Y-82	Kant, Immanuel 1724-1804............. DLB-94	Keeley, James 1867-1934 .... DLB-25
James Joyce Conference Y-85	Kantemir, Antiokh Dmitrievich 1708-1744...................... DLB-150	W. B. Keen, Cooke and Company DLB-49
A Joyce (Con)Text: Danis Rose and the Remaking of *Ulysses*...........Y-97	Kantor, MacKinlay 1904-1977 .... DLB-9, 102	The Mystery of Carolyn Keene............Y-02
The National Library of Ireland's New James Joyce Manuscripts Y-02	Kanze Kōjirō Nobumitsu 1435-1516 ... DLB-203	Keillor, Garrison 1942- Y-87
The New *Ulysses* Y-84	Kanze Motokiyo (see Zeimi)	Keith, Marian (Mary Esther MacGregor) 1874?-1961..................... DLB-92
Public Domain and the Violation of Texts Y-97	Kaplan, Fred 1937- DLB-111	Keller, Gary D. 1943- DLB-82
	Kaplan, Johanna 1942- DLB-28	Keller, Gottfried 1819-1890 ....DLB-129; CDWLB-2
The Quinn Draft of James Joyce's Circe Manuscript Y-00	Kaplan, Justin 1925- DLB-111; Y-86	
Stephen Joyce's Letter to the Editor of *The Irish Times*....................Y-97	Kaplinski, Jaan 1941- DLB-232	Kelley, Edith Summers 1884-1956........ DLB-9
	Kapnist, Vasilii Vasilevich 1758?-1823 ... DLB-150	Kelley, Emma Dunham ?-?............ DLB-221
Ulysses, Reader's Edition: First Reactions . Y-97	Karadžić, Vuk Stefanović 1787-1864 ....DLB-147; CDWLB-4	Kelley, William Melvin 1937- DLB-33
We See the Editor at Work Y-97	Karamzin, Nikolai Mikhailovich 1766-1826..................... DLB-150	Kellogg, Ansel Nash 1832-1886 .... DLB-23
Whose *Ulysses*? The Function of Editing. . Y-97		Kellogg, Steven 1941- DLB-61
Jozsef, Attila 1905-1937..... DLB-215; CDWLB-4	Karinthy, Frigyes 1887-1938........... DLB-215	Kelly, George E. 1887-1974...........DLB-7, 249
Juarroz, Roberto 1925-1995 .... DLB-283	Karsch, Anna Louisa 1722-1791 .... DLB-97	Kelly, Hugh 1739-1777 .... DLB-89
Orange Judd Publishing Company....... DLB-49	Kasack, Hermann 1896-1966 .... DLB-69	Kelly, Piet and Company DLB-49
Judd, Sylvester 1813-1853 .... DLB-1, 243	Kasai Zenzō 1887-1927 .... DLB-180	Kelly, Robert 1935- DLB-5, 130, 165
Judith circa 930...................... DLB-146	Kaschnitz, Marie Luise 1901-1974 .... DLB-69	Kelman, James 1946- DLB-194
Julian of Norwich 1342-circa 1420 ..... DLB-1146	Kassák, Lajos 1887-1967 .... DLB-215	Kelmscott Press DLB-112
	Kaštelan, Jure 1919-1990 .... DLB-147	Kelton, Elmer 1926- DLB-256

Kemble, E. W. 1861-1933 . . . . DLB-188
Kemble, Fanny 1809-1893 . . . . DLB-32
Kemelman, Harry 1908-1996 . . . . DLB-28
Kempe, Margery circa 1373-1438 . . . . . . DLB-146
Kempner, Friederike 1836-1904 . . . . DLB-129
Kempowski, Walter 1929- DLB-75
Claude Kendall [publishing company] DLB-46
Kendall, Henry 1839-1882 . . . . DLB-230
Kendall, May 1861-1943 . . . . DLB-240
Kendell, George 1809-1867 . . . . DLB-43
Kenedy, P. J., and Sons DLB-49
Kenkō circa 1283-circa 1352 . . . . DLB-203
Kennan, George 1845-1924 . . . . DLB-189
Kennedy, A. L. 1965- DLB-271
Kennedy, Adrienne 1931- DLB-38
Kennedy, John Pendleton 1795-1870 . . . DLB-3, 248
Kennedy, Leo 1907-2000 . . . . DLB-88
Kennedy, Margaret 1896-1967 . . . . DLB-36
Kennedy, Patrick 1801-1873 . . . . DLB-159
Kennedy, Richard S. 1920- DLB-111; Y-02
Kennedy, William 1928- DLB-143; Y-85
Kennedy, X. J. 1929- DLB-5
    Tribute to John Ciardi Y-86
Kennelly, Brendan 1936- DLB-40
Kenner, Hugh 1923- DLB-67
    Tribute to Cleanth Brooks Y-80
Mitchell Kennerley [publishing house] DLB-46
Kenny, Maurice 1929- DLB-175
Kent, Frank R. 1877-1958 . . . . DLB-29
Kenyon, Jane 1947-1995 . . . . DLB-120
Keough, Hugh Edmund 1864-1912 . . . . . . DLB-171
Keppler and Schwartzmann DLB-49
Ker, John, third Duke of Roxburghe
    1740-1804 . . . . DLB-213
Ker, N. R. 1908-1982 . . . . DLB-201
Kerlan, Irvin 1912-1963 . . . . DLB-187
Kermode, Frank 1919- DLB-242
Kern, Jerome 1885-1945 . . . . DLB-187
Kernaghan, Eileen 1939- DLB-251
Kerner, Justinus 1786-1862 . . . . DLB-90
Kerouac, Jack
    1922-1969 . . . DLB-2, 16, 237; DS-3; CDALB-1
    Auction of Jack Kerouac's
        On the Road Scroll Y-01
    The Jack Kerouac Revival Y-95
    "Re-meeting of Old Friends":
        The Jack Kerouac Conference Y-82
    Statement of Correction to "The Jack
        Kerouac Revival" Y-96
Kerouac, Jan 1952-1996 . . . . DLB-16
Charles H. Kerr and Company DLB-49
Kerr, Orpheus C. (see Newell, Robert Henry)
Kersh, Gerald 1911-1968 . . . . DLB-255
Kertész, Imre Y-02
Kesey, Ken
    1935-2001 . . . . DLB-2, 16, 206; CDALB-6

Kessel, Joseph 1898-1979 . . . . DLB-72
Kessel, Martin 1901-1990 . . . . DLB-56
Kesten, Hermann 1900-1996 . . . . DLB-56
Keun, Irmgard 1905-1982 . . . . DLB-69
Key, Ellen 1849-1926 . . . . DLB-259
Key and Biddle DLB-49
Keynes, Sir Geoffrey 1887-1982 . . . . DLB-201
Keynes, John Maynard 1883-1946 . . . . DS-10
Keyserling, Eduard von 1855-1918 . . . . DLB-66
Khan, Ismith 1925-2002 . . . . DLB-125
Khaytov, Nikolay 1919- DLB-181
Khemnitser, Ivan Ivanovich 1745-1784 . . . DLB-150
Kheraskov, Mikhail Matveevich
    1733-1807 . . . . DLB-150
Khomiakov, Aleksei Stepanovich
    1804-1860 . . . . DLB-205
Khristov, Boris 1945- DLB-181
Khvoshchinskaia, Nadezhda Dmitrievna
    1824-1889 . . . . DLB-238
Khvostov, Dmitrii Ivanovich 1757-1835 . . . DLB-150
Kidd, Adam 1802?-1831 . . . . DLB-99
William Kidd [publishing house] DLB-106
Kidder, Tracy 1945- DLB-185
Kiely, Benedict 1919- DLB-15
Kieran, John 1892-1981 . . . . DLB-171
Kies, Marietta 1853-1899 . . . . DLB-270
Kiggins and Kellogg DLB-49
Kiley, Jed 1889-1962 . . . . DLB-4
Kilgore, Bernard 1908-1967 . . . . DLB-127
Kilian, Crawford 1941- DLB-251
Killens, John Oliver 1916-1987 . . . . DLB-33
    Tribute to Julian Mayfield Y-84
Killigrew, Anne 1660-1685 . . . . DLB-131
Killigrew, Thomas 1612-1683 . . . . DLB-58
Kilmer, Joyce 1886-1918 . . . . DLB-45
Kilroy, Thomas 1934- DLB-233
Kilwardby, Robert circa 1215-1279 . . . . . . DLB-115
Kilworth, Garry 1941- DLB-261
Kimball, Richard Burleigh 1816-1892 . . . . DLB-202
Kincaid, Jamaica 1949-
    . . . . . . DLB-157, 227; CDALB-7; CDWLB-3
King, Charles 1844-1933 . . . . DLB-186
King, Clarence 1842-1901 . . . . DLB-12
King, Florence 1936- Y-85
King, Francis 1923- DLB-15, 139
King, Grace 1852-1932 . . . . DLB-12, 78
King, Harriet Hamilton 1840-1920 . . . . . . DLB-199
King, Henry 1592-1669 . . . . DLB-126
Solomon King [publishing house] DLB-49
King, Stephen 1947- DLB-143; Y-80
King, Susan Petigru 1824-1875 . . . . DLB-239
King, Thomas 1943- DLB-175
King, Woodie, Jr. 1937- DLB-38
Kinglake, Alexander William
    1809-1891 . . . . DLB-55, 166
Kingsbury, Donald 1929- DLB-251

Kingsley, Charles
    1819-1875 . . . . DLB-21, 32, 163, 178, 190
Kingsley, Henry 1830-1876 . . . . DLB-21, 230
Kingsley, Mary Henrietta 1862-1900 . . . . . DLB-174
Kingsley, Sidney 1906-1995 . . . . DLB-7
Kingsmill, Hugh 1889-1949 . . . . DLB-149
Kingsolver, Barbara
    1955- DLB-206; CDALB-7
Kingston, Maxine Hong
    1940- DLB-173, 212; Y-80; CDALB-7
Kingston, William Henry Giles
    1814-1880 . . . . DLB-163
Kinnan, Mary Lewis 1763-1848 . . . . DLB-200
Kinnell, Galway 1927- DLB-5; Y-87
Kinsella, Thomas 1928- DLB-27
Kipling, Rudyard 1865-1936
    . . . . DLB-19, 34, 141, 156; CDBLB-5
Kipphardt, Heinar 1922-1982 . . . . DLB-124
Kirby, William 1817-1906 . . . . DLB-99
Kircher, Athanasius 1602-1680 . . . . DLB-164
Kireevsky, Ivan Vasil'evich 1806-1856 . . . DLB-198
Kireevsky, Petr Vasil'evich 1808-1856 . . . DLB-205
Kirk, Hans 1898-1962 . . . . DLB-214
Kirk, John Foster 1824-1904 . . . . DLB-79
Kirkconnell, Watson 1895-1977 . . . . DLB-68
Kirkland, Caroline M.
    1801-1864 . . . . DLB-3, 73, 74, 250; DS-13
Kirkland, Joseph 1830-1893 . . . . DLB-12
Francis Kirkman [publishing house] DLB-170
Kirkpatrick, Clayton 1915- DLB-127
Kirkup, James 1918- DLB-27
Kirouac, Conrad (see Marie-Victorin, Frère)
Kirsch, Sarah 1935- DLB-75
Kirst, Hans Hellmut 1914-1989 . . . . DLB-69
Kiš, Danilo 1935-1989 . . . . DLB-181; CDWLB-4
Kita Morio 1927- DLB-182
Kitcat, Mabel Greenhow 1859-1922 . . . . . DLB-135
Kitchin, C. H. B. 1895-1967 . . . . DLB-77
Kittredge, William 1932- DLB-212, 244
Kiukhel'beker, Vil'gel'm Karlovich
    1797-1846 . . . . DLB-205
Kizer, Carolyn 1925- DLB-5, 169
Klabund 1890-1928 . . . . DLB-66
Klaj, Johann 1616-1656 . . . . DLB-164
Klappert, Peter 1942- DLB-5
Klass, Philip (see Tenn, William)
Klein, A. M. 1909-1972 . . . . DLB-68
Kleist, Ewald von 1715-1759 . . . . DLB-97
Kleist, Heinrich von
    1777-1811 . . . . DLB-90; CDWLB-2
Klíma, Ivan 1931- DLB-232; CDWLB-4
Klimentev, Andrei Platonovic
    (see Platonov, Andrei Platonovich)
Klinger, Friedrich Maximilian
    1752-1831 . . . . DLB-94
Kliushnikov, Viktor Petrovich
    1841-1892 . . . . DLB-238
Klopfer, Donald S.

Cumulative Index

Impressions of William Faulkner Y-97
Oral History Interview with Donald S. Klopfer Y-97
Tribute to Alfred A. Knopf Y-84
Klopstock, Friedrich Gottlieb 1724-1803 .... DLB-97
Klopstock, Meta 1728-1758 .... DLB-97
Kluge, Alexander 1932- DLB-75
Kluge, P. F. 1942- Y-02
Knapp, Joseph Palmer 1864-1951 .... DLB-91
Knapp, Samuel Lorenzo 1783-1838 ...... DLB-59
J. J. and P. Knapton [publishing house] .. DLB-154
Kniazhnin, Iakov Borisovich 1740-1791 .. DLB-150
Knickerbocker, Diedrich (see Irving, Washington)
Knigge, Adolph Franz Friedrich Ludwig, Freiherr von 1752-1796 .... DLB-94
Charles Knight and Company DLB-106
Knight, Damon 1922-2002 .... DLB-8
Knight, Etheridge 1931-1992 .... DLB-41
Knight, John S. 1894-1981 .... DLB-29
Knight, Sarah Kemble 1666-1727 .... DLB-24, 200
Knight-Bruce, G. W. H. 1852-1896 ...... DLB-174
Knister, Raymond 1899-1932 .... DLB-68
Knoblock, Edward 1874-1945 .... DLB-10
Knopf, Alfred A. 1892-1984 .... Y-84
Knopf to Hammett: The Editoral Correspondence Y-00
Alfred A. Knopf [publishing house] DLB-46
Knorr von Rosenroth, Christian 1636-1689 .... DLB-168
Knowles, John 1926- DLB-6; CDALB-6
Knox, Frank 1874-1944 .... DLB-29
Knox, John circa 1514-1572 .... DLB-132
Knox, John Armoy 1850-1906 .... DLB-23
Knox, Lucy 1845-1884 .... DLB-240
Knox, Ronald Arbuthnott 1888-1957 ..... DLB-77
Knox, Thomas Wallace 1835-1896 ..... DLB-189
Kobayashi Takiji 1903-1933 .... DLB-180
Kober, Arthur 1900-1975 .... DLB-11
Kobiakova, Aleksandra Petrovna 1823-1892 .... DLB-238
Kocbek, Edvard 1904-1981 .. DLB-147; CDWLB-4
Koch, Howard 1902-1995 .... DLB-26
Koch, Kenneth 1925-2002 .... DLB-5
Kōda Rohan 1867-1947 .... DLB-180
Koehler, Ted 1894-1973 .... DLB-265
Koenigsberg, Moses 1879-1945 .... DLB-25
Koeppen, Wolfgang 1906-1996 .... DLB-69
Koertge, Ronald 1940- DLB-105
Koestler, Arthur 1905-1983 ...... Y-83; CDBLB-7
Kohn, John S. Van E. 1906-1976 .... DLB-187
Kokhanovskaia (see Sokhanskaia, Nadezhda Stepanova)
Kokoschka, Oskar 1886-1980 .... DLB-124
Kolb, Annette 1870-1967 .... DLB-66
Kolbenheyer, Erwin Guido 1878-1962 .... DLB-66, 124

Kolleritsch, Alfred 1931- DLB-85
Kolodny, Annette 1941- DLB-67
Kol'tsov, Aleksei Vasil'evich 1809-1842.. DLB-205
Komarov, Matvei circa 1730-1812 ...... DLB-150
Komroff, Manuel 1890-1974 .... DLB-4
Komunyakaa, Yusef 1947- DLB-120
Kondoleon, Harry 1955-1994 .... DLB-266
Koneski, Blaže 1921-1993 ... DLB-181; CDWLB-4
Konigsburg, E. L. 1930- DLB-52
Konparu Zenchiku 1405-1468? DLB-203
Konrád, György 1933- DLB-232; CDWLB-4
Konrad von Würzburg circa 1230-1287.. DLB-138
Konstantinov, Aleko 1863-1897 .... DLB-147
Konwicki, Tadeusz 1926- DLB-232
Kooser, Ted 1939- DLB-105
Kopit, Arthur 1937- DLB-7
Kops, Bernard 1926?- DLB-13
Kornbluth, C. M. 1923-1958 .... DLB-8
Körner, Theodor 1791-1813 .... DLB-90
Kornfeld, Paul 1889-1942 .... DLB-118
Korolenko, Vladimir Galaktionovich 1853-1921 .... DLB-277
Kosinski, Jerzy 1933-1991 .... DLB-2; Y-82
Kosmač, Ciril 1910-1980 .... DLB-181
Kosovel, Srečko 1904-1926 .... DLB-147
Kostrov, Ermil Ivanovich 1755-1796 ..... DLB-150
Kotzebue, August von 1761-1819 .... DLB-94
Kotzwinkle, William 1938- DLB-173
Kovačić, Ante 1854-1889 .... DLB-147
Kovalevskaia, Sof'ia Vasil'evna 1850-1891 .... DLB-277
Kovič, Kajetan 1931- DLB-181
Kozlov, Ivan Ivanovich 1779-1840 ...... DLB-205
Kraf, Elaine 1946- Y-81
Kramer, Jane 1938- DLB-185
Kramer, Larry 1935- DLB-249
Kramer, Mark 1944- DLB-185
Kranjčević, Silvije Strahimir 1865-1908 .. DLB-147
Krasko, Ivan 1876-1958 .... DLB-215
Krasna, Norman 1909-1984 .... DLB-26
Kraus, Hans Peter 1907-1988 .... DLB-187
Kraus, Karl 1874-1936 .... DLB-118
Krause, Herbert 1905-1976 .... DLB-256
Krauss, Ruth 1911-1993 .... DLB-52
Kreisel, Henry 1922-1991 .... DLB-88
Krestovsky V. (see Khvoshchinskaia, Nadezhda Dmitrievna)
Krestovsky, Vsevolod Vladimirovich 1839-1895 .... DLB-238
Kreuder, Ernst 1903-1972 .... DLB-69
Krėvė-Mickevičius, Vincas 1882-1954 ... DLB-220
Kreymborg, Alfred 1883-1966 .... DLB-4, 54
Krieger, Murray 1923- DLB-67
Krim, Seymour 1922-1989 .... DLB-16
Kripke, Saul 1940- DLB-279

Kristensen, Tom 1893-1974 .... DLB-214
Kristeva, Julia 1941- DLB-242
Kritzer, Hyman W. 1918-2002 .... Y-02
Krleža, Miroslav 1893-1981 .... DLB-147; CDWLB-4
Krock, Arthur 1886-1974 .... DLB-29
Kroetsch, Robert 1927- DLB-53
Kropotkin, Petr Alekseevich 1842-1921 ... DLB-277
Kross, Jaan 1920- DLB-232
Krúdy, Gyula 1878-1933 .... DLB-215
Krutch, Joseph Wood 1893-1970 .... DLB-63, 206, 275
Krylov, Ivan Andreevich 1769-1844 ..... DLB-150
Krymov, Iurii Solomonovich (Iurii Solomonovich Beklemishev) 1908-1941 .... DLB-272
Kubin, Alfred 1877-1959 .... DLB-81
Kubrick, Stanley 1928-1999 .... DLB-26
Kudrun circa 1230-1240 .... DLB-138
Kuffstein, Hans Ludwig von 1582-1656 .. DLB-164
Kuhlmann, Quirinus 1651-1689 .... DLB-168
Kuhn, Thomas S. 1922-1996 .... DLB-279
Kuhnau, Johann 1660-1722 .... DLB-168
Kukol'nik, Nestor Vasil'evich 1809-1868 .... DLB-205
Kukučín, Martin 1860-1928 .... DLB-215; CDWLB-4
Kumin, Maxine 1925- DLB-5
Kuncewicz, Maria 1895-1989 .... DLB-215
Kundera, Milan 1929- DLB-232; CDWLB-4
Kunene, Mazisi 1930- DLB-117
Kunikida Doppo 1869-1908 .... DLB-180
Kunitz, Stanley 1905- DLB-48
Kunjufu, Johari M. (see Amini, Johari M.)
Kunnert, Gunter 1929- DLB-75
Kunze, Reiner 1933- DLB-75
Kupferberg, Tuli 1923- DLB-16
Kurahashi Yumiko 1935- DLB-182
Kureishi, Hanif 1954- DLB-194, 245
Kürnberger, Ferdinand 1821-1879 ...... DLB-129
Kurz, Isolde 1853-1944 .... DLB-66
Kusenberg, Kurt 1904-1983 .... DLB-69
Kushchevsky, Ivan Afanas'evich 1847-1876 .... DLB-238
Kushner, Tony 1956- DLB-228
Kuttner, Henry 1915-1958 .... DLB-8
Kyd, Thomas 1558-1594 .... DLB-62
Kyffin, Maurice circa 1560?-1598 .... DLB-136
Kyger, Joanne 1934- DLB-16
Kyne, Peter B. 1880-1957 .... DLB-78
Kyōgoku Tamekane 1254-1332 .... DLB-203
Kyrklund, Willy 1921- DLB-257

L

L. E. L. (see Landon, Letitia Elizabeth)
Laberge, Albert 1871-1960 .... DLB-68

Laberge, Marie 1950- DLB-60
Labiche, Eugène 1815-1888............DLB-192
Labrunie, Gerard (see Nerval, Gerard de)
La Bruyère, Jean de 1645-1696..........DLB-268
La Calprenède 1609?-1663 ....DLB-268
La Capria, Raffaele 1922- DLB-196
Lacombe, Patrice
   (see Trullier-Lacombe, Joseph Patrice)
Lacretelle, Jacques de 1888-1985.........DLB-65
Lacy, Ed 1911-1968................DLB-226
Lacy, Sam 1903- DLB-171
Ladd, Joseph Brown 1764-1786..........DLB-37
La Farge, Oliver 1901-1963.............DLB-9
Lafayette, Marie-Madeleine, comtesse de
   1634-1693.......................DLB-268
Laffan, Mrs. R. S. de Courcy
   (see Adams, Bertha Leith)
Lafferty, R. A. 1914-2002 ....DLB-8
La Flesche, Francis 1857-1932 ....DLB-175
La Fontaine, Jean de 1621-1695 ....DLB-268
Laforge, Jules 1860-1887 ....DLB-217
Lagerkvist, Pär 1891-1974 ....DLB-259
Lagerlöf, Selma 1858-1940............DLB-259
Lagorio, Gina 1922- DLB-196
La Guma, Alex
   1925-1985 .... DLB-117, 225; CDWLB-3
Lahaise, Guillaume (see Delahaye, Guy)
Lahontan, Louis-Armand de Lom d'Arce,
   Baron de 1666-1715?................DLB-99
Laing, Kojo 1946- DLB-157
Laird, Carobeth 1895-1983 .... Y-82
Laird and Lee DLB-49
Lake, Paul 1951- DLB-282
Lalić, Ivan V. 1931-1996...............DLB-181
Lalić, Mihailo 1914-1992...............DLB-181
Lalonde, Michèle 1937- DLB-60
Lamantia, Philip 1927- DLB-16
Lamartine, Alphonse de 1790-1869 .....DLB-217
Lamb, Lady Caroline 1785-1828........DLB-116
Lamb, Charles
   1775-1834 ...... DLB-93, 107, 163; CDBLB-3
Lamb, Mary 1764-1874 ....DLB-163
Lambert, Angela 1940- DLB-271
Lambert, Betty 1933-1983 ....DLB-60
Lamm, Donald
   Goodbye, Gutenberg? A Lecture at
   the New York Public Library,
   18 April 1995.................. Y-95
Lamming, George
   1927- DLB-125; CDWLB-3
La Mothe Le Vayer, François de
   1588-1672......................DLB-268
L'Amour, Louis 1908-1988......DLB-206; Y-80
Lampman, Archibald 1861-1899.........DLB-92
Lamson, Wolffe and Company DLB-49
Lancer Books.....................DLB-46
Lanchester, John 1962- DLB-267
Lander, Peter (see Cunningham, Peter)

Landesman, Fran 1927-................DLB-16
Landesman, Jay 1919-.................DLB-16
Landolfi, Tommaso 1908-1979 ....DLB-177
Landon, Letitia Elizabeth 1802-1838......DLB-96
Landor, Walter Savage 1775-1864....DLB-93, 107
Landry, Napoléon-P. 1884-1956 ....DLB-92
Lane, Charles 1800-1870 ......DLB-1, 223; DS-5
Lane, F. C. 1885-1984 ....DLB-241
Lane, Laurence W. 1890-1967..........DLB-91
Lane, M. Travis 1934- DLB-60
Lane, Patrick 1939- DLB-53
Lane, Pinkie Gordon 1923- DLB-41
John Lane Company DLB-49
Laney, Al 1896-1988 ....DLB-4, 171
Lang, Andrew 1844-1912 ......DLB-98, 141, 184
Langer, Susanne K. 1895-1985 ....DLB-270
Langevin, André 1927- DLB-60
Langford, David 1953- DLB-261
Langgässer, Elisabeth 1899-1950.........DLB-69
Langhorne, John 1735-1779 ....DLB-109
Langland, William circa 1330-circa 1400..DLB-146
Langton, Anna 1804-1893 ....DLB-99
Lanham, Edwin 1904-1979 ....DLB-4
Lanier, Sidney 1842-1881 ....DLB-64; DS-13
Lanyer, Aemilia 1569-1645 ....DLB-121
Lapointe, Gatien 1931-1983.............DLB-88
Lapointe, Paul-Marie 1929- DLB-88
Larcom, Lucy 1824-1893..........DLB-221, 243
Lardner, John 1912-1960...............DLB-171
Lardner, Ring 1885-1933
   ..... DLB-11, 25, 86, 171; DS-16; CDALB-4
   Lardner 100: Ring Lardner
   Centennial Symposium Y-85
Lardner, Ring, Jr. 1915-2000 .... DLB-26, Y-00
Larkin, Philip 1922-1985 .....DLB-27; CDBLB-8
   The Philip Larkin Society Y-99
La Roche, Sophie von 1730-1807.........DLB-94
La Rochefoucauld, François duc de
   1613-1680 ....DLB-268
La Rocque, Gilbert 1943-1984...........DLB-60
Laroque de Roquebrune, Robert
   (see Roquebrune, Robert de)
Larrick, Nancy 1910- DLB-61
Lars, Claudia 1899-1974 ....DLB-283
Larsen, Nella 1893-1964 ....DLB-51
Larson, Clinton F. 1919-1994 ....DLB-256
La Sale, Antoine de
   circa 1386-1460/1467 ....DLB-208
Lasch, Christopher 1932-1994..........DLB-246
Lasker-Schüler, Else 1869-1945......DLB-66, 124
Lasnier, Rina 1915-1997 ....DLB-88
Lassalle, Ferdinand 1825-1864..........DLB-129
Latham, Robert 1912-1995 ....DLB-201
Lathrop, Dorothy P. 1891-1980 ....DLB-22
Lathrop, George Parsons 1851-1898......DLB-71
Lathrop, John, Jr. 1772-1820 ....DLB-37

Latimer, Hugh 1492?-1555 ....DLB-136
Latimore, Jewel Christine McLawler
   (see Amini, Johari M.)
Latin Literature, The Uniqueness of DLB-211
La Tour du Pin, Patrice de 1911-1975....DLB-258
Latymer, William 1498-1583...........DLB-132
Laube, Heinrich 1806-1884............DLB-133
Laud, William 1573-1645 ....DLB-213
Laughlin, James 1914-1997 ..... DLB-48; Y-96, 97
   A Tribute [to Henry Miller].......... Y-80
   Tribute to Albert Erskine............ Y-93
   Tribute to Kenneth Rexroth Y-82
   Tribute to Malcolm Cowley Y-89
Laumer, Keith 1925-1993 ....DLB-8
Lauremberg, Johann 1590-1658 ....DLB-164
Laurence, Margaret 1926-1987 ....DLB-53
Laurentius von Schnüffis 1633-1702 ....DLB-168
Laurents, Arthur 1918- DLB-26
Laurie, Annie (see Black, Winifred)
Laut, Agnes Christiana 1871-1936........DLB-92
Lauterbach, Ann 1942- DLB-193
Lautréamont, Isidore Lucien Ducasse,
   Comte de 1846-1870...............DLB-217
Lavater, Johann Kaspar 1741-1801 ....DLB-97
Lavin, Mary 1912-1996...............DLB-15
Law, John (see Harkness, Margaret)
Lawes, Henry 1596-1662 ....DLB-126
Lawless, Anthony (see MacDonald, Philip)
Lawless, Emily (The Hon. Emily Lawless)
   1845-1913 ....DLB-240
Lawrence, D. H. 1885-1930
   ..... DLB-10, 19, 36, 98, 162, 195; CDBLB-6
   The D. H. Lawrence Society of
   North America Y-00
Lawrence, David 1888-1973 ....DLB-29
Lawrence, Jerome 1915- DLB-228
Lawrence, Seymour 1926-1994 .... Y-94
   Tribute to Richard Yates Y-92
Lawrence, T. E. 1888-1935 ....DLB-195
   The T. E. Lawrence Society Y-98
Lawson, George 1598-1678 ....DLB-213
Lawson, Henry 1867-1922.............DLB-230
Lawson, John ?-1711 ....DLB-24
Lawson, John Howard 1894-1977 ....DLB-228
Lawson, Louisa Albury 1848-1920 ......DLB-230
Lawson, Robert 1892-1957 ....DLB-22
Lawson, Victor F. 1850-1925............DLB-25
Layard, Austen Henry 1817-1894 ....DLB-166
Layton, Irving 1912- DLB-88
LaZamon flourished circa 1200.........DLB-146
Lazarević, Laza K. 1851-1890 ....DLB-147
Lazarus, George 1904-1997 ....DLB-201
Lazhechnikov, Ivan Ivanovich
   1792-1869 ....DLB-198
Lea, Henry Charles 1825-1909 ....DLB-47
Lea, Sydney 1942- DLB-120, 282

Lea, Tom 1907-2001................DLB-6

Leacock, John 1729-1802..............DLB-31

Leacock, Stephen 1869-1944..........DLB-92

Lead, Jane Ward 1623-1704...........DLB-131

Leadenhall Press..................DLB-106

"The Greatness of Southern Literature":
League of the South Institute for the
Study of Southern Culture and History
...................................Y-02

Leakey, Caroline Woolmer 1827-1881...DLB-230

Leapor, Mary 1722-1746..............DLB-109

Lear, Edward 1812-1888......DLB-32, 163, 166

Leary, Timothy 1920-1996.............DLB-16

W. A. Leary and Company DLB-49

Léautaud, Paul 1872-1956..............DLB-65

Leavis, F. R. 1895-1978...............DLB-242

Leavitt, David 1961-................DLB-130

Leavitt and Allen DLB-49

Le Blond, Mrs. Aubrey 1861-1934......DLB-174

le Carré, John (David John Moore Cornwell)
1931-................DLB-87; CDBLB-8

Tribute to Graham Greene............Y-91

Tribute to George Greenfield.........Y-00

Lécavelé, Roland (see Dorgeles, Roland)

Lechlitner, Ruth 1901-..............DLB-48

Leclerc, Félix 1914-1988..............DLB-60

Le Clézio, J. M. G. 1940-............DLB-83

Leder, Rudolf (see Hermlin, Stephan)

Lederer, Charles 1910-1976..........DLB-26

Ledwidge, Francis 1887-1917..........DLB-20

Lee, Dennis 1939-..................DLB-53

Lee, Don L. (see Madhubuti, Haki R.)

Lee, George W. 1894-1976............DLB-51

Lee, Harper 1926-..........DLB-6; CDALB-1

Lee, Harriet (1757-1851..............DLB-39

Lee, Laurie 1914-1997...............DLB-27

Lee, Leslie 1935-..................DLB-266

Lee, Li-Young 1957-................DLB-165

Lee, Manfred B. 1905-1971............DLB-137

Lee, Nathaniel circa 1645-1692 ....DLB-80

Lee, Robert E. 1918-1994............DLB-228

Lee, Sir Sidney 1859-1926 ....DLB-149, 184

"Principles of Biography," in
Elizabethan and Other Essays......DLB-149

Lee, Sophia (1750-1824)..............DLB-39

Lee, Tanith 1947-..................DLB-261

Lee, Vernon
1856-1935......DLB-57, 153, 156, 174, 178

Lee and Shepard....................DLB-49

Le Fanu, Joseph Sheridan
1814-1873.........DLB-21, 70, 159, 178

Leffland, Ella 1931-................Y-84

le Fort, Gertrud von 1876-1971........DLB-66

Le Gallienne, Richard 1866-1947........DLB-4

Legaré, Hugh Swinton
1797-1843.........DLB-3, 59, 73, 248

Legaré, James Mathewes 1823-1859...DLB-3, 248

Léger, Antoine-J. 1880-1950..........DLB-88

Leggett, William 1801-1839..........DLB-250

Le Guin, Ursula K.
1929-.....DLB-8, 52, 256, 275; CDALB-6

Lehman, Ernest 1920-...............DLB-44

Lehmann, John 1907-1989.........DLB-27, 100

John Lehmann Limited..............DLB-112

Lehmann, Rosamond 1901-1990........DLB-15

Lehmann, Wilhelm 1882-1968..........DLB-56

Leiber, Fritz 1910-1992................DLB-8

Leibniz, Gottfried Wilhelm 1646-1716...DLB-168

Leicester University Press............DLB-112

Leigh, Carolyn 1926-1983.............DLB-265

Leigh, W. R. 1866-1955...............DLB-188

Leinster, Murray 1896-1975............DLB-8

Leiser, Bill 1898-1965................DLB-241

Leisewitz, Johann Anton 1752-1806......DLB-94

Leitch, Maurice 1933-...............DLB-14

Leithauser, Brad 1943-.........DLB-120, 282

Leland, Charles G. 1824-1903..........DLB-11

Leland, John 1503?-1552..............DLB-136

Lemay, Pamphile 1837-1918............DLB-99

Lemelin, Roger 1919-1992.............DLB-88

Lemercier, Louis-Jean-Népomucène
1771-1840......................DLB-192

Le Moine, James MacPherson 1825-1912 .DLB-99

Lemon, Mark 1809-1870..............DLB-163

Le Moyne, Jean 1913-1996.............DLB-88

Lemperly, Paul 1858-1939............DLB-187

L'Engle, Madeleine 1918-............DLB-52

Lennart, Isobel 1915-1971............DLB-44

Lennox, Charlotte 1729 or 1730-1804....DLB-39

Lenox, James 1800-1880..............DLB-140

Lenski, Lois 1893-1974...............DLB-22

Lentricchia, Frank 1940-............DLB-246

Lenz, Hermann 1913-1998.............DLB-69

Lenz, J. M. R. 1751-1792..............DLB-94

Lenz, Siegfried 1926-................DLB-75

Leonard, Elmore 1925-..........DLB-173, 226

Leonard, Hugh 1926-.................DLB-13

Leonard, William Ellery 1876-1944......DLB-54

Leonov, Leonid Maksimovich
1899-1994......................DLB-272

Leonowens, Anna 1834-1914........DLB-99, 166

Leont'ev, Konstantin Nikolaevich
1831-1891......................DLB-277

Leopold, Aldo 1887-1948.............DLB-275

LePan, Douglas 1914-1998.............DLB-88

Lepik, Kalju 1920-1999...............DLB-232

Leprohon, Rosanna Eleanor 1829-1879...DLB-99

Le Queux, William 1864-1927..........DLB-70

Lermontov, Mikhail Iur'evich 1814-1841.DLB-205

Lerner, Alan Jay 1918-1986............DLB-265

Lerner, Max 1902-1992................DLB-29

Lernet-Holenia, Alexander 1897-1976.....DLB-85

Le Rossignol, James 1866-1969........DLB-92

Lescarbot, Marc circa 1570-1642........DLB-99

LeSeur, William Dawson 1840-1917.....DLB-92

LeSieg, Theo. (see Geisel, Theodor Seuss)

Leskov, Nikolai Semenovich 1831-1895..DLB-238

Leslie, Doris before 1902-1982.........DLB-191

Leslie, Eliza 1787-1858...............DLB-202

Leslie, Frank (Henry Carter)
1821-1880.....................DLB-43, 79

Frank Leslie [publishing house].........DLB-49

Leśmian, Bolesław 1878-1937..........DLB-215

Lesperance, John 1835?-1891..........DLB-99

Lessing, Bruno 1870-1940.............DLB-28

Lessing, Doris
1919-......DLB-15, 139; Y-85; CDBLB-8

Lessing, Gotthold Ephraim
1729-1781.............DLB-97; CDWLB-2

The Lessing Society Y-00

Lettau, Reinhard 1929-1996...........DLB-75

The Hemingway Letters Project Finds
an Editor Y-02

Lever, Charles 1806-1872.............DLB-21

Lever, Ralph ca. 1527-1585 ....DLB-236

Leverson, Ada 1862-1933.............DLB-153

Levertov, Denise
1923-1997..........DLB-5, 165; CDALB-7

Levi, Peter 1931-2000................DLB-40

Levi, Primo 1919-1987................DLB-177

Levien, Sonya 1888-1960..............DLB-44

Levin, Meyer 1905-1981.........DLB-9, 28; Y-81

Levin, Phillis 1954-.................DLB-282

Levine, Norman 1923-...............DLB-88

Levine, Philip 1928-.................DLB-5

Levis, Larry 1946-..................DLB-120

Lévi-Strauss, Claude 1908-..........DLB-242

Levitov, Aleksandr Ivanovich
1835?-1877......................DLB-277

Levy, Amy 1861-1889 ....DLB-156, 240

Levy, Benn Wolfe 1900-1973.......DLB-13; Y-81

Lewald, Fanny 1811-1889.............DLB-129

Lewes, George Henry 1817-1878 ....DLB-55, 144

"Criticism in Relation to Novels"
(1863) DLB-21

The Principles of Success in Literature
(1865) [excerpt] DLB-57

Lewis, Agnes Smith 1843-1926..........DLB-174

Lewis, Alfred H. 1857-1914..........DLB-25, 186

Lewis, Alun 1915-1944.............DLB-20, 162

Lewis, C. Day (see Day Lewis, C.)

Lewis, C. I. 1883-1964................DLB-270

Lewis, C. S. 1898-1963
.........DLB-15, 100, 160, 255; CDBLB-7

The New York C. S. Lewis Society Y-99

Lewis, Charles B. 1842-1924..........DLB-11

Lewis, David 1941-2001...............DLB-279

Lewis, Henry Clay 1825-1850 ....DLB-3, 248

Lewis, Janet 1899-1999................Y-87

| Tribute to Katherine Anne Porter Y-80
Lewis, Matthew Gregory
  1775-1818 .... DLB-39, 158, 178
Lewis, Meriwether 1774-1809 ...... DLB-183, 186
Lewis, Norman 1908- DLB-204
Lewis, R. W. B. 1917- DLB-111
Lewis, Richard circa 1700-1734 .... DLB-24
Lewis, Sinclair
  1885-1951 ...... DLB-9, 102; DS-1; CDALB-4
  Sinclair Lewis Centennial Conference ... Y-85
  The Sinclair Lewis Society Y-99
Lewis, Wilmarth Sheldon 1895-1979 ..... DLB-140
Lewis, Wyndham 1882-1957 .... DLB-15
  Time and Western Man
    [excerpt] (1927) DLB-36
Lewisohn, Ludwig 1882-1955 ... DLB-4, 9, 28, 102
Leyendecker, J. C. 1874-1951 .... DLB-188
Lezama Lima, José 1910-1976 ...... DLB-113, 283
L'Heureux, John 1934- DLB-244
Libbey, Laura Jean 1862-1924 .... DLB-221
Libedinsky, Iurii Nikolaevich
  1898-1959 .... DLB-272
Library History Group Y-01
E-Books' Second Act in Libraries Y-02
The Library of America DLB-46
The Library of America: An Assessment
  After Two Decades Y-02
Licensing Act of 1737 .... DLB-84
Leonard Lichfield I [publishing house] ... DLB-170
Lichtenberg, Georg Christoph
  1742-1799 .... DLB-94
The Liddle Collection Y-97
Lidman, Sara 1923- DLB-257
Lieb, Fred 1888-1980 .... DLB-171
Liebling, A. J. 1904-1963 .... DLB-4, 171
Lieutenant Murray (see Ballou, Maturin Murray)
Lighthall, William Douw 1857-1954 ...... DLB-92
Lihn, Enrique 1929-1988 .... DLB-283
Lilar, Françoise (see Mallet-Joris, Françoise)
Lili'uokalani, Queen 1838-1917 .... DLB-221
Lillo, George 1691-1739 .... DLB-84
Lilly, J. K., Jr. 1893-1966 .... DLB-140
Lilly, Wait and Company DLB-49
Lily, William circa 1468-1522 .... DLB-132
Limited Editions Club DLB-46
Limón, Graciela 1938- DLB-209
Lincoln and Edmands DLB-49
Lindesay, Ethel Forence
  (see Richardson, Henry Handel)
Lindgren, Astrid 1907-2002 .... DLB-257
Lindgren, Torgny 1938- DLB-257
Lindsay, Alexander William, Twenty-fifth
  Earl of Crawford 1812-1880 ...... DLB-184
Lindsay, Sir David circa 1485-1555 ..... DLB-132
Lindsay, David 1878-1945 .... DLB-255
Lindsay, Jack 1900-1990 .... Y-84

Lindsay, Lady (Caroline Blanche
  Elizabeth Fitzroy Lindsay)
  1844-1912 .... DLB-199
Lindsay, Norman 1879-1969 .... DLB-260
Lindsay, Vachel 1879-1931 .... DLB-54; CDALB-3
Linebarger, Paul Myron Anthony
  (see Smith, Cordwainer)
Link, Arthur S. 1920-1998 .... DLB-17
Linn, Ed 1922-2000 .... DLB-241
Linn, John Blair 1777-1804 .... DLB-37
Lins, Osman 1924-1978 .... DLB-145
Linton, Eliza Lynn 1822-1898 .... DLB-18
Linton, William James 1812-1897 .... DLB-32
Barnaby Bernard Lintot
  [publishing house] DLB-170
Lion Books DLB-46
Lionni, Leo 1910-1999 .... DLB-61
Lippard, George 1822-1854 .... DLB-202
Lippincott, Sara Jane Clarke 1823-1904 ... DLB-43
J. B. Lippincott Company DLB-49
Lippmann, Walter 1889-1974 .... DLB-29
Lipton, Lawrence 1898-1975 .... DLB-16
Liscow, Christian Ludwig 1701-1760 ..... DLB-97
Lish, Gordon 1934- DLB-130
  Tribute to Donald Barthelme Y-89
  Tribute to James Dickey Y-97
Lisle, Charles-Marie-René Leconte de
  1818-1894 .... DLB-217
Lispector, Clarice
  1925-1977 .... DLB-113; CDWLB-3
LitCheck Website Y-01
Literary Awards and Honors Y-81–02
  Booker Prize Y-86, 96–98
  The Drue Heinz Literature Prize Y-82
  The Elmer Holmes Bobst Awards
    in Arts and Letters Y-87
  The Griffin Poetry Prize Y-00
  Literary Prizes [British] DLB-15, 207
  National Book Critics Circle
    Awards Y-00–01
  The National Jewish Book Awards Y-85
  Nobel Prize Y-80–02
  Winning an Edgar Y-98
The Literary Chronicle and Weekly Review
  1819-1828 .... DLB-110
Literary Periodicals:
  Callaloo Y-87
  Expatriates in Paris DS-15
  New Literary Periodicals:
    A Report for 1987 .... Y-87
    A Report for 1988 .... Y-88
    A Report for 1989 .... Y-89
    A Report for 1990 .... Y-90
    A Report for 1991 .... Y-91
    A Report for 1992 .... Y-92
    A Report for 1993 .... Y-93
Literary Research Archives:
  The Anthony Burgess Archive at

    the Harry Ransom Humanities
      Research Center Y-98
  Archives of Charles Scribner's Sons DS-17
  Berg Collection of English and
    American Literature of the
    New York Public Library Y-83
  The Bobbs-Merrill Archive at the
    Lilly Library, Indiana University ... Y-90
  Die Fürstliche Bibliothek Corvey Y-96
  Guide to the Archives of Publishers,
    Journals, and Literary Agents in
    North American Libraries Y-93
  The Henry E. Huntington Library Y-92
  The Humanities Research Center,
    University of Texas Y-82
  The John Carter Brown Library Y-85
  Kent State Special Collections Y-86
  The Lilly Library Y-84
  The Modern Literary Manuscripts
    Collection in the Special
    Collections of the Washington
    University Libraries Y-87
  A Publisher's Archives: G. P. Putnam ... Y-92
  Special Collections at Boston
    University Y-99
  The University of Virginia Libraries Y-91
  The William Charvat American Fiction
    Collection at the Ohio State
    University Libraries Y-92
Literary Societies Y-98–02
  The Margery Allingham Society Y-98
  The American Studies Association
    of Norway Y-00
  The Arnold Bennett Society Y-98
  The Association for the Study of
    Literature and Environment
    (ASLE) Y-99
  Belgian Luxembourg American Studies
    Association Y-01
  The E. F. Benson Society Y-98
  The Elizabeth Bishop Society Y-01
  The Brontë Society Y-98
  The [Edgar Rice] Burroughs
    Bibliophiles Y-98
  The Byron Society of America Y-00
  The Lewis Carroll Society
    of North America Y-00
  The Willa Cather Pioneer Memorial
    and Education Foundation Y-00
  New Chaucer Society Y-00
  The Wilkie Collins Society Y-98
  The James Fenimore Cooper Society ... Y-01
  The Stephen Crane Society Y-98, 01
  The E. E. Cummings Society Y-01
  The James Dickey Society Y-99
  John Dos Passos Newsletter Y-00
  The Priory Scholars [Sir Arthur Conan
    Doyle] of New York Y-99
  The International Theodore Dreiser
    Society Y-01
  The Friends of the Dymock Poets Y-00

The George Eliot Fellowship. Y-99	The Thoreau Society Y-99	*Locrine and Selimus* DLB-62
The T. S. Eliot Society: Celebration and Scholarship, 1980-1999. . . . . Y-99	The Tilling [E. F. Benson] Society Y-98	Lodge, David 1935- DLB-14, 194
The Ralph Waldo Emerson Society Y-99	The Trollope Societies Y-00	Lodge, George Cabot 1873-1909 . . . . DLB-54
The William Faulkner Society Y-99	H. G. Wells Society Y-98	Lodge, Henry Cabot 1850-1924. . . . . DLB-47
The C. S. Forester Society. Y-00	The Western Literature Association Y-99	Lodge, Thomas 1558-1625. . . . . .DLB-172
The Hamlin Garland Society Y-01	The William Carlos Williams Society . . . Y-99	*Defence of Poetry* (1579) [excerpt] DLB-172
The [Elizabeth] Gaskell Society. Y-98	The Henry Williamson Society Y-98	Loeb, Harold 1891-1974. . . . . DLB-4; DS-15
The Charlotte Perkins Gilman Society . . . Y-99	The [Nero] Wolfe Pack. Y-99	Loeb, William 1905-1981 . . . . .DLB-127
The Ellen Glasgow Society Y-01	The Thomas Wolfe Society Y-99	Loesser, Frank 1910-1969. . . . . DLB-265
Zane Grey's West Society. Y-00	Worldwide Wodehouse Societies Y-98	Lofting, Hugh 1886-1947 . . . . DLB-160
The Ivor Gurney Society Y-98	The W. B. Yeats Society of N.Y. Y-99	Logan, Deborah Norris 1761-1839. . . . . . . DLB-200
The Joel Chandler Harris Association . . . Y-99	The Charlotte M. Yonge Fellowship. Y-98	Logan, James 1674-1751 . . . . DLB-24, 140
The Nathaniel Hawthorne Society Y-00	Literary Theory The Year in Literary Theory Y-92–Y-93	Logan, John 1923-1987. . . . . DLB-5
The [George Alfred] Henty Society Y-98	*Literature at Nurse, or Circulating Morals* (1885), by George Moore. DLB-18	Logan, Martha Daniell 1704?-1779 . . . . . . DLB-200
George Moses Horton Society Y-99	Litt, Toby 1968- DLB-267	Logan, William 1950- DLB-120
The William Dean Howells Society Y-01	Littell, Eliakim 1797-1870 . . . . DLB-79	Logau, Friedrich von 1605-1655 . . . . DLB-164
WW2 HMSO Paperbacks Society Y-98	Littell, Robert S. 1831-1896 . . . . DLB-79	Logue, Christopher 1926- DLB-27
American Humor Studies Association . . . Y-99	Little, Brown and Company. DLB-49	Lohenstein, Daniel Casper von 1635-1683 . . . . DLB-168
International Society for Humor Studies. . Y-99	Little Magazines and Newspapers DS-15	Lo-Johansson, Ivar 1901-1990 . . . . DLB-259
The W. W. Jacobs Appreciation Society. . Y-98	Selected English-Language Little Magazines and Newspapers [France, 1920-1939] DLB-4	Lokert, George circa 1485-1547 . . . . DLB-281
The Richard Jefferies Society Y-98	The Little Magazines of the New Formalism DLB-282	Lomonosov, Mikhail Vasil'evich 1711-1765 . . . . DLB-150
The Jerome K. Jerome Society Y-98	*The Little Review* 1914-1929 . . . . .DS-15	London, Jack 1876-1916. . . . . . .DLB-8, 12, 78, 212; CDALB-3
The Philip Larkin Society Y-99	Littlewood, Joan 1914-2002 . . . . DLB-13	The Jack London Research Center. Y-00
The D. H. Lawrence Society of North America DS-10	Lively, Penelope 1933- DLB-14, 161, 207	The Jack London Society Y-99
The T. E. Lawrence Society Y-98	Liverpool University Press DLB-112	*The London Magazine* 1820-1829. . . . . DLB-110
The [Gotthold] Lessing Society. Y-00	*The Lives of the Poets* (1753). DLB-142	Long, David 1948- DLB-244
The New York C. S. Lewis Society Y-99	Livesay, Dorothy 1909-1996 . . . . DLB-68	Long, H., and Brother DLB-49
The Sinclair Lewis Society Y-99	Livesay, Florence Randal 1874-1953 . . . . DLB-92	Long, Haniel 1888-1956 . . . . DLB-45
The Jack London Research Center. Y-00	Livings, Henry 1929-1998 . . . . DLB-13	Long, Ray 1878-1935 . . . . .DLB-137
The Jack London Society Y-99	Livingston, Anne Howe 1763-1841 . . .DLB-37, 200	Longfellow, Henry Wadsworth 1807-1882. . . . . DLB-1, 59, 235; CDALB-2
The Cormac McCarthy Society Y-99	Livingston, Jay 1915-2001 . . . . DLB-265	Longfellow, Samuel 1819-1892. . . . . DLB-1
The Melville Society Y-01	Livingston, Myra Cohn 1926-1996 . . . . . . DLB-61	Longford, Elizabeth 1906-2002 . . . . DLB-155
The Arthur Miller Society. Y-01	Livingston, William 1723-1790 . . . . DLB-31	Tribute to Alfred A. Knopf. Y-84
The Milton Society of America. Y-00	Livingstone, David 1813-1873 . . . . DLB-166	Longinus circa first century DLB-176
International Marianne Moore Society . . . Y-98	Livingstone, Douglas 1932-1996 . . . . . . DLB-225	Longley, Michael 1939- DLB-40
International Nabokov Society Y-99	Livy 59 B.C.-A.D. 17 . . . . . . DLB-211; CDWLB-1	T. Longman [publishing house] DLB-154
The Vladimir Nabokov Society Y-01	Liyong, Taban lo (see Taban lo Liyong)	Longmans, Green and Company DLB-49
The Flannery O'Connor Society Y-99	Lizárraga, Sylvia S. 1925- DLB-82	Longmore, George 1793?-1867. . . . . DLB-99
The Wilfred Owen Association Y-98	Llewellyn, Richard 1906-1983 . . . . DLB-15	Longstreet, Augustus Baldwin 1790-1870. . . . . .DLB-3, 11, 74, 248
Penguin Collectors' Society. Y-98	Edward Lloyd [publishing house]. DLB-106	D. Longworth [publishing house]. DLB-49
The [E. A.] Poe Studies Association Y-99	Lobel, Arnold 1933- DLB-61	Lonsdale, Frederick 1881-1954. . . . . DLB-10
The Katherine Anne Porter Society Y-01	Lochridge, Betsy Hopkins (see Fancher, Betsy)	Loos, Anita 1893-1981 . . . . .DLB-11, 26, 228; Y-81
The Beatrix Potter Society Y-98	Locke, Alain 1886-1954 . . . . DLB-51	Lopate, Phillip 1943- Y-80
The Ezra Pound Society Y-01	Locke, David Ross 1833-1888 . . . . DLB-11, 23	Lopez, Barry 1945- DLB-256, 275
The Powys Society Y-98	Locke, John 1632-1704 . . . . .DLB-31, 101, 213, 252	López, Diana (see Isabella, Ríos)
Proust Society of America. Y-00	Locke, Richard Adams 1800-1871 . . . . . . DLB-43	López, Josefina 1969- DLB-209
The Dorothy L. Sayers Society. Y-98	Locker-Lampson, Frederick 1821-1895 . . . . DLB-35, 184	Loranger, Jean-Aubert 1896-1942. . . . . . . DLB-92
The Bernard Shaw Society Y-99	Lockhart, John Gibson 1794-1854. . . . . DLB-110, 116, 144	Lorca, Federico García 1898-1936 . . . . . . DLB-108
The Society for the Study of Southern Literature Y-00	Lockridge, Ross, Jr. 1914-1948. . . . . .DLB-143; Y-80	Lord, John Keast 1818-1872 . . . . DLB-99
The Wallace Stevens Society Y-99		Lorde, Audre 1934-1992 . . . . DLB-41
The Harriet Beecher Stowe Center. Y-00		Lorimer, George Horace 1867-1937 . . . . . DLB-91
The R. S. Surtees Society Y-98		

A. K. Loring [publishing house]..........DLB-49
Loring and Mussey...................DLB-46
Lorris, Guillaume de (see *Roman de la Rose*)
Lossing, Benson J. 1813-1891..........DLB-30
Lothar, Ernst 1890-1974..............DLB-81
D. Lothrop and Company..............DLB-49
Lothrop, Harriet M. 1844-1924.........DLB-42
Loti, Pierre 1850-1923...............DLB-123
Lotichius Secundus, Petrus 1528-1560....DLB-179
Lott, Emmeline ?-?...................DLB-166
Louisiana State University Press.........Y-97
Lounsbury, Thomas R. 1838-1915.......DLB-71
Louÿs, Pierre 1870-1925..............DLB-123
Lovejoy, Arthur O. 1873-1962..........DLB-270
Lovelace, Earl 1935-......DLB-125; CDWLB-3
Lovelace, Richard 1618-1657..........DLB-131
John W. Lovell Company.............DLB-49
Lovell, Coryell and Company..........DLB-49
Lover, Samuel 1797-1868.........DLB-159, 190
Lovesey, Peter 1936-.................DLB-87
    Tribute to Georges Simenon..........Y-89
Lovinescu, Eugen
  1881-1943............DLB-220; CDWLB-4
Lovingood, Sut
  (see Harris, George Washington)
Low, Samuel 1765-?..................DLB-37
Lowell, Amy 1874-1925..........DLB-54, 140
Lowell, James Russell 1819-1891
  .....DLB-1, 11, 64, 79, 189, 235; CDALB-2
Lowell, Robert
  1917-1977...........DLB-5, 169; CDALB-7
Lowenfels, Walter 1897-1976.............DLB-4
Lowndes, Marie Belloc 1868-1947........DLB-70
Lowndes, William Thomas 1798-1843...DLB-184
Humphrey Lownes [publishing house]...DLB-170
Lowry, Lois 1937-....................DLB-52
Lowry, Malcolm 1909-1957...DLB-15; CDBLB-7
Lowther, Pat 1935-1975................DLB-53
Loy, Mina 1882-1966...............DLB-4, 54
Loynaz, Dulce María 1902-1997........DLB-283
Lozeau, Albert 1878-1924..............DLB-92
Lubbock, Percy 1879-1965.............DLB-149
Lucan A.D. 39-A.D. 65................DLB-211
Lucas, E. V. 1868-1938........DLB-98, 149, 153
Fielding Lucas Jr. [publishing house]......DLB-49
Luce, Clare Booth 1903-1987..........DLB-228
Luce, Henry R. 1808 1967..............DLB-91
John W. Luce and Company............DLB-46
Lucian circa 120-180.................DLB-176
Lucie-Smith, Edward 1933-.............DLB-40
Lucilius circa 180 B.C.-102/101 B.C.....DLB-211
Lucini, Gian Pietro 1867-1914.........DLB-114
Lucretius circa 94 B.C.-circa 49 B.C.
  ....DLB-211; CDWLB-1
Luder, Peter circa 1415-1472..........DLB-179

Ludlam, Charles 1943-1987...........DLB-266
Ludlum, Robert 1927-2001..............Y-82
Ludus de Antichristo circa 1160.......DLB-148
Ludvigson, Susan 1942-..............DLB-120
Ludwig, Jack 1922-...................DLB-60
Ludwig, Otto 1813-1865..............DLB-129
Ludwigslied 881 or 882.............DLB-148
Luera, Yolanda 1953-................DLB-122
Luft, Lya 1938-.....................DLB-145
Lugansky, Kazak Vladimir
  (see Dal', Vladimir Ivanovich)
Lugn, Kristina 1948-................DLB-257
Lugones, Leopoldo 1874-1938.........DLB-283
Lukács, Georg (see Lukács, György)
Lukács, György
  1885-1971.......DLB-215, 242; CDWLB-4
Luke, Peter 1919-....................DLB-13
Lummis, Charles F. 1859-1928.........DLB-186
Lundkvist, Artur 1906-1991...........DLB-259
Lunts, Lev Natanovich 1901-1924......DLB-272
F. M. Lupton Company...............DLB-49
Lupus of Ferrières circa 805-circa 862...DLB-148
Lurie, Alison 1926-...................DLB-2
Lussu, Emilio 1890-1975.............DLB-264
Lustig, Arnošt 1926-.................DLB-232
Luther, Martin 1483-1546...DLB-179; CDWLB-2
Luzi, Mario 1914-...................DLB-128
L'vov, Nikolai Aleksandrovich
  1751-1803........................DLB-150
Lyall, Gavin 1932-...................DLB-87
Lydgate, John circa 1370-1450........DLB-146
Lyly, John circa 1554-1606........DLB-62, 167
Lynch, Patricia 1898-1972............DLB-160
Lynch, Richard flourished 1596-1601...DLB-172
Lynd, Robert 1879-1949...............DLB-98
Lyon, Matthew 1749-1822.............DLB-43
Lyotard, Jean-François 1924-1998......DLB-242
Lyricists
  Additional Lyricists: 1920-1960.....DLB-265
Lysias circa 459 B.C.-circa 380 B.C......DLB-176
Lytle, Andrew 1902-1995.........DLB-6; Y-95
  Tribute to Caroline Gordon..........Y-81
  Tribute to Katherine Anne Porter.....Y-80
Lytton, Edward
  (see Bulwer-Lytton, Edward)
Lytton, Edward Robert Bulwer
  1831-1891........................DLB-32

M

Maass, Joachim 1901-1972.............DLB-69
Mabie, Hamilton Wright 1845-1916......DLB-71
Mac A'Ghobhainn, Iain (see Smith, Iain Crichton)
MacArthur, Charles 1895-1956.....DLB-7, 25, 44
Macaulay, Catherine 1731-1791........DLB-104
Macaulay, David 1945-................DLB-61
Macaulay, Rose 1881-1958.............DLB-36

Macaulay, Thomas Babington
  1800-1859...........DLB-32, 55; CDBLB-4
Macaulay Company...................DLB-46
MacBeth, George 1932-1992............DLB-40
Macbeth, Madge 1880-1965............DLB-92
MacCaig, Norman 1910-1996...........DLB-27
MacDiarmid, Hugh
  1892-1978..............DLB-20; CDBLB-7
MacDonald, Cynthia 1928-............DLB-105
MacDonald, George 1824-1905....DLB-18, 163, 178
MacDonald, John D. 1916-1986......DLB-8; Y-86
MacDonald, Philip 1899?-1980..........DLB-77
Macdonald, Ross (see Millar, Kenneth)
Macdonald, Sharman 1951-............DLB-245
MacDonald, Wilson 1880-1967..........DLB-92
Macdonald and Company (Publishers)...DLB-112
MacEwen, Gwendolyn 1941-1987....DLB-53, 251
Macfadden, Bernarr 1868-1955.......DLB-25, 91
MacGregor, John 1825-1892............DLB-166
MacGregor, Mary Esther (see Keith, Marian)
Machado, Antonio 1875-1939..........DLB-108
Machado, Manuel 1874-1947...........DLB-108
Machar, Agnes Maule 1837-1927........DLB-92
Machaut, Guillaume de
  circa 1300-1377..................DLB-208
Machen, Arthur Llewelyn Jones
  1863-1947............. DLB-36, 156, 178
MacIlmaine, Roland 1550?-?..........DLB-281
MacInnes, Colin 1914-1976.............DLB-14
MacInnes, Helen 1907-1985............DLB-87
Mac Intyre, Tom 1931-................DLB-245
Mačiulis, Jonas (see Maironis, Jonas)
Mack, Maynard 1909-.................DLB-111
Mackall, Leonard L. 1879-1937........DLB-140
MacKay, Isabel Ecclestone 1875-1928....DLB-92
MacKaye, Percy 1875-1956.............DLB-54
Macken, Walter 1915-1967.............DLB-13
Mackenzie, Alexander 1763-1820........DLB-99
Mackenzie, Alexander Slidell
  1803-1848........................DLB-183
Mackenzie, Compton 1883-1972.....DLB-34, 100
Mackenzie, Henry 1745-1831...........DLB-39
  The Lounger, no. 20 (1785).........DLB-39
Mackenzie, Kenneth (Seaforth Mackenzie)
  1913-1955........................DLB-260
Mackenzie, William 1758-1828.........DLB-187
Mackey, Nathaniel 1947-..............DLB-169
Mackey, Shena 1944-.................DLB-231
Mackey, William Wellington 1937-......DLB-38
Mackintosh, Elizabeth (see Tey, Josephine)
Mackintosh, Sir James 1765-1832......DLB-158
Macklin, Charles 1699-1797............DLB-89
Maclaren, Ian (see Watson, John)
MacLaverty, Bernard 1942-............DLB-267
MacLean, Alistair 1922-1987..........DLB-276
MacLean, Katherine Anne 1925-.........DLB-8

Maclean, Norman 1902-1990 .... DLB-206

MacLeish, Archibald 1892-1982
........DLB-4, 7, 45; Y-82; DS-15; CDALB-7

MacLennan, Hugh 1907-1990 .... DLB-68

MacLeod, Alistair 1936- DLB-60

Macleod, Fiona (see Sharp, William)

Macleod, Norman 1906-1985........... DLB-4

Mac Low, Jackson 1922- DLB-193

Macmillan and Company............ DLB-106

The Macmillan Company DLB-49

Macmillan's English Men of Letters,
First Series (1878-1892) DLB-144

MacNamara, Brinsley 1890-1963 .... DLB-10

MacNeice, Louis 1907-1963 .... DLB-10, 20

Macphail, Andrew 1864-1938 .... DLB-92

Macpherson, James 1736-1796 .... DLB-109

Macpherson, Jay 1931- DLB-53

Macpherson, Jeanie 1884-1946......... DLB-44

Macrae Smith Company................ DLB-46

MacRaye, Lucy Betty (see Webling, Lucy)

John Macrone [publishing house] DLB-106

MacShane, Frank 1927-1999........... DLB-111

Macy-Masius DLB-46

Madden, David 1933- DLB-6

Madden, Sir Frederic 1801-1873........ DLB-184

Maddow, Ben 1909-1992 .... DLB-44

Maddux, Rachel 1912-1983 ...... DLB-234; Y-93

Madgett, Naomi Long 1923- DLB-76

Madhubuti, Haki R. 1942- DLB-5, 41; DS-8

Madison, James 1751-1836 .... DLB-37

Madsen, Svend Åge 1939- DLB-214

Maeterlinck, Maurice 1862-1949 .... DLB-192

Mafūz, Najīb 1911- Y-88
    Nobel Lecture 1988 .... Y-88

The Little Magazines of the
New Formalism DLB-282

Magee, David 1905-1977 .... DLB-187

Maginn, William 1794-1842 .... DLB-110, 159

Magoffin, Susan Shelby 1827-1855 ..... DLB-239

Mahan, Alfred Thayer 1840-1914 .... DLB-47

Maheux-Forcier, Louise 1929- DLB-60

Mahin, John Lee 1902-1984 .... DLB-44

Mahon, Derek 1941- DLB-40

Maikov, Apollon Nikolaevich
1821-1897..................... DLB-277

Maikov, Vasilii Ivanovich 1728-1778 .... DLB-150

Mailer, Norman 1923-
........DLB-2, 16, 28, 185, 278; Y-80, 83, 97;
DS-3; CDALB-6
    Tribute to Isaac Bashevis Singer........ Y-91
    Tribute to Meyer Levin Y-81

Maillart, Ella 1903-1997 .... DLB-195

Maillet, Adrienne 1885-1963 .... DLB-68

Maillet, Antonine 1929- DLB-60

Maillu, David G. 1939- DLB-157

Maimonides, Moses 1138-1204 .... DLB-115

Main Selections of the Book-of-the-Month
Club, 1926-1945 .... DLB-9

Mainwaring, Daniel 1902-1977......... DLB-44

Mair, Charles 1838-1927 .... DLB-99

Mair, John circa 1467-1550........... DLB-281

Maironis, Jonas 1862-1932 .. DLB-220; CDWLB-4

Mais, Roger 1905-1955 .... DLB-125; CDWLB-3

Maitland, Sara 1950- DLB-271

Major, Andre 1942- DLB-60

Major, Charles 1856-1913 .... DLB-202

Major, Clarence 1936- DLB-33

Major, Kevin 1949- DLB-60

Major Books..................... DLB-46

Makarenko, Anton Semenovich
1888-1939 ....DLB-272

Makemie, Francis circa 1658-1708 .... DLB-24

The Making of Americans Contract............ Y-98

Maksimović, Desanka
1898-1993 ....DLB-147; CDWLB-4

Malamud, Bernard 1914-1986
.......DLB-2, 28, 152; Y-80, 86; CDALB-1
    Bernard Malamud Archive at the
    Harry Ransom Humanities
    Research Center Y-00

Mălăncioiu, Ileana 1940- DLB-232

Malaparte, Curzio
(Kurt Erich Suckert) 1898-1957 ..... DLB-264

Malerba, Luigi 1927- DLB-196

Malet, Lucas 1852-1931 .... DLB-153

Mallarmé, Stéphane 1842-1898 .... DLB-217

Malleson, Lucy Beatrice (see Gilbert, Anthony)

Mallet-Joris, Françoise (Françoise Lilar)
1930- DLB-83

Mallock, W. H. 1849-1923...........DLB-18, 57
    "Every Man His Own Poet; or,
    The Inspired Singer's Recipe
    Book" (1877) DLB-35
    "Le Style c'est l'homme" (1892) DLB-57
    Memoirs of Life and Literature (1920),
    [excerpt] DLB-57

Malone, Dumas 1892-1986 .... DLB-17

Malone, Edmond 1741-1812 .... DLB-142

Malory, Sir Thomas
circa 1400-1410 - 1471 ... DLB-146; CDBLB-1

Malpede, Karen 1945- DLB-249

Malraux, André 1901-1976............ DLB-72

Malthus, Thomas Robert
1766-1834..................DLB-107, 158

Maltz, Albert 1908-1985.............. DLB-102

Malzberg, Barry N. 1939- DLB-8

Mamet, David 1947- DLB-7

Mamin, Dmitrii Narkisovich 1852-1912.. DLB-238

Manaka, Matsemela 1956- DLB-157

Manchester University Press DLB-112

Mandel, Eli 1922-1992 .... DLB-53

Mandeville, Bernard 1670-1733 .... DLB-101

Mandeville, Sir John
mid fourteenth century DLB-146

Mandiargues, André Pieyre de
1909-1991 .... DLB-83

Manea, Norman 1936- DLB-232

Manfred, Frederick 1912-1994 ....DLB-6, 212, 227

Manfredi, Gianfranco 1948- DLB-196

Mangan, Sherry 1904-1961 .... DLB-4

Manganelli, Giorgio 1922-1990 .... DLB-196

Manilius fl. first century A.D........... DLB-211

Mankiewicz, Herman 1897-1953 .... DLB-26

Mankiewicz, Joseph L. 1909-1993 .... DLB-44

Mankowitz, Wolf 1924-1998 .... DLB-15

Manley, Delariviere 1672?-1724 ...... DLB-39, 80
    Preface to The Secret History, of Queen
    Zarah, and the Zarazians (1705).... DLB-39

Mann, Abby 1927- DLB-44

Mann, Charles 1929-1998 .... Y-98

Mann, Emily 1952- DLB-266

Mann, Heinrich 1871-1950......... DLB-66, 118

Mann, Horace 1796-1859 .... DLB-1, 235

Mann, Klaus 1906-1949 .... DLB-56

Mann, Mary Peabody 1806-1887 .... DLB-239

Mann, Thomas 1875-1955 ... DLB-66; CDWLB-2

Mann, William D'Alton 1839-1920 ......DLB-137

Mannin, Ethel 1900-1984......... DLB-191, 195

Manning, Emily (see Australie)

Manning, Frederic 1882-1935.......... DLB-260

Manning, Laurence 1899-1972......... DLB-251

Manning, Marie 1873?-1945 .... DLB-29

Manning and Loring DLB-49

Mannyng, Robert flourished 1303-1338.. DLB-146

Mano, D. Keith 1942- DLB-6

Manor Books..................... DLB-46

Mansfield, Katherine 1888-1923........ DLB-162

Mantel, Hilary 1952- DLB-271

Manuel, Niklaus circa 1484-1530 ....DLB-179

Manzini, Gianna 1896-1974 ....DLB-177

Mapanje, Jack 1944- DLB-157

Maraini, Dacia 1936- DLB-196

March, William (William Edward Campbell)
1893-1954 .... DLB-9, 86

Marchand, Leslie A. 1900-1999 .... DLB-103

Marchant, Bessie 1862-1941.......... DLB-160

Marchant, Tony 1959- DLB-245

Marchenko, Anastasiia Iakovlevna
1830-1880 .... DLB-238

Marchessault, Jovette 1938- DLB-60

Marcinkevičius, Justinas 1930- DLB-232

Marcus, Frank 1928- DLB-13

Marcuse, Herbert 1898-1979 .... DLB-242

Marden, Orison Swett 1850-1924 .....DLB-137

Marechera, Dambudzo 1952-1987 ......DLB-157

Marek, Richard, Books................ DLB-46

Mares, E. A. 1938- DLB-122

Margulies, Donald 1954- DLB-228

Mariani, Paul 1940- DLB-111

Marie de France flourished 1160-1178....DLB-208	Martin, David 1915-1997..............DLB-260	Matoš, Antun Gustav 1873-1914........DLB-147
Marie-Victorin, Frère (Conrad Kirouac) 1885-1944......................DLB-92	Martin, Jay 1935- DLB-111	Matsumoto Seichō 1909-1992..........DLB-182
	Martin, Johann (see Laurentius von Schnüffis)	The Matter of England 1240-1400......DLB-146
Marin, Biagio 1891-1985..............DLB-128	Martin, Thomas 1696-1771............DLB-213	The Matter of Rome early twelfth to late fifteenth century................DLB-146
Marinetti, Filippo Tommaso 1876-1944..................DLB-114, 264	Martin, Violet Florence (see Ross, Martin)	
Marinković, Ranko 1913- DLB-147; CDWLB-4	Martin du Gard, Roger 1881-1958.......DLB-65	Matthew of Vendôme circa 1130-circa 1200..............DLB-208
	Martineau, Harriet 1802-1876....DLB-21, 55, 159, 163, 166, 190	Matthews, Brander 1852-1929..DLB-71, 78; DS-13
Marion, Frances 1886-1973.............DLB-44		Matthews, Jack 1925- DLB-6
Marius, Richard C. 1933-1999...........Y-85	Martínez, Demetria 1960- DLB-209	Matthews, Victoria Earle 1861-1907.....DLB-221
Markevich, Boleslav Mikhailovich 1822-1884.....................DLB-238	Martínez, Eliud 1935- DLB-122	Matthews, William 1942-1997...........DLB-5
	Martínez, Max 1943- DLB-82	Matthiessen, F. O. 1902-1950...........DLB-63
Markfield, Wallace 1926-2002........DLB-2, 28	Martínez, Rubén 1962- DLB-209	Matthiessen, Peter 1927- DLB-6, 173, 275
Markham, Edwin 1852-1940........DLB-54, 186	Martinson, Harry 1904-1978..........DLB-259	Maturin, Charles Robert 1780-1824.....DLB-178
Markle, Fletcher 1921-1991........DLB-68; Y-91	Martinson, Moa 1890-1964...........DLB-259	Maugham, W. Somerset 1874-1965 ....DLB-10, 36, 77, 100, 162, 195; CDBLB-6
Marlatt, Daphne 1942- DLB-60	Martone, Michael 1955- DLB-218	
Marlitt, E. 1825-1887..................DLB-129	Martyn, Edward 1859-1923............DLB-10	Maupassant, Guy de 1850-1893........DLB-123
Marlowe, Christopher 1564-1593............. DLB-62, CDBLB-1	Marvell, Andrew 1621-1678.............DLB-131; CDBLB-2	Maupin, Armistead 1944- DLB-278
		Mauriac, Claude 1914-1996............DLB-83
Marlyn, John 1912- DLB-88	Marvin X 1944- DLB-38	Mauriac, François 1885-1970...........DLB-65
Marmion, Shakerley 1603-1639.........DLB-58	Marx, Karl 1818-1883.................DLB-129	Maurice, Frederick Denison 1805-1872....DLB-55
Der Marner before 1230-circa 1287.....DLB-138	Marzials, Theo 1850-1920..............DLB-35	Maurois, André 1885-1967.............DLB-65
Marnham, Patrick 1943- DLB-204	Masefield, John 1878-1967...DLB-10, 19, 153, 160; CDBLB-5	Maury, James 1718-1769..............DLB-31
The *Marprelate Tracts* 1588-1589........DLB-132		Mavor, Elizabeth 1927- DLB-14
Marquand, John P. 1893-1960........DLB-9, 102	Masham, Damaris Cudworth, Lady 1659-1708....................DLB-252	Mavor, Osborne Henry (see Bridie, James)
Marqués, René 1919-1979.............DLB-113		Maxwell, Gavin 1914-1969............DLB-204
Marquis, Don 1878-1937............DLB-11, 25	Masino, Paola 1908-1989..............DLB-264	Maxwell, William 1908-2000............. DLB-218, 278; Y-80
Marriott, Anne 1913-1997.............DLB-68	Mason, A. E. W. 1865-1948............DLB-70	
Marryat, Frederick 1792-1848........DLB-21, 163	Mason, Bobbie Ann 1940- DLB-173; Y-87; CDALB-7	Tribute to Nancy Hale................Y-88
Marsh, Capen, Lyon and Webb.........DLB-49		H. Maxwell [publishing house]..........DLB-49
Marsh, George Perkins 1801-1882..................DLB-1, 64, 243	Mason, William 1725-1797............DLB-142	John Maxwell [publishing house]........DLB-106
	Mason Brothers......................DLB-49	May, Elaine 1932- DLB-44
Marsh, James 1794-1842............DLB-1, 59	The *Massachusetts Quarterly Review* 1847-1850......................DLB-1	May, Karl 1842-1912..................DLB-129
Marsh, Narcissus 1638-1713...........DLB-213		May, Thomas 1595/1596-1650..........DLB-58
Marsh, Ngaio 1899-1982..............DLB-77	Massey, Gerald 1828-1907.............DLB-32	Mayer, Bernadette 1945- DLB-165
Marshall, Alan 1902-1984.............DLB-260	Massey, Linton R. 1900-1974..........DLB-187	Mayer, Mercer 1943- DLB-61
Marshall, Edison 1894-1967...........DLB-102	Massie, Allan 1938- DLB-271	Mayer, O. B. 1818-1891.............DLB-3, 248
Marshall, Edward 1932- DLB-16	Massinger, Philip 1583-1640...........DLB-58	Mayes, Herbert R. 1900-1987..........DLB-137
Marshall, Emma 1828-1899...........DLB-163	Masson, David 1822-1907.............DLB-144	Mayes, Wendell 1919-1992............DLB-26
Marshall, James 1942-1992............DLB-61	Masters, Edgar Lee 1868-1950 .DLB-54; CDALB-3	Mayfield, Julian 1928-1984.....DLB-33; Y-84
Marshall, Joyce 1913- DLB-88	Masters, Hilary 1928- DLB-244	Mayhew, Henry 1812-1887......DLB 18, 55, 190
Marshall, Paule 1929- DLB-33, 157, 227	Mastronardi, Lucio 1930-1979.........DLB-177	Mayhew, Jonathan 1720-1766..........DLB-31
Marshall, Tom 1938-1993.............DLB-60	Matevski, Mateja 1929- ...DLB-181; CDWLB-4	Mayne, Ethel Colburn 1865-1941.......DLB-197
Marsilius of Padua circa 1275-circa 1342.............DLB-115	Mather, Cotton 1663-1728.......DLB-24, 30, 140; CDALB-2	Mayne, Jasper 1604-1672.............DLB-126
		Mayne, Seymour 1944- DLB-60
Mars-Jones, Adam 1954- DLB-207	Mather, Increase 1639-1723............DLB-24	Mayor, Flora Macdonald 1872-1932......DLB-36
Marson, Una 1905-1965..............DLB-157	Mather, Richard 1596-1669............DLB-24	Mayröcker, Friederike 1924- DLB-85
Marston, John 1576-1634..........DLB-58, 172	Matheson, Annie 1853-1924..........DLB-240	Mazrui, Ali A. 1933- DLB-125
Marston, Philip Bourke 1850-1887.......DLB-35	Matheson, Richard 1926- DLB-8, 44	Mažuranić, Ivan 1814-1890............DLB-147
Martens, Kurt 1870-1945..............DLB-66	Matheus, John F. 1887- DLB-51	Mazursky, Paul 1930- DLB-44
Martial circa A.D. 40-circa A.D. 103 .... DLB 211; CDWLB 1	Mathews, Cornelius 1817?-1889 ...DLB-3, 64, 250	McAlmon, Robert 1896-1956...DLB-4, 45; DS-15
William S. Martien [publishing house].....DLB-49	Elkin Mathews [publishing house].......DLB-112	"A Night at Bricktop's"...............Y-01
Martin, Abe (see Hubbard, Kin)	Mathews, John Joseph 1894-1979.......DLB-175	McArthur, Peter 1866-1924............DLB-92
Martin, Catherine ca. 1847-1937........DLB-230	Mathias, Roland 1915- DLB-27	McAuley, James 1917-1976............DLB-260
Martin, Charles 1942- DLB-120, 282	Mathis, June 1892-1927................DLB-44	
Martin, Claire 1914- DLB-60	Mathis, Sharon Bell 1937- DLB-33	Robert M. McBride and Company......DLB-46
	Matković, Marijan 1915-1985..........DLB-181	

McCabe, Patrick 1955- DLB-194	McGahern, John 1934- DLB-14, 231	"*The Nation's* Future," Carey McWilliams's Editorial Policy in *Nation* DLB-137
McCaffrey, Anne 1926- DLB-8	McGee, Thomas D'Arcy 1825-1868 .....DLB-99	
McCann, Colum 1965- DLB-267	McGeehan, W. O. 1879-1933.........DLB-25, 171	Mda, Zakes 1948- DLB-225
McCarthy, Cormac 1933- DLB-6, 143, 256	McGill, Ralph 1898-1969 ....DLB-29	Mead, George Herbert 1863-1931.......DLB-270
The Cormac McCarthy Society Y-99	McGinley, Phyllis 1905-1978 ....DLB-11, 48	Mead, L. T. 1844-1914................DLB-141
McCarthy, Mary 1912-1989........DLB-2; Y-81	McGinniss, Joe 1942- DLB-185	Mead, Matthew 1924- DLB-40
McCarthy, Shaun Lloyd (see Cory, Desmond)	McGirt, James E. 1874-1930............DLB-50	Mead, Taylor ?- DLB-16
McCay, Winsor 1871-1934.............DLB-22	McGlashan and Gill DLB-106	Meany, Tom 1903-1964...............DLB-171
McClane, Albert Jules 1922-1991........DLB-171	McGough, Roger 1937- DLB-40	Mechthild von Magdeburg circa 1207-circa 1282 ....DLB-138
McClatchy, C. K. 1858-1936 ....DLB-25	McGrath, John 1935- DLB-233	
McClellan, George Marion 1860-1934....DLB-50	McGrath, Patrick 1950- DLB-231	Medill, Joseph 1823-1899..............DLB-43
"The Negro as a Writer" DLB-50	McGraw-Hill DLB-46	Medoff, Mark 1940- DLB-7
McCloskey, Robert 1914- DLB-22	McGuane, Thomas 1939- DLB-2, 212; Y-80	Meek, Alexander Beaufort 1814-1865 . DLB-3, 248
McClung, Nellie Letitia 1873-1951 ....DLB-92	Tribute to Seymour Lawrence Y-94	Meeke, Mary ?-1816?...............DLB-116
McClure, James 1939- DLB-276	McGuckian, Medbh 1950- DLB-40	Mei, Lev Aleksandrovich 1822-1862 .....DLB-277
McClure, Joanna 1930- DLB-16	McGuffey, William Holmes 1800-1873 ...DLB-42	Meinke, Peter 1932- DLB-5
McClure, Michael 1932- DLB-16	McGuinness, Frank 1953- DLB-245	Mejia Vallejo, Manuel 1923- DLB-113
McClure, Phillips and Company DLB-46	McHenry, James 1785-1845 ....DLB-202	Melanchthon, Philipp 1497-1560 ....DLB-179
McClure, S. S. 1857-1949 ....DLB-91	McIlvanney, William 1936- DLB-14, 207	Melançon, Robert 1947- DLB-60
A. C. McClurg and Company DLB-49	McIlwraith, Jean Newton 1859-1938 .....DLB-92	Mell, Max 1882-1971 ....DLB-81, 124
McCluskey, John A., Jr. 1944- DLB-33	McIntosh, Maria Jane 1803-1878 ...DLB-239, 248	Mellow, James R. 1926-1997 ....DLB-111
McCollum, Michael A. 1946- Y-87	McIntyre, James 1827-1906............DLB-99	Mel'nikov, Pavel Ivanovich 1818-1883 ..DLB-238
McConnell, William C. 1917- DLB-88	McIntyre, O. O. 1884-1938 ....DLB-25	Meltzer, David 1937- DLB-16
McCord, David 1897-1997 ....DLB-61	McKay, Claude 1889-1948.....DLB-4, 45, 51, 117	Meltzer, Milton 1915- DLB-61
McCord, Louisa S. 1810-1879 ....DLB-248	The David McKay Company...........DLB-49	Melville, Elizabeth, Lady Culross circa 1585-1640 ....DLB-172
McCorkle, Jill 1958- DLB-234; Y-87	McKean, William V. 1820-1903.........DLB-23	
McCorkle, Samuel Eusebius 1746-1811 ... DLB-37	McKenna, Stephen 1888-1967 ....DLB-197	Melville, Herman 1819-1891 .... DLB-3, 74, 250; CDALB-2
McCormick, Anne O'Hare 1880-1954....DLB-29	The McKenzie Trust Y-96	
McCormick, Kenneth Dale 1906-1997 ....Y-97	McKerrow, R. B. 1872-1940...........DLB-201	The Melville Society.................Y-01
McCormick, Robert R. 1880-1955.......DLB-29	McKinley, Robin 1952- DLB-52	Melville, James (Roy Peter Martin) 1931- DLB-276
McCourt, Edward 1907-1972 ....DLB-88	McKnight, Reginald 1956- DLB-234	
McCoy, Horace 1897-1955.............DLB-9	McLachlan, Alexander 1818-1896 ....DLB-99	Mena, María Cristina 1893-1965 ... DLB-209, 221
McCrae, Hugh 1876-1958 ....DLB-260	McLaren, Floris Clark 1904-1978........DLB-68	Menander 342-341 B.C.-circa 292-291 B.C. DLB-176; CDWLB-1
McCrae, John 1872-1918 ....DLB-92	McLaverty, Michael 1907- DLB-15	
McCullagh, Joseph B. 1842-1896 ....DLB-23	McLean, Duncan 1964- DLB-267	Menantes (see Hunold, Christian Friedrich)
McCullers, Carson 1917-1967 ......DLB-2, 7, 173, 228; CDALB-1	McLean, John R. 1848-1916...........DLB-23	Mencke, Johann Burckhard 1674-1732... DLB-168
McCulloch, Thomas 1776-1843 ....DLB-99	McLean, William L. 1852-1931 ....DLB-25	Mencken, H. L. 1880-1956 ....DLB-11, 29, 63, 137, 222; CDALB-4
McDonald, Forrest 1927- DLB-17	McLennan, William 1856-1904 ....DLB-92	"Berlin, February, 1917" Y-00
McDonald, Walter 1934- DLB-105, DS-9	McLoughlin Brothers DLB-49	From the Initial Issue of *American Mercury* (January 1924)................DLB-137
"Getting Started: Accepting the Regions You Own–or Which Own You" DLB-105	McLuhan, Marshall 1911-1980 ....DLB-88	
	McMaster, John Bach 1852-1932 ....DLB-47	Mencken and Nietzsche: An Unpublished Excerpt from H. L. Mencken's *My Life as Author and Editor*. Y-93
	McMurtry, Larry 1936- DLB-2, 143, 256; Y-80, 87; CDALB-6	
Tribute to James Dickey Y-97	McNally, Terrence 1939- DLB-7, 249	
McDougall, Colin 1917-1984 ....DLB-68	McNeil, Florence 1937- DLB-60	Mendelssohn, Moses 1729-1786 ....DLB-97
McDowell, Katharine Sherwood Bonner 1849-1883 .... DLB-202, 239	McNeile, Herman Cyril 1888-1937 ......DLB-77	Mendes, Catulle 1841-1909 ....DLB-217
	McNickle, D'Arcy 1904-1977 .....DLB-175, 212	Méndez M., Miguel 1930- DLB-82
Obolensky McDowell [publishing house] DLB-46	McPhee, John 1931- DLB-185, 275	The Mercantile Library of New York Y-96
	McPherson, James Alan 1943- DLB-38, 244	Mercer, Cecil William (see Yates, Dornford)
McEwan, Ian 1948- DLB-14, 194	McPherson, Sandra 1943- Y-86	Mercer, David 1928-1980............. DLB-13
McFadden, David 1940- DLB-60	McTaggart, J. M. E. 1866-1925 ....DLB-262	Mercer, John 1704-1768 ....DLB-31
McFall, Frances Elizabeth Clarke (see Grand, Sarah)	McWhirter, George 1939- DLB-60	Mercer, Johnny 1909-1976 ....DLB-265
McFarland, Ron 1942- DLB-256	McWilliam, Candia 1955- DLB-267	Meredith, George 1828-1909 ....DLB-18, 35, 57, 159; CDBLB-4
McFarlane, Leslie 1902-1977 ....DLB-88	McWilliams, Carey 1905-1980.........DLB-137	
McFee, William 1881-1966............DLB-153		Meredith, Louisa Anne 1812-1895 .. DLB-166, 230
		Meredith, Owen (see Lytton, Edward Robert Bulwer)

Meredith, William 1919- DLB-5
Meres, Francis
   Palladis Tamia, Wits Treasurie (1598)
   [excerpt]....................DLB-172
Mergerle, Johann Ulrich
   (see Abraham à Sancta Clara)
Mérimée, Prosper 1803-1870.......DLB-119, 192
Merivale, John Herman 1779-1844.......DLB-96
Meriwether, Louise 1923- DLB-33
Merlin Press....................DLB-112
Merriam, Eve 1916-1992..............DLB-61
The Merriam Company...............DLB-49
Merril, Judith 1923-1997..........DLB-251
   Tribute to Theodore Sturgeon.........Y-85
Merrill, James 1926-1995........DLB-5, 165; Y-85
Merrill and Baker....................DLB-49
The Mershon Company...............DLB-49
Merton, Thomas 1915-1968.......DLB-48; Y-81
Merwin, W. S. 1927- DLB-5, 169
Julian Messner [publishing house]........DLB-46
Mészöly, Miklós 1921- DLB-232
J. Metcalf [publishing house].........DLB-49
Metcalf, John 1938- DLB-60
The Methodist Book Concern..........DLB-49
Methuen and Company...............DLB-112
Meun, Jean de (see *Roman de la Rose*)
Mew, Charlotte 1869-1928.........DLB-19, 135
Mewshaw, Michael 1943- Y-80
   Tribute to Albert Erskine.............Y-93
Meyer, Conrad Ferdinand 1825-1898....DLB-129
Meyer, E. Y. 1946- DLB-75
Meyer, Eugene 1875-1959..............DLB-29
Meyer, Michael 1921-2000............DLB-155
Meyers, Jeffrey 1939- DLB-111
Meynell, Alice 1847-1922..........DLB-19, 98
Meynell, Viola 1885-1956............DLB-153
Meyrink, Gustav 1868-1932..........DLB-81
Mézières, Philipe de circa 1327-1405.....DLB-208
Michael, Ib 1945- DLB-214
Michael, Livi 1960- DLB-267
Michaëlis, Karen 1872-1950..........DLB-214
Michaels, Leonard 1933- DLB-130
Michaux, Henri 1899-1984............DLB-258
Micheaux, Oscar 1884-1951............DLB-50
Michel of Northgate, Dan
   circa 1265-circa 1340.............DLB-146
Micheline, Jack 1929-1998............DLB-16
Michener, James A. 1907?-1997..........DLB-6
Micklejohn, George circa 1717-1818.......DLB-31
Middle Hill Press....................DLB-106
Middleton, Christopher 1926- DLB-40
Middleton, Richard 1882-1911........DLB-156
Middleton, Stanley 1919- DLB-14
Middleton, Thomas 1580-1627.........DLB-58
Miegel, Agnes 1879-1964..............DLB-56

Miežalaitis, Eduardas 1919-1997........DLB-220
Mihailović, Dragoslav 1930- DLB-181
Mihalić, Slavko 1928- DLB-181
Mikhailov, A.
   (see Sheller, Aleksandr Konstantinovich)
Mikhailov, Mikhail Larionovich
   1829-1865....................DLB-238
Mikhailovsky, Nikolai Konstantinovich
   1842-1904....................DLB-277
Miles, Josephine 1911-1985...........DLB-48
Miles, Susan (Ursula Wyllie Roberts)
   1888-1975....................DLB-240
Miliković, Branko 1934-1961.........DLB-181
Milius, John 1944- DLB-44
Mill, James 1773-1836........DLB-107, 158, 262
Mill, John Stuart
   1806-1873.......DLB-55, 190, 262; CDBLB-4
   Thoughts on Poetry and Its Varieties
   (1833)......................DLB-32
Andrew Millar [publishing house].......DLB-154
Millar, Kenneth
   1915-1983.........DLB-2, 226; Y-83; DS-6
Millay, Edna St. Vincent
   1892-1950..........DLB-45, 249; CDALB-4
Millen, Sarah Gertrude 1888-1968......DLB-225
Miller, Andrew 1960- DLB-267
Miller, Arthur 1915- DLB-7, 266; CDALB-1
   The Arthur Miller Society.............Y-01
Miller, Caroline 1903-1992..............DLB-9
Miller, Eugene Ethelbert 1950- DLB-41
   Tribute to Julian Mayfield............Y-84
Miller, Heather Ross 1939- DLB-120
Miller, Henry
   1891-1980........DLB-4, 9; Y-80; CDALB-5
Miller, Hugh 1802-1856...............DLB-190
Miller, J. Hillis 1928- DLB-67
Miller, Jason 1939- DLB-7
Miller, Joaquin 1839-1913...........DLB-186
Miller, May 1899-1995................DLB-41
Miller, Paul 1906-1991...............DLB-127
Miller, Perry 1905-1963.........DLB-17, 63
Miller, Sue 1943- DLB-143
Miller, Vassar 1924-1998.............DLB-105
Miller, Walter M., Jr. 1923-1996.........DLB-8
Miller, Webb 1892-1940...............DLB-29
James Miller [publishing house]........DLB-49
Millett, Kate 1934- DLB-246
Millhauser, Steven 1943- DLB-2
Millican, Arthenia J. Bates 1920- DLB-38
Milligan, Alice 1866-1953............DLB-240
Mills, Magnus 1954- DLB-267
Mills and Boon....................DLB-112
Milman, Henry Hart 1796-1868.........DLB-96
Milne, A. A. 1882-1956.....DLB-10, 77, 100, 160
Milner, Ron 1938- DLB-38
William Milner [publishing house]......DLB-106

Milnes, Richard Monckton (Lord Houghton)
   1809-1885..................DLB-32, 184
Milton, John
   1608-1674.....DLB-131, 151, 281; CDBLB-2
   The Milton Society of America.........Y-00
Miłosz, Czesław 1911- DLB-215; CDWLB-4
Minakami Tsutomu 1919- DLB-182
Minamoto no Sanetomo 1192-1219......DLB-203
The Minerva Press..................DLB-154
Minnesang circa 1150-1280............DLB-138
   The Music of *Minnesang*...........DLB-138
Minns, Susan 1839-1938..............DLB-140
Minton, Balch and Company..........DLB-46
Mirbeau, Octave 1848-1917........DLB-123, 192
Mirk, John died after 1414?...........DLB-146
Miron, Gaston 1928-1996.............DLB-60
A Mirror for Magistrates.................DLB-167
Mishima Yukio 1925-1970............DLB-182
Mistral, Gabriela 1889-1957..........DLB-283
Mitchel, Jonathan 1624-1668...........DLB-24
Mitchell, Adrian 1932- DLB-40
Mitchell, Donald Grant
   1822-1908................DLB-1, 243; DS-13
Mitchell, Gladys 1901-1983............DLB-77
Mitchell, James Leslie 1901-1935........DLB-15
Mitchell, John (see Slater, Patrick)
Mitchell, John Ames 1845-1918.........DLB-79
Mitchell, Joseph 1908-1996.......DLB-185; Y-96
Mitchell, Julian 1935- DLB-14
Mitchell, Ken 1940- DLB-60
Mitchell, Langdon 1862-1935............DLB-7
Mitchell, Loften 1919- DLB-38
Mitchell, Margaret 1900-1949...DLB-9; CDALB-7
Mitchell, S. Weir 1829-1914..........DLB-202
Mitchell, W. J. T. 1942- DLB-246
Mitchell, W. O. 1914-1998.............DLB-88
Mitchison, Naomi Margaret (Haldane)
   1897-1999................DLB-160, 191, 255
Mitford, Mary Russell 1787-1855....DLB-110, 116
Mitford, Nancy 1904-1973...........DLB-191
Mittelholzer, Edgar
   1909-1965............DLB-117; CDWLB-3
Mitterer, Erika 1906- DLB-85
Mitterer, Felix 1948- DLB-124
Mitternacht, Johann Sebastian
   1613-1679....................DLB-168
Miyamoto Yuriko 1899-1951..........DLB-180
Mizener, Arthur 1907-1988...........DLB-103
Mo, Timothy 1950- DLB-194
Moberg, Vilhelm 1898-1973..........DLB-259
Modern Age Books..................DLB-46
Modern Language Association of America
   The Modern Language Association of
   America Celebrates Its Centennial..Y-84
The Modern Library.................DLB-46
Modiano, Patrick 1945- DLB-83
Moffat, Yard and Company............DLB-46

Moffet, Thomas 1553-1604 . . . . DLB-136	"The No Self, the Little Self, and the Poets" DLB-105	Morley, John 1838-1923. . . . . DLB-57, 144, 190
Mofolo, Thomas 1876-1948 . . . . DLB-225	Moore, T. Sturge 1870-1944. . . . . DLB-19	Morris, George Pope 1802-1864 . . . . DLB-73
Mohr, Nicholasa 1938- DLB-145	Moore, Thomas 1779-1852. . . . . DLB-96, 144	Morris, James Humphrey (see Morris, Jan)
Moix, Ana María 1947- DLB-134	Moore, Ward 1903-1978 . . . . DLB-8	Morris, Jan 1926- DLB-204
Molesworth, Louisa 1839-1921 . . . . DLB-135	Moore, Wilstach, Keys and Company DLB-49	Morris, Lewis 1833-1907 . . . . DLB-35
Molière (Jean-Baptiste Poquelin) 1622-1673 . . . . DLB-268	Moorehead, Alan 1901-1983 . . . . DLB-204	Morris, Margaret 1737-1816 . . . . DLB-200
Möllhausen, Balduin 1825-1905 . . . . DLB-129	Moorhouse, Geoffrey 1931- DLB-204	Morris, Richard B. 1904-1989 . . . . .DLB-17
Molnár, Ferenc 1878-1952 . . DLB-215; CDWLB-4	The Moorland-Spingarn Research Center DLB-76	Morris, William 1834-1896 . . . . . DLB-18, 35, 57, 156, 178, 184; CDBLB-4
Molnár, Miklós (see Mészöly, Miklós)	Moorman, Mary C. 1905-1994 . . . . DLB-155	Morris, Willie 1934-1999 . . . . Y-80
Momaday, N. Scott 1934- DLB-143, 175, 256; CDALB-7	Mora, Pat 1942- DLB-209	Tribute to Irwin Shaw Y-84
Monkhouse, Allan 1858-1936. . . . . DLB-10	Moraga, Cherríe 1952- DLB-82, 249	Tribute to James Dickey Y-97
Monro, Harold 1879-1932 . . . . DLB-19	Morales, Alejandro 1944- DLB-82	Morris, Wright 1910-1998 . . . . .DLB-2, 206, 218; Y-81
Monroe, Harriet 1860-1936 . . . . DLB-54, 91	Morales, Mario Roberto 1947- DLB-145	Morrison, Arthur 1863-1945 . . . .DLB-70, 135, 197
Monsarrat, Nicholas 1910-1979 . . . . DLB-15	Morales, Rafael 1919- DLB-108	Morrison, Charles Clayton 1874-1966 . . . . DLB-91
Montagu, Lady Mary Wortley 1689-1762. . . . . DLB-95, 101	Morality Plays: *Mankind* circa 1450-1500 and *Everyman* circa 1500 . . . . DLB-146	Morrison, John 1904-1998 . . . . DLB-260
Montague, C. E. 1867-1928 . . . . DLB-197	Morand, Paul (1888-1976) DLB-65	Morrison, Toni 1931- DLB-6, 33, 143; Y-81, 93; CDALB-6
Montague, John 1929- DLB-40	Morante, Elsa 1912-1985 . . . . .DLB-177	Nobel Lecture 1993 . . . . Y-93
Montale, Eugenio 1896-1981 . . . . DLB-114	Morata, Olympia Fulvia 1526-1555 . . . . .DLB-179	Morrissy, Mary 1957- DLB-267
Montalvo, José 1946-1994 . . . . DLB-209	Moravia, Alberto 1907-1990 . . . . .DLB-177	William Morrow and Company. DLB-46
Monterroso, Augusto 1921-2003 . . . . DLB-145	Mordaunt, Elinor 1872-1942 . . . . .DLB-174	Morse, James Herbert 1841-1923 . . . . DLB-71
Montesquiou, Robert de 1855-1921 . . . . . DLB-217	Mordovtsev, Daniil Lukich 1830-1905. . . DLB-238	Morse, Jedidiah 1761-1826 . . . . DLB-37
Montgomerie, Alexander circa 1550?-1598 . . . . DLB-167	More, Hannah 1745-1833 . . . . DLB-107, 109, 116, 158	Morse, John T., Jr. 1840-1937 . . . . DLB-47
Montgomery, James 1771-1854 . . . . . . DLB-93, 158	More, Henry 1614-1687 . . . . DLB-126, 252	Morselli, Guido 1912-1973 . . . . .DLB-177
Montgomery, John 1919- DLB-16	More, Sir Thomas 1477 or 1478-1535 . . . . DLB-136, 281	*Morte Arthure*, the *Alliterative* and the *Stanzaic* circa 1350-1400 . . . . DLB-146
Montgomery, Lucy Maud 1874-1942 . . . . DLB-92; DS-14	Morejon, Nancy 1944- DLB-283	Mortimer, Favell Lee 1802-1878 . . . . DLB-163
Montgomery, Marion 1925- DLB-6	Morency, Pierre 1942- DLB-60	Mortimer, John 1923- DLB-13, 245, 271; CDBLB-8
Montgomery, Robert Bruce (see Crispin, Edmund)	Moreno, Dorinda 1939- DLB-122	Morton, Carlos 1942- DLB-122
Montherlant, Henry de 1896-1972 . . . . . . DLB-72	Moretti, Marino 1885-1979 . . . . DLB-114, 264	Morton, H. V. 1892-1979 . . . . DLB-195
The Monthly Review 1749-1844 . . . . DLB-110	Morgan, Berry 1919- DLB-6	John P. Morton and Company. DLB-49
Montigny, Louvigny de 1876-1955. . . . . . . DLB-92	Morgan, Charles 1894-1958 . . . . . . DLB-34, 100	Morton, Nathaniel 1613-1685 . . . . DLB-24
Montoya, José 1932- DLB-122	Morgan, Edmund S. 1916- DLB-17	Morton, Sarah Wentworth 1759-1846 . . . . DLB-37
Moodie, John Wedderburn Dunbar 1797-1869 . . . . DLB-99	Morgan, Edwin 1920- DLB-27	Morton, Thomas circa 1579-circa 1647 . . . DLB-24
Moodie, Susanna 1803-1885. . . . . DLB-99	Morgan, John Pierpont 1837-1913 . . . . . . DLB-140	Moscherosch, Johann Michael 1601-1669 . . . . DLB-164
Moody, Joshua circa 1633-1697 . . . . DLB-24	Morgan, John Pierpont, Jr. 1867-1943 . . . DLB-140	Humphrey Moseley [publishing house] . . .DLB-170
Moody, William Vaughn 1869-1910 . . . .DLB-7, 54	Morgan, Robert 1944- DLB-120	Möser, Justus 1720-1794 . . . . DLB-97
Moorcock, Michael 1939- DLB-14, 231, 261	Morgan, Sydney Owenson, Lady 1776?-1859 . . . . DLB-116, 158	Mosley, Nicholas 1923- DLB-14, 207
Moore, Alan 1953- DLB-261	Morgner, Irmtraud 1933-1990 . . . . DLB-75	Moss, Arthur 1889-1969 . . . . DLB-4
Moore, Brian 1921-1999. . . . . DLB-251	Morhof, Daniel Georg 1639-1691 . . . . . . DLB-164	Moss, Howard 1922-1987 . . . . DLB-5
Moore, Catherine L. 1911-1987 . . . . DLB-8	Mori Ōgai 1862-1922 . . . . DLB-180	Moss, Thylias 1954- DLB-120
Moore, Clement Clarke 1779-1863 . . . . . . DLB-42	Móricz, Zsigmond 1879-1942 . . . . DLB-215	Motion, Andrew 1952- DLB-40
Moore, Dora Mavor 1888-1979 . . . . DLB-92	Morier, James Justinian 1782 or 1783?-1849 . . . . DLB-116	Motley, John Lothrop 1814-1877 . . . . DLB-1, 30, 59, 235
Moore, G. E. 1873-1958 . . . . DLB-262	Mörike, Eduard 1804-1875 . . . . DLB-133	Motley, Willard 1909-1965 . . . . .DLB-76, 143
Moore, George 1852-1933 . . . . DLB-10, 18, 57, 135	Morin, Paul 1889-1963 . . . . DLB-92	Mott, Lucretia 1793-1880 . . . . DLB-239
Literature at Nurse, or Circulating Morals (1885) DLB-18	Morison, Richard 1514?-1556 . . . . DLB-136	Benjamin Motte Jr. [publishing house] . . . DLB-154
Moore, Lorrie 1957- DLB-234	Morison, Samuel Eliot 1887-1976 . . . . DLB-17	Motteux, Peter Anthony 1663-1718 . . . . . . DLB-80
Moore, Marianne 1887-1972 . . . . DLB-45; DS-7; CDALB-5	Morison, Stanley 1889-1967 . . . . DLB-201	Mottram, R. H. 1883-1971 . . . . DLB-36
International Marianne Moore Society . . . Y-98	Moritz, Karl Philipp 1756-1793 . . . . DLB-94	Mount, Ferdinand 1939- DLB-231
Moore, Mavor 1919- DLB-88	*Moriz von Craûn* circa 1220-1230 . . . . DLB-138	Mouré, Erin 1955- DLB-60
Moore, Richard 1927- DLB-105	Morley, Christopher 1890-1957 . . . . DLB-9	Mourning Dove (Humishuma) between 1882 and 1888?-1936. . . . . .DLB-175, 221

Movies
    Fiction into Film, 1928-1975: A List
      of Movies Based on the Works
      of Authors in British Novelists,
      1930-1959 . . . . .DLB-15

    Movies from Books, 1920-1974 . . . . . . .DLB-9

Mowat, Farley 1921- DLB-68

A. R. Mowbray and Company,
    Limited DLB-106

Mowrer, Edgar Ansel 1892-1977 . . . . .DLB-29

Mowrer, Paul Scott 1887-1971 . . . . .DLB-29

Edward Moxon [publishing house] DLB-106

Joseph Moxon [publishing house] DLB-170

Moyes, Patricia 1923-2000 . . . . .DLB-276

Mphahlele, Es'kia (Ezekiel)
    1919- DLB-125, 225; CDWLB-3

Mrożek, Sławomir 1930- . . .DLB-232; CDWLB-4

Mtshali, Oswald Mbuyiseni
    1940- DLB-125, 225

Mucedorus DLB-62

Mudford, William 1782-1848 . . . . .DLB-159

Mueller, Lisel 1924- DLB-105

Muhajir, El (see Marvin X)

Muhajir, Nazzam Al Fitnah (see Marvin X)

Mühlbach, Luise 1814-1873 . . . . .DLB-133

Muir, Edwin 1887-1959 . . . . . . .DLB-20, 100, 191

Muir, Helen 1937- DLB-14

Muir, John 1838-1914 . . . . .DLB-186, 275

Muir, Percy 1894-1979 . . . . .DLB-201

Mujū Ichien 1226-1312 . . . . .DLB-203

Mukherjee, Bharati 1940- DLB-60, 218

Mulcaster, Richard 1531 or 1532-1611 . . .DLB-167

Muldoon, Paul 1951- DLB-40

Müller, Friedrich (see Müller, Maler)

Müller, Heiner 1929-1995 . . . . .DLB-124

Müller, Maler 1749-1825 . . . . .DLB-94

Muller, Marcia 1944- DLB-226

Müller, Wilhelm 1794-1827 . . . . .DLB-90

Mumford, Lewis 1895-1990 . . . . .DLB-63

Munby, A. N. L. 1913-1974 . . . . .DLB-201

Munby, Arthur Joseph 1828-1910 . . . . . . .DLB-35

Munday, Anthony 1560-1633 . . . . . . .DLB-62, 172

Mundt, Clara (see Mühlbach, Luise)

Mundt, Theodore 1808-1861 . . . . .DLB-133

Munford, Robert circa 1737-1783 . . . . . . .DLB-31

Mungoshi, Charles 1947- DLB-157

Munk, Kaj 1898-1944 . . . . .DLB-214

Munonye, John 1929- DLB-117

Munro, Alice 1931- DLB-53

George Munro [publishing house] DLB-49

Munro, H. H.
    1870-1916 . . . . .DLB-34, 162; CDBLB-5

Munro, Neil 1864-1930 . . . . .DLB-156

Norman L. Munro [publishing house] DLB-49

Munroe, Kirk 1850-1930 . . . . .DLB-42

Munroe and Francis DLB-49

James Munroe and Company DLB-49

Joel Munsell [publishing house] DLB-49

Munsey, Frank A. 1854-1925 . . . . . .DLB-25, 91

Frank A. Munsey and Company DLB-49

Murakami Haruki 1949- DLB-182

Murav'ev, Mikhail Nikitich 1757-1807 . . .DLB-150

Murdoch, Iris 1919-1999
    . . . . .DLB-14, 194, 233; CDBLB-8

Murdock, James
    From *Sketches of Modern Philosophy* DS-5

Murdoch, Rupert 1931- DLB-127

Murfree, Mary N. 1850-1922 . . . . . . .DLB-12, 74

Murger, Henry 1822-1861 . . . . .DLB-119

Murger, Louis-Henri (see Murger, Henry)

Murner, Thomas 1475-1537 . . . . .DLB-179

Muro, Amado 1915-1971 . . . . .DLB-82

Murphy, Arthur 1727-1805 . . . . .DLB-89, 142

Murphy, Beatrice M. 1908-1992 . . . . .DLB-76

Murphy, Dervla 1931- DLB-204

Murphy, Emily 1868-1933 . . . . .DLB-99

Murphy, Jack 1923-1980 . . . . .DLB-241

Murphy, John H., III 1916- DLB-127

Murphy, Richard 1927-1993 . . . . .DLB-40

John Murphy and Company DLB-49

Murray, Albert L. 1916- DLB-38

Murray, Gilbert 1866-1957 . . . . .DLB-10

Murray, Jim 1919-1998 . . . . .DLB-241

John Murray [publishing house] DLB-154

Murry, John Middleton 1889-1957 . . . . . .DLB-149
    "The Break-Up of the Novel"
      (1922) DLB-36

Murry, John Middleton, Jr. (see Cowper, Richard)

Murray, Judith Sargent 1751-1820 . . . .DLB-37, 200

Murray, Pauli 1910-1985 . . . . .DLB-41

Musäus, Johann Karl August 1735-1787 . . .DLB-97

Muschg, Adolf 1934- DLB-75

Musil, Robert
    1880-1942 . . . . .DLB-81, 124; CDWLB-2

Muspilli circa 790-circa 850 . . . . .DLB-148

Musset, Alfred de 1810-1857 . . . . . . .DLB-192, 217

Benjamin B. Mussey and Company DLB-49

Mutafchieva, Vera 1929- DLB-181

Mutis, Alvaro 1923- DLB-283

Mwangi, Meja 1948- DLB-125

Myers, Frederic W. H. 1843-1901 . . . . . . .DLB-190

Myers, Gustavus 1872-1942 . . . . .DLB-47

Myers, L. H. 1881-1944 . . . . .DLB-15

Myers, Walter Dean 1937- DLB-33

Myerson, Julie 1960- DLB-267

Mykolaitis-Putinas, Vincas 1893-1967 . . . .DLB-220

Myles, Eileen 1949- DLB-193

Myrdal, Jan 1927- DLB-257

Mystery
    1985: The Year of the Mystery:
      A Symposium Y-85
    Comments from Other Writers Y-85

The Second Annual New York Festival
    of Mystery Y-00

Why I Read Mysteries Y-85

Why I Write Mysteries: Night and Day,
    by Michael Collins Y-85

N

Na Prous Boneta circa 1296-1328 . . . . . . .DLB-208

Nabl, Franz 1883-1974 . . . . .DLB-81

Nabokov, Véra 1902-1991 . . . . .Y-91

Nabokov, Vladimir 1899-1977 . . .DLB-2, 244, 278;
    Y-80, 91; DS-3; CDALB-1

    International Nabokov Society Y-99

    An Interview [On Nabokov], by
      Fredson Bowers Y-80

    Nabokov Festival at Cornell Y-83

    The Vladimir Nabokov Archive in the
      Berg Collection of the New York
      Public Library: An Overview Y-91

    The Vladimir Nabokov Society Y-01

Nádaši, Ladislav (see Jégé)

Naden, Constance 1858-1889 . . . . .DLB-199

Nadezhdin, Nikolai Ivanovich
    1804-1856 . . . . .DLB-198

Nadson, Semen Iakovlevich 1862-1887 . . .DLB-277

Naevius circa 265 B.C.-201 B.C. DLB-211

Nafis and Cornish DLB-49

Nagai Kafū 1879-1959 . . . . .DLB-180

Nagel, Ernest 1901-1985 . . . . .DLB-279

Naipaul, Shiva 1945-1985 . . . . .DLB-157; Y-85

Naipaul, V. S. 1932- DLB-125, 204, 207;
    Y-85, Y-01; CDBLB-8; CDWLB-3

    Nobel Lecture 2001: "Two Worlds" Y-01

Nakagami Kenji 1946-1992 . . . . .DLB-182

Nakano-in Masatada no Musume (see Nijō, Lady)

Nałkowska, Zofia 1884-1954 . . . . .DLB-215

Joseph Nancrede [publishing house] DLB-49

Naranjo, Carmen 1930- DLB-145

Narezhny, Vasilii Trofimovich
    1780-1825 . . . . .DLB-198

Narrache, Jean (Emile Coderre)
    1893-1970 . . . . .DLB-92

Nasby, Petroleum Vesuvius (see Locke, David Ross)

Eveleigh Nash [publishing house] DLB-112

Nash, Ogden 1902-1971 . . . . .DLB-11

Nashe, Thomas 1567-1601? DLB-167

Nason, Jerry 1910-1986 . . . . .DLB-241

Nasr, Seyyed Hossein 1933- DLB-279

Nast, Condé 1873-1942 . . . . .DLB-91

Nast, Thomas 1840-1902 . . . . .DLB-188

Nastasijević, Momčilo 1894-1938 . . . . .DLB-147

Nathan, George Jean 1882-1958 . . . . .DLB-137

Nathan, Robert 1894-1985 . . . . .DLB-9

National Book Critics Circle Awards Y-00-01

The National Jewish Book Awards Y-85

Natsume Sōseki 1867-1916 . . . . .DLB-180

Naughton, Bill 1910-1992 . . . . .DLB-13

Cumulative Index

Navarro, Joe 1953- DLB-209
Naylor, Gloria 1950- DLB-173
Nazor, Vladimir 1876-1949............DLB-147
Ndebele, Njabulo 1948- DLB-157, 225
Neagoe, Peter 1881-1960 ....DLB-4
Neal, John 1793-1876 ....DLB-1, 59, 243
Neal, Joseph C. 1807-1847 ....DLB-11
Neal, Larry 1937-1981 ....DLB-38
The Neale Publishing Company DLB-49
Nebel, Frederick 1903-1967 ....DLB-226
F. Tennyson Neely [publishing house] DLB-49
Negoițescu, Ion 1921-1993............DLB-220
Negri, Ada 1870-1945................DLB-114
Neihardt, John G. 1881-1973 .....DLB-9, 54, 256
Neidhart von Reuental
  circa 1185-circa 1240 ....DLB-138
Neilson, John Shaw 1872-1942........DLB-230
Nekrasov, Nikolai Alekseevich
  1821-1877.......................DLB-277
Neledinsky-Meletsky, Iurii Aleksandrovich
  1752-1828......................DLB-150
Nelligan, Emile 1879-1941 ....DLB-92
Nelson, Alice Moore Dunbar 1875-1935 ..DLB-50
Nelson, Antonya 1961- DLB-244
Nelson, Kent 1943- DLB-234
Nelson, Richard K. 1941- DLB-275
Nelson, Thomas, and Sons [U.K.] DLB-106
Nelson, Thomas, and Sons [U.S.]........DLB-49
Nelson, William 1908-1978.............DLB-103
Nelson, William Rockhill 1841-1915 .....DLB-23
Nemerov, Howard 1920-1991 .....DLB-5, 6; Y-83
Németh, László 1901-1975 ....DLB-215
Nepos circa 100 B.C.-post 27 B.C. DLB-211
Nėris, Salomėja 1904-1945 .. DLB-220; CDWLB-4
Neruda, Pablo 1904-1973 ....DLB-283
Nerval, Gérard de 1808-1855..........DLB-217
Nesbit, E. 1858-1924 ....DLB-141, 153, 178
Ness, Evaline 1911-1986................DLB-61
Nestroy, Johann 1801-1862 ....DLB-133
Nettleship, R. L. 1846-1892 ....DLB-262
Neugeboren, Jay 1938- DLB-28
Neukirch, Benjamin 1655-1729........DLB-168
Neumann, Alfred 1895-1952 ....DLB-56
Neumann, Ferenc (see Molnár, Ferenc)
Neumark, Georg 1621-1681............DLB-164
Neumeister, Erdmann 1671-1756 ......DLB-168
Nevins, Allan 1890-1971.........DLB-17; DS-17
Nevinson, Henry Woodd 1856-1941 ....DLB-135
The New American Library DLB-46
New Directions Publishing Corporation...DLB-46
The New Monthly Magazine 1814-1884 ....DLB-110
New York Times Book Review...............Y-82
John Newbery [publishing house] DLB-154
Newbolt, Henry 1862-1938 ....DLB-19
Newbound, Bernard Slade (see Slade, Bernard)

Newby, Eric 1919- DLB-204
Newby, P. H. 1918- DLB-15
Thomas Cautley Newby
  [publishing house] DLB-106
Newcomb, Charles King 1820-1894... DLB-1, 223
Newell, Peter 1862-1924...............DLB-42
Newell, Robert Henry 1836-1901........DLB-11
Newhouse, Samuel I. 1895-1979.......DLB-127
Newman, Cecil Earl 1903-1976 ....DLB-127
Newman, David 1937- DLB-44
Newman, Frances 1883-1928 ....Y-80
Newman, Francis William 1805-1897....DLB-190
Newman, John Henry 1801-1890.. DLB-18, 32, 55
Mark Newman [publishing house] DLB-49
Newmarch, Rosa Harriet 1857-1940.....DLB-240
George Newnes Limited...............DLB-112
Newsome, Effie Lee 1885-1979..........DLB-76
Newton, A. Edward 1864-1940 ....DLB-140
Newton, Sir Isaac 1642-1727...........DLB-252
Nexø, Martin Andersen 1869-1954 .....DLB-214
Nezval, Vítěslav
  1900-1958 .... DLB-215; CDWLB-4
Ngugi wa Thiong'o
  1938- DLB-125; CDWLB-3
Niatum, Duane 1938- DLB-175
The *Nibelungenlied* and the *Klage*
  circa 1200......................DLB-138
Nichol, B. P. 1944-1988 ....DLB-53
Nicholas of Cusa 1401-1464...........DLB-115
Nichols, Ann 1891?-1966..............DLB-249
Nichols, Beverly 1898-1983 ....DLB-191
Nichols, Dudley 1895-1960 ....DLB-26
Nichols, Grace 1950- DLB-157
Nichols, John 1940- Y-82
Nichols, Mary Sargeant (Neal) Gove
  1810-1884 ....DLB-1, 243
Nichols, Peter 1927- DLB-13, 245
Nichols, Roy F. 1896-1973 ....DLB-17
Nichols, Ruth 1948- DLB-60
Nicholson, Edward Williams Byron
  1849-1912 ....DLB-184
Nicholson, Geoff 1953- DLB-271
Nicholson, Norman 1914- DLB-27
Nicholson, William 1872-1949 ....DLB-141
Ní Chuilleanáin, Eiléan 1942- DLB-40
Nicol, Eric 1919- DLB-68
Nicolai, Friedrich 1733-1811..........DLB-97
Nicolas de Clamanges circa 1363-1437... DLB-208
Nicolay, John G. 1832-1901 ....DLB-47
Nicole, Pierre 1625-1695 ....DLB-268
Nicolson, Adela Florence Cory (see Hope, Laurence)
Nicolson, Harold 1886-1968........DLB-100, 149
"The Practice of Biography," in
  *The English Sense of Humour and
  Other Essays* DLB-149
Nicolson, Nigel 1917- DLB-155
Niebuhr, Reinhold 1892-1971......DLB-17; DS-17

Niedecker, Lorine 1903-1970 ....DLB-48
Nieman, Lucius W. 1857-1935..........DLB-25
Nietzsche, Friedrich
  1844-1900 ....DLB-129; CDWLB-2
Mencken and Nietzsche: An Unpublished
  Excerpt from H. L. Mencken's *My Life
  as Author and Editor* Y-93
Nievo, Stanislao 1928- DLB-196
Niggli, Josefina 1910-1983 ....Y-80
Nightingale, Florence 1820-1910 ....DLB-166
Nijō, Lady (Nakano-in Masatada no Musume)
  1258-after 1306 ....DLB-203
Nijō Yoshimoto 1320-1388..............DLB-203
Nikitin, Ivan Savvich 1824-1861 ....DLB-277
Nikitin, Nikolai Nikolaevich 1895-1963...DLB-272
Nikolev, Nikolai Petrovich 1758-1815 ... DLB-150
Niles, Hezekiah 1777-1839 ....DLB-43
Nims, John Frederick 1913-1999 ....DLB-5
  Tribute to Nancy Hale Y-88
Nin, Anaïs 1903-1977 ....DLB-2, 4, 152
Niño, Raúl 1961- DLB-209
Nissenson, Hugh 1933- DLB-28
Niven, Frederick John 1878-1944 ....DLB-92
Niven, Larry 1938- DLB-8
Nixon, Howard M. 1909-1983.........DLB-201
Nizan, Paul 1905-1940 ....DLB-72
Njegoš, Petar II Petrović
  1813-1851 ....DLB-147; CDWLB-4
Nkosi, Lewis 1936- DLB-157, 225
Noah, Mordecai M. 1785-1851........DLB-250
Noailles, Anna de 1876-1933 ....DLB-258
Nobel Peace Prize
  The Nobel Prize and Literary Politics Y-88
  Elie Wiesel Y-86
Nobel Prize in Literature
  Joseph Brodsky Y-87
  Camilo José Cela Y-89
  Dario Fo Y-97
  Gabriel García Márquez Y-82
  William Golding...................Y-83
  Nadine Gordimer Y-91
  Günter Grass Y-99
  Seamus Heaney Y-95
  Imre Kertész.....................Y-02
  Najīb Mahfūz Y-88
  Toni Morrison Y-93
  V. S. Naipaul Y-01
  Kenzaburō Ōe Y-94
  Octavio Paz Y-90
  José Saramago Y-98
  Jaroslav Seifert Y-84
  Claude Simon Y-85
  Wole Soyinka Y-86
  Wisława Szymborska Y-96
  Derek Walcott Y-92
  Gao Xingjian Y-00

Nodier, Charles 1780-1844 ....DLB-119
Noël, Marie (Marie Mélanie Rouget)
    1883-1967 ....DLB-258
Noel, Roden 1834-1894................DLB-35
Nogami Yaeko 1885-1985 ....DLB-180
Nogo, Rajko Petrov 1945- DLB-181
Nolan, William F. 1928- DLB-8
    Tribute to Raymond Chandler Y-88
Noland, C. F. M. 1810?-1858............DLB-11
Noma Hiroshi 1915-1991 ....DLB-182
Nonesuch Press DLB-112
Creative Nonfiction Y-02
Noon, Jeff 1957- DLB-267
Noonan, Robert Phillipe (see Tressell, Robert)
Noonday Press........................DLB-46
Noone, John 1936- DLB-14
Nora, Eugenio de 1923 ....DLB-134
Nordan, Lewis 1939- DLB-234
Nordbrandt, Henrik 1945- DLB-214
Nordhoff, Charles 1887-1947............DLB-9
Norén, Lars 1944- DLB-257
Norfolk, Lawrence 1963- DLB-267
Norman, Charles 1904-1996 ....DLB-111
Norman, Marsha 1947- DLB-266; Y-84
Norris, Charles G. 1881-1945 ....DLB-9
Norris, Frank
    1870-1902 ....DLB-12, 71, 186; CDALB-3
Norris, John 1657-1712................DLB-252
Norris, Leslie 1921- DLB-27, 256
Norse, Harold 1916- DLB-16
Norte, Marisela 1955- DLB-209
North, Marianne 1830-1890 ....DLB-174
North Point Press.....................DLB-46
Nortje, Arthur 1942-1970..........DLB-125, 225
Norton, Alice Mary (see Norton, Andre)
Norton, Andre 1912- DLB-8, 52
Norton, Andrews 1786-1853 ....DLB-1, 235; DS-5
Norton, Caroline 1808-1877 ....DLB-21, 159, 199
Norton, Charles Eliot 1827-1908 ....DLB-1, 64, 235
Norton, John 1606-1663 ....DLB-24
Norton, Mary 1903-1992...............DLB-160
Norton, Thomas 1532-1584 ....DLB-62
W. W. Norton and Company DLB-46
Norwood, Robert 1874-1932............DLB-92
Nosaka Akiyuki 1930- DLB-182
Nossack, Hans Erich 1901-1977.........DLB-69
Notker Balbulus circa 840-912..........DLB-148
Notker III of Saint Gall circa 950-1022 ...DLB-148
Notker von Zweifalten ?-1095 ....DLB-148
Nourse, Alan E. 1928- DLB-8
Novak, Slobodan 1924- DLB-181
Novak, Vjenceslav 1859-1905 ....DLB-147
Novakovich, Josip 1956- DLB-244
Novalis 1772-1801 ....DLB-90; CDWLB-2
Novaro, Mario 1868-1944 ....DLB-114

Novás Calvo, Lino 1903-1983..........DLB-145
Novelists
    Library Journal Statements and
        Questionnaires from First Novelists ...Y-87
Novels
    The Columbia History of the American Novel
        A Symposium on................Y-92
    The Great Modern Library Scam Y-98
    The Proletarian Novel DLB-9
    Novels for Grown-Ups...............Y-97
    The Year in the Novel Y-87–88, Y-90–93
Novels, British
    "The Break-Up of the Novel" (1922),
        by John Middleton Murry.......DLB-36
    The Consolidation of Opinion: Critical
        Responses to the Modernists.....DLB-36
    "Criticism in Relation to Novels"
        (1863), by G. H. Lewes.........DLB-21
    "Experiment in the Novel" (1929)
        [excerpt], by John D. Beresford...DLB-36
    "The Future of the Novel" (1899), by
        Henry James DLB-18
    The Gay Science (1866), by E. S. Dallas
        [excerpt].....................DLB-21
    A Haughty and Proud Generation
        (1922), by Ford Madox Hueffer ..DLB-36
    Literary Effects of World War II.....DLB-15
    "Modern Novelists –Great and Small"
        (1855), by Margaret Oliphant DLB-21
    The Modernists (1932),
        by Joseph Warren Beach........DLB-36
    A Note on Technique (1926), by
        Elizabeth A. Drew [excerpts] DLB-36
    Novel-Reading: *The Works of Charles
        Dickens; The Works of W. Makepeace
        Thackeray* (1879),
        by Anthony Trollope DLB-21
    Novels with a Purpose (1864), by
        Justin M'Carthy DLB-21
    "On Art in Fiction" (1838),
        by Edward Bulwer DLB-21
    The Present State of the English Novel
        (1892), by George Saintsbury DLB-18
    Representative Men and Women:
        A Historical Perspective on
        the British Novel, 1930-1960....DLB-15
    "The Revolt" (1937), by Mary Colum
        [excerpts] DLB-36
    "Sensation Novels" (1863), by
        H. L. Manse DLB-21
    Sex, Class, Politics, and Religion [in
        the British Novel, 1930-1959] DLB-15
    Time and Western Man (1927),
        by Wyndham Lewis [excerpts] ...DLB-36
Noventa, Giacomo 1898-1960..........DLB-114
Novikov, Nikolai Ivanovich 1744-1818 ...DLB-150
Novomeský, Laco 1904-1976..........DLB-215
Nowlan, Alden 1933-1983..............DLB-53
Noyes, Alfred 1880-1958...............DLB-20
Noyes, Crosby S. 1825-1908 ....DLB-23
Noyes, Nicholas 1647-1717.............DLB-24
Noyes, Theodore W. 1858-1946........DLB-29
Nozick, Robert 1938-2002.............DLB-279

N-Town Plays circa 1468 to early
    sixteenth century DLB-146
Nugent, Frank 1908-1965 ....DLB-44
Nušić, Branislav 1864-1938..DLB-147; CDWLB-4
David Nutt [publishing house]..........DLB-106
Nwapa, Flora 1931-1993 ....DLB-125; CDWLB-3
Nye, Edgar Wilson (Bill)
    1850-1896...............DLB-11, 23, 186
Nye, Naomi Shihab 1952- DLB-120
Nye, Robert 1939- DLB-14, 271
Nyka-Niliūnas, Alfonsas 1919- DLB-220

O

Oakes, Urian circa 1631-1681 ....DLB-24
Oakes Smith, Elizabeth
    1806-1893 ....DLB-1, 239, 243
Oakley, Violet 1874-1961 ....DLB-188
Oates, Joyce Carol 1938-
    ....DLB-2, 5, 130; Y-81; CDALB-6
    Tribute to Michael M. Rea Y-97
Ōba Minako 1930- DLB-182
Ober, Frederick Albion 1849-1913 ......DLB-189
Ober, William 1920-1993 ....Y-93
Oberholtzer, Ellis Paxson 1868-1936......DLB-47
The Obituary as Literary Form.........Y-02
Obradović, Dositej 1740?-1811 ....DLB-147
O'Brien, Charlotte Grace 1845-1909.....DLB-240
O'Brien, Edna 1932- ...DLB-14, 231; CDBLB-8
O'Brien, Fitz-James 1828-1862...........DLB-74
O'Brien, Flann (see O'Nolan, Brian)
O'Brien, Kate 1897-1974 ....DLB-15
O'Brien, Tim
    1946- DLB-152; Y-80; DS-9; CDALB-7
O'Casey, Sean 1880-1964 .....DLB-10; CDBLB-6
Occom, Samson 1723-1792 ....DLB-175
Occomy, Marita Bonner 1899-1971....DLB-51
Ochs, Adolph S. 1858-1935.............DLB-25
Ochs-Oakes, George Washington
    1861-1931.....................DLB-137
O'Connor, Flannery 1925-1964
    ....DLB-2, 152; Y-80; DS-12; CDALB-1
    The Flannery O'Connor Society Y-99
O'Connor, Frank 1903-1966...........DLB-162
O'Connor, Joseph 1963- DLB-267
Octopus Publishing Group DLB-112
Oda Sakunosuke 1913-1947 ....DLB-182
Odell, Jonathan 1737-1818............DLB-31, 99
O'Dell, Scott 1903-1989................DLB-52
Odets, Clifford 1906-1963............DLB-7, 26
Odhams Press Limited DLB-112
Odio, Eunice 1922-1974...............DLB-283
Odoevsky, Aleksandr Ivanovich
    1802-1839 ....DLB-205
Odoevsky, Vladimir Fedorovich
    1804 or 1803-1869..............DLB-198
O'Donnell, Peter 1920 ....DLB-87
O'Donovan, Michael (see O'Connor, Frank)

O'Dowd, Bernard 1866-1953 . . . . DLB-230

Ōe, Kenzaburō 1935- DLB-182; Y-94

    Nobel Lecture 1994: Japan, the Ambiguous, and Myself Y-94

O'Faolain, Julia 1932- DLB-14, 231

O'Faolain, Sean 1900-1991 . . . . DLB-15, 162

Off-Loop Theatres DLB-7

Offord, Carl Ruthven 1910- DLB-76

O'Flaherty, Liam 1896-1984 . . . .DLB-36, 162; Y-84

Ogarev, Nikolai Platonovich 1813-1877 . . .DLB-277

J. S. Ogilvie and Company DLB-49

Ogilvy, Eliza 1822-1912 . . . . DLB-199

Ogot, Grace 1930- DLB-125

O'Grady, Desmond 1935- DLB-40

Ogunyemi, Wale 1939- DLB-157

O'Hagan, Howard 1902-1982 . . . . DLB-68

O'Hara, Frank 1926-1966 . . . . DLB-5, 16, 193

O'Hara, John
    1905-1970 . . . . . . DLB-9, 86; DS-2; CDALB-5

    John O'Hara's Pottsville Journalism Y-88

O'Hegarty, P. S. 1879-1955 . . . . DLB-201

Ohio State University

    The William Charvat American Fiction Collection at the Ohio State University Libraries Y-92

Okara, Gabriel 1921- DLB-125; CDWLB-3

O'Keeffe, John 1747-1833 . . . . DLB-89

Nicholas Okes [publishing house] DLB-170

Okigbo, Christopher
    1930-1967 . . . . DLB-125; CDWLB-3

Okot p'Bitek 1931-1982 . . . . DLB-125; CDWLB-3

Okpewho, Isidore 1941- DLB-157

Okri, Ben 1959- DLB-157, 231

Old Dogs / New Tricks? New Technologies, the Canon, and the Structure of the Profession Y-02

Old Franklin Publishing House DLB-49

Old German Genesis and *Old German Exodus* circa 1050-circa 1130 . . . . DLB-148

The *Old High German Isidor* circa 790-800 . . . . DLB-148

Older, Fremont 1856-1935 . . . . DLB-25

Oldham, John 1653-1683 . . . . DLB-131

Oldman, C. B. 1894-1969 . . . . DLB-201

Olds, Sharon 1942- DLB-120

Olearius, Adam 1599-1671 . . . . DLB-164

O'Leary, Ellen 1831-1889 . . . . DLB-240

Olesha, Iurii Karlovich 1899-1960 . . . . . DLB-272

Oliphant, Laurence 1829?-1888 . . . . . DLB-18, 166

Oliphant, Margaret 1828-1897 . . DLB-18, 159, 190

    "Modern Novelists–Great and Small" (1855) DLB-21

Oliver, Chad 1928-1993 . . . . DLB-8

Oliver, Mary 1935- DLB-5, 193

Ollier, Claude 1922- DLB-83

Olsen, Tillie 1912/1913-
    . . . . DLB-28, 206; Y-80; CDALB-7

Olson, Charles 1910-1970 . . . . DLB-5, 16, 193

Olson, Elder 1909- DLB-48, 63

Olson, Sigurd F. 1899-1982 . . . . DLB-275

The Omega Workshops DS-10

Omotoso, Kole 1943- DLB-125

Omulevsky, Innokentii Vasil'evich 1836 [or 1837]-1883 . . . . DLB-238

Ondaatje, Michael 1943- DLB-60

O'Neill, Eugene 1888-1953 . . . . . DLB-7; CDALB-5

    Eugene O'Neill Memorial Theater Center DLB-7

    Eugene O'Neill's Letters: A Review Y-88

Onetti, Juan Carlos
    1909-1994 . . . . .DLB-113; CDWLB-3

Onions, George Oliver 1872-1961 . . . . . . DLB-153

Onofri, Arturo 1885-1928 . . . . DLB-114

O'Nolan, Brian 1911-1966 . . . . DLB-231

Opie, Amelia 1769-1853 . . . . DLB-116, 159

Opitz, Martin 1597-1639 . . . . DLB-164

Oppen, George 1908-1984 . . . . DLB-5, 165

Oppenheim, E. Phillips 1866-1946 . . . . . . DLB-70

Oppenheim, James 1882-1932 . . . . DLB-28

Oppenheimer, Joel 1930-1988 . . . . DLB-5, 193

Optic, Oliver (see Adams, William Taylor)

Orczy, Emma, Baroness 1865-1947 . . . . . DLB-70

Oregon Shakespeare Festival Y-00

Origo, Iris 1902-1988 . . . . DLB-155

O'Riordan, Kate 1960- DLB-267

Orlovitz, Gil 1918-1973 . . . . DLB-2, 5

Orlovsky, Peter 1933- DLB-16

Ormond, John 1923- DLB-27

Ornitz, Samuel 1890-1957 . . . . DLB-28, 44

O'Rourke, P. J. 1947- DLB-185

Orozco, Olga 1920-1999 . . . . DLB-283

Orten, Jiří 1919-1941 . . . . DLB-215

Ortese, Anna Maria 1914- DLB-177

Ortiz, Simon J. 1941- DLB-120, 175, 256

Ortnit and *Wolfdietrich* circa 1225-1250 . . . . DLB-138

Orton, Joe 1933-1967 . . . . DLB-13; CDBLB-8

Orwell, George (Eric Arthur Blair)
    1903-1950 . . DLB-15, 98, 195, 255; CDBLB-7

    The Orwell Year Y-84

    (Re-)Publishing Orwell Y-86

Ory, Carlos Edmundo de 1923- DLB-134

Osbey, Brenda Marie 1957- DLB-120

Osbon, B. S. 1827-1912 . . . . DLB-43

Osborn, Sarah 1714-1796 . . . . DLB-200

Osborne, John 1929-1994 . . . . . DLB-13; CDBLB-7

Osgood, Frances Sargent 1811-1850 . . . . . DLB-250

Osgood, Herbert L. 1855-1918 . . . . DLB-47

James R. Osgood and Company DLB-49

Osgood, McIlvaine and Company DLB-112

O'Shaughnessy, Arthur 1844-1881 . . . . . . DLB-35

Patrick O'Shea [publishing house] DLB-49

Osipov, Nikolai Petrovich 1751-1799 . . . . DLB-150

Oskison, John Milton 1879-1947 . . . . . . .DLB-175

Osler, Sir William 1849-1919 . . . . DLB-184

Osofisan, Femi 1946- DLB-125; CDWLB-3

Ostenso, Martha 1900-1963 . . . . DLB-92

Ostrauskas, Kostas 1926- DLB-232

Ostriker, Alicia 1937- DLB-120

Ostrovsky, Aleksandr Nikolaevich
    1823-1886 . . . . .DLB-277

Ostrovsky, Nikolai Alekseevich
    1904-1936 . . . . .DLB-272

Osundare, Niyi 1947- DLB-157; CDWLB-3

Oswald, Eleazer 1755-1795 . . . . DLB-43

Oswald von Wolkenstein
    1376 or 1377-1445 . . . . .DLB-179

Otero, Blas de 1916-1979 . . . . DLB-134

Otero, Miguel Antonio 1859-1944 . . . . . . DLB-82

Otero, Nina 1881-1965 . . . . DLB-209

Otero Silva, Miguel 1908-1985 . . . . DLB-145

Otfried von Weißenburg
    circa 800-circa 875? DLB-148

Otis, Broaders and Company DLB-49

Otis, James (see Kaler, James Otis)

Otis, James, Jr. 1725-1783 . . . . DLB-31

Ottaway, James 1911-2000 . . . . .DLB-127

Ottendorfer, Oswald 1826-1900 . . . . DLB-23

Ottieri, Ottiero 1924- DLB-177

Otto-Peters, Louise 1819-1895 . . . . DLB-129

Otway, Thomas 1652-1685 . . . . DLB-80

Ouellette, Fernand 1930- DLB-60

Ouida 1839-1908 . . . . DLB-18, 156

Outing Publishing Company DLB-46

Overbury, Sir Thomas
    circa 1581-1613 . . . . DLB-151

The Overlook Press DLB-46

Ovid 43 B.C.-A.D. 17 . . . . . . .DLB-211; CDWLB-1

Owen, Guy 1925- DLB-5

Owen, John 1564-1622 . . . . DLB-121

John Owen [publishing house] DLB-49

Peter Owen Limited DLB-112

Owen, Robert 1771-1858 . . . . DLB-107, 158

Owen, Wilfred
    1893-1918 . . . . DLB-20; DS-18; CDBLB-6

    A Centenary Celebration Y-93

    The Wilfred Owen Association Y-98

The Owl and the Nightingale
    circa 1189-1199 . . . . DLB-146

Owsley, Frank L. 1890-1956 . . . . .DLB-17

Oxford, Seventeenth Earl of, Edward
    de Vere 1550-1604 . . . . .DLB-172

OyamO (Charles F. Gordon)
    1943- DLB-266

Ozerov, Vladislav Aleksandrovich
    1769-1816 . . . . DLB-150

Ozick, Cynthia 1928- DLB-28, 152; Y-82

    First Strauss "Livings" Awarded to Cynthia Ozick and Raymond Carver An Interview with Cynthia Ozick . . . Y-83

    Tribute to Michael M. Rea Y-97

P

Pace, Richard 1482?-1536 ....DLB-167
Pacey, Desmond 1917-1975 ....DLB-88
Pack, Robert 1929- DLB-5
Padell Publishing Company............DLB-46
Padgett, Ron 1942- DLB-5
Padilla, Ernesto Chávez 1944- DLB-122
L. C. Page and Company DLB-49
Page, Louise 1955- DLB-233
Page, P. K. 1916- DLB-68
Page, Thomas Nelson
 1853-1922 .... DLB-12, 78; DS-13
Page, Walter Hines 1855-1918 ....DLB-71, 91
Paget, Francis Edward 1806-1882 ....DLB-163
Paget, Violet (see Lee, Vernon)
Pagliarani, Elio 1927- DLB-128
Pain, Barry 1864-1928............DLB-135, 197
Pain, Philip ?-circa 1666.................DLB-24
Paine, Robert Treat, Jr. 1773-1811........DLB-37
Paine, Thomas
 1737-1809 .....DLB-31, 43, 73, 158; CDALB-2
Painter, George D. 1914- DLB-155
Painter, William 1540?-1594 ....DLB-136
Palazzeschi, Aldo 1885-1974 ....DLB-114, 264
Paley, Grace 1922- DLB-28, 218
Palcy, William 1743-1805 ....DLB-252
Palfrey, John Gorham 1796-1881...DLB-1, 30, 235
Palgrave, Francis Turner 1824-1897 ......DLB-35
Palmer, Joe H. 1904-1952 ....DLB-171
Palmer, Michael 1943- DLB-169
Palmer, Nettie 1885-1964 ....DLB-260
Palmer, Vance 1885-1959 ....DLB-260
Paltock, Robert 1697-1767 ....DLB-39
Paludan, Jacob 1896-1975 ....DLB-214
Pan Books Limited....................DLB-112
Panaev, Ivan Ivanovich 1812-1862 ......DLB-198
Panaeva, Avdot'ia Iakovlevna
 1820-1893 ....DLB-238
Panama, Norman 1914- DLB-26
Pancake, Breece D'J 1952-1979 ....DLB-130
Panduro, Leif 1923-1977 ....DLB-214
Panero, Leopoldo 1909-1962..........DLB-108
Pangborn, Edgar 1909-1976...........DLB-8
Panizzi, Sir Anthony 1797-1879 ....DLB-184
Panneton, Philippe (see Ringuet)
Panshin, Alexei 1940- DLB-8
Pansy (see Alden, Isabella)
Pantheon Books.....................DLB-46
Papadat-Bengescu, Hortensia
 1876-1955 ....DLB-220
Papantonio, Michael 1907-1976 ....DLB-187
Paperback Library...................DLB-46
Paperback Science Fiction DLB-8
Papini, Giovanni 1881-1956 ....DLB-264

Paquet, Alfons 1881-1944 ....DLB-66
Paracelsus 1493-1541.................DLB-179
Paradis, Suzanne 1936- DLB-53
Páral, Vladimír, 1932- DLB-232
Pardoe, Julia 1804-1862...............DLB-166
Paredes, Américo 1915-1999 ....DLB-209
Pareja Diezcanseco, Alfredo 1908-1993...DLB-145
Parents' Magazine Press................DLB-46
Parfit, Derek 1942- DLB-262
Parise, Goffredo 1929-1986............DLB-177
Parish, Mitchell 1900-1993 ....DLB-265
Parizeau, Alice 1930-1990 ....DLB-60
Park, Ruth 1923?- DLB-260
Parke, John 1754-1789 ....DLB-31
Parker, Dan 1893-1967 ....DLB-241
Parker, Dorothy 1893-1967........DLB-11, 45, 86
Parker, Gilbert 1860-1932.............DLB-99
Parker, James 1714-1770...............DLB-43
Parker, John [publishing house].........DLB-106
Parker, Matthew 1504-1575............DLB-213
Parker, Stewart 1941-1988.............DLB-245
Parker, Theodore 1810-1860....DLB-1, 235; DS-5
Parker, William Riley 1906-1968 ....DLB-103
J. H. Parker [publishing house] DLB-106
Parkes, Bessie Rayner (Madame Belloc)
 1829-1925 ....DLB-240
Parkman, Francis
 1823-1893 .... DLB-1, 30, 183, 186, 235
Parks, Gordon 1912- DLB-33
Parks, Tim 1954- DLB-231
Parks, William 1698-1750 ....DLB-43
William Parks [publishing house] DLB-49
Parley, Peter (see Goodrich, Samuel Griswold)
Parmenides late sixth-fifth century B.C. ...DLB-176
Parnell, Thomas 1679-1718 ....DLB-95
Parnicki, Teodor 1908-1988 ....DLB-215
Parr, Catherine 1513?-1548............DLB-136
Parra, Nicanor 1914- DLB-283
Parrington, Vernon L. 1871-1929 .....DLB-17, 63
Parrish, Maxfield 1870-1966 ....DLB-188
Parronchi, Alessandro 1914- DLB-128
Parton, James 1822-1891..............DLB-30
Parton, Sara Payson Willis
 1811-1872 .... DLB-43, 74, 239
S. W. Partridge and Company DLB-106
Parun, Vesna 1922- DLB-181; CDWLB-4
Pascal, Blaise 1623-1662...............DLB-268
Pasinetti, Pier Maria 1913- DLB-177
 Tribute to Albert Erskine.............Y-93
Pasolini, Pier Paolo 1922-1975......DLB-128, 177
Pastan, Linda 1932- DLB-5
Paston, George (Emily Morse Symonds)
 1860-1936 .... DLB-149, 197
The Paston Letters 1422-1509 ....DLB-146
Pastorius, Francis Daniel
 1651-circa 1720 ....DLB-24

Patchen, Kenneth 1911-1972 ....DLB-16, 48
Pater, Walter 1839-1894 .. DLB-57, 156; CDBLB-4
 Aesthetic Poetry (1873) DLB-35
 "Style" (1888) [excerpt] DLB-57
Paterson, A. B. "Banjo" 1864-1941 ......DLB-230
Paterson, Katherine 1932- DLB-52
Patmore, Coventry 1823-1896 ....DLB-35, 98
Paton, Alan 1903-1988 .... DLB-225; DS-17
Paton, Joseph Noel 1821-1901...........DLB-35
Paton Walsh, Jill 1937- DLB-161
Patrick, Edwin Hill ("Ted") 1901-1964 ...DLB-137
Patrick, John 1906-1995 ....DLB-7
Pattee, Fred Lewis 1863-1950 ....DLB-71
Patterson, Alicia 1906-1963 ....DLB-127
Patterson, Eleanor Medill 1881-1948......DLB-29
Patterson, Eugene 1923- DLB-127
Patterson, Joseph Medill 1879-1946.......DLB-29
Pattillo, Henry 1726-1801 ....DLB-37
Paul, Elliot 1891-1958 .... DLB-4; DS-15
Paul, Jean (see Richter, Johann Paul Friedrich)
Paul, Kegan, Trench, Trubner and
 Company Limited.................DLB-106
Peter Paul Book Company DLB-49
Stanley Paul and Company Limited DLB-112
Paulding, James Kirke
 1778-1860 .... DLB-3, 59, 74, 250
Paulin, Tom 1949- DLB-40
Pauper, Peter, Press..................DLB-46
Paustovsky, Konstantin Georgievich
 1892-1968 ....DLB-272
Pavese, Cesare 1908-1950 .... DLB-128, 177
Pavić, Milorad 1929- DLB-181; CDWLB-4
Pavlov, Konstantin 1933- DLB-181
Pavlov, Nikolai Filippovich 1803-1864.....DLB-198
Pavlova, Karolina Karlovna 1807-1893 ....DLB-205
Pavlović, Miodrag
 1928- DLB-181; CDWLB-4
Paxton, John 1911-1985...............DLB-44
Payn, James 1830-1898 ....DLB-18
Payne, John 1842-1916 ....DLB-35
Payne, John Howard 1791-1852 ....DLB-37
Payson and Clarke DLB-46
Paz, Octavio 1914-1998................Y-90, 98
 Nobel Lecture 1990 ....Y-90
Pazzi, Roberto 1946- DLB-196
Pea, Enrico 1881-1958 ....DLB-264
Peabody, Elizabeth Palmer
 1804-1894 ....DLB-1, 223
 Preface to Record of a School:
 Exemplifying the General Principles
 of Spiritual Culture DS-5
Elizabeth Palmer Peabody
 [publishing house]..................DLB-49
Peabody, Josephine Preston 1874-1922 ...DLB-249
Peabody, Oliver William Bourn
 1799-1848 ....DLB-59
Peace, Roger 1899-1968 ....DLB-127

Cumulative Index

Peacham, Henry 1578-1644? DLB-151

Peacham, Henry, the Elder
1547-1634 .... DLB-172, 236

Peachtree Publishers, Limited DLB-46

Peacock, Molly 1947- DLB-120

Peacock, Thomas Love 1785-1866 ... DLB-96, 116

Pead, Deuel ?-1727 .... DLB-24

Peake, Mervyn 1911-1968 ..... DLB-15, 160, 255

Peale, Rembrandt 1778-1860 .... DLB-183

Pear Tree Press..................... DLB-112

Pearce, Philippa 1920- DLB-161

H. B. Pearson [publishing house] DLB-49

Pearson, Hesketh 1887-1964 .... DLB-149

Peattie, Donald Culross 1898-1964 ...... DLB-275

Pechersky, Andrei (see Mel'nikov, Pavel Ivanovich)

Peck, George W. 1840-1916 .... DLB-23, 42

H. C. Peck and Theo. Bliss
[publishing house] DLB-49

Peck, Harry Thurston 1856-1914 ..... DLB-71, 91

Peden, William 1913-1999 .... DLB-234

    Tribute to William Goyen Y-83

Peele, George 1556-1596 .... DLB-62, 167

Pegler, Westbrook 1894-1969 .... DLB-171

Péguy, Charles 1873-1914 .... DLB-258

Peirce, Charles Sanders 1839-1914....... DLB-270

Pekić, Borislav 1930-1992... DLB-181; CDWLB-4

Pellegrini and Cudahy DLB-46

Pelletier, Aimé (see Vac, Bertrand)

Pelletier, Francine 1959- DLB-251

Pemberton, Sir Max 1863-1950 .... DLB-70

de la Peña, Terri 1947- DLB-209

Penfield, Edward 1866-1925 .... DLB-188

Penguin Books [U.K.]................ DLB-112

    Fifty Penguin Years.................. Y-85

    Penguin Collectors' Society............ Y-98

Penguin Books [U.S.] DLB-46

Penn, William 1644-1718 .... DLB-24

Penn Publishing Company DLB-49

Penna, Sandro 1906-1977 .... DLB-114

Pennell, Joseph 1857-1926............. DLB-188

Penner, Jonathan 1940- Y-83

Pennington, Lee 1939- Y-82

Penton, Brian 1904-1951 .... DLB-260

Pepper, Stephen C. 1891-1972 ....DLB-270

Pepys, Samuel
1633-1703......... DLB-101, 213; CDBLB-2

Percy, Thomas 1729-1811 .... DLB-104

Percy, Walker 1916-1990........DLB-2; Y-80, 90

    Tribute to Caroline Gordon Y-81

Percy, William 1575-1648............. DLB-172

Perec, Georges 1936-1982 .... DLB-83

Perelman, Bob 1947- DLB-193

Perelman, S. J. 1904-1979 .... DLB-11, 44

Perez, Raymundo "Tigre" 1946- DLB-122

Peri Rossi, Cristina 1941- DLB-145

Perkins, Eugene 1932- DLB-41

Perkins, Maxwell
    The Claims of Business and Literature:
    An Undergraduate Essay Y-01

Perkins, William 1558-1602 .... DLB-281

Perkoff, Stuart Z. 1930-1974........... DLB-16

Perley, Moses Henry 1804-1862 .... DLB-99

Permabooks DLB-46

Perovsky, Aleksei Alekseevich
(Antonii Pogorel'sky) 1787-1836 .... DLB-198

Perrault, Charles 1628-1703............DLB-268

Perri, Henry 1561-1617 .... DLB-236

Perrin, Alice 1867-1934............... DLB-156

Perry, Anne 1938- DLB-276

Perry, Bliss 1860-1954 .... DLB-71

Perry, Eleanor 1915-1981............. DLB-44

Perry, Henry (see Perri, Henry)

Perry, Matthew 1794-1858 .... DLB-183

Perry, Sampson 1747-1823 .... DLB-158

Perse, Saint-John 1887-1975 .... DLB-258

Persius A.D. 34-A.D. 62.............. DLB-211

Perutz, Leo 1882-1957 .... DLB-81

Pesetsky, Bette 1932- DLB-130

Pestalozzi, Johann Heinrich 1746-1827 .... DLB-94

Peter, Laurence J. 1919-1990 .... DLB-53

Peter of Spain circa 1205-1277 .... DLB-115

Peterkin, Julia 1880-1961 .... DLB-9

Peters, Ellis (Edith Pargeter) 1913-1995 ...DLB-276

Peters, Lenrie 1932- DLB-117

Peters, Robert 1924- DLB-105

    "Foreword to *Ludwig of Baviria*" DLB-105

Petersham, Maud 1889-1971 .... DLB-22

Petersham, Miska 1888-1960 .... DLB-22

Peterson, Charles Jacobs 1819-1887 ..... DLB-79

Peterson, Len 1917- DLB-88

Peterson, Levi S. 1933- DLB-206

Peterson, Louis 1922-1998 .... DLB-76

Peterson, T. B., and Brothers DLB-49

Petitclair, Pierre 1813-1860............ DLB-99

Petrescu, Camil 1894-1957 .... DLB-220

Petronius circa A.D. 20-A.D. 66
.... DLB-211; CDWLB-1

Petrov, Aleksandar 1938- DLB-181

Petrov, Evgenii (Evgenii Petrovich Kataev)
1903-1942 ....DLB-272

Petrov, Gavriil 1730-1801 .... DLB-150

Petrov, Valeri 1920- DLB-181

Petrov, Vasilii Petrovich 1736-1799 ..... DLB-150

Petrović, Rastko
1898-1949 ....DLB-147; CDWLB-4

Petruslied circa 854?................... DLB-148

Petry, Ann 1908-1997................ DLB-76

Pettie, George circa 1548-1589 .... DLB-136

Peyton, K. M. 1929- DLB-161

Pfaffe Konrad flourished circa 1172 ..... DLB-148

Pfaffe Lamprecht flourished circa 1150 .. DLB-148

Pfeiffer, Emily 1827-1890 .... DLB-199

Pforzheimer, Carl H. 1879-1957........ DLB-140

Phaedrus circa 18 B.C.-circa A.D. 50 .... DLB-211

Phaer, Thomas 1510?-1560 .... DLB-167

Phaidon Press Limited DLB-112

Pharr, Robert Deane 1916-1992......... DLB-33

Phelps, Elizabeth Stuart 1815-1852....... DLB-202

Phelps, Elizabeth Stuart 1844-1911....DLB-74, 221

Philander von der Linde
(see Mencke, Johann Burckhard)

Philby, H. St. John B. 1885-1960 .... DLB-195

Philip, Marlene Nourbese 1947- DLB-157

Philippe, Charles-Louis 1874-1909 .... DLB-65

Philips, John 1676-1708................ DLB-95

Philips, Katherine 1632-1664 .... DLB-131

Phillipps, Sir Thomas 1792-1872........ DLB-184

Phillips, Caryl 1958- DLB-157

Phillips, David Graham 1867-1911 ..... DLB-9, 12

Phillips, Jayne Anne 1952- Y-80

    Tribute to Seymour Lawrence Y-94

Phillips, Robert 1938- DLB-105

    "Finding, Losing, Reclaiming: A Note
    on My Poems" DLB-105

    Tribute to William Goyen Y-83

Phillips, Stephen 1864-1915 .... DLB-10

Phillips, Ulrich B. 1877-1934.............DLB-17

Phillips, Wendell 1811-1884 .... DLB-235

Phillips, Willard 1784-1873 .... DLB-59

Phillips, William 1907-2002 ....DLB-137

Phillips, Sampson and Company DLB-49

Phillpotts, Adelaide Eden (Adelaide Ross)
1896-1993 .... DLB-191

Phillpotts, Eden 1862-1960...DLB-10, 70, 135, 153

Philo circa 20-15 B.C.-circa A.D. 50......DLB-176

Philosophical Library DLB-46

Philosophy
    Eighteenth-Century Philosophical
    Background DLB-31

    Philosophic Thought in Boston DLB-235

    Translators of the Twelfth Century:
    Literary Issues Raised and
    Impact Created............... DLB-115

Elihu Phinney [publishing house]........ DLB-49

Phoenix, John (see Derby, George Horatio)

PHYLON (Fourth Quarter, 1950),
    The Negro in Literature:
    The Current Scene................ DLB-76

Physiologus circa 1070-circa 1150 .... DLB-148

Piccolo, Lucio 1903-1969 .... DLB-114

Pickard, Tom 1946- DLB-40

William Pickering [publishing house].... DLB-106

Pickthall, Marjorie 1883-1922 .... DLB-92

Pictorial Printing Company DLB-49

Piel, Gerard 1915- DLB-137

    "An Announcement to Our Readers,"
    Gerard Piel's Statement in *Scientific
    American* (April 1948) DLB-137

Pielmeier, John 1949- DLB-266

Piercy, Marge 1936- DLB-120, 227
Pierro, Albino 1916-1995..............DLB-128
Pignotti, Lamberto 1926- DLB-128
Pike, Albert 1809-1891 ....DLB-74
Pike, Zebulon Montgomery 1779-1813 ...DLB-183
Pillat, Ion 1891-1945 ....DLB-220
Pil'niak, Boris Andreevich (Boris Andreevich Vogau) 1894-1938................DLB-272
Pilon, Jean-Guy 1930- DLB-60
Pinckney, Eliza Lucas 1722-1793 ....DLB-200
Pinckney, Josephine 1895-1957 ....DLB-6
Pindar circa 518 B.C.-circa 438 B.C.
.... DLB-176; CDWLB-1
Pindar, Peter (see Wolcot, John)
Pineda, Cecile 1942- DLB-209
Pinero, Arthur Wing 1855-1934 ....DLB-10
Piñero, Miguel 1946-1988 ....DLB-266
Pinget, Robert 1919-1997..............DLB-83
Pinkney, Edward Coote 1802-1828......DLB-248
Pinnacle Books......................DLB-46
Piñon, Nélida 1935- DLB-145
Pinsky, Robert 1940- Y-82
   Reappointed Poet Laureate Y-98
Pinter, Harold 1930- DLB-13; CDBLB-8
   Writing for the Theatre DLB-13
Piontek, Heinz 1925- DLB-75
Piozzi, Hester Lynch [Thrale] 1741-1821 ....DLB-104, 142
Piper, H. Beam 1904-1964...............DLB-8
Piper, Watty DLB-22
Pirandello, Luigi 1867-1936............DLB-264
Pirckheimer, Caritas 1467-1532 ....DLB-179
Pirckheimer, Willibald 1470-1530 ....DLB-179
Pisar, Samuel 1929- Y-83
Pisarev, Dmitrii Ivanovich 1840-1868 ....DLB-277
Pisemsky, Aleksei Feofilaktovich 1821-1881 ....DLB-238
Pitkin, Timothy 1766-1847 ....DLB-30
Pitter, Ruth 1897- DLB-20
Pix, Mary 1666-1709 ....DLB-80
Pixerécourt, René Charles Guilbert de 1773-1844 ....DLB-192
Pizarnik, Alejandra 1936-1972 ....DLB-283
Plaatje, Sol T. 1876-1932 ....DLB-125, 225
Plante, David 1940- Y-83
Platen, August von 1796-1835 ....DLB-90
Plantinga, Alvin 1932- DLB-279
Plath, Sylvia 1932-1963 ....DLB-5, 6, 152; CDALB-1
Plato circa 428 B.C.-348-347 B.C.
.... DLB-176; CDWLB-1
Plato, Ann 1824?-? DLB-239
Platon 1737-1812 ....DLB-150
Platonov, Andrei Platonovich (Andrei Platonovich Klimentev) 1899-1951 ...DLB-272
Platt, Charles 1945- DLB-261

Platt and Munk Company..............DLB-46
Plautus circa 254 B.C.-184 B.C.
.... DLB-211; CDWLB-1
Playboy Press......................DLB-46
John Playford [publishing house]........ DLB-170
Der Pleier flourished circa 1250..........DLB-138
Pleijel, Agneta 1940- DLB-257
Plenzdorf, Ulrich 1934- DLB-75
Pleshcheev, Aleksei Nikolaevich 1825?-1893 ....DLB-277
Plessen, Elizabeth 1944- DLB-75
Pletnev, Petr Aleksandrovich 1792-1865 ....DLB-205
Pliekšāne, Elza Rozenberga (see Aspazija)
Pliekšāns, Jānis (see Rainis, Jānis)
Plievier, Theodor 1892-1955............DLB-69
Plimpton, George 1927- DLB-185, 241; Y-99
Pliny the Elder A.D. 23/24-A.D. 79......DLB-211
Pliny the Younger circa A.D. 61-A.D. 112 ....DLB-211
Plomer, William 1903-1973 ....DLB-20, 162, 191, 225
Plotinus 204-270........... DLB-176; CDWLB-1
Plowright, Teresa 1952- DLB-251
Plume, Thomas 1630-1704 ....DLB-213
Plumly, Stanley 1939- DLB-5, 193
Plumpp, Sterling D. 1940- DLB-41
Plunkett, James 1920- DLB-14
Plutarch circa 46-circa 120....... DLB-176; CDWLB-1
Plymell, Charles 1935- DLB-16
Pocket Books......................DLB-46
Poe, Edgar Allan 1809-1849
.........DLB-3, 59, 73, 74, 248; CDALB-2
   The Poe Studies Association Y-99
Poe, James 1921-1980 ....DLB-44
The Poet Laureate of the United States...... Y-86
   Statements from Former Consultants in Poetry Y-86
Poetry
   Aesthetic Poetry (1873) DLB-35
   A Century of Poetry, a Lifetime of Collecting: J. M. Edelstein's Collection of Twentieth-Century American Poetry Y-02
   "Certain Gifts," by Betty Adcock....DLB-105
   Contempo Caravan: Kites in a Windstorm Y-85
   "Contemporary Verse Story-telling," by Jonathan Holden DLB-105
   "A Detail in a Poem," by Fred Chappell DLB-105
   "The English Renaissance of Art" (1908), by Oscar Wilde DLB-35
   "Every Man His Own Poet; or, The Inspired Singer's Recipe Book" (1877), by H. W. Mallock DLB-35
   "Eyes Across Centuries: Contemporary Poetry and 'That Vision Thing,'" by Philip Dacey DLB-105

A Field Guide to Recent Schools of American Poetry Y-86
"Finding, Losing, Reclaiming: A Note on My Poems, by Robert Phillips" DLB-105
"The Fleshly School of Poetry and Other Phenomena of the Day" (1872) ...DLB-35
"The Fleshly School of Poetry: Mr. D. G. Rossetti" (1871) DLB-35
The G. Ross Roy Scottish Poetry Collection at the University of South Carolina . Y-89
"Getting Started: Accepting the Regions You Own–or Which Own You," by Walter McDonald DLB-105
"The Good, The Not So Good," by Stephen Dunn DLB-105
The Griffin Poetry Prize Y-00
The Hero as Poet. Dante; Shakspeare (1841), by Thomas Carlyle DLB-32
"Images and 'Images,'" by Charles Simic....................DLB-105
"Into the Mirror," by Peter Cooley ..DLB-105
"Knots into Webs: Some Autobiographical Sources," by Dabney Stuart.....DLB-105
"L'Envoi" (1882), by Oscar Wilde ...DLB-35
"Living in Ruin," by Gerald Stern...DLB-105
Looking for the Golden Mountain: Poetry Reviewing Y-89
Lyric Poetry (French) DLB-268
"The No Self, the Little Self, and the Poets," by Richard Moore......DLB-105
On Some of the Characteristics of Modern Poetry and On the Lyrical Poems of Alfred Tennyson (1831) DLB-32
The Pitt Poetry Series: Poetry Publishing Today Y-85
"The Poetry File," by Edward Field....................DLB-105
Poetry in Nineteenth-Century France: Cultural Background and Critical Commentary................DLB-217
The Poetry of Jorge Luis Borges Y-86
"The Poet's Kaleidoscope: The Element of Surprise in the Making of the Poem" by Madeline DeFrees ..DLB-105
The Pre-Raphaelite Controversy DLB-35
"Reflections: After a Tornado," by Judson Jerome DLB-105
Statements from Former Consultants in Poetry Y-86
Statements on the Art of Poetry......DLB-54
The Study of Poetry (1880), by Matthew Arnold DLB-35
A Survey of Poetry Anthologies, 1879-1960 ....DLB-54
Thoughts on Poetry and Its Varieties (1833), by John Stuart Mill DLB-32
Under the Microscope (1872), by A. C. Swinburne DLB-35
The Unterberg Poetry Center of the 92nd Street Y............... Y-98
Victorian Poetry: Five Critical Views.....................DLBV-35
Year in Poetry Y-83–92, 94–01

401

Year's Work in American Poetry Y-82	Pope, Alexander 1688-1744 . . . . . . DLB-95, 101, 213; CDBLB-2	Powell, Anthony 1905-2000 . . . DLB-15; CDBLB-7
Poets		The Anthony Powell Society: Powell and the First Biennial Conference Y-01
The Lives of the Poets (1753) DLB-142	Popov, Aleksandr Serafimovich (see Serafimovich, Aleksandr Serafimovich)	
Minor Poets of the Earlier Seventeenth Century DLB-121	Popov, Mikhail Ivanovich 1742-circa 1790 . . . . DLB-150	Powell, Dawn 1897-1965 Dawn Powell, Where Have You Been All Our Lives? Y-97
Other British Poets Who Fell in the Great War DLB-216	Popović, Aleksandar 1929-1996 . . . . DLB-181	Powell, John Wesley 1834-1902 . . . . DLB-186
Other Poets [French] DLB-217	Popper, Karl 1902-1994 . . . . DLB-262	Powell, Padgett 1952- DLB-234
Second-Generation Minor Poets of the Seventeenth Century DLB-126	Popular Culture Association/ American Culture Association Y-99	Powers, J. F. 1917-1999 . . . . DLB-130
Third-Generation Minor Poets of the Seventeenth Century DLB-131	Popular Library DLB-46	Powers, Jimmy 1903-1995 . . . . DLB-241
Pogodin, Mikhail Petrovich 1800-1875 . . . DLB-198	Poquelin, Jean-Baptiste (see Molière)	Pownall, David 1938- DLB-14
Pogorel'sky, Antonii (see Perovsky, Aleksei Alekseevich)	Porete, Marguerite ?-1310 . . . . DLB-208	Powys, John Cowper 1872-1963 . . . . . DLB-15, 255
	Porlock, Martin (see MacDonald, Philip)	Powys, Llewelyn 1884-1939 . . . . DLB-98
Pohl, Frederik 1919- DLB-8	Porpoise Press DLB-112	Powys, T. F. 1875-1953 . . . . DLB-36, 162
Tribute to Isaac Asimov Y-92	Porta, Antonio 1935-1989 . . . . DLB-128	The Powys Society Y-98
Tribute to Theodore Sturgeon Y-85	Porter, Anna Maria 1780-1832 . . . . . DLB-116, 159	Poynter, Nelson 1903-1978 . . . . DLB-127
Poirier, Louis (see Gracq, Julien)	Porter, Cole 1891-1964 . . . . DLB-265	Prado, Pedro 1886-1952 . . . . DLB-283
Poláček, Karel 1892-1945 . . . DLB-215; CDWLB-4	Porter, David 1780-1843 . . . . DLB-183	Prados, Emilio 1899-1962 . . . . DLB-134
Polanyi, Michael 1891-1976 . . . . DLB-100	Porter, Eleanor H. 1868-1920 . . . . DLB-9	Praed, Mrs. Caroline (see Praed, Rosa)
Pole, Reginald 1500-1558 . . . . DLB-132	Porter, Gene Stratton (see Stratton-Porter, Gene)	Praed, Rosa (Mrs. Caroline Praed) 1851-1935 . . . . DLB-230
Polevoi, Nikolai Alekseevich 1796-1846 . . DLB-198	Porter, Hal 1911-1984 . . . . DLB-260	Praed, Winthrop Mackworth 1802-1839 . . DLB-96
Polezhaev, Aleksandr Ivanovich 1804-1838 . . . . DLB-205	Porter, Henry ?-? DLB-62	Praeger Publishers DLB-46
Poliakoff, Stephen 1952- DLB-13	Porter, Jane 1776-1850 . . . . DLB-116, 159	Praetorius, Johannes 1630-1680 . . . . DLB-168
Polidori, John William 1795-1821 . . . . DLB-116	Porter, Katherine Anne 1890-1980 . . . . . . DLB-4, 9, 102; Y-80; DS-12; CDALB-7	Pratolini, Vasco 1913-1991 . . . . DLB-177
Polite, Carlene Hatcher 1932- DLB-33	The Katherine Anne Porter Society Y-01	Pratt, E. J. 1882-1964 . . . . DLB-92
Pollard, Alfred W. 1859-1944 . . . . DLB-201	Porter, Peter 1929- DLB-40	Pratt, Samuel Jackson 1749-1814 . . . . DLB-39
Pollard, Edward A. 1832-1872 . . . . DLB-30	Porter, William Sydney (O. Henry) 1862-1910 . . . . DLB-12, 78, 79; CDALB-3	Preciado Martin, Patricia 1939- DLB-209
Pollard, Graham 1903-1976 . . . . DLB-201	Porter, William T. 1809-1858 . . . . DLB-3, 43, 250	Préfontaine, Yves 1937- DLB-53
Pollard, Percival 1869-1911 . . . . DLB-71	Porter and Coates DLB-49	Prelutsky, Jack 1940- DLB-61
Pollard and Moss DLB-49	Portillo Trambley, Estela 1927-1998 . . . . . DLB-209	Prentice, George D. 1802-1870 . . . . DLB-43
Pollock, Sharon 1936- DLB-60	Portis, Charles 1933- DLB-6	Prentice-Hall DLB-46
Polonsky, Abraham 1910-1999 . . . . DLB-26	Posey, Alexander 1873-1908 . . . . DLB-175	Prescott, Orville 1906-1996 . . . . Y-96
Polonsky, Iakov Petrovich 1819-1898 . . . . DLB-277	Postans, Marianne circa 1810-1865 . . . . . DLB-166	Prescott, William Hickling 1796-1859 . . . . DLB-1, 30, 59, 235
Polotsky, Simeon 1629-1680 . . . . DLB-150	Postgate, Raymond 1896-1971 . . . . DLB-276	Prešeren, Francè 1800-1849 . . . . DLB-147; CDWLB-4
Polybius circa 200 B.C.-118 B.C. DLB-176	Postl, Carl (see Sealsfield, Carl)	
Pomialovsky, Nikolai Gerasimovich 1835-1863 . . . . DLB-238	Poston, Ted 1906-1974 . . . . DLB-51	Presses (*See also* Publishing)
Pomilio, Mario 1921-1990 . . . . DLB-177	Potekhin, Aleksei Antipovich 1829-1908 . DLB-238	Small Presses in Great Britain and Ireland, 1960-1985 . . . . DLB-40
Ponce, Mary Helen 1938- DLB-122	Potok, Chaim 1929-2002 . . . . DLB-28, 152	Small Presses I: Jargon Society Y-84
Ponce-Montoya, Juanita 1949- DLB-122	A Conversation with Chaim Potok Y-84	Small Presses II: The Spirit That Moves Us Press Y-85
Ponet, John 1516?-1556 . . . . DLB-132	Tribute to Bernard Malamud Y-86	Small Presses III: Pushcart Press Y-87
Ponge, Francis 1899-1988 . . . . DLB-258; Y-02	Potter, Beatrix 1866-1943 . . . . DLB-141	Preston, Margaret Junkin 1820-1897 . . . . DLB-239, 248
Poniatowska, Elena 1933- DLB-113; CDWLB-3	The Beatrix Potter Society Y-98	Preston, May Wilson 1873-1949 . . . . DLB-188
Ponsard, François 1814-1867 . . . . DLB-192	Potter, David M. 1910-1971 . . . . DLB-17	Preston, Thomas 1537-1598 . . . . DLB-62
William Ponsonby [publishing house] DLB-170	Potter, Dennis 1935-1994 . . . . DLB-233	Prévert, Jacques 1900-1977 . . . . DLB-258
Pontiggia, Giuseppe 1934- DLB-196	John E. Potter and Company DLB-49	Price, Anthony 1928- DLB-276
Pony Stories, Omnibus Essay on DLB-160	Pottle, Frederick A. 1897-1987 . . . . . DLB-103; Y-87	Price, Reynolds 1933- DLB-2, 218, 278
Poole, Ernest 1880-1950 . . . . DLB-9	Poulin, Jacques 1937- DLB-60	Price, Richard 1723-1791 . . . . DLB-158
Poole, Sophia 1804-1891 . . . . DLB-166	Pound, Ezra 1885-1972 . . . . DLB-4, 45, 63; DS-15; CDALB-4	Price, Richard 1949- Y-81
Poore, Benjamin Perley 1820-1887 . . . . . . DLB-23	The Cost of the *Cantos*: William Bird to Ezra Pound Y-01	Prichard, Katharine Susannah 1883-1969 . . . . DLB-260
Popa, Vasko 1922-1991 . . . . DLB-181; CDWLB-4	The Ezra Pound Society Y-01	Prideaux, John 1578-1650 . . . . DLB-236
Pope, Abbie Hanscom 1858-1894 . . . . DLB-140	Poverman, C. E. 1944- DLB-234	
	Povich, Shirley 1905-1998 . . . . DLB-171	Priest, Christopher 1943- DLB-14, 207, 261

Priestley, J. B. 1894-1984
...DLB-10, 34, 77, 100, 139; Y-84; CDBLB-6
Priestley, Joseph 1733-1804 ....DLB-252
Prime, Benjamin Young 1733-1791 ....DLB-31
Primrose, Diana floruit circa 1630........DLB-126
Prince, F. T. 1912- DLB-20
Prince, Nancy Gardner 1799-?..........DLB-239
Prince, Thomas 1687-1758.........DLB-24, 140
Pringle, Thomas 1789-1834............DLB-225
Printz, Wolfgang Casper 1641-1717......DLB-168
Prior, Matthew 1664-1721..............DLB-95
Prisco, Michele 1920- DLB-177
Prishvin, Mikhail Mikhailovich
  1873-1954 ....DLB-272
Pritchard, William H. 1932- DLB-111
Pritchett, V. S. 1900-1997 ....DLB-15, 139
Probyn, May 1856 or 1857-1909 ....DLB-199
Procter, Adelaide Anne 1825-1864 ...DLB-32, 199
Procter, Bryan Waller 1787-1874 .....DLB-96, 144
Proctor, Robert 1868-1903 ....DLB-184
Prokopovich, Feofan 1681?-1736........DLB-150
Prokosch, Frederic 1906-1989 ....DLB-48
Pronzini, Bill 1943- DLB-226
Propertius circa 50 B.C.-post 16 B.C.
  ....DLB-211; CDWLB-1
Propper, Dan 1937- DLB-16
Prose, Francine 1947- DLB-234
Protagoras circa 490 B.C.-420 B.C.......DLB-176
Proud, Robert 1728-1813..............DLB-30
Proust, Marcel 1871-1922 ....DLB-65
  Marcel Proust at 129 and the Proust
    Society of America................Y-00
  Marcel Proust's *Remembrance of Things Past*:
    The Rediscovered Galley Proofs....Y-00
Prutkov, Koz'ma Petrovich 1803-1863 ...DLB-277
Prynne, J. H. 1936- DLB-40
Przybyszewski, Stanisław 1868-1927 ......DLB-66
Pseudo-Dionysius the Areopagite floruit
  circa 500 ....DLB-115
Public Lending Right in America
  PLR and the Meaning of Literary
    Property Y-83
  Statement by Sen. Charles
    McC. Mathias, Jr. PLR Y-83
  Statements on PLR by American Writers Y-83
Public Lending Right in the United Kingdom
  The First Year in the United Kingdom ..Y-83
Publishers [listed by individual names]
  Publishers, Conversations with:
  An Interview with Charles Scribner III...Y-94
  An Interview with Donald Lamm Y-95
  An Interview with James Laughlin......Y-96
  An Interview with Patrick O'Connor....Y-84
Publishing
  The Art and Mystery of Publishing:
    Interviews Y-97
  Book Publishing Accounting: Some Basic
    Concepts Y-98

1873 Publishers' Catalogues.........DLB-49
The Literary Scene 2002: Publishing, Book
  Reviewing, and Literary Journalism.....Y-02
Main Trends in Twentieth-Century
  Book Clubs......................DLB-46
Overview of U.S. Book Publishing,
  1910-1945 ....DLB-9
The Pitt Poetry Series: Poetry Publishing
  Today Y-85
Publishing Fiction at LSU Press........Y-87
The Publishing Industry in 1998:
  Sturm-und-drang.com..............Y-98
The Publishing Industry in 1999 ....Y-99
Publishers and Agents: The Columbia
  Connection Y-87
Responses to Ken Auletta............Y-97
Southern Writers Between the Wars ...DLB-9
The State of Publishing Y-97
Trends in Twentieth-Century
  Mass Market Publishing DLB-46
The Year in Book Publishing..........Y-86
Pückler-Muskau, Hermann von
  1785-1871......................DLB-133
Pufendorf, Samuel von 1632-1694 ......DLB-168
Pugh, Edwin William 1874-1930........DLB-135
Pugin, A. Welby 1812-1852............DLB-55
Puig, Manuel 1932-1990 ....DLB-113; CDWLB-3
Pulitzer, Joseph 1847-1911 ....DLB-23
Pulitzer, Joseph, Jr. 1885-1955..........DLB-29
Pulitzer Prizes for the Novel, 1917-1945 ...DLB-9
Pulliam, Eugene 1889-1975 ....DLB-127
Purcell, Deirdre 1945- DLB-267
Purchas, Samuel 1577?-1626 ....DLB-151
Purdy, Al 1918-2000 ....DLB-88
Purdy, James 1923- DLB-2, 218
Purdy, Ken W. 1913-1972.............DLB-137
Pusey, Edward Bouverie 1800-1882 ......DLB-55
Pushkin, Aleksandr Sergeevich
  1799-1837 ....DLB-205
Pushkin, Vasilii L'vovich
  1766-1830 ....DLB-205
Putnam, George Palmer
  1814-1872 ....DLB-3, 79, 250, 254
G. P. Putnam [publishing house] DLB-254
G. P. Putnam's Sons [U.K.]............DLB-106
G. P. Putnam's Sons [U.S.] DLB-49
  A Publisher's Archives: G. P. Putnam ...Y-92
Putnam, Hilary 1926- DLB-279
Putnam, Samuel 1892-1950.........DLB-4; DS-15
Puttenham, George 1529?-1590.........DLB-281
Puzo, Mario 1920-1999 ....DLB-6
Pyle, Ernie 1900-1945 ....DLB-29
Pyle, Howard 1853-1911......DLB-42, 188; DS-13
Pyle, Robert Michael 1947- DLB-275
Pym, Barbara 1913-1980......DLB-14, 207; Y-87
Pynchon, Thomas 1937- DLB-2, 173
Pyramid Books DLB-46
Pyrnelle, Louise-Clarke 1850-1907 ....DLB-42

Pythagoras circa 570 B.C.-?............DLB-176

Q

Quad, M. (see Lewis, Charles B.)
Quaritch, Bernard 1819-1899 ....DLB-184
Quarles, Francis 1592-1644 ....DLB-126
The Quarterly Review 1809-1967..........DLB-110
Quasimodo, Salvatore 1901-1968 ....DLB-114
Queen, Ellery (see Dannay, Frederic, and
  Manfred B. Lee)
Queen, Frank 1822-1882..............DLB-241
The Queen City Publishing House DLB-49
Queneau, Raymond 1903-1976......DLB-72, 258
Quennell, Peter 1905-1993 ....DLB-155, 195
Quesnel, Joseph 1746-1809 ....DLB-99
Quiller-Couch, Sir Arthur Thomas
  1863-1944...........DLB-135, 153, 190
Quin, Ann 1936-1973 ....DLB-14, 231
Quinault, Philippe 1635-1688..........DLB-268
Quincy, Samuel, of Georgia ?-? DLB-31
Quincy, Samuel, of Massachusetts
  1734-1789 ....DLB-31
Quine, W. V. 1908-2000...............DLB-279
Quinn, Anthony 1915-2001..............DLB-122
Quinn, John 1870-1924 ....DLB-187
Quiñónez, Naomi 1951- DLB-209
Quintana, Leroy V. 1944- DLB-82
Quintana, Miguel de 1671-1748
  A Forerunner of Chicano
    Literature....................DLB-122
Quintilian
  circa A.D. 40-circa A.D. 96.........DLB-211
Quintus Curtius Rufus fl. A.D. 35.......DLB-211
Harlin Quist Books DLB-46
Quoirez, Françoise (see Sagan, Françoise)

R

Raabe, Wilhelm 1831-1910 ....DLB-129
Raban, Jonathan 1942- DLB-204
Rabe, David 1940- DLB-7, 228; Y-91
Raboni, Giovanni 1932- DLB-128
Rachilde 1860-1953..............DLB-123, 192
Racin, Kočo 1908-1943 ....DLB-147
Racine, Jean 1639-1699................DLB-268
Rackham, Arthur 1867-1939 ....DLB-141
Radauskas, Henrikas
  1910-1970 ....DLB-220; CDWLB-4
Radcliffe, Ann 1764-1823..........DLB-39, 178
Raddall, Thomas 1903-1994 ....DLB-68
Radford, Dollie 1858-1920 ....DLB-240
Radichkov, Yordan 1929- DLB-181
Radiguet, Raymond 1903-1923..........DLB-65
Radishchev, Aleksandr Nikolaevich
  1749-1802 ....DLB-150
Radnóti, Miklós
  1909-1944.............DLB-215; CDWLB-4
Radványi, Netty Reiling (see Seghers, Anna)

Rahv, Philip 1908-1973 . . . . DLB-137
Raich, Semen Egorovich 1792-1855 . . . . . DLB-205
Raičković, Stevan 1928- DLB-181
Raimund, Ferdinand Jakob 1790-1836 . . . . DLB-90
Raine, Craig 1944- DLB-40
Raine, Kathleen 1908- DLB-20
Rainis, Jānis 1865-1929 . . . . . DLB-220; CDWLB-4
Rainolde, Richard
 circa 1530-1606 . . . . DLB-136, 236
Rainolds, John 1549-1607 . . . . DLB-281
Rakić, Milan 1876-1938 . . . . . DLB-147; CDWLB-4
Rakosi, Carl 1903- DLB-193
Ralegh, Sir Walter
 1554?-1618 . . . . DLB-172; CDBLB-1
Raleigh, Walter
 Style (1897) [excerpt] DLB-57
Ralin, Radoy 1923- DLB-181
Ralph, Julian 1853-1903 . . . . DLB-23
Ramat, Silvio 1939- DLB-128
Ramée, Marie Louise de la (see Ouida)
Ramírez, Sergío 1942- DLB-145
Ramke, Bin 1947- DLB-120
Ramler, Karl Wilhelm 1725-1798 . . . . DLB-97
Ramon Ribeyro, Julio 1929-1994 . . . . DLB-145
Ramos, Manuel 1948- DLB-209
Ramous, Mario 1924- DLB-128
Rampersad, Arnold 1941- DLB-111
Ramsay, Allan 1684 or 1685-1758 . . . . DLB-95
Ramsay, David 1749-1815 . . . . DLB-30
Ramsay, Martha Laurens 1759-1811 . . . . DLB-200
Ramsey, Frank P. 1903-1930 . . . . DLB-262
Ranck, Katherine Quintana 1942- DLB-122
Rand, Avery and Company DLB-49
Rand, Ayn 1905-1982 . . . . DLB-227, 279; CDALB-7
Rand McNally and Company DLB-49
Randall, David Anton 1905-1975 . . . . DLB-140
Randall, Dudley 1914- DLB-41
Randall, Henry S. 1811-1876 . . . . DLB-30
Randall, James G. 1881-1953 . . . . DLB-17
The Randall Jarrell Symposium: A Small
 Collection of Randall Jarrells Y-86
Excerpts From Papers Delivered at the
 Randall Jarrel Symposium Y-86
Randall, John Herman, Jr. 1899-1980 . . . . DLB-279
Randolph, A. Philip 1889-1979 . . . . DLB-91
Anson D. F. Randolph
 [publishing house] DLB-49
Randolph, Thomas 1605-1635 . . . . . . DLB-58, 126
Random House DLB-46
Rankin, Ian (Jack Harvey) 1960- DLB-267
Henry Ranlet [publishing house] DLB-49
Ransom, Harry 1908-1976 . . . . DLB-187
Ransom, John Crowe
 1888-1974 . . . . DLB-45, 63; CDALB-7
Ransome, Arthur 1884-1967 . . . . DLB-160
Raphael, Frederic 1931- DLB-14

Raphaelson, Samson 1896-1983 . . . . DLB-44
Rare Book Dealers
 Bertram Rota and His Bookshop Y-91
 An Interview with Glenn Horowitz Y-90
 An Interview with Otto Penzler Y-96
 An Interview with Ralph Sipper Y-94
 New York City Bookshops in the
  1930s and 1940s: The Recollections
  of Walter Goldwater Y-93
Rare Books
 Research in the American Antiquarian
  Book Trade Y-97
 Two Hundred Years of Rare Books and
  Literary Collections at the
  University of South Carolina Y-00
Rashi circa 1040-1105 . . . . DLB-208
Raskin, Ellen 1928-1984 . . . . DLB-52
Rastell, John 1475?-1536 . . . . DLB-136, 170
Rattigan, Terence
 1911-1977 . . . . DLB-13; CDBLB-7
Raven, Simon 1927-2001 . . . . DLB-271
Rawlings, Marjorie Kinnan 1896-1953
 . . . . DLB-9, 22, 102; DS-17; CDALB-7
Rawlinson, Richard 1690-1755 . . . . DLB-213
Rawlinson, Thomas 1681-1725 . . . . DLB-213
Rawls, John 1921-2002 . . . . DLB-279
Raworth, Tom 1938- DLB-40
Ray, David 1932- DLB-5
Ray, Gordon Norton 1915-1986 . . . DLB-103, 140
Ray, Henrietta Cordelia 1849-1916 . . . . . . DLB-50
Raymond, Ernest 1888-1974 . . . . DLB-191
Raymond, Henry J. 1820-1869 . . . . . . DLB-43, 79
Raymond, René (see Chase, James Hadley)
Razaf, Andy 1895-1973 . . . . DLB-265
Rea, Michael 1927-1996 . . . . Y-97
 Michael M. Rea and the Rea Award for
  the Short Story Y-97
Reach, Angus 1821-1856 . . . . DLB-70
Read, Herbert 1893-1968 . . . . DLB-20, 149
Read, Martha Meredith DLB-200
Read, Opie 1852-1939 . . . . DLB-23
Read, Piers Paul 1941- DLB-14
Reade, Charles 1814-1884 . . . . DLB-21
Reader's Digest Condensed Books DLB-46
Readers Ulysses Symposium Y-97
Reading, Peter 1946- DLB-40
Reading Series in New York City Y-96
Reaney, James 1926- DLB-68
Rebhun, Paul 1500?-1546 . . . . DLB-179
Rèbora, Clemente 1885-1957 . . . . DLB-114
Rebreanu, Liviu 1885-1944 . . . . DLB-220
Rechy, John 1931- DLB-122, 278; Y-82
Redding, J. Saunders 1906-1988 . . . . . . DLB-63, 76
J. S. Redfield [publishing house] DLB-49
Redgrove, Peter 1932- DLB-40
Redmon, Anne 1943- Y-86
Redmond, Eugene B. 1937- DLB-41

James Redpath [publishing house] DLB-49
Reed, Henry 1808-1854 . . . . DLB-59
Reed, Henry 1914-1986 . . . . DLB-27
Reed, Ishmael
 1938- DLB-2, 5, 33, 169, 227; DS-8
Reed, Rex 1938- DLB-185
Reed, Sampson 1800-1880 . . . . DLB-1, 235
Reed, Talbot Baines 1852-1893 . . . . DLB-141
Reedy, William Marion 1862-1920 . . . . . . DLB-91
Reese, Lizette Woodworth 1856-1935 . . . . DLB-54
Reese, Thomas 1742-1796 . . . . DLB-37
Reeve, Clara 1729-1807 . . . . DLB-39
 Preface to *The Old English Baron*
  (1778) DLB-39
 The Progress of Romance (1785)
  [excerpt] DLB-39
Reeves, James 1909-1978 . . . . DLB-161
Reeves, John 1926- DLB-88
Reeves-Stevens, Garfield 1953- DLB-251
Henry Regnery Company DLB-46
Rehberg, Hans 1901-1963 . . . . DLB-124
Rehfisch, Hans José 1891-1960 . . . . DLB-124
Reich, Ebbe Kløvedal 1940- DLB-214
Reid, Alastair 1926- DLB-27
Reid, B. L. 1918-1990 . . . . DLB-111
Reid, Christopher 1949- DLB-40
Reid, Forrest 1875-1947 . . . . DLB-153
Reid, Helen Rogers 1882-1970 . . . . DLB-29
Reid, James ?-? DLB-31
Reid, Mayne 1818-1883 . . . . DLB-21, 163
Reid, Thomas 1710-1796 . . . . DLB-31, 252
Reid, V. S. (Vic) 1913-1987 . . . . DLB-125
Reid, Whitelaw 1837-1912 . . . . DLB-23
Reilly and Lee Publishing Company DLB-46
Reimann, Brigitte 1933-1973 . . . . DLB-75
Reinmar der Alte circa 1165-circa 1205 . . DLB-138
Reinmar von Zweter
 circa 1200-circa 1250 . . . . DLB-138
Reisch, Walter 1903-1983 . . . . DLB-44
Reizei Family DLB-203
Religion
 A Crisis of Culture: The Changing Role
  of Religion in the New Republic . DLB-37
Remarque, Erich Maria
 1898-1970 . . . . DLB-56; CDWLB-2
Remington, Frederic
 1861-1909 . . . . DLB-12, 186, 188
Renaud, Jacques 1943- DLB-60
Renault, Mary 1905-1983 . . . . Y-83
Rendell, Ruth (Barbara Vine)
 1930- DLB-87, 276
Rensselaer, Maria van Cortlandt van
 1645-1689 . . . . DLB-200
Repplier, Agnes 1855-1950 . . . . DLB-221
Reshetnikov, Fedor Mikhailovich
 1841-1871 . . . . DLB-238
Rettenbacher, Simon 1634-1706 . . . . DLB-168

Retz, Jean-François-Paul de Gondi,
    cardinal de 1613-1679 ....DLB-268
Reuchlin, Johannes 1455-1522.........DLB-179
Reuter, Christian 1665-after 1712 ....DLB-168
Fleming H. Revell Company DLB-49
Reverdy, Pierre 1889-1960 ....DLB-258
Reuter, Fritz 1810-1874 ....DLB-129
Reuter, Gabriele 1859-1941.............DLB-66
Reventlow, Franziska Gräfin zu
    1871-1918 ....DLB-66
Review of Reviews Office DLB-112
Rexroth, Kenneth 1905-1982
    ...... DLB-16, 48, 165, 212; Y-82; CDALB-1
    The Commercialization of the Image
        of Revolt DLB-16
Rey, H. A. 1898-1977 ....DLB-22
Reynal and Hitchcock DLB-46
Reynolds, G. W. M. 1814-1870..........DLB-21
Reynolds, John Hamilton 1794-1852.....DLB-96
Reynolds, Sir Joshua 1723-1792........DLB-104
Reynolds, Mack 1917-1983 ....DLB-8
Reznikoff, Charles 1894-1976 ....DLB-28, 45
Rhetoric
    Continental European Rhetoricians,
        1400-1600, and Their Influence
        in Reaissance England DLB-236
    A Finding Guide to Key Works on
        Microfilm...................DLB-236
    Glossary of Terms and Definitions of
        Rhetoic and Logic DLB-236
Rhett, Robert Barnwell 1800-1876........DLB-43
Rhode, John 1884-1964.................DLB-77
Rhodes, Eugene Manlove 1869-1934 ....DLB-256
Rhodes, James Ford 1848-1927 ....DLB-47
Rhodes, Richard 1937- DLB-185
Rhys, Jean 1890-1979
    .... DLB-36, 117, 162; CDBLB-7; CDWLB-3
Ricardo, David 1772-1823 .... DLB-107, 158
Ricardou, Jean 1932- DLB-83
Rice, Elmer 1892-1967.................DLB-4, 7
Rice, Grantland 1880-1954 .... DLB-29, 171
Rich, Adrienne 1929- DLB-5, 67; CDALB-7
Richard, Mark 1955- DLB-234
Richard de Fournival
    1201-1259 or 1260 ....DLB-208
Richards, David Adams 1950- DLB-53
Richards, George circa 1760-1814 ......DLB-37
Richards, I. A. 1893-1979..............DLB-27
Richards, Laura E. 1850-1943 ....DLB-42
Richards, William Carey 1818-1892 .....DLB-73
Grant Richards [publishing house]......DLB-112
Richardson, Charles F. 1851-1913........DLB-71
Richardson, Dorothy M. 1873-1957 .....DLB-36
    The Novels of Dorothy Richardson
        (1918), by May Sinclair........DLB-36
Richardson, Henry Handel
    (Ethel Florence Lindesay Robertson)
    1870-1946 .... DLB-197, 230
Richardson, Jack 1935- DLB-7

Richardson, John 1796-1852 ....DLB-99
Richardson, Samuel
    1689-1761 ....DLB-39, 154; CDBLB-2
    Introductory Letters from the Second
        Edition of Pamela (1741).........DLB-39
    Postscript to [the Third Edition of]
        Clarissa (1751)..................DLB-39
    Preface to the First Edition of
        Pamela (1740) DLB-39
    Preface to the Third Edition of
        Clarissa (1751) [excerpt] DLB-39
    Preface to Volume 1 of Clarissa
        (1747).........................DLB-39
    Preface to Volume 3 of Clarissa
        (1748).........................DLB-39
Richardson, Willis 1889-1977 ....DLB-51
Riche, Barnabe 1542-1617 ....DLB-136
Richepin, Jean 1849-1926 ....DLB-192
Richler, Mordecai 1931-2001............DLB-53
Richter, Conrad 1890-1968 ....DLB-9, 212
Richter, Hans Werner 1908-1993 ....DLB-69
Richter, Johann Paul Friedrich
    1763-1825 ....DLB-94; CDWLB-2
Joseph Rickerby [publishing house].....DLB-106
Rickword, Edgell 1898-1982 ....DLB-20
Riddell, Charlotte 1832-1906...........DLB-156
Riddell, John (see Ford, Corey)
Ridge, John Rollin 1827-1867...........DLB-175
Ridge, Lola 1873-1941.................DLB-54
Ridge, William Pett 1859-1930 ....DLB-135
Riding, Laura (see Jackson, Laura Riding)
Ridler, Anne 1912- DLB-27
Ridruego, Dionisio 1912-1975 ....DLB-108
Riel, Louis 1844-1885 ....DLB-99
Riemer, Johannes 1648-1714 ....DLB-168
Rifbjerg, Klaus 1931- DLB-214
Riffaterre, Michael 1924- DLB-67
A Conversation between William Riggan
    and Janette Turner Hospital Y-02
Riggs, Lynn 1899-1954 ....DLB-175
Riis, Jacob 1849-1914..................DLB-23
John C. Riker [publishing house].........DLB-49
Riley, James 1777-1840................DLB-183
Riley, John 1938-1978 ....DLB-40
Rilke, Rainer Maria
    1875-1926 ....DLB-81; CDWLB-2
Rimanelli, Giose 1926- DLB-177
Rimbaud, Jean-Nicolas-Arthur
    1854-1891 ....DLB-217
Rinehart and Company DLB-46
Ringuet 1895-1960....................DLB-68
Ringwood, Gwen Pharis 1910-1984 .....DLB-88
Rinser, Luise 1911- DLB-69
Ríos, Alberto 1952- DLB-122
Ríos, Isabella 1948- DLB-82
Ripley, Arthur 1895-1961 ....DLB-44
Ripley, George 1802-1880..... DLB-1, 64, 73, 235

The Rising Glory of America:
    Three Poems....................DLB-37
The Rising Glory of America: Written in 1771
    (1786), by Hugh Henry Brackenridge
    and Philip Freneau DLB-37
Riskin, Robert 1897-1955..............DLB-26
Risse, Heinz 1898- DLB-69
Rist, Johann 1607-1667 ....DLB-164
Ristikivi, Karl 1912-1977 ....DLB-220
Ritchie, Anna Mowatt 1819-1870 .....DLB-3, 250
Ritchie, Anne Thackeray 1837-1919 ......DLB-18
Ritchie, Thomas 1778-1854 ....DLB-43
The Ritz Paris Hemingway Award Y-85
    Mario Varga Llosa's Acceptance Speech . Y-85
Rivard, Adjutor 1868-1945 ....DLB-92
Rive, Richard 1931-1989.........DLB-125, 225
Rivera, José 1955- DLB-249
Rivera, Marina 1942- DLB-122
Rivera, Tomás 1935-1984 ....DLB-82
Rivers, Conrad Kent 1933-1968 ....DLB-41
Riverside Press DLB-49
Rivington, James circa 1724-1802 ......DLB-43
Charles Rivington [publishing house] DLB-154
Rivkin, Allen 1903-1990 ....DLB-26
Roa Bastos, Augusto 1917- DLB-113
Robbe-Grillet, Alain 1922- DLB-83
Robbins, Tom 1936- Y-80
Roberts, Charles G. D. 1860-1943 ....DLB-92
Roberts, Dorothy 1906-1993............DLB-88
Roberts, Elizabeth Madox
    1881-1941............... DLB-9, 54, 102
Roberts, Keith 1935-2000 ....DLB-261
Roberts, Kenneth 1885-1957 ....DLB-9
Roberts, Michèle 1949- DLB-231
Roberts, Theodore Goodridge
    1877-1953 ....DLB-92
Roberts, Ursula Wyllie (see Miles, Susan)
Roberts, William 1767-1849.............DLB-142
James Roberts [publishing house] DLB-154
Roberts Brothers DLB-49
A. M. Robertson and Company DLB-49
Robertson, Ethel Florence Lindesay
    (see Richardson, Henry Handel)
Robertson, William 1721-1793..........DLB-104
Robin, Leo 1895-1984.................DLB-265
Robins, Elizabeth 1862-1952 ....DLB-197
Robinson, A. Mary F. (Madame James
    Darmesteter, Madame Mary
    Duclaux) 1857-1944 ....DLB-240
Robinson, Casey 1903-1979 ....DLB-44
Robinson, Derek Y-02
Robinson, Edwin Arlington
    1869-1935 ....DLB-54; CDALB-3
    Review by Derek Robinson of George
        Greenfield's Rich Dust Y-02
Robinson, Henry Crabb 1775-1867 ......DLB-107
Robinson, James Harvey 1863-1936 ......DLB-47

405

Robinson, Lennox 1886-1958 .... DLB-10	Rorty, Richard 1931- DLB-246, 279	Roversi, Roberto 1923- DLB-128
Robinson, Mabel Louise 1874-1962 ..... DLB-22	Rosa, João Guimarães 1908-1967 ...... DLB-113	Rowe, Elizabeth Singer 1674-1737 .... DLB-39, 95
Robinson, Marilynne 1943- DLB-206	Rosales, Luis 1910-1992 .... DLB-134	Rowe, Nicholas 1674-1718 .... DLB-84
Robinson, Mary 1758-1800 .... DLB-158	Roscoe, William 1753-1831 .... DLB-163	Rowlands, Samuel circa 1570-1630...... DLB-121
Robinson, Richard circa 1545-1607 ..... DLB-167	Rose, Reginald 1920-2002 .... DLB-26	Rowlandson, Mary
Robinson, Therese 1797-1870 .... DLB-59, 133	Rose, Wendy 1948- DLB-175	circa 1637-circa 1711........... DLB-24, 200
Robison, Mary 1949- DLB-130	Rosegger, Peter 1843-1918............ DLB-129	Rowley, William circa 1585-1626 .... DLB-58
Roblès, Emmanuel 1914-1995 .... DLB-83	Rosei, Peter 1946- DLB-85	Rowling, J. K.
Roccatagliata Ceccardi, Ceccardo	Rosen, Norma 1925- DLB-28	The Harry Potter Phenomenon......... Y-99
1871-1919...................... DLB-114	Rosenbach, A. S. W. 1876-1952 .... DLB-140	Rowse, A. L. 1903-1997 .... DLB-155
Roche, Billy 1949- DLB-233	Rosenbaum, Ron 1946- DLB-185	Rowson, Susanna Haswell
Rochester, John Wilmot, Earl of	Rosenberg, Isaac 1890-1918 .... DLB-20, 216	circa 1762-1824 .... DLB-37, 200
1647-1680..................... DLB-131	Rosenfeld, Isaac 1918-1956 .... DLB-28	Roy, Camille 1870-1943 .... DLB-92
Rochon, Esther 1948- DLB-251	Rosenthal, Harold 1914-1999.......... DLB-241	The G. Ross Roy Scottish Poetry Collection
Rock, Howard 1911-1976............. DLB-127	Jimmy, Red, and Others: Harold	at the University of South Carolina...... Y-89
Rockwell, Norman Perceval 1894-1978 .. DLB-188	Rosenthal Remembers the Stars of	Roy, Gabrielle 1909-1983.............. DLB-68
Rodgers, Carolyn M. 1945- DLB-41	the Press Box Y-01	Roy, Jules 1907-2000 .... DLB-83
Rodgers, W. R. 1909-1969............. DLB-20	Rosenthal, M. L. 1917-1996 .... DLB-5	The Royal Court Theatre and the English
Rodney, Lester 1911- DLB-241	Rosenwald, Lessing J. 1891-1979 ...... DLB-187	Stage Company DLB-13
Rodríguez, Claudio 1934-1999........ DLB-134	Ross, Alexander 1591-1654 .... DLB-151	The Royal Court Theatre and the New
Rodríguez, Joe D. 1943- DLB-209	Ross, Harold 1892-1951.............. DLB-137	Drama DLB-10
Rodríguez, Luis J. 1954- DLB-209	Ross, Jerry 1926-1955................ DLB-265	The Royal Shakespeare Company
Rodriguez, Richard 1944- DLB-82, 256	Ross, Leonard Q. (see Rosten, Leo)	at the Swan Y-88
Rodríguez Julia, Edgardo 1946- DLB-145	Ross, Lillian 1927- DLB-185	Royall, Anne Newport 1769-1854 ... DLB-43, 248
Roe, E. P. 1838-1888 .... DLB-202	Ross, Martin 1862-1915 .... DLB-135	Royce, Josiah 1855-1916 ....DLB-270
Roethke, Theodore	Ross, Sinclair 1908-1996................ DLB-88	The Roycroft Printing Shop........... DLB-49
1908-1963 .... DLB-5, 206; CDALB-1	Ross, W. W. E. 1894-1966.............. DLB-88	Royde-Smith, Naomi 1875-1964..... DLB-191
Rogers, Jane 1952- DLB-194	Rosselli, Amelia 1930-1996 .... DLB-128	Royster, Vermont 1914-1996..........DLB-127
Rogers, Pattiann 1940- DLB-105	Rossen, Robert 1908-1966 .... DLB-26	Richard Royston [publishing house]......DLB-170
Rogers, Samuel 1763-1855 .... DLB-93	Rosset, Barney Y-02	Różewicz, Tadeusz 1921- DLB-232
Rogers, Will 1879-1935 .... DLB-11	Rossetti, Christina 1830-1894... DLB-35, 163, 240	Ruark, Gibbons 1941- DLB-120
Rohmer, Sax 1883-1959 .... DLB-70	Rossetti, Dante Gabriel	Ruban, Vasilii Grigorevich 1742-1795 ... DLB-150
Roiphe, Anne 1935- Y-80	1828-1882 .... DLB-35; CDBLB-4	Rubens, Bernice 1928- DLB-14, 207
Rojas, Arnold R. 1896-1988............ DLB-82	The Stealthy School of	Rudd and Carleton................. DLB-49
Rolfe, Frederick William	Criticism (1871) DLB-35	Rudd, Steele (Arthur Hoey Davis) DLB-230
1860-1913.................... DLB-34, 156	Rossner, Judith 1935- DLB-6	Rudkin, David 1936- DLB-13
Rolland, Romain 1866-1944........... DLB-65	Rostand, Edmond 1868-1918.......... DLB-192	Rudnick, Paul 1957- DLB-266
Rolle, Richard circa 1290-1300 - 1340 ... DLB-146	Rosten, Leo 1908-1997................ DLB-11	Rudolf von Ems circa 1200-circa 1254 ... DLB-138
Rölvaag, O. E. 1876-1931............ DLB-9, 212	Rostenberg, Leona 1908- DLB-140	Ruffin, Josephine St. Pierre 1842-1924.... DLB-79
Romains, Jules 1885-1972 .... DLB-65	Rostopchina, Evdokiia Petrovna	Ruganda, John 1941- DLB-157
A. Roman and Company DLB-49	1811-1858 .... DLB-205	Ruggles, Henry Joseph 1813-1906 .... DLB-64
Roman de la Rose: Guillaume de Lorris	Rostovsky, Dimitrii 1651-1709........ DLB-150	Ruiz de Burton, María Amparo
1200/1205-circa 1230, Jean de	Rota, Bertram 1903-1966 .... DLB-201	1832-1895 .... DLB-209, 221
Meun 1235-1240-circa 1305........ DLB-208	Bertram Rota and His Bookshop Y-91	Rukeyser, Muriel 1913-1980 .... DLB-48
Romano, Lalla 1906-2001 ....DLB-177	Roth, Gerhard 1942- DLB-85, 124	Rule, Jane 1931- DLB-60
Romano, Octavio 1923- DLB-122	Roth, Henry 1906?-1995 .... DLB-28	Rulfo, Juan 1918-1986 ......DLB-113; CDWLB-3
Rome, Harold 1908-1993 .... DLB-265	Roth, Joseph 1894-1939 .... DLB-85	Rumaker, Michael 1932- DLB-16
Romero, Leo 1950- DLB-122	Roth, Philip	Rumens, Carol 1944- DLB-40
Romero, Lin 1947- DLB-122	1933- DLB-2, 28, 173; Y-82; CDALB-6	Rummo, Paul-Eerik 1942- DLB-232
Romero, Orlando 1945- DLB-82	Rothenberg, Jerome 1931- DLB-5, 193	Runyon, Damon 1880-1946......DLB-11, 86, 171
Rook, Clarence 1863-1915 .... DLB-135	Rothschild Family................. DLB-184	*Ruodlieb* circa 1050-1075 .... DLB-148
Roosevelt, Theodore	Rotimi, Ola 1938- DLB-125	Rush, Benjamin 1746-1813............. DLB-37
1858-1919................ DLB-47, 186, 275	Rotrou, Jean 1609-1650 ....DLB-268	Rush, Rebecca 1779-? DLB-200
Root, Waverley 1903-1982............. DLB-4	Routhier, Adolphe-Basile 1839-1920 ..... DLB-99	Rushdie, Salman 1947- DLB-194
Root, William Pitt 1941- DLB-120	Routier, Simone 1901-1987 .... DLB-88	Rusk, Ralph L. 1888-1962 .... DLB-103
Roquebrune, Robert de 1889-1978...... DLB-68	George Routledge and Sons DLB-106	Ruskin, John
		1819-1900 ..... DLB-55, 163, 190; CDBLB-4

406

Russ, Joanna 1937- DLB-8
Russell, Benjamin 1761-1845 .... DLB-43
Russell, Bertrand 1872-1970 .... DLB-100, 262
Russell, Charles Edward 1860-1941 ...... DLB-25
Russell, Charles M. 1864-1926 .... DLB-188
Russell, Eric Frank 1905-1978 .... DLB-255
Russell, Fred 1906-2003 .... DLB-241
Russell, George William (see AE)
Russell, Countess Mary Annette Beauchamp (see Arnim, Elizabeth von)
Russell, Willy 1947- DLB-233
B. B. Russell and Company DLB-49
R. H. Russell and Son DLB-49
Rutebeuf flourished 1249-1277 .... DLB-208
Rutherford, Mark 1831-1913 .... DLB-18
Ruxton, George Frederick 1821-1848 .... DLB-186
R-va, Zeneida (see Gan, Elena Andreevna)
Ryan, James 1952- DLB-267
Ryan, Michael 1946- Y-82
Ryan, Oscar 1904- DLB-68
Ryder, Jack 1871-1936 .... DLB-241
Ryga, George 1932-1987 .... DLB-60
Rylands, Enriqueta Augustina Tennant 1843-1908 .... DLB-184
Rylands, John 1801-1888 .... DLB-184
Ryle, Gilbert 1900-1976 .... DLB-262
Ryleev, Kondratii Fedorovich 1795-1826 .... DLB-205
Rymer, Thomas 1643?-1713 .... DLB-101
Ryskind, Morrie 1895-1985 .... DLB-26
Rzhevsky, Aleksei Andreevich 1737-1804 .... DLB-150

S

The Saalfield Publishing Company DLB-46
Saba, Umberto 1883-1957 .... DLB-114
Sábato, Ernesto 1911- DLB-145; CDWLB-3
Saberhagen, Fred 1930- DLB-8
Sabin, Joseph 1821-1881 .... DLB-187
Sacer, Gottfried Wilhelm 1635-1699 ..... DLB-168
Sachs, Hans 1494-1576 ..... DLB-179; CDWLB-2
Sack, John 1930- DLB-185
Sackler, Howard 1929-1982 .... DLB-7
Sackville, Lady Margaret 1881-1963 .... DLB-240
Sackville, Thomas 1536-1608 .... DLB-132
Sackville, Thomas 1536-1608 .... DLB-62
Sackville-West, Edward 1901-1965 ..... DLB-191
Sackville-West, V. 1892-1962 .... DLB-34, 195
Sadlier, Mary Anne 1820-1903 .... DLB-99
D. and J. Sadlier and Company DLB-49
Sadoff, Ira 1945- DLB-120
Sadoveanu, Mihail 1880-1961 .... DLB-220
Sáenz, Benjamin Alire 1954- DLB-209
Saenz, Jaime 1921-1986 .... DLB-145, 283
Saffin, John circa 1626-1710 .... DLB-24

Sagan, Françoise 1935- DLB-83
Sage, Robert 1899-1962 .... DLB-4
Sagel, Jim 1947- DLB-82
Sagendorph, Robb Hansell 1900-1970 .... DLB-137
Sahagún, Carlos 1938- DLB-108
Sahkomaapii, Piitai (see Highwater, Jamake)
Sahl, Hans 1902-1993 .... DLB-69
Said, Edward W. 1935- DLB-67
Saigyō 1118-1190 .... DLB-203
Saiko, George 1892-1962 .... DLB-85
Sainte-Beuve, Charles-Augustin 1804-1869 .... DLB-217
Saint-Exupéry, Antoine de 1900-1944 .... DLB-72
St. John, J. Allen 1872-1957 .... DLB-188
St John, Madeleine 1942- DLB-267
St. Johns, Adela Rogers 1894-1988 ..... DLB-29
St Omer, Garth 1931- DLB-117
Saint Pierre, Michel de 1916-1987 ..... DLB-83
St. Dominic's Press DLB-112
The St. John's College Robert Graves Trust .. Y-96
St. Martin's Press DLB-46
St. Nicholas 1873-1881 .... DS-13
Saintsbury, George 1845-1933 ...... DLB-57, 149
    "Modern English Prose" (1876) DLB-57
    The Present State of the English Novel (1892), ... DLB-18
Saiokuken Sōchō 1448-1532 .... DLB-203
Saki (see Munro, H. H.)
Salaam, Kalamu ya 1947- DLB-38
Šalamun, Tomaž 1941- DLB-181; CDWLB-4
Salas, Floyd 1931- DLB-82
Sálaz-Marquez, Rubén 1935- DLB-122
Salemson, Harold J. 1910-1988 .... DLB-4
Salesbury, William 1520?-1584? DLB-281
Salinas, Luis Omar 1937- DLB-82
Salinas, Pedro 1891-1951 .... DLB-134
Salinger, J. D. 1919- DLB-2, 102, 173; CDALB-1
Salkey, Andrew 1928- DLB-125
Sallust circa 86 B.C.-35 B.C. DLB-211; CDWLB-1
Salt, Waldo 1914-1987 .... DLB-44
Salter, James 1925- DLB-130
Salter, Mary Jo 1954- DLB-120
Saltus, Edgar 1855-1921 .... DLB-202
Saltykov, Mikhail Evgrafovich 1826-1889 .... DLB-238
Salustri, Carlo Alberto (see Trilussa)
Salverson, Laura Goodman 1890-1970 ... DLB-92
Samain, Albert 1858-1900 .... DLB-217
Sampson, Richard Henry (see Hull, Richard)
Samuels, Ernest 1903-1996 .... DLB-111
Sanborn, Franklin Benjamin 1831-1917 .... DLB-1, 223
Sánchez, Luis Rafael 1936- DLB-145
Sánchez, Philomeno "Phil" 1917- DLB-122

Sánchez, Ricardo 1941-1995 .... DLB-82
Sánchez, Saúl 1943- DLB-209
Sanchez, Sonia 1934- DLB-41; DS-8
Sand, George 1804-1876 .... DLB-119, 192
Sandburg, Carl 1878-1967 .. DLB-17, 54; CDALB-3
Sanders, Edward 1939- DLB-16, 244
Sanderson, Robert 1587-1663 .... DLB-281
Sandoz, Mari 1896-1966 .... DLB-9, 212
Sandwell, B. K. 1876-1954 .... DLB-92
Sandy, Stephen 1934- DLB-165
Sandys, George 1578-1644 .... DLB-24, 121
Sangster, Charles 1822-1893 .... DLB-99
Sanguineti, Edoardo 1930- DLB-128
Sanjōnishi Sanetaka 1455-1537 .... DLB-203
Sansay, Leonora ?-after 1823 .... DLB-200
Sansom, William 1912-1976 .... DLB-139
Santayana, George 1863-1952 ...... DLB-54, 71, 246, 270; DS-13
Santiago, Danny 1911-1988 .... DLB-122
Santmyer, Helen Hooven 1895-1986 .... Y-84
Sanvitale, Francesca 1928- DLB-196
Sapidus, Joannes 1490-1561 .... DLB-179
Sapir, Edward 1884-1939 .... DLB-92
Sapper (see McNeile, Herman Cyril)
Sappho circa 620 B.C.-circa 550 B.C. DLB-176; CDWLB-1
Saramago, José 1922- Y-98
    Nobel Lecture 1998: How Characters Became the Masters and the Author Their Apprentice Y-98
Sarban (John W. Wall) 1910-1989 ...... DLB-255
Sardou, Victorien 1831-1908 .... DLB-192
Sarduy, Severo 1937-1993 .... DLB-113
Sargent, Pamela 1948- DLB-8
Saro-Wiwa, Ken 1941- DLB-157
Saroyan, Aram
    Rites of Passage [on William Saroyan] ... Y-83
Saroyan, William 1908-1981 ..... DLB-7, 9, 86; Y-81; CDALB-7
Sarraute, Nathalie 1900-1999 .... DLB-83
Sarrazin, Albertine 1937-1967 .... DLB-83
Sarris, Greg 1952- DLB-175
Sarton, May 1912-1995 .... DLB-48; Y-81
Sartre, Jean-Paul 1905-1980 .... DLB-72
Sassoon, Siegfried 1886-1967 .... DLB-20, 191; DS-18
    A Centenary Essay Y-86
    Tributes from Vivien F. Clarke and Michael Thorpe Y-86
Sata Ineko 1904- DLB-180
Saturday Review Press DLB-46
Saunders, James 1925- DLB-13
Saunders, John Monk 1897-1940 .... DLB-26
Saunders, Margaret Marshall 1861-1947 .... DLB-92
Saunders and Otley DLB-106
Saussure, Ferdinand de 1857-1913 ...... DLB-242

Savage, James 1784-1873 .... DLB-30
Savage, Marmion W. 1803?-1872 .... DLB-21
Savage, Richard 1697?-1743 .... DLB-95
Savard, Félix-Antoine 1896-1982 .... DLB-68
Savery, Henry 1791-1842 .... DLB-230
Saville, (Leonard) Malcolm 1901-1982 ... DLB-160
Savinio, Alberto 1891-1952 .... DLB-264
Sawyer, Robert J. 1960- DLB-251
Sawyer, Ruth 1880-1970 .... DLB-22
Sayers, Dorothy L.
  1893-1957..... DLB-10, 36, 77, 100; CDBLB-6
  The Dorothy L. Sayers Society Y-98
Sayle, Charles Edward 1864-1924 ...... DLB-184
Sayles, John Thomas 1950- DLB-44
Sbarbaro, Camillo 1888-1967 .... DLB-114
Scalapino, Leslie 1947- DLB-193
Scannell, Vernon 1922- DLB-27
Scarry, Richard 1919-1994 .... DLB-61
Schaefer, Jack 1907-1991 .... DLB-212
Schaeffer, Albrecht 1885-1950 .... DLB-66
Schaeffer, Susan Fromberg 1941- DLB-28
Schaff, Philip 1819-1893 .... DS-13
Schaper, Edzard 1908-1984 .... DLB-69
Scharf, J. Thomas 1843-1898 .... DLB-47
Schede, Paul Melissus 1539-1602 ...... DLB-179
Scheffel, Joseph Viktor von 1826-1886 ... DLB-129
Scheffler, Johann 1624-1677 .... DLB-164
Schelling, Friedrich Wilhelm Joseph von
  1775-1854 .... DLB-90
Scherer, Wilhelm 1841-1886 .... DLB-129
Scherfig, Hans 1905-1979 .... DLB-214
Schickele, René 1883-1940 .... DLB-66
Schiff, Dorothy 1903-1989 .... DLB-127
Schiller, Friedrich
  1759-1805 .... DLB-94; CDWLB-2
Schirmer, David 1623-1687 .... DLB-164
Schlaf, Johannes 1862-1941 .... DLB-118
Schlegel, August Wilhelm 1767-1845 ..... DLB-94
Schlegel, Dorothea 1763-1839 .... DLB-90
Schlegel, Friedrich 1772-1829 .... DLB-90
Schleiermacher, Friedrich 1768-1834 ..... DLB-90
Schlesinger, Arthur M., Jr. 1917- DLB-17
Schlumberger, Jean 1877-1968 .... DLB-65
Schmid, Eduard Hermann Wilhelm
  (see Edschmid, Kasimir)
Schmidt, Arno 1914-1979 .... DLB-69
Schmidt, Johann Kaspar (see Stirner, Max)
Schmidt, Michael 1947- DLB-40
Schmidtbonn, Wilhelm August
  1876-1952 .... DLB-118
Schmitz, Aron Hector (see Svevo, Italo)
Schmitz, James H. 1911-1981 .... DLB-8
Schnabel, Johann Gottfried 1692-1760 ... DLB-168
Schnackenberg, Gjertrud 1953- DLB-120
Schnitzler, Arthur
  1862-1931 .... DLB-81, 118; CDWLB-2

Schnurre, Wolfdietrich 1920-1989 .... DLB-69
Schocken Books DLB-46
Scholartis Press.................... DLB-112
Scholderer, Victor 1880-1971 .... DLB-201
The Schomburg Center for Research
  in Black Culture DLB-76
Schönbeck, Virgilio (see Giotti, Virgilio)
Schönherr, Karl 1867-1943 .... DLB-118
Schoolcraft, Jane Johnston 1800-1841 .... DLB-175
School Stories, 1914-1960 .... DLB-160
Schopenhauer, Arthur 1788-1860 .... DLB-90
Schopenhauer, Johanna 1766-1838 .... DLB-90
Schorer, Mark 1908-1977 .... DLB-103
Schottelius, Justus Georg 1612-1676 .... DLB-164
Schouler, James 1839-1920 .... DLB-47
Schoultz, Solveig von 1907-1996 ...... DLB-259
Schrader, Paul 1946- DLB-44
Schreiner, Olive
  1855-1920 .... DLB-18, 156, 190, 225
Schroeder, Andreas 1946- DLB-53
Schubart, Christian Friedrich Daniel
  1739-1791 .... DLB-97
Schubert, Gotthilf Heinrich 1780-1860 .... DLB-90
Schücking, Levin 1814-1883 .... DLB-133
Schulberg, Budd 1914- DLB-6, 26, 28; Y-81
  Excerpts from USC Presentation
  [on F. Scott Fitzgerald] Y-96
F. J. Schulte and Company DLB-49
Schulz, Bruno 1892-1942 ... DLB-215; CDWLB-4
Schulze, Hans (see Praetorius, Johannes)
Schupp, Johann Balthasar 1610-1661 .... DLB-164
Schurz, Carl 1829-1906 .... DLB-23
Schuyler, George S. 1895-1977 .... DLB-29, 51
Schuyler, James 1923-1991 .... DLB-5, 169
Schwartz, Delmore 1913-1966 .... DLB-28, 48
Schwartz, Jonathan 1938- Y-82
Schwartz, Lynne Sharon 1939- DLB-218
Schwarz, Sibylle 1621-1638 .... DLB-164
Schwerner, Armand 1927-1999......... DLB-165
Schwob, Marcel 1867-1905........... DLB-123
Sciascia, Leonardo 1921-1989 .... DLB-177
Science Fiction and Fantasy
  Documents in British Fantasy and
    Science Fiction DLB-178
  Hugo Awards and Nebula Awards DLB-8
  The Iconography of Science-Fiction
    Art DLB-8
  The New Wave DLB-8
  Paperback Science Fiction........... DLB-8
  Science Fantasy DLB-8
  Science-Fiction Fandom and
    Conventions.................... DLB-8
  Science-Fiction Fanzines: The Time
    Binders........................ DLB-8
  Science-Fiction Films DLB-8
  Science Fiction Writers of America
    and the Nebula Award DLB-8

  Selected Science-Fiction Magazines and
    Anthologies DLB-8
  A World Chronology of Important Science
    Fiction Works (1818-1979) DLB-8
  The Year in Science Fiction
    and Fantasy Y-00, 01
Scot, Reginald circa 1538-1599......... DLB-136
Scotellaro, Rocco 1923-1953 .... DLB-128
Scott, Alicia Anne (Lady John Scott)
  1810-1900 .... DLB-240
Scott, Catharine Amy Dawson
  1865-1934 .... DLB-240
Scott, Dennis 1939-1991.............. DLB-125
Scott, Dixon 1881-1915 .... DLB-98
Scott, Duncan Campbell 1862-1947 ..... DLB-92
Scott, Evelyn 1893-1963 .... DLB-9, 48
Scott, F. R. 1899-1985................ DLB-88
Scott, Frederick George 1861-1944 ...... DLB-92
Scott, Geoffrey 1884-1929 .... DLB-149
Scott, Harvey W. 1838-1910 .... DLB-23
Scott, Lady Jane (see Scott, Alicia Anne)
Scott, Paul 1920-1978 .... DLB-14, 207
Scott, Sarah 1723-1795 .... DLB-39
Scott, Tom 1918- DLB-27
Scott, Sir Walter 1771-1832
  .... DLB-93, 107, 116, 144, 159; CDBLB-3
Scott, William Bell 1811-1890 .... DLB-32
Walter Scott Publishing Company
  Limited....................... DLB-112
William R. Scott [publishing house] DLB-46
Scott-Heron, Gil 1949- DLB-41
Scribe, Eugene 1791-1861............. DLB-192
Scribner, Arthur Hawley 1859-1932 .... DS-13, 16
Scribner, Charles 1854-1930 .... DS-13, 16
Scribner, Charles, Jr. 1921-1995........... Y-95
  Reminiscences.................... DS-17
Charles Scribner's Sons DLB-49; DS-13, 16, 17
  Archives of Charles Scribner's Sons DS-17
Scribner's Magazine DS-13
Scribner's Monthly DS-13
Scripps, E. W. 1854-1926............. DLB-25
Scudder, Horace Elisha 1838-1902..... DLB-42, 71
Scudder, Vida Dutton 1861-1954........ DLB-71
Scudéry, Madeleine de 1607-1701 ....DLB-268
Scupham, Peter 1933- DLB-40
Seabrook, William 1886-1945 .... DLB-4
Seabury, Samuel 1729-1796 .... DLB-31
Seacole, Mary Jane Grant 1805-1881 .... DLB-166
The Seafarer circa 970................ DLB-146
Sealsfield, Charles (Carl Postl)
  1793-1864 .... DLB-133, 186
Searle, John R. 1932- DLB-279
Sears, Edward I. 1819?-1876........... DLB-79
Sears Publishing Company........... DLB-46
Seaton, George 1911-1979 .... DLB-44
Seaton, William Winston 1785-1866 ..... DLB-43
Martin Secker [publishing house] DLB-112

Martin Secker, and Warburg Limited....DLB-112

Sedgwick, Arthur George 1844-1915......DLB-64

Sedgwick, Catharine Maria
  1789-1867........DLB-1, 74, 183, 239, 243

Sedgwick, Ellery 1872-1960.............DLB-91

Sedgwick, Eve Kosofsky 1950-........DLB-246

Sedley, Sir Charles 1639-1701..........DLB-131

Seeberg, Peter 1925-1999..............DLB-214

Seeger, Alan 1888-1916................DLB-45

Seers, Eugene (see Dantin, Louis)

Segal, Erich 1937-......................Y-86

Šegedin, Petar 1909-..................DLB-181

Seghers, Anna 1900-1983.....DLB-69; CDWLB-2

Seid, Ruth (see Sinclair, Jo)

Seidel, Frederick Lewis 1936-...........Y-84

Seidel, Ina 1885-1974..................DLB-56

Seifert, Jaroslav
  1901-1986.......DLB-215; Y-84; CDWLB-4

  Jaroslav Seifert Through the Eyes of
    the English-Speaking Reader.......Y-84

  Three Poems by Jaroslav Seifert.......Y-84

Seifullina, Lidiia Nikolaevna 1889-1954...DLB-272

Seigenthaler, John 1927-...............DLB-127

Seizin Press...........................DLB-112

Séjour, Victor 1817-1874...............DLB-50

Séjour Marcou et Ferrand, Juan Victor
  (see Séjour, Victor)

Sekowski, Józef-Julian, Baron Brambeus
  (see Senkovsky, Osip Ivanovich)

Selby, Bettina 1934-..................DLB-204

Selby, Hubert, Jr. 1928-.............DLB-2, 227

Selden, George 1929-1989..............DLB-52

Selden, John 1584-1654................DLB-213

Selenić, Slobodan 1933-1995...........DLB-181

Self, Edwin F. 1920...................DLB-137

Self, Will 1961-......................DLB-207

Seligman, Edwin R. A. 1861-1939.......DLB-47

Selimović, Meša
  1910-1982..............DLB-181; CDWLB-4

Sellars, Wilfrid 1912-1989............DLB-279

Sellings, Arthur (Arthur Gordon Ley)
  1911-1968............................DLB-261

Selous, Frederick Courteney 1851-1917...DLB-174

Seltzer, Chester E. (see Muro, Amado)

Thomas Seltzer [publishing house].......DLB-46

Selvon, Sam 1923-1994.....DLB-125; CDWLB-3

Semmes, Raphael 1809-1877............DLB-189

Senancour, Etienne de 1770-1846......DLB-119

Sendak, Maurice 1928-.................DLB-61

Seneca the Elder
  circa 54 B.C.-circa A.D. 40........DLB-211

Seneca the Younger
  circa 1 B.C.-A.D. 65....DLB-211; CDWLB-1

Senécal, Eva 1905-....................DLB-92

Sengstacke, John 1912-1997............DLB-127

Senior, Olive 1941-...................DLB-157

Senkovsky, Osip Ivanovich
  (Józef-Julian Sekowski, Baron Brambeus)
  1800-1858.........................DLB-198

Šenoa, August 1838-1881...DLB-147; CDWLB-4

Sepamla, Sipho 1932-............DLB-157, 225

Serafimovich, Aleksandr Serafimovich
  (Aleksandr Serafimovich Popov)
  1863-1949.........................DLB-272

Serao, Matilde 1856-1927..............DLB-264

Seredy, Kate 1899-1975................DLB-22

Sereni, Vittorio 1913-1983............DLB-128

William Seres [publishing house].......DLB-170

Sergeev-Tsensky, Sergei Nikolaevich (Sergei
  Nikolaevich Sergeev) 1875-1958....DLB-272

Serling, Rod 1924-1975................DLB-26

Sernine, Daniel 1955-.................DLB-251

Serote, Mongane Wally 1944-....DLB-125, 225

Serraillier, Ian 1912-1994............DLB-161

Serrano, Nina 1934-...................DLB-122

Service, Robert 1874-1958.............DLB-92

Sessler, Charles 1854-1935............DLB-187

Seth, Vikram 1952-...............DLB-120, 271

Seton, Elizabeth Ann 1774-1821.......DLB-200

Seton, Ernest Thompson
  1860-1942....................DLB-92; DS-13

Seton, John circa 1509-1567...........DLB-281

Setouchi Harumi 1922-.................DLB-182

Settle, Mary Lee 1918-.................DLB-6

Seume, Johann Gottfried 1763-1810....DLB-94

Seuse, Heinrich 1295?-1366............DLB-179

Seuss, Dr. (see Geisel, Theodor Seuss)

Severin, Timothy 1940-................DLB-204

Sévigné, Marie de Rabutin Chantal,
  Madame de 1626-1696...............DLB-268

Sewall, Joseph 1688-1769..............DLB-24

Sewall, Richard B. 1908-..............DLB-111

Sewall, Samuel 1652-1730..............DLB-24

Sewell, Anna 1820-1878...............DLB-163

Sexton, Anne 1928-1974...DLB-5, 169; CDALB-1

Seymour-Smith, Martin 1928-1998......DLB-155

Sgorlon, Carlo 1930-..................DLB-196

Shaara, Michael 1929-1988..............Y-83

Shabel'skaia, Aleksandra Stanislavovna
  1845-1921.........................DLB-238

Shadwell, Thomas 1641?-1692...........DLB-80

Shaffer, Anthony 1926-................DLB-13

Shaffer, Peter 1926-......DLB-13, 233; CDBLB-8

Shaftesbury, Anthony Ashley Cooper,
  Third Earl of 1671-1713...........DLB-101

Shaginian, Marietta Sergeevna
  1888-1982.........................DLB-272

Shairp, Mordaunt 1887-1939............DLB-10

Shakespeare, Nicholas 1957-..........DLB-231

Shakespeare, William
  1564-1616......DLB-62, 172, 263; CDBLB-1

  The New Variorum Shakespeare.......Y-85

  Shakespeare and Montaigne: A Symposium
    by Jules Furthman................Y-02

$6,166,000 for a *Book!* Observations on
  *The Shakespeare First Folio: The History
  of the Book*........................Y-01

Taylor-Made Shakespeare? Or Is
  "Shall I Die?" the Long-Lost Text
  of Bottom's Dream?...................Y-85

The Shakespeare Globe Trust............Y-93

Shakespeare Head Press...............DLB-112

Shakhova, Elisaveta Nikitichna
  1822-1899.........................DLB-277

Shakhovskoi, Aleksandr Aleksandrovich
  1777-1846.........................DLB-150

Shange, Ntozake 1948-............DLB-38, 249

Shapiro, Karl 1913-2000..............DLB-48

Sharon Publications..................DLB-46

Sharp, Margery 1905-1991............DLB-161

Sharp, William 1855-1905............DLB-156

Sharpe, Tom 1928-................DLB-14, 231

Shaw, Albert 1857-1947...............DLB-91

Shaw, George Bernard
  1856-1950......DLB-10, 57, 190, CDBLB-6

  The Bernard Shaw Society............Y-99

  "Stage Censorship: The Rejected Statement"
    (1911) [excerpts].................DLB-10

Shaw, Henry Wheeler 1818-1885........DLB-11

Shaw, Irwin
  1913-1984........DLB-6, 102; Y-84; CDALB-1

Shaw, Joseph T. 1874-1952............DLB-137

  "As I Was Saying," Joseph T. Shaw's
    Editorial Rationale in *Black Mask*
    (January 1927)...................DLB-137

Shaw, Mary 1854-1929.................DLB-228

Shaw, Robert 1927-1978..............DLB-13, 14

Shaw, Robert B. 1947-................DLB-120

Shawn, Wallace 1943-.................DLB-266

Shawn, William 1907-1992.............DLB-137

Frank Shay [publishing house].........DLB-46

Shchedrin, N. (see Saltykov, Mikhail Evgrafovich)

Shcherbina, Nikolai Fedorovich
  1821-1869.........................DLB-277

Shea, John Gilmary 1824-1892.........DLB-30

Sheaffer, Louis 1912-1993............DLB-103

Sheahan, Henry Beston (see Beston, Henry)

Shearing, Joseph 1886-1952...........DLB-70

Shebbeare, John 1709-1788............DLB-39

Sheckley, Robert 1928-.................DLB-8

Shedd, William G. T. 1820-1894........DLB-64

Sheed, Wilfrid 1930-...................DLB-6

Sheed and Ward [U.S.]................DLB-46

Sheed and Ward Limited [U.K.]........DLB-112

Sheldon, Alice B. (see Tiptree, James, Jr.)

Sheldon, Edward 1886-1946.............DLB-7

Sheldon and Company..................DLB-49

Sheller, Aleksandr Konstantinovich
  1838-1900.........................DLB-238

Shelley, Mary Wollstonecraft 1797-1851
  ....DLB-110, 116, 159, 178; CDBLB-3

  Preface to *Frankenstein; or, The
  Modern Prometheus* (1818).........DLB-178

Shelley, Percy Bysshe
    1792-1822...... DLB-96, 110, 158; CDBLB-3
Shelnutt, Eve 1941- DLB-130
Shenshin (see Fet, Afanasii Afanas'evich)
Shenstone, William 1714-1763 .... DLB-95
Shepard, Clark and Brown.............. DLB-49
Shepard, Ernest Howard 1879-1976 ..... DLB-160
Shepard, Sam 1943- DLB-7, 212
Shepard, Thomas I, 1604 or 1605-1649 ... DLB-24
Shepard, Thomas, II, 1635-1677 .... DLB-24
Shepherd, Luke flourished 1547-1554.... DLB-136
Sherburne, Edward 1616-1702 .... DLB-131
Sheridan, Frances 1724-1766.......... DLB-39, 84
Sheridan, Richard Brinsley
    1751-1816............ DLB-89; CDBLB-2
Sherman, Francis 1871-1926............ DLB-92
Sherman, Martin 1938- DLB-228
Sherriff, R. C. 1896-1975 ..... DLB-10, 191, 233
Sherrod, Blackie 1919- DLB-241
Sherry, Norman 1935- DLB-155
    Tribute to Graham Greene............ Y-91
Sherry, Richard 1506-1551 or 1555 ..... DLB-236
Sherwood, Mary Martha 1775-1851 ..... DLB-163
Sherwood, Robert E. 1896-1955....DLB-7, 26, 249
Shevyrev, Stepan Petrovich 1806-1864 .. DLB-205
Shiel, M. P. 1865-1947 .... DLB-153
Shiels, George 1886-1949 .... DLB-10
Shiga Naoya 1883-1971 .... DLB-180
Shiina Rinzō 1911-1973 .... DLB-182
Shikishi Naishinnō 1153?-1201......... DLB-203
Shillaber, Benjamin Penhallow
    1814-1890................. DLB-1, 11, 235
Shimao Toshio 1917-1986............. DLB-182
Shimazaki Tōson 1872-1943............. DLB-180
Shimose, Pedro 1940- DLB-283
Shine, Ted 1931- DLB-38
Shinkei 1406-1475................... DLB-203
Ship, Reuben 1915-1975 .... DLB-88
Shirer, William L. 1904-1993 .... DLB-4
Shirinsky-Shikhmatov, Sergii Aleksandrovich
    1783-1837.................... DLB-150
Shirley, James 1596-1666 .... DLB-58
Shishkov, Aleksandr Semenovich
    1753-1841.................... DLB-150
Shockley, Ann Allen 1927- DLB-33
Sholokhov, Mikhail Aleksandrovich
    1905-1984 .... DLB-272
Shōno Junzō 1921- DLB-182
Shore, Arabella 1820?-1901 .... DLB-199
Shore, Louisa 1824-1895 .... DLB-199
Short, Luke (see Glidden, Frederick Dilley)
Peter Short [publishing house] DLB-170
Shorter, Dora Sigerson 1866-1918 ..... DLB-240
Shorthouse, Joseph Henry 1834-1903 .... DLB-18
Short Stories
    Michael M. Rea and the Rea Award for the
        Short Story.................... Y-97

The Year in Short Stories Y-87
The Year in the Short Story Y-88, 90–93
Shōtetsu 1381-1459 .... DLB-203
Showalter, Elaine 1941- DLB-67
Shulevitz, Uri 1935- DLB-61
Shulman, Max 1919-1988.............. DLB-11
Shute, Henry A. 1856-1943 .... DLB-9
Shute, Nevil (Nevil Shute Norway)
    1899-1960 .... DLB-255
Shuttle, Penelope 1947- DLB-14, 40
Shvarts, Evgenii L'vovich 1896-1958 .....DLB-272
Sibbes, Richard 1577-1635 .... DLB-151
Sibiriak, D. (see Mamin, Dmitrii Narkisovich)
Siddal, Elizabeth Eleanor 1829-1862 .... DLB-199
Sidgwick, Ethel 1877-1970............ DLB-197
Sidgwick, Henry 1838-1900 .... DLB-262
Sidgwick and Jackson Limited DLB-112
Sidney, Margaret (see Lothrop, Harriet M.)
Sidney, Mary 1561-1621 .... DLB-167
Sidney, Sir Philip 1554-1586.. DLB-167; CDBLB-1
    An Apologie for Poetrie (the Olney edition,
        1595, of Defence of Poesie)....... DLB-167
Sidney's Press...................... DLB-49
Sierra, Rubén 1946- DLB-122
Sierra Club Books.................. DLB-49
Siger of Brabant circa 1240-circa 1284 ... DLB-115
Sigourney, Lydia Huntley
    1791-1865........DLB-1, 42, 73, 183, 239, 243
Silkin, Jon 1930-1997 .... DLB-27
Silko, Leslie Marmon
    1948- DLB-143, 175, 256, 275
Silliman, Benjamin 1779-1864 .... DLB-183
Silliman, Ron 1946- DLB-169
Silliphant, Stirling 1918-1996 .... DLB-26
Sillitoe, Alan 1928- DLB-14, 139; CDBLB-8
    Tribute to J. B. Priestly Y-84
Silman, Roberta 1934- DLB-28
Silone, Ignazio (Secondino Tranquilli)
    1900-1978..................... DLB-264
Silva, Beverly 1930- DLB-122
Silva, José Asunció 1865-1896 .... DLB-283
Silverberg, Robert 1935- DLB-8
Silverman, Kaja 1947- DLB-246
Silverman, Kenneth 1936- DLB-111
Simak, Clifford D. 1904-1988........... DLB-8
Simcoe, Elizabeth 1762-1850........... DLB-99
Simcox, Edith Jemima 1844-1901....... DLB-190
Simcox, George Augustus 1841-1905..... DLB-35
Sime, Jessie Georgina 1868-1958 .... DLB-92
Simenon, Georges 1903-1989.......DLB-72; Y-89
Simic, Charles 1938- DLB-105
    "Images and 'Images'" DLB-105
Simionescu, Mircea Horia 1928- DLB-232
Simmel, Johannes Mario 1924- DLB-69
Valentine Simmes [publishing house] DLB-170
Simmons, Ernest J. 1903-1972 .... DLB-103

Simmons, Herbert Alfred 1930- DLB-33
Simmons, James 1933- DLB-40
Simms, William Gilmore
    1806-1870............DLB-3, 30, 59, 73, 248
Simms and M'Intyre................. DLB-106
Simon, Claude 1913- DLB-83; Y-85
    Nobel Lecture..................... Y-85
Simon, Neil 1927- DLB-7, 266
Simon and Schuster DLB-46
Simons, Katherine Drayton Mayrant
    1890-1969 .... Y-83
Simović, Ljubomir 1935- DLB-181
Simpkin and Marshall
    [publishing house] DLB-154
Simpson, Helen 1897-1940 .... DLB-77
Simpson, Louis 1923- DLB-5
Simpson, N. F. 1919- DLB-13
Sims, George 1923- DLB-87; Y-99
Sims, George Robert 1847-1922 ...DLB-35, 70, 135
Sinán, Rogelio 1904-1994............ DLB-145
Sinclair, Andrew 1935- DLB-14
Sinclair, Bertrand William 1881-1972..... DLB-92
Sinclair, Catherine 1800-1864.......... DLB-163
Sinclair, Jo 1913-1995.................. DLB-28
Sinclair, Lister 1921- DLB-88
Sinclair, May 1863-1946........... DLB-36, 135
    The Novels of Dorothy Richardson
        (1918)....................... DLB-36
Sinclair, Upton 1878-1968 ..... DLB-9; CDALB-5
Upton Sinclair [publishing house]........ DLB-46
Singer, Isaac Bashevis 1904-1991
    ....DLB-6, 28, 52, 278; Y-91; CDALB-1
Singer, Mark 1950- DLB-185
Singmaster, Elsie 1879-1958 .... DLB-9
Sinisgalli, Leonardo 1908-1981......... DLB-114
Siodmak, Curt 1902-2000................ DLB-44
Sîrbu, Ion D. 1919-1989 .... DLB-232
Siringo, Charles A. 1855-1928 .... DLB-186
Sissman, L. E. 1928-1976 .... DLB-5
Sisson, C. H. 1914- DLB-27
Sitwell, Edith 1887-1964 ...... DLB-20; CDBLB-7
Sitwell, Osbert 1892-1969...........DLB-100, 195
Skácel, Jan 1922-1989................ DLB-232
Skalbe, Kārlis 1879-1945.............. DLB-220
Skármeta, Antonio
    1940- DLB-145; CDWLB-3
Skavronsky, A. (see Danilevsky, Grigorii Petrovich)
Skeat, Walter W. 1835-1912 .... DLB-184
William Skeffington [publishing house] .. DLB-106
Skelton, John 1463-1529.............. DLB-136
Skelton, Robin 1925-1997..........DLB-27, 53
Škėma, Antanas 1910-1961 .... DLB-220
Skinner, Constance Lindsay
    1877-1939..................... DLB-92
Skinner, John Stuart 1788-1851 .... DLB-73
Skipsey, Joseph 1832-1903 .... DLB-35

Skou-Hansen, Tage 1925- DLB-214
Škvorecký, Josef 1924- DLB-232; CDWLB-4
Slade, Bernard 1930- DLB-53
Slamnig, Ivan 1930- DLB-181
Slančeková, Božena (see Timrava)
Slataper, Scipio 1888-1915 ....DLB-264
Slater, Patrick 1880-1951 ....DLB-68
Slaveykov, Pencho 1866-1912 ....DLB-147
Slaviček, Milivoj 1929- DLB-181
Slavitt, David 1935- DLB-5, 6
Sleigh, Burrows Willcocks Arthur
    1821-1869 ....DLB-99
Sleptsov, Vasilii Alekseevich 1836-1878... DLB-277
Slesinger, Tess 1905-1945 ....DLB-102
Slessor, Kenneth 1901-1971 ....DLB-260
Slick, Sam (see Haliburton, Thomas Chandler)
Sloan, John 1871-1951 ....DLB-188
Sloane, William, Associates DLB-46
Slonimsky, Mikhail Leonidovich
    1897-1972......................DLB-272
Sluchevsky, Konstantin Konstantinovich
    1837-1904 ....DLB-277
Small, Maynard and Company ,,,,,,,,,DLB-49
Smart, Christopher 1722-1771 ....DLB-109
Smart, David A. 1892-1957 ....DLB-137
Smart, Elizabeth 1913-1986 ....DLB-88
Smart, J. J. C. 1920 ....DLB-262
Smedley, Menella Bute 1820?-1877 ......DLB-199
William Smellie [publishing house] DLB-154
Smiles, Samuel 1812-1904 ....DLB-55
Smiley, Jane 1949- DLB-227, 234
Smith, A. J. M. 1902-1980 ....DLB-88
Smith, Adam 1723-1790 .... DLB-104, 252
Smith, Adam (George Jerome Waldo
    Goodman) 1930- DLB-185
Smith, Alexander 1829-1867 ....DLB-32, 55
    "On the Writing of Essays" (1862) ...DLB-57
Smith, Amanda 1837-1915 ....DLB-221
Smith, Betty 1896-1972 ....Y-82
Smith, Carol Sturm 1938- Y-81
Smith, Charles Henry 1826-1903 ....DLB-11
Smith, Charlotte 1749-1806 ....DLB-39, 109
Smith, Chet 1899-1973.................DLB-171
Smith, Cordwainer 1913-1966...........DLB-8
Smith, Dave 1942- DLB-5
    Tribute to James Dickey Y-97
    Tribute to John Gardner Y-82
Smith, Dodie 1896- DLB-10
Smith, Doris Buchanan 1934- DLB-52
Smith, E. E. 1890-1965 ....DLB-8
Smith, Elihu Hubbard 1771-1798.........DLB-37
Smith, Elizabeth Oakes (Prince)
    (see Oakes Smith, Elizabeth)
Smith, Eunice 1757-1823 ....DLB-200
Smith, F. Hopkinson 1838-1915..........DS-13
Smith, George D. 1870-1920 ....DLB-140

Smith, George O. 1911-1981 ....DLB-8
Smith, Goldwin 1823-1910 ....DLB-99
Smith, H. Allen 1907-1976 ....DLB-11, 29
Smith, Harry B. 1860-1936 ....DLB-187
Smith, Hazel Brannon 1914-1994 ....DLB-127
Smith, Henry circa 1560-circa 1591......DLB-136
Smith, Horatio (Horace)
    1779-1849 ....DLB-96, 116
Smith, Iain Crichton 1928-1998......DLB-40, 139
Smith, J. Allen 1860-1924 ....DLB-47
Smith, James 1775-1839 ....DLB-96
Smith, Jessie Willcox 1863-1935 ....DLB-188
Smith, John 1580-1631................DLB-24, 30
Smith, John 1618-1652.................DLB-252
Smith, Josiah 1704-1781 ....DLB-24
Smith, Ken 1938- DLB-40
Smith, Lee 1944- DLB-143; Y-83
Smith, Logan Pearsall 1865-1946.........DLB-98
Smith, Margaret Bayard 1778-1844......DLB-248
Smith, Mark 1935- Y-82
Smith, Michael 1698-circa 1771 ....DLB-31
Smith, Pauline 1882-1959 ....DLB-225
Smith, Red 1905-1982 ....DLB-29, 171
Smith, Roswell 1829-1892 ....DLB-79
Smith, Samuel Harrison 1772-1845 ....DLB-43
Smith, Samuel Stanhope 1751-1819 ....DLB-37
Smith, Sarah (see Stretton, Hesba)
Smith, Sarah Pogson 1774-1870 ....DLB-200
Smith, Seba 1792-1868..........DLB-1, 11, 243
Smith, Stevie 1902-1971 ....DLB-20
Smith, Sydney 1771-1845................DLB-107
Smith, Sydney Goodsir 1915-1975........DLB-27
Smith, Sir Thomas 1513-1577 ....DLB-132
Smith, Wendell 1914-1972...............DLB-171
Smith, William flourished 1595-1597 ....DLB-136
Smith, William 1727-1803 ....DLB-31
    A General Idea of the College of Mirania
    (1753) [excerpts]................DLB-31
Smith, William 1728-1793 ....DLB-30
Smith, William Gardner 1927-1974 ......DLB-76
Smith, William Henry 1808-1872 ....DLB-159
Smith, William Jay 1918- DLB-5
Smith, Elder and Company DLB-154
Harrison Smith and Robert Haas
    [publishing house].................DLB-46
J. Stilman Smith and Company DLB-49
W. B. Smith and Company DLB-49
W. H. Smith and Son DLB-106
Leonard Smithers [publishing house].....DLB-112
Smollett, Tobias
    1721-1771..........DLB-39, 104; CDBLB-2
    Dedication to Ferdinand Count Fathom
    (1753) DLB-39
    Preface to Ferdinand Count Fathom
    (1753) DLB-39
    Preface to Roderick Random (1748).....DLB-39

Smythe, Francis Sydney 1900-1949......DLB-195
Snelling, William Joseph 1804-1848 .....DLB-202
Snellings, Rolland (see Touré, Askia Muhammad)
Snodgrass, W. D. 1926- DLB-5
Snow, C. P.
    1905-1980.....DLB-15, 77; DS-17; CDBLB-7
Snyder, Gary
    1930- DLB-5, 16, 165, 212, 237, 275
Sobiloff, Hy 1912-1970..................DLB-48
The Society for Textual Scholarship and
    TEXT........................Y-87
The Society for the History of Authorship,
    Reading and Publishing Y-92
Söderberg, Hjalmar 1869-1941 ....DLB-259
Södergran, Edith 1892-1923 ....DLB-259
Soffici, Ardengo 1879-1964 ....DLB-114, 264
Sofola, 'Zulu 1938- DLB-157
Sokhanskaia, Nadezhda Stepanovna
    (Kokhanovskaia) 1823?-1884 ....DLB-277
Solano, Solita 1888-1975 ....DLB-4
Soldati, Mario 1906-1999 ....DLB-177
Šoljan, Antun 1932-1993 ....DLB-181
Sollers, Philippe (Philippe Joyaux)
    1936- ,,,,,,,,,,,,,,,,,,,,,,,,,DLB-83
Sollogub, Vladimir Aleksandrovich
    1813-1882 ....DLB-198
Sollors, Werner 1943- DBL-246
Solmi, Sergio 1899-1981 ....DLB-114
Solomon, Carl 1928- DLB-16
Solway, David 1941- DLB-53
Solzhenitsyn, Aleksandr I. 1918-
    Solzhenitsyn and America............ Y-85
Some Basic Notes on Three Modern Genres:
    Interview, Blurb, and Obituary........ Y-02
Somerville, Edith Œnone 1858-1949.....DLB-135
Somov, Orest Mikhailovich 1793-1833 ...DLB-198
Sønderby, Knud 1909-1966............DLB-214
Song, Cathy 1955- DLB-169
Sonnevi, Göran 1939- DLB-257
Sono Ayako 1931- DLB-182
Sontag, Susan 1933- DLB-2, 67
Sophocles 497/496 B.C.-406/405 B.C.
    ....DLB-176; CDWLB-1
Šopov, Aco 1923-1982................DLB-181
Sorel, Charles ca.1600-1674 ....DLB-268
Sørensen, Villy 1929- DLB-214
Sorensen, Virginia 1912-1991 ....DLB-206
Sorge, Reinhard Johannes 1892-1916 ....DLB-118
Sorrentino, Gilbert 1929- DLB-5, 173; Y-80
Sotheby, James 1682-1742 ....DLB-213
Sotheby, John 1740-1807 ....DLB-213
Sotheby, Samuel 1771-1842 ....DLB-213
Sotheby, Samuel Leigh 1805-1861.......DLB-213
Sotheby, William 1757-1833.........DLB-93, 213
Soto, Gary 1952- DLB-82
Soueif, Ahdaf 1950- DLB-267
Souster, Raymond 1921- DLB-88

The *South English Legendary* circa
  thirteenth-fifteenth centuries........ DLB-146
Southerland, Ellease 1943- DLB-33
Southern, Terry 1924-1995 .... DLB-2
Southern Illinois University Press Y-95
Southern Literature
  Fellowship of Southern Writers Y-98
  The Fugitives and the Agrarians:
    The First Exhibition Y-85
  "The Greatness of Southern Literature":
    League of the South Institute for the
    Study of Southern Culture and
    History........................ Y-02
  The Society for the Study of
    Southern Literature Y-00
  Southern Writers Between the Wars .. DLB-9
Southerne, Thomas 1659-1746.......... DLB-80
Southey, Caroline Anne Bowles
  1786-1854..................... DLB-116
Southey, Robert 1774-1843...... DLB-93, 107, 142
Southwell, Robert 1561?-1595 .... DLB-167
Southworth, E. D. E. N. 1819-1899 ..... DLB-239
Sowande, Bode 1948- DLB-157
Tace Sowle [publishing house] DLB-170
Soyfer, Jura 1912-1939 .... DLB-124
Soyinka, Wole
  1934- DLB-125; Y-86, Y-87; CDWLB-3
  Nobel Lecture 1986: This Past Must
    Address Its Present............... Y-86
Spacks, Barry 1931- DLB-105
Spalding, Frances 1950- DLB-155
Spark, Muriel 1918- ... DLB-15, 139; CDBLB-7
Michael Sparke [publishing house] DLB-170
Sparks, Jared 1789-1866 .... DLB-1, 30, 235
Sparshott, Francis 1926- DLB-60
Späth, Gerold 1939- DLB-75
Spatola, Adriano 1941-1988 .... DLB-128
Spaziani, Maria Luisa 1924- DLB-128
Specimens of Foreign Standard Literature
  1838-1842 .... DLB-1
The Spectator 1828- DLB-110
Spedding, James 1808-1881 .... DLB-144
Spee von Langenfeld, Friedrich
  1591-1635 .... DLB-164
Speght, Rachel 1597-after 1630......... DLB-126
Speke, John Hanning 1827-1864 .... DLB-166
Spellman, A. B. 1935- DLB-41
Spence, Catherine Helen 1825-1910..... DLB-230
Spence, Thomas 1750-1814 .... DLB-158
Spencer, Anne 1882-1975 .... DLB-51, 54
Spencer, Charles, third Earl of Sunderland
  1674-1722..................... DLB-213
Spencer, Elizabeth 1921- DLB-6, 218
Spencer, George John, Second Earl Spencer
  1758-1834..................... DLB-184
Spencer, Herbert 1820-1903 .... DLB-57, 262
  "The Philosophy of Style" (1852).... DLB-57
Spencer, Scott 1945- Y-86
Spender, J. A. 1862-1942 .... DLB-98

Spender, Stephen 1909-1995 .. DLB-20; CDBLB-7
Spener, Philipp Jakob 1635-1705 .... DLB-164
Spenser, Edmund
  circa 1552-1599 .... DLB-167; CDBLB-1
  Envoy from *The Shepheardes Calender* . DLB-167
  "The Generall Argument of the
    Whole Booke," from
    The Shepheardes Calender........ DLB-167
  "A Letter of the Authors Expounding
    His Whole Intention in the Course
    of this Worke: Which for that It
    Giueth Great Light to the Reader,
    for the Better Vnderstanding
    Is Hereunto Annexed,"
    from *The Faerie Queene* (1590) ... DLB-167
  "To His Booke," from
    The Shepheardes Calender (1579) .. DLB-167
  "To the Most Excellent and Learned
    Both Orator and Poete, Mayster
    Gabriell Haruey, His Verie Special
    and Singular Good Frend E. K.
    Commendeth the Good Lyking of
    This His Labour, and the Patronage
    of the New Poete," from
    The Shepheardes Calender........ DLB-167
Sperr, Martin 1944- DLB-124
Spewack, Bella Cowen 1899-1990 ...... DLB-266
Spewack, Samuel 1899-1971........... DLB-266
Spicer, Jack 1925-1965 .... DLB-5, 16, 193
Spielberg, Peter 1929- Y-81
Spielhagen, Friedrich 1829-1911........ DLB-129
"Spielmannsepen" (circa 1152-circa 1500) .. DLB-148
Spier, Peter 1927- DLB-61
Spillane, Mickey 1918- DLB-226
Spink, J. G. Taylor 1888-1962 .... DLB-241
Spinrad, Norman 1940- DLB-8
  Tribute to Isaac Asimov Y-92
Spires, Elizabeth 1952- DLB-120
Spitteler, Carl 1845-1924 .... DLB-129
Spivak, Lawrence E. 1900- DLB-137
Spofford, Harriet Prescott
  1835-1921 .... DLB-74, 221
Sports
  Jimmy, Red, and Others: Harold
    Rosenthal Remembers the Stars
    of the Press Box Y-01
  The Literature of Boxing in England
    through Arthur Conan Doyle Y-01
  Notable Twentieth-Century Books
    about Sports DLB-241
Sprigge, Timothy L. S. 1932- DLB-262
Spring, Howard 1889-1965 .... DLB-191
Squibob (see Derby, George Horatio)
Squier, E. G. 1821-1888 .... DLB-189
Stableford, Brian 1948- DLB-261
Stacpoole, H. de Vere 1863-1951....... DLB-153
Staël, Germaine de 1766-1817...... DLB-119, 192
Staël-Holstein, Anne-Louise Germaine de
  (see Staël, Germaine de)
Stafford, Jean 1915-1979............. DLB-2, 173
Stafford, William 1914-1993 .... DLB-5, 206
Stallings, Laurence 1894-1968 .... DLB-7, 44

Stallworthy, Jon 1935- DLB-40
Stampp, Kenneth M. 1912- DLB-17
Stănescu, Nichita 1933-1983 .... DLB-232
Stanev, Emiliyan 1907-1979 .... DLB-181
Stanford, Ann 1916- DLB-5
Stangerup, Henrik 1937-1998.......... DLB-214
Stanihurst, Richard 1547-1618 .... DLB-281
Stanitsky, N. (see Panaeva, Avdot'ia Iakovlevna)
Stankevich, Nikolai Vladimirovich
  1813-1840 .... DLB-198
Stanković, Borisav ("Bora")
  1876-1927.............. DLB-147; CDWLB-4
Stanley, Henry M. 1841-1904 ... DLB-189; DS-13
Stanley, Thomas 1625-1678 .... DLB-131
Stannard, Martin 1947- DLB-155
William Stansby [publishing house] DLB-170
Stanton, Elizabeth Cady 1815-1902 ...... DLB-79
Stanton, Frank L. 1857-1927........... DLB-25
Stanton, Maura 1946- DLB-120
Stapledon, Olaf 1886-1950 .... DLB-15, 255
Star Spangled Banner Office............ DLB-49
Stark, Freya 1893-1993 .... DLB-195
Starkey, Thomas circa 1499-1538 ...... DLB-132
Starkie, Walter 1894-1976 .... DLB-195
Starkweather, David 1935- DLB-7
Starrett, Vincent 1886-1974 .... DLB-187
Stationers' Company of London, The DLB-170
Statius circa A.D. 45-A.D. 96 .... DLB-211
Stead, Christina 1902-1983............ DLB-260
Stead, Robert J. C. 1880-1959 .... DLB-92
Steadman, Mark 1930- DLB-6
Stearns, Harold E. 1891-1943...... DLB-4; DS-15
Stebnitsky, M. (see Leskov, Nikolai Semenovich)
Stedman, Edmund Clarence 1833-1908... DLB-64
Steegmuller, Francis 1906-1994 .... DLB-111
Steel, Flora Annie 1847-1929 ...... DLB-153, 156
Steele, Max 1922- Y-80
Steele, Richard
  1672-1729.......... DLB-84, 101; CDBLB-2
Steele, Timothy 1948- DLB-120
Steele, Wilbur Daniel 1886-1970 .... DLB-86
Wallace Markfield's "Steeplechase" Y-02
Steere, Richard circa 1643-1721 .... DLB-24
Stefanovski, Goran 1952- DLB-181
Stegner, Wallace
  1909-1993 ....DLB-9, 206, 275; Y-93
Stehr, Hermann 1864-1940 .... DLB-66
Steig, William 1907- DLB-61
Stein, Gertrude 1874-1946
  .... DLB-4, 54, 86, 228; DS-15; CDALB-4
Stein, Leo 1872-1947.................. DLB-4
Stein and Day Publishers DLB-46
Steinbeck, John 1902-1968
  .... DLB-7, 9, 212, 275; DS-2; CDALB-5
  John Steinbeck Research Center,
    San Jose State University Y-85

Skou-Hansen, Tage 1925- DLB-214	Smith, George O. 1911-1981 .... DLB-8	Smythe, Francis Sydney 1900-1949 ...... DLB-195
Škvorecký, Josef 1924- DLB-232; CDWLB-4	Smith, Goldwin 1823-1910 .... DLB-99	Snelling, William Joseph 1804-1848 ..... DLB-202
Slade, Bernard 1930- DLB-53	Smith, H. Allen 1907-1976 .... DLB-11, 29	Snellings, Rolland (see Touré, Askia Muhammad)
Slamnig, Ivan 1930- DLB-181	Smith, Harry B. 1860-1936 .... DLB-187	Snodgrass, W. D. 1926- DLB-5
Slančeková, Božena (see Timrava)	Smith, Hazel Brannon 1914-1994 .... DLB-127	Snow, C. P.
Slataper, Scipio 1888-1915 .... DLB-264	Smith, Henry circa 1560-circa 1591...... DLB-136	1905-1980 ..... DLB-15, 77; DS-17; CDBLB-7
Slater, Patrick 1880-1951 .... DLB-68	Smith, Horatio (Horace)	Snyder, Gary
Slaveykov, Pencho 1866-1912 .... DLB-147	1779-1849 .... DLB-96, 116	1930- DLB-5, 16, 165, 212, 237, 275
Slaviček, Milivoj 1929- DLB-181	Smith, Iain Crichton 1928-1998...... DLB-40, 139	Sobiloff, Hy 1912-1970................. DLB-48
Slavitt, David 1935- DLB-5, 6	Smith, J. Allen 1860-1924 .... DLB-47	The Society for Textual Scholarship and
Sleigh, Burrows Willcocks Arthur	Smith, James 1775-1839 .... DLB-96	*TEXT* Y-87
1821-1869 .... DLB-99	Smith, Jessie Willcox 1863-1935 .... DLB-188	The Society for the History of Authorship,
Sleptsov, Vasilii Alekseevich 1836-1878... DLB-277	Smith, John 1580-1631................ DLB-24, 30	Reading and Publishing Y-92
Slesinger, Tess 1905-1945 .... DLB-102	Smith, John 1618-1652................. DLB-252	Söderberg, Hjalmar 1869-1941 .... DLB-259
Slessor, Kenneth 1901-1971 .... DLB-260	Smith, Josiah 1704-1781 .... DLB-24	Södergran, Edith 1892-1923 .... DLB-259
Slick, Sam (see Haliburton, Thomas Chandler)	Smith, Ken 1938- DLB-40	Soffici, Ardengo 1879-1964 .... DLB-114, 264
Sloan, John 1871-1951 .... DLB-188	Smith, Lee 1944- DLB-143; Y-83	Sofola, 'Zulu 1938- DLB-157
Sloane, William, Associates DLB-46	Smith, Logan Pearsall 1865-1946......... DLB-98	Sokhanskaia, Nadezhda Stepanovna
Slonimsky, Mikhail Leonidovich	Smith, Margaret Bayard 1778-1844 ..... DLB-248	(Kokhanovskaia) 1823?-1884 .... DLB-277
1897-1972..................... DLB-272	Smith, Mark 1935- Y-82	Solano, Solita 1888-1975 .... DLB-4
Sluchevsky, Konstantin Konstantinovich	Smith, Michael 1698-circa 1771 .... DLB-31	Soldati, Mario 1906-1999 .... DLB-177
1837-1904 .... DLB-277	Smith, Pauline 1882-1959 .... DLB-225	Šoljan, Antun 1932-1993 .... DLB-181
Small, Maynard and Company DLB-49	Smith, Red 1905-1982 .... DLB-29, 171	Sollers, Philippe (Philippe Joyaux)
Smart, Christopher 1722-1771 .... DLB-109	Smith, Roswell 1829-1892 .... DLB-79	1936- DLB-83
Smart, David A. 1892-1957 .... DLB-137	Smith, Samuel Harrison 1772-1845 ...... DLB-43	Sollogub, Vladimir Aleksandrovich
Smart, Elizabeth 1913-1986 .... DLB-88	Smith, Samuel Stanhope 1751-1819 ...... DLB-37	1813-1882..................... DLB-198
Smart, J. J. C. 1920 .... DLB-262	Smith, Sarah (see Stretton, Hesba)	Sollors, Werner 1943- DBL-246
Smedley, Menella Bute 1820?-1877 ...... DLB-199	Smith, Sarah Pogson 1774-1870 .... DLB-200	Solmi, Sergio 1899-1981 .... DLB-114
William Smellie [publishing house] DLB-154	Smith, Seba 1792-1868.......... DLB-1, 11, 243	Solomon, Carl 1928- DLB-16
Smiles, Samuel 1812-1904 .... DLB-55	Smith, Stevie 1902-1971................ DLB-20	Solway, David 1941- DLB-53
Smiley, Jane 1949- DLB-227, 234	Smith, Sydney 1771-1845............... DLB-107	Solzhenitsyn, Aleksandr I. 1918-
Smith, A. J. M. 1902-1980 .... DLB-88	Smith, Sydney Goodsir 1915-1975 .... DLB-27	Solzhenitsyn and America............. Y-85
Smith, Adam 1723-1790 .... DLB-104, 252	Smith, Sir Thomas 1513-1577 .... DLB-132	Some Basic Notes on Three Modern Genres:
Smith, Adam (George Jerome Waldo	Smith, Wendell 1914-1972............. DLB-171	Interview, Blurb, and Obituary......... Y-02
Goodman) 1930- DLB-185	Smith, William flourished 1595-1597 .... DLB-136	Somerville, Edith Œnone 1858-1949..... DLB-135
Smith, Alexander 1829-1867 .... DLB-32, 55	Smith, William 1727-1803 .... DLB-31	Somov, Orest Mikhailovich 1793-1833 ... DLB-198
"On the Writing of Essays" (1862) ... DLB-57	*A General Idea of the College of Mirania*	Sønderby, Knud 1909-1966............ DLB-214
Smith, Amanda 1837-1915 .... DLB-221	(1753) [excerpts]................ DLB-31	Song, Cathy 1955- DLB-169
Smith, Betty 1896-1972 .... Y-82	Smith, William 1728-1793 .... DLB-30	Sonnevi, Göran 1939- DLB-257
Smith, Carol Sturm 1938- Y-81	Smith, William Gardner 1927-1974 .... DLB-76	Sono Ayako 1931- DLB-182
Smith, Charles Henry 1826-1903 .... DLB-11	Smith, William Henry 1808-1872 .... DLB-159	Sontag, Susan 1933- DLB-2, 67
Smith, Charlotte 1749-1806 .... DLB-39, 109	Smith, William Jay 1918- DLB-5	Sophocles 497/496 B.C.-406/405 B.C.
Smith, Chet 1899-1973................ DLB-171	Smith, Elder and Company............ DLB-154	.... DLB-176; CDWLB-1
Smith, Cordwainer 1913-1966............ DLB-8	Harrison Smith and Robert Haas	Šopov, Aco 1923-1982................ DLB-181
Smith, Dave 1942- DLB-5	[publishing house]................ DLB-46	Sorel, Charles ca.1600-1674 .... DLB-268
Tribute to James Dickey Y-97	J. Stilman Smith and Company DLB-49	Sørensen, Villy 1929- DLB-214
Tribute to John Gardner Y-82	W. B. Smith and Company DLB-49	Sorensen, Virginia 1912-1991 .... DLB-206
Smith, Dodie 1896- DLB-10	W. H. Smith and Son DLB-106	Sorge, Reinhard Johannes 1892-1916 .... DLB-118
Smith, Doris Buchanan 1934- DLB-52	Leonard Smithers [publishing house]..... DLB-112	Sorrentino, Gilbert 1929- DLB-5, 173; Y-80
Smith, E. E. 1890-1965 .... DLB-8	Smollett, Tobias	Sotheby, James 1682-1742 .... DLB-213
Smith, Elihu Hubbard 1771-1798 .... DLB-37	1721-1771........... DLB-39, 104; CDBLB-2	Sotheby, John 1740-1807 .... DLB-213
Smith, Elizabeth Oakes (Prince)	Dedication to *Ferdinand Count Fathom*	Sotheby, Samuel 1771-1842 .... DLB-213
(see Oakes Smith, Elizabeth)	(1753) DLB-39	Sotheby, Samuel Leigh 1805-1861....... DLB-213
Smith, Eunice 1757-1823 .... DLB-200	Preface to *Ferdinand Count Fathom*	Sotheby, William 1757-1833......... DLB-93, 213
Smith, F. Hopkinson 1838-1915........... DS-13	(1753) DLB-39	Soto, Gary 1952- DLB-82
Smith, George D. 1870-1920 .... DLB-140	Preface to *Roderick Random* (1748) DLB-39	Soueif, Ahdaf 1950- DLB-267
		Souster, Raymond 1921- DLB-88

The *South English Legendary* circa
thirteenth-fifteenth centuries........ DLB-146
Southerland, Ellease 1943- DLB-33
Southern, Terry 1924-1995 .... DLB-2
Southern Illinois University Press Y-95
Southern Literature
  Fellowship of Southern Writers Y-98
  The Fugitives and the Agrarians:
    The First Exhibition Y-85
  "The Greatness of Southern Literature":
    League of the South Institute for the
    Study of Southern Culture and
    History...................... Y-02
  The Society for the Study of
    Southern Literature Y-00
  Southern Writers Between the Wars .. DLB-9
Southerne, Thomas 1659-1746......... DLB-80
Southey, Caroline Anne Bowles
  1786-1854..................... DLB-116
Southey, Robert 1774-1843...... DLB-93, 107, 142
Southwell, Robert 1561?-1595 .... DLB-167
Southworth, E. D. E. N. 1819-1899 ..... DLB-239
Sowande, Bode 1948- DLB-157
Tace Sowle [publishing house] DLB-170
Soyfer, Jura 1912-1939 .... DLB-124
Soyinka, Wole
  1934- DLB-125; Y-86, Y-87; CDWLB-3
  Nobel Lecture 1986: This Past Must
    Address Its Present............... Y-86
Spacks, Barry 1931- DLB-105
Spalding, Frances 1950- DLB-155
Spark, Muriel 1918- ... DLB-15, 139; CDBLB-7
Michael Sparke [publishing house] DLB-170
Sparks, Jared 1789-1866 .... DLB-1, 30, 235
Sparshott, Francis 1926- DLB-60
Späth, Gerold 1939- DLB-75
Spatola, Adriano 1941-1988 .... DLB-128
Spaziani, Maria Luisa 1924- DLB-128
Specimens of Foreign Standard Literature
  1838-1842 .... DLB-1
The Spectator 1828- DLB-110
Spedding, James 1808-1881 .... DLB-144
Spee von Langenfeld, Friedrich
  1591-1635 .... DLB-164
Speght, Rachel 1597-after 1630......... DLB-126
Speke, John Hanning 1827-1864........ DLB-166
Spellman, A. B. 1935- DLB-41
Spence, Catherine Helen 1825-1910..... DLB-230
Spence, Thomas 1750-1814 .... DLB-158
Spencer, Anne 1882-1975 .... DLB-51, 54
Spencer, Charles, third Earl of Sunderland
  1674-1722..................... DLB-213
Spencer, Elizabeth 1921- DLB-6, 218
Spencer, George John, Second Earl Spencer
  1758-1834..................... DLB-184
Spencer, Herbert 1820-1903.........DLB-57, 262
  "The Philosophy of Style" (1852).... DLB-57
Spencer, Scott 1945- Y-86
Spender, J. A. 1862-1942 .... DLB-98

Spender, Stephen 1909-1995 .. DLB-20; CDBLB-7
Spener, Philipp Jakob 1635-1705 .... DLB-164
Spenser, Edmund
  circa 1552-1599 .... DLB-167; CDBLB-1
  Envoy from *The Shepheardes Calender*. DLB-167
  "The Generall Argument of the
    Whole Booke," from
    The Shepheardes Calender........ DLB-167
  "A Letter of the Authors Expounding
    His Whole Intention in the Course
    of this Worke: Which for that It
    Giueth Great Light to the Reader,
    for the Better Vnderstanding
    Is Hereunto Annexed,"
    from *The Faerie Queene* (1590) ... DLB-167
  "To His Booke," from
    The Shepheardes Calender (1579) .. DLB-167
  "To the Most Excellent and Learned
    Both Orator and Poete, Mayster
    Gabriell Haruey, His Verie Special
    and Singular Good Frend E. K.
    Commendeth the Good Lyking of
    This His Labour, and the Patronage
    of the New Poete," from
    The Shepheardes Calender........ DLB-167
Sperr, Martin 1944- DLB-124
Spewack, Bella Cowen 1899-1990 ...... DLB-266
Spewack, Samuel 1899-1971 .... DLB-266
Spicer, Jack 1925-1965 .... DLB-5, 16, 193
Spielberg, Peter 1929- Y-81
Spielhagen, Friedrich 1829-1911........ DLB-129
"Spielmannsepen" (circa 1152-circa 1500) .. DLB-148
Spier, Peter 1927- DLB-61
Spillane, Mickey 1918- DLB-226
Spink, J. G. Taylor 1888-1962 .... DLB-241
Spinrad, Norman 1940- DLB-8
  Tribute to Isaac Asimov Y-92
Spires, Elizabeth 1952- DLB-120
Spitteler, Carl 1845-1924 .... DLB-129
Spivak, Lawrence E. 1900- DLB-137
Spofford, Harriet Prescott
  1835-1921 .... DLB-74, 221
Sports
  Jimmy, Red, and Others: Harold
    Rosenthal Remembers the Stars
    of the Press Box Y-01
  The Literature of Boxing in England
    through Arthur Conan Doyle Y-01
  Notable Twentieth-Century Books
    about Sports DLB-241
Sprigge, Timothy L. S. 1932- DLB-262
Spring, Howard 1889-1965 .... DLB-191
Squibob (see Derby, George Horatio)
Squier, E. G. 1821-1888 .... DLB-189
Stableford, Brian 1948- DLB-261
Stacpoole, H. de Vere 1863-1951....... DLB-153
Staël, Germaine de 1766-1817........ DLB-119, 192
Staël-Holstein, Anne-Louise Germaine de
  (see Staël, Germaine de)
Stafford, Jean 1915-1979 ....DLB-2, 173
Stafford, William 1914-1993 .... DLB-5, 206
Stallings, Laurence 1894-1968 ....DLB-7, 44

Stallworthy, Jon 1935- DLB-40
Stampp, Kenneth M. 1912- DLB-17
Stănescu, Nichita 1933-1983 .... DLB-232
Stanev, Emiliyan 1907-1979 .... DLB-181
Stanford, Ann 1916- DLB-5
Stangerup, Henrik 1937-1998.......... DLB-214
Stanihurst, Richard 1547-1618 .... DLB-281
Stanitsky, N. (see Panaeva, Avdot'ia Iakovlevna)
Stankevich, Nikolai Vladimirovich
  1813-1840 .... DLB-198
Stanković, Borisav ("Bora")
  1876-1927..............DLB-147; CDWLB-4
Stanley, Henry M. 1841-1904 ... DLB-189; DS-13
Stanley, Thomas 1625-1678 .... DLB-131
Stannard, Martin 1947- DLB-155
William Stansby [publishing house] DLB-170
Stanton, Elizabeth Cady 1815-1902 ...... DLB-79
Stanton, Frank L. 1857-1927........... DLB-25
Stanton, Maura 1946- DLB-120
Stapledon, Olaf 1886-1950 .... DLB-15, 255
Star Spangled Banner Office............ DLB-49
Stark, Freya 1893-1993............... DLB-195
Starkey, Thomas circa 1499-1538 ...... DLB-132
Starkie, Walter 1894-1976 .... DLB-195
Starkweather, David 1935- DLB-7
Starrett, Vincent 1886-1974 ....DLB-187
Stationers' Company of London, The DLB-170
Statius circa A.D. 45-A.D. 96 .... DLB-211
Stead, Christina 1902-1983............ DLB-260
Stead, Robert J. C. 1880-1959 .... DLB-92
Steadman, Mark 1930- DLB-6
Stearns, Harold E. 1891-1943...... DLB-4; DS-15
Stebnitsky, M. (see Leskov, Nikolai Semenovich)
Stedman, Edmund Clarence 1833-1908 ... DLB-64
Steegmuller, Francis 1906-1994 .... DLB-111
Steel, Flora Annie 1847-1929 ...... DLB-153, 156
Steele, Max 1922- Y-80
Steele, Richard
  1672-1729.......... DLB-84, 101; CDBLB-2
Steele, Timothy 1948- DLB-120
Steele, Wilbur Daniel 1886-1970 .... DLB-86
Wallace Markfield's "Steeplechase" Y-02
Steere, Richard circa 1643-1721 .... DLB-24
Stefanovski, Goran 1952- DLB-181
Stegner, Wallace
  1909-1993 ....DLB-9, 206, 275; Y-93
Stehr, Hermann 1864-1940 .... DLB-66
Steig, William 1907- DLB-61
Stein, Gertrude 1874-1946
  .... DLB-4, 54, 86, 228; DS-15; CDALB-4
Stein, Leo 1872-1947.................. DLB-4
Stein and Day Publishers DLB-46
Steinbeck, John 1902-1968
  ....DLB-7, 9, 212, 275; DS-2; CDALB-5
  John Steinbeck Research Center,
    San Jose State University Y-85

412

The Steinbeck Centennial Y-02
Steinem, Gloria 1934- DLB-246
Steiner, George 1929- DLB-67
Steinhoewel, Heinrich 1411/1412-1479 ...DLB-179
Steloff, Ida Frances 1887-1989 ....DLB-187
Stendhal 1783-1842 ....DLB-119
Stephen, Leslie 1832-1904 ...... DLB-57, 144, 190
Stephen Family (Bloomsbury Group) DS-10
Stephens, A. G. 1865-1933............DLB-230
Stephens, Alexander H. 1812-1883 ....DLB-47
Stephens, Alice Barber 1858-1932 ....DLB-188
Stephens, Ann 1810-1886 ....DLB-3, 73, 250
Stephens, Charles Asbury 1844?-1931.....DLB-42
Stephens, James 1882?-1950 ....DLB-19, 153, 162
Stephens, John Lloyd 1805-1852 ....DLB-183, 250
Stephens, Michael 1946 ....DLB-234
Stephensen, P. R. 1901-1965 ....DLB-260
Sterling, George 1869-1926 ....DLB-54
Sterling, James 1701-1763..............DLB-24
Sterling, John 1806-1844 ....DLB-116
Stern, Gerald 1925- DLB-105
"Living in Ruin"..................DLB-105
Stern, Gladys B. 1890-1973 ....DLB-197
Stern, Madeleine B. 1912- DLB-111, 140
Stern, Richard 1928- DLB-218; Y-87
Stern, Stewart 1922- DLB-26
Sterne, Laurence 1713-1768 ... DLB-39; CDBLB-2
Sternheim, Carl 1878-1942............DLB-56, 118
Sternhold, Thomas ?-1549..............DLB-132
Steuart, David 1747-1824 ....DLB-213
Stevens, Henry 1819-1886.............DLB-140
Stevens, Wallace 1879-1955....DLB-54; CDALB-5
The Wallace Stevens Society Y-99
Stevenson, Anne 1933- DLB-40
Stevenson, D. E. 1892-1973 ....DLB-191
Stevenson, Lionel 1902-1973 ....DLB-155
Stevenson, Robert Louis
  1850-1894 .... DLB-18, 57, 141, 156, 174;
                                DS-13; CDBLB-5
  "On Style in Literature:
     Its Technical Elements" (1885) ...DLB-57
Stewart, Donald Ogden
  1894-1980 ....DLB-4, 11, 26; DS-15
Stewart, Douglas 1913-1985 ....DLB-260
Stewart, Dugald 1753-1828 ....DLB-31
Stewart, George, Jr. 1848-1906 ....DLB-99
Stewart, George R. 1895-1980 ....DLB-8
Stewart, Harold 1916-1995 ....DLB-260
Stewart, J. I. M. (see Innes, Michael)
Stewart, Maria W. 1803?-1879..........DLB-239
Stewart, Randall 1896-1964............DLB-103
Stewart, Sean 1965- DLB-251
Stewart and Kidd Company DLB-46
Stickney, Trumbull 1874-1904..........DLB-54
Stieler, Caspar 1632-1707..............DLB-164

Stifter, Adalbert
  1805-1868 ....DLB-133; CDWLB-2
Stiles, Ezra 1727-1795 ....DLB-31
Still, James 1906-2001 ....DLB-9; Y-01
Stirling, S. M. 1953- DLB-251
Stirner, Max 1806-1856...............DLB-129
Stith, William 1707-1755..............DLB-31
Stivens, Dal 1911-1997................DLB-260
Elliot Stock [publishing house]..........DLB-106
Stockton, Annis Boudinot 1736-1801.....DLB-200
Stockton, Frank R. 1834-1902 .. DLB-42, 74; DS-13
Stockton, J. Roy 1892-1972 ....DLB-241
Ashbel Stoddard [publishing house]........DLB-49
Stoddard, Charles Warren 1843-1909....DLB-186
Stoddard, Elizabeth 1823-1902 ....DLB-202
Stoddard, Richard Henry
  1825-1903 ....DLB-3, 64, 250; DS-13
Stoddard, Solomon 1643-1729..........DLB-24
Stoker, Bram
  1847-1912 ...... DLB-36, 70, 178; CDBLB-5
  On Writing *Dracula*, from the
     Introduction to *Dracula* (1897) ... DLB-178
Frederick A. Stokes Company DLB-49
Stokes, Thomas L. 1898-1958 ....DLB-29
Stokesbury, Leon 1945- DLB-120
Stolberg, Christian Graf zu 1748-1821.....DLB-94
Stolberg, Friedrich Leopold Graf zu
  1750-1819 ....DLB-94
Stone, Lucy 1818-1893 ....DLB-79, 239
Stone, Melville 1848-1929 ....DLB-25
Stone, Robert 1937- DLB-152
Stone, Ruth 1915- DLB-105
Stone, Samuel 1602-1663...............DLB-24
Stone, William Leete 1792-1844 ....DLB-202
Herbert S. Stone and Company..........DLB-49
Stone and Kimball DLB-49
Stoppard, Tom
  1937- DLB-13, 233; Y-85; CDBLB-8
  Playwrights and Professors DLB-13
Storey, Anthony 1928- DLB-14
Storey, David 1933- DLB-13, 14, 207, 245
Storm, Theodor
  1817-1888 ....DLB-129; CDWLB-2
Storni, Alfonsina 1892-1938............DLB-283
Story, Thomas circa 1670-1742 ....DLB-31
Story, William Wetmore 1819-1895 ...DLB-1, 235
Storytelling: A Contemporary Renaissance... Y-84
Stoughton, William 1631-1701..........DLB-24
Stow, John 1525-1605 ....DLB-132
Stow, Randolph 1935- DLB-260
Stowe, Harriet Beecher 1811-1896......DLB-1,12,
                    42, 74, 189, 239, 243; CDALB-3
  The Harriet Beecher Stowe Center Y-00
Stowe, Leland 1899-1994...............DLB-29
Stoyanov, Dimitr Ivanov (see Elin Pelin)
Strabo 64/63 B.C.-circa A.D. 25 ....DLB-176
Strachey, Lytton 1880-1932......DLB-149; DS-10

Preface to *Eminent Victorians*........DLB-149
William Strahan [publishing house]......DLB-154
Strahan and Company................DLB-106
Strand, Mark 1934- DLB-5
The Strasbourg Oaths 842.............DLB-148
Stratemeyer, Edward 1862-1930 ....DLB-42
Strati, Saverio 1924- DLB-177
Stratton and Barnard DLB-49
Stratton-Porter, Gene
  1863-1924 ....DLB-221; DS-14
Straub, Peter 1943- Y-84
Strauß, Botho 1944- DLB-124
Strauß, David Friedrich 1808-1874 ......DLB-133
The Strawberry Hill Press..............DLB-154
Strawson, P. F. 1919- DLB-262
Streatfeild, Noel 1895-1986 ....DLB-160
Street, Cecil John Charles (see Rhode, John)
Street, G. S. 1867-1936.................DLB-135
Street and Smith.....................DLB-49
Streeter, Edward 1891-1976.............DLB-11
Streeter, Thomas Winthrop 1883-1965...DLB-140
Stretton, Hesba 1832-1911.........DLB-163, 190
Stribling, T. S. 1881-1965 ....DLB-9
Der Stricker circa 1190-circa 1250.......DLB-138
Strickland, Samuel 1804-1867 ....DLB-99
Strindberg, August 1849-1912 ....DLB-259
Stringer, Arthur 1874-1950 ....DLB-92
Stringer and Townsend DLB-49
Strittmatter, Erwin 1912-1994 ....DLB-69
Strniša, Gregor 1930-1987 ....DLB-181
Strode, William 1630-1645 ....DLB-126
Strong, L. A. G. 1896-1958 ....DLB-191
Strother, David Hunter (Porte Crayon)
  1816-1888 ....DLB-3, 248
Strouse, Jean 1945- DLB-111
Stuart, Dabney 1937- DLB-105
  "Knots into Webs: Some
    Autobiographical Sources" DLB-105
Stuart, Jesse 1906-1984 ..... DLB-9, 48, 102; Y-84
Lyle Stuart [publishing house]...........DLB-46
Stuart, Ruth McEnery 1849?-1917 ......DLB-202
Stubbs, Harry Clement (see Clement, Hal)
Stubenberg, Johann Wilhelm von
  1619-1663 ....DLB-164
Studebaker, William V. 1947- DLB-256
Studies in American Jewish Literature....... Y-02
Studio...........................DLB-112
Stump, Al 1916-1995 ....DLB-241
Sturgeon, Theodore 1918-1985 ...... DLB-8; Y-85
Sturges, Preston 1898-1959 ....DLB-26
Styron, William
  1925- DLB-2, 143; Y-80; CDALB-6
  Tribute to James Dickey Y-97
Suárez, Mario 1925- DLB-82
Such, Peter 1939- DLB-60
Suckling, Sir John 1609-1641?.......DLB-58, 126

Suckow, Ruth 1892-1960 . . . . DLB-9, 102
Sudermann, Hermann 1857-1928 . . . . DLB-118
Sue, Eugène 1804-1857 . . . . DLB-119
Sue, Marie-Joseph (see Sue, Eugène)
Suetonius circa A.D. 69-post A.D. 122 . . . DLB-211
Suggs, Simon (see Hooper, Johnson Jones)
Sui Sin Far (see Eaton, Edith Maude)
Suits, Gustav 1883-1956 . . . . DLB-220; CDWLB-4
Sukenick, Ronald 1932- DLB-173; Y-81
    An Author's Response Y-82
Sukhovo-Kobylin, Aleksandr Vasil'evich
    1817-1903 . . . . DLB-277
Suknaski, Andrew 1942- DLB-53
Sullivan, Alan 1868-1947 . . . . DLB-92
Sullivan, C. Gardner 1886-1965 . . . . DLB-26
Sullivan, Frank 1892-1976 . . . . DLB-11
Sulte, Benjamin 1841-1923 . . . . DLB-99
Sulzberger, Arthur Hays 1891-1968 . . . . . DLB-127
Sulzberger, Arthur Ochs 1926- DLB-127
Sulzer, Johann Georg 1720-1779 . . . . DLB-97
Sumarokov, Aleksandr Petrovich
    1717-1777 . . . . DLB-150
Summers, Hollis 1916- DLB-6
Sumner, Charles 1811-1874 . . . . DLB-235
Sumner, William Graham 1840-1910 . . . . . DLB-270
Henry A. Sumner [publishing house] DLB-49
Sundman, Per Olof 1922-1992 . . . . DLB-257
Supervielle, Jules 1884-1960 . . . . DLB-258
Surtees, Robert Smith 1803-1864 . . . . DLB-21
    The R. S. Surtees Society Y-98
Sutcliffe, Matthew 1550?-1629 . . . . DLB-281
Sutcliffe, William 1971- DLB-271
Sutherland, Efua Theodora 1924-1996 . . . DLB-117
Sutherland, John 1919-1956 . . . . DLB-68
Sutro, Alfred 1863-1933 . . . . DLB-10
Svendsen, Hanne Marie 1933- DLB-214
Svevo, Italo (Ettore Schmitz)
    1861-1928 . . . . DLB-264
Swados, Harvey 1920-1972 . . . . DLB-2
Swain, Charles 1801-1874 . . . . DLB-32
Swallow Press DLB-46
Swan Sonnenschein Limited DLB-106
Swanberg, W. A. 1907-1992 . . . . DLB-103
Swedish Literature
    The Literature of the Modern
        Breakthrough DLB-259
Swenson, May 1919-1989 . . . . DLB-5
Swerling, Jo 1897- DLB-44
Swift, Graham 1949- DLB-194
Swift, Jonathan
    1667-1745 . . . . DLB-39, 95, 101; CDBLB-2
Swinburne, A. C.
    1837-1909 . . . . DLB-35, 57; CDBLB-4
    Under the Microscope (1872) DLB-35
Swineshead, Richard floruit circa 1350 . . . DLB-115
Swinnerton, Frank 1884-1982 . . . . DLB-34

Swisshelm, Jane Grey 1815-1884 . . . . DLB-43
Swope, Herbert Bayard 1882-1958 . . . . DLB-25
Swords, James ?-1844 . . . . DLB-73
Swords, Thomas 1763-1843 . . . . DLB-73
T. and J. Swords and Company DLB-49
Swynnerton, Thomas
    early 16th century-1554 . . . . DLB-281
Sykes, Ella C. ?-1939 . . . . DLB-174
Sylvester, Josuah 1562 or 1563-1618 . . . . DLB-121
Symonds, Emily Morse (see Paston, George)
Symonds, John Addington
    1840-1893 . . . . DLB-57, 144
    "Personal Style" (1890) DLB-57
Symons, A. J. A. 1900-1941 . . . . DLB-149
Symons, Arthur 1865-1945 . . . . . DLB-19, 57, 149
Symons, Julian 1912-1994 . . . . . DLB-87, 155; Y-92
    Julian Symons at Eighty Y-92
Symons, Scott 1933- DLB-53
Synge, John Millington
    1871-1909 . . . . DLB-10, 19; CDBLB-5
    Synge Summer School: J. M. Synge
    and the Irish Theater, Rathdrum,
    County Wiclow, Ireland Y-93
Syrett, Netta 1865-1943 . . . . DLB-135, 197
Szabó, Lőrinc 1900-1957 . . . . DLB-215
Szabó, Magda 1917- DLB-215
Szymborska, Wisława
    1923- DLB-232, Y-96; CDWLB-4
    Nobel Lecture 1996:
    The Poet and the World Y-96

T

Taban lo Liyong 1939?- DLB-125
Tabori, George 1914- DLB-245
Tabucchi, Antonio 1943- DLB-196
Taché, Joseph-Charles 1820-1894 . . . . DLB-99
Tachihara Masaaki 1926-1980 . . . . DLB-182
Tacitus circa A.D. 55-circa A.D. 117
    . . . . DLB-211; CDWLB-1
Tadijanović, Dragutin 1905- DLB-181
Tafdrup, Pia 1952- DLB-214
Tafolla, Carmen 1951- DLB-82
Taggard, Genevieve 1894-1948 . . . . DLB-45
Taggart, John 1942- DLB-193
Tagger, Theodor (see Bruckner, Ferdinand)
Taiheiki late fourteenth century DLB-203
Tait, J. Selwin, and Sons DLB-49
Tait's Edinburgh Magazine 1832-1861 . . . . . DLB-110
The Takarazaka Revue Company Y-91
Talander (see Bohse, August)
Talese, Gay 1932- DLB-185
    Tribute to Irwin Shaw Y-84
Talev, Dimitr 1898-1966 . . . . DLB-181
Taliaferro, H. E. 1811-1875 . . . . DLB-202
Tallent, Elizabeth 1954- DLB-130
TallMountain, Mary 1918-1994 . . . . DLB-193
Talvj 1797-1870 . . . . DLB-59, 133

Tamási, Áron 1897-1966 . . . . DLB-215
Tammsaare, A. H.
    1878-1940 . . . . DLB-220; CDWLB-4
Tan, Amy 1952- DLB-173; CDALB-7
Tandori, Dezső 1938- DLB-232
Tanner, Thomas 1673/1674-1735 . . . . DLB-213
Tanizaki Jun'ichirō 1886-1965 . . . . DLB-180
Tapahonso, Luci 1953- DLB-175
The Mark Taper Forum DLB-7
Taradash, Daniel 1913- DLB-44
Tarasov-Rodionov, Aleksandr Ignat'evich
    1885-1938 . . . . DLB-272
Tarbell, Ida M. 1857-1944 . . . . DLB-47
Tardivel, Jules-Paul 1851-1905 . . . . DLB-99
Targan, Barry 1932- DLB-130
    Tribute to John Gardner Y-82
Tarkington, Booth 1869-1946 . . . . DLB-9, 102
Tashlin, Frank 1913-1972 . . . . DLB-44
Tasma (Jessie Couvreur) 1848-1897 . . . . DLB-230
Tate, Allen 1899-1979 . . . . . . DLB-4, 45, 63; DS-17
Tate, James 1943- DLB-5, 169
Tate, Nahum circa 1652-1715 . . . . DLB-80
Tatian circa 830 . . . . DLB-148
Taufer, Veno 1933- DLB-181
Tauler, Johannes circa 1300-1361 . . . . DLB-179
Tavčar, Ivan 1851-1923 . . . . DLB-147
Taverner, Richard ca. 1505-1575 . . . . DLB-236
Taylor, Ann 1782-1866 . . . . DLB-163
Taylor, Bayard 1825-1878 . . . . . DLB-3, 189, 250
Taylor, Bert Leston 1866-1921 . . . . DLB-25
Taylor, Charles H. 1846-1921 . . . . DLB-25
Taylor, Edward circa 1642-1729 . . . . DLB-24
Taylor, Elizabeth 1912-1975 . . . . DLB-139
Taylor, Sir Henry 1800-1886 . . . . DLB-32
Taylor, Henry 1942- DLB-5
    Who Owns American Literature Y-94
Taylor, Jane 1783-1824 . . . . DLB-163
Taylor, Jeremy circa 1613-1667 . . . . DLB-151
Taylor, John 1577 or 1578 - 1653 . . . . DLB-121
Taylor, Mildred D. 1943- DLB-52
Taylor, Peter 1917-1994 . . . DLB-218, 278; Y-81, 94
Taylor, Susie King 1848-1912 . . . . DLB-221
Taylor, William Howland 1901-1966 . . . DLB-241
William Taylor and Company DLB-49
Teale, Edwin Way 1899-1980 . . . . DLB-275
Teasdale, Sara 1884-1933 . . . . DLB-45
Teillier, Jorge 1935-1996 . . . . DLB-283
Telles, Lygia Fagundes 1924- DLB-113
The Temper of the West: William Jovanovich . . . Y-02
Temple, William 1555?-1627 . . . . DLB-281
Temple, Sir William 1628-1699 . . . . DLB-101
Temple, William F. 1914-1989 . . . . DLB-255
Temrizov, A. (see Marchenko, Anastasia Iakov-
    levna)
Tench, Watkin ca. 1758-1833 . . . . DLB-230

Tender Is the Night (Documentary) DLB-273	Writing for the Theatre, by Harold Pinter DLB-13	Eugene O'Neill Memorial Theater Center DLB-7
Tenn, William 1919- DLB-8	The Year in Drama Y-82–85, 87–98	The Goodman Theatre DLB-7
Tennant, Emma 1937- DLB-14	The Year in U.S. Drama Y-00	The Guthrie Theater DLB-7
Tenney, Tabitha Gilman 1762-1837 . . DLB-37, 200	Theater, English and Irish	The Mark Taper Forum DLB-7
Tennyson, Alfred 1809-1892 . . DLB-32; CDBLB-4	Anti-Theatrical Tracts DLB-263	The National Theatre and the Royal Shakespeare Company: The National Companies DLB-13
On Some of the Characteristics of Modern Poetry and On the Lyrical Poems of Alfred Tennyson (1831) DLB-32	The Chester Plays circa 1505-1532; revisions until 1575 . . . . DLB-146	Off-Loop Theatres DLB-7
	Dangerous Years: London Theater, 1939-1945 . . . . DLB-10	The Royal Court Theatre and the English Stage Company DLB-13
Tennyson, Frederick 1807-1898 . . . . DLB-32	A Defense of Actors DLB-263	The Royal Court Theatre and the New Drama DLB-10
Tenorio, Arthur 1924- DLB-209	The Development of Lighting in the Staging of Drama, 1900-1945 . . . . DLB-10	
Tepl, Johannes von circa 1350-1414/1415 . . . . DLB-179	Education DLB-263	The Takarazaka Revue Company Y-91
Tepliakov, Viktor Grigor'evich 1804-1842 . . . . DLB-205	The End of English Stage Censorship, 1945-1968 . . . . DLB-13	Thegan and the Astronomer flourished circa 850 . . . . DLB-148
Terence circa 184 B.C.-159 B.C. or after DLB-211; CDWLB-1	Epigrams and Satires DLB-263	Thelwall, John 1764-1834 . . . . DLB-93, 158
	Eyewitnesses and Historians DLB-263	Theocritus circa 300 B.C.-260 B.C. DLB-176
Terhune, Albert Payson 1872-1942 . . . . DLB-9	Fringe and Alternative Theater in Great Britain DLB-13	Theodorescu, Ion N. (see Arghezi, Tudor)
Terhune, Mary Virginia 1830-1922 . . . . DS-13		Theodulf circa 760-circa 821 . . . . DLB-148
Terpigorev, Sergei Nikolaevich (S. Atava) 1841-1895 . . . . DLB-277	The Great War and the Theater, 1914-1918 [Great Britain] DLB-10	Theophrastus circa 371 B.C.-287 B.C. DLB-176
	Licensing Act of 1737 . . . . DLB-84	Thériault, Yves 1915-1983 . . . . DLB-88
Terry, Megan 1932- DLB-7, 249	Morality Plays: *Mankind* circa 1450-1500 and *Everyman* circa 1500 . . . . DLB-146	Thério, Adrien 1925- DLB-53
Terson, Peter 1932- DLB-13		Theroux, Paul 1941- . . . DLB-2, 218; CDALB-7
Tesich, Steve 1943-1996 . . . . Y-83	The New Variorum Shakespeare Y-85	Thesiger, Wilfred 1910- DLB-204
Tessa, Delio 1886-1939 . . . . DLB-114	N-Town Plays circa 1468 to early sixteenth century DLB-146	They All Came to Paris DS-15
Testori, Giovanni 1923-1993 . . . . DLB-128, 177	Politics and the Theater DLB-263	Thibaudeau, Colleen 1925- DLB-88
Texas	Practical Matters DLB-263	Thielen, Benedict 1903-1965 . . . . DLB-102
The Year in Texas Literature Y-98	Prologues, Epilogues, Epistles to Readers, and Excerpts from Plays DLB-263	Thiong'o Ngugi wa (see Ngugi wa Thiong'o)
Tey, Josephine 1896?-1952 . . . . DLB-77		*This Quarter* 1925-1927, 1929-1932 . . . . . DS-15
Thacher, James 1754-1844 . . . . DLB-37		Thoma, Ludwig 1867-1921 . . . . DLB-66
Thacher, John Boyd 1847-1909 . . . . DLB-187	The Publication of English Renaissance Plays DLB-62	Thoma, Richard 1902- DLB-4
Thackeray, William Makepeace 1811-1863 . . . DLB-21, 55, 159, 163; CDBLB-4	Regulations for the Theater DLB-263	Thomas, Audrey 1935- DLB-60
	Sources for the Study of Tudor and Stuart Drama DLB-62	Thomas, D. M. 1935- DLB-40, 207; CDBLB-8
Thames and Hudson Limited DLB-112		
Thanet, Octave (see French, Alice)	Stage Censorship: "The Rejected Statement" (1911), by Bernard Shaw [excerpts] DLB-10	The Plagiarism Controversy Y-82
Thaxter, Celia Laighton 1835-1894 . . . . . . DLB-239		Thomas, Dylan 1914-1953 . . . . DLB-13, 20, 139; CDBLB-7
Thayer, Caroline Matilda Warren 1785-1844 . . . . DLB-200	Synge Summer School: J. M. Synge and the Irish Theater, Rathdrum, County Wiclow, Ireland Y-93	The Dylan Thomas Celebration Y-99
Thayer, Douglas H. 1929- DLB-256		Thomas, Edward 1878-1917 . . . . DLB-19, 98, 156, 216
Theater	The Theater in Shakespeare's Time . . DLB-62	
Black Theatre: A Forum [excerpts] DLB-38	The Theatre Guild DLB-7	The Friends of the Dymock Poets . . . Y-00
Community and Commentators: Black Theatre and Its Critics DLB-38	The Townely Plays fifteenth and sixteenth centuries DLB-146	Thomas, Frederick William 1806-1866 . . . DLB-202
German Drama from Naturalism to Fascism: 1889-1933 . . . . DLB-118	The Year in British Drama Y-99–01	Thomas, Gwyn 1913-1981 . . . . DLB-15, 245
A Look at the Contemporary Black Theatre Movement DLB-38	The Year in Drama: London Y-90	Thomas, Isaiah 1750-1831 . . . . DLB-43, 73, 187
	The Year in London Theatre Y-92	Thomas, Johann 1624-1679 . . . . DLB-168
The Lord Chamberlain's Office and Stage Censorship in England DLB-10	*A Yorkshire Tragedy* DLB-58	Thomas, John 1900-1932 . . . . DLB-4
New Forces at Work in the American Theatre: 1915-1925 . . . . DLB-7	Theaters The Abbey Theatre and Irish Drama, 1900-1945 . . . . DLB-10	Thomas, Joyce Carol 1938- DLB-33
		Thomas, Lewis 1913-1993 . . . . DLB-275
Off Broadway and Off-Off Broadway . . DLB-7		Thomas, Lorenzo 1944- DLB-41
Oregon Shakespeare Festival Y-00	Actors Theatre of Louisville DLB-7	Thomas, R. S. 1915-2000 . . . . . DLB-27; CDBLB-8
Plays, Playwrights, and Playgoers DLB-84	American Conservatory Theatre DLB-7	Isaiah Thomas [publishing house] DLB-49
Playwrights on the Theater DLB-80	Arena Stage DLB-7	Thomasîn von Zerclære circa 1186-circa 1259 . . . . DLB-138
Playwrights and Professors DLB-13	Black Theaters and Theater Organizations in America, 1961-1982: A Research List DLB-38	
Producing *Dear Bunny, Dear Volodya:* *The Friendship and the Feud* Y-97		Thomason, George 1602?-1666 . . . . DLB-213
		Thomasius, Christian 1655-1728 . . . . DLB-168
Viewpoint: Politics and Performance, by David Edgar DLB-13	The Dallas Theater Center DLB-7	Thompson, Daniel Pierce 1795-1868 . . . . DLB-202

Thompson, David 1770-1857 .... DLB-99
Thompson, Dorothy 1893-1961 .... DLB-29
Thompson, E. P. 1924-1993 .... DLB-242
Thompson, Flora 1876-1947 .... DLB-240
Thompson, Francis
  1859-1907 .... DLB-19; CDBLB-5
Thompson, George Selden (see Selden, George)
Thompson, Henry Yates 1838-1928 ..... DLB-184
Thompson, Hunter S. 1939- DLB-185
Thompson, Jim 1906-1977 .... DLB-226
Thompson, John 1938-1976 .... DLB-60
Thompson, John R. 1823-1873 .... DLB-3, 73, 248
Thompson, Lawrance 1906-1973 ...... DLB-103
Thompson, Maurice 1844-1901 ...... DLB-71, 74
Thompson, Ruth Plumly 1891-1976 ..... DLB-22
Thompson, Thomas Phillips 1843-1933 ... DLB-99
Thompson, William 1775-1833 .... DLB-158
Thompson, William Tappan
  1812-1882 .... DLB-3, 11, 248
Thomson, Cockburn
  "Modern Style" (1857) [excerpt] DLB-57
Thomson, Edward William 1849-1924 ... DLB-92
Thomson, James 1700-1748 .... DLB-95
Thomson, James 1834-1882 .... DLB-35
Thomson, Joseph 1858-1895 .... DLB-174
Thomson, Mortimer 1831-1875 .... DLB-11
Thomson, Rupert 1955- DLB-267
Thon, Melanie Rae 1957- DLB-244
Thoreau, Henry David 1817-1862
  ...... DLB-1, 183, 223, 270; DS-5; CDALB-2
  The Thoreau Society Y-99
  The Thoreauvian Pilgrimage: The
    Structure of an American Cult .. DLB-223
Thorne, William 1568?-1630 .... DLB-281
Thornton, John F.
  [Repsonse to Ken Auletta] Y-97
Thorpe, Adam 1956- DLB-231
Thorpe, Thomas Bangs
  1815-1878 .... DLB-3, 11, 248
Thorup, Kirsten 1942- DLB-214
Thrale, Hester Lynch
  (see Piozzi, Hester Lynch [Thrale])
Thubron, Colin 1939- DLB-204, 231
Thucydides
  circa 455 B.C.-circa 395 B.C. DLB-176
Thulstrup, Thure de 1848-1930 .... DLB-188
Thümmel, Moritz August von
  1738-1817 .... DLB-97
Thurber, James
  1894-1961 .... DLB-4, 11, 22, 102; CDALB-5
Thurman, Wallace 1902-1934 .... DLB-51
  "Negro Poets and Their Poetry" DLB-50
Thwaite, Anthony 1930- DLB-40
  The Booker Prize, Address Y-86
Thwaites, Reuben Gold 1853-1913 ..... DLB-47
Tibullus circa 54 B.C.-circa 19 B.C. DLB-211
Ticknor, George 1791-1871 .. DLB-1, 59, 140, 235
Ticknor and Fields DLB-49

Ticknor and Fields (revived) DLB-46
Tieck, Ludwig 1773-1853 .... DLB-90; CDWLB-2
Tietjens, Eunice 1884-1944 .... DLB-54
Tikkanen, Märta 1935- DLB-257
Tilghman, Christopher circa 1948 ...... DLB-244
Tilney, Edmund circa 1536-1610 .... DLB-136
Charles Tilt [publishing house] DLB-106
J. E. Tilton and Company DLB-49
Time-Life Books DLB-46
Times Books DLB-46
Timothy, Peter circa 1725-1782 .... DLB-43
Timrava 1867-1951 .... DLB-215
Timrod, Henry 1828-1867 .... DLB-3, 248
Tindal, Henrietta 1818?-1879 .... DLB-199
Tinker, Chauncey Brewster 1876-1963 .. DLB-140
Tinsley Brothers DLB-106
Tiptree, James, Jr. 1915-1987 .... DLB-8
Tišma, Aleksandar 1924- DLB-181
Titus, Edward William
  1870-1952 .... DLB-4; DS-15
Tiutchev, Fedor Ivanovich 1803-1873 ... DLB-205
Tlali, Miriam 1933- DLB-157, 225
Todd, Barbara Euphan 1890-1976 ...... DLB-160
Todorov, Tzvetan 1939- DLB-242
Tofte, Robert
  1561 or 1562-1619 or 1620 .... DLB-172
Tóibín, Colm 1955- DLB-271
Toklas, Alice B. 1877-1967 .... DLB-4; DS-15
Tokuda Shūsei 1872-1943 .... DLB-180
Toland, John 1670-1722 .... DLB-252
Tolkien, J. R. R.
  1892-1973 ...... DLB-15, 160, 255; CDBLB-6
Toller, Ernst 1893-1939 .... DLB-124
Tollet, Elizabeth 1694-1754 .... DLB-95
Tolson, Melvin B. 1898-1966 .... DLB-48, 76
Tolstoy, Aleksei Konstantinovich
  1817-1875 .... DLB-238
Tolstoy, Aleksei Nikolaevich 1883-1945 ..DLB-272
Tolstoy, Leo 1828-1910 .... DLB-238
Tomalin, Claire 1933- DLB-155
Tomasi di Lampedusa, Giuseppe
  1896-1957 .... DLB-177
Tomlinson, Charles 1927- DLB-40
Tomlinson, H. M. 1873-1958 ... DLB-36, 100, 195
Abel Tompkins [publishing house] DLB-49
Tompson, Benjamin 1642-1714 .... DLB-24
Tomson, Graham R.
  (see Watson, Rosamund Marriott)
Ton'a 1289-1372 .... DLB-203
Tondelli, Pier Vittorio 1955-1991 ...... DLB-196
Tonks, Rosemary 1932- DLB-14, 207
Tonna, Charlotte Elizabeth 1790-1846 ... DLB-163
Jacob Tonson the Elder
  [publishing house] DLB-170
Toole, John Kennedy 1937-1969 .... Y-81
Toomer, Jean 1894-1967 .. DLB-45, 51; CDALB-4

Tor Books DLB-46
Torberg, Friedrich 1908-1979 .... DLB-85
Torrence, Ridgely 1874-1950 ...... DLB-54, 249
Torres-Metzger, Joseph V. 1933- DLB-122
Toth, Susan Allen 1940- Y-86
Richard Tottell [publishing house] DLB-170
  "The Printer to the Reader,"
    (1557) DLB-167
Tough-Guy Literature DLB-9
Touré, Askia Muhammad 1938- DLB-41
Tourgée, Albion W. 1838-1905 .... DLB-79
Tournemir, Elizaveta Sailhas de (see Tur, Evgeniia)
Tourneur, Cyril circa 1580-1626 .... DLB-58
Tournier, Michel 1924- DLB-83
Frank Tousey [publishing house] DLB-49
Tower Publications DLB-46
Towne, Benjamin circa 1740-1793 ...... DLB-43
Towne, Robert 1936- DLB-44
The Townely Plays fifteenth and sixteenth
  centuries DLB-146
Townsend, Sue 1946- DLB-271
Townshend, Aurelian
  by 1583-circa 1651 .... DLB-121
Toy, Barbara 1908-2001 .... DLB-204
Tozzi, Federigo 1883-1920 .... DLB-264
Tracy, Honor 1913-1989 .... DLB-15
Traherne, Thomas 1637?-1674 .... DLB-131
Traill, Catharine Parr 1802-1899 .... DLB-99
Train, Arthur 1875-1945 .... DLB-86; DS-16
Tranquilli, Secondino (see Silone, Ignazio)
The Transatlantic Publishing Company .. DLB-49
The Transatlantic Review 1924-1925 .... DS-15
The Transcendental Club
  1836-1840 .... DLB-1; DLB-223
Transcendentalism DLB-1; DLB-223; DS-5
  "A Response from America," by
    John A. Heraud DS-5
  Publications and Social Movements ... DLB-1
  The Rise of Transcendentalism,
    1815-1860 .... DS-5
  Transcendentalists, American DS-5
  "What Is Transcendentalism? By a
    Thinking Man," by James
    Kinnard Jr. DS-5
transition 1927-1938 .... DS-15
Tranströmer, Tomas 1931- DLB-257
Travel Writing
  American Travel Writing, 1776-1864
    (checklist) DLB-183
  British Travel Writing, 1940-1997
    (checklist) DLB-204
  (1876-1909 .... DLB-174
  (1837-1875 .... DLB-166
  (1910-1939 .... DLB-195
Traven, B. 1882?/1890?-1969? DLB-9, 56
Travers, Ben 1886-1980 .... DLB-10, 233
Travers, P. L. (Pamela Lyndon)
  1899-1996 .... DLB-160

Trediakovsky, Vasilii Kirillovich
1703-1769. . . . . .DLB-150

Treece, Henry 1911-1966 . . . . .DLB-160

Treitel, Jonathan 1959- DLB-267

Trejo, Ernesto 1950-1991 . . . . .DLB-122

Trelawny, Edward John
1792-1881 . . . . DLB-110, 116, 144

Tremain, Rose 1943- DLB-14, 271

Tremblay, Michel 1942- DLB-60

Trent, William P. 1862-1939. . . . . DLB-47, 71

Trescot, William Henry 1822-1898. . . . . . .DLB-30

Tressell, Robert (Robert Phillipe Noonan)
1870-1911 . . . . .DLB-197

Trevelyan, Sir George Otto
1838-1928 . . . . .DLB-144

Trevisa, John circa 1342-circa 1402. . . . . .DLB-146

Trevor, William 1928- DLB-14, 139

Trierer Floyris circa 1170-1180 . . . . .DLB-138

Trillin, Calvin 1935- DLB-185

Trilling, Lionel 1905-1975 . . . . .DLB-28, 63

Trilussa 1871-1950. . . . . .DLB-114

Trimmer, Sarah 1741-1810 . . . . .DLB-158

Triolet, Elsa 1896-1970 . . . . .DLB-72

Tripp, John 1927- DLB-40

Trocchi, Alexander 1925-1984 . . . . .DLB-15

Troisi, Dante 1920-1989 . . . . .DLB-196

Trollope, Anthony
1815-1882 . . . . DLB-21, 57, 159; CDBLB-4

Novel-Reading: *The Works of Charles
Dickens; The Works of W. Makepeace
Thackeray* (1879) DLB-21

The Trollope Societies Y-00

Trollope, Frances 1779-1863 . . . . . . .DLB-21, 166

Trollope, Joanna 1943- DLB-207

Troop, Elizabeth 1931- DLB-14

Trotter, Catharine 1679-1749. . . . . .DLB-84, 252

Trotti, Lamar 1898-1952. . . . . .DLB-44

Trottier, Pierre 1925- DLB-60

Trotzig, Birgitta 1929- DLB-257

Troupe, Quincy Thomas, Jr. 1943- DLB-41

John F. Trow and Company DLB-49

Trowbridge, John Townsend 1827-1916 . .DLB-202

Trudel, Jean-Louis 1967- DLB-251

Truillier-Lacombe, Joseph-Patrice
1807-1863 . . . . .DLB-99

Trumbo, Dalton 1905-1976 . . . . .DLB-26

Trumbull, Benjamin 1735-1820 . . . . .DLB-30

Trumbull, John 1750-1831. . . . . .DLB-31

Trumbull, John 1756-1843. . . . . .DLB-183

Truth, Sojourner 1797?-1883 . . . . .DLB-239

Tscherning, Andreas 1611-1659 . . . . .DLB-164

Tsubouchi Shōyō 1859-1935 . . . . .DLB-180

Tuchman, Barbara W.
Tribute to Alfred A. Knopf Y-84

Tucholsky, Kurt 1890-1935. . . . . .DLB-56

Tucker, Charlotte Maria
1821-1893 . . . . .DLB-163, 190

Tucker, George 1775-1861. . . . . . .DLB-3, 30, 248

Tucker, James 1808?-1866? DLB-230

Tucker, Nathaniel Beverley
1784-1851 . . . . .DLB-3, 248

Tucker, St. George 1752-1827 . . . . .DLB-37

Tuckerman, Frederick Goddard
1821-1873 . . . . .DLB-243

Tuckerman, Henry Theodore 1813-1871 . .DLB-64

Tumas, Juozas (see Vaizgantas)

Tunis, John R. 1889-1975 . . . . DLB-22, 171

Tunstall, Cuthbert 1474-1559 . . . . .DLB-132

Tunström, Göran 1937-2000 . . . . .DLB-257

Tuohy, Frank 1925- DLB-14, 139

Tupper, Martin F. 1810-1889 . . . . .DLB-32

Tur, Evgeniia 1815-1892 . . . . .DLB-238

Turbyfill, Mark 1896-1991 . . . . .DLB-45

Turco, Lewis 1934- Y-84

Tribute to John Ciardi Y-86

Turgenev, Aleksandr Ivanovich
1784-1845 . . . . .DLB-198

Turgenev, Ivan Sergeevich 1818-1883. . . .DLB-238

Turnbull, Alexander H. 1868-1918 . . . . . .DLB-184

Turnbull, Andrew 1921-1970 . . . . .DLB-103

Turnbull, Gael 1928- DLB-40

Turner, Arlin 1909-1980 . . . . .DLB-103

Turner, Charles (Tennyson) 1808-1879 . . .DLB-32

Turner, Ethel 1872-1958 . . . . .DLB-230

Turner, Frederick 1943- DLB-40

Turner, Frederick Jackson
1861-1932 . . . . DLB-17, 186

A Conversation between William Riggan
and Janette Turner Hospital Y-02

Turner, Joseph Addison 1826-1868. . . . . .DLB-79

Turpin, Waters Edward 1910-1968. . . . . .DLB-51

Turrini, Peter 1944- DLB-124

Tutuola, Amos 1920-1997 . . . DLB-125; CDWLB-3

Twain, Mark (see Clemens, Samuel Langhorne)

Tweedie, Ethel Brilliana circa 1860-1940 . DLB-174

A Century of Poetry, a Lifetime of Collecting:
J. M. Edelstein's Collection of Twentieth-
Century American Poetry Y-02

Twombly, Wells 1935-1977. . . . . .DLB-241

Twysden, Sir Roger 1597-1672 . . . . .DLB-213

Tyler, Anne
1941- DLB-6, 143; Y-82; CDALB-7

Tyler, Mary Palmer 1775-1866 . . . . .DLB-200

Tyler, Moses Coit 1835-1900 . . . . DLB-47, 64

Tyler, Royall 1757-1826. . . . . .DLB-37

Tylor, Edward Burnett 1832-1917. . . . . . .DLB-57

Tynan, Katharine 1861-1931. . . . . . .DLB-153, 240

Tyndale, William circa 1494-1536. . . . . . .DLB-132

U

Uchida, Yoshika 1921-1992 . . . . .CDALB-7

Udall, Nicholas 1504-1556 . . . . .DLB-62

Ugrešić, Dubravka 1949- DLB-181

Uhland, Ludwig 1787-1862 . . . . .DLB-90

Uhse, Bodo 1904-1963 . . . . .DLB-69

Ujević, Augustin ("Tin") 1891-1955 . . . . .DLB-147

Ulenhart, Niclas flourished circa 1600. . . .DLB-164

Ulibarrí, Sabine R. 1919- DLB-82

Ulica, Jorge 1870-1926 . . . . .DLB-82

Ulivi, Ferruccio 1912- DLB-196

Ulizio, B. George 1889-1969 . . . . .DLB-140

Ulrich von Liechtenstein
circa 1200-circa 1275 . . . . .DLB-138

Ulrich von Zatzikhoven
before 1194-after 1214 . . . . .DLB-138

Unaipon, David 1872-1967 . . . . .DLB-230

Unamuno, Miguel de 1864-1936. . . . . . . .DLB-108

Under, Marie 1883-1980 . . . DLB-220; CDWLB-4

Underhill, Evelyn 1875-1941. . . . . .DLB-240

Ungaretti, Giuseppe 1888-1970 . . . . .DLB-114

Unger, Friederike Helene 1741-1813 . . . . .DLB-94

United States Book Company DLB-49

Universal Publishing and Distributing
Corporation .DLB-46

University of Colorado
Special Collections at the University of
Colorado at Boulder Y-98

Indiana University Press Y-02

The University of Iowa
Writers' Workshop Golden Jubilee Y-86

University of Missouri Press Y-01

University of South Carolina
The G. Ross Roy Scottish Poetry Collection
. . . . Y-89

Two Hundred Years of Rare Books and
Literary Collections at the
University of South Carolina Y-00

The University of South Carolina Press Y-94

University of Virginia
The Book Arts Press at the University
of Virginia Y-96

The Electronic Text Center and the
Electronic Archive of Early American
Fiction at the University of Virginia
Library Y-98

University of Virginia Libraries Y-91

University of Wales Press DLB-112

University Press of Florida Y-00

University Press of Kansas Y-98

University Press of Mississippi Y-99

Uno Chiyo 1897-1996 . . . . .DLB-180

Unruh, Fritz von 1885-1970. . . . . .DLB-56, 118

Unsworth, Barry 1930- DLB-194

Unt, Mati 1944- DLB-232

The Unterberg Poetry Center of the
92nd Street Y Y-98

T. Fisher Unwin [publishing house] DLB-106

Upchurch, Boyd B. (see Boyd, John)

Updike, John 1932- DLB-2, 5, 143, 218, 227;
Y-80, 82; DS-3; CDALB-6

John Updike on the Internet Y-97

Tribute to Alfred A. Knopf Y-84

Tribute to John Ciardi. Y-86

Upīts, Andrejs 1877-1970 . . . . .DLB-220

Cumulative Index

Upton, Bertha 1849-1912 .... DLB-141
Upton, Charles 1948- DLB-16
Upton, Florence K. 1873-1922 .... DLB-141
Upward, Allen 1863-1926 .... DLB-36
Urban, Milo 1904-1982 .... DLB-215
Ureña de Henríquez, Salomé
  1850-1897 .... DLB-283
Urfé, Honoré d' 1567-1625 .... DLB-268
Urista, Alberto Baltazar (see Alurista)
Urquhart, Fred 1912-1995 .... DLB-139
Urrea, Luis Alberto 1955- DLB-209
Urzidil, Johannes 1896-1970 .... DLB-85
U.S.A. (Documentary) DLB-274
Usk, Thomas died 1388 .... DLB-146
Uslar Pietri, Arturo 1906-2001 .... DLB-113
Uspensky, Gleb Ivanovich 1843-1902 ....DLB-277
Ussher, James 1581-1656 .... DLB-213
Ustinov, Peter 1921- DLB-13
Uttley, Alison 1884-1976 .... DLB-160
Uz, Johann Peter 1720-1796 .... DLB-97

V

Vadianus, Joachim 1484-1551 ....DLB-179
Vac, Bertrand (Aimé Pelletier) 1914- ... DLB-88
Vācietis, Ojārs 1933-1983 .... DLB-232
Vaculík, Ludvík 1926- DLB-232
Vaičiulaitis, Antanas 1906-1992 .... DLB-220
Vaičiūnaite, Judita 1937- DLB-232
Vail, Laurence 1891-1968 .... DLB-4
Vailland, Roger 1907-1965 .... DLB-83
Vaižgantas 1869-1933 .... DLB-220
Vajda, Ernest 1887-1954 .... DLB-44
Valdés, Gina 1943- DLB-122
Valdez, Luis Miguel 1940- DLB-122
Valduga, Patrizia 1953- DLB-128
Vale Press DLB-112
Valente, José Angel 1929-2000 .... DLB-108
Valenzuela, Luisa 1938- .. DLB-113; CDWLB-3
Valeri, Diego 1887-1976 .... DLB-128
Valerius Flaccus fl. circa A.D. 92 .... DLB-211
Valerius Maximus fl. circa A.D. 31 ..... DLB-211
Valéry, Paul 1871-1945 .... DLB-258
Valesio, Paolo 1939- DLB-196
Valgardson, W. D. 1939- DLB-60
Valle, Víctor Manuel 1950- DLB-122
Valle-Inclán, Ramón del 1866-1936 .... DLB-134
Vallejo, Armando 1949- DLB-122
Vallès, Jules 1832-1885 .... DLB-123
Vallette, Marguerite Eymery (see Rachilde)
Valverde, José María 1926-1996 .... DLB-108
Van Allsburg, Chris 1949- DLB-61
Van Anda, Carr 1864-1945 .... DLB-25
Vanbrugh, Sir John 1664-1726 .... DLB-80
Vance, Jack 1916?- DLB-8

Vančura, Vladislav
  1891-1942 .... DLB-215; CDWLB-4
van der Post, Laurens 1906-1996 .... DLB-204
Van Dine, S. S. (see Wright, Williard Huntington)
Van Doren, Mark 1894-1972 .... DLB-45
van Druten, John 1901-1957 .... DLB-10
Van Duyn, Mona 1921- DLB-5
  Tribute to James Dickey Y-97
Van Dyke, Henry 1852-1933 .... DLB-71; DS-13
Van Dyke, Henry 1928- DLB-33
Van Dyke, John C. 1856-1932 .... DLB-186
Vane, Sutton 1888-1963 .... DLB-10
Vanguard Press DLB-46
van Gulik, Robert Hans 1910-1967 .... DS-17
van Itallie, Jean-Claude 1936- DLB-7
Van Loan, Charles E. 1876-1919 ....DLB-171
Vann, Robert L. 1879-1940 .... DLB-29
Van Rensselaer, Mariana Griswold
  1851-1934 .... DLB-47
Van Rensselaer, Mrs. Schuyler
  (see Van Rensselaer, Mariana Griswold)
Van Vechten, Carl 1880-1964 ...... DLB-4, 9, 51
van Vogt, A. E. 1912-2000 .... DLB-8, 251
Vargas Llosa, Mario
  1936- DLB-145; CDWLB-3
  Acceptance Speech for the Ritz Paris
    Hemingway Award Y-85
Varley, John 1947- Y-81
Varnhagen von Ense, Karl August
  1785-1858 .... DLB-90
Varnhagen von Ense, Rahel
  1771-1833 .... DLB-90
Varro 116 B.C.-27 B.C. DLB-211
Vasiliu, George (see Bacovia, George)
Vásquez, Richard 1928- DLB-209
Vásquez Montalbán, Manuel 1939- ... DLB-134
Vassa, Gustavus (see Equiano, Olaudah)
Vassalli, Sebastiano 1941- DLB-128, 196
Vaugelas, Claude Favre de 1585-1650 ....DLB-268
Vaughan, Henry 1621-1695 .... DLB-131
Vaughan, Thomas 1621-1666 .... DLB-131
Vaughn, Robert 1592?-1667 .... DLB-213
Vaux, Thomas, Lord 1509-1556 .... DLB-132
Vazov, Ivan 1850-1921 ...... DLB-147; CDWLB-4
Véa, Alfredo, Jr. 1950- DLB-209
Veblen, Thorstein 1857-1929 .... DLB-246
Vega, Janine Pommy 1942- DLB-16
Veiller, Anthony 1903-1965 .... DLB-44
Velásquez-Trevino, Gloria 1949- DLB-122
Veley, Margaret 1843-1887 .... DLB-199
Velleius Paterculus
  circa 20 B.C.-circa A.D. 30 .... DLB-211
Veloz Maggiolo, Marcio 1936- DLB-145
Vel'tman, Aleksandr Fomich
  1800-1870 .... DLB-198
Venegas, Daniel ?-? DLB-82

Venevitinov, Dmitrii Vladimirovich
  1805-1827 .... DLB-205
Vergil, Polydore circa 1470-1555 .... DLB-132
Veríssimo, Erico 1905-1975 .... DLB-145
Verlaine, Paul 1844-1896 .... DLB-217
Verne, Jules 1828-1905 .... DLB-123
Verplanck, Gulian C. 1786-1870 .... DLB-59
Very, Jones 1813-1880 .... DLB-1, 243; DS-5
Vian, Boris 1920-1959 .... DLB-72
Viazemsky, Petr Andreevich
  1792-1878 .... DLB-205
Vicars, Thomas 1591-1638 .... DLB-236
Vickers, Roy 1888?-1965 .... DLB-77
Vickery, Sukey 1779-1821 .... DLB-200
Victoria 1819-1901 .... DLB-55
Victoria Press DLB-106
Vidal, Gore 1925- DLB-6, 152; CDALB-7
Vidal, Mary Theresa 1815-1873 .... DLB-230
Vidmer, Richards 1898-1978 .... DLB-241
Viebig, Clara 1860-1952 .... DLB-66
Viereck, George Sylvester 1884-1962 ..... DLB-54
Viereck, Peter 1916- DLB-5
Vietnam War (ended 1975)
  Resources for the Study of Vietnam War
    Literature DLB-9
Viets, Roger 1738-1811 .... DLB-99
Vigil-Piñon, Evangelina 1949- DLB-122
Vigneault, Gilles 1928- DLB-60
Vigny, Alfred de
  1797-1863 .... DLB-119, 192, 217
Vigolo, Giorgio 1894-1983 .... DLB-114
The Viking Press DLB-46
Vilde, Eduard 1865-1933 .... DLB-220
Vilinskaia, Mariia Aleksandrovna
  (see Vovchok, Marko)
Villanueva, Alma Luz 1944- DLB-122
Villanueva, Tino 1941- DLB-82
Villard, Henry 1835-1900 .... DLB-23
Villard, Oswald Garrison 1872-1949 .. DLB-25, 91
Villarreal, Edit 1944- DLB-209
Villarreal, José Antonio 1924- DLB-82
Villaseñor, Victor 1940- DLB-209
Villedieu, Madame de (Marie-Catherine
  Desjardins) 1640?-1683 ....DLB-268
Villegas de Magnón, Leonor
  1876-1955 .... DLB-122
Villehardouin, Geoffroi de
  circa 1150-1215 .... DLB-208
Villemaire, Yolande 1949- DLB-60
Villena, Luis Antonio de 1951- DLB-134
Villiers, George, Second Duke
  of Buckingham 1628-1687 .... DLB-80
Villiers de l'Isle-Adam, Jean-Marie
  Mathias Philippe-Auguste,
  Comte de 1838-1889 .... DLB-123, 192
Villon, François 1431-circa 1463? DLB-208
Vine Press DLB-112
Viorst, Judith ?- DLB-52

Vipont, Elfrida (Elfrida Vipont Foulds,
    Charles Vipont) 1902-1992 .... DLB-160
Viramontes, Helena María 1954- DLB-122
Virgil 70 B.C.-19 B.C. DLB-211; CDWLB-1
Vischer, Friedrich Theodor 1807-1887.... DLB-133
Vitier, Cintio 1921- DLB-283
Vitruvius circa 85 B.C.-circa 15 B.C..... DLB-211
Vitry, Philippe de 1291-1361 .... DLB-208
Vittorini, Elio 1908-1966 .... DLB-264
Vivanco, Luis Felipe 1907-1975 .... DLB-108
Vivian, E. Charles (Charles Henry Cannell,
    Charles Henry Vivian, Jack Mann,
    Barry Lynd) 1882-1947 .... DLB-255
Viviani, Cesare 1947- DLB-128
Vivien, Renée 1877-1909 .... DLB-217
Vizenor, Gerald 1934- DLB-175, 227
Vizetelly and Company DLB-106
Voaden, Herman 1903-1991 .... DLB-88
Voß, Johann Heinrich 1751-1826 .... DLB-90
Vogau, Boris Andreevich
    (see Pil'niak, Boris Andreevich)
Voigt, Ellen Bryant 1943- DLB-120
Vojnović, Ivo 1857-1929 ..... DLB-147; CDWLB-4
Volkoff, Vladimir 1932- DLB-83
P. F. Volland Company DLB-46
Vollbehr, Otto H. F.
    1872?-1945 or 1946 .... DLB-187
Vologdin (see Zasodimsky, Pavel Vladimirovich)
Volponi, Paolo 1924-1994 .... DLB-177
Vonarburg, Élisabeth 1947- DLB-251
von der Grün, Max 1926- DLB-75
Vonnegut, Kurt 1922-
    .... DLB-2, 8, 152; Y-80; DS-3; CDALB-6
    Tribute to Isaac Asimov Y-92
    Tribute to Richard Brautigan Y-84
Voranc, Prežihov 1893-1950 .... DLB-147
Voronsky, Aleksandr Konstantinovich
    1884-1937 .... DLB-272
Vovchok, Marko 1833-1907 .... DLB-238
Voynich, E. L. 1864-1960 .... DLB-197
Vroman, Mary Elizabeth circa 1924-1967 .. DLB-33

W

Wace, Robert ("Maistre")
    circa 1100-circa 1175 .... DLB-146
Wackenroder, Wilhelm Heinrich
    1773-1798 .... DLB-90
Wackernagel, Wilhelm 1806-1869 ...... DLB-133
Waddell, Helen 1889-1965 .... DLB-240
Waddington, Miriam 1917- DLB-68
Wade, Henry 1887-1969 .... DLB-77
Wagenknecht, Edward 1900- DLB-103
Wägner, Elin 1882-1949 .... DLB-259
Wagner, Heinrich Leopold 1747-1779 .... DLB-94
Wagner, Henry R. 1862-1957 .... DLB-140
Wagner, Richard 1813-1883 .... DLB-129
Wagoner, David 1926- DLB-5, 256

Wah, Fred 1939- DLB-60
Waiblinger, Wilhelm 1804-1830 .... DLB-90
Wain, John
    1925-1994 ... DLB-15, 27, 139, 155; CDBLB-8
    Tribute to J. B. Priestly Y-84
Wainwright, Jeffrey 1944- DLB-40
Waite, Peirce and Company DLB-49
Wakeman, Stephen H. 1859-1924....... DLB-187
Wakoski, Diane 1937- DLB-5
Walahfrid Strabo circa 808-849......... DLB-148
Henry Z. Walck [publishing house]....... DLB-46
Walcott, Derek
    1930- DLB-117; Y-81, 92; CDWLB-3
    Nobel Lecture 1992: The Antilles:
    Fragments of Epic Memory........ Y-92
Robert Waldegrave [publishing house] ... DLB-170
Waldis, Burkhard circa 1490-1556? DLB-179
Waldman, Anne 1945- DLB-16
Waldrop, Rosmarie 1935- DLB-169
Walker, Alice 1900-1982 .... DLB-201
Walker, Alice
    1944- DLB-6, 33, 143; CDALB-6
Walker, Annie Louisa (Mrs. Harry Coghill)
    circa 1836-1907 .... DLB-240
Walker, George F. 1947- DLB-60
Walker, John Brisben 1847-1931 .... DLB-79
Walker, Joseph A. 1935- DLB-38
Walker, Margaret 1915-1998......... DLB-76, 152
Walker, Obadiah 1616-1699 .... DLB-281
Walker, Ted 1934- DLB-40
Walker, Evans and Cogswell Company ... DLB-49
Wall, John F. (see Sarban)
Wallace, Alfred Russel 1823-1913....... DLB-190
Wallace, Dewitt 1889-1981 .... DLB-137
Wallace, Edgar 1875-1932 .... DLB-70
Wallace, Lew 1827-1905 .... DLB-202
Wallace, Lila Acheson 1889-1984 .... DLB-137
    "A Word of Thanks," From the Initial
    Issue of Reader's Digest
    (February 1922) DLB-137
Wallace, Naomi 1960- DLB-249
Wallace Markfield's "Steeplechase"......... Y-02
Wallant, Edward Lewis
    1926-1962 .... DLB-2, 28, 143
Waller, Edmund 1606-1687............ DLB-126
Walpole, Horace 1717-1797 ..... DLB-39, 104, 213
    Preface to the First Edition of
    The Castle of Otranto (1764) ,.. DLB-39, 178
    Preface to the Second Edition of
    The Castle of Otranto (1765) ... DLB-39, 178
Walpole, Hugh 1884-1941............. DLB-34
Walrond, Eric 1898-1966 .... DLB-51
Walser, Martin 1927- DLB-75, 124
Walser, Robert 1878-1956 .... DLB-66
Walsh, Ernest 1895-1926.............. DLB-4, 45
Walsh, Robert 1784-1859 .... DLB-59
Walters, Henry 1848-1931 .... DLB-140

Waltharius circa 825 .... DLB-148
Walther von der Vogelweide
    circa 1170-circa 1230............. DLB-138
Walton, Izaak
    1593-1683......... DLB-151, 213; CDBLB-1
Wambaugh, Joseph 1937- DLB-6; Y-83
Wand, Alfred Rudolph 1828-1891 ...... DLB-188
Waniek, Marilyn Nelson 1946- DLB-120
Wanley, Humphrey 1672-1726 .... DLB-213
War of the Words (and Pictures): The Creation
    of a Graphic Novel Y-02
Warburton, William 1698-1779......... DLB-104
Ward, Aileen 1919- DLB-111
Ward, Artemus (see Browne, Charles Farrar)
Ward, Arthur Henry Sarsfield (see Rohmer, Sax)
Ward, Douglas Turner 1930- DLB-7, 38
Ward, Mrs. Humphry 1851-1920 .... DLB-18
Ward, James 1843-1925 .... DLB-262
Ward, Lynd 1905-1985................ DLB-22
Ward, Lock and Company DLB-106
Ward, Nathaniel circa 1578-1652 .... DLB-24
Ward, Theodore 1902-1983 .... DLB-76
Wardle, Ralph 1909-1988 .... DLB-103
Ware, Henry, Jr. 1794-1843............ DLB-235
Ware, William 1797-1852 .... DLB-1, 235
Warfield, Catherine Ann 1816-1877....... DLB-248
Waring, Anna Letitia 1823-1910 .... DLB-240
Frederick Warne and Company [U.K.] DLB-106
Frederick Warne and Company [U.S.]..... DLB-49
Warner, Anne 1869-1913 .... DLB-202
Warner, Charles Dudley 1829-1900 ..... DLB-64
Warner, Marina 1946- DLB-194
Warner, Rex 1905-1986 .... DLB-15
Warner, Susan 1819-1885 .... DLB-3, 42, 239, 250
Warner, Sylvia Townsend
    1893-1978 .... DLB-34, 139
Warner, William 1558-1609 .... DLB-172
Warner Books DLB-46
Warr, Bertram 1917-1943 .... DLB-88
Warren, John Byrne Leicester (see De Tabley, Lord)
Warren, Lella 1899-1982 .... Y-83
Warren, Mercy Otis 1728-1814...... DLB-31, 200
Warren, Robert Penn 1905-1989
    .... DLB-2, 48, 152; Y-80, 89; CDALB-6
    Tribute to Katherine Anne Porter Y-80
Warren, Samuel 1807-1877 .... DLB-190
Die Wartburgkrieg circa 1230-circa 1280 ... DLB-138
Warton, Joseph 1722-1800.......... DLB-104, 109
Warton, Thomas 1728-1790 ...... DLB-104, 109
Warung, Price (William Astley)
    1855-1911 .... DLB-230
Washington, George 1732-1799........ DLB-31
Washington, Ned 1901-1976 .... DLB-265
Wassermann, Jakob 1873-1934 .... DLB-66
Wasserstein, Wendy 1950- DLB-228
Wasson, David Atwood 1823-1887.... DLB-1, 223

Cumulative Index

Watanna, Onoto (see Eaton, Winnifred)
Waterhouse, Keith 1929- DLB-13, 15
Waterman, Andrew 1940- DLB-40
Waters, Frank 1902-1995 .... DLB-212; Y-86
Waters, Michael 1949- DLB-120
Watkins, Tobias 1780-1855 .... DLB-73
Watkins, Vernon 1906-1967 .... DLB-20
Watmough, David 1926- DLB-53
Watson, Colin 1920-1983 .... DLB-276
Watson, Ian 1943- DLB-261
Watson, James Wreford (see Wreford, James)
Watson, John 1850-1907 .... DLB-156
Watson, Rosamund Marriott
 (Graham R. Tomson) 1860-1911.... DLB-240
Watson, Sheila 1909-1998 .... DLB-60
Watson, Thomas 1545?-1592.......... DLB-132
Watson, Wilfred 1911- DLB-60
W. J. Watt and Company DLB-46
Watten, Barrett 1948- DLB-193
Watterson, Henry 1840-1921 .... DLB-25
Watts, Alan 1915-1973 .... DLB-16
Watts, Isaac 1674-1748 .... DLB-95
Franklin Watts [publishing house] DLB-46
Waugh, Alec 1898-1981 .... DLB-191
Waugh, Auberon 1939-2000 ...DLB-14, 194; Y-00
Waugh, Evelyn
 1903-1966 ..... DLB-15, 162, 195; CDBLB-6
Way and Williams DLB-49
Wayman, Tom 1945- DLB-53
Weatherly, Tom 1942- DLB-41
Weaver, Gordon 1937- DLB-130
Weaver, Robert 1921- DLB-88
Webb, Beatrice 1858-1943 .... DLB-190
Webb, Francis 1925-1973 .... DLB-260
Webb, Frank J. ?-? DLB-50
Webb, James Watson 1802-1884 .... DLB-43
Webb, Mary 1881-1927 .... DLB-34
Webb, Phyllis 1927- DLB-53
Webb, Sidney 1859-1947 .... DLB-190
Webb, Walter Prescott 1888-1963 .... DLB-17
Webbe, William ?-1591 .... DLB-132
Webber, Charles Wilkins 1819-1856? ... DLB-202
Webling, Lucy (Lucy Betty MacRaye)
 1877-1952 .... DLB-240
Webling, Peggy (Arthur Weston)
 1871-1949 .... DLB-240
Webster, Augusta 1837-1894 .... DLB-35, 240
Webster, John
 1579 or 1580-1634? DLB-58; CDBLB-1
 The Melbourne Manuscript Y-86
Webster, Noah
 1758-1843 .... DLB-1, 37, 42, 43, 73, 243
Webster, Paul Francis 1907-1984 .... DLB-265
Charles L. Webster and Company DLB-49
Weckherlin, Georg Rodolf 1584-1653 ... DLB-164

Wedekind, Frank
 1864-1918 .... DLB-118; CDWLB-2
Weeks, Edward Augustus, Jr. 1898-1989 . DLB-137
Weeks, Stephen B. 1865-1918 .... DLB-187
Weems, Mason Locke 1759-1825... DLB-30, 37, 42
Weerth, Georg 1822-1856 .... DLB-129
Weidenfeld and Nicolson DLB-112
Weidman, Jerome 1913-1998 .... DLB-28
Weigl, Bruce 1949- DLB-120
Weinbaum, Stanley Grauman 1902-1935 .. DLB-8
Weiner, Andrew 1949- DLB-251
Weintraub, Stanley 1929- DLB-111; Y82
Weise, Christian 1642-1708 .... DLB-168
Weisenborn, Gunther 1902-1969.... DLB-69, 124
Weiss, John 1818-1879 .... DLB-1, 243
Weiss, Paul 1901-2002 .... DLB-279
Weiss, Peter 1916-1982 .... DLB-69, 124
Weiss, Theodore 1916- DLB-5
Weiß, Ernst 1882-1940 .... DLB-81
Weiße, Christian Felix 1726-1804 .... DLB-97
Weitling, Wilhelm 1808-1871 .... DLB-129
Welch, James 1940- DLB-175, 256
Welch, Lew 1926-1971? DLB-16
Weldon, Fay 1931- DLB-14, 194; CDBLB-8
Wellek, René 1903-1995 .... DLB-63
Wells, Carolyn 1862-1942 .... DLB-11
Wells, Charles Jeremiah
 circa 1800-1879 .... DLB-32
Wells, Gabriel 1862-1946 .... DLB-140
Wells, H. G.
 1866-1946 ...DLB-34, 70, 156, 178; CDBLB-6
 H. G. Wells Society Y-98
 Preface to *The Scientific Romances of
  H. G. Wells* (1933) DLB-178
Wells, Helena 1758?-1824 .... DLB-200
Wells, Robert 1947- DLB-40
Wells-Barnett, Ida B. 1862-1931..... DLB-23, 221
Welsh, Irvine 1958- DLB-271
Welty, Eudora 1909-2001 ...... DLB-2, 102, 143;
 Y-87, 01; DS-12; CDALB-1
 Eudora Welty: Eye of the Storyteller Y-87
 Eudora Welty Newsletter Y-99
 Eudora Welty's Funeral Y-01
 Eudora Welty's Ninetieth Birthday Y-99
 Eudora Welty Remembered in
  Two Exhibits Y-02
Wendell, Barrett 1855-1921 .... DLB-71
Wentworth, Patricia 1878-1961 .... DLB-77
Wentworth, William Charles 1790-1872 . DLB-230
Werder, Diederich von dem 1584-1657 .. DLB-164
Werfel, Franz 1890-1945 .... DLB-81, 124
Werner, Zacharias 1768-1823.......... DLB-94
The Werner Company DLB-49
Wersba, Barbara 1932- DLB-52
Wescott, Glenway
 1901-1987 .... DLB-4, 9, 102; DS-15

Wesker, Arnold 1932- DLB-13; CDBLB-8
Wesley, Charles 1707-1788 .... DLB-95
Wesley, John 1703-1791 .... DLB-104
Wesley, Mary 1912-2002 .... DLB-231
Wesley, Richard 1945- DLB-38
A. Wessels and Company DLB-46
Wessobrunner Gebet circa 787-815 .... DLB-148
West, Anthony 1914-1988 .... DLB-15
 Tribute to Liam O'Flaherty Y-84
West, Cheryl L. 1957- DLB-266
West, Cornel 1953- DLB-246
West, Dorothy 1907-1998 .... DLB-76
West, Jessamyn 1902-1984 .... DLB-6; Y-84
West, Mae 1892-1980 .... DLB-44
West, Michelle Sagara 1963- DLB-251
West, Nathanael
 1903-1940 .... DLB-4, 9, 28; CDALB-5
West, Paul 1930- DLB-14
West, Rebecca 1892-1983 .... DLB-36; Y-83
West, Richard 1941- DLB-185
West and Johnson DLB-49
Westcott, Edward Noyes 1846-1898 .... DLB-202
The Western Literature Association......... Y-99
The Western Messenger
 1835-1841 .... DLB-1; DLB-223
Western Publishing Company DLB-46
Western Writers of America Y-99
The Westminster Review 1824-1914 .... DLB-110
Weston, Arthur (see Webling, Peggy)
Weston, Elizabeth Jane circa 1582-1612...DLB-172
Wetherald, Agnes Ethelwyn 1857-1940 ... DLB-99
Wetherell, Elizabeth (see Warner, Susan)
Wetherell, W. D. 1948- DLB-234
Wetzel, Friedrich Gottlob 1779-1819 ..... DLB-90
Weyman, Stanley J. 1855-1928 .... DLB-141, 156
Wezel, Johann Karl 1747-1819 .... DLB-94
Whalen, Philip 1923-2002 .... DLB-16
Whalley, George 1915-1983 .... DLB-88
Wharton, Edith 1862-1937
 ......DLB-4, 9, 12, 78, 189; DS-13; CDALB-3
Wharton, William 1920s?- Y-80
Whately, Mary Louisa 1824-1889 ...... DLB-166
Whately, Richard 1787-1863 .... DLB-190
 Elements of Rhetoric (1828;
  revised, 1846) [excerpt] DLB-57
Wheatley, Dennis 1897-1977 .... DLB-77, 255
Wheatley, Phillis
 circa 1754-1784 .... DLB-31, 50; CDALB-2
Wheeler, Anna Doyle 1785-1848? DLB-158
Wheeler, Charles Stearns 1816-1843 .. DLB-1, 223
Wheeler, Monroe 1900-1988 .... DLB-4
Wheelock, John Hall 1886-1978 .... DLB-45
 From John Hall Wheelock's
  Oral Memoir Y-01
Wheelwright, J. B. 1897-1940 .... DLB-45
Wheelwright, John circa 1592-1679 ..... DLB-24

Whetstone, George 1550-1587.........DLB-136
Whetstone, Colonel Pete (see Noland, C. F. M.)
Whewell, William 1794-1866...........DLB-262
Whichcote, Benjamin 1609?-1683......DLB-252
Whicher, Stephen E. 1915-1961........DLB-111
Whipple, Edwin Percy 1819-1886......DLB-1, 64
Whitaker, Alexander 1585-1617.........DLB-24
Whitaker, Daniel K. 1801-1881..........DLB-73
Whitcher, Frances Miriam
 1812-1852...................DLB-11, 202
White, Andrew 1579-1656..............DLB-24
White, Andrew Dickson 1832-1918......DLB-47
White, E. B. 1899-1985....DLB-11, 22; CDALB-7
White, Edgar B. 1947-.................DLB-38
White, Edmund 1940-.................DLB-227
White, Ethel Lina 1887-1944............DLB-77
White, Hayden V. 1928................DLB-246
White, Henry Kirke 1785-1806..........DLB-96
White, Horace 1834-1916...............DLB-23
White, James 1928-1999...............DLB-261
White, Patrick 1912-1990..............DLB-260
White, Phyllis Dorothy James (see James, P. D.)
White, Richard Grant 1821-1885........DLB-64
White, T. H. 1906-1964............DLB-160, 255
White, Walter 1893-1955...............DLB-51
William White and Company...........DLB-49
White, William Allen 1868-1944......DLB-9, 25
White, William Anthony Parker
 (see Boucher, Anthony)
White, William Hale (see Rutherford, Mark)
Whitechurch, Victor L. 1868-1933.......DLB-70
Whitehead, Alfred North
 1861-1947..................DLB-100, 262
Whitehead, James 1936-................Y-81
Whitehead, William 1715-1785......DLB-84, 109
Whitfield, James Monroe 1822-1871......DLB-50
Whitfield, Raoul 1898-1945............DLB-226
Whitgift, John circa 1533-1604.........DLB-132
Whiting, John 1917-1963................DLB-13
Whiting, Samuel 1597-1679..............DLB-24
Whitlock, Brand 1869-1934..............DLB-12
Whitman, Albery Allson 1851-1901......DLB-50
Whitman, Alden 1913-1990..............Y-91
Whitman, Sarah Helen (Power)
 1803-1878....................DLB-1, 243
Whitman, Walt
 1819-1892....DLB-3, 64, 224, 250; CDALB-2
Albert Whitman and Company..........DLB-46
Whitman Publishing Company..........DLB-46
Whitney, Geoffrey 1548 or 1552?-1601..DLB-136
Whitney, Isabella flourished 1566-1573...DLB-136
Whitney, John Hay 1904-1982..........DLB-127
Whittemore, Reed 1919-1995............DLB-5
Whittier, John Greenleaf
 1807-1892............DLB-1, 243; CDALB-2
Whittlesey House....................DLB-46

Wickham, Anna (Edith Alice Mary Harper)
 1884-1947.....................DLB-240
Wickram, Georg circa 1505-circa 1561...DLB-179
Wicomb, Zoë 1948-..................DLB-225
Wideman, John Edgar 1941-......DLB-33, 143
Widener, Harry Elkins 1885-1912.......DLB-140
Wiebe, Rudy 1934-....................DLB-60
Wiechert, Ernst 1887-1950..............DLB-56
Wied, Martina 1882-1957...............DLB-85
Wiehe, Evelyn May Clowes (see Mordaunt, Elinor)
Wieland, Christoph Martin 1733-1813....DLB-97
Wienbarg, Ludolf 1802-1872...........DLB-133
Wieners, John 1934-...................DLB-16
Wier, Ester 1910-......................DLB-52
Wiesel, Elie
 1928-.........DLB-83; Y-86, 87; CDALB-7
 Nobel Lecture 1986: Hope, Despair and
  Memory......................Y-86
Wiggin, Kate Douglas 1856-1923........DLB-42
Wigglesworth, Michael 1631-1705.......DLB-24
Wilberforce, William 1759-1833........DLB-158
Wilbrandt, Adolf 1837-1911............DLB-129
Wilbur, Richard 1921-....DLB-5, 169; CDALB-7
 Tribute to Robert Penn Warren........Y-89
Wild, Peter 1940-......................DLB-5
Wilde, Lady Jane Francesca Elgee
 1821?-1896....................DLB-199
Wilde, Oscar 1854-1900.....DLB-10, 19, 34, 57,
              141, 156, 190; CDBLB-5
 "The Critic as Artist" (1891).........DLB-57
 "The Decay of Lying" (1889).........DLB-18
 "The English Renaissance of
  Art" (1908)....................DLB-35
 "L'Envoi" (1882)...................DLB-35
 Oscar Wilde Conference at Hofstra
  University......................Y-00
Wilde, Richard Henry 1789-1847......DLB-3, 59
W. A. Wilde Company..................DLB-49
Wilder, Billy 1906-....................DLB-26
Wilder, Laura Ingalls 1867-1957.....DLB-22, 256
Wilder, Thornton
 1897-1975........DLB-4, 7, 9, 228; CDALB-7
 Thornton Wilder Centenary at Yale.....Y-97
Wildgans, Anton 1881-1932............DLB-118
Wiley, Bell Irvin 1906-1980.............DLB-17
John Wiley and Sons..................DLB-49
Wilhelm, Kate 1928-....................DLB-8
Wilkes, Charles 1798-1877.............DLB-183
Wilkes, George 1817-1885..............DLB-79
Wilkins, John 1614-1672...............DLB-236
Wilkinson, Anne 1910-1961.............DLB-88
Wilkinson, Eliza Yonge
 1757-circa 1813.................DLB-200
Wilkinson, Sylvia 1940-.................Y-86
Wilkinson, William Cleaver 1833-1920...DLB-71
Willard, Barbara 1909-1994............DLB-161
Willard, Emma 1787-1870..............DLB-239

Willard, Frances E. 1839-1898.........DLB-221
Willard, Nancy 1936-................DLB-5, 52
Willard, Samuel 1640-1707.............DLB-24
L. Willard [publishing house]..........DLB-49
Willeford, Charles 1919-1988..........DLB-226
William of Auvergne 1190-1249........DLB-115
William of Conches
 circa 1090-circa 1154.............DLB-115
William of Ockham circa 1285-1347.....DLB-115
William of Sherwood
 1200/1205-1266/1271.............DLB-115
The William Charvat American Fiction
 Collection at the Ohio State
 University Libraries..................Y-92
Williams, Ben Ames 1889-1953........DLB-102
Williams, C. K. 1936-...................DLB-5
Williams, Chancellor 1905-1992........DLB-76
Williams, Charles 1886-1945...DLB-100, 153, 255
Williams, Denis 1923-1998.............DLB-117
Williams, Emlyn 1905-1987..........DLB-10, 77
Williams, Garth 1912-1996.............DLB-22
Williams, George Washington
 1849-1891......................DLB-47
Williams, Heathcote 1941-.............DLB-13
Williams, Helen Maria 1761-1827......DLB-158
Williams, Hugo 1942-..................DLB-40
Williams, Isaac 1802-1865..............DLB-32
Williams, Joan 1928-....................DLB-6
Williams, Joe 1889-1972...............DLB-241
Williams, John A. 1925-..............DLB-2, 33
Williams, John E. 1922-1994............DLB-6
Williams, Jonathan 1929-...............DLB-5
Williams, Miller 1930-.................DLB-105
Williams, Nigel 1948-.................DLB-231
Williams, Raymond
 1921-1988..............DLB-14, 231, 242
Williams, Roger circa 1603-1683........DLB-24
Williams, Rowland 1817-1870..........DLB-184
Williams, Samm-Art 1946-..............DLB-38
Williams, Sherley Anne 1944-1999......DLB-41
Williams, T. Harry 1909-1979...........DLB-17
Williams, Tennessee
 1911-1983......DLB-7; Y-83; DS-4; CDALB-1
Williams, Terry Tempest 1955-....DLB-206, 275
Williams, Ursula Moray 1911-.........DLB-160
Williams, Valentine 1883-1946..........DLB-77
Williams, William Appleman 1921-......DLB-17
Williams, William Carlos
 1883-1963........DLB-4, 16, 54, 86; CDALB-4
 The William Carlos Williams Society....Y-99
Williams, Wirt 1921-....................DLB-6
A. Williams and Company.............DLB-49
Williams Brothers....................DLB-49
Williamson, Henry 1895-1977..........DLB-191
 The Henry Williamson Society.........Y-98
Williamson, Jack 1908-..................DLB-8

Cumulative Index

Willingham, Calder Baynard, Jr.
1922-1995 .... DLB-2, 44
Williram of Ebersberg circa 1020-1085 .. DLB-148
Willis, John circa 1572-1625 .... DLB-281
Willis, Nathaniel Parker 1806-1867
.... DLB-3, 59, 73, 74, 183, 250; DS-13
Willkomm, Ernst 1810-1886 .... DLB-133
Wills, Garry 1934- DLB-246
    Tribute to Kenneth Dale McCormick.... Y-97
Willson, Meredith 1902-1984.......... DLB-265
Willumsen, Dorrit 1940- DLB-214
Wilmer, Clive 1945- DLB-40
Wilson, A. N. 1950- DLB-14, 155, 194
Wilson, Angus 1913-1991 ..... DLB-15, 139, 155
Wilson, Arthur 1595-1652 .... DLB-58
Wilson, August 1945- DLB-228
Wilson, Augusta Jane Evans 1835-1909 ... DLB-42
Wilson, Colin 1931- DLB-14, 194
    Tribute to J. B. Priestly Y-84
Wilson, Edmund 1895-1972........... DLB-63
Wilson, Ethel 1888-1980 .... DLB-68
Wilson, F. P. 1889-1963 .... DLB-201
Wilson, Harriet E.
1827/1828?-1863? DLB-50, 239, 243
Wilson, Harry Leon 1867-1939 .... DLB-9
Wilson, John 1588-1667 .... DLB-24
Wilson, John 1785-1854 .... DLB-110
Wilson, John Anthony Burgess
(see Burgess, Anthony)
Wilson, John Dover 1881-1969 .... DLB-201
Wilson, Lanford 1937- DLB-7
Wilson, Margaret 1882-1973 .... DLB-9
Wilson, Michael 1914-1978 .... DLB-44
Wilson, Mona 1872-1954 .... DLB-149
Wilson, Robert Charles 1953- DLB-251
Wilson, Robert McLiam 1964- DLB-267
Wilson, Robley 1930- DLB-218
Wilson, Romer 1891-1930 .... DLB-191
Wilson, Thomas 1524-1581 .... DLB-132, 236
Wilson, Woodrow 1856-1924 .... DLB-47
Effingham Wilson [publishing house].... DLB-154
Wimpfeling, Jakob 1450-1528 .... DLB-179
Wimsatt, William K., Jr. 1907-1975 ...... DLB-63
Winchell, Walter 1897-1972 .... DLB-29
J. Winchester [publishing house] DLB-49
Winckelmann, Johann Joachim
1717-1768 .... DLB-97
Winckler, Paul 1630-1686 .... DLB-164
Wind, Herbert Warren 1916- DLB-171
John Windet [publishing house] DLB-170
Windham, Donald 1920- DLB-6
Wing, Donald Goddard 1904-1972 ..... DLB-187
Wing, John M. 1844-1917 .... DLB-187
Allan Wingate [publishing house] DLB-112
Winnemucca, Sarah 1844-1921 .... DLB-175
Winnifrith, Tom 1938- DLB-155

Winsloe, Christa 1888-1944.......... DLB-124
Winslow, Anna Green 1759-1780...... DLB-200
Winsor, Justin 1831-1897............ DLB-47
John C. Winston Company DLB-49
Winters, Yvor 1900-1968............. DLB-48
Winterson, Jeanette 1959- DLB-207, 261
Winthrop, John 1588-1649.......... DLB-24, 30
Winthrop, John, Jr. 1606-1676 .... DLB-24
Winthrop, Margaret Tyndal 1591-1647 .. DLB-200
Winthrop, Theodore 1828-1861 .... DLB-202
Wirt, William 1772-1834 .... DLB-37
Wise, John 1652-1725................ DLB-24
Wise, Thomas James 1859-1937....... DLB-184
Wiseman, Adele 1928-1992 .... DLB-88
Wishart and Company............... DLB-112
Wisner, George 1812-1849............ DLB-43
Wister, Owen 1860-1938 ....DLB-9, 78, 186
Wister, Sarah 1761-1804............. DLB-200
Wither, George 1588-1667 .... DLB-121
Witherspoon, John 1723-1794......... DLB-31
    The Works of the Rev. John Witherspoon
    (1800-1801) [excerpts] DLB-31
Withrow, William Henry 1839-1908..... DLB-99
Witkacy (see Witkiewicz, Stanisław Ignacy)
Witkiewicz, Stanisław Ignacy
1885-1939 .... DLB-215; CDWLB-4
Wittenwiler, Heinrich before 1387-
circa 1414? DLB-179
Wittgenstein, Ludwig 1889-1951 .... DLB-262
Wittig, Monique 1935- DLB-83
Wodehouse, P. G.
1881-1975......... DLB-34, 162; CDBLB-6
    Worldwide Wodehouse Societies Y-98
Wohmann, Gabriele 1932- DLB-75
Woiwode, Larry 1941- DLB-6
    Tribute to John Gardner Y-82
Wolcot, John 1738-1819 .... DLB-109
Wolcott, Roger 1679-1767 .... DLB-24
Wolf, Christa 1929- DLB-75; CDWLB-2
Wolf, Friedrich 1888-1953 .... DLB-124
Wolfe, Gene 1931- DLB-8
Wolfe, Thomas 1900-1938 ..... DLB-9, 102, 229;
Y-85; DS-2, DS-16; CDALB-5
    "All the Faults of Youth and Inexperience":
A Reader's Report on
Thomas Wolfe's *O Lost*............ Y-01
    Emendations for *Look Homeward, Angel*... Y-00
    Eugene Gant's Projected Works........ Y-01
    Fire at the Old Kentucky Home
[Thomas Wolfe Memorial].......... Y-98
    Thomas Wolfe Centennial
Celebration in Asheville........... Y-00
    The Thomas Wolfe Collection at
the University of North Carolina
at Chapel Hill.................. Y-97
    The Thomas Wolfe Society Y-97, 99
Wolfe, Tom 1931- DLB-152, 185
John Wolfe [publishing house] DLB-170

Reyner (Reginald) Wolfe
[publishing house] DLB-170
Wolfenstein, Martha 1869-1906........ DLB-221
Wolff, David (see Maddow, Ben)
Wolff, Helen 1906-1994................. Y-94
Wolff, Tobias 1945- DLB-130
    Tribute to Michael M. Rea........... Y-97
    Tribute to Raymond Carver.......... Y-88
Wolfram von Eschenbach
circa 1170-after 1220 ....DLB-138; CDWLB-2
    Wolfram von Eschenbach's *Parzival*:
Prologue and Book 3 .... DLB-138
Wolker, Jiří 1900-1924............... DLB-215
Wollstonecraft, Mary 1759-1797
.... DLB-39, 104, 158, 252; CDBLB-3
Women
    Women's Work, Women's Sphere:
Selected Comments from Women
Writers.................... DLB-200
Wondratschek, Wolf 1943- DLB-75
Wong, Elizabeth 1958- DLB-266
Wood, Anthony à 1632-1695.......... DLB-213
Wood, Benjamin 1820-1900........... DLB-23
Wood, Charles 1932-1980 .... DLB-13
    The Charles Wood Affair:
A Playwright Revived............ Y-83
Wood, Mrs. Henry 1814-1887 .... DLB-18
Wood, Joanna E. 1867-1927 .... DLB-92
Wood, Sally Sayward Barrell Keating
1759-1855..................... DLB-200
Wood, William ?-? DLB-24
Samuel Wood [publishing house]........ DLB-49
Woodberry, George Edward
1855-1930 ....DLB-71, 103
Woodbridge, Benjamin 1622-1684....... DLB-24
Woodbridge, Frederick J. E. 1867-1940 ...DLB-270
Woodcock, George 1912-1995.......... DLB-88
Woodhull, Victoria C. 1838-1927 ...... DLB-79
Woodmason, Charles circa 1720-? DLB-31
Woodress, James Leslie, Jr. 1916- ... DLB-111
Woods, Margaret L. 1855-1945........ DLB-240
Woodson, Carter G. 1875-1950.........DLB-17
Woodward, C. Vann 1908-1999 ....DLB-17
Woodward, Stanley 1895-1965 ....DLB-171
Woodworth, Samuel 1785-1842........ DLB-250
Wooler, Thomas 1785 or 1786-1853 .... DLB-158
Woolf, David (see Maddow, Ben)
Woolf, Douglas 1922-1992........... DLB-244
Woolf, Leonard 1880-1969 .....DLB-100; DS-10
Woolf, Virginia 1882-1941
.... DLB-36, 100, 162; DS-10; CDBLB-6
    "The New Biography," *New York Herald
Tribune*, 30 October 1927 ...... DLB-149
Woollcott, Alexander 1887-1943 .... DLB-29
Woolman, John 1720-1772 .... DLB-31
Woolner, Thomas 1825-1892 .... DLB-35
Woolrich, Cornell 1903-1968.......... DLB-226
Woolsey, Sarah Chauncy 1835-1905 ..... DLB-42

Woolson, Constance Fenimore
  1840-1894 . . . . DLB-12, 74, 189, 221
Worcester, Joseph Emerson
  1784-1865 . . . . DLB-1, 235
Wynkyn de Worde [publishing house] . . . DLB-170
Wordsworth, Christopher 1807-1885 . . . . DLB-166
Wordsworth, Dorothy 1771-1855 . . . . DLB-107
Wordsworth, Elizabeth 1840-1932 . . . . DLB-98
Wordsworth, William
  1770-1850 . . . . DLB-93, 107; CDBLB-3
Workman, Fanny Bullock 1859-1925 . . . . DLB-189
World Literatue Today: A Journal for the
  New Millennium Y-01
World Publishing Company DLB-46
World War I (1914-1918) DS-18
  The Great War Exhibit and Symposium at
    the University of South Carolina. . . . Y-97
  The Liddle Collection and First World
    War Research Y-07
  Other British Poets Who Fell
    in the Great War DLB-216
  The Seventy-Fifth Anniversary of
    the Armistice: The Wilfred Owen
    Centenary and the Great War Exhibit
    at the University of Virginia Y-93
World War II (1939–1945)
  Literary Effects of World War II DLB-15
  World War II Writers Symposium
    at the University of South Carolina,
    12–14 April 1995 . . . . Y-95
  WW2 HMSO Paperbacks Society Y-98
R. Worthington and Company DLB-49
Wotton, Sir Henry 1568-1639 . . . . DLB-121
Wouk, Herman 1915- Y-82; CDALB-7
  Tribute to James Dickey Y-97
Wreford, James 1915- DLB-88
Wren, Sir Christopher 1632-1723 . . . . DLB-213
Wren, Percival Christopher 1885-1941 . . . DLB-153
Wrenn, John Henry 1841-1911 . . . . DLB-140
Wright, C. D. 1949- DLB-120
Wright, Charles 1935- DLB-165; Y-82
Wright, Charles Stevenson 1932- DLB-33
Wright, Chauncey 1830-1875 . . . . DLB-270
Wright, Frances 1795-1852 . . . . DLB-73
Wright, Harold Bell 1872-1944 . . . . DLB-9
Wright, James 1927-1980 . . . . DLB-5, 169; CDALB-7
Wright, Jay 1935- DLB-41
Wright, Judith 1915-2000 . . . . DLB-260
Wright, Louis B. 1899-1984 . . . . DLB-17
Wright, Richard
  1908-1960 . . . . . DLB-76, 102; DS-2; CDALB-5
Wright, Richard B. 1937- DLB-53
Wright, S. Fowler 1874-1965 . . . . DLB-255
Wright, Sarah Elizabeth 1928- DLB-33
Wright, T. H.
  "Style" (1877) [excerpt] DLB-57
Wright, Willard Huntington
  ("S. S. Van Dine") 1888-1939 . . . . DS-16
Wrigley, Robert 1951- DLB-256
Writers' Forum Y-85
Writing
  A Writing Life Y-02

On Learning to Write Y-88
  The Profession of Authorship:
    Scribblers for Bread Y-89
  A Writer Talking: A Collage Y-00
Wroth, Lawrence C. 1884-1970 . . . . DLB-187
Wroth, Lady Mary 1587-1653 . . . . DLB-121
Wurlitzer, Rudolph 1937- DLB-173
Wyatt, Sir Thomas circa 1503-1542 . . . . . DLB-132
Wycherley, William
  1641-1715 . . . . DLB-80; CDBLB-2
Wyclif, John
  circa 1335-31 December 1384 . . . . DLB-146
Wyeth, N. C. 1882-1945 . . . . DLB-188; DS-16
Wyle, Niklas von circa 1415-1479 . . . . . . DLB-179
Wylie, Elinor 1885-1928 . . . . DLB-9, 45
Wylie, Philip 1902-1971 . . . . DLB-9
Wyllie, John Cook 1908-1968 . . . . DLB-140
Wyman, Lillie Buffum Chace
  1847-1929 . . . . DLB-202
Wymark, Olwen 1934- DLB-233
Wynd, Oswald Morris (see Black, Gavin)
Wyndham, John (John Wyndham Parkes
  Lucas Beynon Harris) 1903-1969 . . . . DLB-255
Wynne-Tyson, Esmé 1898-1972 . . . . DLB-191

X

Xenophon circa 430 B.C.-circa 356 B.C. . . . DLB-176

Y

Yasuoka Shōtarō 1920- DLB-182
Yates, Dornford 1885-1960 . . . . DLB-77, 153
Yates, J. Michael 1938- DLB-60
Yates, Richard 1926-1992 . . . DLB-2, 234; Y-81, 92
Yau, John 1950- DLB-234
Yavorov, Peyo 1878-1914 . . . . DLB-147
Yearsley, Ann 1753-1806 . . . . DLB-109
Yeats, William Butler
  1865-1939 . . . . DLB-10, 19, 98, 156; CDBLB-5
  The W. B. Yeats Society of N.Y. Y-99
Yellen, Jack 1892-1991 . . . . DLB-265
Yep, Laurence 1948- DLB-52
Yerby, Frank 1916-1991 . . . . DLB-76
Yezierska, Anzia
  1880-1970 . . . . DLB-28, 221
Yolen, Jane 1939- DLB-52
Yonge, Charlotte Mary
  1823-1901 . . . . DLB-18, 163
  The Charlotte M. Yonge Fellowship Y-98
The York Cycle circa 1376-circa 1569 . . . . DLB-146
A Yorkshire Tragedy DLB-58
Thomas Yoseloff [publishing house] DLB-46
Youd, Sam (see Christopher, John)
Young, A. S. "Doc" 1919-1996 . . . . DLB-241
Young, Al 1939- DLB-33
Young, Arthur 1741-1820 . . . . DLB-158
Young, Dick 1917 or 1918 - 1987 . . . . . . DLB-171
Young, Edward 1683-1765 . . . . DLB-95
Young, Frank A. "Fay" 1884-1957 . . . . . . DLB-241
Young, Francis Brett 1884-1954 . . . . DLB-191
Young, Gavin 1928- DLB-204

Young, Stark 1881-1963 . . . . . . DLB-9, 102; DS-16
Young, Waldeman 1880-1938 . . . . DLB-26
William Young [publishing house] DLB-49
Young Bear, Ray A. 1950- DLB-175
Yourcenar, Marguerite 1903-1987 . . . DLB-72; Y-88
Yovkov, Yordan 1880-1937 . . DLB-147; CDWLB-4

Z

Zachariä, Friedrich Wilhelm 1726-1777 . . . . DLB-97
Zagajewski, Adam 1945- DLB-232
Zagoskin, Mikhail Nikolaevich
  1789-1852 . . . . DLB-198
Zajc, Dane 1929- DLB-181
Zālīte, Māra 1952- DLB-232
Zamiatin, Evgenii Ivanovich
  1884-1937 . . . . DLB-272
Zamora, Bernice 1938- DLB-82
Zamudio, Adela 1854-1928 . . . . DLB-283
Zand, Herbert 1923-1970 . . . . DLB-85
Zangwill, Israel 1864-1926 . . . . . DLB-10, 135, 197
Zanzotto, Andrea 1921- DLB-128
Zapata Olivella, Manuel 1920- DLB-113
Zasodimsky, Pavel Vladimirovich
  1843-1912 . . . . DLB-238
Zebra Books DLB-46
Zebrowski, George 1945- DLB-8
Zech, Paul 1881-1946 . . . . DLB-56
Zeidner, Lisa 1955- DLB-120
Zeidonis, Imants 1933- DLB-232
Zeimi (Kanze Motokiyo) 1363-1443 . . . . DLB-203
Zelazny, Roger 1937-1995 . . . . DLB-8
Zenger, John Peter 1697-1746 . . . . DLB-24, 43
Zepheria DLB-172
Zesen, Philipp von 1619-1689 . . . . DLB-164
Zhadovskaia, Iuliia Valerianovna
  1824-1883 . . . . DLB-277
Zhukova, Mar'ia Semenovna
  1805-1855 . . . . DLB-277
Zhukovsky, Vasilii Andreevich
  1783-1852 . . . . DLB-205
G. B. Zieber and Company DLB-49
Ziedonis, Imants 1933- CDWLB-4
Zieroth, Dale 1946- DLB-60
Zigler und Kliphausen, Heinrich
  Anshelm von 1663-1697 . . . . DLB-168
Zil'ber, Veniamin Aleksandrovich
  (see Kaverin, Veniamin Aleksandrovich)
Zimmer, Paul 1934- DLB-5
Zinberg, Len (see Lacy, Ed)
Zincgref, Julius Wilhelm 1591-1635 . . . . . DLB-164
Zindel, Paul 1936- DLB-7, 52; CDALB-7
Zinnes, Harriet 1919- DLB-193
Zinzendorf, Nikolaus Ludwig von
  1700-1760 . . . . DLB-168
Zitkala-Ša 1876-1938 . . . . DLB-175
Ziverts, Mārtiņš 1903-1990 . . . . DLB-220
Zlatovratsky, Nikolai Nikolaevich
  1845-1911 . . . . DLB-238
Zola, Emile 1840-1902 . . . . DLB-123
Zolla, Elémire 1926- DLB-196

Zolotow, Charlotte 1915- DLB-52

Zoshchenko, Mikhail Mikhailovich 1895-1958 .... DLB-272

Zschokke, Heinrich 1771-1848 .... DLB-94

Zubly, John Joachim 1724-1781 .... DLB-31

Zu-Bolton, Ahmos, II 1936- DLB-41

Zuckmayer, Carl 1896-1977 .... DLB-56, 124

Zukofsky, Louis 1904-1978 .... DLB-5, 165

Zupan, Vitomil 1914-1987 .... DLB-181

Župančič, Oton 1878-1949 ...DLB-147; CDWLB-4

zur Mühlen, Hermynia 1883-1951 .... DLB-56

Zweig, Arnold 1887-1968 .... DLB-66

Zweig, Stefan 1881-1942 .... DLB-81, 118

Zwinger, Ann 1925- DLB-275

Zwingli, Huldrych 1484-1531 .... DLB-338

ISBN 0-7876-6821-4

90000